D1428862

OXFORD EC LAW LIBRARY

General Editor: F. G. Jacobs
Advocate General, The Court of Justice
of the European Communities

EC SECURITIES REGULATION

OXFORD EC LAW LIBRARY

The aim of this series is to publish important and original studies of the various branches of European Community Law. Each work will provide a clear, concise, and critical exposition of the law in its social, economic, and political context, at a level which will interest the advanced student, the practitioner, the academic, and government and Community officials.

Other Titles in the Library

The European Union and its Court of Justice
Anthony Arnull

The General Principles of EC Law
Takis Tridimas

EC Company Law
Vanessa Edwards

EC Sex Equality Law
second edition
Evelyn Ellis

European Community Law of State Aid
Andrew Evans

European Community Law
third edition
Daniel G. Goyder

External Relations of the European
Community
I. MacLeod, I. D. Hendry and Stephen Hyett

Directives in European Community Law
Sacha Prechal

EC Tax Law
Paul Farmer and Richard Lyal

The European Internal Market and
International Trade
Piet Eeckhout

Trade and Environment in the
European Community
Andreas R. Ziegler

EC Employment Law
second edition
Catherine Barnard

EC Customs Law
Timothy Lyons

The Law of Money and Financial Services in
the EC
second edition
J. A. Usher

EC Agricultural Law
second edition
J. A. Usher

EC Securities Regulation

NIAMH MOLONEY

OXFORD
UNIVERSITY PRESS

OXFORD

UNIVERSITY PRESS

Great Clarendon Street, Oxford OX2 6DP

Oxford University Press is a department of the University of Oxford.
It furthers the University's objective of excellence in research, scholarship,
and education by publishing worldwide in

Oxford New York

Auckland Bangkok Buenos Aires Cape Town Chennai
Dar es Salaam Delhi Hong Kong Istanbul Karachi Kolkata
Kuala Lumpur Madrid Melbourne Mexico City Mumbai Nairobi
São Paulo Shanghai Singapore Taipei Tokyo Toronto

with an associated company in Berlin

Oxford is a registered trade mark of Oxford University Press
in the UK and in certain other countries

Published in the United States
by Oxford University Press Inc., New York

© Niamh Moloney 2002

British Library Cataloguing in Publication Data

Data available

Library of Congress Cataloging in Publication Data

Data available

ISBN 0-19-826891-2

1 3 5 7 9 10 8 6 4 2

Typeset by Hope Services (Abingdon) Ltd
Printed in Great Britain
on acid-free paper by
TJ International Ltd, Padstow, Cornwall

To My Parents

General Editor's Foreword

The aim of the Oxford EC Law Library is to publish important and original studies of the various branches of EC law. All the previous fifteen titles in the series have served that aim remarkably well. The present title will certainly do the same.

In one respect, however, *EC Securities Regulation* is unique in the series, in that both the subject and the title are novel categories. Indeed this book helps to define and to develop the branch of law with which it deals.

Essentially that law covers securities and investment services: it seeks to introduce a uniform European regime which will both provide better protection for the investor and facilitate cross-border investment, thus contributing also to the integration of the national markets in securities and investment services. The recent development of Community legislation in these areas—the remarkable range of which is apparent from the detailed table of contents—can now be seen as having given birth to a European system of securities regulation.

It is, therefore, easy to see the need for this book. As the author says in her introduction, one of its aims is to characterize EC securities regulation as a discrete subject, liberated from EC financial-services regulation and from EC company law. In the context of the Oxford EC Law Library, this book is appropriately flanked by, on the one hand, Vanessa Edwards' *EC Company Law* and, on the other hand, John Usher's *Law of Money and Financial Services in the EC*.

Although much of the legislation is of very recent origin, the material is already substantial and fully justifies the length of the book, as do the quality and depth of the analysis. The work also appears at an opportune time: if the wishes of the European Council are fulfilled, an integrated securities and investment-services market will be operational in 2003.

FRANCIS G. JACOBS

May 2002

Preface and Acknowledgements

EC Securities Regulation examines the EC's system of securities and investment-services market regulation. The aim of the book is to consolidate and
assess critically those EC rules which address the securities and investment-
services markets and their participants, such as issuers, investors, investment-services providers, and collective-investment schemes, and which aim
to construct an integrated EC securities and investment-services market. EC
securities regulation has steadily increased in sophistication since the adoption of the early issuer-disclosure directives in the late 1970s and early
1980s to the point that it can now be examined as a discrete system of market regulation. While it responds in part, as this book aims to show, to the
traditional objectives of securities regulation, one of the defining characteristics of EC securities regulation is its dual function as a tool of market
regulation and market integration. EC securities regulation must, in addition
to serving the objectives of market regulation, integrate national markets
and manage the particular risks raised by an integrated securities and
investment-services market, all within the institutional, legal and political
constraints of that integrated market.

This book was written over a time of immense and exciting change for EC
securities regulation. Regulation, law-making procedures, market practices,
and market structures are all evolving at a remarkable pace. After a period
during which it endured a rather Cinderella-like existence at the margins of
internal-market policy-making, EC securities regulation has been transformed into an EC policy priority which is exerting a powerful influence on
Member States' regulatory regimes. The process of transformation which
began with the adoption of the Financial Services Action Plan (the FSAP) in
1999, and which was given a new urgency by the seminal 2001 Report of
the Committee of Wise Men on the Regulation of European Securities
Markets (the Lamfalussy Report) and its model for delegated law-making by
the Commission, is continuing and is set to have a far-reaching impact on
the regulation of securities and investment-services markets across the EC.
The pace of regulatory change is matched and regularly outstripped by market-led developments. The integrated EC market-place is fast becoming a
reality, in the wholesale sphere in any event, in the wake of the adoption of
the euro, the emergence of e-commerce, the rise of pan-EC financial conglomerates, the arrival of pan-EC trading systems, and the greater embrace
of market-based finance across the EC, to isolate but five of many developments. As it deals with a target which is not so much moving as accelerat-
ing, this book does not (and could not) provide the reader with an

up-to-the-minute definitive statement of all new developments. It does, however, seek to place the current regulatory system in the context of the reform process, track the major policy initiatives, and analyse the underlying themes which characterize the emerging regime. As such, it is hoped that this book will provide the reader with an examination of the major themes and controversies of this period of change as well as with a consolidation and contextual examination of the regime currently in force.

The analysis takes the securities-regulation regime up to 31 October 2001 and the law in force is stated as known to me at that date. This seemed an appropriate point to stop. By then the Commission had presented its important working paper on the reform of the core Investment Services Directive, the new Lamfalussy-based committee structure (the European Securities Committee and the Committee of European Securities Regulators) which supports the new delegated law-making model had been established, and the first legislative proposals to reflect the new law-making model had appeared. The story continues, however. Where possible, major developments up to 1 December 2001 have been referred to in outline. A number of noteworthy developments have occurred since then. In early February 2002 the inter-institutional tensions engendered by the Lamfalussy Report were eased when the European Parliament voted to accept a Resolution which supported the Lamfalussy delegated law-making model. Central to the Parliament's acceptance of the Lamfalussy model which, as discussed further in Chapter XV of this book, has considerable ramifications for the Parliament's legislative powers in the securities-regulation sphere, was the Commission's February 2002 Declaration to the Parliament. In this Declaration the Commission takes note of the Parliament's intention to limit the duration of any delegation of law-making power to the Commission to four years from the entry into force of the relevant delegating directive, subject to the Parliament and the Council accepting any extension proposed by the Commission. The Commission also declares that it will ensure that the Parliament is granted a three-month period (which may be shortened in urgent cases) in which to examine draft Commission measures. The Declaration includes an assurance that the Commission will ensure full transparency *vis-à-vis* the Parliament during the adoption process and ensure that there is wide public consultation before draft measures are drawn up under the delegated law-making process. The Commission is also to support the Parliament's wish that a market participants group be attached to the Committee of European Securities Regulators, which forms part of the Lamfalussy delegated law-making model. Finally, in a ringing and optimistic assertion of the importance of inter-institutional harmony and balance to the timely delivery of the FSAP, the Commission recalls its political willingness to endeavour that the Parliament benefits from equivalent treatment (with the Council and within the parameters of the current institutional structure) and reaffirms its commitment to take the utmost account of the Parliament's position if the Parliament considers that the Commission has exceeded its implementing powers. It remains to be seen whether the good inter-institutional relations which are critical to the success of the new delegated law-making model will be preserved as the draft delegating directives work through the legislative process, although the Parliament's vote augurs well for the future.

After over two years of difficult negotiations, the Council finally adopted its common position on the Distance Marketing of Financial Services Proposal in mid-December 2001. The common position, which 'reflects a hard-won yet balanced compromise requiring many concessions from most of the Member States',[1] was adopted by a qualified majority vote of the Council. The text of the common position closely follows that of the Council Draft which is discussed in Chapter IX section 9 of this book. The common position represents an abandonment of the minimum harmonization approach which was initially favoured by a number of the Member States and, in the interests of consumer protection and following an analysis by the Commission of national disclosure provisions, harmonizes at a high level the disclosure which must be made in a distance sale of financial services. Member States retain the right to maintain or introduce more stringent disclosure requirements, however, pending further harmonization and as long as such requirements are in conformity with Community law. A truncated disclosure regime applies to 'voice telephony' communications where the consumer expressly consents to this. The withdrawal-rights regime is also more prescriptive than the Commission's original proposal had suggested. Rather than granting the Member States some discretion in this area, the common position sets the standard withdrawal period at fourteen days. The new distance-marketing regime's relationship with other financial-services measures and the e-commerce regime (particularly with respect to that regime's Member-State-of-origin principle which is discussed in Chapter IX section 10 of this book) is also clarified in the common position. The new regime is to apply in conformity with the e-commerce regime, while prior information provisions in Community legislation which governs financial services which are additional to the requirements of the distance-marketing regime are to continue to apply. The distance-marketing regime will also apply without prejudice to host-Member-State control and/or authorization or supervision systems in the Member States where this is compatible with Community legislation. The common position is now awaiting the Parliament's opinion.

---

[1] Communication from the Commission to the European Parliament concerning the common position: SEC (2002) 30 final, 10. The Statement of the Council's Reasons in the common position refers to a 'long and very difficult discussion': [2002] OJ C58/32, Council's Statement of Reasons, para III.

Discussions continue in the marketplace and on an inter-institutional basis on the Commission's controversial 2001 proposal for a new prospectus regime (discussed in Chapter IV section 9.3). Of particular note was the adoption by the European Parliament of a detailed opinion on the proposed new regime in early March 2002. Many of the amendments proposed by the Parliament reflect a concern as to the costs which the new regime could represent for small businesses whose capital-raising activities are domestically-based. They also chime with the hostile reception the proposed regime has received from those sections of the marketplace which regard the new regime as too costly, overly bureaucratic, and insufficiently sensitive to capital-raising on second-tier markets. Among the major changes the Parliament has proposed to the Commission's approach are: changing the shelf-registration system which requires certain issuers to produce an annual update of their prospectus disclosure from a mandatory system to an optional one; giving Member States the option to exempt issuers with an actual or expected market capitalization of less than euro 350 million from the prospectus approval requirement where the application made for an offer to the public or admission to trading on a regulated market is restricted to the home Member State in which the issuer has its registered office; extending the definition of a 'qualified investor' and thereby extending the range of offers which are not considered to be offers to the public and are therefore outside the scope of the new regime; and significantly diluting the Commission's controversial application of the home-Member-State control device to prospectus authorizations by defining the home Member State not only as the Member State where the issuer has its registered office, but also as the State in which the issuer was admitted to trading on a regulated market for the first time or where it intends to offer the securities publicly or apply for admission to trading for other securities, at the choice of the issuer. Given the Parliament's robust defence of its role in the law-making process during the inter-institutional negotiations on the adoption of the Lamfalussy law-making model, it is not surprising that the amendments include detailed guidance as to the principles the Commission should respect when adopting measures under the new prospectus regime in accordance with the Lamfalussy delegated law-making model. The Council's common position is now awaited.

March 2002 also saw the adoption by the European Parliament of opinions on three other FSAP measures: the proposed market-abuse regime (discussed in Chapter XIII section 11.5); the proposed financial-conglomerates regime (discussed in Chapter VIII section 11.3); and the proposal on the application of International Accounting Standards (IAS) (discussed in Chapter IV section 10). Significant amendments to the market-abuse regime include: supplementing the core definition of market manipulation via trading activity with definitions which give more precise examples of market manipulation and removing the Annex of examples which the Commission had suggested; tightening the definition of market manipulation via information dissemination to require that the manipulator or the persons informed of the manipulation derive, directly or indirectly, an advantage or profits from the activity and that the manipulator knew, or could without reasonable doubt be considered to have known, that the information was false or misleading; and, unusually for EC securities regulation which does not, in a reflection of the internal market harmonization project generally, normally venture too far into the realm of remedies or sanctions, requiring the Commission to draw up an indicative list of the administrative measures and sanctions which Member States are to impose on violations of the new regime. The amendments to the financial-conglomerates regime are largely technical but include excluding small and regional financial conglomerates from the regime and permitting financial conglomerates, rather than the competent authorities, to choose the method for calculating capital-adequacy requirements from the options set out in the proposed regime. The suggested amendments to the IAS proposal include: introducing a qualification requirement prior to the adoption of an international accounting standard which would demand that application of the standard result in a true and fair view of the financial position and performance of the company, that it be conducive to the European public good, and that it meet the criteria of understandability, relevance, reliability, and comparability required of financial information; and restricting the IAS adoption requirement to those companies the securities of which are, at their balance sheet date, admitted to trading on a regulated market of any Member State. These three measures are now awaiting the Council's response.

Attempts to relaunch the takeovers project (discussed in Chapter XIV) also continue. The High Level Group of Company Law Experts, which was set up in the aftermath of the July 2001 collapse of the takeover proposal in order to consider how to take the harmonization project forward, presented its extensive report in January 2002. The Group has concluded that the availability of a takeover-bid mechanism is beneficial and its related recommendations for reform include the adoption of a harmonized approach to the equitable price to be paid in a mandatory bid which would allow offerors to predict the equitable price payable. The Group has suggested that the price should, in normal circumstances (Member States would be permitted to apply the rule flexibly), be equal to the highest price paid by the offeror for shares of the relevant class, whether on or off the market, during a certain period (set by the Member States and of between 6 and 12 months) preceding the date of the acquisition of the securities by the offeror which resulted in the change of control. The Group has also suggested the adoption of squeeze-out/sell-out rules which would require a bidder, on acquiring between 90 and 95 per cent of the capital (the threshold to be decided by the Member States), to buy out any remaining shareholders. The fate of takeover-rule harmonization and the liberalization of the market for corporate control remains to be seen. Finally, the Council has adopted a common position on the proposal for financial collateral arrangements (discussed in Chapter XII section 5) and it is awaiting the second reading of the European Parliament prior to its adoption.

This project was initiated with the encouragement of Professor Ewan McKendrick and valuable support was provided throughout its duration by Professor David O'Keeffe. Without the help and incisive analysis of Michel Tison and Jane Welch, some of the more difficult issues raised by the investment-services regime would have remained opaque to me. The staff of the Internal Market Directorate-General at the Commission were helpful and speedy in responding to requests for information, as were the staff of the British Library. My thanks also go to the staff at Oxford University Press and in particular to John Louth and his team, notably Geraldine Mangley, for their professionalism in guiding this book through to publication. Kate Elliott did a fine job in copy-editing the text. More generally, I owe a considerable academic debt to three distinguished scholars, Professors Eddy Wymeersch, Klaus Hopt, and Guido Ferrarini. Their pioneering work in the field of EC securities regulation sparked my interest in this area and has been a source of instruction and inspiration. They have contributed immeasurably to the development of EC securities regulation as a mature academic discipline which may yet come to rival the sophistication of US securities regulation. My greatest debt of gratitude is to Professor Guido Ferrarini who read a number of the book's chapters and who made it possible for me to spend a very fruitful week as a visiting fellow at CEDIF (the Centre for Law and Finance) at the University of Genoa. Any errors or omissions are entirely my responsibility.

Finally, this book would not have been completed without the boundless practical support, unfailing enthusiasm and endless patience of my husband, Iain Donovan.

NIAMH MOLONEY

24 March 2002

Summary Table of Contents

PART VII: THE INSTITUTIONAL STRUCTURE OF
EC SECURITIES REGULATION

Contents

PART IV: THE EC SECURITIES-TRADING MARKETS REGIME

Table of Abbreviations

Am. Econ. Rev.	American Economic Review
Am. J Comp. L	American Journal of Comparative Law
Bell J Econ. and Management Sci.	Bell Journal of Economics and Management Science
BJIBFL	Butterworths Journal of International Banking and Financial Law
Brooklyn J Int'l. L	Brooklyn Journal of International Law
Cal. L Rev.	California Law Review
Col. J T'nal. Law	Columbia Journal of Transnational Law
Col. LR	Columbia Law Review
CESR	Committee of European Securities Regulators
CMLRev.	Common Law Market Review
CFiLR	Company, Financial and Insolvency Law Review
Denver J of Int'l. L and Policy	Denver Journal of International Law and Policy
ECOSOC	Economic and Social Committee
EC	European Community
EBLRev.	European Business Law Review
ECB	European Central Bank
ECR	European Court Reports
EFSL	European Financial Services Law
ELJ	European Law Journal
ELRev.	European Law Review
EMU	European Monetary Union
ESCB	European System of Central Banks
EU	European Union
FSA	Financial Services Authority
Fordham Int. LJ	Fordham International Law Journal
FESCO	Forum of European Securities Commissions
FRR	Financial Regulation Report
Harv. LR	Harvard Law Review
Harv. Int. LJ	Harvard International Law Journal
Hofstra L Rev.	Hofstra Law Review
Ind. LJ	Indiana Law Journal
ICCLJ	International and Comparative Corporate Law Journal

ICLQ	*International and Comparative Law Quarterly*
IFLR	*International Financial Law Review*
IOSCO	International Organization of Securities Commissions
Int'l. Review of L and Econ.	*International Review of Law and Economics*
J of Business	*Journal of Business*
JBL	*Journal of Business Law*
JCMS	*Journal of Common Market Studies*
J Comp. Bus. and Capital Markets L	*Journal of Comparative Business and Capital Markets Law*
J Consumer Res.	*Journal of Consumer Research*
J Corp. L	*Journal of Corporation Law*
J of Econ. Perspectives	*Journal of Economic Perspectives*
J Fin.	*Journal of Finance*
JFRC	*Journal of Financial Regulation and Compliance*
JIBL	*Journal of International Banking Law*
J L and Econ.	*Journal of Law and Economics*
J Legal Studies	*Journal of Legal Studies*
JPE	*Journal of Political Economy*
J Portfolio Mgmt.	*Journal of Portfolio Management*
LIEI	*Legal Issues of European Integration*
LMCLQ	*Lloyd's Maritime and Commercial Law Quarterly*
MoU	Memorandum of Understanding
Mich. LR	*Michigan Law Review*
MLR	*Modern Law Review*
NYU LRev.	*New York University Law Review*
OECD	Organization for Economic Co-operation and Development
OJLS	*Oxford Journal of Legal Studies*
SEC	US Securities and Exchange Commission
So. Cal. L Rev.	*Southern California Law Review*
Stanford LR	*Stanford Law Review*
University of Chicago LR	*University of Chicago Law Review*
University of Colorado LR	*University of Colorado Law Review*
Vanderbilt J Transn'l. L	*Vanderbilt Journal of Transnational Law*
Va L Rev.	*Virginia Law Review*
Washington and Lee LR	*Washington and Lee Law Review*
Yale J Reg.	*Yale Journal of Regulation*
Yale LJ	*Yale Law Journal*
YBEL	*Yearbook of European Law*

Table of Cases

EUROPEAN COURT OF JUSTICE: ALPHABETICAL LIST OF CASES

EUROPEAN COURT OF JUSTICE: NUMERICAL LIST OF CASES

NATIONAL CASES

United Kingdom

United States

Table of Legislation

EC LEGISLATION

Treaties

Decisions

Directives

Recommendations

Regulations

Conventions and Agreements

Draft Legislation

EUROPEAN CONVENTIONS

NATIONAL LEGISLATION

Ireland

Spain

United Kingdom

PART I
Introduction

PART I

Introduction

I

Introduction

I.1 INTRODUCTION AND SCOPE

This book examines the EC's system of securities and investment-services market regulation or EC securities regulation. It is a system in transition, moving from a basic regulatory framework, which has had only limited success in integrating national markets to a considerably more sophisticated and extensive regime which is designed to complete the integration process. Market structures and regulatory regimes alike are evolving. This book examines the current regime and, reflecting this key phase in its evolution, assesses the new proposals and market forces which are changing the shape of EC securities regulation.

In writing this book, parameters had to be set for the scope of EC securities regulation. Indeed, one of the objectives of the book is to try to characterize EC securities regulation as a discrete subject, liberated from EC financial-services regulation and EC company law, in the interstices of both of which it is often to be found.[1] After a slow start, which can be traced back to 1977 and the Commission's Recommendation for a European Code of Conduct Relating to Transactions in Transferable Securities[2] and the early admission to official listing and issuer-disclosure measures adopted in the late 1970s and early 1980s, the subject matter of EC securities regulation has widened steadily since 1993 with the adoption of the cornerstone Investment Services Directive (the ISD).[3] The adoption of the Financial Services Action Plan (the FSAP) in 1999 (see section 7 below) has accelerated the maturing process and, with the exhortation from the Stockholm European Council in 2001 that the key steps for achieving an integrated securities and investment-services market be implemented by 2003, EC securities regulation has now emerged as a fully fledged component of EC law and regulation.

This emergence of EC securities regulation as an independent subject tracks to some extent the development of securities regulation as a discrete discipline on this side of the Atlantic. Securities regulation is a long-established component of the US law-school curriculum while the foundation pillars of US

---

[1] For an analysis of the emergence of EC securities regulation from under the wing of EC company law see Davies, P, 'The European Community's Directive on Insider Dealing: From Company Law to Securities Market Regulation' (1991) 11 *OJLS* 92.

[2] Recommendation 77/534/EEC [1977] OJ L212/37 (the Code of Conduct).

[3] Directive 93/22/EEC on investment services in the securities field. [1993] OJ L141/27.

securities regulation, the Securities Act, 1933 and the Securities Exchange Act, 1934, have produced not only a highly developed regulatory structure but a lively academic debate and voluminous literature on securities regulation. In recent years, securities regulation has begun to generate considerable interest and academic comment across the Atlantic as Member States of the EU have, often under the impetus of EC obligations, moved to introduce sophisticated systems of securities regulation.[4]

The subject matter of this book covers those EC measures which concern the regulation of securities market participants (issuers of securities, collective investment schemes, market intermediaries, and investors) and the operation of the markets themselves. It addresses the regulatory regimes which apply to issuer access to investors and to the securities markets and those which cover activities on the secondary markets in which transactions take place between investors after the initial issuer/investor transaction. After this introduction to EC securities regulation which forms Part I, Part II examines the regulation of issuer access to the securities markets and, in particular, the admission to official listing and issuer disclosure regime (Chapters II–IV) and collective investment schemes (Chapter V). As such, it is broadly concerned with investment products: securities and collective investment schemes. Part III concerns the secondary markets and, in particular, the regulation of investment intermediaries who provide investment services. The twin pillars of investment intermediary regulation, prudential and conduct regulation, are examined, as are compensation schemes (Chapters VI–X). Part IV concerns the securities trading markets on which issuers' securities are traded and investment intermediaries act as a market access channel for investors, particularly retail investors. It addresses the regulation of securities trading markets (Chapter XI) and post-trade settlement systems (Chapter XII). Part V (Chapter XIII) covers the pathology of securities regulation and examines the EC's market abuse regime while Part VI (Chapter XIV) concerns takeover regulation. Finally, Part VII (Chapter XV) examines the institutional structure of EC securities regulation. Those related regulatory areas which impact on the securities markets and their participants but which also have a wider reach, such as the EC's competition rules and money laundering regime, are not covered. Neither does this book cover, for the most part, the private law rights which arise in the interaction between issuers, investors, intermediaries, and markets, nor the EC's company law harmonization programme.[5] Finally, this discussion is con-

---

[4] For an overview of the early development of securities regulation or capital markets law across the EC see Buxbaum, R. and Hopt, K., *Legal Harmonisation and the Business Enterprise* (1988) 189–92.

[5] Although the EC's accounting standards and financial reporting initiatives impact on securities regulation, in so far as they have implications for the type of disclosure which is made by issuers to the market-place, they are primarily concerned with the shareholder/company

cerned with the EC system of securities regulation. The main legislative device used to construct this regime, the directive (section 4 below), requires Member States to implement the rules contained in directives in their national systems. The implementation of EC securities regulation measures in the national systems is not discussed in detail, although reference is made to Member States' regimes to illustrate the difficulties and controversies in the EC framework.

EC securities regulation is at bedrock a device for integrating national securities and investment services markets. A by-product of that integration process has been, as can be seen from the scope of this book, the construction of a discrete system of securities market regulation. This system has, for certain Member States and in respect of particular regulatory areas, resulted not simply in the application of common EC standards but in the imposition of entirely new systems of regulation on national markets which were previously lightly regulated or unregulated; this was particularly the case with the ISD. In recent years, this system has deepened in scope and acquired regulatory sophistication to the extent that it can now be examined as an independent system of market regulation. This system responds to the traditional objectives of securities regulation, albeit, as discussed throughout, that these objectives are often not expressly articulated and must be examined through the sometimes distorting lens of the market integration priority. This priority means that EC securities regulation must also effectively integrate individual national securities markets which display different structural features and cultural approaches to regulation and grapple with the particular risks raised by an integrated securities and investment services market, all within the institutional, legal, and political constraints of that integrated market. This duality is examined throughout the book.

I.2 THE TREATY AND COMPETENCE TO REGULATE

EC securities regulation is based ultimately on the Treaty objective of constructing a common market (Article 2).[6] More specifically, the internal market in securities and investment services, the construction of which has generated the rules of EC securities regulation, is part of a wider project to create a single market comprising 'an area without internal frontiers in

relationship and are usually considered as part of company law rather than securities regulation. The most important of these are the 4th (Directive 78/660/EEC [1978] OJ L222/1), 7th (Directive 83/349/EEC [1983] OJ L193/1) and 8th (Directive 84/253/EEC [1984] OJ L126/20) Company Law Directives which address, respectively, the presentation of annual accounts, consolidated accounts and the qualifications required of statutory auditors.

[6] References to 'the Treaty' are to the EC Treaty as amended by the Treaty of Amsterdam. Art. numbering follows the Amsterdam Treaty. The reference is to EC rather than EU securities regulation, given that the discussion in this book concerns the EC pillar of the EU.

which the free movement of goods, persons, services and capital is ensured [Article 14(2) EC].' A single or integrated investment services and securities market, within which investment services providers and investors can access national markets across the EC and issuers can raise capital, should generate broader and deeper capital markets. As a result, achievement of the Community's market integration objectives should be enhanced by a reduction in the cost of capital for firms, particularly small and medium-sized enterprises, the promotion of growth and employment, and, more specifically, the achievement of greater choice for investors of investment services and investment products: this governing presumption of EC securities regulation can be traced back to 1966 and the seminal Segré Report (see section 6 below). It has received more attention in recent years when, as part of the renewed efforts to complete the single market in this area, the focus on the link between economic growth and investment services/securities market integration has intensified. The starting point for the EC securities regulation regime and the integration of markets, therefore, is that market finance (ie the raising of finance via the capital or securities markets) is a desirable financing mechanism.[7] Indeed, in many respects the evolution of the integration project is a story of the movement of the EC from a predominantly bank-based finance system (as far as continental economies are concerned) to a market-based finance system, although, as discussed in Chapter II, this transformation is very far from complete.[8] The rationales for the measures discussed in the following chapters which support integration can be traced back to these macro objectives, although these measures also have more immediate micro objectives, such as opening up market access across the EC, the efficient functioning of the market-place, market stability and integrity, and investor confidence, which are discussed in more detail in the relevant chapters.

The major obstruction to the internal market in securities and investment services markets and the primary preoccupation of EC securities regulation is the regulatory barrier to market access represented by obstructive and diverging national securities regulation regimes. Investment services and securities markets are traditionally subject to regulation in order to protect investors and the integrity and stability of the market-place itself; a number of factors such as market structures, investor profiles, the maturity of the market-place, saving patterns, and cultural attitudes towards regulation usually dictate the intensity of regulation. As is discussed in greater detail in the following chapters, securities regulation is generally based on the need to correct market failures (ie failures in the market's self-regulatory mecha-

---

[7] The alternative is bank finance, or the raising of finance via credit facilities provided by credit institutions. The relationship between the two and the EC's position on market finance generally is discussed in Ch. II sect. 4.2 below.

[8] Ch. II sect. 9 below.

nism which obstruct the efficient allocation of resources by an otherwise perfect market).[9] Its major preoccupation is with market failures related to asymmetric information and externalities (ie wellbeing-influencing consequences which are visited on one party by the actions of another), such as the instability-generating effects which can be caused when a market participant fails. At the start of the harmonization programme, considerable variations existed across the EC as to how markets were regulated. Even where these rules were not actively obstructionist and designed to protect national markets from competition, the very existence of divergences between rules caused problems for the construction of the single market. Regulatory divergences and the duplication of rules can amount to non-tariff barriers given that the costs they represent for market participants can obstruct access to other Member States' markets and integration. They can distort competition between market participants and prevent the development of the level playing-field on which the internal market is dependent. More positively, uniform rules can generate investor confidence in the stability and efficient functioning of and level of investor protection in the integrated market-place and thus increase the likelihood of cross-border investment.

The Treaty free movement guarantees go some way to removing regulatory obstacles to the construction of the internal market in securities and investment services. In particular, the freedom to provide services (Articles 43–48 EC) and the freedom to establish (Articles 49–55 EC) are the Treaty cornerstones on which the internal market is based. They provide the basis for market access by virtue of the prohibition they place on discriminatory and free-movement-restrictive national rules and have been particularly important in the investment services sphere. They are, however, subject to exceptions which allow Member States to retain free-movement-restricting rules in certain circumstances.[10] Although market regulation is the concern of this book, a single market in securities and investment services free of regulatory barriers cannot operate without the liberalization of capital controls or the free movement of capital. The Treaty capital movement rules are discussed in outline at the end of this introductory chapter.

Where the single market in securities and investment services cannot be achieved by means of the free-movement guarantees alone and regulatory barriers remain in place, the harmonization process steps in by providing for the adoption of harmonized securities regulation rules which are designed to remove the remaining regulatory obstacles to integration by putting common standards in place. Article 3(h) EC provides that the approximation of

---

[9] The market failure doctrine is discussed further in Ch. VI sect. 2.2 below with respect to the investment services regime.

[10] See Ch. VI sect 4 below.

Member States' laws to the extent required for the functioning of the common market is an activity of the Community. All EC measures, including harmonizing measures, must, however, be based on a Treaty provision that empowers the Community to act.[11] Lacking a competence independent of the single market, EC securities regulation is thus based on the single market legislative competences, both the general enabling clauses for the single market and the competence granted in respect of the free-movement guarantees which anchor the single market. For the most part, securities regulation rules have been based on the free movement and barrier removal-related competences set out in Article 44(2)(g) EC (directives designed to co-ordinate the safeguards required by Member States of companies or firms for the protection of members and others), Article 47(2) EC and Article 55 EC (directives designed to co-ordinate Member States' rules on the taking up and pursuit of activities as self-employed persons) and in the two general single market competences, Article 94 EC (directives for the approximation of Member States' rules which directly affect the establishment or functioning of the common market) and Article 95 EC (measures for the approximation of Member States' rules which have as their object the establishment and functioning of the internal market).[12]

The grip exerted by the single market on the securities regulation regime has had an enormous impact on the shape of EC securities regulation; other EC policy areas such as environmental law and, albeit to a limited extent, consumer protection enjoy an existence independent of the single market. On a general level, the overwhelming preoccupation with integration has resulted in a certain philosophical bankruptcy across the regime concerning the underlying regulatory objectives being pursued by the common standards which underpin the single market. While EC securities regulation serves primarily as a lever to open the market-place, it also serves as the regulatory basis for many activities on the market-place. As is discussed throughout, in the rush to harmonize it is not always clear what, for example, underlying regulatory objectives are pursued by the harmonized rules such as the issuer disclosure or capital adequacy controls or whether the common standards should only correct market failures or serve other objectives. In this regard, EC securities regulation is grounded in pragmatism and dictated by market-access requirements rather than by any particular

---

[11] Under Art. 5 EC the Community must act within the limits of the powers conferred upon it by the Treaty and of the objectives assigned to it therein. The choice of legal basis for a measure must be based on objective factors amenable to judicial review: Case 45/86 *Commission v Council* (*Generalized Tariff Preferences*) [1987] ECR 1493.

[12] The residual competence, Art. 308 EC (which activates when action by the Community is necessary to attain, in the course of the operation of the common market, one of the objectives of the Community when the Treaty has not provided the necessary powers) has not played a role in the development of the regime to date.

attachment to the rights and wrongs of market regulation or any particular regulatory philosophy.

The single market focus has also shaped the substantive content of the regime. This is particularly evident in the investment services area, where the single market objective has resulted in a focus on the free movement of the investment firm and its market-access rights and on the stability of the integrated market; limited attention has been given to the proactive protection of the investor who accesses the market-place. Indeed, as a regulatory priority, the investor as a focus for protection has generally been secondary to the investment firm as a beneficiary of liberalization and as an agent for the construction of the internal market. Moreover, one of the themes which emerges strongly from EC securities regulation and which is considered throughout is that it is not entirely clear whether the single market competences on which the regime is based allow for the adoption of measures which seek to raise the level of regulation in order to protect investors or the market-place rather than simply to remove those divergences which are obstructing integration. It appears, however, as discussed throughout this book, that harmonization is increasingly being used for what might be called 'second-generation' purposes and, in particular, to generate investor confidence in the single market and protect the market-place against post-integration risks.

Whether or not the Treaty can sustain the demands which the developing regime is placing on it is in the hands of the Court of Justice which presides over Treaty basis questions. Two important themes emerge from the Court's jurisprudence which are significant for the securities regulation regime. First, the Court has revealed in the past a tendency to defer to the judgement of the Community legislature in respect of the appropriate method for regulating economically complex situations.[13] Secondly, in its seminal 2000 *Tobacco Advertising* ruling,[14] a decision with potentially seismic effects for the development of the securities regulation regime, the Court indicated its intention more aggressively to assert its review powers over the Treaty basis chosen by the Community institutions and its scepticism about the extent to which Treaty competences can be manipulated to accommodate Community action which is deemed necessary. In particular, its finding that, in principle, the single market competences do not confer a general power to regulate the single market may represent a formidable obstacle to the continued development of the regime beyond a market construction device towards a single market regulatory regime.

In addition to being based on a Treaty competence, EC securities regulation must also comply with the Treaty's subsidiarity principle which has

---

[13] Case C–233/94 *Germany v European Parliament and Council* [1997] ECR I–2405, para 56.
[14] Case C–376/98 *Germany v Parliament and Council* [2000] ECR I–8419.

brought about a major shift in EC policy-making and law-making. Set out in Article 5 EC, it provides that, even if the EC has competence to act, before it does so it must assess whether the objectives of the proposed action cannot be sufficiently achieved by the Member States and whether, by reason of its scale or effects, the proposed action can be better achieved by the Community.[15] Although the exact scope of the subsidiarity principle is shrouded in considerable obscurity, it is broadly designed to ensure that action is taken at the most appropriate level and that Community legislation is limited to what is essential.[16] While the regulation of pan-EC actors such as financial conglomerates and pan-EC trading markets fits well with the subsidiarity principle, the principle has the potential to restrict the development of EC securities regulation in other areas, given that local markets tend to display particular cultural and structural features and that local regulators have an in-depth knowledge of their markets. Further, while on the supply side investment firms are increasingly operating on a pan-EC basis, the same is not true on the demand side, particularly with respect to retail investors. The principle has impacted on the form and content of legislation. The EC's currently defunct takeover regime, for example, started life as a detailed directive, but was recast as a framework, minimum standards directive in order, *inter alia*, to reflect the subsidiarity principle. Related to the subsidiarity principle, the proportionality principle (Article 5 EC) must also be respected. It provides that any action taken by the Community must not go beyond what is necessary to achieve the objectives of the Treaty.

Finally, the Charter of the Fundamental Rights of the European Union, adopted in 2000, is appearing as a nascent influence on securities regulation. Recent proposals for a public offer/admission to trading prospectus regime and for a market abuse regime state that their provisions respect the fundamental rights and principles set out in that document.[17] Its influence is likely to grow, given that all the indications are that the reach of EC securities regulation is to extend and that its strengthened supervision and enforcement requirements, in particular, will increasingly have implications for market participants.[18]

---

[15] The subsidiarity principle applies only to areas in which the Community does not exercise exclusive competence. On this question see Ch. IX sect. 12.2.2 below.

[16] The Commission has expressed the view that: '[t]he aim of the subsidiarity principle is to see to it that decisions are taken as close as possible to the citizen, a constant watch being kept to ensure that action taken at Community level is justified in the light of the means available to national, regional or local authorities . . . [it aims] to regulate the exercise of powers and to justify their use in a particular case': Commission Report to the European Council on the Adaptation of Existing Legislation to the Subsidiarity Principle. COM(93)545, 1.

[17] Proposal for a directive on the prospectus to be published when securities are offered to the public or admitted to trading: COM(2001)280, recital 32, and Proposal for a Directive on insider dealing and market manipulation: COM(2001)281, recital 24.

[18] Ch. VI of the Charter concerns the administration of justice.

I.3 HARMONIZATION

I.3.1 *Harmonization and Regulatory Competition*[19]

EC securities regulation has as its underlying objective the construction of a single securities and investment services market via the harmonization of Member States' rules. In principle and outside the EC context, harmonization of rules is, from the economist's perspective, regarded as justified where it is necessary to correct a market failure which extends beyond national boundaries and cannot be corrected by action by individual States. Typical market failures include protectionist barriers, regulatory costs,[20] and externalities which are generated by wellbeing-influencing effects occurring in one State as a result of an activity which is regulated in another State. In the securities regulation sphere, harmonization is typically regarded as justified where markets interact such that intermediaries, investors, and transactions move between them, leading to the potential for cross-border externalities such as fraud[21] and systemic risk.[22] The cost and market-access obstructions generated by securities regulation barriers, as well as the regulatory concerns provoked by cross-border activity, have not only led the EC to take action but have also triggered international moves towards harmonization as participants in the international securities markets increasingly seek access to new markets.[23] While harmonization should deliver a clear regulatory environment in which economic actors can operate with a degree of certainty about which rules apply, harmonization of standards requires international agreement and can be a slow process which may result in the adoption of standards which, given the pace of developments in securities markets, rapidly become obsolete. It also has the potential to restrict regulatory developments which are typically incubated at national level and to limit the extent to which markets can tailor their regimes to reflect different market participant

---

[19] There is a considerable literature on this question and on the relationship between harmonization and regulatory competition. See, eg, Bratton, W, McCahery, J, Picciotto, S, and Scott C (eds), *International Regulatory Competition and Coordination. Perspectives in Economic Regulation in Europe and the United States* (1996).

[20] See HM Treasury's 2000 Report, *Completing a Dynamic Single European Financial Services Market: A Catalyst for Economic Prosperity for Citizens and Business Across the EU* (HM Treasury, July 2000), para 7.

[21] Bentson, G, 'Regulation of Stock Trading: Private Exchanges Versus Government Agencies' (1997) 83 *Va L Rev.* 1501, 1506.

[22] Davis, E, 'Problems of Banking Regulation—An EC Perspective' in Goodhart, C (ed), *The Emerging Framework of Financial Regulation* (1998) 533, 547.

[23] IOSCO (the International Organization of Securities Commissions) is the primary actor in the international harmonization of standards process. The influential US Securities and Exchange Commission (the SEC) is also in favour of international harmonization between regulatory systems: Policy Statement of the Securities and Exchange Commission on the Regulation of International Securities Markets, SEC Exchange Act Release No 6807 (1988).

and transaction profiles. More generally, economic theory teaches that harmonization, like law-making, is vulnerable to regulatory capture or to the demands of the most vocal and influential interest groups. In the EC context, the problem of subsidiarity also arises. An alternative does exist. In principle, the barrier-removing objectives pursued by harmonization can also be achieved through a regulatory competition between States.[24] The regulatory competition model is premised on regulatory arbitrage. This is the assumption that, where regimes differ, consumers will choose products/services which meet their price and quality requirements, but which originate from a State with a regulatory regime that is more efficient and less costly than the domestic regime, over domestic products/services produced under the less efficient domestic regime. Firms may choose to relocate to another regime in response to these signals, while investors may choose to invest their capital in a State in which the regulatory regime reflects, from the investor's perspective, the optimal balance between risk and reward.[25] It has the advantages of easing the informational imbalance under which regulators labour (as compared to industry lobbying groups which benefit from inside knowledge) by allowing signals to be transmitted from the market-place to regulators, reducing the risk of regulatory capture and potentially resulting in the adoption of regulation which reflects a more diverse range of interests,[26] allowing regulatory innovation and the exercise of choice and checking the expansionist regulatory tendencies of government.[27] In the EC context it also appeals to the concept of subsidiarity by shifting the regulatory focus from the centre to the Member States. In the securities regulation sphere, support for regulatory competition[28] is often based on the assumption that it produces regulation which is more sensitive to investors' needs.

[24] See, eg, Kay, J, and Vickers, J, 'Regulatory Reform: An Appraisal' in Majone, G. (ed), *Deregulation or Re-regulation. Regulatory Reform in Europe and the United States* (1990) 242. Regulatory competition has been defined as 'the alteration of national regulation in response to the actual or expected impact of internationally mobile goods, services or factors of national economic activity': Sun, J-M, and Pelkmans, J, 'Regulatory Competition in the Single Market' (1995) 33 *JCMS* 67, 68.

[25] Snell, J, and Andenas, M, 'Exploring the Outer Limits—Restrictions on the Free Movement of Goods and Services' (1999) 10 *EBLRev* 252, 257.

[26] See Bratton, W, McCahery, J, Picciotto, S, and Scott, C, 'Introduction: Regulatory Competition and Institutional Evolution' in Bratton *et al.*, n 19 above, 1, 14: '[g]iven mobility of people and factors [of production], the imposition of costly and restrictive interest group legislation in one jurisdiction benefits a neighbouring jurisdiction with a less costly regime. Individuals and factors of production will vote with their feet, migrating to the less costly jurisdiction. They thereby affect lawmakers' incentives, making inefficient wealth transfers to favoured groups less attractive than regulations that enhance the wealth of the larger population' (references omitted).

[27] See Sun and Pelkmans n 24 above, 82.

[28] See Mahoney, P, 'The Exchange as Regulator' (1997) 83 *Va L Rev.* 1453, Romano, R, 'Empowering Investors: A Market Approach to Securities Regulation' (1998) 107 *YLJ* 2359 and Choi, S, and Guzman, A, 'Portable Reciprocity: Rethinking the International Reach of Securities Regulation' (1998) 71 *So. Cal. L Rev.* 903.

Among the problems generated by regulatory competition are the disadvantages of an uncertain regulatory environment, the risk that protectionist barriers will remain in place, and difficulties concerning the level to which competition drives regulation: the 'race to the bottom'/'race to the top' conundrum. In general, it appears that securities regulation competition tends not to result in a race to the bottom or the setting of standards at an inadequate level, given that market participants tend to favour balanced systems of regulation which support market stability and do not deter investors.[29] It may be, however, that competition in this area is more likely to create a regulatory model which consists of different regimes which tailor their levels of regulation in order to attract different types of securities and investment services business.[30] Effective regulatory competition is, however, dependent on a number of factors, including the mobility of market participants and their ability to choose regulatory regimes, the extent to which regulators can decipher signals from market participants, and the absence of market failures which require intervention in the form of harmonized common standards. The respective merits and drawbacks of harmonization and regulatory competition as single market construction and barrier removal mechanisms vary according to the regulatory sector in question:[31] regulatory competition in the investment services area, for example, raises market-wide systemic or system-wide stability concerns, given that market problems which arise in one Member State may spill over and destabilize the market-place in another. The implications of harmonization/regulatory competition for the different components of EC securities regulation are discussed further in the relevant chapters.[32]

I.3.2 *Integration Devices*

The devices which the EC has used to remove regulatory obstacles via harmonization and the extent to which it has embraced regulatory competition also vary across the securities regulation regime as a whole.[33] The earliest

---

[29] See, eg, Ch. VI sect. 6.4 below on the investment services area.

[30] In the context of issuer disclosure see Choi and Guzman, n 28 above.

[31] See the discussion in Hopt, K, 'Company Law in the European Union: Harmonisation and/or Subsidiarity?' (1999) 1 *ICCLJ* 41, 50–2.

[32] For a broadly based critique of harmonization and regulatory competition in the EC context see Woolcock, S, 'Competition Among Rules in the Single European Market' in Bratton *et al.*, n 19, 289 and Sun and Pelkmans, n 24, both of which support a complementary rather than an antagonistic relationship between the two models.

[33] On the various harmonization methods which have been used in the construction of the single market see the analysis in Slot, P, 'Harmonisation' (1996) 21 *ELRev* 378, 382–7. Among the methods highlighted are: definition of law and policy at Community level; total harmonization (where no derogations from the harmonized rules are allowed); optional harmonization (in which an option is given whether the Member State applies its own rules or the harmonized rules domestically); partial harmonization (where the harmonized rules apply only

securities regulation measures (in the issuer disclosure area) harmonized at a high level of detail and sought to remove obstacles to integration by rendering Member States' regimes equivalent. As discussed further in Chapters II and IV, this approach was not successful largely due to the negotiating difficulties represented by detailed measures and the discretion given to the Member States in implementing the harmonized rules as a result of the derogations and options which these measures contained. A new approach to barrier removal was followed in the wake of the Court of Justice's groundbreaking judgment in *Cassis de Dijon*[34] in which it stated that products legally in circulation in one Member State were to be admitted to other Member States without being required to meet additional regulatory requirements. Member States were, in other words, subject to a 'mutual recognition' rule, or required to recognize the regulatory regimes of other Member States. Member States could, however, impose those requirements which could be classified as 'mandatory requirements', such as consumer protection rules. The single market harmonization project as a whole then switched to the harmonization of these mandatory requirements or public interest rules.

As far as EC securities regulation is concerned, mutual recognition, combined with harmonization of rules at a minimum level and the allocation of primary regulatory control for integrated market activities to the home Member State (very broadly the Member State in which the regulated party is resident or registered) is the touchstone.[35] In principle, mutual recognition levers open the single market once the regulated entity has complied with the minimum harmonized standards which are imposed by the entity's home Member State; costly duplications of regulation are thus avoided. These standards are designed to ensure the stability of the market-place, and, albeit to a lesser extent, the protection of investors and support mutual recognition as Member States can be confident in the regulatory standards applied by each other. While not imposing full harmonization, standards which are harmonized at a minimum level allow a degree of regulatory competition (as to the desirability of the Member State in question as a primary regulator or home Member State) above the minimum level and accommodate flexibility, innovation, and, of particular importance in the EC context,

to cross-border transactions); minimum harmonization (in which minimum rules are set at EC level but Member States may adopt more demanding requirements—market access is protected either by the free movement guarantees or by a mutual recognition clause in the directive); alternative harmonization which allows Member States to choose between alternative methods of harmonization; and mutual recognition of national rules and of national controls.

[34] Case 120/78 *Rewe-Zentral AG v Bundesmonopolverwaltung für Branntwein* (*Cassis de Dijon*) [1979] ECR 649.

[35] The first example of this harmonization model is the 1985 Directive which harmonized the rules applicable to collective-investment schemes: Directive 85/611/EEC on the coordination of laws, regulations and administrative provisions relating to undertakings for collective investment in transferable securities [1985] OJ L375/3.

local market sensitivity. This level of harmonization also places a limit on prejudicial regulatory competition. Regulatory competition is thus built into the harmonization regime which acknowledges, through the mutual recognition system, that national regimes can differ, but minimum standards and home country control place a brake on competition, while harmonization and mutual recognition prise open the single market. This structure and, in particular, the home Member State control anchor component demand considerable levels of co-operation and communication between supervisors across the single market; supervisory co-ordination requirements are thus built into the harmonizing directives in this area. This harmonization device has determined the shape of EC securities regulation, and its implications are discussed further throughout the book in the context of the specific areas of regulation in which it has been used. Indeed, a recurring theme of EC securities regulation is how the integration or harmonization device used has impacted on the substantive regulation adopted for the integrated market.

While the Commission initially promoted this highly influential integration device in its 1985 White Paper on the Internal Market,[36] it is, as outlined above, a creature and creation of the Court of Justice. As such, the mutual recognition of regulation principle applies across Member States' markets regardless of whether harmonization has occurred, and should, in theory, ensure that the securities and investment services market-place is always wedged open. In practice, notwithstanding the harmonization process and the mutual recognition principle, securities regulation in the EC is currently made up of a complex web of common EC rules and diverging national regimes, with the latter continuing to entangle market participants seeking access to the integrated market-place. Persistent obstructions to integration exist not only because EC securities regulation does not extend across the entire complex universe of securities regulation rules, with the result that home country control and mutual recognition are not possible in a number of areas. The mutual recognition principle which should support market access in the absence of harmonization is also subject to exceptions, in particular the ability of Member States to impose public interest legislation on non-national regulated entities.[37] As a result, in the absence of harmonization (or where the level of harmonization does not support full mutual recognition), regulatory obstructions and divergences can arise. Large areas of securities regulation remain unharmonized at present, and in those areas access to the integrated market remains vulnerable to obstructions caused by the imposition of general good or public interest rules by the Member States, whether driven by protectionist or innocent impulses. Even

---

[36] Completing the Internal Market. COM(85)310.

[37] See further Ch. VI sect. 4.6 below which discusses the general good doctrine which allows Member States to plead certain interests to justify the imposition of their rules on regulated entities from other Member States despite the mutual recognition principle.

in those areas which are harmonized divergences persist as Member States implement often opaque rules according to their own national traditions.[38] Accordingly, while EC securities regulation has developed sufficiently as a harmonized regime, such that it can be examined as a distinct market regulation system, the regulation of securities markets across the EC remains fragmented outside this central pillar. Major reforms are currently under way to accelerate the integration process and, in particular, to move the regime more completely towards home Member State control, driven in part by the development of the Internet and the impossibility of subjecting online activities to a host Member State system. The failure of EC securities regulation to date to integrate national securities and investment services markets and their regulatory systems more completely does not of itself condemn the regime as a failure. For certain Member States, the substantive regime which has emerged from the harmonization process has resulted in the adoption of new, enhanced regulatory standards.[39]

I.4 FORMS OF LEGISLATION

Under Article 249 EC, binding EC rules can take three forms: regulations, directives, and decisions. Regulations are self-executing, in that they apply in the Member States once adopted and do not depend on further action at Member State level. In part due to their intrusive and prescriptive nature and the negotiating problems which they can generate, they have not featured widely in EC securities regulation.[40]

Directives are binding as regards the result to be achieved but leave the choice of form and method of implementation to the national authorities. They will contain an implementation date, which will vary according to the severity of the changes required to existing rules or the new rules demanded and the degree of market upheaval which might be expected, by which the

[38] One leading commentator has observed that 'the overall picture of securities regulation at EU level is a partial body of common concepts and regulatory patterns, while a large part of the field remains uncovered, and considerable differences subsist in the rules ultimately applicable, each State having translated the European rules more or less according to its own fancy': Wymeersch, E, *The Harmonisation of Securities Trading in Europe in the New Trading Environment*, WP 2000-16, Working Paper Series of the Financial Law Institute, Universiteit Gent, 2.

[39] eg, before it adopted the national rules required to implement the ISD (the Stock Exchange Act, 1995 and the Investment Intermediaries Act, 1995), Ireland did not have a comprehensive system for the regulation of investment intermediaries. Insider-dealing and public offer disclosure rules have also been driven by harmonization. This outcome reflects the thesis put forward by Buxbaum and Hopt that 'harmonisation—if conceived broadly as an instrument of European legal and economic policy—gets its legitimation less from its results in integration than from the substantive content and effect of the Community law in which it results': n 4 above, 212.

[40] They do appear in EC company law. One high profile example would be the 2001 Council Regulation on a Statute for a European Company (the Societas Europaea), adopted on 8 Oct 2001.

obligations must be implemented by the Member States.[41] The directive is the dominant legislative mechanism used in the securities regulation sphere. This reflects in part the Treaty competences on which EC securities regulation has been based, which mandate the use of directives in certain cases.[42] More generally, however, directives allow for greater flexibility and for a degree of discretion to be conferred on Member States and can, as a result, more easily slot EC obligations into national regimes and structures. In the politically sensitive sphere of market regulation their split competence structure allows room for the exercise of Member State sovereignty.[43] In this respect, they respond well to the dictates of the subsidiarity principle. Conversely, as their effectiveness depends on implementation by Member States, their use has caused problems for the integration project. Harmonization via directives runs the risk that regulatory divergences will remain in place. This is particularly the case where directives give Member States discretion on how to apply provisions or grant options as regards which rules are to be implemented, albeit often in the interests of reaching agreement on contentious issues or in order to respond to particular Member States' market structures and regulatory cultures.[44] Serious divergences can also follow where their provisions are opaque or vague[45] and implementing measures vary as a result across the Member States.[46] This tendency

[41] The implementation date of the proposed and now failed directive on takeovers, eg, emerged as a bone of contention, given that some of its provisions, notably the mandatory bid rule and the prohibition-on-defensive-action rule, required significant changes in certain Member States. One element of the doomed compromise on the measure which was hammered out just weeks before its final collapse in July 2001 was an extension of the implementation deadline to 4 years and the grant of an additional 5th year to implement the defensive-action prohibition. Implementation deadlines will often contain carve-outs for Member States which are thought to need additional time. It was feared that the liberalization of stock exchange access in the wake of the adoption of the ISD, eg, would generate overcapacity in certain Member States' markets. Those Member States that did not permit direct access to stock exchanges by credit institutions, but required them to use a specialized subsidiary and which, on adoption of the ISD, were required to remove this restriction were given additional time to implement the ban on direct access restrictions.

[42] The original internal market competence, Art. 94 EC, for example, requires that harmonization be carried out via directives (Art. 95 EC which has now replaced Art. 94 EC in practice as the dominant internal market competence refers to the adoption of 'measures'), as does Art. 47(2) EC on which the investment services regime has been based. Similarly Art. 44(2)(g) EC which has served as the primary basis for the early official listing and disclosure measures requires that co-ordination of the safeguards required by Member States of companies for the protection of the interests of members and others be carried out via directives.

[43] Buxbaum and Hopt, n 4 above, 233.

[44] The public offers issuer-disclosure regime has been particularly problematic in this regard.

[45] Examples include the failure of the takeover regime to address the concept of 'control' and the omission of a definition of 'public offer' from the public offer prospectuses regime. In both cases, agreement proved impossible. See further Chs IV and XIV below.

[46] The Court of Justice is the final arbiter on the meaning of Community legislation. To date, it has had little opportunity to examine the securities regulation regime, although that situation may change, given that, as discussed in section 7 below, the regime is set to increase dramatically in scope.

towards divergences is exacerbated by the general lack of guiding principles
in EC securities regulation; as is discussed further throughout this book EC
securities regulation measures are often unclear about the objectives which
they serve beyond market integration or the targets of the regulation which
they impose, both of which have a bearing on how rules are transposed in
practice.[47] Minimum standards directives, particularly those adopted or proposed in the wake of the institutionalization of the subsidiarity principle in
the Maastricht Treaty can produce a degree of harmonization so limited that
the need for the directive can be questioned. The charge of ineffective and
inadequate harmonization was levelled by the UK at the proposed Takeover
Directive, for example, which was recast in 1996 from its original incarnation as a detailed measure as a framework directive in light of the subsidiarity principle.[48] Difficulties have also arisen where directives are overly
detailed and give Member States limited room as regards their implementation and become becalmed as a result in the negotiation process. Most seriously perhaps, Member States may simply fail to implement directives or
implement them incorrectly.[49] Should this arise, the Commission, in its role
as guardian of the Treaties, can take enforcement action against the erring
Member State under Article 226 EC which can result in the imposition of
fines on that Member State. In addition, the judicially created direct effect
doctrine permits market participants who may be prejudiced by a Member
State's action to rely on the rights contained in non-implemented or incorrectly implemented directives in their national courts once the implementation date has passed. Reliance on rights contained in directives is dependent,
however, on the rights in question being clear, precise, and unconditional
and on the rights being relied on against the State or part of the State (directives have direct effect only vertically and do not apply to horizontal relationships between individuals).[50] The enforcement structure has also been
bolstered by the State liability doctrine which allows persons to sue a
Member State in damages for failure to implement or incorrect implementa-

[47] Although the Lamfalussy law-making model (see section 7 below), which includes a 'conceptual framework of overarching principles' by reference to which EC securities regulation proposals should be measured, may improve matters in this regard: Final Report of the Committee
of Wise Men on the Regulation of European Securities Markets, Feb 2001 (the Lamfalussy
Report), 22. Since the adoption of the FSAP in 1999 (section 7), a more considered approach
to the objectives of securities regulation can be observed in new proposals and initiatives, with
the Commission increasingly grappling with concepts such as the market failure doctrine,
investor protection, differentiated protection between retail and professional investors, and
interventionist versus disclosure-based regulation.
[48] See Ch. XIV below.
[49] This feature led the Lamfalussy Report to encourage greater reliance on regulations which
are not subject to the risks of the implementation process: n 47 above, 26.
[50] Treaty provisions, by contrast, can have direct effect vertically and horizontally depending on the legal obligation imposed.

tion of a directive where damage has been sustained as a result.[51] Notwith-standing these checks, Member States have a patchy record in implement-ing directives correctly and on time. Although reliance on directives for market regulation harmonization was recommended in the Code of Conduct,[52] as the integration project gathered momentum, particularly after the adoption of the ISD, it became clear that inconsistencies and delays in the implementation process were contributing to the poor pace of market integration.[53] The extent to which directives provide for Member State dis-cretion, however, is likely to change significantly in the future, following the adoption by the EC, in principle at least, of a new model for proposing and adopting securities regulation measures which will significantly increase the level of harmonization.[54]

The final form of binding legislation, decisions, are binding on those to whom they are addressed, often individuals and legal persons, and have limited application in this area. Non-binding recommendations have been used on occasion in EC securities regulation, the most prominent example being the Code of Conduct which contains a comprehensive set of general principles governing activities in the securities markets, many of which have subsequently re-appeared in binding directives, but was, largely, ignored by the Member States.[55]

The process by which these measures are adopted has exerted a decisive and often prejudicial influence on their content. Ultimately, securities regu-lation measures must past through a legislative process which requires, to varying degrees depending on the procedures followed (which depend on the Treaty competence used), agreement between the Member States on the necessity for and scope of the measures. Differences in legal traditions and market structure (such as the extent to which universal banks or specialized investment firms operate on the market-place and the approaches markets take to the transparency of trading), varying emphases on the role of

---

[51] Cases C-6, C-9/90 *Francovich and Others v Italy* [1991] ECR I-5357, Joined Cases C-46/93, C-48/93 *Brasserie du Pêcheur SA v Germany* and *R v Secretary of State for Transport ex parte Factortame Ltd and others* [1996] ECR I-1029.

[52] It stated that harmonization via directives was the only method 'capable of attaining the objective of true European integration': n 2 above, Explanatory Memorandum, para I(4).

[53] It has been observed in the company law context that '[o]nly a small part of European company law is made up of genuine European company law. By far the larger part is deriva-tively European: it is European company law by virtue of transformation. This is true of all the company law directives.' Hopt, n 31 above, 43. A similar point can be made in respect of EC securities regulation, revealing the dependence of the market integration and barrier removing objectives of the regime on the implementation process.

[54] See the discussion of the Lamfalussy Report in section 7 below.

[55] See Hopt, K, 'The European Insider Dealing Directive' in Hopt, K, and Wymeersch, E (eds), *European Insider Dealing* (1991) 132. Recommendations have been relied on more exten-sively in the banking sphere. The Deposit Guarantee Directive (Directive 94/19/EC OJ (1994) L135/5), for example, originated in a 1987 Commission Recommendation, as did the large exposures regime.

market finance, the comparative competitive positions of national markets, varying perspectives on investor protection and corporate governance, as well as old-fashioned political tensions and rivalries, can stymie the progress of legislation or produce legislation which is overly complex.[56] Chapter XV discusses the complex inter-institutional procedures under which EC securities regulation measures are adopted and describes how the delays, political tensions, inertia, and compromises to which they can be subject have weakened the securities regulation regime.

I.5 REGULATORY DEVICES

The regulatory devices traditionally employed by securities regulation appear in the EC regime, even if their use must be looked at through the lens of harmonization and market integration. As discussed throughout, disclosure is the dominant information-based regulatory mechanism for many securities regulation regimes and appears across EC securities regulation. Its *locus classicus* is in the issuer-disclosure sphere, but it is also relied on in the collective investment schemes, investment services, securities-trading markets, market abuse, and (now defunct) takeover regimes. It is likely to increase in importance given that the regime as a whole appears to be moving towards greater reliance on market discipline as a form of control.[57] The regime also relies on more interventionist controls, however, particularly in the investment services regime, in order to set the foundations for market integration via mutual recognition of investment services providers.[58] The emphasis to date has been on the imposition of prudential standards, notably capital adequacy standards and organizational requirements, which safe-

---

[56] The Lamfalussy Report laid part of the blame for the delays in adopting securities regulation measures at the door of the Council 'where there is far too often a tendency to add unnecessary levels of complexity to straightforward Commission proposals (often in an attempt to try to fit 15 sets of national legislation into one Community framework': n 47 above, 14.

[57] eg, the combination of disclosure and market discipline has been canvassed as a supplementary device for managing and monitoring the soundness and risk management policies of investment firms (Commission Services' *Second Consultative Document on Review of Regulatory Capital for Credit Institutions and Investment Firms* (the 2001 Regulatory Capital Review), MARKT/1000/01) while disclosure of transgressions to the market-place has been relied on as a form of deterrent in the Commission's 2001 Market Abuse Proposal, n 17 above.

[58] In this regard the regime differs from US securities regulation which is largely based on disclosure devices (although it does impose more interventionist controls via the Securities Exchange Act, 1934 and the Investment Company Act, 1940 in particular) in that it does not give disclosure the same totemic status. For a comparison of the regulatory devices used in the EC and the USA see Austin, R, 'Commentary 2 on Report on Supervising EU Capital Markets' in Hopt, K, Buxbaum, R, Hertig, G, and Hirsch, A (eds), *European Economic and Business Law* (1996) 209-10 who has noted that the SEC regards itself as a 'disclosure regulator'. The same focus is not apparent in the EC regime; neither is the US level of sophistication as to the objectives of disclosure, particularly in the issuer disclosure sphere, reflected in the EC regime as is discussed further in Ch. IV below.

guard the stability of the integrated market-place. Protective mechanisms (such as conduct-of-business rules), directed to the relationship between the investment firm and the investor, have been less in evidence, in a reflection of the focus on market integration via the free movement of the investment firm and the stability of the new market-place.

A number of trends can be observed in this area. Protection of the retail investor who accesses the integrated market-place and is an agent for integration is emerging, after many years in the doldrums, as a major preoccupation of EC securities regulation. Protection of the integrated market-place against post-integration stability risks such as those posed by increased cross-border activity, and the development of financial conglomerates can also be identified as an influence on the regulatory devices used across the regime.

I.6 THE ROOTS OF EC SECURITIES REGULATION

Broadly speaking, EC securities regulation has evolved in three stages.

In phase 1, efforts were directed towards the construction of a single deep and liquid securities market which issuers across the EC could access for their financing needs. The regulatory focus was on harmonization (via detailed, equivalence-promoting directives initially and subsequently via minimum harmonization and mutual recognition) of Member States' rules on the admission to official listing process and on the disclosure required when an issuer makes a public offer or officially lists securities. In phase 2, attention shifted to the construction of a single market in investment services. The regulatory touchstones here are mutual recognition, minimum standards, and home country control, mediated by the subsidiarity principle which encouraged the use of framework measures, while the preoccupation of the common standards adopted is prudential regulation and the stability of the integrated market-place. A number of core areas were not addressed, however, and others were not subject to harmonization at a level sufficient to support home country control and mutual recognition. Phase 3, which is currently unfolding, is dramatically increasing the scope and sophistication of EC securities regulation as concerted and urgent efforts are being made to complete the single market in securities and investment services. In this phase, securities regulation has assumed a priority it has hitherto not enjoyed on the EC's agenda. This is evidenced not only by a series of path-breaking reports but also by its regular appearance in the conclusions of the biannual European Council meetings which have prioritized the completion of the single market in financial services generally and in investment services and securities in particular. Phase 3 is also distinguished from the earlier phases in that regulatory change is being dictated in many cases by dramatic market practice, technological, and industry-structure developments. In this phase, the considerable gaps in the harmonized rule structure are being filled and earlier measures which have not had the hoped-for success in removing regulatory barriers are being revised. The form in which harmonization is achieved is still evolving: it does seem clear that a more complete transition to home country control will be the outcome of this phase and that mutual recognition will be more fully realized across the single market. The outstanding feature of this phase, however, is the focus on the manner in which common standards are adopted; the new approach, based on a hierarchy of norms principle involving harmonization occurring at two levels (general framework principles and detailed technical measures), amounts to a sea change from the earlier phases, as significant as the initial move towards mutual recognition. Finally, in terms of substantive regulation, the focus has become broader in this phase. In particular, investor protection and protective regulation generally have moved up the agenda to assume the position previously enjoyed by prudential regulation in phase 2. Market integrity, or the protection of the market against abusive practices or a lack of transparency, is also receiving considerably greater attention.

The 1966 Segré Report[59] marks the first significant foray by the EC into securities regulation. It highlighted the poor condition of the EC capital or securities market[60] and the benefits which could follow from the integration of capital markets, identified the obstacles to integration, chief among them the imposition by Member States of diverging and duplicative rules on market participants and proposed remedial measures, notably with respect to the capital-raising process and the harmonization of disclosure standards.[61] Subsequent developments took place on two fronts: the liberalization of capital movements (section I.8) and the harmonization of Member State rules.[62] Although the first securities regulation proposal was presented in 1972 (the proposal which became the listing particulars regime as late as 1980),[63] the Code of Conduct represents the EC's first legislative attempt at setting common standards for an integrated securities and investment ser-

---

[59] Report by a Group of Experts Appointed by the EEC Commission, *The Development of a European Capital Market* (1966). The findings of the Report are discussed throughout this book.

[60] '[Community] savers generally prefer to hold cash or short term assets and it would be difficult to alter that liquidity preference radically in the short term' and '[i]n several Community countries, the equity markets are suffering from a shortage of available capital and from a rather unsatisfactory pattern of business demand for capital . . . business firms often find it hard to obtain risk capital and at the same time the investing public does not always find attractive opportunities on the market': ibid, 17 and 27.

[61] For an overview see Dalhuisen, J, *The New UK Securities Legislation and the EC 1992 Program* (1989) 55.

[62] See Wouters, J, 'EC Harmonisation of National Rules Concerning Securities Offerings, Stock Exchange Listing and Investment Services: An Overview' 4 (1993) *EBLRev.* 199.

[63] [1972] OJ C131/61.

vices market-place. It was followed by the first generation of admission to official listing and disclosure directives, adopted between 1979 and 1982,[64] which sought to construct a single securities market in which issuers could raise capital. This regime focused on stock exchanges and, in particular, on the official listing process, and did not cover public offers of securities.

1985 saw the presentation of the Commission's White Paper on the internal market which set out a programme of measures designed to deliver the single market by 1992 and the Commission's intention to accelerate the harmonization process by means of the mutual recognition/minimum harmonization/home Member State control device. The White Paper's discussion of the investment services and securities sector was linked to a general examination of the financial services area in which the Commission found that 'liberalisation of financial services, linked to capital movements, will represent a major step towards Community financial integration and the widening of the Internal Market'.[65] In the securities/investment services sector the Commission called for the completion of the work which 'still remains to be done to ensure that securities markets operate satisfactorily and in the best interests of investors' and, specifically, for the development of a 'European securities market system' which would provide a Community-wide trading system for securities of international interest.[66] It also broadened the focus of EC securities regulation from its concentration on issuers and the official listing process by including in its 1992 programme the adoption of four measures, two of which took the regime beyond the issuer market access context: the collective investment scheme regime (by 1985, adopted on schedule); a public offer prospectus regime (by 1988, adopted in 1989); a regime concerning the information to be published on the acquisition of major holdings (by 1988, adopted on schedule); and an investment advisers regime (by 1989, adopted as the ISD in 1993). 1985 thus also saw the adoption of the framework for the single market in collective investment schemes. With this regime, the EC gave the passport device, which has come to dominate EC securities regulation, its first airing. The collective investment scheme regime was based on authorization of the collective investment scheme by the home Member State in accordance with the regime's common standards and the conferral of a regulatory passport on the authorized scheme to operate across the EC. It was followed by the second generation of disclosure directives (adopted between 1986 and 1994) which grafted the mutual recognition concept on to the harmonization via

---

[64] A measure harmonizing the disclosure required on the acquisition or disposal of major shareholdings was adopted in 1988.

[65] White Paper on the Internal Market, n 36 above, 27. The White Paper is discussed further in Ch. VI sect. 5.1.3 below.

[66] Ibid, n 36 above, para 197. The evolution of the EC towards a single securities trading market is discussed in Ch. XI sect. 8 below.

the equivalence of standards approach of the first generation measures and introduced harmonized disclosure rules concerning the public offer of securities. These developments moved the issuer disclosure regime closer to becoming a common disclosure system that would enable an issuer to raise capital across the EC in reliance on one integrated disclosure document that could be used in official listing applications and public offers.[67] The scope of EC securities regulation expanded to include the pathology of securities regulation in 1989 with the adoption of an insider dealing regime which was designed to protect the integrity of and confidence in the new market-place. In 1993, after protracted negotiations, EC securities regulation took a major step forward with the adoption of the cornerstone investment services regime. In 1997 this regime was bolstered by the adoption of a directive which required that investor compensation schemes be established in all Member States and setting out common rules. By 1997, which can be seen as the approximate end of phase 2, the harmonized structure contained the basic elements of securities regulation such that a common core of basic rules applied in most Member States. A network of competent authorities had also been established, designed to supervise the harmonized rules and to provide a pan-EC co-operation system on which the supervision of the integrated market could be based. Nonetheless, the regulatory structure supporting the integration process was inadequate: large areas of regulation remained unharmonized (market manipulation, conduct-of-business regulation, and a more detailed consideration of the regulation of securities trading markets, to name but three areas); the existing regimes were deficient in a number of respects (for example, the disclosure regime's mutual recognition structure which was shot through with exceptions and derogations and never worked properly in practice, leaving issuers exposed to the costs represented by varying national regimes); implementation of directives was inconsistent and often badly delayed; and supervisory co-operation was underdeveloped. All in all, the signs were already there that the regime would be ill-equipped to cope with the enormous demands which would be placed on it imminently, notably: the arrival of monetary union, the Internet explosion, and the upsurge in cross-border activity which followed in the wake of these two developments and which was aided by technological developments in the securities-trading environment and market restructuring (best evidenced by the growth of financial conglomerates and the arrival of competition in the securities-trading market environment).

The internal market in securities and investment services is now developing organically at a rate that poses significant challenges for the securities regulation structure. Clearly, the euro removes currency risk and enhances price transparency within the euro zone. It is also leading to

---

[67] As discussed in Ch. IV below, this objective has not been achieved.

changes in investment patterns as investors shift to pan-EC sectoral rather than Member State-based investment patterns. New technologies, particularly the Internet, are increasing the ease with which cross-border investment services can be offered and are also enhancing the dissemination of market information and access to trading, bringing greater numbers of investors to their own national markets and, increasingly, to the integrated market-place. In a related development, technological developments with respect to alternative trading systems (or ATSs) are changing the shape of Community trading by carrying out functions previously the preserve of traditional exchanges, thereby generating competition, reducing transaction costs, and facilitating cross-border trading. Consolidation in the investment services industry on an intra- and inter-Member State basis is continuing, as is the growth of financial conglomerates which offer investment services and securities services along with banking or insurance services. The most high-profile consolidation is arguably taking place between stock exchanges where pan-EC alliances and mergers are taking place on a dramatic scale. Demographic developments and changes in how State-supported pensions schemes are funded are provoking massive growth in the collective investment scheme or investment fund industry and increasing retail investor activity on the market-place. Finally, and perhaps most significantly, market-based finance is beginning to reverse the traditional dominance of bank-based finance in the EC as issuers turn to the securities markets for their financing needs to a much greater extent than previously. All of these developments are discussed further in the following chapters with respect to the different areas of EC securities regulation with which they are most closely implicated.

I.7 THE FSAP AND THE LAMFALUSSY REPORT

Whether the regulatory structure that was in place after phases 1 and 2 would be able to support these greater levels of cross-border activity, respond to the regulatory challenges raised by market developments, and deliver securities and investment services market integration, or whether it would instead hamper integration and frustrate market developments began to come under increasingly closer scrutiny from the end of the 1990s. This period has also produced a considerably more sophisticated articulation from the EC institutions of why the integration of securities and investment services markets should be promoted; the market integration measures adopted up to this stage have tended not to engage in an analysis of why market integration (or the market finance model, support for which is implicit in the securities market integration process) should be encouraged.

In recent years it has become clear that the single market in investment services and securities, which, as part of the single market for financial services generally, was regarded as being critical for growth and job creation, was incomplete. The immediate catalyst for what would be prove to be a tidal wave of reforms and consultations and for a focus of attention on securities regulation and EC securities markets at the highest policy-setting levels appears to have been the then imminent introduction of the euro, which was identified as creating a unique opportunity to equip the EU with a modern and efficient financial infrastructure and as posing new challenges for the regulatory structure of the internal market. Reflecting the UK's focus on financial services market integration as a mechanism for economic reform, the 1998 Cardiff European Council requested the Commission to prepare a framework for action for financial services which would ensure that the full benefits of the euro were realized with respect to financial services generally and that the stability and competitiveness of EU financial markets were ensured. The Commission duly issued a Communication later in 1998 on 'Financial Services Building a Framework for Action'.[68] The Communication emphasized the importance of integrating financial services markets generally, given the employment-generating potential of the financial services industry and the wider choices which would be made available to consumers and investors. More specifically, it found that efficient and transparent markets would optimize the allocation of capital and, by facilitating access to equity financing, would allow small and medium-sized companies to generate growth and employment opportunities. It found, however, that while some progress had been made, financial services markets generally remained segmented and cross-border provision of financial services, particularly in the retail sector, remained low. It highlighted a range of issues which needed to be addressed in order to 'equip the EU with financial markets capable of sustaining competitiveness and weathering financial instability'.[69] Two aspects of financial services market integration were highlighted: the construction of deep and liquid EC capital markets which would serve issuers and investors better and the removal of the remaining barriers to the cross-border supply of retail financial services in order to ensure consumer choice while maintaining consumer confidence and a high level of consumer protection.[70] Five areas were identified for further action: an overhauling of the legislative apparatus in order to ensure more effective responses to regulatory challenges; a market-driven modernization of wholesale markets in order, in particular, to remove the remaining barriers (legal, administrative, and fiscal) to cross-border initial public offers and investment-related activities; completion on an incremental basis of the single

---

[68] COM(1998) 625 (the 1998 Communication).   [69] Ibid, p. 1b.
[70] Ibid, p. 1a.

market for retail financial products in which consumers would benefit from high levels of consumer protection as well as from increased competition and choice; review and clarification of the mechanisms for supervisory and regulatory co-operation; and creation of the general conditions for a fully integrated financial market including construction of an integrated infra-structure with respect to payments, stricter application of the Treaty rules on competition and State aid and progress on tax harmonization. Later in 1998, the Vienna European Council called for the translation of these objec-tives into a specific work programme. Construction of the work programme was undertaken by the newly constituted Financial Services Policy Group, which is comprised of representatives of the Ecofin Council ministers, the European Central Bank, and the Commission, and it was presented by the Commission in its 1999 Communication, 'Implementing the Financial Services Action Plan'.[71] The work programme, or Financial Services Action Plan (FSAP), which should be completed with respect to securities and investment services markets by 2003, sets out a programme of forty-two measures which, if adopted, will radically change the shape of EC financial services and securities regulation. It is as significant for the single market in investment services and securities as the 1992 programme was for the sin-gle market generally. The FSAP's proposals recognize that deficiencies in the harmonized regime are blocking greater integration and are designed to plug the major gaps; in its discussion of the FSAP the Commission noted that although the single market in financial services generally had been under construction since the early 1960s, markets remained fragmented. It also found, however, that the introduction of the euro provided a 'unique win-dow of opportunity' to provide the EC with a modern financial structure in which the cost of capital and intermediation were kept at a minimum.[72] A second theme of the FSAP is the need to protect the market-place against the risks posed by greater integration, to meet the regulatory challenges posed by market developments and to ensure the protection of retail investors in the integrated market-place. The FSAP's investment services- and securities-related proposals (the FSAP generally is designed to serve as 'an aspirational programme for rapid progress towards a single financial market')[73] are grouped around four categories (wholesale markets, retail markets; prudential rules and supervision; and wider conditions for an opti-mal single financial market). They include: revising the ISD to ensure that its mutual recognition principles work more effectively, clarifying the con-duct of business regime which at present is unsatisfactory and results in duplications of regulation, and updating its securities trading market provi-sions to take into account market developments such as the growth of com-petition between markets and the arrival of ATSs; revising the disclosure

---

[71] COM(1999)232 (the FSAP).   [72] Ibid, 1.   [73] Ibid, 2.

regime so that a single prospectus can be used in cross-border capital raising; adopting a market abuse regime; revising the collective investment
scheme in order to update the investment restrictions rules; adopting a
takeover regime; adopting a common set of international accounting standards; addressing investor protection in the cross-border provision of investment services via measures covering, *inter alia*, the distance selling of
financial services; and enhancing co-operation between supervisors.
Together with the 1998 Communication, the FSAP is discussed in greater
detail throughout the text in relation to the specific impact of its proposals
on the various discrete components of EC securities regulation. Progress on
the FSAP is monitored regularly by the Commission in consultation with the
Financial Services Policy Group which issues a series of progress reports. The
2000 Lisbon European Council, the conclusions of which have been
described as bringing about a 'step change' in the movement towards
greater integration,[74] highlighted, in particular, the need for action on the
wholesale markets side, given the contribution they can make to economic
growth, and identified the widest possible access to investment capital on an
EU basis, elimination of barriers to investment in pension funds, further integration of government bond markets, enhancing comparability of companies' financial statements, and intensifying co-operation by regulators as
priority action areas. It also called for action on Internet-related measures,
such as the proposal on the distance selling of financial services.

    The Lisbon European Council also emphasized the crucial role played by
securities markets in generating growth and employment and identified
integration, efficiency, and stability as the benchmarks against which the
performance of EC securities markets should be assessed.[75] As outlined
above with respect to the FSAP and Commission's 1998 pre-FSAP
Communication, the link between economic growth and the integration of
securities and investment services markets regularly appears as the driving
factor behind the push to integrate securities and investment services
markets. In 2000, the Commission elaborated on the benefits of integration, stating that the pooling of national liquidity in an integrated market
would allow private-sector savings to be put to their most productive use
and, in particular, to serve as a complement to statutory pension schemes,
provide companies with a flexible and competitive alternative to bank borrowing, ensure that the potential for the competitive pricing of capital is
optimized by widening the pool of investors available and minimizing inter-

---

[74] Report from the Commission, Progress on *Financial Services. Second Report*
(COM(2000)336) (the Second Progress Report), 2.
[75] For a summary of the Presidency Conclusions see ibid, 1 and the Commission's
Communication on Upgrading the Investment Services Directive (the ISD Communication)
COM(2000)729, 5.

mediation and transaction costs, and, ultimately stimulate growth and job creation.[76]

While the FSAP sets out the substantive measures which must be adopted in order to complete the internal market in securities and investment services and respond to market developments and their related regulatory challenges in the internal market context, its fate, as far as its securities regulation measures are concerned, is bound up with the seminal Lamfalussy Report which was delivered in February 2001[77] and which is a landmark in the history of EC securities regulation. In July 2000 a Committee of Wise Men on the Regulation of European Securities Markets, chaired by Baron Alexandre Lamfalussy, was constituted by the Council in order to assess the current state of integration in the securities and investment services markets and the harmonized structure supporting it, to examine how the mechanisms for regulating the securities markets can best respond to developments such as stock exchange alliances and technological developments and to suggest proposals for adapting current practices in order to ensure greater convergence and co-operation on the markets. Its findings, which are discussed throughout this book, were a searing indictment of the inadequacy of the harmonized structure, its inability to cope with market developments and support greater integration, and the failure of EC legislative procedures to deliver regulation quickly and effectively. It warned that unless steps were taken to complete the regulatory structure and open the market-place and to revise the law-making process, 'economic growth, employment and prosperity will be lower, and competitive advantage will be lost to those outside the European Union. And the opportunity to complement and strengthen the role of the euro and to deepen European integration will be lost.'[78] By contrast, an integrated financial market would, subject to proper prudential safeguards and investor protection, allow capital and financial services to move freely across the single market, with the result on a micro-economic level that European businesses would be in a position to tap deep pools of capital for their financing activities, supplies of capital from EC savings would be matched by demand for capital

---

[76] Ibid, 5 and Second Progress Report, n 74 above, 3. See also the Initial Report of the Committee of Wise Men on the Regulation of European Securities Markets, Nov 2000 (the Initial Lamfalussy Report), which stated at 2 that '[a]n efficient regulatory process for financial services and capital markets is crucial . . . for successful economic reform, for boosting economic growth. Crucial for helping channel the high rate of European savings towards the corporate sector. Crucial for strengthening both the international competitiveness of the European Union in the global economy and for releasing its entrepreneurial potential. Crucial also for job creation and consumer protection'. More specifically, it identified at 4–7 the following benefits: higher returns on ordinary investors' savings in securities, whether directly or via collective investment schemes; enhanced financing opportunities for small and medium-sized companies, and the growth of venture capital funding; lower costs of capital for large companies; and a strengthening of competition and innovation.

[77] N 47 above.   [78] Ibid, 8.

from EC businesses, and consumers would be better able to purchase financial services and securities from the best suppliers. On a macro-economic
level, the Report pointed to the potential for an increase in the productivity
of capital and labour, stronger GDP growth, and enhanced job creation. The
Report found that the development of an integrated securities market was
being held back by a number of factors including: gaps in the harmonized
regulatory regime which were preventing the operation of mutual recognition; an inefficient regulatory system; inconsistent implementation of rules;
inefficiencies in clearing and settlement systems; differences in legal systems
(such as divergences in how bankruptcy proceedings are dealt with); taxation differences; political barriers in the form of creative techniques designed
to assist local suppliers and national markets; external trade barriers; and
cultural barriers such as different entrepreneurial cultures and different attitudes to regulation such as variations in approaches to corporate governance, disclosure, and the importance of competition. Its main concern was
the inability of the law-making process (which is discussed in Chapter XV)
to deliver the required reforms. The Report found that while there was a
strong consensus on the need to deliver the FSAP as soon as possible, the
current regulatory framework was 'too slow, too rigid, complex and ill-
adapted to the pace of global financial market change'.[79] The heavy reliance
on directives, under subsidiarity pressures, was leading to implementation
problems, while consultations with regulators and markets were inadequate.
Its proposed solution was to revise the law-making process such that level 1
principles, or basic political choices, would be adopted in framework measures (in the form of directives or regulations) in accordance with normal
legislative procedures. Level 2 measures, or detailed technical measures,
would be adopted by the Commission under a streamlined and accelerated
law-making procedure, supervised and assisted by two new committees.
Level 3 concerns the implementation process and requires enhanced co-
operation between securities regulators across the EC in order to ensure consistent implementation of level 1 and 2 measures. Level 4 addresses
enforcement and calls for more aggressive enforcement by the Commission
of EC rules.

   The Lamfalussy model is discussed in detail in Chapter XV below. Its
implications for EC securities regulation are enormous. On a procedural
level, the law-making procedure should become considerably more transparent and sensitive to market requirements, given the new model's emphasis on pre-consultation. More generally, it has the potential not only to
accelerate the adoption of securities regulation measures and to enhance
dramatically the ability of the EC to respond to developments in the integrated market-place, but also, by allowing for the adoption of more detailed

[79] Ibid, 7.

technical measures, to transform EC securities regulation from a market integration device based on mutual recognition to a regime which intervenes much more aggressively in national regimes and, in effect, regulates the single market. It may yet prove to be a staging post towards greater centralization of market regulation.[80]

The 2001 Stockholm European Council supported the Lamfalussy Report, noting the 'crucial role' played by financial markets in the overall economy of the EC and emphasizing the importance of creating a 'dynamic and efficient European Securities Market'. In addition to endorsing the Lamfalussy law-making model, it called for every effort to be made to implement the key steps necessary to achieve an integrated securities market by the end of 2003 and called for further convergence of supervisory practices and regulatory standards.[81] Over the summer of 2001, the first package of reforms designed to finalize the integration of the securities market was unveiled and prepared in accordance with the Lamfalussy model, with the Commission presenting proposals for the control of market abuse and for a new prospectus disclosure regime and making two decisions establishing the committees which will streamline the cumbersome legislative process. Overall, it appears from the measures already presented and the consultations being carried out by the Commission on future proposals, that while they are designed to break down the remaining barriers to integration this new generation of measures will also, unlike their precursors, seek to regulate the integrated market to a significantly greater extent.

The FSAP and the Lamfalussy model are the critical influences on the future of EC securities regulation, but the regime will also be shaped by a number of extra-EC influences. Market developments are influencing regulation to a greater extent than ever before; the growth in e-commerce, to take one example, has accelerated the push towards home country control of investment business while the development of ATSs and securities-trading markets alliances and mergers, to take another, is forcing the EC to address sophisticated problems such as how to preserve market transparency in a fragmented trading environment and how best to prevent market manipulation. The extent to which markets and market participants converge in their standards and practices in non-harmonized areas is also likely to play a large part in the evolution of the integrated market. Convergence outside the institutional structures of the EC is already occurring at the level of market regulators. Prior to its incorporation within the EC institutional structure as the

---

[80] One of the favourite preoccupations of securities regulation commentators is to comment on the legal possibility and political likelihood of the establishment of a Euro-SEC wielding powers over the integrated market. This question is discussed in Ch. XV below.

[81] Annexes to the Presidency Conclusion, Stockholm European Council, 23 and 24 Mar 2001, Annex I. Resolution of the European Council on More Effective Securities Market Regulation.

Committee of European Securities Regulators (the CESR), FESCO (the Federation of European Securities Commissions) played a major role in encouraging convergence (see Chapter XV below). EC securities regulation does not take place in a hermetically sealed market-place; in order to ensure the competitiveness of EC market participants and to reflect the global nature of investment services and securities markets, account must be taken of international developments. In particular, the work currently being undertaken by the Basle Committee on Banking Supervision will determine, to a large extent, how the EC's capital adequacy regime will evolve while proposals adopted by IOSCO, the Basle Committee, and the International Association of Insurance Supervisors on the regulation of financial conglomerates have influenced the EC's proposals in this area. In the disclosure sphere, IOSCO and the International Accounting Standards Board are exerting considerable influence on the shape of the new disclosure regime.

As is discussed in Chapter II the full development of an integrated securities and investment services market is, however, dependent on an alteration in patterns of investment behaviour across the Community. Unlike the position in the USA, bank finance remains the predominant source of funding for Community companies.[82] Personal investment in the markets through pension funds and collective investment schemes is also much less developed than in the USA due to the greater embrace of the welfare state in Europe. Where the securities markets are accessed, however, it is not entirely clear that investors will move away from an oft-observed bias towards domestic investment in spite of the benefits of diversification in foreign investments. The retail investor, in particular, has been shown to be reluctant to venture beyond the home market.[83] It seems clear, however, that the internal market in securities and investment services will continue to mature and deepen. The ability of EC securities regulation to respond to this process will be critical.

I.8 CAPITAL CONTROLS

I.8.1 *The Road to Liberalization*

The abolition of capital controls or, more specifically, the removal of restrictions on cross-border financial transactions[84] is a critical horizontal require-

---

[82] Gros, D, and Lannoo, K, *The Euro Capital Market* (2000) 39.

[83] 'Europe is likely to become the home market for institutional investors, but not yet for households': ibid, 163. See also the Initial Lamfalussy Report which noted that while the investment horizons of retail investors (and funds) are becoming more European, 'a strong home bias persists in primary and secondary market activity in the EU markets': n 76 above, 11.

[84] See generally, Bakker, A, *The Liberalisation of Capital Movements in Europe* (1996), Mohamed, S, *European Community Law on the Free Movement of Capital and the EMU* (1999) and

ment for the construction of an EC securities and investment services market.[85] Capital liberalization also forms an essential plank of EMU, which in turn is based on the completion of the internal market. The free movement of capital is enshrined in Chapter 4 of Title III of Part III of the Treaty on capital and payments, Articles 56–60 EC; these provisions were introduced by the Maastricht Treaty. Article 56 EC is the central provision and provides that all restrictions on movements of capital and on payments between Member States and between Member States and third countries are prohibited. The remaining provisions set out the framework within which Article 56 operates. Chapter 4 represents the last stage of a process which has its origins in the original Treaty of Rome free movement of capital provisions. These differed significantly from the current capital and payment provisions and were repealed on their replacement by the Maastricht Treaty. Capital liberalization has been a slow process, not least due to the connection between the free movement of capital and the powers of Member States in the sensitive areas of economic and monetary policy, taxation of capital income, State control of financial entities, and the control of illegal activities related to the free movement of capital.[86]

The first set of original, now repealed, capital movement rules were contained in Chapter 4 of Title II of Part 2 of the Treaty in Articles 66–73 EC.[87] Article 67(1) required Member States progressively to abolish as between themselves all restrictions on the free movement of capital belonging to persons resident in the Member States and any discrimination based on the nationality or on the place of residence of the parties or on the place where such capital was invested. By contrast with the scope of the other fundamental freedoms, however, the Article 67(1) obligation applied only to the extent necessary to ensure the proper functioning of the common market. Article 68(1) EC required Member States to be as liberal as possible in granting any exchange authorizations which were still necessary after the entry into force of the Treaty. The standstill obligation to which Member States were subjected by Article 71 EC required Member States only to endeavour to avoid introducing any new exchange restrictions on the movement of capital and to endeavour not to make the existing rules

Usher, J, *The Law of Money and Financial Services in the European Community* (2nd edn, 2000) 7–38. For an excellent short introduction to capital liberalization see Beaumont, P, and Weatherill, S, *EU Law* (1999) 760–7.

[85] In 1966 the Segré Report called for a review of capital controls in order to assess the 'efficacy of the existing controls, and . . . the gravity of the obstacles which these regulations may place in the way of rational and equitable ordering of financial transactions between countries': n 59 above, 47.

[86] As observed by Judge Kakouris of the Court of Justice, writing extra-judicially in the foreword to Mohamed, n 84 above, 12.

[87] The original Treaty rules are discussed in some detail in Smits, R, 'Some Aspects of the Monetary Law of the European Community' (1983/2) *Legal Issues of European Integration* 39.

more restrictive. Under Article 69 EC the Council was authorized to adopt the necessary directives for the progressive implementation of Article 67 EC. This would prove to be a critical provision for the effectiveness of the free movement of capital given that, as discussed below, the Court of Justice was to find that Article 67 EC did not have direct effect and so could not be relied on directly in the event that the Council had not adopted all the directives which were necessary to liberalize capital movements fully. The freedom of capital movements between Member States and third countries was covered in Articles 70 and 72 EC. Article 73(1) EC allowed Member States to adopt protective measures in the field of capital movements. After consultations, the Commission was empowered to authorize a Member State to take protective measures in the field of capital movements if movements of capital were leading to disturbances in the functioning of that Member State's capital market. The Council could subsequently confirm, revoke, or amend the details of the authorization. In cases of urgency or where secrecy grounds so dictated, Article 73(2) EC permitted Member States in difficulties to take protective measures where necessary without the intervention of the Commission. The Commission could subsequently, after consultations, require that the Member State in question amend or abolish the measures. Finally, Articles 108(3) and 109 EC (which had much greater practical significance for Member States)[88] permitted Member States to adopt restrictive safeguard measures in the event of serious balance-of-payments difficulties.[89] Articles 108(3) and 109 EC have, with certain amendments specific to the establishment of EMU, been retained and now appear in Articles 119(3) and 120 EC and are discussed further in section 8.3 below.

The second set of original and now repealed provisions covered the movement of current payments. Article 106(1) EC was drafted in significantly more imperative terms than Article 67(1) and required Member States to authorize, in the currency of the Member State in which the creditor or the beneficiary resided, any payments connected with the movement of goods, services, and capital and any transfers of capital and earnings, to the extent that the underlying movement of goods, services, capital, or persons between Member States had been liberalized. Article 106(1) EC did not explicitly cover the liberalization of payments made in the currency of the

---

[88] For examples of Art. 108 EC authorisations see n 129 below.

[89] The differences between Arts. 108 and 73 EC were highlighted by the Court in Case 157/85 *Luigi Brugnoni and Roberto Ruffinengo v Cassa di Risparmio di Genova e Imperia* [1986] ECR 2013 where it found that, as the substantive requirements of both provisions differed and as the decisions which could be adopted and authorized under each provision were different, different procedures applied to each provision, such that the adoption of measures under Art. 108 EC did not require compliance with the procedural requirements of Art. 73 EC.

debtor.[90] In contrast with its approach to Article 67 EC, the Court found Article 106(1) EC to have direct effect.[91]

Although classification as a capital movement or current payment had repercussions for the extent to which a financial transaction was liberalized, given the limited liberalization of capital movements under Article 67 EC and the ability of Member States to restrict financial transactions under Article 73 EC, neither term was defined under Article 67(1) or Article 106 EC. In a series of judgments, the Court attempted to draw a distinction between the two forms of financial transaction. The nature of current payments under Article 106(1) EC was discussed in *Casati*,[92] where the Court found that Article 106 EC was designed to ensure the free movement of goods in practice by authorizing all the transfers of currency necessary to achieve that aim. It did not require Member States to authorize the import and export of banknotes for the performance of commercial transactions as such transfers were not necessary for the free movement of goods, given that physical transfers of banknotes did not conform to standard practice for commercial transactions.[93] Article 106 was reviewed again, with a particular emphasis on its relationship with Article 67(1), in *Luisi and Carbone*.[94] The case arose in the context of the prosecution of two Italian nationals for exporting banknotes from Italy, in order to pay for medical treatment and to meet tourism expenses, in breach of an Italian law which limited the amount of currency which could be taken out of Italy by Italian residents. Opening its analysis with the comment that that the Treaty did not specify what was to be understood by the movement of capital, the Court noted that not all physical transfers of financial assets such as banknotes would, in all circumstances, be regarded as movements of capital. Moving on to address the distinction between capital movements and current payments, the Court found that the general scheme of the Treaty and a comparison between Articles 67 and 106 EC confirmed that current payments were transfers of foreign exchange which constituted the consideration within the context of an underlying transaction, while movements of capital were financial

---

[90] Nonetheless, as noted by Smits, n 87 above, 57, on occasion the Court appeared to gloss over this distinction as it seemed to do in *Casati* where it stated that Art. 106 EC was designed to 'ensure the free movement of goods in practice by authorising all the transfers of currency necessary to achieve that aim': Case 203/80 [1981] ECR 2595, para 24. In subsequent cases, however, the Court was more rigorous. See p 36 below.

[91] Cases 286/82 and 26/83 *Luisi and Carbone v Ministero del Tesoro* [1984] ECR 377. In Case 7/78 *R v Ernest George Thomson, Brian Albert Johnson and Colin Alex Norman Woodiwiss* [1978] ECR 2247 the Court emphasized the connection between Art. 106 EC and the liberalization of the underlying transaction which was being paid for. It stated that Art. 106 EC was a derived freedom only. It could apply only where the underlying transactions were liberalized.

[92] N 90 above.

[93] The point has been made that this reasoning of the Court was not wholly sensitive to the practices of small businesses: Usher, n 84 above, 8.

[94] N 91 above.

operations essentially concerned with the investment of the funds in question rather than with remuneration for services. The Court also noted that movements of capital could, of themselves, give rise to current payments. As a result, the physical transfer of banknotes could not be classified as a movement of capital where the transfer in question corresponded to an obligation to pay arising from a transaction involving the movement of goods or services. The payments at issue, accordingly, could not be classified as movements of capital, even where they were effected by the physical transfer of banknotes. Article 106(1) EC thus had the effect of liberalizing the payments which were at issue. The Court did, however, highlight the limitations of Article 106(1) by pointing out that the liberalization it provided for required Member States to authorize payments in the currency of the Member State in which the creditor or beneficiary resided and did not apply to payments made in the currency of a third country. The Court also considered whether Member States still retained power to subject liberalized transfers and payments to foreign-currency-transfer-control measures. It found that while Member States were required to authorize the making of payments, as the free movement of capital had not been completely liberalized, Member States still retained the power to impose controls on transfers of foreign currency in order to verify that the transfers of foreign currency allegedly intended for liberalized payments were not diverted and used for unauthorized movements of capital. The nature of current payments was further examined by the Court in *Lambert*,[95] where the Court again focused on the link between Article 106(1) EC and the ability to make payments in the currency of the creditor's or beneficiary's residence. It found that Article 106(1) simply required Member States to authorize importers to pay exporters in the currency of the Member State in which the exporter resided. Rules which required exporters to receive payments in a particular manner, such as through a bank transfer or by cheque, and prohibited the receipt of payments in the form of banknotes did not obstruct the importer in making the payment in the currency of the State in which the buyer resided or the exporter in receiving that payment and so did not come within the scope of Article 106(1) EC.

Although it subsequently transpired that the full liberalization of capital movements would take a long time to achieve, initially it looked as though progress would be made quite quickly with respect to the implementation of Article 67(1) EC through liberalizing directives. In 1960 the First Capital Liberalization Directive[96] was adopted, which introduced four different levels of liberalization for different types of specified capital movements. Regardless of the degree of liberalization, Member States could still take steps

---

[95] Case 308/86 *Criminal Proceedings Against R Lambert* [1988] ECR 4369.
[96] Directive of 11 May 1960 [1959–62] OJ Spec Ed 49, since repealed.

to verify the nature and genuineness of transactions or transfers and (in what would turn out to be recurring theme in the liberalization programme) could take all requisite measures to prevent infringements of their laws or regulations. It was amended by the Second Capital Liberalisation Directive[97] in 1963. Member States were to grant all foreign exchange authorizations required for the conclusion or performance of transfers or transactions in the capital movements specified in List A. List A included direct investments (excluding financial investments made with a view to giving the investor access to the money or capital markets of another country), real estate investments, specified personal capital movements, short- and medium-term credits granted in relation to commercial transactions or the provision of services, transfers in performance of insurance contracts, and transfers of moneys required for the provision of services.[98] Of most relevance to this book's subject matter is List B which was concerned with operations in securities, in respect of which Member States were to grant a general permission for the conclusion and performance of transactions and transfers in the specified capital movements. The capital movements covered by List B included: the acquisition by non-residents of domestic-listed securities (excluding units of unit trusts); the acquisition by residents of foreign-listed securities (excluding units of unit trusts and bonds issued on a foreign market and denominated in the resident's national currency); and physical movements of the securities covered by List B. In relation to the conclusion and performance of transactions and transfers in respect of the capital movements covered by List C, the degree of liberalization was very limited. Member States could maintain or reintroduce exchange restrictions which were in effect at the time of the entry into force of the First Capital Liberalization Directive as long as the free movement of capital might have obstructed the achievement of the economic policy objectives of the Member State in question. The capital movements listed in List C which were of particular significance to the securities and investment services sector were: the issuing and placing of, first, securities of a domestic undertaking on a foreign capital market and, secondly, securities of a foreign undertaking on a domestic capital market; the acquisition by non-residents of domestic unlisted securities and the acquisition by residents of foreign unlisted securities; the acquisition by non-residents of units in domestic unit trusts and the acquisition by residents of units in foreign unit trusts; the acquisition by residents of foreign bonds dealt in on a stock exchange, issued on a foreign market and denominated

---

[97] Directive 63/21/EEC [1963–64] OJ Spec Ed. 5, since repealed.

[98] The 1st and 2nd Directives both refer in their recitals to Art. 106(2) EC, which provided for the progressive abolition of restrictions on payments, as well as to Art. 69 EC, which empowered the Council to adopt directives for the progressive implementation of Art. 67 EC which accounts for the inclusion of the latter two movements which can be classified as current payments rather than capital movements.

in the national currency of the resident; and physical movements of the securities covered by List C. Also covered in List C were the granting and repayment, subject to certain conditions, of certain long-term and medium-term loans. Member States were not required to liberalize List D capital movements, which included the physical import and export of financial assets such as banknotes, the opening of and placing of funds in current and deposit accounts, and the granting of short-term loans for commercial transactions and the provision of services. Directive 86/566/EEC[99] subsequently amended this structure, merging List A and B into a new List A and adding certain capital movements previously in List C to the new List A. The securities- and investment services-specific additions to the new List A from the old List C included the issue and placing of securities of a domestic undertaking on a foreign capital market and of a foreign undertaking on a domestic capital market[100] and the acquisition of units in unit trusts. What remained of List C became List B and the capital movements it covered were subject to the original List C restriction. Significant investment services and securities inclusions in List B were transactions in securities not dealt in on a stock exchange. Finally, the original List D became List C, with the capital movements subject to List C remaining unliberalized.

The limited liberalization introduced by the First and Second Capital Liberalization Directives meant that the extent to which the free movement of capital was liberalized depended in part on the direct effect or otherwise of Article 67(1) EC. The ruling of the Court of Justice in *Casati* with respect to the direct effect of Article 67(1) was, however, restrictive.[101] The Court found that on the facts Article 67 did not have direct effect. The case arose from the prosecution of an Italian national for attempting to take funds in the form of deutschmarks and lire out of Italy without obtaining the authorization required under Italian law. Neither the First nor the Second Capital Liberalization Directive required Member States to remove controls on the physical import and export of financial assets, including banknotes. Noting

---

[99] [1986] OJ L332/22.

[100] The liberalizing effect of Directive 86/566 with respect to stock exchange official listings was noted in the Preamble to the 1st Mutual Recognition Directive 87/345/EEC [1987] OJ L185/81 (now consolidated in Directive 2001/34/EC on admission of securities to official stock exchange listing and on information to be published on those securities [2001] OJ L184/1 (the Securities Consolidation Directive or SCD). Recital 1 to the Directive noted that in the wake of the adoption of Directive 86/566, the number of cross-border applications for admission to listing was likely to increase (dropped from SCD Preamble). Given the newness of the SCD consolidation (adopted on 28 May 2001), familiarity with the discrete official listing directives as originally adopted and the likelihood of changes to the consolidated regime in any event given the proposals to revise the issuer-disclosure regime, for convenience and ease of reference the original Arts. will be used with the SCD reference given the first time reference is made in a section to an Art. which has been consolidated. On the SCD see Ch. II, n 12 below.

[101] N 90 above. On the ruling see: Louis, J-V, 'Free Movement of Capital in the European Community: the Casati Judgment' (1982) 29 *CMLRev.* 443 and Petersen, M, 'Capital Movements and Payments under the EEC Treaty After Casati' (1982) 7 *ELRev.* 167.

that, at that time, the complete freedom of capital could have undermined the economic policy of Member States and impaired the functioning of the common market, the Court emphasized that, unlike the Treaty provisions on the free movement of goods, persons, and services, the Article 67(1) EC obligation to remove capital controls extended only as far as necessary to ensure the proper functioning of the common market. The Court found that the scope of this qualification could vary over time and that it depended on an assessment of the requirements of the common market and the advantages and risks which capital liberalization would involve, particularly having regard to the level of integration achieved in matters in respect of which capital movements were particularly significant. Such an assessment was, first and foremost, a matter for the Council and the results of that assessment were to be expressed by the adoption by the Council of liberalizing directives. As the Council had not required physical imports and exports of banknotes to be liberalized under the First and Second Capital Liberalization Directives, Article 67(1) was to be interpreted as meaning that restrictions on the export of banknotes were not to be regarded as abolished. The Court also examined the standstill obligation in Article 71 EC and found that the use of the term 'endeavour' was a marked departure from the imperative terms used in similar provisions concerning restrictions on the free movement of goods, persons, and services. It was accordingly apparent to the Court that Article 71(1) EC did not impose an unconditional obligation on Member States which could be relied on by individuals. As a result of *Casati*, the extent to which capital could freely move across borders in the EC was dependent on the Council deciding that abolition of restrictions on a particular category of capital movements was necessary and taking action to liberalize the movements in question. The Court held in a subsequent case, however, that once the Council had acted to liberalize a particular capital movement all restrictions on that movement were prohibited and not simply exchange control restrictions.[102]

Following a period of monetary instability in the 1970s which was aggravated by the oil crisis, many Member States relied on the Treaty safeguard provisions, particularly Article 108(3) EC, to impose restrictions on financial transactions[103] in order to maintain autonomous monetary and credit policies, particularly with respect to interest and exchange rate management.[104]

---

[102] Brugnoni and Ruffinengo, n 89 above. See further Smits, R, 'A Further Step on the Road to Liberalisation' (1986) 11 *ELRev.* 456.

[103] Of these, of considerable significance for the securities and investment services sector were restrictions imposed on the operation of the bond markets and on the ability of domestic investors to move funds into foreign securities and restrictions on raising funds in foreign securities markets.

[104] The discussion in this para is based on the analysis of the evolution of the use of capital controls in the EC in Andenas, M, and Hadjiemmanuil. C, 'Banking Supervision, the Internal Market and European Monetary Union' in Andenas, M, Gormley, L, Hadjiemmanuil, C, and

Restrictions on outward financial transactions, such as investing on a cross-border basis, in the short term help to keep interest rates low. In the long term, they can protect domestic savings and, by concentrating domestic investment funds at home, preserve domestic control over sensitive local industries. Restrictions on inward financial transactions, on the other hand, can help to preserve price stability and avoid increases in domestic exchange rates. These controls can also, however, lead to inefficiencies and distortions to competition. During the 1980s, movements began towards the use of more indirect instruments of monetary and credit policy and the liberalization of economic policy. Combined with this development, in the wholesale investment services and securities markets, at least, the burgeoning currency swaps markets offered professional investors a way of dealing with any outstanding capital controls.[105]

In its 1985 White Paper on the Internal Market the Commission addressed the link between capital controls and the internal market in financial services. It called for greater liberalization of capital movements in order to enable greater integration of financial services markets, as well as to achieve greater monetary stability through the EMS and to promote the optimum allocation of savings. The Commission did not, however, call for the abolition of all capital movement controls but proposed instead that more limited use be made by Member States of the safeguard procedures which allowed them to impose protective measures.[106] Following the White Paper, the amendments to the Treaty introduced by the Single European Act refocused attention on the free movement of capital, promoting it to the same status as the other fundamental freedoms by defining the internal market in what is now Article 14(2) EC as 'an area without internal frontiers in which the free movement of goods, persons, services and capital is ensured'.[107] Article 14(1) also set a time limit of 31 December 1992 for the

---

Harden, I (eds), *European Economic and Monetary Union: The Institutional Framework* (1997) 378–81 and Artis, M, and Lee, N, *The Economics of the European Union* (2nd edn, 1997) 341–3.

[105] Dalhuisen, n 61 above, 40–1. For a discussion of the market forces (particularly in the eurobond market which provided a major impetus to the liberalization of capital controls) which impacted on the liberalization of capital movements independently of the EC measures see the discussion at 38–49.

[106] Up to the end of 1984, however, the Commission had been somewhat lax in authorizing protective measures under Art. 108(3) EC, at times simultaneously issuing authorizations to groups of Member States. It was not until the end of 1984, at the urging of Member States which were more liberal with respect to capital controls, that it began to take a more rigorous approach to the granting of authorizations: Smits, n 102 above, 458. The extent to which Art. 108(3) was relied on can perhaps be best illustrated by the fact that in early 1989 all the Member States, except for Germany, the Netherlands, and the UK, imposed exchange controls to some extent: Dalhuisen, n 61 above, 39. By Sept 1991, however, the position had improved with exchange controls abolished in the UK, Germany, the Netherlands, France, Denmark, Belgium, Luxembourg, and Italy: Department of Trade and Industry, *The Single Market—Financial Services* (Sept 1991) 26.

[107] Case C–101/94 *Commission v Italy* [1996] ECR I–2691, Opinion of the AG, para 19.

implementation of measures to ensure the free movement of capital. As the push towards a single internal market in financial services gathered momentum, the pressures to remove capital controls increased and led in 1988 to the adoption of the Capital Movements Directive[108] which brought the free movement of capital into effect for eight of the then twelve Member States on 1 July 1990.[109]

I.8.2 *The 1988 Capital Movements Directive*

The Capital Movements Directive brought about the free movement of capital and repealed all earlier directives on Article 67 EC (Article 9). It had the effect, accordingly, of liberalizing certain capital movements which had previously been restricted.[110] A significant by-product of the Capital Movements Directive was that it created the environment which made the adoption of the range of liberalizing securities and investment services measures which followed after 1988 possible.[111] Although the Directive has now, for the most part, been superseded by the new chapter on capital movements and payments inserted by the Maastricht Treaty and in force as from 1 July 1994, it is still worthy of coverage as it, rather than the new chapter on capital movements and payments, brought about capital liberalization for most Member States. In addition, given that the Treaty chapter on capital and payments was modelled on the Directive but does not contain an indication of what capital movements and payments are covered, the list of capital movements set out in Annex I to the Directive is a useful illustration of the scope of the free movement of capital principle.[112]

Unlike the earlier directives, the Capital Movements Directive did not adopt a differentiated, incremental approach to liberalization which rendered the degree of liberalization a function of the type of capital movement involved. The central liberalizing provision was Article 1(1) which provided that Member States, subject to the provisions of the Directive, were to abolish restrictions on movements of capital taking place between persons resident in the Member States. In *Bordessa* the Court found Article 1(1) to be

[108] Directive 88/361/EEC for the Implementation of Article 67 of the Treaty [1988] OJ L178/5, hereafter the Capital Movements Directive.

[109] Capital Movements Directive, Art. 6. The link between capital liberalization and EMU can be shown by the commencement of stage 1 of EMU on the date the Capital Liberalization Directive came into force for most Member States.

[110] Cross-border credit operations, eg, had not been liberalized by the 1st and 2nd Capital Liberalization Directives.

[111] See Dassesse, M, 'The European Commission's Interpretative Communication on Freedom of Services and the General Good under the Second Banking Directive' [1997] *Yearbook of International Financial and Economic Law* 45, 47.

[112] See Usher, n 84 above, 19.

directly effective.[113] The financial transactions and operations which constituted capital movements were classified according to the nomenclature set
out in Annex I to the Directive. The list of capital movements set out in
Annex I was non-exhaustive,[114] but nonetheless provided a detailed illustration of the scope of the free movement principle. Although the liberalization the Directive introduced with respect to the opening of and the placing
of funds in bank accounts across the EC and the consequent ability of savers'
funds to be deployed across the EC as a whole received considerable attention, its impact was much wider, given the scale of the liberalization. Of particular importance to the investment services and securities sector was the
statement in the introductory section to Annex I that '[t]he capital movements listed in this Nomenclature are taken to cover . . . access for the economic operator to all the financial techniques available on the market
approached for the purposes of carrying out the activity in question. For
example, the concept of acquisition of securities and other financial instruments covers not only spot transactions but also all the dealing techniques
available: forward transactions, transactions carrying an option or warrant,
swaps against other assets, etc.' Annex I contained a specific section III on
operations in securities normally dealt in on the capital market which covered shares and other securities of a participating nature and bonds.[115] This
section liberalized transactions in securities on the capital markets, including: the acquisition by non-residents of domestic securities dealt in on a
stock exchange; the acquisition by residents of foreign securities dealt in on
a stock exchange; the acquisition by non-residents of domestic securities not
dealt in on a stock exchange; and the acquisition by residents of foreign
securities not dealt in on a stock exchange. It also liberalized the admission
of securities to the capital market, including the introduction of securities on
a stock exchange and their issue and placing on a capital market, and specified that the admission of domestic securities to a foreign capital market and
the admission of foreign securities to a domestic capital market were covered. Section IV applied to collective investment schemes and section V
addressed operations in securities and other instruments normally dealt in
on the money market. Section V was particularly significant for the invest-

[113] Case C-416/93 *Criminal Proceedings Against Aldo Bordessa, Vicente Marí Mellado and
Concepción Barbero Maetre* [1995] ECR I-361. The Court held that under Art. 1 a directly effective right existed to export capital be it in the form of coins, banknotes, or cheques. Art. 1 was
precise and unconditional and did not require specific implementing measures. The ability of
Member States to impose restrictive measures in certain areas specified in Art. 4 (see p 44
below) did not, as the exercise of that power was subject to judicial review, detract from the
ability of individuals to rely on Art. 1.

[114] Annex I stated that the nomenclature was not an exhaustive list of all capital movements and that it should not be interpreted as restricting the scope of the principle of full liberalization of capital movements set out in Art. 1 of the Directive.

[115] The Explanatory Notes to Annex I contained definitions of the expressions used throughout the Annex.

ment services and securities sector in that short-term money-market instruments had not previously been liberalized. Annex I also contained sections on direct investments (section I), investments in real estate (section II), operations in current and deposit accounts with financial institutions (section VI), credits related to commercial transactions or to the provision of services in which a resident was participating (section VII), financial loans and credits not otherwise covered (section VIII), sureties, other guarantees, and rights of pledge (section IX), transfers in performance of insurance contracts (section X), personal capital movements (section XI), physical import and export of financial assets (section XII), and other capital movements (section XIII).[116]

The remaining provisions were, by and large, concerned with exceptions to the free movement principle and with specific derogations for certain Member States. Under Article 2, Member States were permitted to adopt measures regulating bank liquidity even where they impacted on capital transactions carried out by credit institutions with non-residents, subject to compliance with notification requirements. Protective measures were also covered. Under Article 3, Member States were given the power to impose protective measures restricting certain classes of capital movements in exceptional circumstances. Under Article 3(1), where short-term capital movements of exceptional magnitude imposed severe strains on foreign-exchange markets and led to serious disturbances in the conduct of a Member State's monetary and exchange-rate policies, and in particular where substantial variations occurred in domestic liquidity, the Commission could, after consultations, authorize the Member State, but only in relation to the capital movements listed in Annex II,[117] to take protective measures the details of which were to be determined by the Commission. Under Article 3(2), the Member State itself could take the protective measures on grounds of urgency, if such measures were necessary, subject to the Member State notifying the Commission and other Member States. The Commission was empowered, after consultations, to decide whether the Member State could continue to apply the measures or was required to amend or abolish them. The Commission's decisions under Article 3(1) and (2) were subject to the

---

[116] Notwithstanding the detail in Annex I, the scope of the Directive has been the subject of a number of rulings concerning mortgages and housing loans: Case C–484/93 *Svensson and Gustavsson v Ministre du Logement* [1995] ECR I–3955 and Case C–222/79 *Manfred Trummer and Peter Mayer v Bezirksgericht Feldach* [1999] ECR I–1661. For an examination of the *Trummer* judgment see Mohammed, S, ' A Critical Assessment of the ECJ Judgment in Trummer and Mayer' [1999] *BJIBFL* 396.

[117] Annex II covered operations in securities and other instruments normally dealt in on the money market, operations in current and deposit accounts with financial institutions, operations in units in collective investment undertakings, short-term financial loans and credits, personal capital movements concerning loans, physical import and export of financial assets relating to securities normally dealt in on the money market, and means of payment and other capital movements involving short-term operations similar to those listed.

power of the Council under Article 3(3) to revoke or amend the decisions. Any restrictions applied by the Member State were to be defined and applied in such a way as to cause the least possible hindrance to the free movement of persons, goods, and services and could not last longer than six months (Article 3(4)). Article 4 provided that the Directive was without prejudice to the right of Member States to take all requisite measures to prevent violations of their rules in the fields, *inter alia*, of taxation and prudential supervision of financial institutions and to set out procedures for the declaration of capital movements for administrative or statistical purposes. It required, however, that the application of such measures and procedures was not to have the effect of impeding capital movements which were in accordance with Community law. The scope of Article 4 was discussed in *Bordessa* in the context of the compliance with Community law of a Spanish law which imposed a prior authorization requirement on exports of currency over a certain amount in value and which was justified by reference to the effectiveness of tax controls and the fight against illegal activities such as tax evasion, money-laundering, drug-trafficking, and terrorism. Addressing whether these interests could be encompassed within the scope of Article 4, the Court found that while prudential supervision and taxation measures were specifically mentioned, the preceding reference to '*inter alia*' meant that other measures were also permitted in so far as they were designed to prevent 'illegal activities of comparable seriousness, such as money-laundering, drug trafficking or terrorism'. Turning to whether the measures were 'requisite' within the terms of Article 4, the Court found that the authorization requirement amounted to a suspension of the free movement of capital, making exercise of the freedom merely illusory. It also had the potential effect of impeding capital movements carried out in accordance with Community law, contrary to Article 4(2). A system of prior declarations, found the Court, could have achieved the same objectives in a more proportionate fashion. Article 4 aside, specific derogations were set out in Articles 5 and 6(2) and (3) for certain Member States.

In terms of capital liberalization with respect to third countries, Article 7(1) provided that in their treatment of transfers in respect of movements of capital to or from third countries Member States were to try to attain the same degree of liberalization as applied to operations with residents of other Member States. Article 7(1) operated without prejudice, however, to the application to third countries of domestic or Community rules, particularly involving reciprocal conditions, which concerned operations involving establishment, the provision of financial services, and the admission of securities to capital markets. Article 7(2) required Member States to consult with one another on any counter-measures to be taken where large-scale, short-term capital movements to and from third countries seriously disturbed the domestic or external monetary or financial situation of the Member States, or a number of them, or caused serious strains in exchange relations within the Community or between the Community and third countries.

I.8.3 *Free Movement of Capital and Payments: Articles 56–60 EC*

The Maastricht Treaty deleted the original chapter on the free movement of capital, replacing it with a new chapter which came into force on 1 January 1994, when the second stage of EMU commenced. A new approach to capital liberalization, reflecting more closely the liberalization introduced by the Capital Movements Directive and less restrictive in its terms than the original capital movements chapter, was clearly an essential part of the architecture of EMU.[118] Not only is the irrevocable linking of exchange rates and the creation of a single currency area only conceivable in an area where capital controls are removed, as well as being desirable for economic and monetary stability in such an area,[119] the foundation on which EMU is built, the completion of the single market (particularly in financial services), is also dependent on the full liberalization of capital movements and payments.[120]

Article 56 EC is the core provision. Unlike its precursors, it addresses capital movements and current payments together. It provides that, within the framework set out in the chapter, all restrictions[121] on the movement of capital (Article 56(1) EC) or payments (Article 56(2) EC) between Member States are prohibited. Although Chapter 4 does not specify which transactions come within the scope of 'movements of capital' or 'payments', guidance can be taken from the Capital Movements Directive. The Court of Justice made clear in *Trummer and Mayer* that while the Capital Movements Directive implemented Article 67(1) EC which was replaced by Article 56 EC, Article 56 substantially reproduces Article 1 of the Capital Movements

---

[118] Notwithstanding the relationship between capital liberalization and monetary union, the capital movements and payment provisions apply, of course, to all Member States and not simply to those participating in EMU, although the degree to which they apply depends, in certain circumstances, on whether the Member State is a participant in EMU. See the discussion of Arts. 119 and 120 EC below.

[119] It has to be acknowledged, of course, that while the original Treaty provisions of themselves were restrictive in that (for capital movements) they were dependent on Council action for their effectiveness, full liberalization had been achieved by the Capital Movements Directive. For a discussion of why it was still thought necessary to revise the Treaty provisions notwithstanding the liberalization achieved by the Capital Movements Directive see Usher, n 84 above, 24.

[120] Smits, n 87 above, 57.

[121] Although Art. 56 EC does not, unlike Art. 67 EC, specifically refer to the prohibition of discriminatory measures in the field of capital and payments, their prohibition is arguably implicit in Art. 56 EC, particularly since Art. 58(3) EC provides that any measures which may be adopted by Member States in accordance with Art. 58 EC (see p 46 below) must not constitute a means of arbitrary discrimination or a disguised restriction on the free movement of capital and payments.

Directive. Accordingly, the Court found that Annex I of the Capital Movements Directive 'still has the same indicative value, for the purposes of defining the notion of capital movements, as it did before the entry into force of Article 73b et seq. [now Article 56 EC ff.], subject to the qualification, contained in the introduction to the nomenclature, that the list set out therein is not exhaustive'.[122] While largely supplanted by Articles 56–60 EC, therefore, the Capital Movements Directive retains an important interpretative function with respect to the Treaty provisions.

Article 58 EC addresses the extent to which Member States may apply national rules which are not strictly related to but may impact adversely on the free movement of capital and payments. Under Article 58(1)(a) Member States are permitted to distinguish in the application of their tax laws between taxpayers who are not in the same situation with regard to their places of residence or where their capital is invested. Article 58(1)(b) permits Member States to take all requisite measures to prevent infringements of national law particularly in the fields of taxation, the prudential supervision of financial institutions, and the laying down of procedures for the declaration of capital movements for the purposes of administrative or statistical information.[123] Of some significance for securities regulation is the ability of Member States to derogate from the free movement of capital provisions by raising the enforcement of prudential supervision of financial institutions such as providers of investment services.[124] While Article 58(1)(a) does not define 'prudential supervision', at a minimum it must incorporate the soundness and stability rules applied to investment firms in the macro interest of protecting the financial system. Whether or not prudential supervision can encompass micro-protective rules such as conduct rules which operate at the level of the investment firm/investor relationship is less clear. Member States are also permitted under Article 58(1)(b) to adopt measures based on public policy or public security. Although Article 58(1) accordingly specifies a range of interests which may be protected, any measures or procedures adopted under Article 58(1)(a) or (b) must not constitute a means of arbitrary discrimination or a disguised restriction on the free movement of capital and payments. Article 58(1)(b) was considered by the Court of Justice in *Sanz de Lera* in the context of an authorization requirement imposed under Spanish law on the export of banknotes over a certain amount in value and

---

[122] N 116 above, para 21.

[123] The point has been made that this power refers to the ability of Member States to administer and enforce their taxation systems and to supervise financial institutions effectively rather than to actions taken by Member States in order to pursue economic policies, particularly given that balance-of-payments issues are dealt with elsewhere in the Treaty; Usher, n 84 above, 34.

[124] '[The Treaty] recognises the right of Member States to derogate from this Treaty obligation [capital mobility] if they are inconsistent, inter alia, with the national rules on prudential supervision of financial institutions': Mohamed, n 84 above, 182 who terms the right as a 'preferential right over the duty to liberalise capital movements'.

a requirement that a prior declaration be made on the export of banknotes over a lesser amount in value. The frame of analysis adopted by the Court was to consider whether the requirements were 'necessary in order to uphold the objectives pursued and whether those objectives might be attained by measures less restrictive of the free movement of capital'.[125] In an analysis heavily based on its approach in *Bordessa,* which concerned similar restrictions imposed under Article 4 of the Capital Movements Directive, the Court noted that authorization requirements had the effect of suspending currency imports and making them conditional on authorization, making the exercise of the free movement of capital in effect illusory. The objectives of the authorization requirement with respect to monitoring the commission of criminal offences could be effectively achieved without restricting the free movement of capital to that extent by a system of declarations which would not suspend the export of currency but which would nonetheless enable national authorities to carry out, in order to uphold public policy, effective supervision to prevent infringements of national laws. Finally, Article 58(2) EC provides that the free movement of capital rules operate without prejudice to any restrictions on the freedom to establish which are compatible with the Treaty.[126]

While the new Chapter 4 does not contain a safeguard provision specific to capital movements and the disturbance of the functioning of Member States' capital markets parallel to the old Article 73 EC, restrictive protective measures may be taken in the context of balance-of-payments difficulties under Articles 119(3) and Article 120 EC, which reflect the original balance-of-payment provisions set out in the old Articles 108(3) and 109 EC. In both cases the Member State is subject to a number of procedural restrictions. The power to impose restrictive measures forms a part of the Article 119 EC framework which is largely designed to allow for mutual assistance to be provided to a Member State experiencing balance-of-payment difficulties. Under Article 119(1), where a Member State is in difficulties or is seriously threatened with difficulties as regards its balance of payments as a result either of an overall disequilibrium in its balance of payments or the type of currency at its disposal, and where such difficulties are liable in particular to jeopardize the functioning of the common market or the progressive implementation of the common commercial policy, the Commission is to investigate the position of the Member State in question and the action which that Member State has taken or may take in accordance with the Treaty immediately. The Commission is to state what measures it recommends the Member State to take. Article 119(2) sets out the

---

[125] Joined Cases C–163/94, C–165/94 and C–250/94 *Criminal Proceedings Against Lucas Emilio Sanz de Lera and Others* [1995] ECR I–4821, para 23, annotated by de la Torre, F, (1996) 33 *CMLRev.* 1065.

[126] For a discussion of these restrictions see Ch. VI sect. 4 below.

procedure whereby the Council may, on the Commission's recommendation, grant the Member State mutual assistance if the action taken by the Member State and the measures recommended by the Commission do not prove effective in overcoming the difficulties which have arisen or which threaten. Under Article 119(3) EC, if the Council does not grant mutual assistance or the assistance proves ineffective, only then can the Commission authorize the Member State to take protective measures, the details of which are to be determined by the Commission. Article 120(1) EC allows Member States, as a precaution, to take the necessary protective measures where a sudden crisis in the balance of payments occurs and a decision with respect to mutual assistance is not taken immediately.[127] The Commission and the Member States must be informed of the adoption of any such measures under Article 120(2) EC. In accordance with the procedure set out in Article 120(3) EC, the Council may require the Member State to amend, suspend, or abolish the protective measures. Both Articles 119 and 120 EC apply only during stage two of EMU and accordingly may not be relied on by Member States participating fully in EMU.[128] Unlike their earlier counterparts in Articles 108(3) and 109 EC,[129] these safeguard provisions have not been widely used.[130] The Court's discussion of the precursor provisions in its judgment in *Luisi and Carbone*[131] emphasizes the potentially wide reach of Articles 119(3) and 120 EC (for those Member States permitted to rely on those provisions). Examining Articles 108 and 109 EC, the Court found that they remained operative even after the free movement of capital was fully achieved. Articles 119(3) and 120 EC accordingly are available to eligible Member States regardless of the liberalization of capital movements and payments and form a distinct and separate set of rules, independent of the liberalization of financial transactions. The Court stressed, however, that the balance-of-payment safeguards could be relied on only in periods of crisis.[132]

---

[127] Art. 120(1) EC also specifies that any measures adopted must cause the least possible disturbance to the functioning of the common market and must not be wider in scope than is strictly necessary to remedy the sudden difficulties which have arisen.

[128] Arts. 119(4) and 120(4) EC.

[129] See, eg: Decision 68/406/EEC [1968] OJ L251/10 (France, authorization, *inter alia*, to prohibit or require authorization for the conclusion or performance of the capital movements referred to in the 1st and 2nd Capital Liberalization Directives); Decision 78/153/EEC [1978] OJ L45/29 (Ireland, authorization to restrict acquisition by residents of foreign securities and liquidation of the proceeds of same); and Decision 78/154/EEC [1978] OJ L45/30 (UK, authorization, *inter alia*, to restrict direct investments by residents and liquidation of same, capital movements of a personal nature and acquisition of foreign securities dealt in on a foreign exchange). See also Smits, n 87 above, 78–84 for a discussion of the use made of Arts. 108 and 109 EC.

[130] Smits, R, *The European Central Bank, Institutional Aspects* (1997) 60.

[131] N 91. above

[132] The link between measures adopted under Art. 108 EC and 'times of crisis' seems to have been of less concern to the Court in *Brugnoni and Ruffinengo* (n 89 above). One of the issues discussed was the scope of a 1985 Commission decision adopted under Art. 108 EC which authorized Italy to impose protective conditions, including the imposition of a deposit requirement for

Article 56(1) and (2) EC also liberalizes restrictions on capital movements and payments between Member States and third countries, and accordingly is designed to achieve liberalization *erga omnes*.[133] There are, however, a number of restrictions on the application of the free movement of capital principle with respect to third countries which do not apply as between Member States. First, Article 56 EC operates without prejudice to the application to third countries under Article 57(1) EC of any restrictions which existed on 31 December 1993 under national or Community law adopted in respect of the movement of capital to or from third countries involving direct investment (including in real estate), the provision of financial services, or the admission of securities to capital markets.[134] In addition, where, in exceptional circumstances, movements of capital to or from third countries cause, or threaten to cause, serious difficulties for the operation of EMU, under Article 59 EC, the Council may take safeguard measures with regard to third countries for a period not exceeding six months, as long as such measures are strictly necessary. Finally, Article 60 EC sets out the power of the Council to impose restrictions on the movement of capital and payment between the Community and a third country in the context of the imposition by the Community of an economic embargo on that third country in accordance with Article 301 EC.[135] It also permits Member States to take unilateral measures against a third country with respect to capital movements and payments for serious political reasons and on grounds of urgency where the Council has not acted already under Article 60 EC.

The question of the direct effect of Article 56 EC was discussed by the Court in *Sanz de Lera*.[136] The Court found that Article 56 was directly

---

transactions involving the purchase of foreign securities. A similar authorization had previously been granted by the Commission in respect of, *inter alia*, 50% deposit requirements in 1974. The Court relied on statements in the Preamble to the 1985 decision to the effect that the lifting of protective measures should be undertaken gradually and that the decision allowed Italy to continue to apply certain protective measures in order to interpret the 1985 decision as an extension of the earlier 1974 authorization, seemingly without any qualms about the length of time over which Italian protective measures had been authorized by the Commission. The case appears to confirm that the approach of the Commission to authorizations was based on allowing Member States to rely on an authorization previously given to reintroduce safeguard measures, as long as the new measures did not derogate any further than the original measures from the Treaty rules. For a critical examination of this position, arguing that a case-by-case scrutiny was required by the Treaty see Smits, n 87 above, 83–4.

[133] The point has been made that the approach towards capital liberalization with respect to third countries anticipated the need to ensure the external movement and availability of the euro: Usher, n 84 above, 23.

[134] Under Art. 57(2) EC, the Council may adopt measures relating to the areas covered by Art. 57(1).

[135] Art. 301 EC provides that where a common position or a joint action adopted according to the Treaty provisions on a common foreign and security policy requires Community action to interrupt or reduce, in part or completely, economic relations with one or more third countries, the Council shall take the necessary urgent measures.

[136] N 125 above.

effective as it laid down a clear and unconditional prohibition which was not
dependent on further implementing measures. The limitations imposed on
Article 56(1) and (2) EC as regards third countries by Article 57(1) EC do
not, the Court of Justice found, prevent Article 56 from having direct effect.
The exception contained in Article 57(1) EC was, the Court held, so precise
that there was no room for discretion on the part of the Member States or
the Community legislature concerning the date of the applicability of the
restrictions covered by the exception or the classes of capital movement
which may be subject to restrictions. Similarly, the ability of the Council to
impose new restrictions under Article 57(2) EC was strictly confined to the
categories of capital movements to or from third countries listed in that provision. The Court also examined the effect of the exception contained in
Article 58(1)(b) EC and found that it did not prevent Article 56 from having direct effect since the exercise of the Member State's discretion under
Article 58(1)(b) was subject to judicial review, which meant that the ability
of Member States to adopt measures under that provision did not prevent
Article 56 from conferring rights on individuals. In *Sanz de Lera* the question
of direct effect arose in a vertical context, with the Treaty provisions being
relied on against a State. It remains to be seen whether the Court will find
that Article 56 can have direct effect horizontally between private individuals.[137] The response of the Court could have significant practical implication
for the effectiveness of Article 56 as it has been noted that a financial institution could by its independent actions restrict the movement of capital and
payments between Member States.[138]

---

[137] For a discussion of this question see Usher, n 84 above, 25–7.   [138] Ibid, 27.

Capital Raising and Collective-investment Schemes: The EC Investment Products Regime

PART II

Capital Raising and Collective Investment Schemes: The EC Investment Products Regime

II

Introduction to the Securities Directives

II.1 EC SECURITIES REGULATION AND CAPITAL RAISING

While comparisons are often made between the two regimes, EC securities regulation is an entirely different creature from the highly sophisticated and monolithic US federal securities regulation regime. Not least among EC securities regulation's distinctive characteristics are the relative immaturity of the EC regime as compared with its US counterpart, its roots in market integration rather than in the traditional objectives of securities regulation which transforms securities regulation in the EC context from a regulatory device into an integration mechanism, and the absence in the EC regime of a powerful central regulatory authority on the lines of the US Securities and Exchange Commission (the SEC). It does, however, share one feature with its US counterpart. Like the US regime, which is founded on the disclosure-based Securities Act, 1933, which concerns the public offer of securities, EC securities regulation also has its roots in the regulation of the capital-raising process and, in particular, in the imposition of mandatory disclosure requirements on issuers. This chapter is designed to introduce the group of measures which mark this initial foray by the EC into securities regulation and the harmonized admission to official listing and public offer regime which it constructs. The regime is discussed in detail in Chapters III and IV below.

II.2 THE RATIONALE FOR REGULATING THE CAPITAL-RAISING PROCESS

The protection of investors and the promotion of the efficiency of the market-place[1] are the dominant themes in this area.[2]

The regulation of issuer access to the capital markets is designed in large part to promote investor confidence in the securities markets by ensuring that appropriate levels of protection are in place and, thereby, to ensure the effectiveness and efficiency of the market-place. Retail investors are now

---

[1] The rationale for regulating market participants/investment services providers requires, due to the intermediation involved, consideration of a wider range of factors than appears in the capital-raising sphere and is discussed in Ch. VI. The rationale for the regulation of the securities-trading markets on which the securities issued to raise capital are traded is discussed in Ch. XI.

[2] For an overview, see Jennings, R, Marsh, H, Coffee, J, and Seligman, J, *Securities Regulation. Cases and Materials* (8th edn, 1998) 1–6.

turning to the capital markets in greater numbers than ever before.[3] Their
financial wellbeing and, in particular, retirement provision, are as a result
increasingly dependent on the quality of the issuers who access the market-
place and their securities. Further, a weakening in investor confidence consequent on widespread losses by investors can have economy-wide
implications given the role played by the capital markets in financing undertakings (section 4.2 below).

Securities are intangible products which cannot be inspected in the same
way as other consumer products, and their value is largely contingent on
the future performance of the issuer.[4] Like investment services generally,
they are 'experience goods', in that their quality cannot be assessed in
advance.[5] In principle, therefore, investors require information concerning
the issuer (information on the risks represented by the issuer, the issuer's
prospects, financial information, and so on) and the security when making
investment decisions, even if in practice they depend on advice given by a
professional investment intermediary. Indeed, apart from the danger that ill-
informed decisions may result in losses being sustained and a loss in confidence, in the absence of sufficient information investors may leave the
capital markets. While regulation in this area does not seek to insulate
investors from sustaining losses,[6] it does seek to promote investor protection
and investor confidence by ensuring that investors are adequately informed
when making investment decisions, so that they can make efficient resource-
allocation choices and be protected against fraudulent issuers. The regulation of access to the capital markets is thus dominated by disclosure
controls,[7] given that in the absence of a compulsion issuers would, it is
argued, underproduce the relevant information. Information deficiencies in
the capital markets are thus typically regarded as a market failure which jus-

---

[3] For the growth in retail investor activity in the EC see sect. 9 below.

[4] See the discussion in Cox, J, Hillman. R, and Langevoort, D, *Securities Regulation. Cases and Materials* (2nd edn, 1997) 1.

[5] See Page, A, and Ferguson, R, *Investor Protection* (1992) 37.

[6] See, eg, s 5(2)(d) of the UK Financial Services and Markets Act 2000, which provides that in setting standards of consumer protection the Financial Services Authority shall take into account 'the general principle that consumers should take responsibility for their decisions'.

[7] Systems of securities regulation can also regulate the capital-raising process in a more interventionist and paternalistic manner by ensuring that an offer is, eg, fair, just, and equitable before permitting the issuer to access the capital markets. This is the 'merit' form of reg-ulation which is found in certain US States. For an introduction see Steinberg, M, *Understanding Securities Law* (2nd edn, 1996) 117–18. The merit debate also formed part of the discussions which ultimately led to the adoption of the Securities Act, 1933. In favour of a system which would permit only certain approved issuers to access public savings see Douglas, W, 'Protecting the Investor' (1934) 23 *YLJ* (ns) 521. IOSCO (the International Organization of Securities Commissions) is of the opinion that merit regulation is more appropriately associated with developing markets and is not necessary in a fully developed market: IOSCO, *Objectives and Principles of Securities Regulation* (1998), para 10.4, n 31. It may be observed, however, that a streak of paternalism can be observed wherever disclosure requirements emphasize the nega-tive and, in particular, require extensive disclosure of the risks represented by the issuer.

tifies regulatory intervention.[8] Investor protection is also promoted in this area by the imposition of controls on the manner in which the issuer's securities are subsequently traded once the issuer has accessed the capital markets. In particular, the official listing process,[9] a mechanism currently[10] applied to certain securities admitted to trading on securities-trading markets and designed to ensure not only that there is a continual supply of information to the market-place but also that there is sufficient liquidity in the securities traded,[11] is also subject to controls. Here the control of public authorities is less monolithic, with the securities-trading markets themselves playing an important role in setting standards. In the EC, however, public controls have been placed on the admission-to-official-listing process.

Apart from the promotion of investor protection, access to the capital markets is also regulated in order to ensure that, given their central place in market finance economies, securities markets display allocative efficiency in that they allocate resources efficiently to the places where they are most needed. Where a market exhibits allocative efficiency, capital will be supplied most efficiently and, as a result, cheaply to the more efficient issuers, while higher capital costs will be imposed on underperforming issuers. Allocative efficiency depends, however, on securities prices reflecting the intrinsic value of the issuer. Disclosure controls in particular are, somewhat controversially, designed to promote allocative efficiency.

The rationale for mandatory disclosure requirements is discussed further in Chapter IV below, while the other main component of the EC's regulation in this area, the regulation of access to official listing, is discussed in Chapter III below.

II.3 SCOPE OF THE REGIME

For the most part, the focus of the Securities Directives[12] is on the issuer of securities. The Securities Directives are concerned with the capital-raising

---

[8] Disclosure regulation and the existence of a market failure are discussed more fully in Ch. IV sect. 2.1.5 below.

[9] The Official List typically consists of the securities of large and well-established issuers which satisfy certain size and trading record criteria, and in respect of which detailed disclosure is made available to the market. See further Ch. III sect. 1 below.

[10] Moves are afoot at EC level, however, to dismantle the distinction between admission to listing and admission to trading, and apply a common regime to the admission of securities to trading.

[11] Reflecting the fact that '[t]he economic function of the trading markets is to create liquidity—a market characteristic that enables investors to dispose of or purchase securities at a price reasonably related to the preceding price'; Poser, N, 'Restructuring the Stock Markets: A Critical look at the SEC's National Market System' (1981) 56 *NYULRev*. 884, 886.

[12] The securities directives comprise: (1) the admission to listing regime—Directive 79/279/EEC co-ordinating the conditions for the admission of securities to official stock

process: they address the role played by securities-trading markets in bringing securities to the market via the official listing process, as well as the controls placed on issuers who seek funding from the public via the primary public markets (in which securities are sold by the issuer to investors). The Securities Directives also have important implications for the secondary trading markets, where transactions in an issuer's securities occur between investors, in that, by forming a disclosure regime, they play a critical role in efficient price formation and in ensuring liquidity.

Together, the Securities Directives form a harmonized regime covering: admission to official listing, the (now consolidated) Admission Directive; the disclosure required on admission to official listing, the (now consolidated) LPD; the ongoing disclosure required with respect to officially listed securities, the (now consolidated) IRD and the (now consolidated) SSD, as well as the Admission Directive; and the disclosure required on the public offer of securities (the POD). The Securities Directives also establish a mutual recognition of disclosure documents regime in order to facilitate access by issuers

exchange listing [1979] OJ L66/21 (the Admission Directive); (2) the disclosure directives—Directive 80/390/EEC coordinating the requirements for the drawing up, scrutiny and distribution of the listing particulars to be published for the admission of securities to official stock exchange listing [1980] OJ L100/1 (the LPD), Directive 82/121/EEC on information to be published on a regular basis by companies the shares of which have been admitted to official stock exchange listing [1982] OJ L48/26 (the IRD), Directive 88/627/EEC on the information to be published when a major holding in a listed company is acquired or disposed of [1988] OJ L348/62 (the SSD), and Directive 89/298/EEC coordinating the requirements for the drawing-up, scrutiny and distribution of the prospectus to be published when transferable securities are offered to the public [1989] OJ L124/8 (the POD); and (3) the mutual recognition of disclosure documents regime—Directive 87/345/EEC amending the LPD [1987] OJ L185/81 (the MRD I), Directive 90/211 amending Directive 80/390/EEC in respect of the mutual recognition of public-offer prospectuses as stock-exchange listing particulars [1990] OJ L112/24 (the MRD II), and Directive 94/18/EC amending Directive 80/390/EEC coordinating the requirements for the drawing up, scrutiny and distribution of the listing particulars to be published for the admission of securities to official stock exchange listing, with regard to the obligation to publish listing particulars [1994] OJ L135/1 (the Eurolist Directive).

In May 2001 a directive consolidating the Admission Directive, LPD (each as amended), IRD, and SSD was adopted: Directive 2001/34/EC on the admission of securities to official stock exchange listing and on information to be published on those securities [2001] OJ L184/1 (the Securities Consolidation Directive or SCD). Given the newness of the codification (the SCD was adopted on 28 May 2001 and came into force in late July 2001), familiarity with the discrete directives as originally adopted and the likelihood of changes to the consolidated regime in any event, given the proposals to revise the issuer-disclosure regime, for convenience and ease of reference the original Arts will be used with the SCD reference being given the first time reference is made in a section to an Art. which has been consolidated. In the very rare cases where the codification has revised a provision, reference will be made to the 'pre-consolidation' provision. Where the recitals to the original discrete directives are used to illustrate the rationale for the official listing regime, they will be referred to as the pre-consolidation recitals and where the reasoning has been retained in the codification, the parallel reference will be given. Recital 1 to the SCD justifies the codification 'in the interests of clarity and rationality'. It was adopted under a fast-track procedure which permits an accelerated law-making procedure to be followed as long as no changes of substance are made by the codification.

Collectively, all these measures will be referred to as the Securities Directives.

to the capital markets of other Member States and the integration of capital markets across the Community (the (now consolidated) MRD I, MRD II and Eurolist Directives, as well as the POD). There are thus two strands to the regime: the harmonized rules which concern admission to official listing (Chapter III below) and the harmonized disclosure code which applies to issuer access to the capital markets and which covers both officially listed and unlisted securities, albeit to differing degrees (Chapter IV below).

II.4 THE TREATY AND MARKET FINANCE

II.4.1 *The Integration of Capital Markets and the Treaty*

The integration of Community capital markets by the harmonization of Member States' laws, rather than the regulation of access to the capital markets *per se*, lies at the core of the Securities Directives. This transformation of the regulation of capital markets access from a regulatory device to protect investors and market efficiency to a mechanism for market integration is a consequence of the requirement that EC securities regulation must find a basis in the Treaty. The harmonized capital markets regime is, in common with EC securities regulation generally, ultimately based in the foundation Treaty objective of the establishment of a common market (Article 2 EC) in order, *inter alia*, to promote a harmonious, balanced, and sustainable development of economic activities, a high level of employment, sustainable and non-inflationary growth, and a high degree of competitiveness. More immediately, the regime is rooted in Article 3(c) and 3(h) EC which, respectively, highlight the construction of the internal market via the abolition, as between Member States, of obstacles to the free movement of goods, services, and capital, and the approximation of Member States' laws to the extent required for the functioning of the common market as Community activities. Capital- or securities-market integration and the harmonization of Member States' market-access rules are regarded as being essential to the achievement of the Community's internal market construction objectives. The reason for this link lies in the acceptance by the Community of the importance of the securities markets as a source of finance and in the connection made between securities market integration and the objectives of the Community generally.

II.4.2 *Market Finance*

Adherence to a market-finance model is not a *sine qua non* for economic growth.[13] Indeed, the market-finance model can be critiqued, particularly in

---

[13] It has been noted that '[n]ot all industrial societies organise their economies around stock markets; indeed active securities markets may be more the exception than the rule. Germany

the context of the integrated market aspired to by the EC, not least because of systemic risk considerations. Nonetheless its importance to the development of the EC economy and its status as the finance model of choice (as opposed to bank finance via the provision of long-term committed funding by credit institutions via bilateral or syndicated facilities) has been accepted as an article of faith which permeates EC securities regulation.[14] The presumption that the promotion of market finance and the integration of capital markets are central to the attainment of the Community's objectives and the achievement of the benefits of the construction of an internal market is an entrenched element of EC securities regulation generally and runs through the Financial Services Action Plan (the FSAP) and the seminal Lamfalussy Report.[15] It is also a presumption which is hard to deny. The displacement of bank finance by market-based instruments (section 9 below) appears inexorable, not least because credit institutions themselves are encouraging it. No longer content to commit their balance sheet to their clients, they now compete aggressively to promote and lead securities issues which do not tie up their capital.

The 1999 FSAP and the 2001 Lamfalussy Report are of critical importance to the harmonized capital markets or securities regime in that, as part of the wider programme to generate financial market integration, they set out the key revisions which must be made to the Securities Directives and how those measures should be supplemented in order that an integrated capital market can be achieved (section 10 below). They also provide powerful support for the market-finance model and for the integration of capital markets. In its pre-FSAP Communication, the Commission noted generally that a single deep and liquid financial market would serve as the 'motor for growth, job-creation, and improved competitiveness of the European economy' and, specifically, that the integration of capital markets would reduce the cost of capital for industry and facilitate access to equity financing and risk capital and, more generally, benefit the financial services industry by

and Japan represent industrial systems that appear to be more bank-centered than securities market-centered (although each has an active stock market)': Jennings *et al.*, n 2 above, 6. On the extent to which there is a synergy between the capital markets harmonization programme and the convergence of Member States' economies towards a market-finance-based model see sect. 9 below.

[14] It appears that market-finance-based economies experience higher growth, promote a more decentralized economy and a more rapid pace of technological development. See the discussion in Jennings *et al.*, n. 2 above. On the policy debate whether bank- or market-based financial models should be promoted see Dziobek, C, and Garrett, J, 'Convergence of Financial Systems and Regulatory Policy Challenges in Europe and the US' in Blach, S, and Moersch, M (eds), *Competition and Convergence in Financial Markets, The German and Anglo-American Models* (1998) 195. They observe that neither model is optimal from the economic perspective and support a synthesis of the two approaches.

[15] Communication on Implementing the Framework for Financial Markets: Action Plan, COM(1999)(232) (the FSAP) and the Final Report of the Committee of Wise Men on the Regulation of European Securities Markets (Feb 2001) (the Lamfalussy Report), respectively.

generating new opportunities in wider and deeper capital markets.[16] In the FSAP the Commission reiterated the importance of keeping the cost of capital at a minimum in its discussion of issuers' access to the capital market.[17] The Lisbon European Council in March 2000 called generally for the completion of the internal market in financial services and endorsed the importance of market finance, calling for the widest possible access to investment capital across the EU. In its second progress report on the FSAP the Commission explained the rationale for integrating securities or capital markets in more detail than it had previously: '[c]ompanies will benefit from raising capital across the European Union; cheaper and more flexible financing arrangements for corporate borrowers will emerge; innovative start-up companies will find more appropriate funding for [their] needs. . . . Investors will see improved returns: existing savings will be able to work more productively, freeing up resources for other uses. Private sector savings in Europe amount to some 20% of GDP—a valuable asset, if efficiently used, to stimulate growth and job-creation. Against a backdrop of low interest rates, new ways must be found to make this pool of savings yield higher returns for investors and savers. This is particularly important to overcome the medium term public sector debt overhang.'[18] Later in 2000 the Commission would return to the market-finance theme in assertive fashion in its Communication on Upgrading the Investment Services Directive, in which it argued that the pooling of national liquidity would: allow European savings to be put to their most productive use and, in particular, to be used in securities investments in order to complement statutory pensions; provide borrowers with a flexible and competitive alternative to bank finance for financing employment-generating investment; allow companies to fine-tune their financial structures and complete the financing chain from start-up to flotation; and, by promoting access to the widest possible pool of investors, strengthen the price discovery mechanism.[19] It concluded by robustly asserting that '[t]he assessment that market-based financing heralds substantial benefits for European investors and issuers is not overturned by periodic bouts of volatility or occasional market corrections'.[20] Independently of the Commission, the Lamfalussy Report recently endorsed the market-finance model and the integration of capital markets across the Community. It adverted to the danger that a failure to achieve integration could result in the diversion of savings to foreign markets, lower levels of economic growth,

---

[16] Financial Services: Building a Framework for Action, COM(1998)625 (the 1998 Communication) 1. The high cost of capital raising on EC markets as a result of market fragmentation was also highlighted in the Cardiff European Council which, as outlined in Ch. I sect. 6 above, requested the Commission to prepare an action plan for financial services.

[17] N 15 above, 1.

[18] Report from the Commission, Progress on Financial Services. Second Report, COM(2000)336 (the Second Progress Report) 3–4.

[19] COM(2000)729 (the ISD Communication) 5.   [20] Ibid.

employment, and prosperity, and the loss of competitive advantage to those outside the Community, and noted that with capital market integration 'European businesses, large and small will be able to tap deep, liquid, innovative European capital pools centred around the euro for the financing they require to develop these business activities. Competition and choice will drive down the cost of capital'.[21] The benefits of capital market integration were considered more fully by the Wise Men in the Initial 2000 Lamfalussy Report which referred to the benefits which would follow on integration for small and medium-sized companies which, as 'the essential employment creator and backbone of the European economy' would gain if capital markets integrated, such that deeper pools of interconnected capital developed.[22] The benefits for larger companies were also addressed, with the Initial Report noting the higher costs of capital for blue-chip issuers in the Community as compared to the costs of capital raising in the USA, and pointing to the greater possibilities integration would bring for raising equity capital as well as the access which issuers would have to a growing euro corporate bond market in order to securitize their debt.[23]

The roots of the Community's acceptance of the market-finance model and the connection between that model, the Treaty, and harmonization are discussed in section 5 below, while the current status of the market-finance model across the Community is examined in section 9 below.

II.4.3 *Small and Medium-sized Issuers*

The Securities Directives which promote market finance and capital market integration are largely concerned with capital raising via the major securities-trading markets and the official listing process. Although only large and well-established issuers tend to officially list their securities (even if the growth in official listings by dotcom issuers has somewhat dented this received wisdom), the main preoccupation of the admission and disclosure regime, and so of this discussion and the following chapters, is with officially listed securities.[24] Securities are also traded on securities-trading markets without being admitted to the Official List. Many of the markets which either do not form part of the official segment of a securities-trading market or which are independent but do not maintain an official list are second-tier markets designed for smaller and medium-sized enterprises (SMEs), particu-

---

[21] N 15 above, 9.

[22] Initial Report of the Committee of Wise Men on the Regulation of European Securities Markets, Nov 2000 (the Initial Lamfalussy Report) 6.

[23] Ibid, 7.

[24] Access to the capital markets for smaller issuers is a specialized topic which is considered in outline only here. For a full discussion of the problem see, eg, Avgerinos, Y, 'Towards a Pan-European Securities Market for SMEs: the EASDAQ and Euro.NM Models' (2000) 11 *EBLRev.* 8.

larly technology companies.[25] While admission to official listing is covered by the EC regime, at present admission to trading (whether for officially listed or other securities) is not. In addition, the harmonized disclosure and mutual recognition regime for non-Official List securities is underdeveloped even as compared with the unsatisfactory Official List regime, with the result that capital raising across the EC which is not connected to the official listing process can be subject to varying and cumbersome Member State rules. Given that it is accepted that economic growth in the EC is in part a function of the success of SMEs, not least due to their potential for generating employment,[26] the Commission has, for some time, been concerned about the ease with which smaller companies can access the capital markets and rely on market finance for development purposes, as opposed to being compelled to rely on expensive debt financing.[27] It has focused specifically on risk capital and identified weaknesses in the risk capital markets which are hindering the ability of start-up companies to raise finance in a flexible and cost-efficient manner and leading to missed investment and employment opportunities.[28] Access to the capital markets by SMEs is also a feature of

[25] The German Neuer Markt, eg, is not covered by the admission regime. Neither are NASDAQ Europe (previously EASDAQ), the pan-EC market for high-growth smaller issuers based on the US NASDAQ model, the French Nouveau Marché, or the London Stock Exchange's Alternative Investment Market. These markets are designed to make it easier for smaller issuers to access market finance by imposing requirements which are less stringent than those required for established issuers whose securities are officially listed and admitted to trading on the main markets. They also provide a forum in which venture capitalists can exit from investments in smaller issuers; where a flexible exit route is not available, venture capital funding is more difficult to find. For an examination of the role of second-tier markets in raising finance for smaller issuers see Röell, A, 'Competition among European Exchanges' in Ferrarini, G (ed), *European Securities Markets. The Investment Services Directive and Beyond* (1998) 220–2.

[26] The Second Progress Report, eg, highlighted the economic importance of small issuers in contributing to job creation and an entrepreneurial culture, noting that in the 1996–99 period the smaller companies trading on the Neuer Markt and the Nouveau Marché recorded average employment growth of 40% and 47%, respectively: n 18 above, 4.

[27] See its 1993 Communication on the financial problems experienced by small and medium-sized companies, COM(93) 528 (the 1993 SME Communication) and its 1995 Communication on Reporting on the feasibility of the creation of a European Capital Market for smaller entrepreneurially managed companies, COM(95)498 (the 1995 SME Communication)) The 1995 SME Communication was concerned with fast-growing entrepeneurially managed companies and their need for regular injections of equity capital which cannot usually be sourced from private investors ('business angels') or through bank finance and with the establishment and promotion of EASDAQ (now NASDAQ Europe) in order to improve access by SMEs to equity capital. The progress of EASDAQ (and the now defunct Euro.NM) was reviewed in its 1997 Communication on European Capital Markets for Small and Medium Sized Enterprises. Prospects and Potential Obstacles to Progress, COM(97)187. For a review of the difficulties facing SME issuers see also Röell, n 25 above. Among the problems highlighted are the second-class status which can be conferred on the second-tier markets which are run by the main markets, the risk of illiquidity in the shares of smaller issuers, investor distrust, insufficient interest by institutional investors, and the lack of expertise, in some countries, among market professionals in bringing smaller issuers to the market.

[28] Risk Capital: A Key to Job Creation in the European Union. SEC(1998)552. It identified the main obstacles to growth, in risk capital as market fragmentation, regulatory barriers,

the FSAP which incorporates the Risk Capital Action Plan. In its pre-FSAP 1998 Communication, the Commission, as well as promoting the integration of capital markets generally, noted that wider and deeper capital markets would facilitate access to risk capital and equity finance for SMEs, allowing them to access sources of funding other than 'the expensive and inflexible debt financing on which they currently rely'[29] and called for efficient and specialized equity markets to be available for fast-growing, unlisted, innovative start-ups. The FSAP's capital markets measures (see section 10 below), while applicable to the capital markets generally, are also designed, together with the specific measures envisaged in the Risk Capital Action Plan, to eliminate the discrepancies between regulatory regimes which are currently preventing risk capital markets from 'acquiring sufficient critical mass to represent a viable alternative to more costly and inflexible forms of financing' and to 'stimulate the emergence of deeper and more liquid markets at EU level'.[30] In particular, efforts are in train to restructure the disclosure regime so that the capital-raising process is less burdensome.[31]

II.5 HARMONIZATION AND THE TREATY

II.5.1 *Early Developments*

The roots of the Securities Directives lie in the connection between the acceptance of the importance of market finance for the economic development of the Community and the harmonization of capital market rules on the admission of issuers to the market-place and disclosure.

The seminal 1966 Segré Report[32] made an early link between the development of the Community, the integration of national securities markets, and rule harmonization. It found that the financing of economic growth was

fiscal barriers, cultural barriers, the paucity of high-tech companies and insufficiently qualified human resources. This document sets out the Risk Capital Action Plan which is designed to remove these barriers by 2003.

[29] 1998 Communication, n 16 above, 1. It also found at 6 that risk capital financing for innovative start-ups lagged considerably behind US practice.

[30] FSAP, n 15 above, 4–5. As noted above, the Lamfalussy Report also made specific reference to the importance of risk capital for SMEs and emphasized the importance of SMEs to job creation: n 15 above, 10. The Initial Lamfalussy Report considered the impact of integration on the liquidity of SME shares in some detail: n 22 above, 6.

[31] See Ch. IV sect. 9 below. The Risk Capital Action Plan also envisages progress with respect to, *inter alia*, venture capital, pension reform, and patent rules. Risk capital growth is also being promoted by the use of the Community's funding instruments. The revisions to the collective investment scheme regime, discussed in Ch. V, are also designed to promote the risk capital market.

[32] Report by a Group of Experts Appointed by the EEC Commission, *The Development of a European Capital Market* (1966).

dependent on the capital markets and reported that the securities markets 'are . . . markets where efficiency can be notably improved by integration'.[33] In the case of the debt markets, it found that national markets were already overextended domestically, but that foreign investors and borrowers were unable to enter due to exchange controls, discriminatory legislative obstacles, and inefficient techniques for placing securities, all of which were hindering the development of an EC-wide market. Examining the equity markets, it found a shortage in the supply of capital as well as an unreliable market, and called for action to increase the contribution of institutional investors. Establishing a wider market would offer new and varied sources of funding for operating in the common market, align the conditions under which finance could be obtained and so remove competitive distortions, and ultimately increase the supply of capital. The Report set the tenor for later legislative developments by stressing the need for investors in securities traded in EC markets to have access to adequate disclosure. Critically, it also called for the removal of the obstacles faced by issuers of securities wishing to offer or list securities in another Member State. This early support for market finance and the need for the removal of regulatory obstacles to cross-Community funding would lead, ultimately, to the construction of the Securities Directives.

The critical link between the objectives of the Treaty, the development of an integrated capital market, and rule harmonization was formally made in the 1977 Code of Conduct on Transactions in Transferable Securities.[34] While most of its provisions have been overtaken by harmonizing directives, it is useful nonetheless in that it reflects the policies underlying the Community's activities in regulating offers of securities. Equally, while not legally binding,[35] it carries weight as an interpretive aid.[36] The Code of Conduct states that the 'harmonious development of economic activities', as required under Article 2 EC at the time, requires that sufficient capital be available and that sources of capital are sufficiently diversified to enable investments in the common market to be financed as rationally as

[33] Ibid, 5.

[34] Commission Recommendation 77/534/EEC concerning a European Code of Conduct relating to transactions in transferable securities [1977] OJ L212/37 (the 1977 Code of Conduct).

[35] The Commission stated in the Explanatory Memorandum (para IV(13)) that it was 'of course well aware that a recommendation does not bind states as to the results to be achieved' and that successful implementation would depend on the active co-operation of those affected by it. It suggested that in each Member State one body should be responsible for supervising the implementation of the Code.

[36] In cases such as Case 188/91 *Deutsche Shell v Hauptzollamt Hamburg-Harburg* [1993] ECR I-363 the Court of Justice has established that recommendations must be taken into consideration by national courts, particularly where such recommendations are designed to supplement binding Community provisions: Wouters, J, 'EC Harmonisation of National Rules Concerning Securities Offerings, Stock Exchange Listing and Investment Services' (1993) 4 *EBLRev.* 199, 200.

possible.[37] It goes on to acknowledge the allocative role of securities markets, noting that, given that the role of securities markets is to permit the
free interplay of supply and demand for capital, the proper working and
interpenetration of national securities markets is essential to the establishment of a common market in capital.[38] The Commission's objective in this
area emerges as one of encouraging the interpenetration of Member States'
markets via the reduction of the regulatory obstacles which hinder the
access of issuers to securities markets and via the elimination of divergences
between Member States' rules which would otherwise, as a consequence of
the resulting investor confusion about and ignorance of the rules applicable,
restrict investments to domestic securities or to a limited number of very
high-profile international securities.[39] In this early statement of the
Commission's approach to securities regulation therefore, the promotion of
investor protection and investor confidence in the interests of market integration is accordingly pursued in tandem with the removal of the obstacles
faced by issuers.

Prior to the EC's harmonization initiatives, the obstacles faced by issuers
of securities included the regulatory costs imposed by compliance with a
variety of often duplicate regulatory requirements, the existence of which
was criticized by the Segré Report, and restrictions on the admission of foreign securities to national stock exchanges and market-places. A less tangible barrier lay in the absence of a uniform approach towards disclosure
which would enhance investor confidence in investing in foreign securities.
Member State regulatory regimes concerning the offering and listing of securities varied from extensive regulation to none. The position in 1977 was
that 'there cannot be said to be any wide, unified securities market: lack of
transparency, unfamiliarity with other markets or pure absence of interest
contribute to this fragmentation'.[40] The impetus to enhance the interpenetration of national securities markets and deepen the pools of capital available to issuers reflects wider international developments. A range of factors,
including deregulation and regulatory competition between market-places,
developments in technology which have reduced trading costs and facilitated the disclosure of information, the growth of the investment fund industry, privatizations, financing techniques such as the development of
depositary receipts which represent an issuer's shares and facilitate foreign
offerings, and the dismantling of exchange controls, has increased the

---

[37] 1977 Code of Conduct, n. 34 above, Explanatory Memorandum, para 1.   [38] Ibid.
[39] Ibid, paras 2 and 3. Jacobs AG has read the 1977 Code of Conduct as supporting the construction of a regulatory framework in order to 'encourage investment, and so enable the securities markets to perform their economic function, namely the efficient allocation of resources':
Case C–384/93 *Alpine Investments v Minister van Financiën* [1995] ECR I–1141, Opinion of the
AG, para 76.
[40] Wymeersch, E, *Control of Securities Markets in the European Economic Community*,
Collection Studies Competition—Approximation of Legislation Series No 31 (1977) 117.

opportunities available to issuers to access pools of capital globally. In addition, and although EC investors continue to display a home bias in their investments, modern portfolio theory teaches that investments should be diversified across markets and sectors in order to reduce overexposure to the risks of any one market-place. The internationalization of markets allows issuers to widen their shareholder base, increase their sources of funding in a deeper and more liquid international market-place, reduce their costs of funding, and raise their profile.[41]

II.5.2 *The Treaty Competences*

The substantive harmonized rule framework has been built, first, on the competence conferred on the Community to adopt directives in order to attain the freedom of establishment under Article 44 EC (at the time of the Directives' adoption, Article 54 EC) and, more specifically, on Article 44(2)(g) EC (at the time, Article 54(3)(g) EC) which provides for the co-ordination to the 'necessary extent' of 'the safeguards which, for the protection of the interests of members and others, are required by Member States of companies and firms within the meaning of [Article 48(2) EC] with a view to making such safeguards equivalent throughout the Community'. Companies and firms are defined under Article 48(2) EC, as 'companies and firms constituted under civil or commercial law, including cooperative societies, and other legal persons governed by public or private law, save for those which are non-profit-making'. Thus, the regime is in part built on facilitating the inter-Member State establishment of companies and firms. The Treaty establishment guarantee is set out in Article 43 EC and provides that any restrictions on the freedom of establishment, including the right to set up and manage undertakings, in particular companies and firms covered by Article 48(2) EC, are prohibited. The scope of the establishment guarantee is limited to 'companies or firms' formed in accordance with the law of a Member State and having their registered offices, central administrations or principal places of business within the EC (Article 48(1) EC). Secondly, the regime is based more generally in Article 94 EC (at the time, Article 100 EC) which provides for the approximation of national rules that affect the establishment or functioning of the common market.

---

[41] There is an extensive literature on the causes and advantages of the internationalization of securities markets. See from among the earlier literature: Merloe, P, 'Internationalization of Securities Markets: A Critical Survey of US and EEC Disclosure Requirements' (1986) 8 *Journal of Comparative Business and Capital Markets Law* 249, 249–52; Warren, G, 'The Common Market Prospectus' (1989) 26 *CMLRev.* 687, 687–8; and Warren, G, 'The Global Harmonization of Securities Markets: The Achievements of the European Communities' (1990), 31 *Harvard Int. LJ* 185, 185–7. More recently see Cheek, J, 'Approaches to Market Regulation' in Oditah, F (ed), *The Future for the Global Securities Market – Legal and Regulatory Aspects* (1996), 243, 243–4.

These competences have produced a harmonized capital-raising regime which is designed to promote the development of a common capital market. The Treaty competences have produced two interpenetration strategies: the enhancement of investor confidence in securities markets and the integrated securities market via the adoption of common investor protection requirements and, in particular, disclosure requirements and the harmonization of rules in order to remove the regulatory obstacles faced by issuers. The extent to which these strategies relate to their supporting Treaty competences is not without controversy and is discussed further with respect to the constituent measures of the harmonized regime in Chapters III and IV below.

The impact of the freedom to establish guarantee has not, independently of the harmonization it has produced, had as major an impact on the development of the integrated capital market as it (together with the freedom to provide services guarantee) has had in the investment services sphere.[42] In the capital markets area, the importance of the Treaty lies primarily in the harmonization competence it has conferred on the Community. However, the free movement of capital guarantee, discussed in Chapter I, has been critical to the development of an integrated capital market.

II.6 THE DEVELOPMENT OF THE HARMONIZED REGIME

By the early 1970s, work had commenced on proposals for directives designed to harmonize admission and disclosure requirements for officially listed securities. The Commission also issued the 1977 Code of Conduct which addressed, *inter alia*, disclosure requirements for publicly offered and listed securities. Harmonizing directives covering listing requirements and, specifically, setting common minimum standards for the admission of securities to listing (the now consolidated Admission Directive), harmonizing the contents of listing particulars to be published as a condition of admission to listing (the now consolidated LPD), and requiring the ongoing publication of interim reports by issuers whose shares were admitted to listing (the now consolidated IRD) were all in place by the end of the 1980s.

The Commission's 1985 White Paper on the Internal Market moved the Securities Directives into their next phase.[43] Although its main focus, as far as the securities markets are concerned, was on financial services,[44] it refocused attention on the attainment of a single securities market and, in particular, promoted integration via liberalization, rather than detailed har-

---

[42] On the application of the Treaty free-movement rights in the investment services sphere see Ch. VI sect. 4 below.

[43] Completing the Internal Market, COM(85)310 (the Internal Market White Paper).

[44] For this reason the Internal Market White Paper and the mutual recognition/home Member State control device are discussed more fully in Ch. VI sects. 5.1.3 and 6.4 below.

monization, through the use of the mutual recognition technique. As a result, while the White Paper did not present a significant programme for new legislation in the capital markets area,[45] its significance lies in its endorsement of the mutual recognition device which would lead to the mutual recognition of disclosure documents regime. The revisions of the Treaty by the Single European Act increased the speed at which legislative measures were adopted, with the introduction of qualified majority voting and the SSD (now consolidated), the POD, and the mutual recognition directives were adopted soon after.

II.7 DETAILED HARMONIZATION AND MUTUAL RECOGNITION

II.7.1 *The Implementation Problem*

The following chapters will examine the degree of harmonization undertaken by the Securities Directives, but it is worth noting at this point that, unlike the investment services regime which was a later development, they represent a microcosm of the evolution of the Commission's approach to harmonization generally.

In constructing a single market in securities, EC securities regulation does not pursue full liberalization or deregulation. As outlined in Chapter I, harmonization is the touchstone of the regime as a whole and it embraces two forms: the detailed harmonization which is a feature of the early Securities Directives and the minimum harmonization and mutual recognition quasi-liberalization model which is a feature, in particular, of the collective investment scheme system and the later investment services regime. It also appears in a hybrid form (a weak form of mutual recognition tacked on to earlier harmonization) in the securities regime. The early Securities Directives (such as the now consolidated Admission Directive and the LPD) do not liberalize the capital-market-access process but follow the detailed harmonization model, in that they attempt to set out exhaustively the minutiae applicable to the admission of securities to official listing and the publication of listing particulars in the areas harmonized. These directives were designed to operate as a code which could be applied by the Member States without significant further elaboration at national level. Under this approach to harmonization market integration should follow, as the substantive requirements are almost equivalent in each Member State.[46] Although issuers are subject to each

---

[45] The now consolidated SSD was the only capital market measure proposed by the Internal Market White Paper, although the paper set an adoption date of 1988 for the POD which had, at that stage, been in gestation since 1980: n 43 above, Annex, para 1.3.

[46] See generally Wymeersch, E, 'The EU Directives on Financial Disclosure' (1996) 3 *EFSL* 34.

Member State's admission requirements, compliance should not present an onerous burden as the requirements should be very similar.

Despite a high degree of substantive harmonization, these early directives did not succeed in removing the legislative burdens placed on issuers and the harmonization model they pursued is now discredited. Not only did the legislative instrument used, the directive, mean that implementation of the harmonized rules was, in effect, left to the mercy of individual Member States and accordingly rendered vulnerable to misinterpretations, delays, and, though hopefully rarely, wilful misconstructions,[47] the Securities Directives contain substantial escape opportunities for Member States from their harmonizing effects in the form of a network of exemptions, derogations, and generally worded obligations.[48] This meant that the equivalence sought was prejudiced and the harmonized structure distorted as it was filtered through the national legal systems. Particular problems arose with respect to the public offer of securities,[49] although measures are now being taken to scale back Member States' control over public offers of securities by issuers from other Member States. This inbuilt structural problem is, indeed, implicitly acknowledged in the early Securities Directives (namely the now consolidated Admission Directive, the LPD, and IRD), in that they are all monitored by a Contact Committee the functions of which include facilitating consultation between Member States on the extent to which additional or more stringent conditions are being imposed. Real harmonization was also hindered by a certain mutual suspicion which could be observed between European regulators. The detailed approach had, in addition, the unwanted consequence of fossilizing the pace of drafting and negotiations due to level of detail needing agreement.[50] More generally, to the extent that

[47] On directives as instruments for harmonization see Ch. I sect. 4 above.

[48] On the risks involved in 'harmonization by option' see one of the first major reviews of the capital market programme in Buxbaum, R, and Hopt, K, *Legal Harmonisation and the Business Enterprise* (1988) who noted at 234–6 that many options do not simply concern choices of forms and methods, but reflect the success of national lobbying groups in fending off Community rules. While they pointed to the benefits of harmonization by option in terms of its accommodating national rules within EC harmonization (an important benefit, given the links between securities regulation and local conditions), they also noted the risk that Member States would simply use the options to retain their own legal systems and that measures would become petrified in so far as more extensive harmonization further down the line would be ruled out by the Member States.

[49] Ch. IV sect. 9.1 below. On the clog which the options given to Member States have placed on the development of capital markets and the organization and operation of Community stock markets see ECOSOC's opinion on the Commission's Communication on European Capital Markets for Small and Medium-Sized Issuers—Prospects and Potential Obstacles to Progress [1998] OJ C235/13 (the ECOSOC SME Opinion) para 3.4.1.2.2

[50] It has been observed with respect to the early disclosure measures that '[i]n the early directives, the leading idea was to enact similar regulation, which would necessarily be very detailed so that double vetting of the prospectus and other disclosure documents would become unnecessary. This proved unworkable': Wymeersch, E, *The Harmonisation of Securities Trading in Europe in the New Trading Environment*, WP 2000–16, Working Paper Series of the Financial Law Institute, Universiteit Gent, at 2.

regulatory competition can be regarded as beneficial, those benefits can be lost in an equivalence-based system. Detailed harmonization is also a blunt instrument. Where, as in the EC, capital markets are not fully integrated and display national characteristics, it does not provide for the accommodation of local market conditions; the mutual recognition and minimum harmonization regime which underpins the investment services regime allows, to a limited extent, for greater local diversity.[51] The early Securities Directives avoided that particular problem, however, in that they gave Member States considerable discretion in applying the harmonized rules, a feature which, of course, ran counter to the regime's objective in removing barriers via equivalence and generated the problems which have persisted to today.

II.7.2 *Mutual Recognition*

Harmonization at a high level of detail, however, allowed the capital markets programme to move into its second phase. When the Commission's seminal Internal Market White Paper was presented in 1985, the main planks of the market-access and disclosure scheme for officially listed securities were in place. In the wake of the Internal Market White Paper, the regime was fine-tuned to reflect the more flexible harmonization technique of mutual recognition and home-country control. Specifically, once a prospectus or listing particulars have been approved in accordance with the relevant directive's requirements by one Member State (the home State), other Member States (host States) must accept the document although they may impose certain additional information and translation requirements. While mutual recognition requires that Member States place a considerable degree of trust in each other's standards of supervision, each home authority is subject to the minimum harmonized requirements.

As outlined in Chapter IV section 2.2 below, mutual recognition of disclosure documents is not an isolated EC phenomenon. The US/Canada Multijurisdictional System (MJDS), which has been in operation since 1991, operates on principles similar to the EC regime in that it allows Canadian issuers to fulfil US disclosure requirements by filing disclosure documents which satisfy Canadian requirements and vice versa (although the regime is subject to exceptions and exclusions and, in particular, does not apply to initial public offerings).[52] The International Disclosure Standards for

---

[51] Ibid.

[52] SEC Release No 33–6902 (1991). See generally Glennie, D, McKee, R, Unwin, T, and Kalbfleisch, P, 'Canada/US Reciprocal Disclosure System for Securities' [1991] *BJIBFL* 443. The SEC also opened negotiations with the UK concerning its participation in the MJDS. The Commission then approached the SEC, pointing out that individual Member States were no longer free to negotiate with third countries on issues which were the subject of common rules, and that 'there were serious doubts whether the United Kingdom authorities still had the power to negotiate a deal with the United States and Canada': comments of Van Hulle, K, in Wachter,

Cross-Border Offering and Initial Listings by Foreign Issuers adopted in 1998 by IOSCO are also designed to serve as the basis for mutual recognition of disclosure documents. In adopting the IOSCO standards for foreign issuers accessing the US capital markets the SEC claimed that a document prepared in accordance with the standards would serve as an 'international passport to the world's capital market'.[53]

As is further discussed in Chapter IV, considerable difficulties exist with the current mutual recognition of disclosure regime, largely due to the degree to which Member States may legitimately continue to impose requirements on issuers from other Member States. Current proposals to restructure the disclosure regime will replace the mutual recognition with a passport-driven mechanism, although this passport will, if adopted, represent a further step in the evolution of EC securities regulation in that it will not, unlike the investment services passport, be based on minimum standards, but rather on a detailed set of harmonized rules adopted via streamlined and delegated law-making procedures (see Chapter IV section 9.3 below).

II.7.3 *Is the Harmonization Programme Well-founded?*

II.7.3.1 *Harmonization and Regulatory Competition*[54]

Although the Securities Directives rely on harmonization in order to remove regulatory obstacles, barrier removal via regulatory competition remains an alternative method to achieve these objectives.[55] Regulatory competition could arise between Member States and between securities trading markets.

A market of, or competition between, national regulatory regimes[56] or, as proposed by some studies, the apportionment of control to one particular

---

B, Van Hulle, K, Landau, W, Schaafsma, J, and Raaijmakers, M, *Harmonization of Company and Securities Law: The European and American Approach* (1989), Discussion Report, 115–16.

[53] SEC Release No 33–7637 (1999).

[54] For a provoking analysis of this problem (in the public offer disclosure sphere) see Scott, H, 'Internationalization of Primary Public Securities Markets' (2000) 63 *Law and Contemporary Problems* 71. Professor Scott at 75 has suggested a regulatory model which is designed to ease the burden diverging disclosure standards represent for issuers in the international capital markets by eschewing the traditional option of harmonization or the market/competition approach and calling instead for the achievement of optimal standardized disclosure (OSI) via the establishment of an offshore free zone in which countries would permit their investors to participate subject only to minimum disclosure requirements. The analysis thus deals with the problem that 'the SEC believes in the virtues of standardized primary issuance markets, but insists that U.S. law sets the standard'.

[55] On the respective benefits and rationales of harmonization and regulatory competition see Ch. I sect. 3 above.

[56] It may be more accurate to view regulatory competition in this area less in terms of the traditional race to the bottom or race to the top in regulatory standards and more in terms of a process which results in disclosure regimes reflecting certain types of issuer and investor preferences; eg certain regimes may tailor their regimes towards low disclosure, higher risk offerings which will be priced accordingly. See Choi, S, and Guzman, A, 'Portable Reciprocity: Rethinking the International Reach of Securities Regulation' (1998) 71 *So Cal L Rev* 903.

jurisdiction, as opposed to harmonization of standards, has attracted some support in the disclosure sphere in particular.[57] Competition is typically promoted on the ground that it allows regimes to track and be tailored to particular investor preferences.[58] Indeed, although the Securities Directives, unlike the later generation of investment-services measures, aim at a detailed level of harmonization, they are sufficiently open-textured to allow different national implementation regimes to be adopted and for a degree of competition to take place. For a regulatory competition to be effective, of course, it is critical that the national regulators receive signals from the market-place (ultimately via the discounting of securities prices) and respond to those signals free from constraints such as the risk of regulatory capture.[59] Further, effective regulatory competition is dependent on the

---

[57] The internationalization of securities markets has proved to be fertile ground for the regulatory competition discussion. In the USA, eg, 'the threat of foreign competition and capital flight has increasingly become a lobbying tool and political weapon in U.S. regulatory debates': Jennings *et al.*, n 2 above, 76.

[58] Although it does not provide an exact parallel for the EC's harmonized capital markets regime, the treatment of securities regulation and disclosure in the federal US structure has provided a laboratory for the market or competition argument. See Romano, R, 'Empowering Investors: A Market Approach to Securities Regulation' (1998) 107 *Yale LJ* 2359 for a compelling thesis supporting 'competitive federalism', or an expansion in the role of individual States' rules and competition between those rules, such that firms could choose the applicable regulatory regime (via their domicile) as an approach to US securities regulation in the spheres of issuer disclosure, anti-fraud controls, and the registration of securities. Professor Romano's argument is based on the premise that 'competition between sovereigns . . . in the production of securities laws would benefit investors in public corporations by facilitating the adoption of regulation aligned with investors' preferences (2365). Indeed, one empirical study of listing applications has shown that the level of investor protection is a factor which feeds into issuers' decision as to where to list: Pagano, M, Randl, O, Röell, A, and Zechner, J, 'What Makes Stock Exchanges Succeed? Evidence from Cross-listing Decisions' in Ferrarini, G, Hopt, K, and Wymeersch, E (eds), *Capital Markets in the Age of the Euro*, forthcoming. For another model for a degree of regulatory competition or, more accurately, apportionment of disclosure jurisdiction to one State regardless of where the offering is made see Fox, M, 'Securities Disclosure in a Globalizing Market: Who Should Regulate Whom' (1997) 95 *Mich LR* 2498 (disclosure jurisdiction based on the nationality of the issuer, to be determined according to the centre of gravity of the issuer, taking into account the location of the issuer's promoters, the location of the headquarters and the place where most of the issuer's business is carried out, but not the place of incorporation or of the shareholders' residence). For a radical approach to regulatory competition see Choi and Guzman, n 56 above, who have proposed a model of disclosure jurisdiction based on 'portable reciprocity' or the apportionment of disclosure jurisdiction according to the unfettered choice of the issuer. See also Snell, J, and Andenas, M, 'Exploring the Outer Limits—restrictions on the Free Movement of Goods and Services' (1999) 10 *EBLRev.* 253, 257 who have pointed to the benefits competition can bring in terms of allowing investors to choose a regulatory regime based on its balance of risk and reward.

[59] Snell and Andenas in ibid, eg, have pointed to regulatory competition's key function as a 'discovery mechanism'. They have found that 'individual Member States receive signals from private agents engaged in arbitrage and are thus able to determine more easily whether the regulatory system fits their preferences. This is especially important given the imperfect information possessed by public authorities' (258). On whether the market and investors are able to decode choices of regulatory regime and influence issuers' (and ultimately regulators') behaviour see Romano, n 58 above, at 2367. For a challenge to regulatory competition, based in part on the extent to which securities prices effectively signal investors'

absence of other market failures which might otherwise distort the competition.[60]

Whether or not competition in capital market rules should be allowed to take place at a lower level between securities-trading markets is a more difficult question. The EC's admission-to-official-listing and listing disclosure rules are based on a characterization of securities-trading markets as monopolies and on the need to prevent them from exercising their admission to listing powers in a discriminatory and obstructive manner.[61] As is outlined in more detail in Chapter XI on securities-trading market regulation, exchanges and securities-trading markets generally have become exposed to competition in an unprecedented fashion in recent years, such that markets now compete for issuers' business in order to generate greater liquidity[62] and have no incentives to obstruct issuers. Many exchanges have demutualized and become exposed to commercial pressures and shareholders' demands for profits.[63] Technological developments have resulted in traditional exchanges facing competition from new electronic trading markets and pan-EC trading systems. The remote access facility introduced by the Investment Services Directive[64] means that market intermediaries can access markets' trading facilities without the necessity to establish a branch in the Member State in question. As a result, competition for issuers and in trading services is now intense. Whether or not securities-trading markets should be freed from public regulation to set their own standards, and the difficulties raised by diverging requirements such as regulatory obstacles and transactions costs, which are typically dealt with by harmonization, left to a regulatory competition is

positions on different disclosure standards see Cox, J, 'Regulatory Duopoly in US Securities Markets' (1999) 99 *Col. LR* 1200. See also Scott, n 54 above, 76, who has challenged the discounting process.

[60] Cox has argued that this assumption is not met in the disclosure sphere, noting, *inter alia*, that there is a question whether perfect information exists concerning the costs and benefits of disclosure standards: n 59 above, 1231–3.

The regulatory competition model also raises difficult enforcement questions where the rules applying are of a regime entirely different from the one in which the offering occurs (most likely to arise where issuers are given a free choice as to which disclosure standards apply—this is the option canvassed by Choi and Guzman, n 56 above). For an analysis of this question see Scott, n 54 above, 89–92.

[61] The now consolidated Admission Directive is examined from this perspective in Ch. III sect. 2 below.

[62] Largely because 'stock markets . . . attract investors by offering liquidity. As a provider of liquidity, an exchange competes with other exchanges and over-the-counter markets, both to attract companies to list and to induce investors to purchase listed securities': Mahoney, P, 'The Exchange as Regulator' (1997) 83 *Va L Rev.* 1453, 1457. Issuers are also attracted by liquidity, in that it can reduce the cost of subsequent equity capital issues where prices are high. Exchanges also compete for trading business from investors on other factors such as anonymity.

[63] The London Stock Exchange, the Stockholm Stock Exchange, and the Copenhagen Stock Exchanges, eg, are all commercially driven companies.

[64] Directive 93/22/EEC on investment services in the securities field [1997] OJ L141/27. On remote access see Ch. XI sect. 6.4.1 below.

a complex question.[65] The argument against removing public control and allowing competition between markets is based on the assumption that, in seeking to attract issuers and thus the trading business which deepens liquidity, markets will relax rules for the benefit of issuers and prejudice investors. In a competitive situation, a destabilizing race to the bottom could develop. In defence of regulatory competition in this sphere, it can be argued that (as with regulatory competition between Member States) issuers and, in particular, their management, are not given the incentive to exploit investors who may seek alternative investment opportunities if they suspect that prejudicial choices are being made. Exchanges are similarly not likely to be inclined to exploit investors as they would risk a loss of investor confidence in the market. Higher levels of regulation may not always mean that investors are protected to a greater degree.[66] Finally, the arguments in favour of self-regulation as a model for regulation can be called in aid.[67] Not all commentators are convinced, however, that investors' interests and securities-trading markets' interests are always aligned.[68] While the link between securities-trading markets' incentives and investor protection remains unclear and, given that since the adoption of the FSAP and the Lamfalussy Report EC securities regulation has become increasingly focused on investor protection, it is unlikely that markets will be permitted to

[65] For a review of the arguments, in principle, in favour of and opposed to self-regulation see Ogus, A, *Regulation. Legal Form and Economic Theory* (1994) 107–11 and, in the investment services context, Page and Ferguson, n 5 above, 82–4.

[66] In support of competition and greater control by markets see, in the context of whether markets, rather than public authorities, should impose voting rights requirements on issuers, see Fischel, D 'Organized Exchanges and the Regulation of Dual Class Common Stock' (1987) 54 *University of Chicago LR* 119, 127–31. For a broadly based argument in favour of exchange regulation based in part on the premise that the benefits of capital mobility are better achieved through regulatory decentralization to the 'bodies which were the first regulators—the securities exchanges themselves' than greater centralization see generally Mahoney, n 62 above. Exchange control of issuer disclosure is given qualified support in Avougleas, E, 'Financial Market Regulation and the New Market Landscape: In Search of a New Regulatory Framework for Market Abuse' (2000) 2 *ICCLJ* 89, 120–2. While her competitive federalism model does not extend to exchanges, Romano, n 58 above, does refer at 2370 to the possibility of competition between exchanges (in the context, however, of not-for-profit exchanges).

[67] Chief among them arguably are the expertise wielded by such bodies and the flexibility of self-regulation as compared to slower legislative procedures which often produce rigid and rapidly outdated measures.

[68] As noted by Romano, n 58 above, '[i]f there is a conflict between maximising trading volume and investor welfare, the market will not provide exchanges with high-powered incentives.' For an analysis questioning the link between investor protection and exchanges' incentives see Amihud, Y, and Mendelson, H, 'A New Approach to the Regulation of Trading Across Securities Markets' (1996) 71 *NYU LRev.* 1411. For a challenge to the characterization of the exchange as regulator based on, *inter alia*, the extent to which issuers make investor-protection-driven choices, the attractions of sovereign, as opposed to exchange, competition and enforcement issues see Kahan, M, 'Some Problems With Stock Exchange-Based Securities Regulation' (1997) 83 *Va L Rev.* 1509. The argument has also been made that a disclosure regime based on public control is likely to be more effective in combating fraud than a multiple, competitive disclosure system at exchange level: Cox n 59 above, 1235–6.

manage the admission of issuers and the disclosure process without public controls, particularly in light of the recent transformation of traditional exchanges from quasi-public bodies providing public services such as official listing into commercial enterprises. At a minimum, however, the imposition of regulatory requirements on securities-trading markets in a competitive environment should be undertaken with care, and with particular reference to the extent to which the regulation in question addresses a market failure; in the capital markets access sphere, the most compelling market failure which requires public regulatory intervention is, indeed, connected to information asymmetries and deficiencies.[69] A recent important development in this regard has been the decision by the Commission, as part of its 2001 proposal, to restructure the issuer disclosure regime, to require that the review of the disclosure required on a public offer or on admission to trading on a 'regulated market' (as defined by the ISD)[70] must now be carried out by an independent administrative authority and removed from the control of securities trading markets.[71] Underpinning the Commission's position is the concern that securities-trading markets may be exposed to a conflict of interest between their commercial interests and the public interest involved in managing disclosure policy (see Chapter IV section 9.3.8 below). Similarly, moves are afoot to impose admission conditions on all 'regulated markets' (Chapter XI section 9.7 below).

II.7.3.2 *The Rationale for the EC Harmonization Programme*

In addition, the link between harmonization, investor protection/investor confidence, facilitating stock exchange access, and market interpenetration, on which the rationale for the Securities Directives is based, could be challenged. In an early critique of the harmonization programme it was suggested that the statements made in the harmonizing directives on the existence of this link were too general to serve as a convincing rationale.[72] With respect to the investor protection rationale, certainly, as is discussed in the following two chapters, although none of the (now consolidated) Admission Directive, the LPD, nor the IRD is explicit on this link, it appears that investor protection via the establishment of a Community disclosure policy is designed to promote investor confidence which, in turn, feeds into

---

[69] Ferrarini, G, 'The European Regulation of Stock Exchanges: New Perspectives' (1999) 36 *CMLRev.* 569, 572.

[70] See Ch. XI sect. 6.3 below.

[71] Commission proposal on the prospectus to be published when securities are offered to the public or admitted to trading, COM(2001)280 (containing the Prospectus Proposal and the Explanatory Memorandum). See Art. 19(1) of the Commission Proposal.

[72] Buxbaum and Hopt, n 48 above, 200. The point was made that 'it must be more specifically determined what interests this approximation promotes, and how these interests advance, European integration'.

the interpenetration of securities markets.[73] Investor confidence is, however, at best an elusive goal. Although disclosure feeds into investor confidence by enhancing price formation and allowing investors to make rational choices with respect to foreign issuers, it is not the only factor on which investment decisions are made, particularly where foreign investments are concerned.[74] Similarly, rules other than disclosure rules (such as the admission conditions set out in the now consolidated Admission Directive) are unlikely to have an immediate impact on confidence.[75]

Nonetheless, whatever the arguments which can be made as regards the real impact of official listing and disclosure harmonization on investor behaviour or the role of regulatory competition, and even if harmonization no longer appears to be necessary in a competitive environment to remove protectionist barriers, market failures still exist in this area which justify harmonization. In particular, harmonization clearly facilitates cross-border activity by issuers by reducing the transaction costs inherent in diverging regimes (particularly in the disclosure sphere) and provides a bulwark against any destabilizing races to the bottom or regulatory arbitrage which may, all indications to the contrary aside,[76] emerge. It also protects

[73] Recital 1 to the now consolidated Admission Directive, eg, stated only that: 'the coordination of the condition for the admission of securities to official listing on stock exchanges situated or operating in the Member States is likely to provide equivalent protection for investors at Community level, because of the more uniform guarantees offered to investors in the various Member States; whereas it will facilitate both the admission to official stock exchange listing, in each such State, of securities from other Member States and the listing of any given security on a number of stock exchanges in the Community; whereas it will accordingly make for greater interpenetration of national securities markets and therefore contribute to the prospect of establishing a European capital market'. The connecting rationale between the investor protection element and market interpenetration is not made explicit. The parallel codified SCD recital (recital 2) tracks this language but refers additionally to 'greater interpenetration of national securities markets *by removing those obstacles that may prudently be removed* [emphasis added] and therefore contribute [etc]'. The now consolidated IRD supports harmonization in the interests of investor protection, but does not explain how this links back to market construction (IRD recital 2, SCD recital 25). The now consolidated SSD and the POD, by contrast, are more aggressive in promoting investor protection, investor confidence, and market interpenetration. See the SSD recitals 1 and 2 (SCD recital 31 and 32) and the POD Preamble, recitals 1, 3 and 4.

[74] As discussed in sect. 9 above cultural factors and domestic biases can work against investment by retail investors, in particular, in cross-border issuers, regardless of the amount of standardized disclosure which is available.

[75] Buxbaum and Hopt have noted that 'severe abuses will discourage the individual capital investor, but individual legal improvements will not induce him to invest because he will either not know about these improvements or, as a layman, not understand them': n 48 above, 201.

[76] In the listing sphere, in support of the limited likelihood of competition developing which would be prejudicial to investors see Bradley, C, 'Competitive Deregulation of Financial Services Activity in Europe after 1992' (1991) 11 *OJLS* 545, 555. It now appears that compelling evidence does not exist to support the existence of a race to the bottom in either listing standards for equity markets or disclosure requirements for public offerings: Jackson, H, and Pan, E, 'Regulatory Competition in International Securities Markets: Evidence from Europe in 1999—Part I', (2001) 56 *The Business Lawyer* 653.

investors by ensuring that minimum standards apply to issuers who access the capital markets.[77] In any event, harmonization in the disclosure sphere is now regarded as a central feature of EC securities regulation and as critical to the construction of an integrated capital market, as is borne out by the new initiatives currently under consideration in this area (see section 10 below).[78]

II.8 A LIMITED REGIME

In 1985, after the roll-out of the earlier Securities Directives the Commission, somewhat prematurely as it turned out, looked forward to the 'creation of a Community-wide trading system for securities of international interest'.[79] While the Securities Directives in principle facilitate the interpenetration of national securities markets they have not led to the creation of a single integrated European securities market in the sense of a single stock exchange or trading platform for issuers and investors. The regulatory framework established by the Securities Directives has a more modest reach and is designed to facilitate access by issuers to national stock exchanges.[80] They do not deal with the subsequent trading process. As is further discussed in Chapter XI, early efforts to create links between securities-trading markets such as Euro-quote, which was an early attempt to create a common trading platform, and information-based projects such as the Price and Information Project for Europe and the Inter Data Information Service, all foundered. The more limited Eurolist initiative was designed to provide for the simultaneous listing by companies of large-size, high-quality and international standing of their shares on several European exchanges,[81] but was dropped late in 1997. Recent developments have been dominated by a

[77] See Hopt, K, 'Company Law in the European Union: Harmonisation and/or Subsidiarity' (1999) 1 *ICCLJ* 41, 51, who has pointed to the particular difficulties which can arise in an internal market where there is uncertainty and a lack of transparency as to the rules which apply.

[78] For an earlier endorsement of the securities directives harmonization project see Buxbaum and Hopt who found (in 1988) that, by comparison with the company law harmonization programme, 'legal harmonization measures that open up national capital markets or pave the way to a European capital market make a much clearer contribution to European integration. In particular, actions such as the removal of restrictions on the admission of foreign enterprises to national stock exchanges . . . contribute greatly to European integration': n 48 above, 2.

[79] Internal Market White Paper, n 43 above, para 107.

[80] See further Scott-Quinn, B, 'EC Securities Markets Regulation' in Steil, B (ed), *International Financial Market Regulation* (1994) 148.

[81] The Commission has described Eurolist as 'a project promoted by the Federation of Stock Exchanges in the EC which aims at providing deeper and more liquid markets for those EC companies of large size, high-quality and international standing by listing their shares simultaneously in at least six EC Member States': Explanatory Memorandum to Directive 94/18/EC, COM(92)566, 3. See further Ch. IV sect. 8.5 below.

market-driven restructuring of the trading environment involving: cross-border trading via remote access to securities-trading markets; the growth in pan-EC alternative trading systems; and the arrival of new securities trading markets such as NASDAQ Europe, which has established a pan-EC market with a unified infrastructure, a single rulebook and a dedicated trading platform, and has stated its aim of becoming the initial public-offer market of choice. The traditional stock exchanges have begun to establish connections more aggressively, with the creation of Euronext from a merger between the Amsterdam, Brussels, and Paris bourses and the abortive attempt to merge the London Stock Exchange and Deutsche Börse. While the future shape of the trading environment remains to be seen, at the least it can be said that trading is increasingly occurring on a pan-EC basis and in an integrating and competitive securities-trading market landscape.

II.9 ISSUER AND INVESTOR BEHAVIOUR

Of themselves, the Securities Directives can facilitate capital raising across the Community only by easing the regulatory obstacles which issuers face. Issuers and investors may not always choose to access the wider Community market. Not only do issuers and investors often exhibit parochial instincts, despite the fact that diversification into foreign investments is widely recognized as advantageous, market-based finance is only now beginning to become seriously established as a method of corporate funding across the Community.

The extent to which issuers access the capital markets still varies widely across the Community, given that, in continental Europe at least, bank finance has traditionally been dominant. At the outset of the harmonization programme in 1979, market-based finance was by no means the dominant finance model across the Community.[82] Germany is traditionally pointed to as the paradigm example of an economy based on bank finance rather than on market finance. With financing dominated by universal banks, securities exchanges were for some time on the fringes of the capital-raising process.[83] In addition, retail investors across the Community have traditionally preferred to invest in fixed-interest investments rather than in equities.[84]

---

[82] The Initial Lamfalussy Report noted that at the start of the 1980s, over 80% of the external financing of continental European firms was provided by credit institutions: n 22 above, 9.

[83] For an examination of the bank finance/market finance debate in Germany in the context of an analysis of German stock exchange reform see Moran, M, 'Regulation Change in German Financial Markets' in Dyson, K (ed), *The Politics of German Regulation* (1992) 137, 145–9. See also Pagano, M, and Steil, B, 'Equity Trading I: The Evolution of European Trading Systems' in Steil, B, *The European Equity Markets: The State of the Union and the Agenda for the Millennium* (1996) 1, 16.

[84] See, eg, the ECOSOC SME Opinion, n 49 above, para 3.2.6.

Although the capital markets are increasingly being turned to as a source
of finance, the development of the Community equity markets, in particular, still has some way to go, certainly by comparison with the US capital
market. In 1998, for example, total EU stock market capitalization as a percentage of GDP was 80 per cent as compared with 145 per cent in the
USA.[85] As between the Member States, capitalization rates and thus the
importance of the equity markets also vary greatly with, in 1998, stock market capitalization as a percentage of GDP amounting to 156 per cent in the
UK, 46 per cent in Italy, 65 per cent in France, and 49 per cent in
Germany.[86] A considerable degree of convergence has yet to occur in the
extent to which equity capital, in particular, rather than debt financing is
relied on as a source of corporate finance.[87] Nonetheless, in the wake of the
establishment of monetary union and the arrival of the euro, capital markets across the Community have entered a period of considerable change.[88]
Debt markets have developed strongly,[89] while the stock market capitalizations of Member States are showing signs of growth.[90] New companies are
issuing and listing shares to a markedly greater extent than previously,[91]

[85] Gros, D, and Lannoo, K, *The Euro Capital Market* (2000), 166, Table A1.2. An even wider
gulf opens up between the USA and the EU when certain Member States are removed from the
calculation. In its 1998 Communication the Commission reported that stock market capitalization in the EU, excluding the UK and Netherlands, amounted to 32% of GDP: n 16 above,
6.

[86] Gros and Lannoo, n 85 above.

[87] In its 1998 Communication the Commission reported that dependence on debt as a source
of corporate finance varied, at the time, from 50% in the Netherlands to over 70% in France,
Germany, and Italy and 80% in Spain, as compared with 20% in the USA: n 16 above, 1.

[88] Gros and Lannoo have noted that with the establishment of EMU the dominance of universal banks as finance providers should be lessened in favour of market-based disintermediated
finance: n 85 above, p. xiii. For their analysis of whether a more market-based finance system
will, in fact, emerge see 73–8. They have identified the importance of bank credit and regional
differences (including structural differences in legal systems, the development of markets and
institutions, and the role of the State) which lead to divergences in the terms and conditions
under which companies raise finance and the role of intermediaries as potential obstacles to the
emergence of a market-finance system.

[89] The 2nd Progress Report noted that in early 1999 the market value of listed private-sector bond issues represented more than 110% of GDP in Denmark, almost 70% in Germany, and
over 40% in the Netherlands: n 18 above, 4. The Lamfalussy Report also noted the strong
growth in the debt markets, although it pointed to the considerable gap between the euro cor-
porate-bond market and its dollar equivalent: n 15 above, 10. On the integration of the debt
markets, which is progressing more rapidly than the equity markets, see further Gros and
Lannoo, n 85 above, 83–93.

[90] While the stock market capitalization of Member States remains low as compared to the
USA, in 1999 newly admitted companies raised over 130 billion euro in European markets,
more than double the amount raised in 1998. 2nd Progress Report, n 18 above, 4. Gros and
Lannoo have also pointed to the rise in the level of stock market capitalizations since 1997 as
evidence that a more market-finance-based model might be developing: n 85 above, 42. See
also the 1999/2000 FESCO Report at 7 which noted high levels of market activity generally
across the European Economic Area.

[91] One third of the total volume of new shares issued on European stock exchanges in 1999
was issued by newly listed companies: ISD Communication, n 19 above, 6.

although bank finance still continues to dominate as the funding mechanism of choice for Community corporates.[92] In late 2000, however, the Commission could report that 'market-based financing is beginning to over-turn the traditional predominance of bank-based lending in most EU Member States',[93] while in early 2001 the Lamfalussy Report pointed to record levels of turnover on European stock exchanges as 'further evidence of an emerging European equity culture'.[94] These developments are not lim-ited to national markets but, with the elimination of exchange risk, are hav-ing a pan-EC impact.

Assisting the development of market-based funding is the increase in retail investor activity on the equity markets.[95] A number of factors have fed into this development. The introduction of the euro has prompted a drop in interest rates and, in particular, in the rate of return on government secu-rities. A recent trend towards fiscal buoyancy across the Community has also meant that governments have not needed to access the government debt market as much, resulting in a decrease in the supply of government securities. Concerns have arisen about the ability of the public sector to sup-ply adequate State pensions.[96] More positive influences include the growth in the institutional investor sector and investment services industry which are 'mobilising household savings',[97] and a rise in online trading which reduces transaction costs. In particular, although institutional investors do not dominate equity trading to the same extent as they do in the USA, the demand from the institutional sectors (both from pension funds and

[92] The Commission has reported that while financial markets are becoming a more popular way of raising finance, as evidenced by the decline in debt to equity ratios in Community com-panies and the large increases in stock market capitalizations in all Member States (with the exception of Austria and Luxembourg), banks still account for the larger part of corporate financing, with in 1999 bank assets in the EMU Member States amounting to 212% of GDP, as compared with 47.9% for equities. In the USA, the inverse is true, with equities, at the time of the Commission's report, amounting to 160% of GDP and bank assets amounting to 62.5%: 2nd Progress Report, n 18 above, 5.

[93] ISD Communication, n 19 above, 6.   [94] N 15 above, 10.

[95] Of particular note is the change which occurred in investment and savings patterns in Germany towards the end of the 1990s. Shareholder culture has begun to change dramatically. After a long period during which retail investors displayed little interest in the equity markets, equity investments are now rising sharply with, in 2000, one in five Germans holding equities. See Harnischfeger, U, 'ETFs Score Well Against the Fallibility of Managers', *Financial Times*, 5 May 2000. It should be noted, however, that evidence of a backlash by issuers against the equity market has also been observed. In particular, an increasing number of smaller listed issuers are going private, disillusioned in many cases by the failure of their share prices to move even in the face of positive performances and good corporate news: Harnischfeger, U, 'Germany's Growing Listlessness', *Financial Times*, 1 May 2001. In the UK, one in every three adults owns shares: Initial Lamfalussy Report, n 22 above, 11. More generally, the ECOSOC SME Opinion noted that the success of recent privatizations revealed a pent-up demand for equi-ties: n 49 above, para 3.2.6.

[96] See, eg, Röell, n 25 above, 221 (in the context of capital raising by SMEs).

[97] ISD Communication, n 19 above, 6.

collective investment schemes) for market investments is, nonetheless, increasing.[98]

While investment in market instruments is accordingly on the increase, a strong local bias can, nonetheless, still be observed in investment patterns.[99] Movements towards Europe-wide patterns of investments are, however, taking place, following the elimination of exchange-rate risk, the development of investment strategies based on industry rather than national sectors[100] and structural changes in the pan-EC trading environment (described in Chapter XI below) with the Commission reporting in 2000 that '[t]he investment horizons of funds and private investors are becoming more pan-European'.[101]

II.10 REFORM OF THE SECURITIES DIRECTIVES

Notwithstanding the positive effects of the euro on capital-market growth, considerable concerns still exist about the state of integration with the capital market's supporting regulatory structure in the Securities Directives coming under fire.

As outlined in Chapter I, the poor state of capital-market and financial-services market integration became a matter of concern towards the end of the 1990s. The pre-FSAP 1998 Communication highlighted as an imperative for action the elimination of any remaining fragmentation in the Community capital market and the completion of the establishment of 'deep and liquid European capital markets which serve both issuers and investors better'.[102] It recognized that further action was needed to ensure that issuers had easy access to the Community capital markets on competitive terms. In particular, it found that the adoption of 'a coherent programme of action to smooth out the remaining legislative, administrative and fiscal barriers to cross-border flotations and investment-related activities'[103] was still necessary. It expressed concern that the disclosure regime had failed to resolve the problem of national authorities imposing demanding and frequently different disclosure requirements on issuers (a problem which does not seem to have been dealt with effectively at EC level since it was first noted by the Segré Report in 1966), which were ultimately discouraging issuers from

---

[98] Initial Lamfalussy Report, n 22 above, 11. It has pointed to a 20% increase in equity investments by investment funds.

[99] Ibid. See also Gros and Lannoo, n. 85 above, 165, who have noted that while institutional investors are likely to invest on a European basis, individual investors may remain focused on domestic markets. Gros and Lannoo have observed at p. xiv that '[d]espite the single market program, the regulatory framework is still a source of fragmentation, and household savings generally are not internationally diversified'.

[100] The 1999/2000 FESCO Report, n 90 above, 8.

[101] ISD Communication, n 19 above, 6.   [102] N 16 above, 1.   [103] Ibid, 2.

engaging in cross-border share and debt issues to the detriment of both capital formation and investor choice, and called for improvements in the mutual recognition of prospectuses regime.[104] It also raised the problem of divergences in accounting rules and took as an objective the stimulation of cross-border investment through greater transparency and better comparability of accounts. In response, the 1999 FSAP contains proposals to amend the relevant legislation in order to provide for a single passport for issuers and to facilitate repeat access by issuers to the securities markets by introducing a shelf-registration mechanism.[105] It also aims to improve the financial reporting system and enhance comparability of accounts; lack of comparability and the consequent distrust in and uncertainty over accounts were highlighted as discouraging cross-border investment. Since the adoption of the FSAP, the Lisbon European Council has highlighted the widest possible access to investment capital on an EU-wide basis by means of a single passport for issuers as a matter of critical importance for the completion of the internal market in financial services.

The need for reform was also emphasized in the Lamfalussy Report which identified the adoption of a single prospectus scheme for issuers, a mandatory self-registration system, and reform of the accounting rules as priorities. It also called for modernization of the admission to listing requirements and clarification of the distinction between admission to listing and trading.[106]

The momentum for reform has been maintained. A proposal to reform the accounting system was presented in December 2000 and, using the streamlined law-making model proposed by the Lamfalussy Report which has the potential drastically to change the shape of EC securities regulation,[107] a proposal for a revised disclosure regime was presented in June 2001. These measures are considered in Chapter IV. Attempts are also being made to eliminate the difference between admission to listing and admission to trading via the introduction of a generic admission to trading regime (see Chapters III and XI below).

Apart from the regulatory problems generated by the securities regulation framework, diverging attitudes towards taxation (particularly withholding taxes and the imposition of different taxation rates on equities and government securities) and corporate governance and different cultural stances on

---

[104] Ibid, 6.

[105] The FSAP, n 15 above, noted at 4 that 'producing multiple sets of official documentation before issuers can offer securities in other Member States is costly and undoubtedly inhibits pan-EU activity. The application of national rules has thwarted the mutual recognition of prospectuses which the 1989 Public-Offer Prospectus Directive aimed to achieve.'

[106] The Initial Lamfalussy Report noted that the cost of raising capital in the EU was higher than in the USA, even for blue-chip issuers as a result of the complexity of cross-border capital raising and diverging Member State rules which impaired liquidity and efficient pricing. In a worst case scenario it predicted that business might be driven out of Europe to the USA with potentially damaging long-term consequences for the European economy: n 22 above, 7.

[107] See Ch. XV sect. 2.5.3 below on the Lamfalussy law-making model.

entrepreneurial activity still present significant obstacles to the integration of the capital markets. Considerable attention is also being given to pension funds as agents to stimulate the capital markets, with the Commission supporting the role played by pension funds in improving the flow of funds for private-sector investment.[108]

Significant efforts are thus being expended on upgrading the capital markets regime and facilitating access to the capital markets, particularly in the disclosure sphere. It remains to be seen how the new measures will impact on the capital-raising process. The development of a single liquid pool of capital for issuers should be enhanced. More generally, the reforms are likely to result in a considerably more sophisticated capital markets and, in particular, disclosure regime at EC level and accelerate the development of EC securities regulation as a regulatory system, albeit one specifically attuned to the concerns of market integration.

---

[108] The regulation of the pension-fund industry is outside the scope of this work which focuses on issuers, investors, and market intermediaries in the strict sense. The FSAP reforms include, however, the pension-fund sector and, in particular, the easing of restrictions on the type of assets in which funds can invest. The Commission has noted that if, in relative terms, the Member States had as many assets in pension funds as the Netherlands, nearly 3–5 trillion euro more would be available in European capital markets: 2nd Progress Report, n 18 above, 5.

III

The Admission of Securities to Official Listing

III.1 THE OFFICIAL-LISTING PROCESS

As further discussed in Chapter XI, securities-trading markets, whatever their nature, essentially provide a forum in which, in accordance with set rules and procedures, buyers and sellers can interact and instruments which have been admitted to the market can be bought and sold through a trading system. In delivering this basic service, securities-trading markets provide a number of functions including admission to trading, trading or order matching services, price formation, trading information disclosure services, trading supervision, and, possibly, clearing and settlement functions, all of which are, for the most part, concerned with the secondary markets and transactions between investors. The admission to trading function is central to the capital-raising process, however, by providing the issuer of securities with a facility for enhancing the marketability and attractiveness of the issue to investors or capital providers. The success of an offer of securities, and thus of the capital-raising process, is usually dependent on the existence of a market on which the securities can subsequently be traded and which will provide liquidity for the securities[1] and an efficient price formation process, such that any capital gains can be effectively realized. In performing this key conferral-of-marketability function, securities-trading markets play a critical role in the capital-raising process, in promoting investment and in bolstering economy-wide growth.[2]

At present, admission to trading is for many issuers preceded by the admission to official listing process. Many securities-trading markets, typically traditional stock exchanges, provide official listing services as well as trading facilities and will dedicate an official segment of their markets to officially listed securities. In the EC, admission of a security to the Official List is a mechanism, provided either by the stock exchanges themselves (although, as exchanges demutualize and become subject to commercial pressures, this function has been handed over in some cases to independent

---

[1] Liquidity reflects the ease with which buyers and sellers of a security can find a trading counterparty. Trades in an illiquid security carry costs because a seller may have to offer a discounted price in order to find at least one buyer, or a buyer may have to offer a premium price to find at least one seller.

[2] On the extent to which financing in the EC is evolving towards a market model see Ch. II sect. 9 above.

regulatory authorities)[3] or by regulatory authorities, which filters securities through a quality-control process before they are admitted to public trading.[4] The admission to official listing process is an investor-protection mechanism, as well as a device which aids the capital seeker by assisting marketability. It is designed to bolster investors' confidence in the securities admitted to official listing, in the quality of the disclosure available, and in the conduct of the issuer as well as to promote thereby the issue's marketability. Admission to official listing typically implies that the securities have been issued by a well-established issuer which meets certain size and trading-record requirements. In particular, the official listing of a security results in detailed disclosure concerning the securities and the issuer, in respect of which the issuer's management has taken responsibility, being made available such that an informed assessment of the securities can be made, although the official-listing supervisor will not confirm or guarantee the accuracy of the disclosure. In this regard (and when combined with ongoing disclosure obligations), admission to official listing seeks to ensure that a proper market will exist in the securities, in that they can be valued properly on the basis of widely available disclosure.[5] The listing process is also designed to ensure that only those securities which will support liquid trading, which is an important investor-protection mechanism, are admitted to official listing. Devices such as minimum capitalization requirements and restrictions on the non-transferability of securities facilitate smooth trading in securities.[6] In addition, listing usually ensures that investors will be treated fairly as security-holders by the issuer (issuers of listed equity secu-

---

[3] Since May 2000 (under the Official Listing of Securities (Change of Competent Authority) Regulations 2000, SI 2000/968) the UK Financial Services Authority (the FSA) has been the UK Listing Authority (a role previously fulfilled by the London Stock Exchange) and supervises admission to the Official List of the UK Listing Authority. Its operation is governed by the Financial Services and Markets Act 2000.

[4] Admission to listing conditions have been described as 'the front-line of defence in ensuring the quality of the instruments which are traded on markets and adequate disclosure to investors': Commission Communication on Upgrading the Investment Services Directive (93/22/EEC), COM(2000)729 (the ISD Communication), 13.

[5] On the disclosure aspect of admission to official listing see Ch. IV. As outlined in sect. 5.2 below, the Commission has suggested that the current harmonized admission-to-official-listing regime be transformed into a generic admission-to-regulated-markets regime. The emphasis on disclosure is being maintained in the new regime, however, with the Commission finding that the distinguishing feature of a regulated market as compared to other markets is 'the operation of strict controls regarding the "quality" of the instruments admitted to trading so as to render them freely negotiable on the basis of all information which may have an incidence on its fair valuation': *Overview of Proposed Adjustments to the Investment Services Directive*, Working Document of Services of DG Internal Market, Document 1, July 2001 (the ISD Working Paper), 28.

[6] The emphasis on efficient trading is also appearing in the preparatory work for the new admission to regulated markets regime: 'the market operator would be obliged to have arrangements for verifying that issuers have complied with their disclosure requirements and any other conditions for efficient trading in the security (e.g. minimum efficient float)': ibid.

rities, for example, are subject to controls on how major constitutional and business decisions are taken) and that ongoing disclosure to the market and other obligations are imposed on the issuer. Official listing rules also typically include enforcement mechanisms and rules concerning the suspension and cancellation of listing. Once admitted to the Official List, securities are then admitted to trading.[7]

The expense, possible delays, and the onerous requirements of the official-listing process may render it unsuitable for smaller issuers, however, which may choose instead to access the capital markets via an offer of 'unlisted' securities on a second-tier market which subjects issuers and their securities to less onerous admission requirements than those applicable to markets which require their admitted securities to be officially listed. Second-tier markets are often run by the same securities-trading markets which provide official-listing services and operate markets limited to officially listed securities, a feature which can diminish their attractiveness to issuers, who may fear that investors regard the securities as having somehow failed the listing test.[8] There are now a number of fora in the EC in which small and medium-sized issuers may admit their securities to trading which have become particularly important for growth and technology securities. These include second-tier markets run by traditional stock exchanges (which also maintain official segments), such as the Deutsche Börse's Neuer Markt and the London Stock Exchange's Alternative Investment Market,[9] and new markets such as NASDAQ Europe. Second-tier markets admit securities to trading on the basis of less onerous and more flexible requirements than those applicable to admission to listing, particularly with respect to size and trading record and the requirement that disclosure must be pre-vetted or approved.[10] Moves are currently under way, however, to recast the EC's current admission to official

---

[7] Admission to listing on the London Stock Exchange, eg, is a two-stage process. The securities must first be admitted to the Official List by the UK Listing Authority, and then admitted to trading by the London Stock Exchange. The admission to trading rules involve admission and disclosure requirements which work in parallel with the UK Listing Authority's requirements. On completion of the two-stage process, the securities are 'listed' on the London Stock Exchange. To take another UK example, Tradepoint admits securities to trading which have been admitted to listing, but does not itself list securities. Prior to the transfer of the listing function to the UK Listing Authority, Tradepoint admitted securities to trading which had been admitted to listing by the London Stock Exchange.

[8] Röell, A, 'Competition Among European Exchanges: Recent Developments' in Ferrarini, G (ed), *European Securities Markets. The Investment Services Directive and Beyond* (1998) 213, 220.

[9] AIM was launched in 1995 to meet the financing needs of smaller companies, such as venture-capital-backed or family-based companies, which might not qualify for the London Stock Exchange's main market for listed securities.

[10] Although the disclosure requirements imposed are usually stringent: see Röell, n 8 above, 221. The London Stock Exchange's AIM, eg, does not require that disclosure documents be pre-vetted but seeks to deliver investor protection via risk warnings and the ongoing disclosure required when an issuer is admitted to the market. See the London Stock Exchange's response to the Commission Prospectus Proposal, 'Comments from the London Stock Exchange on the Proposed Prospectus Directive', Aug 2001 (the LSE Comment Document), paras 2.5–2.6.

listing regime as an admission to regulated market regime which would harmonize the rules applicable to all 'regulated markets', whether first- (official
segment) or second-tier. This will involve a major change to the current
regime. At the time of writing, the reform is in the preparatory stages only
and is reviewed in outline in Chapter XI section 9.7 on securities-trading markets reform. At present, it appears that some attempts will be made to retain
the distinctive characteristics of particular markets, although the new issuer
disclosure regime discussed in Chapter IV below, which will apply to the new
admission regime, currently applies to admission to all regulated markets and
does not differentiate between official and other market segments. Offers of
securities may take place outside an organized securities-trading market, in
which case the official listing process does not, of course, apply.

III.2 SCOPE AND FEATURES OF THE ADMISSION REGIME

Before an issuer's securities can be admitted to official listing, they and the
issuer must be accepted for listing and meet the listing requirements. At the
outset of the harmonization programme, admission to official listing conditions represented an important interface between Community issuers and a
key access route into the capital markets, the traditional stock exchanges.
Their harmonization was, accordingly, symbolically important in developing
an integrated securities market. More pragmatically, variations in stock
exchange admission-to-official-listing requirements represented a significant
barrier to the creation of an integrated securities market at the start of the
Commission programme in this area, as did the discretion which could be
exercised by competent authorities with respect to foreign issuers.[11] With
the adoption of the now consolidated Admission Directive in 1979,[12] which,
along with the disclosure rules discussed in Chapter IV below, contains the
EC's admission to official listing regime, admission to official listing conditions have been subject to a considerable degree of harmonization, although
the harmonized rules are now regarded as being outdated.[13] The regime is

---

[11] For a summary of admission-to-official-listing procedures across the Community in 1977,
two years before the harmonization of listing conditions, see Wymeersch, E, *Control of Securities
Markets in the European Economic Community*, Collection Studies. Competition—Approximation
of Legislation Series No. 31 (1977) 71–86.

[12] Directive 79/279/EEC coordinating the conditions for the admission of securities to official stock exchange listing [1979] OJ L66/21 (the Admission Directive or the Directive), now
consolidated in Directive 2001/34/EC on admission of securities to official stock exchange listing and on information to be published on those securities [2001] OJ L184/1 (the Securities
Consolidation Directive or SCD). The discussion in this ch. will be based on the Admission
Directive's text but the parallel consolidated references for the SCD are given for the Admission
Directive references.

[13] Final Report of the Committee of Wise Men on the Regulation of European Securities
Market, Feb 2001 (the Lamfalussy Report), 12

also confined to the official listing process; admission to trading generally is not dealt with by the Directive. The failure to deal with the admission to official listing/admission to trading divide has emerged as a weakness in the regime (see section 5.2 below) and is under review.

By imposing controls on the official listing process, the Admission Directive is a creature of a very different securities trading market environment from that of today's competitive trading market-place;[14] it relies on a perception of the traditional stock exchange as a monopoly provider of listing services (which reflected the position of stock exchanges at the time), which would, in the absence of control, abuse its monopolistic position by, for example, discriminating against certain issuers in the application of listing rules.[15] Given this characterization of the stock exchange, barrier removal in the interests of capital-market integration is achieved by harmonization of standards in order to achieve equivalence and non-discrimination. The Directive does not envisage the possibility of a competition for business developing between stock exchanges. Any such competition would make the imposition of discriminatory conditions on issuers highly unlikely.[16] Issuer access to listing aside, as far as investor protection, which, as outlined below, is a major theme of the Directive, is concerned, the Directive appears to operate on the assumption that without external controls, stock exchanges with listing functions would not be given adequate incentives to pursue investor-protection objectives; again, exchanges in a competitive environment are unlikely to prejudice investor protection.[17]

Although market developments have now overtaken the basic premise on which it operates, EC harmonization of the rules applicable to admission to

---

[14] For a review of the conditions which have led to a more competitive environment see Ch. XI sects. 8.2–8.4 below.

[15] For this analysis see Ferrarini, G, 'The European Regulation of Stock Exchanges: New Perspectives' (1999) 36 *CMLRev.* 569, 573–8. On the exchange as monopolist see also Pagano, M, and Steil, B, 'European Equity Markets I: The Evolution of European Trading Systems' in Steil, B (ed), *The European Equity Markets. The State of the Union and an Agenda for the Millennium* (1996) 42 and 51 and the Initial Report of the Wise Men on European Securities Markets, Nov 2000 (the Initial Lamfalussy Report), 12.

[16] It has been argued that 'the European regulation of listing conditions is obsolete. The LCD [Admission Directive] is aimed to protect issuers and investors from the exchanges' market power. However, the competitive nature of today's markets for listing and trading services makes such a regulation redundant . . . exchanges should be free to state the listing conditions best suited to their business purposes and governments should avoid any detailed regulation of the same': Ferrarini , n 15 above, 597.

[17] Listing conditions which promote liquidity in the securities in question are typically regarded as investor-protection devices. On whether external regulation of liquidity-promoting conditions is necessary see Ferrarini, n 15 above, who at 576 has noted that 'from an economic perspective, stock exchanges provide liquidity services and operate in a competitive setting . . . it is difficult to think of an exchange deliberately pursuing the objective of an "illiquid" market'. The proposed new admission to regulated markets regime (section 5.2 and Ch. XI sect. 9.7 below) suggests, however, that EC policy-makers are not yet prepared to embrace the competition argument fully.

official listing is designed to facilitate greater integration and stimulate market-based financing by introducing objective admission standards, such that
cross-border issuers cannot be arbitrarily excluded from listing on domestic
stock exchanges, and by making cross-border and multiple listings across
the EC, and thus capital raising on a Community-wide scale, easier by harmonizing or standardizing admission requirements. The harmonized standards also serve the objective of and reveal a strong emphasis on investor
protection (which reflects the Treaty competence: see section 4.1.2 below).
The philosophical weaknesses which can be observed in the later in time
investment-services regime with respect to investor protection can, however,
be traced back to this first attempt at securities regulation. Investor protection appears as a device for market interpenetration. The admission regime
(both pre- and post-consolidation) does not explain why investors should be
protected in the admission process and why, in particular, investor protection demands that public controls be imposed on the listing process.
Whether market failure-based rationales or more paternalistic motives
underpin the choices made with respect to admission conditions or the need
to impose external investor-protection requirements on exchanges is also not
made apparent.[18] Neither is any attempt made to rationalize the exclusions
from the regime, given the underlying investor-protection theme. This is
arguably a function of the Treaty basis, however, which provides for the
harmonization of the investor-protection safeguards imposed on companies
by Member States in order to promote the freedom to establish of companies,
rather than for investor-protection purposes *per se*. Harmonization and the
provision of 'more equivalent protection' are, however, stated to lead to
'greater interpenetration of securities markets' (Admission Directive, recital
1, SCD, recital 2). The unarticulated assumption appears to be that if
investors are confident about the standards applicable, they will be more
ready to invest. While this analysis links indirectly into the Treaty competence and freedom to establish of companies and their ability to raise
finance, its appearance in the pre-consolidation Admission Directive in 1979
also marks one of the earliest appearances of the characterization of the
investor as capital provider to be encouraged, rather than as vulnerable
investor to be protected, which would dominate the later investment-
services regime in particular.

Disclosure is a key regulatory device in the admission regime. While the
disclosure regime is discussed in more detail in Chapter IV below, disclosure
permeates the Directive both with respect to substantive requirements (such
as the ongoing disclosure of material obligations requirement) and more

---

[18] For the view that in the current competitive securities-trading market environment particular care should be taken not to impose excessive regulation and that regulation should be
linked to market failures such as information deficiencies or transparency problems see
Ferrarini, n 15 above, 572.

generally; the granting of a derogation, for example, is typically linked to the investor having the necessary information to form an informed assessment of the issuer and the securities. Investor protection is also served by the Directive's focus on liquidity and on the smooth operation of the market-place. In particular, the admission conditions are, in part, designed to ensure that a sufficiently liquid market exists in the listed securities; this can be seen in the minimum capitalization requirements (section 4.5.2 below).[19]

III.3 EARLY DEVELOPMENTS

III.3.1 *Market Finance and Issuer Market Access*

The foundations of the EC's harmonized regime for admission to official listing lie in the early initiatives taken in the 1960s concerning the establishment of a European capital market and the promotion of the capital markets and the potentially deep sources of liquidity across the Community as sources of funding for companies. Although the 1966 Report by the Segré Committee[20] stressed the importance of adequate disclosure, such that investors would have appropriate information concerning securities dealt in on other markets, the need to eliminate the obstacles faced by issuers when accessing the markets of a Member State other than their national State was also highlighted.[21] In particular, the Segré Report identified the narrowness of securities markets across the Community, which resulted in sharp price fluctuations and a lack of liquidity, as a considerable obstacle to the development of a European capital market. To alleviate the narrowness problem, it recommended, *inter alia*, a greater degree of co-operation between exchanges and the admission of a greater proportion of foreign securities to listing on domestic exchanges. In particular, it recommended that official stock exchange lists be lengthened by the introduction of foreign securities, given that listing of foreign securities was, at the time, 'one of the principal means which could quickly bring about some measure of market interpenetration'.[22] In a sign of things to come, it identified the application of discriminatory admission-to-listing requirements to foreign securities (usually

---

[19] For an examination of how an illiquid market can prejudice investors see Amihud, Y, and Mendelson, H, 'A New Approach to the Regulation of Trading Across Securities Markets' (1996) 71 *NYU LRev* 1411, 1426–8.

[20] Report of a Group of Experts Appointed by the EEC Commission, *The Development of a European Capital Market* (1966) 239–41 (the Segré Report).

[21] Harmonization measures were also proposed outside the EC. In 1975 and 1977 the International Federation of Stock Exchanges (FIBV) adopted proposals on the multiple listing of securities and proposed minimum admission and disclosure requirements for such listings. See further Wymeersch, E, 'From Harmonization to Integration in European Securities Markets' (1981) 3 *Journal of Comparative Corporate Law and Securities Regulation* 1, 4.

[22] Segré Report, n 20 above, 242.

in order to 'reserve the domestic market's resources for domestic enterprises')[23] as a particular problem and recommended that any discriminatory
provisions which made the admission of foreign securities to listing more difficult or more expensive should be removed and admission procedures harmonized.[24] It is of some interest, given the focus of the regime which would
subsequently emerge on the official-listing process, that the Report placed
considerable emphasis on the role played by markets outside the Official List
which, at that time, involved 'acclimatizing securities until they are ready
for admission to the official market' and recommended greater admission of
foreign securities to these markets.[25]

The enhancement of the efficiency and liquidity of the Community capital
market and the promotion of the market-finance model by facilitating the
access of issuers to listings across the EC are, accordingly, deeply rooted
objectives of the Community's harmonized admission regime. Nonetheless,
investor protection as a function of investor confidence would also emerge
in the harmonized admission regime as a device for furthering the development of the Community capital market.

III.3.2 *The 1977 Code of Conduct*

The original Commission proposal for an admission directive was presented
in 1976.[26] Progress proved slow, and in the interim the European Code of
Conduct relating to transactions in transferable securities[27] was adopted. As
outlined in Chapter II above, it marks a staging point in the development of
the securities regime in that it represents a formal acceptance at Community
level of the vital connection between the 'proper working and interpenetration' of securities markets, the deepening and diversification of sources of
capital, and the achievement of the Community's objectives as set out in the
Treaty; equally significant is its emphasis on the dependence of interpenetration on the removal of divergences between Member States' rules.[28] With
specific reference to admission conditions, while the Code notes the work
which was, at the time, in train on harmonizing admission conditions, certain of its provisions concerning admission to stock exchange listing would

---

[23] Segré Report, n 20 above, 243.   [24] Ibid, 244.   [25] Ibid, 245.
[26] [1976] OJ C56/3. It was preceded by the Commission proposal for a listing particulars
directive [1972] OJ C131/61, which led the European Parliament in its comments on that proposal to bemoan the fact that 'although satisfactory, the arrangements do not alter the need to
co-ordinate in a future Directive, all conditions governing official quotation on a Stock
Exchange for the first time, so that once securities meet the conditions for official quotation on
a Stock Exchange in one Member State, they cannot be prevented by any other legal requirement from being quoted on a Stock Exchange in the territory of another Member State' [1974]
OJ C11/23, para 17.
[27] Commission Recommendation 77/534/EEC concerning a European Code of Conduct relating to transactions in transferable securities [1977] OJ L 212/37 (the 1977 Code of Conduct).
[28] Ibid, Explanatory Memorandum, paras 1–2.

reappear in the now consolidated Admission Directive. These include: the availability of fair, accurate, clear, adequate, and timely information in the interests of effective price formation (Principle 2); publication by the issuer of material information (Supplementary Principle 12); equality of information for all investors (Supplementary Principles 15 and 16) (the disclosure aspects of the Admissions Directive are considered in Chapter IV below); and equal treatment for shareholders (Principle 3).

III.4 THE ADMISSION DIRECTIVE (NOW CONSOLIDATED)

III.4.1 *Objectives, Treaty Basis, and Approach to Harmonization*

III.4.1.1 *Objectives*

Some three years after the presentation of the Commission's 1976 proposal, the Admission Directive was adopted on 5 March 1979[29] and was, by Article 22(1), to be implemented by the Member States by 8 March 1981.[30]

The purpose of the Directive is clear. It applies a harmonized admission conditions regime to securities which are 'admitted to official listing or are the subject of an application for admission to official listing on a stock exchange situated or operating within a Member State' (Article 1(1)) (SCD, Article 2(1)). The reference to 'official listing on a stock exchange' blurs the distinction between admission to listing and admission to trading. Adopted when stock exchanges had a monolithic competitive position, were not shareholder-owned nor subject to commercial pressures, and were typically regarded as public-interest entities competent to oversee the listing process, the Admission Directive does not distinguish between the two functions or address the harmonisation of admission to trading conditions.[31]

While the interpenetration of securities markets is the Directive's dominant rationale, a notable feature of the Directive is its focus on investor protection, which is a function of its Treaty base (see section 4.1.2 below). The co-ordination of conditions for the admission of securities to official listing will, according to recital 1, 'provide equivalent protection for investors at

---

[29] The Directive was amended in Mar 1982 by Council Directive 82/148 [1982] OJ L62/22 which extended the end of the implementation period from 8 Mar 1981 to 30 June 1983 for Member States simultaneously implementing the Admission Directive and the listing particulars and interim reports regime discussed in Ch. IV below. The Commission's proposal is at [1976] OJ C56/2, ECOSOC's comments are at [1976] OJ C204/5 and Parliament's reading is at [1976] OJ C238/38. See generally Morse, G, 'Directive on the Admission of Securities to Official Stock Exchange Listing' (1979) 4 *ELRev.* 201 and Woolridge, F, 'Some recent Community Legislation in the Field of Securities Law' (1985) 10 *ELRev.* 3, 5–10.

[30] Where a Member State was simultaneously implementing the then proposed directive on listing particulars, the deadline was extended by one year.

[31] See further sect. 5.2.

Community level, because of the more uniform guarantees offered to investors in the various Member States' (SCD, recital 2).[32] Investor protection is achieved primarily through disclosure and liquidity requirements, but the protection regime does not extend to conferring directly enforceable rights on investors; investor protection is a function of the relationship between the issuer and the competent authority overseeing the admission conditions.[33] The Admission Directive is also designed to facilitate the admission to official listing in each Member State of securities from other Member States as well as the listing of any given security on a number of stock exchanges in the Community (recital 1) (SCD, recital 2); by establishing common minimum standards, the Directive is designed to reduce the legal costs represented by varying regimes as well as to remove any discriminatory, protectionist barriers faced by issuers seeking listings of securities on exchanges across the EC.[34] Achievement of both of these objectives, common investor-protection standards and the facilitating of cross-border and multiple listings, is stated to encourage the interpenetration of national securities markets and contribute to the development of a European capital market. In addition, although it does not appear in the Admission Directive

[32] In support of the investor-protection function of the Admission Directive see FSA, *The Transfer of the UK Listing Authority to the FSA*, Consultation Paper 37 (1999) (the Listing Authority Transfer Paper), in which the FSA has at 9 described the official listing process as 'the process of being listed in accordance with the relevant European Community directives and UK legislation. This ensures that minimum standards are in place for investor protection and to allow mutual recognition of listing particulars across the EU.' The mutual recognition point refers to the disclosure regime discussed in Ch. IV.

[33] For this perspective see *R v International Stock Exchange, ex parte Else* [1993] QB 534 (discussed in n 65 below). The court took an issuer-centred view of the Directive in responding to the arguments of the investor applicants in that case that the Directive was intended to protect investors, that investors were likely to suffer loss if a listing was cancelled, that investors cannot resist a cancellation decision unless they are informed and can make representations to the competent authority, and that, accordingly, Art. 15 (SCD, Art. 19) (which grants issuers a right of appeal to the courts against cancellation decisions by competent authorities) confers on investors the right to be notified and to make representations. The court at 549 found that: '[the Directive] expressly recognises the responsibility of the competent authorities to protect the interests of investors, which must always be their overriding concern when exercising their powers. But the primary purpose of the Directive is to co-ordinate the listing practice of competent authorities in the various member States with a view to establishing a common market in securities and not, in any direct way to provide additional protection for investors.' Also of interest, given that EC securities regulation has yet to provide a definition of the investor, either in the capital-raising sphere or in the investment-services area (see Ch. IX below), is that the Court focused on the absence of a definition of 'investor' in the Directive as evidence of the fact that the Directive was not designed to confer directly enforceable rights on investors. If it were to grant rights, it would, the Court found at 551, be very important to know who were included in the class of investors.

[34] As was observed in the *Else* judgment, above, at 546: '[t]here could be no truly common market so long as different conditions were imposed by the various member States. Still less could there by a truly common market if it was open to national authorities, under the guise of protecting investors, to make the admission of local securities to listing easier than that of foreign securities'.

Preamble (or in the SCD version), the substantive content of the Directive suggests a strong concern for the smooth operation of the trading markets in the interests of investor protection and in order to facilitate interpenetration. Not only are a number of the Directive's requirements clearly directed towards efficient and smooth secondary trading, the 'smooth operation of the market' is expressly referred to in a number of places.[35]

III.4.1.2 *Legal Basis*

The Directive is based on the freedom to establish (Article 43 EC) and, specifically, on Article 44(2)(g) EC (then Article 54(3)(g) EC) which provides for Commission and Council action 'co-ordinating to the extent necessary the safeguards which, for the protection of the interests of members and others, are required by Member States of companies or firms'. Member State rules imposed on companies concerning the listing of their securities for the protection of investors clearly come within this provision. Article 44(2)(g) EC does not permit the adoption of measures to promote investor protection as an interest of itself; it allows for the harmonization of Member States' investor protection for the purposes of promoting the freedom to establish of companies. It explains, however, the emphasis on investor protection throughout the Directive. The more general competence provided by Article 94 EC (at the time Article 100 EC) was also relied on as a legal basis.[36] The Preamble explains that the co-ordination sought must apply to securities independently of the legal status of their issuers and apply to securities issued by non-member States or their regional or local authorities or international public bodies. These issuers do not, however, come within the scope of Article 44(2)(g) requiring recourse to Article 94 EC as the harmonization introduced by the Admission Directive also directly affects the establishment and functioning of the common market.[37] Indeed, the focus in Article 94 EC

[35] Such as, eg, Art. 13(1) and (2) (SCD, Art. 16(1) and (2)) on the disclosure of information, the suspension power in Art. 14 (SCD, Art. 18) and the requirement in Sch A, para II(2) (SCD, Art. 46(2)) that shares which are not fully paid up must not be treated as negotiable (as required for admission) if open and proper dealing is prejudiced.

[36] Art. 94 EC provides for the issuing of directives 'for the approximation of such laws, regulations or administrative provisions of the Member States as directly affect the establishing or functioning of the common market'.

[37] Art. 44(2)(g) EC only applies to companies or firms within the meaning of Art. 48(2) which is restricted to 'companies or firms constituted under civil or commercial law, including co-operative societies, and other legal persons governed by public or private law, save those which are non-profit making'. The Preamble explains the need for the additional legal basis on the grounds that harmonization 'must . . . apply to securities, independently of their legal status, and must therefore also apply to securities issued by non-member States or their regional or local authorities or international public bodies . . . this Directive therefore covers entities not covered by [Art. 48 EC, then Art. 58 EC] and goes beyond the scope of [Art. 44(2)(g), then Art. 54(3)(g)] while directly affecting the establishment and functioning of the common market within the meaning of Article 100 [now Art. 94 EC]': Recital 2 (SCD, recital 3 (it does n

on the approximation or harmonization of laws which directly affect the establishment or functioning of the common market may seem to render it a more appropriate competence on which to have based the Directive, given that the interpenetration of national securities markets and the construction of a European capital market (and the ancillary objectives of investor confidence/protection and ensuring the smooth functioning of securities markets as preconditions for integration) feeds more directly into the establishment and functioning of the common market than it does into the free movement of companies.[38] It is only in later directives (such as the 1989 Insider Dealing Directive),[39] when the EC began to move into regulating the integrated securities market and away from constructing it by harmonizing stock exchange issuer access (and disclosure) rules, that the link between harmonization and the establishment and functioning of the common market (or the internal market under Article 95 EC) becomes more opaque and, since October 2001 and the *Tobacco Advertising* ruling, more problematic from the perspective of competence to harmonize.[40]

III.4.1.3 *The Harmonisation Device*

As outlined in Chapter II, the now consolidated Admission Directive, in sharp contrast to later liberalizing measures, introduces detailed levels of harmonization in an attempt to remove regulatory barriers by making rules equivalent and to reduce the discretion previously exercised by Member States in this area and, accordingly, the risk of discriminatory treatment of foreign issuers.[41]

include the reference to directly affecting the establishment and functioning of the common market)).

[38] On the limits of Art. 44(2)(g) EC as a capital-market construction measure, given its focus on the establishment rules, see Ch. IV sect. 3.2.3.

[39] Directive 89/592/EEC coordinating regulations on insider dealing [1989] OJ L334/30. It is based on Art. 95 EC (at the time Art. 100a). Art. 95 allows for internal market measures (it provides for the adoption of measures to approximate laws which have as their object the establishment and functioning of the internal market) to be adopted by a qualified majority vote of the Council as compared to the unanimous vote required by Art. 94 EC. On the law making process see further Ch. XV sect. 2.

[40] On the ramifications of the *Tobacco Advertising* judgment (Case C–376/98 *Germany v Parliament and Council* [2000] ECR I–8419) for harmonization designed to promote the internal market see Ch. IX sect. 12.

[41] option of the now consolidated Admission Directive, the German stock exchange which could not refuse an application for listing which fulfor admission: Wymeersch, n 11 above, 71. All other exchanges could retion with respect to admission decisions, although, as Professor at 72, refusals to admit were extremely rare. On the role of the educing the element of discretion in the admission process see also ion and ReRegulation of Cross-Border Financial Services, Part II' 292.

Nonetheless, despite the detailed harmonization introduced by the Directive (albeit in limited areas),[42] the standards are pegged at a minimum level. In practice, admission conditions can vary considerably between Member States as a result of the flexibility granted to them in implementing the Directive: not only are particular provisions subject to derogations and the exercise of discretion, but Member States enjoy a general power to adopt additional and more stringent conditions.[43] Article 5(1) and (2) (SCD, Article 8(1) and (2)) permits Member States to impose more stringent or additional admission conditions either in respect of the admission of securities or in respect of the obligations imposed on issuers of listed securities. Member States may also authorize derogations from these additional conditions, but any such derogations must apply generally for all issuers where the circumstances justifying them are met (Article 5(3)) (SCD, Article 8(3)). The danger of Article 5 being used as a tool to exclude particular foreign securities from listing arbitrarily is minimized by the requirement that, where the conditions concern obligations imposed on issuers of listed securities, they apply generally to all issuers or individual classes of issuer (Article 5(2)). Similarly, where the conditions concern the admission of securities, they must be published before an application is made for the admission of such securities and they must apply generally to all issuers or to individual classes of issuer (Article 5(1)). Full harmonization is weakened further (although the investor-protection theme underlined) by Article 10 (SCD, Article 12) which allows Member States, 'solely in the interests of protecting the investors', to permit competent authorities to subject the listing of a security to such 'special conditions' as they deem appropriate and which have been notified to the applicant issuer.[44] Nonetheless, while in principle

[42] The Directive does not, eg, deal in any detail (save for Sch A, I(4) which deals with the distribution of shares) (SCD, Art. 48) with the conditions which may be imposed on listed securities with respect to how they are brought to the market, such that an open and efficient trading market develops in those securities, having regard to their nature and amount. The UK Listing Authority takes this objective as one of its governing principles in applying its listing rules. Also absent from the Admission Directive's ongoing obligations regime are any controls on directors with respect to dealing in shares of their own companies.

[43] The dangers of this approach were apparent even as the Directive was being negotiated. The European Parliament noted that the harmonizing measures 'still leave a wide margin of discretion to Member States, jeopardizing the very aims of the Directive', and called for the Commission to submit proposals for a common procedure for admission to listing, which would grant an issuer admitted to listing on the stock exchange of one Member State access to the exchanges of other Member States 'without having to fulfil stricter or additional national requirements': n 29 above, paras 1 and 2.

[44] On a strict reading of the Directive, these 'special' conditions, unlike the 'additional' conditions which may be imposed under Art. 5 (SCD, A8), need not be published in advance of the application for listing and are not subject to the requirement of non-discrimination. Member States thus enjoy greater flexibility in imposing additional conditions where investor protection is the rationale. It has been observed that Art. 10 (SCD, Art. 12) provides for the imposition of 'tailor-made' conditions, addressing unique investor-protection issues which may emerge during the application procedure: Wymeersch, n 21 above, 7.

Articles 5 and 10 allow for Member State (and competent authority) discretion in the imposition of listing conditions, that discretion has been drastically curtailed. Not only must the Directive's minimum requirements be complied with, but the non-discrimination principle must be applied with only investor-protection-driven rules benefiting from a less stringent approach.

The Directive is shot through with derogations. Member States may authorize derogations from any additional or more stringent obligations which they may impose, however, only where they 'apply generally for all issuers where the conditions justifying them are similar' (Article 5(3)) (SCD, Article 8(3)). Similarly, the particular admission conditions set out in the Schedules are subject to certain derogations, but under Article 7 (SCD, Article 9) any derogations from the conditions for the admission of securities to official listing which are authorized in accordance with Schedules A and B (SCD, Articles 42–63) must apply generally for all issuers where the circumstances justifying them are similar. Special derogations apply under Article 8 (SCD, Article 10) to debt securities in respect of which repayment and interest payments are guaranteed by a Member State or one of its federal States.[45]

According to recital 7, this flexible approach to harmonization was adopted to reflect the differences in the structures of securities markets in the Member States and to allow Member States to take account of any specific situations which they may have to deal with (SCD, recital 5). The Preamble also acknowledges in recital 9 (SCD, recital 7) that harmonization is only 'partial' and that it 'constitutes a first step towards closer alignment of the rules of Member States in this field'.[46]

III.4.2 *The Core Obligation*

The core obligation imposed on Member States by the now consolidated Admission Directive is to ensure that an issuer applying for the admission of securities will not be admitted to official listing on any stock exchange situated or operating within their territory unless the conditions laid down by the Directive are satisfied, and that issuers of securities admitted to official

---

[45] Specifically, the requirements of Sch B (the admission conditions for debt securities) (SCD, Arts. 52–63) and the requirements of Sch D (A), para 4(a) and (c) (SCD, Art. 81(1) and (3)) (the continuing obligations on issuers to inform the public of major new developments and of any new loan issues, respectively) may be disapplied.

[46] ECOSOC also felt that 'it would be better, in the initial phase, to lay down minimum conditions only, rather than aim for an ideal arrangement': n 29 above, para 1.2. The reference to partial harmonization could also be read, of course, as an indication of intent to address the trading function of stock exchanges, although 14 years would pass before such measures were adopted. See Ch. XI below.

listing are subject to the Directive's obligations (Article 3) (SCD, Article 5).[47]
The admission conditions for shares and debt securities are set out in
Schedules A and B, respectively (Article 4(1)) (SCD, Article 6(1), Articles
42–51 (Schedule A) and Articles 52–63 (Schedule B)). Schedule C (SCD,
Articles 64–69) and D (SCD Articles 78–84) cover the ongoing obligations
imposed on issuers of shares and debt securities respectively, whose securi-
ties are listed on the official list of a stock exchange in a Member State
(Article 4(2)) (SCD, Article 6(2)). Certificates representing shares are subject to a special regime, based on Schedules A and C, under Article 4(3)
(SCD, Article 6(3)). In addition, Article 6 (SCD, Article 7) provides that
Member States may not make the admission to official listing of securities
issued by companies or other legal persons which are nationals of another
Member State subject to the condition that the securities must already have
been admitted to official listing on a stock exchange situated or operating in
one of the Member States.

The effect of the core obligation is sharply to reduce the degree of discretion enjoyed by competent authorities and Member States in admitting securities to official listing and to ensure the non-discriminatory treatment of
foreign securities. Multiple listings are also facilitated, given that admission
conditions are, in theory, rendered broadly equivalent across the
Community, although, as outlined above, the Directive's structure allows for
considerable flexibility in its application.

III.4.3 *Scope*

III.4.3.1 *Securities*

The now consolidated Admission Directive applies to 'securities which are
admitted to official listing or are the subject of an application for admission
to official listing . . . on a stock exchange situated or operating within a
Member State' (Article 1(1)) (SCD, Article 2(1)). 'Securities' is not a defined
term,[48] although the content of the Schedules makes it clear that debt and
equity instruments alike are covered. It is also clear that certificates representing shares are covered as they are subject to a special admission regime

---

[47] Art. 16 of the original proposal authorised competent authorities, in exceptional cases, to
establish official quotation without a formal application where there was, in fact, a market for
the security and it was in the interests of investors to make the relevant dealings subject to the
disciplines and controls of official quotation.

[48] The Commission chose not to follow the example of the earlier 1977 Code of Conduct in
defining transferable securities as 'all securities which are or may be the subject of dealings on
an organised market'. In later securities regulation measures, the definition of securities would
become more sophisticated.

under Article 4(3) (SCD, Article 6(3)),[49] as are debt securities guaranteed by Member States[50] and debt securities issued by public authorities.[51]

In implementing the Directive, Member States may, under Article 1(2) (SCD, Article 2(2)), exclude securities issued by Member States or their local or regional authorities. Units issued by collective-investment undertakings, other than closed-end undertakings,[52] may also be excluded from its requirements by Article 1(2).[53]

III.4.3.2 *Stock Exchange and the Official List*

The Directive applies under Article 1(1) (SCD, Article 2(1)) to securities 'which are admitted to official listing or are the subject of an application for admission to official listing on a stock exchange situated or operating within a Member State'. The key terms 'official list' and 'stock exchange' are not defined by the Directive, despite their acting as triggers for the application

[49] The provisions on certificates representing shares were primarily designed to cover a particular Dutch practice of issuing shares. The legal title to the shares is vested in a subsidiary of a bank or financial institution called an *administratiekantoor*. Certificates (*certificaten*) are then issued by the *administratiekantoor* to investors.

[50] Art. 8 (SCD, Art. 10) allows Member States to derogate from the requirements imposed under Schs B and D, paras. (4)(a) and (c)(SCD, Arts. 52–63 and Art. 81(1) and (3)) (essentially the conditions for the admission of debt securities and the ongoing disclosure obligations in respect of material developments and new issues) in respect of applications for admission to official listing of 'debt securities issued by companies and other legal persons which are nationals of a Member State and which are set up by, governed by or managed pursuant to a special law where repayments and interest payments in respect of those securities are guaranteed by a Member State or one of its federal states'.

[51] Sch B (B), paras 1–4 and Sch D (B), paras 1–2 (SCD, Arts. 60–63 and Arts. 83–84).

[52] Art. 2(a) defines collective investment undertakings other than the closed-end type (on the difference between open- and closed-end undertakings see Ch. V sect. 6.2) as unit trusts and investment companies the object of which is the collective investment of capital provided by the public, which operate on the principle of risk-spreading and the units of which are, at the request of holders, repurchased or redeemed, directly or indirectly, out of the assets of such undertakings (action taken by such undertakings to ensure that the stock exchange value of their units does not vary significantly from their net asset value is to be regarded as equivalent to repurchase or redemption). SCD, Art. 1(b). This definition is similar to the definition of a collective-investment scheme adopted by the UCITS Directive (Directive 85/611/EEC on the coordination of laws, regulations and administrative provisions relating to undertakings for collective investment in transferable securities [1985] OJ L375/3) which liberalizes the market in such collective investment schemes. The definitions are not identical; the UCITS Directive definition, eg, encompasses only undertakings whose sole object is investment in transferable securities (see further Ch. V). Units are defined in Art. 2(b) (SCD, Art. 1(b)) as securities issued by collective investment schemes which represent the rights of participants in the assets of such undertakings.

[53] Exchange-traded funds, both open- and closed-end, are now a regular feature of securities-trading markets. In Apr 2000, eg, the London Stock Exchange announced listings of open-ended exchange-traded funds on the specifically established extraMARK market which forms part of the main London Stock Exchange market and part of the Official List maintained by the UK Listing Authority. The growth in these listings reflects the strong growth in the retail investor market in Europe and the desire of stock exchanges to capture business from that growth.

of the Directive's requirements. It has been suggested that the 'official list' covers that part of a Member State's securities market which offers the maximum guarantees for investors and to which access is most difficult.[54] In practice, the scope of Official Lists across the EC can sometimes be carved out by reference to the other second-tier markets run by the exchanges which do not require that the official listing standard is met. Many Member States have interpreted the Directive as applying to the 'official segment of the national stock exchange'.[55]

The basic features of a 'stock exchange' for the purposes of the Directive can perhaps be distilled from the references in the Schedules to *'another* [emphasis added] regulated, regularly operating, recognised, open market' which suggest that a stock exchange is a regulated market.[56] Stock exchanges as characterized by the Admission Directive are thus regulated markets, but must be distinguished from regulated markets such as the AIM, to which the Directive and its official listing rules do not apply.[57] Changes in the securities-trading market environment, particularly the demutualization of exchanges, are forcing a reassessment of the admission-to-official-listing/admission-to-trading distinction and of the extent to which admission-to-listing functions should be carried out by stock exchanges and whether or not they should maintain official lists. The stock exchange

[54] Wymeersch, E, 'La Directive sur les conditions d'admission en bourse' (1980) 1 Revue de la Banque 17.

[55] Commission's Explanatory Memorandum to the proposal on the prospectus to be published when securities are offered to the public or admitted to trading, COM(2001)280, 7.

[56] This analysis relies on the references to 'another regulated, regularly operating, recognised, open market' in Sch A, para I(2) (this provision concerns derogations from the minimum capitalization requirement) (SCD, Art. 43(3)) and in Sch B (A), para III(2) (SCD, Art. 59) (which refers to conditions imposed on convertible or exchangeable debentures and debentures with warrants): Ferrarini, G, 'Exchange Governance and Regulation: An Overview' in Ferrarini, n 8 above, 245, 259. The approach towards 'stock exchanges' and their functions has since become considerably more certain and sophisticated following the move by EC securities regulation into the regulation of secondary markets and the trading functions supplied by securities trading markets with the adoption of the Investment Services Directive (Directive 93/22/EC [1993] OJ L141/27) (the ISD)) which uses the concept of a 'regulated market' (which is, essentially, one which is designated as such by the Member States, functions regularly, is characterized by the fact that rules issued or approved by the competent authorities define the conditions for the operation of the market, market-access conditions, and, either, where the Admission Directive applies, its listing conditions or, where the Directive does not apply, the conditions which must be satisfied by a financial instrument before it is dealt in on the market, and requires compliance with the ISD's transparency requirements. See further Ch. XI sect. 6.3 below). In the Admission Directive, the categorization of stock exchanges is via their listing functions and is closely connected to the 'public-interest' perspective of exchanges as gatekeepers to the capital markets. The unsatisfactory definition of a stock exchange jars somewhat with the regulated market concept used in the ISD and generates an unnecessary fault-line between the earlier securities directives which focus on capital raising and the later investment-services regime which addresses the secondary markets.

[57] See Ferrarini, n 15 above, 573.

and official list definitions are being revisited in this light (section 5.2 below).[58]

III.4.4 *Competent Authorities and Official-listing Applications*

The effective operation of the now consolidated Admission Directive regime, and thus the achievement of its investor-protection and market-interpenetration objectives, was heavily dependent on the implementation, supervision, and enforcement of its rules. In its first foray into securities regulation with the Admission Directive, the Community established the principle of decentralized supervision and enforcement of the harmonized regime, supported by co-operation between national authorities, which has served as the supervisory model for EC securities regulation as a whole. It also revealed a sensitivity to national models of supervision, be they statutory or self-regulatory, which would continue throughout the regime.[59]

Under Article 9(1) (SCD, Articles 11(1) and 105), Member States are required to designate competent authorities to decide on the admission of securities to official listing on a stock exchange 'situated or operating' in their territory; Member States are also to ensure that the Directive's requirements are applied. While the distinction between 'situated or operating' within a Member State's territory is not explained, it reflects the distinction between centralized exchanges where trading takes place in a particular location and dealer-based markets where trading is decentralized and occurs through a network of dealers.[60] Where duties are allocated between competent authorities, Member States must inform the Commission accordingly. Article 9(1) does not, however, stipulate that the competent authority be responsible for ensuring compliance with the continuing obligations imposed on issuers by the Directive; by contrast Article 3 (SCD, Article 5) requires Member States to ensure that official listing is granted only in accordance with the Directive's provisions and that issuers, once admitted to official listing, are subject to the Directive's obligations.

Despite the pivotal role played by the competent authority in filtering access to the Official List and ensuring that only appropriately qualified issuers benefit from listing, the Directive does not require that the competent authority take a particular legal form. The only stipulation is that, under Article 9(2), the authority have 'such powers as may be necessary for the

---

[58] ISD Communication, n 4 above, 14 and, generally, the ISD Working Paper, n 5 above. See Chs. IV sect. 9.3 and XI sect. 9.7 below on the moves to remove the official-listing concept and to restructure the powers of securities-trading markets.

[59] On the treatment of self-regulatory and statutory or publicly controlled supervision models in EC securities regulation see Ch. XV sect. 3.1.2 below.

[60] Ferrarini, G, 'Securities Regulation and the Rise of Pan-European Equity Markets: An Overview', in Ferrarini, G, Hopt, K, and Wymeersch, E (eds), *Capital Markets in the Age of the Euro* (forthcoming).

exercise of their duties'.[61] The competent authority may, as a result, take a non-statutory or self-regulatory form.[62]

The competent authority is granted a wide degree of discretion under the Directive. As previously noted, it may, under Article 10 (SCD, Article 12), impose special conditions additional to the Directive's requirements which it considers appropriate and which are notified to the applicant as long as the Member State has, solely in the interests of investor protection, granted this power to the competent authority. It may, under Article 9(3) (SCD, Article 11(2)), reject an application if, in its opinion, the issuer's situation is such that a listing would be detrimental to the interests of investors.[63] Competent authorities therefore retain a discretion to refuse admission to securities, even if the formal requirements of the Directive are met, if to do so would be detrimental to the interests of investors. Under Article 11 (SCD, Article 14) an application may also be dismissed if the security is already officially listed in another Member State and the issuer has failed to comply with its admission obligations in that State.

---

[61] The new SCD reference (Art. 105(2)) which reflects later directives in this area is to 'powers necessary for them to carry out their task'. The original proposal was more specific and required that competent authorities have all the authority and powers of verification necessary for their work. In particular, it specified in Art. 19(3) that competent authorities have the authority to require the issuer to furnish any information and produce any documents which they considered necessary in order to decide on the application and that they be empowered to require any audits or inspections which they considered appropriate.

[62] See Wymeersch, E, 'The Implementation of the ISD and CAD in National Legal Systems' in Ferrarini, n 8 above, 3, 7. This provision reflects the reality that, at the time of the Directive's adoption, stock exchange supervisors (the most likely candidates for acting as competent authorities) varied in form across the EC. In the UK the London Stock Exchange was self-regulating, while in France the Commission des Opérations de Bourse was a governmental authority and enjoyed extensive powers. The Belgian Commission Bancaire (which combined the functions of a banking supervisor and securities commission) was also a public body but, unlike its French counterpart, had limited powers. See generally Buxbaum, R, and Hopt, K, *Legal Harmonisation and the Business Enterprise* (1988) 189–92 and Wymeersch, n 11 above, 32–50. Buxbaum and Hopt have observed at 267, however, that while national capital-market supervisory bodies reflected national traditions and were close to the markets they supervised, the decentralized approach carried the danger of triggering discrepancies in supervision and implementation, noting in particular that '[t]here are worlds of difference between, for example, the French Commission des Opérations de Bourse and the Italian CONSOB, each of which is vastly different from the Belgian Commission Bancaire'. These concerns about the adequacy of the underlying supervisory structure have persisted and arise in all areas of EC securities regulation. See Ch. XV sect. 3.

[63] The original proposal took a different approach to the rejection process and placed more emphasis on the obligation to give reasons. Art. 10(1) of the original proposal required competent authorities to give 'explicit reasons' for rejecting an application. In addition, Art. 11(b) of the original proposal permitted Member States to grant competent authorities the power, which could be invoked only for the purpose of protecting the investor, to reject official-listing applications without giving explicit reasons for the rejection. ECOSOC found this latter provision to be 'indefensible' and suggested that competent authorities should be permitted not to provide reasons only when 'it is virtually certain that the legitimate interests of the Member State concerned in general or of investors would be fundamentally affected by such a reason being disclosed': n 29 above, para 2.2.3.

Competent authorities must be made subject to back-stop review by the courts. Article 15(1) (SCD, Article 19(1)) provides that Member States must ensure that decisions of the competent authority refusing the admission of a security to official listing or discontinuing a listing shall be subject to a right to apply to the courts.[64] The right also applies where an application has been automatically rejected following a failure by the competent authority to give a decision within six months of the receipt of the application, or, if the competent authority requires further information, within six months of that request (Article 15(2) and (3)) (SCD, Article 19(2) and (3)). Although recital 3 makes clear that this right must not restrict the discretion of competent authorities (SCD, recital 3), it acts as an external control on the activities of self-regulating competent authorities, in particular.[65]

Consistent with the Directive's focus on adequate disclosure, competent authorities are granted considerable general information-retrieval powers. While specific disclosure obligations are imposed by the Schedules (SCD Articles 42–84), under Article 13(1) (SCD, Article 16(1)), issuers must pro-

---

[64] Art. 10(2) of the original proposal limited the right of appeal to decisions refusing an application. ECOSOC's more radical suggestion that the right to apply to the courts against any decision of a competent authority was, unsurprisingly, not adopted: n 29 above, para 2.2.2.

[65] Challenges under Art. 15 (SCD, Art. 19) can raise difficulties for competent authorities operating in a time-sensitive market environment. Court proceedings may be further delayed if national courts seek clarification on the ambit of Art. 15 by means of the preliminary reference procedure under which national courts may ask the Court of Justice for clarification on questions of EC law (Art. 234 EC). This situation arose in *R v International Stock Exchange, ex parte Else* [1993] QB 534 which, as well as clarifying the scope of Art. 15 also offers a perspective on the purpose of the Directive. The Committee on Quotations of the Stock Exchange upheld a decision of the quotations panel cancelling the official listing of shares in a company in which the applicants were shareholders. Although the company did not challenge the decision, the applicants did on the grounds that they were entitled under Art. 15 to be notified and to be given the opportunity to make representations to the committee prior to the making of any cancellation decision. The judge at first instance decided to make a preliminary reference on the scope of Art. 15 to the Court of Justice. This decision to refer was challenged and overturned on appeal. The Court found that the primary purpose of the Directive was to co-ordinate the listing practices of competent authorities in Member States and not the provision of additional protection for investors. The Court also found that the Directive was concerned with relations between competent authorities and issuers/companies and not with relations between competent authorities and investors. As a result, the Directive did not confer enforceable rights on investors. Companies and issuers alone were the entities against which cancellation decisions could be taken; accordingly, only companies and issuers were granted a right to apply to the courts under Art. 15. The Court also referred to the overriding discretion of competent authorities referred to in recital 7 (SCD, recital 4) and found that in the absence of provision for notifying shareholders (and given that shareholders did not usually act for a company or enforce its rights) Art. 15 did not entitle shareholders to be informed of an impending decision on a listing cancellation. It followed that there was no necessity for a preliminary reference. In reaching its conclusion on the scope of Art. 15, the Court paid particular attention to the position of the competent authorities, finding at 550 that the rights claimed by the applicant investors would 'gravely restrict the discretion of the competent authorities . . . Recent history in more than one field emphasises the need for regulatory authorities to take quick and decisive action where the situation requires it. The Directive, in my view, recognises that need and gives effect to it. The applicants' argument subverts that intention'.

vide the competent authority with all the information considered appropriate by the competent authority in order to protect investors or ensure the smooth operation of the market. In addition, Article 13(2) (SCD, Article 16(2)) provides that, again where the protection of investors or the smooth operation of the market so requires, an issuer may be required to publish such information in the form and within the time limits that the competent authority considers appropriate. Failure to comply with this disclosure requirement will allow the competent authority to publish the information in question (Article 13(2)).

III.4.5 *Admission Requirements and the Schedules*

III.4.5.1 *Introduction*

The conditions set out in the Schedules (SCD, Articles 42–84) are numerous and detailed and introduce a relatively high degree of harmonization. The more significant requirements are highlighted in sections 4.5.2–4.5.5 below. Member States may derogate from certain specified conditions subject to the requirement of Article 7 (SCD, Article 9) that any derogations authorized are non-discriminatory, in that they apply generally to all issuers where the circumstances justifying such derogations are similar.

III.4.5.2 *Conditions Applicable to the Issuer of Shares: Schedule A (SCD, Articles 42–44)*

Under Schedule A, paragraph I(1) (SCD, Article 42), the issuer must be 'in conformity with the laws and regulations to which it is subject, as regards both its formation and its operation under its statutes'. In the interests of investor protection and, in particular, the need to maintain a liquid market in listed securities, a minimum foreseeable market capitalization of one million euro is required (Schedule A, paragraph I(2)) (SCD, Article 43(2)).[66] This condition is flexible. Where the foreseeable market capitalization cannot be assessed, the company's capital assets and reserves (including profit or loss) from the last financial year must amount to not less than one million euro.[67] Member States may provide for admission to official listing when

---

[66] The minimum capitalization figure was originally set by reference to the European Unit of Account (defined in Art. 2(c) as the unit of account defined in Art. 10 of the Financial Regulation of 21 Dec 1977 applicable to the Budget of the European Communities). The European Unit of Account has since been replaced first by the ECU (Regulation 3308/80 [1980] OJ L345/1) and, since 1 Jan 1999, by the euro (Regulation 1103/97 [1997] OJ L162/1, Art. 2). For a discussion of the transition from units of account to the euro see Usher, J, *The Law of Money and Financial Services in the European Community* (2nd edn, 2000) 151–70.

[67] In an early example of delegated law-making by the comitology process which has come to be of critical importance for the adoption of securities regulation measures (Ch. XV sect. 2.5.3), the Directive in Art. 21 (SCD, Art. 109) gives the Commission the power to adjust the

this condition is not met as long as the competent authorities are satisfied that an 'adequate market' (undefined) will be created in the shares concerned. A higher minimum capitalization (or capital assets and reserves requirement) may be imposed by a Member State, but only where another regulated, regularly operating, recognized, open market exists in that Member State and the requirements for it with respect to capitalization or capital and reserves are less than or equal to one million euro. The capitalization requirement does not apply to listing applications in respect of a further block of shares of the same class as those already listed.

Schedule A, paragraph I(3) (SCD, Article 44) imposes an operating history requirement and requires that the issuer must have published or filed audited accounts, in accordance with national law, for the three financial years preceding the application. Competent authorities may derogate from this condition where a derogation is warranted in the interests of the issuer or investors and where the competent authority is satisfied that investors have the information necessary to make an informed judgement on the issuer and the shares.[68] The original proposal required the company to prove that 'it will maintain a profit-making capacity for the current financial year'.[69] This requirement, which would have placed a considerable pressure on competent authorities to assess the financial position of the company substantively, was subsequently dropped, not least because, as

minimum capitalization requirement 'in light of the requirements of the economic situation'. In doing so, the Commission must follow the procedure set out in Art. 21 (SCD, Art. 109) which now, post-consolidation, requires the decision-making process to be supervised by the Contact Committee (sect. 4.8 below), acting as a regulatory committee for the purposes of the comitology process. This power has not been exercised, although the one million euro requirement has been criticized as being too low, particularly given that more than 20 years have passed since the Directive's adoption. See Ferrarini, n 15 above, 575 who has also questioned the link between capitalization requirements and liquidity/investor protection, given that '[e]xperience teaches that even shares with a much higher capitalization often show very low liquidity, if indeed they are not totally illiquid . . . liquidity crucially depends on factors such as market microstructure and transparency . . . a stock exchange should rely more on [measures such as the use of market specialists] than on formal listing conditions'.

[68] The extent to which derogations have been granted from this requirement for dotcom start-ups is a matter of some controversy, with concerns being raised that derogations are allowing poorly managed companies to slip through the listing filter. In the UK, the FSA (in its capacity as the UKLA) is, at the time of writing, to review the listing requirements for dotcoms and, in particular, the concessionary rules which allow innovative high-growth companies and, in practice, dotcoms to enter the London Stock Exchange's main market without a three-year trading record, given the collapse in the share prices of some dotcoms and the consequent damage to retail investor confidence. The reforms include requiring more rigorous disclosure concerning the existing financial record (including start-up and development costs) for such companies, given that the financial record of a business is material to an assessment of the company's financial development, even where the company's value is based, for the most part, on high-growth prospects: FSA, *Proposed Changes to the Listing Rules*, Consultation Paper 81 (2001) 45-6.

[69] Sch A, para I(3).

ECOSOC pointed out, 'it is impossible to give any reliable indications as to profit-making capacity in the following financial year'.[70]

III.4.5.3 *Conditions Applicable to Shares: Schedule A (SCD, Articles 45–51)*

Under Schedule A, paragraph II(1) and (2) (SCD, Articles 45 and 46) shares must be in conformity with the laws and regulations to which they are subject and must be freely transferable or negotiable.[71] Ensuring the free transferability or negotiability of securities is an investor-protection device, in that it facilitates the trading process.[72] The application to list must cover all the shares of the same class already issued.[73] Conditions also apply to the distribution of shares. A sufficient number of the shares[74] must be distributed to the public in one or more Member States by the time of admission to listing.[75] This condition does not apply where the shares are to be distributed to the public through a stock exchange, provided that the competent authority is satisfied that a sufficient number of the shares will be distributed through the stock exchange within a 'short period' (undefined). Where the shares are admitted to official listing in one or more non-Member States, the competent authorities may provide for their admission to official listing if a sufficient number of shares is distributed to the public in the non-Member

---

[70] N 29 above, para 2.4.1.

[71] Shares which are not fully paid up may still be classed as freely negotiable where arrangements have been made to ensure that negotiability is not restricted and that dealing is made open and proper by providing the public with all appropriate information. Where the acquisition of shares is subject to an approval clause, the competent authority may derogate from the requirement of free negotiability only where use of the approval clause does not disturb the market. Sch A, para II(2) (SCD, Art. 46(2) and (3)).

[72] FESCO (the Forum of European Securities Commissions) has stressed the importance of this requirement noting that 'restrictions on transferability [can] impede confidence in the market or its orderly operation': FESCO, *Standards for Regulated Markets under the ISD* (1999) (99–FESCO–C), 21. On FESCO see Ch. XV sect. 2.5.2 below. Negotiability also forms part of the current proposals to restructure the admission to official listing regime: ISD Working Paper, n 5 above, 28.

[73] Sch A, para II(5) (SCD, Art. 49(1)). Member States may provide that this condition be disapplied from applications which do not cover all the shares of the same class already issued, where the shares of that class for which admission is not sought belong to blocks which serve to maintain control of the company or which are not negotiable for a certain time under agreements. The public must, however, be informed of such situations and that there is no danger of them prejudicing the interests of the holders of shares for which admission to official listing is sought: ibid (SCD, Art. 49(2)).

[74] The sufficiency of distribution requirement will be met when the shares in respect of which the application is made are in the hands of the public to the extent of at least 25% of the subscribed capital represented by the class of shares concerned. A lower percentage will fulfil the sufficiency requirement when, in view of the large number of shares of the same class and the extent of their distribution to the public, the market will operate properly with a lower percentage: Sch A para II(5) (SCD, Art. 48(5)).

[75] Sch A, para II(4) (SCD, Art. 48(1)). The SCD provision clarifies that the distribution must be 'not later than the time of admission'. This requirement is designed to ensure that there will be sufficient liquidity in the shares.

state or states where they are listed. Under Schedule A, paragraph II(7)
(SCD, Article 51), where the issuer of the shares is a national of a non-
member state, and the shares are not listed in either the country of origin
or the country in which the major proportion of the shares is held, they may
not be admitted unless the competent authorities are satisfied that the
absence of such a listing is not due to the need to protect investors. The
physical form of shares is also addressed. In an example of the Directive's
non-discrimination theme, where the shares are issued by a company which
is a national of another Member State, it is 'necessary and sufficient' that
their physical form comply with the standards laid down by that other
Member State.[76]

III.4.5.4 *Conditions Applicable to Certificates Representing Shares: Article 4(3)* *(SCD, Article 6(3))*

Certificates representing shares may not be admitted to listing unless the
legal position of the issuer of the shares is in conformity with the applicable
laws and regulations, the minimum capitalization requirements for shares
are met, and the issuer of the shares has published or filed annual accounts
in accordance with national law for the three financial years preceding the
application for official listing.[77] The issuer of the shares must also meet the
conditions set out in Schedule C (SCD, Articles 64–69).[78] The certificates are
subject to the same admission conditions as apply to shares.[79] The issuer of
the certificates is addressed by Article 16 (SCD, Article 15) which provides
that admission to listing applications for certificates are to be considered only
if the competent authorities are of the opinion that the issuer of the certificates is offering adequate safeguards for the protection of investors.

---

[76] Sch A, para II(6) (SCD, Art. 50). Where the shares do not conform to the national
Member State requirements, the competent authority is to make that known to the public.
Interestingly, here we see an appearance for mutual recognition in this, the first securities regulation directive to be adopted, albeit to a very limited extent. In a reiteration of a theme that
runs throughout the Directive, where the issuer is a national of a non-Member State, the physical form of the shares must offer sufficient safeguards for the protection of investors. These conditions also apply to debt securities: Sch B (A), para II (5) (SCD, Art. 57).

[77] Art. 4 (3) (SCD, Art. 6(3)) and Sch A, para I(1)–(3) (SCD, Arts. 42–44). The derogations
from these provisions also apply to certificates representing shares.

[78] Art. 4(3) (SCD, Art. 6(3)). The ongoing obligations are discussed in sect. 4.6 below.

[79] Save for Sch A, para II(7) (SCD, Art. 51) concerning the shares of issuers who are non-
nationals of a Member State which are not listed in the issuer's country of origin or country
where the shares are held in a significant proportion: Art. 4(3) (SCD, Art. 6(3)).

III.4.5.5 *Conditions applicable to the Issuer of Debt Securities and to Debt Securities: Schedule B (SCD, Articles 52–63)*

The Directive does not impose a minimum length of corporate existence, and requires only that the legal position of the issuer be in accordance with the laws and regulations to which it is subject.[80] Issuers of debt securities were, in the original proposal, also required to provide sufficient evidence that they were able to meet their commitments arising from the issue of debt securities.[81]

The legal position of debt securities must be in conformity with the laws and regulations to which they are subject (Schedule B(A) paragraph II(1), SCD, Article 53) and they must be freely negotiable.[82] Any application must cover all debt securities ranking *pari passu*.[83] The minimum size of the debt issue is set at 200,000 euro.[84] Where a public issue precedes admission to listing, the first listing may be made only after the end of the period during which subscription applications may be submitted.[85] Convertible or exchangeable debt securities may be admitted to official listing only where the related shares are already listed on either the same stock exchange or another regulated, regularly operating, recognized stock exchange, or are admitted to such an exchange simultaneously.[86] Particular requirements apply to public debt issuers such as a State, its regional or local authorities, or a public international body.[87] A special derogation is available for official listing applications for debt securities issued by companies and other legal persons which are nationals of a Member State and which are set up by,

---

[80] Sch B (A), para I(1)(SCD, Art. 52).

[81] Sch B (A), para I(2). This requirement, which tracks the profit-making requirement originally imposed on issuers of shares, was also dropped. ECOSOC trenchantly pointed out that not only was it 'not the job of the official authorities to check an issuer's financial status' but it was also unclear how a company could show that it would be able to meet its commitments: n 29 above, para 2.5.1.

[82] Sch B (A), para II(2) (SCD, Art. 54(1)). As with shares, competent authorities may treat debt securities which are not fully paid up as freely negotiable if arrangements have been made to ensure that their negotiability is not restricted and that dealing is made open and proper by providing the public with all appropriate information: ibid (SCD, Art. 54(2)).

[83] Sch B (A), para II(4) (SCD, Art. 53).

[84] Sch B (A), para III (1) (SCD, Art. 58). This requirement does not apply to tap issues where the amount of debt issued is not fixed. Member States may derogate from this minimum requirement where the competent authorities are satisfied that there will be a sufficient market for the securities concerned: ibid (SCD, Art. 58(2)).

[85] Sch B (A), para III(1) (SCD, Art. 61). This requirement does not apply to tap issues when the closing date for subscription is not fixed.

[86] Sch B (A), para III(2) (SCD, Art. 59(1)). In another example of the heavy reliance on disclosure Member States may derogate from this requirement by making admission conditional on the competent authorities' satisfaction that the holders of the debt securities have at their disposal all the information necessary to form an opinion concerning the value of the shares and the securities to which they relate: ibid (SCD, Art. 59(2)).

[87] Sch B (B), paras (1)–(4) (SCD, Arts. 60–63).

governed, or managed pursuant to a special law under which repayments and interest payments in respect of those securities are guaranteed by a Member State or one of its federal States. Member States have the option to disapply the Schedule B conditions for admission of debt securities and the ongoing disclosure obligations set out in Schedule D, paragraph 4(a) and (c) (SCD, Article 81(1) and (3)) with respect to disclosure of material information and new issues (section 4.6.3 below).

III.4.6 *Ongoing Obligations*

III.4.6.1 *Schedules C and D (SCD, Articles 64–84)*

In addition to the ongoing obligations imposed in the body of the Directive, issuers whose listing of shares or certificates representing shares is subject to the Directive must comply with the continuing obligations set out in Schedule C (SCD, Articles 64–69) and issuers with listed debt securities must comply with Schedule D (SCD, Articles 78–84).[88] The ongoing obligations are directed towards how the issuer conducts its affairs with investors and with the market after the admission to listing.[89]

III.4.6.2 *Equal Treatment*

A dominant theme of the ongoing obligations regime is that issuers must ensure that all security holders in the same position are treated equally.[90] Issuers must ensure that, at least in each Member State in which their shares are listed, all the necessary facilities and information are available to enable security holders to exercise their rights. In particular, the issuer must, in the case of shares, inform holders of meetings and enable them to exercise voting rights, publish notices concerning, for example, the allocation and payment of dividends in the case of shares, and the payment of interest

---

[88] In the SCD, the more limited ongoing requirements applicable to listed debt securities issued by a State or its regional or local authorities or by a public international body are set out in Arts. 60–63. Such issuers are subject only to an equal-treatment obligation and a requirement to ensure the publication of the equivalent information at each exchange on which the securities are listed (see sects. 4.6.2 and 4.6.3 below).

[89] The imposition of ongoing obligations on issuers who are admitted to listing has been described as a reflection of the 'stock exchange status' achieved by such issuers who are, accordingly, subject to additional obligations designed to reflect the greater responsibility carried by the issuers with respect to their investors and the market generally: Wymeersch, n 11 above, 73.

[90] Sch C, para 2(a) requires equal treatment for all shareholders in the same position (SCD, Art. 65(1)). Sch D (A), para 1(a) (SCD, Art. 78(1)) applies to debt securities and applies the equal-treatment obligation to all holders of debt securities ranking *pari passu* in respect of all the rights attaching to the securities. The equal-treatment rule does not, however, prevent offers of early repayment of certain debt securities being made to holders by an undertaking in derogation from the conditions of issue and 'in particular in accordance with social priorities'.

and conversion rights, in the case of debt securities, and designate an agent through which they may exercise their financial rights (unless the issuer itself provides financial services).[91]

III.4.6.3 *Disclosure*[92]

Consistent with the Directive's objective of protecting investors and the emphasis on protecting the smooth functioning of the market-place, the ongoing disclosure of key events is a major continuing obligation, as it is essential to promote an orderly market and to ensure that all investors have access at the same time to material information. Article 13 (SCD, Article 16) imposes an obligation on issuers whose securities are admitted to listing to provide the relevant competent authorities with all the information the authority considers appropriate in order to protect investors or ensure the smooth operation of the market. Where the protection of investors or the smooth operation of the market so requires (as may be the case where there is a danger of insider dealing due to a leak of inside information), the competent authority may then, under Article 13(2) (SCD, Article 16(2)), demand the publication of such information to the public in the form and within such time limits as it considers appropriate.[93] Under Article 5(4) (SCD, Article 8(4)), Member States may require issuers of officially listed securities to inform the public on a regular basis of their financial position and the general course of their business. More periodic information obligations are also imposed, with a listed issuer being required to make its most recent annual accounts and its last annual report available to the public as soon as possible.[94]

---

[91] Sch C, para 2(b) (SCD, Art. 65(2)) and Sch D (A), para 1(b) (SCD, Art. 78(2)).

[92] Ongoing disclosure on admission to listing is addressed more fully in the discussion of the EC's disclosure regime in Ch. IV.

[93] This will typically be in the form of an announcement to the market. Where an issuer fails to publish such information, the competent authority may, having 'heard' the issuer, proceed to publish the information. This protection for the issuer seems less robust than the amendment suggested by the ECOSOC that in publishing the information the competent authority 'shall take due account of the issuer's legitimate economic interests': n 29 above, para 2.2.4.

[94] Sch C, para 4(a) (SCD, Art. 67(1)) and Sch D (A), para 3(a) (SCD, Art. 80). The last annual report obligation is, in the case of debt securities, qualified by 'the publication of which is required by national law'. Where a company prepares annual own and consolidated accounts, they must be made available to the public. Competent authorities may authorize the company to make available to the public either own or consolidated accounts as long as the accounts which are not made available do not contain any significant additional information: Sch C, para 4(b) (SCD, Art. 67(2)) and Sch D (A), para 3(b) (SCD, Art. 80(2)). Where the accounts do not comply with rules set out in the EC's accounting directives and if they do not give a true and fair view of the company's assets and liabilities, financial position and profit or loss, more detailed and/or additional information must be provided: Sch C para 4(c) (SCD, Art. 67(3)) and Sch D (A) 3(c) (SCD, Art. 80(3)).

Annual reports aside, the ongoing disclosure theme continues in the now consolidated Schedules.[95] An issuer must inform the public of any major new developments, which are not public knowledge and which may, as a result of their effect on the issuer's assets or liabilities or financial position or the general course of its business, lead to substantial movements in the prices of its shares or, in the case of debt securities, significantly affect the issuer's ability to meet its commitments.[96] This requirement is designed to enhance the price-formation process by requiring disclosure of material information which is not caught by the ongoing obligation to publish the annual report and accounts. The competent authorities may exempt the issuer from this requirement if the disclosure of such information would prejudice the legitimate interests of the company. More specifically, changes in the rights attaching to particular classes of securities must also be disclosed to the public without delay,[97] as must alterations in the structure of the major holdings in the issuer's share capital as compared with information previously published on holdings as soon as these changes come to the notice of the issuer.[98] In the case of debt securities, the issuer must inform the public without delay of any changes in the rights attaching to the shares to which convertible debt securities relate[99] and of any new loan issues (including, in particular, any guarantee or security in respect of such loans).[100]

The Directive uses an effective short-cut to ensure that ongoing disclosure by issuers is at the highest possible level. An issuer must ensure that equivalent information is made available to the market at each of the stock exchanges situated or operating in different Member States where the

---

[95] ECOSOC registered strong dissatisfaction with the ongoing information obligations set out in the Schs. It asked for a thorough re-examination of the ongoing disclosure requirements as the Directive's requirements would 'establish a permanent obligation to provide information which would be dependent on a state of affairs that could be interpreted very broadly': n 29 above, para. 2.6.3. This criticism, however, queries the very appropriateness of ongoing disclosure of material events which is a well-established component of issuer disclosure regimes.

[96] Sch C, para 5(a) (SCD, Art. 68) and Sch D (A), para 4(a) (SCD, Art. 81(1)). The Insider Dealing Directive amended para 5(a) to extend the disclosure obligation beyond official listing to 'companies and undertakings the transferable securities of which, whatever their nature, are admitted to trading on a market [as defined by the IDD]'. See Ch. XIII sect. 4.7 below.

[97] Sch C, para 5(b) (SCD, Art. 68(2)).

[98] This condition applies only to issuers of shares: Sch C, para 5(c) (SCD, Art. 68(3)). With the adoption of Directive 88/627/EEC on the information to be published when a major holding in a listed company is acquired or disposed of [1988] OJ L348/62 (the SSD) (now consolidated in the SCD), issuers subject to its requirements are subject to notification requirements in respect of certain acquisitions and disposals (Ch. IV sect. 5.4). Where an issuer is not subject to the SSD, Art. 5(c) (as modified by the SSD) now requires that it must inform the public within 9 calendar days whenever it comes to its notice that a person or entity has acquired or disposed of shares such that the holding in question exceeds or drops below the SSD threshold (SCD, Art. 68(3)).

[99] Sch D (A), para 4(d) (SCD, Art. 81(2)).

[100] Sch D (A), para 4(c) (SCD, Art. 81(3)).

issuer's securities are officially listed.[101] As a result, disclosure rises to the level imposed by the Member States with the most extensive requirements.[102] As this requirement also applies where an issuer's securities are listed on stock exchanges situated or operating in one or more Member States and in one or more non-Member States,[103] a potential difficulty existed due to the extensive and onerous ongoing disclosure required by the SEC for securities registered in the USA. To avoid the importation of this disclosure burden, when securities are listed on the stock exchange of a non-Member State, equivalent information need only be provided to Member State markets where the securities are listed when 'such information may be important for the evaluation of the securities'.[104]

The information disclosed in accordance with the ongoing obligations requirements must be published in one or more newspapers distributed throughout (or widely distributed in) the Member State or be made available to the public either in writing in places indicated by announcements to be published in one or more newspapers distributed throughout the Member State or widely distributed therein, or by any other equivalent means approved by the competent authorities.[105] There is no requirement that the competent authority vet the disclosure in question before it is released or the means of dissemination.[106] Issuers must also, under Article 17(1) (SCD, Article 102(1)), send such information simultaneously to the competent authorities.

III.4.6.4 *Other Obligations*

Disclosure and equal treatment aside, where the issuer engages in a new public issue of shares of the same class as those already officially listed, it

---

[101] Sch C, para 6(a) (SCD, Art. 69(1)). Sch D (A), para 6(a) (SCD, Art. 82(1)).

[102] See Wymeersch, n 21 above, 8.

[103] Sch C, para 6(b) (SCD, Art. 69(2)). Sch D (A), para 6(b) (SCD, Art. 82).   [104] Ibid.

[105] Art. 17(1) (SCD, Art. 102(1)). Art. 17(2) (SCD, Art. 103) provides that such information must be published in the official language of the Member State concerned or in another language, provided that in the Member State the official language or other language is customary in the sphere of finance and accepted by the competent authorities. The reliance in Art. 17 on the traditional newspaper medium as a channel for the dissemination of information is becoming increasingly outmoded and costly with the development of new technologies and news dissemination systems; the flexibility given to competent authorities to approve other methods of dissemination (which did not appear in the original proposal) has been relied on, with devices such as electronic news services being used by competent authorities. Websites are also likely to be relied on to disseminate information: in the USA, eg, companies provide disclosure via their websites as well as through other channels such as news services. Websites have been built into the new prospectus regime. See Ch. IV sect. 9.

[106] Although Art. 17(1) (SCD, Art. 102(1)) does not specify any criteria against which competent authorities should measure other means of information dissemination, investor protection and the smooth functioning of the market suggest that the alternative means used provide for timely and accurate dissemination in a manner which will reach investors and the market at the same time.

must, where the shares are not automatically admitted, apply for their admission to the same listing not more than a year after their issue or when they become freely negotiable.[107] Finally, both companies whose shares are admitted to listing and companies whose debt securities are listed are required to provide the competent authority of each Member State in which the securities are listed with drafts of any planned amendments to their constitutional documents.[108]

III.4.7 *Enforcement*

Under Article 14(2) (SCD, Article 18(2)) competent authorities may ultimately discontinue a listing where they are satisfied that, owing to special circumstances, normal regular dealings in the security in question are no longer possible. Any decision to discontinue listing a security is subject to a right to apply to the courts (Article 15(1)) (SCD, Article 19(1)). Less drastically, under Article 14(1) (SCD, Article 18(2)) competent authorities may decide to suspend listing where the smooth operation of the market is, or may be, temporarily jeopardized, or where the protection of investors demands suspension. Disclosure appears as an enforcement tool in Article 12 (SCD, Article 17), which provides that competent authorities may make public the fact that an issuer is failing to comply with its admission to listing obligations. This is without prejudice to any other action or penalties which may be contemplated by the competent authorities.

III.4.8 *Contact Committee*

A key feature of the now consolidated Admission Directive (which was adopted in subsequent directives) is the establishment of a Contact Committee by Article 20 (SCD, Article 108).[109] Composed of representatives of the Member States and the Commission and chaired by a Commission representative (Article 20(3)) (SCD, Article 108(1)), it provides a forum through which the operation of the Directive can be monitored and enhanced by co-operation between the Member States and the Commission. It is designed to facilitate the harmonized implementation of the Directive through regular consultations on any practical problems arising from its application and on which exchanges of view are deemed useful, to facilitate the establishment of a concerted attitude between the Member States on the

---

[107] Sch C, para 1 (SCD, Art. 64).

[108] Sch C, para 3 (SCD, Art. 66) and Sch D, para 2 (SCD, Art. 79). In the case of debt securities, the obligation applies only where the revisions will affect the rights of holders of debt securities.

[109] The Contact Committee and its role in the institutional structure of EC securities regulation is discussed in Ch. XV sect. 2.3.2 below.

more stringent or additional conditions and obligations which may be imposed at national level in accordance with Article 5 (SCD, Article 8) and to advise the Commission, if necessary, on any supplements or amendments to be made to the Directive or any adjustments to the minimum capitalization requirement.[110] This formal forum for Member State consultation is a useful antidote to the ample opportunities granted to Member States to derogate from the Directive's requirements and/or impose additional conditions and the resulting weaknesses in the degree of harmonization achieved by the Directive. The Contact Committee is an advisory body only, however, and does not engage in operational decisions: Article 20(2) (SCD, Article 108(2)) expressly provides that it may not appraise the merits of decisions taken by competent authorities in particular cases.[111]

III.5 UPDATING THE ADMISSION DIRECTIVE

III.5.1 *An Admission Passport*

The Directive enhances the position of issuers wishing to officially list securities on a cross-border basis by harmonizing the minimum admission conditions and requiring the application of objective criteria in admission decisions. In practice, cross-border listings, if not necessarily multiple listings, are now common.[112]

---

[110] Art. 20(1)(a)-(c) (SCD, Art. 108(2)).

[111] The original proposal, however, suggested that the Contact Committee could 'deliberate' on refusals to admit securities to listing, where it appears, there was a suspicion of discriminatory treatment. Art. 22(1) of the original proposal provided that competent authorities were to inform the Commission of any decisions (and the supporting reasoning) taken to refuse admission to listing of a security issued within another Member State. Art. 22(2) required the Commission to inform the Contact Committee and went on to provide that '[t]he deliberations of the Committee on this matter shall be covered by the obligation of professional secrecy'. Although Art. 22 was dropped by the Directive's adoption, the device of informing the Commission of certain decisions which might suggest behaviour by competent authorities which runs counter to the aims of the harmonization programme has reappeared in later directives. See Art. 19(10) of the ISD which requires Member States to report on, *inter alia*, the occasions on which a host Member State has taken enforcement action against an investment firm from another Member State operating in its territory.

[112] It has been noted that 'there is a long standing tradition of cross border listing: many major securities have been listed for many years on several European stock exchanges. These were secondary listings, most of the time also of secondary importance, the original market continuing to attract the main trading . . . '[f]oreign listings' whereby issuers from State A list exclusively in State B is a more recent phenomenon and developed especially in the high tech sector': Wymeersch, E, *The Harmonisation of Securities Trading in Europe in the New Trading Environment*, WP 2000-16, Working Paper Series of the Financial Law Institute, Universiteit Gent, 9. Eg, at the end of 1999, of the 2,444 companies listed on the London Stock Exchange's main market (for securities admitted to the Official List) 499 were international (although not necessarily EC-based). Empirical studies have shown that the ratio of foreign listings to total listings varies considerably across the Community, however, with the ratio ranging from almost zero in Milan and Madrid, to around 20% in London and Paris to 50% in Frankfurt,

As a product of the initial approach to harmonization, while the Directive is based on the assumption that cross-border and multiple listings are to be encouraged, it does not, however, provide for mutual recognition of admission to official listing decisions. Admission to the official list of a stock exchange situated or operating in a Member State in accordance with the Directive does not bring with it the right to list automatically on the official list of stock exchanges across the Member States.[113] It is clear from the Preamble to the Admission Directive that, due to differences in the structure of Member States' securities markets, harmonization was limited to establishing minimum conditions for the admission of securities to listing; recital 5 (SCD, recital 6) expressly provides that the Directive's harmonization does not give issuers the right to list on a Member State's stock exchange.

The intricacies of multiple listings applications, to the extent they occur, are eased by Article 18(2) (SCD, Article 13(1)) which requires that where applications are made simultaneously or within short intervals of one another for the admission of the same securities to official listing on stock exchanges situated or operating in more than one Member State, or where an application is made in respect of a security already listed on a stock exchange in another Member State, the competent authorities must communicate with each other and make any arrangements necessary to expedite the application and simplify 'as far as possible' the formalities and any additional conditions required for admission.

As a general principle, under Article 18(1) (SCD, Article 106) competent authorities are to co-operate whenever necessary for the purpose of carrying out their duties and are to exchange any information required for that purpose.[114] In consequence, while professional secrecy requirements are imposed by Article 19(1) (SCD, Article 107)(1)) (which requires that Member States are to provide that all persons employed or formerly employed by the competent authorities are to be bound by professional secrecy, such that any confidential information received in the course of their duties may not be divulged to any person or authority except by virtue of provisions laid down by law), Article 19(2) (SCD, Article 107(2)) provides that the professional secrecy obligation does not preclude the competent

Amsterdam, and Brussels. Pagano, M, Randl, O, Röell, A, and Zechner, J, 'What Makes Stock Exchanges Succeed? Evidence from Cross-Listing Decisions' in Ferrarini *et al.*, n. 60 above. See also the analysis of foreign listing patterns in Gros, D, and Lanoo, K, *The Euro Capital Market* (2000), 42 who have also noted the variations in foreign listing patterns across the Member States.

[113] Although the European Parliament somewhat optimistically amended the Commission proposal to include an art. which provided that within 4 years of the entry into force of the Directive the Commission would submit a proposal which would provide that the admission of securities to official exchange quotation in one Member State would authorize admission to official quotation on other stock exchanges: n 29 above, 40.

[114] In later directives the co-operation procedures would become considerably more sophisticated as harmonization moved into its mutual recognition phase.

authorities of the Member States from exchanging information as provided for in the Directive. Any information exchanged is covered by the professional secrecy obligation to which the persons employed or previously employed by the competent authorities receiving the information are subject. Consistently with the emphasis on co-operation and communication between competent authorities, Article 18(3) (SCD, Article 13(2)) provides that any application for the admission of a security to the official list of a Member State's stock exchange must state whether a similar application is being or has been made, or will be made in the near future, in another Member State.

Although the future shape of EC securities markets remains to be seen, the changes in the trading environment outlined in Chapter XI are likely to impact on the listing process; multiple listings and an 'official listing admission passport' are unlikely to be a feature of the new capital-raising environment. Not only is the official listing concept, as articulated in the EC's regulatory regime, likely to be recast (see section 5.2 below), but multiple listing may ultimately be replaced by what can be called multiple trading supported by a single listing. The listing decision is in part a function of the secondary trading market in the securities in question and its likely depth and liquidity; as liquidity impacts on share prices, a liquid market in an issuer's securities will, all things being equal, reduce the cost of equity capital for the issuer if it decides to access the capital markets through a subsequent share issue.[115] One listing can now, however, support trading in that security across the EC.[116] Issuers can increasingly access foreign capital markets via their domestic markets. The advent of remote access to securities-trading markets for market intermediaries[117] reduces the need for securities to be listed cross-border or on multiple exchanges, as they can be traded across the EC from one market-place, and may ultimately lead to a redirection of trading in an issuer's securities to the issuer's domestic exchange.[118] The trend towards exchange consolidation and the development of pan-EC trading sys-

---

[115] For an analysis of the factors which lead issuers to make cross-border listing decisions see Pagano *et al.*, n 112 above, who have found that issuers are more likely to cross-list in more liquid and larger markets and in markets where several issuers from their industry are already cross-listed. They are also more likely to cross-list in countries with better investor protection and more efficient courts and bureaucracies.

[116] Leading one commentator to observe that the harmonization introduced by the Admission Directive and the listing particulars regime discussed in Ch. IV 'is, to some extent, outdated . . . the "market for markets" is highly competitive and the pan-European markets will soon discard the multiple listing concept': Ferrarini, n 60 above.

[117] See Ch. XI sect. 6.4.1 below.

[118] It has been suggested that adoption of the euro and the remote membership facility will direct equity trades to the domestic exchange where liquidity will be deepest. See Gros and Lanoo, n 112 above, pp xv, 44, 95, and 163. See also the analysis in Ferrarini, n 15 above at 578, who has noted a lack of interest in multiple listings as 'trading will undoubtedly continue to concentrate where the shares are most liquid: ie almost invariably on the home exchange trading system and/or through (largely London-based) international dealing banks'.

tems[119] are also likely to impact on the extent to which multiple listings occur.[120] Indeed, a growing lack of interest in multiple listings could be included among the factors which led to the failure of the Eurolist system in 1997.[121] Designed to facilitate the admission to official listing of blue-chip issuers on the Eurolist group of exchanges, its collapse has been attributed to, *inter alia*, a lack of interest in multiple listings, given the concentration of trading in States where trading is more liquid, as well as to the movement towards consolidation between Community exchanges and, in particular, towards cross-membership, which has facilitated trading across the exchanges.[122]

III.5.2 *Admission to Trading and Admission to Official Listing*

Of arguably more immediate concern is the need to clarify the distinction between admission to listing and admission to trading functions and the role of the now consolidated Admission Directive in this regard.

The role played in the listing process by demutualized stock exchanges, which are profit-driven rather than conforming to the public interest (if monopolistic) model of pre-competition times,[123] is coming under increased scrutiny.[124] Indeed, the appropriateness of conferring the listing function on an exchange with the likelihood of its becoming an instrument of competition in the battle for listing business aside, the costs of running the listing process may place some 'listing' exchanges at a competitive disadvantage to those exchanges which admit securities which have already been listed. As is discussed further in Chapter IV, however, the Commission has recently made its position clear on whether commercially driven exchanges should be engaged in public-interest-motivated activities such as the admission of

[119] Such as the abortive iX project of the London Stock Exchange and Deutsche Börse or Virt-x, the new exchange created by the Swiss Stock Exchange and Tradepoint which provides pan-EC trading facilities.

[120] See Ferrarini, n 60 above, for the view that pan-EC exchanges may ultimately drive listings away from the issuers' home countries to the home country of the pan-EC exchange.

[121] See Ch. IV sect. 8.5 below.   [122] Ferrarini, n 15 above, 578.

[123] On this transformation see Wymeersch, n 112 above, 5–7.

[124] For the UK perspective in the context of the demutualization of the London Stock Exchange see the Listing Authority Transfer Paper, n 32 above, which at 3 has quoted the Chancellor Gordon Brown as stating that: '[i]n light of the Exchange's proposal to demutualise and turn itself into a commercial company, the Exchange has suggested that it would no longer be appropriate for it to continue to exercise its Listing Authority function. I share that view and accordingly I am planning that this function should be transferred to the Financial Services Authority.' It should be noted that not all Member States have responded to the new competitive pressures by relieving stock exchanges of the listing function. In France and Italy, eg, the listing function is carried out by stock exchanges organized as business enterprises. See Ferrarini, G, 'Stock Exchange Governance in the European Union' in Balling, M, Hennessy, E, and O'Brien, R (eds), *Corporate Governance, Financial Markets and Global Convergence* (1998) 139, 142–3 and 153–4.

securities to official listing. In a drastic change to the current position which accommodates self-regulation by the exchanges, if the Commission's proposals to restructure the issuer disclosure regime are successful, the disclosure review required when securities are admitted to trading on a 'regulated market'[125] (including official segments of national markets) will only be carried out by independent administrative authorities and will be removed from the control of the exchanges (Chapter IV section 9.3 below).

The ISD Communication highlighted the need to clarify the distinction between admission to listing and admission to trading and to revisit the Admission Directive.[126] The Community's admission-to-listing regime was also the focus of criticism by the Lamfalussy Report.[127] It identified the introduction of a clear distinction between admission to listing and admission to trading and the modernization of the admission-to-listing requirements (which it described as outdated) as priorities to be achieved by the end of 2003 at the latest.[128] It appears from the Commission's 2001 ISD Working Paper[129] that dramatic action is planned on this front. As discussed in Chapter XI section 9.7.3 below, the Commission has suggested that harmonized admission-to-trading rules be established, based on updated key components of the Admission Directive, which would apply to all securities admitted to trading on a regulated market, such that the basic distinction between admission to trading and admission to official listing would be removed as far as compliance with admission conditions was concerned. The Working Paper does, however, envisage considerable levels of discretion here and different regimes applying depending on the nature of the market. It appears therefore that the current admission-to-official-listing regime will be replaced by an admission-to-regulated-markets regime in which harmonized disclosure requirements will be managed by public competent authorities and that issuer compliance with the disclosure and other harmonized admission conditions will be verified by the markets, subject to supervision by securities-trading markets supervisors; the remaining requirements will be left to the markets as instruments of competition. While attempts are made in the Working Paper to avoid a monolithic approach to the admission process, the fate of this new regime is likely to depend on the extent to which is accommodates the need for different trading venues.

---

[125] See n 56 above.
[126] ISD Communication n 4 above, 13–14.
[127] Lamfalussy Report, n 13 above.
[128] Ibid, 13.
[129] N 5 above.

IV

The Issuer-disclosure Regime

IV.1 EC SECURITIES REGULATION AND DISCLOSURE

This chapter examines the EC's mandatory issuer-disclosure regime. The regime also forms a part of the wider EC disclosure regime which can be tracked through this book, although it represents the most important articulation of disclosure as a regulatory mechanism in EC securities regulation. Staying in the investment products sphere, disclosure appears again in the collective-investment-scheme area where the content of the disclosure document produced to market schemes has recently come under review (see Chapter V below). Disclosure to the market in the interests of encouraging market discipline in the risk-management sphere is, albeit tentatively, appearing in the EC's arsenal of prudential regulation devices (see Chapter VIII below); disclosure in the form of record keeping has long formed a part of prudential regulation. Disclosure also forms part of the regulation of the investor/investment firm relationship, where it appears to be fast becoming the EC's regulatory device of choice in the investment services/investor protection area (see Chapter IX below). It features heavily in the EC's evolving market-abuse regime (see Chapter XIII below) and, in the guise of market transparency requirements, is a major feature of the EC's regulation of securities trading markets (see Chapter XI below).[1] With respect to the latter, the issuer-disclosure regime and the securities-trading-market regime overlap. Market transparency can be regarded as having three elements: efficient price formation, disclosure of material interests in shareholdings (both of which are covered by the issuer-disclosure regime), and pre-/post-trade publicity of trading information which is covered in Chapter XI below. As a matter of first principles, disclosure is an attractive regulatory mechanism, in that it empowers investors to make investment decisions without intervening proactively in the relationship between the investor, the issuer, the investment intermediary, and the market-place.[2] Substantive disclosure

---

[1] For an overview of disclosure as a regulatory device in securities regulation generally and the difficulties attendant on justifying disclosure controls see Ogus, A, *Regulation. Legal Forms and Economic Theory* (1994) 138–41.

[2] It has been observed that 'disclosure regulation seems the perfect complement to the information-driven nature of a capital market, which in turn is congruent with the decentralized decision-making process that characterizes a private market for goods and services': Trachtman, J, 'The Applicability of Law and Economics to Law and Development: The Case of Financial Law' in Norton, J, and Andenas, M (eds), *Emerging Financial Markets and the Role of International Financial Organizations* (1996) 26, 52. See also the analysis in Page, A and

rules aside, issuers of securities who seek access to public funds are also subject to liability and distribution rules, although these aspects of the securities-offering process do not feature to any significant extent in EC securities regulation.

IV.2 MANDATORY ISSUER DISCLOSURE

IV.2.1 *The Rationale for Mandatory Disclosure*

IV.2.1.1 *A Long-running Debate*

Although mandatory issuer disclosure is by now a well-established feature of securities regulation, it is attended, particularly in the USA, by a lively debate on the need for a mandatory-disclosure policy, given that mandatory-disclosure requirements represent a considerable cost for issuers accessing the capital markets. In the USA, mandatory disclosure was initially accepted as having a positive effect on the market, with initial and ongoing disclosure accepted as playing a significant part in allocating capital efficiently. By the 1960s and in the 1970s, however, the SEC's mandatory-disclosure policy was being questioned by leading academics and economists as imposing onerous costs on issuers which were not counterbalanced by benefits.[3] Conversely, an opposing school of thought developed which argued that mandatory disclosure was based on sound policy foundations and generated significant benefits.[4] Although the debate still rages,[5] the SEC holds firm on its mandatory-issuer-disclosure policy, although it has taken significant steps to streamline the disclosure process. This chapter will not attempt to canvass the vast range of arguments and policy tensions which inform the

---

Ferguson, R, *Investor Protection* (1992) who, at 46, characterize the twin benefits of disclosure as a regulatory mechanism in terms of (1) its focus on providing investors with the means to protect themselves (investors may, of course, choose to act imprudently) and (2) the fact that 'freedom of business action is left unimpaired'.

[3] For 2 seminal attacks on the disclosure regime based on the costs of mandatory disclosure as compared to its benefits see Bentson, G, 'Required Disclosure and the Stock Market: An Evaluation of the Securities Exchange Act 1934' (1973) 63 *Am. Econ. Rev.* 132 and Stigler, G, 'Public Regulation of the Securities Markets' (1964) 37 *J Business* 117. Professor Stigler's work, eg, compared issuers' performances pre and post the introduction of the federal disclosure regime and noted that disclosure did not save money for the investor and, as a result of the costs involved, removed some small issuers from the market-place.

[4] See, eg, Coffee, J, 'Market Failure and the Economic Case for a Mandatory Disclosure System' (1984) 70 *Va L Rev.* 717 and Seligman, J, 'The Historical Need for a Mandatory Disclosure System' (1979) 9 *J Corp. L* 1. Professor Seligman has referred to the benefits disclosure brings in terms of investor confidence, fraud prevention, and the control of excessive compensation for underwriters.

[5] Among the major critiques of the mandatory disclosure policy are Kripke, H, *The SEC and Corporate Disclosure: Regulation in Search of a Purpose* (1979) and Easterbrook, F, and Fischel, D, 'Mandatory Disclosure and the Protection of Investors' (1984) 70 *Va L Rev.* 669.

US debate and which underpin the mandatory-issuer-disclosure discussion generally; such an exercise would quite easily sustain a separate work. In order to place the EC's disclosure regime in context, however, and in order to highlight the pragmatic basis of the EC regime in market integration rather than in any deeper attachment to the various roles fulfilled by disclosure policy, the major rationales for imposing disclosure requirements on issuers who access the capital markets and the challenges to those rationales will be identified.

Three justifications, which can overlap, are usually advanced in favour of mandatory issuer disclosure: investor protection and thereby the promotion of investor confidence; the prevention of fraud; and efficient capital allocation. Much of the debate concerns whether and to what extent the disclosure regime in question has balanced the costs and benefits of issuer-disclosure requirements.

IV.2.1.2 *Investor Confidence and Investor Protection*

Investor confidence, which also permeates the EC regime due to the assumed synergy between investor confidence and market interpenetration, is often stated to be at the root of mandatory-issuer-disclosure.[6] If, as a result of the availability of disclosure as regards their investments, investors' confidence in the capital markets is strengthened, the efficiency of the market-place should be enhanced. This equation has been accepted at an international level for some time: in 1976, the OECD recommended that its common disclosure standards for public offerings be adopted by its member States in order to promote investor protection and investor confidence in issuers of securities and in the securities industry and thereby to 'contribute to a progressive development of capital markets, both nationally and internationally'.[7] Investor confidence is achieved by protecting investors in the capital markets by supplying them with information concerning the issuers seeking their capital and the securities offered by those issuers. Armed with the appropriate level of information set by a mandatory disclosure mechanism, so the theory goes, investors should be able to make rational investment choices, compare investments, make appropriate risk assessments, and diversify their portfolios. Disclosure regulation is non-interventionist; based

---

[6] See, eg, an early analysis by Professor Wymeersch in which he noted that investor confidence in the securities system can be considered as an overriding aim of disclosure, while investor protection, the monitoring of company law, the transparency of market operations, and sales promotion can be considered as subsidiary aims: Wymeersch, E, *Control of Securities Markets in the European Economic Community*, Collection Studies, Competition—Approximation of Legislation Series No. 31 (1977) 139–42.

[7] OECD, *Minimum Disclosure Rules Applicable to All Publicly Offered Securities* (1976) (the OECD Disclosure Rules), 67.

on the information available, investors can made a decision about the fairness and worth of the investment in question.[8]

While there is widespread agreement that investors need a certain amount of information when making investment decisions, given the intangible and contingent nature of securities and their value, there are disputes about the extent and nature of the information which should be supplied. In particular, the investor protection via information dissemination rationale can run into difficulties where it appears that the mandatory disclosure required of issuers and directed towards investors exceeds the capacity of the investors to absorb that information, although this argument carries less weight when considered in the context of a burgeoning investment-services industry and the likelihood that investment decisions are taken through the filter which a professional investment adviser in a position to assess the information places on the disclosure. The nature of the disclosure demanded of issuers can also be controversial. The US disclosure regime was criticized throughout the 1970s for its paternalistic focus on rather turgid historic information over all other disclosure and its restriction for years on the use of projections, which can be more valuable to investors given that historic information is not a reliable guide to the future performance of a security.[9] Where the mandatory supply of information is policed by severe sanctions and potentially onerous liability actions, disclosure regimes can produce massive, unwieldy, and ultimately confusing documents which do not inform the investors who are the supposed beneficiaries of the disclosure.[10] Controversy also exists about the extent to which disclosure should be tailored to the needs of particular investors. In particular, there is much debate whether disclosure should be aimed at unsophisticated retail investors and tailored to their needs, or whether it should be addressed instead to investors familiar with financial markets (particularly in view of the reliance which retail investors place on professional advisers), or some variant of both in the form of the reasonable investor. The SEC's position is to direct its disclosure regime towards all market participants, unsophisticated investors, and market professionals alike, although in recent years it has attempted to ensure that disclosure is made accessible, in terms of its presentation, to

---

[8] See Lindsey, R, 'Efficient Regulation of the Securities Market' in McCrudden, C, (ed), *Regulation and Deregulation, Policy and Practice in the Utilities and Financial Services Industries* (1999) 295, 298, who also pointed to the role played by disclosure standards in redressing the imbalance which would otherwise exist between those involved with the offering and the public. The SEC's position is that issuer disclosure is 'premised on the view that investors are best protected in making investments if they are presented with full and fair disclosure of all material information about the investments': SEC Release No 7314, *Securities Acts Concepts and Their Effects on Capital* (1996).

[9] Although the SEC has now changed its position on projections. See n 92 below.

[10] See the discussion in Buxbaum, R, and Hopt, K, *Legal Harmonization and the Business Enterprise* (1988) 219.

retail investors.[11] More controversially, it has been argued that the investor protection via information dissemination assumption is flawed, in that the extent to which investors rely on disclosure when making decisions is not entirely clear. One school of thought suggests that certain investors (noise traders) do not follow disclosure but make investment decisions in a more erratic fashion.[12]

IV.2.1.3 *Prevention of Fraud*

The second function fulfilled by issuer disclosure is linked to the investor protection via information dissemination rationale: disclosure protects investors against fraud. This rationale is based on the famous words of Brandeis: '[s]unlight is said to be the best of disinfectants'.[13] Mandatory disclosure operates to expose fraud and sharp practices by requiring extensive disclosure of corporate activity; in the absence of mandatory disclosure requirements, issuers (and more specifically their managers) may be given incentives to suppress unfavourable information.[14] It also protects against the sale of worthless or fraudulent securities by providing remedies for misrepresentations made in the sale of securities. Fraud also hinders the efficient operation of the market-place (see Chapter IV section 2.1.4 below) in that it can lead to inefficient pricing and an inefficient allocation of resources.[15]

[11] For a discussion of the evolution of the SEC's position on the addressees of disclosure (which moved from one which regarded average retail investors as the target of mandatory disclosure to one which considered disclosure to be directed towards all market participants) see Firtel, K, 'Plain English: A Reappraisal of the Intended Audience of Disclosure Under the Securities Act of 1933' (1998) 72 *So. Cal. L Rev.* 851, 854–62. For one example of this debate see the 1969 Wheat Report on *Disclosure to Investors: A Reappraisal of Administrative Policies under the 33 and 34 Acts* which was produced by a committee established under the auspices of the SEC, and made an extensive study of the SEC's disclosure rules, ultimately representing the SEC's position on disclosure. At 51–2 it asked: '[a]t what audience should disclosure be aimed? Is the literature elicited by the Commission's requirements intended primarily to aid the unsophisticated? Is it, on the contrary, designed to assist the assiduous student of finance who searches for every clue to the intrinsic value of securities? Or should the Commission strive to meet the needs of a hypothetical 'reasonable' investor of 'reasonable' sophistication? Throughout its history, the Commission has struggled with these questions. They may well be unanswerable. A balance must be struck which reflects, to the extent possible, the needs of all who have a stake in the securities markets.' The US regime has been subject to criticism on the ground that at certain stages it has been preoccupied in making detailed disclosure fully comprehensible to a model retail investor, even though in practice such investors did not read the disclosure. See Kripke, H, 'The Myth of the Informed Layman' (1973) 28 *The Business Lawyer* 631.

[12] See n 18 below.

[13] Brandeis, L, *Other People's Money and How the Bankers Use It* (1913) 92.

[14] See Ogus, n 1 above, 140. The role of mandatory disclosure in reducing fraud has been accepted even among certain of the US commentators who question the impact of mandatory disclosure on market efficiency grounds. See the discussion in Cox, J, 'Regulatory Duopoly in U.S. Securities Markets' (1999) 99 *Col. LR* 1200, 1235.

[15] See Avougleas, E, 'Financial Market Regulation and the New Market Landscape: In Search of a New Regulatory Framework for Market Abuse' (2000) 2 *ICCLJ* 89, 96.

IV.2.1.4 *Price Formation and Market Efficiency*

Finally, investor-protection goals aside, mandatory disclosure is often justified by virtue of its function in promoting the efficiency[16] of the capital markets by ensuring the accuracy of securities prices.[17] In particular, it is argued that, where markets are informationally efficient in that information is reflected in prices,[18] disclosure serves to ensure that securities are correctly priced, in that they reflect the intrinsic value of the issuer and, in turn, given the role of securities-trading markets in allocating capital, that capital is efficiently allocated. Investment or capital-allocation decisions are

[16] Capital-market efficiency can be described as having three dimensions: institutional, operational, and allocational efficiency. Institutional efficiency is dependent on the market mechanism, or on the ability of capital seekers and providers to access the market, the flexibility of supply and demand, market stability, and market width (or the ability of the market to accommodate a range of investments and participants). Disclosure is key to institutional efficiency, given the importance of transparency, and the ability of investors to choose between investments, in achieving this form of efficiency. Operational efficiency is largely concerned with the costs of capital acquisition and investment mediation. Finally, allocational or allocative efficiency, which is a major concern of disclosure policy, concerns the extent to which the market will allocate resources efficiently to the places where they are most needed. Disclosure is central here as allocative efficiency presumes that investors are well-informed via accurate securities prices. This discussion is based on the examination of market efficiency in Buxbaum and Hopt, n 10 above, 218-19.

[17] Although investor protection feeds into market efficiency, in that investor confidence ultimately, it is assumed, impacts on the efficiency of the market, the efficiency argument for disclosure can be dissociated from the investor-protection rationale. For an example of this approach see Heiser, K, 'Can Capital Market Law Approaches be Harmonized with Essential Principles of Company Law' (2000) 11 *EBLRev.* 60, 67 and 68.

[18] There is considerable debate on the informational efficiency of markets and the extent to which the efficient capital-market hypothesis (ECMH) should impact on disclosure policy or promote deregulation. At its most basic, the ECMH provides that securities prices fully reflect all available information. On the parameters of the ECMH see Fama, E, 'Efficient Capital Markets: A Review of the Theory and Empirical Work' (1970) 25 *J Fin.* 833. The relationship between information, its processing costs, and market efficiency was subject to a compelling critique in Gilson, R, and Kraakman, R, 'The Mechanisms of Market Efficiency' (1984) 70 *Va L Rev.* 549, in which they examined the extent to which different types of disclosure are efficiently factored into prices, whether mandatory disclosure reduces the cost of processing information, and, in particular, the role of investment bankers in channelling information through to prices. Some commentators challenge the ECMH on the grounds that investors are not always rational and that securities prices also reflect 'noise' from the market-place, representing irrational changes to investor sentiment which are not completely justified by information. See Shleifer, A, and Summers, L, 'New Critiques of the Efficient Market Hypothesis' (1990) 4 *J Econ Perspectives* 19 and Cox, J, Hillman, R, and Langevoort, D, *Securities Regulation. Cases and Material* (2nd edn, 1998) 40-2.

For an examination of the incidence in practice of market efficiency and rational investor behaviour in the context of the dotcom boom and subsequent collapse and the consequent misallocation of capital to unworthy projects see Riley, B, 'Markets Behaving Badly', *Financial Times*, 7 Apr 2001. He noted behavioural theories of investment decision-making which downplay rational behaviour and emphasize the role played by trends and peer pressure (these include a US analysis, which the discussion refers to, which links rising levels of Prozac, overoptimism, and the Wall Street bubble) and concluded that 'the efficient market hypothesis must co-exist with behavioural theory'.

therefore made not on the basis of speculation or advertising but in an allocatively efficient manner, based on the value of the security.[19]

4.2.1.5 *The Market-failure Doctrine*

Some controversy exists, chiefly in the literature of the school of law and economics, with regard to the extent to which the dissemination of issuer information should be mandatory and managed by public rules or left to market forces and the incentives given to issuers and other suppliers of information to provide adequate disclosure. The market-failure doctrine teaches that regulation should be imposed on the market only in order to correct a market failure; it operates on the assumption that a perfect market exists which will allocate resources efficiently and that regulation is a corrective to an imperfect market.[20] Information may represent a market failure in this area in that, the argument goes, in the absence of public control it will not be disseminated, as a result of its 'public-good' nature, and the efficient allocation of resources will accordingly be prejudiced.[21] Alternatively, it has been argued that, left to their own devices, issuers and their management will produce sufficient information for the market ultimately to provide optimum levels of protection/information for investors (in that investors will discount the value of securities in respect of which less disclosure is available as the securities represent a riskier investment when compared to securities in respect of which greater disclosure is available)[22] and that where information would not be produced other than via a mandatory disclosure system the benefits of the information in question are outweighed by the costs

---

[19] The role of disclosure in establishing a pricing mechanism has been highlighted as critical, in that the behaviour of securities prices has a profound effect on the allocative efficiency of securities markets. See Coffee, n 4 above, 734. Not all commentators are convinced that an informationally efficient market, in which prices adjust rapidly to new information, is also efficient from an allocative perspective in so far as adjusted prices also reflect the underlying value of the securities. For a challenge to market efficiency as a regulatory objective, based on the assumption that securities markets do not play as significant a role as is commonly assumed in allocating resources and that the connection between securities prices and the allocation of resources is a weak one, see Stout, L, 'The Unimportance of Being Efficient: An Economic Analysis of Stock Market Pricing and Securities Regulation' (1988) 87 *Mich. LR* 613.

[20] The market-failure doctrine is discussed more fully in Ch. VI as it is central to the regulation of investment services firms. See Ch. VI sect. 2 below.

[21] See the analysis of informational problems as market failures in Page and Ferguson, n 2 above, 36–7. The 'public-good' nature of information—the fact that it becomes public once disseminated, that use of information by one person does not lower its value to others, and that suppliers of information cannot easily control free-riding on information, or restrict its dissemination to those who will directly or indirectly pay for it—means that suppliers of information are not given adequate incentives to supply it. See Ogus n 1 above, 33–5 and 40 and Trachtman, n 2 above, 54.

[22] For a challenge to the discounting theory see Scott, H, 'Internationalization of Primary Public Securities Markets' (2000) 63 *Law and Contemporary Problems* 71, 75–8.

of production.[23] As issuers compete for investors' funds they are, it can be argued, already given adequate incentives to produce information.[24] From the perspective of pragmatism, however, public control over issuer disclosure ensures that disclosure is made available in a standardized manner which facilitates investors in making comparisons;[25] indeed the importance of standardization is emphasized in the reforms which have been proposed to the EC's issuer-disclosure regime.

4.2.1.6 *Forms of Mandatory Disclosure and their Rationales*

(a) *Initial and Ongoing Disclosure*

Traditionally, mandatory disclosure obligations activate on the initial offer of securities or the admission to trading of securities (when a detailed prospectus is required) and on an ongoing basis thereafter, either when particular material events occur or at certain regular intervals.[26]

(b) *Integration of Disclosure and Shelf Registration*

As disclosure concerning an issuer may be available from a number of sources, integrating the disclosure so that the issuer is not required to repeat disclosure already in the public domain can generate cost savings for issuers. Where the information is adequately disseminated to the market-place and

---

[23] See the discussion in Romano, R, 'Empowering Investors: A Market Approach to Securities Regulation' (1998) 107 *Yale LJ* 2359, 2373–80 and Easterbrook and Fischel, n 5 above. An important empirical discussion of disclosure from this perspective can be found in Bentson, n 3 above. Comparing the disclosure produced by US firms pre and post the introduction of the mandatory federal disclosure regime in 1933 and 1934, he found that companies typically voluntarily produced financial statements (albeit in accordance with a listing obligation), which contained, for the most part, a large proportion of the information which would be required subsequently under the mandatory federal regime. For a challenge to the voluntary disclosure argument see Coffee, n 4 above, 738–43.

[24] See Romano, n 23 above at 2374, who has pointed to empirical evidence that managers will voluntarily disclose information where there is an information asymmetry in the market. Professor Romano has also cited at 2375 studies which support the assertion that European stock markets are no less efficient than US markets, even though US requirements are significantly more demanding. Her conclusion is that regulators do not have superior knowledge of the type of information needed by investors: ibid.

[25] Jennings, R, Marsh, H, Coffee, J, and Seligman, J, *Securities Regulation. Cases and Materials* (8th edn, 1998) 4.

[26] The significance of ongoing disclosure as a mechanism for ensuring effective investor protection by ensuring the investor is adequately equipped to make a rational investment decision was recently confirmed by IOSCO in its 1998 *Objectives and Principles of Securities Regulation*. Principle 14 provides that there 'should be full, accurate, and timely disclosure of financial results and other information that is material to an investor's decision' and is justified by reference to the objectives of ensuring investor protection and fair, efficient and transparent markets (para 10.3). See also Davies, P, *Gower's Principles of Modern Company Law* (6th edn, 1997) 483.

investors (under the Efficient Capital Markets Hypothesis), disclosure regimes can be tailored to scale back the formal reporting obligations placed on issuers. If, for example, an annual report has been published, under the ECMH securities prices should reflect that material, and there is no need for the same disclosure to be repeated elsewhere in the formal ongoing reporting structure or in the formal disclosure documents made available to investors. Incorporation-by-reference techniques can be used to refer to formal disclosure reports which have already been filed. In the USA, for example, where the integration of disclosure in order to simplify the complex and onerous disclosure regime and reduce the burden on issuers represents a major component of the SEC's disclosure policy, one aspect of the integration regime provides that ongoing reports required under the ongoing disclosure system can be integrated into the disclosure required on a subsequent offer of securities.[27] While integrated disclosure is more efficient from the issuer's perspective, questions can arise, depending on the design of the system, on the extent to which investors receive sufficient information in a timely manner, so that they can make informed investment decisions.

The shelf-registration process also attempts to streamline disclosure, although, depending on the frequency with which the registration document must be updated, it can be costly for issuers. The preparation and approval by a regulatory authority of a lengthy disclosure document each time an issuer makes an offer of securities to the public or applies for admission of its securities to trading can represent a major burden for those issuers that repeatedly access the capital markets for their financing needs. In order to ease this burden and facilitate the speed with which issuers can access the capital markets and the extent to which they can exploit market conditions, shelf registration is increasingly becoming a feature of disclosure regimes.[28] Shelf-registration schemes will typically require that an initial

---

[27] Explaining the rationale for its integrated disclosure system, the SEC has stated that 'it recognizes that, for companies in the top tier, there is a steady stream of high quality corporate information continually furnished to the market and broadly digested, synthesized and disseminated . . . the widespread market following of such companies and the due diligence procedures being developed serve to address the concerns about the adequacy of disclosure and due diligence and, thus, ensure the protection of investors': SEC Release No. 33-6499 (1983), para I.

[28] The SEC has explained the benefits of shelf registration in terms of 'flexibility to respond to rapidly changing markets, reduced legal, accounting, printing and other expenses and increased competition among underwriters [The latter benefit arises as, in a shelf registration offering, the issuer may, very close to the offering, ask competing underwriters to bid for the offering. This is not possible in a full scale offer as it is necessary to build up a relationship between issuer and underwriter over a period of months as the major disclosure document is prepared]': ibid. It noted that commentators stress that 'by being able to meet 'market windows', registrants are able to obtain lower interest rates on debt and lower dividend rates on preferred stock, thereby benefiting their existing shareholders. The flexibility [of shelf registration] also permits variations in the structure and terms of securities on short notice, enabling registrants to match securities with the current demands of the marketplace . . . Empirical

disclosure document is filed and that supplements are produced each time securities are offered.

IV.2.2 *Disclosure as a Barrier to Capital Raising*

The need to comply with the different disclosure requirements imposed by States can serve as a substantial obstacle to multiple listings and multi-jurisdictional offerings.[29] Exposure to varying and onerous sanctions and liability regimes can also hinder the capital-raising process. Although the former have been addressed by the EC regime, the latter remain subject to Member State control.

In light of the globalization of markets, regulators are increasingly co-operating to bring about the convergence of disclosure standards in order to combat the obstacles created by varying disclosure standards.[30] The foundations of the SEC's US/Canada multi-jurisdictional disclosure system were laid in 1991. In 1998 IOSCO adopted international disclosure standards to be applied to cross-border offerings and initial listings by foreign issuers which were designed to serve as the basis for a disclosure document passport regime which would allow issuers to rely on a document prepared in accordance with the standards for multi-jurisdictional offerings and listings.[31] Although the disclosure standards cover only the more settled aspects of disclosure policy and avoid the more contentious areas,[32] they are likely to have a significant impact on international disclosure standards, not least because the SEC has adopted them for foreign issuers accessing US

studies also support the importance of enhanced financing flexibility in new issue design, market timing and choice of distribution techniques': para IV. In the UK, a shelf-registration system for share issues has been in operation since 1999 and for debt securities since 2000, although it has not been widely used. Shelf registration also operates across other EC Member States but it is not relied on extensively.

[29] A point acknowledged by the SEC in the context of the disclosure requirements applicable to foreign issuers in 1999: SEC Release No. 33-7637 (1999).

[30] For an analysis of recent developments see Steinberg, M, *International Securities Law. A Contemporary and Comparative Perspective* (1999) 1–51, who has isolated the dominant forms of harmonization as (1) co-operation or commonality via the adoption of common rules which result in the production of a standardized disclosure document and (2) reciprocity based on mutual recognition of disclosure documents prepared according to minimum standards. Both these themes can be found in the evolution of the EC disclosure regime. Looking inwards, the pressure to respond domestically to the internationalization of capital markets by providing domestic issuers with an internationally competitive regulatory structure has led one commentator to note memorably that '[a] country seeking to contain its companies and investors by erecting a wall of unreasonable regulatory demands will find a fiber optic tunnel through its ramparts allowing its subjects to escape to more hospitable markets': Cox, n 14 above, 1201.

[31] IOSCO, *International Disclosure Standards for Cross-Border Offerings and Initial Listings by Foreign Issuers* (1998) (the 1998 IOSCO Disclosure Standards). This development (which applies only to offerings of shares) was driven by IOSCO's belief that 'it is important for securities regulators to facilitate cross-border offerings and listing by multinational issuers by enhancing comparability of information while ensuring a high level of investor protection' (at 3).

[32] Chief among these is the difficult area of projections and forecasts.

markets in place of the current system.[33] If the Commission's proposal to restructure the issuer-disclosure regime is adopted, they will also play a critical role in shaping the EC disclosure regime (see section 4.9 below).

IV.3 SCOPE AND FEATURES OF THE EC ISSUER-DISCLOSURE REGIME

IV.3.1 *Scope*

Mandatory disclosure requirements were first imposed on issuers accessing the capital markets by the now consolidated Admission Directive in 1979.[34] Its main concern is to facilitate access to official listing by harmonizing the conditions applicable to admission to official listing; as part of this exercise it also addresses the ongoing disclosure obligations of officially listed issuers which form a part of the listing conditions imposed on issuers. The Listing Particulars Directive (the LPD), the Interim Reports Directive (the IRD), and the Substantial Shareholdings Directive (SSD) (all now consolidated in the SCD), which followed in 1980, 1982, and 1988, respectively, expanded the disclosure regime applicable to officially listed securities.[35] Together with the Admission Directive, they establish an initial and ongoing disclosure code which covers securities during the initial official-listing application and throughout the time they remain officially listed. In 1989 the gap in the disclosure regime was somewhat haphazardly filled when the Public Offers Directive (the POD)[36] introduced a code of disclosure covering issues of secu-

---

[33] The IOSCO standards will replace the disclosure currently required of foreign issuers on Form 20-F which is the basic disclosure document required of foreign issuers: SEC Release No. 33-7745 (1999) and No. 34-41936 (1999).

[34] Directive 79/279/EEC coordinating the conditions for the admission of securities to official stock exchange listing [1979] OJ L66/21 (the Admission Directive), now consolidated in Directive 2001/34/EC on admission of securities to official stock exchange listing and on information to be published on those securities [2001] OJ L184/1) (the Securities Consolidation Directive or SCD). The discussion of the Admission Directive in this chapter will be based on the Admission Directive's text but the parallel consolidated references for the SCD are given for the Admission Directive references.

[35] Directive 80/390/EEC coordinating the requirements for the drawing-up, scrutiny and distribution of the listing particulars to be published for the admission of securities to official stock exchange listing [1980] OJ L100/1 (the LPD), Directive 82/121/EEC on information to be published on a regular basis by companies the shares of which have been admitted to official stock exchange listing [1982] OJ L48/26 (the IRD), and Directive 88/627/EEC on the information to be published when a major holding in a listed company is acquired or disposed of [1988] OJ L348/62 (the SSD), respectively (all now consolidated in the SCD). The discussion of these measures in this chapter will be based on the pre-consolidation texts but the parallel consolidated references for the SCD will also be given.

[36] Directive 89/298/EEC coordinating the requirements for the drawing-up, scrutiny and distribution of the prospectus to be published when transferable securities are offered to the public [1989] OJ L124/8 (the POD).

rities to the public.[37] The basic disclosure framework was subsequently subject to a system of mutual recognition designed to allow issuers to prepare a single disclosure document which, once approved by the relevant Member State's competent authority, could be used for admission applications and public offers throughout the Community without the need for further modification or approval, bar the inclusion of certain local-market-specific information and subject to translation requirements.[38]

While, as outlined in section 3.2 below, the EC's disclosure regime may not reflect the traditional policy debates over and rationales for disclosure, it does cover the traditional components of mandatory issuer disclosure. Disclosure is required on the initial admission to official listing or public offer of securities (LPD and POD) and ongoing disclosure obligations, both regular (IRD and Admissions Directive) and when particular material events occur (Admission Directive and SSD), are also imposed. The regime does not, however, include a disclosure mechanism designed to facilitate repeat access by issuers to the capital markets. It is based on the traditional, static, one-off system of requiring substantial disclosure each time an official-listing application is made or a public offer is launched. In this regard, it has become increasingly apparent that the regime is inappropriate and cumbersome for issuers wishing to raise successive instalments of capital. If current proposals are adopted, however, a more integrated disclosure regime, based on a shelf-registration document supported by supplementary disclosure at the point when the capital markets are accessed by the issuer (section 9.3 below), will be put in place.

IV.3.2 *Rationale: Market Integration*

IV.3.2.1 *The Market Integration Rationale and the Treaty*

Two of the regulatory themes highlighted in section 2 above, disclosure as an investor protection device and as a potential barrier to capital raising, converge in the EC's harmonized disclosure regime in its dominant objective,

[37] The price-formation/disclosure context is somewhat different in the primary public offer market. It has been noted that investors in the public primary market do not benefit from the price-setting mechanisms provided by liquid secondary securities markets. Primary market prices are generally established by the issuer and the underwriters who sell the securities on the issuer's behalf: Scott, n 22 above, 76.

[38] Directive 87/345/EEC amending the LPD [1987] OJ L185/81 (the MRD I), Directive 90/211 amending Directive 80/390/EEC in respect of the mutual recognition of public-offer prospectuses as stock-exchange listing particulars [1990] OJ L112/24 (the MRD II) and Directive 94/18/EC amending Directive 80/390/EEC coordinating the requirements for the drawing-up, scrutiny and distribution of the listing particulars to be published for the admission of securities to official stock exchange listing, with regard to the obligation to publish listing particulars [1994] OJ L135/1 (the Eurolist Directive) (now consolidated in the SCD). The discussion of these measures in this chapter will be based on the pre-consolidation texts but the parallel consolidated references for the SCD will also be given.

the integration of EC securities markets. Based on the rationales expressed in the Preambles to the various (for the most part) SCD-consolidated disclosure directives, EC disclosure policy is designed, first, by creating an integrated disclosure system based on a single disclosure document, to enhance the interpenetration of national securities markets and the creation of a European capital market by reducing the regulatory barriers and costs associated with compliance with varying disclosure regimes. Secondly, it seeks to ensure that EC investors have access to adequate information when deciding to buy securities and that investor protection and thereby investor confidence are enhanced.[39] The achievement of the first objective is inextricably linked with the second, as investors will be more likely to access securities markets across the EC if they have confidence in the degree of disclosure available concerning securities and their issuers. EC disclosure policy is thus driven by rather different objectives from those which traditionally inform disclosure policy.

The regime is based ultimately on Article 2 EC and the construction of a common market and on Article 3(c) EC and Article 3(h) EC which, respectively, now identify (they have been revised since the start of the disclosure programme) the construction of the internal market via the abolition, as between Member States, of obstacles to the free movement of goods, services, and capital, and the approximation of Member States' laws to the extent required for the functioning of the internal market as Community activities. The exigencies of finding an appropriate basis for the regime in the Treaty, which does not refer to investor protection/investor confidence or to capital-markets construction/functioning explicitly, appear to have resulted in the provisions which apply to the freedom to establish of undertakings being called in aid. The discrete pre-consolidation directives of the official-listing disclosure regime were originally based on the removal of obstacles to the freedom to establish of undertakings by means of 'coordinating to the necessary extent the safeguards which, for the protection of the interests of members and others, are required of companies or firms . . . with a view to making such safeguards equivalent throughout the Community' under Article 44(2)(g) EC (then Article 54(3)(g) EC) (Admission Directive, LPD, and IRD). They were also based, more generally, on the adoption of directives 'in order to attain the freedom of establishment' (Article 44 EC, then Article 54 EC) (SSD, MRD I and Eurolist Directive).[40] The POD is also based on Article 44 EC. The SCD, which codifies all these measures bar the POD, now simply refers in an umbrella fashion to Article 44 EC in its Preamble, but it also refers explicitly to the role of Article 44(2)(g) EC in harmonizing

---

[39] See, eg, Reid, D, and Ballheimer, A, 'Exemption for Institutional Investors or Concepts of Non-Public Offerings: the European Community' (1993) 13 *U Penn J Int'l Bus L* 495, 495.

[40] The now consolidated MRD II is based on Art. 44(2) EC (then Art. 54(2) EC) which sets out the various ways in which Art. 44 EC is to be carried out (including Art. 44(2)(g) EC).

interim-report and major-shareholdings disclosure measures in Article 108(2)(iii).

Establishment aside, the discrete directives of the disclosure regime were also based, however, on Article 94 EC (then Article 100 EC) (relied on in the Admission Directive, LPD, and IRD) which provides for the adoption of directives for the approximation of such Member States' laws as 'directly affect the establishment or functioning of the common market'. The SCD is based on Article 95 EC which, since its adoption with the Single European Act, has superseded Article 94 EC, as, unlike Article 94 EC, it does not require unanimous voting. It provides for the approximation of laws which 'have as their object the establishment and functioning of the internal market'. The separate pre-consolidation Preamble to the Admission Directive explains that the co-ordination sought by that directive must apply to securities independently of the legal status of their issuers and to securities issued by non-Member States or their regional or local authorities or international public bodies. These issuers do not, however, come within the scope of Article 44(2)(g) EC[41] requiring recourse to Article 94 EC, as the harmonization introduced by the Admission Directive also directly affects the establishment and functioning of the common market (recital 2) (SCD Preamble, recital 3 (which does not make the establishment/functioning of common market link expressly)). Similarly, the LPD pre-consolidation Preamble states that the co-ordination sought must apply to securities independently of the legal status of the issuing undertaking (recital 5) (SCD Preamble, recital 12). The IRD does not in its pre-consolidation Preamble refer directly to the need to rely on Article 94 EC but states that, in order to ensure effective investor protection and the proper operation of stock exchanges, its regular reporting rules must apply to companies from non-Member States as well as Member State companies (recital 8) (SCD Preamble, recital 30). Implicit in this statement is that recourse to Article 94 EC was therefore required as the establishment provisions do not apply to non-Member-State companies.[42] The disclosure regime is accordingly rooted, first, in the freedom of companies to establish and, specifically, to raise financing in an integrated securities market and, secondly, in the creation of a common market in securities/capital.[43]

The basis of the regime in pragmatism and market integration has obscured the extent to which the traditional objectives of disclosure policy

[41] Which applies only to companies and firms within the scope of Art. 48 EC, or 'companies and firms constituted under civil or commercial law, including cooperative societies, and other legal persons governed by public or private law, save for those which are non-profit-making'.

[42] See also Edwards, V, *EC Company Law* (1999) 239.

[43] See, eg, Reid, D and Ballheimer, A, 'The Legal Framework of the Securities Industry in the European Community under the 1992 Program' (1991) 29 *Col. J T'natl. Law* 103, 123 and Wymeersch, E, 'The EU Directives on Financial Disclosure' (1996) 3 *EFSL* 34.

outlined in section 2 above are articulated in the EC's disclosure regime. Although, reflecting the integration objective, investor confidence and the notion of disclosure as a device to encourage investment feature strongly in the regime, other aspects of the disclosure discussion, such as the correction of market failures in the form of information asymmetries,[44] market efficiency/transparency and the price formation process, and the prevention of fraud are not expressly articulated. For example, while the efficiency (both informationally and from an allocative perspective) of the integrated capital market is, it appears, an implicit goal of the market-construction project, the connection between disclosure and market efficiency is not fully expressed, certainly as far as the earlier foundation measures are concerned.[45] The disclosure and market-efficiency link is not addressed in the Admission Directive, the LPD, or the IRD,[46] although the SSD (recital 1) states that disclosure's role in enhancing investor protection and investor confidence should 'ensure that securities markets function correctly'. This reasoning applies to the official-listing disclosure regime as a whole now by virtue of the SCD, recital 31. The POD also makes a connection between disclosure, investor confidence and 'the proper development and functioning of transferable securities markets'.[47] However, perhaps the transformation of disclosure in the hands of EC policy-makers from a well-established regulatory device to a target for harmonization in the interests of market integration counsels against searching too hard for these themes in the disclosure regime.[48] The debate here is more on the best way of constructing a disclosure regime for an integrating and deepening capital market which is, at the

[44] While it lies at the core of much of regulatory theory, it is perhaps unfair to look for this particular doctrine in these early EC securities-regulation measures. Over 20 years later, and even though EC securities regulation has expanded massively in scope, particularly in the investment-services sphere, this doctrine is only just beginning to make an appearance.

[45] Although the 1977 Code of Conduct (Commission Recommendation 77/534/EEC concerning a European Code of Conduct relating to transactions in transferable securities [1977] OJ L212/37) does make a general connection between the harmonization of laws and the improvement of the safeguards offered to investors and the efficient allocation of resources by the securities markets: Explanatory Memorandum, paras 1 and 2.

[46] Although, as discussed in Ch. III, the now consolidated Admission Directive does, in its substantive provisions, emphasize the smooth operation of the market. In particular, Art. 13 (SCD, Art. 16) requires issuers to produce such information as is thought necessary by the competent authorities in order to 'ensure the smooth operation of the market'.

[47] More recently, however, the Commission has explained the need to harmonize accounting standards by means of the link between common accounting rules and 'an integrated capital market which plays its role effectively, smoothly and efficiently': Proposal for a Regulation of the European Parliament and the Council on the Application of International Accounting Standards, Rev. 13, recital 2. See section 10 below.

[48] This feature is not unique to the EC regime. Examining disclosure policies across the EC prior to the harmonization programme, Professor Wymeersch noted that, at that time, in the Member States 'one rarely comes across any questions about the general purposes of this disclosure policy, its effectiveness, the dissemination of the information and its impact on investors': n 6 above, 140.

same time, regulated by varying national disclosure regimes, and rather less on the deep policy background to mandatory issuer-disclosure.[49] It is perhaps because of this that identification of the disclosure regime's investor-protection objectives is difficult. The nature of the investor targeted by the regime, for example, is not clear. Although the regime pursues investor protection and investor confidence in the interests of market integration, the current disclosure regime is arguably not tailored to the needs of retail investors, as it produces detailed information which may be incomprehensible to investors and is static in nature (as a result of its focus on the production of prospectuses on the offer and official listing of securities) and so does not adequately address investors' needs for a continual flow of information. However, while the regime makes the disclosure/investor-protection connection explicitly and the disclosure/market-efficiency link more obliquely, whether either of these objectives can be pursued under the Treaty is discussed in section 3.2.3 below.

IV.3.2.2 *Market Integration and Harmonization of Disclosure*

The link between disclosure harmonization and the integration of capital markets can be traced back to the seminal 1966 Segré Report[50] on capital-market integration.[51] It found that: '[i]n all Member States an essential factor in the expansion of the capital market is that the public be given better information on securities and familiarised with the machinery of the stock exchange'. It reported that while investments were being made in leading international securities, the lack of sufficient information on the operation and prospects of companies meant that investors were apt to 'tread warily' on the European equity markets.[52] In order to protect public savings and expand the supply of capital it urged that the Community adopt an information policy covering both the information required on a public offering of securities and a continuous flow of information concerning facts and figures. To that end, the Report set out the requirements for a model prospectus for

---

[49] It should be noted at this point, however, that the major reform of the regime currently under way does reveal a more considered approach to how disclosure policy should be managed (section 9.3 below).

[50] The Development of a European Capital Market: Report of a Group of Experts appointed by the European Commission (1966) (the Segré Report), 225.

[51] In addition to the studies undertaken by the EC, a plethora of continental European reports emerged in the early 1960s which noted the link between disclosure and the financing of economic growth such as those of the Lorain Committee (France, 1963) and the De Voghel government commission (Belgium, 1962).

[52] N 50 above, 225. The Report also noted that deficiencies in the supply of information had the consequence that investors were inclined to attach disproportionate importance to the political and taxation aspects of an issue. This investment behaviour aggravated the speculative nature of European stock markets and the general lack of selectivity of the investing public as between different securities.

both public issues and stock exchange admission and, foreshadowing the approach ultimately adopted (an approach which has been conspicuously unsuccessful in the public offers area), suggested that minimum standards be adopted which would allow Member States the freedom to broaden the application of the rules, or enforce different rules, within the limits of the minimum rules.[53] The Segré Report also highlighted the link between ongoing disclosure and increased investment in securities, noting the sharp contrast between US and Member States' disclosure requirements.[54] It was also mindful of the investor-protection dimension, however, noting that while 'information is clearly of particular value when an appeal is made for the public's savings and, even more so, when shares are offered for public subscription and listed on the stock exchange . . . a steady flow of intelligence to shareholders and the public, not limited to the publication of annual accounts, seems indispensable if investors and their advisers are to be enabled to take fully informed investment decisions'.[55] Finding that of all the original Member States only France imposed ongoing information requirements, it recommended that a Community information policy should address the 'permanent flow of information on the operation of companies, in addition to the annual publication of their accounts' and, specifically, the disclosure on a three- or six-monthly basis by company directors of sales and gross profits, the immediate disclosure of any new factor which might have a major bearing on the firm's situation or profits expectations, and the updating of the directors' report produced on the original issue of shares by the company.[56] The Segré Report's key findings on disclosure, namely that differences in disclosure requirements create burdens for issuers and complicate the capital-raising process and, more positively, that appropriate common standards of disclosure can actively promote investment, permeate the EC's disclosure regime.

At the time of the Commission's first major legislative initiative in this area in 1972, with its presentation of a proposal for what would become the now consolidated LPD, disclosure standards varied widely across the Community,[57] resulting in patchy standards of investor protection and high

---

[53] N 50 above, 231.

[54] It found, eg that '[c]ontrary to the practices of other countries, and more especially of the United States, information available on most companies in Member States is still embryonic': ibid, 227.

[55] Ibid, 228.   [56] Ibid, 229 and 238.

[57] Despite the existence of disclosure regimes (albeit of varying degrees of sophistication) in most of the Member States in the early 1970s, in establishing a disclosure code for issuers of securities the EC had to combat an anti-disclosure bias (in continental Europe at least) in European corporate culture. See Buxbaum and Hopt, n 10 above, 169. In this regard the Segré Report had found that, while the information available on companies in most Member States was 'embryonic' the reluctance to disclose could be overcome when access to the US and UK markets was involved: n 50 above, 227.

transaction costs for issuers engaging in multiple issues and/or listings.[58] The LPD proposal languished for some time and was overtaken by the 1977 Code of Conduct.[59] In this early expression of the EC's approach to securities regulation generally, the central importance given to disclosure as a tool for market integration is already apparent. The Explanatory Memorandum to the Code of Conduct points out that, while the differences between the various financial markets in the Member States had not so far constituted an insuperable barrier to a number of financial transactions, 'the lack of full information on the securities themselves and ignorance or misunderstanding of the rules governing the various markets have certainly helped to confine the investment of a great majority of savers to the markets of the countries in which they live or to a few well-known major international securities' (paragraph 1). Accordingly, Principle 2 provides that '[i]nformation should be available to the public which is fair, accurate, clear, adequate and which is given in good time' and goes on to require that 'the information should be provided in such a way that its significance and intent can be easily understood'. This theme is echoed in the Code's Supplementary Principles which have now been overtaken by the directives of the harmonized regime.[60] It is of some interest, however, that the Code also addresses the underlying rationale for disclosure and, in particular, suggests reliance on the market-failure doctrine, noting in paragraph III(11)(B) that 'lack of knowledge is a source of imperfection in any market' and that, if information is not provided, slanted, wrongly interpreted, or incomprehensible, 'prices quoted may well become completely artificial and the market may cease to fulfil its role'.

The link between economic growth, capital raising, and harmonized disclosure requirements has recently been raised again because the weaknesses in the EC disclosure regime have become apparent as the EC securities

---

[58] For a review of the various disclosure regimes see Wymeersch, n 6 above. A summary is provided at 21–3. See also Suckow, S, 'The European Prospectus' (1975) 23 *Am. J Comp. L* 50, 52–4.

[59] The EC was not the first international body to acknowledge the importance of adequate disclosure. In 1974, in its Recommendation concerning Disclosure Requirements and Procedures to be Applicable to all Publicly Offered Securities, the OECD recognized the principle that the investor is entitled to the highest practical degree of protection in respect of standards of securities and that the ultimate responsibility in this area lies with government. This Recommendation was followed by the publication of the OECD Disclosure Rules, n 7 above.

[60] The Supplementary Principles from Supplementary Principle 7 on are concerned with the provision of information to investors. Of particular significance for the issuer-disclosure regime are Supplementary Principle 12, which refers to the publication by companies whose securities are 'dealt in on the market' (defined as official stock exchanges or organized markets) of periodic information concerning their business operations, results, and financial position as well as any fact or important decision capable of having an appreciable effect on the price of securities, and Supplementary Principle 14, which provides that 'it is desirable that a public issue of securities should be preceded by the publication of a prospectus'.

market develops. The 1999 FSAP[61] identified the failure of the mutual-recognition-of-disclosure regime as a factor contributing to the continuing fragmentation of EC securities markets and included review of the disclosure regime in its objectives. As examined further in section 9 below, the disclosure regime is now under intensive review.

IV.3.2.3 *Market Integration and Investor Protection: The Treaty Competences*

(a) *Article 44 EC and Article 44(2)(g) EC*

Although the disclosure regime is at this stage a longstanding feature of the EC securities-regulation landscape and while an excursus into the appropriateness of the legal basis of the regime may seem indulgent at this stage,[62] the Court of Justice has recently raised the profile of the Treaty competence issue in dramatic fashion in its October 2000 *Tobacco Advertising* ruling,[63] warranting, perhaps, a brief revisit to the competence question. In addition, with specific reference to investor protection and disclosure, the somewhat shaky Treaty competence supporting the disclosure regime (from the promotion-of-investor-protection perspective) may explain why a certain ambivalence to the protection of investors can be observed in the disclosure regime. Notwithstanding the oft-repeated protestations on the importance of investor protection in the regime, it displays certain inconsistencies and weaknesses with respect to the identity of the investor who is the object of the disclosure regime and the amount and nature of the information disclosed (section 7 below).

The assumption that mandatory disclosure is an instrument of investor protection is well established. Indeed, in establishing a harmonized disclosure regime the EC was, in certain cases, legislating to address failures by particular Member States to protect investors adequately through an information policy (this was particularly the case with the POD and the now consolidated IRD). However, although the harmonized EC disclosure code is traditionally seen as being rooted in and having made a significant contribution to investor protection across the EC,[64] investor confidence in the securities markets can be highlighted as the underlying and governing

[61] Commission Communication on Implementing the Framework for Financial Markets: Action Plan, COM(1999)(232) (the FSAP).

[62] Buxbaum and Hopt, eg, accepted in 1988 that a degree of pragmatism underpinned the Commission's choices of legal basis when constructing the company and capital markets regime: n 10 above, 204–5.

[63] Case C–376/98 *Germany v Parliament and Council* [2000] ECR I–8419 (the *Tobacco Advertising* ruling).

[64] See, eg, Edwards, n 42 above, 4, Lambrecht, P, and Haljan, D, 'Investor Protection and the European Directives Concerning Securities' in van Houtte, H (ed), *The Law of Cross-Border Securities Transactions* (1999) 257, 269 and Warren, M, 'The Common Market Prospectus' (1989) 26 *CMLRev.* 687.

objective of disclosure. Investor protection is a means to achieve the wider investor-confidence objective which is in turn a function of market integration. Although the relationship between investor confidence and the operation of the markets can be somewhat obscure, the link between investor confidence, disclosure, and, ultimately, the promotion of investment activity on a pan-EC basis and the interpenetration of the capital markets is accepted as given. Indeed, the emerging emphasis on investor confidence in the investment-services regime, which serves as the main rationale for the shift in emphasis towards investor protection which can be observed at present in the EC's investment services regime, can be traced back to the issuer-disclosure regime. Whether investor confidence/investor protection, even in the interests of market integration, can be pursued under either Article 44 EC, on which the SCD and the POD are based, or Article 44(2)(g) EC, on which, pre-consolidation, certain of the discrete disclosure directives were expressly based and which is also referred to in Article 108 of the SCD, is not, however, entirely free from doubt.

Article 44(2)(g) EC (which is relied on in the pre-consolidation Admission Directive, the LPD, and the IRD and in the SCD, Article 108) derives from Article 44 EC, which empowers the Council to adopt directives in order to attain the freedom of establishment and reflects the Community's market-construction objectives. While the scope of the 'safeguards which, for the protection of the interests of members and others' may be co-ordinated is not made explicit (although disclosure requirements clearly come within its scope), it appears that the EC has a clear, if limited, mandate to co-ordinate investor-protection safeguards or measures under Article 44(2)(g) EC as long as those requirements are imposed on companies. This mandate is also subject to the qualification that the co-ordinating investor-protection measure must be characterized as necessary to enhance the right of establishment of companies.[65] Thus, investor protection under Article 44(2)(g) EC is subordinate to and a function of the primary objective of facilitating the freedom to establish of companies: it is not designed to protect investors *per se*.[66] The same can be said of Article 44 EC. Notwithstanding these limitations, an attempt is made to make a more explicit connection between Article 44(2)(g) EC and investor protection in the IRD's pre-consolidation Preamble. As well as stating that the protection of investors in listed securities required that they be supplied with regular information throughout the listing period

---

[65] In Case C–122/96 *Saldanha and MTS Securities Corporation v Hiross Holding* [1997] ECR I–5325 the Court made clear that Art. 44(2)(g) EC empowers the Council only in so far as the measures adopted give effect to the freedom of establishment: para 23.

[66] See the analysis in Fornasier, R, 'The Directive on Insider Dealing' (1989–90) 13 *Fordham Int'l. LJ* 149, 159, who suggested that 'the guarantees referred to in Article 53(3)(g) probably need coordination in order to inspire confidence in a economic agent dealing with a company established in its Member State but registered elsewhere. Article 54 is probably not intended to offer guarantees to investors on the securities markets as such [pre-Amsterdam references].'

and that the IRD was accordingly designed to improve investor protection as well as facilitate the listing of securities on more than one exchange, the IRD states in its Preamble that the LPD sought to ensure improved protection of investors (recitals 1 and 2). This argument has been used to make a connection between the general establishment competence under Article 44 EC and the disclosure regime as now codified in the SCD (SCD, recital 25). Investor protection as a function of investor confidence emerges strongly as a discrete objective in the POD which is based on Article 44 EC (at the time Article 54 EC) and in the now consolidated SSD (also based on Article 44 EC and the reasoning of which now applies to the official-listing disclosure regime as a whole via the SCD, recitals 31 and 32). Interestingly, the pre-consolidation Preambles to the Admission Directive and LPD are more circumspect on the investor-protection rationale for harmonizing disclosure. In the Admission Directive, the co-ordination of admission conditions is stated to provide equivalent protection for investors at Community level in accordance with Article 44(2)(g) EC, but such co-ordination is to attain the Directive's primary objective of facilitating the interpenetration of national securities markets and contributing to the prospect of establishing a European capital market. The LPD Preamble focuses on the connection between the freedom to establish of companies, harmonization under Article 44(2)(g) EC, and harmonization of official-listing-disclosure requirements. It found that the market in which undertakings operated had expanded and triggered a corresponding increase in their financing needs but that, as a result of differences between Member States as regards the content and lay-out of the disclosure required, the financing of undertakings via the official listing of securities (identified as an 'important means of access to the capital markets') was being hindered (recitals 1 and 3) (this has been tracked through to the SCD regime in its recitals 8 and 10). Co-ordinating the rules applicable to listing particulars in order to achieve an adequate degree of equivalence in the safeguards required in each Member State to ensure the provision of information which was sufficient and as objective as possible for actual or potential security-holders would eliminate these obstacles to financing which, although not made explicit, would, presumably, enhance the freedom of establishment (LPD, recital 4) (SCD, recital 11).[67]

All the disclosure directives make a connection between the harmonization of disclosure standards, the interpenetration of securities markets, and the construction of a single securities market. More specifically, the SSD (and thus now the SCD generally as it incorporates the SSD reasoning) and the POD emphasize the macro importance of investor confidence in ensuring that securities markets function correctly, and from there make the link

[67] Although ECOSOC was, nonetheless, of the opinion (examining the LPD proposal) that 'the protection of investors is considered to be one of the main objectives pursued by the Commission in its proposal for a Directive' [1974] OJ C125/1.

between investor confidence, disclosure, and market interpenetration. Again, while securities-market interpenetration may ultimately impact on the freedom to establish of companies, it is not directly connected to facilitating the intra-Community movement of companies. Indeed, it has been argued that the inclusion of Article 94 EC as an additional legal basis is an implicit acknowledgement that the regulation of the securities markets and the promotion of investor confidence, which cannot be pursued directly under Article 44 EC, are the primary objectives of the directives.[68] It should be noted, however, that, although the POD does not rely on Article 94 EC,[69] it refers to the link between the interpenetration of securities markets via the co-ordination-of-disclosure requirements and the establishment of a common market in capital. This suggests that a link is, nonetheless, being made between the free movement of companies and the ease with which they can raise financing in an integrated securities market.

Finally, the POD and the SCD (by virtue of its codification of the SSD and IRD reasoning) may be regarded as claiming a more general competence for the Community via Article 44 EC with respect to the smooth operation of securities markets (and arguably their efficiency), as a subset of the market-construction objective. The IRD Preamble identifies the 'proper operation of stock exchanges' as an objective in recital 8 (SCD Preamble, recital 30) while the SSD and POD refer to the link between disclosure, investor confidence, and the 'proper functioning and development of transferable securities markets' (POD Preamble, recital 3) and ensuring that 'securities markets function correctly' (SSD Preamble, recital 1) (SCD Preamble, recital 31). Again, this general regulatory power over the market-place, even if pursued in order to promote integration, does not fit comfortably with the establishment guarantee.

---

[68] '[T]he recourse to Article 100 to cover entities not contemplated by Article 58 seems rather to show that the real aim pursued by these directives is not to coordinate guarantees according to Article 54—in the framework of the right of establishment—but to regulate the financial market on which all traded securities and all issuers are to be dealt with, whether or not the undertakings concerned enjoy the right of establishment under the Treaty or not [pre-Amsterdam references] [*sic*]': Fornasier, n 66 above, 159.

[69] Even though in the absence of a reference to Art. 94 EC (or Art. 95 EC which had been adopted by then), the POD's scope appears to be limited to the issuers which come within Art. 48 EC's definition of companies or firms. See Edwards, n 42 above, who has noted at 268 that '[f]or no obvious reason the final version [of the POD] simply refers to Article 54 [now Art. 44 EC] although issuers are defined as including 'companies and other legal persons and any undertakings' so that the rationale for the Article 100 recited in the early versions [that the coordination sought must apply to securities independently of the issuer's legal status] would seem to be equally applicable'.

(b) *Articles 94 and 95 EC*

While Article 44(2)(g) EC and Article 44 EC thus appear to require a degree of manipulation before they can accommodate the single securities market construction objective, Articles 94 and 95 EC do permit the Community to harmonize disclosure rules where they represent a barrier to the construction of a single securities or capital market. Since the *Tobacco Advertising* ruling, however, it is clear that where single-market regulation, rather than single-market construction, is at issue, care must be taken with the objectives of harmonization. In that case the Court emphasized that harmonization under Article 95 EC must improve the conditions for the establishment and functioning of the internal market; where it simply regulates the internal market it will not be accommodated within Article 95 EC. The Court focused on the existence of divergences between Member States' rules as a ground for Article 95 harmonization and emphasized that these divergences must be such as to obstruct free movement or cause considerable distortions to competition. In its proposals to restructure the current disclosure regime to eliminate the persisting obstacles to the creation of a single securities market, the Commission relies on Article 95 EC (as well as Article 44 EC). The assumption that the harmonization of disclosure (and the promotion thereby of investor confidence and the smooth functioning of the market) is linked to the improvement of the conditions for the establishment and functioning of the common market thus appears to be a central tenet of the disclosure programme (see further section 9.3 below).

IV.3.3 *The Harmonization Device: Detailed Harmonization and Mutual Recognition*

As outlined in Chapter II, disclosure harmonization was initially attempted via the equivalence route, and latterly via the mutual-recognition device (section 8 below). The articulation of the mutual-recognition device has been somewhat unsatisfactory, however. Indeed, the disclosure regime is widely regarded as having failed in its objective of integrating capital markets, in that issuers remain subject to onerous additional disclosure and related requirements (typically translation requirements) when raising capital cross-border. This is as a result of certain of the structural features of the mutual-recognition regime as well as the open-textured nature of the disclosure regime and its multitude of exemptions, derogations, and options which have resulted in considerably varying interpretations of its requirements across the Member States.

IV.3.4 *The Next Stage*

Having passed through an initial detailed rule-construction phase and a flawed mutual-recognition phase, the third stage of the disclosure regime's evolution is now unfolding and is discussed in section 9. In this phase the cumbersome structure of the current disclosure regime, the primary obligations of which activate on a specific event, be it admission to listing or a public offer, and produce static and rapidly outdated disclosure documents, is under review. An 'issuer passport' will also replace the mutual-recognition regime with a home Member State-control-based system which will allow an issuer to rely on one disclosure document across the Community, be it for an offer of securities to the public or for an application to admit securities to trading, free of intervention from host Member State authorities, which may ask only for a translation of a summary of the document. The following discussion examines the main planks of the mandatory issuer-disclosure regime.[70]

IV.4 DISCLOSURE AND OFFICIALLY LISTED SECURITIES—THE LISTING PARTICULARS DIRECTIVE (LPD)[71]

IV.4.1 *Objectives*

The genesis of the now consolidated LPD lies before that of its actual legislative precursor, the now consolidated Admission Directive, in a Commission proposal presented in 1972.[72] Although the amendments

---

[70] There is an extensive literature on the EC disclosure regime, although much of the material dates from the early 1990s when the disclosure scheme began to take final shape. The following is a representative sample: Merloe, P, 'Internationalization of Securities Markets: A Critical Survey of US and EEC Disclosure Requirements' (1986) 8 *J Comp. Bus. and Capital Markets L* 249; Warren, M, 'Global Harmonization of Securities Laws: The Achievements of the European Communities' (1999) 31 *Harvard Int'l. LJ* 185; Wolff, S, 'Securities Regulation in the European Community' (1991) 20 *Denver J of Int'l. L and Policy* 99; Fama, A, and Im, S, 'Recent Securities Regulation in the European Community and the Integration of European Capital Markets' (1991) 32 *Harvard Int'l. LJ* 553; Reid and Ballheimer, n 43 above; Reid and Ballheimer, n 39 above; Wouters, J, 'EC Harmonisation of National Rules Concerning Securities Offerings, Stock Exchange Listing and Investment Services' (1993) 4 *EBLRev.* 199, 200; and Wymeersch, n 43 above.

[71] See generally Edwards, n 42 above, 251–61; Woolridge, F, 'Some Recent Community Legislation in the Field of Securities Law' (1985) 10 *ELRev.* 3 at 10–17; and Morse, G, 'Sixth Directive on Prospectuses Adopted' (1980) 5 *ELRev.* 316.

[72] [1972] OJ C131/61. The original proposal had two elements: a proposal for a directive concerning the prospectus to be issued in connection with admission to stock exchange quotation and a draft Council recommendation concerning the same where the securities were issued by a State or its regional or local authorities (such securities fell outside the scope of the proposed directive). The proposal is examined in Suckow, n 58 above. The House of Lords Select Committee expressed concern about the scope of the Directive, finding that were the Directive

suggested by the European Parliament and ECOSOC proved to be relatively minor,[73] progress was slow[74] and the LPD was not finally adopted until March 1980.[75]

The introduction of harmonized disclosure standards is linked to the integration of EC securities markets and to the removal of the regulatory obstacles in the form of varying disclosure requirements faced by issuers in raising finance. Different standards of disclosure, varying from Member State to Member State[76] serve 'not only to make it more difficult for undertakings to obtain admission of securities to listing on stock exchanges of several Member States but also hinder the acquisition by investors residing in one Member State of securities listed on stock exchanges of other Member States and thus to inhibit the financing of the undertakings and investment throughout the Community' (recital 3) (SCD, recital 10).[77] Accordingly, the listing-particulars regime co-ordinates Member State requirements concerning the provision of information by issuers at the time of the admission of securities to listing in the form of listing particulars, 'in order to achieve an adequate degree of equivalence in the safeguards required in each Member State to ensure the provision of information which is sufficient and as objective as possible for actual or potential security holders' (recital 4) (SCD, recital 11).[78] The link between disclosure and investor protection in the EC

'to apply to new issues rather than to new listing of securities then the Community would be able to claim some progress towards the provision of surveillance machinery for these more truly international capital markets': House of Lords Select Committee on the European Community, *Report on the Draft Directive on Prospectuses for Company Securities for Stock Exchange Quotation*, HL (1974–75), 21st Report (the HL LPD Report), 6. Despite the weight of comment calling for an extension of the LPD's provisions to public offers, negotiating difficulties would delay the adoption of the POD until 1988.

[73] [1974] OJ C11/24 and [1974] OJ C125/1, respectively,

[74] In its 1980 opinion on the Commission's proposal for the IRD, the European Parliament somewhat wearily expressed its 'regrets that the Council has not yet adopted the Commission's proposal for a Directive on the prospectus to be published when securities are admitted to official stock exchange listing on which Parliament gave its opinion as long ago as the beginning of 1974.' [1970] OJ C85/69, 70.

[75] Member States were to implement the Directive by 19 Sept 1982. The deadline was subsequently modified by Art. 2 of Directive 82/148/EEC [1982] OJ L62/22, which extended the implementation period for States simultaneously implementing the now consolidated Admission Directive and IRD to 30 June 1983.

[76] Recital 3 to the LPD's pre-consolidation Preamble states that disclosure standards 'differ from Member State to Member State, both as regards the contents and layout of the listing particulars and the efficacy, methods and timing of the check on the information given therein': SCD, recital 10.

[77] This argument based on the hindrances faced by investors reflects the investor-confidence point and acknowledges that cross-border investors may be inhibited by differing forms and models of disclosure. In this regard, ECOSOC found that the LPD was 'intended to facilitate the interpenetration of capital markets by improving the quality and comparability of the information published concerning securities quoted on the Community's stock exchanges': n 73 above, recital 3.

[78] Interestingly, although, as outlined in section 3.2.3 above, the LPD's rationale is arguably rooted in market interpenetration rather than in investor protection *per se*, the institutions

securities market is thus acknowledged, even if the harmonization of rules is ultimately directed towards market interpenetration and, in particular, the access of issuers to the capital markets.[79]

IV.4.2 *The Core Obligation and Exemptions*

The listing-particulars regime applies to securities (undefined) which are the subject of an application for admission to official listing on a stock exchange situated or operating within a Member State (Article 1(1)) (SCD, Article 2(1)) and does not apply to units issued by collective investment schemes (excluding closed-end schemes) or to securities issued by a State or by its local or regional authorities (Article 1(2)) (SCD, Article 2(1)). As with the admission-to-official-listing regime with which it is now consolidated, neither 'stock exchange' nor 'official listing' is defined.

Member States must ensure that, as a prerequisite to the admission of securities to official listing on a stock exchange situated or operating in their territory, a disclosure document, termed 'listing particulars', must be published (Article 3) (SCD, Article 20).[80] A competent authority must be appointed by the Member States to approve the listing particulars (Article 18) (SCD, Articles 105 and 35). The LPD does not address the consequence of a failure to produce listing particulars. Sanctions for non-compliance remain the preserve of the Member States.

The publication of listing particulars is not required every time an admission of securities to official listing is sought. In an example of the flexibility given to Member States under the LPD, Member States may allow the

involved in the legislative process read it as an investor-protection measure. The Parliament summarized the LPD's purpose as being 'designed to ensure that in all Member States of the Community the fullest and most objective information is made available on the economic and financial position of the issuing company and the nature of the securities, before they are officially quoted on a stock exchange in the territory of a Member State': n 73 above, 24, point 1. ECOSOC was of the opinion that 'the protection of investors is considered to be one of the main objectives pursued by the Commission in its proposal for a Directive': n 73 above, recital 1. Indeed, ECOSOC would later suggest that the early admission-to-official-listing measures (including the LPD and the Admission Directive) 'were devoted entirely to investor protection' (Opinion of the Economic and Social Committee on Directive 94/18/EC ([1994] OJ L135/1) ([1993] OJ C161/9)) a claim which is not entirely accurate, given the issuer rather than investor focus of the disclosure regime.

[79] The HL LPD Report described the investor-protection/barrier-removal aspects of the LPD's market integration objective as follows: '[t]he purpose is both to simplify the procedure for companies seeking multiple listing in the Member States and to set minimum standards for the quantity and quality of information made available to the investing public. The ultimate purpose of the Directive is therefore to facilitate stock market movements in the Community': n 72 above, 3.

[80] ECOSOC also proposed that the LPD extend to reductions of capital and that listing particulars be required in order to maintain a listing on a reduction of capital. Its rationale was that investors also need to assess the change in an issuer's circumstances following a reduction of capital: n 73 above, para 3.1.1.1.

competent authorities responsible for checking the listing particulars to provide for partial or complete exemption from the obligation to publish listing particulars in specified circumstances (Article 6) (SCD, Article 23). Article 6 contains a detailed list of these circumstances which include: (1) where the securities for which admission to official listing is sought have been the subject of a public issue (now covered by the POD) (Article 6(1)(a)) (SCD, Article 23(1)(a)), issued in connection with a takeover offer (not defined) (Article 6(1)(b)) (SCD, Article 23(1)(b)) or merger (Article 6(1)(c)) (SCD, Article 23(1)(c))[81] and where, not more than twelve months before the admission to official listing, a document which is regarded by the competent authorities as containing information equivalent to that required by the LPD has been published in the same Member State; (2) where the securities for which admission to listing is sought are either shares which been allotted free of charge (Article 6(2)(a)) (SCD, Article 23(2)(a)), shares resulting from the conversion of convertible securities or the exercise of warrants (Article 6(2)(b) and (c)) (SCD, Article 23(2)(b) and (c)), or shares issued in substitution for shares already listed on the same stock exchange if the issuing of the new shares does not involve an increase in the company's issued share capital (Article 6(2)(d)) (SCD, Article 23(2)(d)); (3) where the shares for which admission to official listing is sought form less than 10 per cent of the same class already listed on the same stock exchange (Article 6(3)(a)) (SCD, Article 23(3)(a)); (4) where the securities for which admission to official listing is sought have been issued by certain State monopoly companies or other issuers which benefit from State guarantees (Article 6(3)(b) and (c)) (SCD, Article 23(3)(b) and (c)); and (5) where the shares have been allotted to employees and form part of an already listed class (Article 6(3)(d)) (SCD, Article 23(3)(d)).[82]

As originally adopted, the LPD did not contain a general exemption from the obligation to publish listing particulars where sufficient information was already available concerning the issuer, notwithstanding that in such circumstances the LPD's objectives might have been satisfied, and although that appears to be the rationale underpinning a number of the Article 6 exemptions. It was not until 1994 that a further exemption reflecting this analysis (Article 6(5)) was introduced by an amendment made to the LPD

---

[81] Art. 6(1)(c) refers to 'securities issued in connection with a merger involving the acquisition of another company or the formation of a new company, the division of a company, the transfer of all or part of an undertaking's assets and liabilities or as consideration for the transfer of assets other than cash'.

[82] In line with the disclosure philosophy, however, in all cases the LPD requires the publication of specified information, varying from disclosure of any material change since the previously published disclosure document in the case of the Art. 6(1)(c) (SCD, Art. 23(1)(c)) exemption to the publication of information concerning the number and type of securities to be admitted and the circumstances in which such securities have been listed in exemptions Art. 6(3)(a)–(d) (SCD, Art. 23(3)(a)–(d)).

by Directive 94/18.[83] Article 6(5) (SCD, Article 23(5)) provides that a full or partial exemption from the obligation to publish listing particulars may apply where companies, the shares of which have already been dealt in for at least the preceding two years on a second-tier market which is regulated and supervised by authorities recognized by public authorities, seek to have their securities admitted to official listing in the same Member State.[84] The two-year qualification is designed to prevent companies from abusing the amendment by using it as a short cut to official listing. Adopted in order to ease the passage of companies from junior markets to official listing, the amendment reflects the reality that investor protection is not enhanced by the publication of listing particulars in such circumstances.[85]

IV.4.3 *Information Requirements*

IV.4.3.1 *The General Obligation*

The listing-particulars regime takes a rigorous approach to disclosure, adopting, it appears, the position that investors must be well equipped to make sound and informed investment choices. While listing particulars must contain 'at least the items of information provided for in Schedule A, B, or C' (Article 5(1)) (SCD, Article 22(1)),[86] disclosure by issuers under the LPD is not simply a checking the box exercise; issuers are subject to an overriding obligation to disclose all information which may be required by investors. Article 4(1) (SCD, Article 21(1)) requires that listing particulars contain all information which, according to the particular nature of the issuer and of the securities in question, 'is necessary to enable investors and their investment advisers to make an informed assessment of the assets and liabilities, financial position, profits and losses, and prospects of the issuer[87] and of the

---

[83] Directive 94/18/EC [1994] OJ L135/1. See further section 8.5 below.

[84] The exemption is subject to the proviso that the competent authority must be of the opinion that information equivalent in substance to that required by the LPD is available to investors before the date on which admission to official listing becomes official.

[85] Recital 12 to Directive 94/18 acknowledges that in some cases second-tier markets are regulated and supervised by authorities recognized by public bodies which impose on companies disclosure equivalent in substance to that imposed on officially listed companies (SCD, recital 23). The Federation of European Stock Exchanges supported the amendment and found that a requirement to produce listing particulars on transfer from a second-tier market to official listing was unnecessary, particularly where such companies were already subject to disclosure requirements equivalent to the LPD: Explanatory Memorandum to the Proposal for a Council Directive amending Directive 80/390, COM(92)566, 7.

[86] Schs A, B, and C apply to shares, debt securities, and certificates representing shares, respectively. This differentiated approach reflects the different disclosure requirements applied to debt and equity in certain Member States, such as France: Woolridge, n 71 above, 12. Some Member States, although not all, have tended to subject debt securities to a less onerous disclosure regime.

[87] Under Art. 2(c), 'issuer' covers 'companies and other legal persons and any undertaking whose securities are the subject of an application for admission to official listing on a stock exchange': SCD, Art. 1a.

rights attaching to such securities'. This open-ended requirement introduces an obligation of full disclosure, extending even to the prospects of the issuer, and ensures that any material information[88] does not fall between any gaps which may exist in the Schedules. Article 4(2) (SCD, Article 21(2)) seeks to ensure compliance with this obligation by focusing the minds of the issuer's management on it: Article 4(2) requires Member States to impose responsibility for compliance with Article 4(1) on those persons responsible for the listing particulars.[89] The all-embracing nature of the disclosure obligation is underlined by the requirement that every significant new factor capable of affecting assessment of the securities which arises between the time when the listing particulars are adopted and the time when stock exchange dealings begin is to be covered by a supplement to the listing particulars which is reviewed in the same manner as are the listing particulars (Article 23) (SCD, Article 100). Finally, Article 5(1) requires that all information disclosed must be in 'as easily analysable and comprehensible a form as possible'. The utility of this requirement for ordinary investors is somewhat diminished by Article 4(1) which provides that investment advisers (as well as investors) must be provided with the information necessary to make an assessment of the issuer and the securities. If disclosure is directed towards investment advisers it is unlikely to take a form which is accessible to ordinary investors; although this approach may suggest a disclosure philosophy based more on the promotion of efficient price formation, if the focus of disclosure shifts thereby towards the professional investment community.[90]

IV.4.3.2 *The Schedules (SCD References are in parallel, in SCD Annex I)*

The Schedules set out detailed disclosure requirements (which provide the classic example of the Community's early attempts to harmonize by the equivalence device) which, where inappropriate to the issuer's particular sphere of activity or legal form, can be adapted to reflect the issuer's characteristics, as long as equivalent information is provided (Article 5(3)) (SCD,

---

[88] Notably, the LPD does not use the term material. The overall thrust of Art. 4(1), however, reflects IOSCO's recent finding that 'in addition to . . . specific disclosures . . . most countries rely on an overriding principle that, in connection with a registration or listing of securities or a public offering of securities, a company should disclose all information that would be material to an investor's investment decision and that is necessary for full and fair disclosure': 1998 IOSCO Disclosure Principles, n 31 above, 4.

[89] Ch 1.1 of Schs A and B and C requires disclosure of the names and functions of those responsible for the listing particulars, or part of the listing particulars.

[90] ECOSOC suggested the removal of the reference to investment advisers, given that 'the prime object of a prospectus is to inform the public directly about the circumstances of the issuer . . . supervision of prospectuses, however detailed would not further the protection of savers if investors can neither read nor understand the prospectus and can only base their decision to invest on the recommendation of an financial consultants': n 73 above, para 3.1.2. On the clarity of disclosure question see section 7.2 below.

Article 22(3)). The Schedules' requirements are considered below in outline only. Overall, the disclosure code set out in the Schedules is not all-embracing. It is a framework code. Unlike many national regimes, it does not apply particular requirements to specific industries, apart from requiring specific disclosure in respect of 'mining, extraction of hydrocarbons, quarrying and similar activities' (Schedule A, chapter 4(1)(3)). The disclosure code also avoids an over-emphasis on historic information by requiring disclosure of future prospects. The future-prospects information is based on the assumption that investors are unlikely to accept predictions contained in a disclosure document uncritically.

(a) *Schedule A: Disclosure Requirements for Shares.*

The listing particulars must contain a declaration by those persons disclosed in the listing particulars as responsible for them to the effect that the information contained in the part of the listing particulars for which they are responsible is in accordance with the facts and contains no omissions likely to affect the import of the listing particulars (Schedule A, chapter 1(2)). A statement that the annual accounts have been audited, together with details of any refusals to issue an audit report or any qualified audit reports and of the auditors who have audited the company's annual accounts (defined in Article 2(g) (SCD, Article 1(h)) as the balance sheet, profit and loss account, and the notes to the accounts) for the preceding three financial years is also required (Schedule A, chapter 1(3)).

The disclosure required in respect of the shares is set out in Schedule A, chapter 2. The listing particulars must include a statement that an application for admission to official listing has been made and details of all stock exchanges to which admission to official listing is sought, together with details of any stock exchanges on which shares of the same class are already listed. The reservation of a tranche of shares for marketing in other Member States must also be disclosed. The disclosure required concerning the share issue includes: the rights attaching to the shares; any withholding tax applicable; the arrangements for transfer (including restrictions on transferability); details of any pre-emption rights (including the procedure for their negotiation and any restrictions or withdrawals of such rights); the size of the issue and its price (including the method of payment); details of those persons underwriting or guaranteeing the issue (and their commission); details of the overall charges incurred by the issue; the net proceeds accruing to the issuer and the application of such proceeds; and details of any takeover bids which the issuer initiated or was subject to in the last and current financial year.

General information about the issuer and its capital is covered in Schedule A, chapter 3. The information relating to capital includes: the amount of issued share capital (including the shares into which it is divided); the amount of unissued share capital (including details of any preferential subscription rights relating to it); details of any issues of convertible or exchangeable debt securities or debt securities with warrants; a summary of any changes in capital over the three preceding years; the names of those persons who directly or indirectly, severally or jointly, exercise or could exercise control over the issuer; details of those shareholders who directly or indirectly hold a certain proportion of the issuer's capital specified by the Member States and which may not be set at more than 20 per cent; and, where the issuer belongs to a group, a brief description of the group and the issuer's position within it. The general information to be included concerning the issuer includes an indication of its date of incorporation, legal form, and objects.

The information required concerning the issuer's activities is set out in Schedule A, chapter 4.[91] The disclosure under this heading includes: a description of the issuer's activities, including the main categories of products sold or services performed; a breakdown of net turnover during the past three years by categories of activity and geographical markets (where such categories and markets differ substantially from one another); location and size of the issuer's principal establishment; details of the issuer's degree of dependence on patents or licences, financial or commercial contracts, or new manufacturing processes; information on research and development policy and activities over the past three financial years, where significant; details of any legal or arbitration proceedings which may have or have had a significant effect on the issuer's financial position in the recent past; any interruptions in the issuer's business which may have or have had a similar effect; the average number of employees over the past three years and a breakdown of persons employed by main categories of activity; and details of the issuer's past (during the past three financial years), current, and future investments. Where the issuer is a dominant undertaking forming a group with one or more dependent undertakings, this information must be given for the issuer and the group (Schedule A, chapter 5(5)).

Under Schedule A, chapter 5, financial information is required concerning the issuer's assets and liabilities, financial position, and profits and losses. The issuer must provide in the listing particulars its last three balance sheets and profit and loss accounts, along with the notes to the annual accounts for the last financial year. The draft listing particulars must be filed with the competent authorities not more than eighteen months after the end of the financial year to which the last annual accounts published relate (this period

---

[91] ECOSOC expressed concern about the degree of disclosure required under this heading. In particular it was concerned that disclosure of information with respect to individual products, licences, and patents could 'be tantamount to giving away some of the trade secrets of the issuing company and perhaps also its contracting partners': n 73 above, para 3.5.4.

may be extended in exceptional circumstances). The profit or loss and dividend per share for the last three financial years must also be included. Where more than nine months have elapsed since the end of the financial year to which the published accounts relate, an interim financial statement covering the first six months of the issuer's current financial year must be provided. A table setting out sources and application of funds over the last three financial years must also be supplied, as well as specified details relating to undertakings in which the issuer holds a proportion of the capital likely to have a significant effect on the assessment of its own assets, liabilities, financial position, or profits and losses.

The information required concerning administration, management, and supervision is covered in Schedule A, chapter 6. The listing particulars must disclose the particulars of the members of the administrative, management, and supervisory bodies and of the issuer's promoters (the latter where the issuer has been established for less than five years). Other disclosure required includes: details of the remuneration paid and benefits in kind granted during the last financial year to members of the administrative, management, and supervisory bodies; the total number of shares (and options over shares) in the issuer held by such members, together with details of any outstanding loans or guarantees granted by the issuer to such members; details of the 'nature and extent' of the interests of such members in 'transactions of the issuer which are unusual in their nature or conditions (such as purchases outside normal activity, acquisition or disposal of fixed asset items)' (Schedule A, chapter 6(2)(2)) during the preceding and current financial years; and details of any employee share schemes.

Schedule A, chapter 7 sets out the information required concerning the recent development and prospects of the issuer. This section acts as a counterbalance to the mandatory disclosure of what may often be negative information, such as details of ongoing litigation and information on interruptions to business. Projections and forecasts can be very useful for the investor where they have a reasonable basis in fact, as the past performance of an issuer or a security is not necessarily a reliable indication of its future prospects.[92] The information required here includes general information on the trend of the issuer's business since the end of the financial year to which the last published accounts relate, including, in particular, information

---

[92] The appropriateness of the disclosure of forward-looking or 'soft' information is, however, a matter of some controversy. Originally the SEC would not allow the disclosure of soft information in mandatory disclosure documents on the ground that such information was inherently subjective and unreliable and liable to misuse by unsophisticated investors. Since 1978, however, it has changed its position and now encourages the disclosure of forward-looking information as long as it has a reasonable basis. In a move further to encourage the disclosure of such information it has also introduced a regulatory 'safe harbour', which shields issuers against liability when forward statements are made under certain conditions, which was extended in 1995 by the Private Securities Litigation Reform Act.

concerning the most significant recent trends in production, sales, and stocks and the state of the order book and recent trends in costs and selling prices.[93] The competent authority is expressly permitted to grant a derogation from this requirement. Information must also be supplied, unless a derogation is granted by the competent authority, on the issuer's prospects for at least the current financial year. Where the issuer is a dominant undertaking forming a group with one or more dependent undertakings, this information must be given for the issuer and the group (Schedule A, chapter 5(5)).

(b) *Schedule B: Disclosure Requirements for Debt Securities*

The information requirements for debt securities are broadly similar to those for shares. The main differences are highlighted below.

Schedule B, chapter 2 sets out the information required in respect of the debt securities. The disclosure required under this heading reflects the particular features of debt securities. The details which must be provided include: the conditions of the loan represented by the issue of debt securities; the nature and scope of the guarantees or other commitments designed to ensure that the principal will be repaid and interest payments serviced; taxes withheld in respect of interest payments; arrangements for the redemption of the loan; details relating to the payment of interest; an indication of the debt securities' yield; details of the trustee or other organization responsible for representing the interests of debt security-holders as a body; information on whether the loan is subordinated to other debts of the issuer; and whether the securities are in bearer or registered form.

The general information required about the issuer and its capital is set out in Schedule B, chapter 3. The information required concerning the issuer's share capital is less extensive, but details must be given concerning the amount of any convertible or exchangeable debt securities or debt securities with warrants, along with an indication of the conditions governing the procedure for conversion, exchange, or subscription. Where the issuer belongs to a group of undertakings, a brief description must be given of the group and of the issuer's position within it.

Information concerning the issuer's activities is required under Schedule B, chapter 4. The disclosure required under this heading may be supplied in less detail than is required for shares. In particular, turnover activity may be supplied without a breakdown by category of activity or geographical

---

[93] The EC's approach to soft information is unusual in that it does not require that the projected information be audited. The UK, eg, imposes an auditing requirement (Belgium and Germany require that an indication be made whether the information has been audited) while Spain requires that projections be reviewed by an independent expert. See the 1998 IOSCO Disclosure Standards, n 31 above, paras II-13–II-15.

market (and need be supplied only for the last two financial years) and information on employees, business interruptions, and research and development activities is not required.

The financial information required concerning the issuer's assets and liabilities, financial position, and profits and losses is covered in Schedule B, chapter 5. This information may also be supplied in less detail for debt securities. Of particular note is the requirement that profit and loss accounts and balance sheets be provided for the preceding two financial years only. Issuers of debt securities must, however, provide details of the total amount of loan capital outstanding, all other borrowings and indebtedness (distinguishing between guaranteed and non-guaranteed borrowings) and any contingent liabilities.

Information concerning administration, management and supervision is covered by Schedule B, chapter 6, but the only information requirement imposed on issuers of debt securities under this heading is to disclose details of the members of the administrative, management, or supervisory boards of the issuer. These details (which also apply to issuers of shares) include the name, address, and function of the members, together with an indication of the principal activities performed by them outside the issuer, where these are significant with respect to the issuer.

The requirements imposed in respect of information concerning the recent developments and prospects of the issuer (Schedule B, chapter 7) track the requirements imposed on shares.

(c) *The Modifications*

The disclosure requirements set out in the Schedules do not function as a monolithic code. It has already been noted that, under Article 5(3) (SCD, Article 22(3)), where the Schedule headings are inappropriate to the issuer's legal form or sphere of activity equivalent information is to be provided. In addition, the application of the Schedules is modified in the case of certain categories of securities (Article 5(2)) (SCD, Article 22(2)). These modifications are set out in Articles 8–17 (SCD, Articles 25–34) and take into account the type of issuer, the nature of the securities, and the context in which the securities are issued. The securities subject to an adjusted regime include rights issues (Article 8) (SCD, Article 25), debt securities (without related rights over shares) when the issuer has already listed securities on the same stock exchange (Article 9) (SCD, Article 26), securities issued by financial institutions (Article 11) (SCD, Article 28),[94] debt

---

[94] Member States are to determine the 'financial institutions' covered by this regime and may extend Art. 11 to collective-investment undertakings within the scope of the LPD, finance companies which engage only in capital-raising activities for a parent company, and companies holding portfolios of securities, licences, or patents and whose only activity is the management of such portfolios: Art. 11(2)–(3) (SCD, Art. 28(2)–(3)).

securities issued in a continuous or repeated manner by credit institutions (Article 12) (SCD, Article 29), guaranteed debt securities (Article 13) (SCD, Article 30), debt securities carrying related rights in shares (Article 14) (SCD, Article 31), securities issued in connection with a merger or takeover (Article 15) (SCD, Article 32), certificates representing shares (Article 16) (SCD, Article 33), and State-guaranteed securities (Article 17) (SCD, Article 34). Of particular note is Article 10 (SCD, Article 27), as its rationale for the application of a modified version of the Schedules is the nature of the investor likely to trade in the particular securities concerned; Article 10 thus marks the first appearance of the sophisticated investor in EC securities regulation. By the time of the adoption of the investment-services regime in 1993, the sophisticated investor categorization would have become a useful regulatory device for granting exemptions from regulation. Article 10 contains the so-called euro-bond modification which applies to 'debt securities nearly all of which, because of their nature, are normally bought and traded in by a limited number of investors who are particularly knowledgeable in investment matters'. In the case of these securities, competent authorities may permit the omission of certain information normally required under Schedule B (or allow its inclusion in summary form).[95] Notably, this modification is subject to a materiality requirement. The information excluded or summarized must not be 'material (undefined) from the point of view of the investors concerned'.

The listing-particulars disclosure regime can also be filtered through the competent authority's ability to exercise discretion in applying the Schedules. Although the competent authority may grant a derogation from the detailed information requirements, this power, consistent with the Directive's philosophy of ensuring that investors are provided with 'information which is sufficient and as objective as possible', is limited. Derogations may be granted only where the information concerned is of an immaterial character (Article 7(a)) (SCD, Article 24(a))[96] or in situations where disclosure would be contrary to the public interest or seriously detrimental to the issuer's interest (Article 7(b)) (SCD, Article 24(b)).[97] Power

---

[95] This provision was introduced 'partly to enable the euro-bond market to continue in operation': Wood, P, *International Loans, Bonds and Securities Regulation* (1995) 271. European stock exchanges (in particular London and Luxembourg) have used this modification to reduce the disclosure requirements applicable to specialist debt securities, including euro-bonds. For a discussion of the Luxembourg regime see Schmitt, A, and Hurd, J, 'Caveat Vendor: An Introduction to Listing Procedures for the Luxembourg Stock Exchange' (1995) 12 *JIBL* 502.

[96] Art. 7(a) permits competent authorities to authorize the omission of required information from the listing particulars where it 'is of minor importance only and is not such as will influence assessment of the assets and liabilities, financial position, profits and losses and prospects of the issuer'.

[97] The derogation is subject to the proviso that 'such omission would not be likely to mislead the public with regard to facts and circumstances, knowledge of which is essential for the assessment of the securities in question'. ECOSOC was dubious about the clarity of this

to authorize the omission of mandatory information is also granted to competent authorities in the specific situation of an admission of debt securities to listing coinciding with their public issue, where certain of the terms of the issue are not finalized. In such circumstances, the competent authority may authorize publication of listing particulars which omit such terms, but which indicate how the terms will be publicized (Article 21(3)) (SCD, Article 99(3)). These restrictions on the powers of competent authorities to authorize the omission of information also have the effect of reducing the danger (albeit in today's competitive market-place an unlikely one) of foreign issuers who seek admission to official listing being subject to discrimination.

IV.4.3.3 *Sanctions and the Effectiveness of Disclosure*

The combination of relatively detailed minimum requirements,[98] a catch-all general obligation to make full disclosure, and the limited ability of competent authorities to authorize omissions from the regime's requirements introduced a rigorous disclosure code for admission to official listing[99] and raised pre-existing levels of disclosure.[100] Yet the adequacy and sufficiency of disclosure in practice are typically ensured by imposing sanctions on the issuer and those persons responsible for the disclosure or by making remedies available to investors.[101] In common with the approach taken towards sanctions and liability across EC securities regulation, liability in respect of inadequate or misleading disclosure is left to the discretion of Member States: remedies are, of course, typically the preserve of the Member States under EC law generally. Indeed, under the LPD the 'disclosure relationship', as it were, is between the competent authority imposing the LPD's requirements and the issuer. The investors who are the recipients of the disclosure and

derogation, stating that '[a]lthough a fairly high degree of flexibility can be achieved in some cases by the use of imprecise legal expressions, the accumulation of such expressions here conflicts with the need for legal certainty': n 73 above, para 3.1.5.2.

[98] The LPD has been described as offering 'almost an exhaustive regulation of the topics to be harmonised': Wymeersch, n 43 above, 34.

[99] The success of the disclosure code (from the investor-protection perspective) introduced by the LPD can perhaps be measured by the fact that the SEC relied on it in developing disclosure requirements for foreign issuers. See Pierce, M, 'The Regulation of the Issuance and Trading of Securities in the US and the European Economic Community' (1981) 3 *J Comp. Corp. L and Sec. Reg.* 129, 132–3.

[100] A number of commentators have noted this effect. See, eg, Woolridge, n 71 above, 12–15 on its implications for the UK regime.

[101] 'It is one thing to require full disclosure, another thing to force compliance. The principal mechanism to this end, of course, is the liability scheme': Cox *et al.*, n 18 above, 669. The availability of remedies with respect to faulty disclosure is a complex question, however, and the nature of the remedy can depend on the extent to which the information was disclosed in the context of a specific contractual relationship between the issuer and the investor through, eg, the public-offer prospectus, or was simply made generally available, as is the case with listing particulars. See Wymeersch, n 43 above, 35–3 for a discussion of how inadequate or misleading disclosure may give rise to private remedies for investors.

who seek recovery for losses consequent on misrepresentations or omissions must rely on national remedies, where they exist. Nonetheless, it is interesting that the LPD did not require Member States to ensure either that appropriate sanctions be imposed for non-compliance (with the competent authority playing a role here, perhaps), or, more controversially, that remedies be made available to investors sustaining loss consequent on relying on defective listing particulars.[102] A few years after the adoption of the LPD the EC would (albeit tentatively) grasp the nettle of sanctions in the disclosure context. Article 15 of the now consolidated SSD (SCD, Article 97) requires Member States to provide 'appropriate sanctions' in cases where those subject to the SSD's large-shareholdings disclosure requirements do not comply with its provisions. The requirement to produce a responsibility statement is, however, likely to concentrate the minds of those responsible for collating and reviewing the issuer's disclosure.

IV.4.4 *Publication of Listing Particulars*

Under Article 20 (SCD, Article 98), listing particulars must be published either by insertion in one or more newspapers circulating in the Member State in which admission to official listing is sought (or in wide circulation there) or in the form of a brochure made available free of charge at specified offices.[103] The complete listing particulars or a notice stating where the listing particulars have been published and where they may be obtained by the public must be inserted in a publication designated by the Member State in which admission of the securities to listing is sought (Article 20(2)) (SCD, Article 98(2)).

Listing particulars must be published within a 'reasonable period' before the date on which official listing becomes effective (Article 21(1)) (SCD, Article 99(1)).[104] In the case of a rights issue, where admission is preceded by trading in the pre-emptive subscription rights, the listing particulars must be published within a reasonable period (to be set by the competent authorities) before such trading starts (Article 21(1)). The requirement to publish within a certain time frame is subject to an exemption. In 'exceptional, prop-

---

[102] For a discussion of remedies and their impact on the effectiveness of harmonization see the analysis in Buxbaum and Hopt, n 10 above, 216–17. For a pre-harmonization programme review of the remedies question see Wymeersch, n 6 above, 127.

[103] These are the office of the stock exchange(s) on which the securities are being admitted to official listing, the registered office of the issuer, and the offices of the financial organization designated as the issuer's paying agent in the Member State in which admission is sought.

[104] This period, which is designed to allow wide distribution of the listing particulars and give investors sufficient time to assess the securities to be listed before trading begins, must be set by national legislation or by the competent authority. The original proposal was more precise, requiring publication at least 3 days prior to the opening of officially supervised dealing in the securities.

erly justified cases' the competent authority may allow postponement of publication until, in the case of securities of a class already listed on the same stock exchange and issued in consideration of transfers of assets other than cash, after the date on which official listing becomes effective and, in the case of rights issues, the date of opening of trading in pre-emptive subscription rights (Article 21(2)) (SCD, Article 99(2)).

Any documents designed to generate publicity for the securities and intended for publication by the issuer or on his behalf must be communicated to the competent authorities for a decision on whether they should be reviewed further before publication (Article 22) (SCD, Article 101). These documents must also state that listing particulars exist and where they are being or will be published.

The degree of investor protection represented by the common disclosure code established by the listing-particulars regime is diluted somewhat by the limited dissemination of the listing particulars. The disclosure document is designed to inform investors in the period before the commencement of trading in the securities. There is no requirement to deliver listing particulars to investors at the time of a trade in the securities, although investors will benefit from the continuing disclosure of information under the now consolidated Admission Directive and IRD.

IV.4.5 *Review of Listing Particulars and the Competent Authority*

Member States are required to designate one or more competent authorities (and to notify the Commission of the designation and of any divisions of power between authorities) to approve the listing particulars before publication (Article 18(1) and (2)) (SCD, Articles 35 and 105). Listing particulars may not be published until they have been approved by the competent authority. A competent authority may not approve listing particulars unless it is of the opinion that they satisfy all the LPD's requirements (Article 18(3)) (SCD, Article 35(2)). As approval of the listing particulars is simply a function of compliance with the LPD's requirements, it in no way guarantees the quality of the securities. Nonetheless, given the role of the competent authority in approving the listing particulars, it may appear that it is vulnerable to litigation in situations where approval should not have been granted. Reflecting this concern, the LPD provides expressly that it does not affect the liability of competent authorities and devolves the issue of the liability of competent authorities towards investors and others suffering loss as a result of defective or misleading listing particulars to the Member States (Article 18(4)) (SCD, Article 105(3)).

As with the Admission Directive, the LPD does not impose particular form requirements on competent authorities and allows for self-regulatory bodies to act as competent authorities. Member States must ensure, however, that the competent authorities have the powers necessary to carry out their task (Article 18(3)) (SCD, Article 105(3)). Ultimately, the Member States are to ensure that the LPD is applied (Article 18(1)) (SCD, Article 105(1)). As discussed in Chapter III, however, the arrival of competition between securities-trading markets for listing business and, in particular, demutualization, is prompting a reassessment of the extent to which securities-trading markets, as self-regulatory bodies, should act as competent authorities for the listing process, review disclosure, and manage the exemption scheme. The proposed reforms to the disclosure regime discussed in section 9.3 below will radically change this *laissez faire* approach to the form of the competent authority.

Competent authorities are subject to secrecy obligations under Article 25 (SCD, Article 107). In particular, without prejudice to cases covered by the criminal law, any information received under an exchange with another authority may be used only in the performance of the authority's duties and in the context of administrative appeals or legal proceedings in relation to such performance (Article 25(3)) (SCD, Article 107(3)).

IV.4.6 *Multiple Official Listings and a Common Disclosure Document*

The listing-particulars regime does not explicitly permit Member States to adopt more stringent or additional conditions. The Preamble states, however, that disclosure rules should be co-ordinated 'without necessarily making them completely uniform' (recital 4) (SCD Preamble, recital 11). Equally, the requirements set out in the Schedules, while detailed, are clearly minimum standards, in that Member States are, under Article 5(1) (SCD, Article 22(1)), to ensure that their requirements 'at least' are met. Furthermore, Articles 5 and 10 of the Admission Directive (SCD, Articles 8 and Article 12) allow Member States to impose additional or more stringent conditions on official listing and these conditions would extend to disclosure requirements.[105] As a result, although cross-border and multiple listing of securities were facilitated by the high degree of co-ordination of minimum standards, regulatory barriers still remained as the LPD in its original form did not provide for automatic approval of listing particulars already approved by a competent authority in another Member State.

Multiple listings were initially facilitated by Article 24(1) which provided that, where applications for admission of the same securities to listing on

---

[105] A point noted by the 1998 IOSCO Disclosure Standards, n 31 above, para II-5. Additional requirements imposed by the Member States under Art. 5 are subject to requirements of prior publication and non-discrimination. Under Art. 10, however, Member States may, solely in the interests of investor protection, give competent authorities the power to impose special conditions on an applicant as long as the applicant is explicitly informed of the condition(s).

stock exchanges situated in several Member States were made either simultaneously or within short intervals of each other, the competent authorities involved were required to exchange information and use their best efforts to achieve maximum co-ordination of their listing-particulars requirements. They were also to try to avoid a multiplicity of formalities and to agree on a single text requiring at the most translation and the issue of supplements as necessary to meet the particular local requirements of the Member State concerned.

The original Article 24(2) introduced a significant aid to multiple listings, in that where an application for the admission of securities to listing was made for securities which had been listed in a Member State less than six months previously, the competent authority of the original listing State was to be contacted by the competent authority of the second State and the second Member State's competent authority was, as far as possible, to exempt the issuer of securities from the requirement to publish listing particulars, subject to any updating, translation, or local supplements as the Member State concerned might require.

IV.4.7 *The Contact Committee*

The functions of the Contact Committee originally set up under the Admission Directive (see Chapter III section 4.8 above) were extended by the LPD to include consulting on, establishing a concerted attitude towards, and suggesting possible revisions to the listing particulars regime (Article 26) (SCD, Article 108).

IV.5 ONGOING DISCLOSURE FOR ISSUERS OF OFFICIALLY LISTED SECURITIES

IV.5.1 *Scope*

The ongoing disclosure regime for officially listed securities is a multi-layered one, and covers several (now SCD consolidated) directives. It includes requirements to prepare and distribute regular reports, such as annual accounts and six-monthly interim reports, as well as *ad hoc* disclosure obligations such as the obligation to disclose material new developments.

IV.5.2 *The Admission Directive*

The now consolidated Admission Directive introduced the principle of ongoing disclosure for issuers whose securities have been admitted to official listing and puts in place a framework for periodic reporting. Article 13 (SCD,

Article 16) provides that issuers whose securities are admitted to listing are to provide competent authorities with all the information considered necessary by the competent authority to protect investors or ensure the smooth operation of the market. In order to ensure the dissemination of price-sensitive information to the market-place, issuers are subject to an overriding obligation to report to the public 'any major new development in its sphere of activity which [is] not public knowledge' which may either affect its ability to meet its commitments (in the case of debt securities), or lead to substantial price movements (in the case of shares).[106] In addition, issuers are subject to certain specific disclosure obligations, such as the obligation to disclose any changes to the rights of debt security holders. Financial reporting obligations under the Admission Directive are limited to the distribution, as soon as possible, of the company's most recent annual reports and accounts.[107] Member States may also impose additional or more stringent ongoing disclosure requirements (Article 5(2)) (SCD, Article 8(2)).

IV.5.3 *The Interim Reports Directive (IRD)*

IV.5.3.1 *A Troubled Genesis*

Although the Commission's proposal for an interim reports directive was presented in 1979,[108] the requirement for companies with officially listed securities to produce half-yearly reports first appeared in a mandatory form in the Commission's 1976 proposal for the Admission Directive. Under the proposal, issuers whose shares or debt securities were admitted to official listing were required, periodically and at least half-yearly, to make available to the public 'sufficient information to enable the public to evaluate the assets and financial position of the company and the general progress of its business'.[109] As it proved difficult to reach agreement on this provision, a

---

[106] Sch C, para 5(a) and Sch D, para A4(a)(SCD, Arts. 68(1) and 81(1)). The now consolidated Admission Directive thus adopts a catch-all approach to the disclosure of material information. The US takes a more specific approach. Companies whose securities are listed on a national stock exchange are required to file a particular form with the SEC when certain specific material events occur.

[107] Sch C, para 4 and Sch D (A), para 3 (SCD, Arts. 67(1) and 80(1)). Where the company produces both consolidated and own accounts, both must be made available to the public unless the competent authority grants an exemption. It may do so only where the set which is not published does not contain any significant additional information which is not included in the published accounts. Where the accounts do not comply with the 'provisions of Council directives concerning companies accounts' (the 4th Directive on Annual Accounts and the Seventh Directive on Consolidated Accounts [1978] OJ L222/11and [1983] OJ L193/1, respectively) and if they do not give a true and fair view of the company's assets and liabilities, financial position, and profit or loss, more detailed or additional information must be provided.

[108] [1979] OJ C29/5. Explanatory Memorandum at COM(78)759.

[109] Sch C, para 4 and Sch D, para 3. Notably, the reporting obligation applied to issuers of both shares and debt securities. ECOSOC was of the opinion that 'the obligation to keep the public informed regularly—at least half-yearly—goes far beyond what is required in an interim

decision was made to address interim-reporting obligations in a separately negotiated directive.[110] The European Parliament and ECOSOC delivered their comments in March 1980 and October 1979, respectively.[111] A number of difficulties arose in the course of the negotiations on the proposal, to the extent that a substantially revised proposal was presented by the Commission in June 1980.[112] The original proposal presented two problems in particular. The first of these concerned the nature of the information to be disclosed under the first proposal. Unlike the now consolidated IRD as adopted, the original proposal did not restrict disclosure to, essentially, financial results. In addition to disclosure of financial information such as net turnover, net operating income, operating charges, gross operating results, and any interim dividends paid or proposed (Article 5(2)), an explanatory statement discussing (with supporting figures), *inter alia*, the number of persons employed, the investments carried out and decisions taken on future investments, the state of the order book, the general situation concerning stock of finished products, the degree of capacity utilization, and any new products or activities which exerted a significant effect on turnover was also required under Article 5(4) of the original proposal. Concerns arose that much of this information was only suitable for the manufacturing sector and that its collation would be unduly onerous for companies.[113] A second problem arose concerning the liability of competent authorities in the event of a failure by companies to comply with the reporting obligation. Article 11(1) of the original proposal provided that the designated competent authorities would be 'responsible for ensuring that the rules laid down in the Directive applied'.[114] The London Stock Exchange, in particular, was concerned that, as a result of the mandatory nature of the obligation to publish half-yearly reports, it would be liable for any failures by companies to report or for incomplete reports by companies.

---

report'. In a warning of difficulties to come in negotiating the IRD, it went on to find that '[t]he provision is a difficult one because (i) it is mandatory and (ii) it is not stated what is "sufficient information"'. It suggested that half-yearly reporting requirements be restricted to the publication of the profit and loss account. [1976] OJ C204/6, para 2.6.2.

[110] See generally Edwards, n 42 above, 262–4.

[111] [1980] OJ C85/69 and [1980] OJ C53/54, respectively.   [112] [1980] OJ C210/5.

[113] In its comments on the original proposal, ECOSOC was scathing with respect to the detail required under Art. 5(4): n 111 above, para 2.5. Much of the information requirements went beyond those of the 4th Directive on Annual Accounts (Directive 78/660/EEC [1978] OJ L22/11) with the anomalous result that interim disclosure was, in some respects, more burdensome for companies than the annual reporting requirement. Nonetheless, the extensive disclosure requirements reappeared in the revised proposal.

[114] ECOSOC pointed out that, unlike the Admission Directive which obliged the competent authority not to do certain things (such as admit securities to listing) unless the conditions of the Directive were fulfilled, the proposal imposed a positive obligation on competent authorities to ensure compliance. This obligation, it felt, raised questions about the position of competent authorities were investors to suffer damage following non-compliance: n 111 above, para 1.2.

These concerns were ultimately addressed by a drastic reduction in the information requirements and by the inclusion of an explicit statement to the effect that the primary responsibility for ensuring compliance rested with the Member States. The IRD was finally adopted in February 1982. Member States were to implement the Directive by 30 June 1983.

IV.5.3.2 *Objectives*

The linkage between the now consolidated IRD's harmonization and the listing-particulars regime's objectives is explicitly acknowledged, with the pre-consolidation IRD Preamble stating that the co-ordination of ongoing information requirements by the IRD fulfils similar functions to the LPD's harmonization, in that (in a slight recasting of the LPD's own original characterization of its objectives) it improves investor protection and makes it more equivalent, facilitates the multiple listing of securities on the stock exchanges of different Member States, and contributes to the establishment of a 'genuine Community capital market' (recital 2) (SCD, recital 25).[115] Recital 8 also identifies investor protection and the proper operation of stock exchanges as underlying objectives of the IRD which feed into the dominant market-construction goal (SCD, recital 30).

IV.5.3.3 *The Core Obligation*

Article 2 (SCD, Article 70) supplements the ongoing disclosure obligations already provided for under the admission-to-official-listing regime by providing that Member States are required to ensure that companies publish half-yearly reports[116] on their activities and profit and losses during the first six months of each financial year.[117]

IV.5.3.4 *Scope*

The IRD applies only to companies[118] 'the shares of which are admitted to official listing on a stock exchange situated or operating in a Member State' (Article 1) (SCD, Article 4).[119] The rationale offered for the exclusion of

---

[115] Prior to the adoption of the IRD, the nature of the obligation to produce an ongoing report varied between the Member States while Luxembourg and Denmark did not require the publication of such a report: Wymeersch, n 6 above, 77–9.

[116] By contrast, issuers in the USA are required to report on a quarterly basis.

[117] The Directive does not address whether this period should be altered if the company lengthens or shortens its financial year.

[118] In the interests of ensuring effective investor protection and the proper operation of stock exchanges, the Directive's provisions also apply to companies from non-member States: recital 8. SCD, recital 30.

[119] The Directive also applies to companies which have listed certificates representing shares. It has been noted that the ongoing disclosure requirements imposed on listed companies reflect

issuers of debt securities is that debt-security holders are protected by the rights bestowed on them by the debt securities and do not, consequently, need the additional protection of a six-monthly disclosure report.[120]

IV.5.3.5 *Disclosure Requirements*

Although the report is designed to enable investors to make an informed appraisal of the general development of the company's activities in the period covered by the report, the statement in the Preamble that the report need only contain essential details on the financial position and progress of the company's business (recital 7) (SCD, recital 29) hides the very limited nature of the disclosure required. The report must contain two elements: (1) financial statements and (2) an explanatory statement relating to the company's activities and profits and losses during the relevant six-month period.[121] Where a company publishes consolidated accounts, it may publish the half-yearly report in either consolidated or unconsolidated form (Article 6(1)) (SCD, Article 74), notwithstanding that the consolidated picture is critical to assessing the overall state of the issuer. Member States may, however, allow the competent authorities, where they consider that the form not adopted would have contained certain additional information, to require the company to publish such information; by contrast, the Admission Directive's requirement to produce annual accounts uses the consolidated account as the standard default option unless an exemption is given by the relevant competent authority.[122]

The financial statements (the IRD is couched in terms of figures presented in table form) are required only to cover the company's net turnover and the profit or loss either before or after any deduction of tax (Article 5(2)) (SCD, Article 73(2)); where a Member State implements the IRD without further requirements or where the issuer chooses not to make more extensive disclosure, the investor may, as a result, be provided (in theory) with only two significant financial indicia of the issuer's progress. Where these figures are unsuited to the company's activities, under Article 5(7) (SCD,

---

the 'stock exchange status' of the company and 'the greater corporate responsibility of these as a rule larger undertakings, not only in relation to the financial markets but often also in relation to the community as a whole': Wymeersch, n 6 above, 73.

[120] IRD, recital 5. SCD, recital 28. The Explanatory Memorandum to the original proposal was more forthcoming and explained that holders of debentures are entitled to payment of interest at fixed dates and reimbursement of capital at the end of the period of the loan. Accordingly, the Commission found that it was not necessary to provide the holders of debentures with regular information about the development of the company. It also stressed that the holders of such securities benefited, in any event, from the obligation imposed by the Admission Directive on all issuers of listed securities to disclosure their annual accounts: n 108 above, 3.

[121] Art. 5(1) (SCD, Art. 73(1)). Accounting terms are to be given the same meaning as they have in the company accounts directives.

[122] See n 107 above.

Article 73(7)) the competent authorities are to ensure that appropriate adjustments are made. These limited requirements do not extend to an obligation to publish the interim balance sheet.[123] Where the company has paid or proposes to pay an interim dividend, the financial statements must indicate the profit or loss after tax for the six-month period, as well as the interim dividend paid or proposed (Article 5(4)) (SCD, Article 73(4)). The financial statements must also show, for each figure stated, the corresponding figure for the equivalent period in the preceding financial year. Member States may permit the competent authorities to authorize companies to use estimated figures for profits and losses. Estimates may be used only on an exceptional basis, however, and only where the shares of the company in question are officially listed in one Member State only (Article 5(3)) (SCD, Article 73(3)). Where the company uses estimates, it must disclose this in the report and must not mislead investors.

The explanatory statement must disclose any significant information enabling investors to make an informed assessment of the trend of the issuer's activities and profits or losses (Article 5(6)) (SCD, Article 73(6)).[124] Accordingly, although the specified requirements are not very extensive, this catch-all obligation is potentially far-reaching. Any special factors which have influenced the company's activities and profits or losses during the period in question must also be disclosed. The statement must allow a comparison to be made with the corresponding period of the previous financial year. Article 5(6) also requires that, as far as possible, the issuer's likely future development in the current financial year must also be disclosed. Where the financial information has been audited, the auditor's report and any qualifications included therein must be included in the report (Article 8)) (SCD, Article 75). The IRD does not address whether the half-yearly report must be signed by the company or whether a responsibility statement is required.

The IRD also imposes a language requirement. The half-yearly report must be produced in the official languages or one of the official languages of the Member State concerned, or in another language, provided that in the Member State concerned (the State in which the shares are admitted to official listing), the official languages/other language is customary in the sphere of finance and accepted by the competent authorities (Article 7(2)) (SCD, Article 103).

---

[123] In practice, issuers tend to disclose the interim balance sheet, profit and loss account, and cash-flow statement.

[124] It is designed to 'permit investors to understand the significance of [the financial statements] and generally to appreciate how the company's business has fared': Explanatory Memorandum to the original proposal, n 108 above, 5.

IV.5.3.6 *Publication*

The IRD arguably does not result in a timely transmission of interim information to the market-place. The report must be published within a rather leisurely four months[125] from the end of the relevant six-month period.[126] In 'exceptional, duly substantiated cases', the competent authority may extend the time limit for publication (Article 4(2)) (SCD, Article 72(2)).

The report must be published in the Member State(s) where the shares are admitted to official listing by insertion in 'one or more of the newspapers distributed throughout the State or widely distributed therein or in the national gazette' (Article 7(1) (SCD, Article 102(2)). It may also be made available to the public, either in writing in the places indicated in an announcement to be published in one or more newspapers distributed throughout the State or widely distributed therein, or by other equivalent means approved by the competent authorities (Article 7(1)). A copy of the report must, no later than the time when the report is published for the first time in a Member State, be sent simultaneously to the competent authority of each Member State in which its shares are officially listed (Article 7(3)) (SCD, Article 102(2)).

IV.5.3.7 *The Competent Authority and Review of the Half-yearly Report*

Under Article 9(1) (SCD, Article 105(1)) Member States are to appoint one or more competent authorities, and notify the Commission of their appointment, giving details of any divisions of powers between them. A particular legal form is not imposed on the competent authority; it must simply have the necessary powers to carry out its tasks (Article 9(2)) (SCD, Article 105(2)).

The functions of the competent authority are significantly more circumscribed under the IRD as compared with the functions fulfilled by competent authorities under the Admission Directive and the LPD. In particular, a competent authority is not required to ensure that companies produce half-yearly reports,[127] or to ensure in advance that the contents of the reports comply with the Directive. Its functions are essentially limited to ensuring

[125] The original proposal required speedier publication and imposed a 3-month limit: Art. 4(1). It appears that the period was extended following ECOSOC's recommendation. It felt that the 3-month deadline might result in the interim figures following too soon after the annual results and, in consequence, too long an interval before any further results would be forthcoming: n 111 above, para 2.4.

[126] Art. 4(1) (SCD, Art. 72(1)). The relevant 6-month period is the first 6 months of the financial year in question: Art. 2 (SCD, Art. 70).

[127] It appears from Art. 2 ('Member States shall ensure that the companies publish half-yearly reports') that such responsibility lies with the Member States (SCD, Art. 70). In addition, Art. 9(2) (SCD, Art. 105(2)) provides that Member States are to ensure that the Directive is applied.

that the Directive's requirements are applied appropriately: accordingly it has power to extend the time limit within which the report must be published when the circumstances are exceptional (Article 4(2)) (SCD, Article 72(2)), power to ensure that the language of the report is appropriate (Article 7(2)) (SCD, Article 103), and power under Article 5(3) (SCD, Article 73(3)) to authorize the use of estimated financial figures where appropriate. In addition, under Article 9(3) (SCD, Article 76(3)) it must ensure that adaptations are made to the IRD's requirements where they are unsuitable for a particular company's circumstances,[128] while under Article 9(4) (SCD, Article 76(4)) it may authorize the omission of information from the report where it is of the opinion that its disclosure would be contrary to the public interest or seriously detrimental to the company.[129] The Article 9(3) and (4) powers also apply to any more stringent or additional interim reporting obligations imposed on companies by the Member States, as is permitted by Article 3 (SCD, Article 71).

Despite the limited responsibilities of the competent authority and in a reflection of concerns about the liability of competent authorities which arose during the negotiations, the IRD also makes clear that its provisions do not affect competent authorities' liability, which continues to be governed solely by national law (Article 9(7)) (SCD, Article 105(3)).

Although under Article 2 (SCD, Article 70) the Member States are ultimately responsible for ensuring that the companies publish the IRD report, it, like the LPD, does not require that Member States provide for sanctions to be imposed in cases where the IRD is breached by an issuer or address the question of remedies.

IV.5.3.8 *A Single Half-yearly Report?*

In a formula familiar from the admission-to-official-listing regime, Member States are explicitly empowered to subject companies to obligations which are additional to or more stringent than those set out in the IRD, but any such obligations must apply generally to all companies or to all companies of a given class (Article 3) (SCD, Article 71).[130] Companies with multiple

---

[128] This power was originally designed to ensure that the manufacturing-company-biased disclosure initially required could be adapted for other issuers. The Commission also acknowledged, however, that adaptations to the publication obligations might be needed where the issuer's business was, eg, of a seasonal nature and observance of the publication rules would not permit investors to have a satisfactory picture of the development of the company's business: Explanatory Memorandum to original proposal, n 108 above, 5 and 7.

[129] Where the omission is authorized in the interests of the company, it must not be likely to mislead the public with regard to facts and circumstances, knowledge of which is essential for the assessment of the shares in question.

[130] The Commission adopted this approach as the IRD was simply a 'first step on the road to harmonisation' and 'it did not appear possible to achieve a greater degree of harmonisation at this stage'. It seemed particularly concerned to ensure that Germany could retain its more

listings of shares may, in practice, be required to produce slightly varying reports for different Member States.[131] In particular, if an exemption is required from a particular reporting obligation under Article 9(4) (SCD, Article 76(2)), it appears that the company in question will be required to apply to the competent authority of each official list to which its shares are admitted.

Ironically, an attenuated form of mutual recognition (which would not appear as a principle for disclosure documents until 1987) is introduced for companies governed by the law of a non-Member State. Under Article 9(5) (SCD, Article 76(4)), where a company is governed by the law of a non-Member State and publishes a half-yearly report, the competent authorities may authorize it to publish that report in place of the report required by the IRD, as long as it provides information equivalent to that required by the IRD.

An attempt is made to alleviate matters under Article 10(1) (SCD, Article 106) which requires the competent authorities to co-operate whenever necessary for the purpose of carrying out their duties and to exchange any information required for that purpose. More specifically, under Article 10(2) (SCD, Article 77), where a report must be published in more than one Member State, the competent authorities shall use their best endeavours to accept as a single text that which meets the requirements of the Member State in which the company's shares were admitted to official listing for the first time, or that which most closely approximates to that text.[132] In the case of a simultaneous admission to official listing in two or more Member States, the competent authorities concerned are to use their best endeavours to accept as a single text that which meets the requirements of the Member State in which the company's head office is situated.[133]

IV.5.3.9 *The Contact Committee*

Given the ability of Member States to impose additional or more stringent requirements, the Contact Committee established under the Admission Directive and given further responsibilities for the LPD is also given a

demanding requirement that companies produce two half-yearly reports: Explanatory Memorandum to the original proposal, n 108 above, 4. ECOSOC was unhappy with this approach and pointed out that in the interests of investor protection and a consistent standard of reporting throughout the Community, stricter standards should be imposed, provided they were uniform and reasonable. It expressed concern that the ensuing variety of reporting standards could make it difficult to compare like with like, and lead to distortions in the flow of capital: n 111 above, para 2.2.

[131] In its opinion, the ECOSOC expressed concern that where a company's shares were listed on more than one exchange, it might be required to produce different reports for each exchange. Note 111, para. 2.3.

[132] Art. 10(2) acknowledges that this involves a 'derogation from Art. 3'.

[133] Where the head office is situated in a non-Member State, the competent authorities are, nonetheless, still required to use their best endeavours to accept a single version of the report.

similar role with respect to the IRD (Article 11) (SCD, Article 108(2). In particular, it is to facilitate the establishment of a concerted attitude with respect to the stricter or additional conditions which Member States may impose.

IV.5.4 *The Substantial Shareholdings Directive (the SSD)*

IV.5.4.1 *Background*

The ongoing disclosure obligations imposed on issuers of officially listed securities were further supplemented in 1988 by a directive on the information to be published when a major holding in a listed company is acquired or disposed of.

The roots of the now consolidated SSD lie in the Admission Directive and, to a lesser extent, the LPD.[134] The Admission Directive, as outlined in Chapter III, had already provided that an issuer whose securities were admitted to official listing was required to inform the public 'of any changes in the structure (shareholders and breakdown of holdings) of the major holdings in its capital, as compared with information previously published on that subject as soon as such changes come to its notice'.[135] The LPD requires (although only at the point at which securities are admitted to official listing) disclosure of, 'in so far as they are known to the issuers, [an] indication of the shareholders who, directly or indirectly, hold a proportion of the issuer's capital which the Member States may not fix at more than 20%'.[136] The initial Commission proposal for the SSD was presented in

---

[134] Indeed, so many of the SSD's basic reporting obligations were already in place that the Commission could state in its Explanatory Memorandum that the 'proposal . . . does not impose any new requirements on listed companies . . . the object is merely to clarify the contents of the obligation laid down in [the Admission Directive] and facilitate the implementation of that obligation by requiring persons acquiring or disposing of major holdings to inform that company accordingly': Explanatory Memorandum to original proposal, COM(85)791, 2 and 3. Despite the supposedly uncontroversial content of the SSD, some difficulties did arise during the negotiations. Many interest groups in Germany were opposed to its adoption, claiming that it favoured the speculative investor and engendered uncertainty. In particular, German banks and industry felt that the proposal could not be justified and that private individuals should not be required to disclose their shareholdings. The German stock exchange was 'adamantly opposed to the Directive': Select Committee on the European Communities, Report on the Disclosure of Significant Shareholders, HL (1985–86), 16th Report (the HL SSD Report), para 27.

[135] Sch C, para (5)(c) (SCD, Art. 68(3)). The obligation to notify thus arose only when the change in question came to the notice of the company. The SSD amended the pre-consolidated provision by including a new para which provides that 'a company not subject to [the SSD] must inform the public within nine calendar days whenever it comes to its notice that a person or entity has acquired or disposed of a number of shares such that his or its holding exceeds or falls below one of the thresholds laid down in Article 4 of that Directive'. This amendment was designed to ensure that third-country companies which might otherwise fall outside the scope of the SSD were made subject to reporting obligations which were similar to those imposed on Member State companies.

[136] Sch A, ch (3)(2)(7). This obligation arises only to the extent that such shareholders are known to the issuer.

December 1985.[137] Following the Parliament's comments and the opinion of ECOSOC,[138] a revised proposal was presented in September 1987,[139] which was finally adopted in December 1988. The SSD was to be implemented by the Member States by 1 January 1991.

IV.5.4.2 *Objectives*

In one of the disclosure regime's clearest articulations of the link between disclosure, investor confidence, and market integration, the SSD's pre-consolidation Preamble states in recital 1 that a 'policy of adequate information of investors in the field of transferable securities is likely to improve investor protection, to increase investors' confidence in securities markets and thus to ensure that securities markets function correctly (SCD, recital 31)'. In a familiar pattern, recital 2 also links the co-ordination of investor-protection measures to 'the greater inter-penetration of the Member States' securities markets' and notes that it will 'therefore help to establish a true European capital market' (SCD, recital 32). To that end, according to recitals 3 and 4, investors should be informed of major holdings and of changes to those holdings in Community companies the shares of which are officially listed on stock exchanges situated or operating within the Community and co-ordinated rules concerning the detailed content of the disclosure and the procedures involved should be adopted (SCD, recitals 33 and 34). Prior to the adoption of the SSD, the information received by investors concerning major or substantial shareholdings varied widely across the EC, resulting in different standards of investor protection across the stock exchanges of the different Member States.[140] Many Member States did not impose a shareholdings-disclosure requirement and, among those Member States which did, standards varied.[141]

---

[137] [1985] OJ C351/35. Explanatory Memorandum at COM(85)791.

[138] [1987] OJ CC125/144 and [1986] OJ C263/1, respectively. While broadly in favour of the proposal, both the Parliament and ECOSOC expressed concern at its lack of precision.

[139] [1987] OJ C255/6. Explanatory Memorandum at COM(87)422. The SSD was one of the first securities-regulation measures to be adopted other than through the simple consultation-of-Parliament process. It was adopted under the co-operation procedure which, although now largely defunct since its virtual replacement by the co-decision procedure, gave the Parliament a 2nd reading of legislation (in the form of a Council common position) which was not available to it under the procedure which had applied to the earlier disclosure directives. The Parliament approved the common position in Oct 1998. [1988] OJ C309/44. On the legislative process see Ch. XV sect. 2 below.

[140] The pan-Community significance of the proposal was also emphasized by the London Stock Exchange which pointed out that, for UK investors, the major innovation of the SSD was the assistance and information it gave to UK investors in Community companies, as they were already well protected with respect to disclosure concerning control of UK companies: HL SSD Report, n 134 above, paras 32–33.

[141] According to the Commission, there were 'very marked discrepancies' between Member States' rules in this area: Explanatory Memorandum to original proposal, n 134 above, 3. Eg,

Although the Preamble clearly links the SSD to the overall issuer-disclosure policy, it does not make clear why disclosure of information concerning major shareholdings is required to protect investors or to enhance investor confidence. In its Explanatory Memorandum to the original proposal, the Commission stated that the proposal would 'provide investors with information on the persons liable to influence a company's management, sometimes to a considerable extent, and thus enable them to follow developments in its ownership and gain a clearer idea of what is happening internally'.[142] Looking forward to the prevention-of-market-abuse regime (which supports the disclosure process and, in particular, its anti-fraud objectives by controlling the fraudulent use of information), which would be established one year later in 1989 with the Insider Dealing Directive,[143] it also referred to the importance of making such information public in order to 'prevent uncontrollable rumours and stop misuse of price-sensitive information'.[144]

Reporting obligations of this nature can also be regarded as corporate governance and, specifically, takeover control devices in that they warn the issuer whether a stake is being built up in the company and so reduce the likelihood of surprise takeover bids.[145] In this regard, they have considerable

---

while Germany required disclosure only when shareholdings passed thresholds of 25% and 50% (see the HL SSD Report, n 134 above, para 27), the UK adopted a higher standard under s 199(2) of the Companies Act 1985, requiring (at the time of the original proposal) disclosure of holdings of 5% or more and of each 1% acquired thereafter (in 1989 the threshold was dropped to 3% by the Companies Act 1989, s 134(2)).

[142] N 134 above, 2.

[143] Directive 89/592/EEC coordinating regulations for insider dealing [1989] OJ L334/31 (the Insider Dealing Directive). See Ch. XIII.

[144] N 134 above, 2.

[145] It has been observed that 'the more comprehensively and rigorously such a policy [of compulsory disclosure of beneficial ownership and changes in control] is applied, the more it will tend to cut against the bidder's freedom to establish a pre-announcement stake in the target company': Davies, P, 'The Take-over Bidder Exemption and the Policy of Disclosure' in Hopt, K, and Wymeersch, E (eds), *European Insider Dealing* (1991)) 243, 256. On the EC's approach to the regulation of takeovers see Ch. XIV. The USA provides the classic example of the large-shareholding reporting obligation as an instrument of takeover regulation. Under s 13(d) of the Securities Exchange Act, 1934 any person or group that becomes the owner of more than 5% of any class of securities listed on a national exchange must file with both the issuer of the securities and the SEC within 10 days of the acquisition a statement setting out: the background of the person; the source of the funds used for the acquisition; the purpose of the acquisition; the number of shares owned; and any related contracts, arrangements, or understanding. Any 'material' changes in respect of the original disclosure must also be reported. The US requirements are designed to ensure that 'if [a] person contemplates doing a tender offer to take control of the company, that must be disclosed in advance. Cox *et al.*, n 18 above, 865. The impact of large-shareholding disclosure on the market for corporate control has generated considerable controversy, in that this disclosure limits the ability of bidders to maximize the benefits from the resources they will have expended in investigating the target. While the market-for-corporate-control discussion is outside the scope of this discussion of disclosure and the securities markets, see, eg, Jarrell, G, and Bradley, M, 'The Economic Effects of Federal and State Regulations of Cash Tender Offers' (1980) 23 *J L and Econ.* 371.

impact on the market for corporate control. The SSD's rationale for harmonizing the disclosure of large shareholdings appears to characterize this disclosure more as an aspect of traditional disclosure policy and as serving the interests of investor protection/confidence and, ultimately, the efficient functioning of the securities markets,[146] however, and rather less as being directed to the market for corporate control.[147]

Implementation of the SSD was slow, which has impeded its effectiveness. Major German companies, for example, did not start to disclose their holdings until 1996.[148] This failure of the SSD is of particular concern for small investors in continental Europe, where holdings tend to be concentrated among a few investors and where retail investors need to be informed of changes in such large, concentrated holdings in order to retain their confidence in the equity markets.[149]

IV.5.4.3 *The Core Obligations*

(a) *A Two-track Regime*

The SSD's large-shareholdings disclosure obligation has two strands: (1) notification of the company concerned by holders of voting rights when a disposition or acquisition of voting rights by such holders results in their holdings of voting rights achieving, exceeding, or falling below certain thresholds and (2) the onward dissemination of this information to the public by the company.

(b) *Article 4(1) and the Holder of Voting Rights*

Under Article 4(1) (SCD, Article 89), a natural person or legal entity who acquires[150] or disposes of a holding[151] in a company and whose voting

---

[146] SSD, recital 1 (SCD, recital 31). For an analysis of the SSD as a securities markets disclosure measure see Davies, n 26 above, 486.

[147] For an analysis of the SSD from the corporate-governance perspective, however, see Ferrarini, G, 'Share Ownership, Takeover Law and the Contestability of Corporate Control' in *Company Law Reform in OECD Countries: A Comparative Outlook of Current Trends*, Conference Proceedings (forthcoming). The point is made that while the disclosure of large shareholdings is important for the efficiency of securities markets as an aspect of mandatory disclosure, large-shareholdings disclosure should be examined from the perspective of its impact on the market for corporate control and, in particular, on the extent to which it reduces bidders' incentives and, as a result, the number of takeovers and, ultimately, investor or shareholder protection. The conclusion reached is that policy-makers should, in setting the threshold for disclosure and the time lag before disclosure is required, balance the need for transparency and for corporate-control contestability.

[148] Gros, D, and Lannoo, K, *The Euro Capital Market* (1999) 127.　　　　　　　　[149] Ibid.

[150] The central concept of 'acquiring a holding' is defined under Art. 2 (SCD, Art. 86) as 'not only purchasing a holding, but also acquisition by any other means whatsoever, including acquisition in one of the situations referred to in Article 7.' Art. 7 is examined below.

[151] Where the acquisition or disposal is carried out by means of certificates representing

rights[152] in that company following that transaction exceeds or falls below 10 per cent, 20 per cent, 33.3 per cent, 50 per cent, or 66.6 per cent,[153] must notify the company and the relevant competent authority of the proportion of the voting rights held following the transaction. This obligation does not, of course, fulfil the SSD's objective of informing investors of major holdings and changes in a company's share capital. That is achieved by the publication obligation placed on companies under Article 10 (SCD, Article 91). However, as the Preamble acknowledges, 'companies . . . can inform the public of changes in major holdings only if they have been informed of

shares, the provisions of the SSD apply to the bearers of the certificates, not to the issuer of the certificates. Art. 1(2) (SCD, Art. 85(2)). Where the person or entity acquiring or disposing of a major holding is a member of a group of undertakings which is required to draw up consolidated accounts under Directive 83/349/EEC [1983] OJ L193/1 (the 7th Company Law Directive), that person or entity benefits from an exemption from Art. 4(1) so long as the notification is made by the parent undertaking or, where the parent undertaking is in turn a subsidiary, by its own parent undertaking.

[152] The original and amended proposals both referred to acquisitions or disposals of 'shares' and to percentages of 'subscribed capital' rather than to voting rights. The use of 'holdings' and 'voting rights' in the SSD reflects more fully that the disclosure in the SSD is designed to ensure the publication of information concerning those in a position of control in the company, and that, as such, it is the acquisition of the voting rights attaching to shares, and not simply the shares themselves, which is material.

[153] While the Commission acknowledged that 'the choice of thresholds which trigger compulsory notification are necessarily somewhat arbitrary', the thresholds were chosen to ensure consistency with other Community company law measures: Explanatory Memorandum to the original proposal, n 134 above, 6–7. The 10% threshold is material as the 7th Company Law Directive (83/349/EEC) [1983] OJ L193/1 provides that a 10% holding in an undertaking is significant in connection with an exemption from sub-consolidation. The 20% threshold was included as the 4th Company Law Directive (78/660/EEC) [1978] OJ L222/1 provides that a holding of more than 20% of a company's capital is presumed to constitute a participating interest, establishing a durable link with that company. The 20% threshold also appears in the 7th Company Law Directive as the threshold (in respect of voting rights of shares held) at which an undertaking is presumed to exert significant influence over another. The 33.3% and 66.6 % thresholds feature in several company law directives in relation to company decision-making. For example, the 2nd Company Law Directive (77/91/EEC) [1977] OJ L26/1 imposes a two-thirds majority requirement for general-meeting resolutions in relation to decisions on the increase, decrease or redemption of capital. Similarly, the 3rd Company Law Directive (78/855/EEC) [1978] OJ L 295/36 requires a two-thirds majority for merger decisions, while the 6th Company Law Directive (82/89/EEC) [1982] OJ L 378/47 applies a two-thirds requirements for decisions on divisions. The 50% threshold was included because of its significance for absolute control. Finally, the 90% threshold was included as, under the 3rd Company Law Directive, a 90% holding allows for certain derogations from the rules concerning acquisitions and mergers, in addition to which many Member States allow compulsory acquisition of the outstanding shares once the 90% threshold is reached.

The extensive explanation in the Explanatory Memorandum suggests that the Commission was anxious not to appear to be imposing arbitrary and onerous notification obligations. This can also be seen in its response to the Parliament's suggestion that notification also be required where the percentage of subscribed capital disposed of by a person during any one month exceeded 10% of the subscribed capital, notification to occur within 7 calendar days of the threshold being reached. The Commission rejected this amendment, finding that it 'would needlessly complicate the information process by increasing almost ad infinitum the number of thresholds which trigger the obligation to inform the public': Explanatory Memorandum to revised proposal, n 139 above, 3.

such changes by the holders of those holdings' (recital 5) (SCD, recital 35). The rules governing the attribution of voting rights which are held by one person to another person for the purposes of determining whether an obligation to notify has arisen are complex, and are set out in Articles 7 and 8 (SCD, Articles 87 and 92). Notification must be made within seven calendar days of the time when the owner of the holding learns of the acquisition or disposal, or of the time when, in the circumstances applicable, he should have learnt of it.

(c) *Article 10(1) and the Company's Disclosure Obligation*

Under Article 10(1) (SCD, Article 91), on receipt of such a notification from a shareholder, the company must, as soon as possible and in any event within nine calendar days[154] of receipt of the notification, disclose it to the public in each of the Member States in which its shares are officially listed. Alternatively, Member States may provide that such disclosure is made by the competent authority, possibly in co-operation with the company. Disclosure to the public is achieved by publishing the information in one or more newspapers distributed throughout or widely in the Member State or States concerned or by making it available to the public in writing in places indicated by announcements to be published in one or more newspapers distributed throughout or widely in the Member State(s) concerned.[155] The information may also be published 'by other equivalent means approved by the competent authorities'.

(d) *The Regime for 10 per cent Holdings*

The SSD also includes particular disclosure measures concerning holdings in excess of 10 per cent of a company's voting rights. Under Article 5(1) (SCD, Article 90), Member States are to provide that, at the first annual general meeting of a company taking place after the implementation of the Directive (the SCD sets out the applicable dates), any natural person or legal entity holding 10 per cent or more of the company's voting rights must disclose both to the company and the competent authority the proportion of voting rights actually held, unless that person has already made a declaration under Article 4 (SCD, Article 89). The public must be informed of all

---

[154] The 9-day period is in contrast with the obligation placed on issuers of officially listed securities under the now consolidated Admission Directive to inform the public of changes to major holdings in its capital 'as soon as such changes come to its notice': Sch C para 5(c) (SCD, Art. 68(3)).

[155] Art. 10(2) (SCD, Art. 102(1)). Publication must be made in the official language(s) of the Member State/other language, as long as the language is customary in the sphere of finance and accepted by the competent authorities: ibid (SCD, Art. 103).

holdings in excess of 10 per cent within one month of that general meeting in accordance with the procedures set out in Article 10.

IV.5.4.4 *Scope*

Under Article 1(1) (SCD, Article 85(1)) Member States are required to subject all natural persons and legal entities in public or private law who acquire or dispose of, directly or through intermediaries, holdings meeting the criteria of Article 4(1) (SCD, Article 89(1)) which involve changes in the holdings of voting rights in companies incorporated under their law, the shares of which are officially listed on a stock exchange or exchanges situated or operating within one or more Member States to the SSD's disclosure obligations. The natural persons and legal entities subject to the SSD's requirements are not restricted by reference to a Member State's nationality or residence requirements, but, conversely, the SSD applies only to voting rights in companies incorporated under the law of a Member State, and whose shares are officially listed on one or more Member State exchanges.[156]

The SSD's obligations apply only to companies whose shares are admitted to official listing on a Member State's stock exchange. While this listing requirement ensures symmetry with the reporting obligations concerning voting rights set out in the Admission Directive, the Commission's justification for the restriction was that 'it is shares in listed companies which are dealt in regularly and the general public tends to invest primarily in those shares'.[157] This restriction, along with the weaknesses in the EC disclosure regime which applies to offerings which take place outside the Official List jars somewhat with the growth of trading in non-Official List securities on trading markets which do not operate an Official List, such as NASDAQ Europe. Changes are afoot with respect to the scope of the SSD, however. Had the proposed Takeover Directive been adopted,[158] the scope of the SSD would have been extended so that its requirements applied to shares admitted to trading on a 'regulated market' within the meaning of

---

[156] The SSD does, however, amend Sch C, para 5(c) of the now consolidated Admission Directive (SCD, Art. 68(3)) to provide that a company not subject to the SSD must inform the public within 9 calendar days whenever it comes to its notice that a person or entity has acquired or disposed of a number of shares so that his or its holding exceeds or falls below one of the Art. 4 SSD thresholds.

[157] Explanatory Memorandum to original proposal, n 134 above, 4. Similarly, while the House of Lords Select Committee shared the view of witnesses who gave evidence to the effect that the Directive's obligations should be extended to all companies, it recognized that the preceding Securities Directives were restricted to listed securities. It also pointed out that the Directive set minimum standards only, allowing the UK to continue to monitor dealings in unlisted and over-the-counter markets: HL SSD Report, n 134 above, para. 67

[158] See Ch. XIV below.

the Investment Services Directive.[159] This revision, designed to ensure that the SSD and the proposed Takeover Directive would have an 'identical scope',[160] is likely to appear again via another route, either in a new proposal for a Takeover Directive, which the Commission has decided to pursue in due course, or perhaps in the revisions to the ongoing disclosure regime currently under discussion (section 9.4 below).

Under Article 1(3) (SCD, Article 85(3)) the SSD does not apply to the acquisition or disposal of major holdings in collective-investment undertakings.

IV.5.4.5 *Derogations, Exemptions, and Additional Requirements*

Although the SSD introduces extensive and detailed rules concerning the disclosure of large shareholdings, the Member States, as they do in the disclosure regime generally, retain considerable discretion in this area. Under Article 3 (SCD, Article 88), they may impose additional or more stringent requirements concerning the disclosure of shareholdings, as long as such requirements apply generally to all those acquiring or disposing of holdings, and to all companies or to all those falling within a particular category acquiring or disposing of holdings or of companies. The core reporting obligation in Article 4 (SCD, Article 89) is also subject to derogation by the Member States, in that they need not apply the thresholds of 20 per cent and 33.3 per cent where they apply a single threshold of 25 per cent, and they may disapply the 66.6 per cent threshold where the threshold of 75 per cent is applied. Member States may also exempt 'professional dealers in securities' from the notification obligation, as long as the acquisition or disposal is effected in their capacity as professional dealers and, reflecting the SSD's preoccupation with disclosure of who exercises control over the company, provided that the acquisition is not used by dealers to 'intervene in the management of the company concerned' (Article 9(1)) (SCD, Article 94(1)). The competent authorities are to ensure that professional dealers are either members of a stock exchange situated or operating in a Member State or approved or supervised by a competent authority (Article 9(2)) (SCD, Article 94(2)).[161]

---

[159] Directive 93/22/EEC on investment services in the securities field [1993] OJ L141/27 (the ISD). On the features of a regulated market see Ch. XI sect. 6.3 below.

[160] Council Common Position (EC) No 1/2001 with a view to adopting a Directive on company law concerning takeover bids [2001] OJ C23/1; Statement of the Council's Reasons, para III. Although this revision chimes with the general movement to apply the EC disclosure rules to regulated markets generally rather than simply to the Official List (see the discussion of the proposed restructuring of the issuer disclosure regime in section 9.3 below), this provision also appears to suggest that the SSD forms part of the general takeover regime, as well as part of the disclosure regime.

[161] Art. 7 of the original proposal applied this exemption to a 'market maker in the pursuit of his activity'. In the revised proposal, in 'order to forestall any possible abuse of this exemption',

As may be expected, competent authorities may, as an exceptional matter, exempt companies from the notification obligation where those authorities consider that the disclosure would be contrary to the public interest or seriously detrimental to the companies concerned (Article 11) (SCD, Article 95). Where the application for exemption is based on the disclosure being seriously detrimental to the companies concerned, the omission must not be such as would be likely to mislead the public with regard to the facts and circumstances knowledge of which is essential for the assessment of the transferable securities in question.

IV.5.4.6 *Attribution of Voting Rights*

(a) *Introduction*

As the notification obligation under Article 4(1) (SCD, Article 89(1)) (and, subsequently, Article 10) (SCD, Article 91) is triggered only when the proportion of voting rights held by a person passes or drops below certain thresholds following an acquisition or disposal by that person, the application of the SSD will often hinge on how voting rights are attributed. For the purposes of determining when a person is required to make a notification, Article 7 (SCD, Article 92) sets out in some detail the circumstances in which voting rights will be attributed to a person or legal entity when they are nominally held by another party. These circumstances broadly reflect situations in which a person may control voting rights held by another.

(b) *Trustees, Nominees, and Concert Parties*

Where voting rights are held by other persons or entities in their own names (such as nominees or trustees), but are held on behalf of a person or entity, they shall be attributed to that person or entity (Article 7(1)) (SCD, Article 92(a)), as will voting rights held by third parties with whom the person or entity has concluded a written agreement which obliges them to adopt, by concerted exercise of the voting rights they hold, a lasting common policy towards the management of the company in question (Article 7(3)) (SCD, Article 92(c)). Although the definition has been implemented by the use of even more complex formulations,[162] it is not without its difficulties. It not entirely clear what is meant by a common policy towards the 'management'

---

the term market maker was removed and replaced by a definition of those persons eligible to benefit from the dealers' exemption. This definition referred to dealers in securities who 'undertake[s] to maintain a market in certain securities by buying and selling such securities on own account at a price fixed by [them] in light of the state of the market'.

[162] In the UK ss 204–206 of the Companies Act 1985 set out the circumstances under which parties will be found to be acting in concert. For an examination of these provisions see Davies, n 26 above, 488–92 where the lengthy definition is described as 'tortuous'.

of the company or when a common policy will be sufficiently 'lasting'. The potentially broad sweep of the definition is narrowed by the requirement that the agreement to act in concert be in writing and also by the exclusion of 'one-off' agreements to act in concert on a particular issue, which would presumably not amount to a lasting common policy. Finally, a concerted action for the specific purpose of acquiring control is not necessary.[163]

(c) *Shares held as Security, Life Interests, Agreements to Acquire, and Deposited Shares.*

Account will also be taken of voting rights attaching to shares owned by a person or entity which are lodged as security, but this will not be the case where the person or entity holding the security controls the voting rights and declares his intention of exercising them. In such circumstances they will be regarded as that person or entity's (that is, the security-holder's) voting rights (Article 7(5)) (SCD, Article 92(e)). Voting rights attaching to shares in which the person or entity has a life interest and voting rights attaching to shares deposited with the person or entity which the person or entity can exercise at its discretion in the absence of specific instructions from the holders will also be attributed to that person or entity (Article 7(6) and (8)) (SCD, Article 92(f) and (h)). Finally, voting rights which a person or entity (or any of the persons or entities mentioned in Article 7(1)–(6)) is entitled to acquire, on his own initiative alone, under a formal agreement will also be counted in determining whether that person is obliged to make a notification (Article 7(7)) (SCD, Article 92(g)). In such circumstances, notification to the company under Article 4(1) must occur on the day of the agreement.

(d) *Controlled Undertakings*

Article 7 (SCD, Article 87) employs the device of including voting rights held by a 'controlled undertaking' in the attribution of voting rights to the person or entity controlling the undertaking. In particular, voting rights held by an undertaking controlled by a person or entity (Article 7(2)) (SCD, Article 92(b)) as well as voting rights held by a third party under a written agreement concluded with a person or entity or with an undertaking controlled by a person or entity providing for the transfer for consideration of the voting rights in question (Article 7(4)) (SCD, Article 92(d)) will be attributed to that controlling person or entity. The SSD

---

[163] The concept of concertation has recently been subject to another EC-level definition attempt in the most recent (and rejected) version of the proposed Takeover Directive. See Ch. XIV sect. 4.3 below.

adopts a tripartite approach to defining a 'controlled undertaking', which is based on certain elements of the definition of subsidiary undertaking in the Seventh Company Law Directive. Article 8(1) (SCD, Article 87(1)) provides that 'controlled undertaking' shall mean any undertaking in which a natural person or legal entity '(a) has a majority of the shareholders' or members' voting rights; or (b) has the right to appoint or remove a majority of the members of the administrative, management or supervisory body and is at the same time a shareholder in, or member of, the undertaking in question; or (c) is a shareholder or member and alone controls a majority of the shareholders' or members' voting rights pursuant to an agreement entered into with other shareholders or members of the undertaking'. Article 8(2) (SCD, Article 87(2)) provides that a parent undertaking's rights as regards voting, appointment and removal shall include the rights of any other controlled undertaking and those of any person or entity acting in his own name but on behalf of the parent undertaking or of any other controlled undertaking.

IV.5.4.7 *The Competent Authority*

Under Article 12(1) (SCD, Article 105(1)), Member States are to designate a competent authority (or competent authorities) for the purposes of the SSD and inform the Commission accordingly and, where applicable, of any divisions of responsibility between competent authorities. As with the Admission Directive, LPD, and IRD, form requirements are not imposed, but Member States must ensure that their competent authorities have such powers as may be necessary for the performance of their duties (Article 12(2)) (SCD, Article 105(2)). Competent authorities are to co-operate and exchange information where useful for the performance of their duties under Article 12(3) (SCD, Article 106) but are subject to professional secrecy obligations by Article 14 (SCD, Article 107). In particular, any confidential information which a competent authority may receive under an exchange of information may be used only for the performance of the authorities' duties (Article 14(3)) (SCD, Article 107(30)). Under Article 13 (SCD, Article 96), the powers and duties of competent authorities relate to companies which are governed by the law of the competent authority's Member State.

IV.5.4.8 *Sanctions*

The seriousness of the SSD's notification and disclosure obligation is underlined by Article 15 (SCD, Article 97). It requires Member States to provide for 'appropriate sanctions' for cases where natural persons or legal entities and the companies within the scope of the SSD do not comply with the SSD's provisions. Notably, this provision marks one of the few places in the disclosure regime where sanctions are expressly required of Member States.[164]

IV.5.4.9 *Co-operation Between the Member States*

The SSD does not provide specifically for co-operation between the Member States, but the Contact Committee set up under the Admission Directive is given additional functions in relation to the SSD, including the establishment of a concerted attitude between Member States to the stricter or additional conditions which Member States may impose in accordance with Article 3 (SCD, Article 88) (Article 16)(1)(b)) (SCD, Article 108(2) (c)(iii)).

IV.6 DISCLOSURE AND PUBLIC OFFERS OF SECURITIES: THE PUBLIC OFFERS DIRECTIVE (POD)

IV.6.1 *Background*

Notwithstanding the adoption of the Admission Directive in 1979 and the LPD in 1980, a significant lacuna still existed in the EC's disclosure system. Public offers, where the securities were not, at the time of the offer, also subject to an official listing application, were not subject to a harmonized disclosure regime, despite the assertion made in the 1977 Code of Conduct 'that it is desirable that a public issue of securities should be preceded by publication of a prospectus'.[165] As a requirement to produce a prospectus for a public offer was not required across all the Member States,[166] investor protection, from the perspective of disclosure, was lacking in public offers of securities. Although in the UK public offers were invariably of officially listed securities and so subject to the disclosure requirements of the LPD,[167] in continental Europe offers of unlisted shares were more common, making the

---

[164] Although while the now consolidated Admission Directive does not require Member States or competent authorities to make particular sanctions available, it does, eg, provide in Art. 12 (SCD, Art. 17) that competent authorities may make public the fact that an issuer is not complying with its obligations.

[165] N 45 above, Supplementary Principle 14.

[166] Prospectus requirements were not imposed on public offers in Germany, the Netherlands, Italy, Denmark, and Greece prior to the presentation of the POD proposal. While Belgium, France, Ireland, the UK, and Luxembourg required a prospectus to be published when an offer was made to the public, the disclosure requirements varied and not all of these States required the publication of a prospectus for public offers of unlisted securities.

[167] The UK had, in any event, regulated public offers by requiring publication of a prospectus containing mandatory disclosure requirements and registration of the prospectus (with the Registrar of Companies) since the adoption of the Companies Act 1900.

need for a public-offers disclosure regime more compelling.[168] The apparently precarious position of the investor in a public offer prior to the adoption of the POD can, however, be explained by the fact that, in practice, a public offer in the form of an offering of securities directly to the general public occurred but rarely in continental Europe.[169] In order to plug the gap in the disclosure framework, a directive harmonizing (and, in many cases, introducing) disclosure requirements for public offers was thought necessary, not only to promote investor confidence in the securities markets outside the Official List but also in order to protect the Official Listing process, which, as is clear from the Admission Directive and the LPD, was, at the time, the capital markets access route of choice for Community policy-makers.[170] More recently, however, the EC's harmonized public-offer-disclosure regime and, in particular, its mutual recognition provisions, have become much more high profile and the weaknesses in the regime which was ultimately adopted more apparent as small and medium-sized unlisted issuers increasingly turn to the ex Official List equity markets for their financing needs (see further section 9.1 below).

The tortured genesis of the POD is perhaps best illustrated by the elapse of more than eight years between the publication of the Commission's initial proposal and the adoption of the Directive in 1989. The Commission presented its initial proposal in 1981.[171] The responses of ECOSOC and the European Parliament[172] were followed by the publication of a revised Commission proposal in 1982.[173] The revised version refined the original proposal by including, *inter alia*, provisions on mutual recognition and introducing an exemption from the obligation to produce a prospectus for public offers of euro-bonds. The Directive was finally adopted in April 1989 and was to be implemented by the Member States by 17 April 1991. As discussed in section 9, the disclosure regime applicable to public offers of securities is currently undergoing intensive review.

---

[168] Professor Wymeersch was an early supporter of a disclosure regime for public offers of securities, particularly as in certain Member States disclosure was required only on admission of the securities to listing, noting that 'the most dangerous securities shun daylight': Wymeersch, n 6 above, 125.

[169] See the discussion in Warren, M, 'Regulatory Harmony in the European Communities: The Common Market Prospectus' (1990) 16 *Brooklyn J Int'l. L* 19, 44.

[170] The failure to impose disclosure obligations on non-officially listed securities was thought to have implications for the health of Community stock exchanges. Issuers seeking admission of their securities to official listing were arguably discriminated against, in that they were subject to a more onerous regime. The Commission would later assert in its Explanatory Memorandum to the initial POD proposal that such discrimination might ultimately have driven issuers away from official listing: COM(80)893, 3. This preoccupation with the effects on stock exchange listing also appears in ECOSOC's opinion on the initial proposal: [1981] OJ C310/50 para 2.

[171] [1980] OJ C335/39. Explanatory Memorandum at COM(80)893.

[172] [1981] OJ C310/50 and [1982] OJ C125/176, respectively.

[173] [1982] OJ C226/4. Explanatory Memorandum at COM(82)441.

IV.6.2 *Objectives*

The POD is designed to enhance the then nascent 'Community information policy' by requiring that a prospectus be made available to investors when transferable securities are offered to the public for the first time, and that the contents of this prospectus be co-ordinated across the Member States in order to achieve equivalence of the minimum safeguards afforded to investors in the various Member States (recital 6). Although the familiar rationales for a Community disclosure policy reappear, albeit in a more sophisticated form than in earlier measures,[174] less emphasis is placed on the barriers to integration which are constructed by differing information requirements than in the previous disclosure measures. The function of disclosure in investor protection is, instead, more fully articulated. The Preamble acknowledges that investment in transferable securities involves risks and that the protection of investors requires that they be put in a position to make a correct assessment of such risks so as to be able to make investment decisions in full knowledge of the facts. Full and appropriate information is expressed to be the most appropriate way of protecting investors against such risks (POD, recitals 1 and 2). The LPD is stated to be an important step in the implementation of a 'Community information policy', which also requires that a prospectus be made available where securities are offered to the public for the first time, whether or not they are subsequently listed (POD, recitals 5 and 6).[175]

The level of disclosure applicable to the public offer depends on whether or not the securities are the subject of a listing application at the time of the offer. The POD takes a two-tier approach, adopting more stringent requirements, based on the LPD, for public offers where an official listing is sought but, in the interests of not over-burdening small and medium-sized issuers, imposing a less demanding regime for all other public offers coming within the scope of the Directive (recital 8). The original and the revised proposals presented by the Commission both imposed the same detailed disclosure regime, heavily based on the LPD, on both types of offer. This undifferentiated approach proved very controversial during negotiations, due largely to concerns with respect to the burden such disclosure was thought to place on small and medium-sized businesses, until the Commission bifurcated the

[174] Recitals 3 and 4 provide that a genuine Community information policy promotes the interpenetration of national securities markets and the creation of a European capital market by offering safeguards to investors (and thereby increasing investor confidence) and contributing to the proper functioning and development of transferable securities markets.

[175] In its Explanatory Memorandum on the initial proposal the Commission noted that the need for an information policy concerning the public offer of securities was all the greater in those countries where the stock exchange was not the central market and where, as a result, a substantial number or even the majority of public offers took place outside the central market: n 171 above, 2.

disclosure regime. The proposals to revise the issuer disclosure regime discussed in section 9.3. below do not, notably, tailor the degree of disclosure required on a public offer to the size of the issuer.

IV.6.3 *The Core Obligation*

Under Article 4, Member States are to ensure that any offer of transferable securities to the public within their territories is subject to the publication of a prospectus by the person making the offer. This obligation applies to all public offers, whether or not the securities are contemporaneously or subsequently admitted to official listing.

Prospectuses issued in relation to securities in respect of which an application to official listing is sought are subject to review by a competent authority. Although prospectuses published in relation to securities which are not the subject of such an application are not pre-reviewed, except in certain circumstances, they must nonetheless be communicated to a designated competent authority.

Preparation and, in certain cases, review of the prospectus are but two aspects of the disclosure process. The provision of adequate information to the investing public is achieved by the requirement that the prospectus must be made available to the public (whether or not the securities are the subject of an official-listing application at the time of the offer) not later than the time when the offer is made to the public.[176] In addition, under Article 18 a supplementary prospectus must be published, in certain circumstances, to reflect developments in the period between the publication of the prospectus and the closure of the offer.

Like the LPD, the POD does not require Member States to ensure that appropriate sanctions are imposed on issuers who do not comply with the prospectus requirements.

IV.6.4 *Scope*

IV.6.4.1 *Transferable Securities*

Under Article 1(1), the POD applies to 'transferable securities which are offered to the public for the first time in a Member State provided that these securities are not already listed on a stock exchange situated or operating in that Member State'. In a departure from the now consolidated Admission Directive, LPD, and IRD, the POD applies to offers of 'transferable securities' rather than simply 'securities' and, moreover, defines the term in comprehensive terms. Transferable securities are defined as 'shares in companies

---

[176] Art. 9 (where admission to listing is sought) and Art. 16 (where admission is not sought).

and other transferable securities equivalent to shares in companies, debt securities having a maturity of at least one year and other transferable securities equivalent to debt securities, and any other transferable securities giving the right to acquire any such transferable securities by subscription or exchange' (Article 3(e)).

This all-embracing definition is then scaled back by Article 2(2) which sets out the categories of transferable securities which are excluded from the scope of the POD. Transferable securities issued in denominations of more than 40,000 euro (Article 2(2)(a)) (designed to exempt offers to sophisticated investors) and units issued by collective-investment schemes other than the closed-end type (Article 2(2)(b))[177] are excluded as are securities issued by a State or its regional or local authorities, or by international bodies of which one or more Member States are members (Article 2(2)(c)).

A number of exemptions apply to securities issued in connection with particular transactions. Transferable securities offered in connection with a takeover bid or merger are exempted (Article 2(2)(d) and (e)). So too are shares allotted free of charge in a bonus issue (Article 2(2)(f)), shares issued in exchange for shares in the same company where the offer of new shares does not involve any overall increase in the company's issued share capital (Article 2(2)(g)) and transferable securities resulting from the exercise of conversion or exchange rights (as long as a public-offer prospectus or listing particulars relating to the convertible or exchangeable debt securities was published in the same Member State) (Article 2(2)(i)). Of some practical significance is the exclusion of transferable securities offered by their employer or by an affiliated undertaking to or for the benefit of serving or former employees (Article 2(2)(h)). Finally, transferable securities issued by non-profit-making bodies (as long as the proceeds are to be applied towards the issuer's objectives) (Article 2(2)(j)) and shares or transferable securities issued by building societies, industrial and provident societies, and similar bodies which permit the holder to avail himself of the services offered by such entities (Article 2(2)(k)) are also excluded from the definition of transferable securities.

While it is well-established that sophisticated or professional investors do not need the same degree of protection as retail investors in an offering of securities and that a professional-investor exemption can ease the burdens of the capital-raising process for smaller issuers in particular,[178] the POD does not contain a discrete institutional or professional-investor exemption.

---

[177] The POD adopts the same definitions of 'units in a collective investment scheme' and 'collective investment schemes other than the closed-end 'as used in the listing particular regime: Art. 3(a) and (b).

[178] See, eg, HM Treasury, *Public Offers of Securities. A Consultation Document Proposing Amendments to United Kingdom Legislation on the Public Offers of Securities and Seeking Views on Reforming Public Offers of Securities within the European Union* (1998) (the 1998 Treasury Public Offers Consultation Document), 21.

It does, however, contain a network of exemptions which are based, more or less, on the premise that professional investors do not need the protection of a mandatory prospectus requirement.[179] The final Article 2(1) transferable-securities-related exemption represents one of the clearest of the POD's attempts to exempt offerings to sophisticated investors from the requirement to produce a prospectus. It relates to Euro-securities[180] which are not the subject of 'a generalised campaign of advertising or canvassing' (Article 2(2)(l)). The failure to define what is meant by a 'generalised campaign of advertising or canvassing' allows Member States to set the parameters of this important exemption and has, it appears, prejudiced its widespread use, given that certain Member States have drawn the restricted advertising qualification very widely.[181] The Euro-securities exemption is worthy of a brief excursus in that it was the source of some controversy during the negotiations.[182] Following strong representations from the UK, Luxembourg, France, Germany, and the International Primary Market Association (IPMA), the trade association representing investment firms involved in the syndication of Euro-securities, the Commission introduced an exemption for Euro-bonds in its revised proposal. The primary concern of the lobbyists was that time-sensitive (Euro-securities offerings typically take advantage of interest-rate and currency fluctuations) Euro-securities transactions would be driven out of the Community if they were delayed by the requirement to produce, subject to review and distribute a detailed prospectus.[183] Forceful arguments were also made to the effect that Euro-securities were traded almost exclusively among financial institution and sophisticated private investors who did not need the protections of the POD.[184] Following further

---

[179] This philosophy informs, eg, Art. 2(2)(a)'s exclusion of offers of securities issued in denominations of more than 40,000 euro and a number of the POD's characterizations of offers as not being offers to the public and outside the scope of the POD (section 6.4.2) such as offers to persons in the context of their trade, profession, or vocation (Art. 2(1)(a)) and offers to a restricted circle of persons (Art. 2(1)(b)).

[180] Euro-securities are defined in Art. 3(f) as transferable securities which are to be underwritten and distributed by a syndicate, at least two of the members of which have their registered offices in different States, which are offered on a significant scale in one or more States other than that of the issuer's registered office, and which may be subscribed for or initially acquired only through a credit institution (defined in Art. 3(d)) or other financial institution. Member States have taken varying approaches to the definition of Euro-securities, with some Member States taking a restrictive approach which makes reliance on the exemption more difficult: 1998 Treasury Public Offers Consultation Document, n 178 above, 22.

[181] Ibid. In Germany, however, the canvassing restriction applies to door-to-door sales, while in the Netherlands retail investors may be approached outside a systematic, general campaign: Scott, n 22 above, 84.

[182] For a description of the machinations of the Euro-securities negotiations see Fama and Im, n 70 above, 561–3.

[183] In making its case for exemption from the POD's disclosure requirements, IPMA could also point to the absence of serious defaults or fraud in the Euro-securities market.

[184] However, Belgium's campaign against the exemption was based on the ground that the Euro-securities market was largely retail. This view was supported by Warren, who asserted in

strenuous lobbying efforts, the POD extended the revised proposal's exemption beyond Euro-bonds to include Euro-equities.

The classes of transferable securities which come within the scope of the POD are further reduced by Article 5, which allows Member States to provide for complete or partial exemption from the obligation to publish a prospectus when the transferable securities offered to the public fall within certain categories of debt securities. These categories include debt securities issued in a continuous or repeated manner by credit institutions or institutions equivalent to credit institutions (Article 5(a)) and debt securities issued by companies or other legal entities which are nationals of a Member State and which benefit from State monopolies and are either set up or governed by a special law, or whose borrowings are guaranteed by a Member State or one of a Member State's regional or local authorities (Article 5(b)). A final category consists of debt securities issued by legal persons other than companies which are nationals of a Member State and whose activities are restricted to certain financing operations (Article 5(c)).[185]

IV.6.4.2 *Offered to the Public for the First Time*

The forlorn admission in the Preamble to the POD that 'so far, it has proved impossible to furnish a common definition of the term "public offer" and all its constituent parts' reveals its glaring handicap in harmonizing the disclosure requirements applicable to public offers. A first attempt to define 'offer to the public' was made in the Commission's original proposal which provided that 'securities shall be considered to be offered for subscription or sale to the public where the offer is not addressed exclusively to a restricted circle of persons'.[186] This attempt at a common definition hinged on the meaning attached to a 'restricted circle of persons' but Member States were to determine what this meant, having regard to the number (and, if appropriate, the nature) of persons to whom the offer was addressed, the amount of the

1990 that '[d]espite assertions to the contrary, the euro-securities markets is largely a retail market. Individual investors, even those buying those securities indirectly through fund managers, could be injured seriously by inadequate disclosure in this marketplace': Warren, n 70 above, 230. For an explanation of how the Euro-securities exception can be used to sell securities to retail investors: see Scott, n 22 above at 84, who has noted that the conditions of the exemption could be satisfied (subject to the advertising and canvassing restriction) where a German company issued securities underwritten by a bank syndicate, including Deutsche Bank and Barclays, and sold the securities to banks in London which could then resell them to individual retail investors. In this respect, the exemption '[which] was specifically designed to ease offers of securities in more than one Member State which are not offered directly and indiscriminately to the public at large . . . contains the potential for promoting pan European public offers': 1998 Treasury Public Offers Consultation Document, n 178 above, 21.

[185] Parliament's suggestion that an exemption also be granted where the offer was designed to attract investment primarily from investors within a particular locality was not taken up: n 172 above, 179.

[186] N 171 above, Art. 1(2).

offer, and the means of publicity used for making the offer. This definition did not find favour with either ECOSOC or the Parliament. The former suggested that public offer be defined as an offer to the public, made directly or indirectly by the issuer, excluding offers addressed to a limited number of persons or bodies known to the issuer.[187] By contrast, the Parliament defined a public offer as an offer which was not addressed exclusively to a restricted circle of persons and defined such a circle as 'an identifiable category of persons or bodies known to the offeror, to whom the offer is directly communicated by the offeror or his appointed agent such that only members of that category may accept the offer, and that such members undertake not to resell the securities offered within a specified period of time'.[188] The revised proposal in the end retained the original definition of offer to the public but adopted a definition of a 'restricted circle of persons'. Agreement proved elusive, with the result that the POD as adopted is without a definition of what is arguably its most central concept, although recent developments will lead to significant reforms.

The POD does try to redeem its failure to define a public offer by setting out in Article 2(1) certain categories of offer which will not be an 'offer to the public' for the purposes of its requirements. In particular, offers of securities made to persons in the context of their trade, profession, or occupation (Article 2(1)(a)), offers to a restricted circle of persons (Article 2(1)(b)), offers where the selling price of all the transferable securities does not exceed 40,000 euro (Article 2(1)(c)) and offers where the transferable securities can be acquired only for a consideration of at least 40,000 euro per investor (Article 2(1)(d)) are not offers to the public. Although this large number of exemptions severely restricts the POD's ability to reduce variations in disclosure standards across the Community, the combined effect of many of these exemptions ensures at least that its protections are targeted towards smaller and less sophisticated investors.

IV.6.4.3 *Provided that the Securities are not Already Listed*

The Preamble makes clear in recital 6 that the POD's provisions apply to securities which are not listed at the time of the offer and 'whether or not [the securities] are subsequently listed'.[189] The application of the POD's central prospectus-publication obligation to securities which are subsequently listed and those which are not caused difficulties during the negotiation process. As the original and revised proposals both imposed the same disclosure regime on public offers of securities which were the subject of a

---

[187] N 172 above, para 3.2.3.   [188] Ibid, 178.
[189] See Edwards, n 42 above, 276 for a discussion of the confusion that has arisen concerning the POD's application to securities unlisted at the time of the offer, but subsequently listed.

listing application and those in respect of which a listing would not be sought, concerns were expressed that issuers of shares in respect of which it was not intended to seek a listing would be subject to overly burdensome disclosure requirements. The compromise adopted by the Commission was to create two different disclosure and publication regimes, one applicable to offers of securities the subject of a listing application and incorporating the extensive requirements of the LPD, the other applicable to public offers of other securities and based on the significantly less onerous requirements set out in the POD.

IV.6.4.4 *Other Exemptions*

Apart from the exemptions deriving from its scope as set out in Article 1(1), the POD contains two specific exemptions. First, where the offer to the public is for only a portion of the transferable securities from a single issue, Member States are given the option of not requiring that a prospectus be published when the remaining portion of the issue is subsequently offered to the public (Article 1(2)). Secondly, where a full prospectus has been published in a Member State within the previous twelve months, the prospectus drawn up for a subsequent offering by the same issuer in the same Member State, but relating to different transferable securities, need indicate only those changes likely to influence the value of the securities which have occurred since publication of the full prospectus (Article 6). The truncated prospectus may be made available only when it is accompanied by the full prospectus to which it relates or when it contains a reference to the full prospectus.

IV.6.5 *Prospectus Requirements for Publicly Offered Securities the Subject of an Official-listing Application*

IV.6.5.1 *Disclosure*

Section II of the Directive addresses two scenarios. First, it sets out the prospectus requirements applicable to public offers where the securities are, at the time of the offer, the subject of an official listing application in the same Member State and, secondly, it sets out the prospectus requirements applicable to public offers where the official listing of the securities is sought on an exchange in another Member State.

Where the securities which are the subject of the public offer are also, at the time of the offer, the subject of an application to official listing in the same Member State, the contents of the prospectus must comply with the requirements of the LPD (which are more stringent than the requirements set out in the Directive for other public offers) while the LPD's procedures for distributing and scrutinizing it will also apply, subject in each case to any adaptations appropriate for a public offer (Article 7). In effect, the POD borrows the disclosure code introduced by the LPD for a particular procedure, official listing, and gives it an additional function with respect to public offers.[190]

In addressing the second listing scenario, the POD takes some steps in the direction of establishing a framework for a single, common disclosure document. Where the public offer in one Member State relates to securities which are also the subject of an application to official listing on the stock exchange of a Member State other than the Member State in which the public offer is made, the issuer is given the option under Article 8(1) to draw up the required prospectus in accordance with the LPD, subject, again, to any adaptations appropriate to the circumstances of a public offer. As a public-offer prospectus in this form is subject to the scrutiny and distribution procedures set out in the LPD (Article 8(1)), this option may be availed of by issuers only when the Member State where the offer to the public takes place provides, in general, for the prior scrutiny of public-offer prospectuses (Article 8(2)).

IV.6.5.2 *Communications and Publication*

Where a prospectus prepared in accordance with Article 7 or 8 is, or will be, published, all announcements of the public offer (such as advertisements, notices, posters, or any other documents announcing the offer) must be communicated in advance to the competent authorities (Article 10(1)). All such documents must also mention that a prospectus has been prepared relating to the offer and state where the prospectus is published (Article 10(1)). If the distribution of these documents prior to the publication of the prospectus is authorized by Member States, the documents must state that a prospectus will be published and indicate where it may be obtained by the public (Article 10(2)).

The prospectus itself must be published in one of two ways. It may be inserted in one or more newspapers circulated throughout the Member State in which the public offer is made. Alternatively, it may be made available, free of charge and in the form of a brochure, to the public in the Member State in which the public offer is made and at the registered office of the person making the public offer and the offices of the paying agents in the Member State where the offer is made (Article 10(3)). Additionally, either the complete prospectus or a notice stating where the prospectus has been published and where it may be obtained by the public must be inserted in a

---

[190] This 'tacking on' of the now consolidated LPD regime does not mean, however, that the obligation to produce a prospectus falls away when the LPD exempts a transaction which is covered by the POD. See the discussion in Edwards, n 42 above, 279.

publication designated by the Member State in which the offer is made (Article 10(4)).

IV.6.6 *Prospectus Requirements for Publicly Offered Securities not Subject to an Official-listing Application*

IV.6.6.1 *The Article 11 Prospectus*

(a) *Introduction*

This prospectus must contain all the information which, according to the particular nature of the issuer and of the transferable securities offered, is necessary to enable investors to make an informed assessment of the assets and liabilities, financial position, profits and losses, and prospects of the issuer and of the rights attaching to the securities (Article 11(1)). This overriding obligation is supplemented by the specific disclosure requirements set out in Article 11(2) which must, at a minimum, be included in the prospectus. The disclosure of this information must be made in as easily analysable and comprehensible a form as possible. Where the information specified is inappropriate to the issuer's sphere of activity or its legal form, or to the transferable securities publicly offered, a prospectus giving equivalent information must nonetheless be drawn up (Article 11(6)). The main disclosure requirements are summarized at paragraphs (b)-(h) below.[191]

(b) *Responsibility Statement*

Under Article 11(2)(a), the prospectus must contain the names and functions of those responsible for the prospectus and a declaration to the effect that to the best of their knowledge, the information contained in the prospectus is in accordance with the facts and that the prospectus makes no omissions likely to affect its import.

(c) *The Offer and the Securities*

The disclosure required under this heading (Article 11(2)(b)) covers: the nature of the securities being offered; the amount and purpose of the issue; the number of securities issued and the rights attaching to them; details of

---

[191] The list of mandatory items changed substantially between the Commission's original proposal and the adopted measure. The original requirements were more demanding, largely because the information requirements did not discriminate between public offers of securities the subject of an application to listing and other public offers. In order to meet the concerns raised in respect of small and medium-sized issuers, the requirements as finally adopted are a simpler version of the LPD's disclosure standards. The general principles of that regime are adopted but the detail is omitted.

any withholding tax; the period during which the offer is open; the dates on which entitlements to dividends or interest arise; those persons underwriting or guaranteeing the offer; any restrictions on the transferability of the securities and the markets on which they may be traded; the identity of the paying agents; the offer price, or, if provided for by national law, the procedure and timetable for fixing the price if it is not known when the prospectus is drawn up; methods of payment; procedures for the exercise of preemption rights; and methods of and time-limits for the delivery of the securities.

(d) *The Issuer and its Capital*

This disclosure, required under Article 11(2)(c), includes: the issuer's name, registered office, date of incorporation, and objects; the amount of subscribed capital; the number and main features of the securities of which the capital is made up; any part of the capital still to be paid up; the amount of convertible or exchangeable securities and securities with warrants attached together with details of the conversion procedures; the group of undertakings to which the issuer belongs, where appropriate; the number of shares not representing capital; the amount of authorized capital and the duration of the authorization; and an indication of the shareholders who directly or indirectly exercise or could exercise a determining role in the management of the issuer.

(e) *The Issuer's Principal Activities*

Under Article 11(2)(d) disclosure must be made of: the issuer's principal activities and, where appropriate, any exceptional factors which have influenced its activities; any dependence on patents, licences, or contracts, where they are of fundamental importance; significant investments in progress; and any legal proceedings having an important effect on the issuer's financial position.

(f) *Financial Information*

The financial information which must be disclosed under Article 11(2)(e) includes: the issuer's assets and liabilities, financial position, profits and losses (both own accounts and, where appropriate, consolidated accounts);[192] interim accounts if they have been published since the end of the previous financial year; and, where appropriate, details of any qualifications on or refusals to audit the accounts.

---

[192] Art. 11(2)(e) also addresses which accounts are to be disclosed where both are prepared.

(g) *Management*

Under Article 11(2)(f) disclosure is required of those involved in the issuer's administration, management, and supervision, including names, addresses, and functions. Where the offer is of shares in a limited liability company, details must also be given of the remuneration of members of the issuer's administrative, management, and supervisory bodies.

(h) *Prospects*

Under Article 11(2)(g), disclosure must be made of recent developments in the issuer's business and prospects to the extent that such information would have a significant impact on any assessment that might be made of the issuer. This information must include the most significant recent trends concerning the development of the issuer's business since the end of the preceding financial year and information on the issuer's prospects for at least the current financial year.

If the period of existence of the issuer is less than any period mentioned in Article 11(2)(a)–(g) as set out above, under Article 11(5) the information required need be provided only for the period of the issuer's existence.

(i) *Additional Requirements for Particular Securities*

Article 11(3) provides that where the public offer relates to guaranteed debt securities, the information specified in Article 11(2)(c)–(g) must also be given with respect to the guarantor. Where the offer relates to convertible or exchangeable securities or securities with warrants attached, under Article 11(4) information must also be provided concerning the nature of the shares or debt securities to which the securities relate. Where the issuer of these underlying shares or debt securities is not the issuer of the securities which are publicly offered, the information specified in Article 11(2)(c)–(g) must also be given with respect to that issuer (Article 11(4)).

(j) *Prior Scrutiny*

Unlike section II prospectuses, prospectuses prepared in accordance with Article 11 are not subject to a requirement of prior scrutiny by a competent authority prior to publication. Investors do not as a result benefit from the extra layer of review by a competent authority which is imposed on public offers of securities in respect of which a listing is sought. For issuers wishing to benefit from the mutual recognition provisions of the POD (section 8.3) and rely on the same document for public offers throughout the Community, prior scrutiny of the prospectus is essential.

Accordingly, issuers may choose to draw up the prospectus under Article 12 instead.

IV.6.6.2 *The Article 12 Prospectus*

Under Article 12, Member States may provide that a person making a public offer is to have the option of drawing up a prospectus (which will be pre-vetted) the contents of which, subject to any adaptations appropriate for a public offer, conform to the requirements of the LPD. The significance of this provision lies in the opportunities it gives for mutual recognition of the prospectus.

The prior scrutiny of an Article 12 prospectus drawn up in accordance with the LPD must be carried out by the bodies designated by the Member States, even in the absence of a request for admission to official stock exchange listing (Article 12(2)).

IV.6.6.3 *Supplementary Prospectuses*

In order to ensure the accuracy and timeliness of the disclosure, Article 18 provides that any significant new factor or significant inaccuracy capable of affecting assessment of the securities offered which arises or is noted between the publication of the prospectus and the definitive closure (undefined) of the public offer must be mentioned or rectified in a supplement to the prospectus. The supplement must be published or made available to the public in accordance with at least the same arrangements as were applied when the original prospectus was disseminated, or in accordance with procedures laid down by the Member States or bodies designated by them.

IV.6.6.4 *Exemptions and Derogations*[193]

Member States (or the bodies designated by them) may authorize the omission of certain information from the prospectus if the information is of minor importance only and is not likely to influence assessment of the issuer's assets and liabilities, financial position, profits and losses, and prospects (Article 13(1)(a)). Information may also be omitted if disclosure of that information would be contrary to the public interest or seriously detrimental to the issuer, provided that omission would not be likely to mislead the public with regard to facts and circumstances essential for the assessment of the transferable securities (Article 13(1)(b)). In addition, where the initiator of the offer is neither the issuer nor a third party acting on the issuer's

---

[193] These apply only in respect of prospectuses prepared in accordance with Art. 11. Art. 12 (and, of course, section II) prospectuses will be subject to the now consolidated LPD regime.

behalf, the Member States or bodies designated by them may authorize the omission of information which would not normally be in the possession of the initiator (Article 13(2)). Finally, partial or complete exemption from the obligation to publish a prospectus may be granted by the Member States or bodies designated by them where the information which those making the offer are required to supply by law is available to investors not later than the time when the prospectus must be or should have been published or made available to the public in accordance with the POD, in the form of documents giving information at least equivalent to that required by section III (Article 13(3)).[194]

In addition, where the public offer consists of shares offered on a pre-emptive basis to the issuer's shareholders on the occasion of their admission to dealing on a stock exchange market the Member States (or bodies designated by them) may allow some of the information specified in Article 11(2)(d), (e), and (f) to be omitted, provided that investors already possess up-to-date information about the issuer which is equivalent to that required by section III, as a result of stock exchange disclosure requirements (Article 11(7)). Article 11(8) goes further and allows Member States (or bodies designated by them) to permit partial or complete exemption from the obligation to publish a prospectus where a class of shares has been admitted to dealing on a stock exchange market and the number or estimated market value or the nominal value (or, in the absence of a nominal value, the accounting par value) of the shares offered amounts to less than 10 per cent of the number (or the corresponding value) of the shares of the same class already admitted to dealing. As with section 11(7), the exemption is available only where the investors already possess up-to-date information about the issuer which is equivalent to that required by section III, as a result of stock exchange disclosure requirements.

IV.6.6.5 *Communication and Publication*

Before its publication, the section III prospectus must, under Article 14, be communicated to the bodies designated for that purpose in each Member State in which the securities are offered to the public for the first time. The section III prospectus must be published or made available to the public in the Member State in which an offer to the public is made in accordance with the procedures laid down by that Member State (Article 15). In addition, when a section III prospectus is, or must be, prepared in accordance with Article 11 or 12, under Article 17(1) any announcement of the public offer (such as advertisements, notices, posters, and other documents announcing

---

[194] This derogation was introduced for the benefit of the UK which regulated certain limited classes of offer as investment advertisements under s 57 of the Financial Services Act 1987. See the discussion in Edwards, n 42 above, 270.

the offer) which are distributed or made available to the public by the person making the public offer, must be communicated in advance to the bodies designated under Article 14, but this requirement applies only if such bodies also carry out prior scrutiny of public-offer prospectuses. If such prior scrutiny is undertaken by the designated body, it must determine whether the documents announcing the offer should be checked before publication. In any event, any such documents must state that a prospectus exists and indicate where it is published. If Member States authorize the dissemination of these documents before the prospectus is available, the documents must, in such circumstances, state that a prospectus will be published and indicate where members of the public will be able to obtain it.

IV.6.7 *Co-operation between Member States and Competent Authorities*

Article 19 requires the Member States to designate bodies which will co-operate for the purposes of the proper application of the POD and exchange all the information necessary to that end.[195] Member States must also ensure that the designated bodies have all the powers required for the accomplishment of their tasks. Article 22(1), which in some respects seems to duplicate Article 19,[196] builds on the basic designation obligation and requires all competent authorities to co-operate wherever necessary for the purposes of carrying out their duties and to exchange any information required for that purpose. In particular, Article 22(2) imposes a specific co-operation obligation in relation to public offers of transferable securities which give a right to participate in company capital, either immediately or following a maturity period, made in one or more Member States other than that in which the registered office of the issuer of the related shares is situated, and where the related shares are already admitted to official listing in that Member State. In such circumstances, where the question of scrutiny of the public-offer prospectus arises, the competent authorities of the Member State in which the offer is made may act only once they have consulted the competent authorities of the Member State in which the registered office is situated.

---

[195] The Commission must be notified of the bodies designated and in turn will notify the other Member States. These bodies responsible for co-operation may be the same as the bodies to which a section III prospectus must be communicated and which are designated for that purpose under Art. 14.

[196] For an examination of the relationship between the two provisions see Edwards, n 42 above, 284 who has noted that the Art. 19 provision is designed to make clear that the competent authority which pre-vets prospectuses for securities which are to be officially listed can be different from the competent authority that receives prospectuses for securities which are not to be listed and is concerned with the Member States' designation obligation rather than with the co-operation obligations which are then imposed on the designated authorities via Art. 22.

The role played by the competent authorities in the mutual recognition of prospectuses is discussed in section 8.3 below.

IV.7 AN EC DISCLOSURE CODE

IV.7.1 *Market Integration as a Consistent Objective*

As a code designed to enhance market integration by reducing regulatory divergences between Member States' disclosure regimes and establishing equivalent common standards, the basic EC disclosure regime is far from successful in that Member States may apply exemptions or impose additional or more stringent obligations on issuers. As discussed in section 8 below, however, it was not until the introduction of mutual recognition that this objective began to be more fully realized.

IV.7.2 *Investor Protection as a Consistent Objective*

The uncertain position of investor protection as an objective of EC disclosure policy has arguably contributed to certain inconsistencies and weaknesses in the scheme with respect to how investor protection is achieved.

In the LPD, the combination of detailed minimum requirements and the Article 4(1) (SCD, Article 21(1)) catch-all general obligation to make full disclosure introduced a relatively rigorous disclosure code for admission to official listing and raised pre-existing levels of disclosure. While the POD incorporates the requirements of the LPD, it is possible for a more limited public-offer prospectus containing the less demanding requirements of Article 11(2) to be published. The diluted disclosure regime, which is designed to assist smaller issuers, does not arguably prejudice investors as the issuer is subject to the overriding obligation to disclose all the information necessary to 'make an informed assessment of the assets and liabilities, financial position, profits and losses and prospects of the issuers and of the rights attaching to the securities' (Article 11(1)).

Nonetheless, the focus on adopting a harmonized disclosure code in order to ease the burden on cross-border and multiple issuers and facilitate the interpenetration of securities markets seems to have deflected attention away from establishing what disclosure is necessary in order to enhance investor protection and thereby investor confidence, who the object of the disclosure is, and whether the disclosure is in a form such that it is reaching its targets. By and large the features of the investor who is the beneficiary of the mandatory disclosure are not specified anywhere in the disclosure regime. It is perhaps revealing that the term 'investor' is not defined anywhere in the disclosure regime. The recipients of the LPD's mandatory disclosure (either via the listing particulars or an LPD-based public-offer prospectus) seem to be identified as retail investors, given that Article 5(1) of the LPD (SCD, Article 22(1)) provides that the disclosure must be in 'as easily analysable and comprehensible a form as possible'; this formula also applies to POD Article 11 prospectuses by Article 11(2).[197] The nature of the exemptions from the POD, many of which carve out offers to professional investors, also suggest a focus on the retail investor. The utility of the LPD disclosure document, in particular, for the protection and information of ordinary investors is somewhat diminished, however, by both the scale of the disclosure required[198] and, specifically, by Article 4(1) of the LPD which imposes a catch-all disclosure obligation not just for the benefit of investors, but also for their investment advisers. While this formula has the advantage of requiring issuers to go beyond simply mechanically complying with the disclosure requirements listed in the schedules to the directive, if disclosure is directed towards investment advisers it is unlikely to take a form which is accessible to ordinary investors.[199] Notwithstanding the Article 5(1) exhortation on clarity, too much information may obscure material facts concerning the securities offered and confuse the investor, who may be unable to distil the key information from the prospectus and may, in the face of overwhelming disclosure, ignore important facts;[200] notably, the investment adviser reference does not

[197] Although the Commission's preparatory documents do not contain any discussion of who the LPD's mandatory disclosure is directed to, in its opinion on the original proposal for the LPD, ECOSOC took the stance that disclosure should be directed towards the unsophisticated investor, noting that 'the prospectus should also provide the general public in all Member States of the Community with objective information on the legal and economic situation of the issuer': n 73 above, para 2.2.2. See also the interpretation by IOSCO of Art. 4(1) of the LPD (SCD, Art. 21(1)) (which imposes the overriding catch-all disclosure obligation), as being designed to cover 'information regarding a company's financial position which was not disclosed in a fund raising document and which would have led to an investor of average intelligence and imaginative faculty not acquiring the securities of the company or to have at least influenced the price of the securities': IOSCO 1998 Disclosure Standards. n 31 above, para II-5.

[198] The point has been made that the LPD requirements 'make prospectuses too weighty and difficult to read.' ECOSOC Opinion on Directive 94/18/EC ([1994] OJ L135/1) ([1993] OJ C161/9) para 3.1.

[199] Indeed, writing in 1977 and before the adoption of the LPD or the POD Professor Wymeersch noted that '[t]he issue prospectus, the purpose of which is to induce the investor to purchase the securities, must also in fact enable him to make the decision. In addition, a more sophisticated, less easily readable and more detailed disclosure document can be made available to the financial community, essentially the investment adviser': n 6 above, 141.

[200] 'The capacity of the public investor to absorb information differs greatly according to his class and previous knowledge, constituting a decisive limit on disclosure's effectiveness. Quite simply, if an investor's capacity to absorb information is exceeded, more information does not promote clarity, but only conceals the facts': Buxbaum and Hopt, n 10 above, 220. There is a considerable literature on the adverse effects of excess information on the exercise of choice. See generally Malhotra, N, 'Reflections on the Information Overload Paradigm in Consumer Decision Making' (1984) 10 *J Consumer Res.* 437. More specifically, there is a vast US literature on the value of detailed disclosure to investors. See, eg, Kripke, n 11 above.

More recently, the SEC has become concerned about the clarity of disclosure and adopted the Plain English Disclosure Rules in 1998. The rules are designed to make disclosure documents

appear in the parallel provision for POD Article 11 prospectuses (POD, Article 11(1)). The case for more simplified disclosure has recently been accepted in principle at EC level. A new regime has been adopted which revises the extensive disclosure requirements applicable to collective-investment schemes by the UCITS Directive[201] by introducing a requirement that a 'simplified prospectus', which is investor-friendly and gives 'key information about the UCITS in a clear, concise, and easily understandable way', be offered to the potential investor prior to conclusion of the contract.[202] The new proposals to reform the disclosure regime are, however, encouraging, in that they reflect an underlying assumption that disclosure must be more carefully adjusted to the needs of investors (section 9.3 below).

A similar point could be made in respect of the specific requirements applicable to the contents of listing particulars and prospectuses. For example, while the LPD and the POD do impose detailed requirements with respect to financial information, they do not require specific and highlighted disclosure to be made of the risk factors specific to the issuer or its industry which might render an offering speculative or high risk in nature: in particular, the regime does not require prominent and highlighted disclosure of risk factors in a particular section which would concentrate the attention of investors. The high-technology and 'dotcom' boom, for example, has raised concerns that investors were not sufficiently made aware of the risks attendant on such investments.[203] Indeed, the 1998 IOSCO Disclosure Standards recommend that the disclosure document prominently disclose

---

easier and clearer to read: SEC Release No. 33–7497 (1998). In adopting the Rules the SEC noted at 4 that 'if a prospectus fails to communicate information clearly, investors do not receive that basic protection [of full and fair disclosure]. Yet prospectuses today often use complex, legalistic language that is foreign to all but a few legal experts . . . A major challenge facing the securities industry and its regulators is assuring that financial and business information is reaching investors in a form they can read and understand'. For a critique of the Plain English approach and the risk that comprehensiveness may be sacrificed to simplicity see Firtel, n 11 above, 895–6.

[201] Directive 85/611/EEC on the coordination of laws, regulations and administrative provisions relating to undertakings for collective investment in transferable securities [1985] OJ L375/3.

[202] Amended Proposal for a European Parliament and Council Directive amending Directive 85/611/EEC on the Coordination of Laws, Regulation and Administrative Provisions Relating to Undertakings for Collective Investment in Transferable Securities with a view to Regulating Management Companies and Simplified Prospectuses. COM(2000)331; Common Position at [2001] OJ C297/10. See Ch. V, sect. 8.3, n 105 on the status of the new regime.

[203] The more rigorous disclosure required of dotcoms engaging in initial public offerings as compared with the disclosure demanded in the UK regime (which reflects, of course, the LPD), particularly with respect to risk warnings, has been noted to the extent that one commentator is of the opinion that: '[i]n the UK, and elsewhere in Europe, the rules are much less draconian [than the US rules] and a prospectus is likely to view the world through distinctly rose-tinted lenses': Dickson, M, 'The new issue lessons to be learnt from Uncle Sam', *Financial Times*, 18/19 Mar 2000. See also the discussion of initial public-offer disclosure and the dotcom boom in the IOSCO Technical Committee Bulletin Regarding Investor Protection in the New Economy (2000), para B(1).

risk factors.[204] The extent of the focus on investor protection can also be questioned in light of the requirement imposed on issuers to disclose forward information with respect to business trends and the issuer's prospects for the current financial year.[205] While this requirement acts as a counterbalance to the mandatory disclosure of what may often be historic and negative information, and even though projections and forecasts can be very useful for the investor, the EC's approach to soft information is unusual in that it does not, as previously noted, require that the projected information, the reliability of which is critical, be audited.[206]

The effectiveness of the harmonized ongoing disclosure system has also been subject to criticism. The regime is directed towards officially listed securities for the most part and does not comprehensively address the ongoing information needs of investors in other securities not admitted to official listing or admitted to trading on a market outside the scope of the ongoing disclosure regime. The IRD requires only very limited disclosure which is transmitted to the market-place between relatively long intervals. The view has also been expressed that the ongoing disclosure regime is not efficiently integrated with the disclosure required on official listing of securities. In particular, the argument has been made that if an adequate and regular supply of information to the market-place can be assured, the requirement to prepare full listing particulars when a listed company lists additional securities could be revisited.[207] Difficulties with the ongoing reporting regime were highlighted by the Committee of Wise Men in their Initial Report, in which they referred to the wide divergences which exist across the EC as regards the information which must be disclosed to the market, and where they contrasted the EC regime with the more rigorous disclosure regime prevailing in the USA, where, as a result, more information is often available on EC companies than can be found in the EC market-place.[208] Moves to restructure the disclosure regime so that admission to listing and public offer disclosure is more fully integrated with the ongoing disclosure regime are now underway (sections 9.3 and 9.4 below).

---

[204] N 31 above, para III, D. They are defined as those factors specific to the company or its industry which make an offering speculative or one of high risk.

[205] POD, Art. 11(2)(g), LPD Schs A and B, 7.

[206] It may be that the EC takes a robust approach to the ability of the investor to discriminate between historical financial information and what might be overly optimistic management protections. Professor Romano has noted that the SEC's reluctance to allow projected information was based on 'a bizarre view of investor decisionmaking' in that it assumed that investors do not discount managers' optimism but believe that any figures provided are solid. Note 23, 2379 (referring to H. Kripke, 'Can the SEC Make Disclosure Policy Meaningful?' [1976] *J Portfolio Mgmt.* 32, 40).

[207] Wymeersch, n 43 above, 39.

[208] Initial Report of the Committee of Wise Men on the Regulation of European Securities Markets, Nov 2000 (the Initial Lamfalussy Report), 6.

Investor protection (and the promotion of investor confidence) through issuer disclosure does not extend to ensuring that adequate sanctions or remedies are in place to address non-compliance with the disclosure obligations. As previously noted, the three major disclosure directives, the LPD, the IRD, and the POD, do not address sanctions or remedies even though the adequacy and sufficiency of disclosure in practice are typically ensured by imposing sanctions on the issuer and those persons responsible for the defective disclosure or by making remedies available to investors who suffer loss by relying on the defective disclosure. Although the specific nature of sanctions and remedies is the preserve of the Member States under EC law, the LPD, the IRD, and POD all lack a provision requiring Member States to ensure, at a minimum, that appropriate sanctions be imposed by the competent authorities if the disclosure rules are breached. Devices such as the LPD and POD responsibility statements and the IRD's requirement that the company or its representatives take responsibility for the correctness or relevance of any facts on which an application for exemption from the IRD's information requirements is based (Article 4) (SCD, Article 72), however, at least remind issuers of the seriousness with which the disclosure process must be taken.

IV.8 BEYOND THE CODE: THE REGIME FALTERS

IV.8.1 *Introduction*

The equivalence approach to the removal of the regulatory obstacles represented by varying disclosure requirements was not successful. Not only were the earlier disclosure directives being implemented in different ways across the EC, but a degree of mutual distrust also existed between competent authorities. The second stage of the EC's disclosure project, mutual recognition, was designed to address the problem of varying disclosure rules via mutual recognition. The 'recognizing' competent authority would be required to 'recognize' listing particulars or public-offer prospectuses previously approved by another competent authority, subject to the inclusion of local-market-specific information. Mutual recognition was possible, however, only as a result of the preceding introduction of common standards.

Mutual recognition has two aspects. It permits issuers to prepare one listing particulars or public offers prospectus for use in listing applications or public offers throughout the EC, once it has been approved by the relevant authority. Mutual recognition also serves the additional function of integrating the two-tier disclosure regime for listing applications and public offers and permitting the preparation of a multi-jurisdictional, dual-purpose document by providing that the same document can be used as either listing particulars or a public offer prospectus.

IV.8.2 *Stage 1: Mutual Recognition of Listing Particulars*

IV.8.2.1 *The First Mutual Recognition Directive (MRD I)*

(a) *Background and Objectives*

The principle of mutual recognition of disclosure documents first appeared in the now consolidated MRD I which amended the LPD to apply the mutual recognition principle to listing particulars by recasting the original Articles 24 and 25. The adoption process was relatively painless and speedy.[209] The untroublesome passage of this ground-breaking legislation can be explained by the acceptance of the principle of mutual recognition in the course of the earlier initial negotiations on the POD. In its 1982 opinion on the Commission's first proposal for the POD, the Parliament had suggested that, where a public offer in respect of the same securities was made in two or more Member States, a single public-offer prospectus approved in one Member State should benefit from mutual recognition in all other Member States and a mutual recognition mechanism was introduced in the revised POD proposal.[210] Although negotiating difficulties on other points delayed adoption of the POD until after the coming into force of the MRD I, the principle of mutual recognition had as a result been established since mid-1982 when the revised POD proposal had been presented. In its Explanatory Memorandum to the proposal for the MRD I, the Commission referred to the advances which had been made on the mutual recognition of public-offer prospectuses and found that in order to facilitate cross-border listings and minimize the obstacles to multi-national listings, the principle of mutual recognition should be applied to listing particulars in the same way as to public-offer prospectuses.[211] The MRD I was adopted in June 1987 and was to be implemented by the Member States by 1 January 1990.

The MRD I's pre-consolidation Preamble (which is not completely replicated in the SCD) reveals two reasons in particular for the introduction of the mutual recognition principle for listing particulars. With the adoption of Directive 86/566/EEC[212] and the consequent abolition of capital controls on the admission of securities to stock exchange listing from 1 March 1987, the number of cross-border listing applications was predicted to increase.[213] In

---

[209] Proposal at [1987] OJ C110/4; Explanatory Memorandum at COM(87)129; ECOSOC comments at [1987] OJ C150/18; and the Parliament's comments at [1987] OJ C125/173.

[210] N 173 above, 181. ECOSOC was another early proponent of mutual recognition in the disclosure field: n 170 above, para 3.7.2.

[211] N 209 above, para 4.

[212] Directive 86/566/EEC amending the first Directive for the implementation of Article 67 of the Treaty [1986] OJ L332/22. See Ch. sect. 8 above.

[213] Recital 1. In its Explanatory Memorandum the Commission also referred to 'the increasing internationalisation of securities markets which is currently underway' as reinforcing the trend for an increased number of cross-border listing applications: n 209 above, para 3.

light of the failure of the LPD to provide for the full mutual recognition of listing particulars,[214] however, cross-border and multiple issuers still faced a panoply of differing disclosure requirements and were required to produce different versions of the listing particulars and carry the burden of the attendant costs and inconveniences. Consequently, the purpose of the MRD I is to establish the application of the mutual recognition principle to listing particulars and, in particular, to specify the authorities which are competent to check and approve the listing particulars in the event of simultaneous listing applications in two or more Member States (recitals 4 and 5) (SCD, recitals 13 and 14). Mutual recognition is thus limited to the sphere of simultaneous listing applications or applications made within a short interval of each other.

(b) *The Mechanics of Mutual Recognition*

The key features of the mutual recognition procedure are: approval of the disclosure document by the home competent authority, the identity of which is determined in accordance with harmonized rules; mutual recognition of the disclosure document without further approval requirements by competent authorities in other Member States; and the ability of other Member States to impose translation and additional local-market-disclosure requirements. In the MRD I, mutual recognition is not all-embracing, but is limited to issuers whose registered office is situated in a Member State and whose applications to listing are made either simultaneously, or within a short interval of each other.[215]

(c) *Identification of the Approving Competent Authority*

In order to make mutual recognition of listing particulars an attainable objective, it was imperative that the MRD I provide harmonized rules for determining the competent authority originally responsible for approving the listing particulars which would, subsequently, benefit from mutual recognition. The MRD I introduced a new Article 24 (SCD, Article 37) which provides that where, for the same securities, application to official listing on stock exchanges situated or operating in two or more Member States (including the Member State in which the issuer's registered office is situated) is made

---

[214] Under Art. 24 of the original LPD, where securities were to be admitted to official listing on stock exchanges in two or more Member States, the competent authorities of the Member States concerned were simply to 'use their best endeavours to achieve maximum coordination of their requirements' and 'to agree to a single text' for the listing particulars for use in the Member States concerned.

[215] Art. 24, LPD (SCD, Art. 37). References to Arts. of the LPD are to the amended Arts. of the LPD.

'simultaneously' or 'within a short interval',[216] the listing particulars are (1) to be drawn up in accordance with the rules applicable (such rules being in accordance with the LPD) in the Member State of the issuer's registered office and (2) approved by the competent authority of that Member State. By contrast, where the listing applications are not made in the Member State in which the issuer's registered office is situated, the issuer has a choice of disclosure regime and is required to choose the Member State under the legislation of which the listing particulars will be drawn up and approved.

(d) *The Mutual Recognition Procedure (1): Mutual Recognition of Listing Particulars Where No Prior Prospectus*

The LPD was further amended by the introduction of Article 24a (SCD, Article 38) which sets out the procedure for mutual recognition of listing particulars. Where the listing particulars have been approved in accordance with Article 24 (SCD, Article 37),[217] Article 24a(1) (SCD, Article 38(1)) provides that, subject to any translation requirements, the listing particulars must then be recognized by the other Member States in which an application has been made for admission to official listing without it being necessary to obtain approval of the listing particulars from the competent authorities and without such competent authorities being able to require the inclusion of additional information in the listing particulars. The competent authorities may, however, require the inclusion of information which is specific to the market of the country of admission. In particular, competent authorities may require additional disclosure concerning the income tax system, the issuer's paying agents in the Member State concerned, and the manner in which notices to investors will be published.

The mutual-recognition regime as set out in Article 24a(1) is subject to a number of restrictions. Member States may restrict the availability of mutual recognition to the listing particulars produced by issuers which have a registered office in a Member State (Article 24a(5) (SCD, Article 38(5)). The degree of mutual recognition is also a function of the extent to which the original approval of the listing particulars included permitted derogations from the LPD requirements. Under Article 24a(2) (SCD, Article 38(2)), the listing particulars must be recognized by other Member States, even where

---

[216] The Commission's proposal originally granted mutual recognition in respect of applications made simultaneously or within one month. The Parliament felt that this period was too short and suggested it be amended to 3 months. ECOSOC was of the same opinion, although it did not suggest an appropriate time limit.

[217] In order to ensure that proof can be obtained of approval in accordance with Art. 24, Art. 24a(3) (SCD, Art. 38(3)) provides that the approving competent authorities must provide the competent authorities of the other Member States with a 'certificate of approval'. Consequently, the recognizing Member State may not deny mutual recognition arbitrarily on the ground it is not satisfied that approval has been given to the listing particulars.

the original approval process granted partial exemptions or derogations from the LPD's requirements, as long as two conditions are fulfilled. First, the partial exemption or derogation must be of a type that is recognized in the rules of the recognizing Member State. Secondly, the conditions that justify the partial exemption or derogation in the approving Member State must also exist in the recognizing Member State, and there must be no other conditions concerning the exemption or derogation which may lead the recognizing Member State to refuse to grant the relevant exemption or derogation. The extent to which the MRD I seeks to encourage mutual recognition can be seen in the final paragraph of Article 24a(2), which goes on to provide that even if these two conditions are not met, the recognizing Member State may permit its competent authorities to recognize the listing particulars. In order to facilitate mutual recognition where exemptions or derogations have been granted in respect of the listing particulars, the certificate of approval provided by the competent authorities which have approved the document must state whether permitted derogations or exemptions from the LPD were granted and the reasons for such exemption or derogation (Article 24a(3)) (SCD, Article 38(3)). The mutual-recognition process is further eased by the requirement that the issuer communicate the draft listing particulars which it intends to use to the competent authorities of each Member State in which it is applying for admission of its securities to official listing.

(e) *The Mutual Recognition Procedure(2): Mutual Recognition of Listing Particulars based on a Prior Public Offer Prospectus*

In a portent of future developments in the POD, the MRD I also added Article 24b to the LPD which, in acknowledging that public-offer prospectuses which are published and distributed in advance of an application for admission to listing, may be drawn up in accordance with the LPD and so may be subject to mutual recognition, extends the utility of public-offer documents and moves the Community closer to an integrated disclosure regime. This original version of Article 24b as introduced by the MRD I is now of only historical interest, as it was to be amended by MRD II to reflect the adoption of the POD and the introduction of a harmonized regime for public-offer prospectuses.

(f) *Co-operation between the Competent Authorities*

The success of the nascent mutual recognition structure depended in large part on the degree of co-operation between the competent authorities.[218]

---

[218] ECOSOC summed up the position neatly, stating that 'close and active cooperation, consultation and collaboration is essential to the harmonious operation of the principle, introduced by the Directive, of the mutual recognition of the validity and quality of the powers exercised by such authorities': n 209 above, 18.

The LPD's co-operation procedures were substantially revamped by the MRD I which introduced a new co-operation mechanism (Article 24(c) (SCD, Articles 106 and 40).

Predictably, Article 24c(1) (SCD, Article 106) imposes the basic requirement that competent authorities co-operate wherever necessary for the purpose of carrying out their duties and exchange any information required for that purpose. Article 24c(2) and (3) (SCD, Article 40(1) and (2)) introduces slightly more sophisticated consultation and co-operation requirements in certain specified circumstances. Article 24c(2) tracks Article 22(2) of the POD (section 6.7 above). Under Article 24c(3), particular co-operation requirements are imposed to deal with the position of an issuer whose applications to listing is not made 'simultaneously or within a short interval', but who has made an application for admission to official listing in respect of the same securities in another Member State within the previous six months. In such cases, the competent authorities to which the application for listing is made are to contact the competent authorities which have already admitted the securities to official listing and, 'as far as is possible', exempt the issuers of the securities in question from the requirement to prepare new listing particulars, 'subject to any need for updating, translation or the issue of supplements in accordance with the requirements of the Member State concerned' (Article 24c(3)).

Under Article 25, the competent authorities are, as part of the listing-particulars regime, subject to secrecy obligations (SCD, Article 107) in that all persons employed or previously employed by them are subject to professional secrecy requirements, but they are not precluded from exchanging information as provided for in the Directive. Any information exchanged is covered by the professional-secrecy obligation imposed on the staff of the receiving authority and may be used only in the performance of the authority's duties or in the context of administrative appeals or legal proceedings in relation to such performance.

(g) *Reciprocity and Non-Member States*

The mutual recognition provisions may, by means of agreements concluded by the Community, be extended to listing particulars drawn up and approved in accordance with the rules of non-Member States, on the basis of reciprocity.[219] The rules must, however, give investor protection equivalent to that afforded by the LPD, even where the rules differ.

---

[219] Art. 25a (SCD, Art. 41).

IV.8.3 *Stage 2: Mutual Recognition of Public-offer Prospectuses*

IV.8.3.1 *The POD and Mutual Recognition*

As previously outlined, the mutual recognition of disclosure documents first emerged as a tool for encouraging the creation of a European capital market during the negotiations on the POD. Its mutual recognition provisions for public-offer prospectuses complement those of the MRD I for listing particulars.

IV.8.3.2 *Identification of the Competent Authority*

The importance of providing an approval mechanism for public-offer prospectuses becomes apparent in the context of mutual recognition. Under Article 20, where public offers are made in respect of the same transferable securities either 'simultaneously or within a short interval of one another' in two or more Member States and where a public-offer prospectus is drawn up in accordance with Article 7, 8, or 12 (that is, drawn up in accordance with the LPD and subject to prior scrutiny by a competent authority) the competent authority responsible for approving the prospectus is that of the Member State where the issuer has its registered office, when the public offer or the application for admission to listing is made in that State (Article 20(1)). Where that Member State does not provide for the prior scrutiny of public-offer prospectuses, which can arise where the securities are not to be listed, the person making the public offer must choose the supervisory authority from another Member State in which the public offer is made and which provides in general for the prior scrutiny of prospectuses (Article 20(2)).

IV.8.3.3 *The Mutual Recognition Mechanism*

Once a prospectus has been approved under Article 20, it must (under Article 21(1)), subject to any translation requirements, be recognized as complying with the laws of the other Member States in which the same transferable securities are offered to the public, simultaneously, or within a short interval of one another, without being subject to further approval or additional information requirements in those Member States. Under Article 21(4) Member States may choose to restrict the application of the mutual-recognition principle to issuers whose registered offices are situated in a Member State.

As with the MRD I, the recognizing Member States may impose additional disclosure requirements specific to the market of the country in which the offer is taking place, concerning, in particular, income-tax requirements, the issuer's paying agents in the Member State, and the manner in which notices to investors are publicized (Article 21(1)). In addition, the limitations as set out in the MRD I apply with respect to mutual recognition where the approving competent authority granted derogations and exemptions permitted under the POD (Article 21(2)). Tracking the equivalent requirement of the MRD I, Article 21(3) provides that the person making the public offer must communicate to the bodies designated by the other Member States in which the public offer is to be made the prospectus which it intends to use in that Member State. This prospectus must be the same as the one approved by the competent authority determined under Article 20.

IV.8.3.4 *Co-operation Between Competent Authorities and Reciprocity*

Article 22 tracks Article 24c of the MRD I (SCD, Articles 106 and 40).[220] As with the MRD I, under Article 24 the Community can enter into agreements with non-Member States to provide for the mutual recognition of prospectuses drawn up and approved in accordance with the rules of a non-member State, as long as the applicable rules provide equivalent protection for investors.

IV.8.3.5 *Mutual Recognition for all Public-offer Prospectuses?*

The degree of mutual recognition introduced for public-offer prospectuses is not entirely comprehensive. Mutual recognition is extended only to prospectuses prepared in accordance with the LPD and approved by a designated competent authority. Prospectuses prepared and published in accordance with Article 11 of the POD do not benefit from mutual recognition. Where a Member State does not provide for a public-offer prospectus to be prepared in accordance with the LPD under Article 12, mutual recognition will not apply. Nonetheless, with the POD, the disclosure regime becomes more sophisticated, in that it moves towards becoming an integrated scheme where the two major disclosure documents, the listing particulars and the public-offer prospectus, can be used interchangeably once they have been subject to a process of prior scrutiny. This move towards a single disclosure document is taken a stage further in the now consolidated MRD II.

IV.8.4 *Stage 3: A Single Disclosure Document*

IV.8.4.1 *Background*

The roots of the MRD II lie in the POD which permits issuers to prepare public-offer prospectuses in accordance with the LPD. Given that public-offer

---

[220] Apart from Art. 24c(3) (SCD, Art. 40(2)).

prospectuses which conform to the requirements of the LPD are subject to mutual recognition as public-offers prospectuses under Articles 20 and 21 of the POD when the public offers in different Member States are made within short intervals of one another, it was a logical step from there to propose that such prospectuses also be mutually recognized as listing particulars, where admission to stock exchange listing is requested within a short time of the public offer.[221]

The MRD II was proposed by the Commission in 1989.[222] Comments from ECOSOC and the Parliament[223] were uncontroversial and the MRD II was adopted in April 1990. It was to be implemented by the Member States by 17 April 1991.

IV.8.4.2 *The Mutual-recognition Mechanism*

The MRD II simply replaces the original version of Article 24b of the LPD with a new Article 24b (SCD, Article 39). It provides that where an application for admission to official listing has been made in one or more Member States and the securities have been the subject of a public-offer prospectus drawn up and approved in accordance with Article 7, 8, or 12 of the POD in the three months preceding the application for admission to listing, the public-offer prospectus shall be recognized as listing particulars in the Member State in which the application for admission to official listing is made, without any further approval requirements or additional information requirements. The recognizing Member State may, however, impose translation requirements and require that the prospectus include information specific to the market of the Member State of admission, concerning, as with the other mutual recognition provisions, the income-tax system, the issuer's paying agents in that Member State, and the way in which notices to investors are to be published.

---

[221] MRD II, recitals 1 and 2. In its Explanatory Memorandum to the MRD II Proposal, COM(89)133 at para 4, the Commission reported that in the course of the Council discussions on the POD 'it became clear that the majority of Member States felt that a public offer prospectus complying with Article 7, 8 or 12 of the Directive should be mutually recognised not only for the purposes of public offers in host Member States but also for the purposes of admission to official stock exchange listing there'.

[222] COM(89)133 [1989] OJ C101/13.

[223] [1989] OJ C201/5 and [1989] OJ C304/34 (first Parliament reading under the co-operation procedure) and [1990] OJ C28/409 (second Parliament reading under the co-operation procedure), respectively.

IV.8.5 *The Eurolist Directive*[224]

IV.8.5.1 *Introduction*

Despite the advances made by the three mutual-recognition directives, considerable regulatory obstacles remained. This was of particular concern in the case of cross-border listings as at the time (although, as discussed in Chapter III section 5.1 above, the changed securities-trading market environment may reduce the incidence of cross-border and multiple listings) the assumption was that 'cross-border listing is one of the available means of making . . . interpenetration of [securities markets] a reality'.[225] For one thing, the time constraints within which the mutual-recognition principle operated restricted its utility. Issuers seeking official listing in another Member State some time after an initial listing were still required to produce detailed listing particulars despite the fact that, by virtue of an earlier official listing elsewhere in the Community, significant information concerning the issuer was already in the public domain. In such circumstances, particularly given the Efficient Capital Markets Hypothesis (although it is not discussed in the preparatory materials), the need to produce listing particulars 'to ensure the provision of information which is sufficient and as objective as possible for actual or potential security-holders'[226] was less convincing.

Interestingly, at this point it is the securities industry, rather than the Commission, which appears to drive the further development of the disclosure system. The Eurolist project attempted to alleviate the difficulties caused by the fact that mutual recognition does not apply to the now consolidated Admission Directive and to facilitate multiple admissions by blue-chip issuers to listing on the basis of a single listing document. It was based on the standardization of listing conditions and continuing obligations between the participating Eurolist stock exchange authorities who would agree to grant listings on the basis of a good-conduct certificate granted by the issuer's home authorities. Issuers seeking admission to Eurolist were required to have been listed on a participating stock exchange and to be seeking a secondary listing on, at a minimum, two other stock exchanges, and to have had a market capitalization of at least 1 billion euro.[227] The instigator of Eurolist, the Federation of European Stock Exchanges, suggested that the

---

[224] See generally Edwards, V, 'Taking Stock—A Stop Closer to Cross-Border Listing' (1995) 16 *The Company Lawyer* 54.

[225] Pre-consolidation Preamble to the Eurolist Directive, recital 2.

[226] LPD, recital 4 (SCD, recital 11).

[227] One commentator described its potential (which would not, in the event, be realized) as follows: 'aimed at simplifying the multilisting of the largest, most actively traded European companies in European host markets. The project may be the first step towards greater integration': Smith, W, 'The French View of Cross-Border Securities Offerings 'in Oditah, F (ed), *The Future for the Global Securities Market—Legal and Regulatory Aspects* (1996) 199, 202.

Commission examine the feasibility of simplifying the requirements for cross-border listing and, in particular, whether the requirement to publish full listing particulars for all official listings could be reassessed. Accepting that Eurolist companies were generally well-known, were selected only if, *inter alia*, they were in full conformity with their obligations to provide information to investors in the Member States where they were listed, that such information was widely reported and available, and that the lengthy procedures and costs associated with the publication of listing particulars would be rationalized, the Commission agreed with the Federation's position and proceeded with a proposal 'to take care of the concerns expressed by the securities industry'.[228] Although the Commission succeeding in adopting the necessary revisions to the disclosure regime, ironically, the Eurolist project was not a success and folded in 1997.

IV.8.5.2 *The Eurolist Directive*

The now consolidated Eurolist Directive[229] introduced a significant amendment to the LPD by adding a new Article 6(4) (SCD, Article 23(4)) which gives Member States the option to exempt issuers seeking admission of their securities to official listing from the obligation to produce listing particulars (producing instead a simplified set of documents) where the same securities are already officially listed in another Member State for at least three years. If Member States choose to exercise this option, the need even for mutual recognition is obviated as the basic obligation to produce listing particulars is removed.

---

[228] COM(92)566, 5. But the Commission also pointed out that while 'the EUROLIST project and the proposal aim at simplifying the cross-border listing procedures in the Community of those companies which are most likely to be interested in cross-border listing, i.e. companies of high quality, large size and international standing already listed in the Community, it must be kept in mind that EUROLIST and the proposal are different things, independent of each other and not conceived as alternatives': ibid. In particular, the Commission noted at 6 that while Eurolist was designed to cover multi-listing of shares in a minimum number of Member States, the proposal would apply when cross-border listing was sought for any type of security on just one or several exchanges.

[229] The Commission proposal is at [1993] OJ C23/6; Explanatory Memorandum at COM(92)566. ECOSOC's comments on that proposal are at [1993] OJ C161/31 and those of the Parliament at PE 177-122, Minutes of the Meeting of the sitting of Wednesday, 15 Dec 1993, Apr 1993 and Dec 1993, respectively. An amended version of the proposal taking into account the views expressed during the consultation process as well as the modifications required by the adoption of the co-decision procedure under Art. 189b (now Art. 251 EC) was presented in Feb 1994 ([1994] OJ C88/3, Explanatory Memorandum at COM(94)33) and was quickly followed by the opinion of the Parliament under the co-decision procedure ([1994] OJ C20/78 (first reading) and [1994] OJ C128/163 (second reading)). The Council's common position is at [1994] OJ C137/6. The Directive was adopted in May 1994 and could be implemented by the Member States (if they chose to avail themselves of the optional exemptions it contained) at any time after its publication.

The basic rationale for the Directive and the revision to the LPD, as expressed in the lengthy Preamble (not all of which has been replicated in the SCD), is to accelerate the interpenetration of securities markets in the Community by adapting existing legislative measures to new market needs and realities (recitals 6 and 14). The reduction in disclosure obligations for issuers benefiting from the Directive's cross-border listing exemption is justified by reference to the characteristics of cross-border issuers. The most likely candidates for cross-border listing and the Directive's exemption are stated to be companies which have already been listed in the Community for some time, are of high quality and international standing and in relation to which, as a result, information is widely circulated and available (recital 10) (SCD, recital 20). Although the Directive does not contain conditions on the type of issuer which may benefit from the Directive's exemptions, Recital 12 (SCD, recital 22) urges that Member States 'may find it useful' to establish non-discriminatory minimum quantitative criteria, such as market capitalization, which issuers must fulfil to be eligible for exemption.

IV.8.5.3 *Scope of the Exemption*

Article 6(4) (SCD, Article 23(4)) contains five conditions which are designed to ensure that sufficient information to assess the securities in question is available to the investing public, notwithstanding that the issuer benefiting from the exemption is not required to publish listing particulars. First, under Article 6(4)(a) (SCD, Article 23(4)(a)) the securities, shares, or certificates representing shares for which admission is sought must have been officially listed in another Member State for not less than three years before the application for admission to official listing. Secondly, under Article 6(4)(b) (SCD, Article 23(4)(b)) the competent authorities of the Member States or States in which the securities in question are officially listed must have confirmed, to the satisfaction of the competent authority of the Member State in which admission to listing is sought, that during the three years (or, where the securities have been listed for less than three years, during the entire period the securities have been listed) the issuer has complied with all the requirements concerning information and admission to listing imposed by the 'Community Directives on companies the securities of which are officially listed'. Thirdly, Article 6(4)(c) (SCD, Article 23(4)(c)) imposes limited disclosure requirements which fall well short of the detailed requirements of the now consolidated LPD.[230] The disclosure required, which must be published

---

[230] The emphasis on minimizing the disclosure burden on cross-border issuers can be seen in the Commission's assertion that '[a]ll such documents can easily and relatively cheaply be supplied by the issuer' and that 'the amount of information requested under this point is necessarily short because otherwise another listing prospectus would be created': Explanatory Memorandum to the original proposal, n 229 above, 9.

in the manner stipulated for the publication of listing particulars, includes (i) a document containing certain specified information;[231] (ii) the latest annual report, the latest audited accounts, and the issuer's latest half-yearly statement for the year in question, where it has already been published; (iii) any listing particulars, prospectus, or equivalent document published by the issuer in the twelve months preceding the application for admission to official listing; and (iv) (unless it has already been provided in the documents required under (i), (ii), and (iii)) the composition of the company's administrative, management, and supervisory bodies and the functions performed by individual members, general information about capital, the current situation on the basis of the latest information communicated to the issuer under the (now consolidated) SSD, and any reports concerning the last published accounts by the official auditors required by the national law of the Member State where the issuer's registered office is situated. The fourth condition relates to the publication of the required information. Article 6(4)(d) (SCD, Article 23(4)(d)) provides that the notices, bills, posters, and other documents announcing the admission of the securities to listing and indicating the essential characteristics of the securities, as well as all other documents relating to the admission of the securities and intended for publication by the issuer or on his behalf, must state that the information required under Article 6(4)(c) exists, and indicate where it is being or will be published as required by Article 20 of the LPD (SCD, Article 98). Finally, under Article 6(4)(e) (SCD, Article 23(4)(e)) the information required under Article 6(4)(c) and the documents referred to in Article 6(4)(d) must be sent to the competent authorities before being made available to the public.

This exemption from the obligation to publish listing particulars is only an option, which may be exercised by Member States. Issuers otherwise fulfilling the conditions of the Directive may not avail themselves of the exemption unless the Member State in question has implemented the Directive.

While the Eurolist proposal folded, the basic principle of streamlining disclosure to reflect information already in the public domain has re-appeared in a more sophisticated manner in the recent proposals to amend the issuer disclosure regime.

IV.9 BEYOND MUTUAL RECOGNITION: RADICAL REFORM

4.9.1 *The Failure of Mutual Recognition*

Notwithstanding the detailed legislative framework, mutual recognition is widely regarded as having failed, with fewer than two or three issuers a year

---

[231] The Explanatory Memorandum to the original proposal makes it clear that these requirements are truncated versions of the equivalent requirements in the LPD: ibid, 10.

attempting to use the regime.[232] The implications are perhaps most pronounced for public offers;[233] indeed, as has been noted in Chapter III section 5.1 above, the extent to which the now consolidated LPD's
mutual-recognition regime, which is directed towards multiple official listings, will be relevant in the rapidly evolving EC trading market can be questioned. The insistence of many Community competent authorities on full
translation of the entire approved prospectus or listing particulars is particularly burdensome[234] and restricts the mutual-recognition regime in practice to only the largest of issuers, while the requirement to include local
information with respect to taxation, paying agents, and notification procedures can also represent a significant obstacle. The brunt of these difficulties
falls on the economically critical small and medium-sized unlisted issuers,
who are increasingly relying on equity finance to fund growth and who are
often forced for cost reasons to limit their flotations to one Member State.[235]
They can, admittedly, rely on the POD's exemption regime to avoid the
prospectus requirement. However, many of the exemptions are very specific
and relate to particular securities and specific transactions.[236] Of more general use are the possibilities available under the POD for making private
placements with institutional investors in order to raise capital in other
Member States.[237] Reliance on private placements with institutional
investors results in the exclusion of retail investors, however,[238] and may
prejudice liquidity in the securities. Further, the scope of exemptions can be

---

[232] See, eg, Gros and Lanoo, n 148 above, 129–30. The International Primary Markets
Association has also expressed concern that the mutual-recognition regime is not capable of
delivering an integrated, efficient integrated market.

[233] The 1999 and 2000 Deutsche Telekom pan-Community public offering represents the
exception rather than the rule. See also the 1998 Treasury Public Offers Consultation
Document which pointed to the very low incidence of 'regular pan-European offers of securities': n 178 above, 1 and 18. It found that even where companies make an initial offer of shares
in tandem with the quotation of those shares on a public market in a Member State (such as
AIM), they do not regularly offer their securities throughout the rest of the EU.

[234] Some Member States do, however, accept English-language prospectuses.

[235] The 1998 Treasury Public Offers Consultation Document reported trenchantly that 'the
transaction costs of using the mutual recognition procedure are an expensive and cumbersome
hurdle which very few offerors of securities find worth surmounting. For each additional jurisdiction of offer, the offeror may be required to provide a new translation, a reformatting of the
prospectus and additional information specific to the country (together with any associated
legal advice). In the case of listed securities, there may be (but should not be) complications in
accommodating the offer to the listing rules of the 'host' State. The result is that there is a considerable cost at the margin of extending the offer to each additional country. Given the largely
fixed nature of these transaction costs in relation to the size of the offer, these costs are felt disproportionately by small and medium-sized enterprises': n 178 above, 18.

[236] See sect. 6.4.1 and 6.4.2 above.

[237] See ECOSOC's opinion on the Commission's Communication on European Capital
Markets for Small and Medium-Sized Issuers—Prospects and Potential Obstacles to Progress
[1998] OJ C235/13, para 3.2.9.

[238] Although, under certain conditions, the Euro-securities exemption does allow for sales
on to retail investors. See sect. 6.4.1 above.

unclear. The Euro-securities exemption (one of the more significant of the exemptions), for example, has been implemented in varying ways by the Member States with certain Member States making reliance on the exemption difficult. As a result, it has been reported that the exemption is not widely used in practice.[239] The power of Member States to refuse mutual recognition where the original approval contained exemptions from the requirements of the applicable directive is also problematic. In addition, although, where a Member State does not require that a prospectus be approved on a public offer of securities, an issuer may request the Member State to approve the prospectus to trigger the disclosure regime's mutual-recognition provisions (POD, Article 12) and then use the prospectus in those Member States where a prospectus is required for the type of public offer in question, Member States are not required to provide this facility.[240] Overall, the regulatory burdens which persist reveal that 'the day to day functioning of the mutual recognition of prospectuses shows that there is a need for modernisation and enhanced flexibility. The extension of an offer or a listing to the various EEA States [including the EC Member States] proves to be complex and sometimes is an obstacle to real pan-European strategies'.[241] At a time when the market for initial public offerings is growing as never before,[242] the mutual-recognition regime is widely acknowledged to be failing the market-place.

The disclosure regime is also out of step with market practices with respect to capital-raising operations which are structured on access to securities-trading markets. The foundation measure, the now consolidated LPD, addresses the listing particulars required for admission to official listing. Since its adoption, the securities-trading market environment has changed drastically, with high-tech and innovative growth companies now being traded on second-tier or non-official securities trading markets (such as the Neuer Markt) and with pan-EC markets such as NASDAQ Europe becoming increasingly significant. Indeed, on the regulatory front EC securities regulation has moved on to focus securities-trading market regulation on 'regulated markets'[243] (a status acquired by the Alternative Investment Market (AIM), Tradepoint, and NASDAQ Europe, for example) rather than on traditional stock exchanges and official lists. The Official List focus of the current regime, however, means that Member States are free 'to decide which

---

[239] 1998 Treasury Public Offers Consultation Document, n 178 above, 21–2.

[240] ECOSOC has noted that certain competent authorities will not issue a certificate verifying that they have approved a prospectus: n 237 above, para 3.4.1.2.3.

[241] FESCO, A *'European Passport'* for *Issuers*, A Report for the EU Commission (2000) (the FESCO Issuer Passport Commission Paper), FESCO/00/138b.

[242] In 2000, eg, more initial public offerings were launched on EC securities markets than on the US market.

[243] Ch. XI sect. 6.3 below.

disclosure is required [for these regulated markets] which has implications for the possibility of offering these securities cross border'.[244] Any movement to impose undifferentiated harmonized requirements on second-tier markets runs the risk, however, of prejudicing the flexibility and lower costs of these regimes[245] which makes them attractive to start up, and innovative technology companies in particular, unless, arguably, some attempt is made to carve out a lighter regime for these markets.

Given that the disclosure regime is event-specific and involves the preparation and approval of lengthy disclosure documents on an application for admission to official listing or when a public offer is made, it is slow and cumbersome and not sensitive to the requirements of issuers who make repeated calls on the capital markets. As market conditions can change rapidly in the course of the preparation and approval of the disclosure document, repeat issuers can be hindered in taking advantage of favourable market conditions.

Market integration and the development of a deep and liquid pan-EC market is not only prejudiced by the difficulties faced by issuers. The inbuilt home bias of retail investors, cultural factors, and language difficulties already militate against pan-EC investment activity by these investors. The disclosure regime might be regarded as aggravating the problems which a hesitant Community retail investor base generates for market integration. Investor protection and thereby investor confidence (and, based on accepted wisdom, investor activity across the market-place) is not, arguably, well-served by a disclosure regime based on detailed, event-specific prospectuses supplemented by a limited ongoing disclosure regime[246] which applies, for the most part, to officially listed securities.[247] An integrated system which ensures that an initial disclosure document is updated or supplemented by annual disclosure and on each subsequent occasion on which the capital markets are accessed would ensure a more regular supply of information to the market and investors than is supplied through the current rather spas-

---

[244] Commission proposal on the prospectus to be published when securities are offered to the public or admitted to trading, COM(2001)280 (containing the Prospectus Proposal and the Explanatory Memorandum), 3. See further sect. 9.3 below.

[245] The London Stock Exchange's AIM, eg, does not require that disclosure documents be pre-vetted and seeks to deliver investor protection via risk warnings and the ongoing disclosure required when an issuer is admitted to the market. This looser structure is designed to allows AIM to grant issuers greater certainty over the timing of their admission and reduce both the time-to-market and preparation costs. See the London Stock Exchange's response to the Commission Prospectus Proposal, Comments from the London Stock Exchange on the Proposed Prospectus Directive, Aug 2001 (the LSE Comment Document), paras 2.5–2.6.

[246] The investor-protection-driven reforms to the ongoing disclosure regime are outlined in sect. 9.4 below.

[247] However, since the revisions made by the Insider Dealing Directive, the now consolidated Admission Directive's material disclosure requirements also apply to securities admitted to trading on a regulated market as defined by the ISD.

modic system.[248] As previously noted, wide divergences exist across the EC as regards the information which must be disclosed to the market, with more information often available on EC companies through the US ongoing disclosure regime than can be found in the EC market-place.[249] Disclosure documents also vary in format, making comparability difficult (a problem exacerbated by variations in accounting standards: see section 10 below). More generally, the failure to define 'public offer' has led to disparities in levels of investor protection across the Community, in that the same offering may be treated as a private placement and so as exempt from the requirement to produce a prospectus in one Member State and as a public offer subject to prospectus requirements in another.

IV.9.2 *Movements Towards a Full Disclosure Passport and Shelf Registration*

IV.9.2.1 *The FSAP*

The pre-FSAP 1998 Communication highlighted as an imperative for action the elimination of any remaining fragmentation in the Community capital market and the completion of the establishment of 'deep and liquid European capital markets which serve both issuers and investors better'.[250] It recognized that further action was needed to ensure that issuers had easy access to the Community capital markets on competitive terms. In particular, with respect to disclosure it expressed concern that national authorities were still imposing demanding and differing disclosure requirements on issuers, which were ultimately discouraging issuers from engaging in cross-border issues to the detriment of both capital formation and investor choice, despite the now consolidated LPD and the POD.[251]

In response, the 1999 FSAP[252] contains proposals to amend the relevant legislation in order to provide for a single 'passport' for issuers (akin to the passport available to providers of investment services) and to facilitate repeat access by issuers to the securities markets via a shelf-registration mechanism based on the issuer's annual reports.[253] It also contains a commitment to

[248] FESCO (now the Committee of European Securities Regulators) has noted that 'the full prospectus is an exhaustive document that is not adapted to the needs of all kinds of investors. A document with tailored information will better suit the needs of the various categories of investors': FESCO, *A 'European Passport' for Issuers*, Consultation Paper (2000) (the FESCO Issuer Passport Consultation Paper), Fesco/99-098e, 4. Its shelf-registration system (and the Commission's proposals in this regard) is based on requiring the production of a number of separate disclosure documents containing different types of disclosure.

[249] Initial Lamfalussy Report, n 208 above, 6.

[250] Financial Services: Building a Framework for Action, COM(1998)625 (the 1998 Communication), 1.

[251] Ibid, 6.   [252] N 61 above.

[253] It notes at 4 that 'producing multiple sets of official documentation before issuers can offer securities in other Member States is costly and undoubtedly inhibits pan-EU activity. The

encourage closer co-operation between securities supervisors, who are the gatekeepers of the mutual-recognition scheme.

Since the adoption of the FSAP, the Lisbon European Council has high-lighted the widest possible access to investment capital on an EU-wide basis by means of a single passport for issuers as a matter of critical importance for the completion of the internal market in financial services. In the Second FSAP Progress Report, particular attention was paid to reform of the mutual-recognition regime.[254] The Commission reported rather bluntly that disclosure directives have not worked, citing as obstacles: the tendency of competent authorities to limit the scope of mutual recognition to narrowly defined classes of securities; frequent demands for additional information; concerns that minimum disclosure requirements were insufficient; the unsuitability of traditional systems for listings and public offers of securities for issuers wishing to raise successive instalments of capital; and the failure of the disclosure regime to deal with investor needs for regular updating of market information.

IV.9.2.2 *The Lamfalussy Report*

As previously discussed in Chapter II, the Wise Men appointed to review the state of European securities markets strongly endorsed the market-finance model and called for rapid movement to complete the internal capital/securities market.[255] The unsatisfactory state of the disclosure regime was also given prominence, with the Wise Men identifying as a priority the adoption of a single-prospectus system for issuers and of a mandatory shelf-registration system. They painted a bleak picture of the disclosure regime as a market-integration mechanism: 'the EU passport for issuers is still not a reality. There is not even an agreed definition of a public offer of securities, with the result that the same operation is analyzed as a private placement in some Member States and in others. The current system discourages firms from raising capital on a European basis and therefore from real access to a large, liquid and integrated financial market.'[256]

It is the Lamfalussy Report's decision-making model, however, that is likely to make a permanent impression on EC securities regulation and, in particular, on the disclosure regime. As is further discussed in Chapter XV, it recommended that a bifurcated approach be taken to law-making in order

application of national rules has thwarted the mutual recognition of prospectuses which the 1989 Public-Offer Prospectus Directive aimed to achieve.'

[254] Progress on Financial Services, Second Report, COM(2000)336 (the 2nd FSAP Progress Report).

[255] Initial Lamfalussy Report. n 208 above, and the Final Report of the Committee of Wise Men on the Regulation of European Securities Markets, Feb 2001 (the Lamfalussy Report).

[256] Initial Lamfalussy Report, n 208 above, 16.

to streamline and speed up the current cumbersome procedure. In outline,[257] it proposed that framework principles be adopted according to standard legislative procedures (termed level 1), but that technical details and the rules necessary to adapt measures to market developments be adopted by the Commission via comitology procedures (comitology procedures require, in this instance, that the Commission be supervised by a European Securities Committee and assisted by a Committee of European Securities Regulators) (termed level 2). This model was endorsed by the Stockholm European Council in May 2001 and both committees have been established. The new disclosure regime (section 9.3 below) is based on this model.

IV.9.2.3 *FESCO*

Outside (until summer 2001) the EC institutional structure, FESCO (now the Committee of European Securities Regulators and within the EC institutional structure) has played a major role in this third evolutionary phase of the disclosure regime by laying the groundwork for the new issuer passport and shelf-registration regime.[258] Its issuer passport is based on creating 'the opportunity for an issuer to make European public offers to all European investors or apply for listing in a manner that simplifies regulatory compliance for issuers while at the same time ensuring investor protection'.[259] A marked emphasis on retail investor protection can be observed in the FESCO proposals. Its European passport regime is designed to permit issuers to access the single capital market 'with little more effort than is now necessary to obtain approval for a domestic offering and minimise the risk that an issue gets to the market after market conditions have changed'. Investors would 'have access to securities offered by other European countries [and] have the same information throughout the European market at best practice level'.[260] In particular, the shelf-registration system would ensure that investors 'have various levels of documentation tailored according to their needs [and] obtain annually updated documentation on an issuer at any moment and not only when an offering or a listing is made'.[261]

---

[257] See further Ch. XV sect. 2.5.3 below.

[258] The FESCO Issuer Passport Consultation Paper, n 248 above, and the FESCO Issuer Passport Commission Paper, n 241 above. Although these proposals are non-binding they have been influential in the development of the new regime, with much of the preparatory work for the Commission's issuer passport proposal being carried out by FESCO. On FESCO see Ch. XV sect. 2.5.2 below. In July 2001 it published a follow-up paper considering (i) the 'building block' approach to disclosure and the use of schedules in order to streamline disclosure requirements for new financial products; (ii) *pro forma* financial disclosure and other financial information (including, significantly, profit forecasts and their treatment); and (iii) the disclosure required as to the modalities of the offering (such as pricing, lock-up agreements, and acceptance agreements).

[259] FESCO Issuer Passport Commission Paper, n 241 above, 1.   [260] Ibid, 12.

[261] FESCO Issuer Passport Consultation Paper, n 248 above, 7.

Its European passport is based on permitting issuers to extend their offers or apply for listings of their securities (both equity and debt) in other Member States without being required 'to produce duplicative sets of documentation or respond to numerous and additional national requirements'.[262] FESCO has suggested that once a set of documents has been reviewed by the relevant competent authority in the home Member State or the State of the issuer's primary listing in accordance with the enhanced disclosure requirements proposed by FESCO (based on the 1998 IOSCO Disclosure Standards), those documents would be valid for other jurisdictions subject only to 'notification' to the host Member State authority; mutual recognition would be replaced by simple notification. The notification would be accompanied by the approved prospectus and an 'approval certificate', dated not earlier than three months before the notification was made. Resolution of the multiple language problem is, of course, central to the success of any mechanism designed to streamline the disclosure process. FESCO's approach is to require issuers to produce a summary of the prospectus in the language(s) of the Member State in which the offering takes place or listing is sought, where that is different from the language in which the prospectus is prepared. The summary would provide 'in particular to retail investors, immediate succinct information on the most relevant aspects of the issuer and the proposed operation in a concise format [which] enables investors to make an informed assessment on the situation of the issuer and on the operation itself'.[263] The home authority would verify that the content was consistent with the standard set by FESCO members and approve its contents. Responsibility for the translation would remain with the issuer.

FESCO has also suggested the imposition of a single format on all prospectuses which would assume a common approach to each disclosure item. Investors would, as a result, be in a position to access and compare information more easily. Given the failure of the current regime to engage with risk warnings in any detail, it is of some interest that FESCO has suggested that, were a single format to be used for all prospectuses, care be taken to ensure that facts which would be of particular importance to investors be given prominence at the beginning of the documents.[264] FESCO has also proposed more drastic alterations to the current format of issuer disclosure and endorsed the shelf-registration technique. It has suggested that the disclosure document be split into two documents, one containing basic information concerning the issuer (the registration document) and the other setting out specific information concerning the securities to be offered/listed (the securities note). The registration document could be registered each year by the issuer after the approval of the financial statements. The avail-

---

[262] FESCO Issuer Passport Consultation Paper, n 248 above, 7.
[263] FESCO Issuer Passport Commission Paper, n 241 above, 6.   [264] Ibid.

ability of these documents to retail investors would be required, although FESCO has supported the separate circulation of the registration document, the securities note, and the summary, as long as all documents would be available on request without additional costs. It has also supported the circulation of the documents forming the prospectus in electronic form.

Finally, FESCO has addressed the exemption problem and, in particular, noted that 'the harmonization of the total exemptions and derogations provided for by the present directives is a fundamental issue for the creation of the European passport'.[265] FESCO members have also reached agreement on when a public offer does not take place and a prospectus, accordingly, is not required.

Given the current debate on the extent to which the competent authorities overseeing the disclosure process should be independent of the securities-trading markets in a competitive trading environment, FESCO has noted that any new passport regime depends on mutual confidence between the competent authorities involved. It has recommended, as a result, that care be taken to avoid conflicts of interests and that EC-level measures be adopted in order to deal with standard-setting, supervisory practices, enforcement and sanctioning, and cross-border co-operation.

This influential proposal now forms the basis of the Commission's proposed restructuring of the issuer disclosure regime.

IV.9.3 *The Proposed New Disclosure Regime*

IV.9.3.1 *Objectives, Features, and Treaty Basis*

At the end of May 2001, the Commission finally presented its long-awaited proposal to reform the disclosure regime in light of the developments discussed above.[266] As the proposal has, at the time of writing, just set out on what may be a precarious legislative process, given that it represents the first test of the Lamfalussy Report's streamlined law-making process,[267] only its main features will be outlined here. When and if it comes into force,

---

[265] Ibid, 8.   [266] N 244 above.

[267] Much will depend on how the Parliament reacts to the proposal. Given that the adoption of rules via comitology procedures effectively removes the Parliament from the law-making process (see Ch. XV sect. 2.2.2 below) its agreement on the areas to be devolved to the comitology process (see sect. 9.3.2 below) will be critical. The market-place is also dissatisfied with the proposal. While the market is, in principle, supportive of the single-passport concept (although there is considerable unhappiness concerning the detail of the new regime), initial reaction to the Proposal from the market was not favourable, due in part to what was seen as a failure by the Commission to consult sufficiently widely and to address the issues raised in the submissions requested from the market, even though extensive consultation is at the heart of the Lamfalussy Report's decision-making model: Boland, V, 'Battle looms over Brussels plan for capital markets regulation', *Financial Times*, 11 June 2001. For a robust response from the Commission defending the adequacy of the consultation see *Proposed Prospectus Directive, Frequently Asked Questions*, MARKT F2/HHG/NDB D (2001).

however, the provisions of the now consolidated LPD, MRD I, MRD II, the Eurolist Directive, and the POD will be repealed. Its significance for EC securities regulation's capital-raising and disclosure framework cannot be overstated.

The Proposal is structured around the introduction of an issuer-disclosure passport based on a shelf-registration mechanism which would obviate the need continually to produce major disclosure documents each time an offering is launched or listing application made. It is designed to overhaul the LPD and the POD completely in order to facilitate the widest possible access to investment capital for all issuers, including small and medium-sized enterprises (SMEs). In its Explanatory Memorandum the Commission pointed to the different practices and interpretations across the EC regarding the content and layout of prospectuses, and noted the different methods used and time required to approve disclosure documents. In the absence of reform, it warned that the European financial market would remain fragmented and that 'cross border capital raising will remain the exception, rather than the rule—the antithesis of the logic of the single currency'.[268] The Proposal has five key features: the adoption of enhanced disclosure standards in line with international standards for public offers of securities and admission to trading—the distinction between admission to official listing and admission to other trading markets is thereby removed, and, it appears, a 'one size fits all' approach adopted; the introduction of a registration-document system for issuers whose securities are admitted to trading on a regulated market in order to ensure key issuer information is updated on an annual basis; the possibility for issuers to offer or admit securities to trading on the basis of a simple notification of the prospectus once the prospectus has been approved by the home competent authority; concentration of responsibility in the home competent authority; and extensive use of the comitology process in line with the Lamfalussy Report's findings in developing the regime.

Investor protection is a recurring theme throughout the Proposal. It is clear that investor protection is pursed in the interests of investor confidence. In an unusually clear articulation of the rationale behind the promotion of investor protection at EC level, the Commission stated that 'it is [its] firm belief . . . that increasing investor confidence will deliver significant benefits in terms of lowering the cost of raising capital and at the end of the chain, it will improve job creation and the overall dynamism of the European economy.'[269] The sharper focus on investor protection can be seen most clearly in the deliberate attempts that are made to ensure that the disclosure required in the new regime is tailored to investors' requirements and presented in the format most useful for investors. In this regard, the Proposal marks a major advance on the current regime which makes little attempt to

---

[268] Explanatory Memorandum, n 244 above, 1.   [269] Ibid, 5.

ensure that the much-vaunted connection between disclosure, investor protection, investor confidence, and market interpenetration is actually made.
This more finely tuned approach to disclosure is not only indicative of a
more careful appreciation of how disclosure policy should be managed; it
also chimes with the paradigm shift towards investor protection which can
be observed in the related investment-services regime since the adoption of
the FSAP. More generally, the Proposal also uses disclosure in a considerably more sophisticated manner than previously apparent and in a way
which, given its heightened focus on ongoing disclosure and the updating
of information, suggests a keener appreciation of the effects of disclosure on
market efficiency and price formation. Disclosure aside, the new investor-
protection focus can also be seen in the new advertising rules regime (Article
13 of the Proposal). While the current regime addresses, albeit in a skeletal
manner, the advertising of offers, the Proposal provides that, in order to
ensure common implementation and investor protection, detailed rules be
adopted by the Commission under level 2 comitology procedures (see section
9.3.2). By way of illustration, in its Explanatory Memorandum, the
Commission points to rules setting out guidance on how to advertise the performance of the securities offered without giving retail investors a misleading impression about future gains.[270]

The new regime is based on the passport regime applicable to investment-
service providers and discussed in Chapter VII. Particular features transplanted from the investment-services regime (apart from the basic home
country control/mutual-recognition concept) include the notification obligation and the precautionary-measures principle which allows the host
Member State a degree of supervisory control. The Proposal is, however, a
development on from the investment-services passport. Not only does it not
rely on mutual recognition of minimum standards (detailed rules will flow
from the Proposal via the Lamfalussy Report's decision-making model) but
it harmonizes at a relatively high level of detail the powers which must be
conferred on the competent authority and addresses sanctioning in some
detail. With respect to the latter, Article 23 provides that Member States are
to lay down the rules on 'penalties, including administrative sanctions'
applicable to breaches and requires that sanctions be 'effective, proportionate and dissuasive'. Neither the powers of competent authorities nor sanctioning have been subject to detailed harmonization in EC securities
regulation. Indeed, if the Proposal can be relied on as an indicator of the
future shape of EC securities regulation, the regime is on the verge of being
transformed into a detailed and sophisticated structure which provides considerable operational guidance to the competent authorities supervising the
regime.

[270] Explanatory Memorandum, n 244 above, 12.

The 'basic objective' of the Proposal is 'ensuring the completion of a single securities market' (recital 30). In order to achieve that objective, it tracks the current regime in that it is based on Article 44 EC which provides for the adoption of directives in order to attain the freedom of establishment (see section 3.2.3 above) and Article 95 EC on the adoption of 'measures for the approximation of the provisions laid down by law, regulation or administrative action in Member States which have as their object the establishment and functioning of the internal market'. The removal of the remaining regulatory obstacles to the financing of companies across the EC and the construction of the internal market in securities thus anchors the Proposal to the Treaty. As with the POD and the now consolidated SSD a connection is made between investor protection, investor confidence and the establishment and functioning of the internal market. In a rare example of an explicit focus on investor protection in EC securities regulation, recital 10 to the Proposal states unequivocally that '[o]ne of the objectives of the Directive is to encourage investors' and that, as a result, disclosure should be tailored to reflect the varying characteristics and expertise of investors. Recital 11 goes on to provide that the 'provision of full, appropriate information concerning securities and issuers of such securities promotes the protection of investors . . . such information is an effective means of increasing confidence in securities and thus of contributing to the proper functioning and development of securities markets'. In its *Tobacco Advertising* ruling[271] the Court trenchantly rejected the existence of a general power to regulate the internal market under Article 95 EC, and emphasized that the measure in question must improve the conditions for the establishment and functioning of the internal market; the abstract risk of obstacles or of distortions to competition is not sufficient to activate Article 95. While it is clear that barriers to a single securities market still exist, and that the basis for the Proposal is accordingly sound, whether or not the EC can promote investor confidence under Article 95 in the absence of real regulatory obstacles is less clear.

IV.9.3.2 *The Law-making Model*

The Prospectus Proposal is a landmark measure in that, together with the market-abuse proposal discussed in Chapter XIII section 11.5, it adopts the Lamfalussy Report's decision-making model. The basic rules (or framework principles) are contained in the proposed Directive (level 1 measures), but the fine technical points of the regime (or the non-essential technical measures) are, under Article 22, to be adopted by the Commission under comitology procedures, aided by the European Securities Committee and the Committee of European Securities Regulators (level 2 measures).

---

[271] *Tobacco Advertising* ruling, n 63 above.

Significant control over the substantive detail of the regime is thus delegated to the level 2 procedure including, most significantly, the technical detail needed to develop the disclosure rules (Article 6), but also clarifications and updating of the Directive's definitions (Article 2), clarifications of the exemption regime (Article 3), the incorporation by reference procedure (Article 10), the approval and publication process (Articles 11 and 12), the detail on the advertising rules (Article 13), and rules on third-country issuers (Article 18). A notable feature of the Proposal is the extent to which level 2 powers are granted with respect to supervision of the competent authority's operating methods and, in particular, the adoption of guidance on the management of the approval process (Article 11). In deciding which measures could be left to the level 2 process, the Commission selected areas 'in order to ensure a prompt response to fast changing reality and to ensure proper functioning of the internal market . . . as well as proper protection of retail investors'.[272] In line with the May 2001 Stockholm European Council Resolution which endorsed the Lamfalussy law-making model, the level 2 procedure is subject to deadlines where the measures in question are necessary to ensure the effective operation of the Directive.

IV.9.3.3 *Scope*

The new regime will apply to the prospectus to be published when securities are offered to the public or admitted to trading on a 'regulated market' as defined by the ISD (Article 1). In a major change to the current official-list-focused regime,[273] the distinction between the regime applicable to securities admitted to official listing (the LPD) and securities admitted to trading on markets which do not require official listing (the POD) is removed. Adoption of the admission-to-trading formula is designed to ensure that no loopholes will emerge in the implementation of the Directive. However, as discussed further below, the failure to tailor the disclosure requirements or the pre-vetting condition to fit the features of second-tier markets is likely to generate some controversy.

In a second major change to the current regime and in order to align the disclosure regimes in each Member State, the Prospectus Proposal introduces in Article 2 a definition of a public offer in order to ensure that the current disparities in the imposition of a prospectus requirement, and thus in the treatment of retail investors, are removed.[274] A public offer is now defined as an 'offer, invitation or promotional message, in any form, addressed to

[272] Explanatory Memorandum, n 244 above, 6.

[273] And, it appears, at the request of EC regulators: ibid, 7.

[274] The Commission also noted that it was particularly important that discrepancies in investor protection be avoided given that electronic communications now mean that investors can be reached throughout the EC.: ibid.

the public, whose objective is the sale or subscription of securities including by placing securities through financial intermediaries'.

The Proposal also sets out a new exemptions regime (based on the FESCO exemptions agreement) which, like the public-offer definition, is designed to ensure that a harmonized disclosure regime applies (Article 3). As a result, the Proposal removes the discretion currently enjoyed by the Member States with respect to exemptions which has had such a prejudicial effect on the operation of the mutual-recognition regime. The first group of exemptions concerns offers directed towards particular categories of investor and covers offers to qualified investors (defined by way of a list including credit institutions, investment firms, pensions funds, and other financial institutions), offers addressed to a restricted circle of persons the number of which is below 150 per Member State or below 1,500 in a multinational offer, and offers where the securities offered can be acquired only for a consideration of at least 150,000 euro per investor.[275] Where the securities are subsequently resold to the public, the exemption is lost. As is the case in the current regime, offers of certain types of securities set out in Article 3 (essentially securities offered in exchange for existing securities or securities which result from operations in respect of which equivalent information is or has been made available to the public or to shareholders) are also exempted. Clarifications and adaptations of the terminology and exemptions set out in Article 3 are, in order to take account of developments on the financial markets and to avoid diverging implementations of the exemption regime which could prejudice investor protection, subject to level 2 decision-making.

IV.9.3.4 *The Core Disclosure Obligations*

Under Article 3, Member States are to ensure that any offer of securities to the public within their territories is subject to the publication of a prospectus by the person making the offer. Under Article 4, Member States must ensure that any admission of securities to trading on a regulated market situated or operated within their territories is subject to the availability of a prospectus. In order to encourage multinational trading, Article 4 confirms

---

[275] The London Exchange suggested that the size of offering exemption be set at 500 offerees, regardless of whether the offer is carried out on a single- or multi-jursidictional basis: LSE Comment Document, n 245 above, para 2.10. More generally, and in a reflection of the London Stock Exchange's concerns for second-tier markets, the Proposal's approach to private placements has come under attack by the Euro-bond industry. Participants are concerned that the Proposal's one-size-fits-all approach is not sufficiently tailored to the needs of different markets and different securities, and that Euro-bond offerings (outside the scope of the Proposal's exemptions) would be subject to the same level of detailed disclosure as required of an equity offering to retail investors regardless of the sophistication of the target audience and of the creditworthiness of the issuer: Preston, A, 'Home country rule threat to Eurobond market', *Euromoney*, July 2001, 33.

that the prospectus obligation is satisfied when the issuer has filed the registration document and the securities note (see section 9.3.6 below) with the home competent authority and fulfils the Directive's annual updating-of-disclosure requirement. Regulated markets will thus be required to accept the disclosure documents approved by the issuer's home Member State. Even if multiple listings do not develop, as is often suggested, this provision will nonetheless facilitate issuers who wish to admit their securities to trading (perhaps on a pan-EC trading market) outside their home Member State.

IV.9.3.5 *Enhanced Disclosure Standards*

Operating from the perspective that the now consolidated LPD's disclosure requirements no longer meet the needs of investors in modern global financial markets, the Proposal puts in place a new disclosure code, based on the 1998 IOSCO Disclosure Standards. Under Article 6, the detailed disclosure requirements are to be adopted under level 2 comitology procedures within 180 days of the Directive coming into force. The success of the passport will depend on these standards being put in place quickly, as without them the passport cannot operate. The Article 6 delegation of power to the Commission will thus represent a major test for the Lamfalussy strategy. However, the Commission will be constrained. Not only do the Annexes to the Directive set out the headings in respect of which disclosure requirements are to be adopted, the disclosure requirements are, under Article 6(2), to be in accordance with the 1998 IOSCO Disclosure Standards, albeit adapted, it appears, to reflect the different types of securities offered or admitted to trading as the Standards cover only equities. While the IOSCO Principles reflect 'internationally accepted best practices' (reliance on the IOSCO standards will introduce disclosure of risk factors, related party transactions, corporate governance, and a section on management's discussion and analysis), basing the EC regime on those principles should also mean that documents prepared under the new regime will be acceptable for offerings or admission to trading outside the EC.[276] The benefits of the issuer passport could, in theory, be global, given that the IOSCO standards are designed to promote international mutual acceptance of disclosure documents (albeit only for equities).

By contrast with FESCO's proposals, however, the Prospectus Proposal does not, controversially, appear to be adjusted to alter the disclosure required of SMEs admitted to trading on non-Official List markets. FESCO has suggested that although the disclosure required of SMEs should not be reduced, it should reflect the fact that SMEs can be admitted to regulated markets designed for SMEs on the basis of less rigorous conditions than those

[276] Explanatory Memorandum, n 244 above, 9.

that apply to official listing, which may include a shorter trading record. In such circumstances, FESCO suggested that disclosure items inappropriate to issuers with shorter trading records should be replaced by equivalent information, such as information concerning the issuer's development and the commitment of shareholders to the issuer.[277] Although SMEs are not addressed in the Proposal itself, the annexed impact-assessment form states that, in principle, disclosure standards should not vary according to the size of the issuer. Instead, the prospectus should allow the investor to make a proper assessment of the securities offered or admitted to trading.[278] This feature of the Proposal has generated some resistance from the second-tier market industry and the smaller issuers who use those markets.[279]

IV.9.3.6 *The Proposed Format for Disclosure*

One of the most significant of the many important changes made by the Prospectus Proposal is its drastic restructuring of the format in which issuer disclosure is supplied. The prospectus is to be split into three documents: a registration document which will contain information about the issuer; a securities note containing information on the securities; and a summary note containing a summary of these two documents, which is central to the issuer passport as it is designed to deal with the translation problem (see section 9.3.8 below) (Article 5(4)). The registration document will provide an annual (at least) updating of information to investors (Article 9 requires that

---

[277] FESCO Issuer Passport Consultation Paper, n 248 above, 9.

[278] The Commission noted that the US experience had shown that high levels of disclosure concerning SMEs should improve investor confidence: Impact Assessment Form, para 5.

[279] See the London Stock Exchange's Comment Document, n 245 above, paras 2.3–2.11. It expressed concern that removing the distinction between the official and the second-tier market and requiring approval for all prospectuses 'threatens Europe's secondary markets, including AIM in the UK' (para 2.3). It defended the lighter AIM disclosure regime which, it felt, did not sacrifice regulatory standards (it noted that AIM's failure rate compared favourably with those of other markets) but provided for a flexible regulatory structure for young companies. The Proposal made 'no provision for the range of equity markets which flourish in the UK, supporting companies throughout their life-cycle from private to fully listed' and would, it felt, mean that second-tier markets would be 'virtually impossible to sustain in the framework set out in the Directive' (para 2.7). In order to ensure that a range of markets was available to issuers and investors (who would as a result benefit from the advantages of diversification), it proposed that where issuers raise money in a single jurisdiction, the home Member State should exercise discretion over the need for pre-vetting by the competent authority and that simplified prospectus requirements should be adopted via an exemption process. Considerable resistance has been mounted to the 'one-size-fits-all' approach in the UK, as can be seen from the pages of the *Financial Times*. See, eg, Guerrera, F, and Dickson, M, 'Passport to Discord', *Financial Times*, 22 Nov 2001; Norman, P, and Boland, V, 'LSE Demands Brussels Listens to City Concerns', *Financial Times*, 16 Nov 2001; Letters, *Financial Times*, 16 Nov 2001 (the letter from a group of 56 chairmen, chief executives, and directors of smaller UK companies, claimed that the new regime would cost at least £150,000 a year); the Lex column, *Financial Times*, 16 Nov 2001; and Boland, V, 'Opposition Mounts to EU Securities Directive', *Financial Times*, 7 Sept 2001.

following the first filing it is to be updated on a regular basis by the issuer each year after the approval of the issuer's financial statements) and supplement the current ongoing disclosure regime set out in the now consolidated Admission Directive, IRD, and SSD. It is also designed to allow for a 'fast-track' procedure for new issuers, in that on a new issue only information related to the particular securities offered or admitted to trading will be required, via the securities note and the summary (Article 8). The securities note must, in addition to the items required under Annex III, provide information which would normally be provided in the registration document if there has been a material change or recent development since the registration document was published. The approval process will thus be much quicker for issuers who access the capital markets regularly, as only the securities note will be reviewed. The new regime is, however, likely to generate greater costs for issuers, particularly as they must update the basic registration document whether or not they intend to access the securities markets.

In a sign of the link between disclosure and efficient price formation, this new format is to be mandatory for issuers whose securities are traded on regulated markets (Article 7(1));[280] issuers whose securities are offered to the public but not admitted to trading may continue to use the traditional format (Article 7(2)). The information requirements for each of the registration document, securities note, and summary will be set out in Annexes II, III, and IV, once the detail has been agreed under the level 2 comitology process.

The Proposal also provides in Article 10 for incorporation by reference; the details of the incorporation by reference regime, such as the documents which will be eligible, will be set at level 2. The incorporation-by-reference mechanism allows for the disclosure of information by reference to another document which has already been filed and approved by the home competent authority (Article 10(1)). In an attempt to integrate the disclosure regime further, Article 9 provides that the issuer may use the registration document, which is updated annually, as the basis for the annual report. Not only will this reduce issuers' costs still further, it should also contribute to further harmonization of the annual report required by the EC accounting regime[281] (on accounting disclosure see section 10 below).[282]

---

[280] The London Stock Exchange also expressed reservations on the costs and utility of the registration scheme, arguing that it 'presents an significant additional burden to all companies, but particularly SMEs. It takes no account of the capital raising intentions of the company or the needs of its investor base', and suggested that its use be optional where an offer is made in a single jurisdiction: LSE Comment Document, n 245 above, paras 2.12–2.11.

[281] 4th Company Law Directive 78/660/EEC on the annual accounts of certain types of companies (essentially public and private companies limited by share or by guarantee) [1978] OJ L222/1, Art. 46 and 7th Company Law Directive 83/349/EEC on consolidated accounts [1983] OJ L193/1, Art. 36.

[282] Ferrarini, G, 'Securities Regulation and the Rise of Pan-European Equity Markets: An Overview' in Ferrarini, G, Hopt, K, and Wymeersch, E, Capital *Markets in the Age of the Euro* (forthcoming) (in the context of the parallel FESCO proposal).

Finally on the format of the prospectus, the Proposal's prospectus circulation rules (Article 12) update the current rules and encourage the circulation of prospectuses by means of electronic means of communication, such as the Internet.[283] Under Article 12(1), once the prospectus is approved it is to be filed, in a reflection of technological developments, in an electronic format with the competent authority and must also be made available to the public immediately by the issuer or the offeror. Under Article 12(2) the prospectus is deemed to be made available where it is circulated in a newspaper, made available in the form of a brochure, or made available in electronic form on the issuer's website, in each case in accordance with Article 12(2)'s conditions. In an innovative development, Article 12(2) requires that prospectuses must be published on the competent authority's website. Not only would this ease the burden disclosure represents for issuers, but 'investors would have effective and free access to information on a real-time basis'.[284] The detailed technical rules on the publication and circulation of prospectuses are to be adopted by the Commission under the level 2 comitology procedures.

Although the main importance of the new regime lies in the practical impact it is likely to have on capital raising, it is also of some interest that in relying on shelf registration and incorporation-by-reference techniques, the Commission appears to be implicitly at least accepting the validity of the Efficient Capital Markets Hypothesis (ECMH). Under this hypothesis, there is no need to repeat disclosure each time an offering or an application for admission to trading is made where the information has been supplied through another reporting process, as the information has already been fed through to the market-place.[285] Consistently with the pragmatism of EC securities regulation, the relationship between the new regime and the validity (or otherwise) of the ECMH is not addressed. A concern for adequate investor protection can be seen, however, in Article 10(2), which provides that where information is incorporated by reference a cross-reference list must be provided in order to enable investors to identity specific items of information easily, and in Article 12(4) which provides that the various documents constituting the shelf-registration prospectus can be published

---

[283] Electronic filing is now well-established in the USA under the SEC's EDGAR (Electronic Data Gathering, Analysis and Retrieval System).

[284] Explanatory Memorandum, n 244 above, 5.

[285] In the admittedly different context of the highly complex US mandatory-disclosure regime the SEC has relied on efficient market concepts to justify its integrated and shelf-registration disclosure regime in which the disclosure required on an offer of securities can, for top-tier issuers, be supplied via incorporation by reference techniques: '[the relevant forms] recognise the applicability of the efficient market theory to those companies which provide a steady stream of high quality corporate information to the marketplace and whose corporate information is broadly disseminated': SEC Release No. 33-6499 (1983) para IV(B)(1).

and circulated separately but the documents must be made available, free of charge, according to the Article 12(2) publication arrangements.

IV.9.3.7 *Approving the Passport*

The mechanics of the issuer passport require that all prospectuses be approved by the home Member State authority (Article 11); in this regard, the Proposal represents a significant change from the current system which does not subject all public-offer prospectuses (or the documents required on admission to trading on second-tier markets) to approval, although, of course, pre-vetting is required under the current regime for all prospectuses in respect of which mutual recognition is sought. A particular innovation of the Proposal, however, is to subject the approval process to time guillotines in order to ensure that approval operates smoothly and that the speed benefits of the shelf-registration process are fully realized (Article 11 (2)–(4)). The periods imposed depend on the type of issuer involved. The standard deadline to which the competent authority is subject is fifteen days from submission of the draft prospectus or, where the competent authority finds that the submission is incomplete or requires additional information, fifteen days from the supply of the required information. A forty-day deadline applies where the securities offered are not already admitted to trading and where the issuer will not, as a result, be known to the market-place or the competent authority. The securities note must be approved within seven days of submission. Detailed technical rules with regard to the scrutiny of the prospectus and the adaptation of deadlines in order to take account of developments on financial markets are to be adopted by the Commission in accordance with level 2 comitology procedures. Significantly, given the impact this level 2 delegation could have on the autonomy of competent authorities, the Commission has explained this delegation to level 2 in terms of 'guidance'. It has stated that under the level 2 procedure the Commission will issue guidance on the best practice to be followed by national competent authorities when checking prospectuses and guidance on the relevant deadlines.[286]

IV.9.3.8 *Home Member State Control*

(a) *The Mechanism*

The Prospectus Proposal replaces the current mutual-recognition system with a simple notification and home Member State-control system, similar to that which applies to investment firms under the ISD. At the core of the new system is the ousting of host Member States from the prospectus-review

---

[286] Explanatory Memorandum, n 244 above, 11.

process and, in particular, the ban placed on host Member States from requesting additional information. Under Article 2 the home Member State is defined as the Member State where the issuer has its registered office[287] or, where the issuer is incorporated in a third country, the Member State where the securities have been admitted to trading for the first time. The host Member State is the State in which an offer to the public is made or admission to trading is sought where that State is different from the home Member State. Article 14 provides that in the case of multinational offerings or multiple trading, the prospectus approved by the home competent authority must be accepted in all the Member States concerned. Additional information, or the approval of that information, may not be required. The host Member State competent authority may exceptionally refuse to accept the prospectus, but only if the information specific to the relevant host market under the Article 6 disclosure rules is contained in neither the securities note nor, where the traditional format is followed, the prospectus. The new mutual recognition is subject to time limits, however, given that information can rapidly become out of date, and so dangerous for investors. Under Article 15(2), if more than three months have passed since approval of the prospectus, the host Member State's competent authority is entitled to require the publication of an updated securities notes and summary note or, where the traditional format is used by an issuer, an updated prospectus.

The current burdensome, if perhaps politically inevitable, translation regime is replaced by a new regime under Article 16. Where an offer is made or admission to trading is sought in more than one Member State, the prospectus or, where appropriate, the registration document and the securities note must be made available in a language customary in the sphere of

---

[287] This core feature of the proposal, review by the home Member State as designated via the issuer's registered office, has caused concern in the Euro-bond market, the participants in which fear that home Member State control has the potential to inflict heavy damage on the London and Luxembourg markets which are at the centre of the Euro-bond market: Preston, n 275 above. The London Stock Exchange also challenged this core feature of the regime. It argued that issuers should be free to choose the competent authority responsible for the supervision of its disclosure. It raised two concerns in particular: the implications for competent-authority resources and expertise; and the lack of incentive for competent authorities to provide more efficient services. Pointing to the degree of specialization by competent authorities (it noted the expertise of London and Luxembourg in the debt and depositary-receipts markets), it argued that intermediaries are required to be familiar only with the practice and requirements of a small number of jurisdictions and that expertise in complex areas is concentrated, bringing efficiency gains. The home Member State regime would, it argued, require intermediaries to become familiar with a much wider range of jurisdictions, place strains on the resources of competent authorities, and 'result in fragmentation rather than harmonization, particularly in markets for specialised securities, and lead to increased costs and delays': LSE Comment Document, n 245 above, paras 4.4–4.5. It also argued that the Proposal would create a domestic monopoly for each competent authority and provide little incentive for improvements in services or efficiency savings. Its solution to the risk-of-regulatory-arbitrage problem was the harmonization of standards introduced by the Proposal and a new requirement that issuers disclose the reason for avoiding the home competent authority: ibid, paras 4.6–4.7.

finance which is generally accepted by the competent authority of the host Member State. In that case, the host competent authority may require only that the summary note be translated into its domestic language: whether or not the Member States will accept this limited translation requirement remains to be seen.[288] The strong investor-protection theme which permeates the Proposal is borne out by the purpose of the summary (which under Annex IV 'should give in a few pages the most important information included in the prospectus') which is to 'provide, in particular to retail investors, immediate succinct information on the most relevant aspects relating to the issuer and the proposed operation in a concise format'.[289]

The investment-services passport regime, somewhat controversially, contains notification requirements. The notification concept has, in the interests of investor protection, now been transplanted to the new issuer passport regime. Under Article 17, the competent authorities of the home Member State are to provide the competent authority of the host Member State with the prospectus and a certificate of approval confirming that the prospectus has been drawn up in accordance with the Directive. The passport is also subject to a 'precautionary measures' principle by Article 21. If the host Member State's authority finds that irregularities have been committed by the issuer or by the financial institutions running the public offer, or finds breaches of the issuer's obligations, it is to refer those findings to the home authority. Where measures are taken by the home competent authority but the violations in question persist, the host authority may, after informing the home authority, take all the appropriate measures to protect investors.

More generally, in order to promote the necessary degree of trust required between competent authorities and on which the successful operation of the notification and home Member State control regime depends, as outlined below, the Proposal requires the home Member State's authorities to be responsible for ensuring equivalent treatment of investors and for supervising ongoing disclosure of material information.

(b) *The Competent Authority*

The Proposal addresses head on the current controversies swirling around the role which should be played by commercially driven securities-trading markets in the disclosure process and the extent to which they should be allowed to act as competent authorities responsible for the review of disclosure. In a seismic change from the current position, the Proposal takes the view that independent 'administrative authorities' whose independence from

---

[288] Much will depend on how Member States interpret the 'generally accepted' qualification. See Scott, H, 'Internationalization of Primary Public Securities Markets Revisited' in Ferrarini *et al.*, n 282 above.

[289] Explanatory Memorandum, n 244 above, 4.

economic actors is guaranteed (recital 24) are better placed than commercially driven stock exchanges to ensure market and investor protection: 'exchanges which are not for-profit entities are subject to a conflict of interest and should not be in charge of ensuring any longer "public functions", such as the approval of prospectuses. At the same time exchanges and markets, relieved of the duty to perform such functions, will be free to compete solely on the basis of commercial efficiency'.[290] Article 19(1) accordingly requires that each Member State is to designate the 'competent administrative authority' competent to carry out the duties provided for in the Directive.

Article 19(2) requires, like the current disclosure directives, that the competent authority have all the powers necessary for the performance of its functions. Unusually for EC securities regulation, Article 19(2) specifies in some detail the powers which a competent authority must have at its disposal. These range from inspection and investigatory powers, such as the ability to carry out on-site inspections and to require auditors and managers to provide information, to enforcement powers such as the power to prohibit a public offer if it finds the Directive has been infringed, to suspend, or ask the relevant trading market to suspend, trading (for a maximum of ten days) if it has grounds for suspecting that the provisions of the Directive have been infringed and to prohibit trading if it finds that the Directive has been infringed. Article 19(3) also makes clear that competent authorities must have powers with respect to the ongoing behaviour of the issuer, and in particular to: require the issuer to disclose all material information which may have an effect on the assessment of the securities offered to the public or admitted to trading on a regulated market in order to ensure investor protection or the smooth operation of the market (Article 19(3)(a)); and suspend or ask the relevant regulated market to suspend trading if, in its opinion, the issuer's situation is such that trading would be detrimental to investors' interests (Article 19(3)(b)). Under Article 19(3)(c) competent authorities are to ensure that issuers whose securities are traded on a regulated market comply with the obligations provided for under Article 17 of the now consolidated Admission Directive (that is, the obligation to publish the information required to be disclosed to the public under Schedules C and D of the Admission Directive) and that equivalent information is provided to investors and equivalent treatment is granted by the issuer to all securities holders in all Member States where the offer is made or the securities are traded.

IV.9.3.9 *The Future*

While the fate of the Proposal remains to be seen, it does appear to be a dramatic improvement on the current system. The single-passport regime, in

---

[290] Explanatory Memorandum, n 244 above, 4.

principle, should reduce transaction costs for issuers and generate greater enthusiasm for pan-EC capital raising. More specifically, the shelf-registration system will also reduce costs by removing the burdens attendant on the preparation of a major disclosure document each time access to the markets is sought. It will also give issuers considerably greater flexibility in planning their financing needs and in responding to market movements as the approval process will be much speedier. Integration of the annual update of the registration document with the annual report will also bring cost savings. Investor protection via disclosure is enhanced by a more sophisticated management of disclosure policy. Not only will more modern disclosure standards apply, ongoing disclosure is considerably enhanced via the annual update of the registration document, while the circulation of disclosure via the website of the relevant competent authority is a technical development which should substantially improve the dissemination of information and appears to reflect a commitment that the disclosure be, in practice, read and assessed by retail investors. Once the level 2 disclosure standards operation is complete, comparability should be significantly enhanced, given that all EC prospectuses will follow a similar pattern with respect to format as well as the information disclosed.

Its status (and the extent to which it will survive unscathed) as one of the two first illustrations of the Lamfalussy law-making model, however, is where its importance for EC securities regulation as a whole is immeasurable. Here, the Proposal reveals an early declaration of intent from the Commission that more detailed harmonization can be expected. Not only are the level 1 principles contained in the Proposal highly specific, but the scale of the rule-making powers proposed to be delegated to level 2 is not insignificant, extending well beyond the setting of disclosure standards; indeed, a certain nervousness from the Commission may be inferred from the softening of the references to the delegation of 'detailed technical rule'- or 'technical rule'-making powers in the Proposal by the Explanatory Memorandum's illustration (with respect to the Article 11 (approval), Article 13 (advertising), and Article 18 (third-country issuers) delegations) of the scope of the rule-making powers by way of the 'guidance' which those rules will offer. Much will depend on how the Parliament, which has shown itself to be sceptical as to the Lamfalussy model (see Chapter XV section 2.5.3) and which has recently demonstrated its willingness to assert its independence and its law-making powers with devastating consequences for the fate of the proposed Takeover Directive, reacts to the scale of the delegation involved. It also remains to be seen how national competent authorities, which will remain in control of the new disclosure regime, will respond to their limited discretion once the level 2 procedures get under way. Although the earlier FESCO proposals suggest a willingness to make the regime work, the national competent authorities could yet be the Achilles heel of the new regime.

IV.9.4 *Reform of the Ongoing Disclosure Regime*

As part of the FSAP the Commission is reviewing the now consolidated IRD and the ongoing disclosure regime generally in order to ensure that 'more frequent and better quality information' is made available to the markets.[291] At the heart of the Commission's review is the need to ensure that regular updating of market information takes place. Any formal proposal in this area is likely to follow the Lamfalussy decision-making model. Indeed, the Lamfalussy Report used a level 1 revision of the IRD, adapted to provide for level 2 law-making, as an illustration of its proposals.[292] The focus of the ongoing disclosure review thus far appears to be more on the quality of ongoing disclosure and on investor protection (and, as a result, on integration via investor confidence) and rather less on facilitating issuer access to the Community capital market; indeed, certain of the reforms proposed, such as the move to quarterly reporting, are likely to increase the disclosure burden on issuers.

As part of the review process, in July 2001 the Commission produced a 'without prejudice' consultation document on the ongoing disclosure regime.[293] It found that the IRD's interim-report regime, in particular, did not adequately assist investors to make an informed judgement of an issuer's development and activities, was outdated, and had led to varying interpretations across the Member States, with reports differing in content and format across the Community. It suggested that a new, consolidated regime for all ongoing and regular disclosure was necessary in order to ensure that all Community investors, regardless of their residence, were protected by adequate disclosure safeguards. At the core of the review (which, unusually, the Commission stated was not designed to search for perfection) is the premise that investor protection and confidence are contingent on upgraded information. Smaller issuers were singled out for particular attention, with the Commission emphasizing the link between investment activity and regular information, given that, by comparison with their larger counterparts, smaller issuers are less well known and their securities tend to be less liquid.

The review document suggested seven proposals. The first of these was a consolidation of the regime (the Admission Directive's ongoing obligations, the IRD, and the SSD) in a single text (carved out from the current SCD consolidated version) in the interests of accessibility and clarity. Apart from mechanically consolidating the various texts, the consolidation exercise would also align the common rules which currently diverge across the three directives, such as the rules on scope, publication, competent authorities,

---

[291] FSAP, n 61 above, 17.   [292] Lamfalussy Report, n 255 above, 52.
[293] *Towards an EU Regime on Transparency Obligations of Issuers Whose Securities are Admitted to Trading on a Regulated Market* (the Transparency Report), MARKT/11/.07.2001.

enforcement, and language requirements, and revise them to reflect the approach taken in the Prospectus Proposal. The Commission's second proposal was, in line with a theme running through EC securities regulation generally at present, to apply the ongoing regime to issuers of securities (debt and equity) traded on regulated markets. As the Commission highlighted, the current regime, which is tied to issuers of officially listed equities for the most part, does not apply to issuers, typically start-up and high-tech companies, traded outside the Official List. The third proposal concerned the upgrading of the current disclosure requirements. A significant change proposed here would move the IRD regime to a quarterly cycle. In support of this change, the Commission noted that the quarterly regime represented international best practice, with several Member States already requiring this frequency of reporting and with certain global issuers being subject to such a regime for decades. It also adverted to commercial reality, pointing out that some investment firms forbid investments in securities of issuers which do not report on a quarterly cycle. The enhanced disclosure standards would include a requirement for condensed consolidated financial statements (prepared in accordance with IAS—see section 10 below) for each period, which would be subject to a limited review by the statutory auditor, given that a full statutory audit on a quarterly basis would be too onerous, a management report, and an acceleration of the publication deadline from the current four months after the end of the six-month period to not later than sixty days after the end of the interim period. The fourth proposal concerned the alignment of the Admission Directive's material-information obligation with the approach taken by the LPD (Article 4(1)) (SCD, Article 21(1)) and the POD (Article 11(1)) to what constitutes material information (the informed assessment formula). The fifth proposal addressed electronic publication of information and the impact of the Internet. Tracking the approach of the Prospectus Proposal, the Commission suggested that all ongoing information be made available on the issuer's official website and filed with the home Member State's competent authority in an electronic format, so that the authority could make the information available to the public speedily. The sixth proposal concerned the competent authorities. The Commission recommended that one competent authority, which would be the independent securities regulator responsible for investor protection and market transparency, be established for each Member State and given power to require additional disclosure, obtain information from auditors and managers, suspend or request the suspension of trading, and carry out on-site inspections. Member States would also be required to impose sanctions for violations of the new regime. Finally, the Commission proposed that the Lamfalussy model be adopted, with level 2 implementing measures being used to adapt and clarify the regime in order to reflect market developments.

IV.10 HARMONIZATION OF ACCOUNTING STANDARDS

IV.10.1 *The Market-integration Link*

The weaknesses in the EC's issuer-disclosure regime and the consequences
for the development of an integrated EC securities market, efficient capital
raising, and investor protection do not derive solely from defects in the disclosure directives. While the directives of the disclosure regime set out
requirements concerning the categories of financial information which must
be disclosed on the official listing or offer of securities and the dissemination
of annual and interim reports, significant divergences exist across the
Member States with respect to how the required financial information must
be presented. From the issuer's perspective harmonized accounting standards would facilitate the cross-border listing and offer of securities. The
transparency and comparability of financial information in the integrated
securities is also of critical importance for investor protection in the integrated market-place.

IV.10.2 *The Current Position*

A series of company law directives already addresses the harmonization of
accounting standards. The most important of these are the Fourth,[294]
Seventh,[295] and Eighth[296] Company Law Directives which address, respectively, the presentation of annual accounts, consolidated accounts, and the
qualifications required of statutory auditors.[297] Significant leeway is given
to Member States in their implementation, however, particularly with
respect to local legal and tax requirements, such that they do not introduce
common EC accounting standards.[298] Considerable differences have also
arisen between Member States on the interpretation of the accounting directives. The accounting directives are not comprehensive in their coverage,
with the result that Member States' accounting rules perform a gap-filling
function in many cases. Finally, Member States and national supervisory

---

[294] 4th Company Law Directive on the annual accounts of certain types of companies (essentially public and private companies limited by share or by guarantee), Directive 78/660/EEC
[1978] OJ L222/1.

[295] 7th Company Law Directive on consolidated accounts, Directive 83/349/EEC [1983] OJ
L193/1.

[296] 8th Company Law Directive on the approval of persons responsible for carrying out the
statutory audits of accounting documents, Directive 84/253/EEC [1984] OJ L126/20.

[297] For an in-depth analysis of the accounting directives see Edwards, n 42 above, 117–211.

[298] It has also been noted that the varying policies underlying the rules on the presentation
of financial information across the Member States have led to differences in accounting practices and standards. Gros and Lanoo have noted that, while in the UK and Ireland accounting
requirements are driven by the needs of the financial markets, in a number of continental
Member States they are driven by legal requirements: n 148 above, 114.

authorities may permit companies to prepare their accounts in accordance with internationally accepted standards (International Accounting Standards (IAS) or the US Generally Accepted Accounting Principles (US GAAP)), rather than national standards, as long as they comply with the requirements of the accounting directives.

While these differences in accounting standards have limited impact where investors tend to invest in domestic securities, variations in accounting standards across the Member States create a number of problems as investors diversify into cross-border investments. Fragmentation in accounting standards can discourage investors from investing in securities of non-domestic companies where the accounts are presented in an unfamiliar or confusing format. Transparency of information and the comparability of companies' financial statements can be adversely affected. The ability of companies to distribute financial information on the Internet is also leading to growing pressure for standardized financial information in order that investors can easily compare the relative performance of different companies. The parallel existence of different standards makes efficient supervision of financial reporting requirements more difficult. Finally, the professional investment management and analysis community prefers the presentation of financial information in accordance with an accepted international standard in the interests of comparability. Overall, varying accounting standards have been acknowledged by the Commission in its 2000 financial Reporting Strategy Communication[299] to be an obstacle to the development of a deep and liquid EC securities market and its global competitiveness. Pressure has therefore been growing for the adoption of a single standard for financial reporting across the EC which would also facilitate the preparation of disclosure documents for multiple cross-border offerings and listings of securities. The need for progress on accounting standards was underlined by the finding of the Lamfalussy Report that variations in accounting standards and the failure to adopt IAS were among the factors which were particularly damaging to the construction of an integrated securities market and which needed urgent attention.[300]

IV.10.3 *International Convergence*

The accounting-standards harmonization problem has been compounded in recent years by the growing use by EC companies of one of the two international reporting frameworks, either US GAAP or IAS, in respect of their international offerings and listings. In particular, a number of large EC issuers report under US GAAP, which is the dominant international

---

[299] Communication on 'The EU Financial Reporting Strategy: The Way Forward' (the Financial Reporting Strategy Communication) COM(2000)359, 3 and 5.
[300] N 255 above, 13.

standard, in order to fulfil US listing requirements. The variations between
US GAAP and domestic EC standards can lead to very different sets of financial statements being produced in respect of the same set of financial information, leading to investor confusion and a lack of transparency. Adding to
the confusion is that, while some Member States allow companies to report
solely on the basis of US GAAP as long as the requirements of the accounting directives are also met, others require that the national standards be followed in parallel, while still others have permitted companies to report
under IAS. IAS have been developed by the International Accounting
Standards Committee (IASC) and IOSCO in order to create a single set of
financial reporting standards. Despite the broad acceptance worldwide of
convergence in accounting standards, the adoption of IAS was a difficult and
controversial process due to the SEC's resistance to the standards. In May
2000, however, a significant step forward in the acceptance of IAS was
taken when IOSCO recommended to its membership that they permit multinational issuers to use IAS when preparing financial statements. The IASC
(now the International Accounting Standards Board or IASB) has also
undergone a major structural reorganization in order to enhance the extent
to which IAS (future standards isued by the IASB will be known as IFRS)
are adopted across the major securities markets. In the EC, as the need for
a single set of reporting standards became compelling, the debate turned to
which of the two international standards, US GAAP or IAS, should form the
basis of the EC harmonization.

IV.10.4 *The Approach to Harmonization*

While increasingly aware of the need for comparability of financial statements and the adoption of a single reporting standard, the EC has displayed
a resistance to the adoption of US GAAP, despite its dominance as the internationally accepted accounting standard, as adoption would involve the
acceptance of an accounting standard outside the influence of the EC and its
Member States and under the control of the USA. In 1995, the Commission
recommended that IAS, which were at that point under negotiation, be followed and accepted by stock exchanges as part of their listing requirements.[301] In the FSAP, while the Commission noted generally that any
solution adopted with respect to comparability must reflect international
developments, the bias towards IAS was evident, with the Commission
finding that IAS seemed to provide the most appropriate benchmark for
a single set of financial reporting requirements. The FSAP also contains a
commitment by the Commission to present a strategy for enhancing the

---

[301] Commission Communication on Accounting Harmonisation: A New Strategy vis-à-vis
International Harmonisation, COM(95)508.

comparability of financial reports issued by listed EC companies, including consideration of a mechanism for reviewing international standards to facilitate their use, without national variations, by listed EC companies.

In June 2000 the Commission finally presented its Financial Reporting Strategy Communication. It reiterated the connection between deepening EC securities markets and common financial reporting standards. The central objective of the strategy is to ensure that securities can be traded on EC and international financial markets. While the predominant theme of the report is the development of a deep and liquid EC securities market, it is notable that the Commission placed considerable emphasis on the role of financial information in safeguarding the interests of investors, as well as other stakeholders such as creditors. While it noted that accounting standards were essential for an efficient market-place, it also observed that financial information underpins the entire system of market information and represents a critical link between the issuer and the investor. Acknowledging that both US GAAP and IAS provide generally equivalent levels of investor protection, the report emphasized the need to opt for one approach, given that while market forces could determine the preferred standards, any such competition between systems would cause a delay in achieving comparability. It confirmed its earlier preference for IAS, pointing to the international perspective of IAS as compared to the US focus of US GAAP, the detailed training needed to use US GAAP, and the inability of the EC to exert any influence over the development of US GAAP. At the nub of the report, accordingly, was the Commission's decision to present a proposal which would require that all EC companies listed on a regulated market prepare consolidated accounts in accordance with IAS, and that within two years of this requirement coming into force, it be extended to all companies preparing a public offer prospectus in accordance with the now consolidated LPD.

The Commission is also in the process of reviewing the accounting directives in order to take into account the needs of the integrated market, the demands from investors for greater disclosure and transparency, and developments in international accounting standards. It has also encouraged greater co-operation among securities supervisors, through the medium of FESCO, in order to discourage regulatory arbitrage with respect to accounting standards.[302]

IV.10.5 *The Proposed IAS Regulation*

IV.10.5.1 *The Adoption of IAS*

In December 2000, the Commission presented a proposal for a Regulation on the Application of International Accounting Standards which closely

---

[302] Financial Reporting Strategy Communication, n 299 above, 9.

reflects the Financial Reporting Strategy.[303] In its Explanatory Memorandum, the Commission pointed to the weaknesses of the accounting directives as a means of delivering comparability, transparency, and an appropriate level of disclosure for investors. In particular, it noted that the ability of Member States to adapt minimum EC rules to reflect national practices, which was appropriate when investors and other stakeholders were of the same nationality as the company, was outmoded in the context of an integrated financial market where securities could be held by a diverse group of investors. Market forces were rejected as a means of determining common accounting standards and IAS recommended as a 'comprehensive and conceptually robust set of standards specifically intended to serve the needs of the international business community'.[304]

The Regulation is designed to close out national differences and achieve a high degree of comparability between national accounting regimes. It is based on Article 95 EC, confirming the connection between the establishment and functioning of the single securities market and disclosure, in this case financial disclosure, harmonization. Recital 2 to the Preamble states in this regard that 'in order to contribute to a better functioning of the internal market, publicly traded companies must be required to apply a single set of high quality international accounting rules . . . [this] will also ensure a high level of transparency and comparability of financial reporting by all publicly traded companies as a necessary condition for building an integrated capital market which plays its role effectively, smoothly and efficiently'. The investor protection/confidence connection is made in recital 3 which states that '[t]he protection of investors and the maintenance of confidence in the financial markets is also an important aspect of the completion of the internal market in this area'. The Regulation is also designed to reinforce the freedom of movement of capital in the internal market and assist companies in competing on an equal basis for financial resources.

At the core of the proposed Regulation is the requirement in Article 4 that, for the financial year starting on or after 1 January 2005, all EC companies traded on a regulated market,[305] as well as EC companies whose securities are offered to the public in view of their admission to trading on a regulated market in accordance with the LPD's conditions, prepare consolidated accounts in accordance with IAS[306] adopted for the EC in

---

[303] Proposal for Regulation of the European Parliament and the Council on the Application of International Accounting Standards. [2001] OJ C154/285. ECOSOC's opinion is at [2001] OJ C260/86.

[304] Ibid, 3.   [305] As defined in Art. 1(3) of the ISD.

[306] While the Regulation is designed the provide for the adoption of IAS, the definition of international accounting standards in Art. 2 is somewhat broader, covering IAS, subsequent amendments to and interpretations of IAS, future standards and interpretations produced by the IASB, and 'equivalent accounting standards, which are standards that ensure a high degree of transparency and comparability of financial reporting and are as close as possible to [IAS]'.

accordance with the Regulation's procedures. Under Article 5, Member States have the option to require or permit non-Article 4 companies to publish financial statements in accordance with IAS or to require or permit Article 4 companies to use IAS when preparing individual accounts. The Regulation will operate alongside the pre-existing accounting directives which will continue to provide a basic minimum level of comparability for all companies.

IV.10.5.2 *The Endorsement Mechanism*

The controversial endorsement procedure, which has a wider significance for decision-making for the integrated securities market generally,[307] is set out in Article 6. The use of IAS carries with it certain institutional difficulties. Any changes to IAS need to be accommodated within the EC accounting regime without the need for a full-scale amendment of the relevant accounting directives each time IAS are modified. In addition, as the Commission stated in the Financial Reporting Strategy Communication, adoption of IAS cannot involve the delegation of responsibility for setting financial reporting requirements to a non-governmental third party. In order to ensure that IAS are overseen at EC level and altered where necessary to cater for the EC environment, the proposed Regulation sets out an endorsement mechanism which would confirm that IAS conform with the overall EC approach to financial reporting and, specifically, with the accounting directives. The endorsement mechanism is designed so that it will intervene to change new IAS standards only where necessary to reflect the particular economic and legal features of the integrated market.

The Commission is the engine of the IAS endorsement procedure which, like the adoption of technical rules under the Prospectus Proposal, is based on the EC's comitology procedures. Under Article 3, the Commission is to identify and adopt the IAS that are to be made mandatory in the EC regime, by reference to the need to ensure a high degree of transparency and comparability of financial statements. In the first instance, the Commission is to propose IAS to a comitology committee, the Accounting Regulatory Committee. Under Article 6, the Committee, composed of representatives of the Member States and chaired by a Commission representative, is to assist the Commission in accordance with the general comitology rules and procedures laid down in the Comitology Decision 1999/468/EC.[308] Based on these procedures, the Committee would examine the Commission's proposal, and, within one month, decide whether to accept the proposal on the basis

---

[307] See Ch. XV sect. 2.5 below, where the endorsement mechanism is placed in the wider context of the current debate on how rule-making for the single securities and investment services market should be pursued.
[308] [1999] OJ L184/23.

of a qualified majority vote. If the Committee does not support the Commission, the Commission will then return the proposal to an expert technical committee (the Accounting Regulatory Committee) or bring the proposal before the Council. At all stages the European Parliament must be fully informed, and it may intervene if it feels that the Commission has exceeded its powers.

The Accounting Regulatory Committee provides the institutional and political check on the Commission. A further layer is added to the endorsement process by the Accounting Technical Committee, which is to provide the initial technical review of IAS and to ensure that users of IAS, the accounting profession, and national standard setters are involved in the endorsement process. This two-tier structure of institutional controls and expert advice is also a feature of the Lamfalussy law-making model.[309] The endorsement mechanism has its critics, who claim that it may result in over-interference with IAS and obstruct international efforts to establish common accounting rules. Nonetheless, when considered in the context of the Lamfalussy law-making model and the structure of the Prospectus Proposal it represents a decisive shift in EC securities regulation, and, in particular disclosure regulation, towards more sophisticated and detailed rules set centrally through more flexible and speedier delegated law-making functions.

---

[309] See Ch. XV sect. 2.5.3 below.

V

Collective-investment Schemes

V.1 COLLECTIVE-INVESTMENT SCHEMES

Chapters II, III and IV have examined the rules applicable to the capital-raising process, in particular the mandatory issuer-disclosure regime, and how the EC has sought to establish an integrated securities market. Retail investors are likely to access this market indirectly through an investment vehicle in the form of a collective investment scheme.[1] A collective investment scheme is a popular form of investment vehicle which allows investors with limited funds to access the capital markets through a fund which pools investors' funds and spreads risk across a range of investments according to defined asset-selection and risk criteria. Collective-investment schemes are currently enjoying a period of extraordinary growth and now hold a significant proportion of public savings.[2] Valued at £1,845 billion and representing 35 per cent of the EU's GDP in mid-2000,[3] the collective investment scheme industry represents an important channel for retail saving in the Community, largely as a result of the structure of the continental pension-fund industry. Although the situation is changing, certain Member States do not have a significant private-pension-fund industry as pensions are largely financed by the State through the taxation system. As a result, savings are channelled into other forms of organized savings such as collective investment schemes.[4] As an important savings vehicle and a

---

[1] Although pension funds can be considered as a form of collective-investment scheme they are the subject of specialized regulation and do not traditionally form part of securities regulation, and so will not be considered in this ch. Given the importance of pension funds as institutional investors on the securities markets and their ability to mediate between issuers and public savings, pension fund reform forms a major part of the Community financial-services market-integration plan. See the Commission's Occupational Retirement Pensions Proposal, COM(2000)207.

[2] eg, in May 2001 AUTIF (the Association of Unit Trusts and Investment Funds) reported net growth of 24% in sales on the previous year at the same time: AUTIF, Press Release, May 2001. For a discussion of the US explosion in collective-investment scheme or mutual-fund (as they are termed in the USA) saving and its economy-wide ramifications see Hale, D, 'Our Mutual Revolution' [1998] *JIBFL* 219. Between 1979 and 1999 the assets under management by mutual funds in the USA rose from US$134.8 billion to $6.8 trillion, a 4,900% increase. 49% of US households hold investments in mutual funds: SEC (US Securities and Exchange Commission), *Mutual Funds Fees and Expenses* (2001), para A. For an examination of the factors feeding the growth in the asset-management industry generally, including the collective-investment scheme sector see Walter, I, 'The Global Asset Management Industry: Competitive Structure and Performance' (1999) 8 *Financial Markets, Institutions and Instruments* 1.

[3] Hargreaves, D, 'Brussels Boost for Cross-Border Investment', *Financial Times*, 1 June 2000.

[4] See Gros, D, and Lannoo, K, *The Euro Capital Market* (2000) 61–3 and 66.

complement to State-supported pension funds, the collective investment scheme industry's success and the ease with which schemes can access an efficient and liquid securities market has been identified as critical to the health of the EC's economy; they have, as a result, acted as an important trigger for the promotion of a liquid single securities market.[5] In consequence, an important component of the FSAP[6] has been a review of the investment-management rules under which collective-investment schemes operate in order to allow for greater choice with respect to the investments which schemes can make (section 8.2 below).

Collective-investment schemes operate by collecting funds from investors which are then invested in securities or other assets. While they can take a myriad different forms, two predominant types can be identified. In the first structure, which has a separate legal personality, the scheme assets are owned by a company in which investors are given a share representing their investment. In the second, where the establishment of the scheme does not create a separate legal personality, the scheme assets are held on behalf of investors, whose proportionate holdings are represented by a unit, by a trustee.[7] In both cases the management and investment of the assets by a manager[8] will be separate from the custody of the assets.[9] The share or unit gives the investor the right to participate in the profits or income which arise from the scheme's investment activities. Contractual schemes represent a third form of collective investment scheme. They are closely related to the trust structure, in that an independent legal personality is not created on establishment of the scheme. The multiplicity of forms collective investment schemes can take include unit trusts, limited partnerships, and open-ended investment companies.

---

[5] See, eg, the Commission's Communication on Upgrading the Investment Services Directive (93/22/EEC) COM(2000)729, 1, and the analysis in the Initial Report of the Committee of Wise Men on the Regulation of European Securities Markets, Nov 2000 (the Initial Lamfalussy Report), 5. The latter has emphasized that in an integrated securities-market the real return on investors' savings through funds would be higher. The equation works both ways, with collective-investment schemes impacting on the development of the EC capital market. Walter has noted that the current growth in the institutional asset-management industry generally will, if it continues, mean that 'the capital markets will increasingly be the major source of external financing for European corporations in the future. . . . fiduciary asset pools managed against performance benchmarks by mutual funds and pension funds will create increasingly fluid sources of capital for industry, and a fundamental shift in the accountability of management and the monitoring of corporate performance in Europe': n 2 above, 72.

[6] Commission Communication on Implementing the Framework for Financial Markets: Action Plan, COM(1999)232 (the FSAP).

[7] For an examination of the features of a unit trust in the UK industry see Franks, J, and Mayer, C, Risk, *Regulation and Investor Protection* (1989) 23–4.

[8] In addition to overseeing the fund's investments, the manager is also responsible for the administration of the assets, which involves tasks such as the supervision of the reinvestment of dividends on equity investments.

[9] The custodian of the assets may also act as a transfer agent, managing the buying and selling of investments.

Collective investment schemes offer a number of advantages to investors. They benefit from economies of scale in that they can access a wide spread of investments[10] and thus benefit from portfolio diversification, irrespective of the scale of their investment in the scheme. Scheme investment decisions are taken by market professionals who compare and examine appropriate investments in a manner that would be very difficult for the small investor to emulate, particularly where the investments are made in foreign markets. Transaction costs are also lower, as scheme managers who buy assets in large tranches can pass on the cost reductions to the unit-holders.[11] Collective-investment schemes also offer economy-wide advantages as they encourage saving and can stimulate and finance economic growth by deepening sources of capital.

V.2 RATIONALE FOR AND FORMS OF REGULATION

It has long been recognized that collective-investment schemes should be regulated in the interests of investor protection,[12] particularly as collective-investment schemes are often directed at unsophisticated and inexperienced investors[13] who do not exercise control over the investments made by the scheme or the scheme assets: the regulation of those who control large pools

[10] Investors can chose between a wide range of schemes, offering differing investment policies. A broad distinction can be drawn between growth funds, which focus on capital appreciation and may be risky, conservative growth funds, which adopt less adventurous investment policies, and income funds, which are managed to provide a reliable income from the fund assets.

[11] In short: '[collective-investment schemes] offer expertise, economies of scale and a level of diversification far superior to that obtainable by the typical investor constructing a portfolio': Langbein, J, 'The Secret Life of the Trust' (1997) 107 *Yale LJ* 165, 170.

[12] See generally Clark, R, 'The Four Stages of Capitalism' (1981) 94 *Harv. LR* 561, 564–5 and 571 on the rise of investment intermediation and its ramifications. The legal techniques for controlling the riskiness of intermediaries such as investment companies are examined in Clark, R, 'The Soundness of Financial Intermediaries' (1976) 86 *Yale LJ* 1. As early as 1936 a report was commissioned by the Board of Trade into the activities of unit trusts in the UK, where they had first been introduced in 1931: *Fixed Trusts: Report of the Departmental Committee Appointed by the Board of Trade* (1936) (Cmnd 5259). On the history of the regulation of collective-investment schemes in the UK see generally Page, A, and Ferguson, R, *Investor Protection* (1992) 182–5. Mutual funds have been regulated in the USA since 1940 when the Investment Company Act, 1940 was passed to address a number of serious abuses in the operation of investment funds which were highlighted by a wide-ranging study submitted by the SEC to Congress in 1938–9.

[13] The dangers faced by retail investors in some of the more esoteric schemes which have been constituted can be illustrated by the then UK Securities and Investment Board's Annual Report for 1997, in which the Chairman's Statement referred to the significant proportion of inquiries received concerning schemes promising high returns and relating to sales of ostriches and investments in greyhounds. Industry-wide problems can also arise. The 1998 Korean financial crisis revealed abuses in the collective-investment scheme industry including conflicts of interests and price manipulation.

of liquid capital is usually irresistible to regulators fearful of abuse.[14] More broadly, inadequate regulation can lead to economy-wide instability as collective-investment schemes have the potential through their investment policies to create instability in the securities markets.[15] Typical components of collective investment scheme regulation include investment-policy and risk-management rules, controls on the valuation methods used to value units and the assets they represent, structural rules separating the functions of asset management and custody, and prudential and conduct requirements (imposed on the custodian and manager).[16]

V.3 SCOPE AND FEATURES OF THE EC REGIME

The Community's collective-investment scheme regime is set out in the UCITS Directive.[17] The EC's approach to the regulation of collective-investment schemes stems from the predominant market-integration objective which underpins EC securities regulation generally; the regime is directed towards liberalizing access by collective investment schemes to investors across the Community. The focus thus far has been on the UCITS (the particular collective-investment scheme which comes within the scope of the Directive) as a product and on the market access of that product, rather than on the market access and regulation of those who manage the collective-investment scheme, although the new UCITS regime represents a major step forward in the regulation of those who manage collective-investment schemes (section 8.3 below).

Although the UCITS Directive, for the most part, concerns an investment product it also, albeit to a very limited extent, regulates investment-services providers in the more traditional sense.[18] It stands, as a result, on the cusp

---

[14] See Cox, J, Hillman, R, and Langevoort, D, *Securities Regulation, Cases and Materials* (1997) 1164.

[15] See Riley, B, 'Demystifying Collective Investment Schemes', *Financial Times*, 24 May 2000.

[16] Convergence is being achieved internationally in the regulatory treatment and supervision of collective-investment schemes. In 1998 IOSCO adopted principles for the regulation of collective-investment schemes as part of its Objectives and Principles of Securities Regulation (the 1998 IOSCO Principles). They cover eligibility criteria for scheme managers, conduct supervision, conflicts of interests and delegations, legal form and structure, disclosure to investors, asset protection, asset valuation, and pricing and redemption requirements. See generally the reports by the IOSCO Technical Committee on *Investment Management* (1994), on *Guidance on Custody Arrangements for Collective Investment Schemes* (1996) and on *Principles for the Supervision of Operators of Collective Investment Schemes* (1997).

[17] Directive 85/611/EEC on the coordination of laws, regulations and administrative provisions relating to undertakings for collective investment in transferable securities [1985] OJ L375/3 (the UCITS Directive or the Directive).

[18] The Directive imposes a very limited degree of regulation on the depositary and manager of the collective-investment scheme.

between the official-listing/public-offer regime, which focuses on the capital-raising process and trade in securities, and the investment-services regime which would follow. Its harmonization technique places it with the later investment-services regime, however. Its market-integration mechanism of mutual recognition, home-country control, and the conferment of a regulatory 'passport' is sharply different from the detailed harmonization mechanism used by the official-listing regime in the initial phase of harmonization. Indeed, the UCITS Directive serves as the template in the securities-regulation field for the regulatory passport which would come to dominate the regulation of investment services;[19] concepts central to the regulatory passport, such as authorization by the home Member State according to set criteria, are articulated here for the first time in the securities and investment-services field. The mutual-recognition structure, and specifically home Member State control, also impacts on the substantive content of regulation, in that the supervision mechanisms are more sophisticated than those set out in the early official-listing regime; the adequacy of supervision and co-operation structures is also a key feature of the investment-services regime.

V.4 THE ROOTS OF THE REGIME

The potential of collective investment schemes as agents to stimulate and integrate the European capital market was noted by the Segré Report in 1966. Analysing the shortage of capital across the Community and, in particular, 'the inadequate supplies of capital from private investors', the Report recognized that 'institutional investors are best suited to manage the savings of a large section of the public with no practical experience of direct and judicious investment in securities', but reported that they were hindered in attracting public funds by regulation and needed to be stimulated if the Community equity markets were to attract the saving of the public at large.[20] In a harbinger of later developments, the Report recommended that the expansion of investment-company activity across the Community be encouraged by the alignment of Member States' rules on the investment policies, management, and supervision of investment companies. It also suggested that harmonization of the widely varying information made available concerning investment companies would increase public confidence in investment companies as a form of saving.[21]

---

[19] Directive 93/22/EEC on investment services in the securiti[ISD). See Ch. VII.
[20] Report by a Group of Experts Appointed by the EEC Con *European Capital Market* (1966).
[21] Ibid, 207–8.

V.5 EARLY DEVELOPMENTS

By 1976, collective-investment schemes with a corporate structure, that is in the form of investment companies in which investors hold shares, were operating in Denmark, France, Luxembourg, and the Netherlands. Of these Member States, only France specifically regulated the activities of investment companies; the other Member States simply relied on the provisions of general company law. Collective-investment schemes without a corporate form operated in most of the Member States. These collective investment vehicles typically consisted of a management company, a depositary which acted as custodian of the scheme assets, and a fund which collected the funds invested by unit-holders. They were subject to specific regulation in Germany, Belgium, France, and the United Kingdom.[22]

The Commission first presented a proposal for the harmonization of collective-investment scheme regulation across the EC in 1976.[23] Co-ordination of Member State rules was deemed to be necessary in order to ensure uniform safeguards for investors and to eliminate the competitive distortions caused by different regulatory regimes. Achievement of these objectives would in turn bring about greater interpenetration of securities markets. More generally, the exclusion of units or shares in collective-investment schemes from the two early free-movement-of-capital directives,[24] arising from concerns that divergences in Member States' laws were such that equivalent safeguards for savers and equivalent competitive conditions between schemes did not exist, restricted the free movement of such schemes. The proposal was designed to remove this objection to the free movement of collective investment schemes by co-ordinating Member States' legislation.

A striking feature of the 1976 proposal is the manner in which market interpenetration is achieved. Article 1(2) of the proposal provided that

---

[22] Although regulation was, at that point, being planned in Ireland, Italy, Luxembourg, the Netherlands, and Denmark. Generally, transactions in UCITSs across the EC were restricted in the wake of a number of celebrated frauds in the 1960s; the most notorious of which concerned the Investors Overseas Service. See Scott Quinn, B, 'EC Securities Markets Regulation' in Steil, B, *International Financial Market Regulation* (1994) 121, 148.

[23] [1976] OJ C171/1, Explanatory Memorandum at COM(76)152. The proposal was lightly amended by COM(77)277. Collective-investment schemes are not specifically mentioned in the foundation Commission Recommendation 77/534/EEC concerning a European Code of Conduct relating to transactions in transferable securities [1977] OJ L212/37.

[24] [1960] JO 43/921 and [1963] JO 9/62. Member States could maintain exchange restrictions on cross-border purchases and sales of units in unit trusts where such a free movement of capital might form a barrier to the achievement of the economic policy objectives of the Member State in question. The free movement of units in collective investment schemes was liberalized by Directive 86/566 [1986] OJ L332/22. These provisions are now of largely ical interest. On the free movement of capital see Ch. I sect. 8 above.

Member States could not apply 'any provisions whatsoever' to collective-investment schemes situated in another Member State. In a very early example of mutual recognition, which would not become widespread until the presentation of the Commission's 1985 Internal Market White Paper,[25] Member States were required to permit schemes authorized in another Member State in accordance with the proposal's requirements to operate within their territory without further regulation, except for local marketing rules. Underlying the proposal was the principle that schemes located in any Member State should be subject to a single set of legal provisions, regardless of where they operated. Accordingly, only the competent authorities of the Member State in which the UCITS was situated could authorize it and supervise its activities, even where the activities were carried out in another Member State. The Commission justified this approach, which would come to dominate financial-services legislation some ten years later, by stating that 'the minimum rules laid down . . . would appear to form an adequate basis for safeguarding savers and ensuring sound conditions of competition . . . the single system of authorisation . . . is based on the mutual confidence which the competent authorities should extend to each other as regards the diligence with which each of them will ensure that the Directive is properly applied and, generally speaking, that all investors will be adequately protected'.[26] Although both the European Parliament and ECOSOC responded in 1977,[27] the proposal languished for some time while the measures which formed the official listing regime slowly came into force.

By 1985, however, the single-market programme intervened to expedite matters. The Internal Market White Paper observed that, with respect to 'participation in collective investment schemes', along with other 'financial products' such as mortgages and insurance policies, 'it should be possible to facilitate the exchange of such "financial products" at Community level, using a minimal coordination of rules (especially on such matters as authorization, financial supervision and reorganisation, winding up, etc) as the basis for mutual recognition by Member States of what each does to safeguard the interests of the public'.[28] The White Paper pointed to the weaknesses of the equivalence regime and endorsed a new approach to harmonization (although its antecedents can be seen in the 1976 proposal)

[25] Completing the Internal Market, COM(85)310 (the Internal Market White Paper).
[26] N 23 above, 10.
[27] [1977] OJ C57/31 and [1977] OJ C75/10, respectively. Neither the European Parliament nor the ECOSOC gave the proposal a ringing endorsement. The Parliament found that the co-ordination measures were 'incomplete', while ECOSOC was concerned that the ability of Member States to impose stricter rules than the proposal's requirements on schemes situated in their territory, the numerous opportunities to derogate from the proposal, and the failure to harmonize marketing rules would all limit the effectiveness of the proposal as a harmonization measure.
[28] N 25 above, para 102.

based on the mutual recognition by each Member State of the regulatory regimes of other Member States, with the home Member State regulatory regime anchoring the regime: 'harmonisation, particularly as regards the supervision of ongoing activities should be guided by the principle of 'home country control' . . . the authorities of the Member State which is the destination of the services, whilst not deprived of all power, would have a complementary role'.[29] In order to ensure mutual trust and confidence, mutual recognition would be subject to a 'minimum harmonisation of surveillance standards'.[30] More specifically, it highlighted adoption of the UCITS proposal by the end of 1985 as part of its Financial Services Timetable for Completing the Internal Market By 1992.[31] The measure was finally adopted in December 1985 and was to be implemented by the Member States by October 1989.

V.6 THE UCITS DIRECTIVE

V.6.1 *Objectives and Treaty Basis*

The UCITS Directive[32] is designed to promote the free movement of collective-investment schemes and, in particular, to make it easier for a collective-investment scheme situated in one Member State to market its units in another Member State (recital 2). Article 47(2) EC (at the time Article 57(2) EC), on which the Directive is based, forms part of the Treaty's free-movement structure and is designed to facilitate the freedom to establish. It applies to the freedom to provide services by Article 55 EC. It provides for the co-ordination of Member States' laws with respect to the taking-up and pursuit of activities as self-employed persons and has been described by the Court of Justice as permitting the adoption of measures which 'contribute to the abolition of obstacles to free movement which may result in particular from a divergence between the provisions laid down by law,

---

[29] N 25 above, para 103.

[30] Ibid. On the White Paper and the mutual recognition/home Member State control 'passport' device see Ch. VI sects.5.1.3 and 6.4 below, where they are discussed in the context of the investment-services harmonization programme on which they have had a profound impact.

[31] Ibid, Annex, para 1.3.

[32] See generally, Woolridge, F, 'The EEC Directive on Collective Investment Schemes' [1987] *JBL* 329 and Ciani, D, 'European Investment Funds: The UCITS Directive of 1985 and the Objectives of the Proposal for a UCITS II Directive' (1996) 4 *JFRC* 150. The Commission's internal 1988 Report on the UCITS Directive provides a thorough examination of the Directive. 'Towards a European Market for the Undertakings for Collective Investment in Transferable Securities—Commentary on the Provisions of Council Directive 85/611/EEC of 20 December 1985' (the 1988 UCITS Report). For an interesting comparison between the Directive and the US Investment Company Act, 1940 see Paul, P, 'The European Community's UCITS Directive: One Model for US Regulatory Change in a Globalised Securities Market' (1992) 25 *Vanderbilt J Transn'l. Law* 61.

regulation or administrative action in Member States concerning the taking-up and pursuit of activities as self-employed persons'.[33] Recital 1 makes clear that the laws of the Member States with respect to collective-invest-ment undertakings 'differ appreciably from one State to another' and that co-ordination will make it easier for a collective-investment undertaking to market its units in other Member States (recital 2). Harmonization is also justified by reference to the need to remove the distortions to competition created by the diverging Member States' rules by harmonizing the rules in question and 'approximating the conditions of competition between those undertakings at Community level' (recital 2). Free movement of the UCITS apart, investor protection is offered as what must be a subsidiary rationale for harmonization, with recital 1 stating that the diverging rules 'do not ensure equivalent protection', and recital 2 finding that co-ordination will 'at the same time ensur[e] more effective and more uniform protection for unit-holders'.[34] This emphasis on investor protection reflects the largely unsophisticated and inexperienced UCITS investor base. While the major objective of the UCITS Directive is clearly rooted in Article 47(2) EC, nonetheless, as is discussed in more detail with respect to investment ser-vices in Chapter IX section 12 below, it is questionable whether investor pro-tection can be pursued as a regulatory objective under Article 47(2) EC. Article 47(2) is directed toward the removal of barriers to free movement which arise as a result of the diversity or obstructive nature of the non-har-monized rules. It does not accommodate investor protection *per se* as a justification for the adoption of protective rules under Article 47(2), although investor-protection harmonization can be justified where the investor-protection rules in question restrict free movement. Finally, the free movement of UCITSs and the enhancement of investor protection are both linked to the free circulation of the units of collective investment schemes and thus to the construction of a European capital market (recital 3).

The Directive's objectives are to be attained by adopting common rules for the authorization, supervision, structure, and investment policies (with respect to asset quality and risk-spreading) of collective-investment schemes and the disclosure which they must provide. These rules support the Directive's mutual recognition mechanism and thus its market-integration objectives by ensuring that a common rule-base is in place in all the Member States. The Directive's identification of the areas in respect of which com-mon standards were necessary reflects a strong commitment to investor protection; something which cannot be said of the standards chosen to

---

[33] Case C-233/94 *Germany v Parliament and Council* [1997] ECR I-2405, para 15.

[34] The Directive has no impact on Member States' rules concerning the admission of units of UCITS to listing. As this was a sensitive issue, a statement was made in the Council minutes placing on record that the Directive has no effect on the jurisdiction of Member States with regard to the admission of UCITS units to listing: the 1988 UCITS Report, n 32 above, 91.

underpin the mutual-recognition regime which applies to investment services. While the Directive's primary aim is to permit units of a UCITS to be freely marketed across the Community, and its regulatory structure and substantive provisions reflect this objective, its provisions apply to all UCITS which come within the scope of the Directive, whether or not their units are marketed outside the Member State in which they are situated. Two themes run through the Directive's regulatory framework: first, regulation of a scheme's structure and management and secondly, disclosure.

V.6.2 *Scope*

Under Article 1(1), the Directive applies to undertakings for collective-investment in transferable securities (UCITSs). UCITSs are further defined as undertakings the sole object of which is the collective-investment in transferable securities of capital raised from the public[35] and which operate on the principle of risk-spreading.[36] In addition, the units of the UCITS must, at the request of the unit-holder, be capable of repurchase or redemption, directly or indirectly out of the UCITS's assets.[37] Article 1(3) provides that a UCITS may be constituted according to the law of contract (as common funds without a separate legal personality and managed by management companies)[38] trust law (as unit trusts), or under statute (as investment companies).[39] Under Article 1(5), Member States must prohibit UCITSs which

---

[35] This provision reflects the Directive's emphasis on protecting the retail investor, but the meaning of 'the public' is not entirely clear. Would, eg, a marketing campaign directed at a particular sector of the public, such as teachers, through the medium of their professional journal, be sufficient? The 1988 UCITS Report (ibid) suggested at 11 that marketing to a large sector of the public such as all the professions would be sufficient, but that targeting specific sectors, such as one profession, would not be, as the intention behind the Directive is to regulate UCITSs which are marketed to the public at large. In the interests of maximum investor protection, however, a wide approach to this definition must be preferred. This reluctance to grapple with the key notion of how to define the public which is protected by the measure was also side-stepped (albeit with more serious consequences) in the Public Offers Directive (Directive 89/298/EEC coordinating the requirements for the drawing-up, scrutiny and distribution of the prospectus to be published when transferable securities are offered to the public [1989] OJ L124/8).

[36] A scheme which does not operate on the principle of risk-spreading is one which, eg, seeks to exercise control over the undertakings in which it invests.

[37] For clarification, Art. 1(2) of the Directive also provides that any action taken by a UCITS to ensure that the stock exchange value of its units does not vary significantly from their net asset value is regarded as equivalent to repurchase or redemption.

[38] eg, French *fonds commun de placement*.

[39] eg, French SICAVs and, in the UK, OEICs or open-ended investment companies. On OEICs see Thomas, M, 'Open-Ended Investment Companies: a Hybrid Form of Investment' (1998) 19 *The Company Lawyer* 26 and Lomnicka, E, 'Open-ended Investment Companies—A New Bottle for Old Wine' in Rider, B (ed), *The Corporate Dimension: An Exploration of Developing Areas of Company and Commercial Law* (1998) 47. OEICs have an overt EC focus in that they were set up as a response to the difficulties faced by the UK fund-management industry in fully exploiting the UCITS passport, as continental investors were wary of the trust form of collective-

are subject to the Directive's provisions from transforming themselves into collective investment schemes which fall outside the Directive's scope.

Article 2(1) sets out the specific exclusions from the Directive's scope. One of the most significant exclusions, which follows from the Directive's definition of a UCITS as a scheme in which units can be redeemed or repurchased, are UCITSs 'of the closed-end type'. Collective-investment schemes can be broadly divided into the closed-end type and the open-ended type. In a closed-end scheme, restrictions apply to the redemption of the units representing the capital of the scheme.[40] By contrast, in an open-ended scheme of whatever form units are issued continuously, or at short intervals, at a price related to current net asset value[41] and may be redeemed by unitholders on request, again at current net asset value, or a price related to it. The Directive's restriction to open-ended schemes reflects the popularity of open-ended schemes at the time of the Directive's adoption. In addition, as open-ended schemes often lie outside the safeguards of company law they were seen as more susceptible to failure unless specific rules were applied. The other exclusions from the scope of the Directive are UCITSs which raise capital without promoting the sale of their units to the public within the Community, or any part of it, UCITSs whose units may be sold only to the public in non-Community countries, and categories of UCITS which must be prescribed by the Member States and in respect of which the Directive's investment and borrowing rules are inappropriate.

Although applicable to UCITSs generally, the Directive suggests that UCITSs can be constituted in two forms, investment companies or unit trusts,[42] depending on whether or not they are in a corporate form. A unit trust under the Directive consists of three entirely separate entities, the

---

investment scheme, being more familiar with corporate or contractual schemes. See the original proposal in *Financial Services in the UK: A New Framework for Investor Protection* (Cmnd 9432, 1985) para 9.8 and the SIB's foreword to the Proposed Regulations for Open-Ended Investment Companies (1996) where it stated that OEICs were to be 'welcomed as providing a modern and flexible vehicle that would enable the UK industry to expand its operations elsewhere in the EU and further afield'.

[40] These typically take the form of fixed-capital funds, an example of which is the French *société d'investissement à capital fixé*. The misleadingly named UK 'investment trusts' (they are companies, not trusts) are also closed-end in that the manager of the scheme is not obliged to buy back the original investment by the subscriber (who holds a share in the company which owns the fund assets). As a result, liquidity can be provided only by the investor selling on the open market and, depending on market forces of supply and demand, the price obtained may not relate to the value the share represents of the assets held in the trust.

[41] Current net asset value is the current market value of the scheme's portfolio, divided by the number of units outstanding.

[42] 'Unit trusts' as regulated by the Directive are not limited to trust structures. The Directive includes contractual arrangements such as common funds or *fonds commun de placement* under the umbrella of unit trusts. The defining feature of a unit trust in this context is that the common fund or the trust is managed by a management company.

capital raised from unit-holders, the management company which manages the trust's assets and markets the trust, and the depositary which has custody of the trust's assets. In an investment company, the company is also the management company (or it may designate a separate management company), but the assets are held by a depositary. Crucially, in a unit trust, unit-holders do not have direct control over the management company as they hold units in the trust, not shares in the management company, while shareholders in an investment company as shareholders exercise control over the investment company.[43] Investment companies, management companies, and depositaries are all regulated by the Directive.

V.6.3 *The UCITS Passport*

The Directive encourages greater interpenetration of securities markets by granting a UCITS a regulatory passport to operate across the Community (in host Member States), without further regulation apart from local marketing rules, once it has been authorized by the Member State in which is situated (the home Member State) in accordance with the Directive's requirements.

Under Article 4(1), a UCITS may not carry on any activities unless it has been authorized by the competent authorities of the Member State in which it is situated. Once authorization has been granted, it is valid for all Member States. Article 1(6) reinforces this point by making clear that, subject to the powers given to host Member States in the Directive, a host Member State may not apply any other provisions whatsoever in the field covered by the Directive to a UCITS situated in another Member State where the UCITS markets its units within its territory. A Member State may apply requirements stricter than or additional to those set out in the Directive to UCITSs which are situated in its territory, as long as such requirements are of general application and do not conflict with the provisions of the Directive (Article 1(7)). Of key importance therefore is the identification of the Member State in which the UCITS is situated. Article 3 provides that a UCITS is deemed to be situated in the Member State in which the investment company or the management company of the unit trust has its registered office. Member States must require that the head office be situated in the same Member State as the registered office.[44]

Once authorized, the UCITS may operate across the Community, subject to certain notification requirements and local advertising rules. Article 46

---

[43] For ease of reference, holders of units in collective-investment schemes, whether in the form of an investment company or a unit trust, will be collectively referred to as unit-holders, unless the distinction is material.

[44] This requirement is designed to prevent 'letter box UCITSs' whose management and administration are predominantly outside the Community from benefiting from the passport, and to facilitate supervision of UCITSs. See the 1988 UCITS Report, n 32 above, 6. This is also a feature of the investment services regime: Ch. VII sect. 4.2 below.

requires that prior to marketing its units in a host Member State, the UCITS must inform the competent authorities of that Member State. This notification obligation requires the UCITS to send the following documents to the competent authorities of the host Member State: an attestation by the competent authorities that it fulfils the conditions imposed by the Directive; its fund rules or instruments of incorporation; its prospectus; its latest annual report and any subsequent half-yearly reports, where appropriate; and details of the arrangements made for marketing the units in the host Member State. A UCITS may begin to market its units two months after this notification unless the competent authorities of the host Member State establish, in a reasoned decision taken before the expiry of the two-month period, that the arrangements made for the marketing of its units do not comply with the requirements of its local advertising rules or other generally applicable rules which do not fall within the field covered by the Directive or do not fulfil the requirements of Article 45 (section 6.9 below) concerning the marketing of the units.

The mutual-recognition and home-country-control principles at the heart of the Directive are carried through to the supervision structures by Article 49(3). The competent authorities of the Member State in which the UCITS is situated have jurisdiction to supervise that UCITS. Supervision of compliance with marketing rules (both local and as set out in the Directive) is the responsibility of the competent authorities in which the UCITS markets its units. While the competent authorities of the home Member State have power to take action if the UCITS infringes any law or any regulation set out in the fund rules or the instruments of incorporation, the host Member State's authorities retain power to take action against the UCITS if it infringes any of the Directive's marketing rules, local advertising rules, or local rules which apply generally and fall outside the scope of the Directive (Article 52(1) and (2)). Given the mutual confidence on which the mutual-recognition principle is based, Article 52(3) requires the competent authorities of the home Member State to communicate any decisions concerning a withdrawal of authorization, any serious measures taken against a UCITS, or any suspension of repurchase or redemption imposed on it to the competent authorities of the host Member State.

The UCITS passport currently applies only to the scheme itself and is designed to facilitate the marketing of scheme units. It does not cover the financial institutions 'behind' the scheme. Management companies and depositaries must each obtain a separate authorization in each Member State in which they operate, as they also fall outside the investment-services passport available under the ISD passport. The new UCITS regime remedies this weakness as far as the managers of a UCITS are concerned (section 8.3 below).

V.6.4 *The Authorization Process*

As the passport mechanism and home-country control are dependent on other Member State competent authorities having confidence in the authorization standards applied by the competent authority with jurisdiction over the UCITS, the Directive establishes common standards which must apply to all UCITS. The authorization standards cover both unit trusts and investment companies specifically, and also set out the requirements applicable to UCITSs generally. In the case of unit trusts, the competent authorities must have approved the management company, the fund rules, and the choice of depositary (Article 1(2)). For investment companies, the competent authorities must approve the instruments of incorporation and the choice of depositary (Article 1(2)). Approval of the fund rules or the instruments of incorporation is an essential investor-protection mechanism as these documents will set out the management and investment rules of the scheme.

More generally, for all types of UCITS the Directive imposes standards of competence and character on persons managing the UCITS. The competent authorities may not authorize a UCITS if the directors (under Article 1(3) those persons who, under the law or the instruments of incorporation, represent or effectively determine the policy of the management company, the investment company, or the depositary) of the management company, the investment company or the depositary are not of sufficiently good repute or lack the experience required for the performance of their duties.[45] The Directive does not give any guidance on how reputation and experience are to be measured, leaving the competent authorities with flexibility in this area.[46] Ongoing supervision of the UCITS is required by Article 4(4) which requires that neither the management company nor the depositary may be replaced, or the fund rules of the investment company's instrument of incorporation amended, without the approval of the competent authorities.

The competent authorities are required to give reasons for any decision to refuse authorization (and for any negative decision taken in implementation of the general measures adopted in application of this Directive) and communicate them to applicants (Article 51(1)). Further, any decisions taken in respect of a UCITS under laws adopted in accordance with the Directive must be subject to the right to apply to the courts. This right also

---

[45] To that end the competent authorities must be provided with the names and addresses of the directors (and of any successors) of the management company, the depositary, and the investment company.

[46] The parallel provisions in the investment-services field benefit from FESCO's (FESCO is now the Committee of European Securities Regulators) activities in promoting convergence. See Ch. VII sect. 4.4 below.

applies where the competent authorities have not responded within six months of the submission of an authorization application (Article 51(2)).

V.6.5 *Structural Requirements*

V.6.5.1 *Unit Trusts*

Under Article 5, a management company must have sufficient resources at its disposal to enable it to conduct its business effectively and to meet its liabilities. In order to maximize the protection of unit-holders by requiring a high degree of specialization by management companies, the management company may not engage in activities other than the management of unit trusts and investment companies (Article 6). This provision also seeks to prevent any potential conflicts of interests which might arise were the management company to engage in other activities.

Article 7(1) requires that a unit trust's assets must be entrusted to a depositary for safekeeping. As it is the custodian of the trust's assets and responsible for essential technical procedures relating to the administration of the assets (such as collecting income and redeeming units), regulation of the depositary is central to protecting the interests of unit-holders. The choice of depositary is regulated by Article 8(2), which provides that the depositary must be an institution which is subject to public control. The Member States are to designate which categories of institutions are eligible to act as depositaries. In addition, the application of a single supervision system to the management company and the depositary is emphasized by Article 8(1), which requires that a depositary must either have its registered office in the same Member State as that of the management company or, alternatively, be established in that Member State if its registered office is in another Member State. Article 8 was also designed to reflect the reality that the depositary must remain in close contact with the management company in order to supervise it effectively. It had the effect, however, of restricting the freedom of depositaries to offer their services across the single market. Apart from these limitations on choice, however, the depositary is not subject to approval or authorization controls apart from the requirement, also applicable to the management company, that it furnish sufficient financial and professional guarantees to be able effectively to pursue its business as a depositary and meet the commitments inherent in that function (Article 8(2)). It appears that the reason behind this omission was a pragmatic acknowledgement that depositaries will generally be credit institutions which are already subject to approval by the banking authorities.

The duties of the depositary are set out in Article 7(3). These duties, which are designed to ensure that vital tasks related to the administration of the assets are carried out and that the management company is supervised to ensure it operates within the law and the fund rules, include ensuring that the sale, issue, repurchase, redemption, and cancellation of units are carried out in accordance with the law and with fund rules; ensuring that the value of units is calculated in accordance with fund rules; carrying out the instructions of the management company, unless they conflict with the law or with fund rules; ensuring that any consideration from transactions in the unit trust's assets is remitted to it within the usual time limits; and ensuring that a unit trust's income is applied within the law and the fund rules.

Unusually in the EC securities-regulation field where remedies and redress are not typically addressed, Article 9 renders the depositary liable, in accordance with the law of the Member State in which the management company's registered office is situated, to the management company and unit-holders for any loss suffered by them as a result of its 'unjustifiable failure' to perform its obligations or its improper performance of them.[47] The position of unit-holders is specifically addressed with the requirement that liability to unit-holders may be invoked directly or indirectly through the management company, depending on the legal nature of the relationship between the depositary, the management company, and the unit-holders.

Article 10 addresses the key issue of independence and provides that a single company may not act as both a management company and a depositary. The management company and the depositary are also required to act independently and solely in the interests of unit-holders. Ongoing stability is addressed by Article 11, which requires that the law or the fund rules must lay down the conditions for the replacement of the management company and the depositary and rules to ensure the protection of unit-holders in the event of such replacement.

V.6.5.2 *Investment Companies*

A similar regime is applied to investment companies. The legal form of investment companies remains outside the scope of the Directive. Article 12 directs the Member States to determine the legal form which an investment company must take, but provides as a minimum that an investment company must have sufficient paid-up capital to enable it to conduct its business effectively and to meet its liabilities. An investment company may not engage in activities other than managing the collective investment scheme in question and must entrust its assets to a depositary (Articles 13 and 14(1)).

Depositaries of investment companies are subject to broadly the same regime as applies to depositaries of unit trusts, but there are some differ-

---

[47] Liability is not affected where the depositary entrusts all or some of the assets in its safe-keeping to a third party.

ences. The same restrictions on location and public control apply, as do the same independence and depositary replacement requirements (Articles 15 and 17). The depositary of an investment company is also subject to the same liability regime as applies to depositaries of unit trusts (Articles 16 and 14(2)). Its duties, however, are less onerous (Article 14(3)). In particular, a depositary is not required to ensure that the value of units is calculated in accordance with the law and fund rules,[48] nor to ensure that any instructions given to it by the management company are not in conflict with the law or fund rules.[49] This lessening of the depositary's supervisory function arises as shareholders in investment companies benefit from the protections of company law, and, as shareholders, can exert an influence over the management of the investment company, unlike unit-holders in unit trusts who do not have any control over the activities of the management company. Member States are also given more discretion with respect to the treatment of investment-company depositaries than they can exercise in respect of unit trust depositaries. Under Article 14(4) and (5) Member States are given the opportunity to derogate from the requirement that an investment company entrust its assets to a depositary in two circumstances. The first of these (Article 14(4)) is where the investment company situated in the territory of the Member State markets its units exclusively though one or more stock exchanges on which its units are admitted to official listing. The second arises under Article 14(5), under which a Member State may exempt investment companies from the depositary requirement where the investment company situated in its territory markets at least 80 per cent of its units through one or more stock exchanges which are designated in its instruments of incorporation. The units of such an investment company must also be admitted to official listing on the stock exchanges of those Member States within which its units are marketed. In addition, any transactions undertaken by an investment company eligible for this exemption, which are conducted outside the relevant stock exchanges, must be effected at stock exchange prices only. Finally, the company's instruments of incorporation must specify the stock exchange in the country of marketing the prices on which are to determine the prices at which the company will effect any transactions outside the stock exchanges in that country. Reflecting the Directive's investor-protection roots, a Member State may exercise this option only if it considers that unit-holders have protections equivalent to those of unit-holders which have depositaries. Investment companies benefiting from either exemption[50] are also subject to measures designed to

---

[48] Imposed on unit trust depositaries by Art. 7(b).

[49] Art. 7(d) effectively requires this of unit trust depositaries by requiring that they carry out the instructions of the management company, unless they conflict with the law or fund rules.

[50] The identity of such investment companies must be forwarded by the Member States to the Commission.

regulate the net asset value of their units. Under Article 14(4), such invest-ment companies must, in the absence of a provision in law, state in their instruments of incorporation the methods of calculation of the net asset val-ues of their units, intervene on the market to prevent the stock exchange values of their units from deviating by more than 5 per cent from their net asset values, and establish the net asset values of their units, communicate them to the competent authorities at least twice a week, and publish them at least twice a month.[51]

Despite the fact that investment companies and management companies are entrusted with the investment of investors' savings, the Directive does not impose authorization controls (such as specific capital requirements)[52] or prudential controls on the manager. Such requirements as are imposed are a function of the authorization of the UCITS product, and are not designed to subject the manager of the UCITS to detailed review. Investor protection is largely achieved through rules such as the investment-policy controls which regulate the UCITS product, rather than the manager. This gap in the Directive would become more pronounced as the fund industry grew. Questions of regulation aside, the UCITS Directive is also inadequate in that it does not grant a passport to managers of UCITSs who must be authorized in every Member State in which they offer services. This require-ment, as well the restrictions of their activities to UCITS management only, places severe restrictions on managers of UCITSs from fully benefiting from the internal market (on the remedial measures being taken in this respect see section 8 below).

V.6.6 *Investment Policies*

The most extensive and restrictive rules contained in the Directive concern the investment policies of the UCITS. These investment-policy rules are designed to protect unit-holders by regulating the quality of scheme assets and ensuring that appropriate risk-spreading methods are adopted. Under the new UCITS regime, UCITS will be permitted to invest in a substantially wider range of instruments (section 8.2 below).

---

[51] Further monitoring is imposed by the requirement that an independent auditor must, at least twice a month, ensure that the calculation of the value of units is effected in accordance with the law and the company's instruments of incorporation. The auditor must also on those occasions ensure that the company's assets are invested in accordance with the law and the company's instruments of incorporation.

[52] A number of Member States sought the inclusion of capital requirements in the Directive during negotiations, but the vast range of capital requirements from minimal to extensive in force at the time across the Community was thought to render any protections which the Directive might be able to achieve illusory for certain Member States with sophisticated capital regimes: the 1988 UCITS Report, n 32 above, 21. More extensive authorization requirements, including capital requirements, will be required of investment companies and management companies under the new UCITS regime: sect. 8.3.3 and Ch. VII sect. 9.3.1 below.

As a matter of first principles, it is clear from Article 1(1) that UCITSs may invest only in 'transferable securities',[53] a key term which is not defined. Member States are entitled to adopt their own definition which could result in variations in the investment policy restrictions placed on UCITSs in different Member States.

The first group of investment policy restrictions concerns dealing and listing qualifications and is designed to ensure that the UCITS' assets are easily realizable and assessable. Article 19(1) requires that the transferable securities must be admitted to an official list or dealt in on a regulated market. The transferable securities must be admitted to official listing on a stock exchange in a Member State, or dealt in on another regulated market in a Member State which operates regularly and is open to the public, or admitted to official listing on a stock exchange or dealt in on a regulated market in a non-Member State, provided that the stock exchange or regulated market has been approved by the competent authorities or is provided in law, the fund rules, or the instruments of incorporation, or, finally, must consist of recently issued transferable securities. Where the UCITS invests in recently issued transferable securities, the terms of the issue must include an undertaking that application will be made for admission to official listing on a stock exchange or to another regulated market. Again, the stock exchange or regulated market in a non-Member State must be approved by the competent authorities or provided for in law, the fund rules, or the instruments of incorporation. The admission must take place within a year of the issue. A UCITS may invest no more than 10 per cent of its assets in transferable securities which fall outside these categories (Article 19(2)(a)).

Article 19(2)(b) is somewhat delphic, in that it provides that a UCITS may invest no more than 10 per cent of its assets in 'debt instruments' which are treated, due to their characteristics 'as equivalent to transferable securities'. The failure to define transferable securities makes this provision difficult to unravel,[54] but an indication of the nature of these debt instruments is given by the requirement that they be 'transferable, liquid and have a value which can be accurately determined at any time or at least with the frequency

---

[53] The original proposal was less strict and limited UCITSs to investing 'mainly in transferable securities and liquid assets'. 'Mainly' was further defined as at least 80% of the UCITS' assets. The Directive does not prohibit UCITS from taking the form of 'umbrella UCITS', which operate a number of separate investment funds, each specializing in transferable securities from different geographical and market sectors. Investors may usually swap their investment between the different 'compartments' of the UCITS. The new UCITS disclosure regime includes specific disclosure requirements on umbrella UCITSs: sect. 8.3.2 below.

[54] The 1988 UCITS Report, n. 32 above at 43–4, noted, however, that this provision was designed to take account of the situation obtaining in some Member States where UCITSs were permitted to invest in debt instruments such as options, treasury bonds, debt certificates and promissory notes.

stipulated in Article 34'.[55] Under Article 20, Member States are to inform the Commission of the debt instruments they plan to treat as equivalent to transferable securities. An attempt is made to address the divergences which could open up in investment-policy regulation between the Member States by Article 20(2), which permits the Commission to forward this information to the other Member States with any comments it may have. These communications may also be discussed by the Contact Committee (section 6.11 below). UCITSs are also banned from acquiring either precious metals or certificates representing them (Article 19(2)(d)). Given the overriding restriction of investing only in transferable securities, Article 19(2) pragmatically clarifies that investment companies are permitted to acquire movable and immovable property which is essential for the direct pursuit of their business and Article 19(3) acknowledges that both unit trusts and investment companies may hold ancillary liquid assets.[56]

A further group of restrictions applies in respect of the diversification of investments; these rules attempt to ensure risk-spreading in the portfolio of assets.[57] The diversification rules are designed to limit the impact which a bankruptcy or a failure to make payments (such as interest payments on debt securities) on the part of a single issuer may have on a portfolio of assets and operate by imposing quantitative limits on the securities held. The general rule under Article 22(1) is that a UCITS may not invest more than 5 per cent of its assets in transferable securities issued by the same issuer. Any increased risk which may be incurred by investing in several issuers in the same group is not addressed. In certain circumstances, however, issuers in the same group may represent the same risk so that allowing investment of up to 5 per cent in each may be significantly increasing risk rather than spreading it. The 5 per cent rule is subject to a significant number of derogations. Member States have a general discretion to raise the 5 per cent limit to 10 per cent, but in those circumstances, the total value of transferable securities held by a UCITS in issuers in which it invests more than 5 per cent must not exceed 40 per cent of the total value of its assets.[58] More

---

[55] For Art. 34 see sect. 6.8.1 below. Despite this relaxation, the total of these debt instruments, together with any transferable securities which do not fall within Art. 19(1), must not, under any circumstances, amount to more than 10% of a UCITS' assets.

[56] Such as cash and bank deposits at sight which provide liquidity for the UCITS. It may be necessary for the UCITS to hold ancillary liquid assets where, eg, investment in securities must be suspended due to unfavourable market conditions or where cash is held for a short time between selling an investment and re-investing the proceeds.

[57] In a wide-ranging discussion of the legal implications of modern portfolio-management theory for investment managers, diversification has been described as 'the most powerful device for reducing risk in a portfolio . . . its long-standing attractiveness to investors is what gave major impetus to modern portfolio theory': Bines, H, 'Modern Portfolio Theory and Investment Management Law: Refinement of Legal Doctrine' (1976) 76 *Col. LR* 721, 794.

[58] Art. 22(2). This derogation is aimed at UCITSs which invest in small markets (such as the Irish market) in which there are relatively few quoted issuers in which a UCITS can invest.

specifically, Member States may raise the limit to 35 per cent if the transferable securities are issued or guaranteed by a Member State, its local authorities, a non-Member State, or a public international body of which one or more Member States are members (Article 22(3)). Directive 88/220/EEC[59] added an additional derogation which raised the limit to 25 per cent in respect of mortgage credit bonds issued by credit institutions to address a particular situation obtaining in Denmark (Article 22(4)). Holdings of transferable securities in the latter two categories are not included for the purposes of applying the overall 40 per cent of total value limit (Article 22(5)). In addition, where a Member State, its local authorities, a non-Member State, or public international body of which one or more Member States are members issues or guarantees more than one type of transferable security, Member States may authorize UCITSs to invest up to 100 per cent of their assets in such an issuer or guarantor, in accordance with the principle of risk-spreading (Article 23(1)). The securities must, however, be from at least six different issues, securities from any single issue must not account for more than 30 per cent of the UCITS' total assets and the competent authorities may grant the derogation only to a particular UCITS where they are satisfied that unit-holders have protection equivalent to those unit-holders in UCITSs which comply with the investment limits set out in Article 22. Further protection is given to unit-holders by the disclosure requirements. The UCITS must make express mention in either the fund rules or the instruments of incorporation (which must be approved by the competent authorities) of any entity outlined above in which it intends to invest more than 35 per cent of its assets and include a 'prominent statement' referring to this authorization and the entities concerned in its prospectus and any promotional literature (Article 22(2) and (3)).

In what turned out to be a controversial restriction, UCITSs may not acquire the units of other open-ended collective-investment schemes, unless they fall within the Directive's definition of a UCITS and, in any event, may not invest more than 5 per cent of their assets in the units of such collective investment schemes.[60] Additional restrictions apply in respect of investments in unit trusts managed by the same management company as manages the investing unit trust or in investment companies to which the investing company is linked (Article 24(3) and (4)).

[59] [1988] OJ L100/31.

[60] Art. 24(1) and (2). UCITSs of UCITSs (or funds of funds) carry certain risks for investors, in that investors may not be aware of the composition of the investment which they ultimately acquire through the 2nd UCITS and the original UCITS may be in a position to circumvent the rules prohibiting acquisition of a 'significant influence' in any undertaking (on which see ahead). Conversely, they have a number of advantages, the principal one being the ability of the original UCITS to benefit from the sector and geographic expertise of a 2nd UCITS without incurring the related costs, and to pass on the benefit of such diversification to unit-holders. The Directive ultimately takes a cautious approach.

In order to encourage appropriate risk-spreading and to prevent a UCITS from pursuing control over the issuers in which it invests, which is outside the function of a UCITS, restrictions are placed by Article 25 on the voting rights and management control which a UCITS may acquire through its investment activities. The central requirement is that the investment company or the management company (acting in connection with all of the unit trusts which it manages and which fall within the scope of the Directive), may not acquire any shares carrying voting rights which would enable it to exercise significant influence over the management of an issuing body (Article 25(1)). The Directive neither defines 'significant influence' nor introduces detailed harmonizing rules, but simply requires Member States to take account of other Member State rules in this area. To this end, the Council issued a Recommendation in 1985 recommending that where the investment company or management company of a UCITS acquires voting rights issued by a company established in a Member State which applies a percentage limit to represent the acquisition of a 'significant influence', its competent authorities should ensure, if so requested by that Member State where the percentage limits apply, that the limits are observed by the management company or investment company.[61] Article 25(2) sets out additional limits on acquisitions of transferable securities which do not carry voting rights. An investment company or unit trust may not acquire more than 10 per cent of the non-voting shares of any single issuing body, 10 per cent of the debt securities of any single issuing body, and 10 per cent of the units of any single UCITS. Again, Member States are given extensive opportunities to depart from these rules. Article 25(3) provides that Member States may waive both requirements in respect of a list of different types of transferable securities, which includes transferable securities issued or guaranteed by a Member State or its local authorities or a non-Member State, or issued by public international bodies of which the Member State is a member.[62] Article 25(3)(e) is of some significance in that it concerns the use of subsidiaries by UCITSs. Article 25 provides that the waiver can apply to shares held by an investment company in the capital of subsidiary companies which carry on the business of management, advice, or marketing exclusively on its behalf. This provision implies that UCITSs may use subsidiaries to carry out certain functions, a strategy which can generate transparency and supervisory risks. The new UCITS regime addresses this difficulty (see section 8.2.7 below).

Generally, Member States may authorize a UCITS to employ 'techniques and instruments relating to transferable securities' under the conditions and within the limits which they lay down, provided that such techniques and

---

[61] [1985] OJ L375/19.   [62] Art. 25(3)(a)–(e) for the full list.

instruments are used for the purpose of efficient portfolio management.[63] Likewise, Member States may authorize UCITSs to use techniques and instruments to protect against exchange risk in managing their assets and liabilities (Article 21(2)).

The investment policy rules do not apply where a UCITS is exercising subscription rights attaching to transferable securities which form part of its assets (Article 26(1)). In addition, Member States may permit recently authorized UCITS to derogate from the investment limits imposed by Articles 22 and 23 for the six months following their authorization, as long as the principle of risk-spreading is observed. The Directive does not require liquidation of assets where the investment-policy limits have been breached unintentionally. Where the limits imposed by the section are exceeded by a UCITS for reasons beyond its control (such as, for example, a sudden contraction in the size of the UCITS following a number of redemptions or repurchases) or as a result of the exercise of subscription rights, the UCITS must instead adopt as a priority objective for its sale transactions the remedying of that situation, taking into account the interests of unit-holders (Article 26(2)).

V.6.7 *General Obligations*

Apart from the investment policy rules, the Directive imposes a number of prudential requirements on UCITSs in terms of the management of the scheme, which are broadly designed to protect the UCITS' assets for the benefit of unit-holders. Investment companies and management companies and depositaries acting on behalf of a unit trust are prohibited from borrowing under Article 36(1). In addition to the specific investment-policy rules, this general ban also impacts on a UCITS' investment policy. Member States may derogate from this rule by authorizing a UCITS to borrow up to 10 per cent of its assets (in the case of an investment company) or 10 per cent of the value of the fund (in the case of a unit trust) but the borrowing may only be on a temporary basis. A Member State may, additionally, authorize an investment company to borrow up to 10 per cent of its assets where the borrowing is for the acquisition of immovable property essential for the direct pursuit of its business. Where such borrowing is authorized, it may not, together with any borrowings under the first derogation, exceed in total 15 per cent of the investment company's assets (Article 36(2)). Conversely, neither an investment company nor a management company or

---

[63] Art. 21(1). This convoluted provision is designed to cover the use of derivative instruments such as futures and options. Considerable difficulties arose in the course of the negotiations over the treatment of options traded on a regulated option market (the main ones at the time were in London and the Netherlands) and whether they would be treated as transferable securities. The unhappy solution was Art. 21(1).

depositary of a unit trust may grant loans or guarantees.[64] The last of these prudential requirements prohibits the investment company and the management company or depositary acting on behalf of a unit trust from carrying out uncovered sales of securities (Article 42).

The core redemption and repurchase procedures are also regulated. The basic obligation set out in Article 37(1) requires that a UCITS must repurchase or redeem its units at the request of any unit-holder.[65] Two derogations apply to this rule. First, a UCITS may temporarily suspend the repurchase or redemption of units in the cases and according to the procedures set out by law, the fund rules, or the investment company's instruments of incorporation (Article 37(2)(a)). Suspension may be provided for only in exceptional cases and must be justified having regard to the interests of unit-holders or the public.[66] Secondly, the Member States may allow the competent authorities to require the suspension of repurchase or redemption in the interests of unit-holders or the public (Article 37(2)(b)).[67]

Although fair and accurate valuations of scheme property are critical for investor protection, the Directive does not set out harmonized rules on asset or unit valuation. Article 38 simply requires that asset-valuation rules as well as issue, sale, redemption, and repurchase-price calculation rules must be laid down in law, the fund rules, or the instruments of incorporation of the investment company. Similarly, the distribution or reinvestment of income must be effected in accordance with the law, the fund rules, or the instruments of incorporation of the investment company (Article 39). Under Article 40, UCITS units may not be issued unless the equivalent of the net issue price is paid into the assets of the UCITS within the 'usual time limits', although this provision does not preclude the distribution of bonus units.

Finally, although the Directive does not harmonize remuneration and expenditure rules, Article 43 requires that the law or the fund rules must prescribe the remuneration and the expenditure which a management company may charge to a unit trust and the way in which such remuneration is to be calculated, and provides that the law or an investment company's instruments of incorporation prescribe the nature of the costs to be borne by the company.

---

[64] Art. 41, although this prohibition does not prohibit the acquisition of transferable securities which are not fully paid.

[65] This obligation is the essence of an open-ended scheme. The disclosure requirements (see sect. 6.8 below) reinforce Art. 37(1) by requiring disclosure of the manner and the conditions under which redemption or repurchase is carried out.

[66] Given the significance of such a decision by a UCITS it is unsurprising that Art. 37(3) requires that the decision to do so be communicated without delay to the competent authorities and to the authorities of all Member States in which it markets its units.

[67] In addition, Art. 37 does not apply to investment companies which are not required to use a depositary because of their stock exchange status (Art. 14(4)).

V.6.8 *Disclosure*

V.6.8.1 *General Principles*

Although investor protection is addressed by the authorization, structural, and investment-policy controls, disclosure is central to the Directive's investor-protection regime. Indeed, collective-investment schemes are particularly suitable for regulation via disclosure, in that their performance is regularly evaluated by the media, accurate and comparable data describing market share and average returns on investment over a significant period of time are generally available, and it appears that the investing public readily absorbs this information.[68] The mandatory disclosure required by the Directive is, however, somewhat arcane, and arguably does not fully utilize the sensitivity of the investing public to disclosure in an accessible form.

The central disclosure obligation is imposed by Article 27(1) which requires investment companies, and, for each of the unit trusts managed, management companies to publish a prospectus, an annual report for each financial year, and a half-yearly report covering the first six months of the financial year. These documents must each be sent to the relevant competent authorities, but prior scrutiny is not required.[69]

Distribution of these documents to potential investors is addressed by Article 33 which requires that the prospectus, the latest annual report, and any subsequent half-yearly reports published must be offered to subscribers free of charge before the conclusion of a contract. In addition, under Article 35, all publicity comprising an invitation to purchase the units of a UCITS must indicate that a prospectus exists and the places where it may be obtained by the public. Ongoing disclosure of financial information is

---

[68] In the USA, the degree to which the mutual-fund industry should be regulated, given the sensitivity of investors to disclosure has been questioned: Ippolito, R, 'Consumer Reaction to Measures of Poor Quality: A Study of Mutual Fund Performance 1965–84' (1992) 35 *J L and Econ.* 45. He has found that regulatory intervention should be limited to ensuring that timely and accurate information about performance is reported and has concluded (at 68) that 'the mutual fund industry provides one compelling observation in favor of an information approach to regulation'. Disclosure must, however, be accessible and digestible to be effective. For a perspective on how investors react to collective-investment scheme disclosure see the FSA (UK Financial Services Authority), *Informing Consumers: a Review of Product Information at the Point of Sale*, Discussion Paper, (2000). It examined the key features document (or KFD) required under the UK system when packaged products are sold and found that in general consumers had difficulty in understanding the material and often did not read it.

[69] Art. 32. The original proposal provided in Art. 37 that the prospectus and any changes to it were to be checked by the competent authorities prior to publication, and that any comments were to be taken into account by the UCITS. The competent authorities were also to check the annual and six-monthly reports. In all cases the proposal rather unrealistically expected the competent authorities to ensure that the prospectus and reports did not contain any information or omissions which might mislead the public. This provision was dropped after a number of Member States objected to the potential liability which might be imposed on public authorities: 1988 UCITS Report, n 32 above, 73.

achieved by Article 33(2) which requires that the financial reports be made available to the public at the places specified in the prospectus, and Article 33(3) which provides that the reports must be supplied to unit-holders free of charge on request.

Apart from these specific requirements, a UCITS is required to make other material information available periodically. Under Article 34, the issue, sale, repurchase, or redemption price of its units must be made public 'in an appropriate manner' each time it issues, sells, repurchases, or redeems units, and, in any event, at least twice a month. A derogation is available here, in that competent authorities may permit a UCITS to reduce the reporting frequency to once a month, as long as such a derogation does not prejudice the interests of unit-holders.

V.6.8.2 *The Prospectus*

In a formula familiar from the current issuer-disclosure regime, the prospectus must contain the information necessary for the investor to make an informed judgement of the investment proposed to them (Article 28). This catch-all disclosure obligation is supplemented by the requirement that the prospectus contain at least the information set out in Schedule A and the obligation to keep all 'essential elements' of the prospectus up to date (Article 30). Where the information in question is already contained in the fund rules or the investment company's instruments of incorporation, which must be annexed to the prospectus (Article 29(1)),[70] it need not be repeated (Article 28(1)). Schedule A sets out extensive disclosure requirements covering the unit trust, the management company, and the investment company. The requirements range from basic requirements such as name and address, management information, and particulars concerning the auditor, to detailed requirements concerning the units, such as their tax treatment, their characteristics, issue, sale, repurchase, and redemption procedures, and the rules for determining and applying income, to descriptions of the unit trust's or investment company's investment objectives. Information must also be provided on how UCITS assets are valued and how the sale, issue, redemption, and repurchase price of units are determined. Information requirements also apply to the depositary including disclosure of the material provisions of its contract with the management company or investment company which may be relevant to unit-holders. Disclosure is also required concerning any advisory firms or external investment advisers who give advice under contract which is paid for out of the assets of the UCITS.

---

[70] Under Art. 29(2) these documents need not be annexed, however, where the unit-holder is informed that, on request, the documents will be sent or is told where, in each Member State in which the units are placed on the market, the documents may be consulted.

The current UCITS disclosure requirements do not, however, appear to be sensitive to the needs of investors. In particular, there is no requirement that the prospectus specifically address the risk posed by an investment in the collective-investment scheme. This is a significant weakness in the disclosure structure, given that retail investors should be made aware of the relationship between return and risk when investing in a collective-investment scheme. Disclosure of fees and other charges is also omitted from the mandatory requirements. Further, unlike in the issuer-disclosure regime it is not necessary that the disclosure be in as 'easily analysable and comprehensible a form as possible'. The Schedule A requirements have led to the production of detailed prospectuses, the utility of which for ordinary retail investors has been questioned. The new UCITS regime drastically overhauls the prospectus rules, however, and is discussed in section 8.3.2 below.

V.6.8.3 *The Financial Reports*

The annual report must be published within four months of the end of the period to which it relates and the half-yearly report within two months of the end of such period (Article 27(2)). The annual report must contain a balance sheet or statement of assets and liabilities, a detailed income and expenditure account for the financial year, a report on the activities of the financial year, and the information required by Schedule B,[71] as well as 'any significant information which will enable investors to make an informed judgment on the development of the activities of the UCITS and its results' (Article 28(2)). The financial information must be audited and the auditor's report included in full in the annual report (Article 31). The information required in the half-yearly report is less extensive. Where the UCITS has paid or proposes to pay an interim dividend, the figures supplied must indicate the results after tax for the half-year concerned and the interim dividend paid or proposed (Article 28(3)).

V.6.8.4 *Liability for False or Misleading Disclosure*

As with the issuer-disclosure regime, the Directive does not impose any minimum requirements concerning sanctions or remedies in respect of false or misleading disclosure. Although the audit requirement imposes an external

---

[71] The Sch B requirements include a statement of assets and liabilities, the number of units in circulation, the net asset value per unit, and detailed information concerning the composition of the portfolio of assets. Additional requirements include a statement of developments concerning the assets of the UCITS during the relevant period, a comparative table covering the last 3 financial years and including for each financial year the total net asset value and the net asset value per unit at the end of the financial year, and details of all efficient portfolio management transactions carried out and the degree of commitment involved.

control on the quality of the information contained in the annual report, the harmonized rules do not protect investors against incomplete, misleading, or false disclosure. In particular, unlike the other disclosure directives which require the distribution of a prospectus, a responsibility statement in respect of the disclosure in the prospectus is not required.

V.6.9 *Marketing Rules*

Although the central principle of the Directive is that a UCITS is regulated by the Member State in which it is situated and may not be subject to further regulation by any Member State in which it markets its units, unless such regulation falls outside the field governed by the Directive (Article 44(1)), marketing rules are a major exception to this principle. Under Article 44(2), any UCITS may advertise its units in the Member State in which they are marketed, but the UCITS must comply with the 'provisions governing advertising' in that Member State as well as any rules applicable which fall outside the field covered by the Directive.[72] These rules must be applied by the host Member State without discrimination. The explanation given for the lack of co-ordination of marketing rules in the original 1976 proposal was that any attempt to harmonize such rules would, in view of marked differences between Member States, have significantly delayed the Directive. In the intervening decade or so between the proposal's presentation and the adoption of the Directive, those differences remained insuperable.[73] Notwithstanding the passport, UCITSs offering their units in Member States other than the home State face the obstacles represented by fifteen different marketing regimes.[74] The new UCITS regime does not harmonize the regulation of UCITS advertising by host Member States any further, but, in an alignment of the UCITS Directive with the ISD, does add a provision

[72] The original proposal took a more detailed approach and gave host Member States jurisdiction under Art. 54 in respect of UCITS situated in another Member State but marketing or intending to market units within their territory in respect of 'marketing regulations'. These were defined as covering rules relating to entries in trade registers, sales promotions, unfair competition, canvassing and other form of marketing techniques, and rules concerning the form of savings plans. During the negotiations, listing the rules covered was seen as a potential source of confusion and was replaced by the wider formula ultimately adopted. The general formula ultimately adopted includes, according to the 1988 UCITS Report, n. 32 above at 96, rules concerning the marketing of units, rules prohibiting direct sales, and rules on trade names.

[73] Interestingly, the original proposal recommended that the marketing issue should be dealt with in a more comprehensive manner and suggested that the marketing of transferable securities, and not just units of UCITSs, be addressed. ECOSOC called on the Commission to submit a proposal on the marketing of securities: n 27 above, para 1.4. Some 25 years on, the marketing of investments remains largely unco-ordinated. See Ch. IX.

[74] For a review of the range of national marketing rules to which a passporting UCITS is potentially subject see Little, T, 'Marketing Investment Funds in some Major European Markets Part 1 and Part 2' (1994) 1 *EFSL* 170 and 199.

which requires that any advertising rules adopted must be in the 'interests of the general good'.[75] The 'general good' concept has considerable importance in the investment services sphere and is discussed further in Chapter VI section 4.6.2 below.

Although the Directive therefore leaves the regulation of the marketing of UCITSs largely to the discretion of the Member States, under Article 45, a UCITS must, in accordance with the laws of the Member State in which it is marketing its units, take the measures necessary to ensure that facilities are available in that Member State for making payments to unit-holders, repurchasing or redeeming units, and making available the information which UCITSs are obliged to provide.

Finally, Article 47 currently (on the new regime see section 8.3.2 below) requires a UCITS, where it markets its units in a Member State other than that in which it is situated, to distribute in that other Member State, in at least one of that other State's official languages, the documents and information which it must publish in the Member State in which it is situated, in accordance with the same procedures as provided for in the Member State in which it is situated. These translation requirements have proved burdensome in practice for collective-investment schemes. UCITSs are permitted by Article 48 to use the same generic name (ie investment company or unit trust) in the Community as they use in the Member State in which they are situated. Host Member States are permitted to require that the name be accompanied by explanatory particulars in order to avoid confusion.

V.6.10 *Supervision and the Competent Authorities*

As previously outlined, supervision of UCITSs is split between the home and host Member States, with the home Member State responsible for the primary supervision of the UCITS. The host authorities have supervisory responsibility in relation to advertising rules and other rules of general application which fall outside the scope of the Directive.[76]

Article 49 requires Member States to designate the authorities responsible for supervision which must be 'public authorities or bodies appointed by public authorities'.[77] They must also have all the powers necessary to carry out their tasks.[78]

---

[75] N 105 below, Art. 6(a)(4). [76] Art. 44.

[77] The preceding admission to official listing measures did not require this element of public control, but simply required that the competent authorities have such powers as were necessary to carry out their functions. Arguably the difference in approach is predominantly a reflection of the sophisticated mutual-recognition structure and home-country control mechanism pioneered by the UCITS Directive and the need to ensure confidence in Member State supervisory systems. It might also be a reflection of the role played by private securities-trading markets in the admission to listing of securities.

[78] Art. 49(1), (2), and (4).

Article 50(1) acknowledges that effective co-operation is at the heart of successful mutual recognition and requires that the competent authorities collaborate closely in order to carry out their tasks and, for that purpose alone, communicate to each other all information required. As originally adopted, the UCITS Directive imposed a blanket professional-secrecy obligation on the competent authorities, although it also provided that the professional-secrecy obligation did not preclude communication between the competent authorities. The professional-secrecy and information-exchange rules have since been replaced and refined by amendments which were introduced by the Prudential Supervision Directive in 1995.[79] The basic professional-secrecy obligation now extends to all persons who work or have worked for the competent authorities, as well as auditors or experts instructed by the competent authorities. The professional-secrecy obligation itself has also been recast, and it now takes the form of a prohibition, without prejudice to cases covered by criminal law, on the divulging of any confidential information received in the course of duty to any person or authority whatsoever, save in summary or aggregate form such that it is not possible to identify individually any particular UCITS, depositary, or management company. On the winding-up of a UCITS or any undertaking contributing towards its business activities, confidential information which does not concern third parties involved in rescue attempts may be disclosed in civil or commercial proceedings (Article 50(2)).

Under the amended Article 50(3) competent authorities may exchange information (which on exchange is subject to professional secrecy) in accordance with the Directive or any other directives applicable to UCITSs or to undertakings contributing towards their business activity. The information exchanged may be used only to monitor compliance with authorization conditions and to facilitate supervision of the conduct of business by the UCITS, its administrative and accounting procedures, and its internal control mechanisms, to impose sanctions, and in administrative appeals or court proceedings involving the UCITS and the competent authority (Article 50(5)). The new provisions also set out (Article 50(6)) a list of the bodies with which, and the circumstances under which, confidential information may be exchanged. These final amendments partly align the Directive with the ISD and partly introduce the specific innovations with respect to prudential supervision and information exchange contained in the Prudential Supervision Directive which were also applied to the ISD.[80] Most recently,

---

[79] European Parliament and Council Directive 95/26 amending Directives 77/780/EEC and 89/646/EEC in the field of credit institutions, Directives 73/239/EEC and 92/49/EEC in the field of non-life insurance, Directives 79/267/EEC and 92/96/EEC in the field of life assurance, Directive 93/22 in the field of investment firms and Directive 85/611/EEC in the field of undertakings for collective investment in transferable securities (UCITS) with a view to reinforcing prudential supervision (the Prudential Supervision Directive) [1995] OJ L168/7.

[80] See Ch. VII sect. 8.4 below for these information-exchange rules.

Article 50(4) on information exchange with third countries, which was added by the Prudential Supervision Directive to reflect the ISD's original approach to information exchanges with third-country competent authorities, has been amended again by Directive 2000/64/EC.[81]

V.6.11 *Derogations and the Contact Committee*

Throughout the Directive Member States are given opportunities to derogate from its requirements.[82] This feature and the express ability of Member States to, conversely, impose requirements 'stricter than or additional to' the Directive's requirements on UCITSs situated within their territories (Article 1(7)) prejudices the degree of uniformity achieved by the Directive, but is a common feature of the current official-listing/public-offer regime.[83] The general mutual-recognition principle, however, protects a passporting UCITS from the imposition of certain additional requirements.

Partly to alleviate this failure to achieve uniformity, as with the previously adopted Securities Directives, the UCITS Directive provides in Article 53 for the establishment of a Contact Committee. Its functions are to facilitate the harmonized implementation of the Directive through regular consultations, to facilitate consultations between Member States on the additional requirements Member States may adopt or the local rules which may apply in host Member States, and to advise the Commission on any amendments necessary.

V.7 THE ISD

UCITSs, together with their depositaries and managers are excluded from the scope of the ISD.[84] Providing investment services such as investment advice, portfolio management services, and broking services in relation to units in collective-investment undertakings does, however, come within the scope of the ISD.[85] The ISD passport will therefore be significant for the distribution of units of a UCITS, although it will have no application to the constitution, operation, and marketing of the UCITS itself, and the activities of its

---

[81] [2000] OJ L290/27. The parallel ISD provision has also been revised. See Ch. VII sect. 8.4 below on the revision.

[82] In the area of investment policy, eg, Luxembourg has chosen to implement the most permissive requirements of the Directive and has taken advantage of the many derogations. See generally Schmitt, A, 'Investment Funds in Luxembourg' (1993) 2 *JIBL* 48.

[83] Sensitive to the competitive distortions possible, ECOSOC hoped that Member States would make as little use as possible of this facility and that alignment would occur voluntarily: n 27 above, para 1.2.2.

[84] ISD, Art. 2(2)(h).   [85] Art. 1(1) and (2) and Annex, Section A and B.

depositary and manager. Significant variations exist across the EC in the distribution networks for units of UCITS. The ISD passport is likely to be significant in the UK, Ireland, and Italy where investment-services intermediaries are the preferred method of distribution, while in other continental European Member States the banking directives will be more significant for distribution.[86]

V.8 REFORM

V.8.1 *The Push for Reform*

Notwithstanding the introduction of the passport, integration of the UCITS market has been slow.[87] This is partly due to diverging practices in the European fund industry. To take one example, different investment policies are pursued by UCITSs across the various national lines. Although variations in investment choices are in the main a function of the preferences of the institutional investors who invest in collective-investment schemes, the investment patterns and biases of local investors are also significant. In the UK, for example, collective-investment schemes tend to invest more heavily in equities; in Germany fixed-interest securities are the dominant form of investment; while in France money-market funds are the most important.[88] The varying structures which can be adopted by UCITSs can also slow the process of integration as investors tend to be suspicious of unfamiliar structures. In addition, dissatisfaction arose with the UCITS Directive as an integration vehicle. In particular, concerns were expressed that the investment restrictions placed on UCITS which limited investment opportunities to investments in transferable securities were preventing the collective-investment scheme industry and investors from fully exploiting the benefits of the UCITS passport and of collective investment schemes as investment vehicles. Variations in the implementation of the Directive also began to emerge, threatening the harmonization introduced by the Directive.[89]

---

[86] Banks are the dominant channels of distribution in Germany, France and Spain, holding market shares of between 60 and 80%: Gros and Lannoo, n 4 above, 67 and Walter, n 2 above, 14.

[87] The adoption of the UCITS Directive, however, significantly raised expectations. On the passing of the implementation deadline in Oct 1989, it was heralded as 'the first tangible indication of a single European market in retail financial services': Gartland, 'UCITS are running but hurdles lie ahead', *Financial Times*, 14 Oct 1989, cited in Poser, N, *International Securities Regulation. London's Big Bang and the European Securities Markets* (1991) 364.

[88] Overall, across the EU funds investing in debt securities form the largest group: Gros and Lannoo, n 4 above, 67.

[89] Although not all commentators would agree. It has been observed that, by contrast with the admission to official-listing/public-offer regime, 'the harmonised legal regime has worked for unit trusts': Gros and Lannoo, n 4 above, 34.

In 1993 the Commission presented a proposal to extend the scope of the UCITS Directive.[90] After widespread consultation of the industry, the Commission issued a revised proposal to amend the Directive in 1994.[91] The final 1994 proposal contained a number of significant amendments to the UCITS Directive which were predominantly concerned with the UCITS product and designed, *inter alia*, to widen the range of assets in which a UCITS could invest. The investment-policy revisions included amending the basic definition of a UCITS to include undertakings engaged in collective investment in deposits with credit institutions up to 25 per cent of the value of scheme assets. In addition, three new categories of UCITS were added. These were cash funds, which invest solely in deposits with credit institutions, funds of funds, which invest solely in units of other UCITSs, and master-feeder funds, which invest solely in the units of a single UCITS. Little progress was made in the Council where the provisions on feeder funds and cash funds proved controversial, and the proposal ultimately foundered.

Added to concerns over the restrictions placed on the investment policies of UCITSs and the consequent inability of UCITSs to reflect developments in the capital markets, as the popularity of collective-investment schemes as a form of saving grew across the EC, the adequacy of the Directive's supervision of the management companies entrusted to make investments on behalf of investors also came under scrutiny. In particular, with the adoption of the ISD it became obvious that the regulation of management companies with respect to authorization and operating standards was out of kilter with the regulation of investment firms generally. Management companies were also unable to benefit from the advantages of the harmonization of regulation, in that they were ineligible for the ISD passport and could not operate across the single market on the basis of home Member State authorization.

Progress on a proposal to amend the Directive remained stalled for some time over difficulties concerning whether to direct the amendments predominantly towards the UCITS product or the UCITS manager. In 1998 the Commission resolved the dilemma by bifurcating the proposed amendments and presenting two proposals, one focusing on the UCITS product and extending the range of funds which can benefit from the UCITS passport, the other addressing the UCITS manager as well as the UCITS prospectus. In the FSAP, the Commission highlighted progress on the proposals as an urgent political priority in the interests of maximizing the ability of investors to exploit the benefits of the single market fully and to access a wide range of competitive investment products.[92] Clearly, promoting and facilitating the transfer of retail investor savings to the capital markets via collective-investment undertakings will contribute to the deepening and liquidity of the Community capital markets. But the need to ensure that this changing

[90] COM(93)37.   [91] COM(94)329.   [92] FSAP, n 6 above, 3.

market-place is subject to appropriate prudential regulation in the interests of the stability of the single market in investment services generally has also emerged as a strong theme of the liberalizing amendments to the current regime.

V.8.2 The UCITS Product Regime

V.8.2.1 Objectives

The UCITS Directive contains the seeds of the Product Proposal[93] in that recital 6 of the Preamble states that collective-investment undertakings falling outside its scope are to be the subject of co-ordination at a later stage. The new product regime which, like the UCITS Directive, is based on Article 47(2) EC, now addresses that co-ordination and is designed to extend the UCITS passport to collective investment schemes investing in financial assets other than transferable securities. Its objective is to offer more opportunities to the European collective investment undertakings industry and greater choice to the investor. In particular, it widens the investment objectives of UCITSs in order to permit them to invest in financial instruments, other than transferable securities, which are sufficiently liquid (recital 2). While the revisions are designed to render the regulatory structure for UCITSs more flexible and to enhance their ability to respond to developments in the capital markets, in order to ensure that the investor remains appropriately protected with respect to the more diverse investments possible and their attendant

---

[93] Amended Proposal for a Directive amending Directive 85/611/EEC on the Coordination of Laws, Regulation and Administrative Provisions Relating to Undertakings for Collective Investment in Transferable Securities. COM(2000)329 (the Revised Product Proposal). The Council's Common Position is at [2001] OJ C297/35. The measure was adopted by the Council as a directive on 4 Dec 2001. This discussion is based on the Common Position (references to the Product Proposal are to the Common Position text, while references to Articles are to the revised Articles of the UCITS Directive introduced by the new regime). At the time of writing, the final text of the adopted measure had not been published in the Official Journal and had not yet come into force. The European Parliament did not, however, materially amend the Common Position during its second reading prior to the adoption of the measure. Its only amendments (which were to request the Commission to undertake a review of the UCITS regime with a view to undertaking further modifications within 3 years of the coming into force of the Directive and to insert a 60-month transitional period which would allow Member States to grant a UCITS existing on the entry into force of the Directive 60 months (or 5 years) from that date to comply with the new national legislation) were accepted by the Commission (COM(2001)686).

The original proposal is at COM(1998)449 (the Original Product Proposal). ECOSOC's opinion on the Original Product Proposal is at [1999] OJ C116/11. The European Parliament examined the Original Product Proposal in some detail. Both the Committee on Economic and Monetary Affairs and the Committee on Legal Affairs and the Internal Market delivered extensive opinions, proposing a number of amendments: A5-0025/2000. The European Central Bank's (ECB) opinion (Art. 105(4) EC gives the ECB a consultative role with respect to Community proposals) at [1999] OJ L285/9.

risks, new disclosure and transparency requirements are introduced with respect to the new range of investments,[94] as are risk-management and diversification rules. Overall, despite earlier speculation that the new regime would take the form of a framework directive, instead it takes a relatively intensive approach to regulation, applying quite detailed rules in the interests of investor protection.[95] Nonetheless, Member States retain the discretion to impose additional and more stringent investment-policy rules under Article 1(7) of the UCITS Directive which has not been revised. In addition, in line with the subsidiarity principle, considerable responsibility is devolved on the competent authorities with respect to the development and execution of the new regime's principles.

V.8.2.2 *Broadening the Scope of Permissible Investments*

Rather than setting out new categories of UCITS (as the 1994 proposal did), the new regime recognizes that it is for each UCITS to chose its own investment profile and its degree of specialization in particular securities, economic sectors, or geographic areas. Accordingly, the central revision contained in the new regime is to expand the definition of a UCITS as an undertaking 'the sole object of which is the collective investment in "transferable securities of capital raised from the public"' to include collective investment in the 'other liquid financial assets mentioned in Article 19(1)'. Article 19(1) has also been significantly amended to specify which additional 'liquid financial assets' are now available as potential investments for a UCITS.

The basic investment-restriction provision, Article 19(1)(a), is revised in three respects. First, the concept of a 'regulated market' is imported from the ISD and, consequentially, Article 19(1)(a) which currently includes 'transferable securities admitted to official stock exchange listing' as permissible investments, is amended to refer to transferable securities admitted to or dealt in on a regulated market within the meaning of the ISD.[96] Secondly, the foundation definition of 'transferable securities' in Article 1(8) is amended to cover shares in companies and other securities equivalent to shares in companies, bonds, and other forms of securitized debt, and any other negotiable securities which carry the right to acquire any such

---

[94] In this respect, regulation seems to be moving towards the US disclosure-based model which emphasizes regular reporting obligations but does not impose significant investment restrictions on mutual funds.

[95] In this way, the new regime resembles the evolution of the Distance Marketing of Financial Services Proposal [2000] OJ C177/21 which was developed at the same time. The industry was also expecting quite light regulation of distance-marketing of financial services but a relatively detailed scheme was presented by the Commission. See Ch. IX sect. 9 below.

[96] See Ch. XI sect. 6.3 below. This revision also reflects the general movement of EC securities regulation away from the official-listing concept.

transferable securities by subscription or exchange, excluding the techniques and instruments referred to in Article 21 (which concerns derivatives and efficient portfolio management, see section 8.2.6 below).[97] The third, and most significant, revision is the inclusion of money-market instruments (admitted to or dealt in on a regulated market) within the scope of Article 19(1)(a), (b), and (c). Money-market instruments are defined under Article 1(9) as instruments normally dealt in on the money market which are liquid and have a value which can be accurately determined at any time. A clear distinction is maintained, however, between money-market instruments traded on regulated markets which are liquid and whose value can be easily determined, and those traded on the money markets. Under Article 19(h) money-market instruments other than those dealt in on a regulated market (such as treasury and local authority bills, certificates of deposit, commercial paper, and bankers' acceptances) which fall under Article 1(9) are permitted as investments, but only if they meet certain liquidity and valuation standards. The issue or issuer of the instruments must be regulated for the purpose of protecting investors and savings, and only certain issuers' instruments will be eligible. The eligible issuers are: eligible institutions (the list includes central, regional, and local authorities, central banks of Member States, the European Central Bank, the European Union, the European Investment Bank, non-Member States, and public international bodies to which one or more Member States belong); undertakings any securities of which are dealt in on the regulated markets covered by Article 19(1)(a), (b), and (c); establishments subject to prudential supervision in accordance with criteria defined by Community law or subject to and complying with prudential rules considered by the competent authorities to be at least as stringent as those laid down by Community law; and other bodies belonging to the categories approved by the UCITS' competent authorities. This last case is designed to catch particularly specialized issuers and is subject to a number of qualifications which include that the issuer's capital and reserves amount to at least 10 million euro and that the issuer is an entity which, within a group of companies which includes one or several listed companies, is dedicated to the financing of securitization vehicles which benefit from a banking liquidity line.

Article 19(1)'s treatment of investments made by a UCITS in units of other collective-investment undertakings is also revised. The new regime recognizes that investments in other collective-investment schemes can provide liquid investments and reduce transaction costs by allowing a UCITS to construct a diversified scheme without creating a new fund to invest directly in

---

[97] Recital 3 of the Product Proposal additionally clarifies that 'transferable securities' covers negotiable instruments only and so does not include securities such as shares issued by building societies, ownership in which cannot be transferred except through repurchase by the issuing body.

a diversified range of financial assets and so should be facilitated. Under Article 19(1)(e), a UCITS may invest in the units of a UCITS authorized under the Directive and/or other collective-investment undertakings within the meaning of Article 1(2) (whether or not they are situated in a Member State) as long as these other collective investment undertakings meet the eligibility conditions of Article 19(1)(e). These conditions, which are designed to ensure that investor protection is not prejudiced as a result of this investment activity, require that they be authorized under laws which subject them to supervision considered by the investing UCITS' competent authority to be equivalent to that required under Community law and that co-operation between authorities is sufficiently ensured. The level of protection for unit-holders in the non-UCITS collective-investment undertaking must be equivalent to that provided for unit-holders in a UCITS. In particular, the rules on asset segregation, borrowing, lending, and uncovered sales of transferable securities and money-market instruments must be equivalent to those set out in the UCITS Directive. Finally, the business of the collective-investment undertaking must be reported in half-yearly and annual reports to enable an assessment to be made of its assets and liabilities and income and operations over the reporting period.

A third major revision concerns investment in deposits. Currently, cash may only be held by a UCITS as an ancillary liquid asset.[98] In order to take market developments into account and in consideration of the completion of EMU (recital 8), Article 19(f) provides that investments in deposits with credit institutions which are (in order to ensure adequate liquidity) repayable on demand or have the right to be withdrawn and mature in no more than twelve months are permissible. The credit institution with which the deposit is made must, however, have its registered office in a Member State or, where the registered office is in a non-Member State, must, alternatively, be subject to prudential rules considered by the investing UCITS' competent authority to be equivalent to those applicable under Community law.

Article 19(1) is also revised to include financial derivative instruments in the list of permissible investments (Article 19(1)(g)). Under the current regime, derivatives may not form part of the investment policy of a UCITS. The new Article 19(1)(g) provides that investments may be made in financial derivative instruments, including equivalent cash-settled instruments, dealt in on a regulated market and/or financial derivative instruments dealt

---

[98] Art. 19(4). Accordingly, recital 9 to the Product Proposal recognizes that, in addition to holding deposits as investments, a UCITS is also permitted to hold ancillary liquid assets such as deposits at sight and/or cash where it is justifiable to do so in order to cover current or unexpected payments, to reinvest, after a sale, in transferable securities or other permissible investments or where, due to unfavourable market conditions, investments must be suspended.

in over-the-counter (OTC derivatives).[99] Financial derivatives are subject to
a number of prudential conditions designed to address the liquidity and valuation difficulties and counterparty risk problems which investing in OTC
derivatives, in particular, may involve and to provide investors with a level
of protection which is close to that applicable to investments in derivatives
which are dealt in on regulated markets. For both types of derivative instrument the underlying asset must consist of instruments covered by Article
19(1), financial indices, interest rates, foreign exchange rates, or currencies,
in which the UCITS may invest according to its investment objectives as
stated in its fund rules or instruments of incorporation. Counterparties to
OTC derivatives transactions must be institutions subject to prudential
supervision and belong to the categories approved by the investing UCITS'
competent authorities. Finally, the OTC derivatives must be subject to reliable and verifiable valuation and must be capable of being 'sold, liquidated
or closed by an offsetting transaction at any time at their fair value at the
UCITS' initiative'.

V.8.2.3 *Risk-spreading Rules and Investment Limits*

In light of the expanded range of possible investments the new regime
contains a number of revisions to the risk-spreading rules contained in
Article 22.

The revised Article 22(1) provides that a UCITS may invest no more than
5 per cent of its assets in transferable securities or money-market instruments issued by the same body. As far as deposits are concerned, under
Article 22(1) a UCITS may not invest more than 20 per cent of its assets in
deposits made with the same body. Article 22(1) also provides that the risk
exposure to a counterparty of the UCITS in an OTC derivative transaction
may not exceed 10 per cent of its assets when the counterparty is a credit
institution (as referred to in Article 19(1)(f)) or, in all other cases, 5 per cent
of its assets. For transferable securities and money-market instruments, the
5 per cent limit may, under Article 22(2), be raised to 10 per cent, but the

---

[99] In the Original Product Proposal the Commission restricted investments in derivative
instruments to standardized derivatives (described as standardized financial-futures contracts
and standardized options) traded on regulated markets, and excluded OTC instruments on prudential grounds. This exclusion was strongly criticized by ECOSOC (which raised the problem
of the restrictions which would be placed on UCITSs operating in countries with under-devel-
oped derivatives exchanges), the Parliament, and the ECB. All the institutions accepted that
prudential controls over the use of OTC derivatives were desirable but felt that prudential regulation was a more measured response to investments in OTC derivatives than a blanket prohibition: n 93 above, para 3.4, at 30, and para I. 10, respectively. The Council Working Group
also favoured the inclusion of OTC derivatives. Accordingly (but also as a result of developments
in financial markets), the new regime now includes OTC derivatives, but subjects investments
in these instruments to a number of prudential controls.

total value of these instruments held by the UCITS in the issuing bodies in each of which it invests more than 5 per cent of its assets must not then exceed 40 per cent of the value of its assets (this limit does not apply to deposits and OTC derivative transactions made with financial institutions subject to prudential supervision). In addition, a UCITS may not combine investments in transferable securities or money-market instruments issued by, deposits made with, or exposures arising from OTC derivative transaction undertaken with a single body in excess of 20 per cent of its assets. The basic 5 per cent limitation can be raised to 35 per cent for securities issued by public authorities and by 25 per cent for bonds issued by credit institutions where, in each case, certain conditions are met. (Article 22(3) and (4)). The limits provided for under Article 22(1)–(4) may not be combined: as a result, investments in transferable securities or money-market instruments issued by the same body or in deposits or derivative instruments made with this body in accordance with Article 22(1)–(4) may not, in any circumstances, exceed in total 35 per cent of the assets of the UCITS (Article 22(5)); it also provides that the transferable securities and money-market instruments referred to in Article 22(3) and (4) are not to be taken into account for the purposes of applying the Article 22(2) 40 per cent limit.[100] Finally, Article 22(5) brings a new dimension to the investment-policy rules, and enhances effective and transparent management of risk-spreading, by addressing groups. It provides that companies included in the same group for the purposes of consolidation are to be regarded as a single body for the purpose of the investment limits. Member States may allow cumulative investment in transferable securities and money-market instruments within the same group up to a limit of 20 per cent.

V.8.2.4 *Particular Investment Policies*

(a) *Tracker Funds*

Article 22 of the UCITS Directive currently restricts a UCITS to investing no more than 10 per cent (where Member States opt to use their discretion to impose the higher limit) of its assets in securities issued by the same issuer. This requirement has denied the UCITS passport to collective-investment schemes which track the composition of stock or debt securities indices by investing in securities of different issuers according to the same proportions

---

[100] The overall limit of 35% was a matter of some controversy. The ECB noted that 'it seems questionable whether the investment of up to 35% of the assets of a fund in instruments of one issuer can be reconciled with the principle of risk spreading': n 93 above, para I, 4. The UK Association of Unit Trusts and Investment Funds has also warned of the risks involved in increasing investments in a single issuer over 10% given that most funds are sold to retail investors: Hargreaves, n 3 above.

used in the basket of securities on which the particular index is based.[101] Although index-tracking is now widely used as an investment-management technique and carries, as well as the benefits of diversification, the added benefit for investors of lower transaction costs, UCITS which track stock or securities indices may breach the 10 per cent rule where a particular issuer accounts for more than 10 per cent of the market on which the index is based.

The new Article 22(a) is designed to reflect the popularity of tracker funds and to encourage greater investment in equities. It permits Member States to adopt a limit of up to 20 per cent of assets for investments in shares or debt securities issued by the same body when, according to the fund rules or instruments of incorporation, the aim of the UCITS' investment policy is to 'replicate' (or track) the composition of a certain stock or debt-securities index which is recognized by the competent authorities according to the criteria set out in Article 22a. These criteria, which are designed to ensure that the replication technique is not abused, require that the index is sufficiently diversified, that it represents an adequate benchmark for the market to which it refers and that it is published in an appropriate manner. The 20 per cent limit may, under Article 22a(2), be raised to 35 per cent where this is justified by 'exceptional market conditions in particular in regulated markets where certain transferable securities or money market instruments are highly dominant'.[102]

(b) *Funds of Funds*

While the revised Article 19(1)(e) sets new requirements for funds of funds, further specific requirements are set out in Article 24 which has been substantially revised by the new regime to facilitate the establishment of UCITSs in the form of funds of funds. The current ceiling on investments in other collective-investment schemes of 5 per cent of total assets is removed and a new ceiling of 10 per cent of total assets is placed on investments in

---

[101] Index-tracking is an investment strategy which attempts to deal with the theory posited by the efficient capital-markets hypothesis, that is, that the stock market already reflects all the known disclosure which is material to the valuation of listed companies and that the market cannot be 'beaten' without recourse to inside information.

[102] Although this limit is subject to a market-conditions proviso, it does not reflect the concerns raised during the negotiating process about the desirability in principle of a 35% limit. The Original Product Proposal provided for a basic limit of 35% in respect of which ECOSOC, the Parliament, and the ECB all expressed concerns: n 93 above, para 3.6, at 31, and para I.3, respectively. ECOSOC called for a lower limit of 20%, given that one of the effects of the euro has been the creation of geographically more extensive indices in which issuers which previously would have represented more than 10% of the capitalization of national stock exchanges now account for much lesser proportions. A 20% limit was also proposed by the Parliament on the ground that a 35% rule would not ensure sufficient diversification and so would breach the fundamental principle of appropriate risk-spreading underlying the Directive.

a single collective investment undertaking, which Member States may raise to 20 per cent (Article 24(1)). Feeder funds which invest all their assets exclusively in the units of one UCITS (the master fund) are not, as result, permitted under the Directive. Investments made in units of collective investment undertakings other than UCITSs may not exceed, in aggregate, 30 per cent of the assets of the UCITS;[103] a UCITS may, however, invest 100 per cent of its funds in units of other UCITSs.

A rule designed to protect investors against cascades of investments in collective-investment undertakings, which may result in opaque cross-investments in other collective-investment undertakings, is introduced under Article 19(1)(e). It provides that a UCITS may not invest in units of another UCITS or collective-investment undertaking which invests itself more than 10 per cent of its assets in units of other UCITSs and/or collective-investment undertakings.

Finally, particular rules are introduced under Article 24(3) to protect investors where the UCITS invests in a UCITS or other collective-investment undertaking which is managed by the same management company (or by any other company with which the management company is linked by common management or control or by a substantial direct or indirect holding). That management company or other company may not charge subscription or redemption fees on account of the UCITS' investment in the units of such other UCITS and/or collective-investment undertaking. Article 22(3) also provides that a UCITS that invests a substantial proportion of its assets in other UCITSs and/or collective-investment undertakings is to disclose in its prospectus and annual report the maximum level of the management fees that may be charged to both the UCITS itself and the other UCITSs or collective investment undertakings in which it intends to invest.

(c) *Cash Funds*

Under Article 19(1)(f), the current prohibition on investing in bank deposits is removed as long as that Article's new eligibility criteria and the risk-spreading rules set out in the revised Article 22 are met. Of particular significance for investments in deposits is the amendment to Article 22(1) which provides that investments in the various companies of a group are to be treated collectively as investments a single body for the purposes of the risk-spreading rules (section 8.2.3 above).

---

[103] The Original Product Proposal's approach permitted UCITSs to invest up to 100% of their assets in non-UCITS schemes, an option which was strongly criticized by Parliament on the ground that it would allow a UCITS to circumvent the UCITS Directive's provisions on investor protection and risk-spreading by investing all of its assets in the units of non-UCITS schemes and could endanger the integrity of the single-market collective-investment scheme industry. Note 93, 28 and 36. In response to these concerns the new regime contains qualitative tests for non-UCITS schemes as investments under the revised Art. 19(1)(e) (see sect. 8.2.2 above).

V.8.2.5 *Disclosure of Investment Policies*

The prominence of disclosure as a regulatory technique in EC securities regulation can be seen in the new investment-policy regime which includes risk assessment by investors as part of its regulatory arsenal. The new Article 24a requires that specific disclosure be made with respect to the new investment opportunities, given the increased risks to which investors may be exposed. Under Article 24a(1) the prospectus must indicate in which categories of assets a UCITS is authorized to invest. In particular, if it is authorized to engage in derivatives transactions, it must include a 'prominent statement' indicating that these transactions may be carried out for the purposes of hedging or with the aim of meeting investment goals, and the possible outcome of the use of financial derivatives instruments on the risk profile. Under Article 24a(2), when a UCITS invests principally in assets other than transferable securities and money-market instruments or when it replicates an index, its prospectus and, where necessary, any other promotional literature must include a prominent statement drawing attention to the investment policy. Similarly, when the net asset value of a UCITS is likely to have a high volatility due to its portfolio composition or the portfolio-management techniques that may be used, its prospectus/promotional literature must include a prominent statement drawing attention to this fact (Article 24a(3)). Finally, under Article 24a(4), on the request of an investor, the management company must provide supplementary information relating to the quantitative limits which apply in the risk management of the UCITS, to the methods chosen to this end, and to the recent evolution of the risks and yields of the main instrument categories.

V.8.2.6 *Managing Derivatives Exposure*

With the introduction of the use of derivatives as investments and not simply as general hedging or portfolio-management devices, the Article 21 portfolio-management regime has been completely recast. In order to ensure a constant awareness of the risks and commitments arising from derivative transactions, Article 21(1) requires that the management or investment company must have a risk-management process in place which enables it, at any time, to monitor and measure the risk of the positions held and their contribution to the overall risk profile of the portfolio. A process for the accurate and independent assessment of the value of OTC derivative instruments must also be in place. With respect to each UCITS, the competent authorities must be informed regularly and in accordance with rules to be set by the competent authorities of the types of derivative instruments involved, the underlying risks, the quantitative limits and the methods chosen to estimate risk.

In a throw-back to the earlier position, Article 21(2) provides that Member States may authorize UCITSs to 'employ techniques and instruments relating to transferable securities and money market instruments' under the conditions and limits they lay down for the purposes of efficient portfolio management but, where derivatives are involved, the conditions and limits must conform with the Directive. Any techniques and instruments used may not cause the UCITS to diverge from its investment objectives as laid down in its constitutional documents or prospectus.

Under Article 21(3), a UCITS must ensure that its global exposure relating to derivative instruments (the calculation of which must be carried out in accordance with the Directive's general guidelines) does not exceed the total net value of its portfolio. As far as investment limits are concerned, Article 21(3) also provides that, as part of its investment policy and within the Article 22(5) limit, a UCITS may invest in financial derivative instruments provided that the exposure to the underlying assets does not exceed in aggregate the Article 22 investment limits. However, where a UCITS invests in index-based financial derivative instruments, these investments do not have to be combined to the limits laid down in Article 22. At all times, where a transferable security or money market instrument embeds a derivative, the latter must be taken into account when complying with Article 21. Member States are required under Article 21(4) to provide the Commission with full information concerning the specific methods used to calculate risk exposures and of any changes. This information will be forwarded by the Commission to the other Member States and be discussed within the Contact Committee.

V.8.2.7 *Subsidiaries*

Consequential amendments have been made to Article 25 in order to take into account the increased range of potential investments. In addition, the exemption available in Article 25(3)(e) in respect of shares held by a UCITS in the form of an investment company in the capital of a subsidiary company which carries on the business of management, advice, or marketing exclusively on behalf of the UCITS has been refined and now covers subsidiary companies the shares of which are held by more than one investment company. It now applies 'to shares held by an investment company or investment companies in the capital of subsidiary companies carrying on only the business of management, advice, or marketing in the country where the subsidiary is located, in regard to the repurchase of units at unit-holders' request exclusively on its or their behalf'. This provision, which continues to permit the use of non-Member State subsidiaries, is designed to ensure that UCITSs covered by the Directive are not used for any purposes other than the collective investment of money raised from the public.

Subsidiaries may, as a result, be used only when they are necessary to carry out the activities specified in the Directive on behalf of the UCITS. Recital 15 to the Product Proposal states in uncompromising fashion that 'the general obligation to act solely in the interests of unit-holders and, in particular, the objective of increasing cost efficiencies, never justify a UCITS undertaking measures which may hinder the competent authorities from exercising effectively their supervisory functions'.

V.8.2.8 *Lending*

The restrictions on lending activities set out in Articles 41 and 42 have also been subject to revisions consequential on the increased range of investments now permissible.

V.8.2.9 *Comitology and the Contact Committee*

The last of the revisions relates to the powers of the Contact Committee and, in line with the current move to delegate securities-regulation law-making powers to comitology procedures, confers law-making powers on the Contact Committee in its guise as a Regulatory Committee.[104] Article 53a provides that in addition to the functions provided for in Article 53(1), comitology powers be given to the Contact Committee, as a Regulatory Committee, in order to assist the Commission with respect to technical modifications in relation to clarifying definitions to ensure uniform application throughout the Community and aligning terminology and definitions in accordance with subsequent acts on UCITSs and related matters.

V.8.3 *The Management Company and Prospectus Regime*

V.8.3.1 *Introduction*

Currently, investors in UCITSs are protected only by the imposition of standards on the UCITS as an investment product and the limited regulation of the UCITS manager and depositary by the UCITS Directive. The Management Proposal[105] is designed to improve investor protection by reg-

---

[104] On the comitology process and its increasing importance for EC securities regulation, particularly in the wake of the Lamfalussy Report, see Ch. XV sect. 2.5.3 below.

[105] Amended Proposal for a Directive amending Directive 85/611/EEC on the Coordination of Laws, Regulations and Administrative Provisions Relating to Undertakings for Collective Investment in Transferable Securities with a view to Regulating Management Companies and Simplified Prospectuses (the Revised Management Company Proposal), COM(2000)331. The Council's Common Position is at [2001] OJ C297/10. The measure was adopted by the Council as a directive on 4 Dec 2001. This discussion is based on the Common Position (references to the Management Proposal or Management Company Proposal are to the Common Position text, while references to Articles are to the revised Articles of the UCITS Directive introduced by the

ulating the management companies which manage UCITSs and by enhancing the regulation of UCITSs which take the form of investment companies which do not designate a separate management company. Based on Article 47(2) EC, its primary purpose, however, is to introduce management-company market-access conditions, as well as operating controls and prudential safeguards, so bringing the regulation of management companies into line with the system for other financial-service providers such as credit institutions, investment firms, and insurance companies; these rules allow for the conferment of a regulatory passport on management companies. Management companies are currently regulated very lightly by the Directive and do not benefit from the UCITS passport. They are also excluded from the passport available to firms providing investment services as Article 2(2)(g) of the ISD specifically excludes 'the depositaries and managers of [collective investment schemes].' In addition, the Management Proposal further liberalizes the UCITS market by removing the restrictions placed on management companies from engaging in any activities other than the management of the UCITS (currently imposed by Article 6 of the Directive) and introduces important provisions concerning the delegation of management activities.

Unlike the 1994 UCITS Proposal, the Management Proposal does not address the position of the depositary. Depositaries therefore remain tied to being established or having their registered offices in the Member State in which the management company has its registered office. They do not benefit from a passport and cannot freely offer their services as depositaries across the Community to a wide range of UCITSs.[106]

Management-company issues aside, the Proposal also streamlines and enhances the disclosure which must be provided by a UCITS.

As the provisions concerning the management-company passport are not related specifically to trading in the UCITS product and belong more appropriately with the discussion of the EC's investment-services regime, they are further considered, along with investment firms, in Part III which examines the investment-services regime. The main features of the Management

new regime). At the time of writing, the final text of the adopted measure had not beenpublished in the Official Journal and had not yet come into force. The Parliament did not, however, materially amend the Common Position text during its second reading prior to the adoption of the measure. Its only amendment (which was to shorten the Common Position's 5-year time frame from the entry into force of the new regime, at the end of which the Commission was to review the capital requirements imposed on management companies, to 3 years) was accepted by the Commission (COM(2001)687).

The original version of the proposal which, like the Original Product Proposal, was the subject of extensive comment is at COM(1998)451 (the Original Management Proposal). See n 93 above for the comments of the ECB and the first reading of the Parliament. The ECOSOC opinion is at [1999] OJ C116/1.

[106] It is envisaged, however, that the Commission will produce a report for the Council on the appropriate treatment of depositaries: Communication from the Commission to the Parliament on the Common Position (the Common Position Communication), SEC 2001/1004, para 3.2.2.2.

Proposal's treatment of the UCITS prospectus and investment companies which do not designate a separate manager, which are the other main changes to the UCITS regime introduced by the Proposal, are outlined in sections 8.3.2 and 8.3.3 below.

V.8.3.2 *The UCITS Prospectus*

(a) *Disclosure and UCITS*

The huge growth in the UCITS industry in recent years has refocused attention on the disclosure on the basis of which investors are purchasing units in schemes. Indeed, a UCITS prospectus is likely to be used to a much greater extent by the average investor than a listing particulars or a prospectus; retail investors are significantly more active in investing in UCITSs than in accessing the securities markets directly. UCITS disclosure policy should reflect the fact that the UCITS ultimately acts as an intermediary between the investor and the securities markets; disclosure should, accordingly, be directed towards informing the retail investor who relies heavily on this form of intermediation. The Directive currently, however, requires publication of an extensive and detailed prospectus in order to allow investors to make an informed assessment of the UCITS. Too much information may obscure material facts concerning the UCITS, however, and confuse the investor who may be unable to distil the key information from the prospectus and may, in the face of overwhelming disclosure, ignore important facts. The view has been growing in recent years that a simplified prospectus, containing clear and essential information, and, crucially, facilitating comparisons between different schemes, would more appropriately address the needs of the average investor.

(b) *Revisions to the Disclosure Regime*

The Management Company Proposal dramatically revises the disclosure regime by introducing a requirement in Article 27 that a 'simplified prospectus', which is investor-friendly and gives 'key information about the UCITS in a clear, concise, and easily understandable way',[107] must be produced in addition to the full prospectus, annual report, and half-yearly report.[108]

[107] Recital 15. This reflects the approach taken by the SEC which subjects mutual-fund prospectuses (both full and abbreviated: see n 108 below) to its Plain English Requirements.

[108] The EC is not alone in revamping its disclosure rules for collective-investment schemes. A similar approach has recently been taken by the SEC which has become increasingly concerned, that, as the disclosure document relied on most heavily by retail investors, mutual-fund prospectuses have become unwieldy, unhelpful documents which do not address the needs of the average unsophisticated retail investor who invests in mutual funds. One extensive study of disclosure by mutual funds reported trenchantly that '[w]hile mutual fund companies are catering directly to bakers and sales clerks, mutual fund prospectuses appear intelligible to only

Mandatory distribution of the full UCITS prospectus (which must still be prepared and is likely to be requested by professional investors and advisers) to potential investors is no longer required. The revised Article 33 now provides that only the simplified prospectus must be offered to subscribers free of charge before the conclusion of the contract. The full prospectus and the latest published annual and half-yearly reports must, however, be supplied free of charge to subscribers on request (Article 33(1)).

Under Article 28(1), the simplified prospectus must contain the information necessary for the investor to be able to make an informed judgement of the investment proposed and, in particular, of the risks attached thereto. This new focus on the link between investor protection and risk disclosure is also tracked through to the full prospectus which must, in addition, include a clear and easily understandable explanation of the fund's risk profile. As well as providing in summary form the information set out in the new Schedule C annexed to the Directive, Article 28(3) also requires that the prospectus be written and structured in such a way that it can be easily understood by the average investor. Member States are given the option of permitting the simplified prospectus to be attached to the full prospectus as a removable part, possibly as a summary of, or as a guide to, the full prospectus. Both the full and simplified prospectuses can be presented either as written documents 'or in any other durable medium having an equivalent legal status approved by the competent authorities (Article 28(4))'. The simplified prospectus is subject to the same regime as the full prospectus in terms of keeping its essential elements up to date and sending it, and any amendments, to the competent authorities.

The information which must be included in the simplified prospectus under Annex C is divided into a number of sections: brief presentation of the UCITS; investment information; economic regime; commercial information; and additional information. In terms of the brief presentation of the UCITS, disclosure is required on: when the unit trust or investment company was created and in which Member State it has been registered or incorporated; an indication that a UCITS has different investment compartments, where

---

bankers and securities lawyers': New York City Office of the Public Advocate, *Making Sense of Mutual Fund Prospectuses* 3, quoted in Robertson, R, 'In Search of the Perfect Mutual Fund Prospectus' (1999) 54 *The Business Lawyer* 461, 475. The SEC's response has been two-pronged: Release No. 33–7513 (1998) permits mutual funds to offer a new disclosure document, an abbreviated prospectus called a 'profile', in place of the extensive prospectus required under the Securities Act, 1933. The profile summarizes key information concerning the mutual fund such as its investment strategies, the risks involved, its performance over a 10-year period, fees, redemption, and purchase procedures. The profile must follow a standardized format to facilitate comparison between different funds. The full prospectus must also be supplied on confirmation of purchase of a unit. In addition, the SEC has amended its disclosure rules for full mutual-fund prospectuses as it is concerned that prospectuses are often 'legalistic disclosure documents that are difficult to read, hard to understand and prepared with litigation in mind': SEC Release No. 33–7512 (1998).

this is the case; the management company (where applicable, as an investment company may be self-managed); the expected period of existence; the
depositary; the auditors; and the financial group promoting the UCITS. The
investment information must include: a short definition of the UCITS' objectives; a description of the UCITS' investment policy and a brief assessment
of the fund's risk profile (including, where applicable, information according
to Article 24a and by investment compartment); details of the historical performance of the UCITS and a warning that this is not an indicator of future
performance;[109] and, in a creative requirement, a discussion of the profile
of the typical investor the UCITS is designed for. This last requirement is
likely to be of significant assistance to retail investors. The economic regime
information required includes a description of the tax regime applicable, and
details of entry and exit commissions together with information on any
other possible expenses or fees, which should distinguish between those paid
by the unit-holder and those paid out of the UCITS' assets; the new focus on
expenses can also be seen in Article 24(3) of the Product Proposal which
imposes disclosure requirements on funds of funds with respect to management fees).[110] The mandatory commercial information includes practical

---

[109] Past-performance information has recently attracted the attention of regulators concerned about its impact on investor behaviour. The SEC issued Mutual Fund Tips in Jan 2000
advising investors that past performance is not the only guide and, in particular, that fees
should be carefully considered as they can sharply impact on the return from a mutual fund.
The FSA floated the idea of prohibiting the use of performance statistics in the marketing of
retail collective-investment schemes in 2000 due to the lack of consistency between past and
future performance and the danger that retail investors could be misled by past-performance
statistics, but withdrew from this proposal in light of fierce industry opposition. It is, however,
concerned by past-performance statistics and decided against using them in its Comparative
Tables (n 110 below) which it has made available for investors and which compare the features of various types of investments. See the discussion in the FSA, *Response to Consultation
Paper 28* (2000) at paras 6.48–6.57 and the report produced by M Rhodes under the aegis of
the FSA on *Past Imperfect: The Performance of UK Equity Managed Funds*, Occasional Paper 4
(2000). While the FSA has accepted that investors want past-performance information and that
it is regarded as an important marketing tool, it is, at the time of writing, to review the past-
performance-information regulatory scheme in order to ensure that its use is not unfair,
unclear, or misleading. See the Sept 2001 *Report of the FSA Task Force on Past Performance* and
the FSA's response (Press Release, 26 Sept 2001).

[110] The extent to which prospectuses clarify fees and expenses has also become an issue of
concern for regulators. Investors seem unconsciously to choose funds with high fees as an indication of reliability which in turn acts as an incentive for more aggressive charges: Financial
Services Authority, *Price of Retail Investing in the UK*, Occasional Paper 6 (2000). The SEC has
emphasized the importance of fee and expense disclosure given the impact these charges can
have on fund returns and highlighted the importance of investor education in this regard: SEC
Mutual Fund Report, n 2 above, para B(2). Revisions to the SEC disclosure rules now mean
that prospectuses must show the effect of an increase in costs on a $1000 mutual-fund invest-
ment over set time periods. Investors can therefore assess how, for example, a 1% increase in
fees will affect their return from the mutual fund. The failure of the new regime to deal with
this issue represents a lost opportunity for practical investor protection. A concern with fee disclosure can be seen in the FSA's Comparative Tables which set out the key features of certain
investment products, including unit trusts, across a range of providers, and which provide
information on, *inter alia*, price and the cost of exercising any flexibility options built into the

information on how to buy and sell units as well as information on how to pass investments from one compartment of an umbrella UCITS to another. Also required are details of when and how dividends are distributed and the frequency of and where/how prices are published. The final additional information category includes a requirement that a statement be made that, on request, the full prospectus and financial reports may be obtained free of charge before the conclusion of the contract. This category also requires that information be made available concerning a contact point from which additional explanations can be obtained.

The information requirements applicable to the full prospectus have also been revised to reflect the summary prospectus requirements concerning schemes which have different investment compartments, the historical performance information, the profile of the typical investor for which the scheme is designed, and information on fees and expenses.

(c) *Marketing and Disclosure Rules: A Full Disclosure Passport*

The new prospectus regime is based on the principle of maximum harmonization which ousts the jurisdiction of host Member States. Article 28(3) is a core market-integration measure, and represents a new departure for the current EC disclosure regime (although the proposed issuer-disclosure proposal also builds on this approach), in that it provides that the simplified prospectus may be 'used as a marketing tool designed to be used in all Member States without alteration except translation. Member States may therefore not require that further documents or additional information be added'. The simplified prospectus has, as a result, been described by the Commission as: 'a benchmark marketing tool, the culmination of the Commission's maximum harmonization approach in this matter'.[111]

Article 35 has been revised to provide that all publicity comprising an invitation to purchase UCITS units must indicate that both prospectuses exist and specify the places where they may both be obtained by the public. Article 47 has also been revised to provide that if a UCITS markets its units in a Member State other than that in which it is situated, it must distribute in that other Member State, in accordance with the same procedures as provided for in the home Member State, the full and simplified prospectuses, the annual and half-yearly reports and the other information required under Articles 29 and 30. These documents are to be provided in 'the or one of the official languages of the host Member State or in a language approved by the competent authorities of the host Member State'. The Article 46

product. The Tables are not designed to offer advice but to enhance the disclosure regime. See the discussion in FSA, *Comparative Information for Financial Services* (1999), Consultation Paper 28.

[111] Common Position Communication, n 106 above, para 3.2.2.7.

pre-marketing regime has also been revised to refer to the simplified prospectus and to provide that an 'investment company or management company'
(rather than a UCITS as under the current regime) may market its units
following completion of the Article 46 procedure.

The new regime's recognition that detailed disclosure is not necessarily
in the best interests of investor protection chimes with an overall trend
towards greater sophistication in the disclosure regime. By highlighting the
information needs of the 'average investor' and adopting a two-tier disclosure system, the proposal introduces a more discriminating approach to disclosure. A similarly sensitive (and 'full passport' driven) approach to
disclosure can also been seen in the current proposal to restructure the
issuer disclosure regime (Chapter IV section 9.3 above). It would appear that
EC securities regulation is increasingly becoming an internally consistent
regime.[112]

V.8.3.3 *Self-managed Investment Companies*

A striking revision introduced by the Management Company Proposal concerns the regulation of the UCITS product where it takes the form of an
investment company. As discussed in Part III, the Proposal puts in place a
new regulatory regime, encompassing prudential and protective regulation,
for stand-alone management companies. A major theme of the new UCITS
regime is that a similar system should apply to self-managed investment
companies which do not designate an independent management company,
albeit adjusted to reflect the particular characteristics of investment companies.[113] Under Article 4(3), a UCITS may not be authorized unless the management company or investment company complies with the new regime.

Article 12 now provides that access to the business of investment companies is to be subject to 'prior official authorisation', granted by the home
Member State's competent authorities. The current authorization process is
considerably expanded by Article 13a(1) to track the new management-
company regime which is, in turn, based on the investment-services regime.
Authorization is, accordingly, dependent on the investment company sub-
mitting a programme of activity which sets out, *inter alia*, the organizational
structure of the company, and on a more stringent review of the directors.
In particular, investment-company directors (defined as, as at present, those
persons who under the law or the instruments of incorporation represent the

---

[112] This trend can also be seen in the market abuse area. See See Ch. XIII sect. 11.6 below.
[113] The Commission has explained that '[t]he logic underlying the common position . . . [on
this revision] is that the provisions applicable to management companies must be applicable
mutatis mutandis to self-managed investment companies, taking into account the latter's
specific characteristics': Common Position Communication, n 106 above, para 3.2.2.6.

investment company or effectively determine the policy of the company) must be of sufficiently good repute and sufficiently experienced in relation to the type of business carried out by the investment company. The investment services regime's 'four-eyes' requirement is imposed: the conduct of an investment company's business must be decided by at least two persons who meet the reputation/competence qualification. The transparency rule is also transplanted from the investment-services regime: where close links exist between the investment company and other natural or legal persons, authorization may only be granted if those links do not prevent effective supervision.[114] Authorization must also be refused where the laws, regulations, or adminstrative provisions of a non-Member State governing one or more natural or legal persons with which the investment company has close links, or difficulties in their enforcement, prevent the effective exercise of supervision. Competent authorities are also to require investment companies to provide them with the information they require. In a major change to the current requirement that the investment company have 'sufficient paid-up capital' to allow it to carry out its business effectively and to meet its liabilities, the new authorization process requires self-managed investment companies to have an initial capital of at least 300,000 euro.[115] The procedural requirements and protections applicable to authorization under the investment-services regime are also grafted on to the investment-company regime (Article 13a(2)–(4)).[116]

Investment companies are subject to a tailored version of the operating regime imposed on management companies and examined further in Chapters VIII and IX. While, for example, the new delegation system for management companies applies,[117] investment companies may not manage assets for third parties: Article 13b provides that investment companies may manage only assets of their own portfolio and may not, under any circumstances, receive a mandate to manage assets on behalf of a third party. Similarly, self-managed investment companies are subject to the new conduct regime which applies to management companies.[118] A stand-alone

---

[114] Close links are defined by reference to the Prudential Supervision Directive. Directive 95/26/EC amending Directives 77/780/EEC and 89/646/EEC in the field of credit institutions, Directives 73/239/EEC and 92/49/EEC in the field of non-life insurance, Directives 79/267/EEC and 92/96/EEC in the field of life assurance, Directive 93/22 in the field of investment firms and Directive 85/611/EEC in the field of undertakings for collective investment in transferable securities, with a view to reinforcing prudential supervision [1995] OJ L168/7. See Ch. VII sect. 4.5 below.

[115] This requirement is designed to 'safeguard shareholders' interests and to secure a level playing field in the market for harmonized collective investment undertakings': recital 13. The additional own-funds requirement imposed on management companies (Ch. VII sect. 9 below) will not apply unless an independent management company is appointed.

[116] See Ch. VII sect. 4.6 below.   [117] See Ch. VIII sect. 6.3 below.
[118] See Ch. IX sect. 7 below.

prudential regime applies, however, and is set out in Article 13c.[119] Home Member States are required to draw up prudential rules to be observed at all times by self-managed investment companies. These rules must, having regard to the nature of the investment company, require that the company has: sound administrative and accounting procedures; control mechanisms for electronic data-processing; adequate internal control mechanisms including employee transaction rules, rules 'for the holding or management of investments in financial instruments in order to invest its initial capital', record-keeping rules, and transactions reconstruction procedures; and that the assets of the company are invested according to the instruments of incorporation and the laws currently in force.

---

[119] A distinct regime was required as the internal organization of an investment company (with variable capital under the EC regime) is quite different from that of a management company.

PART III
The EC Investment-services Regime

VI

The Regulation of Investment-services Providers: The EC Regime

VI.1 INVESTMENT INTERMEDIARIES AND TRADING MARKETS

Part II of this book is concerned with the regulation of the offer of securities in the primary markets and their admission to Official Listing and with the regulation of UCITSs. Part III (Chapter VII on the investment services passport, Chapter VIII on prudential regulation, Chapter IX on protective regulation, and Chapter X on investor compensation schemes) and Part IV (Chapter XI on the securities trading market regime and Chapter XII on clearing and settlement) concern the secondary markets in which securities and investment products are traded between investors after the initial transaction between the issuer and investors.[1] There are two strands to this discussion: the regulation of the intermediaries who participate in the secondary trading markets by providing investment services (Part III) which, due to the substantive scope of the regime, forms the larger part of this examination of the EC's regulation of secondary markets; and the regulation of the operation of the trading markets themselves (Part IV) which is, at present, a less extensive regime.[2]

This chapter introduces Part III by: examining the underlying rationales for and features of investment-services regulation (the extent to which the EC regime reflects these rationales and features is considered in relation to the different areas of investment-services regulation in the following chapters); exploring the roots of the regime; reviewing the relationship between the Treaty and the provision of investment services in the EC; and identifying the major features of the harmonized investment-services regime which are further developed with respect to the discrete elements of the regime throughout Part III.

---

[1] The primary markets concern the bringing of securities to the market for the first time and transactions between the issuer seeking capital and the investor providing capital. The secondary markets have been described as involving 'all transactions in securities which take place after their issue, or after the initial distribution. Both the stock exchange market and the markets outside the stock exchanges, or parallel markets, are considered to belong to the secondary securities trade': Wymeersch, E, *Control of Securities Markets in the European Economic Community*, Collection Studies. Competition—Approximation of Legislation Series No. 31 (1977) 31. For a similar approach to the distinction see the OECD's 1987 Report on International Trade in Services—Securities, 7–8.

[2] The regulation of market abuses, such as insider trading and market manipulation, which tracks across Parts II, III and IV, is considered in Part V (Ch. XIII) below.

VI.2 THE RATIONALE FOR REGULATION[3]

VI.2.1 *Investment Intermediaries*

Market intermediaries or investment intermediariën play a critical role in the operation of the securities markets by providing a market-access channel for investors and capital seekers.[4] By providing services such as investment advice, discretionary portfolio management, and brokerage services,[5] investment intermediaries act as a bridge between investors and the securities markets; through activities such as underwriting, own-account trading and corporate finance advice they facilitate market access for companies seeking capital.

The importance of the regulation of investment intermediaries has been recognized by the Court of Justice in one of its rare excursions into the investment services arena in *Alpine Investments*, where it found that 'the existence of professional regulations serving to ensure the competence and trustworthiness of the financial intermediaries on whom investors are particularly reliant' was critical to ensure investor confidence in the securities markets.[6] In a similar vein, Advocate General Jacob noted in his Opinion that '[a]n investor in securities or in commodities markets is more dependent on the advice of an intermediary than, say, a person who invests in real property, both as regards the choice of investment which is suitable to his needs and as regards the appropriate time when an investment should be made. That is why all countries with developed financial markets have sought to regulate them by adopting rules not only concerning the issuers of investments but also the financial intermediaries.'[7] These references to investor protection,[8] investor confidence, and the sensitivity of the investor/investment intermediary relationship all echo well-established rationales for regulating investment intermediaries.

---

[3] The rationale for regulating trading markets and market conduct is discussed in Chs. XI and XIII below, respectively. The dominant rationale for regulating trading markets is market integrity or ensuring that markets are stable, transparent, and efficient and engender confidence. The differing rationales which drive the two regimes give rise to distinct regulatory regimes which can provoke problems where the two regimes intersect. This has occurred recently with the development of alternative trading systems (ATSs) which can be classified as investment intermediaries or trading markets. See Ch. XI sect. 8.4 below.

[4] On the rise of market intermediaries as a dominant economic influence see Clark, R, 'The Four Stages of Capitalism' (1981) 94 *Harv. LR* 561.

[5] Broking involves a number of stages: accepting a buy or sell order; execution of that order on an exchange or off the market in an over-the-counter (OTC) transaction; and ensuring that settlement (or the transfer of payment and instruments post-trade) occurs correctly.

[6] Case C-384/93 *Alpine Investments v Minister van Financiën* [1995] ECR I-1141, para 42.

[7] Ibid, Opinion of the AG, para 72.

[8] The clients of investment intermediaries who are the concern of much of the regulation in this field will be referred to throughout as investors or clients.

VI.2.2 *Investor Protection and Systemic Stability*[9]

While numerous rationales are offered for the regulation of investment intermediaries, two broad themes can be identified. The first of these is the micro-protection of investors on an individual basis, but in the interests of wider investor confidence[10] and market efficiency, through the correction of market failures, predominantly information failures, which can result in prejudice to investors, damage to competition, and an inefficient allocation of resources.[11] The second theme is concerned with bolstering the soundness of investment intermediaries, the macro-management of systemic stability, and the avoidance of system-wide financial crises. These two themes[12] are, however, closely related and can overlap. Confidence in the market-place generally could be said to lie at the root of both investor-protection and systemic-stability objectives.[13] In addition, investors are protected generically by the prevention of systemic instability and, on an individual basis, by many of the mechanisms which promote soundness and protect against

[9] Investor protection and systemic stability and their relationship to the various elements of investment-intermediary regulation are further discussed in the relevant chs on prudential regulation (Ch. VIII), protective regulation (Ch. IX) and compensation schemes (Ch. X).

[10] While, as discussed further in Part III generally, it is an ever-strengthening undercurrent in EC securities regulation, investor confidence is a nebulous concept, and the validity of its use as a basis for regulation has been challenged, particularly in the context of insider dealing. Regardless of the particular rules which it produces, investor confidence is generally linked to liquidity and the efficiency of the wider securities markets. For one characterization see the UK Financial Services Authority's view that 'market users are most likely to feel confident in markets when those markets operate fairly, efficiently and safely': FSA, *The FSA's Approach to Regulation of Market Infrastructure*, Discussion Paper (2000) 10.

[11] Paternalism is sometimes additionally raised as a justification for investor-protection regulation. See further Ch. IX.

[12] For the investor-protection/soundness and stability rationale see the 1998 IOSCO Objectives and Principles of Securities Regulation (the 1998 IOSCO Principles), the first two core principles of which are investor protection and the reduction of systemic risk. The third core principle, ensuring that markets are fair, efficient, and transparent relates to the regulation of securities-trading markets. See also Cesarini, F, 'Economics of Securities Markets Regulation: Some Current Issues' in Ferrarini, G (ed), *European Securities Markets—The Investment Services Directive and Beyond* (1998) 65, 65 who finds that the 'ultimate purpose of securities market regulation is twofold: . . . the protection of investors . . . and . . . the stability of financial intermediaries' and Goodhart, C, 'Some Regulatory Concerns' in Goodhart, C (ed), *The Emerging Framework of Financial Regulation* (1998) 215, 220.

[13] eg, market confidence is identified as one of the general regulatory objectives in accordance with which the UK Financial Services Authority (FSA) must act. The protection of consumers, which impacts on market confidence, is split out as a separate objective, but arguably also feeds into this objective indirectly: Financial Services and Markets Act 2000 (the FSMA), s 2(2)(a) and (b). The Lamfalussy Report has used confidence as an objective which cuts across regulation horizontally. Recommending the adoption of a 'conceptual framework of overarching principles' on which all EC Financial-services and securities regulation should be constructed, it included among the principles the maintenance of confidence in European securities markets: Final Report of the Committee of Wise Men on the Regulation of European Securities Markets, Feb 2001 (the Lamfalussy Report) 22.

systemic instability.[14] Finally, while market-failure correction could be regarded as being at the heart of investor protection, systemic risk is also a market failure against which both investors and the market-place need to be protected.[15] The theory that market failures and their correction lie at the root of regulation generally is therefore also reflected in both rationales for investment-services regulation.[16]

Without venturing too far into regulatory theory, market-failure arguments are based on the premise that in a perfect market[17] resources will be efficiently allocated and that regulation corrects an imperfect market. In the investment-services area these arguments produce the assumption that regulatory interventions on the market-place are justifiable only in order to correct market failures (failures in the market's self-regulatory mechanisms or a mismatch between actual market conditions and the assumptions on which a perfect market is based) which obstruct the efficient allocation of resources by an otherwise perfect market and prejudice the meeting of investors' preferences through competition between investment intermediaries and by rational investor choice.[18] Market failures are generally characterized in terms of resulting in risks not being correctly priced in the market-place. Accordingly, the achievement of investor-protection and

[14] '[A]nything that threatens solvency will imperil both systemic stability and investors' funds': Goodhart, n 12 above, 220. This approach was also followed by Jacobs AG in his *Alpine Investments* Opinion, where he noted that 'the need to protect investors and the need to ensure the integrity of the financial markets are related objectives': n 6 above, para 75.

[15] Page, A, and Ferguson, R, *Investor Protection* (1992) 35 and 39, and Franks, J, and Mayer, C, *Risk, Regulation and Investor Protection. The Case of Investment Management* (1989) 156–9.

[16] Ibid, 3 and Page and Ferguson, n 15 above, 35. The market-failure doctrine was explicitly referred to in para 7 of the HM Treasury Report on *Completing a Dynamic Single European Financial Services Market: A Catalyst for Economic Prosperity for Citizens and Business Across the EU* (July 2000) (the Treasury Report). Informational asymmetries in the customer/financial-services providers relationship and externalities leading to system-wide instability were among the market failures identified as requiring to be addressed in order to ensure markets operate effectively and efficiently.

[17] A perfect market is generally regarded by economists as requiring: numerous buyers and sellers; an absence of barriers to market entry and exit; the possession of perfect information by buyers and sellers on the products on the market-place; homogenous products; and an absence of externalities, in that the cost of producing goods is borne by the producer and the cost of consuming goods is borne by the consumer. Perfect markets also assume rational behaviour by market actors. This assumption is frequently questioned on the grounds of 'bounded rationality' or the phenomenon that consumers are limited in their ability to decode information and will make acceptable choices rather than optimal ones. For a summary see Scott, C, and Black, J, *Cranston's Consumers and the Law* (3rd edn, 2000) 34–5.

[18] A full discussion of the theories, economic and otherwise, underlying the imposition of regulation is outside the scope of this work. See Ogus, A, *Regulation, Legal Form and Economic Theory* (1994) and, on the market failure argument, Kay, J, and Vickers, J, 'Regulatory Reform: An Appraisal' in Majone, G (ed), *Deregulation or Re-regulation. Regulatory Reform in Europe and the United States* (1990) 221. For a summary of the market-failure argument see Cartwright, P, 'Consumer Protection in Financial Services: Putting the Law in Context' in Cartwright, P (ed), *Consumer Protection in Financial Services* (1999) 7–9.

systemic-stability objectives and the management of their associated risks requires regulatory intervention where a market failure prejudices the attainment of these objectives or where the risks involved are associated with market failures. For example, with respect to the investor-protection rationale, imperfect information has been highlighted as a market failure which impacts seriously on the risks to which investors are exposed in the market-place and which triggers the need for investor protection.[19] Market failures arise in relation to information in the investment-services markets as, to take one example and broadly speaking, the process of collecting information is costly and complex, as it is not usually sufficiently disseminated[20] and its interpretation requires specialist skills.[21] The resulting imperfection as to the investor's possession of information concerning the specific transactions concerned and the overall stability of the investment firm may mean that the investor is not fully informed or aware of the degree of risk being carried, or not aware of or in a position to protect against, or monitor the risk of, fraudulent behaviour, conflicts of interests, or negligence in the conduct of the investor/investment intermediary relationship.[22] As these risks are not sufficiently reflected in prices due to imperfect information, investment intermediaries do not have adequate incentives to avoid these risks and investors may make inefficient choices or exit from the market-place. But as these risks are associated with an information-related market failure and prevent an efficient allocation of resources, market-failure theory suggests that they are open to regulation.[23] While the correction of information-based market failures is at the root of much of investment-services regulation, the correction of another classic category of market

[19] Fraud is another related market failure which has triggered a strong regulatory response.

[20] The 'public good' nature of information—the fact that it becomes public once disseminated, that use of information by one person does not lower its value to others, and that suppliers of information cannot easily control free-riding on information, or restrict its dissemination to those who will directly or indirectly pay for it— means that suppliers of information are disincentivised from supplying it. See Ogus, n 18 above, 33–5 and 40.

[21] A second problem related to information and the supply of investment services is that information alone will not inform the investor as to the future performance of the investment or control the future behaviour of the investment intermediary. In this respect, investment products and the services provided by investment intermediaries are termed 'experience goods' by economists.

[22] Information-based market failures in the financial services and investment services sphere have been very widely examined from the economic perspective. See, for example, the 1992 OECD Report on Consumer Information About Financial Services, 11–14 and Dermine, J, 'EC Banking Regulation' in Steil, B (ed), *International Financial Market Regulation* (1994) 95, 109–11.

[23] Private rules can correct certain market failures but '[w]here, then, "market failure" is accompanied by "private law failure" . . . there is a prima facie case for regulatory intervention in the public interest': Ogus, n 18 above, 30. Private rules are usually regarded as being inadequate to deal with market failures linked to investor-protection and soundness objectives.

failure, externalities, can also be traced through the regulatory structure.[24] In particular, the investment-services market-place is vulnerable to an externality in the form of systemic risk, or the risk that the failure of one investment firm could have domino effects through the whole system and result in a catastrophic system failure, although the extent to which systemic risk exists in the investment-services market is a matter of some debate. In general, investment intermediaries are more prone to information-based market failures which implicate investor protection directly than they are to market failures which are primarily concerned with systemic risk.[25] The content of regulation is accordingly directed more towards the correction of information and fraud-based market failures.

The degree to which investor-protection or systemic-stability concerns are raised by the particular activities carried out by investment intermediaries tends to shape the content of the regulation imposed. Intermediaries which only provide investment advice and do not hold investor assets are unlikely to raise systemic-stability concerns.[26] The activities of brokers and dealers, on the other hand, may have systemic consequences as well as investor-protection implications. If, for example, a market-maker fails, system-wide problems may develop.[27]

VI.2.3 *Regulatory Techniques*

The techniques used to regulate investment intermediaries are largely a function of the rationale for regulating.

In terms of the investor-protection rationale, the regulatory techniques include the disclosure mechanisms which dominate the regulation of issuer access to the markets, but extend beyond disclosure to include more proactive regulation which attempts to limit or reduce the risks which reliance on investment intermediaries can trigger for investors.[28] While disclosure techniques can go part of the way in protecting investors and in re-

---

[24] An externality (and a justification for regulation) arises 'when the well-being of one economic agent (consumer or firm) is directly affected by the actions of another': Kay and Vicker, n 18 above, 226. A third category of market failure, which is not directly addressed by securities regulation (although it appears in competition law) concerns monopolies and market power.

[25] Mayer, C, and Neven, D, 'European Financial Regulation: A Framework for Policy Analysis' in Giovanni, A, and Mayer, C (eds), *European Financial Market Integration* (1991) 112, 113.

[26] IOSCO, eg, has recommended light regulation of investment advisers, given their limited activities: 1998 IOSCO Principles, n 12 above, para 12.8.

[27] Franks and Mayer distinguish between the lesser systemic risk posed by investment managers who give discretionary portfolio management advice and on whom the effective operation of the market-place is not dependent (pointing to countries which operate effectively without an investment-management industry) and the greater risk posed by broker-dealers given their more central role in the operation of markets: n 15 above, 158.

[28] See generally Page and Ferguson, n 15 above, 59–77.

adjusting the information imbalance, investors may not be in a position to assess disclosure of the risks posed by an investment intermediary or, indeed, inclined to seek it out.[29] Devices beyond disclosure such as quality-assurance mechanisms in the form of authorization and licensing rules[30] become necessary to spare the clients of investment intermediaries the burden of obtaining and analysing the information which will help them to minimize the risks inherent in dealing with investment intermediaries.[31] Indeed the point has been made, in the context of the supply of portfolio-management services, that, given that investors have chosen to pass the risk assessment of specific investments on to the intermediary, it makes little sense on efficiency grounds to re-impose another set of risk-assessment obligations relating to the investment intermediary.[32]

In terms of the wider systemic-stability rationale, which also feeds into individual investor protection, more aggressive regulatory strategies are needed.[33] Specific techniques relating to ensuring the soundness of the investment intermediary are used to protect the stability of the financial system against any adverse consequences following on default by investment intermediaries.

Overall, a wide variety of regulatory techniques are used in investment-intermediary regulation,[34] but they can be divided broadly into four categories: access regulation or authorization controls; protective regulation; prudential supervision; and compensation mechanisms. Market-access or authorization controls are a form of quality-assurance mechanism which relieve investors of the burden of assessing complex disclosure concerning the risks represented by the intermediary by allowing them to rely instead on a licensing process which reflects the judgement of an objective supervisor on the intermediary.[35] They represent more than disclosure filters, however, as they are designed to protect investors and market integrity by weeding out in advance intermediaries which may potentially be incompetent, fraudulent, or unable to meet their commitments by imposing

[29] On the weaknesses of disclosure in the investment services sphere see Gower, L, *Review of Investor Protection* (1982) para 2.01.

[30] See the discussion in Page and Ferguson, n 15 above, 36–8.

[31] On the interaction between disclosure and other regulatory techniques see generally Sah, M, and Cameron, G, 'Controlling the Quality of Fiduciary Advice: The Use of the Regulatory Form to Satisfy Fiduciary Obligations' [1997] *JBL* 142.

[32] Clark, n 4 above, 571.

[33] See Heremans, D, 'Economic Aspects of the Second Banking Directive and of the Proposal for a Directive on Investment Services in the Securities Field' in Stuyck, J (ed), *Financial and Monetary Integration in the European Economic Community, Legal, Economic and Institutional Aspects* (1994) 37, 44.

[34] For a challenge to the adequacy and efficiency of the traditional regulatory response to systemic risk and information problems see Ford, C, and Kay, J, 'Why Regulate Financial Services' in Oditah, F (ed), *The Future for the Global Securities Markets—Legal and Regulatory Aspects* (1996) 145.

[35] See Page and Ferguson, n 15 above, 38.

competency, character, and capital adequacy requirements. Protective regulation has a micro focus on the relationship between the investor and the intermediary. It addresses the conduct of the investment intermediary in its relations with its clients or investors and imposes standards of good behaviour which are designed to protect the investor against the imbalances in the intermediary/client relationship. Prudential regulation has a somewhat wider macro focus. It seeks to ensure the soundness of investment intermediaries in order to protect, on a micro level, the assets of investors and, on a macro level, the wider stability of the financial system against the risks of systemic failure and multiple-investment intermediary collapses and is largely concerned with capital adequacy controls. Finally, compensation mechanisms, which are often associated with paternalism, act as a safety net against failures of regulation and may provide redress for investors when regulatory controls fail and losses are sustained. The constituent elements of protective and prudential regulation are discussed in more detail in Chapters VIII and IX which deal with these forms of regulation.

VI.2.4 *Moral Hazard and Efficient Regulation*

Moving beyond disclosure regulation involves costs.[36] Regulation imposes burdens on investment intermediaries in terms of resources (particularly where capital-adequacy controls are concerned) and in terms of the restrictions it imposes on their freedom of action. The proactive regulation of intermediaries also carries with it the problem of moral hazard: the risk that investors exercise less care than they otherwise would in the belief that regulation removes the need to take care in making investments or dealing with investment intermediaries by guaranteeing the reliability and soundness of investment intermediaries.[37] Regulatory techniques beyond disclosure also ultimately limit investor choice, albeit in the interests of investor protection, by regulating market entry and controlling the behaviour of investment

---

[36] The costs of regulation have been subject to exhaustive analysis in the economics literature. Among the more famous discussions of this problem are the seminal works by Stigler (see, eg, Stigler, G, 'The Theory of Economic Regulation' (1971) 2 *Bell J Econ. and Management Sci.* 3). For an outline of the costs of regulation see Llewellyn, D, 'Consumer Protection in Retail Investment Services: Protection Against What' (1995) 3 *JFRC* 43, 44 and Gowland, D, *The Regulation of Financial Markets in the 1990s* (1990) 21–35.

[37] '[B]y promising something [competence] which cannot, in reality, be delivered, the regulatory system undermines the inevitable fundamental responsibility which consumers must take for their own decisions. As a result, when things go wrong, investors believe they are entitled to compensation, almost irrespective of the quality of the advice received': Ford and Kay, n 34 above, 150. The FSMA explicitly acknowledges the moral-hazard problem by stating that in considering the degree of consumer protection which is appropriate, the FSA is to take into account 'the general principle that consumers should take responsibility for their decisions': FSMA 2000, Pt I, s 5(2)(d). The EC regime has, in general, tended to avoid addressing moral-hazard problems. It articulates moral-hazard concerns most fully in the compensation scheme sphere. See Ch. X.

intermediaries.[38] Overly burdensome regulation can also distort competition and obstruct innovation, while inflexible rules can rapidly become obsolete as markets and investment techniques develop.[39] The effective regulation of investment intermediaries accordingly requires that an attempt be made to identify a rationale for regulating and to balance the benefits and objectives of regulation designed to support this rationale against these costs in order to reach the appropriate minimum level of regulation.[40] A common device used in the area of investor-protection regulation is to distinguish between the investors protected by the regulation in question, typically using a classification based on professional and retail investors, and to tailor the burden imposed accordingly (section 6.3 below)

VI.2.5 *The Rationale for Regulation and the EC Regime*

All of these elements and themes can be found in the EC's investment-intermediaries' regime and are discussed in the next four chapters. The regulatory issues raised by the peculiar sensitivities of the investment-services market to regulation and the distinctive need for investors and the system as a whole to be adequately protected must, however, be regarded in a regulatory context in which a powerful influence is exerted by the dominant market-integration objective; this transforms investment-services regulation from a public-regulation mechanism into a market-integration device. Regulation is also complicated by the particular and increased risks to investors and to systemic stability involved in moving beyond national markets and in establishing a single EC-wide market for investment services.[41]

While the focus of the EC regime has hitherto been on the construction of the single market and, consequently, on the protection of the soundness of investment intermediaries and the stability of the market-place, a sea change currently underway is redirecting the regulatory focus towards investor confidence and its maintenance through harmonized investor-

[38] The impact of behaviour-influencing regulation on the free market has long been observed to be a consequence of moving beyond disclosure regulation. See, eg, Page and Ferguson, n 15 above, 38 and Sah and Cameron, n 31 above, 145 who describe the choice between disclosure and other forms of regulation as 'a choice between the free market and one which is paternalistic and administered'.

[39] 'The market may not actually rule but it plays a much more important role as a driving force in any answer to the search for an optimal regulatory model': Scott-Quinn, B, 'A Model of Financial Regulation' in McCrudden, C (ed), *Regulation and Deregulation. Policy and Practice in the Utilities and Financial Services Industries* (1999) 313, 316.

[40] 'Ideally, regulation and competition should be complementary, the one providing a framework within which the other can then be allowed to operate safely': UK Report of the Wilson Committee to Review the Functioning of Financial Institutions (1980) para 1071.

[41] eg, in its opinion on the Commission proposal for what would become the Investor Compensation Schemes Directive (Directive 97/9/EC [1997] OJ L84/22) ECOSOC noted that any increase in competition arising from the construction of the single market might exacerbate the financial and operational difficulties of investment firms [1994] OJ C127/1 para 1.3.

protection rules. Evidence is also emerging of a more considered approach to the rationales for and objectives of investment-services regulation beyond its use as a market-integration device. Not only are objectives such as investor confidence and investor protection gaining currency (section VI.6.6), the market-failure doctrine as an underlying rationale for regulation is also, albeit to a limited extent, being explicitly articulated.[42]

The main features of the EC regime track the main components of investment-services regulation generally, and include authorization, operational, and capital-adequacy controls as well as protective conduct-of-business controls, with disclosure, and the promotion of rational investor choice, increasingly playing an important role in protective regulation, in particular.[43] The regime is, however, considerably more developed at present with respect to capital adequacy than it is with respect to conduct of business controls.

VI.3 THE DEVELOPMENT OF AN EC SYSTEM OF INVESTMENT-INTERMEDIARY REGULATION

VI.3.1 *Introduction*

The harmonized EC system of investment-intermediary regulation represents a compromise. It mediates between, on the one hand, the imperatives of regulating investment intermediaries, as outlined above, in the interests of investor protection and systemic stability and of respecting national interests in imposing such regulation and, on the other, the conflicting need to remove regulatory obstacles to the creation of an EC market in investment services. Ultimately, the achievement of an integrated market is at the heart of the EC's regulation of investment intermediaries and shapes the form and substance of the harmonized regulatory regime which is, in effect, the by-product of the integration process.

The investment-services regime is based ultimately on the Treaty objective of constructing an internal market (Article 2 EC and Article 14(2) EC) and, more immediately, on the free-movement rights granted under the Treaty to investment intermediaries in respect of the freedom to establish and the freedom to provide services (Articles 43-48 EC and 49-55 EC, respectively). These free-movement guarantees provide the two supporting pillars of the investment-services regime. The first pillar of the regime, the liberalizing, but reregulating, substantive regulatory regime which articu-

---

[42] See, eg, the Commission Communication on Upgrading the Investment Services Directive 93/22/EC COM(2000)729 (the ISD Communication) where the Commission noted at 5 that '[r]emoving regulatory obstacles to free circulation will not be sufficient. Regulatory action is also needed to correct market failure and to facilitate the effective interaction of supply and demand for capital'.

[43] See Ch. IX sect. 13 below.

lates the internal market principles of mutual recognition, minimum harmonization, and home-country control in the investment-services area, is
based on the power of the EC to adopt harmonizing directives in order to
ensure the achievement of these free-movement guarantees. The substantive
framework has been built, first, on the removal of obstacles to the free movement of investment firms by the harmonization of national rules on the functioning of investment-services markets under Article 47(2) EC and, secondly,
and more generally, on the approximation of national rules that affect the
functioning of the common/internal market under Articles 94 and 95 EC.
These foundation Articles reflect the cornerstone Treaty objective of establishing a common market (Article 2 EC) and find a basis in Article 3(c) and
3(h) EC which, respectively, highlight the construction of the internal market and the approximation of Member States' laws as required for the functioning of the common market as Community activities. The Treaty
competences which have acted as the basis for the harmonized regime are
discussed further in relation to the various elements of the harmonized
regime in the following chapters. As the EC matures as a securities regulator and moves into addressing the investor-protection and stability risks
which have arisen post-integration and which, due to their system-wide
implications, call for attention at EC level in accordance with the subsidiarity principle, considerable strains are being placed on Articles 47(2) and 95
EC. There is a second dimension to the Treaty rights. As they provide the
basis for the access by investment intermediaries to the markets of other
Member States, independently of any harmonizing measures adopted by the
EC, by virtue of the prohibition they place on discriminatory and free-
movement-restrictive national rules, they provide the second pillar of the
investment-intermediary regime. The substance of these access rights and
their articulation by the Court are discussed in this chapter.

The relationship between the Treaty rights and the harmonized regulatory regime has two key facets. First, the Treaty structure has acted as a
powerful agent for the development of the regime. On a fundamental level,
the Court's articulation of the scope of the free-movement guarantees, and,
in particular, its development of the mutual-recognition concept via its case
law on the prohibition of measures which are non-discriminatory but
restrict free movement, has provided the conceptual underpinning for the
liberalizing harmonization regime. Additionally, the Court has interpreted
the Treaty rights to allow Member States, in certain circumstances, to maintain regulatory requirements which in practice restrict market access,
thereby lending a greater urgency and impetus to the harmonization
programme. Secondly, the Treaty rights perform a critical gap-filling function. Where the EC has failed to harmonize an aspect of the regulatory structure applicable to investment intermediaries, where an aspect of the
harmonized structure is unclear, or where only limited harmonization has

been undertaken,[44] the Treaty rights and their explanatory case law serve an essential back-up role in mediating between the application of different Member States' regulatory systems. Indeed, the harmonization programme has borrowed particular concepts developed by the Court in interpreting the core Treaty freedoms, in particular the notion of regulation in the interests of the general good,[45] to bridge gaps in the system which might otherwise arise as a result of political deadlock.[46]

VI.3.2 *The Roots of the Regime*

While the predominant focus of the seminal Segré Report was on the integration of securities markets and the capital-formation process, it also examined the role of intermediaries. It found that while the participation of market intermediaries was critical in the creation of a European capital market,[47] market intermediaries were hampered by the varying rules and supervisory controls applicable to them across the EC.[48] From an early stage, therefore, fragmentation of national investment-services markets was believed to impede the efficient allocation of capital and economic growth in the EC. The establishment of a single market for the supply of investment services would, over the next thirty years, form part of the wider project to

[44] See the discussion of Case C–222/95 *Société Civile Immobilière Parodi v Banque H. Albert de Bary et Cie* [1997] ECR I–3899 in sect. 4.6.2 below.

[45] Particularly striking examples of the interrelationship between harmonized regulation and the jurisprudence of the Court on the free-movement guarantees can be found in the main harmonizing measure for investment-intermediary regulation, the Investment Services Directive (Directive 93/22/EEC [1993] OJ LL141/27 (the ISD)). It does not, eg, harmonize advertising regulation but in Art. 13 permits any Member State in which an investment intermediary within the scope of the ISD advertises to impose its advertising rules 'adopted in the interests of the general good'. The Treaty rights have also formed the cornerstone of a recent attempt by the Commission to explain the operation of Art. 11 of the ISD (which allows Member States to impose conduct rules on investment firms which provide services in the Member State): Commission Communication on the Application of Conduct of Business Rules under Article 11 of the Investment Services Directive (93/22/EEC) COM(2000)722 (the Art. 11 Communication), 14.

[46] See generally, Andenas, M, 'The Interplay of the Commission and the Court of Justice in giving effect to the Right to Provide Financial Services' in Craig, P, and Harlow, C, *Law Making in the EU* (1998) 332.

[47] This view was echoed some 30 years later by a senior Commission official who (unofficially) spoke of the need to create a strong and unified European securities market which would require 'a strong European investment management industry to provide efficient matching between the investment products created by issuers on the one hand, and the need for investors to have efficiently managed and well-balanced portfolios on the other': Clarotti, P, 'The Completion of the Internal Market: Current Position and Outlook' in Andenas, M, and Kenyon-Slade, S (eds), *EC Financial Market Regulation and Company Law* (1993) 8.

[48] The Report found that 'active participation by various types of institution in the creation of a European capital market may be hampered by the rules under which they operate and the supervisory controls to which they are subject. Differences in rules are liable to distort competition and impede integration': Report by a Group of Experts Appointed by the EEC Commission, *The Development of a European Capital Market* (the Segré Report) 32 (1966).

ensure the 'proper working and the interpenetration of these [securities] markets [as an] essential aspect of the establishment of a common market in capital' which would allow sources of capital to be 'sufficiently diversified to enable investments in the common market to be financed as rationally as possible'.[49]

From an economic perspective, it has often been observed that an efficient, integrated market in investment services, operating free of anti-competitive regulatory controls and market structures, will enhance the efficient distribution of capital across the EC and generate the associated economy-wide benefits.[50] The efficiency of the financial-services sector generally, and the investment-services sector in particular, has a direct bearing on the overall performance of the economy. In relation to the provision of financial services generally, the 1985 Cecchini Report,[51] which also highlighted the increased efficiency, heightened competition, greater consumer choice, and higher non-inflationary growth which would follow the establishment of a single market, quantified the benefits of a single market in financial services as being in the region of 11–12 billion euro.[52] The parochial tendencies of retail clients, in particular, to prefer service providers in their home Member States for reasons based on reputation and security can, however, have a depressing effect on cross-border trade in financial services, notwithstanding the overall gains such trade can bring to the EC economy.[53] Given that natural tendency against which financial-service providers must operate, the anti-competitive effects of additional regulatory barriers become critical and the regulatory treatment of investment intermediaries across the EC central to the competitiveness of the EC investment-services market.

[49] Commission Recommendation 77/534/EEC concerning a European Code of Conduct Relating to Transactions in Transferable Securities [1977] OJ L212/37 (the 1977 Code of Conduct), Explanatory Memorandum, paras 1 and 2.

[50] In the context of the still emerging EC capital market, the observation that 'capital markets do not emerge from scratch. In the early phase, strong intermediaries are needed to channel savings to productive investments' has some resonance: Gros, D, and Lannoo, K, *The Euro Capital Markets* (2000) 39. The efficiency with which intermediaries respond to market demands and provide for an efficient market mechanism and, on an operational level, set the costs of investment intermediation and capital acquisition are important considerations in achieving an efficient capital market. See the discussion in Hopt, K, and Buxbaum, R, *Legal Harmonisation and the Business Enterprise* (1988) 218–19.

[51] Cecchini, P, *The European Challenge 1992: The Benefits of a Single Market* (1988).

[52] The Cecchini Report was based on examining the beneficial effects of reducing prices to their lowest level in the EC, which the Report predicted would happen on liberalization due to increased competition. For a critique of the Cecchini Report's conclusions with respect to financial services see Chakravarty, S, and Molyneux, P, 'The Single European Market in Financial Services' (1996) 96 *European Business Review* 43.

[53] See Gros and Lannoo, n 50 above, 1–2 and 72.

VI.3.3 *Investment Intermediaries and Regulatory Obstacles*

Prior to the harmonization programme, Member States across the EC regulated investment intermediaries (in order to protect the investor-protection and systemic interests outlined in section 2 above) to widely varying degrees and in very different ways. Regulation varied according to whether the intermediary was a credit institution, a dealer registered with a stock exchange, or an intermediary operating outside the structure of a stock exchange and engaged in ancillary investment services such as investment advice or portfolio management. Credit institutions engaged in securities or investment-services activities were, by and large, subject only to general banking regulation.[54] Dealers in securities who were admitted to stock exchanges were subject to some form of regulation, usually by virtue of stock exchange membership, although the nature of the regulation differed, causing difficulties for market integration.[55] The greatest divergence in regulatory treatment was evident in the supervision of intermediaries who did not deal in securities and were not regulated through stock exchange membership but were engaged in the provision of ancillary investment services.[56] While the regulatory requirements of certain Member States hindered the ability of undertakings from other Member States to offer investment services,[57] conversely the lack of any substantial regulation in certain Member States[58] operated to impede

---

[54] Wymeersch, n 1 above, 129.

[55] Neither France, Belgium, nor Italy imposed minimum initial capital requirements on dealers, in comparison to the minimum capital levels required by the UK, Germany, Denmark, and Luxembourg: Wymeersch. n 1 above, 59. The Wymeersch report concluded at 131 that, although most Member States apart from Belgium and Italy had well-developed systems for regulating brokers, '[t]here are considerable differences among the Member States so that harmonisation appears necessary. Harmonization ought furthermore appreciably strengthen the status of this category of intermediaries in order to strengthen their continued long-term existence in the market as strong and solvent market participants who, together with the banks, ensure the carrying out of securities dealings.'

[56] 'All sorts of portfolio managers and investment consultants frequently exert a decisive influence on stock exchange orders. In countries where their activity is not forbidden they are usually outside the scope of any legal or regulatory provisions. In the past abuses have developed from the activities of these ancillary participants in securities business': ibid, 63.

[57] In Germany, eg, investment services could be carried out only through a credit institution incorporated in Germany.

[58] Professor Wymeersch's 1977 description of the regulatory landscape is illuminating, if somewhat alarming in these more regulated days: '[t]he present approach as regards regulation differs fairly considerably. In France, the passing-on of stock exchange orders, as well as portfolio management, is subject to some measures of investor protection. In the United Kingdom, some investment consultants and intermediate brokers could come within the scope of the Prevention of Fraud (Investments) Act . . . there are many exceptions to this rule . . . In Belgium and the Netherlands only securities brokerage is reserved to the recognized securities business: investment advisory services or portfolio management are offered absolutely freely . . . In Luxembourg the question is solved by the application of the Order controlling the opening of new business, while in Germany problems have arisen both with portfolio managers or consultants and with sellers of securities from their own portfolios. In Italy there is complete freedom': n 1 above, 60–1.

the development of an integrated market, given the dangers to investor protection and market integrity such regimes posed to the development of a single market. Altogether, these variations in the regulation of investment intermediaries acted as an obstacle to greater integration and caused fragmentation of the national investment-services markets.

The structural features of the national stock markets, to which the activities of investment intermediaries are closely connected, also varied widely.[59] The dominance of large universal banks which provided investment and securities services as well as traditional banking services in some continental markets, particularly Germany, made market penetration by specialist investment-services providers more difficult.[60] By contrast, other markets, such as Belgium, permitted credit institutions to take orders only, and required all trades to be handled by brokers who had exclusive rights to operate as intermediaries.[61] The structure of national stock exchanges, the market mechanisms used for trading in securities, and the degree of control on access to trading would subsequently make the negotiation of harmonizing measures difficult.

The problems caused by variations in regulation[62] became particularly acute during the late 1980s and early 1990s when an explosion of regulatory activity took place across the EC[63] with, many, although not all,[64] Member States, with varying degrees of success, adopting laws or regulations

[59] See Wymeersch, n 1 above, 54–64 and 89–92. See also Scott-Quinn, B, 'EC Securities Markets Regulation' in Steil, n 22 above, 121, 123–31 and Dalhuisen, J, *The New UK Securities Legislation and the EC 1992 Program* (1989) 73–8. The issues raised by the variations in the structure and operation of stock exchanges and the EC's response are discussed further in Ch. XI.

[60] See the discussion by Farmery, P, 'Looking Towards a European Internal Market in Financial Services: Some Paradoxes and Paradigms: A Survey of Current Problems and Issues' (1992) 3 *EBLRev.* 94.

[61] Wymeersch, n 1 above at 54 described the distinction as one between 'brokers' stock exchanges' and mixed stock exchanges. The former permitted only stockbroking firms, and not credit institutions, to deal on the exchange, even where most orders were in practice received from credit institutions. This market structure was found in the UK, Belgium, Ireland, and Denmark and, with slight modifications, in France and Italy. The mixed stock exchange structure permitted credit institutions as well as stockbroking firms to deal and was found in, eg, the Netherlands, and Luxembourg.

[62] Regulatory barriers are not, of course, limited to supervisory controls but include foreign-exchange capital controls. These barriers have been dismantled since the liberalization of capital and the introduction of the euro. See Ch. I sect. 8 above. For an outline of barriers to integration in financial services markets generally, including investment-services markets, see the Commission of the European Communities, *Research on the 'Cost of Non-Europe'*, Basic Findings, vol 9, The Cost of Non-Europe in Financial Services' (1988) 62.

[63] In his Opinion in Case C–101/94 *Commission v Italy* [1996] ECR I–2691, Lenz AG noted at para 40 that '[i]n a period of less than 10 years the legislatures of the Member States of the European Communities evidently recognised a need for regulation'.

[64] Ireland, eg, would not introduce a systematic regime for the regulation of investment intermediaries until 1995 when, as part of its implementation of the ISD, it passed the Investment Intermediaries Act 1995.

for the supervision of their investment markets.[65] The new regimes in certain cases simply imposed additional non-discriminatory regulatory costs on investment intermediaries wishing to enter the national market in question,[66] but in other cases actively shielded domestic market participants from outside competition. In 1991 Italy, which hitherto had left investment intermediaries which were not also credit institutions largely unregulated, adopted a securities law which introduced licensing requirements for securities firms which, controversially, included an establishment requirement. Indeed, in its submissions to the Court during the subsequent action against Italy the Commission expressed its general concern with respect to the impact of such abruptly introduced rules, particularly given their adoption after the liberalization of capital movements.[67]

The degree to which the regulatory obstacles (where the measure actually protected the national market) and costs (arising from the requirement to comply with a different system of supervision) arising from these different systems had the potential to impede the development of an EC market in investment services[68] was exacerbated by the extent to which Member States could legitimately impose restrictive measures on investment intermediaries as a result of the interpretation by the Court of the otherwise market-opening measures in the Treaty giving investment intermediaries the freedom to provide services and to establish in all Member States of the EC.

[65] The UK in 1986 introduced the Financial Services Act which changed the regulation of investment services from a self-regulatory regime to a statutory system, while in 1988 France introduced a major reform of the regulation of stockbrokers. Also in 1988, Spain adopted a Securities Markets Act which radically restructured its securities markets. Earlier, in 1985, the Netherlands introduced a general licensing requirement, which was introduced in the wake of problems with the trading practices of firms which were not part of an exchange and so not subject to any authorisation requirements or supervision. The state of regulation across the EC immediately prior to the adoption of the harmonization measures is summarized in Scott-Quinn, n 59 above, 123–30. See also Poser, N, *International Securities Regulation. London's 'Big Bang' and the European Securities Markets* (1991) 379–441.

[66] 'Even though the basic notions of these domestic protections were not always so different, there was a great variety in the technical details and sophistication in various countries': Dalhuisen, J, 'Liberalisation and ReRegulation of Cross-Border Financial Services Part II' (1999) 10 *EBLRev.* 284, 290.

[67] *Commission v Italy*, n 63 above, Opinion of the AG, para 38.

[68] On these two distinct types of obstacle see, eg, Warren, M, 'Global Harmonisation of Securities Laws: The Achievements of the European Communities' (1991) 31 *Harv. Int'l. Law J* 185.

VI.4 THE FREEDOM TO ESTABLISH AND THE FREEDOM TO PROVIDE SERVICES[69]

VI.4.1 *Introduction*

Investment intermediaries seeking to operate on a cross-border basis benefit from the fundamental EC Treaty protections of the freedom to establish (Articles 43–48 EC) and the freedom to provide services (Articles 49–55 EC).[70] These generic provisions, respectively, allow investment intermediaries based in one Member State (the home Member State) to set up or establish a business or provide cross-border investment services in other Member States (host Member States). Crucially, they also set the parameters within which these other Member States may impose their investment-services rules on visiting investment intermediaries.

VI.4.2 *The Freedom to Establish*

VI.4.2.1 *Scope*

Article 43 EC provides that 'restrictions on the freedom of establishment of nationals of a Member State in the territory of another Member State shall be prohibited'. Although the freedom to establish (and the freedom to

---

[69] See generally Usher, J, *The Law of Money and Financial Services in the EC* (2nd edn, 2000) 89–112; Van Gerven, W, and Wouters, J, 'Free Movement of Financial Services and the European Contracts Convention' in Andenas and Kenyon-Slade, n 47 above, 43; and Tison, M, *Unravelling the General Good Exception. The Case of Financial Services*, WP 2000-03, Working Paper Series of the Financial Law Institute, Gent Universiteit. (forthcoming in Andenas, M, and Roth, W-H (eds), *Free Movement of Services*).

[70] The individuals employed by investment intermediaries benefit from the free movement of workers (Arts. 39–42 EC). These provisions are not considered here as they apply generally to all workers and do not have specific implications for investment-intermediary regulation. The relocation by an investment intermediary of employees in another Member State seems to come within the freedom to provide services. See Usher, n 69 above, 89, discussing Case C-113/89 *Rush Portugesa v Office National d' Immigration* [1990] ECR I-1417 and Case C-43/93 *Vander Elst v OMI* [1994] ECR I-3803. The other main freedom, the free movement of goods (the application of the free movement of capital is considered in sect. 4.3.3 below), which is set out in Arts. 28–30 EC is of secondary importance here, as it is largely concerned with the cross-border movement of tangible material products. The intangible investment products provided by investment intermediaries tend to be treated as services provided by the investment intermediary. The free movement of goods and services rights do not, however, exist in hermetically sealed compartments, depending on whether the product is material or intangible. The Court has transposed concepts from the free movement of goods area to the services area, as in Case 62/79 *Coditel v Ciné Vog* [1980] ECR 881. See the discussion in Björkland, M, 'The Scope of the General Good Notion in the Second EC Banking Directive According to Recent Case-Law' (1998) 9 *EBLRev.* 227, 228. This integrated approach does not always apply, however. In *Alpine Investments* (n 6 above) the Court famously refused to apply its free movement of goods jurisprudence with respect to selling arrangements to the provision of services.

provide services) is drafted primarily in terms of natural persons,[71] this prohibition is explicitly applied to 'restrictions on the setting up of agencies, branches or subsidiaries by nationals of any Member State established in the territory of any Member State'.[72] Article 43 EC also specifies that the freedom to establish covers the right to 'set up and manage undertakings, in particular companies and firms' as well as the right to take up activities as a self-employed person. The companies or firms which can, in addition to natural persons, benefit from the freedom to establish are defined under Article 48 EC as 'companies or firms constituted under civil or commercial law, including cooperative societies, and other legal persons governed by public or private law, save those which are non-profit-making'. In order to benefit from the freedom to establish, companies must, under Article 48, be formed in accordance with the law of a Member State and have their registered offices, central administrations, or principal places of business within the Community. A company will not be deprived of the freedom to establish, however, if its principal place of business is in a Member State other than the one in which it has its registered office and in accordance with the laws of which it is formed, even if it conducts all of its business through a form of establishment in that other Member State.[73]

In terms of when the freedom to establish is triggered, the Court has found that 'a national of a Member State who pursues a professional activity on a stable and continuous basis in another Member State where he holds himself out from an established professional base to, amongst others, nationals of that State comes under the provisions of . . . the right of establishment and not those . . . relating to services'.[74] It is clear from Article 43 EC that setting up a branch, agency, or subsidiary can constitute an establishment. The Court's statement that maintaining a 'permanent presence in

[71] Usher, n 69 above, 90. The harmonized regime clearly contemplates that natural persons can provide investment services. See Art. 1(2) of the cornerstone ISD, discussed in Ch. VII sect. 3.2 below.

[72] Member States may not discriminate in respect of the various forms of establishment in their territory by imposing, eg, different requirements on branches or agents from those imposed on subsidiaries: Case C–270/83 *Commission v France* [1986] ECR 273. See further Usher, n 69 above, 93.

[73] Case C–212/97 *Centros v Ervhervs- og Selskabsstyrelsen* [1999] ECR I–1459. The seminal *Centros* case clarified that the freedom to establish would still exist even if the company carried out all of its activities through a branch and never conducted business in the Member State of its primary establishment. As a result, Member States may not restrict secondary establishments even where the purpose of the establishment is to allow the company to conduct all of its business through the secondary establishment. While companies accordingly benefit from the freedom to establish, they do not, under the establishment rules, have the freedom to transfer their central management and control or head office from their State of incorporation and registration to another Member State, free of any restriction imposed by the Member State of registration, while maintaining an establishment in that Member State: Case 81/87 *R v HM Treasury ex parte Daily Mail* [1988] ECR 5483.

[74] Case C–55/94 *Gebhard v Consiglio dell'Ordine degli Avvocati e Procuratori di Milano* [1995] ECR 4165, para 25.

the Member State in question comes within the scope of the provisions of the Treaty on the right of establishment, even if that presence does not take the form of a branch or agency, but consists merely of an office managed by an undertaking's own staff or by a person who is independent but authorized to act on a permanent basis for the undertaking'[75] suggests that a limited presence in another Member State may therefore activate the establishment rules, rather than the services provisions.[76]

That the freedom to establish applies to investment intermediaries is clear from *Commission v Italy*, where the Court confirmed that the protections of the freedom to establish applied to restrictions placed by Italy on the form of establishment which firms dealing in transferable securities could take.[77]

Although Article 44 EC imposes a general obligation on the Council to adopt directives in order to attain the freedom of establishment of particular activities,[78] the freedom to establish has direct effect in that it can be relied on by an individual at national level and is not dependent on the adoption of a directive.[79] In *Commission v Italy* recourse was had to the freedom to establish under the Treaty precisely because the ISD (see section 5.2 below), which now provides a mechanism under which investment intermediaries can exercise the freedom to establish, had not been in force at the time of the action.

---

[75] Case 205/84 *Commission v Germany* [1986] ECR 3755 (the *German Insurance* case), para 20.

[76] For an analysis of when use of an independent intermediary triggers the Treaty rules see the Commission's Interpretative Communication on Freedom to provide services and the interests of the general good in the Second Banking Directive (the General Good Communication) [1997] OJ C209/6, 10–12.

[77] N 63 above, examined by Andenas, M, 'Italian Nationality Requirement and Community Law' (1996) 17 *The Company Lawyer* 219.

[78] The original version of Art. 44 required the Council to produce a general programme for the removal of restrictions on the freedom to establish. The General Programme for the Abolition of Restrictions on the Freedom of Establishment ([1962] OJ 36/62, [1974] OJ Spec Ed 2nd Series IX) which was adopted in 1961 focused on the removal of discriminatory restrictions on the freedom to establish and included the removal of discriminatory licensing requirements, tax requirements, and residence requirements. Although the Amsterdam Treaty amendments removed the reference to the programme from Art. 44 EC, it retains the detailed series of instructions set out in Art. 44(2)(a)–(h) on how the Council and the Commission should approach the adoption of directives in this area.

[79] Case 2/74 *Reyners v Belgium* [1974] ECR 631. Before the Court confirmed that the freedom to establish (and the freedom to provide services) had direct effect, the Council, operating from the standpoint that it was not directly effective, adopted Directive 73/183/EEC on the Abolition of Restrictions on Freedom of Establishment and Freedom to Provide Services in respect of Self-Employed Activities of Banks and Other Financial Institutions [1973] OJ L194/1. The directive, which has since been overtaken by specific investment-services harmonizing measures, required under Art. 3(1) the abolition of certain restrictions on the freedom to establish and to provide services including restrictions on establishing in the host country under the same conditions as nationals and administrative practices which resulted in discriminatory treatment by comparison with the treatment of nationals. A wide range of financial institutions was included within the Directive including banks, savings and loan undertakings, syndicates (including underwriting syndicates), brokers (including stock exchange brokers, outside brokers, stock jobbers and brokers in transferable securities), financial consultancies, and stock exchanges.

VI.4.2.2 *Prohibited Restrictions*

The freedom to establish is designed to ensure that nationals of Member States are granted equal treatment and not discriminated against on grounds of nationality when establishing in another Member State.[80] To that end, Article 43 EC provides that freedom of establishment is to be exercised under the conditions laid down for its own nationals by the law of the Member State where the establishment is effected. Accordingly, investment intermediaries may, legitimately, be subject to the same conditions and regulatory requirements as apply to nationals of the Member State in which establishment is sought, as long as these measures do not amount to a restriction on the freedom to establish.

Although the reference in Article 43 EC to the 'conditions laid down for its own nationals' suggests that only discriminatory restrictions on the freedom to establish are prohibited, it is now clear from *Gebhard* that where measures 'hinder or make less attractive' the freedom to establish they will be prohibited under Article 43 EC, even if they are non-discriminatory, unless otherwise justified.[81] *Gebhard*, which applies to the Treaty free-movement rules generally, has had the effect of aligning the treatment of non-discriminatory rules under the freedom to establish and the freedom to provide services, as the non-discriminatory rule approach was initially developed in the services context (see section 4.3.2 below).[82] One important effect of *Gebhard* is that where non-discriminatory formal-qualification and knowledge requirements are imposed on the investment intermediary seeking to establish, the Member State in question must take into account the equivalence of any knowledge and qualifications already obtained and compare the national-law requirements with the knowledge and qualifications of the intermediary.[83] The investment-services regulation-specific measures which

[80] Case C-168/91 *Konstantinidis* [1993] I ECR I-1191.

[81] N 74 above. The Court found that 'where the taking-up or pursuit of a specific activity is subject to [national rules such as those relating to organisation, qualifications, professional ethics, supervision and the holding of formal qualifications] in the host Member State, a national of a Member State intending to pursue that activity must in principle comply with them'. It went on to find, however, that any national measure 'liable to hinder or make less attractive' the fundamental Treaty freedoms would be permitted only if it was applied in a non-discriminatory manner, was justified by imperative requirements in the general interest, was suitable for securing the attainment of the objective in question, and did not go beyond what was necessary to achieve that objective: paras 36–7. See section 4.6.2 on the extent to which a restrictive, non-discriminatory measure may be justified.

[82] On the development of the non-discriminatory rules jurisprudence see, eg, Beaumont, P, and Weatherill, S, *EU Law* (3rd edn, 1999) 679–88 and Craig, P, and de Búrca, G, *EU Law. Text, Cases and Materials* (2nd edn, 1998) 744–8. The early approach to establishment and services was to protect exercise of the freedoms from discriminatory restrictions. See the discussion in O'Leary, S, 'The Free Movement of Persons and Services' in Craig, P, and de Búrca, G (eds), *The Evolution of EU Law* (1999) 377, 400–1.

[83] N 74 above, para 38. See also Case C-340/89 *Vlassopoulou* [1991] ECR I-2357. This case law led Lenz AG in *Commission v Italy* to note in the context of whether a duplication of

may be imposed under the *Gebhard* approach on investment intermediaries exercising the Treaty establishment rights are outlined in section 4.4 below.

VI.4.3 *The Freedom to Provide Services*

VI.4.3.1 *Scope*

Article 49 EC, which also has direct effect,[84] provides that 'restrictions on freedom to provide services within the Community shall be prohibited in respect of nationals of Member States who are established in a State of the Community other than that of the person for whom the services are intended'. Under Article 52 EC, companies and firms also benefit from the freedom to provide services but must be established in a Member State of the Community.

In addition to the governing definition of services as those residual activities which are not covered by the Treaty provisions relating to freedom of movement for goods, capital, and persons, services are also defined in Article 50 EC as those services 'normally provided for remuneration'. Activities of a commercial character are specifically mentioned as included within the definition of services. It is clear from *Alpine Investments BV v Minister van Financiën*,[85] which concerned restrictions on the ability of an investment intermediary to make cold calls in respect of the supply of investment advice, portfolio management, and the transmission of orders in relation to commodity futures, that the freedom to provide services applies to the supply of investment services.[86]

The Court also found in *Alpine Investments* that the prior existence of an identifiable recipient, or a pre-existing relationship with the recipient, was not necessary for the freedom to provide services to apply.[87] Offers of services or the use of marketing techniques could constitute 'services' for the

---

authorization controls on securities dealers could be justified that 'in the absence of harmonization it is ultimately the rules of the Member State alone which form the criterion, and there is merely a duty on the part of the Member State to examine for comparability and accept things done in the context of the legal system of another Member State in the person of an applicant for authorisation': *Commission v Italy*, n 63 above, Opinion of the AG, para 52.

[84] Case 33/74 *Van Binsbergen v Bestuur van de Bedrijfsvereniging voor de Metaalnijverheid* [1974] ECR 1299.

[85] N 6 above. The case generated significant comment. See in particular Andenas, M, 'Cross Border Cold-calling and the Right to Provide Services' (1995) 16 *The Company Lawyer* 249, Annotation by Hatzopoulos, V, in (1995) 32 *CMLRev.* 1427 and Ross, M, 'A59 and the Marketing of Financial Services' (1995) 20 *ELRev.* 507.

[86] See also Case 15/78 *Société Générale Alsacienne de Banque SA v Koestler* [1978] ECR 1971 where the Court found that 'services such as those at issue which consist in a bank having orders carried out on a stock exchange . . . constitute the provision of services within the meaning of the first paragraph of Article 60 of the Treaty which refers generically to all activities of a commercial character': para 2.

[87] Neither is it necessary that the specific nature of the services to be supplied to the recipient be identified: Case 186/87 *Cowan v Trésor Public* [1989] ECR 195.

purposes of Article 49 EC, as otherwise 'the freedom to provide services would become illusory if national rules were at liberty to restrict offers of services'.[88] Accordingly, in that case the ability to use a marketing technique and, specifically, to make cold calls to potential investors with respect to offers of commodity futures (despite the fact that the majority of any subsequent transactions would be executed outside the Community on the Chicago commodities exchange) could benefit from the freedom to provide services.

The nature of the cross-border element required before the protections of the freedom to provide services are triggered is also fluid. The basic requirement under Article 49 EC is that the service provider be established in a Member State other than that of the service recipient.[89] This relationship can be achieved in a number of ways, all of which benefit from Article 49 EC.[90] The service provider can move to another Member State in order to provide services,[91] the recipient can move to another Member State to receive the services,[92] or the provider and recipient may be established in the same Member State but the provider can move to another Member State to offer the service in question.[93] In addition, the cross-border element can be created through the provision of distance services, which are supplied without the physical movement of either the recipient or the provider and are of particular importance for investment intermediaries due to developments in telecommunications (such as the Internet), and still benefit from Article 49. In *Alpine Investments*, the Court applied the freedom to provide services to services offered by the provider by telephone to recipients outside the provider's State of establishment.[94]

---

[88] *Alpine Investments*, n 6 above, para 19.

[89] As the critical factor for Art. 49 EC is establishment in two different Member States, the freedom to provide cross-border services in another Member State applies to branches of investment intermediaries (Art. 43 clearly provides for establishment through branches), as well as to their head offices, as long as the recipient is established elsewhere.

[90] The following categorization is based on the Opinion of Jacobs AG in *Alpine Investments*, n 6 above, para 28.

[91] See Commission v Italy n 63 above.

[92] Joined Cases 286/82 and 26/83 *Luisi and Carbone v Ministero del Tesoro* [1984] ECR 277. See also *Koestler* (n 86 above), which concerned the execution of stock exchange orders and other financial transactions by a bank established in France for a customer who was also established in France. Notwithstanding that the bank providing services and the recipient of the services were established in the same Member State, the freedom to provide services applied as the customer established himself in Germany before the contractual relationship with the bank ended.

[93] As in the *Tourist Guide* cases. See, eg, Case C-180/89 *Commission v Italy* [1991] ECR I-709.

[94] The Court saw no difficulty in bringing distance services within the scope of Art. 49 EC as, on the facts, the offers of services were 'made by a provider established in one Member State to a potential recipient established in another Member State' and stated unusually expressly (possibly to acknowledge the key role distance methods play in the financial services sector generally) that 'Article 59 [now Art. 49 EC] of the EEC Treaty covers services which the provider offers by telephone to potential recipients established in other Member States': n 6 above, paras 21–22.

VI.4.3.2 *Prohibited Restrictions*

The freedom to provide services is subject, under Article 50 EC, to the broad limitation that the activity in question is to be exercised under the same conditions as are imposed by that State on its own nationals. In principle therefore Member States may impose requirements on service providers, as long as they are not discriminatory. As with establishment, the objective of the freedom to provide services is to ensure equal treatment for those providing services in the host Member State with nationals of that State.

The Court has, however, taken a broad approach with respect to what measures constitute a restriction on the freedom to provide services. Article 49 EC is not simply restricted to discrimination based on nationality, but also covers any restrictions on the freedom to provide services which are imposed on the service provider as a consequence of the fact that the service provider is established in a Member State other than the one in which the services are provided. In *Säger v Dennemeyer* the Court found that Article 49 required 'the abolition of any restriction, even if applied without distinction to national providers of services and to those of other Member States, when it is liable to prohibit or otherwise impede the activities of a provider of services established in another Member State where he lawfully provides similar services'.[95] The types of investment-services regulation rules likely to be caught by this rule are discussed in section 4.4 below.

Alpine Investments contains an important analysis in the context of investment services of whether non-discriminatory marketing rules imposed by the provider's Member State of establishment, rather than, as is more usual, the recipient's, can constitute a restriction on the freedom to provide services. The case concerned the imposition of a condition which prohibited the making of cold calls in connection with investment services related to commodity futures on the exemption from authorization of a Dutch commodity-futures broker. The condition prohibiting the use of cold calls was based on a Dutch law which, in the wake of a number of complaints by investors who suffered loss following investments made after cold calls, imposed a general ban on cold-calling and applied to all financial intermediaries established in the Netherlands and operating either within or outside the territory. The broker, who had clients across Europe, argued that this prohibition was a restriction on its freedom to provide services to clients established in other Member States, contrary to Article 49 EC. Critical to the Court's finding that the measure could, while non-discriminatory, constitute a restriction contrary to Article 49 was that the ban on cold-calling deprived service providers of a 'rapid and direct technique for marketing and for contacting potential clients in other Member States' and could restrict the freedom to

---

[95] Case C-76/90 *Säger v Dennemeyer & Co Ltd* [1991] ECR 221, para 12.

provide cross-border services.[96] The Court found that notwithstanding that the measure was non-discriminatory and did not have the object or effect of placing the national market at an advantage over providers of services from other Member States, it affected not only offers to recipients established in the Member State and those who moved there to receive services, but also potential recipients in other Member States. As a result, it directly affected access to the market in services in other Member States and was a restriction on the freedom to provide services.[97] The prohibition on non-discriminatory but restrictive measures thus extends to measures imposed by the home Member State which restrict the export of services.[98] Restrictions imposed by Member States on their own nationals from providing services in other Member States, such as the marketing restriction in *Alpine Investments*, are likely to be comparatively rare, but will come within the scope of Article 49 EC.

In terms of the degree of hindrance or difficulty required to be imposed by the restrictive measure before Article 49 EC is implicated, the *Säger* approach that the measure must 'prohibit or otherwise impede' the exercise of the freedom to provide services seems to have been overtaken by the Court's ruling in *Gebhard* that the measure simply 'hinder or make less attractive' the freedom to provide services (and the freedom to establish).[99] This lower threshold accords with the *Alpine Investments* analysis of the cold-calling prohibition simply as one which 'directly affected' access to the markets of other Member States.[100] Restrictive effects are typically represented

---

[96] *Alpine Investments*, n 6 above, para 28.

[97] On this point the case is significant in that the Court refused to apply the *Keck* (Cases C-267-268/91 *Keck and Mithouard* [1993] ECR I-6097) line of cases which applies to the parallel Treaty rules on the free movement of goods. The *Keck* jurisprudence takes outside the scope of the Treaty rules which prohibit Member State restrictions on the free movement of goods any 'selling arrangements that apply in the same manner, both in law and in fact, to all traders within the national territory'. Although the non-discriminatory and 'selling arrangement' features of the cold-calling prohibition suggested that it could be classified as a selling arrangement rule under *Keck* (and this argument was made by both the Dutch and the UK government which intervened in the case) the Court declined to apply the *Keck* analysis to the freedom to supply services. The Court stressed in particular that the cold-calling prohibition applied to offers made outside the Member State: paras 35–39. Jacobs AG was also opposed to the *Keck* analysis on the grounds that a functional criterion on whether or not the measure in question substantially impedes the freedom to provide services should govern generally the assessment whether a rule amounted to restriction on the freedom to provide services: Opinion of the AG, para 47.

[98] Earlier case law on the free movement of goods had suggested that only discriminatory restrictions on exports which benefited the national market would infringe the Treaty. See Case 15/79 *Groenveld* [1979] ECR 3409.

[99] Although *Gebhard* concerned a restriction on the freedom to establish, it formulates the nature of the restriction very broadly in terms of '[n]ational measures which hinder or make less attractive the exercise of fundamental freedoms guaranteed by the Treaty': n 74 above, para 37.

[100] In Case C-3/95 *Reisebüro Broede v Sandker* [1996] ECR I-6511 the Court simply referred in para 25 of its Judgment to any restrictions which are 'liable to prohibit, impede or render

by increases in the cost of providing the service in question, arising from mandatory compliance with an additional set of rules which may prevent an intermediary from adopting cost-effective uniform procedures, or by onerous market-access requirements, such as establishment conditions.[101]

VI.4.3.3 *The Freedom to Provide Services and the Free Movement of Capital*

Given that Article 50 EC provides that the freedom to provide services applies only where the activity in question is not covered by the free movement of capital, it might have been expected that the Court would first analyse the activity involved to determine whether it simply involved the free movement of capital,[102] rather than a service connected with the movement of capital and to assess whether the freedom to provide services was actually implicated in the first place. The demarcation can be difficult. In the investment-services arena, the nature of the services provided, in terms of services related to securities, for example, clearly lies in the grey area between the provision of services and the free movement of capital. Although the Court has not specifically examined this question in the context of investment services and products in any detail,[103] it has displayed a tendency to blur the question whether a transaction involves the free movement of capital or the

---

less advantageous' the provision of services. Similarly in *Parodi*, n 44 above, the Court did not impose a high threshold, finding in para 19 that, notwithstanding that the French restriction appeared to be non-discriminatory, 'nonetheless it makes it more difficult for the credit institution' to, in that case, grant a mortgage in France. The low threshold required for a breach of Art. 49 EC to be found (as compared to the degree of restriction required for the establishment guarantee to be breached) has been highlighted as one of the differences in an otherwise broadly uniform treatment of establishment and services in terms of non-discriminatory restrictions. See Hatzopoulos, V, 'Recent Developments of the Case Law of the ECJ in the Field of Services' (2000) 37 *CMLRev.* 43, 71. On the difference between establishment and services restrictions see sects. 4.4 and 4.5 below.

[101] See, eg, the *German Insurance* case, n 75 above, para 28.

[102] On which see Ch. I sect. 8 above.

[103] In *Koestler*, n 86 above, the Court simply stated in para 3 that 'there is no doubt that services such as those at issue which consist of a bank having orders carried out on a stock exchange and in current account transactions in conjunction with the opening of a credit constitute the provision of services within the meaning of the first paragraph of Article 62 of the Treaty which refers generically to all activities of a commercial nature'. The Court did not examine any potential overlap with the capital provisions or explain why the activities constituted a service. Indicators of how the characterization might be undertaken by the Court may be found in the Opinion of Lenz AG in *Commission v Italy*, n 63 above. He found at para 14 that '[i]t is appropriate to keep the matters separate as the Treaty provides for exceptions to the general rules on both freedom of establishment and freedom to provide services, with respect to the movement of capital'. He also draws a useful distinction between services and capital, suggesting in para 24 that the freedom to provide services is clearly involved where the question is whether or not services may be carried out in principle and not whether certain types of transaction may occur.

freedom to provide services where the service provided displays certain characteristics of a capital movement.[104]

Under Article 51(2) EC, the liberalization of banking and insurance services connected with the movement of capital is to be effected in step with the liberalization of the free movement of capital. This provision suggests that movement of the underlying financial products involved must already have been liberalized before the freedom to provide services can apply. If the service involves the movement of capital which has not been liberalized, the freedom to provide services is not available. In this respect, the freedom to provide services is an accessory freedom to the underlying and governing free movement of capital. The freedom to establish is also interrelated by the Treaty to the free movement of capital by Article 43 EC which provides that the freedom to establish is 'subject to the provisions of the Chapter relating to capital'. Advocate General Lenz in *Commission v Italy*, in the context of restrictions on the freedom of securities dealers to establish and restrictions on the freedom to provide services related to dealing in transferable securities, examined the possible application of Article 51(2) EC (even though it does not specifically refer to securities and investment services, explicitly referring only to banking and insurance services) and Article 43 EC. He found that neither the freedom to establish nor the freedom to provide services was restricted in its scope, as Directive 88/361 liberalized operations in securities normally dealt in on the capital market.[105] More generally, the combination of Articles 43 and 51(2) EC led Advocate General Lenz to find that the freedom of establishment and the freedom to provide services were subject under the Treaty to exceptions with respect to the movement of capital and that 'those provisions of the Treaty suggest that freedom of establishment and freedom to provide services are to a certain extent acces-

---

[104] See: Case C–484/93 *Svensson and Gustavsson v Ministre du Lôgement* [1995] ECR I–3955; Case C–410/96 *Ambry* [1998] ECR I–7875; and Case C–118/96 *Safir v Skattemyndigheten i Dalarnas Län* [1998] ECR I–1897. Tesauro AG was more forthright in his Opinion in the last case (at 1905–7), finding that the freedom to provide services and the free movement of capital catered for different situations and should be dealt with on a mutually exclusive basis. He also noted that a combined application of both Arts. 'would not, to say the least, be a very rigorous approach'. More recently, in Case C–222/97 *Manfred Trummer and Peter Mayer v Bezirksgericht Feldbach* [1999] ECR I–1661, which involved a prohibition in Austrian law on the creation of mortgages to cover a pre-existing foreign-currency (Deutschmark) denominated debt, by contrast, the Court displayed a greater readiness to characterise a transaction as a capital movement. The validity of the distinction made in Art. 50 EC between the freedom to provide services and the free movement of capital in light of the operation of the single market and the jurisprudence of the Court is questioned in Usher, n 69 above, 98. On the inconsistent approach of the Court to whether a transaction involves the free movement of capital or the freedom to provide services see generally Mohamed, S, 'A Critical Assessment of the ECJ Judgment in Trummer and Mayer' (1999) *JIBFL* 396, 396–8.

[105] [1988] OJ L 178/5, Annex I, III. Directive 88/361, rather than the free movement of capital provisions contained in the Treaty, was at issue as the restrictive legislation was adopted in 1991 before the introduction of Arts. 56–60 EC which fully liberalized the free movement of capital and payments by the Maastricht Treaty in 1992.

sory to the liberalization of the free movement of capital . . . the question is to what extent the respective degree of liberalization of movement of capital sets a limit to the applicability of the freedom of establishment and freedom to provide services'.[106] The liberalization of capital movements by, in the first instance, the 1988 Capital Movements Directive and, at Treaty level, the Maastricht amendments to the free movement of capital provisions has reduced the impact of this interaction.[107]

VI.4.4 *Non-discriminatory Rules*

The effect of the Court's development of a non-discriminatory restriction rule is to place a very broad prohibition on Member State measures which 'hinder or make less attractive the exercise of' the freedom to establish and the freedom to provide services. National rules which apply without discrimination but involve, *inter alia*, access controls such as authorization requirements (for example, establishment or capital-adequacy rules)[108] or protective marketing or conduct rules[109] can potentially have restrictive effects and may be subject to the Treaty prohibitions. Controls on the taking up of business and operating or conduct conditions which affect the pursuit of business have both been accepted as potentially constituting restrictions on the freedom to provide services,[110] whether via indirect discrimination through residence or establishment conditions or via 'genuinely even-handed rules that tend to partition the market simply because of diversity between national regimes'.[111] Notwithstanding the general approach taken

---

[106] *Commission v Italy*, n 63 above, Opinion of the AG, para 17. *Parodi* (n 44 above) provides another example of where the Court examined whether the capital movement involved in the provision of the service in question had been liberalized before it moved on to consider whether the freedom to provide services could apply.

[107] For a critique of the current effectiveness of Art. 51(2) EC see Mohamed, S, *European Community Law on the Free Movement of Capital and the EMU* (1999) 184.

[108] On capital-adequacy and establishment restrictions see *Commission v Italy*, n 63 above. Establishment conditions are usually treated aggressively by the Court, given that 'if . . . authorisation constitutes a restriction on the freedom to provide services, the requirement of a permanent establishment is the very negation of that freedom': *German Insurance* case, n 75 above, para 52. See also Van Binsbergen, n 84 above and *Parodi*, n 44 above.

[109] *Alpine Investments*, n 6 above. See also Case C–288/89 *Gouda v Commissariat voor de Media* [1991] ECR I–4007 where the Court found that restrictions could arise 'as a result of the application of national rules which affect any person established in the national territory to persons providing services established in the territory of another Member State who already have to satisfy the requirements of that State's legislation': para. 12, and Cases C–34–36/95 *Konsummentombudsmannen v De Agostini Forlag AB and TV—Shop i Sverige AB* [1997] ECR I–3843. For the view that conduct rules could amount to a prohibited restriction see Wouters, J, 'Rules of Conduct, Foreign Investment firms and the ECJ's Case Law on Services' (1993) 14 *The Company Lawyer* 194 and Andenas, M, 'Rules of Conduct and the Principle of Subsidiarity' (1994) 15 *The Company Lawyer* 60.

[110] See generally Chalmers, D, and Szyszczak, E, *EU Law*, vol II, 'Towards a European Polity' (1998) 403–16.

[111] Beaumont and Weatherill, n 82 above, 682.

towards restrictions on free movement generally in *Gebhard*, it appears that host Member States retain more freedom to impose controls on the freedom to establish, given the greater degree of integration into the host Member State involved. Applying the free movement of services treatment (which implies a 'wide principle of equivalence and mutual recognition') would 'entail reverse discrimination against the professionals of the host State, spoil the reputation of foreign professionals and provoke the reaction of the regulatory and judiciary authorities of the host Member State'.[112] In particular, the extent to which restrictions which affect the pursuit of economic activity rather than its taking up could constitute a restriction on the freedom to establish, given that establishment is primarily concerned with the movement of undertakings and persons and thus access to other Member States, is questionable.[113]

VI.4.5 *The Interaction Between the Freedom to Provide Services and the Freedom to Establish*

While the general principle that non-discriminatory rules can, in certain circumstances, be imposed applies to both freedoms, and *Gebhard* suggests a common treatment,[114] identifying how the cross-border activity is charac-

---

[112] Hatzopoulos, n 100 above, 73. See also Beaumont and Weatherill who have noted that under the freedom to establish Member States seem to have slightly more leeway to impose non-discriminatory restrictions, such as qualification rules, given that the undertaking in question which is exercising the Treaty right is more closely integrated in the Member States' legal and economic infrastructure: n 82 above, 680–1, 682.

[113] In Case C–70/95 *Sodemare SA et al. v Regione Lombardia* [1997] ECR I–3395, eg, the Court refused to find that an Italian law prohibiting the Italian subsidiary of a Luxembourg company from entering into contracts with public authorities as it was not a non-profit-making business was a restriction on the freedom to establish by affecting the subsidiary's ability to carry on business, as the rule was 'not liable to place profit-making companies from other Member States in a less favourable factual or legal situation than profit-making companies in the Member State in which they established': para 33. On this question see further: Hatzopoulos, n 100 above, 72–4; Hansen, J, 'Full Circle: Is there a Difference Between the Freedom of Establishment and the Freedom to Provide Services' (2000) 11 *EBLRev.* 83; Tison, n 69 above, 6–8 and 28–9 (who has also suggested that the *Centros* judgment, in which the Court (albeit in the particular context of preventing fraud by foreign companies) emphasized the objective of the freedom to establish as a guarantee of the possibility for companies to set up subsidiaries, branches, and agencies and distinguished between rules which concern the creation of companies and rules which address the exercise of professional activities, indicates the Court's willingness to consider the proper scope of each Treaty guarantee); Roeges, L, 'Banking Activities Through a Branch in Another Member State After the Second Banking Directive' (1993) 13 *YBEL* 295, 320–3; and Cranston, R, and Hadjiemmanuil, C, 'Banking Integration in the European Community: The European Commission's Unfinished Agenda' in Norton, J, Andenas, M, and Footer, M (eds), *The Changing World of International Law in the Twenty-first Century* (1998) 341, 372–3.

[114] 'The Court's case law on free movement . . . and freedom of establishment . . . is similar to the well-established case law on services and oriented towards the abolition of restrictions, not just discriminations': Hatzopoulos, n 100 above, 71 who has also noted at 70 that the Court 'seems to be reasoning in a unitary way for all the personal freedoms (free movement, freedom of establishment, freedom to provide services)'.

terized for the purposes of the Treaty, is nonetheless important due, not least, to the uncertainty as to the extent to which the freedom to provide services can be relied on once the freedom to establish has been activated and the greater leeway given to Member States to impose non-discriminatory restrictions on the freedom to establish (and the nature of the rules addressed by the freedom to establish).[115] The distinction between the freedom to provide services and freedom to establish can be problematic, however, as under Article 50 EC 'services' are defined in a residual manner as those 'not governed by the provisions relating to freedom of movement for goods, capital and persons'. While Article 50 attempts to draw a distinction between the freedom to provide services and the freedom to establish, by providing that in order to provide a service an undertaking may 'temporarily pursue the activity in question in the State where the service is provided' and while the establishment provisions, by contrast, are designed to cover activities involving a more permanent integration into the economy of the host Member State, there is potential for overlap between establishment of a limited nature and the provision of services. The distinction between providing a services and establishment ultimately involves an assessment of whether the undertaking is participating 'on a stable and continuous basis, in the economic life of a Member State other than his State of origin' and profiting therefrom, in which case establishment is indicated or whether, given the temporary nature of the activities, 'determined in the light, not only of the duration of the provision of the service, but also of its regularity, periodicity or continuity', the provision of services is indicated.[116] In determining whether establishment or services is implicated, the fact that the services are supported by 'the infrastructure necessary for the purposes of performing the services in question' will not take the activity outside the services characterisation.[117]

Characterization as coming within the freedom to establish is significant as there is some controversy whether the freedom to establish and the freedom to provide services may be exercised simultaneously by the same undertaking in a Member State. This situation could arise if an investment intermediary established a branch in a Member State, but also wished to

---

[115] See n 113 above.

[116] *Gebhard*, n 74 above, paras 25 and 27.

[117] Ibid, para 27. The Commission has interpreted the *Gebhard* position (in the context of the cross-border activities of credit institutions but, in terms of the application of the *Gebhard* rule, its analysis could equally apply to investment intermediaries generally) as providing that: 'an employee of a credit institution coming to work within the territory of a Member State in order to carry out a limited number of specific tasks in connection with existing customers could . . . have the infrastructure necessary to perform these tasks without the bank being deemed to be "established" within the meaning laid down by Community law. If, on the other hand, he went beyond the bounds of these specific tasks by using that "*pied-à-terre*" to approach nationals of the host Member State, e.g. to offer them banking services as a branch would do, the bank could fall within the scope of the right of establishment': General Good Communication, n 76 above, 10.

continue to provide investment services on a cross-border basis in that Member State from the Member State in which its head office was situated. The 'cumulation theory' of services and establishment suggests that the cumulative exercise of both freedoms is not possible. Cumulation theory seems to have its roots in the insurance sector.[118] In particular, support for a rule prohibiting the cumulative exercise of both freedoms has been taken from the *German Insurance* case where the Court, in the context of an examination of a German rule requiring all providers of direct and co-insurance to be established and authorized in Germany, stated that an undertaking would be deemed to be established in another Member State once it maintained a permanent presence in that State, even if only though a branch or a permanent agency,[119] and that, once established in that Member State, it could not, given the residual nature of the definition of services, rely on the freedom to provide services in relation to its activities in that Member State.[120] Although it is limited to credit institutions and does not cover investment intermediaries generally, in its General Good Communication the Commission seemed confident that the Court's statement in the *German Insurance* case does not amount to a restriction on cumulation, finding that 'there is nothing in the Treaty, Directives, or case-law to prevent a credit institution from carrying on its activities under the freedom to provide services and, at the same time, through some other form of establishment (branch or subsidiary) even if the same activities are involved'.[121] It did note, however, that, from a taxation and regulation perspective, the activities in question must be clearly connected to one of the two forms of operation.[122]

VI.4.6 *Permitted Restrictions*

VI.4.6.1 *Discriminatory Rules*

Discriminatory measures which restrict the freedom to establish can be justified only under Article 46 EC which allows Member States to impose discriminatory restrictions on grounds of public policy, public health, and public security. Article 46 EC applies to the freedom to provide services by virtue of Article 55 EC. The nature of these exceptions allows Member States min-

---

[118] See Dassesse, M, '1992: An EEC Update' [1991] *JIBFL* 384, 387.

[119] The Court specified that an office managed for a company by an independent person on a permanent basis could amount to establishment.

[120] N 75 above, para 20. There are indications in the judgment that this finding is limited to the provision of insurance services. The statement quoted which seems to restrict cumulation is contained in a section entitled 'the provision of services in the context of insurance'.

[121] N 76 above, 12.

[122] This observation bears out the point made in Dassesse, n 118 above, that regulatory bodies may be unhappy with cumulation given the greater difficulty in tracking activities carried out though the cross-border provision of services, particularly for tax purposes.

imal room to impose discriminatory restrictions in the financial-services area generally, and the investment-services sector in particular. Of the three, the exception which is most likely to apply is the public-policy exception, but the scope of this exception has been interpreted very restrictively by the Court. In *Bouchereau* it found that 'recourse by a national authority to the concept of public policy pre-supposes, in any event, the existence, in addition to the perturbation to the social order which any infringement of the law involves, of a genuine and sufficiently serious threat affecting one of the fundamental interests of society'.[123] In the investment-services area this condition is likely to prove almost impossible to fulfil. Indeed, *Commission v Italy* makes clear that even if investor protection can be regarded as an aim of public policy, and the Judgment is not conclusive on this point, a strict proportionality test applies.

IV.4.6.2 *Non-discriminatory Rules and the General Good*[124]

(a) *The General-good Rule*[125]

The limited ability of Member States to impose regulation on those exercising free movement rights as a result of the extent of the prohibition on non-discriminatory but restrictive legislation sits uneasily with Member States' legitimate interests in imposing public-interest regulation. In the investment-services area, achievement of the objectives of investor protection and systemic stability, the risks to each of which are aggravated by integration, and political commitment to these objectives have led most States to construct regulatory regimes of varying sophistication. Undiluted application of the Treaty freedoms would, thus, have jarred with prevailing regulatory philosophies. On the other hand, the spectre of protectionism is often present when regulatory systems are designed, as was arguably the case with the legislation at issue in *Commission v Italy*. In order to accommodate the interests of Member States in imposing non-discriminatory but restrictive regulation which furthers legitimates social and public interests and the exercise of the Treaty freedoms, the Court, expanding the mandatory-requirements jurisprudence developed in the context of the free movement of goods, has developed the concept of non-discriminatory regulation adopted 'in the

---

[123] Case 30/77 *R v Bouchereau* [1977] ECR 1999, para 35.

[124] The general-good justification for restrictive measures also applies to the free movement of capital. Case C–148/91 *Veronica v Commissariaat voor de Media* [1993] ECR I–487. On the general good jurisprudence and its application see the authorities at n 69 above and: Katz, S, 'The Second Banking Directive' (1992) 12 *YBEL* 249, 264–81 and Björkland, n 70 above.

[125] The general-good rule is also discussed in the context of investor protection, where it is of considerable importance, in Ch. IX.

interests of the general good' the imposition of which would be permitted, even where it hindered the exercise of the Treaty freedoms.

The general rule was initially applied by the Court to the freedom to provide services in *Van Binsbergen* where it found that '[t]aking into account the particular nature of the services to be provided, specific requirements imposed on the person providing the service cannot be considered incompatible with the Treaty where they have as their purpose the application of professional rules justified by the general good—in particular rules relating to organisation, qualifications, professional ethics, supervision and liability —which are binding upon any person established in the State in which the service is provided, where the person providing the service would escape from the ambit of those rules being established in another Member State'.[126] To pass the *Van Binsbergen* test, the measure in question must, accordingly, be adopted in the interests of the general good, but, in addition, the Court found that the measure must also be non-discriminatory, objectively justified, and proportionate in that the Member State imposing the restriction must not be able to use less restrictive measures to achieve its objective in imposing the measure.[127] An additional requirement that the service provider must not be subject to comparable rules in his own Member State was added to the *Van Binsbergen* test by later cases.[128] The test was expressed in more general terms, which bring the freedom to establish squarely within the reach of the general good test, in *Gebhard*[129] where the Court stated that: '[n]ational measures liable to hinder or make less attractive the exercise of the fundamental freedoms guaranteed by the Treaty must fulfil four conditions: they must be applied in a non discriminatory manner; they must be justified by imperative requirements in the general interest; they must be suitable for securing the attainment of the objective which they pursue;[130] and they must not go beyond what is necessary in order to attain

---

[126] N 84 above, para 12.

[127] Ibid, paras 14–16.

[128] This condition, which is significant given the reluctance of Member States to rely on the supervisory standards imposed elsewhere as adequate controls on undertakings operating in their domestic markets in the financial services area, was added by Cases 110 and 111/78 *Ministère Public v Van Wesemael* [1979] ECR 35 and subsequently refined by Case 279/80 *Criminal Proceedings Against Webb* [1981] ECR 3305.

[129] N 74 above, para 37.

[130] In other words there must be a causal link between the measure in question and the policy objective it serves. There have been cases where, although the Court has accepted that a legitimate general-good interest has been raised, in principle, by the Member State justifying the measure, it has gone on to find that the measure did not, in fact, fulfil its objectives with respect to the interest at stake. See Case C-362/88 *GB-INNO-BM v Confédération du Commerce Luxembourgeois* [1990] ECR I-667 (discussed in Ch. IX sect. 11.2 below).

that objective'.[131] It also consistently been held that the restrictive measure must not already have been harmonized.[132]

The Court of Justice has not, as yet, given a conclusive definition of what constitutes the 'general good' (or, as expressed in *Gebhard*, 'imperative requirements in the general interest'). It is unlikely that it will; maintaining the flexibility of the concept in order to respond to changing circumstances and the evolving priorities of Member States by developing the concept on a case-by-case basis will probably trump any certainty gains which might flow from a definition. Although the concept is therefore a dynamic one, making it impossible to draw up a finite list of interests which the Court will accept as being in the general good,[133] the case law of the Court contains a number of indications of the interests likely to be raised in the investment-services sector to justify restrictive measures which are also likely to be accepted by the Court as being in the general good. Generally, in applying the general-good rule to the highly regulated financial-services sector where an absence of restrictions may render a market more competitive and the cost of services less costly but could, at the same time, expose service recipients to a greater risk of loss,[134] the Court's approach is, by and large, sensitive to the particular features of financial market regulation.

[131] This condition involves an assessment of whether or not less restrictive means are available to achieve the general-good objective. While the Court's assessment of compliance with the proportionality requirement will often involve a comparative review of the measures in force in other Member States (as in *Commission v Italy*, n 63 above), a measure will not fail the proportionality test simply because less strict rules are in force in another Member State. In *Alpine Investments* the Court ruled that 'the fact that one Member State imposes less strict rules than another Member State does not mean that the latter's rules are disproportionate and hence incompatible with Community law': n 6 above, para 51. The proportionality review may also involve an assessment of whether the service is supplied through a branch or under the freedom to provide services: 'a restriction could more readily be considered to be proportionate in the case of an operator working permanently within a territory than in the case of the same operator working only temporarily. The Court has recognised this difference by imposing a less restrictive and more "light weight" legal framework for suppliers of services operating in a temporary capacity than for established suppliers': General Good Communication, n 76 above, 19. The Commission stressed, however, that this analysis could not apply to consumer protection rules as the level of consumer protection should be identical in each case. For a critique of this differentiated approach see Tison, n 69 above, 29.

[132] *German Insurance* case, n 75 above.

[133] The following interests have been recognized as being in the general good: protection of the recipient of services (*Van Wesemael*, n 128 above); protection of workers (*Webb*, n 128 above); social protection of workers (Case C-272/94 *Guiot* [1996] ECR I-1905); consumer protection (*German Insurance* case, n 75 above); preservation of the good reputation of the domestic financial market (*Alpine Investments*, n 6 above); prevention of fraud (Case C-275/92 *HM Customs and Excise v Schindler & Schindler* [1994] ECR I-1039); protection of intellectual property (Case 62/79 *Coditel v Ciné Vog* [1980] ECR 881); cultural policy (Case C-353/89 *Mediawet* [1991] ECR I-4069); preservation of national historical and artistic heritage (Case C-180/89 *Commission v Italy* [1991] ECR 709); and protection of creditors and protection of the proper administration of justice (*Reisebüro*, n 100 above). This list is based on part on the Commission's discussion of the scope of the Court's general good jurisprudence in its General Good Communication, n 76 above.

[134] Usher, n 69 above, 102.

(b) *The General Good and Financial Services: Three Examples*

Worthy of some attention, given its treatment of a highly regulated financial-services sector, is the judgment of the Court of Justice in the *German
Insurance* case.[135] The Court examined the application of the general-good
rule in the context of restrictions imposed on the provision of insurance in
Germany. Its Judgment suggests that in the financial-services sector an
expansive approach to the general-good exception might be tolerated. Two
of the German requirements at issue are of interest: a rule that those providing direct insurance (other than transport insurance) in Germany be
established in Germany and authorized under German law; and a requirement that those providing co-insurance and acting as the lead insurer be
established in Germany and authorized as the sole insurer of the risk. The
Court acknowledged that these requirements imposed a restriction on the
freedom to provide services, in that they increased the cost of providing
insurance services in Germany, particularly where the insurance services
were provided on an occasional basis. The requirements would only, accordingly, comply with the freedom to provide services where, in a slight refor-
mulation of the *Van Binsbergen* test, 'in the field of activity concerned there
are imperative reasons relating to the public interest which justify restrictions on the freedom to provide services, that the public interest is not
already protected by the rules of the State of establishment, and that the
same result cannot be achieved by less restrictive rules'.[136] Before examining the particular measures at issue, the Court broadly accepted the existence of a public interest in protecting the consumer, both as policy-holder
and as the insured, and in regulating the insurance sector. Showing a willingness to engage with the special features of financial services, the Court
referred to the specific nature of insurance services which made it difficult
for the consumer to assess whether payment would be made in the event of
a claim and the difficult position in which the consumer might be placed on
a failure to pay, and noted that insurance had become a 'mass phenomenon', with effects on a population-wide scale. In the case of the direct insurance requirements, the Court found that the additional authorization

---

[135] N 75 above. This judgment is one of a series of insurance judgments delivered by the
Court in 1986 which followed a series of Art. 226 EC enforcement actions taken by the
Commission against the regulation by Member States of insurance providers and which had a
profound impact on the liberalization of the EC insurance market by kick-starting the harmonization programme. Member States were given an incentive to reach agreement on harmonized standards as a result of the Court's ruling in these cases that certain regulatory
requirements imposed in the general interest could, nonetheless, be set aside as being in con-
travention of the Treaty. See also Case 220/83 *Commission v France* [1986] ECR 3663, Case
252/83 *Commission v Denmark* [1986] ECR 3713, and Case 206/84 *Commission v Ireland*
[1986] ECR 3817.
[136] N 75 above, para 29.

requirements, particularly with respect to insurance conditions and levels of technical reserves,[137] were justified in the interests of the general good. The Community had not harmonized those requirements for insurance providers, broadly equivalent conditions did not prevail across the EC, and authorization was a proportionate method of ensuring compliance with technical reserves and conditions of insurance requirements.[138] That the Court adopts a discriminating approach to any general-good justification raised by a Member State and will assess the appropriateness of the measure in light of its objective, is evident from its rider to the effect that the consumer-protection justification will not apply with equal importance in all cases due to the nature of the risk and/or the insured party, and in some cases may not be valid. In examining the validity of establishment requirements in general, the Court found that, given that 'the requirement of a permanent establishment is the very negation of [the freedom to provide services]' and that 'it has the result of depriving Article 59 [now Article 49 EC] of the Treaty of all effectiveness', it must be shown that such a requirement was indispensable for attaining the objective pursued.[139] This test was not met in the case of direct insurance as the objective pursued, the monitoring of the insurance provider, could have been achieved by other methods of supervision, including co-operation with the other Member States involved. As co-insurance was taken out only by large undertakings which were in a strong position to protect their own interests, the consumer-protection interests applicable to the direct insurance sector did not apply. In addition a greater degree of harmonization had taken place in relation to co-insurance. Accordingly, both the authorization and establishment requirements were in breach of Article 49 EC.

In *Alpine Investments* the Court examined the application of the general-good rule to the investment-intermediaries sector for the first time. While the Court held that the cold-calling prohibition was a restriction on Article 49 EC, it accepted the arguments of the Dutch government and introduced a new general-good justification, finding that the maintenance of a good reputation for the domestic securities market was an imperative reason for justifying a restriction. The Court justified the domestic-market-protection argument by reference to the importance of investor confidence in ensuring the smooth operation of the financial markets, particularly given the 'speculative nature and the complexity of commodities futures contracts', and the dependence of such confidence on 'the existence of professional regulations serving to ensure the

---

[137] The fund required to be set aside by law to meet insurance payouts.

[138] The Court found that notwithstanding that harmonization had taken place with respect to the provision of insurance with the adoption of the first Non-Life Insurance Directive 73/239/EEC [1973] OJ L228/3 and the first Life Assurance Directive 79/267/EEC [1973] OJ L63/1, the directives covered neither technical reserves nor the conditions of insurance.

[139] N 75 above, para 52.

competence and trustworthiness of the financial intermediaries on whom investors are particularly reliant'.[140] Investor protection was raised by the Court, but only in so far as it was a function of investor confidence: 'the nature and extent of [investor protection] does nonetheless have a direct effect on the reputation of Netherlands financial services'.[141] Although consumer protection was by then a well-established general-good interest, and while protection of investors was raised in justification by the Dutch government, the investors protected by the measure were not Dutch nationals, but nationals of other Member States. Investor protection in other Member States was clearly a matter for those Member States and could not be raised as an independent general interest by the Netherlands. Moving to the second stage of the general-good analysis, the Court found that the ban was proportionate in that the commodities futures markets was highly speculative and difficult to understand for non-expert investors, and a ban was necessary to protect them and ensure confidence in the market. Not only does the ruling suggest that the Court will be liberal in its interpretation of what interests come within the scope of the general good in the investment services arena, it also indicates that the proportionality test may not be as stringently applied in the investment services sector as in other areas. In rejecting submissions by Alpine Investments to the effect that, even if the ban was justified in the general interest, it was disproportionate, the Court found that the use by other Member States of less restrictive means to control cold-calling (such as tape-recording in the UK) did not prevent a Member State from imposing more stringent restrictions.[142] The extent to which measures designed to regulate investment intermediaries may be tolerated under this general domestic-market-reputation justification will depend on how the Court develops this general-good justification. While the protection of the reputation of domestic financial markets might appear to give Member States significant leeway to impose restrictive measures, the judgment was firmly rooted in the peculiar features of and dangers posed by the commodity-futures markets.[143] It might also be argued, however, that the willingness of the Court to construct the reputation-based general-good justification suggests that the Court may be reluctant to interfere with Member States' regulation of investment intermediaries.

Supervision in the interests of investor protection and the stability of the market-place were squarely raised as general good justifications in 1996 in *Commission v Italy*.[144] At issue was an Italian law[145] which restricted deal-

---

[140] N 6 above, para 42. [141] N 6 above, para 43. [142] Ibid, para 51.

[143] The Court specifically noted in para 46 'that the commodities future market is highly speculative and barely comprehensible for non-expert investors'. See also the analysis of the case in Andenas, M, 'Current Developments: EC Law', (1996) 45 *ICLQ* 230, 232.

[144] N 63 above.

[145] Act 1 of 2 Jan 1991 which regulated the activity of dealing in securities and the organization of the securities markets (known as the SIMs law after the form, *società di intermediazione mobiliare* (SIM), which dealers were required to take).

ing in transferable securities to securities firms which were authorized under Italian law and which required, as a condition of authorization, that a firm dealing in transferable securities have its registered office in Italy. Other authorization conditions included initial capital-adequacy, ongoing capital-adequacy, and probity of management requirements. At the time of its adoption the legislation was widely regarded as protectionist and, following complaints by certain Member States, the Commission brought an Article 226 EC enforcement action against Italy on the ground that the registration requirement breached both Articles 43 and 49 EC. The Article 43 violation arose as dealers from other Member States were prevented from using other forms of establishment, such as branches or agencies; it was also discriminatory, in so far as it imposed the costs of setting up a new company on dealers established outside Italy. The Italian government claimed that the registration and authorization requirements were objectively justified in the interests of investor protection and market stability[146] and that it was not possible to compare the regulatory conditions imposed by other Member States with those applicable under Italian law, particularly in the case of capital-adequacy requirements.[147] It also claimed that a dealer could not be adequately supervised and sanctioned unless its principal establishment was in Italy, allowing easy access to all the information necessary for supervision. The Court gave short shrift to both of these arguments without discussing whether investor protection and market stability were legitimate general-good interests.[148] It found that comparability between the relevant Italian and foreign rules was attainable and was even envisaged in the contested Italian legislation.[149] Significantly, as investment-intermediary regulation can vary widely with respect to regulatory techniques, the Court was also impressed by the Commission's point that while Member State methods to determine capital requirements varied, overall each afforded equivalent protection. It is also clear that achieving the highest level of protection possible will not avail a Member State as an objective justification, as the Court noted that while certain Member States' systems for determining capital gave greater protection in certain cases, the key factor was that overall the levels of protection were equivalent. The second justification was dispatched

[146] N 63 above, Opinion of the AG, paras 8 and 30.

[147] At that time, prior to the harmonization of capital-adequacy requirements, Italy calculated own-funds requirements by a method different from that in operation in other Member States.

[148] Its only comment on the type of regulation which could come within the scope of the general good was a general comment noting that '[a]ccess to and the exercise of certain self-employed activities may thus be conditional on compliance with provisions laid down by law, regulation or administrative action justified by the general interest, such as rules relating to organisation, qualifications, professional ethics, supervision and liability': para 10.

[149] Art. 20(8) of the contested law provided that the Italian regulator, the CONSOB, was entitled to conclude mutual-recognition agreements with the supervisory authorities of other States.

equally quickly, with the Court finding that establishment in Italy was not the only way in which effective supervision and sanctioning could be ensured. Specifically, the Court referred to the possibility of requiring dealers to supply the Italian authorities with the information necessary for effective supervision, imposing financial-guarantee requirements in respect of solvency concerns in relation to the operations of dealers in Italy, and concluding co-operation agreements with other supervisory authorities. In respect of the breach of Article 59 EC (now Article 49 EC) the Court simply stated in robust terms that the obligation imposed on dealers to set up their principal establishment in Italy was 'the very negation of the freedom to provide services'[150] and, for the same reasons as applied to the breach of Article 43 EC, could not be objectively justified.

(c) *The Impact of Harmonization*

Once the EC has acted to harmonize the rules which otherwise might be justified by reference to the general good, however, the ability of Member States to plead the general good falls away, as the general good will be, or should be, protected by the harmonized rules, as long as the harmonization has taken place at an appropriate level.[151] The mere fact that harmonization has taken place will not, of itself, oust the power of a Member State to regulate.

The scope available to Member States to impose general-good regulation where a degree of harmonization has already been undertaken was examined in the context of the banking sector in *Parodi v Banque de Bary*.[152] The contested measure was a French rule which required that before a Dutch credit institution could grant a Deutschmark mortgage to a French real-estate property company, it had to be authorized in accordance with French law, notwithstanding that the Dutch credit institution was already authorized by its home Member State in accordance with the minimum authorization requirements introduced by the now consolidated first Banking Co-ordination Directive.[153] As the loan was made in 1984, the additional harmonization

---

[150] N 63 above, para. 31.

[151] See, eg, the *German Insurance* case, n 75 above. As has been observed by Tison: 'the underlying idea is that the exercise by the Community of its regulatory powers will be regarded as the codification at Community level of the Member States' powers under the general good': n 69 above, 12.

[152] N 44 above.

[153] 1st Council Directive 77/780/EEC on the coordination of laws regulations and administrative procedures relating to the taking up and pursuit of the business of credit institutions [1977] OJ L322/30 (the BCD I). Its provisions have been consolidated with the other banking regime measures by Directive 2000/12/EC relating to the taking up and pursuit of the business of credit institutions [2000] OJ L126/1 (the CBD). For ease of reference, the discrete banking directives will be referred to throughout this text but the reference of the parallel provisions in the CBD will be given.

with respect to authorization which came into effect with the now consolidated Second Banking Co-ordination Directive[154] did not apply. The minimum authorization requirements set out in the BCD I were, under Article 3(2) of that directive, stated to operate without prejudice to other conditions laid down by national law. Applying the general-good analysis to the French requirement, the Court accepted that the banking sector was particularly sensitive from the perspective of consumer protection, given the need to protect consumers from the harm which they could suffer in transacting with institutions which did not comply with solvency requirements or whose management did not possess the necessary integrity or professional qualifications. Examining the extent to which those interests were already covered by the BCD I the Court found that the 'the first banking directive was no more than a first step . . . towards the mutual recognition by Member States of authorisations issued by each of them to credit institutions'.[155] It accepted that, at the time, in the area of banking activities, there were imperative reasons relating to the public interest which could justify the imposition of authorization and supervision requirements beyond the minimum conditions which were already imposed on credit institutions by their home Member States by virtue of the harmonization already undertaken by the BCD I. As it did not have enough information concerning the purpose of the French authorization conditions, it left it to the national court to determine whether the additional conditions were, in fact, justified, but noted that there might be cases where, due to the nature of the loan and the status of the borrower, there would not be a need to apply the protective rules of the host Member State.

In the investment-services sphere, while prudential regulation is subject to relatively comprehensive harmonization standards,[156] the same is not true of protective regulation. For example, as is discussed further in Chapter IX, the 'harmonization' achieved at present by Article 11 of the ISD, which sets out general principles which Member States must observe in their conduct-of-business regimes, is highly attenuated, such that is has been observed that it does not present an obstacle to the imposition, in principle, of general-good rules.[157]

---

[154] 2nd Council Directive 89/646/EEC on the coordination of laws regulations and administrative procedures relating to the taking up and pursuit of the business of credit institutions and amending Directive 77/780/EEC [1989] OJ L386/1 (the BCD II). As with the BCD I the BCD II has been subsumed into the CBD.

[155] Para 24.

[156] To the extent that it has been observed that host Member States will not be able to impose prudential general good rules, even where the rules in question fall outside the scope of the particular directive: Cranston and Hadjiemmanuil, n 113 above, 370–1 and Andenas, M, 'Cross Border Calling and the Right to Provide Services' (1995) 16 *The Company Lawyer* 249, 251 n 2. See also Tison, n 69 above, 25.

[157] See ibid, 31 who has noted that 'the only useful function of Article 11(1) in the general good test may be to create a refutable presumption of equivalence between the Member States' conduct of business rules'.

(d) *Investment Services and the General Good*

Although the case law is particularly sparse, some tentative conclusions can be drawn on the treatment by the Court of non-harmonized investment-intermediary regulation by Member States which hinders market access by investment intermediaries.

As is further discussed in Chapter IX section 11 below, investor protection has yet to be directly accepted by the Court as an interest which can be protected in the interests of the general good; neither has the Court examined the specific interests which investor protection incorporates.[158] It is also clear from *Alpine Investments* that the protection of investors in other Member States will not be accepted as an interest in the general good capable of justifying restrictive measures. Nonetheless the case law contains some indications of how investor protection might be treated and, in particular, reveals that a differentiated approach, which reflects the traits of the investor and the market-place, is likely to be followed. It is also clear from the Court's blunt analysis of Italy's justification that, notwithstanding the leeway it appears to grant Member States in financial regulation, it is prepared to grapple with the complex interplay of interests and of regulation in this area and that investor protection will not be allowed to act as a mask for protectionist measures. While the extent to which the Court will permit reliance on investor protection as a justification remains to be seen, its acceptance, in principle, of investor protection as a general-good interest to justify restrictive measures is arguably a practical necessity, given that harmonization measures in this area are, to date, sparse and that pressure on Member States to ensure sufficient standards of investor protection is even more acute, given the integration of the market-place following the liberalization introduced by the ISD.

Investor protection is not, of course, the only policy which underlines the regulation of investment intermediaries. Protecting the stability of the market-place is the second major rationale for regulating in this area. The Court has yet to decide that this is an interest which may be safeguarded in the interests of the general good. The signs are that it is likely to accept that it is,[159] not least because it has already acknowledged in *Alpine Investments*

---

[158] The Court does not specifically refer to investor protection in *Commission v Italy* (n 63 above) and investor protection was not directly at issue in *Alpine Investments*. Lenz AG noted in *Commission v Italy*, however, that 'the "protection of investors, the stability of the markets and the transparency of dealing," which the Italian government invokes are indisputably worth protecting. The question is only whether the contested provision is suitable for pursuing those aims, and, if so, whether it is proportionate': n 63 above, Opinion of the AG, para 46.

[159] See also Van Gerven and Wouters, n 69 above, 65. This also seems to be the position of Lenz AG, who found in his Opinion in *Commission v Italy* that ' "the stability of the markets and the transparency of dealing", which the Italian Government invokes, are indisputably worth protecting': n 63 above, Opinion of the AG, para 46. The Court's awareness of the importance of market stability can also be inferred, in the banking context (although stability is more

that 'financial markets play an important role in the financing of economic operators' and based its acceptance of the protection of the reputation of the national financial sector as a general-good interest on the dependence of the smooth operation of the financial markets, in part, on the confidence of investors.[160] The ability of Member States to rely on protecting the stability of national investment markets as a justification for imposing restrictive measures will, however, be constrained by the considerable degree of harmonization which has taken place in relation to prudential regulation (see Chapter VIII below).

Overall, in the absence of harmonization, it appears that Member States retain quite considerable freedom to impose market-stability and investor-protection requirements, due to the sensitive nature of investment services and the need to protect investors, in particular where the restrictive measures used do not involve establishment requirements.[161]

VI.5 THE EVOLUTION OF THE HARMONIZED REGIME

VI.5.1 *The Approach to Harmonization Emerges*

VI.5.1.1 *The Limitations of the Treaty*

The Treaty provisions are therefore limited as market-integration devices in the investment-services sector. As the interpretation by the Court of the freedom to provide services and the freedom to establish allowed Member States to impose restrictive regulation, action at EC level was necessary to deal with divergences in the regulation by Member States of investment intermediaries and the consequent market-access restrictions.[162] The Court itself had

directly implicated in banking regulation), from Case C–441/93 *Panagis Pafitis v TKE AE* [1996] ECR I–1347 where it stated that '[c]onsiderations concerning the need to protect the interests of savers, and, more generally, the equilibrium of the savings system, require strict supervisory rules in order to ensure the continuing stability of the banking system': para 49.

[160] N 6 above, para 42.

[161] The position is summed up by Jacobs AG in his Opinion in *Alpine Investments* where he found that 'in the absence of harmonization rules, each Member State enjoys some discretion in determining the level of investor protection in its territory. Otherwise it would follow that, in the absence of harmonization rules, Member States would need to align their legislation with that of the Member State which imposed the least onerous requirements. That might have the effect of undermining rather than promoting investor confidence': n 6 above, Opinion of the AG, para 90.

[162] More pragmatically, the Treaty provisions are not a very efficient means of bringing about market integration. They operate in a negative fashion, removing barriers to market access though incremental judicial pronouncements of illegality under EC law, and do not necessarily ensure certainty as to which rules can apply in a given circumstance, which is critical in commercial situations. Harmonization by directives is a more positive mechanism for removing barriers to integration and can create a more certain legal environment more quickly. See Weatherill and Beaumont, n 82 above, 554–5.

indicated in the *German Insurance* case in the context of the insurance market that the Treaty freedoms could go only so far in integrating marketplaces before Community harmonization was required.

VI.5.1.2 *Early Developments*

In 1977, with the adoption of the Code of Conduct[163] the EC took its first steps towards establishing an investment-services regime. As previously outlined, the Recommendation is non-binding although Member States were to 'ensure that those who are in a position to influence the workings of securities markets comply with the principles of the code of conduct'.[164] The Code's substantive principles for the provision of investment services, which include protective conduct rules such as dealing rules and conflict-of-interest rules, are discussed in the following chapters. Its objective in the investment-services sphere was market integration and the reduction of disparities in the rules governing markets as this would 'tend to encourage the interpenetration of the member countries' markets, particularly if this is accompanied by improving the safeguards available to savers'.[165] Very little progress would be made following the 1977 Code of Conduct in harmonizing the rules applicable to investment intermediaries until the early 1990s.

VI.5.1.3 *The 1985 White Paper*

(a) *Minimum Standards and Mutual Recognition*

As outlined in Chapter II, the original approach of the harmonized admission-to-official-listing regime to the regulatory barriers created by different national regimes was to introduce detailed harmonized rules such that the standards applicable in each Member State would be equivalent. From its inception, the treatment of the regulation of investment intermediaries benefited from a change in approach by the Commission. In 1985, in its White Paper, 'Completing the Internal Market', the Commission noted, albeit in the context of the free movement of goods, that 'experience has shown that the alternative of relying on a strategy based totally on harmonization would be over-regulatory, would take a long time to implement, would be inflexible and could stifle innovation'.[166] Rather than introduce detailed equivalent rules, it built into its harmonization strategy the reality that each Member State would retain its own system of regulation and proposed instead an alternative strategy of mutual recognition of the regulation carried out by each Member State, anchored by the home Member State's regulatory regime. In the financial-services sphere, in respect of which the

---

[163] N 49 above.   [164] Ibid, Explanatory Memorandum, section II, 6.
[165] Ibid, para 2.   [166] COM(85)310 (the Internal Market White Paper), para 64.

Commission noted that 'liberalisation of financial services, linked to that of capital movements, will represent a major step towards Community financial integration and the widening of the Internal Market': ' harmonisation, particularly as regards the supervision of ongoing activities, should be guided by the principle of "home country control". This means attributing the primary task of supervising the financial institution to the competent authorities of its Member State of origin, to which would have to be communicated all information necessary for supervision. The authorities of the Member State which is the destination of the service, whilst not deprived of all power, would have a complementary role. There would have to be a minimum harmonization of surveillance standards, though the need to reach agreement on this must not be allowed to delay the necessary and overdue decisions.'[167] Mutual recognition depends on the acceptance by Member States of the adequacy of the regulation carried out by other Member States. Thus, critical to the new approach to harmonization was the adoption of minimum harmonization standards in key areas of regulatory concern which would form the core of every Member State's system of regulation in the relevant area. Member States would remain free to impose regulation beyond the minimum on institutions for which they were the home State.

This regulatory technique has shaped the substantive content of investment-services regulation by the EC and, accordingly, the quality of market regulation and investor protection in the EC investment-services markets. It has also determined the largely decentralized shape of investment-services market supervision through the home-country control device. Notwithstanding its far-reaching effects, the technique is not based on any consideration of the requirements of the investment services markets, but on what might be termed a ruthless pragmatism: '[m]utual recognition, as the Commission's White Paper made clear, was considered an inferior integration mechanism, made necessary only by Council obstructionism in the Commission's pursuit of common rules'.[168]

---

[167] Ibid, paras 101 and 103. The adoption by the Commission of the mutual-recognition technique for financial-services harmonization built on the groundbreaking Court ruling in Case 120/78 *Rewe-Zentral AG v Bundesmonopolverwaltung für Branntwein* (the Cassis de Dijon ruling) [1979] ECR 649, which applied mutual recognition to the free movement of goods. As well as endorsing the mechanism which has shaped the investment-services regime, the Internal Market White Paper included in its annexed Timetable For Completing the Internal Market by 1992 the intriguingly entitled 'Proposal for a Directive concerning investment advisors' which was to be presented in 1989 and adopted in 1989 (para 1.3). In the event, the ISD, the scope of which extends considerably beyond investment advice and, ironically, which does not extend a regulatory passport to investment firms which only give investment advice, would not be adopted until 1993.

[168] Steil, B, *Regional Financial Market Integration: Learning From the European Experience* (1998) 3.

(b) *A Renewed Focus on Financial Services*

The White Paper and the repositioning of the approach to harmonization were partly triggered by concerns that the EC was, in the early 1980s, losing its competitive position with respect to Japan and the USA as a result of the failure to integrate the EC's national markets fully.[169] The financial-services sector generally was highlighted in the White Paper as an area in which movement towards a single market had been slow and where progress was essential in order to strengthen the competitive position of the EC and to benefit consumers of financial services. Three objectives can be identified in its securities/financial-services programme, which was to be completed by 1992: the complete liberalization of capital movements (see Chapter I); the interlinking of stock exchanges (Chapter XI); and the establishment of a common regulatory structure for financial institutions, in order to support home Member State control and mutual recognition. Of these three objectives, the foundation of the single market ultimately lay in the first of these, with the liberalization of capital movements in 1988 making the subsequent liberalization of financial services possible.

(c) *The Single European Act*

The White Paper fulfilled a third important function in kick-starting the EC's investment-services programme in that it fed into the Treaty amendments contained in the 1987 Single European Act (SEA). The SEA acted as a spur to further action in that it facilitated the adoption of legislation by introducing qualified-majority voting in respect of the adoption of directives concerning the free movement of services and the freedom to establish. It also contained the basis for economic and monetary union.

VI.5.2 *The Main Planks of the Regime are Set in Place*

In 1989, with the adoption of the now consolidated BCD II the EC took its first, if sideways, steps towards establishing a single market for investment services and regulating investment intermediaries. The BCD II follows the White Paper's mutual-recognition and home-country-control structure and

---

[169] The integration (or internationalization) of, and the consequent competitive pressures in, the financial services sector globally began to increase significantly at this time due, in part, to: technological developments; trends towards greater diversification in the range of services offered by financial institutions; the development of increasingly more sophisticated and internationally-oriented financial products (such as global depositary receipts); and deregulation in areas such as exchange controls and more specifically, commission structures. See, eg, the introduction to Morgan, G, and Knights, D (eds), *Regulation and Deregulation in European Financial Services* (1997) 1–6 and Bradley, C, 'Competitive Deregulation of Financial Services Activity in Europe after 1992' (1991) 11 *OJLS* 545, 545–7.

grants a 'passport' to credit institutions in respect of the activities set out in the BCD II, which include the provision of investment services by credit institutions.[170] The BCD II also imposes minimum harmonization requirements in relation to authorization and operating conditions. It is, however, predominantly a banking measure and applies to undertakings which take deposits or other forms of repayable funds from the public. The cornerstone of the regulation of the investment-services market is the Investment Services Directive or ISD,[171] adopted in 1993 and applicable to a wide range of investment intermediaries. In addition to granting a passport to firms which engage in the activities within its scope, it imposes minimum authorization and operating requirements on investment firms. The ISD also addresses access to regulated markets across the EC. The Capital Adequacy Directive,[172] adopted in 1993, is a key ancillary measure to the ISD and sets out the harmonized capital-adequacy requirements applicable to investment firms and credit institutions in respect of their investment-services activities. This regulatory framework is being expanded by a new regime to regulate the management companies of collective investment schemes.[173]

The basic investment-intermediary regulatory regime has been supplemented by the Investor Compensation Schemes Directive,[174] which also follows the minimum harmonisation and mutual recognition model, and, more recently, by a Proposal for a Directive on the Distance Marketing of Financial Services and a Proposal on the Supplementary Supervision of Financial Conglomerates.[175]

These measures, together with a number of ancillary general consumer-protection measures (Chapter IX) and the market-abuse provisions which are of more general application (Chapter XIII) form the basis of the EC's investment-services-regulation scheme.

---

[170] See Ch. VII. The initial focus on credit institutions can be explained by the dominance of credit institutions as service providers in the financial-services sector in continental Europe. Banking supervision was also a long-established feature of all Member States' supervisory systems. The same could not be said of investment-services firms which did not provide traditional banking services. See generally Blair, W, Allison, A, Palmer, K, Richards-Carpenter, P, and Walker, G, *Banking and Financial Services Regulation* (2nd edn, 1998) 374.

[171] N 45 above.

[172] Directive 93/6/EC on the capital adequacy of investment firms and credit institutions [1993] OJ L141/1 (the CAD).

[173] See Ch. VII sect. 9 below.

[174] Directive 97/9/EC on investor compensation schemes [1997] OJ L84/22 (the ICSD).

[175] Amended Proposal for a directive concerning the distance marketing of consumer financial services and amending Directives 97/7/EC and 98/27/EC [2000] OJ C177/21 (the Distance Marketing Proposal) and Proposal for a Directive on the supplementary supervision of credit institutions, insurance undertakings and investment firms in a financial conglomerate and amending Council Directives 73/239/EEC, 79/267/EEC, 92/49/EEC, 92/96/EEC, 93/6/EEC and 93/22/EEC, and Directives 98/78/EC and 2000/12 of the European Parliament and the Council, COM(2001)213 [2001] OJ C213/227 (the Supplementary Supervision Proposal), respectively.

VI.5.3 *Further Progress*

VI.5.3.1 *The Financial Services Action Plan*

As described in Chapter I, towards the end of the 1990s it became apparent
that the investment-services framework was neither keeping pace with market developments nor delivering an integrated investment-services market
with its associated benefits of a reduction in the costs of capital raising, stimulation of investment and employment, and other economy-wide advantages.
The unsatisfactory state of investment-services market integration formed a
major part of the Commission's 1998 Communication on 'Financial Services:
Building a Framework for Action'.[176] which found that the benefits of the
single market in investment services had not been fully realized. Further
progress was reported as being necessary both in the wholesale investment-
services markets and in the retail sector, where investment services were
rarely supplied on a cross-border basis, in order that full advantage could be
taken of the euro and of the market-driven modernization of the investment-
services market-place. The 1998 Communication was followed in 1999 by
the Commission's Financial Services Action Plan (FSAP) which sets out the
key measures which must be implemented in order to achieve a single market in financial services, including investment services.[177] The FSAP's
specific objectives are grouped around three strategic objectives: a single EU
wholesale market, open and secure retail markets, and state-of-the-art prudential rules and supervision, each of which contain a number of investment-
services-specific measures which are considered throughout Part III.

A single market in investment services will not, of course, be delivered
simply by enhancing the regulatory regime applicable to investment firms
and the efficacy of the investment-services passport. A number of other
difficulties remain to be resolved. Legal questions surrounding the infrastructure underpinning the investment-services markets, the payment and
settlement systems for cross-border securities transactions, and, in particular, the treatment of cross-border collateral need to be addressed.[178]
Differences in the taxation of investment-services and investment-services
providers still represent a barrier to market integration.[179] Retail market

---

[176] COM(1998)625 (the 1998 Communication).   [177] COM(1999)232 (the FSAP).
[178] See Ch. XII.

[179] Particularly as Case C–204/ 90 *Bachmann v Belgium* [1992] ECR I–249 permits, in principle, the imposition of taxation measures which restrict the exercise of the Treaty freedoms to
establish and provide services where the taxation measure in question is justified in the interests of the coherence of the tax system. This justification for restrictive differential tax treatment
will not always be accepted by the Court. See Case C–80/94 *Wielockx* [1995] ECR I–2493 and
Case C–190/94 *Asscher v Stäatssecretaris van Financiën* [1996] ECR I–3089. On the fiscal barriers to market integration see Zavvos, G, 'EC Financial Markets: Regulation for Stability and
Openness' in Wymeersch, E (ed), *Further Perspectives in Financial Integration in Europe* (1994)
27, 30. Taxation reform forms part of the FSAP.

integration faces particular difficulties with respect to the cultural preferences of clients who gravitate naturally to home-Member-State firms, language difficulties and the importance of establishing a reputation in the host
State, which can take time.[180]

VI.5.3.2 *The Lamfalussy Report*

The regulatory framework for the single market in investment services was
subject to scathing criticism in the Lamfalussy Report as part of its overall
finding that 'the status quo would entrench the continuation of European
financial market fragmentation'.[181] While the wider financial-services and
securities regulation regime was condemned as being 'too rigid, complex and
ill-adapted to the pace of global financial market change',[182] specific reference was made to numerous weaknesses in the investment-services regime
and, in particular, to the inadequate articulation of the home-country
control principle which was prejudicing the proper operation of mutual
recognition. If the Report's central recommendation, adoption of a two-tier
legislative procedure designed to facilitate the adoption of general principles
through normal legislative procedures and the adoption of detailed rules
through an enhanced comitology process in order to ensure delivery of the
FSAP,[183] is fully implemented, major changes both as to the scope and the
content of the investment-services regime can be expected.

VI.5.4 *The E-commerce Challenge*

The development of the Internet is posing a particular challenge to the
developing regulatory structure. While EC investors have yet to take to the
Internet in huge numbers, trades executed online are increasing steadily,[184]
leading to concerns that investor protection is not being sufficiently

---

[180] Added to these difficulties is the problem that the failure of prices of financial services to
converge more closely to a lower level 'has certainly contributed to consumer disenchantment
with the single financial market and provoked calls for more regulation': Gros and Lannoo,
n 50 above, 36. They concluded (at 163) that 'Europe is likely to become the home market for
institutional investors, but not yet for households. Remaining regulatory differences are likely
to be more of a deterrent for households than for institutional investors'. Their conclusions
appear to be supported by the recent finding from the Commission that significant disparities
exist in respect of fixed commissions for private equity transactions, with fees in the most expensive Member State being 17 times more than those applying in the least expensive Member
State: 1998 Communication, n 176 above, 10.

[181] N 13, 8.   [182] Ibid, 7.   [183] See further Ch. XV sect. 2.5.3 below.

[184] In its 2nd report on progress on the FSAP (Progress on Financial Services, Second
Report, May 2000, COM(2000)336) the Commission reported at 7 that while EC investment
firms were only recent entrants to the e-commerce market-place, the number of online
European trading accounts was expected to increase tenfold by 2004. Similarly, the Interim
Report of the Committee of Wise Men on European Securities Regulation (Nov 2000) noted at
11 the development of electronic brokerage which was driving down transaction costs and leading to a rapid increase in the number of online brokerage accounts.

supported in the Internet market-place. On the supply side, the Internet represents a potentially powerful marketing and delivery tool for investment firms, given the dematerialized nature of investment services and products and is a critical market-integration device.

The EC's response to the interaction between the Internet and the provision of investment services is still evolving. It originally adopted a bifurcated approach—applying liberalization-driven free-movement and market-integration principles to the provision of e-commerce services generally (best seen in the E-commerce Directive)[185] and incrementally filling in that basic structure with financial-services-specific measures designed to enhance investor protection and market stability. Chief among the latter is the current proposal for a distance marketing regime discussed in Chapter IX. However, e-commerce-specific investment-services regulation runs counter to the general rule that regulation should be technology-neutral. The neutrality policy now appears to be driving Commission policy.[186]

More generally, legislative measures and principles developed in order to respond to the e-commerce environment, chiefly the Member-State-of-origin principle of regulation, are exerting a profound influence on the development of the harmonized investment-services regime as a whole and provoking further convergence in key areas of investor-protection regulation.

VI.6 THE MAIN THEMES OF THE REGIME

VI.6.1 *Market Integration and Substantive Reregulation*

The regulation by the EC of investment intermediaries has two dominant features. First, as is discussed in Chapter VII, it is designed to integrate national investment-services markets by liberalizing regulation and allowing a regulatory passport, based on home-Member-State control, to be used by investment-services providers. Secondly, in order to support the passport device, it goes beyond liberalization to reregulate by introducing a substantive code of harmonized regulation, both prudential and protective, applicable to investment intermediaries. As will be outlined further in the specific discussions of prudential and protective regulation in Chapters VIII, IX, and X, these harmonized standards are designed to protect the systemic stability of the new market-place and enhance confidence in its operation by ensuring the protection of investors. Accordingly, even though a certain philosophical bankruptcy can be observed in the regime's rationale for investor

---

[185] Directive 2000/13 on certain legal aspects of information society services, in particular electronic commerce, in the Internal Market [2000] OJ L178/1 (the ECD).

[186] See the Commission Communication on E-commerce and Financial Services, COM(2001)66, discussed in Ch. IX.

protection, in particular, reregulation at EC level reflects a broader trend internationally away from challenging the need for regulation in light of the inefficiencies and distortions to competition it can create, as was popular during the internationalization and deregulatory period of the late 1980s and early 1990s, towards consideration of what substantive components of regulation are necessary.[187] The harmonized rules, their content and rationale, have significance beyond the integrated market-place in that they apply to investment intermediaries regardless of whether they operate outside their home Member States. Indeed, for certain Member States the harmonized standards represent entirely new regimes of supervision.[188] In such circumstances, the stakes are high and the consequences of inadequate regulation far-reaching. The next chapters will examine the devices used to facilitate the establishment of a single market in investment services but will also assess the substantive code of investment-intermediary regulation produced and its supporting rationale.

VI.6.2 *Functional Regulation*

The regulation by the EC of investment intermediaries and investment services is carried out on a functional, rather than an institutional, basis.[189] Regulation applies to the provision of investment services, and is not dependent on the organizational or legal status of the investment intermediary. In particular, it does not depend on whether the investment-services provider is a credit institution or an investment intermediary without any connections to traditional banking business. This approach dovetails with the structure of the EC investment-services industry in which investment services are

---

[187] See Scott-Quinn, n 39 above, 313, 313.

[188] In the context of the EC investment-services regime, the comment that 'harmonization— if conceived broadly as an instrument of European legal and economic policy—gets its legitimation less from results in integration than from the substantive content and effect of the Community law in which it results . . . it may also be that the hopes placed in Community laws are even higher precisely because the national law-makers either in some or all Member States have not been able to find convincing solutions for certain problems': Buxbaum and Hopt, n 50 above, 212, has a particular resonance given the uneven regulatory treatment of investment services across the EC prior to the harmonization programme. The adoption of the ISD, in Germany eg, required the imposition of an entirely new regulatory structure for investment firms. See Kusserow, B, 'Germany Implements ISD and CAD: The 6th Amendment to the German Banking Act' 11 (1996) *JIBL* 477 who noted (at 493) that 'investment service providers . . . for the first time in Germany, will be heavily regulated'.

[189] This approach to regulation is particularly appropriate, given that it has been noted that the reregulation which occurs as national markets draw closer together on a global basis in order to ensure adequate supervision and fair competition (of which the EC's programme is one example) 'in itself contributes to an 'attenuation of institutional differences' [ref omitted] among financial systems and their regulatory organs': Coleman, W, and Underhill, G, 'Globalization, Regionalism and the Regulation of Securities Markets' (1995) 2 *Journal of European Public Policy* 488, 493.

provided by investment firms specialized in investment services, universal banks, and financial conglomerates.[190]

The functional approach adopted by the EC in regulating investment services can be illustrated by its treatment of credit institutions which provide investment services as well as the traditional banking services of accepting deposits and providing credit. The authorization under EC law of a credit institution which comes within the harmonized EC banking regime can extend beyond traditional banking functions to cover the provision of investment services in relation to transferable securities and other financial instruments. Where the authorized credit institution engages in such investment-services activities, it also comes, however, within the scope of the investment-services regime applicable under the ISD, which applies to the provision of investment services, and not to particular types of institution. The credit institution is not required under EC law to segregate its investment-services activities from its traditional banking functions. In order to avoid duplication of common rules, such as licensing rules, the ISD disapplies those of its rules which duplicate the banking-regime rules but subjects credit institutions which supply investment services to the specialized conduct-of-business rules and prudential requirements set out in respect of investment services in the ISD. These rules apply in addition to the harmonized rules applicable to credit institutions generally.[191] Similarly, the same capital-adequacy requirements apply to investment firms as apply to credit institutions providing investment services. In adopting this functional approach, the EC regulatory regime appears to be designed to encourage the establishment of an integrated banking and investment-services market by not favouring a particular form of organization, be it credit institution or investment intermediary, over another.[192]

---

[190] Ferrarini, G, 'Towards a European Law of Investment Services and Institutions' (1994) 21 *CMLRev.* 1283, 1284. It also allows the investment-services regime to reflect the continued dominance of credit institutions in continental Europe. For an analysis of the importance of credit institutions in the single market see Gros and Lannoo, n 50 above, 58–61.

[191] Certain rules relating to liquidity and capital are specific to the deposit and credit functions of credit institutions and do not appear in the investment-services regime. These rules will continue to apply to credit institutions which also provide investment services by virtue of their falling within the basic definition of what constitutes a credit institution (on which see BCD I Art. 1 (CBD Art. 1(1)) which focuses on the deposit-taking and credit-granting functions).

[192] The functional approach is not without its detractors. It has been noted that '[t] he regulatory interface between banking and securities markets that results from these overlapping directives has important implications for systemic stability, competitive equality and the efficiency of markets': Dale, R, 'The Regulation of Investment Firms in the European Union (Part 1)' (1994) 10 *JIBL* 394. He has pointed in particular to the problems which arise as a consequence of imposing common capital-adequacy requirements on a functional basis on investment firms and credit institutions in relation to their respective investment-services activities, instead of on an institutional basis and of failing to differentiate between the different risks posed by an investment firm and a credit institution, even where they both provide investment services. See further Ch. VIII.

The next chapters will deal, for the most part, with the investment-firm model of investment-services provider. Rules which are designed to address the traditional credit and deposit-taking functions of credit institutions will not be addressed.

VI.6.3 *Wholesale and Retail Markets*

The distinction between retail and professional investors plays an important role in the investment-services regime. Investment-services regulation traditionally distinguishes between the wholesale and retail markets in order to avoid the imposition of unnecessary and burdensome regulation, particularly protective regulation, on investment firms where the beneficiaries are sophisticated professional investors.[193] The wholesale/retail divide is one which the investment-services industry in the EC is keen to preserve and it has reacted strongly against any attempts to apply traditional investor-protection rules to the wholesale market.[194] In the EC context, the wholesale/retail distinction also allows the effects of harmonization to be tempered in areas where rule harmonization is controversial (particularly in conduct of business regulation) due to the perception that it is not responding to particular cross-border or market-integration concerns such as systemic risk.

The distinction appears as an underlying theme in the EC investment-services regime, appearing in the ISD, the ICSD, and in the Distance Marketing Proposal. More generally, considerations of the need to facilitate the development of the wholesale investment-services market by insulating it from undue regulation inform the Commission's current plans for investment-services regulation and can be seen in the clear distinction made in the FSAP between the specific measures necessary for the wholesale investment-services market and the retail market-place.[195] The articulation

---

[193] 'The expanding role of large institutional investors has been accompanied by demands for lessened regulation of these entities, because institutions are said to have the sophistication to protect themselves from fraud and overreaching. Regulators have been receptive to such demands . . . many institutional traders have been freed of the regulatory shackles imposed in markets where the proverbial widows and orphans invest. The result amounts to a virtual two-track regulatory system': J. Markham, 'Protecting the Institutional Investor—Jungle Predator or Shorn Lamb' (1995) 12 *Yale Journal on Regulation* 345.

[194] Early discussions on the Distance Marketing Proposal which suggested that the Commission was minded to extend its protections to professional investors were met by vocal opposition from the investment-services industry and heavy lobbying by trade associations. By the time the first proposal was formally presented to the Council, professional investors had been dropped from its coverage.

[195] The Commission has expressed the opinion that over-regulation of the wholesale market could stymie the development of an integrated, competitive, and liquid securities market as well as limit the development of innovative financial products by the wholesale market: Art. 11 Communication, n 45 above, 11. For a good example of the difference in the Commission's approach towards both market-places see the FSAP, n 177 above, at 3 which discusses the wholesale market in terms of stripping away the 'present mass of legal and administrative

of the wholesale/retail distinction has been problematic, however, with the directives adopting a variety of often unclear and confusing approaches. The treatment of conduct-of-business regulation under the ISD has been particularly difficult in this regard.

VI.6.4 *The Market-integration Device*

An underlying theme of EC securities regulation generally is how the regulatory device used to achieve market integration has significant consequences for the shape and substantive content of regulation. In the investment-services arena, integration through liberalization, minimum harmonization, and home-Member-State control has been the dominant influence.[196] As a result, the regime is, in general, lighter on substantive content than the earlier official-listing regime and Member States are given considerable room, subject to the controls exerted by the minimum standards and the competitive consequences of imposing overly onerous regulation which are attendant on the passport structure, in implementing the harmonized standards.

As discussed with respect to the issuer-disclosure regime, the market-integration technique of full harmonization, combined with reliance on options and Member State discretion, has caused problems in relation to the effectiveness of that regime. Difficulties also arise in the investment-services area. The home-Member-State control and minimum-standards approach may not be regarded as appropriate in that it may inappropriately skew the substantive content of the regime's minimum reregulation. Minimum-standards directives may reflect political compromises and so may not provide an appropriate basis for regulation. The Commission has never been entirely clear about how it decides what standards are essential and subject to minimum harmonization.[197] Existing standards will vary across the EC according to the maturity of a State's market-place, the profile of its investors, government priorities on the distribution of savings, and so on. If minimum standards are, after negotiation, set at levels which reflect the optimum reduction in regulatory costs, rather than a choice of the appropriate minimum level for investor protection and systemic stability, investors' interests may be compromised. The single-market environment exposes investors to an increased level of risk. If the minimum level of

barriers . . . lest . . . the benefits of access to EU-wide capital markets [be] denied' and at 8 where the focus of the retail market discussion is on re-regulation and 'the progressive harmonisation of marketing and information rules'.

[196] On harmonization generally see Ch. I sect. 3 above.

[197] It has been noted that 'the determination of essentials among a group of nations is likely to proceed as much by horse-trading as by a rational consideration of de minimum requirements': Scott-Quinn, n 59, 133.

investor protection does not reflect this risk but is simply a function of the need to remove regulatory barriers, protection may not be adequate. Similarly, in the interests of systemic stability, minimum prudential controls must be set at sufficiently stringent levels. Failure to regulate at an appropriate level raises the spectre of regulatory arbitrage or the infamous 'race to the bottom' as Member States compete to adopt the loosest regulatory controls consistent with the terms of the directive in order to attract investment business as home regulators.[198] While Member States may choose to impose more onerous requirements on their home investment firms, in doing so they may be placing their own firms at a competitive disadvantage to firms authorized in States with less stringent systems of regulation. This competitive disadvantage can arise both in the home Member State with respect to firms authorized elsewhere and when home-authorized firms compete in host Member States with host Member State firms subject to less onerous standards of regulation.

Minimum harmonization, home-country control, and mutual recognition is, of course, but one way of harmonizing standards in order to achieve the benefits of integration. Although the full harmonization of the pre-White Paper era might provide more effective regulation in the investment-services area by ensuring (depending on the negotiation process) a high standard of investor protection and of systemic protection and limiting the possibility of a competition in laxity, it is, politically much more difficult to achieve.[199] An alternative approach to achieving the benefits of integration and the removal of regulatory obstacles would be to allow a competition between regulators to take place (which has the advantage of avoiding entrenched negotiating positions—national positions on the regulation of securities-trading markets bedevilled the progress of the ISD) and each market to compete for business by lowering regulatory barriers and thus promoting lower costs and integration.[200] This may well remove obstacles to regulation but, in the investment-services sphere, could prejudice systemic stability and investor protection were the competition to result in regulation at too low a

---

[198] On the race to the bottom problem see the analysis in Bradley, n 169 above, 551–6 and in Charny, D, 'Competition among Jurisdictions in Formulating Corporate Law Rules: An American Perspective on the "Race to the Bottom" in the European Communities' (1991) 32 *Harv LR* 423.

[199] The point has been made that 'the political dynamics of the Council have since illustrated that harmonization of rules and standards generally operates to curtail liberalization, whereas the combination of mutual recognition and home country control has proven reasonably effective in muting the influence of protectionist lobbies': Steil, n 168 above, 3.

[200] Regulatory competition has some considerable support; while 'there might once have been blind belief in the desirability of, or perhaps even the necessity for legal unification [with respect to company law, banking stock exchange and capital market regulation], but this has recently given way to a more sceptical basic position, supported by the concept of the competition between legislators': Hopt, K, 'Company Law in the European Union: Harmonisation and/or Subsidiarity?' (1999) 1 *ICCLJ* 41, 50.

level, particularly given the increased danger of systemic risk as markets
become increasingly interdependent.[201] Regulatory competition has, however, the advantage of allowing for greater regulatory innovation and flexibility in the development of common standards; it also permits systems to
compete on different regulatory platforms and reflect different types of market composition and regulatory orientations.[202] In addition, the real likelihood of a destabilizing race to the bottom developing is probably overstated
with a broad convergence in standards or a 'struggle to the top' being more
likely.[203] The well-established argument that, in principle, harmonization
should be used only to address market failures (such as the existence of protectionist trade barriers immune to competitive forces or, in the case of
investment services, in particular, the risk of systemic instability) which
spread across borders and so cannot be left to regulatory competition and
can only be dealt with effectively by harmonization, has been applied to the
investment-services sphere.[204] In the investor protection area, for example,
it might be argued that in the absence of systemic consequences and
entrenched protectionism impervious to competition, regulatory competition, subject to disclosure of the regulatory regime applicable and the level

---

[201] Risks to systemic stability are traditionally associated with competition among regulators in the financial-services arena generally. Where systemic risks are involved, regulatory
competition will not achieve an optimum solution, in that national regimes will not take into
account the impact of firm failures outside the Member State. See, eg, Goode, R, *Commercial
Law in the Next Millennium* (1998) 84 and Davis, E, 'Problems of Banking Regulation—An EC
Perspective' in Goodhart, n 12 above, 533, 547. See also the (unofficial) comments of one
Commission official who, at an early stage in the harmonization programme, pointed to the
dangers of migration by market participants to lax regulatory centres and the consequent need
to harmonize regulation at an EC level to ensure appropriate minimum standards of prudential
supervision and investor protection: Fitchew, G, 'Towards a Complete Internal Market in
Financial Services: The White Paper and Beyond' in Castello Branco, M, and Pelkmans, J (eds),
The Internal Market for Financial Services (1987) 127.

[202] For vigorous support of the case for a 'market-oriented approach of competitive federalism' to US securities regulation see Romano, R, 'Empowering Investors: A Market Approach to
Securities Regulation' (1998) 107 *Yale LJ* 2359. Professor Romano's thesis is based on the
issuer-disclosure regime and its antifraud controls and does not extend to the provision of
investment services by market professionals.

[203] '[T]here are some natural limitations on how much standards can deteriorate. For example, some or all market participants will generally demand a minimum level of regulation in
order to guarantee some order in the markets . . . examples of jurisdictions tailoring their standards in an overt effort to entice market participants are comparatively rare. Indeed, far from
constituting a "race to the bottom" of constantly lowered standards, the competition among
the world's major financial centres—London, New York, Tokyo and Frankfurt—has seen more
of a convergence of standards': Green, E, Braverman, D, and Schneck, J, 'Concepts of
Regulation—the US Model' in Oditah, n 34 above, 157, 175. See also Bradley, n 169 above,
555 who has examined the possibility of a 'struggle to the top' between regulators. See also (in
the issuer-disclosure sphere) Jackson, H, and Pan, E, 'Regulatory Competition in International
Securities Markets: Evidence from Europe in 1999—Pact 1' (2001) 56 *The Business Lawyer*
653.

[204] See Ferrarini, G, 'Securities Regulation and the Rise of Pan-European Equity Market: An
Overview' in Ferrarini, G, Hopt, K, and Wymeersch, E (eds), *Capital Markets in the Age of the
Euro* (forthcoming).

of protection afforded,[205] might result in the most efficient market-driven solutions and permit Member States to attract different types of investor, reflecting different levels of protection.[206] Indeed, the close link between protective regulation and local market conditions makes the competition argument all the more compelling in the protective sphere. Prior to its transformation into the Committee of European Securities Regulators, FESCO presided over a form of co-ordinated regulatory competition in that it developed common principles in areas in which the EC had yet to act.[207] Nonetheless, it should not be overlooked that the regulatory competition argument is often made most forcefully with respect to issuer disclosure. It has been observed that the owners of investment-services providers who, under regulatory competition theory, need to have an incentive to choose a home Member State on regulatory competition grounds are not subject to the same market forces as are issuers and that their interests will not necessarily coincide with the interests of their investor clients (who are the beneficiaries of the legislation in question) when making regulatory choices.[208] Overall, whatever the attractions of the regulatory-competition argument and however confined its operation, failure to harmonize in the special environment of the single market in investment services can provoke difficulties due, amongst other factors, to the interaction between EC and national law and uncertainty about the legal situation in other parts of the market.[209]

Mutual recognition of minimum standards and home-Member-State control represents a compromise between the full harmonization and regulatory-competition mechanisms as means for achieving the benefits of removing regulatory obstacles. Negotiations are needed only on core principles.[210] The minimum standards, while not imposing full harmonization, allow a degree of regulatory competition and thus flexibility, innovation, and local market sensitivity but, theoretically, place a limit on any 'race to the bottom' prejudicial to the integrated investment-services market and the

---

[205] Disclosure of the regime in question is necessary to allow regulatory competition to take place effectively and the regulatory choices which feed into the competition process to be made. See, eg, Romano , n 202 above, 236.

[206] Davis has pointed to the argument that 'as information asymmetries have no implications for other firms, there is not a case for harmonization of conduct of business rules': n 201 above, 546.

[207] On FESCO, its importance to the harmonization process and its place in the institutional structure of EC securities regulation, see Ch. XV sect. 2.5.2 below.

[208] See the analysis in Romano, n 202 above, 2369–70.

[209] Hopt, n 200 above, 51 who has also noted that 'European legal harmonization is particularly appropriate where individual Member States use their legal systems to erect or maintain barriers to market access'. The Italian SIM litigation (*Commission v Italy*, n 63 above) bears out the existence of market failures in the form of protectionism which, under harmonization/regulatory competition theory, require intervention.

[210] On the 'political impossibility' of achieving full harmonization and the need for 'gradual convergence' see Cranston and Hadjiemmanuil, n 113 above, 354.

rationale for its regulation which might emerge.[211] Conversely, the home-Member-State-control device[212] controls the proliferation of excessive regulation above the minimum standards due to the risk of driving away firms which might, in the face of heavy regulatory burdens, opt to transfer their operations and be subject to the regime in another Member State.[213] Regulatory competition is thus built into the harmonization system which reflects, through the mutual-recognition device, the reality that national regimes differ,[214] but minimum standards and home-country-control place a brake on the competition.[215] From a pragmatic perspective, whatever the arguments against harmonization, concerns are repeatedly expressed about the link between increased integration and interdependence and systemic instability, and the Commission is committed to a programme of harmonization, as witnessed by the FSAP. Indeed, if the Lamfalussy Report's law-making recommendations are adopted, harmonization is likely to increase in scope and in detail.

[211] '[The] EC approach of setting minimum harmonized standards may be seen as a compromise between these approaches, in that competition between regulators will determine the precise level at which standards will be set in relation to the minimum': Davis, n 201 above, 547. See also the comment that harmonization is 'at the very least a peg against further downward progress, or . . . a cordon sanitaire around the body of regulation. It provides a middle ground of regulation between the extremes of laissez faire . . . and a precisely defined and complete set of rules': contribution by Wilkinson, R, in Carosio, G, *Financial Regulation in Europe*, Special Paper No 34, LSE Financial Markets Group, Special Papers Series (1990).

[212] It is worth noting at this point that mutual recognition and home county control are rarely absolute in the directives applicable to investment services. As discussed in Ch. VII, under the ISD host Member States retain significant control over the activities of investment services firms, which are otherwise subject to the control of the home Member State, in their territories. Similarly, the home-Member-State-control principle is also diluted in the ICSD. The Court of Justice has, in this regard, made the point (in the context of banking services and the parallel Deposit Guarantee Directive (Directive 94/19 on deposit-guarantee schemes [1994] OJ L135/5) that 'it has not been proved that the Community legislature laid down the principle of home State supervision in the sphere of banking law with the intention of systematically subordinating all other rules in that sphere in that to that principle . . . since it is not a principle laid down by the Treaty, the Community legislature could depart from it': Case C–233/94 *Germany v European Parliament and Council* [1997] ECR I–2405, para 64.

[213] For the view that mutual recognition and home-country control can generate beneficial competition between regulators in that overly cautious regulators are given an incentive not to over-regulate given the risk of losing supervisory business see Wymeersch, E, *The Harmonisation of Securities Trading in Europe in the New Trading Environment*, WP 2000–16, Working Paper Series of the Financial Law Institute, Universiteit Gent, 3. It has also been observed that in the area of prudential supervision, in order to avoid a competitive disadvantage, there seems to have been a convergence of prudential standards to the minimum level, which has not, nonetheless, weakened supervision as the harmonized prudential requirements, in general, led to the adoption of higher standards across the Member States: Tison, n 69 above, 22.

[214] 'The EU legislative framework for financial markets is grounded in a concept widely referred to as "competition among rules", which takes the continuing reality of separate and distinct national legal and regulatory systems as given': Steil, n 168 above, 1.

[215] The point has been made that: '[t]he success of some market centres is partly based on differences in regulatory burdens: if it stays within limits of overall prudence, this is not necessarily an evil feature': Wymeersch, n 213 above, 3.

Notwithstanding its attractions as an integration device, the articulation of home-Member-State control in the areas of prudential supervision and protective regulation has been complex. In particular, home-Member-State control in the investment-services area raises difficult questions about the effectiveness of supervision as its success, in supervisory terms, is heavily reliant on co-operation between supervisors. The effectiveness of home-Member-State driven prudential supervision, an area in which home control is well established, has come under review (see Chapter VIII section 10 below). Home-Member-State control has also caused difficulties in the compensation-scheme sphere, where its introduction was thought to carry the risk of market disruptions and resulted in the adoption of transitional remedial measures (Chapter X section 4.7 below). Home-Member-State control cannot, as yet, be achieved in the sphere of protective regulation due to weaknesses in the harmonized regime. However, developments in e-commerce are, due to the difficulties in locating the place where an online service is provided and the impracticability of applying myriad host-Member-State rules for each Member State from which an online service can be accessed, intensifying the pressure to move away from host-Member-State control and have produced a third-Member-State control device: the Member State of origin, or the Member State in which the firm is established. In the absence of fuller harmonization, the Member State of origin device, which applies horizontally across all online services and catches investment services, poses considerable problems for effective investor protection (Chapter IX section 10 below).

VI.6.5 *Post-liberalization Regulatory Trends (1)*

In the wake of the ISD and investment-services market liberalization, a preoccupation with systemic concerns has become a core feature of EC investment-services regulation. The ICSD discussed in Chapter X is one of the first illustrations of how managing the stability of the liberalized market has influenced the shape of substantive regulation. It marks the start of a regulatory development which has led to the Supplementary Supervision Proposal on financial conglomerates (Chapter VIII section 11.3 below) which attempts to deal with a new post-integration threat to stability and, beyond the provision of investment services, to the prudential regulation of settlement systems (Chapter XII). More generally, the prudential regulation regime is increasingly concerned with enforcement and the effectiveness of the supervisory structure supporting the prudential rules. Overall, prudential supervision is becoming increasingly more sophisticated both in its mechanisms (particularly with respect to capital adequacy) and its objectives (particularly with respect to post-integration risks).

VI.6.6 *Post-liberalization Regulatory Trends (2)*

Since the adoption of the FSAP it has become clear that the EC's renewed commitment to constructing an integrated investment-services market as part of a single financial-services market includes a commitment to substantive reregulation. One of the outcomes of this is a redirection of attention towards investor protection.

In the investment-services sphere the market integration benefits of liberalization collide head-on with the costs represented by regulation in the interests of investor protection.[216] Similarly, investors' interest in competition and increased choice, which are best served by liberalization, can conflict with their interests in being protected against risk when exercising that choice. This uneasy dynamic between liberalization and regulation is not unusual, being a specific expression of the general tension between the removal of barriers to integration, which permeates Community action under the Treaty, and reregulation in order to protect the integrated market-place. In the investment-services regime, the promotion of investor protection has generally been secondary to the construction of the single market. The controls exerted on investment firms by the ISD, for example, are largely a function of market-integration imperatives; it regulates only to the extent necessary to ensure the success of the passport device. In particular, while the operating controls which it imposes include harmonized prudential rules designed to protect the financial stability of investment firms and the systemic stability of the wider market-place, there is only limited coverage of the conduct of the relationship between the investment firm and the client.[217] Further, the development of new investment services with EC-wide ramifications, such as the trading services provided by alternative trading systems, and new methods for the delivery of investment services, exemplified by the e-commerce revolution, are subjecting the EC's basic protective regime to new stresses and strains as its basic principles are grafted on to new risk environments. As the single market matures, however, the regulatory regime has become more pro-investor in its focus, encompassing the establishment of investor-compensation schemes (the ICSD) and more sophisticated regulation of the conduct of business by investment intermediaries (the Distance Marketing Proposal). Indeed, while the investment firm and the investment-firm passport were the priorities in the pre-ISD liberal-

---

[216] The uneasy dynamic between market integration and protection was reflected in the Commission's statement in its 1998 Communication that 'the need to ensure a high level of consumer protection should be proportionate and not be used as an excuse to hinder cross-border business': n 176 above, 12.

[217] This unevenness in the regulatory regime seems to be acknowledged by the Commission in its 1998 Communication where it found that '[t]he EU framework of prudential controls provides a substantial first line of defence for consumer interests' but called for further 'targeted action' to enhance protection and hence confidence in the marketplace: ibid, 11.

ization stage, post-ISD, the regulatory focus is now, as can be seen in the 2001 ISD Working Paper,[218] being redirected towards the investor and the encouragement of investor participation in the market-place.

In managing post-liberalization risks, however, the EC, as a quasi-securities regulator, moves from market construction into market regulation as investment-services harmonization changes its focus from liberalization to regulation and moves increasingly towards becoming a system of regulation rather than an integration device. As is discussed in the following chapters (see, for example, Chapters VIII section 11.3.3 and IX section 12 below), in the wake of the Court's landmark *Tobacco Advertising*[219] ruling on the limits of internal-market competences there is a question over the extent to which the Treaty can accommodate this next evolutionary stage of investment-services regulation.

VI.7 GUIDING PRINCIPLES FOR INVESTMENT-SERVICES REGULATION

The investment-services regime which is examined in the next four chapters reflects one consistent principle: the integration of investment-services markets. Beyond that, inconsistencies exist with respect to the rationale for adopting reregulation in the investment-services sphere, the relative coverage of prudential and protective regulation, the features of the investors the subject of the legislation, and even in relation to the articulation of the dominant liberalization principle, as there are considerable structural difficulties with the passport regime and, in particular, problems with the control exercised by host Member States which hinder integration. The pressures on the regime will only increase, not only on the foot of further integration and the consequent strains on systemic stability and investor protection, but also as it attempts to accommodate new market participants, such as financial conglomerates and investment firms which provide trading market services (ATSs). In addition, the different developmental stages of the regime mean that different areas are provoking very different concerns; in the prudential sphere the focus is on the effective enforcement and supervision of relatively well-established rules, while in the protective sphere attention is being directed to constructing substantive standards and protections. Although the investment-services regime is thus currently under siege from different directions, it seems clear from the FSAP, the Lamfalussy Report, and the 2001 ISD Working Paper that the substantive content of the regime as a whole

---

[218] Overview of Proposed Adjustments to the Investment Services Directive. Working Document of Services of DG Internal Market. Document, 1 July 2001 (the ISD Working Paper—considered throughout Part III).

[219] Case C–376/98 *Germany v Parliament and Council* [2000] ECR I–8419 (the *Tobacco Advertising* case).

will increase. It is less clear that the regime will be refined such that it reflects appropriately the strains on the system discussed in the following chapters. The danger would then exist that an unwieldy body of disjointed regulation would emerge (a risk that has already arisen in relation to the interaction between e-commerce measures and the investment-services regime). If the regime is amended and supplemented on the scale suggested by the FSAP and the Lamfalussy Report, the risk of incoherence could be minimized were the 'conceptual framework of overarching principles', which the Lamfalussy Report suggested be adopted as a Regulation or in an amendment to the Treaty, to be adopted. These principles fuse the traditional rationale for investment-services regulation outlined at the start of this chapter with the particular features of the single market. They are: to maintain confidence in European securities markets; to maintain high levels of prudential supervision; to contribute to the efforts of macro and micro prudential supervisors to ensure systemic stability; to ensure appropriate levels of consumer protection proportionate to the different degrees of risk involved; to respect the subsidiarity and proportionality principles of the Treaty; to promote competition and ensure that the Community's competition rules are fully respected; to ensure that regulation is efficient as well as encouraging, not discouraging, innovation; and to take account of the European, as well as the wider international, dimension of securities markets.[220]

---

[220] Lamfalussy Report, n 13 above, 22.

VII

The Investment-services Passport

VII.1 INTRODUCTION

The Investment Services Directive[1] dominates the EC investment-services landscape. The year of its adoption, 1993, marks the emergence of an extensive, if embryonic, securities-regulation regime at EC level, covering not simply the offer of and admission to official listing of securities and insider-dealing issues, but also addressing the wider secondary market-place and its participants.[2] Not only does the ISD, by way of its passport device, provide the regulatory mechanism which unlocks the single market in investment services, it also sets out the harmonized substantive prudential and protective rules which underpin the new investment-services market-place which it constructs. The former, market-integration function of the ISD will be considered in this chapter; the latter function is considered in Chapters VIII and IX. The ISD also plays a key role in liberalizing access to securities trading markets which is considered in Part IV.

Although it broke new ground in EC securities regulation and in the integration of investment-services markets, the gestation of the ISD, although undoubtedly troublesome (particularly with respect to its liberalization of access to securities-trading markets provisions, difficulties with which ultimately prevented the adoption of the ISD in time for the end of

---

[1] Council Directive 93/22/EEC on investment services in the securities field [1993] OJ L141/27 (the ISD or the Directive). The ISD has generated a considerable literature. Of the general reviews see, eg, Theil, R, 'A Review of the Financial Services Directives' (1992) 7 *JIBL* 500; Dassesse, M, 'The Investment Services Directive' [1992] *JIBFL* 5; Abrams, C, 'The Investment Services Directive' in Campbell, D (ed), *Financial Services in the New Europe* (1992) 311; Lomnicka, E, 'The Internal Financial Market and Investment Services' in Andenas, M, and Kenyon-Slade, S (eds), *EC Financial Market Regulation and Company Law* (1993) 81; Ashall, P, 'The Investment Services Directive: What Was the Conflict All About' in ibid, 91; Cremona, M, 'A European Passport for Investment Services' (1994) *JBL* 195; Carbon de Lichtbuer, M, 'The Investment Services Directive, An Analysis' in Wymeersch, E (ed), *Further Perspectives in Financial Integration in Europe* (1994) 79; Ferrarini, G, 'Towards a European Law of Investment Services and Institutions' (1994) 31 *CMLRev.* 1283; O'Neill, N, 'The Investment Services Directive' in Cranston, R (ed), *The Single Market and the Law of Banking* (2nd edn, 1995) 189; Blair, W, Allison, A, Palmer, K, Richards-Carpenter, P, and Walker, G, *Banking and Financial Services Regulation* (2nd edn, 1998) 373–92; Tison, M, *The Investment Services Directive and its Implementation in the EU Member States*, WP 1999-17, Working Paper Series of the Financial Law Institute, Universiteit Gent; and Usher, J, *The Law of Money and Financial Services in the European Community* (2nd edn, 2000) 141–4.

[2] Recital 14 makes clear that the ISD does not affect Community rules or national provisions regulating public offers of the instruments covered by the ISD or any such rules concerning the marketing and distribution of such instruments.

1992 single-market deadline), was not as protracted as that of other securities-regulation directives; indeed by comparison with the now notorious progress of the failed proposed takeover regime the ISD was a speedy arrival on the securities-regulation landscape. The original proposal was presented by the Commission in 1989.[3] Following the comments of the European Parliament and ECOSOC a revised proposal was presented in 1990.[4] The ISD was finally adopted by the Council in May 1993.[5] The text as finally adopted is significantly more detailed than the original rather open-textured proposal presented by the Commission with the bulk of changes reflecting a combination of politically driven amendments and refinements borrowed from the Second Banking Co-ordination Directive,[6] which was adopted during the ISD negotiations.

This chapter will focus on the integration of investment-services markets from the perspective of the ISD and the investment firm. Credit institutions which provide investment services can access the single market in investment services through the banking passport. The banking passport will not be discussed in this chapter as it reflects the particular features of banking regulation, although the extent to which the investment-services regime is grafted onto the banking passport for such credit institutions, in order to address the particular regulatory concerns posed by the investment-services market-place, will be identified. The single-market-construction discussion will also include an outline of the new passport regime for management companies of collective-investment schemes.

VII.2 SINGLE-MARKET MAKING: THE END AND THE MEANS

VII.2.1 *Article 47(2) EC*

Based on Article 47(2) EC (at the time of its adoption Article 57(2) EC), the ISD's market-integration objectives fit naturally with the grant of competence by that Article to the Community to 'issue directives for the coordination of the provisions laid down by law, regulation or administrative action

---

[3] [1989] OJ C43/7, Explanatory Memorandum at COM(88)778.

[4] [1989] OJ C304/39, [1989] OJ C298/6, [1990] OJ C42/7 (Explanatory Memorandum at COM(89)629), respectively.

[5] Notice of the adoption of a Common Position is at [1993] OJ C18/1. The ISD was adopted under the co-operation procedure as then required by Art. 47(2) EC. Art. 47(2) EC measures are now adopted under the co-decision procedure discussed in Ch. XV sect. 2.2.1 below. The ISD was to be implemented by the Member State by 1 July 1995.

[6] 2nd Council Directive 89/646/EEC on the coordination of laws regulations and administrative procedures relating to the taking up and pursuit of the business of credit institutions and amending Directive 77/780/EEC [1989] OJ L386/1 (the BCD II). Its provisions have been consolidated with the other banking regime measures by Directive 2000/12/EC relating to the taking up and pursuit of the business of credit institutions [2000] OJ L126/1 (the CBD).

in Member States concerning the taking-up and pursuit of activities as self-employed persons'. Article 47(2) EC forms part of the Treaty framework on the freedom to establish. The Article 47(2) EC competence is extended to the freedom to provide services by Article 55 EC, which is not referred to explicitly in the ISD; the movement of investment firms across the market by means of the provision of cross-border services is, however, clearly contemplated by the ISD. As the investment-services regime moves beyond market integration into market regulation the relationship between the Treaty and the regime becomes a less happy one, as is outlined in later chapters.

The Preamble to the ISD describes it in recital 1 as being 'essential to the achievement of the internal market . . . from the point of view both of the right of establishment and of the freedom to provide financial services, in the field of investment firms' and links it directly to the Commission's White Paper on Completing the Internal Market.[7] From the outset the primary purpose of the ISD is made clear: the removal of the regulatory barriers faced by investment-services providers when operating across the EC either by providing services on a cross-border basis or through the establishment of a branch. As outlined in subsequent chapters, market stability and investor protection also underpin the ISD but they are a function of the dominant market-integration objective.

VII.2.2 *Essential Features*

The ISD's integration strategy is to liberalize investment-services markets by subjecting an investment firm to the regulatory system of one Member State, regardless of where it carries out its activities. It grants a 'passport' to investment firms authorized in one Member State (the home Member State) to provide investment services in any other Member State (the host Member State) either by providing services on a cross-border basis or by establishing a branch in the host State, without the need for re-authorization. The investment firm remains subject to the ongoing prudential rules of the home Member State. The host Member State may not require re-authorization but has a complementary, if secondary, role in ongoing regulation.[8] The ISD is therefore an expression of the mutual-recognition principle which has been developed by the Court of Justice.[9]

---

[7] COM(85)310.

[8] Although the ISD's focus is on the investment firm and its ability to operate across the EC rather than on the investor, recital 34 provides that a Member State may not limit the right of investors habitually resident or established in that Member State to avail themselves of any investment service provided by an investment firm covered by the Directive situated outside that Member State and acting outwith that Member State.

[9] Mutual recognition under the Treaty and as part of the jurisprudence on the freedom to provide services and to establish free from duplicative regulatory controls (discussed in Ch. VI sect. 4 above) can be distinguished from mutual recognition under the ISD. While the Treaty

Unlike the earlier original admission and disclosure regime, the ISD does not seek to co-ordinate the law. In order to achieve its objectives, it uses the devices of minimum harmonization, home-country control, and mutual recognition: 'the approach adopted is to effect only the essential harmonization necessary and sufficient to secure the mutual recognition of authorization and of prudential supervision systems, making possible the grant of a single authorization valid throughout the Community and the application of the principle of home-country control' (recital 13).[10] Its harmonization of the rules governing the provision of investment services is selective. Only those aspects of regulation which infringe to the requisite degree the passport mechanism are harmonized. Harmonization of authorization rules was critical to the success of the ISD as the grant of authorization serves as the gateway to the single market.[11] The second stage of the regulatory process, ongoing supervision, is also harmonized and subject to home-Member-State control but the focus is on prudential rather than protective supervision. As with the minimum authorization conditions, the home Member State is free to impose more stringent standards (recital 27) but these may apply only to investment firms established and authorized in the home Member State. A Member State which adopts authorization and prudential requirements which are more stringent than the minimum requirements of the ISD must allow investment firms authorized in Member States which adopt the ISD minimum requirements to operate in its territory. Accordingly, the imposition of more stringent conditions with their associated regulatory costs may place its own investment firms at a competitive disadvantage.[12] Full mutual recognition or full reliance on the home State passport breaks down, however, in that the host State retains a role outside the prudential sphere (and, in particular, with respect to the regulation of the conduct of business and advertising, areas which are not harmonized by the Directive) but is con-

rules allow for mutual recognition to be 'trumped' in effect by the general-good justification, the ISD regime provides, in certain cases, for 'perfect mutual recognition' in that the minimum harmonized standards oust the general-good justification. For this analysis see Tison, M, *Unravelling the General Good Exception*, WP 2000–03, Working Paper of the Financial Law Institute, Universiteit Gent (forthcoming in Andenas, M, and Roth, W-H (eds), *Free Movement of Services*) 22.

[10] On mutual recognition, minimum harmonization, and home-country control as integration devices see Ch. VI sect. 6.4 above.

[11] The Commission's original proposal described the main objective of the proposal in the following terms: '[t]he main aim of the proposal is to lay down an authorisation procedure for any person wishing to provide one or more of the services coming within the Directive's scope . . . on the basis of such authorisation the person in question . . . will be allowed to provide the service in question on a cross-border basis within the Community or to set up branches in the other Member States without needing to be authorised again': Explanatory Memorandum to original proposal, n 3 above, 1.

[12] It has been noted that this feature of mutual recognition in the ISD is 'meant to speed the process of harmonization of standards and procedures by making it uncompetitive to over-regulate domestic investment firms': Theil, n 1 above, 501.

trolled nonetheless by the general-good principle which is institutionalized in the ISD.

An underlying objective of the ISD is non-discrimination in the application of regulation to investment firms, regardless of whether they are providing services in their home Member State or elsewhere. The non-discrimination principle is expressly acknowledged in Article 28 which provides that Member States shall ensure that the Directive is implemented without discrimination.

VII.2.3 *Relationship with the Banking Regime*

The technique used by the ISD to achieve market integration is derived from earlier harmonization and integration in the banking sector, which led the way with the now consolidated BCD II. The structure of the BCD II, with its central concepts of home-country control and the grant of a passport on authorization, acted as a template for the ISD. It, in turn, built on the First Banking Co-ordination Directive which paved the way for mutual recognition by requiring Member States to establish an authorization procedure for credit institutions, in accordance with the minimum standards of that directive.[13] Indeed, the competitive advantage accruing to credit institutions in the field of investment services as a result of the adoption of the BCD II in 1989 was a spur to the adoption of the ISD.[14] This advantage arose as the passport provided by the BCD II for duly authorized credit institutions is based on the wide range of activities carried out by banks under the universal bank model,[15] and extends beyond traditional commercial banking services.[16] In particular, a differentiation is not made between commercial and investment banking. The passport also covers activities which form the

[13] 1st Council Directive 77/780/EEC on the coordination of laws, regulations and administrative provisions relating to the taking up and pursuit of the business of credit institutions [1977] OJ L322/30 (BCD I), now part of the consolidated banking regime set out in the CBD.

[14] Although the need to strengthen the position of investment firms with respect to credit institutions had been noted in 1977: '[s]o long as measures to strengthen the financial and economic position of brokers have not been fully implemented, the organization of competition between the two sectors would appear likely to bring about too unequal a struggle, which can only lead to domination by the banks': Wymeersch, E, *Control of Securities Markets in the European Economic Community*, Collection Studies, Competition—Approximation of Legislation Series No. 31 (1977) 130.

[15] See generally Clarotti, P, 'The Implementation of the Second Banking Coordination Directive and its Aftermath' in Wymeersch, n 1 above, 43, 46.

[16] The Annex to the BCD II (CBD, Annex I), which sets out the activities which benefit from the banking passport, lists the main commercial banking activities including the acceptance of deposits and other repayable funds from the public, lending (including, *inter alia*, consumer credit, mortgage credit, factoring (with or without recourse), and financing of commercial transactions (including forfaiting)), financial leasing, money transmission services, issuing and administering means of payment (such as credit cards, travellers' cheques, and bankers' drafts), guarantees and commitments, money broking services, credit reference services, and safe custody services.

basis of investment-firm activity: trading for the bank's own account or for the account of customers in a wide range of instruments;[17] participation in share issues and the provision of services related to such issues; advice to undertakings on capital structure, industrial strategy and related questions and advice related to mergers and the purchase of undertakings; portfolio management and advice; and the safekeeping and administration of securities. The banking passport is available only to credit institutions which are defined as undertakings 'whose business it is to receive deposits or other repayable funds from the public and grant credits for its own account'.[18] This anomaly was not of great significance in continental Europe where the universal bank structure meant that banking and investment services were carried out by credit institutions and, indeed, that separate regulatory regimes for investment firms did not exist in certain Member States as investment services were regulated as part of the overall regulation of the credit institution. In the UK, in particular, however, where investment-services firms were often unaffiliated to credit institutions as the UK regime regulates on a functional basis, requiring separate authorization in respect of banking and investment-services activities (although not prohibiting one institution from carrying out both activities),[19] investment firms and the investment-services industry were, as a result of differences in structure,[20] placed at a competitive disadvantage to continental credit institutions with respect to investment services. UK investment-service providers could not establish branches and provide cross-border services across the Community with the same freedom with which credit institutions carrying out the same activities could provide services and establish branches in the UK.[21] Apart from the distortion in competition created by the banking passport, a specific investment-services measure was also needed to address the prudential and conduct regulation specific to the supply of investment services and essential to the integrity of the single market in investment services which was missing from the banking regime.

[17] S 7 of the Annex lists trading in money-market instruments, foreign exchange, financial futures and options, exchange and interest rate instruments and transferable securities.

[18] Art. 2(1) BCD II and Art. 1 BCD I (CBD, Arts. 1(1) and 2(1)).

[19] See generally Blair *et al.*, n 1 above, 373–4 and Cranston, R, *Principles of Banking Law* (1997) 21–3 who has also noted a gradual encroachment of the universal bank structure into the London banking market since the late 1980s.

[20] The now consolidated BCD II did not address these differences in structure although the wide range of activities which a credit institution may carry out under the banking passport suggests that it supports the universal bank model: ibid, 104.

[21] See the discussion in Dassesse, M, Isaacs, S, and Penn, G, *EC Banking Law* (2nd edn, 1994), 30–1. For an analysis querying the extent to which the now consolidated BCD II gave an advantage to credit institutions providing investment services over investment firms which did not form part of a banking group in light of the own-funds requirements imposed on credit institutions see O'Neill, N, 'Investment Services and the Single Market—Beyond 1992' [1993] *JIBFL* 17.

The BCD II does provide in Article 18(2) (CBD, Article 19) that a 'financial institution'[22] may benefit from the passport as long as it a subsidiary of a credit institution or of two or more credit institutions, its memorandum and articles of association permit the carrying on of the activities in question, and it fulfils five other conditions. These require that the parent undertaking is authorized as a credit institution in the Member State by whose law the subsidiary is governed, the activities in question are actually carried on in the territory of the same Member State, the parent undertaking holds 90 per cent of the voting rights attaching to shares in the subsidiary's capital, the parent undertaking has satisfied the competent authorities about the prudent management of the subsidiary and has declared, with the consent of its home-Member-State authorities, that it jointly and severally guarantees the commitments entered into by the subsidiary; and that the subsidiary is included, for the activities in question in particular, in the consolidated supervision of the parent undertaking. Failure to comply with any of these conditions will subject the subsidiary to the legislation of the host Member State. This provision was introduced to ensure that the banking passport could apply to certain activities (such as dealing in securities) which, in certain Member States, credit institutions could not carry out directly, but in respect of the carrying out of which they were required to incorporate separate subsidiaries. As the subsidiaries could not be categorized as credit institutions for the purposes of the banking-regime passport such activities would, unless an exception was created, have fallen outside the banking regime's liberalization.[23] Nonetheless, the restrictive terms of the financial-institution passport and the link required to a credit institution made it unavailable for stand-alone UK investment-services firms. Indeed, even for the investment-services subsidiaries of credit institutions which were supposedly the beneficiaries of this provision, the severity of these conditions meant that reliance on the banking passport for the activities of the investment-services subsidiaries of credit institutions was very difficult and, in certain cases, that reliance on the Treaty freedoms was a more attractive option for such undertakings.[24]

---

[22] An undertaking other than a credit institution the principal activity of which is to acquire holdings or carry out banking passport activities other than the acceptance of deposits or other repayable funds.

[23] Explanatory Memorandum to the original proposal for the BCD II COM(87)715, 14.

[24] Roeges, L, 'Banking Activities Through a Branch in another Member State after the Second Banking Directive' (1993) 13 *YBEL* 295, 304.

VII.3 SCOPE

VII.3.1 *A Functional Approach*

Agreeing on the scope of the ISD was a key issue during its preparatory stages. Not only are the core activities of investment firms not as readily identifiable as those of credit institutions,[25] the drafters did not have the advantage of being able to draw on an earlier approaches to delimiting an investment firm's core activities.[26] Rather than use a broad definition, the mechanism used by the ISD is to specify in some detail the type of investment services covered by the Directive. Function rather than form is the key to the ISD's approach.

VII.3.2 *Investment Firms*

Under Article 2(1), the provisions of the ISD apply to all investment firms. An investment firm is defined in Article 1(2) as any legal person the regular occupation or business of which is the provision of investment services to third parties on a professional basis.[27]

Member States may choose to include investment firms which are not legal persons in the scope of the Directive, but their inclusion is subject to their meeting certain eligibility conditions.[28] In particular, their legal status

[25] See Ashall, n 1 above, 93.

[26] The 1977 Code of Conduct (Commission Recommendation 77/534/EEC concerning a European code of conduct relating to transactions in transferable securities [1977] OJ L212/37 (the 1977 Code of Conduct), which might otherwise have provided a useful basis for regulation, adopts a somewhat unsophisticated approach, imposing its requirements on 'financial intermediaries' which it defines as 'all persons professionally concerned in transactions in transferable securities'. At an international level, at that time IOSCO was achieving only limited agreement with respect to principles of regulation by comparison with its more recent achievements. The 1998 Principles and Objectives of Securities Regulation (the 1998 IOSCO Principles), eg, now defines 'market intermediaries' as including 'those who are in the business of managing individual portfolios, executing orders, dealing in or distributing securities and providing information relevant to the trading of securities': para 12.2.

[27] The definition of investment firms changed considerably as the proposal evolved. The definition in the Commission's original proposal simply covered 'any natural or legal person whose business it is to engage in one or more of the activities set out in the Annex': n 3 above, Art. 1. The reference to providing investment services to third parties in a professional basis was added in order to emphasize that the proposal's provisions did not apply to persons dealing exclusively on their own account.

[28] The treatment of natural persons was somewhat contentious, given that most Member States required the provision of investment services to be undertaken by companies. A small number of Member States, including the UK, however, allowed investment services to be provided by partnerships or sole traders and argued that, as investors' assets could be protected by mechanisms other than the protections offered by the structure of a company with separate personality, they be included within the scope of the ISD. The compromise reached was to allow investment firms to take the form of natural persons, but to subject them to additional prudential requirements. On the negotiations on this point see Bell, R, 'A Single Passport for EC Investment Services' [1992] *JIBFL* 410, 411.

must ensure a level of protection for third parties' interests which is at least equivalent to that afforded by legal persons, and they must be subject to equivalent prudential supervision appropriate to their legal form. Additional and rather onerous conditions, which are designed to protect client assets and funds on an insolvency or the death of a sole proprietor, apply to natural persons where they provide services involving holding third parties' funds or transferable securities. In such cases, they may be considered as investment firms for the purposes of the ISD only if, without prejudice to the other requirements of the ISD and the Capital Adequacy Directive,[29] the following conditions are complied with: the ownership rights of third parties in instruments and funds belonging to them are safeguarded, especially in the event of the insolvency of the firm or of its proprietors, seizure, set-off, or any other action by creditors of the firm or of its proprietors; the firm must be subject to rules designed to monitor the firm's solvency and that of its proprietors; the annual accounts of the firm must be audited by one or more persons empowered under national law to audit accounts; and, where the firm has only one proprietor, that person must make provision for the protection of investors in the event of the firm's cessation of business following his death, his incapacity, or any other such event. Article 1(2) provides, however, in its final paragraph that, where a person provides broking services (section A(1)(a) of the Annex to the ISD) and where that service is carried out 'solely for the account and under the full and unconditional responsibility of an investment firm, that activity shall be regarded as the activity not of that person but of the investment firm itself'.

The Commission is required under the ISD to report on the application of a certain number of its articles and to propose modifications where necessary. Although this obligation arises, for the most part, in relation to the ISD's securities-trading markets provisions it also covers the operation of Article 1(1). The Commission reported in 1998 that most Member States have not exercised the possibility of authorizing persons other than legal persons as investment firms and that there was no need to amend or delete the eligibility conditions set out in Article 1(1).[30]

Credit institutions[31] which are authorized and supervised under the banking regime, but whose banking authorization covers one or more of the ISD core investment services (see section 3.3 below) and who accordingly also come within the scope of the ISD, are exempted from a number of the ISD's provisions which duplicate those of the banking regime, but remain

---

[29] Directive 93/6/EEC on the capital adequacy of investment firms and credit institutions [1993] OJ L141/1 (the CAD).

[30] Report from the Commission to the Council. COM(1998)780 (the 1998 ISD Report), 2.

[31] Defined under Art. 1(3) by reference to the now consolidated BCD I, Art. 4 which defines credit institutions as undertakings whose business is to receive deposits or other repayable funds from the public and to grant credits for their own account (CBD, Art. 1(1)).

subject to those requirements of the ISD which are additional to the banking regime and are specifically designed to regulate investment firms.[32] Accordingly, while many banks will gain their passports for investment services through the banking regime, the ISD will nonetheless exert a considerable regulatory influence, notably with respect to conduct of business and prudential regulation.

VII.3.3 *Investment Services*

The critical element of the definition of investment firm is what is deemed to constitute an investment service. Investment service is defined in Article 1(1) as any of the services listed in section A of the Annex to the ISD, relating to any of the instruments listed in Section B of the Annex, which are provided for a third party.

VII.3.3.1 *Section A Services*

The services listed in Annex A are: reception and transmission on behalf of investors of orders in relation to one or more of the instruments listed in Section B (this includes the bringing together of two or more investors for the purposes of enabling them to conclude a contract—recital 13) and execution of such orders other than for own account; dealing in any of the Section B instruments for own account; managing portfolios of investments in accordance with mandates given by investors on a discriminatory, client-by-client basis where such portfolios include one or more of the Section B instruments; and underwriting in respect of issues of Section B instruments, and or the placing of such issues.[33] It is clear that the basic business model behind the ISD is the traditional broker-dealer. Both the market-integration devices and the substantive regulation introduced by the ISD reflect this choice.[34] The inclusion of underwriting and placing services emphasizes,

---

[32] Specifically, only Art. 2(4) (counterparty to State entities engaging in monetary activities exception), Art. 8(2) (compliance with capital adequacy rules), Art. 10 (application of prudential rules), Art. 11 (application of conduct rules), Art. 14(3) and (4) (performance of transactions on regulated markets), Art. 15 (access of investment firms to regulated markets) (the latter two provisions are covered in Ch. XI), Art. 19 (information-gathering and enforcement powers of host Member State) and Art. 20 (reporting requirements imposed on investment firms concerning regulated market transactions (see Ch. XI)) apply to credit institutions.

[33] The original and revised proposals took a wider view of the range of services which could be carried out by passporting investment firms and included giving professional investment advice as well as safekeeping and administration services related to the instruments covered by the proposal. Investment advice and custody services were subsequently demoted to non-core services.

[34] See the Commission's 2000 Communication on Upgrading the Investment Services Directive (93/22/EEC) COM(2000)729 (the ISD Communication), 7. This model is being placed under some strain given the demands placed on it to accommodate the regulatory concerns raised by alternative trading systems (ATSs). See sect. 10.3.2 below and Ch. XI.

however, that wholesale investment-services business is also covered by the ISD.

The Directive contains a second tier of 'non-core' activities which are defined in Section C of the Annex. Although authorization may be granted to investment firms which, in addition to Section A activities, also cover one or more of such non-core activities, authorization may not be granted to investment firms which provide only non-core services (Article 3(1)).[35] Of particular note is the inclusion of the provision of investment advice on the non-core list.[36] Notwithstanding the need to protect investors from the dangers posed by investment advisers, particularly in relation to conflicts of interests, investment firms which engage solely in the provision of advice fall outside the ISD's regulatory structure.[37] The investor-protection issue raised by the absence of an authorization requirement is, of course, mitigated by the inability of an investment adviser to benefit from the ISD passport and operate across the EC, thereby accessing a wider group of investors (although the Treaty free-movement provisions and the general-good control will apply). Where the investment adviser also engages in a core activity, the benefits of the passport are available and the adviser may be subject to the conduct regime set out in Article 11 in respect of any investment advice given. The treatment of non-core services is currently under consideration in light of the ISD Communication's finding that certain non-core

[35] These non-core activities are: safekeeping and administration in relation to Section B instruments; safe custody services; granting credits or loans to an investor to allow that investor carry out a transaction in one or more of the Section B instruments where the firm granting the loan is involved in the transaction (margin-trading services); advice to undertakings on capital structure, industrial strategy, and related matters and advice and services relating to mergers and the purchase of undertakings; underwriting services; investment advice concerning Section B instruments; and foreign-exchange services provided in connection with the supply of investment services. Negotiations on the scope of the non-core services were difficult with banking organizations lobbying for the scope of the investment-services passport to be restricted. Evidence of this can be seen in recital 7 which states that investment firms may not rely on the ISD to carry out spot or forward exchange transactions other than as services connected with the provision of investment services and that the use of a branch solely for the purpose of carrying out such transactions would be a misuse of the ISD. Credit institutions, by contrast, have a full passport for these activities.

[36] It has been suggested that the reason for this treatment of investment advisers is that advisory services were not subject to authorization in all Member States. Ferrarini, n 1 above, 1289.

[37] Even though it was noted as early as 1977 that '[a]buses which have often severely shaken the confidence of investors were found in several Member States due to certain advisory practices engaged in by persons who do not enjoy the legal status of recognised security dealers but present themselves as investment consultants, portfolio managers, etc. Conversely there is a need in certain—not necessarily the most well-to-do—strata of the population for serious and above all independent advice': Wymeersch, n 14 above, 136. The ISD's hands-off approach to investment advisers is, however, reflected in the 1998 IOSCO Principles (n 26 above) which suggest in para 12.7 that licensing of investment advisers may not be strictly necessary, and that where investment advisers are subject to regulation 'a disclosure based regime designed to permit potential advisory clients to make an informed choice of advisers' would be adequate.

services should, in the interests of greater market integration and enhanced investor protection, benefit from the passport.[38]

VII.3.2.2 *Section B Instruments*

Given the pace of change in the investment-services industry and the continually evolving nature of investment products, the ISD lists a wide range of broadly categorized and, where they are defined, broadly defined instruments[39] in Section B. The list covers: transferable securities;[40] units in collective investment undertakings; money market instruments;[41] financial

---

[38] The Commission Communication on E-Commerce and Financial Services, COM(2001)66 (the E-commerce and Financial Services Communication) at 13 also expressed concern with respect to certain non-core activities, including investment advice, and suggested that consideration would be given to the need for further harmonization. See sect. 10.3.2 below.

[39] The ISD was the first securities measure to use the broad category of 'instruments' rather than a definition of 'securities' or 'transferable securities'. See, by contrast, the use of 'transferable securities' (albeit broadly defined as shares and debt securities, as well as securities equivalent to shares and debt securities, contracts or rights to subscribe for, acquire, or dispose of such securities, futures contracts, options, and financial futures in respect of such securities and index contracts in respect of such securities) in the Insider Dealing Directive 89/592 [1989] OJ L334/31, Art. 1(2). 'Transferable securities' is also used in the Public Offers Directive (Directive 89/298/EEC coordinating the drawing-up, scrutiny and distribution of the prospectus to be published when transferable securities are offered to the public [1989] OJ L124/8) Art. 3(e) and in the 1977 Code of Conduct (although defined in a somewhat limited fashion in each case as, respectively, 'shares in companies and other transferable securities equivalent to shares in companies, debt securities having a maturity of at least one year and other transferable securities equivalent to debt securities, and any other transferable security giving the right to acquire any such transferable securities by subscription or exchange' and 'all securities which are or may be the subject of dealings on an organised market'). Directive 80/390/EEC coordinating the requirements for the drawing up, scrutiny and distribution of the listing particulars to be published for the admission of securities to official stock exchange listing [1980] OJ L100/1 (the LPD) simply refers to 'securities', as does the Admission Directive (Directive 79/279/EEC coordinating the conditions for the admission of securities to official stock exchange listing [1979] OJ L66/21) (both now consolidated in Directive 2001/34/EC on admission of securities to official stock exchange listing and on information to be published on those securities [2001] OJ L184/1) (the Securities Consolidation Directive or SCD)). Neither defines the term but it is clear from their provisions (specifically the Annexes) that shares, certificates representing shares, debt securities, and convertible or exchangeable debentures and debenture with warrants are covered.

[40] Defined in Art. 1(4) as (1) shares in companies and other securities equivalent to shares in companies and bonds and other forms of securitized debt which are negotiable on the capital markets and (2) any other securities normally dealt in giving the right to acquire any such transferable securities by subscription or exchange or giving rise to a cash settlement, excluding instruments of payment. Further clarification is provided by recital 9 which explains that transferable securities covers government securities, shares in companies, negotiable securities giving the right to acquire shares by subscription or exchange, depositary receipts, bonds issued as part of a series, index warrants, and securities giving the right to acquire such bonds by subscription. Negotiability is a key factor. It is clear from recital 11 that shares and other securities issued by bodies such as building societies and industrial and provident societies which cannot in practice be transferred except through a repurchase by the issuing body do not come within the ISD.

[41] Defined in Art. 1(5) as those classes of instruments which are normally dealt in on the money market. These include treasury bills, commercial paper, and certificates of deposit.

futures contracts (including equivalent cash-settled instruments); forward interest-rate agreements; interest-rate, currency, and equity swaps; and options to acquire or dispose of any of the aforementioned instruments, including equivalent cash-settled instruments and, in particular, options on currency and interest rates.[42]

VII.3.4 *An Expansive Approach to Interpreting the Scope of the ISD?*

Some guidance on the approach the Court may take in interpreting the scope of the ISD, should difficulties arise, may be taken from its approach to the banking regime. In *Re Criminal Proceedings against Massino Romanelli and Paolo Romanelli*,[43] the Court examined the meaning of 'repayable funds'. Under Article 3 of the BCD II (CBD, Article 3) only credit institutions within the terms of the banking regime can take 'repayable funds' from the public. The Romanellis, who were not a credit institution under the banking regime, sold instruments representing an amount receivable which were immediately repurchased at a price which included agreed interest and warrants representing an option to acquire debentures. In their defence they argued that the prohibition on taking repayable funds extended only to intrinsically repayable funds or credit capital, such as certificates of deposit and bonds, and did not cover risk capital which was not invested on the basis of a repayment guarantee but with the aim of speculative gain. The Court took a broad approach in interpreting Article 3, ruling that, given that one of objectives of the banking directives was the protection of consumers from the harm which they could suffer at the hands of inadequately authorized undertakings and, given the sensitivity of the banking sector generally, 'repayable funds' included not only intrinsically repayable funds but also funds which were the subject of a contractual agreement to repay. The Court is likely to take a similarly purposive approach with respect to the interpretation of the ISD, although the extent to which a parallel can be drawn with this consumer protection-driven approach to interpretation is debatable in light of the difficulties in classifying the ISD as protective measure.

---

[42] Derivative instruments (but not commodity derivatives) therefore come within the ISD's regulatory structure although no particular provision is made for them. Derivatives and transactions concerning derivatives have been subject to ongoing review by the EC. In 1995, eg, ECOSOC published a report on derivatives [1996] OJ C18/1, addressed to the European Parliament and the Parliaments of the Member States, which was designed to dispel concerns with respect to derivatives which might otherwise arise from a lack of knowledge of the derivatives industry. It concluded that the risks and dangers associated with derivatives were neither new nor greater than those associated with other sectors of the capital markets, and that, by making transactions in securities less unpredictable, derivatives contributed to a real economic need.

[43] Case C–366/97 [1999] ECR I–855.

VII.3.5 *Exclusions*

The potentially wide sweep of the definition of investment firm is scaled back by Article 2(2)[44] which lists a number of undertakings and persons which are excluded from the scope of the Directive.[45]

The largest group of exclusions apply to firms providing investment services in particular circumstances. Firms which provide investment services exclusively for their parent undertakings, for their subsidiaries, or for other subsidiaries of their parent are excluded, for example, as they are not providing services for third parties (Article 2(2)(b)), as, for the same reason, are firms that provide investment services consisting exclusively in the administration of employee-participation schemes (Article 2(2)(d)) and firms engaging in both these activities (Article 2(2)(e)). Article 2(2)(g) excludes firms that may not hold clients' funds or securities (and thus may not place themselves in debt to their clients), who only engage in receiving and transmitting orders in transferable securities and units in collective-investment undertakings, who may transmit orders only to the specific counterparties listed in Article 2(2(g),[46] and whose activities are governed by rules or a code of ethics at national level. Finally, in this vein, under Article 2(2)(j), 'locals' or firms that provide investment services consisting exclusively in dealing for their own account on financial futures or options markets, or which deal for the accounts of other members of those markets, or make prices for them, and which are guaranteed by clearing members of the same markets are excluded from the scope of the ISD. Responsibility for ensuring the performance of contracts entered into by such firms must be assumed by clearing members of the same market.

Predictably, also excluded are persons providing investment services in an incidental manner in the course of a professional activity (such as solicitors) where that activity is regulated by legal or regulatory provisions or a code of ethics governing the profession, which provisions or codes do not exclude the provision of that service (Article 2(2)(c)). This provision is designed to take outside the ISD persons who do not, as part of their regular occupation

---

[44] An additional exclusion is contained in recital 8 which provides that the door-to-door selling of transferable securities is not covered by the ISD. It also excludes tied agents.

[45] Notably, neither the original nor the revised Commission proposal provided for a list of exclusions.

[46] The listed institutions are: firms authorized under the ISD; credit institutions authorized in accordance with the banking regime; branches of investment firms and credit institutions which are authorized in a third country and which are subject to and comply with prudential rules considered by the competent authorities to be at least as stringent as those laid down in the EC's investment-services or banking regime; collective-investment undertakings authorized under the law of a Member State to market units to the public and the managers of such undertakings; and investment companies with fixed capital (as defined in the 2nd Company Law Directive 77/91/EEC [1977] OJ L26/1), the securities of which are listed or dealt in on a regulated market in a Member State.

or business, engage in the provision of investment services to third parties on a professional basis. Article 2(2)(i) excludes from the scope of the ISD persons whose main business is trading in commodities amongst themselves or with producers or professional users of such products and who provide investment services only for such producers and professional users to the extent necessary for their main business.[47]

A significant exclusion relates to collective investment undertakings. Under Article 2(2)(h), whether co-ordinated at Community level or not, collective investment undertakings (undefined) are excluded from the ISD. Although collective investment undertakings which come within the scope of the UCITS Directive already benefit from a passport,[48] the exclusion also covers the depositaries and managers of collective investment undertakings. Failure to include management companies in the ISD placed them at a considerable disadvantage in the nascent single market for investment services and hindered the development of the single market for collective investment schemes. This gap is being closed by the new regime which amends the UCITS Directive to grant a passport to managers (section 9 below).

Insurance undertakings[49] which already benefit from a passport and are subject to authorization and supervision under the insurance directives, and do not in any event provide investment services 'on a professional basis', are excluded by Article 2(2)(a). Central banks of Member States and other national bodies performing similar functions and other bodies charged with or intervening in the management of the public debt are excluded by Article 2(2)(f).

Two exclusions relate to Member-State-specific situations. Under Article 2(2)(k) associations set up by Danish pension funds with the sole aim of managing the assets of the pensions funds which are members of such associations are excluded,[50] as are, under Article 2(2)(i), Italian *agenti di cambio*, regulated under the relevant Italian laws.

---

[47] Although the treatment of commodity dealers was highly controversial during the ISD negotiations with a number of Member States in favour of including commodity dealers within its scope (the Netherlands has, in its implementation of the ISD, included commodity derivatives within its revised system of investment-services regulation (Speigel, M, 'New Securities Litigation in the Netherlands' (1996) 11 *JIBL* 180)—other Member States to do the same include Spain and Ireland), their exclusion was retained at the insistence of the UK.

[48] Directive 85/611/EEC on the coordination of laws, regulations and administrative provisions relating to undertakings for collective investment in transferable securities [1985] OJ L375/3. See Ch. V.

[49] As defined in the 1st Non-life Insurance Directive (Directive 73/239/EEC [1973] OJ L228/3) or the 1st Life Assurance Directive (Directive 79/267/EEC [1979] OJ L63/1).

[50] As these associations only manage the assets and do not provide investment services to third parties, and as the pension funds are separately regulated in any event, subjecting these undertakings to the provisions of the ISD was thought to be unnecessary.

Finally, Article 2(4) addresses monetary policy activities and provides that the rights conferred by the ISD do not extend to the provision of services as counterparty to the State, the central bank, or other Member State national bodies performing similar functions in the pursuit of the monetary, exchange-rate, public debt, and reserves management policies of the Member State concerned.[51]

Under Article 2(3), the Commission was to report on the application of Article 2(2) in conjunction with the application of the list of services set out in Section A of the Annex, in the first instance by 31 December 1998 and at regular intervals thereafter and, where appropriate, propose amendments to the definitions of the exclusions and the services covered in light of the operation of the ISD. In its first report, although three Member States raised some queries about the correct interpretation of Article 2(2), the majority reported no difficulties in applying the exemptions or in relation to the scope of Article 2(2), leading the Commission to conclude that no specific amendments to either Article 2(2) or the list of services was necessary.[52] Nonetheless, two years later, in its ISD Communication, the Commission would find that the scope of the Article 2(2) and (4) exemptions was too wide and call for a reconsideration of their relevance (section 10 below).

VII.4 THE AUTHORIZATION PROCESS

VII.4.1 *Introduction*

The authorization conditions and procedure are at the heart of the ISD's investment-services regime, in terms of both its primary market-integration purpose and its complementary, if secondary, market-stability and investor-protection objectives. Generally, authorization controls and procedures act as a gateway to the market-place through which prospective market intermediaries such as investment firms must pass, and form a key component of most systems of securities regulation. The introduction by the ISD of harmonized minimum authorization requirements allows Member States to permit investment firms from other Member States to operate in their territories confident that the firm has been through an agreed vetting process designed to remove inappropriate persons from the market-place. Notwithstanding the ISD's stated primary objective of facilitating the integration of the single market in investment services by granting a passport to authorized investment firms, the core authorization provisions impose the authorization

---

[51] This provision seeks to ensure that the rights conferred on investment firms by the ISD are without prejudice to the right of Member States, central banks, and other national bodies performing similar functions to choose their counterparties on the basis of objective, non-discriminatory criteria: recital 25. This provision must now be considered in the context of EMU.

[52] 1998 ISD Report, n 30 above, 4.

requirement on all investment firms which are subject to the ISD, regardless of whether they intend to provide cross-border services or establish branches in other Member States. Accordingly, the ISD has a wider significance beyond market integration in that, for certain Member States, it imposed a new system of investment-firm regulation. The imposition of an authorization requirement and authorization conditions covering suitability, competence, and initial capital should reduce the risk of investors suffering loss due to illegal or incompetent behaviour by an investment firm or through the inadequate capitalization of a firm. Accordingly, although authorization is essentially the device upon which the passport mechanism is based and is a particular feature of investment-services regulation, its introduction on a mandatory harmonized basis for investment firms across the EC represents a considerable shift in regulatory direction for EC securities regulation, which hitherto had been based on disclosure-based regulation, as exemplified by the disclosure and admission-to-official-listing regime, towards a more interventionist approach to regulation.

VII.4.2 *Jurisdiction to Authorize and the Home Member State*

Article 3(1) provides that each Member State is to make access to the business of investment firms subject to authorization.[53] The authorization responsibility imposed on the Member State applies only to investment firms for which it is the 'home State'. Two tests apply to determine whether the Member State is an investment firm's home State. Where the firm is a natural person, the Member State in which the head office is situated is the home State (Article 1(6)(a)). Where the firm is a legal person, the home State is either the Member State in which the firm's registered office is situated or, if under its national law it has no registered office, the Member State in which its head office is situated.

The allocation of the authorization process to the home Member State opens up the possibility of regulatory arbitrage as the ISD is a minimum-standards directive. Home Member States may choose to impose authorization conditions and other controls within their remit at a higher level on their home firms. Investment firms may, as a result, have an incentive to incorporate in another jurisdiction in order to benefit from a more relaxed regulatory regime; although in all cases the ISD's minimum requirements will apply. The authorization process is subject to a number of checks

---

[53] Art. 30(1) contains the basic 'grandfathering provision' which, in order to ensure that adoption of the ISD did not trigger a reduction in the number of investment firms providing investment services, provided that investment firms already authorized in their home States to provide investment services before 31 Dec 1995 (the deadline for implementation of the ISD) were to be deemed to be authorized for the purposes of the ISD.

designed to provide a defence to this type of forum-shopping by investment firms.

In an attempt to prevent investment firms from opening up 'letter box' registered offices or head offices in order to evade stricter authorization standards in force in another Member State where the firm actually carries on all or the greater part of its activities, Article 3(2) requires that a legal person which, under its national law, has a registered office must have its head office in the same Member State as its registered office and that, where a registered-office requirement does not apply, the head office must be situated in the Member State in which the firm's authorization was issued and in which it actually carries on its business.[54] This requirement also attempts to ensure that the home Member State supervisor, as lead supervisor, can make contact easily with the firm's top management which will be involved in key decision-making and setting firm policy. Although it is a critical term for the purposes of identifying the home Member State and central to the letter-box avoidance system, 'head office' is not defined. Arguably, the term implies that a significant amount of firm management (such as personnel functions and risk management) as well as a considerable degree of high level, central decision-making occurs in the Member State in which the 'head office' is situated.[55]

In a similar vein, recital 4 provides that authorization should not be granted (or should be withdrawn) where factors such as the content of programmes of operations, the geographical distribution or the activities actually carried on indicate clearly that an investment firm is choosing the legal system of one Member State in order to evade the standards imposed by the Member State in which it intends to carry on or does carry on the greater part of its activities.[56] In practice, this means that operation within the investment services industry and business environment of the authorizing Member State is an authorization requirement.

[54] ECOSOC was sceptical about the inclusion of this provision, noting that it was 'up to the Commission and the Council to bring in such a degree of harmonisation that there is absolutely nothing to be gained from using a letter box company': n 4 above, para 2.9.

[55] A possible rationale for the failure to define the term can be found in the Council's common position on the Prudential Supervision Directive (see sect. 4.5 below), which, *inter alia*, applies the Art. 3(2) requirement to credit institutions and insurance companies. Rejecting the suggestion of the Parliament that 'head office' be defined, the Council stated that it would be inappropriate to use a rigid definition, as that would limit the range of factors which could be taken into account and could increase the scope for evading the provision [1994] OJ C213/29, Statement of the Council's Reasons, para III.3.

[56] In practice, there may well be occasions where a home Member State competent authority would choose not to authorize a firm where a large number of activities are carried on elsewhere, given the significant responsibilities imposed on the home-Member-State as lead regulator and, in particular, that home Member State compensation schemes (see Ch. X) must cover activities carried on in other Member States. This argument is made in respect of the parallel provision in the now consolidated BCD II in Dassesse *et al.*, n 21 above, 52–3.

VII.4.3 *Authorization Conditions: Minimum Initial Capital*

Under Article 3 authorization may not be granted unless the investment firm has sufficient initial capital as laid down in the CAD, having regard to the nature of the investment service in question.[57] This is a minimum requirement. Member States may adopt more stringent initial capital standards.

Minimum capital standards ensure that investment firms enter the market-place with sufficient financial resources.[58] Initial capital requirements should not, however, be so stringent as to deter competition and stultify the market-place itself by imposing unnecessary barriers to the entry of new firms. The CAD mediates between these concerns in Article 3 which sets out the minimum initial capital levels for trading for investment firms.[59]

The level applicable is a function of the activities which the investment firm undertakes and reflects the range of activities which an investment firm may be authorized to carry out, some of which do not require that the firm be subject to onerous capital requirements. An initial minimum capital of 125,000 euro is imposed by Article 3(1) where the firm does not deal for its own account, holds clients' money and/or securities,[60] and offers one or more of the following services: reception and transmission of investors' orders; execution of investors' orders; and individual portfolio management. Under Article 3(2), a Member State may reduce the 125,000 euro level to 50,000 euro where the investment firm is not authorized to hold clients' money or securities, to deal on its own account, or to underwrite on a firm-commitment basis. Finally, under Article 3(3), all other investment firms are subject to an initial minimum capital level of 730,000 euro.[61]

This minimum initial capital level for investment firms is lower than that required of credit institutions which engage in investment services[62] in

---

[57] The CAD also imposes detailed ongoing capital requirements on investment firms and is discussed in detail in Ch. VIII.

[58] They also filter out 'fly-by-night' operations by requiring that the owners of the investment firm have a direct financial stake in the business: 1998 IOSCO Principles, n 26 above, para 12.3.

[59] Art. 3 also sets out grandfathering provisions in Art. 3(5), (6), and (7) in respect of the capital requirements applicable to investment firms in existence before the application of the ISD.

[60] Competent authorities may permit an investment firm which executes investors' orders to hold the instruments in question for its own account where: such positions arise only as a result of the failure of the firm to match investors' orders precisely; the total market value of all such positions is subject to a ceiling of 15% of the firm's initial capital; such positions are incidental and provisional in nature and strictly limited to the time required to carry out the transaction in question; and the firm meets the risk-capital and large-exposure requirements set out in Art. 4 and Art. 5 of the CAD. This exemption is designed to reflect the reality that the operational rules of markets usually require orders to be made in homogenous, rounded amounts, which means that, at various times, brokers who would not otherwise do so, may be required to hold small, residual amounts of securities on their own accounts for short periods.

[61] A fourth level of 50,000 euro applies to certain specialized firms. Art. 3(4).

[62] Credit institutions are subject to a minimum initial capital level of 5 million euro under Art. 4 of the now consolidated BCD II (CBD, Art. 5).

recognition of the fact that investment firms are more specialized and carry out a narrower range of activities undertaken by credit institutions.

VII.4.4 *Authorization Conditions: Management Requirements*

Under Article 3(3), authorization may not be granted unless the persons who 'effectively direct the business' are of sufficiently good repute and sufficiently experienced. The imposition of reputation/suitability and experience requirements in order to ensure that investment firms are prudently and honestly managed is a standard feature of many systems of investment-services regulation. The ISD does not clarify, however, which members of the firm's management are subject to the test,[63] what is meant by 'of sufficiently good repute' or 'sufficiently experienced', or set out any benchmarks by which these requirements may be measured. The failure to set out the qualifications by which reputation and experience could be assessed led ECOSOC to conclude in its comments on the original proposal that the authorization conditions were insufficient.[64] This minimal approach arguably reveals the authorization process to be, primarily, an integration device designed to support the passport and liberalization rather than an investor-protection mechanism. While the basic authorization process is set at sufficiently detailed levels for the home-country-control and passport mechanism to be accepted by Member States, investor protection might have been better served by more detailed guidance on the application of the standards, given the wide variation in standards which may arise across the EC and, with liberalization, the ability of investors across the EC to access services provided by investment firms authorized in another Member State where lower authorization standards may apply than in their Member State of residence.[65] The authorization standards also omit certain principles. With the continuing professionalization of the investment-services industry and the proliferation of award-granting bodies,[66] a surprising omission is any requirement that managers possess appropriate professional

---

[63] Amendments recently proposed by the Commission to the fitness and propriety test which are designed to address the supervision of financial conglomerates would ensure that it applies to co-directors of the firm's business appointed in another legal entity and persons appointed in another legal entity who exercise a material influence on the direction of the firm's business. See Ch. VIII sect. 11.3 below.

[64] N 4 above, para 2.11.

[65] This problem is, however, simply an expression of the basic difficulty of using minimum standards in the investment services area. See Ch. VI sect. 6.4 above. Whether the EC could have adopted standards beyond the minimum required to operate the passport mechanism and remove obstacles to the freedom to provide services and to establish is, however, debatable. On the difficulties investor protection poses as a legislative objective see Ch. IX sect. 12 below.

[66] eg, the London Society of Investment Professionals (LSIP), an affiliate of the US Association of Investment Management and Research was established in London as recently as 1997: Riley, B, 'European Analysts in Retreat from Merger', *Financial Times*, 17 May 2000.

qualifications.[67] It may perhaps be explained by the fact that the ISD imposes authorization requirements only on those who direct the business of the firm and not on those employed by the investment firm and actually engaged in the provision of investment services. Although the effectiveness of authorization controls is dependent on a comprehensive review of the candidate for authorization, Article 3 does not require that the prospective investment firm provide the competent authority with biographical information on which an assessment can be made, although disclosure to the competent authority of a programme of operations is required. Confirmation of the Commission's unwillingness to revisit the fitness and propriety issue can be taken from its recent review of the supervision of financial conglomerates, in the course of which it stated that it was not of the view that further harmonization should be pursued, given, in particular, the benefits of having a flexible concept of 'fit and proper' which could adapt to different circumstances.[68]

The harmonization initiatives undertaken by FESCO may, however, result in considerable convergence in how competent authorities apply these authorization standards. It has adopted standards which are to be applied by FESCO members when assessing and monitoring fitness and propriety.[69] The standards are designed to improve mutual understanding of how the ISD's minimum standards apply and to establish agreed minimum standards for the assessment of fitness and propriety. Adoption of the standards was driven by the need to ensure the effective operation of the internal market and the protection of investors, investment firms, and markets. In particular, supervisors across the EC participating in FESCO were concerned that, in the absence of consistent supervisory practices and guidance on the ISD standards, there was a risk that investment firms which fail the 'fit and proper' test for authorization in one Member State were being authorized under a different Member State's regime and thereby obtaining a passport to operate across the EC.[70] FESCO's amplification of the ISD standards is based on the principle that the fit and proper test requires that the individuals subject to it are expected to meet high standards of personal integrity in all respects and to be competent and capable of performing the functions or role

---

[67] For a robust argument for testing and professional requirements see Gower, L, *Review of Investor Protection* (1982) paras 9.18–9.19.

[68] Towards an EU Directive on the Prudential Supervision of Financial Conglomerates. Consultation Document. MARKT/3021/2000 (the Financial Conglomerates Paper), 33. The Commission's July 2001 ISD Working Paper discussed in sect. 10.3.2 below does contain proposals to modernize the authorization process, but does not address the 'fit and proper' issue in any detail.

[69] FESCO, *European Standards on Fitness and Propriety to Provide Investment Services,* Apr 1999, 99-FESCO-A (the FESCO Standards). FESCO's standards are non-binding. On FESCO (now the Committee of European Securities Regulators) see Ch. XV sect. 2.5.2 below.

[70] Ibid, 2.

currently performed, or which it is proposed they should perform in the investment firm. It has recommended that the fit and proper requirement, which the ISD applies vaguely to those who 'effectively direct the business', be expected of directors (executive and non-executive), senior management (as defined by national law), and, significantly, officers and employees who carry out key functions (including those with power to commit the investment firm or to advise or trade on behalf of firm customers). FESCO has noted that not all competent authorities will apply the test directly to the last group but may require instead that their fitness and propriety are monitored by management. Its recommendations on the application of the fit and proper test also apply to qualifying shareholders (see section 4.5 below). To facilitate supervisors in applying this test, FESCO has suggested minimum information requirements which should be required of directors, senior managers and qualifying shareholders but has left it to the discretion of each supervisor whether face-to-face meetings are required. It has also suggested that failure to co-operate with the supervisor should be grounds for a refusal of authorization.

Standards apart, the ISD adopts the 'four-eyes' principle by requiring that the direction of a firm's business must be decided by at least two persons fulfilling the reputation and experience requirements. This requirement is designed to enhance investor protection by ensuring that, on an insolvency, the investment firm's assets are separated from those of its proprietors and by removing the particular risks attendant in having one individual directing the investment firm. Where an appropriate arrangement ensures the same result as the 'four-eyes' principle, competent authorities may authorize investment firms which are natural persons or, taking account of the nature and volume of their activities, legal persons, where such firms are managed by single natural persons in accordance with their articles of association and national laws.

VII.4.5 *Authorization Conditions: Organization and Shareholders*

The assessment of the firm also encompasses its organizational structure. Article 3(4) provides that a programme of operations which details the organizational structure of the investment firm and the type of business to be undertaken must be provided prior to authorization.[71]

---

[71] The FESCO Standards amplify Art. 3(4) and set out the basic information which must be contained in the business plan: ibid, 5. The FESCO Standards at 6 also cover the information required in respect of the firm's organizational structure. These requirements include: details of the management structure, division of responsibilities and operational procedures; internal controls and monitoring systems; operational requirements; outsourcing arrangements, where applicable; where the firm has a sole proprietor, the coverage provided to protect investors where the business ceases as a result of the proprietor's death, incapacity, or other similar event; and the appointment of compliance officers.

Authorization procedures typically extend beyond a review of the investment firm itself and its management to an assessment of those who can exercise control over or materially influence the investment firm. The ISD authorization procedure limits the extent of this wider review to an assessment of significant shareholders. Before a competent authority grants an authorization it must be informed of the identities of the shareholders or members, whether direct or indirect,[72] and whether natural or legal persons, that have qualifying holdings[73] and of the amount of those holdings (Article 4). Authorization must be refused if, taking into account the need to ensure the sound and prudent management of an investment firm, the competent authority is not satisfied about the suitability of the qualifying shareholders. The failure to define suitability is more serious in this context as while what constitutes suitability in the context of the managers of the investment firms might be broadly similar across all the Member States, the criteria against which the suitability of shareholders should be assessed are less clear and could lead to distortions in the way in which authorizations are granted across the EC.[74]

Apart from the review required of qualifying shareholders, prior to the adoption of the Prudential Supervision Directive,[75] ISD authorization procedures largely focused on the investment firm as an independent entity and, in particular, did not address the group (where relevant) within which the investment firm operates. With the adoption of the PSD, competent authorities are required to ensure, before authorization is granted, that the group structure within which the investment firm operates is sufficiently transparent such that

[72] Supervisors are accordingly required to look through the direct shareholder to the ultimate beneficial holder. The ultimate owners of the investment firm must, therefore, be identified prior to authorization.

[73] Qualifying holdings are (Art. 1(10)) direct or indirect holdings in an investment firm which represent 10% or more of the capital or of the voting rights or which make it possible to exercise a significant influence over management. Included in the calculation of the percentage of voting rights held are the voting rights listed in Art. 7 of Directive 88/627/EEC on the information to be published when a major holding in a listed company is acquired or disposed of [1988] OJ L348/62 (the SSD, now consolidated in the SCD). The qualifying holding requirement was a new one for many Member States.

[74] FESCO has recommended that where the shareholders are institutional or corporate entities, the annual reports and accounts should be reviewed: FESCO Standards, n 69 above, 7. Its recommendations on fitness and propriety are also applied to qualifying shareholders, although it has recommended that competence not be a factor for review where the shareholder is not involved in the management of the investment firm.

[75] Directive 95/26/EC amending Directives 77/780/EEC and 89/646/EEC in the field of credit institutions, Directives 73/239/EEC and 92/49/EEC in the field of non-life insurance, Directives 79/267/EEC and 92/96/EEC in the field of life assurance, Directive 93/22 in the field of investment firms and Directive 85/611/EEC in the field of undertakings for collective investment in transferable securities, with a view to reinforcing prudential supervision [1995] OJ L168/7 (the PSD). It was adopted as a consequence of the acknowledgement by the regulatory community in the wake of the catastrophic world-wide collapse of BCCI that financial-services supervision in the EC needed to be reinforced. It is discussed further below in the context of the ISD's information-exchange mechanisms (sect. 8) and in Ch. VIII.

the firm can be effectively supervised. Article 2(2) of the PSD introduces a new transparency-based provision to Article 3(3) which requires that, where 'close links' exist between an investment firm and other natural and legal persons, the competent authorities may grant authorization only if those links do not prevent the effective exercise of their supervisory functions; underlying this requirement is the concern that complex or opaque group structures could potentially raise problems for supervision. 'Close links' are defined as links where two or more natural or legal persons are linked by 'participation'[76] or 'control'.[77] Close links also exist under Article 2(2) where two or more natural or legal persons are permanently linked to one and the same person by a control relationship. Competent authorities must also refuse authorization if the laws, regulations, or administrative provisions of a non-Member State governing one or more natural or legal persons with which the undertaking has close links, or difficulties involved in their enforcement, prevent the effective exercise of their supervisory function. In order that they can effectively police these provisions, the competent authorities are empowered to require investment firms to supply them with the information they require to monitor compliance with these provisions on a continuous basis. Discretion is granted to the competent authority to decide what information can be required of investment firms. Despite the refinements made by the PSD, authorization for the purposes of the ISD remains possible without any assessment of the nature of the influence exercised by key employees (although widespread adoption of the FESCO Standards might bridge this gap) and major creditors which could, in certain circumstances, adversely effect the prudent management of the investment firm.

VII.4.6 *Authorization: Process and Protections*

In order to ensure that the nature and extent of the investment firm's authorization to access the market-place is clear, the authorization must specify the investment services listed in Section A of the Annex which the investment firm is authorized to provide (Article 3(1)). The authorization may

---

[76] Defined in Art. 2(1) of the PSD as the ownership, direct or by way of control, of 20% or more of the voting rights or capital of an undertaking. Acquisition of a temporary investment forming a significant proportion of the firm's capital will not constitute a participation, however, as long as the temporary nature of the investment does not make it possible to exercise influence over the structure or financial policy of the investment firm: PSD, recital 5.

[77] Defined extensively in Art. 2(1)(b) as encompassing the relationship between a parent undertaking and a subsidiary, as described in Art. 1(1) and (2) of the 7th Company Law Directive on consolidated accounts 83/349/EEC [1983] OJ L193/1 and similar relationships between any natural or legal person and an undertaking (for this definition see Ch. VIII sect. 9.5 below). The effect of this definition is to ensure that a control relationship exists whenever a Member State's legal regime requires the preparation of consolidated accounts. Art. 2(1)(b) also provides that a subsidiary undertaking of a subsidiary undertaking shall be considered to be a subsidiary of the parent undertaking which is at the head of both undertakings.

cover the provision of non-core investment services, but authorization, for the purposes of the ISD, may not be granted to investment firms which only engage in non-core services.

In certain circumstances, competent authorities are required to consult the competent authorities of other Member States before granting an authorization. Under Article 6 such consultation is required where the applicant is a subsidiary of an investment firm or credit institution authorized in another Member State, a subsidiary of a parent undertaking[78] of an investment firm or credit institution authorized in another Member State, or controlled[79] by the same natural or legal persons as control an investment firm or credit institution authorized in another Member State. This consultation requirement is designed to provide a bulwark against the regulatory arbitrage which could occur by an investment firm transferring the business of a parent in one Member State to a subsidiary in another Member State and thereby achieving the same result as transferring its registered office. The authorities of the parent may not veto the establishment of the subsidiary, although the Member State charged with the subsidiary's authorization would be required to take into account the Preamble's injunction on avoiding the stricter rules of a Member State which would normally apply.[80]

The authorization rules extend beyond setting minimum conditions for the grant of authorization and include procedural protections for applicants. Under Article 3(5), an applicant for authorization under the ISD must be informed within six months of the submission of a complete application whether or not authorization has been granted. Reasons must be given whenever an authorization is refused. Under Article 26, Member States are required to ensure that decisions taken in respect of investment firms under the national measures adopted in accordance with the ISD, including, accordingly, authorization decisions, must be subject to the right to apply to the courts. Investment firms must also have the right to apply to the courts where an authorization decision has not been made within six months of submission by the investment firm of an authorization application containing all the information required by the national provisions adopted by the Member State in accordance with the ISD.

---

[78] Parent undertaking and subsidiary are defined in Art. 1(11) and (12), respectively, by reference to the 7th Company Law Directive, n 77 above. This provision is likely to be restructured to reflect the growth of financial conglomerates and to require greater co-operation between competent authorities concerning the information required to assess qualifying shareholders and management: Ch. VIII sect. 11.3 below.

[79] Control is also defined by reference to Art. 1 of the 7th Company Law Directive, n 77 above.

[80] See the discussion in Cruikshank, C, 'Regulatory Arbitrage, Harmonization and Financial Innovation' in Jeunemaître, A (ed), *Financial Markets Regulation. A Practitioner's Perspective* (1997) 173, 176–7.

Competent authorities are also prevented from arbitrarily withdrawing authorization. Article 3(7) sets out the circumstances in which authorization may be withdrawn. Withdrawal may take place where the investment firm in question does not make use of the authorization within twelve months, expressly renounces the authorization or ceased to provide investment services more than six months previously, unless the Member State concerned has provided for authorization to lapse in such cases (Article 3(7)(a)). Withdrawal is also possible under Article 3(7)(b) where the authorization has been obtained by means of false statements or by any other irregular means. Withdrawal is, of course, permitted as a disciplinary measure. Article 3(7) provides for withdrawal in respect of failure to fulfil the conditions under which authorization was granted, failure to comply with the CAD and serious and systematic infringement of the prudential-regulation and conduct-supervision measures adopted by Member States under Articles 10 and 11 (Article 3(7)(c)–(e)). Finally, an authorization may be withdrawn in any of the cases where national law provides for withdrawal (Article 3(7)(f)).

VII.4.7 *Authorization: Relations with Third Countries*

Branches of investment firms which are authorized in third countries do not benefit from the freedom to provide services or to establish outside the Member State in which they are established and authorized and must, accordingly, be separately authorized in each Member State in which they operate.[81] In respect of both the commencing and carrying on of business by such branches, Member States must not, however, under Article 5 apply provisions which result in a more favourable treatment of branches of investment firms whose registered offices are outside the Community than that accorded to branches of investment firms whose registered offices are in a Member State.

Subsidiaries of third-country undertakings, which will, by definition, 'be formed in accordance with the law of a Member State' and have their registered offices in a Member State, as required by Article 48 EC before the freedoms to establish and to provide services are made available, may be granted authorization under the Directive and benefit from the ISD passport.[82] The

---

[81] Recital 30 confirms this position which arises from the Treaty. Art. 48EC provides that a legal person must either be formed in accordance with the laws of a Member State or have either its registered office, its central administration, or its principal place of business within the Community in order to benefit from the freedom to provide services and to establish.

[82] During the negotiations on the now consolidated BCD II reciprocity provisions, on which the ISD regime is closely based, the USA severely criticized the difference in treatment between branches and subsidiaries of US banks. It was made clear by the Commission that granting the BCD II passport to branches of US banks would imply recognition of the US banking licence as issuing a licence to a US branch would not ensure prudential regulation of the US parent of

ISD contains detailed provisions concerning the authorization of subsidiaries of investment firms which are authorized in third countries.[83] These provisions are designed to provide a flexible framework for assessing relationships with third countries and to ensure that Community investment firms are afforded reciprocal treatment in the third countries in question. The stated objective of the ISD in this respect is not to close Community financial markets, but to keep Community markets open to the rest of the world and to improve the liberalization of global financial markets (recital 31).

The third-country rules are based in the first instance on notification requirements, subsequently on negotiation procedures, and, finally, on enforcement measures. Competent authorities must inform the Commission when they authorize a firm which is a direct or indirect subsidiary of a parent undertaking which is governed by the law of a third country (Article 7(1)(a)). The notification must specify and describe the group structure to which the authorized investment firm belongs. Notification is also required where a parent undertaking acquires a holding in a Community investment firm which results in that firm becoming a subsidiary of the parent (Article 7(1)(b)). The Commission is then required to inform the Council accordingly.[84] In addition to the specific requirements imposed on competent authorities, more generally the Member States are required to inform the Commission of any general difficulties which their investment firms experience in establishing or providing services in any third country (Article 7(2)).

The supervision of third-country relations by the ISD is, however, predominantly the domain of the Commission. Under Article 7(3), the Commission is required to draw up periodic reports examining the treatment accorded to Community investment firms in third countries as regards establishment, the carrying on of investment services, and the acquisition of holdings in third-country investment firms. These reports are to be submitted to the Council together with any appropriate proposals. If, either on the basis of these reports or on the basis of other information, it appears to the Commission that a third country does not grant effective market access to

which the branch was a legally dependent element and of which it might form only a very small part, and that such mutual recognition was not possible as the USA did not recognise the EC licence. At that point the controversy died down: Bömcke, N, 'External Aspects of the Second Banking Directive' in Stuyck, J (ed), *Financial and Monetary Integration in the European Economic Community, Legal, Institutional and Economic Aspects* (1993) 95, 100. On US–EC tensions during the drafting of the reciprocity provisions see also Katz, S, 'The Second Banking Directive' 12 (1992) *YBEL* 249, 251–2.

[83] For an examination of the now consolidated BCD II reciprocity regime on which the ISD system is closely based see Scott, H, 'Reciprocity and the Second Banking Directive' in Cranston, n 1 above, 97.

[84] Art. 7(1) provides that the Council is to be informed 'until such time as a committee on transferable securities is set up by the Council acting on a proposal from the Commission'. The equivalent provisions under the banking regime, by contrast, provide for notification to the Banking Advisory Committee. On the Securities Committee question see Ch. XV sect. 2 below.

Community investment firms which is comparable to that granted by the Community to investment firms from that third country, the Commission may submit proposals to the Council with respect to engaging in negotiations to obtain comparable competitive opportunities for investment firms (Article 7(4)).[85] The Commission's mandate in respect of third-country relations also extends to supervising whether Community firms receive national treatment in third countries. Where it appears to the Commission (from the same sources) that Community investment firms in a third country are not granted national treatment which affords the firms the same competitive opportunities as are available to domestic investment firms, and that, in addition, the conditions of effective market access are not fulfilled, the Commission (this time without the need to acquire Council approval) 'may initiate negotiations in order to remedy the situation' (Article 7(5)). Ultimately, Member State competent authorities may, under Article 7(5), be required to limit or suspend their decisions with respect to pending authorization applications or acquisitions of holdings by direct or indirect parent undertakings governed by the law of the third country in question (Article 7(5)).[86] Where problems emerge in respect of either market access or national treatment, the Commission may, in order to be in a position to propose any Article 7(5) measures necessary, also require Member States to inform it of any applications for the authorization of any firms which are direct or indirect subsidiaries of a parent undertaking governed by the law of the third country in question and whenever the Member States are informed that such a parent undertaking proposes to acquire a holding in a Community investment firm which would result in the Community firm becoming its subsidiary (Article 7(6)).[87] Any measures taken under Article 7, however, must comply with the Community's obligations under any international agreements (bilateral or multilateral) governing the taking-up and pursuit of the business of investment firms (Article 7(7)).

[85] Although the ISD does not define what is meant by 'effective market access', in the context of the parallel provision in the now consolidated BCD II it has been noted that, as the sanction for not providing effective market access is simply the opening of negotiations by the Commission this provision does not represent significant dangers for third countries: Bömcke, n 82 above, 102.

[86] Failure to provide national treatment combined with market-access problems will therefore trigger more serious consequences for third countries, although the sanctions apply only to pending authorizations and do not provide for the revocation of authorizations already granted. This difference in treatment, combined with the fact that investment firms (including third-country subsidiaries) authorized by their home Member States before the implementation deadline for the ISD passed were deemed to be authorized for the purposes of the ISD, was a significant incentive for investment firms to avoid the reciprocity provisions by establishing subsidiaries in the EC before the implementation date passed.

[87] The disclosure obligation accordingly lapses as soon as agreement is reached with the third country or when any restrictive measures imposed in accordance with Art. 7(5) cease to apply.

VII.5 SINGLE-MARKET MAKING AND THE ISD PASSPORT

VII.5.1 *Authorization and Prudential Supervision*

Article 14, which is at the heart of the ISD's single-market construction mechanism, requires Member States to ensure that investment services (including core and non-core services)[88] may be provided within their territories either by the establishment of a branch[89] or under the freedom to provide services by any investment firm authorized and supervised by the competent authorities of another Member State in accordance with the Directive, provided that the services provided are covered by the authorization.[90]

In particular, Article 14(2) specifically prohibits Member States from making the establishment of a branch or the provision of investment services subject to any authorization requirement, to any requirement to provide endowment capital, or to any measure having equivalent effect. Article 3(1) dovetails with Article 14(2) by allocating jurisdiction to grant authorization to the competent authorities of the home Member State, as does Article 8(1), which requires the home Member State to ensure that investment firms which it has authorized comply at all times with the authorization conditions set out in Article 3(3). Accordingly, the provision by an investment firm of services subject to an authorization granted in accordance with the ISD must be permitted in the host Member State, even where the host Member State does not permit investment firms for which it is the home Member State to carry out those activities.

Authorization represents but one element of the regulation of investment firms. The ISD's single market-making mechanism extends beyond home-country-control and mutual recognition of authorization to ongoing regulation, and includes mutual recognition of the quality and suitability of supervision by the home Member State's competent authority. In terms of the ISD's priorities in harmonizing ongoing supervision requirements and bringing them within the scope of the ISD passport, the harmonization of prudential supervision requirements was deemed to be critical for the

[88] Although the use of a branch to provide non-core services only might be considered to be an abuse of the passport mechanism by analogy with recital 7 on foreign exchange activities.

[89] The ISD defines branch in Art. 1(8) as a place of business which is part of an investment firm, which has no legal personality, and which provides investment services in respect of which the investment firm has been authorized. All places of business set up in the same Member State by an investment firm which maintains its headquarters in another Member State are to be regarded as forming a single branch.

[90] Recital 3 reflects Art. 14(2) by stating that 'by virtue of mutual recognition, investment firms authorized in their home Member State may carry on any or all of the services covered by this Directive for which they have received authorization throughout the Community by establishing branches or under the freedom to provide services'.

stability of the single market in investment services.[91] The home Member State is, for example, required under Article 10 to draw up prudential rules which are to be observed by investment firms at all times, even when providing investment services in the host Member State (these cover: rules for the sound and prudent management of investment firms which include sound administrative and accounting procedures; rules on the protection of investors' ownership rights; rules on record-keeping; and rules on the avoidance of conflicts of interests), while the CAD sets out the capital adequacy framework. Accordingly, Article 8(3) provides that prudential supervision of an investment firm is to be the responsibility of the competent authorities of the home Member State, whether the investment firm establishes a branch or provides services in another Member State (although a special rule applies to conflict-of-interest management) while Article 8(2) specifies that the home competent authorities must ensure that the investment firms which they have authorized comply with the capital adequacy requirements set out in the CAD.[92]

The ISD passport and the parallel responsibilities of the home Member States cover, accordingly, authorization, supervision of ongoing compliance with authorization conditions, and prudential supervision, and harmonization in the area of ongoing supervision is, accordingly, limited to those areas.[93]

VII.5.2 *Restrictions on the Article 14 Passport*[94]

VII.5.2.1 *Article 14 Restrictions*

(a) *Identity of Passported Activities with Home-Member-State Authorization*

The mutual recognition applicable under Article 14 is restricted to services covered by an authorization from the home Member State. Investment firms

---

[91] Explanatory Memorandum to original proposal, n 3 above, 1–2.

[92] The prudential-supervision regime is discussed in Ch. VIII. For a discussion of the extent to which the prudential-supervision passport or mutual recognition is 'perfect' in so far as the host State's role in prudential supervision is ousted completely or whether it is perfect only where prudential rules are harmonised see Tison, n 9 above, 25–7. See also the Commission's Interpretative Communication on the freedom to provide services and the interest of the general good in the 2nd Banking Directive [1997] OJ C209/6 (the General Good Communication), 17.

[93] As explained in recital 3: 'the approach adopted is to effect only the essential harmonisation necessary and sufficient to ensure mutual recognition of authorization and prudential supervision systems'.

[94] Apart from the restrictions on the passport specifically set out in the ISD, the passporting firm could also possibly face restrictions from its home Member State with respect to exercising the passport. Although concerned on the facts with marketing rules and commodity derivatives (which are not harmonized by the ISD) Case C–384/93 *Alpine Investments v Minister van Financiën* [1995] ECR I–1141 confirms the general principle that restrictions on exporting services outside a Member State can amount to a breach of the Treaty unless they are justified under the general-good rule. See Lomnicka, E, 'The Single European Passport in Financial Services' in Rider, B, and Andenas, M (eds), *Developments in European Company Law vol 1, 1996* (1997) 181, 186.

whose activities in the host Member State fall outside the scope of the home-Member-State authorization or whose home-Member-State authorization covers activities which do not come within the scope of authorization under the ISD (as would be the case with investment firms which provide only advisory functions) will not benefit from the authorization passport in respect of those activities. Such firms will, of course, still benefit from the independent Treaty guarantees concerning the freedom to establish and the freedom to provide services.[95]

(b) *The Branch and Provision of Cross-border Services Limitation*

It is also clear from Article 14 that the benefit of the passport and mutual recognition of authorization is limited to where the firm is either establishing a branch or providing services on a cross-border basis. Where an investment firm provides services which come within the scope of the ISD in another Member State, but uses a subsidiary under the freedom to establish to do so, it will not benefit from mutual recognition of authorization, and will be subject to the authorization rules of the Member State in which the subsidiary is established, although that State is required to consult with the competent authorities of the parent undertaking's home Member State under Article 6.[96] Neither the ISD nor its preparatory materials reveal the reason for this discriminatory treatment of subsidiaries.[97] It may be that the differential treatment is a reflection of the fact that branches are the Commission's preferred vehicle for movement across the Community, given

[95] As is acknowledged by recital 28. Host Member States will be constrained by the general-good rule in applying rules which restrict the freedom to provide services and to establish. In particular, account must be taken of any authorization procedures or prudential rules to which the firm has been subject in its home State. Where these obligations track those set out in the ISD, it is unlikely that the general-good justification would be available, as its harmonization supposedly represents a codification of the general good. See Tison, n 9 above, 27 and the discussion in Cranston, R, and Hadjiemmanuil, C, 'Banking Integration in the European Community: The European Commission's Unfinished Agenda' in Norton, J, Andenas, M, and Footer, M (eds), *The Changing World of International Law in the Twenty-first Century* (1998) 341, 370–1.

[96] The point has been made that this discrimination in the application of the home-Member-State-control principle flies in the face of general Community law which, according to the Court of Justice in Case 270/83 *Commission v France* [1986] ECR 273, requires that Member States may not discriminate between the various form of establishment when imposing requirements on undertakings established in their territory, but with a State of origin in another Member State. See Usher, n 1 above, 94. See also the analysis in Van Gerven, W, 'The Second Banking Directive and the Case-law of the Court of Justice' (1990) 10 *YBEL* 61–2.

[97] In the context of the banking regime, it has been suggested that the distinction in treatment and the need for separate authorization can be justified on consumer-protection grounds as claims against a subsidiary may be brought only against the subsidiary and not, as in the case of branches, against the parent undertaking: Roth, W-H, 'General Introduction to the Second Banking Coordination Directive and the Proposal for a Directive on Investment Services' in Stuyck, n 82 above, 57, 74.

the economic inefficiencies involved with setting up subsidiaries. The fact remains that, for tax and commercial reasons, many investment firms will continue to operate in other Member States through subsidiaries, and that the denial of the passport to subsidiaries may weaken the practical effectiveness of the ISD as a market-integration measure.[98]

VII.5.2.2 *Establishment of a Branch in Combination with the Provision of Services under the Passport?*

The mutual-recognition-of-authorization procedures do not specify whether a passporting firm may both establish a branch and provide cross-border services in the same host Member State by relying on the ISD passport. As a result, it is not clear whether, where an investment firm has already established a branch in a host Member State, another branch of the investment firm established in a second host Member State or the head office of the firm in the home Member State is precluded from offering services on a cross-border basis in the first host Member State.[99] As outlined in Chapter VI,[100] however, despite a certain opaqueness in the case law, the Commission appears confident that such a prohibition does not exist under the Treaty.[101]

VII.5.3 *Relying on the Article 14 Passport: The Procedures*

VII.5.3.1 *Advance Requirements*

Although authorization becomes effective immediately (Article 3(6)), investment firms are subject to notification and review requirements before they can exercise the passport rights granted by Article 14. These requirements, the bureaucratic nature of which, particularly where the passport is used to exercise the freedom to provide cross-border services, seem to be at odds with the point of granting the passport in the first place,[102] vary depending on

---

[98] See generally Ashall, n 1 above, 100.

[99] On this question of formulation see Dassesse *et al.*, n 21, 56–7 who have noted, in the banking context, that there may be many commercial reasons relating to commercial organization, internal organization, and product range for why a credit institution may opt to provide certain services in a host Member State not through a branch which it has established in the host State but through its head office, or a branch in another Member State.

[100] See Ch. VI sect. 4.5 above.

[101] General Good Communication, n 92 above, 12. It did note, however, that, from a taxation and regulation perspective, the activities in question must be clearly connected to one of the two forms of operation. This point may go some way to addressing the observation which has been made that regulatory bodies may be unhappy with cumulation, given the greater difficulty in tracking activities carried out though the cross-border provision of services, particularly for tax purposes. See Dassesse, M, '1992: An EEC Update' [1991] *JIBFL* 384, 387.

[102] It has been observed that as 'Member States have prohibited the exercise of certain activities or the sale of certain products on their territory, alleging . . . that the notification procedure was not duly respected', the notification requirements have 'proved to be serious barriers to integration': Gros, D, and Lanoo, K, *The Euro Capital Markets* (2000) 35.

whether the passport rights are being exercised through the establishment of a branch or under the freedom to provide services.

VII.5.3.2 *Establishing a Branch*

When an investment firm wishes to establish a branch within the territory of another Member State a notification requirement arises under Article 17(1). Although, unlike its sister provision in respect of the provision of services the exact scope of which is bedevilled with uncertainties, this obligation has the merit of being relatively straightforward, it being reasonably clear under the ISD what constitutes establishment through a branch, the administrative burden represented by notification[103] jars somewhat with the underlying objectives of the ISD and its basis in the freedom to establish. Although it is not clear from either the ISD's preparatory materials or the Preamble what purpose the notification procedure is designed to serve (although notification is a feature of the passport structure generally—it also applies to the banking and insurance passport regimes), its potentially restrictive impact should be balanced against the benefits it brings to supervision and ensuring compliance with, in particular, the applicable host-Member-State rules.

The investment firm must first notify the competent authorities of the home Member State of its intention to establish in the host Member State (Article 17(1)—the grandfathering regime is set out in Article 30(3)). This apparently eccentric choice, the host Member State arguably being the State most immediately concerned by the investment firm's decision to establish in its territory, is a reflection, however, of the home Member State's position as primary supervisor. For the purposes of prudential supervision and enforcement, which are the concern of the home Member State, it is critical that the home Member State's competent authorities are made aware of the use of the passport by investment firms which they have authorized. In addition, the home Member State is required under Article 17(2) to ensure that every notification in respect of exercising the right to establish in another Member State details the Member State within which the firm intends to establish a branch, a programme of operations, including a description of the types of business envisaged and the organizational structure of the branch, the address in the host Member State from which documents can be obtained, and the names of those responsible for the management of the branch.

Exercise of the right to establish under the ISD passport is not automatic on supply of the relevant information. Article 17 allows the home Member State to prevent an investment firm from establishing a branch in another

[103] See Smits, J, 'Banking Regulation in a European Perspective' (1989) 1 *LIEI* 61, 70.

Member State under the ISD passport. The home competent authority must, within three months of its receipt of this information, communicate the information to the host Member State's competent authorities, together with details of any compensation scheme intended to protect the branch's investors, and inform the firm accordingly (Article 17(3)). Since the adoption of the ISD, Directive 97/9/EC on investor-compensation schemes has come into force and Article 12 of the ISD (which requires investment firms to inform investors of the scheme applicable or whether there is no cover) has been repealed. Directive 97/9 does not expressly repeal Article 17(3) which arguably continues to have the same importance, even though compensation schemes are now subject to harmonization, given that branch investors are, under Directive 97/7, protected by the home scheme. Notification would also dovetail with Directive 97/7's Article 10 information requirements. This communication of information acts as the initial trigger for the ability of the investment firm to establish in the host Member State, with the host Member State playing an essentially passive role in the process. The home competent authority may, however, refuse to communicate the information where there is reason to doubt the adequacy of the administrative structure or the financial situation of the firm, in each case taking into account the investment-services activities envisaged by the firm. Any refusal to communicate the information must be reasoned and the reasons communicated to the investment firm within three months of the home State's competent authority's receipt of the relevant information. Such refusals, together with failures to respond to investment firms within the three-month period, are subject to the right to apply to the courts of the home Member State. As refusals to notify the host competent authorities could severely prejudice the operation of the ISD passport, provision is made in the Directive to monitor the application of the refusal procedure under Article 19(1). Where the home Member State's authorities refuse to forward the notification, it appears that the investment firm could still attempt to establish a branch in the host Member State, subject to the non-discriminatory conditions imposed by the host Member States, as long as these were justified by reference to the general good. It seems unlikely that the refusal to forward the information could also have the draconian effect of preventing the investment firm from relying on the freedom to establish, which exists, in any event, independently of the ISD.

Before the investment firm may commence business, however, under Article 17(4) the host Member State's competent authorities have two months from their receipt of the information from the home competent authorities to prepare for the supervision of the firm and, where applicable, indicate the conditions, including the rules of conduct under which, in the interests of the general good, that business of the firm must be carried on in the host Member State (see section 6.2 below). It is only on receipt of a communication from the host Member State's competent authorities or, failing which, the expiry of the two-month period without receipt of any communication from the host competent authorities, that the branch may be established and commence business (Article 17(5)). Any change in the information which is required to be communicated to the home competent authorities under Article 17(2) must be notified in writing to the home and host competent authorities at least one month before the change is implemented (Article 17(6)). This month-long advance-notice procedure is provided to enable the home authorities to make a re-assessment of the administrative structure and financial situation of the firm (Article 17(7)). Similarly, the host authorities may, on receipt of written notice of the change, take a decision concerning supervision and the general-good rules applicable to the branch under Article 17(4). Changes in the details originally communicated in respect of the compensation schemes available for investors at the branch must also be communicated by the home Member State's competent authority to those of the host Member State (Article 17(7)).

VI.5.3.3 *Freedom to Provide Services*

(a) *The Article 18 Notification Problem*

Firms relying on the ISD passport to provide services on a cross-border basis are also subject to a notification regime under Article 18. Notification under Article 18 raises two difficulties in particular. First, the administrative burden posed by the notification procedure sits somewhat uneasily with the fundamental Treaty freedom to provide services. The tension between the Treaty and the notification procedure is even more apparent under Article 18 than under Article 17 as Member States usually impose less stringent regulation on firms providing services in their territory than on firms setting up a secondary establishment, and notification requirements are often not imposed.[104] An investment firm's presence in the host Member State is less intrusive and less permanent than the establishment of a branch, raising the question whether an additional notification requirement is necessary and what purpose it serves.[105] Secondly, the burden posed by the requirement

---

[104] See, eg, Smits, n 103, 72. See also Usher, n 1 above, 131.

[105] The preparatory materials do not reveal why this requirement was introduced. At the least it can be said that the notification requirement reflects the host Member State's powers (see sect. 6 below) and reinforces the ISD's supervision and co-operation procedures. A similar position was taken by ECOSOC in its comments at para 3.2.3.1 ([1996] OJ L204/44) on the Commission's Draft Communication on the freedom to provide services and the interest of the general good in the 2nd Banking Directive [1995] OJ C/291/7: 'the notification procedure enables national authorities to exercise supervision over foreign institutions operating on their territory, particularly with respect to [the] application of the rules adopted in the interest of the general good for the protection of consumers'.

to notify is exacerbated by the diffuse nature of the territorial trigger for notification. As notification is required when a service is provided 'within the territory of a Member State' for the first time, the question arises whether activities involving marginal contact with the host Member State, as would be the case with the provision of investment services via telecommunications, where the fact that the counterparty to the service/transaction in question is located there is the only real connection back to the host Member State, trigger the notification requirement. In fact, the Article 18 procedure has been identified as an obstacle to the integration of the wholesale market in investment services. Prior to the adoption of the ISD, the provision of investment services on a cross-border basis through telecommunications in the wholesale market was, for the most part, largely unregulated due to the experience of and resources available to participants in that market. With the adoption of the ISD, the extent to which the supply of investment services to a wholesale-market client or counterparty in another Member State came within the Article 18 notification obligation became a question of considerable practical significance. A failure to notify, albeit inadvertently where the investment firm may not have believed that the obligation had been triggered, might have exposed the investment firm to the risk that investors would seek to annul securities transactions where the market had, after execution, moved against the investor, on grounds of breach of the notification requirement.[106] Accordingly, risk-averse investment firms generally notified under Article 18 whether or not they were convinced they were carrying on business in the particular Member State. As well as amounting to an administrative burden, notification typically carried with it the application of the putative host Member State's conduct of business rules (see section 6.4 below), leading to costs for investment firms in the wholesale market.[107]

The Article 18 notification procedure is, however, less onerous than that imposed by Article 17. In particular, the home Member State is not given the power to prevent an investment firm from providing investment services under the freedom to provide services. While the investment firm is again subject to a requirement to communicate information to the home competent authority, the information required is limited to details about the Member State in which the firm intends to provide services and a pro-

---

[106] The obligation to notify under the banking regime was, in a number of cases, seized upon by clients of credit institutions to avoid their contractual obligations where the notification requirement was not complied with by the credit institution. See the analysis by Dassesse, M, 'The European Commission's Interpretative Communication on Freedom of Services and the General Good Under the Second Banking Directive' in Norton, J (ed), *1997 Yearbook of International Financial and Economic Law* (1999) 49. The Commission's position in the General Good Communication was that notification should not 'be considered a procedural condition affecting the validity of a banking contract': n 92 above, 9.

[107] See generally Welch, J, 'The Sophisticated Investor and the ISD' in Ferrarini, G, Hopt, K, and Wymeersch, E (eds), *Capital Markets in the Age of the Euro* (forthcoming).

gramme of operations, which must, in particular, set out the investment service or services the firm intends to provide. On communication of the particulars, or at the end of that month, although the ISD is not clear on this point, the investment-services firm may start to provide investment services in the host Member State.[108] The host Member State must, however, where applicable, communicate to the investment firm, on receipt of the particulars from the home competent authority, the conditions, including the rules of conduct imposed in the interests of the general good which the investment-services firm must comply with when providing services in the host Member State. The investment firm is also required to give advance written notice of any changes to the particulars communicated to the home and host competent authorities before implementing any such changes in order that the host competent authorities, in particular, can inform the investment firm of any changes to the conditions applicable to the firm in the host Member State as a result.

(b) *Carrying on Business Within the Territory of another Member State*

Notification is required only where the investment firm wishes to carry on business 'within the territory' of another Member State for the first time. As previously outlined, the provision of services through telecommunications raises difficulties in assessing whether services are provided 'within the territory' of another Member State where there is no physical connection to that Member State apart from the fact that the investor is resident in that Member State. The requirement to notify may appear superfluous where the main features of the investment service in question are to be carried out outside the investor's Member State. Factors such as whether the transaction is executed in the home Member State of the investment firm and whether it concerns home-Member-State investments also feed into the determination of the territory within which the service is provided. Changing one factor, such as where the security is admitted to trading or the place of settlement could potentially change the result.[109] The problem of whether or not notification is required can be further exacerbated where an investor from a Member State in which the investment firm has not previously operated initiates the relationship, through a telephone call or an e-mail. As solicitation of services by investors may become more common[110] if price competition

---

[108] Art. 18(2) provides that '[t]he competent authorities of the home Member State shall, within one month of receiving the information . . . forward it to the competent authorities of the host Member State. The investment firm may then start to provide the investment services in question in the host Member State.'

[109] Haines, P, 'The Investment Services Directive—Progress to Date' (1995) 2 *EFSL* 30, 31.

[110] Hertig, G, 'Imperfect Mutual Recognition for EC Financial Services' (1994) 14 *Int'l. Review of L and Econ.* 177, 183.

in investment services develops more fully across the EC than it has to date, the extent to which notification will be required in Member States in which the investor receiving the services is resident but where the investment firm has not previously operated, and where the transaction is carried out without any physical connection to the investor's Member State requires clarification.

(c) *Article 18 and the Commission's Approach*

Some light was thrown on the extent of the notification obligation by the Commission's General Good Communication which set out, *inter alia*, the Commission's position on the meaning of the phrase 'within the territory of another Member State' contained in the banking regime's services-notification mechanism—Article 20 of the BCD II (CBD, Article 21).[111] Since then, the context has changed again with the 2000 Commission Communication on the Application of Conduct of Business Rules under Article 11 of the Investment Services Directive[112] and the introduction of the principle of Member State of origin (or Member State of establishment) control by the E-commerce Directive (ECD).[113]

Although the General Good Communication is useful in interpreting Article 18, it addressed the banking regime and the position of credit institutions thereunder and can provide only an indication of the Commission's position on Article 18.[114] In a comment which could equally apply to the ISD, the Communication acknowledged that the banking services covered by the banking regime passport are 'difficult to pin down to a specific location . . . and are increasingly provided in an intangible form' and noted that '[t]he growth of distance services, particularly those using electronic means, will undoubtedly soon result in excessively strict criteria on location becoming obsolete'.[115] Indeed the possibility of abolishing the notification requirement if the procedure becomes obsolete with the growth in e-commerce was explicitly raised in the Communication. Until that occurs, the tenor of the Communication was to minimize the burdens created by the notification requirement. Its key finding was that for the purposes of triggering the

---

[111] See generally Dassesse, M, 'A Courageous Initiative and an Important Precedent, The Commission's Interpretative Communication on the Second Banking Directive: the Single Market in Financial Services May, At Long Last, Become a Reality' [1997] *JIBFL* 339 and Abrams, C, 'The Second Banking Directive and the Investment Services Directive: When and How Can the Single European Passport be Used for Cross Border Services' (1997) 4 *EFSL* 248.

[112] COM(2000)722 (the Art. 11 Communication).

[113] Directive 2000/31/EC on certain legal aspects of information society services, in particular electronic commerce, in the internal market [2000] OJ L178/1 (the ECD).

[114] More generally, the General Good Communication is not binding on the Member States and does not prejudge the view of the Court of Justice.

[115] N 92 above, 7.

Article 20 notification requirement, the place where the activities are carried out is to be determined by reference to the 'characteristic performance' of the service; the characteristic performance of a service is the 'essential supply for which payment is due'.[116] More specifically, the Communication provided that temporarily visiting a Member State will not trigger the notification procedure, as long as the visits do not involve the characteristic performance of a service. It also suggested that where the service is supplied to a recipient who has, in order to receive the service, gone in person to the Member State in which the credit institution is established, this does not amount to providing a service within the territory of the recipient's Member State, and notification is not required. The provision of distance banking services was specifically addressed, with the Commission finding that distance banking services cannot require prior notification as the supplier of distance services cannot be deemed to be providing a service within the territory of the recipient's Member State.[117] The characteristic performance device is a somewhat cumbersome one, however, which requires, as acknowledged by the Commission, a case-by-case analysis, making any decision by an investment firm not to notify a risky one.

The General Good Communication was not, however, favourably received in all quarters. Member States were not prepared to accept the 'characteristic performance' formula and continued to apply a variety of different approaches to the notification requirement, with some Member States applying the Commission's original solicitation test. The Article 11 Communication, which is discussed further in section 6.4.2 below, addressed how the 'Member State in which the service is provided' was to be determined for the purpose of the imposition of conduct-of-business rules. Adopting a bifurcated approach which is designed to ensure that the most appropriate regulatory regime applies in light of the particular investor protected by the conduct-of-business rules, it suggested that the home Member State was the State in which the cross-border service is provided for professional investors, while in the case of retail investors, the Member State in

[116] In 1995 the Commission circulated for comment a draft communication which relied instead on an assessment of whether the credit institution or the client originally solicited the services in question. Where the credit institution took the initiative, the service would be provided within the territory of the Member State of the client's residence and where the client made the initial approach, the service was to be viewed as provided within the Member State where the credit institution was located. This approach was criticized as being unworkable due to the difficulties in ascertaining whether and when solicitation had occurred.

[117] It is not entirely clear how this analysis fits with, or has since been overtaken by, the ECD. While the ECD submits investment services to the rules of the Member State of origin of the service provider, a derogation in the interests of consumer and investor protection is given to host Member States rules under Art. 3(4). In the event that internet services are not provided within the territory of another Member State, the basis for host-country intervention may seem precarious. The ECD approach chimes more easily with recent developments in the regulation of e-commerce, however.

which the investor is located was recommended. While the Article 11 Communication is an attempt to deal with one of the consequences of notification, the indiscriminate application of conduct-of-business rules, it does not expressly address the notification question but is grounded in the particular context of conduct regulation. The notification procedure, however, is not necessarily simply a function of investor protection, which underlies the Article 11 Communication. Notification requirements also apply in the banking and insurance areas where conduct regulation is not at issue. Indeed, in the General Good Communication, the Commission noted that notification under the BCD II 'pursues a simple objective of exchange of information between supervisory authorities and is not a consumer-protection measure'.[118] The ECD may increase the pressure to remove the notification requirement from those lobbying for its removal. Its governing principle, that the rules of the Member State of origin of the provider of the e-commerce-delivered service apply to those services (including investment services), certainly sets the scene for a regulatory environment unhindered by notification requirements, although, of course, it is concerned with a particular method of service delivery. The response to notification and its role in a telecommunications-driven market-place appears to be still evolving; notification is not addressed in the Communication on E-commerce and Financial Services. It is, however, covered in the ISD Working Paper, discussed in section 10.3.2 below.

VII.6 HOST-MEMBER-STATE CONTROL

VII.6.1 *Mutual Recognition Diluted*

The ISD does not articulate its underlying mutual-recognition principle so as to grant investment firms which rely on the passport complete freedom from the regulatory reach of the host Member States in which they operate. Mutual recognition is at its strongest in relation to authorization and prudential supervision, with the minimum harmonization ousting the host State's role. The inability of the EC to introduce minimum harmonized standards in all areas of ongoing supervision at the time of the ISD's adoption limited the extent to which home Member States could remain the exclusive regulator, however, and, accordingly, the extent to which investment firms exercising passport rights could be subject to one system of regulation. The host Member State is explicitly given jurisdiction in relation to conduct rules (Article 11), is permitted to impose its form and content advertising rules as long as they are justified in the interests of the general good (Article 13) and has a general residual jurisdiction to impose other legal or regulatory mea-

[118] N 92 above, 9.

sures in the interest of the general good (recital 33, Article 17(4), Article 18(2), and Article 19(5)). The repeated use throughout the ISD of the qualification that only those rules which are adopted in the interests of the 'general good' simply institutionalises in the ISD the underlying free-movement jurisprudence which limits the application of mutual recognition in the absence of harmonization, as the general-good justification may be more easily raised. Ultimately, the Court of Justice, through its 'general-good' jurisprudence is likely to play a significant role in demarcating the regulatory control which can be exercised beyond the home Member State.

VII.6.2 *General Residual Jurisdiction in the Interests of the General Good*

VII.6.2.1 *Scope under the ISD*

The ISD expressly builds into its allocation of jurisdiction between home and host Member States the residual general-good jurisdiction which all host Member States may exercise under the Treaty rules on the freedom to establish and the freedom to supply services. Authorization and prudential supervision do not qualify for the residual general-good jurisdiction, being harmonized by the ISD to reflect general-good interests.

Under Article 19(6) host Member States have the power to take enforcement action in respect of breaches of conduct rules adopted under Article 11 and 'other legal or regulatory provisions adopted in the interest of the general good'. Articles 17(4) and 18(2) both provide that a host Member State may indicate the conditions, including the rules of conduct, under which in the interests of the general good business may be carried out in the host State through the establishment of a branch or under which a investment firm may provide services under the freedom to provide services.

Recital 33 also contains a general reference to the general-good jurisdiction stating that 'Member States must ensure that there are no obstacles to prevent activities that receive mutual recognition from being carried on in the same manner as in the home Member State, as long as they do not conflict with laws and regulations protecting the general good in force in the host Member State'. Measures concerning the 'manner in which' an activity is carried out have been characterized, in the context of the provision of banking services under the banking regime, as 'product-related provisions' which regulate banking services as a product.[119] In the case of the investment services covered by the ISD, these measures would typically cover rules on commercial practices, such as advertising, which is already placed within the control of the host Member State subject to the general-good restriction.[120]

---

[119] Roth, n 97 above, 80–1.   [120] See Tison, n 9 above, 27.

VII.6.2.2 *The 'General Good' and the Court of Justice*[121]

Although the ISD does not define what is meant by the general good,[122] and, in particular, does not refer specifically to the case law of the Court of Justice, the consensus is that it refers to the general-good rule as developed by the Court.[123] The general-good device has been developed by the Court to allow Member States, once certain conditions are met, to impose measures on persons exercising the freedom to establish and the freedom to provide services, even where those requirements restrict the exercise of those freedoms, where important objectives are at stake. It allows the Court to mediate between the Community interest in ensuring that the fundamental Treaty protections of the freedom to establish and the freedom to provide services are not hindered by restrictive Member State rules and the interests of Member States in protecting important domestic interests such as, in the investment-services arena, the stability and integrity of their markets and the protection of investors. Investment firms subject to a restrictive rule imposed by a host Member State in accordance with its general-good jurisdiction may, notwithstanding that the Member State claims it to be in the interests of the general good, challenge that rule if it does not comply with the general-good jurisprudence of the Court. In this respect the general good is a device which restricts, rather than extends, a host Member State's power over passporting firms. The Court plays a central role in setting these limits to the power of host Member States to impose general-good rules on passporting firms; its general-good case law is discussed in Chapter VI.

The interaction between the general-good rule and the ISD illustrates how the Treaty rules and their supporting case law can be used to address failures in the harmonization regime. Although the Court generally takes a

---

[121] For an examination of the general-good rule in the context of the ISD see Tison, n 9 above, 22–36. The interplay between the concept of the general good as developed by the Court and the ISD's parallel general-good provisions in the banking regime has received considerable attention. See, eg, Van Gerven, n 96 above; Dassesse, n 111 above; Katz, n 82 above; and Björkland, M, 'The Scope of the General Good Notion in the Second EC Banking Directive According to Recent Case-Law' (1998) 9 *EBLRev.* 227.

[122] Addressing the reason for the failure to define the general good in the now consolidated BCD II, the Commission explained that 'in non-harmonised areas, the level of general good involved depends on the assessment of the Member States and can vary substantially from one country to another according to national traditions and the objectives of the Member States': General Good Communication, n 92 above, 15.

[123] In the General Good Communication, eg, the Commission stated that the lack of a definition of the general good and the failure of the BCD II to specify within what limits and under what conditions the host Member State may impose its general-good rules meant it was necessary to refer to the relevant case law of the Court: ibid, 15. There is no reason to suppose that a different approach is to be taken in relation to the parallel general-good provisions in the ISD. Giving host Member States sole authority to determine which of their rules could be applied to passporting investment firms in the interests of the general good would not only compromise the market-integration objectives at the core of the ISD, but fly in the face of general Community law.

robust approach to measures restrictive of financial services, in the absence of further harmonization, the general-good jurisdiction and the danger that it may be used as a veil for protectionist action nonetheless represents a significant obstacle to market integration.[124]

VII.6.2.3 *The Requirement to Notify Rules*

The difficulties which a passporting investment firm may otherwise face in isolating which of a host Member State's rules can be characterized as general-good rules, given the dynamic nature of the concept and its dependence on the evolving jurisprudence of the Court, are assuaged somewhat by the notification requirements set out in Articles 17(4) and 18(2) in respect of investment firms operating under the freedom to establish and the freedom to provide services, respectively. Under Article 17(4), the host Member State's competent authorities are required, 'if necessary', to indicate 'the conditions, including the rules of conduct, under which, in the interests of the general good', business is to be carried on in that Member State; this must be done before a branch of an investment firm commences business within its territory and within two months of receiving the information which the home Member State must send before the firm may establish a branch. Under Article 18(2), once the host Member State's competent authorities have received the information which the home competent authority is required to forward to them in relation to an investment firm which wishes to carry on business in the host Member State for the first time under the freedom to provide services, it must, 'where appropriate', indicate to the investment firm the conditions with which in the interests of the general good the providers of the investment services in question must comply.

The extent to which the notification obligation is a mandatory one is a potentially significant question, given that investment firms may otherwise find it difficult to establish the rules to which they are subject. The somewhat vague terms in which the notification obligation is couched suggest it is not a compulsory requirement. While Article 18(2) provides explicitly that notification be made to the investment firm, it is not clear from Article 17(4) to whom the notification is to be made. More significantly, the references to 'if necessary' in Article 17(4) and to 'where appropriate' in Article 18(2) could each be read as granting a discretion to host-Member-State authorities whether or not the rules should be notified. Support for the non-obligatory nature of the notification requirement can be taken from the General Good Communication which found, with respect to the parallel

---

[124] Lambrecht, P, and Haljan, D, 'Investor Protection and the European Directives Concerning Securities' in van Houtte, H (ed), *The Law of Cross-Border Securities Transactions* (1999) 257, 265. See also Wouters, J, 'Rules of Conflict, Foreign Investment Firms and the ECJ's Case Law on Services' (1993) 14 *The Company Lawyer* 195.

notification requirement contained in Article 19(4) of the BCD II (CBD, Article 20(4)) (in relation to credit institutions seeking to establish a branch in host Member States), that it was 'difficult to infer' that it imposed an obligation on the host Member State due to the qualification of the Article 19(4) requirement by the term 'if necessary'.[125] Also significant for notification under the ISD is the Commission's opinion that 'it would be inconceivable' that a failure to notify a general-good rule could result in the inability of the host Member State to enforce the measure against the credit institution.[126]

VII.6.3 *Host-Member-State Control and Advertising Rules*

Article 13 provides that while investment firms may advertise their services through all available means of communications in host Member States, they will be subject to any rules governing the form and content of such advertising adopted in the interest of the general good. Advertising rules covering the provision of investment services are accordingly not harmonized and may be imposed by host Member States as long as the general-good requirement is met. While it is clear from the context of Article 13 that host-Member-State advertising rules may be imposed, it is arguable that compliance by investment firms with home-Member-State rules in relation to advertising outside the Member State is also required by Article 13.[127]

VII.6.4 *Host-Member-State Control and Conduct-of-Business Rules*

VII.6.4.1 *The Article 11 Problem*

Of much greater complexity than Article 13 is the treatment by the ISD of the extent to which host Member States may, under Article 11, apply their conduct-of-business rules to passporting investment firms. In its original proposal, the Commission noted that such rules 'are not brought within the competence of the home-country authorities at this stage. At present there are considerable divergences between Member States in the content of such rules and the way in which they are applied. A considerable further effort of harmonization will be needed to permit the application of these rules to

---

[125] The Commission's dissatisfaction with Art. 19(4) is only too clear from its statement that 'the optional nature of notification by the host Member State of its general-good rules may constitute a risk to the exercise of the right of establishment. How can a credit institution know rules it has to observe if a Member State refuses to notify it of those rules? . . . The Commission will make every attempt to remedy the situation': n 92 above, 14.

[126] The extent to which failure to notify general-good rules means that the host Member State is estopped from enforcing those rules against a credit institution has been the subject of some discussion. See Dassesse. n 101 above, 385 and Katz, n 82 above, 262.

[127] Usher, n 1 above, 132.

pass under home-country control.'[128] Notwithstanding these difficulties, it was felt imperative, in the interests of sustaining and developing investor confidence in the single market in investment services, that some provision be made in respect of conduct-of-business regulation. The approach taken is set out in Article 11 which specifies in paragraph (2) that conduct-of-business regulation, in terms of implementation and compliance, remains within the jurisdiction of the State 'within which the service is provided'. The ISD does not simply specify which Member State has jurisdiction, however, but, in an uneasy compromise between minimum harmonization and home-country control (as is the case with prudential supervision) and no harmonization and host-country control (as is the case with advertising regulation) requires all Member States to ensure a conduct-of-business regime is in place and sets out the principles which must be reflected in these conduct regimes.[129]

In terms of operating the passport, the Article 11 combination of allocating jurisdiction to the State in which the service is provided and failing to harmonize the conduct rules covered by Article 11 in any detail creates, in principle at least, a fundamental difficulty for passporting investment firms and has been identified as a major weakness in the ISD. Investment firms are potentially subject to, at the moment, fifteen different interpretations of the general principles set out in Article 11 and the associated regulatory costs if they choose to provide investment services within all the Member States. The Commission's important Article 11 Communication revealed that while Member States' conduct regimes are broadly similar, particularly in their treatment of professional investors, considerable variations exist in relation to the best execution, churning, allotment, conflicts of interest, documentation rules, and execution-only requirements imposed with respect to transactions involving retail investors. Clearly, the complexities of this regime, together with the costs involved in complying with a series of different regimes in terms of adjusting internal systems to ensure compliance with different rules, difficulties in ascertaining what the applicable rules are where the relevant Member State does not specify which rules apply to passporting firms, translation burdens, and variations in the ways in which conduct rules may be enforced against investment firms by investors, potentially amount to significant obstructions to market integration.[130]

Apart from the multiplicity of conduct regimes possible, at the core of the Article 11 problem is that it does not clarify when an investment firm can

---

[128] Explanatory Memorandum to original proposal, n 3 above, 3.

[129] The substantive content of conduct regulation under the ISD is discussed in Ch. IX.

[130] For a discussion of how diverging conduct rules can raise compliance costs and cause conflicts between rules see generally Avougleas, E, 'The Harmonisation of Rules of Conduct in EU Financial Markets: Economic Analysis, Subsidiarity and Investor Protection' (2000) 6 *ELJ* 72, 76–85.

be deemed to provide services within a particular Member State and to be subject to its conduct-of-business regime. Article 11(2) does not specify whether a physical or territorial connection between the Member State in which the recipient of an investment service is located and the investment firm, such as the temporary presence of representatives of the investment firm, is necessary before that Member State can be characterized as the Member State in which the service is provided and its rules can apply. The distance supply of investment services through telecommunications raises questions as to whether a telephone call or an e-mail from an investment firm to a client in another Member State can trigger that other Member State's conduct rules. With respect to internet transactions, however, the adoption of the ECD (section 11 below) has clarified matters: the rules of the Member State of origin of the service provider (the State of establishment, which can include the State in which an investment firm has a branch), including conduct-of-business rules, will apply regardless of the condition of harmonization. Internet transactions aside, considerations relating to where the transaction is executed and settled can also feed into the determination of the place 'in which a service is provided' and could, theoretically at least, bring a number of other regimes into play. The extent to which the conduct rules of the Member State of a client who contacts the investment firm are triggered when the transaction is carried out without any physical connection to the client's State, and where the investment firm has not actively solicited the client, is unclear. Article 11(2) is also silent on whether a service can be characterized as provided in a Member State when that Member State is involved simply because the investor or service recipient has moved there from another Member State, in which the service has already been provided by the investment firm but the contractual relationship had not been terminated, perhaps due to the actions of the recipient, when the service recipient moved.[131] Finally, it is not entirely clear from Article 11 whether jurisdiction is given exclusively to the 'State in which the service is provided' or whether that State's rules apply in addition to the conduct rules of the investment firm's home Member State.[132]

As a result of these ambiguities, Member States apply a varying range of tests, ranging from the General Good Communication's characteristic performance formula to case-by-case systems, in order to assess whether their conduct-of-business rules apply in a given situation. In practice, a Member State's conduct rules are usually automatically applied when services are provided to investors located in the territory of that Member State, regardless of whether the service is provided on a temporary or permanent basis, even where the home country applies equivalent conduct rules, leading to

---

[131] Case 15/78 *Société Générale Alsacienne de Banque SA v Koestler* [1978] ECR 1971.
[132] For this analysis see Lomnicka, n 94 above, 191.

a complex and costly legal environment for investment firms.[133] The problem is exacerbated by the heavy supervision usually exercised by the home Member State in relation to, in particular, record-keeping. The Article 11 Communication reported that it is relatively rare for a Member State to interpret Article 11(2) such that it could result in a disapplication of its domestic investor-protection controls, finding that only two Member States operated an interpretation of Article 11(2) which could result in domestic rules being suspended.

This fundamental difficulty is aggravated by the failure of Member States to abide by the Article 11(1) requirement to tailor their conduct regimes to the professional or retail status of the investor involved.

VII.6.4.2 *The Article 11 Communication*

(a) *Purpose*

The Article 11 Communication attempted to clarify which Member State controls conduct-of-business regulation under the current regime. It also revealed the Commission's preference for moving conduct-of-business control to the home Member State, although this must now be viewed through the distorting lens of the ECD and the Member-State-of-origin option which has exploded onto the home/host-country control debate. The Communication was designed to 'suggest how conduct of business protection can be tailored to prevailing market reality . . . [and] outline a possible orientation for overcoming one of the main stumbling blocks to the operation of the ISD'.[134] It was stated not to impose new obligations or prejudge any interpretation which the Court might place on Article 11, but to represent a first step towards eventual revision of Article 11 as part of the process currently underway to update the ISD.

(b) *Retail Investors and Host Control*

The Communication, in an analysis heavily based on the general-good jurisprudence of the Court, took as its starting point the proposition that the Treaty and the ISD create a clear presumption in favour of the free provision of services on the basis of home-Member-State authorization. It also noted, however, the power of Member States to impose general-good rules under Articles 17(4) and 18(2) and found that this meant that host Member States wishing to impose conduct rules which extend beyond the minimal harmonization achieved by Article 11 can do so if it is in the interests of the general good. Relying on the recent case law of the Court with respect to general-good rules the Commission concluded that, in deciding whether to

---

[133] Art. 11 Communication, n 112 above, 3 and 10.   [134] Ibid, 5.

apply their conduct-of-business rules, host Member States could take into account 'whether or not the home State of the service provider implements conduct of business rules which offer equivalent protection and whether the imposition of conduct rules is a proportionate response to the preserving of the underlying "general good"'.[135] In assessing proportionality, the Commission went on to find that the need for investor protection was a possible criterion of assessment. In the case of retail investors, the Commission acknowledged that '[g]iven the present fragmented state of contractual and extra-contractual frameworks and enforcement systems, national administrators may have concerns about the exposure of their retail investors to legal uncertainty or counterparty risk'.[136] Accordingly, it concluded that, under Article 11(2), the investor's domestic regime be applied, as long as the Treaty free-movement rules and Community legislation were respected. The need for greater harmonization in this area was supported by the Commission, and, indeed, work on harmonizing the conduct standards applicable to the protection of retail investors is ongoing.[137] What is clear from the Communication is that the current state of conduct-of-business harmonization precludes a move away from host-country control.

(c) *Wholesale Investors and Home Control*

A different approach was suggested for wholesale investors, which was based on the Article 11(1) proviso that Member States are to apply their conduct rules to passporting firms 'in such a way as to take account of the professional nature of the person for whom the service is provided'.[138] Article 11(3) specifies that where an investment firm executes an order placed by another investment firm on behalf of an investor, the professional nature of the investor is to be assessed with respect to the investor from whom the order originates. This proviso is designed to protect the wholesale investment-services market against over-regulation and is based on the assumption that professional investors are less in need of regulatory protection due to their market experience, bargaining power, and the resources which they have at their disposal. Consideration of the professional nature of the

---

[135] Art. 11 Communication, n 112 above, 15.   [136] Ibid, 18.

[137] See sect. 10.3.2 below on the proposals for a conduct-of-business regime in the Commission's July 2001 ISD Working Paper and Ch. IX. In support of the move away from host-country control see the view of Gros and Lannoo that '[f]urther harmonisation in conduct-of-business rules in the ISD is required to ease cross-border provision of services. This would allow firms to provide services across under home country conduct-of-business rules, rather than under host rules': n 102 above, 130.

[138] Art. 11(1) reflects the general principle set out in recital 32 that investor-protection controls should take account of 'the different requirements for protection of various categories of investors and of their levels of professional expertise'. Differential treatment of retail and professional investors is a recurring theme in EC securities regulation. See further Ch. IX.

investor is not an exercise to be carried out at the discretion of the Member States. It is a binding obligation and must be carried out before the conduct rules in question are imposed on the investment firm.[139] A glaring anomaly in this proviso, given its importance to the wholesale markets and the connection between the integration of wholesale markets and the success of investment-services market integration generally, is the failure to define or even suggest what is meant by the 'professional nature' of the investor. This anomaly has had far-reaching consequences.

Clearly, inappropriate application of host-Member-State conduct rules has the potential to impede integration of the wholesale investment-services market and, in cases where Member States did not impose conduct-of-business rules prior to the adoption of the ISD, result in an increase in the regulatory requirements imposed on investment firms by host Member States. It has become strikingly apparent that compliance with the professional-investor limitation on Article 11 has been variable, in part due to failures by the Member States but also in part due to the absence of a uniform approach in the ISD towards the classification of professional investors. In its assessment of the wholesale investment-services market prior to the adoption of the FSAP the Commission noted that 'rigid and unqualified insistence on local trading rules leads to a patchwork of widely differing requirements'.[140] In the FSAP which followed the Commission found that, despite the professional-investor qualification, 'host country authorities are unwavering in applying their conduct of business rules'.[141] While most Member States tailor their conduct rules where the investors involved in a particular transaction are classed by the Member State as professional and, in practice, all Member States offer broadly equivalent protection to professional investors, a recurring problem in achieving appropriate application of conduct rules has been the varying interpretations taken by Member States to the central question of how professional investors can be distinguished from retail investors. Differences also exist with respect to the extent to which Member States permit investors to choose less rigorous protection and to which Member States apply different conduct rules according to the type of investment service or instrument. The problem is aggravated by the tendency, previously discussed, of Member States to apply their conduct regimes whenever an investor is located on their territory. Investment firms dealing with professional investors in the wholesale market may as a result be

---

[139] Cruikshank, C, 'Is There a Need to Harmonise Conduct of Business Rules' in Ferrarini, G (ed), *European Securities Markets. The Investment Services Directive and Beyond* (1998) 131, 134.

[140] Commission Communication on Financial Services: Building a Framework for Action, COM(1998)625 (the 1998 Communication) 9.

[141] Communication on Implementing the Framework for Financial Markets: Action Plan, COM(1999)232) (the FSAP) 4.

subject to widely varying conduct-of-business regimes in respect of similar transactions and counterparties.

The Article 11 Communication, which is heavily based on work on the categorization of investors carried out by FESCO, sought to tackle the professional-investor problem by giving guidance both on how the professional status of an investor could be assessed and on when services provided to a professional investor should be considered as being provided within a particular Member State. It first of all confirmed that the obligation to take into account the professional status of an investor is mandatory and is not conditional on the prior harmonization of conduct-of-business rules. While the Commission acknowledged that the ISD did not contain a clear definition of the professional nature of the investor, it did not take a direct position on this question, but recommended instead that the Member States implement the common definition agreed by FESCO for classifying professional investors.[142] FESCO's important paper on the classification of professional investors was designed, together with its complementary work on the standardization of conduct-of-business rules,[143] to increase the flow of financial services across the European Economic Area by making regulation more uniform and less prescriptive for professional investors. The FESCO definition has divided professional investors into three categories. The first category covers investors who are considered as professional without further formalities or checks by the firm providing the investment service. These are: entities required to be authorized to operate in the financial markets (including ISD-authorized investment firms and credit institutions authorized under the banking regime, insurance companies, and collective investment schemes); and sovereigns and international organisations (including national governments, central banks, and international or supranational institutions such as the IMF, the World Bank, the ECB, and similar organizations). While institutions in this category are automatically considered to be professional, they may request non-professional treatment and be subject to a higher level of protection. The second category consists of those large and institutional investors who may be treated as professional investors on request, but in respect of whom an investment firm should not assume the same level of knowledge and experience which would be expected of the investors in the first group. This second group includes large and institutional investors (including large companies and partnerships, institutional investors whose corporate purpose is to invest in financial instruments, commodity dealers, and issuers of listed instruments). It also includes other expert or sophisticated individual investors who may be treated as professional on request.

---

[142] FESCO, Categorisation of Investors for the Purpose of Conduct of Business Rules (2000). 00–FESCO A.

[143] FESCO, Standards and Rules for Harmonizing Core Conduct of Business Rules for Investor Protection. Consultative Paper (2001). Fesco/00-124b.

Categorization as a professional investor is subject to the investment firm being reasonably assured, in light of the investor's expertise and experience, that the investor can make independent investment decisions and assess risk. This assessment must be undertaken in accordance with specific quantitative criteria for assessing transaction experience, size of investment portfolio, and length of time the investor has been involved with the financial markets. Compliance with a number of procedural requirements, designed to ensure that the investor is aware of the consequences of being treated as a professional, is also required. In the event that the recent suggestions for the reform of the ISD put forward by the Commission for consultation are adopted a definition of the professional investor will be adopted as part of a revised ISD (section 10.3.2 below).

With respect to the related question of when a service provided to a professional investor can be regarded as being provided within a particular Member State, the Commission's position, which supports home-country control, was built upon the general analytical framework it proposed for Article 11(2). It suggested that, given the need to take into account whether the imposition of host-country rules was proportionate with respect to the investor's need for protection and the fact that all Member States offer comparable protection to professional investors, investment services provided to professional investors could be governed exclusively by the conduct-of-business regime of the home Member State of the investment-services provider.

(d) *Home, Host, or State of Origin?*

The tenor of the Article 11 Communication and more recent developments suggest that the Commission is pushing away from host-Member-State control for all conduct-of-business rules in the wholesale and retail sectors. Pointed references to movements towards greater harmonization in the Article 11 Communication and in the 2001 E-Commerce and Financial Services Communication[144] also indicate that conduct-of-business regulation will be moved from host Member State control when greater convergence has been achieved: currently, 'significant differences persist in the level of protection afforded [to] retail investors by national rules' which preclude any move away from host-country control, given that investors would be exposed to unfamiliar and possibly less stringent regimes than those in place in their Member States.[145] What is less clear is where conduct control is likely to end up. Traditionally, the choice has been between home and host States. The ECD will on its coming into force however, subject online

---

[144] Nn 112 and 38 above, at 18 and 12, respectively.
[145] E-Commerce and Financial Services Communication, n 38 above, 12.

conduct-of-business regulation, even in its current unharmonized state, to the control of the Member State in which the service provider is established. Attempts are made to protect investors exposed to unfamiliar regimes by means of the investor-protection derogation given to host Member States under Article 3(4). It remains to be seen whether the Member State of origin, which includes in practice the Member State from which a branch operates, will ultimately govern conduct-of-business regulation. The Article 11 Communication is couched in terms of the need for a future examination of the role of host Member States (as far as retail investors are concerned) and, of course, applies the home-Member-State principle to the wholesale sector. The influence of the ECD can be seen, however, in the inclusion of a specific reference to branches and the conclusion that '[t]he authorities in the country where the branch is established are best-placed to assume a front-line role for supervising the compliance of both categories of investor'.[146] In support of this conclusion the Article 11 Communication noted the requirement, set out in the context of Article 10's prudential conflict-of-interest rule, that 'where a branch is set up the organizational arrangements may not conflict with the rules of conduct laid down by the host Member State to cover conflicts of interest'. The E-Commerce and Financial Services Communication which followed in 2001 is more opaque. Although it strongly supported greater convergence of conduct-of-business standards, it referred to the need for a 'smooth transition to a home coun-try approach',[147] even though the ECD and the Article 11 Communication in combination suggest that home-country control of branches is not envis-aged. Elsewhere, however, it referred to the need for 'oversight of the firm/client relationship' to shift to the country of origin of the service provider.[148] A degree of resolution appears to have been reached in July 2001 with the ISD's Working Paper. While it remains to be seen whether it will survive in its current very early form, the suggestions canvassed in the Working Paper (discussed in section 10.3.2 and Chapter IX section 13.7 below) provide considerably more clarity in this complex area and suggest a treatment involving the branch Member State.

VII.6.4.3 *Imposition of Conduct Rules Limited by the General Good Restriction?*

The ISD does not specify whether a Member State with jurisdiction under Article 11(2) may apply all of its conduct rules or whether it may impose

---

[146] N 112 above, 19. This conclusion was reached as '[b]ranches in other Member States generally operate customer handing systems which are autonomous from that of the parent company. Supervisors in the country of the branch are on-site, have direct access to audit trail and record keeping of the branch and are better positioned to check the handling of the direct relationship between the branch and its clients.'

[147] N 38 above, 12.   [148] Ibid, 18.

only those which are in the interests of the general good. Article 11 does not explicitly refer to a general-good condition. The difficulty arises as a result of Articles 17(4) and 18(2) which require the host Member State to notify an investment firm which is exercising its ISD passport in that host Member State either through a branch (Article 17(4)) or under the freedom to provide services (Article 18(4)) of the conditions including the rules of conduct under which, in the interests of the general good, the branch must carry on its business or with which the service provider must comply in the host Member State. These provisions seem to indicate that conduct rules imposed on passporting firms by host Member States must be in the interests of the general good. Article 19(6), however, permits a host Member State to take appropriate measures to prevent or penalize irregularities committed within the host Member State which are contrary to the rules of conduct introduced under Article 11 'as well as . . . other regulatory provisions adopted in the interests of the general good'. This latter formula may suggests that conduct rules are not subject to a general-good limitation. The question therefore arises whether only those conduct rules which are in the general good may be imposed on passporting firms.

The preparatory legislative materials suggest that the Commission wished conduct rules to be subject to the general-good limitation. Article 13(1) of the original proposal[149] provided that host Member States could require compliance with legal provisions in force in the host Member State 'which are justified on the grounds of the general good'. As all restrictions on the freedom to establish and the freedom to provide services are subject to this general proviso, it seems that, as a matter of general EC law, the host State can impose those conduct rules which are justified in the interests of the general good.[150] This position has been endorsed by the Commission in its Article 11 Communication in respect of conduct rules which 'are more prescriptive than the minimal harmonisation of principles . . . achieved under Article 11'.[151]

Application of the general-good test to Article 11 is most likely to involve considerations of the extent to which investor protection interests (which appear to be the driving force for the inclusion of Article 11) can be constituted as 'general-good' interests (see further Chapter IX section 11 below). Given its very limited degree of harmonization, it is unlikely that Member States will be prevented from raising the general-good justification on the ground that the area is already harmonized.[152]

---

[149] N 3 above.

[150] See, eg, Wouters, n 124 above; Cruikshank, C,' The Investment Services Directive' in Wymeersch, n 1 above, 73, 75 and Tison. n 9 above, 30.

[151] N 112 above, 15.

[152] There is a considerable body of opinion to the effect that Art. 11 does not harmonize conduct-of-business regulation, but is designed to give Member States autonomy on how they implement their conduct regimes in light of local investor profiles and market conditions. See Ch. IX sect. 5.2.2 below.

VII.6.4.4 *Overlapping Rules*

The extent of the ability of host Member States to impose their conduct rules on passporting firms is further muddied by the overlap between prudential rules, which are subject to home control, and conduct-of-business rules.[153] Although both sets of rules can be distinguished in principle on the basis of their differing functions with respect to prudential organizational matters (Article 10) and protective transactional conduct matters (Article 11), the borderline between the two is not clear, given that one rule can serve both functions. The ISD itself has confused the area by classifying conflict-of-interest rules as both prudential rules (where they concern organizational issues) and conduct-of-business rules (where they manage conflicts which arise in the course of the investor/firm relationship and cannot be avoided by organizational controls), with the potential for a conflict of jurisdiction between the home Member State and the host Member State thus arising. Article 11 attempts to rationalize the overlap by providing that, in the case of a branch, the home-Member-State conflict-of-interest rules with respect to the organizational structure of the branch may not conflict with the host State's conflict-of-interest rules. The Commission has also highlighted an overlap between Articles 11 and 13, in that many Member States include advertising regulation in their conduct-of-business regime which can lead to confusion as Articles 13 and 11 follow different approaches in determining regulatory jurisdiction.[154]

VII.6.4.5 *Application to Non-core Services Where Appropriate*

A final problem with respect to the effectiveness of Article 11 concerns its application to non-core services. A host Member State may apply its conduct rules to a passporting firms when it engages in non-core activities, but only where it is appropriate to do so. The Directive does not specify what is meant by appropriate in these circumstances, leading to the possibility of vastly differing interpretations by the Member State and the imposition of varying burdens of regulation on passporting firms according to the Member State in which the service is provided. This is not a formula which accords with the Directive's market-integration objectives.

---

[153] Although it has recently been highlighted by the Art. 11 Communication which referred to 'complementarity and overlap in the application of Articles 10 and 11' (n 112 above, 8) this problem is not new. In its comments on the original proposal, ECOSOC was particularly concerned by the blurred boundary between the two sets of rules: n 4 above, para 1.5.1.

[154] Art. 11 Communication, n 112 above, 8.

VII.7 HOST-MEMBER-STATE CONTROL: REPORTING REQUIREMENTS AND THE ENFORCEMENT PROCESS

VII.7.1 *Reporting Requirements*

The reporting obligations which may be imposed on passporting investment firms are expressed in permissive rather than mandatory terms. Article 19(1) permits host Member States to require all investment firms which have branches in their territories 'to report periodically on their activities' in those host Member States to the host competent authorities, but only for statistical purposes. The extent of this reporting obligation is not clear from Article 19(1). The danger for the operation of the passport is that this reporting obligation, even for statistical purposes, could be onerous, particularly where the investment firm operates in several Member States.[155] More generally, in discharging their responsibilities under the ISD, under Article 19(2) Member States may require branches of investment firms in their territories to provide the same particulars as national investment firms. A similar requirement may be imposed under Article 19(2) on investment firms which operate in the host Member State under the freedom to provide services. In this case, the host Member State may require the investment firm to provide the information necessary to monitor compliance with the applicable rules of the host Member State. These reporting requirements may not, however, be more stringent than those which the host Member State imposes on established firms in order to monitor their compliance with its rules.

VII.7.2 *Enforcement and the Host Member State*

The mutual-recognition and home-Member-State-control structure is placed under some strain in the context of enforcement. While jurisdiction in respect of monitoring compliance with the ISD's rules is split, albeit unevenly, between the host and home Member States, the home Member State is the primary enforcer under the ISD. Given its role in conduct-of-business and general-good regulation the host Member State does have certain important enforcement powers in order to ensure compliance with these rules. Clearly, host Member States and their governments, accountable to a constituency of investors and protective of the financial stability and integrity of their financial systems, could not be required to surrender

---

[155] Specific reference is made in Art. 19(1) to the responsibilities of Member States in respect of their conduct of monetary policy. In connection with such obligations and for that purpose, host Member States may require all branches of investment firms within their territories to provide the same particulars as those required of national investment firms. This must now be read in the context of EMU.

enforcement powers in respect of violations of host rules committed by pass-porting firms in their territories.[156] Nonetheless, ensuring compliance with host-Member-State rules often requires the intervention of the home Member State's competent authority which may, through its contact with the head office and its knowledge of firm-wide practices, be in a better position to detect breaches and demand compliance.[157] Accordingly, as well as allocat-ing powers to take enforcement action, in the interests of effective supervi-sion the ISD also establishes co-operation and notification mechanisms which apply to the enforcement process.

The home Member State clearly enjoys enforcement powers in respect of breaches of the authorization conditions and violations of the prudential-supervision requirements (Article 8(1) and (3)). In particular, the home Member State may withdraw authorization where the investment firm no longer fulfils the authorization conditions, does not comply with the capital-adequacy requirements of the CAD or seriously and systematically infringes the prudential rules adopted under Article 10 (Article 3(7)(d) and (e)). The home Member State may also withdraw authorization, however, where the investment firm seriously and systematically infringes the conduct rules adopted under Article 11 (Article 3(7)(e)). It appears that this power is also granted in respect of violations of Article 11 which are committed outside the home Member State. The effectiveness of the withdrawal power is, of course, dependent on co-operative action being taken by the host competent authority to prevent the firm from operating in its territory. Under Article 19(9), where an authorization is withdrawn, the host Member State's com-petent authority must be informed, following which it must take appropri-ate measures to prevent the investment firm from initiating further transactions within its territory.

Of critical importance, however, is the allocation of enforcement powers between the home and host Member States in respect of violations of host-Member-State rules. Article 19 sets out a series of rules for determining this allocation of enforcement powers. As a general rule, the home Member State is the lead enforcer in respect of breaches of the rules applicable in the host Member State. In this respect, Article 19(3) provides that where the com-petent authorities of a host Member State find that an investment firm that has a branch or provides investment services in its territory is in breach of 'the legal or regulatory provisions adopted in that State pursuant to those provisions of the Directive which confer powers on the host Member State's

---

[156] Recital 41 notes that 'the stability and sound operation of the financial system and the protection of investors presuppose that a host Member State has the right and the responsibil-ity both to prevent and to penalize any action within its territory by investment firms contrary to the rules of conduct and other legal or regulatory provisions it has adopted in the interest of the general good and to take action in emergencies'.

[157] See Biancheri, C, 'Cooperation Among Supervisory Authorities under the ISD' in Ferrarini, n 139 above, 363, 363.

competent authorities', it shall require the firm to put an end to the irregular situation. If the investment firm fails to take the necessary corrective action, under Article 19(4) the host competent authorities are to inform the home competent authorities accordingly, and the latter must, at the earliest opportunity, 'take all appropriate measures' to ensure that the investment firm puts an end to its irregular situation. Consistently with the theme of co-operation that underlies the ISD's approach to relations between home and host Member States, the home competent authority must inform the host competent authority of the nature of the measures which it takes. In the event that the measures taken by the home Member State do not induce the investment firm to remedy the situation (or where the measures taken are inadequate or are not available in the host Member State)[158] the host Member State may then step in (Article 19(5)). Having informed the competent authorities of the home Member State, it may take 'appropriate measures' to prevent or penalize further irregularities and, so far as necessary, to prevent the investment firm from initiating any further transactions within its territory. Host Member States must be permitted to serve legal documents necessary for the imposition of such measures in other Member States (Article 19(5)). In parallel with this procedure, however, in cases of emergency the host Member State may, before taking any of these steps, take any precautionary measures necessary for the protection of investors and others to whom the service is provided, but the Commission and the competent authorities of any other Member State involved must be informed of the measures at the earliest opportunity (Article 19(8)).[159] One other strand to the enforcement powers of host Member States can be isolated in the ISD. The co-operation procedure and the requirement imposed on the host Member State to defer, in the first instance, to measures taken by the home Member State do not affect the general power expressed in Article 19(6) of host Member States to take 'appropriate measures'[160] to prevent or penalize irregularities committed within their territories which are contrary to the Article 11 conduct rules and any provisions adopted in the general

[158] With the exception of Art. 19(9) which requires the host Member State to take appropriate measures to prevent an investment firm whose authorization has been withdrawn by the home Member State 'from initiating any further transactions within its territory and to safeguard investors' interests', the ISD does not contain any specific provisions (apart from the general obligation set out in Art. 23(3) to 'collaborate closely in order more effectively to discharge [the competent authorities'] respective responsibilities') designed to ensure that the measures adopted by the home competent authorities actually take effect in the host Member State.

[159] Discriminatory or protectionist use of this power is guarded against by the power given to the Commission, after consultation with the competent authorities of the other Member States concerned, to require that the host Member State abolish or amend the measures. It appears, however, that divergences have opened up between the Member States in their interpretations of Art. 19(8) which have been identified by the Commission in its ISD Communication as weakening the effectiveness of the ISD. See below sect. 10.3 below.

[160] Art. 19(6) specifies that these measures may include preventing the investment firm from initiating any further transactions within host Member States' territories.

good. The general-good restriction on Article 19(6) precludes its application
to questions of authorization and prudential supervision. The host Member
State's competent authority is not required to inform the home Member
State's competent authority before it imposes measures under Article 19(6).
Under the co-operation requirement set out in Article 23(3), however, and
only 'in so far as it is necessary for the purposes of exercising their powers
of supervision', home Member States' competent authorities are to be
informed by the host Member State's competent authorities of any measures
taken by the latter under Article 19(6) which involve the imposition of
penalties on the investment firm or restrictions on an investment firm's
activities.

Both host and home Member States are subject to the requirement that
any enforcement measures taken under the procedures outlined above
(apart from Article 19(8) measures) which involve penalties or restrictions
on the activities of an investment firm must be properly justified and communicated to the investment firm concerned, and subject to the right to the
apply to the courts in the Member State which adopted them (Article 19(7)).

VII.8 SUPERVISION OF THE LIBERALIZED MARKET-PLACE[161]

VII.8.1 *The ISD Supervisory Framework*

Critical to the success of the ISD passport and its home-Member-State-driven
supervisory framework was the establishment of an institutional supervisory
structure to police the ISD's authorization mechanism and ongoing control
structure and manage cross-border investment services activity in the
liberalized market-place.[162] In particular, the effective management of all
authorization and prudential supervision from the home Member State
demanded a high degree of institutionalised supervisory co-ordination and
co-operation. The ISD's supervision structure is based on a network of competent authorities. This network is responsible under the ISD for authorizing
investment firms, for supervising both the operation of the passport and the
integrity of the single market in investment services it constructs, and for
ensuring the effectiveness of the supervisory framework by supervising and
enforcing rules according to the division of responsibilities set out in the ISD,
and by following co-operation and consultation procedures. The supervisory
framework is based on a number of elements: the designation of competent
authorities in each Member State responsible for supervision; the allocation
of regulatory jurisdiction and enforcement powers between Member States in

---

[161] See generally Biancheri, n 157 above.

[162] Supervision is also discussed in the context of the supervision superstructure applicable
to the EC investment-services and securities market generally in Ch. XV sect. 3 below.

order to deal with particular events; and the establishment of co-operation and consultation mechanisms, primarily based on the information-exchange mechanism, which are the *sine qua non* of supervisory co-operation.[163] Although the ISD's supervision structure is decentralized, and, arguably, inherently unstable, particularly in light of deepening market integration, the ISD's supervisory mechanisms have been credited with triggering some convergence of regulatory and supervisory practices.[164]

VII.8.2 *Competent Authorities*

Article 22(1) requires Member States to designate and inform the Commission of the competent authorities which are to carry out the duties provided for in the ISD, indicating, where necessary, where duties are divided between authorities. The requirement to designate and, where necessary, establish regulatory authorities was essential for the success of the passport. More generally, it also formalised investment-services supervision across the single market. Considerable latitude is given to the Member States in respect of the form taken by the designated competent authorities by Article 22(2). Competent authorities can be constituted as either: public authorities; bodies recognized by national law; or bodies recognized by public authorities expressly empowered for that purpose by national law.

While the ISD does not specify the particular powers (investigatory, enforcement, or remedial) which a competent authority must be able to wield when fulfilling its duties under the ISD, it must, under Article 22(3), have 'all the powers necessary for the performance of [its] functions'. Enforcement powers are given particular, if non-specific, attention, with Member States being required under Article 27 to ensure that their competent authorities may adopt or impose on investment firms, and those who control their business, measures or penalties which are designed to prevent and end violations of laws concerning the supervision and carrying on of activities by investment firms. It is clear from Article 3(7) that competent authorities must, at a minimum, have the power to withdraw authorizations.

Whatever information-retrieval powers are granted under national law, all competent authorities benefit from the 'whistle-blowing' duty imposed on statutory auditors[165] by the new Article 25a(1) (added by the

---

[163] Financial Conglomerates Paper, n 68 above, 35.

[164] ISD Communication, n 34 above, 8.

[165] The duty is imposed on 'any person authorized within the meaning of Directive 84/253/EEC, performing in a financial undertaking the task described in Article 51 of Directive 78/660/EEC, Article 37 of Directive 83/349/EEC or Article 31 of Directive 85/611/EEC or any other statutory task'. Directive 84/253/EEC [1984] OJ L126/20, is the 8th Company Law Directive on statutory auditors and sets out the conditions under which statutory auditors are to be approved. The task referred to in Arts. 51, 37 and 31 of the relevant directives is the auditing of accounts.

PSD)[166] to 'report promptly' to the competent authorities any fact or decision concerning the investment firm of which they have become aware and
which is liable to constitute a material breach of the authorization conditions or the rules specifically applicable to the conduct of the investment
firm's activities, affect the continuous functioning of the investment firm, or
lead to either a refusal to certify or a reservation concerning the
accounts.[167] The original proposal also included facts which were likely to
'imperil the protection of clients'.[168] Given the PSD's specific focus on prudential supervision rather than on protective investor protection the removal
of this ground for 'whistle-blowing' is not entirely surprising, although it
does provide an illustration of the overall imbalance in the EC regime
between prudential and protective supervision discussed in later chapters.[169]
As a result of their special access to financial information, statutory auditors
are thus formally brought into the supervisory and enforcement framework
as supplementary watchdogs who can provide the competent authorities
which wield supervisory and enforcement powers with valuable information.[170] Statutory auditors who make this disclosure in good faith are protected from liability by Article 25(a)(2).

Where there are two or more competent authorities in the same Member
State, they are required under Article 23(1) to collaborate closely in supervising the activities of investment firms operating in that Member State. The
increasing tendency among financial-market participants to undertake a wide
variety of functions and the need for effective supervision to respond to the
proliferation of financial conglomerates is acknowledged by Article 23(2),
which requires Member States to ensure that collaboration takes place
between the competent authorities and the public authorities responsible for
the supervision of financial markets, credit and other financial institutions,
and insurance undertakings, as regard the entities those authorities supervise.

---

[166] This provision is one of the elements introduced to strengthen prudential supervision and
promote systemic stability.

[167] This whistle-blowing duty extends to similar facts or decisions in respect of an undertaking having close links resulting from a control relationship with the investment firm.

[168] [1993] OJ C229/10. Also included were facts likely to impair development gravely or
which indicated that principles of sound management had been seriously violated.

[169] Recital 15 to the PSD does, however, refer to the whistle-blowing device as being
required 'for the purpose of strengthening the prudential supervision of financial undertakings
and protection of clients of financial undertakings'.

[170] The preparatory materials reveal considerable nervousness about the consequences of
imposing a whistle-blowing duty on auditors. In its comments on the original proposal, ECOSOC
was concerned that the duty brought into play a conflict between auditors as being responsible to shareholders and their increasing use as an arm of the supervisory structure, and called
for a comprehensive review of their professional obligations and to whom they were responsible, and for a code of practice to assist auditors in deciding when to report to the competent
authorities [1994] OJ C91/61 paras 2.4 and 3.6.2. Similarly, the Council in its Common
Position noted that precise criteria were required to define exactly when a report was required
[1994] OJ C213/29: Statement of the Council's Reasons, para III, 5.

VII.8.3 *Co-operation Between Competent Authorities*

Important general principles concerning co-operation between home and host competent authorities, which are designed to facilitate effective execution by the competent authorities of their respective supervision and enforcement responsibilities, are set out in Articles 23 and 24. These general principles, together with the enforcement and supervision jurisdiction allocation system, are essential for preserving investor protection and market integrity across the integrated investment-services market and its decentralized supervisory structure.[171] They have, to a large extent, obviated the need for the conclusion of Memoranda of Understanding, which usually set out the framework within which supervisory authorities co-operate, between competent authorities.

The core requirement, set out in Article 23(1), is that all the competent authorities concerned with the provision of investment services by an investment firm collaborate closely in order to discharge more effectively their respective responsibilities under the ISD. In particular, they are to supply one another on request with all the information concerning the management and ownership of the relevant investment firm that is likely to facilitate their supervision, as well with all information likely to facilitate the monitoring of such firms.[172] Article 6, which requires home-Member-State competent authorities, in specified circumstances, to consult with the competent authorities of other Member States prior to granting authorization is an illustration of this general principle. Consultation requirements also apply with respect to the ISD's shareholder-notification provisions.[173] As a practical matter, Article 24(1) facilitates the effective exercise of home-Member-State supervision by requiring each host Member State to ensure that, where an investment firm is operating in its territory through a branch, the home Member State's competent authorities may either themselves, or through an intermediary, carry out on-the-spot verifications of the information they require to discharge their supervision responsibilities.[174] Unusually, the ISD neither provides for joint inspections nor sets out the procedures to be followed in the conduct of inspections, although both of these areas are often

[171] ISD Communication, n 34 above, 8.

[172] eg, FESCO has pointed to the need for effective information exchange in order to ensure the effective supervision of an investment firm's initial and ongoing compliance with the fit-and-proper standards as it evolves and its business develops: FESCO Standards, n 69 above, 2 and 9. The standards are designed in part to strengthen the arrangements for co-operation and sharing of information on firms and individuals.

[173] Discussed in Ch. VIII sect. 7.2 below.

[174] The introduction of the parallel power in the banking regime in 1989 marked a significant departure from the general principle of international law that the operations of administrative agencies, such as competent authorities, are limited to activities carried out in the territory of the agencies' State: Roth, n 97 above, 65.

covered in co-operation agreements between supervisors.[175] Alternatively the home Member State's competent authorities may request the competent authorities of the host Member State to carry out such a verification.[176] Host competent authorities may also carry out on-the-spot verification of branches established in their territory for the purposes of discharging their responsibilities under the ISD (Article 24(3)).

General principles of co-operation aside, the ISD specifically addresses the position of the host Member State and its information requirements. The core questions of authorization and its withdrawal are addressed by Article 19(9), which requires that in the event of a withdrawal of authorization the competent authorities of the host Member State be informed. The host Member State is then required to take appropriate measures to prevent the investment firm from initiating any further transactions in its territory and to safeguard investors' interests. Additionally, Articles 18 and 19 set out the particular information-exchange procedures which must be followed when an investment firm exercises its passport rights in another Member State. Indeed, the philosophy underlying the relationship between the dominant home Member State's supervisor and the host Member State can be illustrated by the view that, while it is not specifically mentioned in the ISD, the co-operation procedures may be read to provide that the home Member State is required to inform the host Member State whenever it detects a problem with an investment firm operating within the territory of the host Member State.[177]

VII.8.4 *The Information Gateways*

Ensuring effective co-operation between supervisors meant that the traditional confidentiality restrictions imposed on such authorities had to be addressed by the ISD.

Professional-secrecy requirements are imposed on competent authorities' employees and ex-employees and on auditors and other experts instructed by the competent authorities by Article 25(1) which, in essence, prohibits such persons from divulging confidential information received in the course of their duties to any person or any authority whatsoever, without prejudice to cases covered by criminal law. Confidential information may be disclosed, however, as long as it is in summary or aggregate form so that individual investment firms cannot be identified from the disclosure.

---

[175] See Biancheri, n 157 above, 368. For a discussion of Memoranda of Understanding see Bergsträsser, S, 'Cooperation Between Supervisors' in Ferrarini, n 139 above, 373, 376–8.

[176] Art. 24(2). If a competent authority receives such a request, it must either act upon it itself, allow the requesting authority to carry out the verification, or allow auditors or other experts to do so.

[177] Biancheri, n 157 above, 367.

Overly rigorous confidentiality requirements, however, risk prejudicing effective supervision and communication between supervisors, in particular where an investment firm is part of a wider group involved in a range of regulated financial activities and operates across several Member States. Accordingly, the ISD provides for information exchange in particular circumstances by nominating a series of specified 'gateways' through which otherwise confidential material can be passed.

The first gateway, which also represents a basic recognition of the importance of information exchange in the split-supervision system set up by the ISD, is contained in Article 25(2) which provides that secrecy requirements do not apply to the exchange of information between competent authorities in accordance with the ISD or other directives applicable to investment firms. The information exchanged is, on receipt, subject to the professional-secrecy restrictions (Article 25(2)). On receipt of confidential information, competent authorities may use it only in the course of their duties and for the specific purposes set out in Article 25(4): in order to monitor compliance with authorization conditions and conduct-of-business requirements (particularly those concerning capital adequacy, administrative and accounting procedures, and internal control mechanisms), to impose sanctions, and in relation to administrative appeals against decisions by the competent authorities and in court proceedings initiated by investment firms against such decisions.

Under Article 25(5)(a), the ISD, as originally adopted, simply permitted competent authorities to exchange information with other competent authorities within the same Member State. In addition, under Article 25(5)(b) exchanges could also be made, either within a Member State or between Member States, with authorities responsible for the supervision of credit institutions, other financial organizations and insurance undertakings and the authorities responsible for the supervision of financial markets, bodies responsible for the liquidation and bankruptcy of investment firms and other similar procedures, and, finally, persons responsible for carrying out statutory audits of investment firms and other financial institutions and organizations responsible for administering compensation schemes. Under Article 25(7) the professional-secrecy restrictions do not apply so as to prevent competent authorities from disclosing confidential information to organizations which are recognized under national law to provide clearing and settlement services, if the competent authorities are of the opinion that disclosure is necessary in order to ensure the proper functioning of those organizations in relation to defaults or potential defaults by other parties.[178]

---

[178] Any information received under this provision is subject to professional-secrecy requirements and, in addition, Member States must ensure that any information which has originally been disclosed to the disclosing competent authority through an exchange with a 2nd competent authority may not be disclosed to clearing and settlement agents under this provision, unless the express consent of the 2nd competent authority has been received.

Finally, Article 25(8) permits Member States, where disclosure is necessary in the interests of prudential supervision, to authorize the disclosure of information to other departments of their central government which are responsible for legislation concerning the supervision of providers of financial services.[179]

The ISD's information-exchange restrictions have, in the interests of maintaining systemic stability across the EC, now been overhauled and supplemented by the PSD amendments, which are based on the premise that, notwithstanding the importance of confidentiality, exchanges of information between competent authorities and other authorities which help to strengthen the stability of the financial system are appropriate and necessary for effective supervision.[180] The amendments are designed to ensure that prudential information can be transferred between competent authorities and a wider range of supervisory authorities, and that competent authorities as a result have access to a deeper pool of information. Information exchanges were already possible between competent authorities and statutory auditors and liquidators; the amendments additionally allow competent authorities to examine whether the liquidators and statutory auditors have been carrying out their functions correctly.[181] A new Article 25(5a) now provides additionally that Member States may authorize exchanges of information between the competent authorities and (1) authorities responsible for overseeing the bodies involved in the liquidation and bankruptcy of financial undertakings and other similar procedures, and (2) authorities responsible for overseeing persons charged with carrying out statutory audits of credit institutions, insurance undertakings, and investment firms. Information exchange between these bodies is subject to the restriction that it must be authorized by the Member States in question.[182] In addition, Member States which permit information exchange under Article 25(5a) are to require that exchanges of information with these bodies are subject to the requirement that the information is for the purposes of

---

[179] Information which has been received through an exchange with another competent authority or an authority specified in Art. 25(5) or from an on-the-spot verification under Art. 24 may not be disclosed in this manner except with the consent of the authority which originally disclosed the information or the authority of the Member State in which the verification was carried out.

[180] Art. 25(9) of the ISD as originally adopted referred to the pending co-ordination of all provisions governing the exchange of information between authorities for the entire financial sector. This co-ordination has now been achieved by the PSD.

[181] Explanatory Memorandum to the Commission's Proposal for the PSD, COM(93)363, 3.

[182] The prior authorization requirement, which did not appear in the original proposal and does not apply to information exchange under the original ISD information-exchange provisions, was included due to fears that the information-exchange powers were overly wide, affected too many bodies and might have been used for purposes beyond those of prudential supervision: Viegneron, P, Steinfeld, P, and Counye, D, 'Lessons of the BCCI Collapse' (1993) 13 *YBEL* 263, 285.

carrying out the overseeing functions of the bodies in question, that any information received is subject to professional secrecy, and that, where the information originates in another Member State, it may be disclosed only with the express agreement of, and for the purposes assented to by, the competent authorities which disclosed the information. Member States are also to communicate to the Commission and the other Member States the names of the authorities which may receive information under this section. Under the new Article 25(5b), Member States may, with the aim of strengthening the stability and integrity of the financial system, authorize the exchange of information between competent authorities and the authorities responsible for the detection and investigation of company-law violations.[183] Article 25(6) has also been amended to provide that a competent authority may transmit to central banks and other bodies with a similar function, in their capacity as monetary authorities, and, where appropriate, other public authorities responsible for the supervision of payment systems, information intended for the performance of their duties.[184]

Information exchange was further strengthened in 2000 by the adoption of Directive 2000/64/EC on Exchange of Information with Third Countries.[185] It amends Article 25(3) to bolster the information-exchange mechanism for third countries and to align it with the new exchange regime set out in the PSD. Previously, Article 25(3) permitted Member States to conclude information-exchange agreements with third-country competent authorities only if the information exchanged was covered by professional-secrecy guarantees at least equivalent to those set out in the original version of Article 25. It now provides that Member States may conclude information-exchange co-operation agreements with third-country competent authorities or with third-country bodies or authorities covered by Article 25(5) and (5a) if the information disclosed is subject to guarantees of professional secrecy at least equivalent to those set out in Article 25. Any exchange of information must be intended for the performance of the supervisory tasks of the authorities or bodies concerned. Where the information originates in another Member State, disclosure is prohibited unless the

---

[183] Exchange in this situation is also subject to the conditions applicable to Art. 25(5a). The exchange authorization can extend to exchanges with persons not employed in the public sector but appointed by the authorities to aid in the detection and investigation of violations. The inclusion of authorities responsible for overseeing companies generally (rather than financial-services institutions) is a reflection of the fact that, as flagged in recital 9 of the Preamble to the PSD, fraud and insider-dealing in or by companies can affect the stability and integrity of the financial system.

[184] Art. 25(6) as originally adopted provided only for disclosure to 'those central banks which do not supervise credit institutions or investment firms individually'.

[185] [2000] OJ L290/27. It was to be adopted by the Member States by 17 Nov 2002. The Directive also amends the UCITS Directive's third-country information-exchange provisions, as discussed in Ch. V above, as well as those in the 3rd Non-Life Insurance (Directive 92/49/EEC [1992] OJ L228/1) and 3rd Life Assurance Directive (92/96/EEC [1992] OJ L360/1).

express agreement of the competent authorities which originally disclosed the information has been obtained, and it may be disclosed only for the purposes for which those competent authorities gave their agreement.

VII.9 EXTENSION OF THE INVESTMENT-SERVICES PASSPORT: THE MANAGEMENT-COMPANY PASSPORT

VII.9.1 *Introduction*

The ISD passport excludes a significant proportion of investment-services providers from its scope, in that under Article 2(h) the managers of collective investment schemes are excluded.[186] As discussed in Chapter V, collective investment schemes as an investment product already benefit from a passport when they comply with the requirements of the UCITS Directive which harmonizes the rules applicable to collective investment undertakings and grants a passport to eligible collective investment schemes or UCITSs. The ineligibility of the management companies which manage the passporting UCITS product to benefit from a passport has been highlighted as an obstruction to the full development of the single market in collective-investment schemes. The new management-company regime, set out in the Management Company Proposal,[187] will provide management companies of collective investment schemes with an ISD-type passport. The objective of

---

[186] As are the depositaries of collective investment schemes and collective investment schemes whether co-ordinated at Community level or not. For a discussion of the structure of collective investment schemes and functions of management companies and depositaries see Ch. V.

[187] Amended Proposal for a European Parliament and Council Directive amending Directive 85/611/EEC on the Coordination of Laws, Regulation and Administrative Provisions Relating to Undertakings for Collective Investment in Transferable Securities with a view to Regulating Management Companies and Simplified Prospectuses (the Management Company Proposal or the Proposal). COM(2000)331 (including the Explanatory Memorandum). The Council's Common Position is at [2001] OJ C297/10. The measure was adopted by the Council as a directive on 4 Dec 2001. This discussion is based on the Common Position (references to the Management Company Proposal are to the Common Position text, while references to Articles are to the revised Articles of the UCITS Directive introduced by the new regime). At the time of writing, the final text of the adopted measure had not been published in the Official Journal and had not yet come into force. The Parliament did not, however, materially amend the Common Position text during its second reading prior to the adoption of the measure. Its only amendment (which was to shorten the Common Position's 5-year time frame from the entry into force of the new regime, at the end of which the Commission was to review the capital requirements imposed on management companies, to 3 years) was accepted by the Commission (COM(2001)687).

The original version of the proposal (and the Commission's Explanatory Memorandum), which was the subject of extensive comment, is at COM(1998)451 (the Original Management Company Proposal). For the comments of the ECB see [1999] OJ L285/9 and for the first reading of the Parliament under the co-decision procedure see A5-0025/2000. The ECOSOC opinion is at [1999] OJ C116/1.

the new regime is to harmonize the market-access rules and operating conditions applicable to management companies. As with the ISD, harmonization is limited to the essential harmonization necessary to secure mutual recognition and make possible the grant of a single authorization or passport and home-country control. The new regime will greatly enhance the single market in collective-investment schemes by allowing a home Member State-authorized management company to engage in a host Member State in, *inter alia*, the distribution of units of the unit trusts/common funds managed by the company in its home Member State and the distribution of shares of similarly managed investment companies, and the performance of all the other functions and tasks included in the activity of collective portfolio-management (recital 7). It will also be permitted to manage the assets of investment companies incorporated in Member States other than its home Member State and to perform, on the basis of mandates, on behalf of management companies incorporated in Member States other than its home Member State, the functions included in the activity of collective portfolio management (recital 7). The passport also extends beyond collective portfolio management to include discretionary or individual portfolio management, investment advice, and custody services.[188] As with the ISD, the Management Company Proposal's requirements are proposed as minimum standards with Member States permitted, as a general rule, to adopt more stringent conditions (recital 11).

Given that management companies act as investment intermediaries and raise similar concerns as investment firms generally with respect to prudential supervision and investor protection, albeit in the particular context of collective portfolio-management, it is hardly surprising that the Management Company Proposal is closely modelled on the ISD as supplemented by the particular requirements needed for the regulation of collective portfolio management. As with the ISD, the Management Company Proposal not only serves the interests of market integration by establishing the framework for the passport, it also enhances investor protection by introducing substantive harmonization. While the authorization conditions are considered at section 9.3 below, the substantive harmonization of ongoing prudential and conduct rules is considered along with the prudential and protective supervision of investment firms in Chapters VIII and IX below.

---

[188] The benefits of the harmonization proposed by the Management Company Proposal have been summarized by ECOSOC as providing for 'a "single licence" regime equivalent to that enjoyed by other financial services, increas[ing] investor protection and enabl[ing] management companies to carry out the management of collective investment undertakings and portfolios on behalf of both private and institutional investors, including pension funds': n 187 above, para 1.1.2.

VII.9.2 *Scope*

VII.9.2.1 *Management Companies*

As the UCITS Directive does not define 'management company', and as classification as a management company under the revised UCITS Directive has considerable regulatory consequences in terms of eligibility for the management company passport, authorization requirements, and, in particular, initial and ongoing capital requirements, this core definition is added by Article 1a. It covers any company the regular business of which is the management of the assets of UCITSs in the form of unit trusts/common funds and/or investment companies. The definition is designed to cover all management companies which undertake the collective portfolio management of UCITSs, regardless of the legal form the UCITS may take.

VII.9.2.2 *Management Activities*

The UCITS Directive currently restricts management-company activities to the management of UCITSs. The reason for this enforced specialization is to protect investors by ensuring that the management company is focused on the business of collective investment-scheme management. It does not, however, clarify the exact scope of this restriction. As a result, considerable confusion has arisen about whether a UCITS management company is limited to investment management only, or whether it can legitimately engage in marketing or administrative activities as well. Further difficulties have arisen concerning whether management activities can be delegated to third parties; certain Member States, for example, do not permit management companies to delegate asset-management and accounting activities. Elimination of this 'grey zone' has been highlighted as critical, given that the introduction of the euro and a single monetary policy has increased the need to prevent financial crises and irregularities, and that any regulatory confusion destructs the maintenance of a level playing field between companies, hinders effective supervision and investor protection, and undermines the stability and reliability of the financial system.[189] In addition, the industry has called for a removal of the restriction on management companies from carrying out, in addition, individual portfolio management, as this restriction has prevented 'important economies of scale and create[d] irrational segmentation between collective and individual portfolio management'.[190]

In recognition of these multiple difficulties, Article 5(2) of the UCITS Directive is revised by the Management Company Proposal to provide that

---

[189] Explanatory Memorandum to Original Management Company Proposal, n 187 above, 6.
[190] Ibid, 5.

no management company may engage in activities other than the 'management' of UCITSs in the form of unit trusts/common funds and of investment companies, except the additional management of other collective-investment undertakings which are not covered by the UCITS Directive and for which the management company is subject to prudential supervision but which cannot be marketed in other Member States under the UCITS passport. The activity of 'management' is further defined as including the activities listed in Annex 2 (which is not exhaustive), which covers investment, marketing, and administrative activities. Investment administration is elaborated on in some detail and includes: legal and fund management accounting services; customer inquiries; valuation and pricing, including tax returns; regulatory compliance monitoring; maintenance of the unit-holder register, distribution of income; unit issues and redemption; contract settlements, including certificate dispatch; and record keeping.

Management companies are not, however, restricted to collective portfolio-management activities. Article 5(3) significantly widens the range of activities which may be undertaken by management companies under the UCITS Directive. Member States may authorize management companies to engage in individual portfolio management, including the management of pension funds, in accordance with mandates given by investors on a discretionary, client-by-client basis, as long as the portfolios include one or more of the instruments covered by Section B of the Annex to the ISD. Management companies may also be authorized to provide non-core services with respect to, first, investment advice in relation to ISD instruments and, secondly, safekeeping and administration in relation to units of collective-investment undertakings as these services are linked to the core service of investment management. Consistently with the approach taken by the ISD with respect to non-core services, management companies may not be authorized to provide non-core services unless they also provide discretionary portfolio-management services. Management-company authorization is also dependent on collective portfolio-management being carried out. The introduction of discretionary portfolio management, investment advice, and custody services as services which may be provided by management companies, however, allows management companies to engage in these services which are regulated by the ISD. Accordingly, in order to ensure a homogeneous regulatory treatment, under Article 5(4) management companies which offer discretionary portfolio-management services, investment advice, and custody services are, in addition to the revisions to the UCITS Directive's requirements proposed by the Management Company Proposal, subject to the ISD's ongoing requirements with respect to these activities. In this respect, a parallel can be drawn with the treatment of credit institutions which provide investment services. The ISD's Article 2(4) exclusion for monetary operations also applies.

VII.9.3 *The Authorization Process*

VII.9.3.1 *Authorization: Jurisdiction to Authorize and Authorization Conditions*

The new authorization procedure for management companies is, like ISD authorization, designed to provide a basis for the mutual recognition of authorization and the operation of the passport and to ensure investor protection and the stability of the financial system by harmonizing authorization conditions at a minimum level. Under Article 5(1), 'prior official authorization' is necessary before a management company can carry on business as such, and is the responsibility of the management company's 'home Member State', defined as the Member State in which the management company has its registered office (Article 1a(3)). Once authorization is granted in accordance with the revised UCITS Directive it will be valid for all Member States.

Authorization is subject to a number of conditions set out in a new Article 5a which are aimed at ensuring sufficient levels of investor protection and which reflect those set out in the ISD, being broadly divisible into capital, competence, and organizational or regulatory arbitrage-prevention requirements. The capital requirements (Article 5a(1)(a)) mark the greatest point of divergence from the ISD. They are designed to ensure a distinction is maintained between the activities of collective and individual/discretionary portfolio management and 'are based as much as possible on the reference values established in the CAD in order to guarantee equality of treatment with investment firms (whose core business is individual portfolio management)'.[191] A basic initial capital requirement of 125,000 euro applies to both activities.[192] An additional own-funds[193] requirement based on the value of the assets under management, is, however, imposed on collective portfolio-management activities in order, in part, to reflect the possibility open to UCITSs under the new investment policy regime[194] to invest in derivatives which demand a greater degree of risk management and more sophisticated valuation techniques.[195] The additional requirement is trig-

[191] Communication from the Commission to the Parliament concerning the Common Position, SEC/2001/1004 (the Common Position Communication), para 3.2.2.4.

[192] Art. 5(4) (which applies the CAD to the ISD-type activities) and Art. 5a(1).

[193] The own-funds definition tracks the CAD definition (see Ch. VIII sect. 9.3.5 below).

[194] See Ch. V sect. 8.2 above.

[195] This requirement, *per* the Commission, 'is in no way intended to constitute a minimum "safety net" for compensating investors, which would be illusory given the volumes and types of assets managed. Market and credit risks are borne by investors in UCITS unaided and are charged direct to the value of the UCITS portfolio and hence to their units in the unit trust/common fund or their shares in the investment company. The management company must, however, bear the operational risk associated with the management of UCITS . . . an own funds "cushion", therefore is needed for this purpose': Common Position Communication, n 191 above, para 3.2.2.4.

gered when the value of the portfolios of the management company exceeds 250 million euro; it amounts to 0.02 per cent of the amount by which the value of the management company's portfolios exceeds 250 million euro. The initial capital and additional capital requirements together are subject to a ceiling of 10,000,000 euro. Care is taken to set parameters concerning the types of portfolios which are to be taken into account for this calculation; essentially, the calculation applies to those portfolios for which the management company is liable. The portfolios to be included are: unit trusts/common funds managed by the management company, including portfolios for which it has delegated the management function but excluding portfolios that it is managing under a delegation; investment companies for which the management company is the designated management company (delegations will not apply here); and other collective investment undertakings managed by the management company including portfolios for which it has delegated the management function but excluding portfolios that it is managing under a delegation. In a new departure for the EC's capital-adequacy regime, Member States may, however, reduce the additional own-funds requirement by 50 per cent if the management company benefits from a guarantee covering this amount from a credit institution or insurance company having its registered office in a Member State or, if in a non-Member State, subject to prudential rules considered by the competent authorities to be equivalent to those in the EC regime. Finally, the own funds of a management company may never be less than the amount required by Annex IV of the CAD (one quarter of the previous year's fixed overheads).

With respect to competency and reputation, Article 5a(1)(b) broadly tracks the ISD requirements, although the sufficient experience requirement is qualified by reference to experience with respect to the type of UCITS managed by the management company. Provision is expressly made for the transmission of the names of relevant persons to the competent authorities.

On the organizational side, as with the ISD, the management company's head office and registered office must be located in the same Member State and the authorization application must set out the company's programme of activities and describe its organisational structure (Article 5a(1)(c) and (d)). Where close links exist between the management company and other natural or legal persons, the competent authorities may grant an authorization only where such links do not prevent the effective exercise of their supervisory functions and must refuse authorization where the laws, regulations, or administrative provisions of a non-Member State governing one or more natural or legal persons with which the management company has close links, or difficulties with their enforcement, prevent the effective exercise of their supervisory functions (Article 5a(2)). Article 5b(1) addresses qualifying shareholders while Article 5b(3) tracks Article 6 of the ISD, adjusted to reflect financial-conglomerate structures.

VII.9.3.2 *Authorization: Process, Protections, and Third-country Relations*

Applicants must be informed of the outcome of their application within six months of the submission of a complete application and may commence business as soon as authorization is granted (Article 5a(3) and (4)). Authorization may be withdrawn in a number of specified circumstances set out in Article 5a(5) which track the parallel requirements of the ISD, and include where the company no longer fulfils the authorization conditions or where the company has seriously and systematically infringed the UCITS Directive's provisions. Relations with third countries in respect of management-company authorization are subject to broadly the same third-country provisions as apply in the ISD (Article 5b(2) and 5c).

VII.9.3.3 *Authorization: The ISD Overlap*

Investment firms authorized under the ISD to carry out discretionary portfolio-management services, investment advice, and custody services only may obtain authorization as management companies under the revised UCITS Directive and give up their ISD authorization under Article 2(1) of the Management Company Proposal.

VII.9.4 *The Management-company Passport*

VII.9.4.1 *Mutual Recognition*

Once a management company has been authorized by the home Member State, it may, under Article 5(1) (authorization valid for all Member States) and Article 6(1) and (2) operate throughout the internal market on the basis of that authorization, either by the establishment of a branch or under the freedom to provide services. Under Article 6(1), authorized management companies may carry on within the territories of other Member States the activities for which they have been authorized via a branch or under the freedom to provide services. In particular, under Article 6(2), Member States may not make the establishment of a branch or the provision of services subject to authorization or capital requirements or any other measures having equivalent effect. Home Member States are, accordingly, responsible for ensuring that the management companies which they have authorized comply at all times with the authorization conditions (Article 5d(1)).

As under the ISD, mutual recognition is also extended to prudential supervision of management companies by virtue of Article 5d(2), which provides that prudential supervision of the management company is the responsibility of the home Member State, without prejudice to the provisions of the UCITS Directive which give responsibility to the host-country authorities. As effective mutual recognition of prudential supervision is dependent on mutual trust and confidence between Member States, the Management Company Proposal introduces a number of harmonized prudential rules which must be imposed on management companies and which are discussed in Chapter VIII. A conduct regime for management companies is introduced under Article 5h (see Chapter IX below), while the ISD's prudential, advertising, and conduct regimes apply to the ISD-type activities of the management company.

VII.9.4.2 *Using the Passport*

Exercise of the management-company passport in order to establish a branch or to provide services is subject to the notification of specified information to the home Member State's competent authority and the completion of certain formalities which closely track the parallel procedures set out for exercise of the ISD passport. Management companies wishing to establish a branch are subject to Article 6a, which tracks Article 17 of the ISD, while those wishing to provide cross-border services are subject to Article 6b, which tracks Article 18 of the ISD.

While Article 6a and b and Articles 17 and 18 are, respectively, closely aligned,[196] they are adjusted to take into account the effect of the UCITS passport which, independently of the management-company passport, applies to the UCITS in respect of which the management company carries out management functions. The UCITS product passport is governed separately by section VIII of the UCITS Directive and is subject to separate notification, marketing, and administrative requirements.[197] Article 6a and b makes specific reference to these supplementary requirements.[198] Article 6a and b also reflects the range of activities beyond collective portfolio-management which may potentially be carried out by management companies. As these additional services come within the scope of the ISD, in order to level the playing field between investment firms and these management companies, host Member States are required to inform management companies of the conduct rules which apply to discretionary portfolio-management, investment advice, and custody services. Article 6b also

[196] Although Art. 6b, unlike Art. 18, requires that the services notification from the home Member State forward details of any applicable compensation scheme.

[197] See Ch. V.

[198] As explained by the Commission, '[t]he passport for the product is now solely governed by Article 46 and is available for the shares of harmonised investment companies and the units of UCITS managed by management companies. Consequently, Articles 6a and 6b cover the passport for management companies in regard to the provision of functions included in the activity of collective portfolio management and the selected ISD services . . . The marketing of their UCITS in other Member States is possible but subject to the regulation of Article 46 to which Articles 6a and 6b refer': COM(2000)331, 7.

provides that a management company is subject to the notification procedure where it entrusts a third party with the marketing of units in a host
Member State.

VII.9.5 *Reporting, Home/Host Enforcement, and Supervisory Co-operation*

The ISD's Article 19 reporting requirements are tracked through the
Management Company Proposal by Article 6c. The enforcement procedure
is also contained in Article 6c and closely reflects that set out in Article 19
of the ISD. Where a passporting management company breaches host-
Member-State rules, the home Member State's competent authority is to take
all appropriate measures to ensure that the company puts an end to the
breach. Only if the home competent authority fails or is unable to take adequate action and the violations persist may the host authority take penaliz-
ing measures and/or prevent the management company from entering into
any further transactions in the host Member State. This procedure is without prejudice to the power of host Member States to take measures to prevent or penalize any breaches of legal or regulatory provisions adopted in
the interest of the general good.

The supervision and cooperation system is broadly similar to that of the
ISD, although founded on the structure of supervision set up for UCITSs by
the UCITS Directive in Articles 49–52 (see Chapter V). As with the ISD, the
system is based on a network of competent authorities. The Management
Company Proposal's revisions to the UCITS Directive do not, unlike Article
27 of the ISD, specifically require that Member States must ensure that competent authorities have powers to take measures or impose penalties in
respect of rule violations, but do provide under Article 5a(5) that authorization may be withdrawn in the event of systematic and serious infringement of the UCITS Directive.

The co-operation structures are expanded to take into account the operation of the management-company passport by the introduction of Article
52a and b which supplements the current regime with the supervisory powers and cooperation procedures and structures contained in Articles 23(3)
and 24 of the ISD. The collaboration provision is drafted in simpler terms
than the parallel ISD provision (Article 23(3)) and simply requires 'the competent authorities of all the Member States concerned' to collaborate closely
(Article 52a(1)). The same inspection and verification powers as are given
to home Member States' competent authorities under the ISD apply in
respect of the supervision of management companies (Article 52(b)). The
original information-exchange provisions of the UCITS Directive were
amended by the PSD which both aligned the original information-exchange
requirements with those of the ISD, as originally adopted, and added the
specific refinements introduced by the PSD itself.

VII.10 THE SUCCESS OF THE ISD
AS A MARKET-INTEGRATION MEASURE

VII.10.1 *Reliance on the ISD Passport*

It is not disputed that the ISD has succeeded, at a basic level, in breaking down investment-services market segmentation at the level of the investment firm. Significant numbers of Article 18 notifications have been recorded in a number of Member States, with Italy, Sweden, Belgium, Ireland, and Luxembourg, in particular, reporting high numbers of passporting investment firms providing investment services on a cross-border basis.[199] Perhaps one of the most significant indicators of the ISD's success is that in a number of Member States the number of passporting investment firms exceeds the number of domestic authorized investment firms.[200]A number of problems have arisen, however, which call into doubt the extent to which the ISD can efficiently deliver an integrated market.

VII.10.2 *Implementation Problems*

Implementation of the ISD by Member States was both slow and, in certain cases, faulty, and hampered the integration of national investment-services markets.[201] In its 1998 Communication the Commission launched a scathing attack on the implementation record of Member States, finding that '[t]he delayed implementation of the Investment Services Directive has caused market rigidities as a result of lack of competition and difficult market access. Market innovation has been stifled whilst investment firms are less than optimally prepared for the readjustment and enhanced competition that the euro will bring.'[202]

---

[199] 825, 845, 843, 795, and 814, respectively, as at Sept 2000. The number of branch notifications under Art. 17 is significantly lower, however, with the same Member States recording 16, 6, 8, 2, and 2 notifications. These figures do not include credit institutions providing investment services: ISD Communication, n 34 above, 22.

[200] Ibid, 7.

[201] On the implementation process see McAll, S, 'Implementation of the Investment Services Directive: Progress to Date' (1996) 3 *EFSL* 83. In its *15th Annual Report on Monitoring the Application of Community Law* for the year 1997, the Commission reported that during 1997 it commenced legal proceedings against Spain for failure to implement the ISD and against Luxembourg and Germany in respect of their incomplete implementation of the ISD, COM(98)317, para 2.2.4.5. Spain finally implemented the ISD 2 years after the deadline with the adoption of its Securities Markets Law in Nov 1998. In June 1999, the Court of Justice in Case C–417/97 *Commission v Luxembourg* [1999] ECR I–3247 declared that Luxembourg was in breach of its Treaty obligations by failing to implement the ISD fully.

[202] 1998 Communication, n 140 above, 4.

VII.10.3 *Structural Weaknesses in the ISD and Reform*

VII.10.3.1 *The 2000 ISD Communication*

Difficulties with implementation aside, a deeper problem has become apparent. The continuing segmentation of investment-services markets is seen as being in part a consequence of fundamental weaknesses in the market-integration devices used by the ISD.[203] Accordingly, its review has been identified as a core element of the FSAP, with the Commission stating in 1999 that '[t]he Investment Services Directive is in urgent need of upgrading if it is to serve as the cornerstone of an integrated securities market'.[204] As part of the FSAP, the Commission is undertaking a wide-ranging review of the ISD to assess its suitability as the basis for an integrated and efficient market for investment services. This led in 2000 to the publication of the ISD Communication, which acknowledged that the ISD had eliminated only the 'first set of legal obstacles' to the single market and that a 'wide-ranging overhaul of the ISD' was required.[205] The Lamfalussy Report also identified weaknesses in the ISD regime, including the failure to make the passport work fully for the wholesale sector and the confusion surrounding Article 11.[206]

Although the ISD Communication was primarily concerned with the ISD's provisions on securities-trading markets, it identified a number of areas in which the investment-firm passport was deficient. A core problem highlighted was the 'extensive dilution of the home country philosophy' via Article 13, the residual general-good provisions, and Article 11's conduct rules mechanism: the 'failure to provide for effective mechanisms to smooth a transition to [the] home country principle or to circumscribe the scope of [the] host country principle' was identified as a 'shortcoming of the present Directive'.[207] Unclear provisions in the ISD were also identified as leading to widespread discrepancies.

More specifically, the Communication highlighted the limited scope of the ISD passport. Not only did it raise the possibility that certain of the non-core services should be able to benefit from the passport, the number of exclusions set out Article 2(2) and (4) was identified as being too wide. The Communication acknowledged, however, that any move to grant non-core services a full passport would require a reconsideration of the adequacy of

---

[203] For an early perspective on the ISD's weaknesses see Hall, M, 'The Investment Services and Capital Adequacy Directives: Further Steps Towards Completion of the Single European Market in Financial Services' (1995) 3 *JFRC* 358, 367–9.

[204] N 141 above, 3.   [205] N 34 above, 1 and 9, respectively.

[206] Final Report of the Committee of Wise Men on the Regulation of European Securities Markets (Feb 2001) (the Lamfalussy Report), 12.

[207] N 34 above, 8.

the ISD's supervisory provisions.[208] The prevalence of unclear provisions and definitions was charged with leading to wide-ranging divergences in the implementation of the ISD. The Commission reported that Member States differed, for example, in their interpretations of the critical definition of what constituted a core service and in how the emergency powers available to host Member States under Article 19(8) were to be exercised. More generally, it had become clear that significant differences existed between Member States in the manner in which they tailored the requirements of the ISD depending on the nature of the investment service provided. Of particular concern to the Commission were the wide variations in the extent to which Member States tailored the Article 11 conduct-of-business requirements where the service provided is delivered on an 'execution only' basis.[209]

Considerable attention was given to the structural split in the ISD between home and host regulation. Home-country control, the touchstone for successful market integration, has been achieved, for the most part, in the area of prudential regulation due to the relatively high degree of rule harmonization. Conduct-of-business regulation and marketing controls are, conversely, subject to host-Member-State control, with the result that investment firms are subject to a duplication of regulation. Even in the prudential regulation area, however, the Communication noted that the home-country-control principle had been diluted with a number of host Member States applying organizational prudential controls with respect to client money to passporting investment firms. It found that cross-border broking and dealing services were being particularly badly affected by the duplication of regulation.[210] The residual general-good jurisdiction of host Member States explicitly acknowledged in the ISD was also identified as representing an obstacle to integration. At the core of the Commission's response to these difficulties was its view that 'a single passport will requirement systematic reliance on the home country principle for supervision of firms' obligations to the market and fair dealing with clients'.[211] While home-country control (or Member-State-of-origin control) with respect to the wholesale market is achievable and has been supported by the Commission in its Article 11 Communication, the higher degree of protection needed by retail investors makes a move away from host control an unrealistic goal under the current regime, given the immature state of protective harmonization (although this argument did not weigh heavily on the application of the Member-State-of-origin rule to online investment services). Retail investment-services markets are still heavily fragmented as Member States apply their investor-protection

---

[208] The E-commerce and Financial Services Communication also suggested that further harmonization might be considered in non-core areas which have become of particular concern, such as investment advice and planning and commodity broking: n 38 above, 13. This now forms part of the Commission's proposals to reform the ISD (sect. 10.3.2 below).

[209] N 34 above, 9.   [210] Ibid, 10.   [211] Ibid.

regimes in the absence of harmonization. This problem was acknowledged in the ISD Communication which noted that '[a]s regards retail investors, the transition to home country supervision of investment services will need to be carefully managed' and that, given the current state of harmonization, 'investors may derive benefit and confidence from the possibility of seeking redress within their own jurisdiction'.[212] A number of initiatives are under way (see section 10.3.2 and Chapter IX below) which are likely to result in greater harmonization of protective rules and facilitate the abandonment of host-Member-State control. As well as standardising the regulatory environment and removing regulatory obstacles, further harmonization would, if carried out at an appropriate level, also increase investor confidence in the single market and aid integration.

VII.10.3.2 *The 2001 ISD Working Paper*

Action on the ISD is clearly a Commission priority: '[u]pdating of the ISD can facilitate European progress towards enhanced liquidity, efficiency and stability. Inaction risks undervaluing the positive externalities and public goods that efficient securities markets, characterized by transparency and integrity, embody for the overall economic system'.[213] Many of the initial suggestions for reform have now been subject to further elaboration in the Commission's important July 2001 ISD Working Paper.[214] This document is designed to give an indication of the Commission's 'preliminary orientations' on how the ISD should be reformed and to allow for further consultation. Its detailed provisions are, as a result, considered in outline only, with only the most striking features of the Commission's current thinking isolated here.

The first group of investment services/investment firm reforms concerns the scope of the ISD.[215] The Commission has suggested that the current distinction between core and non-core services be retained, but has proposed a number of modifications to the current regime. In particular, the definition of 'investment services' would be revised to include a new definition of 'mediation and arranging of client orders', which would be a core service. This new definition is designed to cover those services which 'mediate client orders to authorized investment firms for execution; and/or facilitate the posting, communication or identification of trading interests by clients'.[216] It reflects the Commission's decision to treat alternative trading systems or

---

[212] N 34 above.   [213] Ibid, 19.

[214] Overview of Proposed Adjustments to the Investment Services Directive. Working Document of Services of DG Internal Market. Document 1, July 2001

[215] Ibid, 10–15. The paper addresses all aspects of the ISD and is discussed further in the following chs.

[216] Ibid, Annex 1, 1.

ATSs as investment firms, which is discussed more fully in the context of securities-trading market regulation in Chapter XI below, and would cover order-routing services, bulletin boards, and introducing brokers. The common features of entities providing 'arranging services' are, according to the Commission, the fact that they do not hold client money or assets or enter into a client relationship which would entail fiduciary obligations, but assist in the execution of transactions without becoming a party to the transaction; an authorized investment firm would be required to execute the transaction.[217] In a similar vein, the brokerage definition would be revised to include new developments such as automated matching of countervailing client orders. The growth in retail investor activity has triggered an additional suggestion that investment advice be upgraded from a non-core to a core service. This transfer is designed to catch only independent, impartial investment advice, tailored to the needs of particular investors, and not the advice provided by investment firms promóting their own products and ' "bundled" with the performance of other investment services'.[218] In particular, tied agents selling the products of one investment firm would not be covered by this provision. The definition would require that the client paid a fee for the advice in order to remove tied agents from its scope and minimize the potential for conflicts of interest. This approach reflects the concern that investors' interests may be prejudiced if the adviser is encouraged to promote certain products and services by commission structures and other inducements. The Commission has also proposed that the current approach to financial instruments be revised to include instruments whose current status is unclear and, in a major change to the current regime, to include commodity derivatives. This would have the effect of bringing specialist commodity-derivative brokerage and dealing services into the ISD and its sister CAD regime. Finally, the Commission has suggested an ISD-based definition of a 'professional investor' for the purposes of Article 11, based on the categorization used in the Investor Compensation Schemes Directive[219] which would 'establish a straightforward binary split between professionals and retail investors . . . [and] avoid the creation of intermediate categories whose ultimate treatment would be ascertained subject to additional checks or formalities'.[220] Professional investors would, as a result, include: (1) professional and institutional investors, including investment firms, credit institutions, collective-investment undertakings, and other professional and institutional investors authorized under national law; (2) supranational

---

[217] N 214 above, 10.   [218] Ibid, 11.

[219] Directive 97/7/EC on investor compensation schemes [1997] OJ L84/22. The Commission's position was that the type of investor targeted by the protections of the EC's investor-compensation regime was also likely to be an appropriate beneficiary of high levels of investor protection.

[220] N 214 above, Annex 1, 15.

institutions, government bodies, and, possibly, local and regional bodies; (3) firms in the same group as the firm providing the investment services; and (4) companies whose securities are offered to the public.[221] As with the FESCO regime, investors would be able to request that a categorization as a professional or retail investor could be changed by an investment firm. Any such recategorization would be for the purposes of the application of conduct-of-business rules and would apply only to the private contract between the two parties.

The second group of major investment-firm/investment-services-related revisions concern the ISD's authorization and supervisory regimes;[222] the latter have profound implications for the home/host-Member-State-control structure. With respect to authorization conditions, the Commission has proposed that the current regime be modernized[223] and, in particular, that the CAD's capital adequacy requirements be revised as necessary to reflect the new core-investment-services regime, given that neither arranging nor providing investment advice involves the holding of client assets or funds. The more dramatic revisions concern the ongoing supervision regime (Articles 10 and 11) and, in particular, the conduct-of-business regime. While these revisions are considered in Chapters VIII and IX, respectively, the most significant revision is the suggestion by the Commission to recast and update the Article 11 regime, based on the standards-convergence work which is being carried out by FESCO (now the CESR) in this area, so that it provides a more intensive harmonization of conduct-of-business regulation. This is designed to pave the way for conduct-of-business regulation to shift to home-Member-State or Member-State-of-origin control. The Commission has suggested that home-Member-State control should follow for retail investors once the new conduct-of-business regime is in place. However, branches of investment firms would, with respect to the investment firm/investor relationship, be subject to the regime in place in the country in which the branch was established. The new regime would be differentiated in its application and would specify in detail how the application of the conduct regime would vary where services were supplied to professional investors. The conduct-of-business regime would also take into account the nature of the services provided and, in particular, whether they were execution only. It is clear from the ISD Working Paper that detailed harmonization, adopted in all likelihood according to level 2 Lamfalussy comitology procedures and based on level 1 high-level principles can be expected.

---

[221] An alternative proposal suggested was to base the professional/retail distinction on the size of the company's treasury function.

[222] N 214 above, 16–25.

[223] The suggestions include: specifying the information to be included in the programme of operations; requiring that an independent compliance function be established; and requiring that those who direct the business of the firm possess the relevant skills and expertise.

The third group of revisions which impact on the ISD's investment firm/investment-services structure concern tied agents. At present, recital 8 permits investment firms to use tied agents when carrying on business throughout the single market; each Member State can impose its own rules on their authorization. In a related provision, Article 2(2)(g) takes outside the scope of the ISD firms whose only business consists of receiving and transmitting orders to authorized financial institutions. In order to clarify the position of tied agents (which would not be treated as investment firms under the ISD), the Commission has proposed that when tied agents act on behalf of investment firms in other Member States via remote (typically online) means, they should be subject to the regime in operation in the Member State in which they are established and suggested a framework for a common licensing regime. The tied agent would also be required to comply with the relevant conduct-of-business rules with respect to its communications with investors.[224]

Finally, the Commission has suggested that the notification process be streamlined in line with the planned shift to home-Member-State control. While notification would be required for cross-border investment services, it would no longer be used to impose host-Member-State requirements but would focus on simply informing the host Member State of the nature of the passporting firms operating on their market-place. Information would also be transmitted directly from the firm to the host Member State. Similarly, branch notification would be used to confirm the role of the host Member State in conduct-of-business supervision.

VII.11 INVESTMENT-SERVICES MARKET INTEGRATION AND THE INTERNET: THE ECD[225]

The rapid growth in the use of the Internet to supply investment services is one of the most striking features of the recent development of EC securities markets. The extent to which Internet or online services can be provided freely throughout the EC has a significant impact on investment-services market integration. Uncertainties as to which Member States' rules apply to online services and divergences in how Member States regulate online services have the potential to hinder the use of the Internet by investment firms

---

[224] The utility of this provision might be questioned given the EC's e-commerce regime (see sect. 11 below), a point acknowledged by the Commission.

[225] The Commission's original proposal is at [1999] OJ C30/4, Explanatory Memorandum at COM(1998)586. ECOSOC's comments are at [1999] OJ C169/36, the Parliament's first reading (the measure was adopted under the co-decision procedure) at [1999] OJ C279/389 and the Council's common position at [2000] OJ C128/32.

across the EC.[226] The inability of the ISD to deliver efficient market-integra-
tion-promoting solutions for the e-commerce environment is particularly
marked, for example, with respect to Articles 18 and 11. The ECD, which
was to be adopted by the Member States by 17 January 2002 now sets out
the internal market framework for services delivered online.

While the ECD does not specifically address investment services, it is
designed to contribute to the creation of a legal framework for the online
provision of financial services (recital 27). It is based on two principles: first,
that, in order to ensure the effective protection of (undefined) 'public interest objectives', e-commerce services should be supervised at the source of the
activity; and, secondly, that in order to guarantee the freedom to provide
services, e-commerce services should in principle be subject to the law of the
Member State in which the service provider is established (recital 22). The
ECD accordingly recognizes that e-commerce services which do not have a
physical connection to another Member State are most effectively supervised
by the Member State in which the service provider is established[227] and that
e-commerce service providers should be protected from the imposition of regulation by each Member State in which the services are accessible.[228] Its primary objective under Article 1 is to contribute to the proper functioning of
the internal market by ensuring the free movement of information-society
services (which include investment services)[229] between the Member States.
This objective is achieved through the 'country of origin principle' set out in
Article 3(1) and (2).[230]

---

[226] In its Explanatory Memorandum the Commission pointed to the potential application of
all Member States' rules to the provision of e-commerce services, a lack of certainty about the
rules applicable and the danger of new rules being adopted by Member States as all amounting to legal barriers which gave rise to considerable uncertainty and economic costs and which
hampered the exercise of the Treaty free-movement guarantees by both service providers and
consumers. As a result, investment opportunities were being lost, competitiveness prejudiced,
and consumer confidence compromised: n 225 above, 7–10.

[227] The Communication on E-commerce and Financial Services noted that control could be
exercised more rapidly and more efficiently in the Member State in which the service provider
was established and from which it operated its website, not least because other Member States
could have difficulties in enforcing measures against service providers located outside their territory: n 38 above, 7.

[228] This principle is based on the argument that given that services available over a website
are 'automatically and simultaneously accessible in all Member State [i]t would be unjustifiably
burdensome if a financial service provider had to comply with fifteen different sets of rules and
regulations . . . service providers would be forced to design different services in order to comply with different Member State requirements, discouraging the use and take up of e-commerce
throughout the European Union': ibid. The Communication also noted that if a variety of regulatory regimes applied, providers might tend to focus on major markets to the detriment of
smaller Member States.

[229] Information-society services broadly cover any service normally provided for remuneration, at a distance, by means of electronic equipment for processing and storage of data: Art.
1(a) and Recital 17.

[230] The ECD's substantive rules and its implications for investor protection are discussed in
Ch. IX sect. 10 below.

Under Article 3(1), each Member State is to ensure that the information-society services provided by a service provider[231] 'established on its territory' comply with the national provisions applicable in the Member State in question which fall within the 'co-ordinated field'. Notably, the ECD does not use the home-Member-State formula relied on by the ISD, which is connected to the location of the firm's head or registered office, but uses the concept of establishment, or what has been termed the 'Member State of origin principle'. While Article 3 does not specify how the key connecting factor of establishment is to be determined,[232] Article 2(3) provides that an 'established service provider' is a service provider which effectively pursues an economic activity using a fixed establishment for an indefinite period. It further provides that the presence and use of the technical means and technology required to provide the service does not, of itself, constitute establishment. The concept of establishment is further amplified by recital 19 which clarifies that the establishment determination is to be made in accordance with the case law of the Court of Justice, according to which establishment involves the actual pursuit of economic activity through a fixed establishment for an indefinite period. More specifically, recital 19 suggests that the place of establishment of a company is not the place at which the technology supporting its website is based, but the place from which it pursues its economic activities.[233] The 'co-ordinated field' is broadly defined in Article 2(i) and (h) as those Member State requirements applicable to information-society services or service providers in respect of, first, the taking up of the activity of an information-society service such as authorization and notification requirements and, secondly, the pursuit of such activity such as requirements concerning the behaviour of the service provider and the quality or content of the service provided (including those applicable to advertising and contracts).

The cornerstone provision is Article 3(2), which has been termed the internal-market clause. It provides that Member States may not, for reasons falling within the co-ordinated field, restrict the freedom to provide information-society services from another Member State. As a result, investment firms may, when relying on the ECD passport, provide investment services online to investors across the EC on the basis of Member-State-of-origin rules. Under Article 3(4), Member States may derogate from the Member-

---

[231] Under Art. 2(b), a natural or legal person providing information-society services.

[232] Even though the Commission acknowledged in its Explanatory Memorandum to the original proposal that determining the place of establishment of an online service provider was difficult: n 225 above, 10.

[233] Underlying the approach to establishment are two principles: that the Member State and its supervisory authorities have flexibility in applying the concept; and that Member States can effectively exercise authority and wield enforcement powers over service providers: Explanatory Memorandum to original proposal, n 225 above, 20.

State-of-origin principle on a number of grounds including, significantly for investment services, the protection of consumers, including investors.

The use of establishment as the market-integration device does, however, involve potential problems in relation to which Member State can impose its rules. Nothing in the ECD appears to prohibit an investment firm from choosing to provide e-commerce investment services through a particular branch in order to benefit from a less rigorous regulatory regime. Accordingly, while it minimizes investment firms' regulatory burdens by nominating one Member State's regime as governing the supply of investment services via the Internet, the considerable gaps which still exist in the harmonized investment-services regime suggest that the ECD may prejudice investor protection in the online investment-services market.[234] In this regard, the new conduct-of-business regime envisaged by the ISD Working Paper will be critical.

[234] See Ch. IX sect. 10 below.

VIII

The Prudential Regulation of Investment-services Providers

VIII.1 THE RATIONALE FOR PRUDENTIAL REGULATION

The prudential regulation of investment firms primarily addresses those areas where '[an] investment firm's capital, client money and public confidence may most be put at risk'.[1] Prudential rules are concerned with risk management; they address the solvency of individual investment firms as well as systemic stability, and broadly cover 'safety and soundness policies'.[2] They are designed to reduce, but not eliminate, the risk of investment-firm failure by managing the levels of risk assumed by firms.[3] Where failure does occur, prudential rules seek to contain it and minimize its systemic impact, as well as soften its more immediate impact on individual investors and clients and their assets.

Prudential regulation supports investor-protection objectives by bolstering the soundness of investment firms. Most investment services, apart from pure advisory services, will involve an investment firm holding funds and instruments belonging to investors or clients. An insolvency, particularly where there has been fraud or inadequate protection of client assets, will place those assets at risk, prejudicing investor protection on an individual basis and, ultimately, investor confidence in the market-place as a whole. In addition, and to a significantly greater degree than protective regulation, prudential regulation also addresses the soundness and stability of the market-place and, in particular, the control of systemic risks which can result in the instability of and a loss of confidence in the financial system. Due to the interdependence of investment firms, the failure of one firm can have adverse consequences for others, provoke a domino effect, and result in

---

[1] IOSCO, *Objectives and Principles of Securities Regulation* (1998) (the 1998 IOSCO Principles), para 12.2.

[2] Ferrarini, G, 'Introduction' to Ferrarini, G (ed), *Prudential Regulation of Banks and Securities Firms, European and International Aspects* (1995) 3, 4. The UK's Financial Services Authority (FSA) has described its prudential-supervision regime as consisting of rules which 'will reduce the risk of investment firms being able to meet their liabilities and their commitments to investors and counterparties as they fall due': FSA, *The Investment Business Interim Prudential Sourcebook*, Consultation Paper 54 (2000) (the FSA Prudential Sourcebook Paper) Annex B, 1.

[3] See generally the OECD Report on Risk Management in Financial Services (1992) which examines the causes of risk and the risk-management strategies followed by financial-services undertakings.

large-scale failure in the market-place.[4] More generally, the failure of a firm may cause a wider loss of confidence in the investment markets and a reduction in liquidity. From a market-failure perspective, prudential regulation addresses information-based market failures by protecting investors against solvency risks of which they may not be aware and manages systemic risks which cannot be corrected by market forces.[5]

The particular degree of risk posed by an investment firm to investor protection/confidence and market stability, the likely impact of an insolvency, and the degree of prudential supervision imposed accordingly will vary depending on the nature and complexity of the activities carried out. Market stability is unlikely to be threatened by the provision of investment advice, while dealing in securities and market-making, which can impact on the soundness of an investment firm, may pose more of a threat to the system depending on the importance of the firm and its place in the financial system. Similarly, the provision of investment advice does not raise investor-protection concerns on grounds of firm soundness although the supply of portfolio-management or broking services does, given the losses which the investor may suffer if the firm fails. The nature of the instruments dealt in by investment firms is also a factor. Heavy derivatives exposure can, for example, pose a risk to the soundness of a firm. As outlined further in section 9 below, the link between risk and regulation is particularly critical in the controversial area of capital-adequacy requirements which impose costs on investment firms.

VIII.2 THE SCOPE OF PRUDENTIAL REGULATION

VIII.2.1 *Macro and Micro Preventive and Protective Regulation*

Prudential supervision therefore has two rationales: it is concerned with investor protection, in that it protects investors against the consequences of insolvency and bolsters investor confidence in the market-place, but it is also concerned with the market-place as a whole and its protection against systemic risk and instability.[6] Overall, both rationales are ultimately directed

---

[4] The OECD's 1991 Report on Systemic Risks in Securities Markets (the OECD Systemic Risk Report) at 14 describes a systemic crisis as one 'which severely impairs the working of the system; and at the extreme causes a complete breakdown in it'. It went on to find at 45 that 'the failure of a large player in the securities markets could seriously affect other firms, clearing systems, and lenders as well as the overall functioning of the financial system'. Not all are agreed about the gravity of the systemic risk posed by investment firms. On the controversy about the extent to which investment firms raise systemic risk concerns and how capital adequacy rules should be designed accordingly see sect. 9.1.2 below.

[5] See, eg, the analysis of market failures in Page, A, and Ferguson, R, *Investor Protection* (1992) 36–9.

[6] For this dual rationale see Goodhart, C, 'Some Regulatory Concerns' in Goodhart, C (ed), *The Emerging Framework of Financial Regulation* (1998) 213, 220. See also Cesarini, F,

towards macro regulatory concerns: the protection of the soundness of the market-place and the preservation of confidence in the market-place. Prudential regulation is thus directed to the macro protection of the market as a whole, rather than to the micro protection of individual investors in their relationships with investment firms, although it does impact on those relationships, particularly where operational prudential controls are concerned.[7] Prudential supervision can also be characterized as preventive regulation, in order to contrast it with protective regulation which is concerned with the micro investor/investment firm relationship.[8]

VIII.2.2 *Forms of Prudential Regulation*[9]

Authorization requirements form a part of prudential regulation. Not only do they protect individual investors against information asymmetries by putting potential investment-services providers through a filter designed to keep riskily-structured, ill-equipped, and under-capitalized entities from the market, they also serve a systemic purpose in that, by limiting market access, they protect incumbent firms from increased competition and so reduce the number of firm failures which arise from competitive pressures.[10] Both as part of the authorization process, and throughout the life of the investment firm, capital adequacy controls form a major element of prudential supervision. Capital adequacy requirements are designed to ensure that an investment firm has sufficient financial resources to meet its commitments, survive certain risk-events such as major adverse market movements, and wind down its operations in an orderly manner.[11] They are particularly controversial due to their costs and what is sometimes regarded as the shaky foundation for their imposition; doubts have been cast on their investor-protection function (in that capital does not protect against the most common soundness-related risk to which an investor is exposed—fraud

'Economics of Securities Markets Regulation: Some Current Issues' in Ferrarini, G (ed), *European Securities Markets. The Investment Services Directive and Beyond* (1998) 65, 66.

[7] For this classification in terms of macro prudential controls which protect clients' money and the financial system against systemic crises and which are of importance to the financial system in general and micro financial controls, such as conduct-of-business controls, which operate at the level of the firm see Gros, D, and Lannoo, K, *The Euro Capital Market* (2000) 122.

[8] See, eg, Page and Ferguson, n 5 above, 39 and Ferrarini, n 2 above, 4. The prudential-preventive/protective divide is a fluid one in that investor-compensation schemes which usually activate when investment firms fail and have a protective function traditionally also come within the prudential-supervision framework. Prudential supervision which is entirely preventive in nature has been criticized as being inadequate, given that no amount of prudential supervision will prevent defaults from ever happening and that safety nets are accordingly required to ensure effective containment in the event of an insolvency. See the analysis by Szegö, G, 'The CAD and Competitive Distortion' in Ferrarini, n 2 above, 63, 65.

[9] For one view of the various forms of soundness regulation see Clark, R, 'The Soundness of Financial Intermediaries' 86 (1976) *Yale LJ* 1, 10.

[10] Ibid, 40.   [11] 1998 IOSCO Principles, n 1 above, para 12.4.

in dealing with assets) and on their connection to systemic risk control (in that the link between investment-firm failure and systemic instability is not completely made out). Prudential regulation also extends to structural and operational risk-management controls. These typically cover internal systems and controls (such as asset-protection and record-keeping rules), organizational structures, and ownership oversight requirements.

Successful prudential supervision involves the effective interplay of all of these risk-management techniques. It also must be sufficiently flexible to permit investment firms to engage in controlled risk-taking, which is essential for the operation of the investment-services and securities markets.[12]

VIII.3 THE EC AND PRUDENTIAL SUPERVISION

VIII.3.1 *Scope of the Regime*

The system of harmonized prudential supervision and risk management adopted by the EC for authorized investment firms broadly reflects the above formulation of prudential supervision. Unlike protective regulation which is only just emerging at EC level, the prudential regime is relatively well-established. Harmonized rules apply to the authorization process, initial and ongoing capital-adequacy levels, the protection of client assets, and other operational matters affecting firm stability, firm ownership, and the powers of supervisory authorities to monitor compliance with prudential requirements.

Authorization, operational, and capital-adequacy prudential rules are at the heart of the Investment Services Directive (the ISD), which has been strengthened by the Prudential Supervision Directive (the PSD).[13] The ISD's prudential-supervision regime for investment firms is supplemented by the capital-adequacy rules contained in the Capital Adequacy Directive (the CAD), which is a key ancillary measure to the ISD.[14] Investor-compensation schemes which traditionally form a part of prudential supervision but stand on the cusp between prudential and protective regulation are covered by the Investor Compensation Schemes Directive, examined in Chapter X.[15]

---

[12] 1998 IOSCO Principles, n 1 above, para 4.2.3.

[13] Directive 93/22/EEC on investment services in the securities field [1993] OJ L141/27 (the ISD) and Directive 95/26/EC amending Directives 77/780/EEC and 89/646/EEC in the field of credit institutions, Directives 73/239/EEC and 92/49/EEC in the field of non-life insurance, Directives 79/267/EEC and 92/96 in the field of life assurance, Directive 93/22 in the field of investment services and Directive 85/611/EEC in the field of undertakings for collective investment in transferable securities (UCITS), with a view to reinforcing prudential supervision [1995] OJ L168/7 (the PSD), respectively.

[14] Directive 93/6/EEC on the capital adequacy of investment firms and credit institutions [1993] OJ L141/1 (the CAD).

[15] Directive 97/9/EC on investor compensation schemes [1997] OJ L84/22 (the ICSD).

Finally, considered separately in Chapter XII in the context of clearing and settlement, the Settlement Finality Directive,[16] which seeks to bolster settlement systems against the systemic risk and legal risks attendant on the insolvency of a settlement-system participant, also forms part of the prudential supervision regime which supports the integrated investment-services market-place.

The prudential supervision regime will be discussed with reference to investment firms authorized to provide investment services under the ISD and subject to the ISD/CAD regime. Credit institutions authorized to provide investment services under the banking regime are, in relation to their invest-ment-services activities, subject to a broadly similar prudential regime, either via the direct application of the ISD or through replacement of ISD rules (such as authorization controls) by broadly similar measures in the banking regime. While brief reference will be made to the particular rules which apply to credit institutions providing investment services under the banking regime to illustrate how a broadly similar functional investment-services prudential regime applies, this chapter will not consider credit insti-tutions in detail and, in particular, will not consider the prudential controls (particularly capital adequacy controls) which apply to the traditional credit services provided by credit institutions. A review will also be carried out of the regime applicable to the most recent arrival on the EC's investment-services regulatory landscape, management companies providing services under the management-company passport.[17] In particular, reference will be made to the operational prudential rules of the new management-company regime as these rules represent a new departure for the EC prudential super-vision regime.

---

[16] Directive 98/26/EC on settlement finality in payment and securities settlement systems [1998] OJ L166/45 (the Settlement finality Directive).

[17] Amended Proposal for a European Parliament and Council Directive amending Directive 85/611/EEC on the coordination of laws, regulation and administrative provisions relating to undertakings for collective investment in transferable securities [the UCITS Directive [1985] OJ L375/3] with a view to regulating management companies and simplified prospectuses (the Management Company Proposal). COM(2000)331. The Council's Common Position is at [2001] OJ C297/10. The measure was adopted by the Council as a directive on 4 Dec 2001. This discussion is based on the Common Position (references to the Management Company Proposal are to the Common Position text, while references to Articles are to the revised Articles of the UCITS Directive introduced by the new regime). At the time of writing, the final text of the adopted measure had not been published in the Official Journal and had not yet come into force. The Parliament did not, however, materially amend the Common Position text during its second reading prior to the adoption of the measure. Its only amendment (which was to shorten the Common Position's 5-year time frame from the entry into force of the new regime, at the end of which the Commission was to review the capital requirements imposed on management companies, to 3 years) was accepted by the Commission (COM(2001)687).

VIII.3.2 *Features of the Regime*

The dominant influence of investment-services market integration on the substantive development of the EC investment-services regime is thrown into sharp focus by the prudential supervision regime. The market-integration objectives of the Treaty Articles on which the investment-services regime is based have resulted in the adoption of a relatively comprehensive harmonized prudential supervision regime as a means for constructing the integrated market through the passport device (as agreement on the passport and home-Member-State control would have been impossible in the absence of harmonization) and for protecting the stability of the integrated market-place post-liberalization. Where the link between market integration and the protection of the liberalized market-place is less clear, harmonization is much less advanced, as discussed in Chapter IX.[18]

Article 47(2) EC, which is the legal basis for the main directives which form the prudential supervision regime (ie the ISD, the CAD, and the PSD) is designed to facilitate the freedom to establish (and applies to the freedom to provide services via Article 55 EC), and provides for the harmonization or co-ordination of Member States' laws with respect to the taking-up and pursuit of activities as self-employed persons. While it is a market-liberalization device, in that it is designed to remove regulatory obstacles to free movement, Article 47(2) EC has been relied on to reregulate and harmonize prudential rules in order to operate the liberalizing investment-firm passport and mutual-recognition regime (although, as discussed in section 11.3.3 below the proposed financial-conglomerates regime might represent a new departure for Article 47(2) EC as a basis for prudential regulation). The harmonization of prudential rules is thus driven first and foremost by market-integration concerns. As can be seen from the statement in recital 3 to the ISD Preamble that 'the approach adopted is to effect only the essential harmonization necessary and sufficient to secure the mutual recognition of authorization and of prudential supervision systems, making possible the grant of a single authorization valid throughout the Community and the application of the principle of home Member State supervision', harmonization of prudential rules was a *sine qua non* for home-Member-State control and the success of the passport. It was also essential to ensure the stability of the new market-place which became more vulnerable to instability and

---

[18] Indeed, in discussing the pre-Accession strategies and preparations in the area of financial-services regulation to be undertaken by the associated countries of Central and Eastern Europe, the Commission's emphasis seems to be on soundness and prudential regulation rather than on protective supervision. See Clarotti, P, 'The EU As A Model for Financial Market Reform' in Norton, J, and Andenas, M (eds), *Emerging Financial Markets and the Role of International Financial Organisations* (1996) 22.

systemic shocks on liberalization.[19] As investment firms operate on a cross-border basis they become enmeshed with other markets and other firms to a much greater extent and their exposure to risk, and that of the integrated market-place, is heightened.[20] Indeed, the systemic implications of prudential supervision are typically raised in support of the harmonization of prudential standards over a regulatory competition as a means of removing regulatory obstacles.[21] Notwithstanding the dominant characterization of prudential supervision harmonization as a market-integration mechanism, the traditional twin themes of prudential supervision—the dominant theme of market stability and the secondary theme of investor protection (both of which feed into market integration)—appear in the directives which form the substantive harmonized prudential-supervision regime. Authorization standards are harmonized under the ISD in order to 'protect investors and the stability of the financial system' (recital 3), while prudential asset-protection rules are designed to protect investors (recital 29). The CAD's capital-harmonization rules are necessary in order to 'ensure the continuity of institutions and to protect investors' (recital 8), while the PSD's standards are directed to ensuring the stability and integrity of the financial system as well as to investor protection (recitals 8, 9, and 15). More recently, the Commission has acknowledged that 'the role of prudential regulation is to enhance and protect financial stability and soundness, including the protection of the individual depositor and investor'.[22]

The basis of the regime in market integration is also reflected in the emphasis in the prudential regime on ensuring competitive equality between credit institutions and investment firms when providing investment services. This is particularly the case with capital-adequacy regulation due to the anti-competitive effects of differing capital requirements. Levelling the investment-services market playing-field between credit institutions and investment firms as far as capital requirements are concerned is a major theme of the CAD and, as discussed in section 9.2.2 below, made for difficult and protracted negotiations. More recently, competitive equality has emerged as a

---

[19] As recently expressed in the Commission's Communication on Implementing the Framework for Financial Market—Action Plan (COM(1999)232) (the FSAP) at 10, 'the EU's supervisory and regulatory regime has provided a sound basis for the emergence of a single financial market which goes hand in hand with prudential soundness and financial stability'.

[20] See, eg, Federal Trust, *Towards an Integrated European Capital Market* (1993) 21.

[21] See Hertig, G, 'Imperfect Mutual Recognition for EC Financial Services' (1994) 14 *Int'l. Review of L and Econ.* 177, 180, and, albeit in the somewhat different context of credit institutions, the analysis in Davis, E, 'Problems of Banking Regulation—An EC Perspective' in Goodhart , n 6 above, 533, 547.

[22] Commission Services' Second Consultative Document on Review of Regulatory Capital for Credit Institutions and Investment Firms (the 2001 Regulatory Capital Review), MARKT/1000/01, 7.

central pillar of the review of the capital adequacy regime currently underway (section 9.6.3 below).[23]

The market-integration, systemic-stability and investor-protection interests which are declared to be served by the harmonized prudential supervision regime are addressed by a variety of supervisory mechanisms with a
common basis in managing soundness. The prudential regulation mechanisms used include: authorization controls; operational and organizational
prudential controls; ownership requirements; and, most controversially,
capital-adequacy requirements. Disclosure does not feature largely in the
prudential supervision regime, although the potential role of disclosure and,
accordingly, the market and market discipline in giving incentives to investment firms to adopt sound risk-management and stability policies and in
supplementing the capital-adequacy regime is now being canvassed (section
9.6.3 below).

The relatively secure basis of prudential supervision and systemic stability within the dominant market-integration objective of EC securities regulation has allowed harmonization to develop in a more sophisticated and
comprehensive manner than it has in the related protective supervision
sphere. This distinction between the regimes can be seen in the different
challenges which each regime is facing. While the major controversies
underlying the protective regime concern the characterization of investor
protection as a regulatory objective, the rationale for harmonization, the
extent to which further substantive harmonization should be undertaken,
and the regulatory mechanisms which should be used, the prudential supervision regime is grappling with problems associated with a more mature system. Among these is the extent to which the supervisory structure policing
the harmonized substantive rules is effective (section 10 below). In addition,
there is concern about whether the regime is sufficiently well adapted to
cope with the new strains integration and market developments are placing
on the regime's soundness and systemic risk controls. While the protective
regime is evolving to cope with the 'supply side' and the protection of
investors, the prudential regime is adapting to deal with the evolution of
'demand side' market participants, such as the development of financial conglomerates operating on a pan-EC basis (section 11 below). Prudential
supervision techniques are also evolving. Prudential regulation can be burdensome and costly. As understanding deepens as to how risks can best be
managed and how capital can be most effectively structured, revisions to the
regime will be required to ensure that it is flexible, effective, and cost-
efficient. Finally, to a greater degree than in the protective sphere, inter-

---

[23] At the heart of the revision is the need to ensure that 'the revised framework . . . [is] suitable to be applied to institutions of a wide range of scale and sophistication and who compete
in a variety of arenas . . . [t]he competitive equity between firms must be preserved but at the
same time opportunities for capital arbitrage avoided': ibid, 6.

national developments and innovations are having a significant impact on the evolution of the Community prudential supervision regime. In particular, recent work by the Basel Committee on capital adequacy and by the Joint Forum on Financial Conglomerates is being reflected in the EC regime (sections 9.6.3 and 11.3 below).

However, certain themes are common to the prudential and protective regimes. Differentiated regulation can be seen in both. In the prudential sphere, this operates in two directions: first, ensuring that investor-protection-based prudential rules (such as asset-protection rules) are not imposed on firms where the beneficiary of the protection is sophisticated and not in need of such protection and, secondly, ensuring that prudential regulation adequately reflects the risks to investor protection and systemic stability which are actually posed by the investment firm. With respect to the latter, the regime makes some attempts to differentiate in the application of capital-adequacy controls to investment firms based on the activities engaged in. It does not, however, fully engage with an assessment of the exact role which should be played by capital requirements, given the risks posed by investment firms, and accepts the imposition of capital requirements as an essential part of prudential supervision (section 9.6.3 below). The capital regime will become significantly more sensitive to risk, however, if current proposals for change are adopted (section 9.6.3). Moral hazard also appears as a potential danger in the prudential-supervision regime in two areas in particular. As far as investment firms are concerned, for example, excessively demanding capital requirements bolstering against insolvency may make an investment firm less careful in managing client assets. On the demand side, over-reliance by investors on authorization procedures and operating controls may diminish the extent to which investors assess the risk represented by a particular investment firm and its activities. Moral hazard is not, however, explicitly dealt with, save under the ICSD.

VIII.4 THE ROOTS OF THE REGIME

Although, as discussed in Chapter VI, the 1966 Segré Report[24] identified financial intermediaries as critical agents for the construction of an integrated capital market, it did not deal in any great detail with the liberalization of investment services, the devices which might be used to that end, or the soundness and risk-management controls which might be required to make integration effective. It did, however, note that divergences in operating controls were liable to distort competition and obstruct integration, and

---

[24] Report by a Group of Experts Appointed by the EEC Commission, *The Development of a European Capital Market* (1966).

called for the removal of fundamental rule-divergences through harmonization.[25] The early securities-regulation measures were concerned with the
securities-trading markets and access by issuers and were not focused on
investment firms and soundness questions. The 1977 Code of Conduct,
which was an incubator for much of the current securities-regulation
regime, did not deal with soundness and systemic stability questions, focusing instead on the conduct of securities transactions and the fairness and
efficiency of securities-trading markets.[26] It was not until the adoption of the
ISD/CAD regime and the arrival of the investment-firm passport that a tailored harmonized prudential supervision regime for investment firms began
to emerge.

VIII.5 PRUDENTIAL REGULATION AND AUTHORIZATION

VIII.5.1 *The ISD Regime*

The authorization conditions imposed by the ISD on investment firms form
a key element of prudential supervision, as well as forming the basis for the
ISD passport, by filtering out under-capitalized, inadequately experienced,
and potentially badly or fraudulently managed investment firms. These
entry-level soundness controls reduce the risk of loss of investor assets, as
well as the risk of any wider systemic instability which might follow, by
reducing the risk of firm default. The minimum initial capital requirement
set out in Article 3(3) is designed to ensure that the investment firm has adequate resources as well as to encourage sound and prudent management by
requiring the firm's owners to make a financial commitment to the firm.
Similarly, the review under Article 3 of the fitness and propriety of management, the assessment under Article 4 of the suitability of qualifying
shareholders in light of the need to ensure the sound and prudent management of the investment firm, and the Article 3 examination of the firm's
business activities and organizational structure provides an initial check on
the prudence and soundness of the investment firm.[27] These conditions do
not apply to credit institutions which supply investment services under a

[25] Report by a Group of Experts Appointed by the EEC Commission, *The Development of a
European Capital Market* (1966), 269–71. It also examined capital-adequacy controls in the context of credit institutions, noting that rules diverged considerably and that competition problems were likely to arise and, at 274, recommending, as a result, the 'gradual alignment of
laws prescribing rules for balancing the composition of the banks' liabilities and assets'.

[26] Commission Recommendation 77/534/EEC concerning a European code of conduct relating to transactions in transferable securities [1977] OJ L212/37 (the 1977 Code of Conduct).
It did, however, cover in General Principle 6 conflicts of interest management which also
appears in the ISD's operational prudential-supervision regime.

[27] See further Ch. VII, sects. 4.3–5 above on the authorization process. While the fitness and
propriety filter is an important element of prudential supervision it can be a burdensome
requirement from the perspective of the regulator, depending on the number of investment-

banking regime authorization (ISD, Article 2(1)), but prudential requirements as to initial capital, the fitness of management, and suitability of qualifying shareholders apply to the authorization of credit institutions under the BCD II[28] and BCD I[29] (CBD, Articles 5, 6, 7, and 8).

The authorization process carries a moral hazard, however, in that investors may associate an authorization with a State-sponsored guarantee and exercise less care than is warranted in their dealings with the firm. To that end, a harmonized requirement that authorized investment firms disclose that authorization does not mean that investments are guaranteed might have diluted the moral hazard while retaining the prudential benefits of authorization.

Since the adoption of the ISD, the authorization conditions have been supplemented by the PSD (for its part in the development of prudential supervision see section 10.3.1 below) which has added an authorization condition designed to ensure that the effective supervision of the investment firm will not be prejudiced or prevented by any close links between the investment firm and any other natural or legal persons. Article 2(2) of that directive introduces a new provision to Article 3(3) requiring that, where 'close links' exist between an investment firm and other natural and legal persons, the competent authorities may grant authorization only if those links do not prevent the effective exercise of their supervisory functions. This revision also applies to the authorization conditions set out for credit institutions authorized under the banking regime.

Supervision and enforcement of the authorization conditions and ongoing compliance by the investment firm with them is the responsibility of the home Member State (Article 8(1), see further section 10 below).

VIII.5.2 *The Management-company Regime*

With the exception of the initial capital requirements and the scope of the authorization, the authorization conditions imposed on the management companies of collective-investment schemes by the Management Company Proposal are broadly similar to the ISD conditions and reflect the same

services providers in a Member State. See Blair, W, Allison, A, Palmer, K, Richards-Carpenter, P, and Walker, G, *Banking and Financial Services Regulation* (2nd edn, 1998) 390.

[28] 2nd Council Directive 89/646/EEC on the coordination of laws regulations and administrative procedures relating to the taking up and pursuit of the business of credit institutions and amending Directive 77/780/EEC [1989] OJ L386/1 (the BCD II). Now part of the consolidated banking regime established by Directive 200/12 relating to the taking up and pursuit of the business of credit institutions [2000] OJ L126/1 (the CBD). For ease of reference, the original measures and the CBD will be referred to.

[29] 1st Council Directive 77/780/EEC on the coordination of laws regulations and administrative procedures relating to the taking up and pursuit of the business of credit institutions [1977] OJ L322/30 (the BCD I) (now consolidated in the CBD).

objectives with respect to investor protection and market stability.[30] Supervision of these requirements on an ongoing basis and enforcement lies with the home Member State (Article 5d).

VIII.6 PRUDENTIAL REGULATION AND OPERATIONAL PRUDENTIAL RULES

VIII.6.1 *Operational Prudential Rules*

Operational prudential rules impose risk-management standards on investment firms and their management with respect to internal organization and operational controls in order to protect investors and market stability. While they are not designed to impose a particular organizational or management model on investment firms, they provide a bulwark against poor risk-management and inadequate control systems. Poor internal-control systems can expose an investment firm to the risk of failure and aggravate the consequences of an insolvency.

The distinction between operational prudential controls and protective conduct-of-business rules is not always clear. Certain prudential rules, while connected with soundness and thus with the stability of the system in general, have a strong relationship with investor protection and may be classed as being directed towards the regulation of the relationship between the investment firm and the investor and as protective. Asset-protection rules, for example, are classed as conduct-of-business rules in some regimes,[31] while in the ISD itself, conflict-of-interest rules appear as both prudential controls under Article 10 and conduct-of-business rules under Article 11. Indeed, Article 11(3), which requires an investment firm to have and employ effectively the resources and procedures necessary for the proper performance of its business activities, may be regarded as a prudential rule. Classification of a rule as prudential for the purposes of Article 10 is, however, critical with respect to determining whether the home-Member-State (Article 10) or the host-Member-State (Article 11) rules apply.[32]

---

[30] Management Company Proposal, n 17 above, Art. 5, 5a and 5b. See further Ch.. VII sect. 9.3 above. Self-managed investment companies which do not designate a management company are also subject to authorization requirements, but as these concern the UCITS regime rather than the investment-services regime they are considered briefly in Part I, in Ch. V.

[31] In the UK, eg, client-asset rules form part of the conduct-of-business regime: FSA, Conduct of Business Sourcebook, Policy Statement (2001). COB 9. The FSA has stated in this regard that allocation of client-asset rules to the home Member State 'is in marked contrast to most other areas of conduct of business regulation where the rules of the host State apply': FSA, The Conduct of Business Sourcebook, Consultation Paper 45a, (2000) (the FSA Conduct of Business Paper) 82.

[32] The potential overlap between Arts. 10 and 11 rules has been identified as a problem for the efficacy of the ISD passport. See Ch. VII sect. 10.3 above.

VIII.6.2 *The ISD and Operational Prudential Rules*

VIII.6.2.1 *Article 10*

Article 10 requires each home Member State to draw up prudential super-vision rules to be observed at all times by investment firms. Under Article 2(1), Article 10 also applies to credit institutions which provide investment services under the banking-regime passport in relation to the provision of those services, as the banking regime's operational prudential requirements reflect the traditional functions of credit institutions and are not sufficiently adapted to the provision of investment services. While Article 13(2) of the BCD II (CBD, Article 17) obliges home Member States to require that credit institutions have sound administrative and accounting procedures and ade-quate internal-control mechanisms, the banking regime does not, for exam-ple, address the safeguarding of investor assets or conflicts of interests. The deposit-taking function of credit institutions is acknowledged, however, by the lifting of the Article 10 ban on own-account use of investors' funds, which applies to investment firms only.

Where the Article 10 prudential requirements are directed towards investor protection, such as the conflict-of-interest and asset-protection rules, they are not, unlike the conduct-of-business requirements set out in Article 11, explicitly subject to a differentiated protection requirement and do not expressly distinguish between professional and retail investors; this is largely a function of their organizational nature. Nonetheless, recital 32 pro-vides that it is 'appropriate to take account of the different requirements for protection of various categories of investors and of their levels of professional expertise'. Implementation of the Article 10 requirements should accord-ingly reflect this basic principle.

Broadly speaking, the rules protect against operational risk, or the risk of loss arising through some form of internal system failure (operational risk is, controversially, also likely to be managed via capital-adequacy require-ments—section 9 below). The scope of Article 10 evolved considerably dur-ing negotiations on the ISD from a loose-textured set of principles (which left Member States considerable discretion in their implementation) to the more tightly drafted set of mandatory prudential rules which the ISD now con-tains.[33] While questions could be raised about the sufficiency and stringency of the Article 10 standards, they are certainly more rigorous than the pro-tective regime's conduct-of-business 'principles' set out in Article 11. The

---

[33] In the original ISD proposal [1988] OJ C43/7 (the Original Proposal), Member States were given the option in Art. 9(3) of adapting or disapplying the prudential rules if they were not appropriate, given the nature of the investment service in question. Following the objections of the European Parliament [1989] OJ C304/35, 39 and ECOSOC [1989] OJ C296/6 para 2.20, this discretion was removed, although it has arguably been replaced by the injunction in recital 32 to apply regulation sensitively.

level of harmonization reflects the home-Member-State control principle (under Article 8(3) prudential supervision is the responsibility of the home Member State: see section 10 below) and the systemic stability implications of the adequacy of prudential supervision. While a regulatory competition could develop in operational prudential rules, it would be subject to the Article 10 floor. There is, of course, room for the reverse to occur. A race to the top is possible, given that Article 10 sets out minimum requirements only. Member States are free to introduce more stringent standards (ISD, recital 27).

VIII.6.2.2 *Article 10 and Internal Controls*

The home-Member-State's prudential rules must require each investment firm to have sound administrative and accounting procedures, control and safeguard arrangements for electronic data-processing,[34] and adequate internal-control mechanisms including, in particular, rules for personal transactions by its employees. This first Article 10 requirement is significantly more sophisticated than its predecessor in the original ISD proposal, which simply provided in Article 9 that 'sound administrative and accounting procedures and internal control mechanisms' be required of investment firms.

Although this first requirement is relatively wide-ranging, it does not make explicit the types of internal procedures and systems needed to manage risk effectively, leaving the exact determination of the risk-management rules required to the home Member State. Notwithstanding that this is in accordance with the minimum-standards nature of Article 10, as well as reflecting the impossibility of setting out in sufficient detail comprehensive risk-management rules, some further elucidation of the minimum standards would have strengthened the ISD's prudential regime. For example, the internal-control mechanism rule might have included the segregation of key functions which, where carried out by the same person, might result in errors or abuses which could expose the investment firm to increased risk.[35] Margin provision might also, due to its implications for soundness, have come within the administrative and internal-control requirements. Where investment firms provide credit facilities to investors, prudent risk management suggests that they be monitored closely.

As far as ongoing supervision of investment firms is concerned, while the Commission's July 2001 Working Paper on the ISD[36] is primarily focused

---

[34] While accounting and administration rules are standard in most regulatory regimes, the requirement in respect of electronic data-processing created new obligations for some Member States: Securities and Investment Board, *Implementation of the Investment Services Directive and Capital Adequacy Directive*, Discussion Paper (1994) (the SIB Paper) 24.

[35] 1998 IOSCO Principles, n 1 above, para 12.5.

[36] Overview of Proposed Adjustments to the Investment Services Directive, Working Document of Services of DG Internal Market, Document 1, July 2001 (the ISD Working Paper).

on conduct-of-business regulation, it has also addressed prudential controls. The reforms illustrate the general move by the EC into more sophisticated prudential regulation. The suggested revisions to Article 10 are largely related to internal controls (although the Working Paper suggests that more detailed rules implementing Article 10 can be expected as the Commission has suggested that level 2 measures be adopted where necessary to clarify or achieve convergence in national measures). They include the extension of Article 10 to cover the increased dependence on information-technology systems and, specifically, 'systems resilience and contingency arrangements',[37] as well as outsourcing functions. In particular, the Commission has suggested that outsourcing should be subject to the competent authority being satisfied that service provision is not subject to undue additional operational risk and subject to particular controls where the outsourcing has implications for the core business of the firm.

VIII.6.2.3 *Asset Protection*[38]

(a) *Rationale*

Proper protection of the investor assets which are held by an investment firm through segregation or identification procedures and own-account trading prohibitions is central to protecting investors' assets from an investment firm's insolvency and to recovering those assets in an orderly and timely fashion in the event of an insolvency occurring.[39] They also protect client assets from being misused by investment firms for their own account.[40] Ring-fencing or asset-protection rules also have a wider systemic importance in maintaining confidence in the operation of the financial markets.[41]

---

[37] Ibid, Annex 2, Art. 12.

[38] The asset-protection rule is garbled in the ISD as published in the Official Journal. A corrigendum is published at [1993] OJ L170/32.

[39] 'Client money regulation is specific to investment firms . . . it is designed to mitigate the impact of insolvency on investors, . . . by seeking to ensure that client money is not available to meet the claims of creditors in the event of a firm's insolvency but is preserved for distribution among clients': Page and Ferguson, n 5 above, 256. The dangers associated with inadequate segregation of investor assets became apparent in the USA in the late 1960s and early 1970s, when due to an extraordinary expansion in investment business generally, many investment firms (broker-dealers) were unable to keep up with the volume of transactions and failed to segregate assets properly. On the subsequent insolvency of several firms (in what was termed the 'back room crisis'), large-scale losses were experienced by investors, which resulted in a review of the segregation rules and the adoption of a federal compensation scheme.

[40] It has been noted that '[i]n the face of financial difficulties, the line between client and company funds is easily blurred, and the prospect of company failure provides an incentive to use accessible client funds to support the company's operation': Franks, J, and Mayer, C, *Risk, Regulation and Investor Protection. The Case of Investment Management* (1989) 77.

[41] The FSA has noted that one of the benefits of an effective client money system is 'increased consumer confidence arising from a perceived enhancement of investor protection, which consequently provide a spur to business': FSA, *Protecting Client Money on the Failure of an Authorised Firm*, Consultation Paper 38 (2000) (the FSA Client Money Paper) 26.

Article 10 aside, client assets are also protected in the EC regime at a more general level by the CAD's capital adequacy rules. Capital adequacy rules arguably indirectly reduce the risk to investor assets by helping an investment firm to withstand risk events which might lead to an insolvency and the loss of assets, although a moral hazard may arise if investment firms are as a result less likely to manage investor assets properly in the belief that they can ultimately buy their way out of any problems which may emerge.[42] Accounting and administrative procedures and internal controls designed to minimize fraud also support the asset-protection rules. Indeed, for investors, losses are most likely to follow on an insolvency which is combined with fraudulent dealings in investor assets.

Member State rules implementing the asset protection principles should, in accordance with Recital 32, be tailored according to the sophistication of the investors involved and use should accordingly made of devices such as rule waivers where appropriate.[43] Article 10 contains separate requirement with respect to the protection of client securities and client funds.[44] In both cases, the treatment is limited. The variety of ways in which Member States may, as a result, construct asset protection systems combined with home Member State control arguably leaves investors prey to considerable confusion as to how their assets are protected.

(b) *Investor Securities*

In relation to investor securities, the home-Member-State rules must provide that the investment firm makes adequate arrangements for instruments (the ISD does not specifically define 'instruments', but presumably the rules cover the instruments listed in the Annex to the ISD and in respect of which investment services are provided) belonging to investors in order to safeguard investors' ownership rights, particularly in the event of the investment firm's insolvency. The latter reference to the importance of safeguard

---

[42] See, in the context of imposing additional capital requirements on firms that hold investor money, FSA Client Money Paper, n 41 above.

[43] The original proposal gave an express discretion in Art. 9(3)(which was condemned by the Parliament and ECOSOC and was subsequently removed in the revised proposal) to Member States to disapply the ringfencing rules in respect of funds and securities owned by professional and business investors.

[44] The original proposal aggregated the treatment of funds and securities and simply provided that the investment firm 'arranges for securities belonging to investors to be kept separately from its own securities and for money belonging to investors to be placed in an account or in accounts which are separate and distinct from the firm's own account': Original proposal, n 33 above, Art. 9(2). By the time of the revised proposal [1990] OJ C42/7, the securities and funds requirements were split out by Art. 11(1). An investment firm was to arrange 'for securities belonging to investors to be kept separately from its own securities' and, in respect of client moneys, except in the case of an investment firm that was a credit institution, was to arrange for 'money belonging to investors to be placed in an account or accounts which are separate and distinct from the firm's own account'.

arrangements in the event of an insolvency is not made with respect to investor funds. The ISD does not specify what constitute 'adequate arrangements' for the purposes of Article 10. At the heart of this requirement, however, is that measures are in place to ensure that no confusion arises between investor and investment-firm securities. At a minimum, 'adequate arrangements' seem to require that client securities are identifiable as such and segregated. Article 10 does not deal with the out-sourcing of these arrangements by investment firms. As long as the arrangements entered into by the investment firm and permitted by home-Member-State rules are 'adequate', they appear to be permitted under Article 10.

(c) *Investor Funds*

In terms of investor funds,[45] the rules must ensure that 'adequate arrangements' are made to safeguard funds belonging to investors. Again, the nature of these 'adequate arrangements' is not specified, although the original proposal specified in Article 9 that separate and distinct accounts be used for investor moneys. The manner in which rights are safeguarded will typically involve a separate account held at a designated institution, but will depend to a large extent on the Member State's legal regime and the use of legal devices, such as the trust in the UK. Arguably the effectiveness of recording and accounting obligations with respect to the funds held will impact on the 'adequacy' of the arrangements, as will the methods used to distribute protected funds on an insolvency. Investor 'funds' are not defined, even though the scope of what constitutes client funds can be problematic, particularly with respect to when moneys become due and payable to the investment firm on its own account.

(d) *Own-account Trading*

Asset protection rules typically also involve the regulation of proprietary or own-account trading by the investment firm and usually set clear parameters within which proprietary trading can take place. Article 10 provides that provision must be made in home-Member-State rules for a prohibition on investment firms using investors' instruments for their own-account trading, except with investors' express consent and (with the exception of credit institutions) for a prohibition on using investors' funds for their own account. The asset-protection rules are not, however, designed to prevent an investment firm from doing business for its own account but on behalf of the investor where this is required by the nature of the transaction, as would be the case, for example, with stocklending (recital 29).

---

[45] For an analysis of the risks to which investor funds are exposed in the investment-management process see Franks and Mayer, n 40 above, 44, 47–50.

(e) *The Home-State-supervision Problem*

The imposition and supervision by the home Member State of its asset-protection rules will be more complex where the assets are held outside the home Member State through, for example, a branch, when the firm exercises its ISD passport rights.[46] Despite the difficulties associated with the imposition of a Member States' rules on assets held outside the Member State,[47] home-Member-State supervision dovetails with the ICSD which makes the home Member State's compensation scheme responsible for all losses sustained by investors across the EC as a result of the investment firm's activities.[48] As host Member States are not permitted to apply their asset-protection rules, effective investor protection and prudential supervision in this area will be heavily dependent on effective co-operation and information-sharing between the host- and home-Member-State authorities.[49]

VIII.6.2.4 *Record-keeping*

Records must be kept of the transactions executed by investment firms and must be sufficient to enable the home Member State's competent authorities to monitor compliance with the prudential rules. Records must also be retained for the periods which are laid down by the competent authorities.

VIII.6.2.5 *Conflicts of Interests*

The organizational theme which runs through Article 10 continues with its treatment of conflicts of interests. Article 10 requires that home-Member-State rules must provide that investment firms are structured and organized in such a way as to minimize the risk of clients' interests being prejudiced by conflicts of interests between the firm and its clients or between one of its clients and another. This rule is designed to reduce the conflicts of interests which may arise from the range of activities carried out by investment firms. It overlaps with the transactional conflicts-of-interests rule in Article 11, which requires Member States to include in their conduct-of-business rules a requirement that firms try to avoid conflicts of interests and, where they are unavoidable, to ensure that clients are fairly treated. The overlap has

---

[46] Prior to the adoption of the ISD, the UK client-money regime, eg, applied on a host-State basis and did not apply to assets arising from investment services provided outside the UK. See generally Haines, P, 'The Investment Services Directive—Progress to Date' (1995) 2 *EFSL* 30, 31.

[47] Difficulties may arise where the home Member State bases its regime on legal concepts which are unfamiliar to the host Member State's legal system: O'Neill, N, 'The Investment Services Directive' in Cranston, R (ed.), *The Single Market and the Law of Banking* (2nd edn, 1995) 189, 205.

[48] See Ch. X.   [49] On the co-operation mechanisms see sect. 10 below.

been acknowledged by the Commission which has stated that there is 'complementarity and overlap in the application of Articles 10 and 11'.[50] The overlap is also recognized in the exception to the home Member State's control of prudential rules which is made for host-Member-State conflict-of-interest rules. Where a branch is set up in a host Member State, its organizational structure and arrangements may not conflict with rules of conduct laid down by the host Member State to cover conflicts of interests.

VIII.6.3 *The Management Company Proposal and Operational Prudential Controls*

The Management Company Proposal imposes operational prudential requirements on management companies of collective-investment schemes. These requirements, which are subject to home-Member-State control (Article 5d), reflect the prudential controls introduced by the ISD but also address the particular collective portfolio-management activities of management companies. The scope of application of the harmonized rules depends on whether the management companies engage solely in collective portfolio-management activities (UCITS management) or also provide ISD-type services.

Article 5(f), which broadly reflects Article 10 of the ISD, requires home Member States to draw up prudential rules which management companies, with regard to the activity of the management of UCITSs authorized under the UCITS Directive, are to observe at all times. The first group of rules concerns internal procedures. In particular, the rules must require the company to have sound administrative and accounting procedures and control and safeguard arrangements for electronic data-processing. Adequate internal control mechanisms must also be required of management companies including, *inter alia*, the transparency-driven requirement that each transaction involving the fund may be reconstructed according to its origin, the parties to it, its nature, and the time and place at which it was effected. Management companies must also have rules in place concerning employee transactions and own-account investing. Finally, the rules must provide that the assets of the unit trust/common fund or investment company managed by the management company are invested according to the fund rules or the instruments of incorporation and the legal provisions in force. The second group of rules concerns conflict-of-interest management and break out in some detail the possible incidences of conflict. Management companies must be structured and organized in such a way as to minimize the risk of UCITSs'

---

[50] Communication from the Commission on the Application of Conduct of Business Rules under Art. 11 of the Investment Services Directive (93/22/EEC). COM(2000)722, 8. See the discussion of Art. 11 in Ch. IX sect. 5.2.5 below for a fuller discussion of conflict-of-interests regulation.

or clients' interests being prejudiced by conflicts of interest between the company and its clients, between one of its clients and another, between one of its clients and a UCITS, or between two UCITSs. The organizational arrangements of a branch may not conflict with the rules of the host Member State concerning conflicts of interest. The specialist nature of the prudential requirements applicable to management companies is underlined by the requirement that, in applying prudential rules, the home Member State must have regard to the nature of the UCITSs managed by the management company.

The organizational and operational structures of management companies are subject to additional prudential regulation by the delegation rules (Article 5g). The UCITS Directive does not currently address the delegation of functions by management companies. This is a widespread practice in the funds industry, and regulation of delegation has been identified as an urgent priority by the Commission, in view of the differences in the regulation of delegation practices across the Community.[51] Member States retain an overriding discretion as to whether delegation is permitted. Under Article 5g, however, where a Member State does permit a management company to delegate certain functions to third parties for the purposes of more efficiently conducting the company's business, a number of preconditions must be met. The competent authority must be notified in an appropriate manner. The mandate must also comply with certain conditions which are designed to address investor protection by controlling the categories of persons to whom a delegation may be made, and to ensure that the management company retains appropriate control over the delegation. In the case of the core function of investment management, management companies may delegate specific investment decisions only to intermediaries which are authorized or registered for the purpose of asset management and subject to prudential supervision, in accordance with investment-allocation criteria periodically laid down by the management company. Where investment-management mandates are given to a third-country intermediary, co-operation between the prudential supervisory authorities concerned must be ensured. Finally, in order to prevent a conflict of interest, investment-management mandates must not be given to the depositary or to any other undertaking whose interests may conflict with those of the management company or the unit-holders. More generally, delegation must not prevent the effectiveness of supervision over the management company, and in particular it must not prevent the management company from acting or the UCITS from being managed in the best interests of its investors, and measures must exist which enable those persons who direct the business of the management company

---

[51] Some Member States require certain activities such as asset management and fund accounting to be carried out by the management company; others allow delegation of all functions and impose conflicts-of-interests restrictions.

to monitor effectively at any time the activity of the person to whom the mandate is given. In addition, the mandate must not prevent the persons who direct the business of the management company from giving, at any time, further instructions to the person to whom functions are delegated or from withdrawing the mandate at any time. Having regard to the nature of the functions to be delegated, the person to whom the functions are delegated must be qualified and capable of performing the functions in question. Finally, the UCITS prospectus must list the functions which the management company has been permitted to delegate. In no case shall the management company's and the depositary's liabilities be affected by any delegation by the management company to third parties. In unusually picturesque language for a substantive provision, a management company is also prohibited from delegating functions to the extent that it becomes a 'letter-box entity'.

Where the management company also provides ISD services (essentially discretionary portfolio-management services), it must, partly in the interests of ensuring a 'homogeneous regulatory framework in this area',[52] comply with the operational prudential requirements set out in the ISD under Article 10 (Article 5(4)). In addition, special conflicts-of-interests rules apply where a management company is authorized to provide both collective and individual portfolio-management services. Under Article 5f, a management company which has been granted a dual authorization covering discretionary portfolio management may not invest all or part of an investor's portfolio in units of the unit trusts, common funds, or investment companies under its management unless it receives prior approval from the investor.[53]

VIII.7 PRUDENTIAL REGULATION AND OWNERSHIP CONTROLS

VIII.7.1 *Introduction*

Supervision of major shareholders is a well-established aspect of prudential supervision. Ownership controls are usually designed to allow supervisors to review the suitability of potentially dominant shareholders and prevent adverse influences on the conduct of the investment firm's business. They also seek to ensure that supervisors are aware of the position an investment firm may have in large complex conglomerates following changes in its shareholding.

---

[52] Recital 51.

[53] Self-managed investment companies are also subject to operational prudential controls. These are considered briefly in Ch. V as they form part of the UCITS regime, rather than the investment-services regime.

VIII.7.2 *Ownership Controls and the ISD*

In addition to requiring that the suitability of qualifying shareholders be assessed in light of their influence on the sound and prudent management of the investment firm as part of the initial authorization process under Article 4, the ISD also imposes notification obligations with respect to the acquisition and disposal of certain holdings in investment firms post-authorization.[54] Member States may impose notification obligations which are more stringent than the minimum harmonized requirements set out in the ISD (recital 27). As with Article 4, the rules apply in respect of a 'qualifying holding' which is defined as any direct or indirect holding in an investment firm which represents 10 per cent or more of the capital or of the voting rights,[55] or which makes it possible to exercise a significant influence over the management of the investment firm in which the holding subsists.

Under Article 9(1) (acquisitions) and (3) (disposals) Member States are to require that any person who proposes, directly or indirectly, to acquire or dispose of a qualifying holding in an investment firm must first inform the competent authorities and notify them of the size of the intended holding (in the case of an acquisition) or the actual holding (in the case of a disposal). Any such person must also inform the competent authorities if he proposes to increase or reduce his qualifying holding so that the proportion of the voting rights or capital held reaches, exceeds, or falls below 20, 33, or 50 per cent or so that the investment firm becomes or ceases to be a subsidiary of that person. Under Article 1(12) 'subsidiary' is defined by reference to Directive 83/349; Article 1(12) also provides that any subsidiary of a subsidiary undertaking is to be regarded as a subsidiary of the ultimate parent.[56]

The regulation of qualifying holdings is not restricted simply to notification. An important element of prudential supervision lies in the power of competent authorities to oppose acquisitions of qualifying holdings. Under Article 9(1) competent authorities have up to three months from the date of the notification 'to oppose' the planned acquisition if, in view of the need to ensure the sound and prudent management of the investment firm,

---

[54] These requirements which are set out in Art. 9 did not change greatly during the ISD negotiations and were based on the notification requirements of the BCD II (CBD, Art. 16).

[55] Voting rights are defined by reference to Art. 7 of Directive 88/627/EEC on the information to be published when a major holding in a listed company is acquired or disposed of [1988] OJ L348/62 (the Substantial Shareholdings Directive or SSD, now consolidated in Directive 2001/34/EC on admission of securities to official stock exchange listing and on information to be published on those securities [2001] OJ L184/1 (the Securities Consolidation Directive or SCD)). See Ch. IV.

[56] The 7th Company Law Directive 83/349/EEC on consolidated accounts [1983] OJ L193/1 defines subsidiary (and parent) in Art. 1(1). These definitions are outlined in sect. 9.5 below on consolidated supervision.

they are not satisfied of the suitability of the persons acquiring the qualifying holding. Where the competent authority does not oppose the acquisition plan, it may fix a deadline for its implementation. The opposition conditions, which track the Article 4 requirements applicable to qualifying shareholders during the authorization process, are vague. No guidance is given on what constitutes 'suitability' or 'sound and prudent management'. Widely varying interpretations of this provision are possible across the Member States, although FESCO's (now the CESR) work in harmonizing fitness and propriety standards and its criteria for how 'suitability' is to be established with respect to qualifying shareholders is likely to result in some convergence.[57] The acquirer and investment firm may, of course, defy the opposition by the competent authority. In such cases, the hitherto vague parameters of the opposition power harden as Article 9(5) provides that if a holding is acquired despite the opposition of the competent authorities, regardless of any other sanctions which may also be adopted, Member States shall provide for: the exercise of the corresponding voting rights to be suspended; the nullity of the votes cast; or for the possibility of their annulment. More generally, under Article 9(5) Member States are to require that, where the influence exercised by a person covered by Article 9(1) is likely to be prejudicial to the sound and prudent management of an investment firm, the competent authorities take 'appropriate measures' to put an end to that situation. These measures are listed as including injunctions, sanctions against directors and those responsible for management, and suspension of the exercise of the voting rights attaching to the shares held by the shareholders or members in question. These measures also apply to persons covered by Article 9(1) who fail to make a notification.

Where the acquirer is an investment firm authorized in another Member State (or the parent undertaking of, or a person which controls, such a firm) and where, as a result of the planned acquisition, the firm in which the acquirer proposes to acquire a holding would become the acquirer's subsidiary or come under his control, in reviewing the acquisition, the competent authority must consult with the competent authorities of that other Member State (Article 9(2)).

The notification obligations are not restricted to those making the regulated disposals or acquisitions. Article 9(4) places on obligation on investment firms, 'on becoming aware' of the relevant disposals or acquisitions, to inform the competent authority to that effect. In addition, at least once a year investment firms are to inform the competent authorities of the names of the shareholders and members who possess qualifying holdings and the sizes of such holdings. Although this information is typically available

---

[57] FESCO, *European Standards on Fitness and Propriety to Provide Investment Services* (1999), 99-FESCO-A See further Ch. VII sect. 4.4 above.

through the share register, Article 9(4) also refers to this information as being that 'as shown, for example, by the information received at annual general meetings of shareholders and members or as a result of compliance with the regulations applicable to companies listed on stock exchanges'. In this regard, the Substantial Shareholdings Directive imposes notification and disclosure obligations with respect to holdings in listed companies which reach or fall below certain thresholds (see Chapter IV above).

Since the adoption of the PSD, where the investment firm is part of a group or has close links with other entities, the ownership-control regime now extends to including an assessment of whether the group structure or the close links will obstruct effective supervision. This requirement is directed towards structural transparency, however, and not to assessing the suitability of shareholders.

Credit institutions which provide investment services under the banking-regime authorization are subject to a very similar notification regime under Article 11 of the BCD II (CBD, Article 16). Credit institutions are also subject to additional ownership controls which restrict the types of institutions within which a credit institution may invest, given that holdings in non-credit institutions may represent a risk to the soundness of a credit institution as a result of the increased danger of contagion or the risk that the stability of the credit institution may be threatened by activities carried out by another group entity. While these controls are primarily a matter of banking law rather than investment-services regulation they are outlined briefly in the context of financial conglomerates in section 11 below.

VIII.7.3 The *Management-company Regime and Ownership Controls*

Acquisitions and disposal of qualifying holdings in management companies will, under the new regime, be subject to the same notification and approval requirements as apply to investment firms under the ISD (Article 5e).

VIII.8 INVESTOR-COMPENSATION SCHEMES

Investor-compensation schemes represent an important element of prudential regulation, in that they provide redress when prudential rules fail and losses are sustained by investors. Due to difficulties in reaching agreement with respect to compensation-fund harmonization, the ISD simply provided in Article 12 that investors be informed which compensation fund or equivalent protection applied to the transaction in question, the degree of cover offered, or whether any compensation scheme would be available. In 1997, the ICSD was adopted and has introduced harmonized rules in this area, as discussed in Chapter X.

VIII.9 PRUDENTIAL SUPERVISION AND CAPITAL ADEQUACY

VIII.9.1 *Rationale*

VIII.9.1.1 *Loss Absorption, Systemic Stability, and Investor Protection*

The controversy which surrounds the imposition of capital-adequacy requirements on investment firms warrants some discussion, given that they form the central plank of the EC prudential supervision regime. The imposition of capital-adequacy requirements on investment firms is usually justified, in part, by reference to systemic risks and the danger posed to the financial system generally by the inability of investment firms to absorb, in an orderly manner, unexpected losses and, in particular, losses arising from market-risk events, usually adverse market movements.[58] A widespread failure of investment firms following a systemic securities-market collapse could impact severely on confidence in the market-place and have serious consequences for liquidity.[59] In the investment-services and securities markets, transactions take place involving a number of parties and funding/trading relationships, with each transaction often being dependent on the ability of the other party to pay. If a party is insolvent, or is simply facing a funding difficulty and cannot settle his obligations, but is forced into insolvency during a general liquidity crisis, a domino effect may arise, causing a series of failures, including consequent failures in clearing and settlement systems.[60] As the risk profile of investment firms increases through increased derivative-based activities, the dangers to stability become even more pronounced, as revealed by the efforts made to rescue the Long Term Capital Management hedge fund in 1998. Capital requirements seek to ensure that firms are better placed to sustain market risks and that if losses are sustained and lead to an insolvency, a firm can be liquidated in an orderly fashion, positions closed, and liabilities met without further disruption to the market-place. Capital-adequacy regulation also seeks to ensure that market participants have confidence in each other's ability to settle transactions and relieves investment firms of some of the necessity to check the financial position and integrity of counterparties on a continual basis.[61] Finally, capital-adequacy

---

[58] Steil, B, 'International Securities Market Regulation' in Steil, B (ed), *International Financial Market Regulation* (1994) 197, 204.

[59] See the discussion in the OECD Systemic Risk Report, n 4 above, 15.

[60] See Steil, n 58 above, 215.

[61] The SEC has noted that, in addition to enhancing investor confidence in the financial integrity of securities firms, its capital adequacy requirements 'promote transactions between broker-dealers, lenders and creditors, on the one hand and the counterpart broker-dealers on the other, because those entities are more likely to consider a broker-dealer creditworthy if it must comply with a liquidity based capital adequacy standard': 1934 Securities Exchange Act Release No. 27, 249.

rules work with operational prudential rules to protect investors whose assets are held by an investment firm against loss by cushioning the firm against losses and, if an insolvency arises, ensuring that the firm is wound up in an orderly fashion.[62]

In the EC, capital-adequacy requirements have an additional dimension, in that they serve as a device for market integration. However, while they support the passport device and the removal of individual Member States' rules, they also promote the traditional stability rationale in the altered risk environment of the expanded integrated market created post-liberalization.

VIII.9.1.2 *The Challenge to the Rationale*

The imposition of capital-adequacy rules on investment firms is a matter of some controversy. It seems to be generally accepted that credit institutions should be subject to capital requirements due to their central role in the economic infrastructure, their liabilities to depositors, and their vulnerability to destabilizing runs. With respect to the provision of investment services by investment firms, however, the opinion has been expressed that investment firms pose little threat in terms of systemic risk, as the marketable securities which tend to make up the asset base of investment firms allow for an orderly winding-up to take place and there is limited risk of contagion. Any remaining concerns raised by insolvency in terms of investor protection and counterparty assurance, the argument runs, can be dealt with, respectively, by investor-protection rules requiring the ring-fencing of assets and providing compensation schemes and settlement procedures which require delivery versus payment.[63] The nature of the activity engaged in and the importance of the firm may also weaken the argument for capital requirements.[64] In the case of portfolio-management services, for example, the point has been made that, while investment firms providing these services

---

[62] Overall, '[a]n appropriately designed capital standard should ensure that if a firm suffers losses, it continues to operate in a financially sound manner. It should protect counterparties, customers, and creditors by reducing the possibility that financial problems at a firm will cause it to default on its obligations': OECD Systemic Risk Report, n 4 above, 45. For the regulator's perspective, see the FSA's explanation of the purpose of capital requirements: '[c]apital principally provides a buffer that enables a firm to absorb unexpected losses without adversely affecting either the interests of consumer or market confidence': FSA, *The FSA's Approach to Setting Prudential Standards*, Consultation Paper 31 (1999) (the FSA Prudential Standards Paper), Annex C, para 2.1.4.

[63] See generally Dale, R, 'The Regulation of Investment Firms in the European Union' in Ferrarini, n 2 above, 27, 28–30. See also the discussion in Goodhart, C, Hartmann, P, Llewellyn, D, Rojas-Suarez, L, and Weisbrod, S, *Financial Regulation—Why, How and Where Now* (1998) 12–13 and, with reference to the effects of the 1987 stock market crash, Benston, G, *Regulation of Financial Markets. A Critique and Some Proposals* (1999) 29–30.

[64] For the view that capital requirements should differ depending on the impact of failure on the financial system and on the extent to which investors are exposed to losses on an insolvency see the FSA Prudential Standards Paper, n 62 above, 16.

are vulnerable to market movements and consequent failure, this vulnerability primarily arises through own-account trading. Not only should any risks to the stability of the financial system following on failure be addressed, as a result, through less costly own-account trading rules and the separation of own-account trading from the portfolio-management business, it has also been argued that portfolio managers are not as crucial to the financial system as broker dealers and their failure is less likely to be disruptive.[65]

Whatever the controversies about the appropriate role of capital adequacy in the regulation of investment firms, in the EC regime its connection to systemic stability and investor protection appears to have been accepted as an article of faith,[66] although the application of the regime is tailored, albeit to a limited extent, to reflect the different risks posed by the various activities carried on by investment firms and by allowing the use of internal risk-assessment models. The EC's approach to capital-adequacy regulation is not, however, entirely monolithic. Delivery of the traditional objective for capital-adequacy regulation, the promotion of soundness, is now increasingly being seen as a function of other operational and management controls and risk-management techniques which create a stable operating environment and not simply as a function of the adequacy of an investment firm's capital cushion. This wider movement can be seen in the EC capital-adequacy regime, particularly through the emphasis placed on risk-management procedures in the capital-adequacy review (section 9.6.3 below).

VIII.9.1.3 *Investment Services, Capital Adequacy, and Risk Management*

Capital-adequacy rules operate by permitting a financial institution to take on risk assets proportionate to the amount of capital the institution holds. The amount of capital required to be maintained by an institution will accordingly be a function of the risk assets held by the institution and is thus designed to ensure that an investment firm can withstand a variety of different risks. The primary risk to which investment firms are exposed to in relation to their investment-services activities is market risk. Market risk or position risk relates to the exposure of an investment firm to losses which may be sustained from open positions in price-sensitive financial instruments. It involves a number of elements, including the risk of the market moving against a particular instrument, risks inherent in the instrument itself, and general market movement risk (eg interest-rate movement risk) which could affect that security. Some securities will carry more risk than others. There

[65] Franks and Mayer, n 40 above, 156–9.

[66] For the different emphasis placed on capital controls as a means of regulating investment firms in the USA see Mayer, C, and Neven, D, 'European Financial Regulation: A Framework for Policy Analysis' in Giovanni, A, and Mayer, C (eds), *European Financial Market Integration* (1991) 112, 114.

are a number of ways in which capital requirements in respect of market risk can be assessed. The 'building block' approach, which has been adopted by the EC, divides market risk into risk that is specific to a particular issuer or security and general market risk and aggregates the two requirements.[67] A second significant risk for investment firms is counterparty or settlement risk. This is the risk that a counterparty will fail or delay in performing a contract (the extent to which investment firms engage in the practice of 'free deliveries' of securities before the payment funds have been received raises particular concerns for counterparty-risk management) or that the integrity of the clearing or settlement system being used will be compromised with adverse effects. Finally, investment firms are also exposed to base risks or core risks. These risks are administrative or commercial in nature and would cover, for example, overheads, expenses, and administrative errors such as execution mistakes. Capital-adequacy regimes address these risks by setting appropriate capital levels to cushion investment firms against their occurrence.

VIII.9.2 *Capital-adequacy Regulation of Investment Firms and the EC*

VIII.9.2.1 *The Rationale for the CAD*[68]

Adopted as an ancillary measure to the ISD,[69] the CAD lays down minimum rules in relation to the capital or own funds which investment firms must maintain as provision against the risks they incur. Although the CAD does not set out a considered rationale for the imposition of capital requirements on investment firms, notwithstanding the controversies outlined above, and does not, surprisingly, refer explicitly to the symbiotic relationship between greater integration and capital-adequacy harmonization,[70] own funds are

---

[67] At an international level, the 1993 Basel Committee on Banking Supervision proposals in respect of the market risk of credit institutions also adopted a building-block approach and this method was retained in the final Market Risk capital standards which were adopted in 1996. The building-block approach has been criticized for presuming that specific and general risk when added together will amount to market risk. See generally, Dale, R, 'International Banking Regulation' in Steil, n 58 above, 167, 176 and Hall, M, 'The Capital Adequacy Directive: An Assessment' 10 (1995) *JIBL* 78, 80.

[68] See, eg: Lavoie, C, 'Consensus on the EC Capital Adequacy Directive: What Will be the Future Costs of Securities Trading?' [1992] *JIBFL* 361; Dale, n 63 above; Haines, P, 'The Capital Adequacy Directive—Key Points' (1995) 2 *EFSL* 64; Hall, n 67 above; and Dassesse, M, Isaacs, S, and Penn, G, *EC Banking Law* (2nd edn, 1994) 185–97.

[69] The original proposal was presented by the Commission in 1990 [1990] OJ C152/6. The Commission's Explanatory Memorandum is at COM(90)141. Comments from ECOSOC and the Parliament followed in early and late 1991, respectively [1991] OJ C69/1 and C326/89. The Commission presented a revised proposal in 1992 [1992] OJ C50/5, Explanatory Memorandum at COM(92)13. The Council's common position was adopted later in 1992 (C3–361/92–SYN 257). The European Parliament's comments on the common position (at the 2nd reading of the co-operation procedure) are at [1992] OJ C337/114.

[70] Although the Explanatory Memorandum to the Original Proposal stated that the main objective of the proposal was to 'ensure that both the health of the general financial system and individual investors are adequately protected in the new integrated European market': ibid, 1.

recognized as a 'key feature in an internal market in the investment services sector since own funds serve to ensure the continuity of institutions and to protect investors' and the need for a 'common framework for monitoring the risks incurred' by investment firms is acknowledged (recitals 8 and 2, respectively). Although the solvency link is highlighted, the immediate motivation for harmonizing capital requirements is the ISD passport. The adoption of a capital-adequacy regime is linked to the 'essential harmonization that is necessary and sufficient to secure the mutual recognition of authorization and of prudential supervision systems' and is regarded as an 'essential aspect . . . of the harmonization necessary for the achievement of mutual recognition within the framework of the internal market' (recital 3).

Capital-adequacy regulation also fulfils a role beyond its traditional remit of solvency and stability protection. The CAD and its capital requirements are designed to maintain a level playing-field between credit institutions and investment firms by subjecting them to the same capital-adequacy regime in respect of their investment services and other businesses (recitals 9 and 10).[71]

VIII.9.2.2 *A Functional Approach*

Prior to the adoption of the CAD, credit institutions were already subject to a capital-adequacy regime with respect to the supervision and monitoring of credit risks (broadly speaking, the risk of counterparty default) via the now consolidated Solvency Ratio Directive (SRD) and the Own Funds Directive (OFD).[72] Their requirements are designed to guard against systemic risks and the threat of depositor loss by strengthening the long-term solvency of a credit institution and are not fine-tuned to the particular market risks arising in respect of assets deriving from investment-services or securities activities.

Credit institutions and investment firms were traditionally subject to different capital requirements owing to their different activities. The traditional

---

[71] Leading one commentator to note that 'the regulatory constraints imposed on European investment firms is the price to be paid for making the universal banking model a central plank of the European financial market regime': Dale, n 63 above, 37.

[72] Directive 89/647/EEC on a solvency ratio for credit institutions [1989] OJ L386/14 (the SRD) and Directive 89/299/EEC on the own funds of credit institutions [1989] OJ L124/16 (the OFD), both now consolidated in the CBD. These requirements which, respectively, impose harmonized credit-risk capital requirements and a harmonized definition of the sources from which a credit institution may meet its capital or own-funds requirements, are based on the internationally agreed standards for credit risk capital adopted in 1989 (Basel Committee on Banking Supervision, International Convergence of Capital Measurement and Capital Standards (the Basel Accord)). The basic credit-risk capital requirement is that credit institutions maintain a minimum ratio of 8% of eligible own funds to risk-weighted balance sheet and off-balance sheet items. Arts. 6–8 of the now consolidated SRD (CBD, Arts. 43–45) categorizes how assets are to be risk-weighted and applies weightings of 0%, 20%, 50%, and 100% according to the category to which the asset belongs.

argument for imposing capital requirements on credit institutions is based on their asset and liability structure. Given that loans form a major part of a credit institution's asset base and that in an insolvency or a liquidity crisis they are not readily marketable, and that, on the other side of the equation, the major component of a credit institution's liabilities consists of repayable-on-demand deposits, if a credit institution experiences difficulties, or if a rumour to that effect is circulated, the possibility of destabilizing 'runs' on that individual credit institution and on other institutions in the system arises. Bolstering the soundness of credit institutions through capital requirements is also regarded as necessary, given the range of activities credit institutions engage in and their central role in the economic infrastructure. Investment firms are not subject to large-scale withdrawals of funds and provide a much narrower range of services. They can also be wound down in a more orderly fashion as their asset base consists of liquid assets. The type of capital required by investment firms and credit institutions is also broadly different. Credit institutions require permanent capital (such as share capital and reserves) which protects against insolvency. An investment firm's capital cushion is typically designed to ensure that an investment firm's asset base is sufficiently liquid to meet its claims as they fall due and, in the event of a winding down of its activities, to allow for an orderly liquidation which does not cause systemic or investor-protection difficulties. Investment firms need greater flexibility in meeting their funding and capital requirements which can change rapidly due to the volatile nature of the securities markets and their rapidly changing balance sheets. Of particular importance for investment firms is the ability to rely on more temporary sources of capital (such as subordinated debt) which can be raised more easily.

Notwithstanding these differences, and unlike the original proposal which was based on two discrete regimes for credit institutions and investment firms (although it is clear from the preparatory material that the Commission was unsure as to the appropriateness of this approach),[73] the CAD adopts a functional approach to capital adequacy.[74] It provides a framework of common harmonized rules which set out the capital-adequacy requirements imposed on investment firms and credit institutions alike, and which apply depending on whether the activities subject to the capital requirements are banking-related or investment-services- and securities-related. The trading book device is used to differentiate between traditional banking and investment services and their different capital requirements. The basis of the functional approach (which has had a significant impact on how the

---

[73] Explanatory Memorandum to original proposal, n 69 above, 5.

[74] The functional approach has been criticized as ignoring the systemic risk connected with particular types of financial institutions. See, eg, Scott Quinn, B, 'EC Securities Regulation' in Steil, n 58 above, 205.

CAD is structured and its level of harmonization)[75] in the desirability of a level playing-field can be seen from the CAD Preamble: 'in a common financial market, institutions, whether they are investment firms or credit institutions, engage in direct competition with one another . . . it is therefore desirable to achieve equality in the treatment of credit institutions and investment firms' (recitals 9 and 10). This theme recurred consistently throughout the evolution of the CAD. Even while the original proposal introduced two streams of capital-adequacy regulation for investment firms and credit institutions, the Explanatory Memorandum made clear that a level playing-field was intended and that the capital rules were not designed to give firms an incentive to adopt one institutional structure over another.[76] The EC was not alone at the time in trying to achieve parity in the treatment of credit institutions and investment firms. Although the co-operative effort would later collapse, in the early 1990s IOSCO and the Basel Committee began to co-ordinate their efforts in this area in order to reach a common position on capital-adequacy requirements in respect of market risk for investment firms and credit institutions; the Basel Committee was concerned that the imposition of capital requirements on credit institutions in respect of their investment-services activities would, in the absence of a similar move by the securities regulators, divert investment-services business away from credit institutions to less well-regulated investment firms.[77] Notwithstanding the impact the level-playing-field objective has had on the development of the regime, the equal treatment meted out in the CAD is not sufficient, of itself, however, to ensure a level playing-field in terms of capital adequacy between credit institutions and investment firms.[78]

The negotiations on the CAD reflect the difficulty in levelling the playing-field between investment firms and credit institutions with respect to capital adequacy. Germany wished to protect the competitive position of its universal banks, which were subject in respect of all their activities, including investment-services activities, to heavy capital requirements which reflected credit risk and the need to ensure solvency. It favoured the imposition of the credit-institution model of capital-adequacy regulation on the provision of investment services. The UK, which imposed a less onerous and more

---

[75] The substantive rules of the CAD have been described as amounting to 'nothing more than a framework', an outcome that was 'perhaps unavoidable in a piece of legislation that attempts to provide common rules for entities that, traditionally at least, have had fundamentally different capital requirements': Dassesse *et al.*, n 68 above, 192–3.

[76] Explanatory Memorandum, n 69 above, 2.

[77] Steil, n 58 above, 201.

[78] In practice, investment firms and credit institution tend to maintain capital levels significantly higher then those imposed by law (as high capital levels are rewarded by the stock markets). As a result, regulatory requirements, of themselves, are not as significant as they otherwise might be for the competitiveness of investment firms and credit institutions: Dale, R, and Wolfe, S, 'Capital Standards' in Steil, B (ed), *The European Equity Markets. The State of the Union and an Agenda for the Millennium* (1996) 265, 230.

flexible regime on investment firms and, in particular, permitted much greater reliance on short-term subordinated loan capital (which was excluded from the German definition of own funds), sought to protect the competitiveness of its investment firms. It was concerned that the high capital standards in the German model would drive the investment-services industry away from London unless a less onerous model which reflected more closely the activities of investment firms was adopted.[79] The deadlock was finally broken by the decision to apply the same capital standards to both credit institutions and investment firms and to use the 'trading book' device as a means of isolating the investment activities of credit institutions and investment firms for the purposes of calculating market risk.

VIII.9.3 *The CAD: Capital Requirements*

VIII.9.3.1 *The Basic Framework and the Trading Book*

Article 8(2) of the ISD requires the competent authorities of the home Member State to ensure that investment firms comply with the requirements of the CAD. By virtue of Article 2(1) of the ISD, the CAD requirements also apply to credit institutions which provide investment services within the scope of the ISD. Under Article 1(2) of the CAD, Member States may impose additional or more stringent requirements than those set out in the Directive.

A key feature of the CAD is the imposition of capital requirements in respect of the 'trading-book business' of investment firms and credit institutions. The 'trading-book business' device was developed to allow an assessment to be made of the market risk posed by the activities of investment firms and credit institutions, and to ensure a level playing-field in respect of capital-adequacy regulation of the market risks incurred by either type of institution. The trading book consists of instruments which are held for trading purposes (and thus have a 'short-term holding horizon')[80] and is designed to leave longer-term investments to the credit-risk capital rules of the now consolidated SRD. It covers 'positions in securities and other financial instruments [which are defined in Article 2(5) by reference to the instruments listed in the Annex to the ISD] which are held for trading purposes and are subject mainly to market risks and exposures relating to certain financial services provided to customers' (recital 13). The constituents of the trading book are defined in great detail in Article 2(6); revisions to the trading-book definition are expected from the capital adequacy review discussed in section 9.6.3 below.

---

[79] See Poser, N, *International Securities Regulation. London's 'Big Bang' and the European Securities Markets* (1991) 351.
[80] 2001 Regulatory Capital Review, n 22 above, 45–6.

Its components are: proprietary positions in financial instruments which are held for resale and/or which are taken on with the intention of benefiting in the short term from actual and/or expected differences between their buying and selling prices or from other price or interest-rate variations, and positions in financial instruments arising from matched principal broking, or positions taken in order to hedge other elements of the trading book; exposures due to unsettled transactions, free deliveries, and OTC derivatives;[81] exposures due to securities lending[82] and repurchase agreements[83] and exposures due to reverse repurchase agreements and securities-borrowing agreements;[84] and exposures in the form of fees, commission, interest, dividends, and margin on exchange-traded derivatives which are directly related to the items included in the trading book. All positions must be marked to market on a daily basis.

Under Article 2(6), inclusion or exclusion of particular items from the trading book is to be undertaken in accordance with objective procedures including, where appropriate, accounting standards in the institution concerned. These procedures and their consistent implementation are subject to review by the competent authorities. As the CAD's capital-adequacy requirements for the trading book are lower than the requirements applicable to non-trading-book activities by the now consolidated SRD under Article 4(1)(iii), it is critical that the constitution of the trading book is carried out correctly and in accordance with the CAD's requirements, as the two different regimes create the danger that a credit institution engaged in the provision of investment services may move assets from the non-trading book to its trading book. Particular care was taken in drafting the CAD to ensure that securities borrowing and reverse repurchase agreements, for example, which could be used by institutions as a disguised form of secured lending

[81] OTC derivatives are defined in Art. 2(10) by reference to Annex II of the now consolidated SRD (CBD, Annex IV) which lists various types of off-balance-sheet items including interest-rate contracts and foreign-exchange contracts.

[82] Securities lending and securities borrowing transactions are defined in Art. 2(18) as any transaction in which a credit institution or an investment firm or its counterparty transfers securities against appropriate collateral, subject to a commitment that the borrower will return equivalent securities at some future date or when requested to do by the transferor. The transaction will constitute securities-lending for the party transferring the securities and securities-borrowing for the party to which they are transferred.

[83] Repurchase and reverse repurchase agreements are defined in Art. 2(17) as any agreement in which a credit institution or an investment firm or its counterparty transfers securities or guaranteed rights relating to title to securities where that guarantee is issued by a recognized exchange which holds the rights to the securities, and the agreement does not allow an institution to transfer or pledge a particular security to more than one counterparty at one time, subject to a commitment to repurchase them (or substituted securities of the same description) at a specified price on a future date specified, or to be specified, by the transferor, being a repurchase agreement for the party selling the securities and reverse repurchase agreement for the party buying them.

[84] These items are to be included in the trading book only if the competent authorities approve and a number of additional conditions set out in Art. 2(6)(b)(i)–(v) are met.

and should, in such circumstances be subject to the credit-risk-based non-trading book regime, are included in the trading book only when the conditions set out in Article 2(6)(b)(i)–(iv) are met.[85] To that the end, competent authorities are specifically required to have the necessary powers to oversee compliance with the trading book rules (Article 9(3)).

VIII.9.3.2 *Scope*

Under Article 1(1), the capital requirements of the CAD apply to credit institutions as defined by Article 1 of the BCD I (CBD, Article 1(1)) (an undertaking whose business it is to receive deposits or other repayable funds from the public and to grant credits for its own account) and which are subject to the capital requirements of the now consolidated SRD. They also apply to investment firms as defined by the ISD, with the exception of credit institutions, 'local firms', and firms which only receive and transmit orders from investors without holding money or securities belonging to their clients, and which for that reason may not at any time place themselves in debit with their clients. A local firm is defined by Article 2(2) as a firm dealing only for its own account on a financial futures or options exchange or for the account of or making a price to other members of the same exchange and guaranteed by a clearing member of the same exchange. Responsibility for ensuring the performance of contracts entered into by such a firm must be assumed by a clearing member of the same exchange, and such contracts must be taken into account in the calculation of the clearing member's overall capital requirements so long as the local firm's positions are entirely separate from those of the clearing member. These last two forms of investment firm reflect the risk-sensitive approach to capital adequacy. The Commission was of the reasonably held opinion that the main risks such firms represent for investors concern fraud- and negligence-related risks, which are not best addressed by capital requirements, but are more effectively dealt with by the fitness and propriety requirements which are imposed by the ISD and professional-indemnity insurance.[86]

VIII.9.3.3 *Initial Capital Requirements and Investment Firms*

Article 3 of the CAD imposes initial minimum capital requirements on investment firms and sets out the conditions under which 'grandfathering' is permitted. In another illustration of the risk-sensitive approach to regula-

---

[85] Although it has been noted that defining the trading book by reference in part to trading intention (Art. 2(6)(a)) will make policing of the trading book difficult: Dale and Wolfe, n 78 above, 236. The revisions to the trading book which have been suggested by the Commission reflect this concern and tighten up the allocation process (sect. 9.6.3 below).

[86] Explanatory Memorandum to revised proposal, n 69 above, 3.

tion, the requirements apply on a graduated scale, given that 'it is appropriate to establish different amounts of initial capital depending on the range of activities that investment firms are authorized to undertake' (recital 4). These requirements are discussed in Chapter VII.

VIII.9.3.4 *Article 4*

Under Article 4(1) of the CAD, investment firms are required to hold 'own funds' which are always more than or equal to the sum of a number of different capital requirements. If the own funds maintained by an investment firm fall below the requirements imposed by Article 4(1), the competent authorities are required to ensure that the 'institution in question takes appropriate measures to rectify its situation as quickly as possible' (Article 4(3)).

The different risks set out in the Annexes to the CAD against which an investment firm is required to maintain capital requirements which, aggregated together, form the total capital required of investment firms are outlined in section 9.3.6 below.

VIII.9.3.5 *Own Funds and Investment Firms*

Any capital-adequacy regime's characterization of own funds should ensure that the own funds held serve the objectives of the capital-adequacy regime in that they are able to absorb losses. The CAD defines own funds by reference to the now consolidated OFD but also provides an alternative definition of own funds (Annex V).

(a) *The (now consolidated) OFD Regime*

Article 2(1) of the now consolidated OFD (CBD, Article 34(2)) sets out an extensive list of the elements which may be included within the calculation of own funds, and is considered in outline only here. The elements of own funds can be divided into two categories—core and supplementary. In general, core capital is permanent. Core capital includes: paid-up share capital including share premium accounts but excluding cumulative preferential shares (which can, however, go to supplementary capital) (Article 2(1)(1)) (CBD, Article 34(2)(1)); reserves and profits or losses brought forward as a result of the application of the final profit or loss (Article 2(1)(2)) (CBD, Article 34(2)(2)); and funds for general banking risks (Article 2(1)(4)) (CBD, Article 34(2)(3)). Supplementary capital includes: revaluation reserves (Article 2(1)(3)) (CBD, Article 34(2)(4)); value adjustments (Article 2(1)(5)) (CBD, Article 34(2)(5)); and fixed term cumulative preferential shares and subordinated loan capital (Article 2(1)(8)) (CBD, Article

34(2)(8)). Under Article 4(3) (CBD, Article 36(3)), inclusion of the latter
two items is dependent on the existence of binding agreements which, in the
event of the bankruptcy or liquidation of the credit institution, provide that
they rank after the claims of all other creditors and are not to be repaid until
all other outstanding debts have been settled. Subordinated loan capital is
subject to additional conditions including the following: it must be fully paid
up; it must have an original maturity of at least five years; the extent to
which it can rank as own funds must be gradually reduced during at least
the last five years before repayment; and the loan agreement must not contain any clause providing that, in specified circumstances other than the
winding up of the institution, the debt will become repayable before the
agreed payment date. Member States are given a considerable degree of discretion by Article 2(1)(6) (CBD, Article 34(2)(6)) which permits the inclusion of 'other items' which are defined in Article 3 (CBD, Article 35) as funds
with the following characteristics: they are freely available to the credit institution to cover normal banking risks where revenue or capital losses have
not yet been identified; their existence is disclosed in internal accounting
records; and their amount is determined by the management of the credit
institution, verified by independent auditors, made known to the competent
authorities and placed under their supervision. Finally, under Article 2(1)(7)
(CBD, Article 34(2)(7)) the commitments of members of credit institutions
set up as co-operative societies and the joint and several commitments of the
borrowers of certain institutions which are organized as funds may be
included as supplemental own funds.

Article 2(1) (CBD, Article 34(2)) also sets out the items which are
specifically excluded from comprising own funds in accordance with Article
6 (CBD, Article 38) (see below). These include: own shares at book value
held by a credit institution (Article 2(1)(9)) (CBD, Article 34(2)(9)); intangible assets (Article 2(1)(10)) (CBD, Article 34(2)(10)); and material losses
of the current financial year (Article 2(1)(11)) (CBD, Article 34(2)(11)).
Also excluded under Article 2(1)(12) and (13) (CBD, Article 34(2)(12) and
(13)) are holdings, subordinated claims, and 'other items' in other credit
and financial institutions which meet certain thresholds. Parent companies
which are subject to consolidated supervision need not deduct their holdings
in other credit institutions or financial institutions which are included in the
consolidation.

Under Article 6(1) (CBD, Article 38(1)), thresholds are placed on the
extent to which supplementary capital can be used to meet own-funds
requirements. In particular, total supplementary capital elements cannot
under Article 6(1)(a) (CBD, Article 38(1)(a)) exceed 100 per cent of core
capital minus the deductions under Article 2(1)(9)–(11) (CBD, Article
34(2)(9)–(11)) and, under Article 6(1)(b) (CBD, Article 38(1)(b)), commitments of members of credit institutions set up as co-operative societies and

funds and fixed-term cumulative preferential shares and subordinated loan capital cannot together exceed 50 per cent of that amount. Under Article 6(1)(c) (CBD, Article 38)(1)(c)), the deductions under Article 2(1)(12) and (13) (CBD, Article 34(2)(12) and (13)) must be made from the own funds total.

(b) *The Alternative Regime*

The approach taken by the CAD to the critical definition of own funds is flexible. An alternative definition is offered to the OFD definition of own funds, as the latter was drafted for credit institutions and accordingly reflects the largely illiquid nature of credit-institution assets and the need for permanent capital to protect against threats to deposits. The alternative definition takes into account the particular characteristics of the activities carried on by investment firms which predominantly involve market risk and the greater liquidity demands on investment firms. Competent authorities may accordingly permit investment firms which are required to meet the capital requirements set out in Annexes I (position risk), II (settlement and counterparty risk), III (foreign exchange risk), IV (other risks), and VI (large exposure risk) to use an alternative definition of own funds for the purposes of meeting those requirements only (Annex V, paragraph 2). In particular, the conditions placed on the use of subordinated loan capital are less stringent. The alternative definition allows for the use of short-term fully paid-up subordinated loan capital with a minimum maturity of two years as own funds, provided that the debt is not subject to any requirement that it is repayable in certain circumstances (other than in the case of a winding up) before the agreed date, unless repayment is approved by the competent authorities, and that it is subject to a lock-in clause which requires that neither principal nor interest be repaid, if to so do would bring the investment firm's capital below 100 per cent of its overall requirements. The credit institution or investment firm is required to inform the competent authorities of all repayments on subordinated loan capital as soon as its own funds fall below 120 per cent of its total requirements. The use of subordinated loan capital as own funds is also subject to ceilings. Short-term subordinated debt, which can be issued with greater ease than share capital, allows investment firms to meet their trading-book requirements more easily, given that their funding requirements can change drastically owing to the volatile nature of securities markets. Another significant feature is the option given to competent authorities to require that illiquid assets be deducted in full from own funds.[87] This requirement reflects the greater liquidity demands of trading-book activities. Illiquid funds are traditionally not favoured in the

---

[87] Annex V(2)(d).

constitution of an investment firm's own funds due to the liquidity demands placed on investment firms by their market activities.

The components of own funds (illiquid assets being deducted at the discretion of the competent authority) under the alternative definition in full are: (1) now consolidated OFD own funds subject to a modification of the list of exclusions from own funds in Article 2(1) (CBD, Article 34(2)) where investment firms are required to deduct illiquid assets from own funds, in that, in such cases, only the items under Article 2(12) and (13) (CBD, Article 34(2)(12) and (13)) in respect of holdings in other institutions need be deducted; (2) an institution's net trading-book profits net of any foreseeable charges or dividends, less net losses on its other business, provided that none of these amounts has already been included in the calculation of own funds under the OFD and, in particular, under Article 2(1)(2) (CBD, Article 34(2)(2)) (reserves) or Article 2(1)(11) (CBD, Article 34(2)(11) (deduction of material losses); and (3) subordinated loan capital (subject to the additional conditions set out above) and/or the supplementary components of own funds under Article 2(1) OFD (CBD, Article 34(2)). Competent authorities may under paragraph 5 of Annex V permit credit institutions and investment firms to replace subordinated loan capital with the supplementary components of own funds.

VIII.9.3.6 *The Capital-adequacy Requirements for Investment Firms*

(a) *Trading-book Capital Requirements*

The first of these requirements concerns the main risks addressed by the CAD. Under Article 4(1)(i) capital requirements are imposed in respect of the trading-book business of the investment firm and, specifically, in relation to position or market risk, settlement and counterparty risk, and large exposure risk. Annexes I, II, and VI of the Directive, respectively, set out detailed instructions on how the capital requirements are to be calculated in respect of each of these risks. Two assumptions support the capital adequacy assessment: '(i) extensive use of market value, supported by the availability of market prices for the instruments or the relevant risk factors; and (ii) active management of [trading book] items under a short-term horizon'.[88]

The position or market-risk requirements set out in Annex 1 are extensive. Broadly speaking, position risk on a security is to be established on a 'building-block' basis[89] by assessing both the specific risk (or the risk of a

---

[88] 2001 Regulatory Capital Review, n 22 above, 45.

[89] The Commission originally followed the 'comprehensive' approach according to which a single factor which assesses both general and specific risk is assigned to each instrument: Explanatory Memorandum to original proposal, n 69, 3. By adopting the building-block approach rather than the comprehensive approach, the EC took a different approach from that of the USA and exacerbated the difficulties at international level in agreeing common

price change in the instrument concerned due to factors related to its issuer or, in the case of a derivative, the issuer of the underlying instrument (per Annex I)) and general risk (or the risk of a price change in the instrument due to a change in interest rates (in relation to debt instruments or debt derivatives) or (in the case of equities or equity derivatives) broad equity market movement unrelated to any specific attributes of individual securities (per Annex I)) attached to the security. Annex I sets out detailed requirements for the assessment of specific and general risk in relation to traded debt instruments and equities and includes special requirements for stock-index futures and the underwriting of debt and equity instruments. As the calculations are partly based on applying a percentage capital-requirement to an assessment of the net position (specific risk requirements apply on a gross basis and general risk requirements on a net basis) held in the securities with which the trading book is constituted, the Annex also includes instructions on how netting is to be carried out, both generally and in relation to particular instruments. The net position is essentially the excess or deficit of an institution's long or short positions over its short or long positions in the same security. One consequence of home-Member-State control is that long positions in one geographical location can be offset against short positions in another location, which allows institutions to keep their capital requirements to a minimum. Under Article 4(5), institutions are required to satisfy their competent authorities that they employ systems which can calculate their financial positions with reasonable accuracy at any time.

Capital requirements in respect of trading-book settlement and counter-party risk are set out in Annex II which, essentially, in respect of counter-party risk at least, involves a credit-risk analysis. The settlement-risk requirements apply in respect of transactions in which debt instruments and equities (excluding the special rules which apply in Annex II to repurchase and reverse repurchase agreements and securities lending and borrowing transactions and OTC derivatives) are unsettled after their due delivery dates.[90] The counterparty-risk rules apply where the investment firm has paid for securities before receiving them or has delivered securities before receiving payment for them and, in the case of cross-border transactions, one day or more has elapsed since it made that payment or delivery. The capital requirements necessary are assessed in respect of the credit risk posed

---

capital-adequacy standards in respect of market risk. See Lomnicka, E, 'The Single European Passport in Financial Services' in Rider, B, and Andenas, M (eds.) *Developments in European Company Law vol 1 1996* (1997) 181, 199–200.

[90] Broadly speaking, the settlement-risk capital-requirements are calculated by multiplying the price difference (or the difference between the agreed settlement price for the debt or equity instrument and its current market value where the difference could involve a loss for the institution) by the appropriate factor set out in para 2 of Annex II.

by the counterparty. Settlement and counterparty risk is to a large extent dependent on the integrity of the clearing and settlement system relevant to the transactions and whether the system allows funds and securities to move at the same time, reducing the risk of loss. Although the ISD/CAD system does not impose requirements with respect to the operation of clearing and settlement systems, harmonized measures have, since their adoption, been taken in this direction (see Chapter XII).

The third and final element involved in calculating the total capital requirements applicable to the trading book is an assessment of the large-exposure capital requirements which are set out in Annex VI and are based on the reporting requirements and large-exposure ceilings imposed by the Large Exposures Directive (CBD, Articles 48–50),[91] as modified by Annex VI in order to reflect the smaller risk which is posed by the short-term exposures represented by trading-book assets.

(b) *Foreign-exchange Risk in Respect of Business Activities*

The second element of the provision required against risk of investment firms is the capital requirement in respect of foreign-exchange risk in relation to all the business of an investment firm (Article 4(1)(ii)). Annex III sets out how these capital requirements are to be assessed.[92]

(c) *SRD (now consolidated) Requirements*

The third element of the risk provision required of investment firms is designed to ensure parity with the treatment of credit institutions. The now consolidated SRD imposes capital requirements on credit institutions with respect to credit risk. Under Article 4(1)(iii) investment firms are required to meet the capital requirements imposed in respect of credit risk by the SRD for all their business activities, but excluding their trading-book business and illiquid assets. By imposing these requirements on all non-trading-book activities, the CAD seeks to ensure complete equality of treatment between investment firms and credit institutions, even though, in practice, credit institutions will, of course, have significantly larger non-trading books than investment firms, due to their deposit-taking and lending activities.

---

[91] Annex VI para 1 provides that the large-exposure capital requirements arising in connection with the trading book of credit institutions and investment firms in relation to individual clients and groups of connected clients are to be calculated according to the Large Exposures Directive 92/121/EEC [1992] OJ L 29/1 (the LED), now consolidated in the CBD.

[92] The capital requirement is calculated by multiplying the extent to which the credit institution's or investment firm's overall net foreign-exchange position exceeds 2% of its total own funds by 8%. Detailed rules apply to the calculation of the overall net position.

(d) *Other Capital Requirements*

The final element which goes into the calculation of total own funds required to be maintained by investment firms is to be established by the competent authorities. Under Article 4(1)(iv) and (2) competent authorities are to require investment firms to cover the risks arising in connection with business that is outside the scope of the CAD and the now consolidated SRD but considered to be similar to the risks covered by those two directives by adequate own funds.

(e) *Minimum Overall Levels of Own Funds and Annex IV*

Once the total capital requirement in respect of which own funds must be maintained has been calculated by adding together these four elements, a final assessment of the level of own funds necessary is required. Irrespective of the total amount of capital required following the addition of the four elements, the own-funds requirement for investment firms may never be less than the amount prescribed in Annex IV. Annex IV covers the capital requirement in respect of 'other risks' and requires that investment firms are to hold own funds equivalent to one quarter of their preceding year's fixed overheads. The competent authorities may adjust that requirement in the event of a material change in a firm's business since the preceding year. This minimum threshold is designed to act as a cushion against all other risks.[93]

(f) *Interest-rate Risk Monitoring*

Interest-rate risk assessment forms part of the general risk assessment applicable to securities as part of Annex I's requirements with respect to the trading book. Additionally, under Article 4(4), the competent authorities are to require that investment firms set up systems to monitor and control the interest-rate risk on all their business and that these systems are subject to supervision by the competent authorities.

---

[93] In its Explanatory Memorandum to the original proposal, the Commission referred to 'the risk that market turnover collapses reducing a firm's broking income to a level insufficient to cover its expenses': n 69 above, 3. More recently the Commission has explained that 'this expenditure-based requirement was introduced to allow investment firms to withstand a short-term drop in their activities, and functions as a backstop ratio, i.e. investment firms should meet the higher of this expenditure-based requirement and the risk based requirement for credit risks and market risks': 2001 Regulatory Capital Review, n 22 above, 7. This requirement is likely to be adjusted in the event that proposals to impose capital requirements in relation to operational risk are adopted: sect. 9.6.3 below.

(g) *Article 5: Large Exposure Risk and Investment Firms*

Investment firms are required under Article 5(1) to monitor their large exposures in respect of all business carried out (trading book and non-trading book) in accordance with the requirements of the now consolidated LED. Large-exposure risk provision is designed to cover the risks incurred in having a substantial proportion of an investment firm's capital exposed to a single counterparty and reflects the risk of default by that counterparty and the occurrence of a loss which could destabilize the investment firm. The LED is not, however, designed to monitor large exposures in activities which are subject to market risk. Accordingly, where a credit institution or an investment firm calculates its trading-book capital requirements in accordance with the CAD, it must monitor and control all of its large exposures in accordance with the requirements of the now consolidated LED, as modified by Annex VI. As investment firms' large exposures will be related to their trading-book business, this requirement does not, in practice, add to the requirements with respect to large exposures already imposed under Article 4(1)(i) in respect of trading-book business.

VIII.9.3.7 *The Capital-adequacy Requirements for Credit Institutions*

As already outlined, credit institutions are subject to the requirements of the CAD. The core provisions against risk set out in Article 4(1) apply to credit institutions, except that the minimum level of capital required of investment firms and calculated by reference to their fixed overheads under Annex IV does not apply to credit institutions.[94] Article 4(1) pulls together the requirements of the now consolidated SRD and the requirements of the CAD. Credit institutions are required, accordingly, to provide own funds which are always more than or equal to the sum of the amounts already required by: the SRD (Article 4(1)(iii)); the requirements of Article 4(1)(i) in respect of position risk, settlement, and counterparty risk, and large exposures in relation to their trading-book activities; the requirements of Article 4(1)(ii) in respect of foreign-exchange risk in relation to all their business activities; and any additional requirements imposed by the competent authorities in respect of risks arising in connection with business which is outside the scope of the SRD and the CAD, where the risks are considered to be similar to those covered by those Directives (Article 4(1)(iv)). Credit institutions may also benefit from the more flexible approach taken to the definition of

---

[94] As the risks against which this requirement provides protection are deemed to be *de minimis* in respect of the wide range of activities carried out by credit institutions but of potentially paramount importance for investment firms: Explanatory Memorandum to the original proposal, n 69 above, 8.

own funds in Annex V, although investment firms and credit institutions are subject to different ceilings on the use of subordinated loan capital.

Under Article 4(6) credit institutions (and investment firms) may be exempted from the CAD's trading-book requirements where their trading-book business does not normally exceed 5 per cent of their total business and never exceeds 6 per cent. In addition, their total trading-book positions must not normally exceed 15 million euro and never exceed 20 million euro (Article 4(6)(i)–(iii)). Capital requirements for their trading-book business will be calculated in accordance with the SRD.

Prior to the adoption of the CAD, credit institutions were already subject to the requirements of the now consolidated LED. While that obligation is reiterated in Article 5(1), Article 5(2) provides that where a credit institution calculates its trading-book capital requirements in accordance with the CAD, it must monitor and control its large exposures in accordance with the LED, as modified by Annex VI.

VIII.9.3.8 *Capital Adequacy and Management Companies*

Management companies which are authorized to carry out discretionary portfolio-management services and ISD-type services will, under the Management Company Proposal, be subject to the CAD's requirements (Article 5(4)). Where the management company carries out only collective portfolio-management, the CAD does not apply. Under Article 5d, however, management companies will be required to maintain own funds which must not fall below the level specified in Article 5a(1)(a); these requirements are outlined in Chapter VII section 9 above. Where that level is breached, the competent authorities may, where circumstances justify it, allow the management company a limited period in which to rectify their actions or cease their activities.

VIII.9.4 *Supervision and Enforcement of the CAD*

VIII.9.4.1 *Reporting Requirements*

Mandatory reporting requirements are essential in ensuring that compliance with capital-adequacy rules is monitored effectively. Under Article 8(1), Member States are to require that investment firms and credit institutions provide the competent authorities of their home Member States with 'all the information necessary for the assessment of their compliance with' the CAD's rules. Similarly, Member States are to ensure that an institution's internal control mechanisms and administrative and accounting procedures allow the competent authorities to verify compliance with the CAD's rules. The exact nature and content of the report are at the discretion of the competent authority. The frequency of the reporting obligation varies according to the minimum initial capital required of investment firms from once a month (730,000 euro) to once every three months (125,000 euro) to once every six months (50,000 euro) (Article 8(2)). Credit institutions are subject to the reporting obligations which apply under the banking regime (SRD Article 3, now consolidated CBD, Article 40). Special reporting obligations are imposed by Article 8(5) in respect of repurchase and reverse repurchase agreements and securities-lending and -borrowing agreements. The competent authorities must require institutions which engage in these transactions to report any case in which their counterparties default on their obligations.

VIII.9.4.2 *Supervision and Enforcement by the Competent Authority*

Article 8(2) of the ISD (which also applies to credit institutions authorized under the banking regime to provide investment services) gives the home Member State's competent authorities jurisdiction to ensure compliance with the CAD rules (see also section 10 below).

Article 9(1) of the CAD requires Member States to designate competent authorities responsible for carrying out the duties provided for in the Directive. These must be public authorities or bodies officially recognized by national law or by public authorities as part of the supervisory system in operation in the Member State. In a formula familiar from the ISD, under Article 9(3) they must be granted all the powers necessary for their tasks, but a specific reference is made to the need to have the powers necessary to oversee the constitution of trading books.

Given that responsibility for compliance with the CAD's requirements lies with the home Member State of an investment firm, Article 9(4) requires the competent authorities of the various Member States to collaborate closely in performing duties under the CAD, in particular where investment services are provided on a services basis or through the establishment of a branch. As monitoring compliance with the requirements of the CAD is required of the home Member States under Article 8(2) of the ISD, competent authorities benefit from the enforcement and co-operation systems contained in the ISD (Chapter VII section 8 above). Article 9(4) specifies additionally, however, that competent authorities are to supply one another on request with all information likely to facilitate the supervision of the capital adequacy of investment firms and credit institutions. Information exchange is subject to the requirements of the ISD.

VIII.9.5 *The CAD and Consolidation*[95]

The CAD's requirements apply on a consolidated basis[96] in accordance with Article 7. Consolidation of capital requirements is a central principle of the EC's capital-adequacy regime. It allows risk assessment to be carried out on a group-wide basis and can prevent arbitrage in capital requirements where it is possible to allocate financial activities to different undertakings within a group.[97]

The EC's consolidation regime for capital requirements is contained in two directives: the CAD and the (now CBD consolidated) Consolidated Supervision Directive (CSD).[98] Together, these directives cover homogeneous financial-services groups and provide for the consolidation of, essentially, financial holding companies, credit institutions, investment firms, and financial institutions. The CSD sets out the basic consolidation regime for credit-institution-based groups. The CAD applies the consolidation principles and mechanics which are set out in the CSD to groups which include investment firms but do not contain a credit institution.

Under Article 7(1) of the CAD, the Article 4 and 5 CAD rules on provisions against risk and large exposures apply on a solo basis where the institution concerned, whether credit institution or investment firm, is not a parent undertaking or a subsidiary. Article 7(2) provides that the Article 4 and 5 capital requirements apply on a consolidated basis for: (1) any institution (a credit institution or investment firm) which has a credit institution within the meaning of the CSD, an investment firm, or another 'financial institution' as a subsidiary, or which holds a participation in such an entity; and (2) any institution the parent undertaking of which is a 'financial holding company'. A credit institution for the purposes of Article 7(2) is any undertaking whose business is to receive deposits or other repayable funds from the public and to grant credits for its own account or any private or public undertaking which corresponds to that definition and has been

---

[95] This section concerns the consolidated supervision of largely homogeneous groups of credit institutions, investment firms, and credit institutions and investment firms. Much consideration is currently being given to the broader question of how to supervise heterogeneous groups which encompass areas which are traditionally separately regulated and which, in particular, mix banking, insurance, investment services, and other activities. See sect. 11 below.

[96] Consolidated supervision has been expressed in the context of credit institutions as meaning 'that the authority supervising the credit institution group will apply the financial data of the whole group in monitoring compliance with its supervisory standards': Grunson, M, and Feuring, W, 'A European Union Banking Law: The Second Banking and Related Directives' in Cranston, n 47 above, 25, 41.

[97] For a discussion of the rationale for consolidation in the EC capital-adequacy regime see the Commission's Consultation Document on *A Review of Regulatory Capital Requirements for EU Credit Institutions and Investment Firms*, MARKT/1123/99-EN (the 1999 Regulatory Capital Review) 8. See also Dale and Wolfe, n 78 above, 242.

[98] Directive 92/30/EEC on the supervision of credit institutions on a consolidated basis [1992] OJ L110/52, now consolidated in the CBD.

authorized in a third country. A 'financial institution' is an undertaking, other than a credit institution, the principal activity of which is to acquire holdings or carry on certain of the activities covered by the BCD II Annex (CBD, Annex I).[99] A 'subsidiary' for the purposes of the consolidation requirement is defined by reference to Article 1 of the CSD (CBD, Article 1(13)).[100] Participation is also defined by reference to that directive.[101] With respect to the second route into the consolidation process, or via the parent company, a 'financial holding company' is defined under the CAD as a financial institution the subsidiary undertakings of which are either 'exclusively or mainly' (not defined) credit institutions, investment firms, or other financial institutions, one of which at least is a credit institution or an investment firm. A parent undertaking is defined by reference to the CSD (CBD, Article 1(12)) as any undertaking which, in the opinion of the competent authorities, effectively exercises a dominant influence over another undertaking or which is covered by Directive 83/348/EEC.[102]

The CAD's Article 4 and 5 capital requirement for undertakings which qualify under Article 7(2) will be applied on a consolidated basis in accordance with the CSD's consolidation principles. In outline,[103] the CSD's principles include rules on: how to determine the competent authority (the determining factor will be the nature of the undertaking at the head of the

---

[99] The relevant activities are: lending; financial leasing; money transmission services; issuing and administering means of payment; guarantees and commitments; investment services-type activities involving trading for own account or for the account of customers in money-market instruments, foreign exchange, financial futures and options, exchange and interests instruments and transferable securities; participation in share issues and the provision of related services; corporate finance advice; money broking; portfolio management; and advice.

[100] Art. 1 (CBD, Art. 1(13)) defines a subsidiary as any undertaking over which, in the opinion of the competent authorities, a parent undertaking effectively exercises a dominant influence and provides that all subsidiaries of subsidiary undertakings are also to be considered subsidiaries of the undertaking that is the original parent, as well as defining subsidiary by reference to the Consolidated Accounts Directive 83/349/EEC [1983] OJ L193/1. That Directive defines the relationship between parent and subsidiary by reference to a number of factors including: having a majority of the shareholders' or members' voting rights in another undertaking (the subsidiary undertaking); having the right to appoint or remove a majority of the members of the administrative, management, or supervisory boards of another undertaking (the subsidiary undertaking) in which the undertaking has a shareholding; having the right to exercise a dominant influence over an undertaking (the subsidiary undertaking) of which it is a shareholder, pursuant to a contract or a provision in that undertaking's constitutional documents, where this is permitted by the governing law of that undertaking; and having a shareholding in an undertaking (the subsidiary undertaking) in which a majority of the members of the administrative, management, or supervisory board of that undertaking who have held office during the financial year have been appointed solely as a result of the exercise of its voting rights or in which the undertaking controls alone, pursuant to an agreement with other shareholders or members, a majority of shareholders' or members' voting rights.

[101] Defined in Art. 1 as the ownership, direct or indirect, of 20% or more of the voting rights or capital of an undertaking (CBD, Art. 1(9)).

[102] See n 100 above.

[103] For a full discussion see Dassesse *et al.*, n 68 above, 80–98.

group (Article 4 (CBD, Article 53))); the form and extent of consolidation and whether it is full or proportional (Article 5 (CBD, Article 54)); and competent authority co-operation mechanisms (Article 7 (CBD, Article 56)). It also contains particular rules for a 'mixed activity holding company' (a parent undertaking other than a financial holding company or credit institution which has at least one credit institution subsidiary). Mixed-activity holding companies are not subject to consolidation but are subject to information-provision requirements and to on-the-spot information-verification inspections (Article 6 (CBD, Article 55)). In addition, Article 7(7)–(14) of the CAD applies to Articles 4 and 5. These provisions include waiver provisions in respect of the application of capital requirements on a solo and sub-consolidated basis (the consolidation of sub-groups within the wider group) where the group is already supervised on a consolidated basis by the Member State granting the waiver and other conditions are met (Article 7(7) and (9)) and the rules on how the consolidated requirements are to be calculated (Article 7(10)–(14)).

Where a group covered by Article 7(2) does not contain a credit institution, the CSD continues to apply but is subject to a number of largely technical modifications (Article 7(3)). The CAD also provides in Article 7(4)–(6) for a waiver from the consolidation requirements for investment-firm groups which do not contain credit institutions, subject to certain conditions. The consolidation waiver, like the approach to the alternative definition of own funds for investment firms in relation to subordinated debt, reveals that the CAD is sensitive to the differences in the risks faced by credit institutions and investment firms, notwithstanding the CAD's stated objective of treating credit institutions and investment firms in the same way.[104] The conditions imposed on a waiver include that each investment firm in the group meets the Article 4 and 5 requirements on a solo basis, that each firm sets up systems to monitor and control the sources of capital and funding of all other financial institutions in the group, and that certain items of own funds are deducted (Article 7(4)). Grant of a waiver is also subject to a number of safeguards designed to ensure that the group structure does not compromise the capital levels of the investment firm. All investment firms in a group which has been granted a waiver must notify the competent authority of those risks (including those linked to the composition and sources of their capital and funding) which could undermine their financial position (Article 7(5)). If on notification the competent authority considers that the positions of the

---

[104] The waiver appears to be based on the assumption that investment firms, unlike credit institutions, can be protected from financial difficulties elsewhere in the group by, eg, restrictions on intra-group capital transfers, and that credit institutions, owing to the possibility of 'runs' on deposits, are uniquely vulnerable to contagion risks: Dale and Wolfe, n 78 above, 242. The capital-adequacy review has proposed, however, that, in the interests of prudent supervision, the waiver be abolished. See sect. 9.6.3 below.

investment firm are not adequately protected, it must require the investment firm to take measures which may include, if necessary, limitations on the transfer of capital from the investment firm to other group entities (Article 7(5)). Competent authorities are also required, on granting a waiver, to take 'other appropriate measures' to monitor the risks, specifically large exposures, of the whole group, including any undertakings not located in a Member State (Article 7(6)).

VIII.9.6 *Review of the CAD*

VIII.9.6.1 *In-house Value at Risk Models*

In-house value-at-risk models (VARs) are sophisticated computer models which allow an institution to use its own in-house models to assess its capital requirements in respect of market risk, rather than using standardized regulatory models. They have the dual advantage of allowing a more accurate risk assessment to be carried out and of being cheaper to operate than standardized risk-assessment models, in that their accuracy leads to lower capital requirements. They can also contribute to a greater identity between statutory capital requirements and internal compliance rules, which strengthens capital regulation generally. The incentive to create models which reduce capital requirements is, of course, obvious and represents a significant drawback. Customized VARs also lessen the uniformity of capital requirements.

On its adoption, the CAD did not provide for the use by investment firms of VARs in assessing position risk. The use of VARs was, however, subsequently examined in 1995 by the Basel Committee as part of its ongoing work on market risk-capital requirements and by 1998 the Basel Committee VAR requirements had come into effect as part of the Basel Committee's final capital standards for market risk for credit institutions.[105] By 1998 IOSCO had also agreed a position on VARs.[106] These developments and the implications for the competitiveness of the EC investment-services industry, as EC institutions were placed at a competitive disadvantage owing to their inability to benefit from the lower capital-funding costs associated with VARs, prompted a review of the CAD. The Commission's initial proposal for reform

---

[105] See Elderfield, M, 'Basle Publishes Market Risk Capital Standards' [1996] *JIFBL* 125.

[106] See the 1998 report by IOSCO's Technical Committee on 'Methodologies for Determining Minimum Capital Standards for Internationally Active Securities Firms Which Permit the Use of Models Under Prescribed Conditions' and its 1998 Consultation Paper on 'Risk Management and Control Guidance for Securities Firms and their Supervisors'. In 1999 it adopted a Report on 'Recognising a Firm's Internal Market Risk Model for the Purpose of Calculating Required Regulatory Capital: Guidance to Supervisors'.

was presented in 1997[107] and Directive 98/31[108] was adopted mid-way through 1998.

Directive 98/31 amends the CAD by adding a new Annex VIII which, in paragraph 1, allows Member States to recognize a credit institution's or investment firm's VARs for the purposes of calculating their capital requirements in relation to position risk, foreign-exchange risk, and commodities risk. VARs may be used instead of or in combination with the methods set out in the CAD for calculating these risks. The amendments recognize that credit institutions and investment firms have, since the adoption of the CAD's standardized models for capital-adequacy assessment, developed their own risk-management systems which measure market risk more accurately than standardized models and that the use of such models should be encouraged to enhance the competitive position of EC investment firms and credit institutions (recitals 2, 3, and 5). A number of conditions must be fulfilled before a competent authority may grant recognition to an institution's VAR (Annex VIII, paragraph 2). The basic requirement is that the institution's risk-management system is conceptually sound and implemented with integrity, and a number of qualitative standards are imposed in order to ensure that this objective is met. Institutions are also required to monitor the accuracy and performance of the VAR model by back-testing. Additional requirements apply to VARs used in the assessment of specific risk-capital requirements. This emphasis on tailored internal risk assessment models is also a feature of the capital adequacy review (section 9.6.3 below).

VIII.9.6.2 *Commodities*

Directive 98/31 also introduced a new Annex VII to the CAD which sets out specific rules for the calculation of market risk in relation to commodity derivatives. Commodity derivatives were not covered in the CAD as originally adopted and so were subject to the now consolidated SRD regime, which is not sensitive to market risks. In addition the Commission was becoming increasingly concerned at the level of serious fraud perpetrated by certain commodity-futures traders and the threat it posed to the image and integrity of the commodity-futures business. The amendments extend the definition of the trading book to include positions in commodities or commodity derivatives which can be held for trading purposes and are subject

---

[107] [1997] OJ C240/24, Explanatory Memorandum at COM(97)71. The comments of ECOSOC and the European Parliament are at [1998] OJ C19/9 and C14/172, respectively . The European Monetary Institute also delivered an opinion. A Revised Proposal was presented by the Commission later in 1998 which incorporated many of the comments made by ECOSOC and the European Parliament [1998] OJ C118/16, Explanatory Memorandum, COM(98)90. The Council's common position is at [1998] OJ C135/7 and the European Parliament's comments on the common position at [1998] OJ C19/9.

[108] [1998] OJ L204/13.

mainly to market risk. The specific commodity risk capital requirements set out in Annex VII apply, in respect of the overall business of the investment firm or credit institution.

Directive 98/13 also contains a number of specific amendments relating to the treatment of the netting of exchange-traded futures and options and OTC derivatives under Annex I.

VIII.9.6.3 *Future Revisions and the Basel Proposals*

As part of the FSAP's[109] strategic objective 3—State of the Art Prudential Rules and Supervision—a major re-examination of the EC capital-adequacy regime is currently under way to bring the system up to date with current market and supervisory trends. The review is being undertaken in parallel with discussions in the Basel Committee, with the Commission's review being both influenced by and having an effect on, the Basel proposals (eight Member States sit on the Basel Committee while the Commission is an observer). Proposals are under discussion for a new Basel Capital Accord on assessing credit risk which would allow credit institutions to adjust asset-risk-weightings to reflect more closely the actual economic risks incurred by the credit institutions and address the criticism that the current approach of classifying assets according to four broad risk of default categories is too crude and costly.[110] The proposals also address capital requirements for operational and other risks which are not currently covered and examine the supervision structure, including the extent to which disclosure and market discipline can be used to manage risk. Overall, the new regime is based on a three-pillar structure which is designed to ensure that the capital-adequacy regime adequately reflects the risks to which credit institutions and the financial system are exposed. The three pillars are: minimum capital requirements; supervisory review; and market discipline.

In line with its FSAP objectives and the Basel Accord developments, the Commission first presented a paper on the review of regulatory capital requirements in 1999 which was followed by second paper in 2001, issued after the revised Basel Accord proposals were presented.[111] These papers, which reflect the Basel proposals while fine-tuning them to the Community environment (and to the application of the Community capital regime to

---

[109] N 19 above.

[110] The 1st set of proposals was issued in June 1999 and was followed by a 2nd set in Jan 2001. Adoption of the proposals is not expected until 2005 and is likely to be held up by negotiations on translating the proposals into the EC capital-adequacy regime for credit risk. It is expected that the revised EC framework and the new Basel Accord will be implemented at the same time in the interests of financial stability and in order to ensure that a level playing-field is maintained.

[111] The 1999 Regulatory Capital Review, n 97 above and the 2001 Regulatory Capital Review, n 22 above, respectively.

credit institutions and investment firms, in particular), are designed to provide the basis for a proposed directive for a new capital-adequacy framework and facilitate the ongoing development of the internal market. Underlying the review is the need to update the capital regime to ensure that standards reflect market developments, accurately reflect the risks run by credit institutions and investment firms, and allow for a comprehensive assessment to be made of the risks to which credit institutions and investment firms are exposed. A more sensitive and tailored application of capital standards is envisaged. Also emphasized is the need to provide firms with incentives to adopt higher standards of risk management and move beyond the standard capital-assessment requirements to more risk-sensitive methodologies. In line with the current regime, ensuring competitive equality is also a major theme of the review, with the new structure being designed to be suitable for a wide range of institutions of varying size and sophistication competing in different arenas. Although the major focus of the review is on credit risk and thus on a firm's non-trading-book (or banking) activities which are outside the scope of securities regulation, investment firms will be affected by a number of other proposals including: the introduction of capital requirements for operational risk; revisions proposed to the consolidated-supervision regime; a new approach to defining the trading book; the supervisory review process and the use of internal risk management techniques; and the new focus on disclosure. These will be considered here in outline only, given that, at the time of writing, a proposal has yet to be presented.

The review has recognized that while credit and market risk are the predominant focus of the capital regime, a range of other significant risks is not subject to capital requirements. To that end, a key and controversial feature of the review is the proposal that capital requirements be introduced for risks other than credit and market risk as part of the overall objective to produce a more comprehensive and risk-sensitive approach to risks. The 2001 Regulatory Capital Review has proposed a minimum capital requirement for operational risks, defined as 'the risk of direct or indirect loss resulting from inadequate or failed internal processes, people and systems or from external events' which will apply to investment firms and credit institutions.[112] Examples of operational risk include fraud and computer-system failure. Considerable controversy has already arisen as to the extra costs this capital charge may impose on investment firms and the competitive disadvantage at which they may be placed in relation to investment firms based outside the Community and not subject to the Basel framework, given that the concept of operational risk was developed by the Basel Committee in the context of large international credit institutions. The Commission has made clear, however, that a differentiated approach to operational risk is

[112] Ibid, 36.

envisaged, and that the regime will accommodate different levels of sophis-tication and risk profile. Standarized and, depending on the sophistication of the institution's risk-management policies, internal measurements for assessing operational risks are envisaged. Investment firms are, of course, at the moment subject to capital requirements in respect of 'other risks' under Annex IV of the CAD. This requirement, which is based on expenditure, is likely to be revised to reflect the adoption of a new risk-based operational-risks regime.

On consolidated supervision, the review has focused on the extent to which waivers can be granted from solo and consolidated capital require-ments (see section 9.5 above). It has been suggested that the waiver regime be aligned for both credit-institution and investment-firm groups and, in par-ticular, that the waiver from consolidation currently available for homoge-neous investment firm groups under Article 7(4) of the CAD be removed.

With respect to the trading book, the 2001 Regulatory Capital Review has confirmed that the current approach to market risk is satisfactory and is not to be substantially modified. It has recommended that the definition of the trading book be refined with regard to how items are allocated. In par-ticular, the revised definition would affirm the responsibility of credit insti-tutions and investment firms in allocating and valuing items between the trading book and the banking regime, while also setting out the conditions which should assist this process. It has also been suggested that allocation of items in the trading book should be based on 'trading intent' and 'prudent valuation'. Trading intent would be evidenced through risk-management policies (following criteria set out in the new regime) and doc-umentation. Prudent valuation requirements would also be introduced in order to enhance accuracy and flexibility in valuation. Documented internal controls and policies on the management of trading intent and prudent val-uation would be required (as part of the Supervisory Review process: see the next paragraph). The new regime would be flexible as regards liquidity, however, with neither the liquidity of the market in a particular position nor the expected holding horizon (as long as it is short term) being an absolute criterion for allocating or excluding items. The revised regime would also define 'financial instruments', which, in the current regime, are defined by reference to the ISD's Annex, Section B list of instruments, given that this list does not easily address financial innovation (the 2001 Regulatory Review referred to weather derivatives, for example). It has been proposed that the list approach be dropped and that an enlarged general definition, which would encompass 'practically any kind of item—[*sic*] that can be held by a bank or an investment firm',[113] be adopted for the purposes of consti-

---

[113] The 1999 Regulatory Capital Review, n 97 above and the 2001 Regulatory Capital Review, 47.

tuting the trading book. Investment firms and credit institutions would be required, as part of the Supervisory Review process, to maintain documentation policies in respect of the trading book.

Also important to the investment-services regime is the discussion on supervision and the emphasis on the Supervisory Review Process. Supervisory Review is designed to ensure that firms not only comply with the capital requirements but also, as part of the process of refining the capital-adequacy regime's focus on risk, develop and use enhanced risk-management techniques in monitoring and managing risk. Supervisory Review requires institutions to assess and manage their risk profile and satisfy the competent authority that their assessment and management are adequate. It also feeds into the extent to which and how a competent authority imposes differentiated capital requirements above the minimum standards (as they are permitted to do under the EC regime and will be encouraged to do under the new regime) on institutions depending on their particular risk profile and risk-management policies.

Disclosure (and so market discipline)[114] has emerged from the review as a supplementary regulatory device for monitoring and managing soundness. Underlying the disclosure approach is the premise that enhanced transparency in financial-disclosure practices will enable market participants to assess an institution's risk profile and strengthen market discipline, thereby improving an institution's market strategy, its risk control, and its internal management and organization. In order to achieve this, the proposed disclosure regime would include mandatory core-disclosure obligations designed to guarantee disclosure of 'accurate, timely and relevant information relative to the capital structure of the institution . . . on at least an annual basis'.[115] In relation to the trading book and market risk specifically, the 2001 Regulatory Capital Review has suggested that information on the level of sophistication and complexity of trading-book business and exposure to risk within the trading book should be disclosed.

---

[114] The use of disclosure and market discipline in managing risk and promoting systemic stability has been supported in the Group of 30 study on *Global Institutions, National Supervision and Systemic Risk* (1997). See the discussion in Coakley, J, 'Trends in Financial Services and Influences on Approaches to Regulation' in McCrudden, C (ed), *Regulation and Deregulation. Policy and Practice in the Utilities and Financial Services Industries* (1999) 343, 352–3.

[115] 2001 Regulatory Capital Review, n 22 above, 57.

VIII.10 ENFORCEMENT AND SUPERVISION OF
THE PRUDENTIAL REGIME[116]

VIII.10.1 *Enforcement Powers*

As is the case with the protective rules discussed in Chapter IX, neither the
ISD nor the CAD (nor the Management Company Proposal) specifies what
measures the home Member State should take in enforcing the prudential
regime. While home Member States are required under the ISD (Article
19(4)) to 'take all appropriate measures to ensure that the investment firm
concerned puts an end to its irregular situation' in respect of breaches of
rules adopted in the host Member State pursuant to the ISD, no similar
explicit injunction to take 'appropriate measures' is imposed on the home
Member State in respect of breaches of the prudential rules. This difference
in treatment between prudential and other rule breaches can be explained,
however, by the need to ensure that breaches of rules in the host Member
States are appropriately dealt with by the home Member State which, as the
primary enforcer, is a step removed from the breach. More generally, under
Article 27 of the ISD Member States are to provide that their competent
authorities may adopt or impose measures or penalties aimed specifically at
ending observed breaches or the causes of such breaches by investment
firms, or those who effectively control them, of laws, regulations, or administrative provisions concerning their supervision or the carrying on of their
activities. Although the ISD does not specify the nature of the measures
which must be taken, it does provide under Article 3(7) that the home
Member State may withdraw authorization where the investment firm no
longer meets the conditions under which authorization was granted, no
longer complies with the CAD, or has 'seriously and systematically'
infringed the rules adopted under Article 10 (Article 3(7)(c), (d) and (e))
(the Management Company Proposal also covers authorization withdrawals
for serious and systematic infringements of the UCITS Directive). Article 9 is
an exception to an otherwise 'hands-off' approach, in that it addresses the
type of sanctions which should be used to deal with breaches of Article 9
and the devices which may be employed to control ownership related risks
to the stability of an investment firm.

VIII.10.2 *Supervision through a Network of Home-Member-State Supervisors*

Prudential supervision of investment-service providers is allocated to the
home Member State. Allocation of jurisdiction to the home Member State

---

[116] See also the discussion of prudential supervision in the context of centralized supervision
generally and the likelihood of a single regulator in Ch. XV.

was critical to ensure the effectiveness of the passport mechanism for both investment firms and credit institutions providing investment services.[117] While devolving prudential supervision to one Member State eases the regulatory burden on investment-services providers and facilitates the integration of the investment-services market-place, it also enhances effective supervision, in that there is less opportunity for firms to fall between any gaps in supervision which could arise if a number of host Member States were responsible for prudential supervision.[118] The ISD and the CAD contain co-operation and information-exchange requirements and procedures (see Chapter VII sections 7–8 and section 9.4 above) designed to facilitate effective prudential supervision of investment firms, as does the Management Company Proposal (Chapter VII section 9.5 above). The central plank of the basic co-operation structure is the requirement that competent authorities co-operate to discharge their respective responsibilities and supply one another on request with all information on the management and ownership of firms which is likely to facilitate their supervision of investment firms. Home competent authorities also benefit from the power to carry out on-the-spot verifications of this information.

Supervision of the EC prudential-regulation regime is accordingly dependent on a network of home-Member-State competent authorities required to exercise solo supervision as well as consolidated supervision but supported by a co-operation network. In principle, effective prudential supervision, which is directed towards solvency and organizational soundness, does not require the dominant home Member State's competent authority to be close to and familiar with the particular conditions of and participants in all the market-places on which the investment firm is operating. The same cannot be said of protective regulation which requires regulators to be familiar with the minutiae of investor/investment-firm transactions and with the conduct of investment firms. Nonetheless, the effectiveness of this diffuse and decentralized system and its ability to cope with greater market interdependence and vulnerability to instability and systemic risks, as cross-border activities increase and cross-border financial conglomerates continue to develop (section 11 below), will be a function of the extent to which these authorities co-operate with one another. Even if the co-operation mechanisms work

---

[117] In its Explanatory Memorandum to the original proposal for the ISD, the Commission stated that 'it is desirable for the creation of a true internal market in financial services that (i) the monitoring of the financial soundness of the investment firm; and (ii) its compliance with other major prudential . . . rules should also, so far as possible, be within the exclusive regulatory competence of the home Member State supervisors', COM(88)778, 3. Home-Member-State supervision required substantial changes to the working practices of competent authorities across the EC owing to extension of responsibility with respect to home firms and the requirement to withdraw from the prudential supervision of firms operating in the Member States but authorized elsewhere: SIB Paper, n 34 above, 10.

[118] See Lomnicka, n 89 above, 186.

efficiently, a single robust and coherent standard of prudential supervision protecting the integrated market against solvency and stability risks is unlikely, unless convergence of standards and supervisory practices occurs. Convergence faces two difficulties. In the first place, it may be argued that while effective prudential supervision, particularly in the area of capital adequacy, requires that competent authorities are able to tailor the rules to particular risk profiles, the prudential rules are overly open to varying interpretations.[119] The internal control rules contained in Article 10 of the ISD, for example, operate at a high level of generality and give Member States substantial leeway in their operation. Secondly, the quality of supervision is likely to be variable. Different supervisory cultures, varying levels of resource allocation to competent authorities, and the tendency to designate different types of institutions as competent authorities all cloud the supervisory picture and obstruct convergence of supervisory practices.[120]

VIII.10.3 *Future Directions for the Supervisory Structure*

VIII.10.3.1 *The Impact of the BCCI Collapse*

The extent to which a prudential-supervision structure which was dependent on home-Member-State supervision and co-operation between sectoral supervisors could amount to effective supervision received its first major challenge in the wake of the 1991 worldwide failure of the Bank of Credit and Commerce International SA (BCCI).[121] The failure of supervisors to deal with BCCI before its fraudulent activities triggered a major crisis launched a number of inquiries, including one by the Banking Advisory Committee at EC level, into the adequacy of the supervisory structure.[122] Although the conclusion at EC level was that the home-country control and co-operation structure was essentially sound,[123] weaknesses were identified in the ability of the EC regime to manage the supervision of complex groups of companies effectively. The inability of competent authorities to decipher the opaque

---

[119] Supervisory discretion, however desirable, creates its own problems: '[a] consistent application of supervisory discretion across the EU is a key challenge in the integrated market for banking and investment services': 2001 Regulatory Capital Review, n 22 above, 36.

[120] See generally Andenas, M, and Hadjiemmanuil, C, 'Banking Supervision, the Internal Market and European Monetary Union' in Andenas, M, Gormley, L, Hadjiemmanuil, C, and Harden, I (eds), *European Economic and Monetary Union: The Institutional Framework* (1997) 373, 386.

[121] See generally, Vigneron, P, Steinfeld, P, and Counye, D, 'Lessons of the BCCI Collapse' (1993) 13 *YBEL* 263 and Magliaveras, K, 'The Attempts of the European Community to Introduce Effective Financial Supervision in the Financial Services Sectors' in Caiger, A, and Floudas, D, *1996: Onwards: Lowering the Barriers Further* (1996) 81.

[122] The Banking Advisory Committee consists of representatives of the Commission and of the Member States and advises the Commission on a range of banking matters. See further Ch. XV.

[123] Sir Leon Brittan reported to the Ecofin Council to this effect in Nov 1992.

BCCI structure had been identified as one of the factors which made the fraudulent activity possible.

In 1993 the Commission presented a proposal designed to enhance the prudential supervision of insurance undertakings, collective-investment schemes, and credit institutions as well as investment firms.[124] The PSD was adopted in 1995.[125] It is designed to reinforce prudential supervision and ensure the stability of the financial system by addressing the risks to effective supervision and systemic stability posed by opaque group structures and the ability of supervisors to detect fraud and other irregularities in the financial-services sector which could destabilize the financial system. It does not drastically overhaul the prudential supervision regime; its revisions are better described as fine-tuning the system. It contributes to the prudential supervision of investment firms by: strengthening effective prudential supervision by requiring an assessment of whether the links between an investment-services firm and other undertakings might prejudice effective supervision to be made before authorization is granted; widening the range of authorities with which competent authorities may exchange otherwise confidential information beyond the tradition home/host competent authority axis, thereby increasing the information available to competent authorities; and imposing a 'whistle-blowing obligation' on auditors (these provisions are discussed in Chapter VII in the context of the ISD's passport mechanism).

VIII.10.3.2 *The FSAP*

The adequacy and effectiveness of the prudential supervision infrastructure have been reviewed since then by the Commission which, by and large, appears reluctant to alter the co-operation-based *status quo* substantially. It has, on a number of occasions, called on supervisors to enhance co-operation and communication and highlighted market developments which demand more careful co-ordination between supervisors. In its 1998 Communication on financial services, it explicitly supported the co-operation structure, finding that co-operation between competent authorities was key

---

[124] [1993] OJ C229/10. The Explanatory Memorandum is at COM(93)363. The initial drafts of the proposal covered banking activities only, as the difficulties raised by the BCCI collapse were seen primarily in terms of the bankruptcy of a credit institution. It was subsequently decided that the revisions needed in respect of prudential supervision in the light of the BCCI collapse should apply across all financial sectors: Vigneron *et al.*, n 121 above, 276. ECOSOC's opinion and the Parliament's first reading are at [1994] OJ C91/61 and C52/15, respectively. The Commission's subsequent revised proposal is at COM(94)549 and the Council's common position is at [1994] OJ C213/29. The decision of the European Parliament on the common position is at [1994] OJ C323/56.

[125] [1995] OJ L168/7. For a review of the legislative process see Magliaveras, n 121 above, 86–96.

to the management of institutional and prudential risk, although it called for more effective and efficient co-operation, particularly with respect to the detection of solvency problems and in the designation of the supervisor with responsibility for managing solvency crises where the entity in question was structured on a cross-border basis.[126] The Commission called for a 'well-developed approach to co-ordination' and to that end suggested that a 'supervisors co-operation charter' be drawn up which would clearly assign responsibilities for supervising on a cross-border basis and set out mechanisms for addressing particular supervisory problems.[127] In the FSAP, the supervision of financial conglomerates (section 11 below) emerged as the Commission's main prudential-supervision concern, although it did note that industry consolidation and greater integration of markets generally called for 'careful consideration of structures for containing and supervising institutional and systemic risk'.[128] The FSAP, which contains a specific strategic objective on 'State of the Art Prudential Rules and Supervision', does not address in any great detail the basic investment-firm prudential-supervision framework although, in the substantive regulatory area, it does contain a commitment to revise the capital-adequacy regime (section 9.6.3 above).[129]

Of some interest for the EC's approach to prudential supervision, however, are the proposals made under the FSAP as part of the capital-adequacy review to enhance the role of disclosure in soundness regulation (section 9.6.3 above). In addition, as part of the FSAP the Commission has adopted a Recommendation on the Disclosure of Financial Instruments.[130] The Recommendation is designed to 'allow investors and market participants to take well-informed decisions, thus fostering market transparency and market discipline as a most valuable complement to supervision' (recital 5); to that end it introduced recommendations for the disclosure to be made by financial institutions concerning their activities relating to 'financial instruments'.[131] A supervisory approach seems to be developing which combines traditional public supervision by competent authorities with market control and disclosure. While prudential control will, owing to its systemic implica-

[126] Commission Communication on Financial Services: Building a Framework for Action (the 1998 Communication), COM(98)625, 16.

[127] Ibid.   [128] FSAP, n 19, above 10.

[129] Progress reports on the FSAP reflect the fundamental focus on the co-operation model of supervision. The Commission's Second Progress Report of May 2000 on the Financial Services Action Plan (the 2nd Progress Report) COM(2000)336, eg, highlighted at 12 the exchange of information as a key element in strengthening co-operation.

[130] Commission Recommendation 2000/408/EC concerning disclosure of information on financial instruments and other items complementing the disclosure required according to Council Directive 86/635/EEC on the annual accounts and consolidated accounts of banks and other financial institutions [2000] OJ L154/36.

[131] Financial instruments are defined as including primary financial instruments and derivative instruments, including commodity derivatives.

tions, always need strong supervision by dedicated agencies, the market-place can play a useful ancillary role in supplementing that supervision.

Prudential regulation emerged largely unscathed from the Lamfalussy Report's review at a substantive level but the adequacy of the current supervision structure was questioned.[132] Raising the spectre of systemic instability in the integrated market, the Wise Men warned that the efficiency benefits of an integrated market-place would not necessarily be accompanied by similarly enhanced stability. The Wise Men reiterated the original rationale for the Community's move into prudential regulation in stark terms: increased integration involves greater connection between intermediaries on a cross-border basis and increases their exposure to common shocks. With the growing links between securities markets and intermediaries it saw an urgent need to strengthen co-operation between supervisors. Divergences in supervisory practices are, however, likely to be addressed by the new Committee of European Securities Regulators, established in the wake of the Report, and the more detailed Article 10 prudential rules, adopted as level 2 measures, which, the Commission has indicated in its ISD Working Paper, are likely to be forthcoming.

Strengthened co-operation structures thus appear to be the preferred option for managing prudential supervision on a pan-EC basis as integration deepens and the risk of systemic instability increases accordingly. Nonetheless, and while the Commission has stated that its 'vocation in the financial services field is regulatory' rather than supervisory, and appears to be reluctant to enter into a debate on the need for a single regulator to monitor the prudential supervision of investment services by either investment firms or credit institutions,[133] the potential role which could be played by the European Central Bank or another centralized agency in the prudential regulation of the provision of investment services remains an intriguing question (Chapter XV).

VIII.10.3.3 *E-commerce and Prudential Supervision*

While the e-commerce revolution is having considerable impact on the protective regime's regulatory model by moving the regime away from host-Member-State control to home-Member-State/Member-State-of-establishment control and, in consequence, by triggering a move towards greater harmonization, its impact on how prudential supervision is managed in the internal market has been much less pronounced. However, in its Communication on E-commerce and Financial Services,[134] the Commission

---

[132] Final Report of the Committee of Wise Men on the Regulation of European Securities Markets, Feb 2001 (the Lamfalussy Report), 17.

[133] FSAP, n 19 above, 11.

[134] COM(2001)66.

noted that the emergence of new financial-services risk profiles associated with electronic business models was being fed into the review of the capital-adequacy regime currently under way. More specifically, it addressed the interaction between the home-country-control model of prudential supervision and the Member-State-of-origin principle established by the E-commerce Directive.[135] It is clear from the Communication that the home-country-control principle will not be diluted in the case of prudential supervision in the e-commerce environment. The ECD seems to raise difficulties in this respect, in that the Member State responsible for rule enforcement where the supply of e-commerce-delivered services is concerned is the Member State in which the e-commerce services provider is 'established'. This allocation of responsibility might seem to indicate that branches of investment firms would become subject under the e-commerce regime to the supervisory regime of the Member State in which they were established, rather than the home Member State in which the head office of the investment firm was situated, as per the ISD/CAD model. Given that prudential supervision addresses the structure and operation of the investment firm on a global basis, it seems quixotic that a directive addressing a particular method of delivering services could interfere with this model. It is not surprising therefore that the Communication stated that existing allocations of responsibility between Member States as regards prudential regulation do not change as a result of the ECD. Indeed, the 'co-ordinated field' to which the ECD's Member-State-of-origin principle applies (Articles 2(i) and 3), is concerned with service delivery and so does not appear to extend to prudential supervision.

More generally, in its ISD Working Paper the Commission suggested that its proposal that conduct of business regulation should be the responsibility of the branch from which investment services activities are carried out should not affect the primary allocation of Article 10 responsibilities to the home Member State. In particular, it found that 'for systems integrity and trading processes, centralised supervision of all back-office activities of the investment firm will be sufficient in ensuring the sound operation of the branch [and] more effective in identifying and redressing any supervisory concerns'.[136] However, the Working Paper did acknowledge that for other ongoing organizational requirements, specifically those rules which impact on investor-facing activities such as the asset-protection and conflict-of-interest management rules, the Member State in which the branch was established might be the more appropriate supervisor.[137]

---

[135] Directive 2000/13 on certain legal aspects of information society services, in particular electronic commerce, in the internal market [2000] OJ L178/1 (the ECD).

[136] ISD Working Paper, n 36 above, Annex 2, Art. 12.

[137] The Commission's thinking on how best to supervise conflict-of-interest management is still evolving. The Working Paper has suggested that all organizational requirements,

VIII.11 PRUDENTIAL SUPERVISION OF FINANCIAL CONGLOMERATES

VIII.11.1 *The Regulatory Challenge*

The EC regime deals with the consolidated supervision of largely homogeneous groups consisting of credit institutions, investment firms, and credit institutions and investment firms together. An increasingly more pressing challenge to the effectiveness of the Community's prudential-supervision structure concerns its ability to cope with the emergence and growth of more heterogeneous financial conglomerates which provide investment, banking, and insurance services within a group structure.[138] Indeed, financial conglomerates have now been identified as the 'mainstay of the EU financial system'.[139] From the varying perspectives of supervision, substantive regulation of new prudential risks and competition, the effective treatment of financial conglomerates, whether homogeneous or heterogeneous, places considerable demands on the current prudential-supervision structure and the construction of a suitably tailored regime represents a major challenge to policy-makers.

The supervisory difficulties posed by financial conglomerates centre on ensuring the effective supervision of constituent entities which generate a variety of risks that impact on the group as a whole. Risks can be aggravated, given the likelihood of considerable divergences in supervisory approaches across the different regulatory sectors.[140] Particular supervisory challenges include: how to ensure effective co-operation between supervisors, given that

conflict-of-interest management, should remain with the home Member State, notwithstanding the possibility currently available under Art. 10 for the host Member State to have a role. However, conflict-of-interest management is also included in the group of rules which impact on investor-facing activities and which, the Commission has suggested, could be subject to branch-Member-State control.

[138] The 2nd Progress Report reported that more than 250 financial conglomerates have been created since 1995: n 129 above, 6. For a discussion of the market conditions which encourage the growth of conglomeration see the 1993 OECD Report on Financial Conglomerates (the OECD Financial Conglomerates Report).

[139] Commission Report on the Financial Services Action Plan, First Progress Report, Oct 1999, 3. The homogeneous/heterogeneous classification is one used by the Commission.

[140] The current trend towards bringing banking, insurance, securities and investment-service supervisors (or a combination of these supervisors) together in one financial-services supervisor may alleviate the difficulties involved in supervising conglomerates. The introduction of a single financial-services regulator in the UK with the establishment of the Financial Services Authority is but one example of a trend which includes the establishment of single regulators for the banking, insurance, and securities sectors in Norway (1986), Sweden (1991), and Denmark (1998). Luxembourg introduced a single regulator for banking and securities in 1999, while discussions are currently under way in Ireland with respect to the establishment of a single financial-services regulator.

difficulties in one part of the conglomerate can impact severely on other operations leading to contagion risks; whether a lead or co-ordinating supervisor should be appointed from the different sectoral insurance, banking, and investment and securities supervisors involved in the supervision of the conglomerate; how to provide for adequate information flows from the group to the various sectoral supervisors; how to ensure that a complete risk profile of the group as a whole can be established; how to ensure conflict of interest management within the group; how to prevent supervisory arbitrage in the re-allocation of business between group entities to avoid sectoral supervisory rules which may otherwise apply; and how best to supervise overly complex and non-transparent group structures where management control may be too thinly dispersed.[141] These difficulties are clearly exacerbated where the conglomerate operates on a cross-border basis.

In terms of substantive regulation and risk control, capital-adequacy regulation requires fine-tuning to ensure that the financial conglomerate structure does not prejudice the capital adequacy of the different entities within the group which are subject to capital requirements. Controls are required to ensure that 'double gearing' or the use of the same capital simultaneously in two or more entities in a financial conglomerate does not occur. A related capital-adequacy problem is 'excessive leveraging' or the issuing of debt by the conglomerate parent which is then passed down the group as equity to the entities in the group. Management of intra-group transactions (such as trading operations between group entities, central management of liquidity, and the purchase or sale of assets with other group entities) and risk exposure (management of the exposures carried by entities within a financial conglomerate which could threaten the solvency of other entities in the group) may also require the imposition of particular management structures and reporting requirements. However, finding the appropriate regulatory response to intra-group transactions and risk-exposure management can be difficult. Intra-group transactions represent an important management tool, which should not be cavalierly treated by supervisors as they often create supervisory problems only where they introduce interdependencies between group entities. Considerable difficulties can arise in developing a common approach to the risk exposure for financial conglomerates as different philosophies drive the management of risk concentration in the different sectors. Large-exposure rules apply to risk concentrations in credit institutions and investment firms and measure exposures by reference to capital, while

---

[141] For an examination of the supervisory issues raised by financial conglomerates see generally Carton de Tournai, G, 'A few Reflections on Financial Conglomerates and their Supervision' in Wymeersch, E (ed), *Further Perspectives in Financial Integration in Europe* (1994) 65, Schneider, U, 'The Supervision of Financial Conglomerates' in Ferrarini, n 2 above, 77 and Nobel, P, 'Evolution of Regulation and the Company Law of Groups' (2000) 21 *The Company Lawyer* 98.

asset-spread rules apply to insurance undertakings and apply to the insurer's technical provisions.

From a competition perspective, financial conglomerates should not be subject to more onerous regulation, and accordingly to a competitive disadvantage, as compared with the regime applicable to their sectoral competitors, simply because of their corporate structure. Where regulation in excess of that imposed on the relevant sectoral service providers is imposed, it should reflect only the particular and additional risks represented by the financial conglomeration structure.[142]

Their systemic implications and cross-border operation make the development of a regulatory and supervisory approach to financial conglomerates a natural target for international-level discussions. In 1992, for example, IOSCO produced its Principles for the Supervision of Financial Conglomerates. In 1996 a Joint Forum on Financial Conglomerates was set up at international level and constituted by representatives of IOSCO, the Basel Committee on Banking Supervision, and the International Association of Insurance Supervisors. It was established to build on the work of the Tripartite Group of Banking, Insurance, and Securities Regulators which was established in 1993. In 1999 the Joint Forum produced a number of extensive papers concerning the supervision of financial conglomerates which cover: capital adequacy; the application of 'fit and proper' principles; a framework for information sharing; supervisory co-ordination; intra-group transactions and exposures principles; and risk-concentration principles. The Joint Forum papers form the basis of the Commission's approach to the supervision of financial conglomerates.[143]

VIII.11.2 *The Current Approach*

VIII.11.2.1 *Controls on the Development of Financial Conglomerates*

The basic concept of financial conglomeration is a familiar one in the Community. The universal bank model is well established in continental Europe with respect to the provision of banking and investment services within the same institution, and there is general acceptance of the *banc-assurance* model of providing insurance and banking services within the same group.[144]

---

[142] HM Treasury, *Completing a Dynamic Single European Financial Services Market: A Catalyst for Economic Prosperity for Citizens and Businesses Across the EU* (July 2000) para 62.

[143] Supervision of Financial Conglomerates, papers prepared by the Joint Forum on Financial Conglomerates and jointly released by the Basel Committee on Banking Supervision, IOSCO, and the International Association of Insurance Supervisors, Feb 1999 (the Joint Forum Papers). On the international initiatives see Coakley, n 114 above, 347–8.

[144] See Cranston, R, *Principles of Banking Law* (1997) 38–9. The 2nd Progress Report, eg, noted that in France, Finland, Spain, and Ireland more than 50% of life-assurance products are provided by insurance companies which form part of a banking group: n 129 above, 6.

The transformation of investment firms and credit institutions which provide investment services into financial conglomerates has not been subject to obstructive regulatory controls at EC level. While it imposes reporting and review requirements on the acquisition and disposition of holdings under Article 9, the ISD does not restrict the extent to which an investment firm can acquire holdings in credit institutions, insurance companies, or life-assurance companies, creating the possibility of the growth of financial conglomerates. Article 12 of the BCD II (CBD, Article 51) imposes restrictions on the extent to which a credit institution can acquire holdings in other undertakings but does not restrict the development of investment-firm/credit-institution groups. Article 12(1) (CBD, Article 51(1)) provides that a credit institution may not have a qualifying holding (defined in Article 1(10) (CBD, Article 1(10)) as a direct or indirect holding in an undertaking which represents 10 per cent or more of the capital or of the voting rights or which makes it possible to exercise a significant influence over the management of the undertaking in which the holding subsists) which exceeds 15 per cent of its own funds in an undertaking which is not a credit institution, a subsidiary of a credit institution whose activities are a direct extension of banking or concern services ancillary to banking such as leasing, factoring, the management of unit trusts, the management of data processing services, or any other similar activity, or a 'financial institution'. Financial institutions are defined in Article 1(6) (CBD, Article 1(5)) as undertakings other than credit institutions the principal activities of which are to acquire holdings or to carry on one or more of the activities listed in the Annex to the BCD II (CBD, Annex I), bar the acceptance of deposits and other repayable funds from the public. Further, Article 12(3) permits Member States to disapply the Article 12(1) and (2) holding restrictions from life-assurance and non-life insurance companies.

VIII.11.2.2 *Supervision of Financial Conglomerates*

Aspects of the current prudential supervision regime impact on the supervision of financial conglomerates. As outlined in section 9.5 above, the principle of consolidated supervision with respect to capital adequacy has been established for groups containing credit institutions and investment firms. The PSD has enhanced the supervisory regime for financial conglomerates via the generic Article 2(2) 'close links' rule, which provides, *inter alia*, that the authorization of financial undertakings with close links to other natural or legal persons be contingent on those close links not preventing the 'effective exercise' of supervisory functions, and by strengthening information-exchange obligations. More specifically, the 'effective exercise' of supervision is defined by reference to the effectiveness of consolidated supervision in recital 6 to the PSD. It provides that where the supervisory functions concerned include supervision on a consolidated basis, the authorities applied to for authorization must be able to identify the authorities competent to exercise supervision on a consolidated basis over the entity seeking authorization.

The limitations of this generic supervision regime in dealing with the particular risks posed by and supervisory difficulties involved with financial conglomerates have been thrown into sharp relief by the independent action of supervisors. Outside the formal requirements of the prudential supervision directives, supervisors across the single market have entered into Memoranda of Understanding, specially tailored to address the particular concerns raised by financial conglomerates, which have provoked considerable co-ordination of supervisory practices.[145]

VIII.11.3 *The Supplementary Supervision Proposal*

VIII.11.3.1 *Emergence of the Proposal*

Ensuring appropriate and adequate supervision of financial conglomerates has emerged in recent years as the dominant theme of discussions on reform of the prudential regime. In its 1998 Communication, the Commission noted that the dividing lines between different financial-services activities and their related supervision were becoming increasingly blurred and called for a reinforcement of co-operation between sectoral supervisors,[146] while the FSAP's prudential regulation proposals include a commitment to developing prudential rules for financial conglomerates. The Commission published an extensive consultation document on its approach to the supervision of financial conglomerates in 2000.[147] This was followed in mid-2001 by a proposal for a directive on the supplementary supervision of financial conglomerates.[148]

---

[145] Wymeersch, E, *The Harmonisation of Securities Trading in Europe in the New Trading Environment*, WP 2000–16, Working Paper Series of the Financial Law Institute, Universiteit Gent, 3.

[146] N 126 above, 16. This reflects the position of the OECD that '[t]he traditional prudent concerns of the banking, securities and insurance supervisors will still have to be satisfied, but it is recognised that each of these supervisory functions will have to take place in a rapidly evolving market place with considerable erosion of traditional functional categories': OECD Financial Conglomerates Report, n 138 above, 21.

[147] Commission, *Towards an EU Directive on the Prudential Supervision of Financial Conglomerates*, Consultation Document, MARKT/3021/2000 (the Consultation Paper).

[148] Proposal for a directive on the supplementary supervision of credit institutions, insurance undertakings and investment firms in a financial conglomerate and amending Council Directives 73/239/EEC, 79/267/EEC, 92/49/EEC, 92/96/EEC, 93/6/EEC and 93/22/EEC, and Directives 98/78/EC and 2000/12 of the European Parliament and the Council, COM(2001)213 ([2001] OJ C213/227) (the Supplementary Supervision Proposal or Proposal). A broadly supportive opinion has been delivered by the European Central Bank ([2001] OJ C271/10). As at the time of writing the Proposal is at a relatively early stage in the legislative process, its provisions will be considered in outline only.

Placing the problem of financial conglomeration in its EC context, in its Explanatory Memorandum the Commission noted that, while homogeneous groups of financial institutions were already covered for specific prudential purposes (the CAD and the now consolidated CSD regime for credit institution groups, investment firm groups and credit institution/investment firm groups and the Directive 98/78[149] regime for insurance groups), heterogeneous groups, such as credit institutions or investment firms with insurance subsidiaries or mixed activity groups (groups carrying out mainly non-financial activities but which contain at least one credit institution or investment firm),[150] were covered only to a very limited extent. Prudential questions which were addressed at group level on a sectoral basis for credit institution, investment firm, and insurance groups (such as the control of double-gearing) were, as a result, not being addressed where the group structure did not fall within the existing regime. Even though financial conglomerates consisting of credit institutions, investment firms, and insurance companies had the potential significantly to destabilize the financial system and affect individual depositors, policy-holders, and investors, the Commission found there was no group-wide prudential supervision framework addressing capital, risk concentration, intra-group transactions, and the suitability of management. This uneven treatment of conglomerates had, per the Commission, led to prudential deficiencies in the regulatory framework and competitive distortions. As a result, the development of a level playing-field was being hindered while supervised entities and competent authorities were unclear about which rules applied.

The substantive recommendations of the Consultation Paper and the subsequent Supplementary Supervision Proposal are based, as was flagged in the FSAP, on the recommendations already made at international level on the supervision of financial conglomerates by the Joint Forum on Financial Conglomerates. Reflecting the areas highlighted by the Joint Forum they cover: capital adequacy; intra-group transactions and risk concentration; fit and proper principles for management, directors, and major shareholders; appointment of a co-ordinator; information exchange; and convergence of supervisory practices.

VIII.11.3.2 *Substantive Requirements*

Of particular practical significance for the shape and scope of the new regime

---

[149] Directive 98/78/EC on the Supplementary Supervision of Insurance Undertakings in an Insurance Group [1998] OJ L330/1.

[150] A useful diagram representing the types of groups excluded is provided at the Consultation Paper, n 147 above, 8. It also clarifies how the form of the group's parent company can take a group outside the current supervision framework.

is the Commission's characterization of a 'financial conglomerate'. In order to distinguish the proposed financial-conglomerate regime from that already applicable to homogeneous financial groups, the Commission has proposed a definition of a financial conglomerate based on cross-sector activity (Articles 2 and 3). It has defined a financial conglomerate as a group the activities of which mainly consist of providing financial services in the financial sector (while financial services are defined broadly as including banking, insurance, and investment-services activities, collective portfolio-management services do not appear to be covered), which includes at least one regulated undertaking, is comprised of at least one insurance or reinsurance undertaking and at least one other entity of a different financial sector and which engages in 'significant' cross-sectoral activity. The Proposal sets out a threshold test (based on 50 per cent financial services activity) for assessing whether the group is a financial conglomerate for the purposes of the Proposal or a non-financial group. The 'significant' cross-sector activity requirement, assessed by means of a 10 per cent cross-sector activity threshold, is designed to ensure that supervisors are not subject to unnecessary burdens, given the limited additional prudential risk posed by groups whose cross-sector activity is minimal.

Article 4 sets out the scope of the supplementary-supervision regime, which operates without prejudice to the sectoral rules. The Proposal's supplementary requirements apply to every regulated entity at the head of a financial conglomerate, every regulated entity the parent undertaking of which is a mixed financial-holding company (a parent undertaking which is not a regulated entity and which, together with its subsidiaries, of which at least one is a regulated entity that has its head office in the Community, and other entities forms a financial conglomerate) that has its head office in the Community and every regulated entity in a financial conglomerate linked by virtue of unified management.

The capital-adequacy regime (Article 5 and Annex I) is designed to facilitate the assessment of capital adequacy on a group-wide basis and to identify and to suggest technical mechanisms for dealing with particular problems, such as double-gearing, which can result in a distorted view of group capital and impact adversely on the individual entities within the group. More generally, financial conglomerates are required to have adequate capital-adequacy policies and internal control mechanisms in place at group level. A common supervisory approach to intra-group transactions and risk concentration, both of which raise concerns with respect to contagion risk, conflicts of interests, supervisory arbitrage, and the degree of transparency as to the overall group-risk profile, is covered by Article 6 and Annex II. Given the difficulties in addressing intra-group transactions and risk concentrations outlined above, the Proposal's approach is based on using a light regulatory touch rather than on imposing quantitative limits.

The regime is based on requiring regulated entities within the financial conglomerate to have effective internal risk-management processes and internal control mechanisms in order to manage intra-group transactions within the conglomerate and risk concentration at the level of the conglomerate.

The Proposal also addresses the application of fit and proper rules within financial conglomerates. While the Commission noted that specific legislation was not required in that the current sectoral rules provided a sufficient legal basis to contain financial conglomerate structures, it proposed that the sectoral rules be amended to reflect the reality that financial conglomerates are often managed along business lines rather than on legal-entity lines. To take the example of the ISD's fitness and propriety regime, Article 23 of the Proposal amends Article 3(3) of the ISD to require that where the business of an investment firm is co-directed by persons appointed in a different legal entity or where persons appointed in a different legal entity have a material influence on the direction of an investment firm, the fitness and propriety rules should also apply to those persons.[151]

One of the Commission's core recommendations is the requirement that the competent authorities involved in the supervision of a financial conglomerate must appoint from among themselves a co-ordinator or a co-ordinating supervisor (Article 7). This requirement is designed to ensure that, given that the prudential supervision of financial conglomerates is split between a number of sectoral supervisors, it is still possible to ensure that a mutual understanding of the risk profile of the group as a whole exists between supervisors, such that there are no gaps in prudential supervision, that supervisory tasks are not duplicated, and that contradictory measures are not imposed on group entities. Appointment of a co-ordinator should also ensure that the overall prudential risk to which a financial conglomerate is exposed is managed and supervised. Article 7 sets out the criteria according to which the co-ordinator is to be identified in the absence of agreement, while Article 8 sets out four core supervisory tasks to be fulfilled by the co-ordinator: co-ordination of information-gathering and dissemination; capital-adequacy assessment and monitoring of the Article 5 and 6 rules; assessment of the financial conglomerate's structure, organization, and internal control systems; and planning and co-ordination of supervisory activities in going concern and emergency situations in co-operation with

---

[151] Other ISD revisions include amending the Art. 6 notification procedure and Art. 9 acquisition/disposal rules to reflect the structure of financial conglomerates. In particular, the Art. 6 procedure is revised to require the competent authorities involved to consult with each other when assessing the suitability of shareholders and the reputation and experience of directors involved in the management of another entity of the same group. They are to provide each other with information as regards the suitability of shareholders and the reputation and experience of directors that are of relevance for the granting of authorization as well as for monitoring compliance with operating conditions.

the relevant competent authorities. It is clear from the Commission's Consultation Paper and Article 8 that the allocation of co-ordinating functions to the co-ordinator under the Proposal is not designed to result in a transfer of responsibilities from established sectoral supervisors, involve the construction of a new institutional model of supervision, or extend supervision to unsupervised entities in financial conglomerates.

In line with the current trend to devolve financial/investment-services law-making to specialized committees,[152] the Proposal provides that the Commission can adopt 'technical amendments' to the Proposal, once it is adopted, in certain areas. These areas are limited, for the most part, to the clarification of definitions (although the clarification and adaptation of the capital-adequacy requirements in light of developments on financial markets and in prudential techniques are included) and the alignment of terminology. The regulatory committee procedure set out in Article 5 of Comitology Decision 99/468/EC[153] will apply and, in this regard, the Commission will be supervised and assisted by a 'Financial Conglomerates Committee' composed of representatives of the Member States and chaired by a representative of the Commission.

VIII.11.3.3 *The Treaty Basis*

The choice of Article 47(2) EC as the Treaty basis for the Proposal has a wider significance for the development of the prudential regime as a whole. Article 47(2) provides for the co-ordination of Member States' laws with respect to the taking-up and pursuit of activities as self-employed persons, and has been described by the Court as permitting the adoption of measures which 'contribute to the abolition of obstacles to free movement which may result in particular from a divergence between the provisions laid down by law, regulation or administrative action in Member States concerning the taking-up and pursuit of activities as self-employed persons'.[154] The Proposal is not directly connected with free movement and the removal of obstacles to free movement in the same way as the ISD and the CAD are; it is not immediately concerned with the removal of obstacles via the passport device and reregulation in order to support the passport. It is concerned more generally with protecting the stability of the liberalized market-place 'post-passport' as it evolves and, in particular, as it becomes vulnerable to new 'integration risks' as the shape of the integrated market changes—in

---

[152] See the discussion of comitology and the Lamfalussy Report in Ch. XV sects. 2.5.3 and 2.5.4 below.

[153] Council Decision Laying Down the Procedures for the Exercise of Implementing Powers Conferred on the Commission [1999] OJ L184/23.

[154] Case C–233/94 *Germany v Parliament and Council* [1997] ECR I–2405 (the *Deposit Guarantee* case), para 15.

this case via the growth of financial conglomerates. It appears from the Proposal, however, that ensuring the stability of the integrated market as it develops following the introduction of the passport is suggested as a legitimate target for Article 47(2) measures, in so far as the Proposal improves the functioning of the internal market by promoting wider market stability even if free movement is not directly implicated. Indeed, the continual references to 'supplementary supervision' suggest that the Proposal is regarded as an extension of the original free-movement-related prudential requirements set out in the ISD/CAD regime. This reading of Article 47(2) as a basis for measures which deal with post-integration risks could render it a powerful regulatory tool for the Commission.[155]

Also of interest is the absence of references in the Proposal and its preparatory materials to disparities between national rules which hinder the internal market. Whether the objective of the measure is the removal of obstacles to free movement, or, more generally, improving the functioning of the internal market, this analysis normally features heavily in the investment-services measures. Here, the focus is on inconsistencies and gaps in the EC prudential regime itself, rather than on difficulties with the regime at national level, although passing reference is made to the adoption of new supervisory mechanisms at Member State level to deal with financial conglomerates.[156] Arguably, protecting the stability of the integrated market against the risks caused by financial conglomerates whose cross-border operation has been made possible by the free-movement provisions is sufficiently connected with facilitating free movement to come within Article 47(2) EC. Nonetheless, the Court has frequently stressed the connection between the removal of obstructive regulatory divergences and Article 47(2). In the *Deposit Guarantee* case, for example, the Court found that Article 47(2) was an appropriate basis for the Deposit Guarantee Directive,[157] in that the effect of the Directive was to prevent Member States from invoking depositor protection in order to impede the activities of credit institutions authorized in other Member States and to eliminate fundamental differences between deposit-protection schemes. More seriously, in the *Tobacco Advertising* ruling, the Court quelled any moves towards characterizing Article 47(2) (and Article 95 EC) as general enabling powers conferring power on the EC to regulate the internal market generally and laid considerable emphasis on the removal of real regulatory barriers to integration as a qualification on

[155] The current capital-adequacy review is similarly based on the development of the single market and on the enhancement of prudential standards, although there is a clearer connection to free movement and the passport in the capital-adequacy regime: 1999 Regulatory Capital Review, n 97 above, 6.

[156] Proposal, n 148 above, 3.

[157] Directive 94/19/EC on deposit-guarantee schemes [1994] OJ L135/5.

[158] Case C–376/98 *Germany v Parliament and Council* [2000] ECR I–8419 (the *Tobacco Advertising* case). On the ruling in more detail see Ch. IX sects. 12.3 and 12.4.2 below.

reliance on Article 47(2).[158] In particular, it found that 'a mere finding of disparities between national rules and of the abstract risk of obstacles to the exercise of fundamental freedoms' would not be sufficient to justify reliance on Article 47(2).[159] It may be, however, that the particular features of the investment-services market, its sensitivity to regulation and the stability risks provoked by integration strengthens the case for legislation designed to improve the functioning of the market-place by supporting (rather than facilitating) free movement and the passport by protecting the stability of the integrated market-place within which the passport is exercised. Some nervousness about the connection between the market-functioning/stability argument and Article 47(2), given the distance between the Proposal and the original conferral of passport rights, might be inferred, however, from the references in the Explanatory Memorandum (they do not appear in the Proposal itself) to the need to level the playing-field between different types of financial conglomerates and avoid competitive distortions. These arguments reflect more closely traditional free-movement and internal-market-construction objectives and chime with the *Tobacco Advertising* ruling's emphasis on the removal of distortions to competition and obstructions to free movement under Article 47(2) and Article 95EC.[160]

Although the choice of Treaty basis may be somewhat problematic, what is uncontroversial is that the requirements of Article 5EC with respect to subsidiarity and proportionality seem to be met. As the Proposal points out, the establishment of rules for the supervision of financial conglomerates which operate on an EC-wide basis is best undertaken at EC level. Equally, as a minimum-standards directive largely focused on co-ordinating supervisory action rather on adopting substantive rules the Proposal appears to meet the proportionality requirement.

[159] Ibid, para 87.
[160] N 148 above, 3.

IX

The Protective Regulation
of Investment-services Providers

IX.1 THE RATIONALE FOR PROTECTIVE REGULATION

Investor protection in relation to the provision of investment services[1] is often justified by reference to the need to protect the efficient functioning of the market-place. Investor protection is viewed as a matter of public interest and as essential, on a macro basis, for the proper functioning of the market-place by promoting the efficient transfer of funds from investors to the market. This is because investor confidence, as a by-product of protection, is regarded as central to the efficient allocation of resources in the market-place.[2] Investor protection can also be driven by more paternalistic concerns and the assumption that investors should be protected from themselves.[3]

The scope of investor-protection regulation (see section 2 below) depends on the extent to which the underlying rationale for regulation requires that investors should be protected and its characterization of the risks from which regulation should shield investors. Paternalistic regulation takes a broad view of the extent to which the investor should be protected and intervenes beyond the simple correction of market failures. Paternalistic regulation may, for example, withdraw investors from the market-place by preventing

---

[1] This chapter addresses investor protection in the investor/investment-firm relationship. Investors are also protected through the market-integrity rules which impact on that relationship, such as the market-abuse rules discussed in Ch. XIII, and securities-trading market controls such as the transparency rules, concentration requirements and market standards discussed in Ch. XI.

[2] See, eg, the 1984 Gower Report on Review of Investor Protection: Part I, which, at para 1.16 found that regulation is necessary 'to protect reasonable people from being made fools of. That degree of confidence is essential if people are to have the justified confidence to invest.' See also Heiser, K, 'Can Capital Market Law Approaches be Harmonized with Essential Principles of Company Law' (2000) 11 *EBLRev.* 60, 67–8, Lindsey, R, 'Efficient Regulation of the Securities Market' in McCrudden, C, (ed), *Regulation and Deregulation, Policy and Practice in the Utilities and Financial Services Industries* (1999) 295, 296, Mahmood, S, 'Regulatory Challenges Posed by Investor Protection' (1998) 5 *EFSL* 193, 193, Llewellyn, D, 'Consumer Protection in Retail Investment Services: Protection Against What' (1995) 3 *JFRC* 43 and Page, A, and Ferguson, R, *Investor Protection* (1992) 33.

[3] Paternalistic regulation operates from the perspective that, regardless of wider market-efficiency concerns, certain investors are in a weak position *vis-à-vis* investment firms and should be prevented from making mistakes and suffering losses. It is typically challenged on the ground that investors should not be insulated from all risks or from the consequences of their actions in the context of the inherent risks of the investment-services market-place. For the market efficiency/paternalism distinction see Page and Ferguson, n 2 above, 35 and 39 and Clark, R, 'The Soundness of Financial Intermediaries' (1976) 86 *Yale LJ* 1, 19–20.

investment firms from providing highly sophisticated services to retail investors.[4] In its most extreme form it may intervene to protect small investors from all the risks, including the risk of making an unwise decision, of the investment-services market-place.[5] Market-driven investor protection, by contrast, seeks to address and protect investors from market failures which hinder the efficient allocation of resources by the market.[6] The main market failure usually concerns informational imbalances in the investor/investment-firm relationship. Imperfect information may mean that investors are not fully aware of the degree of risk they are carrying with respect to the investment firm and not in a position to monitor or impose discipline on the firm.[7] Clearly, the investment-firm/investor transaction can involve varying degrees of risk; the provision of investment advice, the supply of one-off execution-only brokerage services, and the provision of discretionary portfolio-management services all have different risk profiles. Imperfect information may mean that investors are exposed to risks which can arise in some or all of these areas with respect to the solvency of the firm, the likelihood of fraud or misuse of investor funds, conflicts of interests, and the competence of the firm in advising on and executing deals appropriately. As far as solvency is concerned, investors' funds and instruments are typically held by investment firms as part of the investment-firm/investor relationship, either as part of a portfolio-management service or while a transaction is settled; the failure of an investment firm, the danger of which can be aggravated as a result of positions taken by the firm in own-account transactions, may expose the investor to loss in the absence of prudential

[4] Less extremely, suitability rules which require investment firms to assess the appropriateness of an investment in light of the investor's characteristics and experience have been classed as paternalistic: Markham, J, 'Protecting the Institutional Investor—Jungle Predator or Shorn Lamb?' (1995) 12 *Yale J Reg.* 345, 369.

[5] Many securities regulators explicitly reject this approach. The UK Financial Services and Markets Act 2000 (the FSMA), eg, states in s 5(2)(d) that in pursuing its consumer protection objectives under the FSMA, the Financial Services Authority (FSA) must be mindful of 'the general principle that consumers should take responsibility for their actions'. On an international level, IOSCO has stated that 'the mission of IOSCO members is not to guarantee that investors will avoid losses, but to see that investors are armed with the information they need to make informed investment decisions': IOSCO Technical Committee Bulletin, *Regarding Investor Protection in the New Economy* (2000) (the IOSCO New Economy Bulletin) 11.

[6] On the market-failure approach see Dermine, J, 'EC Banking Regulation' in Steil, B (ed), *International Financial Market Regulation* (1994) 95, 109–11 and Llewellyn, n 2 above, 45. See also the analysis in Page and Ferguson, n 2 above, 35–8 and in Franks, J, and Mayer, C, *Risk Regulation and Investor Protection. The Case of Investment Management* (1989) who noted at 152 that '[i]ntervention by a regulatory authority is justified only in circumstances in which market failures can be identified. Market failures occur when prices and incentives to not fully reflect the costs and benefits of goods and services provided'. The arguments in support of and against the market-failure approach are discussed in the context of consumer protection in Scott, C, and Black, J, *Cranston's Consumers and the Law* (3rd edn, 2000) 26–36.

[7] 'The most important class of market failures that arises in the financial markets is imperfect information': Franks and Mayer, n 6 above, 152.

controls. The control exercised by firms over investor assets also carries with it the risk of investor loss through fraud and dishonesty in the absence of full information on the firm's activities. Lack of awareness of potential conflicts of interests can result in exposure to prejudicial dealing practices on the part of the investment firm, such as front-running or the provision of biased advice to place funds in investments in which the firm has a position or is otherwise interested. The technicalities involved in the dealing and transaction-settlement process may also result in losses for investors. Best execution rules, for example, which essentially require investment firms to obtain the best price available for investor orders, are based on the imbalance between investor and firm as to price information.

Overall, the scope of an investor-protection regime will typically suggest a combination of philosophies, which are often not overtly expressed, as well as cultural attitudes to regulation.[8] Even if a consistent rationale for regulation or a combination of rationales cannot be detected, the scope of an investor protection regime and the risks it addresses will almost always reflect policies concerned with the costs of regulation; these include competitiveness concerns, the appropriateness of imposing regulatory burdens on investment firms,[9] and the desirability or otherwise of a light regulatory touch.[10]

IX.2 THE SCOPE OF PROTECTIVE REGULATION

IX.2.1 *Prudential and Protective Rules*

The investor-protection mechanisms used to address these risks can be broadly divided into preventive prudential rules and protective rules. Alternatively, as noted in the context of prudential supervision in Chapter VIII, this classification can be made in terms of macro controls, which pro-

---

[8] Regulation is often composed of a combination of paternalistic and market-failure-based measures. Clark (in the context of financial intermediaries which pool investors' funds such as unit trusts) found that paternalism can never be a complete rationale as protective regulation typically falls far short of compensating for all errors in risk-taking, that market imperfections (such as information deficiencies) are often regulated beyond what is necessary to correct imperfections, and concluded that 'it is assumed that at least the smaller capital suppliers somehow must be protected against personally serious losses caused by the failures of financial intermediaries, regardless of the degree of perfection of market forces': n 3 above, 26.

[9] It is not axiomatic that investment firms will resist the imposition of investor-protection regulation. The point has been made that investment firms are not in principle adverse to protective and, in particular, conduct regulation as it is in their interest to develop long-term relationships with investors and to manage the relationship appropriately. Langevoort, D, 'Selling Hope, Selling Risk: Some Lessons for Law from Behavioural Economics About Stockbrokers and Sophisticated Customers' (1996) 84 *Cal. L Rev.* 627, 629. Compliance with investor-protection rules can also protect a firm against liability and enhance its reputation.

[10] See, eg, FSMA, s 2(3).

tect the financial system and investors in general, and micro controls, which focus on the individual investment-firm/investor relationship.[11]

IX.2.2 *Prudential Regulation*

As discussed in Chapter VIII, prudential controls, which include authorization rules, capital-adequacy requirements, and operational prudential controls such as asset-protection and record-keeping rules, safeguard the systemic stability of the wider financial system, and address the soundness of firms and their risk-management policies. Investor protection can also be identified as a purpose of these rules.

IX.2.3 *Protective Regulation*

Protective regulation, by contrast, addresses the conduct of the investment-firm/investor relationship and is the concern of this chapter. It imposes standards of behaviour on secondary market practices and transactions. Adequate disclosure and transparency in the conduct of the investment-firm/investor relationship, designed to ensure that investors are informed and can make rational decisions, is the foundation for much of protective regulation. But disclosure alone is not usually regarded as sufficient to protect investors in the investor/investment-firm relationship, particularly given that investors access investment firms' services, particularly advice and portfolio-management services, precisely because they do not wish to interpret complex disclosure and want instead to trust in the reputation, expertise, and professional standards of that firm.[12] In addition, the bounded rationality problem emerges: investors may not be in a position to interpret disclosure which is designed to protect them and assist them in making rational decisions.[13] Accordingly, protective regulation extends to the conduct of the investment-firm/investor relationship. Marketing regulation extends beyond

---

[11] Gros, D, and Lannoo, K, *The Euro Capital Markets* (2000) 122. Franks and Mayer refer to 'firm-specific risks' and 'systemic risks': n 6 above, 156. See also Wymeersch, E, 'The Implementation of the ISD and the CAD' in Ferrarini, G (ed), *European Securities Markets: the Investment Services Directive and Beyond* (1998) 3, 15.

[12] The extent to which investors rely on professional investment advice and the dangers this reliance can hold was highlighted by IOSCO during the 'new economy' stocks boom. It noted that '[w]hile market professionals . . . normally perform valuable gate-keeping and advisory functions for the benefits of investors, the euphoria associated with new technology investments may have caused some of these market professionals to lose their perspective and to compromise the judgments that they normally provide to the market place and investors': IOSCO New Economy Bulletin, n 5 above, 4.

[13] The FSA has produced a number of studies on the varying abilities of investors to decipher disclosure and their vulnerability to confusion in the financial services area. See, eg, FSA, *Better Informed Consumers*, Consumer Research Paper 1 (2000) and FSA, *Informed Decisions*, Consumer Research Paper 5 (2000).

pure disclosure and intervenes more pro-actively in the relationship by regulating the use of marketing devices such as cold calls. Conduct-of-business rules[14] also form a part of protective regulation. While these typically have a large disclosure component (including risk-warning requirements and rules concerning the provision of written agreements and the disclosure they must contain) they can also include: honesty, loyalty and fairness requirements, including suitability-based 'know your client' obligations; diligence and skill rules; rules on commissions, charges, and fees; dealing rules such as best-execution requirements and execution-only rules; and conflicts-of-interests rules.[15] These disclosure and conduct rules presuppose that the investor is rational and, once in possession of adequate disclosure and protected by conduct rules, will make an informed investment decision. They do not paternalistically intervene directly in investor/investment-firm bargaining nor, except arguably in the case of suitability rules, exclude the investor from making certain decisions.

Moving away from protective measures which are connected to market failures with respect to disclosure and fraud to more paternalistic mechanisms, compensation mechanisms could also be classed as protective, as could rules which intervene in contractual relationships to prevent abuses of greater bargaining power by firms (such as rules regulating contract performance, withdrawal rights, and termination).

Finally, extending protective regulation from the traditional components of investor protection, general consumer-protection rules, particularly procedural rules with respect to redress and complaint procedures which are particularly significant in cross-border situations, could also be identified as protective.[16] Public regulation of the investment-firm/investor relationship aside, protective controls can also be imposed through private law via, for example, principal/agent, trustee and confidence-relationship-based

---

[14] Marketing rules can form a part of conduct-of-business regulation. In the UK regime, eg, the FSA's detailed Conduct of Business Sourcebook includes rules on financial promotion: FSA, *The Conduct of Business Sourcebook*, Policy Statement (2001) (the FSA Conduct of Business Sourcebook).

[15] For an illustration of the wide reach of conduct-of-business regulation see the FSA's Draft Conduct of Business Sourcebook, Consultation Paper 45a (2000) (the FSA Draft Conduct of Business Sourcebook Paper) which at 6–7 has described the primary purpose of the conduct-of-business regime as 'to set and reinforce business standards for various aspects of firms' relationships with their customers. There are therefore rules to cover information flows between the firm and the customer, advising the customer or acting for the customer at discretion . . . and executing transactions'.

[16] The 1998 IOSCO Objectives and Principles of Securities Regulation (1998 IOSCO Principles) at para 4.2.1 stress that '[i]nvestors should have access to a neutral mechanism (such as courts or other mechanisms of dispute resolution) or means of redress and compensation for improper behaviour'.

fiduciary responsibilities, breach of which can impose liability on the investment firm and sound in damages.[17]

IX.3 THE EC AND PROTECTIVE REGULATION

IX.3.1 *Scope of the Regime*

The traditional elements of protective regulation outlined above appear, if, at present, in a skeletal fashion, in the Community's protective regime.[18] This chapter will consider the extent to which the harmonized investment-services regime addresses protective regulation, but it will also, given that this area is characterized by a light approach to harmonization by comparison with the prudential regime, review the jurisprudence of the Court of Justice on the extent to which the Treaty permits Member States to retain national investor-protection controls in the absence of harmonization.[19] The Investment Services Directive,[20] the Investor Compensation Schemes Directive[21] (discussed in Chapter X), and, most recently, the Distance Marketing Proposal[22] all form part of the investment-services protective framework. The investor/investment-firm relationship is also supervised via a number of horizontal consumer-protection directives which impact on the

[17] Private-law remedies will not be considered in this ch. See generally the discussion in Cranston, R, *Principles of Banking Law* (1997) 199–237.

[18] On the protective regime generally, see Lambrecht, P, and Haljan, D, 'Investor Protection and the European Directives Concerning Securities' in van Houtte, H (ed), *The Law of Cross-Border Securities Transactions* (1999) 257; Cranston, R, and Hadjiemmanuil, C, 'Banking Integration in the European Community: The European Commission's Unfinished Agenda' in Norton, J, Andenas, M, and Footer, M (eds), *The Changing World of International Law in the Twenty-first Century: A Tribute to the Late Kenneth R. Simmonds* (1998) 341; Cremona, M, 'Freedom of Movement of Financial Services' in Caiger, A, and Floudas, D (eds), *1996 Onwards: Lowering the Barriers Further* (1996) 65; Tridimas, T, 'Investor Protection in the European Community: An Assessment of the Harmonisation Programme' in Feldman, D, and Meisel, F (eds), *Corporate and Commercial Law: Modern Developments* (1996) 105 and Van Crombugghe, N, 'Consumer Protection and Free Movement of Financial Services' in Campbell, D (ed), *Financial Services in the New Europe* (1992) 349.

[19] This review was not carried out in Ch. VIII above on prudential supervision as the coverage of the prudential regime has significantly reduced the opportunities for Member States to rely on the general good exception.

[20] Directive 93/22/EC on investment services in the securities field [1993] OJ L141/27 (the ISD)

[21] Directive 97/9/EC on investor-compensation schemes [1997] OJ L84/22 (the ICSD).

[22] [2000] OJ C177/21. Explanatory Memorandum at COM(1999)385 (the Distance Marketing Proposal). Political agreement was reached on the Proposal in Sept 2001 but, at the time of writing, a common position has yet to be published in the Official Journal.

behaviour of the investment firm in its relations with investors,[23] including the E-commerce Directive.[24]

The protective regime will be discussed in relation to investment firms authorized under the ISD. Credit institutions authorized to provide investment services under the banking regime are, in relation to their investment-services activities, subject to a similar protective regime, via the application of the ISD. Attention will also be given to the new regime for the most recent arrival on the EC's investment-services regulation landscape, management companies/self-managed investment companies providing investment services under the management-company passport.[25] The general consumer-protection measures tend to apply to investment-services providers generically.

IX.3.2 *Features of the Regime*

In the EC regime, investor protection is a function of market integration. Investor-protection interests are generally aligned with those of investment-services market-integration. The EC investor typically appears in the harmonized regime as a supplier of capital to, and a beneficiary of increased choice and competition in, the integrated market, but only rarely as a focus for protection against the risks of the integrated market-place.[26] Indeed, as

[23] eg, the Unfair Contract Terms Directive (Directive 93/13/EEC on unfair terms in consumer contracts [1995] OJ L95/29), while a general consumer-protection measure, has implications for the investment-firm/investor contract and is discussed at sect. 8.2.2 below. Consumer-protection measures which do not have a significant impact on the standard services provided in the course of the investment-firm/investor relationship are not discussed in this ch. Perhaps the most significant of these is the Consumer Credit Directive (Directive 87/102/EEC for the approximation of the laws, regulations and administrative provisions of the Member States concerning consumer credit [1987] OJ L42/48, as amended by Directive 90/088/EEC [1990] OJ L 61/14).

[24] Directive 2000/31/EC [2000] OJ L178/1 (the E-commerce Directive or ECD).

[25] Amended Proposal for a European Parliament and Council Directive amending Directive 85/611/EEC on the Coordination of Laws, Regulation and Administrative Provisions Relating to Undertakings for Collective Investment in Transferable Securities [1985] OJ L375/3 (the UCITS Directive) with a view to Regulating Management Companies and Simplified Prospectuses (the Management Company Proposal), COM(2000)331. The Council's Common Position is at [2001] OJ C297/10. The measure was adopted by the Council as a directive on 4 Dec 2001. This discussion is based on the Common Position (references to the Management Company Proposal are to the Common Position text, while references to Articles are to the revised Articles of the UCITS Directive introduced by the new regime). At the time of writing, the final text of the adopted measure had not been published in the Official Journal and had not yet come into force. The Parliament did not, however, materially amend the Common Position text during its second reading prior to the adoption of the measure. Its only amendment (which was to shorten the Common Position's 5-year time frame from the entry into force of the new regime, at the end of which the Commission was to review the capital requirements imposed on management companies, to 3 years) was accepted by the Commission (COM(2001)687).

[26] In its comments on the Commission's Green Paper on Financial Services: Meeting Consumers' Expectations, COM(96)209 (the Green Paper on Financial Services Consumers— sect. 13.1 below), the Parliament noted the primacy of the single-market construction objective in financial-services measures and trenchantly observed that 'consumer protection should

a regulatory priority, the investor as a focus for specific protection has been subsidiary to the investment firm as a beneficiary of integration.[27]

Nonetheless, there is a natural affinity between the objectives of market integration, on the one hand, and investor protection as a device to enhance investor confidence and the effectiveness of the integrated market-place, on the other.[28] This macro function of investor protection is articulated in the protective regulation model which emerges indirectly from the Treaty-based investment-services market-liberalization regime and in the protective regulation model the Court is developing by identifying the national investor-protection rules which can apply in cross-border situations. The sparse coverage of protective regulation, as compared to the detailed harmonization of prudential regulation, underlines, however, that the market-integration objectives of the Treaty have resulted in the harmonized investment-services regime being sharply skewed towards prudential regulation and the protection of the market-place generally.[29] The Treaty's ability to sustain a more extensive protective harmonization policy is, however, questionable (section 12 below).

In line with the underlying concern of EC securities regulation with market integration and liberalization, a preoccupation with avoiding costly regulatory burdens can be identified throughout the regime.[30]

be a fundamental political and legal priority for national and Community legislators; such protection cannot be left to the automatic operation of single market mechanisms' [1997] OJ C65/76, para 3.4.1.

[27] One Commission official (speaking unofficially) has stated that in the securities field, 'we have focused our efforts on two types of player in these markets, i.e., issuers of securities on the one hand and intermediaries or investment firms on the other': Cruikshank, C, 'Cooperation and Convergence: The View from Brussels' in Oditah, F (ed), *The Future for the Global Securities Market—Legal and Regulatory Aspects* (1996) 268. The Commission has recently endorsed this view in its 2001 Communication on E-commerce and Financial Services, COM(2001)66 (the E-commerce and Financial Services Communication) stating at 10 that '[t]he Union's financial services legislation is in large part geared toward providing financial institutions with access to Community markets on the basis of a European passport'.

[28] To take a recent example, the central role of investor confidence in achieving market integration was acknowledged by the Initial Report of the Wise Men which linked the conditions for attaining the benefits of an integrated market to 'the attainment of broad public confidence in European financial markets': Initial Report of the Committee of Wise Men on the Regulation of European Securities Markets, Nov 2000 (the Initial Lamfalussy Report) 6. As noted in Ch. VI, the Final Report of the Wise Men went further and recommended that 'the conceptual framework of overarching principles', on which, it suggested, all EC financial-services and securities regulation should be constructed, include the maintenance of confidence in European securities markets: Final Report of the Committee of Wise Men on the Regulation of European Securities Markets, Feb 2001 (the Lamfalussy Report) 22.

[29] The Commission has acknowledged the soundness bias of the financial-services regime generally and its focus on financial strength, probity, and reliability: Green Paper on Financial Services Consumers, n 26 above, 3.

[30] The Commission has noted that achieving a single market for retail financial services requires the need for consumer safeguards to be balanced against the need to increase competition and widen consumer choice, and that the latter can be prejudiced by disproportionately high levels of protection: Commission Communication on Financial Services: Building a Framework for Action, COM(1998)625 (the 1998 Communication) 12.

On a more general level, the dominance of market integration as the underlying objective of EC investment-services harmonization has resulted in a certain philosophical bankruptcy. Where investor protection is alluded to, coherent reasons why investors should be protected, be it generally or at EC level, are rarely given.[31] A coherent rationale for the adoption of regulation, be it market-failure correction and the efficient operation of the market-place as a whole, paternalism or a considered combination of both, is essential in establishing the appropriate minimum level of protection and ensuring that the measures adopted are not overly obstructive of the market-place.[32] This is particularly true of EC protective regulation, given the pro-investor feelings that are typically invoked by the investor/investment-firm relationship,[33] the sensitivity of the evolving single investment-services market to regulation, and the difficulties in reaching an appropriate level of protection which accommodates local market regulation and deals with the specific risks represented by an integrated market. Paternalism, and the extent to which it governs the EC's characterization of risk has an important bearing on whether the regulatory regime is coherent, as do market-failure theories.[34]

The regulatory devices used to achieve investor protection in the internal market are heavily based on prudential requirements and, in particular, on solvency-based capital-adequacy requirements. More specifically, there are striking omissions from the harmonized regime including concrete conduct-of-business and advertising controls, contractual requirements designed to protect the weaker bargaining position of investors, and remedies. The remedies deficiency may, however, reflect the well-established principle that remedies for breach of Community law are the preserve of the Member States, although the Distance Marketing Proposal is a considerable step forward in this regard.

The investment-services protective regime is, for the most part, limited to the traditional investor/broker model which underpins the ISD, although the

---

[31] The most glaring example of this is the ISD which, despite numerous references to investor protection, does not offer a rationale for investor-protection regulation (sect. 5.1 below). By contrast, the ICSD, discussed in Ch. X relies on investor confidence.

[32] 'If we can identify the objective accurately, then perhaps the least cost remedy will become apparent': Goodhart, C, 'Some Regulatory Concerns' in Goodhart, C (ed), *The Changing Framework of Financial Regulation* (1998) 215, 224.

[33] See Franks and Mayer, n 6 above, 198. In a similar vein see Clark. n 3 above, 21 who has found that 'it is hard to accept an undifferentiated desire to avoid suffering on the part of capital suppliers as a basis for governmental action. The urge to help the little fellow cries out for deeper justification'.

[34] While the EC rarely uses the language of market failure, the position of the UK Treasury is that EC (and Member State) legislation should, in relation to protective measures, effectively address market failures concerning informational asymmetries in order to strengthen competition in retail markets: HM Treasury, *Completing a Dynamic Single European Financial Services Market: A Catalyst for Economic Prosperity for Citizens and Business Across the EU* (2000) (the Treasury Report) para 7.

new management-company regime will expand the reach of protective regulation. While firms which engage exclusively in services such as investment advice and custody do not benefit from the ISD passport, they benefit from the Treaty free-movement rights, subject to the general-good rule. It could be argued that the importance of these functions in the investment-services market generally demands that common minimum investor-protection standards apply. Similarly some services, such as commodity broking fall completely outside the EC regime.[35]

Finally, the supervisory regime underpinning the protective regime and, in particular, the allocation of jurisdiction to the home or host Member State has had a significant influence on the shape of protective regulation in the integrated market. In principle, there are sound investor-protection grounds for allocating protective regulation to host-Member-State control. It can be argued that protective rules should reflect local market conditions and regulatory cultures and traditions, and that host-Member-State competent authorities are best placed to detect and respond to breaches of protective rules. Under host Member State control, investor complaints, which are much more likely to arise in connection with protective as opposed to prudential rules and on which competent authorities rely to a much greater extent for effective enforcement than in the prudential area,[36] may be made in the Member State in which the investor is located and with whose complaints and redress system the investor is most familiar. One of the strongest arguments in favour of host-Member-State control, however, is that for as long as protective rules remain unharmonized, as is the case with conduct-of-business and marketing regulation for example, and the possibility exists of divergences between the levels of protection offered by Member States' regimes, investors should remain subject to their local controls. Nonetheless, from the perspective of market integration, host-Member-State control is problematic. But while home-Member-State control drastically reduces regulatory obstacles, it can also be supported from an investor-protection perspective. The home Member State may, in certain circumstances, be in a better position to monitor and assess the investment firm's conduct.[37] Some support for this general proposition, albeit in the specific context of cold-calling regulation, comes from *Alpine Investments v Minister van Financiën*

---

[35] The Commission's July 2001 ISD Working Paper (Overview of Proposed Adjustments to the Investment Services Directive. Working Document of Services of DG Internal Market. Document 1, July 2001) suggests that some developments can be expected in this regard. See Ch. VII sect. 10.3.2 above.

[36] Köndgen, J, 'Rules of Conduct: Further Harmonisation' in Ferrarini, n 11 above, 115, 125.

[37] It has been argued, eg, that compliance with conduct-of-business regulation is largely dependent on the internal-control mechanisms and corporate culture of the investment firm globally which cannot be effectively controlled by the host Member State in which services are provided: Avougleas, E, 'The Harmonisation of Rules of Conduct in EU Financial Markets: Economic Analysis, Subsidiarity and Investor Protection', (2000) 6 *ELJ* 72, 83.

where the Court of Justice stated that '[t]he Member State from which the telephone call is made is best placed to regulate cold calling. Even if the receiving State wishes to prohibit cold calling or to make it subject to certain conditions, it is not in a position to prevent or control telephone calls from another Member State without the co-operation of the competent authorities of that State'.[38] A third option would involve the application of the protective rules of the branch from which the investment services are provided. This option is attractive from an investor-protection perspective, given that investors may have direct contact with branches and that supervision can be carried out effectively.[39] It has also emerged as the integration device for online investment services in the ECD. Although host-Member-State control currently features strongly in the protective regime (which is why the adequacy of the supervisory and co-operation structure does not play as central a role in this chapter as it did in Chapter VIII with respect to prudential supervision and home-Member-State control: indeed, in the protective area the supervisory concern is, arguably, more with the existence of effective remedies for investors), all the indications are that protective regulation will be moved to a combination of home-Member-State and branch-Member-State control following the adoption of a more extensive harmonized protective regime (sections 13.5–7 below).

IX.3.3 *The Need for Harmonization*

It is important to address at the outset why an argument can be made for protective regulation at EC level. A strong case can be made for harmonized prudential regulation on the ground that systemic stability and home control of prudential supervision are prerequisites for market integration. The need for protective measures is less obvious, given that investor protection is usually characterized as a matter for local market regulators who are close to the domestic market and the individual investors in that market. From an economic perspective it could be argued that harmonization should go no further than harmonization of those rules which address externalities in that they also impact on the soundness and systemic stability of the Community financial system, given that soundness is compromised by the greater risks represented by integration.[40] A number of arguments can be made, however, in support of the harmonization of protective measures.

---

[38] Case C–384/93 *Alpine Investments v Minister van Financiën* [1995] ECR I–1141, para 48.

[39] The Commission has adverted to the benefits of direct access by supervisors to audit trails and records, their ability to monitor the firm/investor relationship and the fact that supervisors are on-site: Commission Communication on the Application of Conduct of Business Rules Under Article 11 of the Investment Services Directive (93/22/EEC), COM(2000)722 (the Art. 11 Communication), 19.

[40] See, eg, Heremans, D, 'Economic Aspects of the Second Banking Directive and of the Proposal for a Directive on Investment Services in the Securities field' in Stuyck, J (ed),

As the single market in investment services matures, retail investors, in particular, do not simply benefit from an increased choice of investment products and intermediaries and greater price competition. They also face risks. The increased danger of systemic instability aside, increases in the range of investment products and investment firms on the market-place may not only diminish transparency and aggravate the possibility of investor confusion; they may also expose investors to risks to which they were not previously subject due to the relative immaturity and structure of the domestic investment-services market as compared with the integrated market and consequent weaknesses in their domestic protective regime.[41] Integration could result in changes in market behaviour which a Member State may not be adequately prepared for. For example, aggressive marketing techniques such as cold-calling may be used by passporting firms and may not be appropriately regulated where such techniques were not previously widely used in the Member State in question. Conversely, investors may also be exposed to increased risks arising from the disapplication of their domestic investor-protection controls through the operation of certain of the jurisdiction allocation rules which underpin the integrated market.[42] Investors may be prejudiced as their domestic rules, particularly where the rules in question have not been harmonized, may be more stringent than those of the Member State whose rules are applied instead. Accordingly, while the debate continues about the appropriate intensity of harmonization, whether it should replace or supplement Member State rules, and the specific components of investor protection which are susceptible to harmonization, support exists in principle for the desirability of common minimum investor-protection standards.[43] The specific weaknesses in the regime are discussed throughout this chapter. To take one example, however, common disclosure standards,

---

Financial and Monetary Integration in the European Economic Community, Legal, Institutional and Economic Aspects (1993) 37, 45 and Davis, E, 'Problems of Banking Regulation—An EC Perspective' in Goodhart, n 32 above, 533, 547.

[41] See Hertig, G, 'Imperfect Mutual Recognition for EC Financial Services' (1994) 14 *Int'l. Rev. of L and Econ.* 177, 182; Farmery, P, 'Looking Towards a European Internal Market in Financial Services: Some Paradoxes and Paradigms: A Survey of Current Issues and Problems' (1992) 3 *EBLRev.* 94, 97; Van Crombrugghe, n 18 above, 350; and Bradley, C, 'Competitive Deregulation of Financial Services Activity in Europe After 1992' (1991) 11 *OJLS* 545, 547.

[42] Such as the 'internal market' rule contained in the ECD, which places the supply of services via e-commerce means under the control of the 'Member State of origin' of the service provider and Art. 11 of the ISD which places conduct-of-business regulation under the control of the Member State in which the service is provided.

[43] The Commission's perspective, eg, is that 'appropriate and progressive harmonization of marketing and information rules throughout the Union together with a pragmatic search for non-legislative solutions offers the prospect of a truly integrated retail market fully respecting the interests of consumers and suppliers': 1999 Commission Communication on Implementing the Framework for Financial Markets: Action Plan, COM(1999)232 (the FSAP) 8. As discussed in sect. 13 below, the Commission also supports conduct-of-business-rule harmonization. The UK Treasury favours agreement on core standards for conduct of business and consumer protection: Treasury Report, n 34 above, paras 37–54.

whether as marketing controls or as part of conduct-of-business regulation, have a particular appeal, given the danger of investor confusion as the market-place opens up and the range of products and investment firms increases. To take another, given the expense, inconvenience, and delay associated with judicial proceedings, enhancing the availability of less costly and quicker alternative dispute-resolution mechanisms on a market-wide basis would also enhance the protective regime.[44]

More generally, while retail investors have yet to flood into the integrated market,[45] the extent to which the harmonized regime supports a coherent investor-protection policy for the integrated market will surely become an increasingly higher profile question if national markets begin to diminish as the dominant regulatory focus. Such a diminution may well be the ultimate outcome of the growth in distance technologies, industry consolidation, stock exchange alliances, the development of new trading platforms, and the impact of the euro. In such changed circumstances, combined with the heightened appreciation at EC level of the pivotal role of the retail investor (section 13 below), the device of addressing the regulation of the integrated market with respect to investor-protection controls by simply allocating regulatory jurisdiction without substantive harmonization (used in, for example, the ISD with respect to advertising (Article 13) and conduct of business (Article 11)) may be exposed as wanting.

Finally, the dominant market-integration objective of the harmonized regime can be supported by investor protection as a device to enhance investor confidence and, accordingly, the effectiveness of the integrated market-place. The Commission has already noted that cross-border activity will thrive only if investors are confident about the integrity of the service and the selling techniques used, the credentials of the supplier, and the existence of cross-border redress procedures.[46] Indeed, investor protection as an interest worth protecting aside, the failure to harmonize protective measures prejudices market integration, in that variations in protective regimes can obstruct the free movement of investment firms. At present, home-Member-State control under the ISD operates for authorization and prudential controls. Greater reliance on home-Member-State control is, however, dependent on further harmonization, given the variations in protective regulation across the Member States.

Whatever the controversies about whether more harmonization is appropriate, in one of the most dramatic of the seachanges which EC securities regulation is experiencing at present, the EC now appears to be moving

---

[44] Access to justice has been identified by the Court of Justice as a corollary of the internal market: Case C-43/95 *Data Delecta Aktiebolag and Ronny Forsberg v MSL Dynamics* [1996] ECR I-4661.

[45] See the 1998 Communication, n 30 above, 1a and Gros and Lannoo, n 11 above, 163.

[46] FSAP, n 43 above, 7.

inexorably towards significantly greater levels of protective harmonization, home/branch-Member-State control as the integration touchstone and, finally, a much more sophisticated appreciation of the role of the retail investor as an agent for integration and of the need for protective measures as bulwarks against the risks of the integrated market (section 13 below).

IX.3.4 *Retail and Sophisticated Investors*

Protective regulation traditionally responds to the features of the investor who is the object of protection by distinguishing between retail and whole-sale investors. Retail investors transfer their own savings to the market while wholesale or institutional investors transfer significant amounts of capital to the market-place as part of their professional business and are con-sidered to be less in need of protection because of their experience and mar-ket power.[47] Differentiated regulation which reflects the features of these two investor groups and the market-places in which they operate has the advantage of enhancing investor confidence by tailoring protective require-ments to investors' needs and of maximizing the efficiency with which scarce supervisory resources are used. It also ensures that the regulatory burdens imposed on investment firms are proportionate with respect to the protec-tion granted and needed by the beneficiary of the regulation. Recent experi-ence in the derivatives markets, however, reveals that care needs to be taken in making the distinction, as erstwhile sophisticated investors have been shown themselves to be in need of considerable protection in that market-place.[48]

Differentiated regulation with respect to protective regulation is a recur-ring theme in the harmonized investment-services regime.[49] Differentiated protection is articulated in different ways, however, resulting in a certain incoherence about the characteristics of the investor who is the object of EC protective regulation. The Distance Marketing Proposal and the general con-sumer-protection directives which impact on the investor/investment-firm relationship (with the exception of the protections of the ECD which apply to all recipients of e-commerce services, including investment services[50]) are directed towards natural persons acting outside their trade or profession. While the ISD explicitly acknowledges that 'it is . . . appropriate to take account of the different requirements for protection of various categories of

---

[47] For one description of the traits of the retail investor see *The Protection of the Small Investor—A Report by Justice* (1992) para 2.15.

[48] See Markham, n 4 above, 359. See also Langevoort, 9 above, and the discussion of the *Metallgesellschaft* case in Edwards, F, 'Derivatives Can Be Hazardous To Your Health' in Goodhart, n 32 above, 215, 220, and 351.

[49] It has also been supported by the Lamfalussy Report, n 28 above, 22.

[50] Although it does rely on a form of differentiated regulation in that contractual obligations concerning consumers are excluded from the Member State of origin principle.

investors and of their levels of investor protection' (recital 32), it does not define what is meant by 'investor'. Its key protective provision, Article 11 on conduct-of-business rules, provides, however, for differentiated protection by requiring that it is to be applied having regard to the 'professional nature' of the investor protected by the conduct rules in question;[51] it does not, at present, contain any guidance on which of the wide range of conduct rules should apply to the professional market.[52]

It certainly cannot be said with any confidence that EC protective regulation follows a particular strategy in that conduct, disclosure, and other protective rules are directed to an 'EC investor' exhibiting distinctive characteristics and capabilities and exposed to particular EC risks.[53] This is particularly the case given the continued reliance on national rules in the absence of harmonization and on national perceptions of the varying capabilities and protective requirements of investors. The emphasis on disclosure as a protective regulation device, which, while always evident in the protective regime, has emerged strongly as the dominant protective mechanism since the adoption of the FSAP, does, however, suggest an awareness that the EC investor in the integrated market-place is particularly vulnerable to disclosure-based risks and confusion, given the expansion of the market-place and the wide range of investment products and investment services potentially on offer.

Although the regime does attempt to differentiate between the investors which should benefit from protective regulation, it does not, consistently with its being a relatively unsophisticated regime, directly address the extent to which moral-hazard problems may be raised by protecting particular classes of investor.

---

[51] A similar approach is taken in Art. 14(4) of the ISD which relies on whether investors are professional or institutional investors 'able to act in their own best interests' as a qualifying filter on whether a Member State can grant a waiver to the concentration of trades on a regulated market rule when the concentration rule is applied by the Member State and a waiver is sought by investors. See further Ch. XI sect. 6.5 below.

[52] Revisions are in train, however, both of the professional/retail classification and of how conduct rules should apply. See sect. 13.7 below.

[53] While investors will, of course, exhibit different levels of market activity, understanding and discrimination in all markets, it is possible to confer certain characteristics on the EC investor for the purposes of regulation. The retail/professional categorization marks a limited attempt to do so. In the consumer-protection and free movements of goods sphere the Court has relied on the notion of the 'reasonably circumspect' consumer in assessing the extent to which Member States can apply protective rules which limit the exercise of Treaty freedoms in the interests of consumer protection. See the discussion in Weatherill, S, 'Consumer Policy' in Craig, P, and de Búrca, G, *The Evolution of EU Law* (1999) 693, 699–702 and Stuyck, J, 'European Consumer Law After The Treaty of Amsterdam: Consumer Policy In Or Beyond The Internal Market' (2000) 37 *CMLRev.* 367, 391–2.

IX.4 THE ROOTS OF THE PROTECTIVE REGIME

While it highlighted the dependence of the future growth of the EC capital market on investment firms and the efficiency with which they could channel funds from investors to the market-place, the seminal 1966 Segré Report did not deal in any detail with investor protection and the harmonization of protective regulation.[54] The first formal attempt to regulate the relationship between the investor and the investment firm at EC level was made in the 1977 Code of Conduct.[55] It makes an early connection between the objectives of the Treaty and the activities of the Community, on the one hand, and harmonized protective regulation, on the other. In its Explanatory Memorandum, the Commission observed that the objectives of Article 2 of the Treaty of Rome with respect to the 'harmonious development of economic activities in the Community',[56] could be achieved only if sufficient capital were available, and found that the proper working and interpenetration of the securities markets was an essential aspect of the establishment of a common market in capital (paragraph 1). Noting that confusion about the rules governing securities markets was confining investment within the Member State of the investor's residence, the Commission concluded that a reduction in these disparities would encourage market interpenetration and the creation of a common market in capital (paragraph 2). The investor is thus identified as critical to the achievement of Article 2 EC and the delivery of a common market in capital in the guise of a source of capital. Investor protection appears as a function of the primary interpenetration objective, with the Commission stating that a reduction in market-rule disparities would encourage interpenetration 'particularly if this is accompanied by improving the safeguards available to savers' (Explanatory Memorandum, paragraph 2). This approach, which characterizes the investor and investor protection as tools of market integration, is a recurring theme in the relationship between investor protection and the harmonized regime. Investor confidence is also suggested as the underlying rationale for investor protection. Supplementary Principle 1 provides that all persons dealing regularly on the securities markets are under a duty to

[54] Perhaps because at that time 'in continental Europe stockbrokers and other dealers are not organised in such a way as to facilitate contacts with the public at large. As for investment consultants, they are still far removed from the developed stage they have attained on the capital markets of some non-member countries': Report by a Group of Experts Appointed by the EEC Commission, *The Development of a European Capital Market* (1966) (the Segré Report) 204.

[55] Commission Recommendation 77/534/EEC concerning a European code of conduct relating to transactions in transferable securities [1977] OJ L212/37 (the 1977 Code of Conduct).

[56] Art. 2 EC now refers to the 'harmonious, balanced and sustainable development of economic activities'.

'promote investors' confidence in the fairness of the market' by following best standards of commercial probity and of professional conduct.

The Code's Principles are designed to 'establish standards of ethical behaviour on a Community-wide basis, so as to promote the effective functioning of securities markets' (Code of Conduct, Fundamental Objective paragraph). While predominantly concerned with disclosure, the fair treatment of shareholders, and protecting the integrity of the market-place, the General Principles reflect a classic conduct-of-business requirement by providing that financial intermediaries (defined in the definitions section as all persons professionally concerned in transactions in transferable securities) endeavour to avoid all conflicts of interests between themselves and their clients and between their clients and other third parties with whom they have a fiduciary relationship (General Principle 6). If the conflict cannot be avoided, financial intermediaries are required not to seek to gain from the situation and to avoid any prejudice to clients or other persons with whom they are in a fiduciary relationship. The Supplementary Principles contain a number of principles which traditionally form part of conduct-of-business regulation. Supplementary Principles 1–6 are designed to 'indicate a number of aspects of what the expression "fair behaviour" by financial intermediaries is to be taken to mean' and 'describe a number of rules of conduct specific to intermediaries' (Explanatory Memorandum, paragraph III, 12). Supplementary Principle 1, for example, imposes on all persons dealing regularly on the securities markets a duty to promote investors' confidence in the fairness of the market by observance of the best standards of commercial probity and professional conduct. More specifically, Supplementary Principle 4 imposes a best-execution requirement by requiring financial intermediaries to seek out and recommend the best conditions for their clients for the execution of orders given to them, while Supplementary Principle 5 requires that financial intermediaries refrain from encouraging sales or purchases with the sole object of generating commission.

IX.5 PROTECTIVE REGULATION AND THE ISD

IX.5.1 *Investor Protection as an Objective*

Based on Articles 47(2) and 55 EC, which root the ISD in facilitating the freedom to provide services and the freedom to establish and in removing obstacles to those freedoms, the ISD is predominantly a market-integration and liberalization measure. Its primary addressee and beneficiary is the investment firm.[57] As discussed in Chapter VIII in the context of prudential

---

[57] As is illustrated by the Capital Adequacy Directive's (Directive 93/6/EEC on the capital adequacy of investment firms and credit institutions [1993] OJ L141/1 (the CAD)) characterization

supervision, the ISD is also designed to support the ISD passport by reregulating and adopting minimum standards. The Preamble explicitly states that these standards reflect, in part, the interests of investor protection.[58] The rationale behind this subsidiary investor-protection objective, whether it is a tool to correct market failures in the interests of wider confidence, directed towards individual investors' interests or designed to serve paternalistic objectives, is not specified. The indirect focus on investor protection in the ISD's substantive provisions and the emphasis throughout on market integration might imply, however, that investor protection is to be pursued as a tool of investor confidence, which in turn feeds into market integration.

Whatever the ISD's rationale for protecting investors, for a number of reasons it cannot be asserted with any confidence that the ISD takes investor protection as a primary objective. The investor-protection regime which emerges from the reregulation introduced by the ISD (and the sister CAD) is almost entirely prudential in nature and is largely consequential on the protection of the integrity of the new market-place and the need to harmonize soundness standards, without which Member States would not have agreed to the ISD's and CAD's mutual-recognition regime. Together, the ISD and CAD introduce minimum authorization standards as well as ongoing prudential supervision standards, including capital-adequacy rules, operational prudential controls, and ownership controls.[59] While these rules are important for investor protection by protecting against institutional failure and systemic instability, particularly where they raise the pre-existing level of prudential supervision, they serve a critical function in ensuring the wider stability and integrity of the market-place. Protective rules with respect to advertising and conduct of business receive scant attention while the investment-firm/investor contract is not covered at all, notwithstanding the importance of these rules for the average retail investor.[60] This weakens somewhat the recent assertion by the Commission that the ISD contains a 'heavy emphasis on transaction requirements designed to protect investors

of the 'main objective' of the ISD as to permit investment firms to operate across the internal market on the basis of home-Member-State authorization: recital 1. On Art. 47(2) EC as basis for an investor protection policy see sect. 12.2 below.

[58] The ISD refers in recital 2 to the need to subject investment firms within its scope to authorization requirements 'in order to protect investors and the stability of the financial system'. In addition, recital 5 provides that investor protection requires that internal supervision be guaranteed, recital 29 raises investor protection as the justification for the asset-protection rules and recital 32 (in the context of the differentiated protection requirement) provides that 'one of the objectives of this Directive is to protect investors'.

[59] Respectively: ISD, Arts. 3 and 4, CAD, Art. 3; ISD, Art. 8(2), CAD, Arts. 4–6, and 8; ISD, Art. 10; and ISD, Art. 9.

[60] '[T]he core concern [for investors] is . . . the transaction, and the organisation and regulation of the issuer or broker constitutes a more peripheral concern' Lambrecht and Haljan, n 18 above, 259.

from abusive or improper conduct by the investment firm'.[61] At a basic level, despite the repeated Preamble references to 'investor protection', the ISD nowhere defines what is meant by the 'investor'. Indeed, the co-ordination of authorization and prudential standards might suggest a model of investor protection which reflects the interests of the sophisticated wholesale investor, who arguably is sufficiently protected by prudential controls and is less in need of controls on the investment-firm/investor relationship, rather than the interests of the retail investor. Overall, the ISD reflects an expression of investor protection which (at best) aligns or (at worst) subsumes the interests of the investor within the larger soundness needs of the investment firms targeted by the ISD and the newly-integrated market-place as a whole. The failure to address protective controls in the ISD can, however, be regarded as an expression of political realities and a recognition at policy-making level that harmonization of prudential controls was critical due to the burdens represented by such rules and their role in protecting against systemic risk. It might also be regarded as an unconscious illustration of uncertainty about whether investor protection, as an interest distinct from market integration, can be legitimately pursued under the Treaty (section 12 below).

IX.5.2 *Conduct-of-business Rules and Article 11*

IX.5.2.1 *The Roots of Article 11*

Although earlier working drafts were based on harmonization and home-country control, the original ISD proposal omitted conduct-of-business regulation completely apart from to allocate jurisdiction to the host Member State.[62] ECOSOC, in particular, objected to the failure to deal with conduct regulation and recommended the inclusion of a number of conduct rules, based on the 1977 Code of Conduct's principles but also including suitability and disclosure requirements, among the harmonized prudential requirements.[63] Nonetheless, the revised proposal also largely ignored conduct-of-business regulation[64] and it was not until the Council negotiations that a list of principles to be followed by Member States in drawing up conduct-of-business rules was set out, following the concerns of certain Member States that the ISD did not contain sufficient investor protection measures.[65]

[61] 2000 Commission Communication on Upgrading the Investment Services Directive, COM(2000)729, 7 (the ISD Communication).
[62] [1989] OJ C43/7; Explanatory Memorandum, COM(88)778. Art. 13 of the original proposal simply gave host Member States jurisdiction with respect to rules 'justified on grounds of public good'.
[63] [1989] OJ C298/6. The coverage of conduct regulation was, it felt, 'inadequate': paras 1.5, 1.5.1, and 2.19.5.
[64] [1990] OJ C42/7; Explanatory Memorandum, COM(89)629.
[65] C. Cruikshank, 'Is There a Need to Harmonise Conduct of Business Rules' in Ferrarini. n 11 above, 131, 131.

IX.5.2.2 *The Degree of Harmonization*

Article 11 provides that Member States are to draw up rules of conduct which investment firms are to observe at all times. The rules are required to implement at least the principles set out in Article 11. By comparison with the capital-adequacy rules set out in the CAD or even with the less technical operational prudential controls contained in Article 10, Member States are given considerable discretion in implementing Article 11, as the principles operate at a high level of generality. The extent to which the requirement to draw up conduct rules, combined with the principles set out in Article 11, harmonizes conduct-of-business regulation is questionable. There is a considerable body of opinion to the effect that Article 11 does not harmonize conduct-of-business regulation but is designed instead to give Member States autonomy as to how they implement their conduct-of-business regimes in light of local investor profiles and market conditions.[66] In its Article 11 Communication the Commission formally concurred with this view, finding that 'Article 11 (1) does not prescribe, in detail, the content or structure of conduct of business regimes in Member States. Instead, it confines itself to a statement of general principles which should inform such regimes'.[67] Whether or not Article 11 harmonizes conduct-of-business rules is not an entirely academic question. The extent to which Member States may, under the general-good rule, apply their national rules where they restrict the Treaty free-movement guarantees depends in part on whether or not the rule imposed has been subject to harmonization. It appears illogical, however, specifically to grant the host Member State jurisdiction over conduct-of-business regulation, state that the Member States must 'at least' implement the principles contained in Article 11, and then eliminate the ability of Member States to impose detailed rules which go beyond the terms of Article 11 on passporting investment firms. It appears more likely that conduct rules have to meet the other requirements of the general-good test: that the rule promotes a legitimate interest, is proportionate, and does not duplicate a rule already imposed by the home Member State.

IX.5.2.3 *Article 11, Investor Protection, and Market Integrity*

In common with the treatment of investor protection by the ISD generally, the purpose of Article 11 is not made explicitly clear although, as suggested

---

[66] See O'Neill, N, 'The Investment Services Directive' in Cranston, R, *The Single Market and the Law of Banking* (2nd edn, 1995) 189, 202; Tison, M, 'Unravelling the General Good Exception. The Case of Financial Services' in Andenas, M, and Roth, W-H (eds), *Free Movement of Services* (forthcoming) and Cruikshank, n 65 above, 132. For the view that the principles set out in Art. 11 correspond to the continental concept of 'general clauses' or 'statutory provision with a built-in potential for development', see Köndgen, n 36 above, 115, 120.

[67] Art. 11 Communication, n 39 above, 6.

above, investor confidence in the integrated EC market-place and, accordingly, protection of the wider market-place generally, might be identified as the underlying philosophy. The Article 11 principles closely follow the IOSCO conduct-of-business principles[68] which provided the Member States with a useful model with which to work in the final stages of the ISD negotiations. The Article 11 principles are thus based on addressing informational imbalances in the investor/investment-firm relationship through disclosure, fairness, diligence, and skill requirements, suggesting that the link between informational market failures and protective regulation is, in principle, accepted by the Commission as one basis for regulation in the interests of investor confidence.[69]

Investor protection aside, the Article 11 conduct-of-business regime could also be designed to play a role in protecting the stability of the financial system which appears as an ISD objective throughout the Preamble. While the stability of the financial system is typically regarded as a function of prudential regulation, it can also be analysed by reference to the effectiveness of the price-formation process and the integrity of securities markets generally. Protecting the investor/investment-firm relationship against market abuses, such as market manipulation and fraud (discussed in Chapter XIII) which, as outlined below (section 5.2.5), could be contained within the Article 11 principles, has a wider impact on the protection of the price-formation process and the effectiveness of the trading market in securities. This interpretation would also be consistent with the identity between the substantive content of the Article 11 principles and the IOSCO conduct-of-business regime. In addition to pursuing investor protection, the IOSCO principles are also expressly designed to set high standards of behaviour in financial markets and enhance market integrity.[70] A distinction is usually made, however, between market-conduct rules, which are designed to prohibit abusive practices in the trading of securities in order to protect investors and the integrity of the market-place as a whole and conduct-of-business rules, which are usually confined to the management of individual bilateral investor/investment-firm relationships.[71] Nonetheless, the open-ended nature of the Article 11 rules, together with the references therein in Principles 1 and 2 to the duty of the firm to act in the best interests of the integrity of the market (which might simply emphasize the connection

---

[68] IOSCO Technical Committee Report, *International Conduct of Business Principles* (1990).

[69] Unusually, clear evidence of the market failure rationale informing Art. 11 can be inferred from the Commission's comment in the Art. 11 Communication that '[t]he rationale for these safeguards is that there is a danger that certain investors may be disadvantaged by their lack of access to, or capacity to correctly process, financial information': n 39 above, 6.

[70] N 68 above, pt I, paras 16 and 19. Market integrity is also an objective of the conduct-of-business regime set out in the 1998 IOSCO Principles, n 16 above, para 12.5.

[71] For a discussion of the distinction between market-conduct rules and conduct-of-business rules see Avougleas, n 37 above, 74.

between investor protection/investor confidence and the protection of the market-place as a whole), blurs the dividing line between the two sets of rules and arguably dilutes the investor-protection rationale,[72] even if traditional conduct-of-business rules remain the dominant concern of Article 11.

IX.5.2.4 *Scope*

Article 11 specifies that the principles apply to the supply by an ISD investment firm of core services as well as, 'where appropriate', non-core services. This clarification is particularly important, given the potential losses which can be generated by incompetence, dishonesty, or conflicts of interests in the provision of investment advice, which is a non-core service.

In stark contrast to the approach adopted by FESCO (now the Committee of European Securities Regulators) in elaborating on Article 11 (section 13.3.3 below), the principles set out in Article 11 do not, at present, take into account the varying degrees of risk to which an investor is exposed depending on the nature of the core service provided although, as discussed at section 5.2.6 below, a differentiated approach based on the nature of the investor, rather than the service, is required. A 'where appropriate' qualification does apply to non-core services, but this may simply reflect the differentiation on the basis of the investor requirement. Execution-only services, for example, require a different degree of regulation from discretionary portfolio-management services, which as well as involving transaction execution services also involve the provision of advice and the exercise of judgement in the management of the portfolio as well as custody services, and this distinction is typically made in conduct-of-business regimes. Article 11 does not, however, reflect this distinction.[73]

IX.5.2.5 *Substantive Content*

The Principles operate at a high level of generality. This discussion will attempt to identify the substantive rules which may be implied by the various Principles.

---

[72] Although it has given Art. 11 considerable flexibility. In its study of the regulation of alternative trading systems FESCO identified a number of the Art. 11 principles as providing a basis for the management of market integrity risks: *The Regulation of Alternative Trading Systems in Europe*, a paper for the EU Commission (2000) (Fesco/00-064c) 20–1.

[73] The investment-services industry generally favours a differentiated approach to regulation. For an example of this, see the industry consultations for the FSA Draft Conduct of Business Sourcebook Paper which revealed dissatisfaction with a harmonized approach to the application of conduct-of-business rules across the full range of investment services and a preference for specialized treatment of particular activities and functions: n 15 above, 8.

(a) *Principles 1–4*

The first four principles concern the degree of skill and care which an investment firm should exercise in its relations with clients, and seek to address the risk faced by investors that, as a result of incompetence on the part of the investment firm, they may sustain a loss.

Principle 1 forms part of the ISD's general anti-fraud regime. Other anti-fraud controls are set out in more detail in the prudential rules contained in Article 10, particularly the client-money rules. Principle 1 requires an investment firm to act honestly and fairly in conducting its business activities in the best interests of its clients and the integrity of the market. Clearly, fraud in the investment-firm/investor relationship exposes the investor to direct losses if investor assets are stolen or misused. Principle 1 also brings into play, however, wider market-conduct prohibitions on market abuse and price manipulation, discussed further in Chapter XIII given that honesty and fairness must be pursued in the wider interests of the 'integrity of the market'.

Principle 2 provides that the investment firm must act with due skill, care, and diligence, in the best interests of its clients and the integrity of the market. The specific reference to the integrity of the market again suggests that market conduct generally should also be addressed by Principle 2. With respect to the investor/investment-firm relationship, however, investors are particularly vulnerable to loss where there is a lack of care, skill, and diligence in the provision of investment advice and in the execution process. With respect to the execution process, the potential for error is large, from the initial receipt of the order through to the final settlement process which involves other parties such as market-makers and custodians.[74] Although a best-execution rule could be inferred from this principle (the guidance on the equivalent IOSCO principle states that it includes best execution), this fundamental protective conduct requirement is not made explicit. However it is formulated, the best-execution rule is usually aimed at 'requiring firms to exercise reasonable care in the execution of orders' and 'requires firms to obtain for clients the best price available to the firm (given the dimensions of the customer order)'. [75] Care and skill take on a further dimension where

---

[74] The most common errors appear to involve the purchase or sale of incorrect amounts of securities, selling instead of purchasing and vice versa, and delays in executing orders: Franks and Mayer, n 6 above, 34.

[75] FSA, *Best Execution*, Discussion Paper (2001) (the FSA Best Execution Discussion Paper) 3 and 4. Best execution generally requires that once the best price has been ascertained for the size and type of the transaction concerned, the transaction must be carried out at that price unless it is in the investor's interests not to do so. Exercising reasonable care is not limited to finding the best price, however, but also demands that consideration be given to, eg, the soundness of the counterparty to the transaction. See Rider, B, Abrams, C, and Ashe, M, *Guide to Financial Services Legislation* (3rd edn, 1997) 204.

the service in question involves the giving of investment advice or the discretionary management of a portfolio on behalf of an investor. In particular, the exercise of due care and skill with respect to discretionary portfolio management brings into play questions of whether the firm should speculate, when assets should be sold, and the extent to which diversification policies should be followed.[76]

Principle 3 is particularly non-specific and addresses organizational matters, requiring the investment firm to have and employ effectively the resources and procedures necessary for the proper performance of its business activities. It seems to be directed more towards organizational matters than transactional/relationship management issues and as such may appear to be more akin to the Article 10 rules than the Article 11 principles.

Principle 4 is a 'know your client' provision and requires investment firms to seek from their clients information regarding their financial situation, investment experience, and objectives as regards the investment service requested. While this requirement is of particular importance where the investment firm is providing specific, tailored advice to an investor with whom a close relationship has been established, as would be the case with discretionary portfolio-management services, it is also essential to the provision of appropriate investment-advice services, particularly where speculative investments are involved. Principle 4 does not explicitly refer to the 'suitability' rule which typically partners the 'know your client' requirement in conduct-of-business regimes.[77] Reflecting the dependence of the unsophisticated investor on the investment firm and the informational asymmetries in that relationship, suitability rules usually require that an investment firm supply a client only with investment products and services which are suitable for and tailored to that client's needs, given that client's degree of sophistication in investment matters, appetite for and understanding of risk, and financial resources.[78] Suitability and know-your-client rules in combination require that an assessment be made of the investor's investment objectives, experience, and any other details of the investor's financial position which the firm reasonably believes it needs to know in order to make a suitability assessment. An effective suitability rule would, however, have required agreement during the ISD negotiations on a basic standard of what

[76] See the analysis in Bines, H, 'Modern Portfolio Theory and Investment Management Law: Refinement of Legal Doctrine' (1976) 76 *Col. LR* 721.

[77] The FSA, eg, is of the opinion that '[a] cornerstone of present regulatory standards is that a firm should know its customer so that it is able to give advice, or effect a transaction, which is suitable to each customer's circumstances': FSA Draft Conduct of Business Sourcebook Paper, n 15 above, 50.

[78] The suitability doctrine originated in the USA where it was developed as a response to the high-pressure sales techniques used by broker-dealers to push investors into making immediate decisions. See generally Cox, J, Hillman, R, and Langevoort, D, *Securities Regulation. Cases and Materials* (2nd edn, 1997) 1104–10.

'suitability' entails; this was not even possible, however, with respect to the core authorization process discussed in Chapter VI. Clearly, varying market conditions, patterns of investor behaviour, and regulatory cultures have considerable potential to stymie agreement on this question. A basic requirement for a suitability regime could, nonetheless, be read into Article 11 through a combination of Principle 4 and Principles 1 and 2. Indeed, the Commission's position is that 'suitability' rules are required under Article 11.[79] The application of Principle 4 to the 'service requested' appears to catch the full range of investment services from execution-only services to discretionary portfolio-management services, even though execution-only services, which dominate the burgeoning market in online investment services, are typically not subject to the full weight of suitability and know-your-client rules. Principle 4 applies, however, only in respect of the investment services 'requested'. Accordingly, if an investor requests execution-only services, the information-gathering obligation and any suitability requirement would apply, it appears, only to the initial determination of whether the investor is suitable for execution-only services and not to the investments subsequently bought or sold by the investor.[80] FESCO's position (section 13.3.3 below) is to facilitate execution-only business and the growing number of online investors who do not wish their investment firms to make a judgement on a transaction's suitability, by tailoring the suitability rules and ensuring that they are sufficiently flexible for online execution-only business.

(b) *Principle 5 and Disclosure*

Disclosure makes an appearance in the ISD's conduct-of-business regulation scheme as the dominant theme of Principle 5. Principle 5 requires an investment firm to make adequate disclosure of relevant material information in its dealings with clients. Principle 5 does not, however, make explicit the purpose of the disclosure, although presumably it is to ensure that investors have sufficient information to make an informed assessment of the investment service or advice in question. Neither does Principle 5 specify the nature of the disclosure. Notwithstanding the wide use of risk warnings as an investor-protection technique, particularly in relation to derivatives, it does not specify that adequate disclosure be made by the investment firm with respect to the particular risks involved in the transaction. Neither does it specify that any risk disclosure made reflect the experience of the investor in question.[81] Risk warnings also play an important role in ensuring that

---

[79] Art. 11 Communication, n 39 above, 17.

[80] See further Köndgen, n 36 above, 128–9.

[81] The Art. 11 Communication has suggested, however, that risk-warning controls are required by Principle 5: n 39 above, 6. It is also possible that an obligation to implement a

investors take responsibility for their own decisions and, in particular, assess whether their own appetite for risk dovetails with the riskiness of the investment or service in question; in this regard their exclusion from Article 11 reflects the protective regime's underdeveloped approach towards moral hazard. Another omission from this general disclosure requirement is that the disclosure be timely, which is consistently a feature of disclosure rules where they are used as regulatory tools. Periodic disclosure is particularly important in relation to discretionary portfolio-management where the assets under management change frequently. If a portfolio contains derivatives, disclosure in relation to open positions in the portfolio and their status becomes critical. Although Article 11 sets out general principles only, these fundamental requirements with respect to the effectiveness of disclosure to investors could arguably have been included in Principle 5.

The disclosure-based requirement that the client receive a written confirmation of the contract, or, at a minimum, information setting out the nature of the services received and the terms of the contract does not appear explicitly in Principle 5.[82] While the Unfair Contract Terms Directive supplements Principle 5, it does so only to a very limited extent, by providing that contractual terms must be in plain and intelligible language; it does not require that contract terms be in a particular form or that specific disclosure be made (section 8.2.2 below). While mandatory contract requirements carry the risk that investors would be subject to a bomdardment of detailed, overly complex, and ultimately unhelpful documents, minimum requirements to the effect that an investor be adequately informed of the nature of the service contracted for serve an important investor-protection function, as does the issue of contract notes which set out the central features of the trade at the conclusion of particular transactions. This is particularly important in the discretionary portfolio-management sphere where the agreement between the investor and the firm should set out the basis on which the services are provided, including the firm's understanding of the investor's objectives.

A final significant omission from the disclosure principle is any provision in respect of the disclosure of fees and charges, both direct and indirect.[83] Disclosure aside, the fairness and reasonableness of fees can form part of more interventionist conduct-of-business regimes. Regulation of fees can

---

risk-disclosure requirement could be inferred from the IOSCO guidance on the equivalent foundational IOSCO principle which has suggested that the client be provided with information on the risks involved so that an informed assessment of the transaction may be made.

[82] The investor-protection benefits of such a requirement are recognised internationally. See the 1998 IOSCO Principles, n 16 above, para 12.5.

[83] The impact of information on fees, penalties, and charges on the ability to make an effective choice was highlighted in the OECD's 1992 *Report on Consumer Information About Financial Services Report* (the OECD Consumer Information Report) 8.

raise the charge of undue interference with commercial freedom. On an EC wide level, agreement on the desirability of fee controls is unlikely.

(c) *Principle 6, Conflicts of Interests and Chinese Walls*

Principle 6 overlaps with the prudential requirements of Article 10 in that it requires investment firms to avoid conflicts of interests and, when they cannot be avoided, to ensure that their clients are fairly treated. Article 10, by contrast, requires that firms be organized and structured in such a way as to minimize the risk of clients' interests being prejudiced by conflicts of interests between the firm and its clients or between one of its clients and another. Accordingly, organizational conflicts of interests are caught by Article 10 while Article 11 deals with particular transactional conflicts which can arise notwithstanding the organization of the investment firm.

Informational asymmetries with respect to the existence of conflicts of interests which may colour the service being provided by the investment firm are a particular problem for investors and have long been addressed through the requirements of the investor/investment-firm fiduciary relationship as well as through regulatory rules.[84] The variety of activities engaged in by investment firms and insufficient separation between those activities and the advice, brokerage, and investment-management services provided to investors creates an environment in which conflicts of interests which prejudice investors can be easily triggered.[85] An investment firm may, for example, have a material interest in a particular securities transaction which it recommends to an investor. The firm may wish to rebalance positions in securities which have arisen through, for example, underwriting or market-making activities by offloading them on investors through investment-advice services or by purchasing them for investors as part of discretionary portfolio-management services.[86] Another area potentially ripe for conflict-of-interest difficulties is investment advice, in the context of mergers and acquisitions, where information on the affairs of two competing companies flows between their advisers in the same investment firm. An emerging conflicts problem for the professional investment community concerns

---

[84] A full discussion of the complex issues raised by conflict-of-interest regulation, particularly with respect to controlling the flow of confidential information and the role of fiduciary duties in this regard, is outside the scope of this book. See, eg, Coates, S, 'Conflicts of Interest in the Securities Industry' in Rider, B, and Ashe, T (eds) *The Fiduciary, The Insider and the Conflict* (1995) and Rider, B, 'Conflicts of Interest: An English Problem' in Ferrarini, n 11 above, 149.

[85] For a list of the potential conflicts of interests which can arise (in the context of multi-function credit institutions), see Hopt, K, 'European Insider Dealing: Inside Information and Conflicts of Interests Between Banks—Part 2' [1991] *JIBFL* 499, 500–1 and, from an Anglo-American perspective, Poser, N, *International Securities Regulation. London's 'Big Bang' and the European Securities Markets* (1991) 186–8.

[86] See the discussion in Cranston, n 17, 24.

the provision of supposedly disinterested investment-research and trading recommendations by investment analysts who may face a conflict of interest in providing independent advice with the commercial interests of their investment firm's trading, underwriting, and corporate advice units. The fund-management industry, which relies on such objective research to manage funds, is increasingly concerned that the independence of research reports is threatened by the extent to which the investment firm is already commercially connected, or hoping to enter into commercial relationships, with the companies in question.[87]

Under Article 10, firms are to be 'organised and structured' so that conflicts of interests are avoided, but no specific guidelines are given, resulting in the potential for a wide variety of approaches to the problem. The creation of separate subsidiaries for potentially conflicting areas represents a blunt solution which may not be adequate where the conflict involves information flows between divisions. The Commission has suggested, however, that the Article 10 requirement could be met by Chinese walls, or the creation of separate departments within investment firms for each type of activity with barriers on exchange of information between them.[88] Chinese walls have been widely used to manage conflicts of interests and the flow of confidential and sensitive information since their initial introduction to the securities regulation arsenal by the US SEC in the late 1960s as a mechanism for controlling the transmission of inside information and insider-dealing. A full discussion of the operation of and legal issues raised by the operation of Chinese walls is outside the scope of this work. Suffice it to say that their operation can raise difficulties for investment firms as a Chinese Wall may, itself, result in a violation of another conduct-of-business rule and that their effectiveness in managing conflicts and controlling information flows has been questioned.[89] They are often buttressed by other methods of conflict-of-interest management which can include refusal-to-act policies (based on 'stop lists' of companies whose securities become restricted for recommendation, brokerage, and dealing purposes due to the nature of their relationship with the investment firm), internal client- and service-approval mechanisms designed to head off potential conflicts and staff-dealing rules.

[87] See Silverman, G, 'Wall Street Research Questioned' and Targett, S, 'When the Desire is to Accentuate the Positive', *Financial Times*, 22 Feb 2001.

[88] *Single Market News*, Feb 1996, no. 2. For a description of Chinese walls see Cranston, R, 'Insider Dealing—Informational Imbalances and Financial Businesses' in Hopt, K, and Wymeersch, E (eds), *European Insider Dealing* (1991) 203, 216.

[89] Attribution of knowledge to the investment firm and its impact on the fulfilment by an investment firm of its fiduciary (and regulatory) duty to act in the best interests of its clients is a particular problem. The Commission's Explanatory Memorandum to the 1977 Code of Conduct suggests that confidential information may be used to give informed advice against an investment (without revealing the grounds for the advice) to an investor, when the aim of the advice is to avoid a loss on the part of the investor rather than to generate a profit: Explanatory Memorandum, III, D.

The Article 11 approach towards conflicts of interests acknowledges that conflicts of interests, where unavoidable, can be managed, as long as appropriate steps are taken to ensure that investors are 'fairly treated'. On what is meant by fair treatment, the IOSCO guidance on the equivalent IOSCO conduct of business principle suggests that conflicts of interests may be managed by a combination of disclosure, internal confidentiality rules, and other appropriate methods. An emphasis on disclosure as a means of ensuring fair treatment dovetails with the approach taken in many Member States, which is to outlaw conflicts of interests unless they are disclosed to the client.[90]

(d) *Principle 7*

Finally, principle 7 is a catch-all provision which requires an investment firm to comply with all regulatory requirements applicable to the conduct of its business activities so as to promote the best interests of its clients and the integrity of the market.

(e) *The Omissions*

Certain rules which would traditionally form part of conduct regulation appear to fall outside Article 11 in so far as they cannot easily be connected back to the high-level Principles. Withdrawal or cancellation rights which give investors the benefit of 'cooling-off' periods after contracting for investment services are not mentioned anywhere in Article 11, despite the fact that they form a key component of the protection given to investors by conduct-of-business regulation. The failure to cover withdrawal rights, even at the basic general-principles level represented by Article 11, is particularly striking, given that withdrawal rights provide an important antidote to high-pressure marketing techniques, such as cold-calling, the regulation of which is also omitted from Article 11.[91] In the portfolio-management area, investors may be vulnerable to 'soft dollar' trading practices which involve the portfolio manager extracting a higher commission for executing transactions for the investor than that which has been charged by the broker who undertook the transaction for the portfolio manager.[92] Soft-dollar arrangements can also threaten best-execution practices in that, where a particular broker offers a portfolio manager incentives (such as research reports, information technology, or custody services) for passing on orders, the portfolio manager may be less inclined to search for the best deal for the investor.

---

[90] See Ferrarini, G, 'Towards a European Law of Investment Services and Institutions' (1994) 31 *CMLRev.* 1283, 1305.

[91] Withdrawal rights will form part of the protective regime, however, albeit in the limited context of distance marketing, if the Distance Marketing Proposal is adopted. See sect. 9 below.

[92] On 'soft dollar' practices see Franks and Mayer, n 6 above, 78–9.

Soft-dollar practices require careful regulation, however, as the research or technology which is passed on may ultimately be to the benefit of the investor.[93] It is not clear whether the appropriate management of soft-dollar practices can be identified as a requirement under Article 11, although these arrangements may place the firm in a conflict of interest, covered by Principle 6. Similarly, 'churning' a portfolio, or engaging in an excessive number of transactions to generate portfolio-management fees (or as a result of soft-dollar practices) also exposes investors to losses but is not directly addressed by Article 11. Article 11 is also silent with respect to the fair and timely execution of orders, unless order practices can be implied into the honesty/fairness and care/skill/diligence Principles. In particular, Article 11 does not expressly require the investment firm to deal fairly, in turn, and as soon as reasonably practicable (unless a delay is in the best interests of the investor) with investor orders and to allocate executed orders promptly.[94] As the order in which transactions are executed can, depending on the size of the order, move the market price, most conduct regimes include in their dealing rules requirements that orders be taken in turn and prohibitions on 'front-running' or the practice of giving priority to particular orders in order to benefit from an expected movement in prices.[95] Where orders are aggregated for execution purposes, investor protection demands fairness as between orders in the post-trade allocation process in that, particularly where there is a mismatch between the securities actually bought or sold and order requirements, the manner in which the allocation is made is decided in advance.[96] Neither is any reference made in Article 11 to margin trading or lending by the investment firm to the investor, although these activities can place the unwary investor in a precarious position if the investor is not made aware of any fees and of the consequences of default. These omissions arguably leave a significant gap at EC level in the regulation of the conduct of the investor/investment-firm relationship.

---

[93] As a result, they are usually permitted if certain conditions are met, such as that any benefits are provided under a written agreement, adequate disclosure is made to investors, best execution is not prejudiced, and that the arrangement ultimately enhances the services provided by the firm to investors. Soft dollar practices in the UK pension-fund industry have been subject to extensive review by the Treasury-commissioned Myners Report 2001, which has called for fund managers to be required to absorb the costs of share-dealing and research.

[94] The time at which an order is executed also feeds into best-execution in that liquidity and thus prices vary at different times of the day.

[95] Front-running, and in particular the front-running of research (or trading in advance of a market-sensitive recommendation), also raises market integrity concerns and has been addressed in the Commission's Market Abuse Proposal. See Ch. XIII sect. 11.5 below.

[96] While allocation rules in the context of the secondary trading market investor/investment-firm relationship are not addressed, save to the extent that they may come within a Member State's Art. 11 regime, an attempt has been made to standardize allotment rules in relation to investment firms' behaviour in the primary markets. See the FESCO European Code on Allotment, set out in FESCO, Stabilisation and Allotment, A European Supervisory Approach, Consultative Paper (2000). Fesco/00-099b.

(f) *The Adequacy of the Regime*

The level of detail needed to make conduct-of-business rules effective, particularly with respect to dealing rules[97] and conflict-of-interest rules, the difficulties inherent in defining concepts such as 'suitability' or 'speculative' or in establishing standards of due care and skill and the close relationship between conduct-of-business rules and the features of the domestic market all combine to makes full conduct harmonization at EC level difficult (subsidiarity and Treaty competence questions also raise problems: section 12 below). High-level principles also have the advantage of flexibility, a particularly important feature, given the impact e-commerce is having on the way in which investment services are delivered and how conduct-of-business rules should apply. In principle, the rate at which market and investors' practices change and the need for conduct regimes to adapt may also make detailed harmonization impractical, given the current slow pace of law making at EC level.

Nonetheless, basic mandatory requirements at EC level as to the type of disclosure needed and the principles to be followed in dealing in securities would contribute to establishing a more robust set of conduct-of-business principles for the protection of investors across the EC and reduce investor confusion about the level of protection applicable in those cases where domestic rules do not apply.[98] Indeed, in certain areas market-integration developments are forcing a reconsideration of how basic conduct rules should apply. This might suggest a role for a common approach to developing rules for this new market-place. There is, for example, an increased need

---

[97] eg, while a minimum degree of harmonization may be possible and desirable, best-execution rules involve the interplay of a number of elements (including decisions about where trades will be executed and how those decisions are managed, the role of price benchmarks in establishing that best execution has occurred, the role of disclosure in informing investors of a firm's execution policies, the relevant market structure (including the extent to which data consolidation (of various markets' trading information) is pursued), and the nature of the order placed) which would make detailed harmonization difficult. Harmonization of best-execution rules is also sensitive in that, depending on the level of harmonization, it could impact on competition between firms and influence the flow of orders towards particular markets and trading venues. As discussed in Ch. XI, the EC is generally reluctant to engage in harmonization which influences market structure. The Commission has, however, proposed revisions to the transparency regime which should promote best execution, Ch. XI sect. 9.7 below.

[98] FESCO (now the Committee of European Securities Regulators) is of the opinion that divergences in conduct-of-business regulation: 'hinder . . . the provision of an adequate level of protection to European investors': FESCO, *Standards and Rules for Harmonizing Core Conduct of Business Rules for Investor Protection*, Consultative Paper (2001), Fesco/00-124b (the FESCO Conduct Standards), 6. Significant divergences exist across the EC as to the extent to which Member States have gone beyond the basic principles set out in Art. 11 and imposed detailed codes of conduct. The Commission has reported that considerable variations exist in relation to best-execution, churning, allotment, conflicts of interests, documentation rules, and execution-only requirements (with respect to transactions involving retail investors). Art. 11 Communication, n 39 above, 9 and 11. For an overview of the different approaches to best execution, in particular, see the FSA Best Execution Discussion Paper, n 75 above, Annex B, 1.

for clear disclosure as the range of services and products on offer increases as the market-place integrates. Best-execution is another area in which EC developments are placing new demands on basic conduct rules. The development of EC-wide trading and the evolution of ATSs, which together are producing a number of fora in which prices are formed, is increasingly making the best-execution obligation more difficult to interpret and to satisfy.[99] Indeed, best-execution is increasingly appearing as a regulatory mechanism at EC level in the context of securities-trading markets. In endorsing FESCO's approach to the supervision of ATSs, the Commission has implicitly emphazied the role of best-execution in ensuring that ATSs are adequately supervised, and it has also highlighted the role of 'strict enforcement' of best-execution in ensuring investor protection in the absence of securities-trading market concentration rules.[100] In these circumstances a common approach seems sensible. Ultimately, even if full harmonization is not realistic, at a minimum the Article 11 Principles need to be supplemented by more specific sub-principles or rules which would require Member States to implement rules which would ensure that the main investor-protection mechanisms inherent in each high-level Principle, as outlined above (such as the risk-warning requirements inherent in Principle 5), are implemented in each Member State.

The law-making proposals set out in the Lamfalussy Report for the adoption of general framework principles through the usual legislative process (level 1) and the adoption of detailed implementing technical rules through an expedited comitology-based rule-making mechanism (level 2) look set, however, to provide a solution to the difficulties of harmonizing conduct rules. In July 2001, after a series of indications that it supported fuller harmonization, the Commission took a major step towards revising the Article 11 regime by including in its working paper on the proposed reforms it has suggested for the ISD a framework for a new conduct-of-business regime. At this embryonic stage, it is premature to comment extensively on the Commission's suggested conduct-of-business framework. It does appear clear, however, that harmonization will reflect the Lamfalussy model and contain a combination of high-level principles and detailed implementing rules and that the substantive content of the regime will be considerably expanded and updated (section 13.7 below).

IX.5.2.6 *Differentiated Protection*

Unlike prudential rules which have wider systemic implications and, in general, protect all investors in a similar fashion, conduct-of-business rules are,

---

[99] See the discussion of ATSs in Ch. XI sect. 8.4 below.
[100] ISD Communication, n 61 above, 12 and 14.

for the most part, designed to protect small investors in their dealings with investment-services firms which possess superior market knowledge. Appropriate conduct regulation should therefore be sufficiently flexible to differentiate between the level of protection given to retail and professional investors.[101] Indeed, market integrity, rather than investor protection, is the main regulatory concern raised by the professional investor/investment-firm relationship in the wholesale market.

Article 11 reflects this distinction and recognizes that professional investors should not be protected by superfluous conduct-of-business rules which impose a burden on the investment firm as these investors are adequately protected by the authorization process and by the prudential supervision of the investment firm. It provides that conduct-of-business rules must be applied 'in such a way as to take account of the professional nature of the person for whom the service is provided'.

As discussed in Chapter VII, the Commission attempted to deal with the difficulties faced by the wholesale investment-services market as a result of the uneven compliance by Member States with the professional-investor qualification by suggesting in its Article 11 Communication that professional investors are, even in the absence of fuller harmonization, adequately protected by the conduct rules of the investment firm's home Member State. It also suggested that the FESCO definition of a professional investor be adopted by Member States when applying Article 11 (Chapter VII section 6.4.2 above).[102] The Commission's approach thus represents a compromise between ensuring that professional investors receive a certain level of protection while, at the same time, keeping the wholesale investment-services market free from unduly burdensome host-Member-State conduct regulation primarily designed for retail-investor protection. The extent to which particular rules such as suitability and know-your-client rules should apply to the wholesale market is problematic, however, not least given the evidence that professional investors are not always aware of the risks certain investments, such as derivatives, represent. FESCO's initial approach was to apply a diluted suitability/know-how principle which simply required an investment firm to obtain information from the professional investor relevant for money-laundering identification requirements and as regards any trading restrictions imposed on the professional investors.[103] As is discussed in section

---

[101] Not least because '[c]onsumers of financial services are more likely to retain confidence in a market where regulatory protections are tailored to their needs': FSA, *Customer Classification*, Consultation Paper 43 (2000) (the FSA Customer Classification Paper) 4.

[102] The revisions to the ISD will, based on current indications, include a definition of a professional investor: Ch. VII sect. 10.3.2 above.

[103] FESCO Conduct Standards, n 98 above, pt IV, para 4. Pt IV sets out the core conduct-of-business rules for professionals. The revised standards issued by FESCO's new incarnation (the Committee of European Securities Regulators) for consultation in Oct 2001 take a more rigorous approach and require that information be sought concerning the customer's financial

13.7 below, it appears that the Commission will take a sophisticated approach to the treatment of professional investors in designing the new conduct regime; its orientations on how the future conduct-of-business regime will develop reflect a concern to ensure that regulation is appropriately tailored.

IX.5.2.7 *Host-Member-State Control*

While the respective merits of home- and host-Member-State control from the investor-protection perspective can be debated, Article 11 currently appears to represent the worst of both worlds. Regulatory control is not granted to the host Member State in which the investor is based, but to the Member State 'in which the service is provided'. This somewhat delphic formula could, particularly with telecommunications and unsolicited services, be interpreted to mean that the home-Member-State rules of the investment firm apply where the service is not characterized as being provided within the Member State. Accordingly, home-Member-State control, without the protection of minimum harmonization, is one potential outcome, in theory at least (per the Commission it rarely happens in practice) of the Article 11 formula. Although the Article 11 Communication supports, in principle, the application of domestic rules to retail investors, investors are in theory exposed to the potential risk of losing their domestic controls and being subject to a protective regime which is less rigorous.[104]

It appears clear, however, that, driven by market-integration pressures, home-Member-State control remains the ultimate objective. As discussed in Chapter VII section 6.4.2 above, the Commission has attempted to resolve the Article 11 conduct-of-business problem by suggesting that rules designed to protect professional investors be subject to home-Member-State control and that retail investors, in the absence of further harmonization, remain subject to their domestic controls. The Commission has acknowledged that 'as regards retail investors, the transition to home country supervision . . . will need to be carefully managed', given that in the absence of common standards it cannot be presumed that investors will receive comparable investor protection to that of their domestic regime when covered by the

---

situation, investment experience, and objectives. They also require that investment advice and professional recommendations be suitable, although the suitability/know-your-client requirement is not imposed on counterparty relationships: CESR, Standards and Rules for Harmonizing Core Conduct of Business Rules for Investor Protection, CESR/01-014 (the Revised FESCO Conduct Standards), pt IV, para 3.

[104] It has been suggested that where an investor's domestic conduct rules are disapplied in a particular transaction, the investor should be informed accordingly by the investment firm: Abrams, C, 'The Investment Services Directive—Who Should be the Principle Regulator of Cross-Border Services?' (1995) 2 *EFSL* 317.

rules of an investment firm's home Member State.[105] This transition is now under way.

IX.5.3 *Advertising and Marketing Regulation under the ISD*

IX.5.3.1 *Article 13*

Article 11 does not address the advertising or marketing of investment services, being concerned with the conduct of a transaction or the relationship between a particular investor and an investment firm. Article 13 simply provides that the ISD does not prevent investment firms from advertising their services through all available means of communication in host Member States, subject to national rules governing the form and content of such advertising adopted in the interest of the general good.[106] Advertising rules are therefore not harmonized by the ISD and appear to be subject to the jurisdiction of the Member State in which the authorized investment firm advertises.[107]

Rules concerning specific marketing practices such as cold-calling and door-to-door sales (see section 5.3.2 below) are thus not subject to common EC standards. Neither are rules designed to regulate the content of investment-services advertising specifically such as requirements as to clarity, risk-warnings both as to the securities market generally and as to particular or unusual risks, fairness, use of certain terms which might cause confusion such as 'guaranteed', and rules concerning the use of past performance figures. Given that transparency may be the first casualty in the single market in investment services and that investment products and services require special treatment in order to ensure that disclosure is sufficient, clear, and not misleading, the failure to impose common advertising standards amounts to a significant gap in the ISD. This is all the more a problem, given that the general consumer protection in advertising measures discussed in section 8 below do not deal with the particular disclosure needs of retail investors or the increased risks to which they are subject, given the nature of the investor/investment-firm relationship.

IX.5.3.2 *Cold Calls and Door-to-door Sales*

'Real-time' advertising strategies where the investor is approached directly (as opposed to permanent advertising strategies which depend on permanent

---

[105] Art. 11 Communication, n 39 above, 11.

[106] See sect. 11 below for a discussion of the Court's approach to general-good regulation.

[107] See the Opinion of Jacobs AG in *Alpine Investments* that '[i]t is notable that the directive does not harmonise the rules of the Member States concerning the marketing of investments': n 38 above, para 14.

hard-copy or electronic advertisements and communications)[108] through, for example, cold calls or door-to-door sales place the retail investor, in particular, in a particularly vulnerable position. Aggressive marketing strategies may be used, the opportunity for reflection may be short, disclosure may be limited, and the investor may not feel in control of the situation or in a position to terminate the contact made by the investment firm.[109] This problem is exacerbated in the single market due to the potentially increased range of products and services and the related dangers of confusion and lack of transparency which are aggravated if a particular Member State does not, perhaps due to the late development of its investment markets and the hitherto infrequent use of such marketing strategies, regulate to protect investors against such practices.

Nonetheless, neither cold-calling rules nor door-to-door selling rules are harmonized by the ISD. Door-to-door sales are specifically excluded from the scope of the ISD by recital 8. With respect to cold-calling, in his Opinion in *Alpine Investments*, Advocate General Jacobs found, after a review of the ISD and other relevant legislation, that 'at present, Community legislation neither prohibits cold calling by telephone or in person nor prevents Member States from prohibiting it'.[110] Member States will be subject to the jurisprudence of the Court of Justice on the extent to which the imposition of these rules can constitute a prohibited restriction on the free-movement guarantees. While *Alpine Investments* confirmed that prohibitions on cold-calling can, in principle, come within the prohibition on restrictions on the freedom to provide services, it also found that as long as such measures are non-discriminatory, proportionate, and in the interests of the general good they can be justified under Article 49 EC. Cold-calling controls vary widely across the single market, however, from outright bans to permission-based regimes,[111] depending on the regulatory traditions of the Member State. Given the wider array of products to which investors are exposed in the single market and the possibility that investors based in Member States

---

[108] For this distinction between real time and permanent advertising see the FSA Draft Conduct of Business Sourcebook Paper, n 15 above, 39.

[109] With respect to door-to-door sales, the point has been made that it involves 'a particularly aggressive selling technique [used] in a sphere in which purchasers are often ill informed and exceptionally credulous': Van Gerven, W, 'The Second Banking Directive and the Case-law of the Court of Justice' (1990) 10 *YBEL* 57, 68. As far as cold calls are concerned, in one reported example German investment intermediaries cold-called French domestic households with offers of investment products on the Chicago Stock Exchange in commodities such as cacao and maize with promises of extraordinary profits. After aggressive selling strategies (some households being called several times over several weeks) a number of investors sent payments by cheque to a post office box. Predictably, the profits never materialized: (1998) 2351 *European Report* II 2. Admittedly, commodity derivatives are not, as yet, covered by the ISD, but the example illustrates nonetheless the dangers of cold calls.

[110] N 38 above, Opinion of the AG, para 23.

[111] FESCO Conduct Standards, n 98 above, 3.

which may not have dealt with cold-calling due to the immaturity of the domestic market-place may be vulnerable to aggressive marketing tactics in the liberalized market-place, cold-calling may be regarded as an appropriate candidate for harmonization.

IX.5.4 *Dispute Resolution, Sanctions, and Enforcement under the ISD*

The competent authorities responsible for supervision under the ISD are simply required under Article 22(3) to have all the powers necessary for the performance of their functions. Under Article 27, Member States must provide that their competent authorities may adopt or impose on investment firms measures or penalties aimed specifically at ending observed breaches or the causes of such breaches. The ISD does not specify what measures may be taken by either the home or host Member State to enforce conduct-of-business rules, whether they should take the form of criminal or civil sanctions, or whether they should involve financial penalties or other forms of sanction, save to provide that authorization may be withdrawn by the home State where the firm has seriously and systematically infringed conduct rules adopted under Article 11 (Article 3(7)(e)). Consistently with its primary objective as a market integration and macro market-protection measure, protective regulation under the ISD does not include the conferment of private rights of action on individual investors when its protective rules are breached. Indeed, the sole inclusion of withdrawal of authorization as a mechanism to control rule breaches is another indication of the ISD's focus on protecting the market-place and investors as a collective body. While public control and sanctions are essential, given that investors may lack the capacity to take private actions against investment firms for breach of regulatory conduct-of-business rules (where such rights of action are made available outside the contractual/fiduciary framework of the firm/investor relationship), private remedies for breach of publicly imposed obligations supplement the enforcement process.[112] Specific remedies for breach apart, the ISD does not require that procedures be put in place for the resolution of disputes between investors and firms or that complaint mechanisms be put in place. Given that conduct rules are not harmonized and that the ISD is not an investor-protection measure *per se*, these omissions are hardly surprising, but are weaknesses nonetheless. Indeed, retail-investor confidence in the integrated market and, consequently, the integration process is unlikely to be enhanced by the variety of ways in which Article 11 has been

---

[112] The view has been expressed that Art. 11 does require Member States to confer direct rights of action on investors against investment firms who breach the conduct-of-business principles: Tison, M, 'Conduct of Business Rules and their Implementation in the EU Member States' in Ferrarini, G, Hopt, K, and Wymeersch, E (eds), *Capital Markets in the Age of the Euro* (forthcoming).

implemented and the widely diverging remedies which exist across the Member States for breach of conduct-of-business rules.[113]

As a market-integration measure, the ISD does, however, set out in some detail the extensive co-operation procedures which must be followed and the inspection powers which may be exercised by Member States (Chapter VII sections 7–8 above). Specifically, host Member States may, under Article 19(6), 'take appropriate measures to prevent or penalize irregularities committed within their territories which are contrary to the rules of conduct introduced pursuant to Article 11 as well as to other legal or regulatory provision adopted in the interests of the general good'. These measures may include preventing the offending investment firm from initiating any further transactions within their territories.

IX.5.5 *Investor Protection and the ISD*

While, at present, the ISD's protective regime can be regarded as insubstantial, it does contribute to investor protection at a basic level by requiring Member States to ensure that conduct-of-business regimes are in place. In addition, notwithstanding the variety of ways in which the ISD has been implemented, conduct regulation has been placed on a public-law footing and investment firms' conduct of the investment-firm/investor relationship made subject to supervision and enforcement by competent authorities.[114] In this respect, Article 11 has ensured that control of the investor/investment-firm relationship has moved beyond the realm of fiduciary duties and now includes regulatory requirements enforceable by public authorities.

IX.6 THE BANKING REGIME AND PROTECTIVE REGULATION

Although the banking regime provides a passport for credit institutions which provide investment services, it does not cover protective regulation expressly, save to provide in Article 21(11) of the BCD II (CBD, Article 22(11))[115] that credit institutions can advertise their services through all available means of communication in the host Member State, subject to any rules governing the form and content of such advertising adopted in the interest of the general good. Credit institutions which provide investment

---

[113] On the variety of remedies available in respect of conduct-rule violations see Wymeersch, n 11 above, 35–6.

[114] See generally Wymeersch, n 11 above, 15–30 and 33–40.

[115] Second Council Directive 89/646/EEC on the coordination of laws regulations and administrative procedures relating to the taking up and pursuit of the business of credit institutions and amending Directive 77/780/EEC [1989] OJ L 386/1 (the BCD II) now consolidated as part of the banking regime by Directive 2000/12 relating to the taking up and pursuit of the business of credit institutions [2000] OJ L126/1 (the CBD).

services under the banking regime passport are, however, subject to Article 11 and to the host-Member-State enforcement regime under Article 19 by virtue of Article 2(1) of the ISD.

IX.7 THE MANAGEMENT-COMPANY REGIME

Under Article 5(h), the Management Company Proposal imposes specific conduct-of-business rules on management companies which engage in collective portfolio-management. These generic conduct rules are broadly similar in content to Article 11 of the ISD, although a home-Member-State control principle applies. Member States are to draw up rules of conduct which management companies authorized in that Member State are to observe at all times and which must implement the Article 5h principles.[116] These are: that a management company acts honestly and fairly and with due care, skill, and diligence in conducting its business activities in the best interests of the UCITSs it manages and the integrity of the market; has and employs effectively the resources and procedures that are necessary for the proper performance of its business activities; tries to avoid conflicts of interests and, when they cannot be avoided, ensures that the UCITSs it manages are fairly treated; and complies with all regulatory requirements applicable to the conduct of its business activities so as to promote the best interests of its investors and the integrity of the market.[117]

Where the management company is authorized to provide ISD-type services such as discretionary portfolio-management services, Article 11 (and Article 13) of the ISD applies to those activities (Article 5(4)) (although

---

[116] The Commission has described the new conduct regime as a 'striking judicious innovation': Communication from the Commission to the Parliament on the Common Position. SEC/2001/1004, para 3.2.2.5. As far as detailed implementing rules are concerned, a different set of conduct rules would typically apply to collective portfolio-management (as is reflected in Art. 5h, suitability rules, eg, do not apply to the individual investment decisions taken with respect to the scheme's composition, as these are taken in accordance with the scheme's objectives—suitability rules would apply to the investment firm advising an investor to invest in a particular scheme). The 1998 IOSCO Principles, eg, provide that '[o]perators should not benefit to the unfair disadvantage of investors in a scheme. Generally this will require regulation covering topics such as best execution, appropriate trading and timely allocation of transactions, commission and fees, related party transactions and underwriting arrangements': n 16 above, para 11.4. The FSA also takes the position that collective-investment scheme operators should be subject to a special conduct-of-business regime: FSA Conduct of Business Sourcebook, n 14 above, 100. It remains to be seen how the proposed revisions to Art. 11 will impact on the management-company regime.

[117] As far as the UCITS regime is concerned, as noted in Ch. 5 UCITS in the form of self-managed investment companies which do not have a designated management company must, under Art. 13b of the Management Company Proposal, also comply with Art. 5h. Recital 14 explains that the conduct regime should always be complied with by authorized investment companies, either by the company directly, or indirectly where it designates a management company.

Article 11 is not tailored to reflect the particular risks involved in discretionary portfolio management).

IX.8 GENERAL CONSUMER-PROTECTION MEASURES

IX.8.1 *Marketing Rules*[118]

IX.8.1.1 *The Misleading Advertising Directive*

The Misleading Advertising Directive's[119] objectives are not limited to consumer protection; it is designed more generally to protect 'consumers, persons carrying on a trade or business or practising a craft or profession and the interests of the public in general' against misleading advertising 'and the unfair consequences thereof' (Article 1). Like the ISD, albeit in a different context, single-market construction underpins the Directive's provisions; advertising is stated to have a direct effect on the common market, misleading advertising is identified as a source of distortions of competition, and divergences in Member States' rules are highlighted as leading to inadequate levels of consumer protection and to obstructions to free movement (recitals 2 and 4).[120]

Retail and sophisticated investors, professional and non-professional, it appears, benefit from its protections which also protect the market-place and investor confidence in general. Its potential application to the investment-services area can be seen from the wide definition of 'misleading' advertising as any advertising (broadly defined in Article 2(1) as 'the making of a representation in any form in connection with a trade, business, craft or profession in order to promote the supply of goods or services including immovable property rights and obligations') which in any way, including its presentation, deceives or is likely to deceive the persons to whom it is addressed or whom it reaches and which, by reason of its deceptive nature, is likely to affect their economic behaviour or injure a competitor (Article 2(2)). In determining whether advertising is misleading, account is to be taken under Article 3 of all its features, including the characteristics of the

---

[118] The Commission has produced a number of initiatives on commercial communications generally. See its 1996 Green Paper on Commercial Communications in the Internal Market, COM(96)192 (the Green Paper on Commercial Communications), which covers all forms of advertising, direct marketing, sponsorship, sales promotion, and public relations promoting products and services, and the subsequent Communication on the Follow-Up to the Green Paper on Commercial Communications in the Internal Market, COM(98)121. For a discussion see Dickie, J, *Internet and Electronic Commerce Law in the European Union* (1999) 65–8.

[119] Directive 84/450/EEC relating to the approximation of the laws, regulations and administrative provisions of the Member States concerning misleading advertising [1984] OJ L250/17 (the Misleading Advertising Directive or the Directive).

[120] For a discussion of its legal basis see sect. 12.3 below.

service, the price of the service, and the conditions on which it is supplied and the nature, attributes, and rights of the advertiser. Under Article 6, Member States are to ensure that court and administrative authorities dealing with breaches of the Directive's provisions can require the advertiser to furnish evidence of the accuracy of factual claims in advertising. Proof of deception is not required; the likelihood of deception is sufficient to bring the Directive into play (Article 2(2)).

Unlike the ISD, where the consequences of breach by investment firms of national measures implementing its protective provisions are not dealt with in any great detail, Article 4 sets out extensive procedures which Member States are required to adopt to ensure that advertisers comply with the Directive and that breaches are sanctioned. These include a requirement that persons or organizations with a legitimate interest in prohibiting misleading advertising be permitted to take legal action or institute administrative proceedings against such advertising (Article 4(1)). As a minimum-standards measure, the Directive does not prevent Member States from retaining or adopting rules 'with a view to ensuring more extensive protection' for those targeted by the Directive (Article 7).

In 1997 the scope of the Misleading Advertising Directive was extended to include comparative advertising,[121] and it now covers the conditions under which comparative advertising (defined as any advertising which explicitly or impliedly identifies a competitor or goods or services offered by a competitor (Article 2a)) is permitted. Investment-services advertising which compares growth or yields, for example, will therefore be subject to its requirements. These include that the advertising is not misleading, that it compares goods or services meeting the same needs or intended for the same purposes, and that it objectively compares one or more material, relevant, verifiable, and representative features of those goods and services (including price) (Article 3a)). Recital 22 to the amending Directive makes clear, however, that where Member States maintain or introduce bans on marketing methods or advertising 'which target[s] vulnerable consumer groups', they are not required to permit comparative advertising for goods or services covered by such prohibitions. Under Article 7(2), Member States may not adopt more stringent comparative-advertising conditions than those laid down in the Directive.

The Misleading Advertising Directive does not, however, address the specific informational asymmetries at stake in the investor/investment-firm relationship, which, even where the marketing is not misleading *per se*, demand that marketing be regulated to ensure that the investor is not subject to undue pressure and is adequately informed of the risks being taken.

---

[121] Directive 97/55/EC amending Directive 84/450/EEC concerning misleading advertising so as to include comparative advertising [1997] OJ L290/18.

IX.8.1.2 *The Doorstep Sales Directive*

Unlike the Misleading Advertising Directive, the Doorstep Sales Directive[122] is addressed to consumers, a consumer being defined as a 'natural person who, in transactions covered by [the] Directive is acting for purposes which can be regarded as outside his trade or profession' (Article 2). Consumer protection is not the explicit objective of the Doorstep Sales Directive. While its provisions protect consumers against unfair practices in respect of doorstep selling, its stated purpose is to harmonize doorstep selling rules as any disparities may affect the functioning of the common market (recital 2).

It applies to contracts which are concluded during a visit by a trader (a person acting in a commercial or professional capacity with respect to the transaction in question) to a consumer's home or place of work, or during an excursion organized by the trader away from his business premises (Articles 2 and 1(1)). Its core provision is not to prevent doorstep sales, but to require that consumers subject to such marketing techniques benefit from (and be notified of the existence of) a 'cooling-off period' of at least seven days (Articles 4 and 5) in order to enable the consumer to assess the obligations arising under the contract (recital 5). As with the Misleading Advertising Directive, the Directive is a minimum standards measure with Member States free to adopt 'more favourable provisions to protect consumers in the field which it covers' (Article 8), subject to compliance with the Treaty free-movement guarantees and the application of the general-good exception in particular. Consumers may not waive the protections granted by the Directive (Article 7).

Notwithstanding the dangers doorstep sales pose for investors, given that high-pressure tactics may be exercised, and although the Directive recognizes that in a doorstep sale the trader 'initiates the contract negotiations, for which the consumer is unprepared or which he does not expect . . . the consumer is often unable to compare the quality and price of the offer with other offers' (recital 4), the Directive does not regulate the investment-services sector. Article 3(2)(e) specifically excludes 'contracts for securities'.[123]

---

[122] Directive 85/577/EEC to protect the consumer in respect of contracts negotiated away from business premises [1985] OJ L 372/31 (the Doorstep Selling Directive or the Directive). Its legal basis is discussed in sect. 12.3 below.

[123] In his Opinion in *Alpine Investments*, Jacobs AG examined the Doorstep Selling Directive to see whether it might have any application to the cold-calling problem at issue but concluded that, as it applied neither to contracts concluded by telephone nor 'contracts for securities', it did not. He did note that it allowed Member States to adopt more stringent requirements in order to protect consumers: n 38 above, para 20. The Commission's original proposal did not exclude contracts for securities but did not impose a tailored regime for such contracts. In its Explanatory Memorandum, the Commission acknowledged that certain contracts such as contracts for shares might require particular protections, but suggested that these would be covered in subsequent proposals and, as a result, particular provision would not be made in the proposed Directive, COM(76)544, para I, 3. In its 1977 comments on the original proposal,

IX.8.2 *Harmonized Contract Requirements*

IX.8.2.1 *From Conduct to the Contract*

The EC has been very slow to venture into the private-law field to redress the balance between the investment firm and the investor in terms of imposing specific contractual conditions, notwithstanding the weak bargaining position of the retail investor and the informational imbalances in the retail investor/investment-firm relationship. As discussed above, the ISD does not address contract-formation issues. There appears to be an ingrained assumption that the retail investor is operating rationally in a co-equal situation with the investment firm and will make appropriate choices and negotiate contracts accordingly.[124] Investors do, however, benefit from the horizontal protections afforded by the harmonization of unfair-contract-term rules. While contributing, if indirectly, to investor protection, it may be more significant that the Unfair Contract Terms Directive suggests that investor-protection harmonization could move beyond the regulatory framework for investment business suggested by the ISD and extend into more interventionist rule-making with respect to the contractual framework of the service provided, involving a more paternalistic approach to investor protection than has hitherto been apparent.

IX.8.2.2 *The Unfair Contract Terms Directive*

The Directive is designed to eliminate disparities in Member States' unfair terms in consumer contracts laws and to remove unfair terms from consumer contracts in order to facilitate the establishment of the single market by removing the distortions to competition experienced by sellers of goods and suppliers of services when they operate in other Member States due to these disparities (recitals 2 and 3).[125] It also has the objective of protecting consumers when they contract under a law of a Member State other than their own by introducing uniform rules in relation to unfair terms, given that consumers are not generally familiar with laws of other Member States and may be deterred, as a result, from entering into transactions to purchase goods and services in other Member States (recitals 4 and 5).

The Directive covers contracts concluded between a 'seller and supplier' and a 'consumer' (Article 1(1)). Consumers are broadly defined in Article 2(b) as any persons who, in contracts covered by the Directive, are acting

---

the Parliament called on the Commission to regard as a priority proposals for harmonizing the particular rules applicable to doorstep sales involving contracts for securities [1977] OJ C241/26.

[124] See also Cranston and Hadjiemmanuil, n 18 above, 341 and 361.
[125] Its legal basis is discussed in sect. 12.3 below.

for purposes which are outside their trade, business, or profession. Retail investors and sophisticated but not professional investors (professional investors are excluded) would come within this definition. Investment firms also clearly come within the scope of 'sellers or suppliers', defined in Article 2(c) as natural or legal persons who, in contracts covered by the Directive, act for purposes relating to their trade, business, or profession, whether publicly or privately owned.

The core protection for consumers is contained in Article 3 of the Directive, which is limited to terms which have not been individually negotiated. It provides in Article 3(1) that a term which has not been individually negotiated will be regarded as unfair if, contrary to the requirement of good faith, it causes a significant imbalance, to the detriment of the consumer, in the parties' rights and obligations under the contract. Under Article 3(2) a contract term will always be regarded as not having been individually negotiated where it has been drafted in advance and the consumer has not been able to influence the substance of the term, particularly in the context of a pre-formulated standard contract (where a seller or supplier claims that a standard term has been individually negotiated, the burden of proof lies with him). Under Article 6, Member States are to provide that unfair terms in a contract concluded with a consumer by a seller or supplier will not, as provided for under their national law, be binding on the consumer and that the contract will continue to bind the parties on the agreed terms if it is capable of continuing in existence without the unfair term. The extent to which standard terms and contracts are used will be critical to the impact of the Directive on relations between investment firms and retail investors.

Article 4(1) provides that in assessing the unfairness of a term account must be taken of the nature of the goods or services provided, all the circumstances attending the conclusion of the contract and all the other terms of the contract, and any other contracts on which it is dependent. The Annex to the Directive sets out an 'indicative and non-exhaustive' list of the terms which may be regarded as unfair. Where certain of these terms are used by suppliers of 'financial services',[126] in order to reflect the rapidly changing conditions of financial markets the Directive contains exemptions which allow financial services to use these otherwise unfair terms, although the exemptions are subject to conditions designed to protect the consumer. Section 1(g) of the Annex designates as unfair any term which enables the seller or supplier to terminate a contract of indeterminate duration without reasonable notice except where there are serious grounds for doing so. Under section 2(a) financial-services suppliers may nonetheless reserve the right to

---

[126] The term is not defined but it is unlikely that it does not incorporate the range of activities traditionally undertaken by investment firms.

terminate unilaterally a contract of indeterminate duration without notice, as long as there is a valid reason to do so and the supplier informs the other contracting party immediately. Similarly, while section 1(j) deems as unfair any term which enables the seller or supplier to alter the contract terms unilaterally and without a valid reason which is specified in the contract, under section 2(b) suppliers of financial services may reserve the right to alter the rate of interest payable by the consumer or due to the supplier or the amount of other charges for financial services without notice. The exemption is subject to the alteration being for a valid reason, the supplier informing the contracting party immediately and the contracting party being permitted to dissolve the contract immediately. A supplier of financial services is also entitled to alter unilaterally the terms of a contract of indeterminate duration without falling foul of section 1(j) as long as the supplier informs the consumer with reasonable notice and the consumer is free to dissolve the contract. Finally, under section 2(c) sections 1(g), 1(j) and 1(l) (the last of which provides that a term, which states that the price of goods is to be determined at the time of delivery or allows a seller of goods or supplier of services to increase his or her price without giving the consumer the corresponding right to cancel the contract if the final price is too high in relation to the price agreed at the time the contract was concluded, is unfair) do not apply to transactions in transferable securities,[127] financial instruments, and other products or services where the price is linked to fluctuations in a stock exchange quotation or index or a financial market rate that the seller or supplier cannot control.[128]

Apart from the unfair terms protection, of particular significance for retail investors is the Article 5 requirement that where a contract is in writing, the terms must be drafted in 'plain, intelligible language' and that, where there is doubt about the meaning of a term, the interpretation most favourable to the consumer will prevail.

With respect to remedies, sanctions, and enforcement, a significant additional control is imposed by Article 7(2), which requires Member States to ensure that persons or organizations with a legitimate interest under national law in consumer protection may take action, according to the national law concerned, before courts or competent authorities for a decision on whether contractual terms drawn up for general use are unfair, so that they can apply appropriate and effective means to prevent the continued use of such terms. Its inclusion is in stark contrast to the lack of

---

[127] Undefined, despite the fact that the ISD, which was at the time of the Unfair Contract Terms Directive's adoption a month away from adoption, contained a relatively comprehensive definition.

[128] Also excluded from ss 1(g), 1(j), and 1(l) are contracts for the purchase and sale of foreign currency, traveller's cheques, or international money orders denominated in a foreign currency.

investor- or client-specific enforcement measures in the ISD in relation to its conduct rules. More generally, under Article 7(1), Member States are to ensure that adequate and effective means are in place to prohibit the continued use of unfair terms in contracts covered by the Directive.

As with the other consumer-protection directives outlined above, the Unfair Contract Terms Directive is a minimum-standards measure. Member States may adopt or retain more stringent provisions 'to ensure a maximum degree of protection for the consumer', subject to compliance with the Treaty (Article 8).[129]

IX.9 THE DISTANCE MARKETING PROPOSAL

IX.9.1 *Background*

The protective-regulation regime will be significantly enhanced if and when the Distance Marketing Proposal[130] is adopted. It represents a significant step forward in harmonized protective regulation, in that it harmonizes protective rules with respect to, *inter alia*, marketing techniques, pre-contract disclosure, and contractual rights and obligations (such as withdrawal rights) (albeit in the limited context of distance marketing).[131] A particular strength of the Distance Marketing Proposal is its recognition of the pivotal role of disclosure in the protection of consumers of financial services.[132] Its main weakness, from the investment-services perspective, is that it is a

---

[129] Further developments with respect to unfair contract terms in financial-services contracts, specifically, may be on the horizon. In its 2000 Report on the Implementation of the Unfair Contract Terms Directive, COM(2000)248, the Commission noted at 27 that financial-services contracts 'consumed' a large quantity of contractual terms and that the financial community had misgivings about different degrees of protection within the Member States and supported the need for a clear and standard contractual framework in the field of cross-border provision of financial services. It should be noted, however, that the Commission reported at 45 that unfair terms in investment contracts formed only 2% of the unfair terms reported.

[130] Moloney, N, 'Distance Marketing of Financial Services: The Approach to Harmonisation Emerges' (2000) 21 *The Company Lawyer* 198. The following discussion is based, in part, on this article. On 27 Sept 2001, the Council reached political agreement on the Distance Marketing Proposal but a common position has, at the time of writing, yet to be published in the Official Journal. The most recent discussion draft available in the Council's Access to Document Registry (the Council Draft) suggests, however, that the common position is likely to differ from the Proposal in a number of respects, particularly with respect to disclosure and withdrawal rights. While this discussion is based on the Commission's Proposal, brief reference will be made to the Council Draft where it differs materially from the proposal.

[131] It may have significant consequences for investor protection, in that the Commission is optimistic that the Proposal may ultimately lead to harmonization of the rules which apply to the marketing and advertising of investment services generally: Art. 11 Communication, n 39 above, 18. See also sect. 13.7 below.

[132] Although disclosure has long been a central plank of EC consumer-protection policy generally. See, eg, Council Resolution 89/C 294/01 on Future Priorities for Relaunching Consumer Protection Policy [1989] OJ C294/1.

horizontal measure and applies to financial services generally. Accordingly, while it contains some important protections for investors, its provisions are not fully tailored to the specific context of the investment-firm/investor relationship. The Council Draft suggests that a more nuanced common position can be expected, however, in that the Draft includes, for example, risk-warning requirements.

In a distance contract, offer, negotiation, and acceptance take place at a distance without the simultaneous presence of the two parties to the contract; the post, telephone, fax, and Internet are typically employed. These contracts expose consumers to a number of risks. They may be placed at an informational disadvantage as a result of the lack of direct face-to-face contact and given the potentially aggressive nature of the marketing (particularly in the case of telephone calls).[133] The consumer may not, as a result, be in a position to examine the nature of the service or product offered, to compare it with comparable offers, or assess the nature of the rights and obligations involved. Difficulties may arise in establishing with whom the consumer is contracting and what evidences the contract in the event of a dispute. The ephemeral quality of contracts entered into by electronic methods may mean that there is no permanent record of the contractual rights and obligations. The cross-border nature of distance contracts may create problems for consumers in respect of judicial or administrative redress. Protection may also be needed to safeguard consumer privacy against aggressive marketing strategies and inertia selling. Apart from the issues raised by distance selling as a marketing technique *per se*, the additional complexity of investment products and services and the financial consequences which can be visited on the unwary investor make a strong case for harmonized rules to ensure that investors located in all Member States are appropriately protected in the single market.

Directive 97/7[134] harmonizes Member States' rules on distance selling generally. It is designed to ensure legal certainty and appropriate levels of protection for consumers irrespective of the Member State in which they reside, enhance confidence in distance selling, and ensure freedom of movement for consumers and suppliers by ensuring that diverging national laws do not hinder distance selling across the EC. It provides a number of protections for consumers in a distance-selling situation including pre-contract information rights, withdrawal rights, and inertia selling and unsolicited

---

[133] Distance-selling techniques in the sale of financial services and products have been a matter of concern for some time. The OECD Consumer Information Report, n 83 above, emphasized the need for transparency in distance sales of financial services.

[134] Directive 97/7/EC on the protection of consumers in respect of distance contract [1997] OJ L144/19 (Directive 97/7). See generally Cremona, M, The Distance Selling Directive' (1998) *JBL* 613 and Howells, G, 'A Consideration of Proposals to Regulate Distance Selling' in Lonbay, J (ed), *Enhancing the Legal Protection of the European Consumer* (1996) 146.

communications controls. Financial services, including investment services, are, however, specifically excluded from the scope of Directive 97/7 (Article 3(1)). Although they were included in the original proposal, this was strongly resisted by several Member States, including France, Germany, the Netherlands, and the UK.[135] Despite intensive lobbying by consumer groups, the Council removed financial services from the scope of the proposal, deciding that a review of the pre-existing financial-services directives was necessary to see whether they already contained provisions similar to those contained in the proposed directive. In addition, the complexities of financial services were deemed to warrant special attention. The Commission finally adopted its first proposal for a directive on distance selling of financial services in 1998.[136] A substantially revised proposal reflecting amendments proposed by the European Parliament and the comments of the Council and the Economic and Social Committee was adopted in 1999.[137]

IX.9.2 *The Investor-protection Objective*

Unlike the ISD which, notwithstanding assorted Preamble references to the contrary, is not designed as an investor-protection measure, the Distance Marketing Proposal explicitly takes the adoption of a high level of protection for consumers of financial services as a central objective in recital 3.[138] Like the ISD and the general consumer-protection measures, however, market integration underlies the Proposal, in so far as the need for the Proposal is rooted in the link between consumer protection and consumer confidence in distance marketing, on the one hand, and the potential of distance marketing as a tool of market integration on the other. It also appears as an explicit objective in recital 8, which states that the Proposal is designed to prevent the adoption by Member States of conflicting consumer-protection rules with respect to distance marketing which could impede the functioning of the internal market.

---

[135] The UK felt that Directive 97/7was drafted with the distance sale of goods in mind and did not, as a result, deal appropriately with the specific characteristics of financial services (notably with respect to withdrawal rights), that the inclusion of financial services raised questions of overlap and conflict with the financial-services directives already adopted, and that, accordingly, financial services should be dealt with vertically in a specific directive: House of Lords Select Committee on the European Communities, Session 1992–93, 16th Report, 'Distance Selling', 1, 4.

[136] [1998] OJ C385/10; Explanatory Memorandum at COM(98)468. The delay in producing a proposal led the consumer lobbying group BEUC to accuse the Commission of 'a grave lack of courage and consistency': (1998) 2350 *European Report* II, 1.

[137] ECOSOC's comments are at [1999] OJ C169/45. The European Parliament's comments are at [1999] OJ C279/197.

[138] Its Treaty basis is discussed in sects. 12.2 and 12.3 below.

IX.9.3 *Scope*

'Financial services' are simply defined in Article 2(b) as 'any banking, insurance, investment or payment measure' and clearly include investment services and products. Article 1(2) clarifies that where a financial-services contract comprises several successive operations or a series of separate operations performed over time, the proposed Directive applies only to the first operation. A distance contract is defined by Article 2(a) as one 'concluded between a supplier and a consumer under an organized distance sales or service-provision scheme run by the supplier, who, for the purpose of this contract, makes exclusive use of means of distance communication up to and including the moment at which the contract is concluded'. Combinations of distance-selling methods, such as use of the Internet and telephone, will fall within this definition. Distance sales conducted on an infrequent, *ad hoc* basis are not covered. An investor who, through a distance mechanism, approaches a supplier of investment services or products who does not ordinarily engage in distance sales, and concludes a contract at a distance may not therefore be eligible for the proposed Directive's protections. The broad definition of 'means of distance communication' in Article 2(e) as 'any means which, without the simultaneous physical presence of the supplier and consumer, may be used for the conclusion of a contract between those parties' clearly accommodates future technological developments.[139] 'Suppliers of financial services' covers under Article 2(c) 'any natural or legal person who, acting in his commercial or professional capacity, is the actual provider of services subject to contracts covered by [the] Directive or acts as intermediary in the supply of those services or in the conclusion of a distance contract between those parties'. The reference to acting as an intermediary acknowledges that the formation of a distance contract involves a number of marketing stages and ensures that suppliers at all stages of process (offer, negotiation, and conclusion) are subject to the proposed Directive's obligations.

Reflecting the differentiated approach to regulation the Distance Marketing Proposal is designed to protect 'consumers' of financial services, of which investors or consumers of investment services are clearly a subset, although the term 'investor' is not used. In a definition which reflects the definition of 'consumer' in Directive 97/7 and the Unfair Contract Terms Directive, a consumer is defined in Article 2(d) as 'any natural person who, in contracts covered by this Directive, is acting for purposes which are outside his trade, business or profession'. These consumers are given two important protections; the right to prior information and the right to withdraw.

---

[139] By contrast, the parallel Art. 2(4) of Directive 97/7 includes in Annex I an indicative list of means of distance communication.

IX.9.4 *Prior Information*

Ensuring that the consumer is appropriately informed lies at the heart of the Distance Marketing Proposal. There are two stages to information disclosure. Specified material information must be supplied before contract conclusion, after which written confirmation of the terms and conditions must follow. Article 3 sets out a list of information which must be communicated to the consumer 'in good time' prior to the conclusion of the contract. These include: a description of the main characteristics of the financial service; the total price of the financial service, including all taxes; and an indication, where relevant, of the possibility that prices may vary between the time the information is supplied and the contract is concluded, together with particulars allowing the consumer to verify the price at the time of conclusion of the contract if this is the case. Other provisions address the performance of the contract and require information to be supplied on: the period for which the offer or the price remains open; the minimum duration of the contract, in the case of financial services to be performed permanently or recurrently; information on contract cancellation; the existence of withdrawal rights, if any, and the price paid by the consumer on withdrawal; and arrangements for payment, delivery, or performance of the contract. The importance of dispute-resolution mechanisms in a distance sale is addressed with the following requirements: the identity and address of the supplier and the identity and address of the representative of the supplier in the consumer's country of residence whom he can consult, if such a representative exists; the law applicable to the contract; the court having jurisdiction in the event of a dispute; the supervisory authority with jurisdiction over the supplier, where applicable; and out-of-court complaint and redress procedures. The information must, as might be expected, 'be provided in a clear and comprehensible manner', a requirement of particular significance for investment-services transactions. The Proposal is flexible in that the information may be supplied in any way appropriate to the means of distance communication. Less predictable is the requirement in Article 3(2) that the information provided should 'comply with the principle of fairness in commercial transactions and the principles that govern the protection of persons who are legally incapable under national law, such as minors'. While this is also a feature of Directive 97/7, it introduces a level of investor protection some way beyond the aspirations concerning the conduct of the investor/investment-firm set out in Article 11 of the ISD.

Where the information requirements overlap with other directives in the financial-services field, they are disapplied by Article 3(1), (2) which sets out the particular items of Article 3(1) which apply to the supply of certain services. The manner in which this has been achieved for investment services is perplexing. In the case of 'services covered by the [ISD]', the basic requirements as to the supplier's name and address, total price for the service, the arrangements for payment, delivery, or performance, the characteristics of the service, and information on contract cancellation are disapplied, although this information is surely material for the distance sale of investment services or products to retail investors. Only the requirements concerning dispute resolution, certain performance-related matters such as the existence of withdrawal rights, duration, as well as disclosure of price fluctuations and the cost of using distance communication are required. It is not entirely clear why. The wording of Article 3(1), (2), which provides that the specified information requirements apply 'without prejudice to Article 11', suggests that Article 11 already covers the information which is excluded.[140] But whether Article 11 already requires Member States to ensure that the excluded information is provided is highly questionable. The fundamental limitation on the Distance Marketing Proposal making a significant contribution to protective regulation, namely its orientation as a general consumer-protection measure, is made strikingly apparent here. It does not cover the specific disclosure concerns raised by the investor/ investment-firm relationship such as the appropriateness of risk warnings, disclosure of how fees and commissions are calculated, and the use of past performance statistics as an indicator of future performance. The approach adopted by the Council Draft to disclosure, however, is considerably more nuanced. Under Article 3 of the Council Draft, the information required is set out according to four distinct categories: the supplier; the financial service; the contract; and redress. The substantive disclosure required under these categories also differs from the Proposal. Of particular note is the inclusion by Article 3(1)(h)(h) of the Council Draft of a requirement that a risk warning be given where the financial service is related to instruments which involve special risks or where the price depends on fluctuations in the financial markets which are outside the control of the supplier and a requirement that the supplier give notice that historical performances are not a guide to future performance. A less onerous information regime applies to telephone communications under Article 3(3) of the Council Draft. Unlike the Proposal, the Council Draft does not provide that the information supplied comply with the principle of fairness in commercial transactions but refers instead in Article 3(2) to the principle of good faith in commercial transactions. The approach taken in the Draft to the interaction between the disclosure requirements of the sectoral directives and the new distance-marketing regime is more sophisticated. Under Article 3(a)(1) of the Council Draft, additional disclosure requirements already applicable under Community law continue to apply.

---

[140] This interpretation is bolstered by the Commission's statement that 'the information provided under this Directive should only include information which is not yet required by the sectoral directives': Explanatory Memorandum, n 136 above, 5.

This information must be provided 'in good time' before conclusion of the contract. This ambiguous formula may cause difficulties in application, but the right to withdraw suggests that this period is not designed to act as a substitute for a reflection period. Under Article 3a(1), the supplier is also required to communicate all the contractual terms and conditions (including the information specified in Article 3(1)) to the consumer, on paper or in a 'durable medium' (defined broadly as any instrument enabling the consumer to store information addressed personally to him), once the contract has been concluded. An exemption is available under Article 3(a)(2) where this obligation is fulfilled prior to the conclusion of the contract. This requirement provides consumers with a durable record of their rights and obligations, which may otherwise be absent, given the ephemeral nature of certain forms of electronic communication. Transparency both before and after contract conclusion is thus addressed. The Council Draft takes a different (and more pro-consumer) approach, however, to the question of when the information should be supplied. Article 3(b) of the Council Draft provides that the supplier is to communicate all the contractual terms and conditions as well as the disclosure required by the new distance-marketing regime on paper or on another durable medium in good time before the consumer is bound by any distance contract or offer.

IX.9.5 *Withdrawal Rights*

The Distance Marketing Proposal grants consumers a general right to withdraw from distance contracts in certain circumstances. This mechanism provides a cooling-off period during which consumers can assimilate information and consider the purchase decision, given the difficulties in comparing and assessing offers in a distance contract. These difficulties are compounded in the case of financial services where the financial commitment may be long term and significant and the consumer may be inexperienced.

A general right to withdraw is set out in Article 4. In line with the Proposal's emphasis on transparency, exercise of the right to withdraw is interconnected with the provision of information. Where the contractual terms and conditions and the information required by Article 3(1) have been provided prior to the conclusion of the contract, the withdrawal period runs from the date of conclusion of the contract. If the contract has been concluded at the express request of the consumer before the contractual terms and conditions and the Article 3(1) information have been communicated to him, the withdrawal period runs from the date of receipt of these particulars, or the last of such particulars, as required under Article 3(a)(1).

In order to reflect appropriately the contract's degree of complexity and financial commitment, Article 4(1) provides that the withdrawal period may vary from fourteen to thirty days, 'depending on the nature of the financial service concerned'.[141] The exact period is to be determined by the Member States and will depend on the degree of consumer protection required. As a supplier could potentially be subject to different withdrawal periods across the Member States in respect of the same service and so restricted in the freedom to provide distance financial services, jurisdiction is granted to the home State. Article 4(1) provides that the supplier is subject only to the withdrawal period required by the Member State in which he is established.

Withdrawal rights are given a somewhat different treatment in the Council Draft. Reflecting the Draft's requirement that the disclosure be supplied in advance of contract conclusion, under Article 4 the withdrawal period runs from the conclusion of the contract. The approach to the length of the withdrawal period is less flexible. Under Article 4 of the Council Draft, the Member States' discretion is removed with the withdrawal period running for fourteen days, except in the case of life insurance and personal pension contracts which are subject to a thirty-day withdrawal period.

The Proposal's withdrawal right is subject to a number of exceptions in Article 4(1)(a). A withdrawal right could clearly lead to a risk of speculation in the case of products subject to fluctuations in price due to market conditions. Accordingly, foreign-exchange services and dealing services in respect of money-market instruments, transferable securities, UCITSs and other collective investment schemes, financial futures and options, and exchange and interest rate instruments whose price depends on market fluctuation outside the supplier's control are not subject to withdrawal rights. Investors using these services or investing in such products in a distance sale will not have the luxury of a change of mind. The extensive information required prior to contract conclusion should, however, significantly reduce the risks of a distance sale for the unsophisticated investor. In particular, under Article 3(1)(2), where the price of the instrument is likely to vary between the provision of the information and the conclusion of the contract, the final price must be verified to the investor at the conclusion of the contract. While the extensive exclusions appear to nullify the benefit of the withdrawal provisions for investors, contracts for general investment services such as portfolio-management and investment advice remain subject to withdrawal rights with respect to the general service provided. Specific contracts concluded under such contracts would, however, be protected by the exclusions.

The existence of a withdrawal right in law offers little protection in practice if those exercising the right are subject to stringent penalties or conditions. Mindful of this, consumers may not be required to indicate grounds for withdrawal, and, under Article 5(1), the costs borne by consumers on

---

[141] Directive 97/7 by contrast adopts a uniform approach towards withdrawal using a standard period of 7 days and 30 days.

withdrawal are limited to the costs incurred by the supplier in providing the service prior to withdrawal. Specifically, only two types of payment may be demanded and, in each case, payment must be made without any undue delay. The consumer may be required to pay a lump sum corresponding to the price of the financial service effectively provided by the supplier before the right to withdraw was exercised. Where the cost of the financial service is based on the number of days during which the service was rendered and so depends on the time at which the right of withdrawal was exercised, a more complex payment calculation is set out. Any sums received by the supplier on conclusion of the distance contract (apart from withdrawal payments) must be returned to the consumer within thirty days of withdrawal. Under Article 4(5) consumers are to exercise withdrawal rights by notifying the supplier on paper or in a durable medium available and accessible to the supplier.

Without prejudice to the right to withdraw, where the consumer has been 'unfairly induced'[142] to enter into the distance contract, the contract may, under Article 4(2), be annulled. Annulment also operates without prejudice to the consumer's right to seek compensation for the harm suffered under national law. This protection against unfair inducement does not appear in the Council Draft.

IX.9.6 *Intrusive Marketing Techniques and Cold-calling*

Although the Distance Marketing Proposal stops of short of banning cold calls, the use of the aggressive and intrusive selling strategies which can accompany distance sales is curtailed.[143] Inertia sales are addressed by Article 9, which requires Member States to take the 'necessary measures' to prohibit the supply of financial services to a consumer without a prior request on his part, when this supply includes a request for immediate or deferred payments, and to exempt the consumer from any 'obligations' in the event of an unsolicited supply. Article 9 also provides that the absence of a reply does not constitute consent. The Proposal does not specify what form these measures may take, leaving the regulation of inertia sales essentially to the discretion of Member States.

---

[142] This term is not defined, save for the proviso that the communication to consumers of objective information on prices of financial services that depend on market fluctuations does not constitute an unfair inducement. In its Explanatory Memorandum to the original proposal the Commission offered limited guidance, stating only that unfair inducement must not be confused with the rules governing unfair competition between professionals and that '[t]he unfairness must be assessed from the consumer's perspective and not from that of the professionals inter se': n 136 above, 13.

[143] These provisions are stated to reflect Arts. 8 and 10 of the European Convention on Human Rights.

Article 10 requires the consumer's prior consent before the use of automatic-calling machines and fax machines is permitted. The Proposal does not specify the manner in which prior consent may be given. In the case of other methods of distance marketing, such as telephone calls and e-mail,[144] the Proposal is not clear about whether prior consent is required. Article 10(2) appears to leave the issue of prior consent to the discretion of the Member States, providing that such means of distant communication 'shall not be authorised unless the consent of the consumers concerned has been obtained or may only be used if the consumer has not expressed his manifest objection'. The precise meaning of 'manifest objection' is also questionable. Although Article 10(2) allows Member States to permit cold calls via telephone to consumers who have not actively registered their objection, the conduct of telephone communications is regulated. Under Article 10(4) the identity of the supplier and the purpose of the call must be made clear at the beginning of the call, in order to provide the consumer with enough information to decide whether or not to carry on the call. Specific reference is made to the consequences of non-compliance. Under Article 10(5), Member States 'shall provide for appropriate penalties' in the event of a supplier's failure to comply with Article 10. The Council Draft essentially follows the Proposal's approach to unsolicited communications. A special information regime is applied to telephone calls under Article 3 of the Council Draft, however, while under Article 10(a) of the Council Draft, the sanctioning requirement set out in Article 10(5) of the Proposal is applied to breaches of the new distance-marketing regime generally.

IX.9.7 *Dispute Resolution*

The Distance Marketing Proposal represents a step forward in protective harmonization in that, albeit to a limited extent, it introduces redress procedures and procedural protections for consumers in respect of distance contracts for financial services. Article 12 requires Member States to ensure that 'adequate and effective complaints and redress procedures' for the settlement of disputes between suppliers and consumers are put in place. These procedures are to include measures which permit particular bodies to take action under national law to ensure the national provisions for the implementation of the Proposal are applied. These bodies are public bodies or their representatives; consumer organizations having a legitimate interest in protecting consumers; and professional organizations having a legitimate interest in acting. The out-of-court resolution of cross-border disputes is facilitated by Article 12(a), which invites dispute-settlement bodies to co-operate

[144] The European Parliament's proposed amendment to this provision extended the automatic calling machine and fax machine ban to the use of telephones and electronic mail in marketing financial services at a distance: n 137 above, 205.

in the resolution of cross-border disputes. Further, although Community law rarely ventures beyond substantive law into the field of procedural rights, the application of the provisions of Directive 98/27/EC on injunctions for the protection of consumer interests[145] to the proposed Directive by Article 16 means that public and non-governmental bodies whose purpose it is to protect collective consumer interests may bring an action for injunctive relief against a supplier who is breaching the proposed Directive. In addition, the mandatory imposition of the burden of proof in respect of the supplier's obligation to inform the consumer and the consumer's consent to conclusion of the contract and, where appropriate, performance, on the supplier by Article 13 is a further encroachment into the traditional sphere of Member States in the interests of the consumer of financial services.[146] Under Article 13, any attempt to shift this burden to the consumer would be an unfair contract term under the Unfair Contract Terms Directive. Finally, the imperative nature of the proposed Directive's protections is asserted by Article 11, which provides that consumers may not waive the rights conferred on them by the Directive.

IX.9.8 *Maximum Harmonization*

One of the more striking features of the Distance Marketing Proposal is that the traditional options of minimum harmonization of essential standards and home-country control (Article 10 of the ISD, for example) or, in the absence of harmonization, host-country control (Article 11 of the ISD, for example) have been eschewed in favour of maximum harmonization in the fields covered by the Proposal.[147] Recital 9 provides that, given the high level of consumer protection guaranteed by the proposed Directive, and with a view to ensuring the free movement of financial services, Member States may not adopt provisions other than those laid down by the proposed Directive in the fields it harmonizes.[148] In theory, consumers of financial services are assured

---

[145] [1998] OJ L166/51. It also applies to the Misleading Advertising Directive (n 119 above), the Doorstep Selling Directive (n 122 above), and the Unfair Contract Terms Directive (n 23 above).

[146] A similar burden-of-proof rule is set out in Art. 3(2) of the Unfair Contract Terms Directive with respect to proving whether a contract is individually negotiated.

[147] The Council's view was that '[w]ith this proposal, the Commission is intending to introduce a new regulatory model into European consumer protection law: whereas the general Directive on distance contracts 97/7 and other consumer protection directives . . . lay down only minimum standards and allow the Member States to lay down more stringent consumer protection rules, the purpose of this proposal is to lead to complete harmonization of salesmanship rules for the distance marketing of financial services': Council Meeting Consumer Affairs, 13 Apr 1999, IP 7212/99.

[148] The extent to which host Member States would be able to control the content of offers of financial and investment services proved to be a controversial point in negotiating the proposal. It was reported that DG XV (internal market) was in favour of allowing a service provider to make the same offer across the EC without additional regulation on compliance with the

of a high standard of protection, while service providers benefit from uniform marketing rules. From the perspective of investor protection, however, the inability of Member States to adopt higher levels of protection in the fields harmonized by the Proposal may potentially result in a reduction in levels of investor protection in certain Member States. Indeed, while the Proposal is heavily based on Directive 97/7, that Directive adopts minimum standards and in Article 14 permits Member States to lay down more stringent consumer-protection rules. However, the maximum harmonization rule is not absolute. In the case of withdrawal rights, full harmonization is accompanied by a degree of Member State discretion. Local market conditions are catered for by the choice given to Member States in relation to the length of the withdrawal period, although this flexibility is absent from the Council Draft.[149]

The Council Draft also adopts the maximum harmonization model, but takes a more flexible approach. In particular, it provides in Article 2 that, pending further harmonization, Member States may maintain or introduce more stringent prior information requirements as long as the requirements are in accordance with Community law.

IX.10 PROTECTIVE REGULATION AND THE INTERNET: THE E-COMMERCE DIRECTIVE

IX.10.1 *The Internet and Investor Protection*

The growth in the use of the Internet in the provision of investment services is, by now, a well-recognized phenomenon.[150] Given their dematerialized nature, the Internet is an attractive marketing and delivery mechanism for investment services and products. One of the most pressing challenges facing the Community is the development of a legal framework for the online investment-services market which accommodates the potentially conflicting interests of market integration and investor protection. Online investment services raise particular investor-protection concerns, in that investors can easily access investment services and initiate transactions with investment firms without being in possession of sufficient information. Indeed, the overconfidence exhibited by certain investors with respect to day trading is a

home-State rules. DG XXIV (health and consumer protection), however, was reported to be of the view that all distance-selling offers should be subject to the control of the host Member State.

[149] At the time of writing, negotiations on the detail of the common position are ongoing. In order to facilitate the negotiation process, particularly with respect to the disclosure rules, the Commission has undertaken an inventory of the various information requirements currently imposed by the Member States: Third Report on Financial Services Priorities and Progress, Nov 2000, COM(2000)692 (the 3rd Progress Report), 18.

[150] On the explosion in e-commerce and the Community response, see generally Dickie, n 118 above.

matter of some regulatory concern.[151] While it is generally accepted that investment-services regulation should be technology neutral,[152] careful application of neutral protective rules is required. In particular, adequate and clear pre-contract disclosure is required. The need for stringent controls on advertising and marketing techniques also arises, given the ease with which potential investors can be targeted over the Internet. The rigorous application of appropriate conduct-of-business rules is essential, given, for example, the danger that a product offered on a generally accessible website may not be suitable for the investor in question.[153] The extent to which the full range of conduct rules has a particular significance for online transactions will depend, of course, on whether online investment services develop beyond the provision of execution-only services, as a wider array of conduct rules apply to the provision of investment advice and discretionary or tailored investment services.[154]

IX.10.2 *The E-commerce Directive*

IX.10.2.1 *Investor Protection as an Objective*

The ECD aims to establish a single market in information-society services by removing legal obstacles to the free movement of information-society services providers and eliminating legal uncertainty by establishing a clear and

---

[151] IOSCO has identified a number of the features of the 'new economy' which provoke concerns. These include the rapid development of short-term trading over the Internet and its impact on investors' risks. It has recommended that investors who trade online be made aware that an order may not be executed more quickly than it would be were it given to a broker in the traditional manner, that investors be clear about the risks and costs involved, and that online brokers, notwithstanding the different relationship they have with investors, continue to be subject to the duty to act in the best interests of the investor: IOSCO New Economy Bulletin, n 5 above.

[152] Principle 1 of the 1998 IOSCO Principles on Securities Trading and the Internet asserts that '[t]he fundamental principles of securities regulation do not change with the medium'. Similarly, the SEC's position on e-mail communications from brokers is that the content and audience of the message are key and not the manner in which it is delivered: Securities Act Release No. 33-7288 (1996) on Use of Electronic Media by Broker-Dealers, Transfer Agents and Investment Advisers for Delivery of Information.

[153] Many investment firms use website access programmes which request the investor to provide information on his or her sophistication and which, based on the information received, tailor the investments or services which the investor may access through the website. In the USA, the NASD has recommended that where investment recommendations are transmitted via e-mail to a wide group of investors of varying sophistication, the suitability of the investment should be assessed in relation to each investor who responds. See generally Bartholomew, D, and Murphy, D, 'The Internet and Securities Regulation: What's Next?' (1997) 25 *Securities Regulation Law Journal* 177. The importance of suitability rules is also stressed by the 1998 IOSCO Principles on Securities Trading and the Internet in Principle 8. The IOSCO New Economy Bulletin highlighted the need for online brokers to comply with conduct-of-business rules, particularly best execution and, where applicable, suitability rules, in an environment in which dealings with investors can occur on a much faster basis: n 5 above, 9.

[154] See the discussion of suitability in sect. 5.2.5 above.

general legal framework for the e-commerce internal market (recitals 5–7 and Article 1). It has the additional aim of striking a balance between the different interests at stake. To that end it takes consumer confidence as an objective of the new legal framework and states that the Directive's provisions must ensure a high level of consumer protection (recitals 7 and 41 and Article 10).[155]

IX.10.2.2 *Disclosure and Marketing Rules*

The main purpose of the ECD is to introduce the Member-State-of-origin principle, whereby online services are regulated only by the Member State in which the provider is established. It applies only to online services; where investment services are supplied partly online and partly by traditional means, it will not apply. Accordingly, it is a regulatory jurisdiction-allocation measure, driven by market-integration concerns, rather than a measure which introduces substantive harmonization. In addition, it is a horizontal measure which does not address investment services specifically. It does, however, introduce some limited harmonization, largely with respect to disclosure and marketing requirements, which, while applicable horizontally to all providers and recipients of online services, may be of some significance for the investor/investment-firm relationship. Unlike the ISD and the Distance Marketing Proposal, most of these protections are not limited to consumers but apply generally to recipients of online services, defined as 'any natural or legal person who for professional ends or otherwise, uses an information society service'(Article 2(d)).

With respect to disclosure, Article 5(1) requires that, in addition to any other information requirements applicable under Community law, the service provider must provide the recipient and the competent authorities with certain basic information, including the name of the service provider, the address at which the provider is established, contact details and, importantly for investment services, the particulars of the relevant supervisory authority where the activity is subject to authorization. In addition, under Article 5(2), Member States must ensure that where information-society services refer to prices, they must be indicated clearly and unambiguously and indicate whether tax is included.

Marketing is addressed by the transparency rules set out in Article 6 which provide that any commercial communications[156] which constitute

---

[155] The ECD's scope and its market integration mechanism are discussed in Ch. VII sect. 11 above.

[156] Defined broadly by Art. 2(f) as any form of communication designed to promote, directly or indirectly, the goods, services or image of the provider. The definition excludes information which allows direct access to the company, such as a domain name or e-mail address and communications relating to the service provider which have been independently compiled.

part of an online service must be clearly identifiable as such, the natural or legal person on whose behalf the commercial communication is made must be clearly identifiable, and promotional offers must be clearly identifiable as such and the conditions required to be met to qualify for them set out clearly. Unsolicited communications are subject to further regulation under Article 7 which, reflecting the treatment of cold calls by the Distance Marketing Proposal, provides that Member States which permit unsolicited commercial communications by e-mail ('spam') must ensure that any such communications by service providers established in their territory are identifiable clearly and unambiguously as soon as they are received by the recipient. Member States are also to take measures to ensure that service providers which send unsolicited e-mails regularly consult and respect the opt-out registers in which natural persons not wishing to receive such communications can register.

The ECD also introduces rules on the conclusion of contracts by electronic means which are designed to ensure that contracts concluded by e-commerce are electronically workable (Articles 9–11).

IX.10.2.3 *Dispute Resolution, Sanctions, and Enforcement*

As with the Distance Marketing Proposal, dispute resolution is addressed, with Article 17 providing that Member States must ensure that the use of out-of-court schemes is not hampered. Member States are also to encourage bodies responsible for out-of-court settlement of consumer disputes to operate in a manner which provides adequate procedural guarantees for the parties concerned.

The adequacy of sanctions for breach of national implementing measures adopted pursuant to the ECD is also addressed, with Article 20 providing that Member States must take all measures necessary to ensure that national requirements are enforced and provide for effective, proportionate, and dissuasive sanctions. Judicial remedies are specifically addressed by Article 18 which requires that court actions must allow for the rapid adoption of measures, including interim measures, in order to terminate any alleged breaches or prevent any further impairment of the interests at stake.

Given the reliance on the Member-State-of-origin principle, Article 19 imposes formal co-operation requirements. Member States are to have adequate means of supervision and investigation and to ensure that they are provided with all necessary information by the service providers. They are also to co-operate with other Member States and provide, in accordance with national law, any assistance and information requested by other Member States or the Commission. Of considerable practical importance for the investor/investment-firm relationship is the requirement imposed on Member States to establish contact points, accessible by electronic means, which set out general information on contractual rights and obligations, complaints and redress mechanisms, and details of any organizations from which further assistance and information can be obtained.

IX.10.2.4 *The Member State of Origin*

Although it is not an investment-services-specific measure, the ECD has important implications for the single market in investment services. Its 'internal market clause' greatly facilitates the ease with which an investment firm can provide online services throughout the EC by placing the supply of investment services online under the control of the Member State of origin (Articles 3 and 4) and freeing the investment firm from compliance with multiple host-Member-State rules.[157] The dangers of applying a horizontal measure to the investment-services sector are clearly illustrated, however, by the uneasy fit between the Member-State-of-origin principle and investment-services market harmonization. Hitherto, while reliance on the close relation of the Member State of origin, the home Member State, has been acknowledged, in the investment-services arena, as the most effective market-integration device, its use has been dependent on a satisfactory level of minimum harmonization in order to ensure both market stability and investor protection. Harmonization of protective investment-services regulation is, as yet, still in its infancy, and, accordingly, the host Member State generally governs protective regulation. The *locus classicus* of this approach is Article 11 of the ISD. By introducing the Member-State-of-origin principle to govern online investment services, the ECD breaks the connection between home-Member-State control and minimum harmonization. While conduct-of-business, marketing, disclosure, and contract-formation rules remain largely unharmonized, the possibility can arise of an investor's stringent domestic investor-protection controls being replaced by less demanding requirements in force in the Member State of origin. The ECD by its terms seems to acknowledge that much still needs to be achieved in this area. Recital 27 states that the Directive only 'contributes' to the construction of a legal framework for online financial services and does not pre-empt future initiatives in the area of financial services, particularly with respect to conduct-of-business rule harmonization. Investment firms may choose to operate their online services from a branch established in a Member State where, perhaps due to domestic savings patterns, investment activity by retail investors is limited and protective rules minimal. The conclusion which can be drawn from this is that, notwithstanding the balancing of interests which

---

[157] The Member State of origin is essentially the Member State in which the service provider is established. This can be the Member State in which the firm has established a branch from which online investment services are provided. See Ch. VII sect. 11 above.

supposedly permeates the ECD, market-integration interests are to the fore.[158]

The difficulties which the Member-State-of-origin principle raises for investor protection are reflected in Article 3(4)(a) which allows Member States to derogate from that principle if, *inter alia*, the measure in question is necessary for 'the protection of consumers, including investors'. Any derogation on grounds of investor protection will be permitted only where the service provided either prejudices investor protection or presents a serious and grave risk of prejudice and the measure imposed is proportionate. Under Article 3(4)(b) (which does not apply in cases of urgency, in which case the Commission and the Member State of origin must simply be notified), before a Member State may impose its investor-protection rules, a Member State must have asked the Member State of origin to take measures and that Member State must either have refused to do so or taken inadequate action and, in addition, have notified the Commission and the Member State of origin of its intention to act. Article 3(4) aside, three other important areas of protective regulation are excluded from the Member-State-of-origin principle by Article 3(3), which provides a derogation from the internal-market clause for the areas listed in the ECD Annex. Contractual obligations concerning consumer contracts and rules concerning the permissibility of unsolicited communications by e-mail are included in the Annex, as are rules concerning the marketing of UCITSs in accordance with Article 44(2) of the UCITS Directive.

Overall, although the Member State of origin has considerable advantages with respect to market integration over the alternative devices of host-Member-State control or the 'significant effects' rule promoted by IOSCO,[159] its application, given the current immature state of protective harmonization, is problematic from the perspective of investor protection. It also adds to the perception that the investor is secondary to the provider of investment services and is regarded more as a beneficiary of the advantages of the single market than as a target for protective measures, although this interpretation must now be regarded in light of the efforts being made to improve the state of protective harmonization.

[158] The hazards of the Member-State-of-origin approach were highlighted during the Directive's passage. In its comments on the Commission's original proposal ECOSOC expressed concern about the risks which the Member-State-of-origin principle posed to consumers [1999] OJ C169/36, paras 3.6.3–3.6.6.

[159] The IOSCO Securities Trading and the Internet Principles (1998) suggest in Principle 15 that if a country can demonstrate that an investment service delivered by the Internet has significant effects on investors or markets in that country, it should impose its rules.

IX.10.3 *The Commission Communication on E-commerce and Financial Services*

As the E-commerce and Financial Services Communication has important implications for the future development of protective regulation in general, it is discussed in section 13.6 below.

IX.11 THE COURT OF JUSTICE, THE GENERAL GOOD, AND PROTECTIVE CONTROLS[160]

IX.11.1 *Investor Protection and the General Good*

Given the limited coverage of protective harmonization, Member States retain considerable control over this area, subject to compliance with the Treaty free-movement guarantees. Accordingly, the Court's articulation of the degree to which Member States can impose protective rules in the interests of the general good, and its assessment of how the increased choice and cost-efficiency benefits to investors of the integration of investment-services markets are to be balanced against the benefits of protective national regulation, is critical to the quality of investor protection in the integrated market.[161] The general-good test, which requires the identification of a legitimate interest for acting and compliance with a proportionality test, was expressed in general terms in *Gebhard* as follows: '[n]ational measures liable to hinder or make less attractive the exercise of the fundamental freedoms guaranteed by the Treaty must fulfil four conditions: they must be applied in a non discriminatory manner; they must be justified by imperative requirements in the general interest; they must be suitable for securing the attainment of the objective which they pursue; and they must not go beyond what is necessary in order to attain that objective'.[162] It has also been consistently held that the general-good interest must not be protected by duplicate rules in the service provider's home Member State and that the restrictive measure must not already have been harmonized.

---

[160] See further Moloney, N, 'Investor Protection and the Treaty: An Uneasy Relationship' in Ferrarini, G, Hopt, K, and Wymeersch, E (eds), *Capital Markets in the Age of the Euro* (forthcoming), on which this discussion is based.

[161] On the general-good test see generally Ch. VI sect. 4.6.2 above. As noted by Weatherill in the free movement of goods context, 'the perception that the law of product market integration is designed to serve the consumer interest by breeding more efficient market structures has met its sharpest test in case law which has pitted the consumer interest in market integration and deregulation against the consumer interest in market regulation, albeit at national level': Weatherill, S, 'Recent Case Law Concerning the Free Movement of Goods: Mapping the Frontiers of Market Deregulation' (1999) 36 *CMLRev.* 51, 54.

[162] Case C–55/94 *Gebhard v Consiglio dell'Ordine degli Avvocati e Procuratori di Milano* [1995] ECR 4165, para 37.

While the protection of the consumer of complex financial products and services was accepted as a general-good interest in the *German Insurance* case,[163] in its ruling the Court characterized consumer protection as an interest which varied depending on the complexities of the financial product involved and the sophistication of the consumer. As a result, the extent to which consumer protection can, based on the *German Insurance* case, encompass the protection of investors as a class of consumers is somewhat unclear. Investor protection has yet to be directly accepted by the Court as a discrete interest which can be protected in the interests of the general good; nor has it examined the specific interests which investor protection incorporates. Investor protection was not addressed until the Court's 1995 ruling in *Alpine Investments*,[164] and then only in a tangential manner. The case concerned a challenge by a Dutch commodity broker to a Dutch rule prohibiting the making of cold calls to potential clients on the ground that the prohibition restricted the freedom of the broker to provide services to investors in other Member States. Investor protection arose indirectly in the context of the protection of investors in other Member States in respect of activities carried out from the Netherlands. Immediately apparent from the Court's analysis is the connection it makes between investor protection and investor confidence. Noting that financial markets play an important role in the financing of economic operators and the speculative nature and complexity of commodities derivatives, it found that 'the smooth operation of financial markets is largely dependent on the confidence they inspire in investors' and that confidence 'depends in particular on the existence of professional regulations serving to ensure the competence and trustworthiness of the financial intermediaries on whom investors are particularly reliant'.[165] While the Netherlands could not justify the measure by raising the protection of investors in other Member States, the Court found that the nature and extent of that protection in the Netherlands did have a direct effect on the good reputation of Dutch financial services, and that protection of that reputation could amount to a general-good interest. Investor protection can accordingly be pursued under the general-good rule as a function of market reputation.[166] The other major investment-services case to date, *Commission v Italy*,[167] contains only limited guidance on how the Treaty interacts with national investor-protection rules. While Italy argued that the contested legislation served the protection of general interests including investor protection as well as the stability of the capital markets, the Court

---

[163] Case 205/84 *Commission v Germany* [1986] ECR 3755 (the *German Insurance* case).
[164] N 38 above.   [165] Ibid, para 42.
[166] This characterization might not necessarily stunt the development of investor protection as a general-good justification. See the Annotation by Hatzopoulos, V, in (1995) 32 *CMLRev.* 1427, 1443.
[167] Case C–101/94 *Commission v Italy* [1996] ECR I–2691.

did not further examine whether investor protection constituted a 'general-good' interest or highlight the particular objectives which must be served by investor-protection measures in order to be legitimate,[168] confining its analysis to whether the legislation was necessary and proportionate. Justifications linked to market reputation are, accordingly, the safer ones for a Member State to raise, although the protection of ill-informed investors will surely also be accepted,[169] not least because of the connection between the two.

The *German Insurance* case suggests that it will be, although the complexities of the investment service or product and the features of the investor are likely to be critical factors. The Court in that case referred to the complexities of insurance contracts and to the imbalances in the relationship between the insured and the insurer which gave rise to a general-good interest in regulating the financial condition of the insured and the terms of insurance contracts. It also found that these concerns would not always be paramount, and that the nature of the risks insured and the party seeking insurance could obviate the need for protection. This differentiated approach, which the Court has also adopted in the banking field,[170] was a feature of *Alpine Investments*, where the Court made clear that the application of the general-good justification will be influenced by the specific characteristics of the particular market, the type of person protected by the restrictive measure, and the degree of risk at issue. The Court laid considerable emphasis on the fact that the ban concerned highly complex commodity futures and that it was designed to protect non-expert investors who were likely to find the commodities market 'barely comprehensible'.[171] Similarly, in concluding that the restrictive Italian rules imposed on foreign securities firms were in breach of the Treaty and not justified by the general-good rule in his Opinion in *Commission v Italy*, Advocate General Lenz distinguished between the 'private customer' protected by the restrictive rules in *Alpine Investments* and the 'economic operators or organisations who are familiar with the sector and are not defenceless before the bargaining power of financial institutions', who were the likely clients of the regulated investment firms and who were protected by the restrictive Italian requirements.[172] He

---

[168] Although in his Opinion, Lenz AG accepted that 'the "protection of investors, stability of the markets and the transparency of dealing" which the Italian government invokes, are indisputably worth protecting. The question is only whether the contested provision is suitable for pursuing those aims, and, if so, whether it is proportionate': ibid, para 46.

[169] See Van Gerven, W, and Wouters, J, 'Free Movement of Financial Services and the European Contracts Convention' in Andenas, M, and Kenyon-Slade, S (eds), *EC Financial Market Regulation and Company Law* (1993) 65 and Katz, S, 'The Second Banking Directive' (1992) 12 *YBEL* 249, 291.

[170] Case C-222/95 *Banque de Bary v Parodi* [1997] ECR I-3899, para 20.

[171] As did Jacobs AG in his Opinion, n 38 above, para 71.

[172] N 167 above, Opinion of the AG, para 83.

went so far as to say that 'the consumer who deserves protection, in the person of the private saver, does not appear in deals of this type'.[173] Although a differentiated approach which excluded the wholesale sector completely would be insensitive to market realities, given that wholesale investors have shown themselves on occasion to be as equally ill-equipped as retail investors to assess the complexities and risks attendant on investing in certain securities, it is clear, at a minimum, that the nature of the investor protected is likely to appear as a filter (one mandated by Article 11 of the ISD in any event in relation to conduct regulation) on the restrictive measures that a Member State may impose. In this regard, investor-specific investment-services regulation, which discriminates on two counts (the nature of the protected person and the type of services market involved) might benefit from what has been described as the Court's tendency to be influenced by 'the fact that the regulator had already unpicked the universal category of the consumer and chosen to protect a specific group' and the fact that broad-brush regulatory approaches seem to be 'vulnerable to the Court's perception that most consumers are sufficiently robust and well-informed to take care of themselves in the marketplace'.[174]

It is also clear from the Court's blunt analysis of Italy's justification in *Commission v Italy* that, notwithstanding the leeway it appears to grant Member States in financial regulation, it is prepared to grapple with the complex interplay of interests and regulation in this area and that investor protection will not be allowed to act as a mask for protectionist measures.

Finally, *Alpine Investments* makes clear that the Court will not lightly sacrifice Member State choices regarding the appropriate level of investor protection to the Treaty free-movement provisions and the internal market. In particular, Member States need not comply with the lowest standards applicable across the EC when applying their protective rules in order to comply with Treaty obligations.[175] Rejecting the defendant's arguments in *Alpine Investments* that other Member States simply required the recording of cold calls and did not impose an outright ban, the Court held that the fact that one Member State imposed less strict rules than another did not mean that the stricter rules were disproportionate and in violation of Treaty obligations. Inherent in the Court's position appears to be the argument that a requirement to align with the lowest standards in place might compromise investor confidence.[176] In this respect, the Treaty free-movement rules can be read as sustaining, in the absence of harmonization, different national models of protective regulation, each of which responds to different market cultures and structures, within the integrated market.

---

[173] Ibid, para 84.   [174] Weatherill, n 161 above, 58–9.

[175] See also Cases 286/81 *Oosthoek's Uitgeversmaatschappij* [1982] ECR 4575 and C–3/95 *Reisebüro Broede v Gerd Sandker* [1996] ECR I–6511.

[176] See the Opinion of Jacobs AG, n 38 above, para 90.

IX.11.2 *Particular Protective Mechanisms and the General Good*

For the most part, it remains to be seen which protective mechanisms, where they are not yet harmonized and so are eligible for the general-good jurisdiction, will be encompassed within the model of acceptable national investor protection being developed by the Court under the Treaty free-movement rules and the general-good rule. The non-harmonized protective rules most likely to be considered under the general-good rules include, for example, marketing rules outside the scope of the limited harmonization of the Distance Marketing Proposal and the ISD (such as detailed cold-calling rules and pre-vetting requirements) and specific conduct rules (such as dealing rules and disclosure rules with respect to fees and expenses and risk warnings).

In all cases, the proportionality requirements as to the suitability of the restrictive measure to attain the objective in question and its necessity, as well as the non-duplication condition, must be met. This may be difficult given that the Court has shown that it places considerable faith in the effectiveness of co-operation and communication between supervisors as an alternative to restrictive rules, it can be sceptical of arguments based on the non-comparability of other Member State rules, finding that comparisons can be made where other methods are equivalent overall, even if not as protective on a case-by-case basis, and it is quite ready to suggest alternative mechanisms of investor protection.[177]

Since *Alpine Investments*[178] it appears that marketing rules can be applied to cross-border activity by the Member State of origin, at least where market reputation is at stake. *Buet* might suggest that restrictive rules for the protection of investors in door-to-door sales of securities could be justifiable on grounds of investor protection (this seems to be implicit in recital 8 of the ISD, in any event). Although the case concerned the free movement of goods and a French prohibition on doorstep sales of English-language educational products, the Court's ruling that the prohibition was justified on consumer-protection grounds, given that purchasers of educational products were particularly vulnerable to doorstep sales, could be transposed to the investment-services sector.[179] The Court may not always, however, accept investor protection as a general-good justification in the marketing sphere. *GB-INNO-BM*,[180] where the Court found that trade-restrictive rules which prevented consumers from accessing information could not be justified on grounds of consumer protection, given that Community consumer-

---

[177] *Commission v Italy*, n 167 above, paras 16–18, 23, and 24.
[178] N 38 above.   [179] Case 382/87 *Buet v Ministère Publique* [1989] ECR 1235.
[180] Case C-362/88 *GB-INNO-BM v Confédération du Commerce Luxembourgeois* [1990] ECR I-667. See also Case C-126/91 *Schutzverband gegen Unwesen in der Wirtschaft eV v Yves Rocher GmbH* [1993] ECR I-2361.

protection policy linked protection to the provision of information, suggests that investment firms advertising in other Member States may not be subject to advertising restrictions which limit the information made available (such as prohibitions on past performance figures or predictions). This ruling should, however, be read subject to the special considerations that apply in the investment-services sector in respect of the ability of investors to interpret often complex information.[181] In this respect, the general tendency of the Court to assume that a consumer is capable of making an informed choice once supplied with the relevant information and to strike down overly protective trade-restrictive rules where the consumer is adequately informed[182] may not translate well to the investment-services area. The model of the investor as a rational decoder of disclosure is, indeed, balanced by the Court's acceptance in *Alpine Investments* of restrictive marketing rules which remove the investor from potentially risky decision-making contexts in which the ability to decode information may be impeded.

IX.12 INVESTOR PROTECTION AND THE TREATY

IX.12.1 *The Problem*

As illustrated by the foregoing review of protective regulation at EC level, a number of gaps can be identified in the EC investment-services regime with respect to protective harmonization, notably in areas of marketing, conduct-of-business regulation, disclosure, contract formation, and dispute resolution. Further harmonization of protective measures in order to enhance investor protection, which is already under discussion in the conduct area, faces a fundamental difficulty, however, in that the promotion of investor protection is not of itself a specific Treaty competence.[183]

IX.12.2 *Article 47(2) EC*

IX.12.2.1 *Diverging Rules, Free Movement, and Investor Protection*

As the basis for the ISD, Article 47(2) EC is the dominant Treaty competence in the investment-services area; it has also been used, along with Article 95 EC, as the basis for the Distance Marketing Proposal. It is designed to

---

[181] The new UCITS prospectus regime also reflects this concern. See Ch. V.

[182] On the Court's rather bracing view of the consumer's ability to deal with information and avoid confusion see Case 407/85 *Drei Glocken v USL Centro-Sud* [1988] ECR 4233, Case C–315/92 *Verband Sozialer Wettbewerb eV v Clinique Laboratories SNC* [1994] ECR I–317, Case C–470/93 *Verein gegen Unwesen in Handel und Gewerbe Köln eV v Mars GmbH* [1995] ECR I–1923, Case C–210/96 *Gut Springenheide* [1998] ECR I–4657, and Case C–303/97 *Verbraucherschutzverein eV v Sketkellerei GC Kessler GmbH und Co* [1999] ECR I–513.

[183] See further Moloney, n 160 above.

facilitate the freedom to establish (and applies to the freedom to provide services via Article 55 EC) and provides for the co-ordination of Member States' laws with respect to the taking-up and pursuit of activities as self-employed persons. It has been described by the Court as permitting the adoption of measures which 'contribute to the abolition of obstacles to free movement which may result in particular from a divergence between the provisions laid down by law, regulation or administrative action in Member States concerning the taking-up and pursuit of activities as self-employed persons'.[184] Harmonization under Article 47(2) involves liberalization, through the reduction of the panoply of Member State rules to one common standard, and reregulation, through the adoption of common rules which reflect Member States' regulatory priorities and make liberalization possible by governing the liberalized market-place. Thus, although the formal, constitutional purpose of Article 47(2) in the investment-services area is to remove regulatory obstacles to the free movement of investment-services providers, an important side-effect has been the adoption of a limited harmonized protective regime as part of the strategy for reregulating the investment-services single market.

While investor protection *per se* is not a justification for the adoption of protective rules under Article 47(2) EC, investor-protection harmonization can be justified where either the diversity or obstructive nature of the investor-protection rules which regulate the pursuit of investment-services activity in other Member States restricts free movement. The restrictive effect of marketing rules banning cold-calling was noted in *Alpine Investments*, while the Commission has noted the obstacles to free movement created by marketing rules as well as by protective rules such as disclosure and contract-based rules.[185] A case for a more intensive minimum harmonization of conduct rules could be based on a similar argument, not only due to divergences in the content of conduct rules and the costs involved in complying with a series of different regimes which could impede market access, but also due to variations in the way conduct rules may be enforced against investment firms by investors across the EC and the consequent legal costs.[186] While the harmonization case may be more difficult to sustain, given the connection between conduct rules and local market conditions, some degree

---

[184] Case C-233/94 *Germany v Parliament and Council* [1997] ECR I-2405 (the *Deposit Guarantee* case), para 15. Similarly, the AG in his Opinion in that case described co-ordination under Art. 47(2) EC in terms of 'eliminating any differences which constitute unjustified obstacles': Opinion of Léger AG, para 40.

[185] FSAP, n 43 above, 7-9. Earlier, in the Green Paper on Commercial Communications, the Commission had noted the difficulties caused by disparities in the rules governing commercial communications for financial services, particularly pre-vetting rules: n 118 above, 28.

[186] For a discussion of how diverging conduct rules can raise compliance costs and cause conflicts between rules see generally Avougleas, n 37 above, 76-85 and the Art. 11 Communication, n 39 above, 11.

of consensus can be observed with respect to conflicts-of-interests rules and dealing rules which might, accordingly, be susceptible to harmonization.[187]

The validity of further protective harmonization under Article 47(2) EC is, however, open to to challenge. Where the harmonized rules appear to enhance levels of protection across the EC rather than simply remove obstacles and smooth out divergences that impede free movement, reliance on Article 47(2) EC may be prejudiced. The Court has on occasion taken quite a broad approach, however, to the harmonization permissible under Article 47(2). In the *Deposit Guarantee* case Germany challenged the Deposit Guarantee Directive,[188] which harmonizes at a minimum level the requirements applicable to deposit-protection schemes across the Community, on the grounds that, *inter alia*, the DGD's basis in Article 47(2) was incorrect as the DGD went beyond the objective of market integration by seeking to increase the level of depositor protection across the Community. This was an objective divorced from market integration and could only be implemented under Article 308 EC, the general enabling clause.[189] Finding that Article 47(2) was an appropriate basis in that the effect of the DGD was to prevent Member States from invoking depositor protection in order to impede the activities of credit institutions authorized in other Member States and to eliminate fundamental differences between deposit-protection schemes, the Court also stressed that, in eliminating obstacles to free movement, the Community was to have regard to the public-interest aims of the various Member States and to adopt a level of protection for those interests which seemed acceptable in the Community. The judgment suggests that as long as divergences between rules are creating an obstacle to the operation of the internal market and to free movement the Community may, under Article 47(2), adopt measures which, as well as removing barriers to free movement, reregulate in order to reflect the public interest behind the restrictive measures and adopt a Community level of protection for that interest.[190] One other point significant for protective harmonization can be drawn from the ruling. Although the Court does not emphasize the point, it appears from the ruling that the Court assumed that consumer protection is relevant to the free- movement objectives of Article 47(2) EC. Germany had challenged

---

[187] For an argument questioning whether harmonization is necessary in practice see Hertig, n 41 above, 184–5. In light of the Court's ruling in the *Tobacco Advertising* case (n 194 below), arguments based on the practical impact of conduct-rule divergences on the internal market will have considerable force in the future.

[188] Directive 94/19/EC [1994] OJ L135/5 (the DGD).

[189] Unlike Art. 47(2) EC this required a unanimous vote of the Council (effectively giving Germany a veto).

[190] Léger AG noted that an increase in protection was a natural consequence of harmonization and that it would require a distinct legal basis only 'if it did not, on the contrary, appear as part of a general systematic aim of coordinating legislation, which improved the position of certain depositors only as an additional effect': n 84 above, para 51.

the DGD's controversial export ban (now defunct but which, when the DGD was adopted, prevented passporting credit institutions from offering higher levels of deposit protection than were available in the host Member State) on the grounds that it disadvantaged savers in Member States in which a minimal level of cover was available who held deposits at a branch of a credit institution authorized in a Member State which required a higher level of protection. This rule, per the German argument, was contrary to the Treaty objective of achieving a high level of consumer protection (Article 3(t) EC (activities of the Community include contributing to the strengthening of consumer protection) and Article 153 EC (competence to promote consumer interests and ensure a high level of consumer protection via Article 95 EC and via measures to support, supplement and monitor the policy pursued by the Member States)). Even though Article 153 does not refer to Article 47(2) the Court found that while the DGD 'aims to promote the right of establishment and the freedom to provide services in the banking sector . . . there must be a high level of consumer protection concomitantly with those freedoms'.[191] It appears therefore that while free movement is the engine for Article 47(2), consumer-protection concerns (and, it seems, investor-protection interests) cannot be disregarded. This approach seems to be mandated, in any event, by Article 153(2) EC, which provides that consumer-protection requirements 'shall be taken into account in defining and implementing other Community policies and activities'.[192] The Court also made clear, however, that consumer protection is not the sole objective of the Community and that the Community legislature was not obliged to adopt the highest level of protection prevailing in a Member State.[193]

The Court has recently revealed, however, that it will not always accept that the divergences between national rules which a harmonizing measure is designed, in theory, to remove exist in practice. In its judgment in the *Tobacco Advertising* case (see further section 12.3 below)[194] the Court sounded a note of caution.[195] While the Court found that Article 47(2) addresses measures 'intended to make it easier for persons to take up and pursue activities by way of services' and noted that as a result it 'confers on the Community legislature specific power to adopt measures intended to

---

[191] Para 48.

[192] See also Roth, W-H, Annotation of Deposit Guarantee Case (1998) 35 *CMLRev.* 459, 465, and 472–3. He suggested at 473 that the Court's approach is correct in so far as any differentiation between Art. 95EC (which, under Art. 153(3)(a) EC, can be used to attain the consumer-protection objectives of Art. 153 EC) and Art. 47(2) EC is unjustified.

[193] Para 48.

[194] Case C–376/98 *Germany v Parliament and Council* [2000] ECR I–8419 (the *Tobacco Advertising* case).

[195] Although the Court focused primarily on the scope of and limits to Art. 95 EC as a legal basis for harmonizing measures, it stated that its findings with respect to Art. 95 EC also applied to Art. 47(2) EC and Art. 55 EC: para 87.

improve the functioning of the internal market',[196] it is clear from the ruling that unless disparities between protective rules have a real and obstructive impact on the exercise of the Treaty free-movement guarantees, the Court will not look kindly on the simple existence of disparities *per se* as a ground for harmonization.

IX.12.2.2 *Article 47(2) EC and Subsidiarity*

While neither the Treaty in general, nor Article 47(2) in particular, mandates the level at which or form in which protective harmonization should occur, the Article 5 EC subsidiarity doctrine has a bearing on this question. Article 5(2) requires that in areas in which the Community does not have exclusive competence, the Community must take action in accordance with the subsidiarity principle, such that action may be taken only where the objectives of the proposed action cannot be sufficiently achieved by the Member States and, by reason of the scale and effects of the proposed action, are better achieved by the Community. Categorizing an area of activity as one in which the Community has exclusive competence (and as falling outside the scope of the subsidiarity doctrine) is a bedevilled question. The view has been expressed that the Community has exclusive competence with respect to actions taken in order to implement the freedom to establish and to provide services under Article 47(2).[197] Indeed, the Commission is of the opinion that it has exclusive competence with respect to the removal of barriers to the free movement of goods, persons, services, and capital.[198] The Distance Marketing Proposal, while based on Article 47(2), nonetheless refers to the subsidiarity principle, stating in recital 11 that 'the objectives of this Directive cannot be sufficiently achieved by the Member States and can therefore be better achieved by the Community' due to the impediments which the adoption by Member States of diverging consumer-protection rules governing distance marketing could place on the functioning of the

---

[196] Ibid.

[197] See Léger AG in the *Deposit Guarantee* case, n 184 above, para 82. See also Toth, A, 'A Legal Analysis of Subsidiarity' in O'Keeffe, D, and Twomey, P (eds), *Legal Issues of the Maastricht Treaty* (1994) 37, 39–43, who is of the view that subsidiarity cannot apply to any matter covered by the original EEC Treaty and, in particular, to the development of the internal market. For the more restrictive view that the Community has exclusive competence only in those areas in which it has already legislated see Steiner, J, 'Subsidiarity under the Maastricht Treaty' in ibid, 49, 55–8 and the arguments of the German government in the *Deposit Guarantee* case, Opinion of the AG, para 79. See also Emiliou, N, 'Subsidiarity: Panacea or Fig Leaf' in O'Keeffe and Twomey (above), 65, 74–5 and Schilling, T, 'A New Dimension of Subsidiarity: Subsidiarity as a Rule and a Principle' (1994) 14 *YBEL* 203, 217–32. On the view that conduct harmonization designed to give effect to the freedom to provide services or the freedom to establish is within the exclusive competence of the Community see Köndgen, n 36 above, 123.

[198] The Principle of Subsidiarity, COM Doc SEC(92) 1990, 27 Oct 195, 5. See also the Commission's 1994 *Report to the European Council on the Application of the Subsidiarity Principle* (the 1994 Subsidiarity Report) COM(94)533, 3.

internal market and on competition between firms. Similarly, the ECD, which is based on Article 47(2), as well as Article 55 and Article 95, notes in recital 6 that by 'clarifying certain legal concepts at Community level to the extent necessary for the proper functioning of the internal market [and] by dealing only with certain specific matters which give rise to problems for the internal market, this Directive is fully consistent with the principle of subsidiarity'.[199] The difficulties with the sphere of application of the doctrine suggest that any harmonization of protective rules under Article 47(2) would be more safely undertaken in compliance with the subsidiarity doctrine. On the application of the subsidiarity principle and the difficulties further harmonization of protective rules may involve in relation to the 'sufficiently achieved' and 'scale and effects' elements of the subsidiarity principle see section 13.5 below.

IX.12.3 *Articles 94 and 95 EC*

The second source for protective harmonization has been the pair of general internal-market provisions—Articles 94 and 95 EC. These provisions have been relied on as the legal basis for a series of general consumer-protection measures, including the Misleading Advertising Directive, the Unfair Contract Terms Directive, the ECD, and the Distance Marketing Proposal. Articles 94 and 95 provide for the adoption of directives which approximate laws which directly affect the establishment or functioning of the common market (Article 94) or for the adoption of measures to approximate laws which have as their object the establishment or functioning of the internal market (Article 95). A fundamental difference between both provisions is that Article 95 provides for the adoption of measures by a qualified majority vote of the Council while Article 94 requires unanimity. As with Article 47(2) EC, the subsidiarity doctrine falls to be considered here. While the competence of the Community with respect to the development of the internal market has been characterized as an area of exclusive competence,[200] the extent to which exclusive competence is at stake is even more debatable than with respect to Article 47(2) given, in particular, that Article 95(4) specifically envisages the possibility of Member State action in certain circumstances, even when the area in question has been harmonized under Article 95.

---

[199] The Court's approach to whether the DGD complied with the duty to give reasons in the *Deposit Guarantee* ruling also seems to suggest that compliance with the subsidiarity principle is required under Art. 47(2) EC: n 184 above, paras 24–29. See also Roth, n 192 above, at 468, who has noted additionally that the subsidiarity principle fulfils an important function in dampening a tendency towards over-regulation in the internal-market sphere.

[200] See, eg, the Commission's Explanatory Memorandum to its proposal for a directive on settlement finality and collateral security, COM(96)193, where at 2 it describes Art. 100A EC (now Art. 95 EC) in terms of exclusive competence.

Although now somewhat obsolete since the adoption of Article 95, Article 94 EC has been used as a basis for harmonizing consumer-protection laws on the grounds that divergences between national rules distort competition and affect the functioning of the common market (Misleading Advertising Directive). This connection between affecting the functioning of the common market and the removal of distortions to competition caused by differences between Member States' laws, gives it a potentially wide reach, given that almost all divergences between national rules can be argued to distort competition in the internal market,[201] although the impact of the *Tobacco Advertising* ruling must now be considered.

Like Article 94, Article 95 EC has acted as a source for harmonizing measures on the potentially elastic ground that disparities between Member State laws can result in distortions to competition (Unfair Contract Terms Directive and Distance Marketing Proposal). It represents, however, a comparatively richer seam to be mined for protective harmonization rules than Article 94. Article 94 harmonization has largely avoided engaging with the investment-services sector, as illustrated by the Doorstep Selling Directive. It is also secondary in importance to Article 95 owing to its unanimity requirement. Further, while the sole consideration behind Article 94 harmonization is the effective functioning of the internal market, Article 95 allows under Article 95(3) for direct cognizance to be taken of consumer protection in the adoption of internal-market legislation. It provides that the Commission in its Article 95 proposals, which concern consumer protection, is to take as a base a high level of protection. Similarly, Article 153(3)(a) EC requires the Community to contribute to the promotion of the interests of consumers and to ensure a high level of consumer protection through the adoption of measures adopted under Article 95 in the context of the completion of the internal market. As it applies 'save where otherwise provided in this Treaty' Article 95 may be used, however, only where Article 47(2) is not the appropriate legal basis or does not cover all the rules harmonized by the measure. Thus, investor-redress and dispute-resolution procedures could come under Article 95 as they do not, it is suggested, come within the sphere of rules which govern the taking-up and pursuit of business by self-employed persons envisaged by Article 47(2). The Distance Marketing Proposal relies on Article 95 in addition to Article 47(2), primarily, it is suggested, as certain of its more general proposals (eg dispute resolution) extend beyond the harmonization of rules applicable to the taking-up and pursuit of business. Market integration still dominates as the objective of Article 95 harmonization, however, as shown by the Court's finding in the *Deposit Guarantee* case that, even though the DGD had the effect of reducing deposit-protection in

[201] Usher, J, *The Law of Money and Financial Services in the European Community* (2nd edn, 2000) 109.

certain Member States, consumer protection was simply one of the Community's objectives and the DGD's policy of market integration was valid.

Articles 94 and 95 EC have not, so far, contributed significantly to protective harmonization. They have produced, for the most part, general consumer-protection measures, although the Distance Marketing Proposal is directed to consumers of financial services, if not investors. What does emerge from the harmonization choices made under these Treaty provisions is a focus on advance disclosure of contractual terms and material information as a means of enhancing choice and thereby promoting competition and the functioning of the internal market (Distance Marketing Proposal).[202] Beyond disclosure, an emphasis on regulating marketing techniques that might prejudice rational choice and decision-making (Misleading Advertising Directive and Distance Marketing Proposal) can also be noted. With the exception of the Unfair Contract Terms Directive and, more recently, the Distance Marketing Proposal, both of which (to different degrees) impose requirements on the substance of the contractual relationship, harmonization has tended to treat the consumer as a rational decision-maker by enhancing disclosure and has not intervened proactively in the consumer's relationships with suppliers to address any substantive unfairness in the contract. Although marketing and disclosure rules play an important role in enhancing investor protection and, in particular, dovetail with the model of the investor as rational capital supplier and beneficiary of enhanced choice, they place a high degree of reliance on the protection of the investor through disclosure. In this respect they are not entirely sensitive to the peculiar characteristics of the investor/firm relationship, the varying abilities of unsophisticated investors to decipher disclosure and the role played by interventionist conduct regulation in investor protection, all of which could be further developed under Articles 47(2) and 95 EC in combination. More generally, Article 95 clearly has significant potential in developing cross-border dispute-resolution and redress procedures for investors in receipt of cross-border services, given the ease with which rule harmonization in this area could be shown to affect the establishment and functioning of the internal market.[203]

Any role which Article 95 EC may play in the development of harmonized protective rules must now be considered in light of the Court's ruling in the *Tobacco Advertising* case, the seismic effects of which are likely to reverber-

---

[202] Another disclosure measure which impacts more tangentially on the investor/investment-firm relationship is the Cross-Border Credit Transfers Directive (Directive 97/5/EC [1997] OJ L43/25). Based on Art. 95 EC, it harmonizes, *inter alia*, rules on the information which must be disclosed before and after a credit transfer.

[203] The FSAP specifically adverts to the role of Art. 95 EC in framing single-market legislation which has as its basis a high level of consumer protection: n 43 above, 15.

ate for some time to come, and which could have considerable consequences for investment-services regulation, given the signs that the EC regime appears to be moving into a market-regulation phase in the wake of the initial market-liberalization phase.[204] Although the Court had previously indicated that Article 95 EC is not an endlessly malleable legal basis,[205] in this ruling it forcefully set out the limitations on Article 95. It found that the 'measures referred to in Article 100a(1) EC [Article 95] are intended to improve the conditions for the establishment and functioning of the internal market. To construe that it vests in the Community a general power to regulate the internal market would not only be contrary to the express meaning of [Articles 3(1)(c) and 14 EC] but would also be incompatible with the principle . . . that the powers of the Community are limited to those specifically conferred on it'.[206] It went on to find that a measure adopted under Article 95 must genuinely have as its object the improvement of the conditions for the establishment and functioning of the internal market and warned that a mere finding of disparities between national rules and of the abstract risk of obstacles to the Treaty free-movement guarantees or of distortions to competition, would not suffice. The Court specifically addressed the connection between Article 95 and the removal of distortions to competition, which has hitherto been used somewhat perfunctorily as a justification for Article 95 consumer-protection measures, finding that such distortions must be 'appreciable', as otherwise, as divergences in national laws usually had an impact, albeit often minimal, on competition, the 'powers of the Community legislature would be practically unlimited'.[207] Reliance on Article 95 in the area of investor protection will thus require careful consideration of the impact of the measure on the functioning of the internal market in investment services. Measures which are in reality designed to regulate the market in the interests of investor protection, while nominally removing divergences between national rules, may face an

---

[204] N 194 above.

[205] Case C-155/91 *Commission v Council* (*Framework Directive on Waste*) [1993] ECR I-939, para 19.

[206] N 194 above, para 83.

[207] Ibid, para 107. The significance of the ruling has been described in an editorial to the *CMLRev.* as follows: '[t]he great importance of the judgment . . . lies in the fact that the Court actually exercises its powers to check whether the conditions for the power to enact legislation on the basis of Article 95 (ex 100a) have been met; it resists the temptation to practice judicial restraint vis-à-vis the Council and Parliament, not leaving it to these institutions to check whether the preconditions of the relevant legal bases are fulfilled. The Court becomes serious on the *limits of competences* [emphasis in original]' and '[h]armonization can no longer be taken as an end in itself. All legislative measures will have to pass a test of judicial scrutiny as to whether the purported object is *actually* [emphasis in original] pursued by the legislative measures . . . The competence relating to the establishment and the functioning of the internal market does not allow overly broad legislation going beyond the specific obstacles or appreciable distortions in a specific fact-setting': 'Editorial Comments. Taking (the Limits of) Competences Seriously' (2000) 37 *CMLRev.* 1301, 1303, and 1304, respectively.

uncertain future unless they also meet the *Tobacco Advertising* ruling's market-based criteria.

IX.12.4 *Beyond the Internal Market: Investor Confidence and Article 153 EC*

IX.12.4.1 *Advantages*

It appears therefore that while Articles 47(2), 94, and 95 EC all allow for the harmonization of investor-protection rules as a by-product of market integration, and while consumer-protection and investor-protection concerns should be 'taken into account' (Article 153(2) EC) and, in relation to Article 95, pursued under that competence (as long as the internal market link is preserved (Article 153(3)(a) EC)), investor protection as a coherent EC policy of itself, divorced from internal-market considerations, does not appear to be justifiable under these provisions.

Specific competence with respect to investor protection would allow a harmonized protective regime to develop with an overall coherence, designed to respond to the investor-protection needs of the integrated market, rather than to be simply an agent for its construction. Greater focus could be trained on the protection needs of the investor rather than on, as is the current position, the free-movement rights of the investment firm and the enhancing of the investor's position as a beneficiary of enhanced choice and competition. Such harmonization would also enhance the position of investors subject to an investor-protection regime (either their own domestic regime or the regime of another Member State which may apply to them via jurisdiction-allocation rules) whose regulatory traditions and cultures might result in sub-optimal protection in the integrated market-place.

The lack of an explicit investor-protection competence also appears to be influencing a creeping movement towards more diffuse and undirected harmonization, which either addresses 'consumers of financial services' generally or the manner in which services are delivered (such as the ECD), or is designed to address a combination of both, as exemplified by the Distance Marketing Proposal. If this trend continues, it may not augur well for investor protection. Merging the interests of investors with those of financial-services consumers generally may ultimately dilute the special degree of protection needed by investors. The common concerns raised by distance selling as a method of marketing financial services do certainly lend themselves to a single treatment. The degree of complexity, commitment, and risk faced by consumers of financial products and services does, however, vary widely. The Distance Marketing Proposal assimilates the interests of investors in relatively complex investment products, such as transferable securities and collective-investment schemes, with those of consumers buying mortgages, placing cash on deposit, entering into consumer-credit loans, and taking out health-insurance and life-assurance policies. While the Proposal's advance disclosure requirements, for example, are to be supplemented by the specialized requirements of the sectoral directives although the Council Draft is more tailored to investment services, the ISD, the predominant sectoral measure for investors, does not at present impose specific requirements as to disclosure in the firm/investor relationship. In the future, if investors and consumers of standard financial services or products such as bank deposits or mortgages are subject to the same protective measures, the need to find the lowest common denominator may result over time in a downgrading of protection at EC level. With respect to the trend towards technology or mode of delivery-specific legislation, while it can be explained on the ground of the link between the encouragement of e-commerce and the development of the single market, it seems somewhat eccentric to have a set of marketing, disclosure, and contract-formation rules apply to the investor/investment-firm relationship but only in the context of distance sales when their protections are equally necessary in face-to-face transactions, given the principle of technology-neutral regulation (see sections 13.6. and 13.7 below on the measures being taken to address these imbalances).

IX.12.4.2 *Article 95 EC and Investor Confidence*

While Article 95 EC is an internal market competence, it may be open to an interpretation which allows for more extensive investor-protection harmonization by switching the internal market focus of Article 95 from the investment firm to the investor. As outlined at the outset of this chapter, investor protection is often connected with the promotion of investor confidence. Article 95 could be regarded as the legal basis for protective measures which promote investor confidence in the single market and thereby enhance its functioning, but are not necessarily linked to the removal of obstructions to free movement.[208]

Whether the restrictive approach the Court has taken to Article 95 EC in the *Tobacco Advertising* case means that investor confidence, of itself, is sufficient to bring a harmonization measure within the scope of Article 95 remains to be seen. Certainly, the case suggests an emphasis on the removal of genuine obstacles to free movement and real distortions to competition.[209]

---

[208] See Weatherill, n 53 above, 716–20. He has argued at 718 that 'the vital element of breeding confidence among both consumers and traders in the viability of the integrated market' could be considered as coming within the scope of Art. 95 EC. See also Stuyck, n 53 above, 395–7.

[209] N 194 above, para 84. In para 95 the Court seems to regard the Art. 95 analysis solely in terms of whether the contested measure eliminates obstacles to free movement or removes distortions to competition. This approach is also taken by Fennelly AG in para 93 of his Opinion where he states that the internal market qualification must be satisfied by the existence of diverging rules which obstruct free movement or distort competition.

The Court did not, however, directly address harmonization which promotes the establishment and functioning of the internal market via the enhancement of consumer or investor confidence and which, as a result, is not simply a manifestation of a general regulatory power over the internal market, the existence of which was trenchantly rejected by the Court. The Court's major concern, expressed in paragraph 83 of its Judgment, appears to be with ensuring that the measure 'genuinely has its object the improvement of the conditions for the establishment and functioning of the common market'. The unusually close connection which is thought to exist between investor confidence and investment activity in the market-place (despite the difficulties in establishing the link on an empirical basis)[210] generally, and the specific interaction between investor activity and the growth of the integrated market, might suggest that this route to harmonization is not, as yet, barred. The connection between investor confidence and investor protection has already been explicitly acknowledged by the Court in *Alpine Investments*, while Advocate General Jacobs also stated in that case that 'although the harmonization directives provide minimum rules, they seek to ensure a high level of investor protection. They recognize that ensuring investor confidence in the securities markets will promote the smooth operation of those markets.'[211] As is discussed further in section 13 below, retail investors, rather than investment firms, are increasingly being targeted as critical to the success of the internal market in investment services. As a result, measures which encourage their participation in the market-place by bolstering protection and confidence might appear to be as essential to the post-ISD phase of market construction as the investment firm passport was to the pre-ISD phase.

The investor-confidence link and the consequent focus on the investor rather than on the investment firm as the agent for internal-market construction has, of course, been used before.[212] The Insider Dealing

---

[210] See Lee, R, *What is an Exchange? The Automation, Management, and Regulation of Financial Markets* (1998), 252. For a challenge to the link between investor confidence and the functioning of the market-place (in the context of insider-dealing regulation) see Hetherington, J, 'When the Sleeper Awakes: Reflections on Corporate Governance and Shareholders' Rights' (1979) 8 *Hofstra LR* 183, 226–9 and Dalhuisen, J, *The New UK Securities Legislation and the EC 1992 Program* (1989) 138. Investor confidence has also been challenged as a justification in the ICSD context: Landsmeer, A, and Van Empel, M, 'The Directive on Deposit-guarantee Schemes and the Directive on Investor Compensation Schemes in View of Case C-233/94' (1998) 5 *EFSL* 143, 147. More generally on the difficulties in examining market psychology see Hill, A, 'Tangled Link Between Stock Markets and Consumer Optimism', *Financial Times*, 29 Mar 2001.

[211] N 38 above, Opinion of the AG, para 76.

[212] In the consumer-protection field, for the focus on the consumer see recital 4 to the Unfair Contract Terms Directive and recital 2 of Directive 97/55/EC amending the Misleading Advertising directive so as to include comparative advertising [1997] OJ L290/18 (both these directives also refer to the distortion of competition rationale). See also the analysis of the price-indication directives (Directive 88/314/EEC on consumer protection in the indication of prices

Directive,[213] adopted under Article 95 EC, and the ICSD, adopted under Article 47(2) EC, both make a direct connection between the promotion and preservation of investor confidence and the need for EC action.[214] Of these two, the Insider Dealing Directive may be the more compelling example, given its basis in the broadly based Article 95 rather than in the more specific free-movement competence of Article 47(2) and because the ICSD is rooted in the free movement of investment firms and the removal of the obstacles to free movement represented by varying compensation regimes. Investor-confidence-based measures may, however, in the absence of convincing evidence of the link between investor confidence and the functioning of the internal market, sail perilously close to giving the Community a general power to regulate the internal market under Article 95 EC. Nonetheless, it may be that the Court would be reluctant to second-guess the Commission's assessment of the extent to which a link existed between harmonization of diverging rules and the generation of investor confidence, particularly given its broadly 'hands-off' approach to policy makers' choices in the investment services sphere which can be read in *Alpine Investments*.[215] In principle, however, *Tobacco Advertising* suggests that the Court will now review the legal basis for measures much more aggressively; as against that, the securities and investment-services sphere is uniquely sensitive to regulation and the internal market in investment services uniquely vulnerable to post-integration risks in terms of investor protection/confidence and, as discussed in Chapter VIII, systemic stability. The fate of investor protection under Article 95 EC remains to be seen.

IX.12.4.3 *Article 153 EC and Protective Harmonization*

Alternatively, Article 153 EC could potentially serve as the basis for protective harmonization divorced from internal-market considerations. Article 153(1) provides that '[i]n order to promote the interests of consumers and to ensure a high level of consumer protection, the Community shall contribute to protecting the health, safety and economic interests of consumers,

---

of non-foodstuffs [1988] OJ L142/19 and Directive 88/315/EEC on consumer protection in the indication of prices of foodstuffs [1988] OJ L142/23) in Usher, n 201 above, 110, who has pointed to their underlying rationale of ensuring greater consumer protection.

[213] Directive 89/592/EC coordinating regulations on insider dealing [1989] OJ L334/30.

[214] Investor confidence is also a feature of the securities directives and the disclosure regime they construct which is discussed in Ch. IV. Directive 89/298/EEC coordinating the requirements for the drawing-up, scrutiny and distribution of the prospectus to be published when transferable securities are offered to the public [1989] OJ L124/8, eg, makes an explicit connection between the promotion of investor confidence via disclosure and 'the proper functioning and development of transferable securities markets': recital 3.

[215] N 38 above. A similar inference might be drawn from the *Deposit Guarantee* ruling, n 184 above, paras 55–56.

as well as to promoting their right to information, education and to organise themselves in order to safeguard their interests'. The Community is to 'contribute to the attainment' of these objectives in two ways: first, under Article 153(3)(a) through internal-market measures adopted under Article 95 EC and, secondly, in a loosening of the internal market Gordian knot, under Article 153(3)(b), which provides that the Community shall adopt 'measures which support, supplement and monitor the policy pursued by Member States'. Article 153(3)(b) thus begs the question whether it can act as a legal basis for harmonization specifically designed to enhance investor protection. Although the borderline as to content between market integration measures under Article 95/Article 47(2) EC and investor protection measures under Article 153(3)(b) may be a fine one, competence to act independently of market-integration objectives would, on a symbolic basis at least, be significant.

One question raised by Article 153(3)(b) EC is whether protective measures of the type missing from the current framework would 'contribute to the attainment' of the consumer-protection objectives set out in Article 153(1), in that the interests of investors as a broad class of 'consumers of investment services' and 'consumers' as envisaged by the terms of Article 153(1) can be aligned.[216] The emphasis on information and education in Article 153(1) suggests that it is designed to protect consumers in situations where they are in an unequal position with respect to the service provider, particularly with respect to information. Investor protection under Article 153(1) may thus be confined to the protection of retail investors. It is suggested that such a restriction is not mandatory under Article 153(3)(b). It is more likely, however, that the emphasis on information in Article 153(3)(b) requires that protection be discriminate and directed only to those who, as a result of an information imbalance, are in an unequal position *vis-à-vis* the investment firm.

A second question concerns the restriction of measures adopted under Article 153(3)(b) EC to those which 'support, supplement and monitor the policy pursued by Member States'. By its terms it seems capable of encompassing measures designed to ensure co-operation by, for example, establishing mechanisms for co-operation, enforcement, and investor redress in

---

[216] It has been argued that 'the argument that an investor is not a consumer requires us to adopt too narrow an interpretation of the concept of the consumer. The analogies between investor and consumer have long been recognised': Cartwright, P, 'Consumer Protection in Financial Services: Putting the Law in Context' in Cartwright, P (ed), *Consumer Protection in Financial Services* (1999) 2, 6. See also Köndgen, n 36 above, 122. For a compromise view see Tridimas, n 18 above, who has noted at 106 that '[a]lthough investors can be seen as a specific category of consumers, in view of the distinctive characteristics of investments in the financial markets, legislation aiming at investor protection has developed, both at national and Community level, independently from legislation aiming at consumer protection'.

cross-border disputes.[217] The extent to which the Community can take the initiative with respect to substantive investor-protection rules, however, is unclear. The Distance Marketing Proposal, which does impose substantive standards, does not rely on Article 153(3)(b), notwithstanding that the ECOSOC in its comments on the original proposal had suggested that 'express mention' be made of the provision.[218] The Commission did not respond directly to this comment, but in rejecting the Parliament's suggestion that Article 153 EC generally be included as a legal basis, it stated that it would be superfluous, given that Article 95 EC was already included.[219] This suggests that the Commission addressed the use of Article 153 as a legal basis only in connection with its Article 153(3)(a) internal-market function and did not consider the potentially wider use of Article 153 under Article 153(3)(b). The use of maximum harmonization in the Proposal and the removal of the ability of Member States to apply more restrictive rules, which under Article 153(5) is not permissible where Article 153(3)(b) is used as a legal basis, may suggest that the harmonization technique adopted played a role in the Commission's choice of legal base. Conversely, although the Court did not discuss the question, Advocate General Léger in the *Deposit Guarantee* case felt that the pre-Amsterdam version of Article 153(3)(b) (Article 129a(1)(b) EC) could have acted as an alternative legal basis for the Directive, given that it supplemented the policy pursued by Member States as a whole in the general area of the protection of the economic interests of consumers.

Finally, the subsidiarity doctrine impacts on Article 153(3)(b) EC. Not only does it add a new area to Community competences (Article 153 was added by the Maastricht Treaty), which suggests that it is not an area of exclusive Community competence, the very terms of Article 153(3)(b) envisage a shared competence between the Community and the Member States. Any harmonization of investor-protection rules would thus need to be justified on the ground that the objectives of the proposed action cannot sufficiently be achieved by the Member States and, by reason of the scale or effects of the proposed action, are better achieved by Community action. Co-ordinating co-operative action by national supervisors, for example, or addressing the ability of investors to take legal action on a cross-border basis are likely to meet the subsidiarity requirement. As discussed in section 13.5 below, the adoption of specific investor-protection standards may not sit easily with subsidiarity.

---

[217] See also Weatherill. n 53 above, 719.   [218] N 137 above, para 2.4.
[219] Explanatory Memorandum to the Revised Proposal, n 22 above, 1.

IX.13 THE NEW FOCUS ON INVESTOR PROTECTION

IX.13.1 *The Green Paper on Consumer Protection in Financial Services*

The first significant move in the direction of investor protection in the wake of the ISD came in 1996 when the Commission presented its Green Paper on Financial Services Consumers.[220] Its objective was to consider the position of private users of financial services who, while benefiting from greater competition on price and quality and from increased choice, also required protection in the market-place. Although its focus was on the consumer as an instrument of integration and as a beneficiary of choice, the Green Paper highlighted a number of consumer-protection concerns, including: the refusal of financial services to non-residents; obstructions to the provision of cross-border services by Member State rules which restricted the range of services offered; the poor quality of services offered; lack of information; aggressive sales tactics by unregulated investment firms; contract enforcement problems; and the outweighing of the benefits of cross-border shopping for investment services by disparities in national tax regimes. The Green Paper engendered a widespread debate, the results of which were presented in a follow-up paper by the Commission in 1997[221] which revealed, unsurprisingly, that the financial services industry was concerned with the correct functioning of the single market and with the encouragement of innovation and was suspicious of the strengthening of consumer rights through legislation, preferring voluntary initiatives. Consumer groups, by contrast, were critical of the quality of consumer protection in the financial-services directives. Although the Commission committed itself to addressing distance-marketing problems, the lack of comprehensive information, and the adequacy of cross-border redress mechanisms, the Green Paper was soon overtaken by the FSAP.

IX.13.2 *Investor Confidence as a Policy Priority*

While the Green Paper on Financial Services Consumers did not take up the investor-protection cause entirely enthusiastically, notwithstanding the Treaty difficulties clear evidence is emerging of a new interest in the retail investor and in protective harmonization as policy priorities in the investment-services area. While the investor has always been characterized as a capital supplier to the single market and as a tool of market integration, the potential of retail investors, in particular, as agents to stimulate the single

---

[220] N 26 above.   [221] COM(97)309.

market is now much more apparent, as is the connection between protective harmonization and investment activity by retail investors.[222]

While the FSAP contains a number of investor protection measures, perhaps one of the most striking examples of this new focus is that the major review of the ISD currently underway, which will play a significant role in defining the future shape of EC investment-services regulation, holds as a guiding principle that 'the promotion of the Treaty freedoms must not come at the expense of investor protection, market integrity and stability. This will require judicious harmonization of key regulatory standards-particularly for the protection of retail investors.'[223] The Lamfalussy Report also prioritized the protection of the retail investor. Not only did it note the absence of 'high and equivalent levels of consumer protection and no efficient methods for resolving cross border consumer disputes', it also recommended that 'the conceptual framework of overarching principles', on which, it suggested, all EC financial-services and securities regulation should be constructed, include the maintenance of confidence in European securities markets and a commitment to ensuring 'appropriate levels of consumer protection proportionate to the different degrees of risk involved'.[224]

The strategy behind this renewed focus on the retail investor appears clear: investor protection generates investor confidence which stimulates market integration. The Commission made this explicit with its 1998 statement that '[t]here is . . . a need to find pragmatic ways of reconciling the aim of enhancing consumer confidence by promoting full financial market integration while ensuring high levels of protection'.[225] Investor confidence as the basis for a new direction in investment-services harmonization raises a number of issues. One difficulty which faces EC policy-makers in constructing a harmonized protective regime is how to identify the elements of protective regulation which have a direct impact on investor confidence. Aside altogether from the empirical difficulties inherent in any such exercise, although the Commission appears to be taking the investor-confidence argument as an article of faith, policy choices concerning the extent to which investor confidence is to be pursued will be required. As discussed at the start of this chapter, protective measures can encompass measures which broadly address market failures and are disclosure and prevention of fraud-based and paternalistic measures which intervene directly in contractual relationships

---

[222] The Commission has noted that '[p]rivate sector savings in Europe amount to some 20% of GDP—a valuable asset, if efficiently used, to stimulate growth and job-creation': *Progress on Financial Services—Second Report*, May 2000, COM(2000)336, 3 (the 2nd Progress Report). The link between improving retail investor protection and greater market integration and efficiency was also highlighted in the 3rd Progress Report, n 149 above, 1.

[223] ISD Communication, n 61 above, 20.

[224] Lamfalussy Report, n 28 above, 12 and 22.

[225] 1998 Communication, n 30 above, 1a. See also sect. 13.6 below on the E-commerce and Financial Services Communication.

or seek to remove the investor entirely from risky decision-making contexts. The piecemeal and indirect development of protective regulation thus far has meant that these choices have not been made explicit by policy-makers— certainly it is very difficult to identify a coherent philosophy of investor protection in the harmonized regime apart from the dominant market-integration objective. The very limited use of more paternalistic contract-formation regulatory techniques to date might suggest that non-interventionist disclosure mechanisms, which allow the rational investor to make informed choices, will dominate.[226] Finally, the promotion of investor confidence must find a basis within the Treaty which may be problematic.

IX.13.3 *Protective Harmonization and the FSAP*

IX.13.3.1 *Disclosure*

Disclosure can be identified as a recurring theme throughout the FSAP, particularly in the proposed revisions to the ISD's conduct regime.[227] The Commission expressly acknowledged in the FSAP that '[c]onsumers need information to assess the characteristics of the contract, the service provider, and the proposed investment'.[228]

IX.13.3.2 *Investor Redress*

Out-of-court settlement procedures have been identified at EC level as having a critical role to play in establishing consumer confidence,[229] and efforts are being made to agree procedures for effective out-of-court redress on a cross-border basis.[230] In 1998 the Commission adopted a recommendation on the principles applicable to bodies responsible for out-of-court settlement

---

[226] A preference for non-interventionist disclosure-based controls in the conduct-of-business sphere can be inferred from the Commission's statement in its Art. 11 Communication that 'investors—or their advisors—have to make their own assessment as to the particular features of the proposed investment. Conduct of business rules only seek to ensure that investors are not induced to undertake unsuitable investments and to protect investors against abuse and misconduct. Legislation in the investment services/securities area is therefore heavily centred on the principles of disclosure of information to enable rational investors to reach informed decisions': n 39 above, 16.

[227] Disclosure was also emphasized in the Green Paper on Financial Services Consumers and forms the core of the Distance Marketing Proposal.

[228] N 43 above, 8.

[229] Access to justice in the internal market generally has been on the Commission's agenda in recent years. See the Commission's Green Paper on Access of Consumers to Justice and the Settlement of Disputes in the Single Market, COM(93)576, and the subsequent Action Plan, COM(96)13, which highlights out-of-court dispute settlement and simplified access to court procedures as priorities.

[230] More generally, a European Consumer Complaint Form has been introduced to facilitate individual complaints. See the discussion in the Commission Report on Consumer Complaints in respect of distance selling and comparative advertising, COM(2000)127, 87–8.

of consumer disputes which sets out seven principles (independence, transparency, adversarial procedures, effectiveness, legality, liberty, and representation) which should be followed by out-of-court settlement mechanisms in order to ensure that disputes are settled fairly.[231] The principles are designed to enhance confidence in out-of-court settlement procedures and, in particular, to promote their use in cross-border disputes. In addition, a Memorandum of Understanding on a Cross-Border Out-of-Court Complaints Network for Financial Services in the European Economic Area (the MoU) is now in place. The MoU, the parties to which include national ombudsmen and complaint authorities, sets out the mechanisms (including information-exchange procedures) according to which parties will co-operate in order to facilitate out-of-court settlement of cross-border disputes in the financial-services area. The MoU supports FIN–NET (the Financial Services Complaints Network) which, reflecting the prevalence of out-of court settlement procedures in the financial-services sector, provides a redress network for disputes involving financial services. It links together the bodies which provide for out-of-court settlement at national level in an EC-wide network. All bodies participating in FIN–NET are to comply with the 1998 Commission Recommendation on Out-Of-Court Settlement. Attention is now being directed to enhancing the diversity and flexibility of out-of-court settlement procedures and, specifically, to promoting procedures which are not based on the resolution of the dispute by a third party but which facilitate the parties in reaching a solution by common consent, and to enhancing confidence in such procedures by establishing common standards for their operation.[232]

The approach thus far appears to be on the establishment of settlement mechanisms rather than on assessing the extent to which out-of-court procedures deliver appropriate standards of investor protection for the integrated market. There is a question whether out-of-court settlement or arbitration clauses of themselves require attention. Mandatory out-of-court arbitration clauses can be a matter of concern, given that retail investors are unlikely to be aware of the significance of, or in a position to challenge, the content of the clause and may not be aware of the implications an arbitration may have for the size of any damages award or the type of interests represented by those reviewing the dispute, for example. The Unfair Contract Terms Directive does, however, regard as an unfair term any term which 'excludes or hinders the consumer's right to take legal action or exercise any other legal remedy, particularly by requiring the consumer to take disputes exclusively to arbitration not covered by legal provisions' (Annex 1(q)). In

[231] Commission Recommendation 98/257 [1998] OJ L115/31 (the 1998 Commission Recommendation on Out-of-Court Settlement).

[232] Commission Communication on Widening Consumer Access to Alternative Dispute Mechanisms, COM(2001)161.

addition, the standards set by the 1998 Commission Recommendation on Out-of-Court Settlement include a liberty standard (principle VI) which provides that a consumer's recourse to the out-of-court procedure must not be the result of a commitment, prior to the materialization of the dispute, which deprives the consumer of the right to bring an action before the courts. Article 6 of the European Convention on Human Rights, of course, enshrines the principle of access to the courts as a fundamental right, while access to justice is also covered in the EU's 2000 Charter of Fundamental Rights.

IX.13.3.3 *Conduct-of-business Regulation and the FESCO Standards*

Although the FSAP does not address conduct-of-business regulation directly, it has, since the adoption of the FSAP, been a recurring feature of policy discussions in this area, given the implications conduct regulation has for efficient market integration.[233]

Work on harmonizing conduct-of-business rules is now under way as part of the general reform of the ISD (section 13.7 below). It is clear from the Commission's July 2001 ISD Working Paper that FESCO (now the Committee of European Securities Regulators) will be a key player in this process by virtue of its work on standardizing conduct rules which, it appears, will be incorporated into any new regime. The aim of the FESCO Conduct Standards and the Revised Conduct Standards is to ensure a high level of investor protection at a reasonable cost. While broadly reflecting the scope of Article 11, the Standards go further, in that they suggest additional principles and rules for specific services such as discretionary portfolio-management services and execution-only services and for particular securities such as derivatives. They also make particular provision for investment services provided at a distance, be it through traditional mechanisms such as the telephone and fax or through the Internet.

FESCO's rationale for standardizing conduct rules is illuminating. While it has reiterated the familiar Commission mantra that diversity in conduct regulation represents an obstacle to integration, it has also referred to the role harmonization plays in ensuring an adequate standard of investor protection. The proposed FESCO Conduct Standards (and the Revised FESCO Conduct Standards) under discussion also chime with the recent changes to the Commission's approach to investor protection, however, in that they emphasize the connection between investor protection and investor confidence.[234] The two sets of Standards are based on a series of high-level

---

[233] eg, as previously noted, recital 27 of the ECD refers to possible harmonization of conduct-of-business rules while the Commission acknowledged in its Art. 11 Communication that further work was needed to clarify and refine the application of the Art. 11 principles to the protection of retail investors: n 39 above, 12.

[234] FESCO Conduct Standards, n 98 above, 6 and Revised FESCO Conduct Standards, n 103 above, 13.

Principles which are supplemented by detailed Rules which clarify the Principles. As well as providing a detailed catalogue of conduct-of-business rules, which of itself addresses the transparency problems and other risks represented by the single market, the Principles also specifically address the cross-border context of single-market investment-firm/investor relationships.[235] The Principles can be divided into groups. General principles are set out in relation to honesty and fairness, the taking of appropriate care in relation to outsourcing services, not doing business with firms which are not duly authorized, conflicts-of-interests management, the disclosure of inducements received or given in connection with services supplied to investors,[236] and the establishment of compliance procedures. Disclosure principles are provided in relation to: (1) the basic elements of disclosure (such as that information must be fair and not misleading, all relevant information necessary for the investor to make an informed decision must be supplied, and disclosure must be timely); (2) marketing disclosures; (3) firm-specific disclosure (including disclosure of any conflicts of interest); (4) financial-instrument and investment-services-specific disclosure (including past performance data requirements);[237] (5) commission and fees disclosure; (6) risk warning requirements;[238] and (7) reporting requirements (including principles on the reporting of open positions on derivatives and the information to be supplied on the execution of transactions).[239] Know-your-customer and suitability principles (including principles on the operation of the suitability principle with respect to execution-only services) are also covered,[240] as are customer agreement principles (including principles on

[235] See, eg, Rule 35 of the FESCO Conduct Standards which requires that investment firms inform investors of the languages in which they may communicate with the investment firm, FESCO Conduct Standards, n 98 above, 15. This is also covered in Rule 41 of the Revised FESCO Conduct Standards: n 103 above, 23.

[236] To give one example of the Principle/Rule mechanism, the Revised FESCO Conduct Standards principle on inducements is supported by Rule 8 which requires disclosure of soft commissions: Revised FESCO Conduct Standards, n 103 above, 18.

[237] In both the FESCO Conduct Standards (n 98 above, 13–19) and the Revised FESCO Conduct Standards (n 103 above, 21–5), the Rules set out in detail the kind of disclosure necessary and how certain information such as past performance figures and forecasts should be expressed.

[238] The Rules in both sets of Conduct Standards set out the situations in which risk warnings are necessary, including transactions in derivatives, high-volatility instruments and securities not dealt in on a regulated market: FESCO Conduct Standards, n 98 above, 18 and Revised FESCO Conduct Standards, n 103 above, 25.

[239] The FESCO Conduct Standards (n 98 above, 19–21) and the Revised FESCO Conduct Standards (n 103 above, 25–6) provide detailed rules on confirmations, periodic information, and derivatives-specific reporting

[240] These principles are supplemented by detailed rules on what information should be obtained from investors and how suitability is to be assessed and followed in practice. In relation to execution-only services, Ibid., at 28–9 address execution-only services in some detail. Customers must, eg, be made aware of the limited nature of the service before a transaction takes place. The firm's obligations include defining the investment parameters (based on information provided by the customer) and warning the customer when an order is placed which is outside these parameters.

agreements relating to derivatives transactions). Finally, the Principles include dealing requirements (including best-execution[241] and orderly-allotment principles) and specific principles on discretionary portfolio management (including customer agreement, disclosure, and management principles).

FESCO's initiative thus marks a significant step forward from Article 11 and is an important indicator of how harmonization may ultimately proceed, notably with respect to the detailed treatment of disclosure, marketing practices, and dealing rules. The emphasis FESCO has placed on disclosure throughout the various stages of the investor/investment-firm relationship, from marketing to agreement to ongoing relationship and transaction management, is particularly striking. Not only does it fit with the disclosure theme which underpins the current approach to protective regulation, but, by reflecting a particular risk posed by the integrated market—lack of transparency and investor confusion—it may, if ultimately adopted at EC level, avoid any charge of harmonization in this area being unnecessary, overly detailed, and insufficiently sensitive to local market conditions.

IX.13.4 *Protective Harmonization and Supervision*

By contrast with prudential regulation, where the combination of a relatively high degree of harmonization and home-Member-State control has allowed the supervision and harmonization debate to move a stage further towards considering whether a single EC prudential supervisor is necessary to achieve effective supervision, the protective harmonization debate is at a significantly more immature stage. Indeed, discussions on the need for a single regulator tend to focus almost exclusively on prudential regulation, acknowledging that the relatively unsophisticated state of harmonization and the connection between protective regulation and the protection of individual investors, which requires that supervision be close to the marketplace, makes supervision of protective regulation by an EC supervisor unrealistic at present.[242]

IX.13.5 *Home and Host Control, Levels of Harmonization, and Subsidiarity*

Protective harmonization lies on the faultline between market integration and investor protection. Host-Member-State control may facilitate investor redress and the application of an investor's domestic rules, but home-

---

[241] Principle 108 of ibid. (at 32) defines the best-execution requirement as an obligation 'to take care to obtain the best possible result for the customer with reference to price, costs borne by the customer, size, nature of the transaction, time of reception of orders, speed and likelihood of execution and trading venues, taking into account the state of the relevant market(s)'.
[242] See further Ch. XV.

Member-State control is clearly beneficial from a market-integration perspective, although potentially prejudicial to investor protection unless accompanied by minimum harmonization at an appropriate level. The home/host decision must also reflect the Treaty competence concerned. The point has been made, for example, that Article 11 of the ISD does not comply with the barrier-removal objectives of Article 47(2) EC, given that Member States retain a wide discretion as to how the general principles set out in Article 11 are implemented and that they are not subject to home-Member-State control.[243]

The Commission appears to be committed to moving away from host-Member-State control, and to a combination of home-Member-State/branch-Member-State control. If host-Member-State control is to be abandoned, the form and level of harmonization becomes critical. The appropriate intensity of harmonization is a matter of some debate. Certain forms of protective regulation may not be susceptible to a high degree of harmonization. The full harmonization of conduct rules, in particular, may not be realistic, given their local bias and tendency to reflect national cultural traditions of market regulation. The critical influence here, however, is the Lamfalussy Report.[244] Its legislative proposals provide for the adoption of general measures setting out broad principles (level 1 measures) which would be supplemented by detailed rules setting out the technical requirements needed to implement the broad principles (level 2 measures). Indeed, the Report used conduct-of-business regulation to illustrate its proposed law-making model. Although it does not make the demarcation of general and detailed rules clear, the conduct-of-business framework suggested by the Commission's July 2001 ISD Working Paper is based on this structure.

Notwithstanding the signs that relatively detailed levels of harmonization via level 2 are under consideration, the subsidiarity principle will exert a strong influence on the level of harmonization undertaken. Whether investor protection is based on Article 47(2), Article 95, or Article 153 EC (the other options, Article 94 EC and the general enabling power contained in Article 308 EC, are unlikely to be widely used owing to their unanimity requirement), as outlined above the harmonization will need to be justified under Article 5(2) EC on the grounds that the objectives of the proposed action cannot sufficiently be achieved by the Member States and, by reason of the scale or effects of the proposed action, are better achieved by Community action. Even though the Distance Marketing Proposal eschews minimum harmonization, a minimum approach to any harmonization would certainly reflect a central aspect of the subsidiarity doctrine. The Protocol on the Application of the Principles of Subsidiarity and Proportionality attached to the Amsterdam Treaty emphasizes that Community action

---

[243] Köndgen, n 36 above, 119.   [244] N 28 above.

should be as simple as possible, that framework directives are to be preferred over detailed instruments, and that as much scope as possible should be left for national decision-making. Minimum harmonization, where appropriate, may also be necessary to comply with the proportionality principle set out in Article 5(3) EC, which requires that Community action must not go beyond what is necessary to achieve the objectives of the Treaty. Protective harmonization may be vulnerable to the argument that the protection of investors is in part a function of local market conditions and culture and is thus most effectively dealt with at Member State level. Harmonization arguments based on protection in the integrated market may also be difficult to sustain at the moment, given that retail investors have still fully to embrace the integrated market. It may be possible to argue, however, that as the market for retail investment services becomes more integrated, aided by the introduction of the euro, growth in e-commerce, and consolidation among market participants, common investor-protection standards set at Community level respond most effectively to transnational investment activities and investor protection in the integrated market. Community action 'would produce clear benefits by reason of its scale or effects', given that investors would be better protected in the integrated market by Community action than Member State action where certain Member States do not apply rigorous protective rules. In addition, investor protection in the integrated market may be prejudiced if, where protective standards are left to the Member States, they become an instrument of competition, resulting in the notorious regulatory 'race to the bottom'.[245]

IX.13.6 *The Commission Communication on E-commerce and Financial Services*

IX.13.6.1 *Objectives*

As part of the FSAP, the Commission committed itself to producing a policy document on the interaction between e-commerce and financial services. Presented in early 2001, the policy direction set out in the Communication,[246] in particular the commitment to the Member-State-of-origin principle for all financial services and, as a result, to further protective harmonization, marks an important staging post in the development of protective regulation.

---

[245] The point has been made that 'those who wish to use the concept of subsidiarity in order to show that as much regulatory power as possible remains at the nation, or sub-national level, will also need to show that competition among rules may be applied without significant problems': Woolcock, S, 'Competition Among Rules in the Single European Market' in Bratton, W, McCahery, J, Picciotto, S, and Scott, C (eds), *International Regulatory Competition and Coordination* (1996) 289, 292. On the extent to which a race to the bottom is likely see Ch. VI sect. 6.4 above.

[246] N 27 above.

The Communication was designed to clarify how the horizontal ECD interacts with the financial-services directives. Its central objectives were to: build on the ECD's approach in order to establish a fully functioning internal market for retail financial services (via wider use of the Member-State-of-origin rule, although the home-Member-State device is also referred to); provide coherence between financial-services legislation and the ECD and between the treatment of the online and traditional provision of financial services; and examine how the ECD's Member-State-of-origin clause applies in area where rules diverge significantly to avoid exposing consumers and investors to legal regimes which may differ considerably from their own. In order to achieve these objectives a three-pronged policy has been proposed. First, measures will be adapted to bring about convergence in consumer- and investor-protection rules for contractual and non-contractual obligations in order to pave the way for a Member-State-of-origin approach for all financial sectors and all distance-trading mechanisms. Secondly, measures will be developed to provide secure payment systems and out-of-court redress on a cross-border basis. Finally, enhanced supervisory co-operation is to be pursued. Of these, the convergence policy has the most significance for the wider protective regime.

IX.13.6.2 *Convergence of Protective Rules*

The Communication can be regarded as a milestone, in that it contains an express acknowledgment of the need for further convergence of protective rules, including conduct-of-business rules. The push for convergence does not appear to be motivated by a concern to develop a coherent policy of EC protective regulation but by narrower concerns that, without convergence, the application of the Member-State-of-origin principle, in general, and the supply of online services, in particular, may be prejudiced. Specifically, the convergence policy has been largely designed to address the danger that Member States will rely heavily on the derogations to the Member-State-of-origin principle set out in Article 3(4)–(6) of the ECD in order to protect investors and consumers where the Member State of origin's rules are not regarded as offering adequate protection. Nonetheless, the convergence policy has a wider significance in that the Communication, reiterating the strongly emerging confidence theme, has noted that consumer confidence is dependent on the existence of sufficiently harmonized levels of protection, such that consumers are as effectively and transparently protected in other Member States as they are in their own. It is also encouraging from the investor-protection perspective that the new convergence policy is not limited to online services. The Communication explicitly referred to the need to establish a coherent set of rules for all methods of trading, on and offline.

The convergence strategy, which is described as a major policy initiative for the financial-services sector, has three elements: high-level harmonization of core marketing rules; convergence in sector-specific and service-specific rules, in particular in relation to the content and presentation of information; and a review of rules relating to retail financial-services contracts. The Communication did not propose further initiatives in the marketing sphere, save that the Distance Marketing Proposal be adopted rapidly. With respect to sector-specific and service-specific measures, the Communication identified conduct-of-business regulation as an area in which significant divergences existed across the Member States in the level of protection afforded to retail investors and highlighted the need for further convergence in order to facilitate the transition to home-Member-State control of investment services (although the Member State of origin is also referred to). The Communication's coverage of financial-services contracts is particularly striking. While the Communication focused in particular on banking and insurance contracts, the review to be carried out of mandatory contractual obligations, in order to ensure that retail financial services can be offered across the EC in a framework of legal certainty, may mark a movement towards greater intervention in the investor/investment-firm contract.

Although the Communication does not contain any significant new commitments to the development of protective regulation beyond those highlighted in the FSAP, the acceptance of the need for protective harmonization, the explicit recognition of the link between confidence and protective regulation and the acknowledgment of the need for greater action in the conduct area all augur well for the protection of the investor at EC level.

IX.13.7 *The 2001 ISD Working Paper*

In July 2001, the various indications that the Commission would act in the conduct sphere were borne out. Its ISD Working Paper,[247] which is a preliminary document only, has suggested that Article 11 be extensively revised and a comprehensive conduct-of-business regime established. The features of the proposed conduct regime are considered here in outline only; the regime is very far from final adoption at this stage, and has yet to be cast as a formal proposal. Even at this early stage, however, the Commission's thinking suggests a major shift in the treatment of investors by EC securities regulation and a decisive move by the regime into more sophisticated investor protection.

The Commission has suggested that the Article 11 principles be extended and updated based on FESCO's work on standards harmonization. The suggested revamped version of Article 11 provides that competent authorities

---

[247] N 35 above.

are to ensure that investment firms, in their dealings with clients or potential clients, comply with the principles set out in the Article. These follow the FESCO model and include: requirements as to marketing communications and their disclosure; disclosure obligations concerning the service provided and designed to ensure investors understand the precise nature of the service provided; a suitability/know-your-client obligation; the obligation to establish a documentary record of the firm/client agreement; conflicts-of-interests management obligations based on the principle that the investment firm must take all reasonable steps to ensure that conflicts of interests are managed in such a way that the interests of investors are not adversely affected (this principle includes a requirement to disclose inducements); guidance on and warning requirements as to the risks and other attributes associated with investments in particular instruments, tailored to reflect the knowledge and experience of investors; an obligation to disclose, on a timely basis, information on financial instruments, proposed investments, and execution venues which is fair, clear, and not misleading, such that an investor can take an informed decision and react promptly to actual or potential losses; a best-execution obligation, framed by reference to the time, size, and nature of the order;[248] and an obligation to report on the progress of execution and the performance of portfolios. Detailed technical rules implementing these principles would be adopted as level 2 measures. While it is too early to attempt an analysis of what these rules reveal of the EC's characterization of the objectives of investor protection, the emphasis on disclosure and the empowerment of the investor to take rational decisions is marked.

This harmonization process would, per the Commission, allow the conduct regime, including protections for retail investors, to move to full home-Member-State control. However, in an interesting development, which appears to be based on considerations of administrative efficiency and the fact that branches conduct 'autonomous client-facing operations'[249] the Commission has followed the ECD Member-State-of-origin principle and suggested that, in the case of activities carried out by a branch, the Member State in which the branch is established should supervise the investment-firm/investor relationship. It was made clear, however, that the branch-Member-State principle was intended only to apply to conduct-of-business regulation and would not be extended to organizational or prudential matters, currently covered by the home Member State.

---

[248] Stated in terms of the obligation to '[p]rocess and execute a client's order in the best interests of the customer so as to obtain the best possible result with reference to the time, size and nature of customer orders. To this end, investment firms shall implement procedures and arrangements which together form a systematic, repeatable and demonstrable approach to ensure that investment firms are consistently seeking best execution for clients': ibid, Annex 2, 14.

[249] Ibid, 16.

A number of governing principles for the new regime have been suggested. The application of the regime would differentiate between professional and retail investors.[250] Detailed measures implementing the principles set out in the ISD (level 2 measures) would clarify how the conduct rules should apply to professional investors. The regime would also distinguish between the types of services provided and indicate clearly how the conduct requirements would apply to particular core services. In principle, a graduated scheme, based on the key risks associated with the activity, would apply. More specifically, own-account dealing between dealers would not be subject to the conduct regime.[251] Execution-only services would also be subject to a specialized regime. Firms engaging in such services would be required to seek information from investors regarding their financial situation, investment expertise, and objectives and to provide investors with information on the financial instruments concerned and any relevant risk warnings. Firms would be prevented from accepting orders for execution until they had received an acknowledgment from the investor that the investor was aware of the limited nature of the services provided and understood the information/risk warnings communicated and, in addition, until they had verified that the investor had sufficient financial resources to complete the transaction. Given the Working Paper's characterization of certain ATSs as investment firms (see Chapter XI section 9.7 below), particular rules would apply to trading-related services; tailored rules would also be required for investment-advice services, which, the Commission suggested, should become a core ISD activity.[252] The regime would also specify which party was responsible for obligations such as best-execution in chain transactions involving, for example, tied agents, investment advisers, and order-matching service providers.

IX.14 INVESTOR PROTECTION: A BRAVE NEW WORLD?

Protective regulation thus emerges as the Cinderella of the EC investment-services regime. Lacking a specific Treaty competence and, unlike prudential regulation which has systemic implications, a direct connection to the construction of the single market, EC-level investor protection for the integrated market-place has, up to now, suffered an uneasy and uncertain

---

[250] On the proposed classification see Ch. VII sect. 10.3.2 above. As it is based on the ICSD, it would also introduce more coherence into this area.

[251] The Working Paper has noted that dealers do not gain any additional protections via the conduct-of-business regime but rely instead on litigation or other defences based on contractual arrangements: n 35 above, Annex 2, 15.

[252] Ch. VII sect. 10.3.2 above. The tailored rules for the supply of investment advice would include the obligation to disclose soft-dollar commissions.

existence at the market-integration faultline between liberalization and reregulation.

The sparseness of the current regime might be criticized for resulting in an over-dependence on national systems which are based on domestic market practices and regulatory cultures and do not respond to the specific EC risks of the integrated market-place. The regime might also be charged with lacking an overall coherence as a result of its connection to a market-integration rather than an investor-protection rationale, although recent developments suggest that a protective model based on the investor as a rational decoder of information is emerging. Casting off the shackles of the single market would liberate investor protection in the integrated market as a policy in its own right and provide a firmer basis for the new protective regime which appears to be emerging. Article 153(3)(b) EC is, however, a weak agent for change. It might be suggested that, given the pace of developments in EC investment-services markets and the increase in investment activity by retail investors, the time has come for a more explicit recognition of the investor's current and potential role in the integrated investment-services market and the inclusion of investor protection as a Community competence. Political sensitivities may be such, however, that an explicit EC competence, albeit explicitly circumscribed (and implicitly controlled by the subsidiarity principle), may be too much of a hostage to fortune.

Nonetheless, investor protection in the investment-services sphere may be on the verge of following the trajectory of its close relation, consumer protection. From a very slow start, consumer protection has now emerged from the constraints of the internal market as an established and independent EC policy.[253] While the 1975 First Programme for Consumer Protection and Information (which emerged two years before the 1977 Code of Conduct) did not have a significant impact, the energy which was instilled into the consumer-protection project in 1985 with the Commission Communication on a New Impetus for Consumer Protection Policy, which proposed a range of measures, was maintained. Although the Single European Act did not grant specific competence in consumer protection, it did demand that notice be taken of consumer protection in adopting internal-market legislation and was followed by the introduction of a specific competence in consumer protection, divorced from the internal market, by the then Article 129a of the Maastricht Treaty (now Article 153 EC). Since then, a wide range of consumer protection measures have been adopted and proposed. Institutionally, by 1995, consumer protection had moved into a specific Directorate General and the involvement of consumer groups in the law-making process through the Consumer Consultative Committee was well-developed. Indeed, in 2000 consumer protection was elevated to the status of a fundamental principle

---

[253] For an account of the development of consumer policy see Weatherill, n 53 above.

and included in the EU's Charter of Fundamental Rights: Article 38 provides that Union policies are to ensure a high level of consumer protection. While investor protection is unlikely to achieve such particular prominence, the ISD Working Paper may yet be an augury of a development phase similar to that enjoyed by consumer protection in recent years.

X

Investor-compensation Schemes

X.1 THE RATIONALE FOR COMPENSATION SCHEMES

X.1.1 *The Case For*

Notwithstanding the soundness protections afforded by prudential regulation, investors may still sustain losses due to the financial or operational difficulties of the investment firm to which they have entrusted funds or securities and systemic stability may be prejudiced if, in consequence, investor confidence is weakened on a large scale. Compensation schemes, by now a well-established if somewhat controversial feature of the securities regulation landscape,[1] act as an additional safety net for investors and, accordingly, investor confidence and systemic stability, when investment firms fail. They are reactive rather than preventive, responding to actual insolvency crises and failures of regulation and refunding rather than protecting investor assets.

Many regulatory systems choose to shield clients of financial intermediaries who have entrusted assets or funds to such intermediaries from the consequences of insolvency. Supporters of deposit-guarantee schemes, in particular, can present a compelling justification based on the need for depositor protection and the dangers of systemic risk. Depositors are not in a position to assess the soundness of credit institutions to which they often have no option but to entrust funds. In addition, their unusual combination of liquid liabilities (customers can withdraw their deposits at short notice) and illiquid assets (loans make up the greater part of a credit institution's assets) renders credit institutions liable to mass withdrawals when a default on deposit repayments is

---

[1] As far back as 1950, the London Stock Exchange established a compensation fund for investors dealing with its members. In the USA, compensation schemes did not form part of the reforming New Deal package of securities legislation which included the foundation Securities Act, 1933 and the Securities and Exchange Act, 1934. The collapse of one of its largest members prompted the New York Stock Exchange to introduce a compensation fund in 1963. Other exchanges followed with similar schemes. They proved inadequate to deal with the large number of financial scandals in the late 1960s which followed a fatal combination of a massive increase in trading volumes and large-scale operational weaknesses in record-keeping and transaction processing. At this point Congress intervened and passed the Securities and Investor Protection Act, 1970 (the SIPA) which established the Securities Investor Protection Corporation (the SIPC). See, eg, Woo, T, 'Who Watches the Watchers? The Securities Investor Protection Act, Investor Confidence, and the Subsidization of Failure' (1999) 72 *So. Cal. LR* 1070 and Bloomenthal, H, and Salcito, D, 'Consumer Protection from Brokerage Failures: The Securities Investor Protection Corporation and the SEC' (1983) 54 *University of Colorado LR* 161.

suspected. Such a 'run' on a credit institution could lead to wider systemic problems. Deposit-guarantee schemes reduce the incentive for depositors to withdraw funds, thereby supporting the integrity of the banking system as well as strengthening depositor protection.[2] The rationale for investor-compensation schemes is less clear-cut. Unlike depositors, investors are not obliged to use investment firms and typically entrust firms with surplus, discretionary funds. The dangers of systemic instability in the event of a loss of investor confidence are, while typically raised as a justification, also less apparent as compared to the risk of depositors provoking a run.

Nonetheless, from an investor-protection perspective, however, investors are vulnerable to firm failure in that investment firms' activities extend to holding and controlling investors' securities and funds; the amounts held will often be in excess of the amounts placed on deposit with a credit institution. In these circumstances, a degree of protection or a safety net for small investors, in particular, against a firm's insolvency is generally recognized as appropriate.[3] Firms acquire custody of investors' assets in a number of ways. Investors' money may be held by a firm following its receipt of the proceeds of a sale of securities, dividends, or interest payable on securities. Cash deposits may be made by investors with a firm before a purchase order is made. Fully-paid securities may be entrusted by the investor to a firm for safe-keeping as a matter of convenience. Where securities have been purchased on the margin, the firm may advance part of the price of the securities and then hold the securities as collateral for loans and re-pledge the securities to a third party to secure its own future borrowings. On the insolvency of a firm, investor funds and securities should be available if the firm has complied with asset-protection rules and own-account trading rules. In reality, funds may have been fraudulently misappropriated. The investor will then simply have a claim in bankruptcy over part of the assets of the bankrupt firm. In circumstances where, due to fraud or negligence, investors' claims are pooled with those of other creditors, compensation schemes will typically intervene to short-circuit bankruptcy proceedings, which are likely to be lengthy as well as to produce uncertain outcomes in terms of retrieving assets, and return cash and/or securities to investors.[4]

---

[2] See, eg, Campbell, A, and Cartwright, P, 'Banks and Consumer Protection: the Deposit Protection Scheme in the United Kingdom' [1998] *LMCLQ* 128, Macey, J, and Miller, G, 'Towards a Regulatory Analysis of Deposit Insurance' in Ferrarini, G (ed), *Prudential Regulation of Banks and Securities Firms* (1995) 209–39, Cranston, R, *Principles of Banking Law* (1997) 80–1 and Hadjiemmanuil, C, *Banking Regulation and the Bank of England* (1996) 375–7. Deposit protection across the EC is now harmonized: Directive 94/19/EC on deposit guarantee schemes [1994] OJ L135/5 (the DGD).

[3] Gower, L, *Review of Investor Protection* (1982) 85.

[4] An alternative approach is to introduce quasi-bankruptcy proceedings which give investors preferential claims over the assets of the firm. This is the approach of the US SIPA under which

From a market-failure perspective, this dilution of insolvency and fraud risk in the interests of investor protection is usually justified by the vulnerability of the investor to fraud and by the informational imbalance between firm and investor. A small investor is unlikely to be in a position to assess the soundness of a firm and to minimize the risk of fraud and insolvency. Although information concerning the firm's financial position may be in the public domain, the small investor will probably not be in a position to interpret it.[5] Likewise, such a small investor will not be aware of the firm's probity, much less be able to monitor it. As a result, compensation schemes address loss or theft of assets by the investment firm but rarely compensate for fluctuations in the value of a security or investment.

Micro investor-protection objectives aside, compensation schemes also serve the wider macro objective of enhancing investor confidence in the investment-services markets,[6] even if investment firms do not display the same systemic risks as credit institutions. Investor losses (or the potential for losses) sustained through operational and financial failures can bring the investment-services industry into disrepute and provoke market-wide problems.[7] By reassuring investors in advance that their assets will benefit from some protection,[8] compensation schemes, it is often contended, increase confidence and encourage investors to invest more funds than they would in the absence of such schemes.[9]

X.1.2 *The Case Against*

Critics of compensation schemes point to the danger that the existence of a safety net for investors creates a moral hazard, in that investors may not

the SIPC supervises the liquidation of the firm under the SIPA, rather than under the US Bankruptcy Code. The advantage of this approach is that calls on the compensation fund are limited to the shortfall remaining once the firm's bankruptcy assets have been distributed among investors.

[5] See,eg, Clark, R, 'The Soundness of Financial Intermediaries' (1976) 86 *Yale LJ* 1, 91–3.

[6] For the dual investor-protection and macro-systemic stability rationale for compensation schemes see FSA (UK Financial Services Authority), *Consumer Compensation*, Consultation Paper 5 (1997) (the FSA 1997 Compensation Paper) 6–8 and FSA, *Financial Services Compensation Scheme Draft Rules*, Consultation Paper 58 (2000) (the FSA 2000 Compensation Paper) 10 and, on investor confidence, 35 and 43–4.

[7] The US Senate hearings on SIPA emphasized the wider systemic consequences for the soundness of the economy were investors to lose confidence in the investment markets as a result of a failure to address the consequences of broker-dealer insolvencies adequately. SIPA was, as a result, designed to promote investor confidence in the securities markets: hearings on S.2348, S.3988, and S.3989 Before the Subcomm. on Securities of the Senate Comm. On Banking and Currency, 91st Cong., 2d Sess. s 143 (1970).

[8] Funding arrangements typically ensure that compensation schemes rarely fail to pay (within scheme limits). Compensation schemes accordingly provide protection in a 'comprehensive and non volatile way': Clarke, n 5 above, 99.

[9] See generally, Block, C, 'Overt and Cover Bailouts: Developing a Public Bailout Policy' (1992) 67 *Ind. LJ* 951 and Page, A, and Ferguson, R, *Investor Protection* (1992) 71.

exercise due care in selecting a financially sound investment firm and in assessing its performance.[10] Risk, so the argument runs, is an inherent part of any investment decision and investors are not obliged to purchase investment services. Investors are not unprotected from risk; they can rely on the panoply of prudential and conduct rules imposed on investment firms which are intended to reduce the risk of investment-firm failure or fraud. In return, they are required to accept responsibility for their choice of investment firm[11] (although this mutuality of obligations between investor and investment firm can be distorted through an inadvertent or fraudulent failure to comply with prudential and conduct controls). This danger of moral hazard is most likely to arise where there is a 100 per cent guarantee against risk and the compensation scheme operates in effect as an indemnity against loss.[12] While the extent to which compensation schemes pose a moral hazard in practice is debatable,[13] moral hazard is by now a well-established element of the compensation-scheme discussion. In particular, compensation schemes are usually capped to provide an incentive for investors to take care in making investment decisions.

Compensation schemes may weaken competition and ultimately investor protection in that their mandatory nature may reduce the extent to which firms can compete in terms of investor security and their incentive to do

---

[10] Moral hazard is a concept drawn from 19th century insurance practices. It referred originally to the risk that an insured party would take less care to prevent the insured event occurring owing to the existence of the insurance safety net. There is an extensive literature on the moral-hazard problem, particularly in the context of deposit insurance where, in the absence of the threat of mass depositor withdrawals (due to the insurance of deposits) the danger arises that credit institutions will adopt riskier strategies such as acquiring high-risks assets in the hope of higher returns. See, eg, the discussions by Miller, G, 'Deposit Insurance for Economies in Transition' *1997 Yearbook of International Financial and Economic Law* (1999) 103–38, McKenzie, G, and Khalidi, M, 'The EU Directive on Deposit Insurance: A Critical Evaluation' (1994) 32 *JCMS* 171 and Schoenmaker, D, *Home Country Deposit Insurance*, Special Paper No. 43, LSE Financial Markets Group Special Paper Series.

[11] Adams, G, 'Beware Moral Hazard' (1995) 2 *EFSL* 258.

[12] For the regulator's perspective see the FSA's view that a complete safety net could 'undermine the encouragement which we would otherwise wish to give to individuals to enter into transactions in financial services only after proper consideration, to the best of their ability, of the balance of risk and reward': FSA 1997 Compensation Paper, n 6 above, 6.

[13] The FSA has noted that initial research it reported on in 1999 suggested that 'consumers' general awareness of compensation arrangements [across all financial sectors] is very low and that it is not a factor to which consumers attach much significance when making savings or investment decisions or decisions about purchasing insurance cover, which might suggest that the incentive effect of the co-insurance element [scheme limits] in the existing schemes is limited': FSA, *Consumer Compensation: A Further Consultation*, Consultation Paper 24 (1999) 16. It reiterated this view in the FSA 2000 Compensation Paper, reporting that there was no evidence to support the view that the existence of compensation schemes discourages consumers from taking care and that the financial security of a firm was considered to be far more important than the existence of a compensation scheme, with reliance being placed on brand recognition and reputation as indicators of financial security: n 6 above, 44. Nonetheless, the FSA has decided to take the risk of moral hazard into account in capping compensation pay-outs.

so.[14] Competition may be further distorted in that, where schemes are funded by a mandatory industry-wide levy, this quasi-taxation may result in sound, prudent firms underwriting improvident and reckless firms which might otherwise attract fewer investors or be required to discount their riskier services.[15] Indeed, where a scheme levies a flat minimum initial levy without reference to the size of the firm, it could operate as a barrier to new entrants. The extent to which a compensation scheme could generate a moral hazard on the supply side, in that certain investment firms might be inclined to take less care given the existence of a safety net, is questionable, however, particularly given the prudential controls imposed on firms.[16]

X.2 SCOPE AND FEATURES OF THE REGIME

Whatever the controversies, at a minimum, investor-compensation schemes enhance investor protection. They also increase investor confidence in that they are a visible and predictable form of regulation. Compensation schemes now form part of the harmonized investment-services framework, with the adoption of a Directive on Investor Compensation Schemes (the ICSD) in 1997 after difficult and protracted negotiations.[17]

The micro investor-protection and macro investor-confidence and market-stability objectives underlying compensation schemes also appear in the EC regime, although they must be examined through the lens of the dominant market-integration objective which has had a significant impact on the shape of the harmonized compensation regime. The regime also represents one of the relatively few attempts in EC investment-services regulation to deal with securities regulation on a sophisticated level as a system of market regulation in itself, divorced from its role as a market-integration device, in that it deals expressly with moral hazard. Evidence of a more sophisticated approach to investment-services regulation can also be drawn from the differentiated approach taken to protection via compensation; the EC regime is specifically directed to small retail investors. By contrast with the Investment

---

[14] Page and Ferguson, n 9, above 71.

[15] While the Wilson Committee noted, in the context of the introduction of deposit protection in the UK, the Committee of the London Clearing Bankers' position that 'requiring sound businesses to underwrite the activities of their less sound competitors was a thoroughly bad principle', it found that 'this point overlooks the externalities involved in ensuring public confidence': Report of the Committee to Review the Functioning of Financial Institutions (1980) 294. Likewise Gower was of the opinion that, although inequitable, it was ultimately in the interests of honest and prudent firms to pay, as otherwise the failure of dishonest firms would taint the reputation of the whole industry: n 3 above, 86.

[16] See the discussion in the FSA 2000 Compensation Paper, n 6 above, 45.

[17] Directive 97/9/EC on investor compensation schemes [1997] OJ L84/22 (the ICSD).

Services Directive in its present form,[18] the ICSD also displays a sharper awareness of the risks to which investors are exposed in the internal market. While the ICSD's main concern is with compensation schemes as an instrument of market integration and investor protection, it also relies on disclosure. The ICSD acknowledges the danger that investors may be confused or misled (and macro investor confidence and market stability prejudiced: recital 21) by the range of compensation schemes available throughout the market-place or by compensation-scheme advertising and introduces disclosure-based controls. More generally, the adoption of a compensation-scheme regime, albeit driven, as discussed in section 4.1 below, by the need to support the ISD passport, marks a move into more interventionist and, arguably, paternalistic investor protection at EC level. Recent moves by the EC into investor protection under the FSAP appear to be grounded in the connection between investor protection and macro investor confidence. The compensation regime arguably represents the start of this next evolutionary stage of the investment-services regime, even if it marks a transition point in that it is ultimately grounded in single-market construction and the removal of obstacles to the free movement of investment firms. Finally, a concern for the wider stability of the investment services in the wake of ISD liberalization emerges clearly from the ICSD. Numerous examples of this concern appear throughout the ICSD: for example, the funding of schemes must not jeopardize the stability of the financial system, and advertising controls are justified by reference to market stability. The ICSD is one of the first illustrations of how, in the wake of the ISD and investment-services market liberalization, a preoccupation with systemic concerns and greater sophistication in prudential regulation have become core features of EC investment-services regulation. In this regard it marks the start of a regulatory development which has led to the Supplementary Supervision Proposal on financial conglomerates (Chapter VIII section 11.3 above), the prudential regulation of settlement systems (Chapter XII section 4 below), and the changes to the prudential regime envisaged by the ISD reforms and the capital-adequacy review: see Chapter VIII sections 6.2 and 9.6.3 above.

X.3 THE ROOTS OF THE REGIME

X.3.1 *Early Developments*

Compensation schemes do not appear in the early attempts to construct an investment-services regime. The 1977 Code of Conduct expressly refers to the importance of investor confidence, but does so in the context of fairness

---

[18] Directive 93/22/EEC on investment services in the securities field [1993] OJ L141/27 (the ISD).

in the securities markets.[19] Its rules for the management of the investor/investment-firm relationship are directed to the conduct of business and do not focus on soundness and prudential regulation, much less on compensation schemes.[20]

Arrangements for compensation schemes were included among the prudential rules to be drawn up and enforced by the Member States in the Commission's original proposal for the ISD.[21] Each investment firm was to be a member of a 'general compensation scheme designed to protect investors who are prevented from having claims satisfied because of the bankruptcy or default of the investment firm' (original proposal, Article 9). This provision did not survive the negotiating process. In particular, Member States were opposed to the difference in treatment between compensation arrangements for investment services carried out on a services basis, which were subject to the home-Member-State regime, and compensation arrangements for investment services carried out through branches, which were subject to the host-Member-State regime. Member States favoured home-country control and early harmonization of compensation schemes. Given that home-Member-State authorities were responsible for authorization and prudential control it was felt that they should also carry the consequences of the failure of firms under their control. The complexities involved in harmonizing compensation schemes meant, however, that to avoid further delays to the adoption of the ISD compensation schemes were excluded from its scope and reserved for a future directive. Article 12 of the ISD as finally adopted simply provided that 'a firm shall inform investors which compensation fund or equivalent protection will apply in respect of the transactions envisaged, what cover is offered by whichever system applies, or if there is no fund or compensation'. The ISD did not leave investors without protection against the insolvent default of investment firms. Among the prudential rules to be adopted and enforced by Member States under Article 10 were adequate arrangements for safeguarding investors' ownership rights in instruments and funds. These rules do not, of course, protect investors against losses consequent on breaches of these rules occurring through fraud or negligence.

---

[19] Commission Recommendation 77/534/EEC concerning a European code of conduct relating to transactions in transferable securities [1977] OJ L212/37. Supplementary Principle 1.

[20] This focus is clear from the Code's expressed objective which is 'to establish standards of ethical behaviour on a Community-wide basis, so as to promote the effective functioning of securities market . . . and to safeguard the public interest': Fundamental Objective, para 2.

[21] Original Proposal at [1989] OJ C43/7; Explanatory Memorandum at COM(88)778.

X.3.2 *Further Delays and the DGD*

The Commission's original 1993 proposal for the ICSD[22] proved relatively uncontroversial, not least because at the time of the proposal's presentation all but two of the Member States had some form of compensation scheme in place.[23] The adoption of the DGD in mid-1994[24] triggered a substantial re-working of the proposal, leading in late 1994 to the presentation of an amended proposal which aligned the original proposal with the DGD.[25] The parallel discussions on the DGD complicated and delayed the adoption of the ICSD and also as heavily influenced its contents; the ICSD as adopted is modelled on the DGD,[26] although rather different rationales apply to compensation in the context of protecting credit-institution deposits, with the systemic stability rationale, in particular, being arguably more compelling.[27]

The Council's common position adopted in late 1995 went further to align both measures, including the introduction of the problematic export ban (section 4.7 below).[28] The measure remained stalled due to the Parliament's concerns that the measure did not adequately protect

[22] [1993] OJ C321/15. Explanatory Memorandum at COM(93)381.

[23] Explanatory Memorandum to Original Proposal, n 22 above, 14–15. The Parliament and ECOSOC were broadly supportive of the measure and their comments were, on the whole, adopted by the Commission in its subsequent amended proposal [1994] OJ C128/85 and [1994] OJ C127/1, respectively. Given that the Directive's provisions are triggered when an investment firm is unable to meet its obligations, it is of some interest to note that ECOSOC did express a general reservation concerning the adoption of the Directive in the absence of a detailed review of the conflict-of-law rules applicable to bankruptcy. It recommended at para 1.4 that a principle of 'single and universal failure' be adopted, such that a single judgement of failure by the country in which the company was principally established would be binding on all Member States. See now the approach taken in Directive 2001/24/EC on the reorganisation and winding up of credit institutions [2001] OJ L125/15.

[24] See generally, Andenas, M, 'Directive on Deposit Guarantee Scheme Challenged' (1995) 16 *The Company Lawyer* 18; Hadjiemmanuil, n 2 above, 377–83; McKenzie and Khalidi, n 10 above; Andenas, M, 'Deposit Guarantee Schemes and Home Country Control' in Cranston, R (ed), *The Single Market and the Law of Banking* (2nd edn, 1995) 105, Le Brun, J, 'The Directive on the Protection of Depositors' in Ferrarini, n 2 above, 241–9 and Dassesse, M, Isaacs, S, and Penn, G, *EC Banking Law* (2nd edn, 1994) 365–72.

[25] [1994] OJ C382/27. Explanatory Memorandum COM(94)585.

[26] The identity between the ICSD and DGD provisions became very significant when the Commission came to review the operation of the ICSD's controversial export ban, when it relied heavily on experience of the operation of the parallel ban in the DGD, not least because the Commission characterized the ICSD as amounting to a transposition of the DGD's principles in the securities field: Report on the Application of the Export Prohibition Clause, Article 7(1) of the Directive on investor-compensation schemes (97/9/EC). COM(2000)81 (the ICSD Report).

[27] ECOSOC recognized the need for harmonization of investor-compensation provisions, but saw it as a 'very different problem' to the harmonization of deposit-guarantee schemes, as, first, investors tended to be better informed than cash depositors and, secondly, the ISD already contained a number of provisions (such as client money requirements) protecting investors against the consequences of failure: n 23 above, para 3.1.

[28] Common Position (EC) No 26/95 [1995] OJ C320/9. The ICSD was adopted under the co-decision procedure.

investors,[29] and was further delayed by Germany's challenge to the DGD. Following the Advocate General's rejection of Germany's challenge in late 1996,[30] a compromise between the Parliament and the Council was finally reached in the Conciliation Committee which was convened as part of the co-decision legislative procedure (on which see Chapter XV section 2.2.1 below) and the Directive was finally adopted in March 1997. It was to be adopted by 28 September 1998.

X.4 THE ICSD

X.4.1 *Treaty Basis and Objectives*

The ICSD,[31] which follows the minimum harmonization and home-country-control template of the ISD, is, like the ISD, based on Article 47(2) EC which provides for the adoption of measures for the co-ordination of the provisions laid down by law, regulation, or administrative action in Member States concerning the taking-up and pursuit of activities as self-employed persons. Article 47(2) is the Treaty basis for measures designed to remove obstacles to free movement which arise, in particular, from regulatory obstacles.[32] The link between Article 47(2) and single market construction underpins the ICSD which is designed to 'complete the single market in investment services and ensure its proper functioning'.[33]

Unlike in the ISD, however, there is a strong emphasis on investor protection throughout the Preamble. Nonetheless, while it is at the core of most compensation regimes, investor protection under the ICSD is not pursued as an independent policy (which was not feasible in any event under Article 47(2) EC due to the single market shackle: see Chapter IX section 12 above)

---

[29] Many of the Parliament's objections to the Common Position [1996] OJ C96/28 were rejected by the Commission in order to ensure consistency with the DGD: Opinion of the Commission on the European Parliament's amendments to the Council's common position regarding the proposal for a European Parliament and Council Directive on Investor Compensation Schemes, COM(96)169, 4.

[30] The Court would not deliver its judgment rejecting the challenge until May 1997: Case C-233/94 *Germany v Parliament and Council* [1997] ECR I-2405 (the *Deposit Guarantee* case).

[31] See generally Lomnicka, E, 'EC Harmonisation of Investor Compensation Schemes' (1994) 1 *EFSL* 17, Cruikshank, C, 'The Draft Directive on the Protection of Investors' in Ferrarini, n 2 above, 27; Gonzalez, M, and Scherer, P, 'Directive on Investor Compensation Schemes' (1997) 12 *JIBL* 388, Marquand, C, 'Investor Compensation and the Small Investor', (1996) 140 *SJ* 892, Landsmeer, A, and van Empel, M, 'The Directive on Deposit-guarantee Schemes and the Directive on Investor Compensation Schemes in View of Case C-233/94' (1998) 5 *EFSL* 143, 146 and Wessel, N, 'Directive on Investor Compensation Schemes' (1999) 10 *EBLRev*. 103.

[32] *Deposit Guarantee* case, n 30 above, para 15.

[33] Council Common Position, n 28 above, Statement of the Council's Reasons, para II. Similarly, in its Explanatory Memorandum to the original proposal the Commission stated that 'first and foremost, it constitutes a necessary supplement to the single licence system based on home country control established by the Investment Services Directive': n 22 above, 5.

but serves the pre-eminent interest of market integration. The market-integration connection is made by bringing EC-wide systemic stability into the rationale and connecting micro investor protection with macro investor confidence, both of which are described as important to the proper functioning of the internal market (recitals 4 and 25). Referring to the prudential asset-protection controls already established by the ISD, the Preamble acknowledges that no system of regulation can provide complete protection, particularly where fraud is concerned, and identifies the existence of an investor-compensation scheme in each Member State, offering a minimum level of protection, as essential to the achievement of investor confidence and to the proper functioning of the common market. At the crux of the analysis is the argument that small investors will be able, due to the existence of harmonized compensation schemes, to purchase investment services from investment firms across the EC as confidently as they would purchase them from domestic firms (recital 5). Investor protection is thus articulated as investor confidence and the macro effects of compensation schemes emerge as a market-integration device. At the core of the rationale for harmonizing compensation schemes is the premise that, in the absence of harmonization, small investors may be discouraged by the absence of, or conversely confused by the varying nature of, compensation schemes across the EC and, as a result, be slow to access the single market in investment services (recitals 5 and 21).[34] Investor confidence is, however, a nebulous concept and the link between the existence of compensation schemes and investor confidence difficult to establish.[35] Its use here serves to underline the EC's concern with investor protection as a market-integration device, rather than as an independent policy, and with the investor as capital supplier to be encouraged, rather than as beneficiary of protection against the risks of the integrated market. Much less apparent from the ICSD's rationale is the need to protect investors against the consequences of firm failure in the riskier environment of the internal market.

Harmonization of compensation schemes also serves a purpose linked more directly to the removal of obstacles to free movement which is typically pursued under Article 47(2) EC. By introducing minimum harmonized rules for compensation schemes, the ICSD aims to eliminate the competitive distortions which could arise and prejudice the operation of the internal market were Member States to impose their compensation-scheme requirements on visiting firms (recital 6). There is an incentive for Member States

---

[34] ECOSOC also emphasized investor confidence and noted that 'losses suffered by investors as a result of the insolvency of an investment firm have an impact on public opinion. The whole of a Member State's financial sector risks being brought into disrepute': n 23 above, para 1.1.

[35] Landsmeer and Van Empel have questioned the Commission's investor-confidence rationale and suggested that market participants would have acted to provide compensation schemes were they really necessary to ensure investor confidence: n 31 above, 147.

to do so under the general-good justification and in the interests of investor protection where, in the absence of harmonization, investors are not deemed to be adequately protected by the coverage provided by visiting firms under their home-Member-State schemes. At the time the ICSD was proposed, the amount of cover varied across the Member States. In addition, even though most Member States operated some form of compensation scheme, investment firms subject to the ISD and able to benefit from its passport were not universally covered (recital 7). For example, while the UK had a comprehensive scheme, certain Member States such as Portugal and Denmark did not provide any cover, while other schemes were limited in scope, by, for example, restricting the scope of the coverage to the activities of stock exchange members (Luxembourg and the Netherlands). Harmonizing compensation-scheme requirements, placing them under home-Member-State control and further liberalizing the investment-services market for investment firms covered by the ISD thus dovetails with the initial liberalization framework set up by the ISD and supports the ISD passport. The link to the ISD passport is made clear by the ICSD's making membership of a compensation scheme in accordance with the ICSD a condition for ISD authorization (Article 2(1)); if a firm is not covered by a compensation scheme, ISD authorization will be withdrawn under Article 5(4).

In order to comply with the subsidiarity principle, the ICSD's scope is limited to the essential harmonization necessary to ensure a minimum level of protection for all users of authorized investment firms. Member States are free to prescribe wider or higher coverage than the minimum requirements, while rules concerning the structure, funding, and operation of compensation schemes are not harmonized (recital 25).

The ICSD's basis in Article 47(2) EC, and thus in the construction of the single market, seems to be safe from challenge even though its objectives are not limited to removing regulatory obstacles as is usually the case under Article 47(2). The *Deposit Guarantee* case rejected a challenge to the legal basis of the DGD in Article 47(2) (based on the argument that the DGD went beyond the objective of market integration by seeking to increase the level of depositor protection across the Community). The Court of Justice found that Article 47(2) was the correct legal basis, in that the DGD prevented Member States from invoking depositor protection to protect their markets and abolished obstacles to free movement. It also confirmed that in removing regulatory obstacles under Article 47(2) the Community could reregulate and impose standards and that notice could and was to be taken of the public-interest aims of the various Member States and a level of protection adopted for those interests which seemed acceptable in the Community.[36] Since then, the *Tobacco Advertising* case has warned that Article 47(2) does

[36] The judgment is discussed in Ch. IX sect. 12.2 above.

not grant a general power to regulate the internal market.[37] Notwith-standing its references to investor confidence, the ICSD is likely to be regarded as sufficiently grounded in removing real divergences between compensation schemes and in the risk of Member States using compensation schemes as barriers to the ISD passport (in the *Tobacco Advertising* judgment the Court stressed that where Article 47(2) is raised in connection with the removal of divergences, they must represent real obstacles to the internal market), to be vulnerable to challenge.

X.4.2 *The ICSD Framework*

X.4.2.1 *Recognition and Membership*

Article 2(1) provides that each Member State must ensure that one or more investor-compensation schemes are introduced and officially recognized within its territory. An investment firm authorized in that Member State may not carry on 'investment business' (defined under Article 1(2) by reference to the core investment services covered by section A of the ISD Annex, but including the non-core services of safe-keeping and administration in relation to the instruments covered by the ISD) unless it belongs to such a scheme.[38]

Where a Member State has admitted a branch of an investment firm the head office of which is outside the Community, it must under Article 11 ensure that the branch has cover equivalent to that prescribed by the ICSD. If equivalent cover is not available, then, subject to Article 5 of the ISD which requires that branches with non-Community head offices are not afforded more favourable treatment than their Community counterparts, the Member State may require the branch to join an investor-compensation scheme within its territory. Investors using the services of these branches

---

[37] Case C-376/98 *Germany v Parliament and Council* [2000] ECR I-8419 (the *Tobacco Advertising* case).

[38] Germany objected to mandatory membership as membership of the German compensation scheme, which applied to credit institutions (which were also the largest suppliers of investment services) and covered all deposit losses, was voluntary. (On the German compensation fund, see generally Deller, P, 'The Deposit Guarantee Directive of the European Community and Germany's Challenge' in Norton, J (ed), *1997 Yearbook of International Financial and Economic Law* (1999) 317, 318–22.) Germany's objections can be illustrated by reference to its parallel objections to the mandatory nature of the DGD. Before the Court of Justice, Germany invoked a breach of the principle of proportionality. In particular, it argued that, by disregarding a well-established practice of one Member State (Germany) and failing to allow Member States to adopt different approaches in regard to the application of the DGD, the DGD breached the proportionality principle. The Court's robust rejoinder was that it was neither possible nor necessary to take all well-established national practices into account and that a compulsory membership requirement was necessary for a harmonized minimum level of protection for all deposits: *Deposit Guarantee* case, n 30 above, paras 75–85.

must be supplied with all relevant information concerning the applicable compensation scheme.

Under Article 2(1), a Member State may exempt a credit institution from the obligation to join an investor-compensation scheme where that credit institution is already exempt under Article 3(1) of the DGD (which essentially provides that membership of a guarantee scheme is not necessary where the credit institution belongs to a system which ensures the credit institution's liquidity and solvency) but it must inform the Commission when it does so. Exemption is dependent on the credit institution providing investors with the same protection and information as are given to depositors and on investors enjoying protection which is at least equivalent to that afforded by an investor-compensation scheme. The Commission must also be informed of the characteristics of the protective scheme in question. A further exemption from mandatory membership of a recognized scheme is available under Article 5(3) which provides that, where an investment firm is excluded from a compensation scheme (section 4.9.3) it may, nonetheless, continue to provide investment services where, before its exclusion, it made alternative compensation arrangements which ensure that investors enjoy cover at least equivalent to that offered by the officially recognized scheme and which have similar characteristics to the officially recognized scheme.

X.4.2.2 *Home-Member-State Control and Mutual Recognition*

Under Article 7(1), an investor-compensation scheme recognized in a Member State also covers investors at branches set up by investment firms belonging to that compensation scheme in other Member States. The ISD established home-country control and mutual recognition as the dominant principles of supervision for investment firms, allocating jurisdiction for authorization and prudential control to the home Member State. The ICSD's approach is consistent with this principle. Home-Member-State control has the advantage of providing the home Member State's authorities with an incentive to ensure adequate supervision as the home-Member-State scheme will carry the consequences of firm failure.[39] By allocating the responsibility for compensation to the Member State with the closest regulatory relationship with the investment firm, the ICSD also lessens the exposure of host Member States to inadequate home-Member-State supervision.

---

[39] It has been argued in the context of deposit protection that home control could have the corrective effect of ensuring that home Member States' supervisory regimes generally are robust: Schoenmaker, D, 'Home Country Deposit Insurance' in Arestis, P (ed), *Money and Banking* (1993) 95, 103. See also Andenas in Cranston, n 24 above, 111–12.

X.4.3 *Scope of the Scheme*

X.4.3.1 *Firms Covered*

As might be expected, given the ICSD's objective of enhancing the ISD pass-port, the scheme applies to 'investment firms' as defined by the ISD, and either authorized in accordance with the ISD or authorized as a credit insti-tution under the banking regime to carry out the core investment-services activities listed in the ISD (Article 1(1)).[40] Investors using the services of unauthorized investment firms will not be protected by the ICSD regime. Management companies which benefit from a passport under the new man-agement-company regime will be subject to the ICSD in respect of their ISD services.[41]

As collective-investment schemes are excluded from the scope of the ISD (Article 2(2)(h)) losses sustained in connection with the management of col-lective-investment schemes, such as unit trusts, will not be covered by the Directive. Collective-investment schemes do, however, benefit from a single licence under the UCITS Directive and, in view of the ICSD's objective in enhancing the single market, might have been thought appropriate for inclusion in the ICSD. Given the particular complexities of such schemes, the Commission was of the opinion that compensation arrangements for collec-tive-investment schemes should be considered in the context of the special arrangements applicable to such schemes and not in the context of a direc-tive designed to enhance the ISD licence.[42] Preparation of the new man-agement-company regime provided the Commission with an opportunity to revisit the compensation question for UCITSs. On the basis of the ICSD

---

[40] Despite this limitation, the ICSD has acted as a catalyst for wider change. Ireland took the opportunity on implementing the ICSD to 'put in place a comprehensive system of compensa-tion for the entire investment intermediary sector': 155 Seanad Debates col. 991. In particu-lar, insurance intermediaries are brought within the scope of the Irish investor-compensation scheme.

[41] Amended Proposal for a European Parliament and Council Directive amending Directive 85/611/EEC on the Coordination of Laws, Regulation and Administrative Provisions Relating to Undertakings for Collective Investment in Transferable Securities [the UCITS Directive [1985] OJ L375/3] with a view to Regulating Management Companies and Simplified Prospectuses (the Management Company Proposal), COM(2000)331. The Council's Common Position is at [2001] OJ C297/10. The measure was adopted by the Council as a directive on 4 Dec. 2001. This discussion is based on the Common Position (references to the Management Company Proposal are to the Common Position text, while references to Articles are to the revised Articles of the UCITS Directive introduced by the new regime). At the time of writing, the final text of the adopted measure had not been published in the Official Journal and had not yet come into force. The Parliament did not, however, materially amend the Common Position text during its second reading prior to the adoption of the measure. Its only amendment (which was to shorten the Common Position's 5-year time frame from the entry into force of the new regime, at the end of which the Commission was to review the capital requirements imposed on management companies, to 3 years) was accepted by the Commission (COM(2001)587). Art. 5(f) subjects management companies to the ICSD regime.

[42] Explanatory Memorandum to Original Proposal, n 22 above, 11.

Report,[43] however, it concluded that it was not in a position to propose the introduction of a compensation scheme for unit-holders of UCITSs; this assessment may change given market developments.[44] Similar arguments apply with respect to pension-holders. The ISD passport covers investment services provided to pension funds or their trustees (discretionary portfolio-management is covered by the ISD) who will, in theory, be able to mount a claim under the ICSD against their investment advisers (although this is unlikely to arise in practice as pension funds are among the entities listed in Annex I as 'institutional and sophisticated investors' who may be excluded from the ICSD). The extent of any compensation rights of individual pension-holders where a pension fund defaults, on the other hand, is a complex issue which clearly goes beyond the scope of the ICSD.

X.4.3.2 *Investors Covered and Differentiated Protection*

Despite the ICSD's bias towards small and unsophisticated investors,[45] the explicit reference in recitals 4, 5, and 11 to 'small investors' (undefined) as being the target for the ICSD's protections, and the relatively low amounts of minimum compensation available under the ICSD, all of which suggest a focus on small retail investors, it extends cover, in principle, to an 'investor', broadly defined under Article 1(5) as 'any person who has entrusted money or instruments to an investment firm in connection with investment business'. The reference to 'in connection with investment business' ensures that compulsory compensation cover extends only to those investors whose relationship with the investment firm encompasses those activities covered by the ISD passport. Under Article 4(2), however, Member States may exclude certain investors from the scheme completely or limit their degree of protection. These investors are listed in Annex I. Section 1 of the list refers to 'professional and institutional investors' and sets out examples including investment firms, collective-investment undertakings, pension funds, and insurance undertakings and 'other professional and institutional investors'.[46] Governmental, local, and municipal authorities may also be excluded under sections 2 and 3, as may directors, managers, and persons holding 5 per cent or more of the capital of investment firms (section 4). Companies with more than fifty employees, a total balance sheet in excess of 2.5 million euro, and net turnover in excess of 5 million euro may also

---

[43] N 26 above.   [44] Management Company Proposal, n 41 above, 7.

[45] The Commission referred to the 'need to ensure investor protection and thus encourage the small investor in particular to invest in securities': Explanatory Memorandum to original proposal, n 22 above, 5.

[46] The Commission has proposed that the ICSD definition serve as the basis for a new definition of a 'professional investor' to be included in a revised ISD. See Ch. VII sect. 10.3.2 above.

be excluded (section 8). Also open to exclusion, albeit with a somewhat different motivation, are investors who have any responsibility for or have taken advantage of certain factors related to an investment firm which gave rise to the firm's financial difficulties or contributed to its deterioration. It remains to be seen whether this list will prove effective or whether the alternative approach of excluding certain types of transactions according to their degree of complexity is a more realistic way of reserving the ICSD's protections for the small investor.[47]

X.4.4 *The Compensation Trigger*

The right to compensation under the ICSD is triggered when the relevant competent authority (defined by reference to the ISD or, where applicable, to the consolidated supervision regime (Article 1(7)) determines that an investment firm appears for the time being, for reasons directly related to its financial circumstances, to be unable to meet its obligations arising out of investor claims and has no early prospect of being able to do so (Article 2(2)). The original version of Article 2(2) referred simply to the firm being 'unable to meet is obligations', prompting ECOSOC to query whether a supervisory authority 'fearing criticism of the quality and efficiency of its work' might activate the compensation process prematurely.[48] The qualification that there must be 'no early prospect' of the firm being able to meet its obligations mitigates this danger somewhat. Compensation is also payable where a judicial authority makes a ruling, for reasons directly related to an investment firm's financial circumstances, which has the effect of suspending the ability of investors to make claims against it (Article 2(2)). Where both the competent authority and the judicial authority have made such a declaration, the earlier in time activates the compensation process. By severing the compensation process from formal bankruptcy procedures in this way the ICSD speeds up the payment process. Significantly, the determination of the existence of a default is made by the relevant competent authority or the courts, and not the compensation scheme.[49]

The obligation to pay compensation is limited to situations where the investment firm is in financial difficulties. Claims arising from minor

---

[47] ECOSOC recommended that Member States be empowered to exclude sophisticated instruments, such as financial futures, options, and swaps, from compensation schemes: n 23 above, para. 4.1. Although the ICSD does not address explicitly the exclusion of certain types of instruments, recital 17 provides that a 'Member State must be able to exclude certain categories of specifically listed investments . . . if it does not consider that they need special protection'.

[48] N 23 above, para 4.2.

[49] Parliament sought to amend the Common Position to include the compensation scheme, as the body most concerned with the consequences of the existence of a default, among the bodies making such a determination. In rejecting this amendment, the Commission emphasized the importance of avoiding disputes between regulators and the compensation scheme: n 29 above, 5.

instances of fraud or negligence, for example, where the investment firm remains solvent do not come within the ICSD as such claims are more appropriately dealt with by the investment firm itself.[50]

X.4.5 *Claims Covered*

Compensation will be available in respect of two types of claim. Investors may request compensation for claims arising out of a firm's inability to repay money owed or belonging to investors and held on their behalf in connection with investment business (Article 2(2)). Under Article 8(1), Member States may provide that funds held in currencies other than those of the Member States and the euro be excluded from cover. Claims may also be made under Article 2(2) in respect of the inability of an investment firm to return to investors any instruments belonging to them and held, administered, or managed on their behalf in connection with investment business. In each case, the existence of an inability to return money or instruments is to be determined in accordance with the legal and contractual conditions applicable. The requirement that claims must arise in connection with 'investment business' as defined in the ISD is again consistent with the ICSD's link to the ISD passport.

Compensation is accordingly available only for a loss of money or instruments arising from the inability of the firm to meet its obligations to investors. Investors may not claim in respect of damages for negligence, breach of statutory or fiduciary duty, or other forms of civil liability. A claim will not lie against the scheme for a reduction in the value of instruments through, for example, the negligence of the firm. Claims in respect of mis-selling or misleading advertising (which, given that fraudulent investment-firm failure with a consequent loss of money and/or funds, is hopefully the exception rather than the norm, are likely to be of greater significance to most investors), to take another example, are also excluded from the scope of the ICSD. In all these cases, investors will simply have a claim over the assets of the bankrupt firm. Claims arising in connection with a transaction in respect of which a money-laundering conviction under Directive 91/308/EEC[51] has been delivered must also be excluded from compensation by any compensation schemes recognized under the ICSD.

---

[50] In its comments on the Common Position, the Parliament sought to remove the restrictive wording concerning the existence of 'financial difficulties' in order to extend the application of compensation schemes to all defaults, insolvent or otherwise, by investment firms. In its response, the Commission stressed that intervention by the scheme would not be necessary where the firm was solvent, as in such circumstances it would be 'up to [the firm] to repair the damage caused to investors': n 29 above, 5.

[51] Directive 91/308/EEC on prevention of the use of the financial system for the purpose of money laundering [1991] OJ L166/77.

X.4.6 *Payment of Compensation and Procedures*

X.4.6.1 *Levels of Compensation and Moral Hazard* [52]

Consistently with the ICSD's focus on the small investor, a relatively low minimum level of compensation of 20,000 euro per investor was adopted (Article 4(1)) as this level was regarded as being 'sufficient to protect the interests of the small investor' (recital 11).[53] This figure can be traced to the original proposal where the Commission noted that a figure of 20,000 euro would only be significant for the small investor. The Commission also relied on evidence that individual holdings of securities in investment accounts tended on average to be greater than individual holdings of cash held on deposit with credit institutions. In order to protect the small investor, it was therefore essential that the level of compensation be at least as high as that set out in the DGD (20,000 euro).[54] Investors who have lost cash deposits are not discriminated against; the minimum amount applies to both cash and securities. Any risk of moral hazard is reduced as the degree of cover is not extensive. Given the emphasis on small investors, the danger of excessive compensation costs being passed on to the investor through higher fees is also minimized. Likewise, any undue burden on Member States introducing schemes for the first time (Portugal and Denmark did not have compensation schemes) or offering a lower level of protection (the Luxembourg regime provided coverage of only 2,500 euro) was avoided. Article 4(3) explicitly acknowledges the possibility of higher standards being imposed by Member States by stating that the adoption or retention of higher standards by Member States is not precluded.

Under Article 4(4), Member States may, in the interests of promoting a degree of co-responsibility amongst investors and 'in order to encourage investors to take due care in their choice of investment firms' (recital 13), limit the cover to a specified percentage of an investor's claim. The percentage covered, however, must be equal to or in excess of 90 per cent of the claim where the amount claimed is under 20,000 euro. This measure goes some way, in principle, to addressing the moral-hazard problem. Moral hazard may also be addressed by reducing payments to investors where they might otherwise be receiving unfair benefits if they consciously took an excessive risk in their choice of investment firm, but the ICSD does not allow for payments to reduced in this way.

---

[52] For a review of how the Member States have implemented the ICSD's minimum level of coverage and capping provisions see the ICSD Report, n 26 above, Annex, para 1.2.

[53] This amount appears to reflect the reality of small investor claims. In the UK, the FSA reported in 2000 that up to that date over 60% of claims on the UK Investor Compensation Scheme were below £10,000 and over 80% were below £20,000: FSA 1997 Compensation Paper, n 6 above, 26.

[54] Explanatory Memorandum to original proposal, n 22 above, 8 and 10.

X.4.6.2 *Calculation and Payment of Claims*

The amount of the money or the value of the instruments owed to the investor is to be calculated as at the date on which the firm was found to be unable to meet its obligations (Article 2(4)). In the case of securities, their value is to be determined, where possible by reference to the market value, the 'where possible' qualification reflecting that a market value may be difficult to obtain for illiquid securities or that there may be several markets from which a market value may be taken or, conversely no organized market. For money and instrument claims the claim is to be calculated in accordance with the legal and contractual conditions (such as set-off and counter-claim) applicable to the assessment.

The cover provided extends to the investor's aggregate claim in respect of the same firm, regardless of the number of accounts, currencies or firm locations affected (Article 8(1)). Investors may seek to maximize cover by spreading investments around a number of firms, but those likely to engage in such practices are unlikely to be the small investors targeted by the ICSD. Specific provisions cover joint investment business. The basic principle is that claims will be divided equally between investors (Article 8(2)). The position of investors who are not absolutely entitled to the funds or securities claimed is also addressed by the ICSD. Article 8(3) provides that the person who is absolutely entitled is to receive the compensation provided such a person has been or can be identified before the determination under Article 2(2) that the firm is unable to meet its obligations.

Once the ICSD's conditions have been met, payment of compensation is mandatory and does not lie within the discretion of the compensation scheme (investors are additionally protected, in that Article 13 provides that Member States must ensure that the investor's right to compensation may be the subject of an action by the investor against the compensation scheme).[55] As a result, it appears that schemes may not reduce payments once the claim has been established. In particular, the ICSD does not allow Member States to adjust claims where it is equitable to do so, although, as outlined in section 4.5 above, claims arising from transactions related to money-laundering convictions are excluded and Member States may choose to exclude those who have contributed to the firm's difficulties. Under Article 9(1), the compensation scheme must inform investors of a default by the investment firm and it may set a period within which investors are required to present their claims. Any such period may not be less than five months from the date on which the determination of a firm's inability to meet its obligations is made or the date on which such a determination is made

---

[55] Discretionary schemes have been criticized in the past and are now rare. See, eg, Gower's comments (n 3 above, 96–9) on the original London Stock Exchange Compensation Fund, payments from which were at the absolute discretion of the Council of the Stock Exchange.

public. Expiry of this period may not, however, be used to deny compensation to an investor who has been 'unable' to make a claim in time. As the concept of a claim period would otherwise be negated, this requirement presumably involves a determination that the investor was in some way prevented by external circumstances from making a claim. Claims must be paid 'as soon as possible' and in any event within three months of the establishment of the eligibility and amount of the claim (Article 9(2)). This period grants compensation schemes time to locate and examine records and establish the legitimacy of claims. This can take some time where there has been fraud or significant operational failures. In wholly exceptional circumstances, the compensation scheme may apply to the competent authorities for an extension of the time limit although the extension may not be for more than three months. Where the investor seeking compensation has been charged with an offence relating to money laundering, payment may be suspended pending judgment on the offence (Article 9(3)). Otherwise, the mechanisms for making payments are largely left to the discretion of the Member States. The ICSD does not, for example, address whether interim payments or payments on account may be made. In the absence of a prohibition, it appears such payments are possible as long as full payment is made by the three-month deadline. The procedures for administering claims arising from branch activities could prove problematic, although Annex II provides that compensation schemes should co-operate in order to ensure that investors are paid properly and in the correct amount, albeit in the context of the management of the top-up procedure (section 4.7.2 below).

X.4.7 *Topping-up and the Export Ban*

X.4.7.1 *Introduction*

The application by the ICSD of the home-Member-State control principle, whereby investors using the services of a branch of an investment firm in a host Member State are covered by the compensation scheme of the investment firm's home Member State, has proved to be controversial.

Home-Member-State control and minimum harmonization allow Member States to introduce coverage above the minimum level of the ICSD (recitals 14 and 25), but alleviate the competitive distortions which could arise were an investment firm subject to different requirements in each Member State. It also places the burden of administering compensation on the scheme of the Member State with the closest regulatory relationship with the firm through authorization and prudential regulation. That Member State will also be in a better position to assess the appropriate premium. It follows, however, that investors in the same Member State may be protected to varying degrees (even where these investors are using similar services and buying similar products) depending on whether the investment firm is authorized in that State or passporting from another Member State, although in all cases the minimum compensation level of 20,000 euro is assured. Branches may suffer from a competitive disadvantage if they cannot offer the same level of coverage in an insolvency as home firms; although the cost of more extensive coverage, while carried by the industry (recital 23), is likely to be ultimately passed on to the investor in the form of higher fees, arguably reducing, over time, any real competitive distortions. In any event, the impact of the scale of compensation available on the exercise of investor choice is debatable. Nonetheless, in an attempt to mediate between these merits and demerits of home-Member-State control in the sensitive context of investor compensation, the ICSD relies on a compromise which dilutes the operation of home-Member-State control and adjusts the level of compensation available, in certain circumstances, by reference to the host-Member-State scheme.

X.4.7.2 *Topping-up*

Where the level or scope of the scheme offered by the host Member State exceeds the coverage of the home Member State's scheme, the host Member State must, in order to address 'disparities in compensation and unequal conditions of competition between national investment firms and branches of firms from other Member States' (recital 15) provide that visiting branches may voluntarily join the host scheme (Article 7(1)). The cover available to host-Member-State investors using the services of the branch may therefore be supplemented or 'topped-up'.[56] Although the top-up provision is rooted in market integration and in avoiding the development of unequal competition conditions as a result of the imposition of home-Member-State control, it has the effect of increasing investor protection (unlike its sister competition-levelling measure, the export ban, which has the effect of downgrading protection). Despite its investor-protection benefits (which also include minimizing investor confusion about the levels of compensation available), the top-up rule represents, nonetheless, a distortion of the home-Member-State control principle. More generous host schemes are exposed to claims in respect of firms the solvency of which they are not in a strong position to monitor. Claims may be made on the host scheme which have arisen due to a failure of supervision by the home authority responsible for prudential control. In addition, the host scheme faces the additional costs of

[56] The ICSD Report notes that as Member States have tended to converge with respect to levels of coverage the top-up provision is not likely to be widely used although it reported that the UK scheme (its coverage level of 73,000 euro is significantly higher than the EC average) has had a number of top-up applications: n 26 above, Annex, para 1.5.

assessing the appropriate premium to charge the branch.[57] The ICSD does, however, reduce the risks faced by host schemes, in that a host scheme may subject the branch to objective and generally applied membership conditions and may, after a twelve-month notice period, expel the branch from the scheme if it does not meet its obligations (Article 7(1) and (2)). From an administrative perspective, the top-up regime presents complex issues both for investors seeking compensation (as the payment of claims will be split between two schemes) and for the administration of the host scheme with respect to the additional premium charged to branches voluntarily joining the scheme. Annex 1 sets out guiding principles applicable to the procedures to be adopted by home and host Member States where a branch applies to join a host Member State's scheme for supplementary cover. In particular, the determination of the existence of a default remains with the home Member State's competent authority. In charging for supplementary cover, the host scheme will be entitled to assume that its liability will be limited to the excess of the cover it has offered over the cover provided by the home Member State, regardless of whether the home scheme actually makes payments to investors in the host Member State.

X.4.7.3 *The Export Ban*

(a) *Scope and Rationale*

Although the ICSD's export ban is now of only historical interest, in that it has been discontinued as of 31 January 1999, a discussion of the ban and the reasons taken to discontinue it is warranted, not only as its inclusion in the ICSD caused considerable controversy, but also because the treatment of the export ban reveals the extent to which single-market construction drives the ICSD.

The export ban was introduced at the common position stage in order to ensure consistency between the ICSD and the DGD, which contained an export ban in Article 4(1).[58] Under the export ban (Article 7(1)), which was designed from the outset to be a transitional measure, where the home Member State's scheme was more extensive in scope than that offered in the host Member State in which a branch provided services, the cover provided by that branch's scheme to its investors in the host Member State was not

---

[57] Such as obtaining information concerning the branch. In the context of deposit guarantee schemes, see see Landsmeer and van Empel, n 31 above, 146.

[58] Common Position, n 28 above, Statement of the Council's reasons, para III(2)(a). ECOSOC had recommended its inclusion in its opinion on the original proposal without offering a rationale for why it was appropriate, apart from referring to the parallel provision in the DGD (n 23 above, para 4.6). The European Parliament, by contrast, objected to its inclusion and deleted it from the Council's common position, but supported the top-up provisions (n 29 above, Amendment 6).

permitted to exceed the cover provided by the host Member State's scheme. This was despite the fact that the general rule of the ICSD is that the firm's compensation scheme cover all its investors, both at home and across the EC. As a result of the export ban, investors across the EC using the services of firms which were members of more extensive compensation schemes could not benefit from the higher standard of compensation, and would have been subject to discriminatory treatment, as compared with investors in the investment firm's home Member State, in the event of an insolvency and pay-outs under the scheme. The export ban was also to the disadvantage of investors holding portfolios with investment firms in a Member State with a high level of compensation and who wished, for whatever reason (personal, administrative, or otherwise), to transfer to a branch in a Member State where the level of compensation was lower. Its discriminatory effects made the export ban an anomalous feature of the ICSD.

The avoidance of a market in compensation schemes and the prevention of related market disturbances as the ICSD was implemented and home-Member-State control established over schemes subject to only minimum harmonization (particularly with respect to levels of coverage which would not, in principle, be uniform across the EC under the ICSD) were the reasons offered for the introduction of the export ban (recital 16). Its origins lie in the DGD negotiations in the course of which concerns were raised that market disturbances would occur were deposits to flood from domestic credit institutions to branches of foreign credit institutions. In the absence of evidence of how depositors were likely to behave, a temporary export ban was thought necessary to manage the market-place. The temporary nature of the DGD export ban (it was due to expire on 31 December 1999) represented a compromise between the Commission, which did not support the ban, other delegations which favoured the ban, and the Legal Service which felt that only a temporary ban would be valid.[59] In the context of investment services, however, it is not at all clear why a competitive market in investor security is necessarily a bad thing. Indeed, as outlined in section 1.2 above, an argument sometimes made against the introduction of compensation schemes *per se* is that they tend to reduce competition in security to the detriment of investors. It also seems unlikely that severe market disturbances would arise were competition to develop. Investors traditionally operate on the basis of the overall cost of the investment service and the firm's reputation. The less immediate factor of the cover provided by the relevant compensation scheme in an insolvency is not usually a critical issue in investor choice.[60] Large-scale movements of portfolios and investments tracking the

[59] For a review of the negotiations see the Commission Report on the Application of the export prohibition clause, Art 4(1) of the Directive on deposit-guarantee schemes (94/19/EC), COM(99)722 (the DGD Report), para 2.1

[60] Lomnicka, n 31 above, 19. See also n 13 above.

level of cover and of sufficient magnitude to create market disturbances appear to be unlikely. Further, there are alternative ways of protecting against any disturbances. A particular branch could be prevented from offering a scheme with greater coverage when, in the opinion of the host Member State authorities, market disturbances were, in fact, imminent.[61]

(b) *The Court of Justice*

The export ban was examined by the Court of Justice in the *Deposit Guarantee* case in the context of an action for annulment of the DGD taken by Germany.[62] A counterpart to the ICSD, the DGD provides for compulsory membership of an officially recognized deposit-protection scheme for deposit-taking institutions and subjects branches to home-country control. At the time of its adoption, the DGD prohibited the export of a more generous home-Member-State scheme to the host Member State in which a branch was operating. The major grounds for annulment raised by Germany were that the DGD was adopted on the wrong legal basis (section 4.1 above) and that there was a failure to state adequate reasons concerning the compatibility of the DGD's adoption with the subsidiarity principle.[63] Germany also challenged the export ban and the top-up provisions of the DGD, each of which it had vigorously opposed during the DGD negotiations.

The export ban was challenged on four grounds. Germany claimed that the export ban violated the duty to state reasons, in that the justification offered, that it would avoid market disturbances, was inadequate in not specifying the circumstances which would cause such disturbances. This was rejected by the Court, which found that the references in the DGD Preamble to the danger that market disturbances could arise were branches of credit institutions to offer higher levels of protection than credit institutions authorized in the host Member State and to the undesirability of deposit protection becoming an instrument of competition were sufficient to fulfil the duty to give reasons.[64] Germany's next claim was that, in requiring branches to reduce the amount of their guarantee, the export ban was restricting rather than facilitating the freedom to establish and hindering the reduction of differences between national schemes. Specifically, Germany argued that the obligation on German credit institutions to establish different contribution

---

[61] A similar argument was made by the German government in challenging the proportionality of the export ban in the Deposit Guarantee case: n 30 above, 2459.

[62] See generally Deller, n 38 above, and the annotation of the ruling by Roth, W-H, (1998) 35 *CMLRev.* 459.

[63] The Court found that the recitals to the DGD adequately set out the Community legislature's view that the aims of the DGD could be best achieved at Community level: n 30 above, para 26.

[64] Ibid, para 36.

rates for branches operating in other Member States gave rise to considerable difficulties. The Court found that as the DGD was designed to harmonize deposit-scheme requirements and eliminate fundamental differences between Member States, the export ban could not be contrary to Article 47(2) EC, simply because of the existence of conditions which might not be to the advantage of branches authorized in certain Member States. On harmonization, certain traders might lose the benefit of national legislation which was particularly favourable to them. The Court accepted that the export ban was an exception to the principle of minimum harmonization and mutual recognition but recognized that due to the complexity of the issue and the differences existing in Member States, the Council and Parliament were entitled to harmonize progressively. It also noted that compliance with the export prohibition was less onerous than compliance with the requirements of varying deposit protection schemes.[65] Germany's third ground for challenge was that the export ban was incompatible with a high level of consumer protection. The Court responded that although consumer protection was a Community objective it was not the sole objective. While it acknowledged that the export ban might result in a reduction in the level of consumer protection in certain circumstances, overall the DGD represented a considerable improvement in the protection of Community depositors. The Court also pointed out that the Treaty did not require that the highest level of protection in a particular Member State be adopted.[66] Infringement of the proportionality principle, the final argument advanced by Germany, was also dispatched by the Court. Germany claimed that the export ban was not necessary to prevent market disturbances arising from a deposit-protection-scheme-driven transfer of deposits; less burdensome means were available, such as a rule authorizing intervention only where disturbance was imminent. The reluctance of the Court to second-guess the Community legislature on complex matters of market regulation is clear in its response that it would not substitute its assessment for that of the Community legislature in economically complex situations.[67] It noted that, as deposit-guarantee schemes did not exist in all Member States prior to the adoption of the DGD, the Community legislature needed to assess the future effects of its action. In so doing, it was permitted to choose between risk prevention and the establishment of a system of specific protection. In opting to avoid market disturbances the occurrence of which could not be entirely ruled out, the Community legislature was pursuing a legitimate objective and the restriction imposed by the ban was not manifestly disproportionate.

[65] Ibid, paras 41–44. [66] Ibid, para 48.
[67] Ibid, paras 54–57. Roth's analysis is particularly critical of the Court's acceptance of the market-disturbance justification on the grounds that the market-disturbance objective was pursued in the DGD as an end in itself and was not sufficiently connected to free movement objectives: n 62 above, 475–6.

The challenge to the top-up provision also failed. The Court rejected Germany's claim that the Community was bound by the principle of home-Member-State supervision, finding that it was neither a Treaty principle nor a rule subordinating all others in the banking sphere and that the Community could depart from it, provided that the legitimate expectations of those concerned were not infringed.[68] Germany also claimed a breach of the proportionality principle, in that the obligation on host schemes to provide supplemental cover for branches the solvency of which they were not in position to supervise involved significant risks for host schemes which could be avoided were home Member States to provide supplemental cover. As in the case of the export ban, the Court rejected the proportionality argument, referring, *inter alia*, to the provisions of the DGD designed to reduce the burdens on the host Member State.[69]

(c) Review

The controversial nature of the export ban and its function in protecting the market-place against initial disturbances as compensation schemes were placed under home-Member-State control meant that it was introduced on a temporary basis only.[70] Article 7(1) provided that the export ban was to remain in place until 31 December 1999, but that before that date the Commission was to draw up a report reviewing the application of the ICSD's export ban and the DGD's export ban and considering the need to continue these provisions. The Commission duly presented its report and recommended that the export ban be discontinued.[71]

In presenting its conclusions, the Commission stressed the temporary nature of the ban and the requirement set out in Article 7(1) (and Article 4(1) DGD) that the export ban report be drawn up 'on the basis of experience acquired in applying' the export ban, noting that there was a trade-off between those two factors. It also noted that the ICSD export-ban report was to take into account experience gained in relation to the DGD export ban, which was considerably more extensive, given that the ICSD did not have to be implemented until September 1998 and limited information was available on its operation (the DGD should have been in place in the Member

---

[68] N 30 above, para 64.

[69] Ibid, paras 70–72. As with the ICSD, the DGD permits host schemes to require branches to fulfil certain conditions and to pay a fee and contains provisions for the co-ordination of information between home and host schemes.

[70] In its response to the Parliament's rejection of the export ban, the Commission argued that, while elimination of the export ban would in principle increase competition between and the efficiency of investment firms, it could also introduce volatility and instability in the investment markets. Given these difficulties, it found it advisable to maintain the ban over a short transitional period and monitor any adverse developments closely: n 29 above, 5.

[71] ICSD Report, n 26 above.

States since July 1995).[72] The Commission first identified the argument proposed by the Member States in support of the ban: that there was insufficient
experience of the effects of the export ban in that, during the transitional
period, no defaults leading to an ICSD or DGD claim were experienced by
credit institutions or investment firms with branches in other Member
States. As a result, the possibility of market disturbances arising could not
be ruled out.[73] In support of removing the export ban,[74] the Commission
pointed to the argument that, as the export ban created an obstacle to free
movement and discriminated between investors of the same firm, it could
only be a transitional measure justified by reference to the uncertain situation existing before the ICSD was adopted. The financial sector had, however, developed considerably, such that the large differences which had
existed between Member States at the adoption of the ICSD, and which had
justified the export ban, no longer existed. In particular, a minimum level of
coverage was in place and considerable convergence on the level of compensation had occurred.[75] In addition, the export ban was a 'residual element which splits the Single Market into national markets' while the process
of financial integration, driven by technological developments, consolidation
of market participants, the FSAP's initiatives,[76] and the introduction of the
euro, was continuing; accordingly, it should be eliminated. Finally, as far as
market disturbances were concerned, experience in the banking sector had
not produced any concrete evidence that market disturbances might occur
on removal of the export ban. The Commission's conclusion was that, given
the harmonization undertaken by the ICSD, 'it seems disproportionate to
prolong the export prohibition clause in order to avoid market disturbances
that nobody could estimate or specify and which seem highly unlikely to
happen' and that a remote risk of disturbances could not be considered as
more important than completion of the single market in financial services.[77]
The Commission also emphasized that retaining the export ban for the ICSD
would be difficult to justify as far as consumer protection was concerned in
light of the removal of the DGD ban,[78] given that, as some schemes cover
both depositors' and investors' claims, discrimination would be introduced
between depositors and investors at the same foreign branch of an institution. The Commission is to monitor the situation closely, however, and propose appropriate remedial measures if necessary in the event that serious
market disturbances do develop.

---

[72] Ibid, para 3.1.   [73] Ibid, para 3.2.   [74] Ibid, para 3.3.
[75] The Commission noted that all Member States but 4 had, at that time, a compensation
level of between 20,000 and 28,000 euro: ibid.
[76] 1999 Commission Communication on Implementing the Framework for Financial
Markets: Action Plan, COM(1999)232 (the FSAP).
[77] Ibid, para 4.   [78] See the DGD Report, n 59 above.

X.4.8 *Disclosure and Advertising*

Foreshadowing the emphasis which has recently emerged on disclosure as an instrument of investor protection in the investor/investment-firm relationship and in the internal-market risk environment, the ICSD introduces information requirements designed to ensure disclosure of key information for the benefit of investors. Member States are required to ensure that each investment firm takes 'appropriate measures' so that 'actual and intending' investors are aware of the compensation scheme to which the firm belongs (Article 10(1)). This requirement extends to any alternative arrangements adopted under Article 2(1) (alternative arrangements for credit institutions) or Article 5(3) (arrangements applicable on exclusion of an investment firm from a scheme). In addition, information must be made available concerning the provisions of the compensation scheme, including the amount and scope of the cover provided. Although not required by the ICSD, it is particularly important that it be made clear to investors that a scheme does not cover losses arising from a stock market decline. Information must be available, although only 'on request', concerning the conditions and formalities applicable to any compensation scheme pay-outs. Actual and intending investors at branches of an investment firm established outside the Community must be supplied with 'all relevant information' concerning the compensation arrangements applicable to their investments (Article 11(2)).

Disclosure will be particularly important where the branch has opted for supplemental cover under the host (the investor's home) scheme. In such circumstances the potential for confusion is considerable, as investors may be faced with a byzantine maze of information concerning compensation for a single holding of securities or funds. Although the information is to be 'made available in a readily comprehensible manner', it remains to be seen whether the ICSD's requirements will be sufficiently adequate to inform investors, without undue confusion, where two compensation schemes apply to their assets. The only express concession made to investors using the services of branches is that the prescribed information be supplied in the official language of the State in which the branch is established (Article 10(2)).

One notable feature of the ICSD is its awareness of the vulnerability of investors to advertising; as discussed in Chapter IX above, investment-services advertising has not been specifically addressed at EC level, and it is only recently that moves have been taken to control advertising in the context of distance sales. Advertising membership of an investor-compensation scheme by an investment firm could lead investors to believe that the firm has been included in the scheme following a review of its soundness or a determination that the firm is an acceptable risk. They could accordingly be lulled into a false sense of security in their dealings with the firm. Acknowledging these dangers, and in another illustration of the ICSD's characterization of investor protection as a function of wider market stability, the ICSD requires Member States to establish rules limiting the use in advertising of information relating to compensation schemes in order to prevent such advertising from affecting the stability of the financial system or investor confidence (Article 10(3)). In particular, Member States may restrict such advertising to factual references to the schemes to which the firm belongs.

X.4.9 *Management and Structure*

X.4.9.1 *Formal Basis*

The ICSD does not require that the compensation scheme be placed on a statutory footing, but leaves the form of the scheme to the Member States. One reason for this flexible approach is provided in recital 18 which states that divergences in legal status between compensation schemes (as between schemes run under the aegis of professional organizations and statutory schemes, for example) become critical only (in relation to the ICSD's purposes) with respect to whether membership is compulsory and when members are excluded. Both these issues are covered by the ICSD in Article 2(1) (mandatory membership), Article 5(2) (exclusion of members which do not meet scheme requirements), and Article 7(2) (exclusion of branches which do not meet the obligations imposed in respect of topping-up). It appears that self-regulatory and private, contractual arrangements will be sufficient for the purposes of the Directive.[79] Nonetheless, Article 13 stipulates that Member States must ensure that the investor's right to compensation may be the subject of an action by the investor against the compensation scheme, and its legal form must therefore allow such an action to be taken.

Although compensation schemes should balance the interests of investors and the firms that fund the scheme,[80] the composition of the board or other governing body of the scheme and the extent to which investors' interests should be represented is not addressed. The rights of investors to compensation once the eligibility criteria are met and to sue the scheme if payment is not forthcoming, should, however, be sufficient to protect the investor against any institutional bias.

---

[79] This flexible approach to legal status can be seen across the EC securities-regulation regime with respect to the treatment of competent authorities, although a seachange is underway. See Ch. XV sect. 3.1.2 below.

[80] Where a scheme is funded by the industry the cost-effectiveness of the scheme is likely to be a bone of contention between the scheme and its members.

X.4.9.2 *Funding*

Sound funding arrangements are critical to the effectiveness of compensation schemes. The financing of compensation schemes can be controversial,
particularly where prudent firms are obliged to pay for the misdeeds of less
sound firms. The ICSD does not lay down minimum rules on the funding of
compensation schemes. Schemes may as a result levy fixed or variable premiums. They may alternatively operate without premiums and levy charges
based on the actual commitments to be met by the scheme. Risk-weighting
may or may not be adopted by schemes in assessing contributions. An argument sometimes made for reducing moral hazard at the level of the investment firm is that firm contributions should be risk-weighted, reflecting the
degree of risk represented by a particular firm. Funding requirements might
also reflect cross-sector risk profiles and assess contributions on a sectoral
basis, given that within the universe of investment services, some activities
are likely to generate more claims than others and cross-subsidies may
emerge between sectors engaged in different activities, such as the discretionary portfolio-management and brokerage sectors, for example.

Compliance with the subsidiarity principle suggests, however, that setting
compensation-scheme rules at this level of detail falls outside the competence
of the Community, unless it can be shown that variations in funding
arrangements are threatening to obstruct the single market. For example,
moral-hazard and competitive distortions are possible where schemes are
underwritten by governments. Excessive scheme expenditure, wholly paid
for by members, poses another threat, in that it can jeopardize the solvency
of otherwise sound members and ultimately the stability of the wider market in investment services.[81] In seeking to address these concerns, recital 23
establishes the principle that the cost of funding schemes be borne by the
investment firms themselves. It also provides that the funding capacities of
schemes must be in proportion to their liabilities and that the funding
arrangements adopted must not jeopardize the stability of the financial system of the Member State in which the scheme is recognized.

The right of investors under Article 13 to sue compensation schemes
where compensation is not forthcoming may suggest that schemes must be
in a position to meet all investors' claims up to the ICSD's minimum threshold and, accordingly, that they may not impose maximum pay-out limits for
particular time periods. It is possible (but not likely) that a catastrophic series
of investment-firm failures might drain the resources of a scheme completely
and place considerable funding strains on member firms. It is not entirely

---

[81] ECOSOC was particularly concerned that the wider Community financial system might be
threatened by the form of funding adopted: n 23 above, para 4.5.

clear in such circumstances how the requirement that funding arrangements must not jeopardize the stability of the financial system and the apparent obligation on a scheme to meet all claims can be reconciled. Two
solutions seem possible. Recital 23 refers to the self-funding requirement in
terms of costs 'in principle' being borne by investment firms. This formula
may leave room for last-resort intervention by government in the form of a
line of credit to the scheme when funding costs become unsustainable by the
industry. Alternatively, it has been suggested that the obligation on deposit-
protection schemes to pay out under the DGD applies only to reasonably
foreseeable defaults and crises in the banking system. This argument might
also apply to investor-compensation schemes recognized under the ICSD.[82]
The Commission has reported that it is investigating funding practices to
ensure that funding principles are observed. In particular, it is monitoring
the provision of borrowing facilities by central banks or political bodies. It is
also to examine funding via contributions linked to actual calls on the
scheme as it is concerned that compensation schemes which are not funded
by periodic levies may not be able to pay out without delay when calls are
made on the scheme.[83]

X.4.9.3 *Internal Controls*

Article 5(1) provides that where an investment firm does not meet the obligations of the scheme, the competent authorities which authorized that firm
shall, in co-operation with the compensation scheme, take all measures
appropriate to ensure that the firm meets its obligations. If the default continues, the compensation scheme may (where permitted under national law
and with the express consent of the competent authorities) give not less than
twelve months' notice of its intention to exclude the firm from the scheme
(Article 5(2)). In the interests of investor protection the scheme must continue to provide cover in respect of investment business transacted during
this twelve-month period. The ultimate sanction for failure to comply with
scheme obligations is loss of authorization as Article 2(1) sets out that an
authorized investment firm may not carry out investment business unless it
is a member of a recognized compensation scheme. Withdrawal of authorization may be avoided and investment business may be carried on by the
excluded firm where (when national law permits and with the express consent of the competent authorities which issued the authorization) the firm,
before its exclusion, made alternative compensation arrangements which
ensure that investors enjoy at least the same level of cover as that offered by
the officially recognized scheme (Article 5(3)). If such arrangements are not

---

[82] Le Brun, n 24 above, 247.   [83] ICSD Report, n 26 above, Annex, para 1.4.

made, the competent authority must withdraw the firm's authorization (Article 5(4)). Under Article 6, compensation cover must extend to cover all business transacted by the firm up to the point at which authorization was withdrawn.

X.4.9.4 *Subrogation*

Subrogation rights are usually granted to investor-compensation schemes in respect of investors' claims against the defaulting firm. This right is established for all compensation schemes under Article 12, in relation to the rights of investors in liquidation proceedings for amounts equal to the payments made by the schemes.

X.4.10 *Competent Authorities and Supervision*

The ICSD does not require that specific competent authorities be established to supervise compensation schemes, but relies on the competent authorities which exercise supervision over investment firms under the ISD or exercise consolidated supervision in accordance with the Community's consolidated supervision framework (Article 1(7)). Throughout the ICSD, the competent authorities exercise back-stop control. They determine when a firm is unable to meet its obligations, triggering the compensation procedure (Article 2(2)). They must ensure, through the imposition of penalties, if necessary, that a firm complies with scheme obligations (Article 5(1)) (including firms which have joined supplemental schemes in host Member States (Article 7(2)) and they must be consulted before a firm is expelled from a scheme (including host-Member-State supplemental schemes (Article 7(2)) and also where a firm is permitted to make equivalent, alternative compensation arrangements (Article 5(2) and (3)). Ultimately, they withdraw authorization where a firm is no longer a member of a recognized or equivalent scheme (Article 5(4)). They also have the power to authorize extensions to the time limit within which payments must be made under a compensation scheme (Article 9(3)).

X.4.11 *Co-operation and Communication: Cross-border Claims*

The application of the principle of home-Member-State control means that investors may find it necessary to make claims against schemes in other Member States. Apart from the Article 10 disclosure requirements, the ICSD does not facilitate such cross-border claims. In particular, apart from the top-up context which is addressed in Annex II, the ICSD does not establish formal procedures for communication and co-operation between compensation schemes. A requirement that every scheme maintain a point of contact in each Member State where its members operated might have been of practical assistance to investors.[84]

X.4.12 *Relationship with the DGD*

The scope of the definition of the 'investment firms' which are subject to the ICSD's requirements extends to credit institutions authorized under the banking regime to provide investment services. Credit institutions supplying these services are also subject to the requirements of the DGD. Where a single scheme meets the requirements of both the ICSD and the DGD, it is not necessary that a credit institution belong to two separate schemes (recital 9). Where an investment firm is also a credit institution, it may be difficult to distinguish between funds held on deposit covered by the DGD and funds held in connection with investment business which are covered by the ICSD (recital 9). In such cases, it is within the discretion of the Member State to decide which scheme applies. In addition, double recovery is prohibited. A claim may not be eligible for compensation under both the ICSD and the DGD (Article 2(3)).

---

[84] See also Marquand, n 31 above, 892.

PART IV

The EC Securities-trading Markets Regime

XI

The Regulation of Securities-trading Markets

XI.1 THE EC CAPITAL-RAISING REGIME
AND SECURITIES-TRADING MARKETS

This chapter concerns the regulation of securities-trading markets by the EC and the integration of trading systems.[1] It is related to the examination of capital raising in Chapters II, III, and IV above, in that the current admission-to-listing and disclosure regime addresses access by issuers to the Official List of securities-trading markets (as well as public-offer disclosure) and the role of securities-trading markets in bringing securities to the market. This chapter deals with the trading services supplied by the securities-trading markets which support the secondary trading market in which the issuer's securities can trade between investors. Disclosure forms one bridge between the two regimes; while it is at the heart of the securities directives, it also features in the EC securities-trading market regime. The focus of disclosure broadens beyond the issuer to encompass market transparency; this is central to efficient price formation on the market. The two regimes are also linked by their distinct contributions to the development of an integrated securities market. While the securities directives facilitate access by issuers to listing and to the securities-trading markets, they do not, of themselves, address the integration of trading mechanisms or facilitate greater liquidity in pan-EC securities trading. The integration of trading and its associated benefits is dependent on liberalizing access to trading on national securities-trading markets and on generating competition and co-operation between markets. This chapter will examine the rationale for and the basis of the EC's regulation of securities-trading markets, the extent to which regulation supports competition between and ultimately the integration of

---

[1] A full discussion of the trading mechanics, market structure, and economic issues underlying securities-trading markets and their integration is outside the scope of this ch. For a detailed review of securities-trading markets in the EC see generally Pagano, M, and Steil, B, 'Equity Trading I: The Evolution of European Trading Systems' in Steil, B (ed), *The European Equity Markets. The State of the Union and an Agenda for the Millennium* (1996) 1, Schwartz, R, 'Equity Trading II: Integration, Fragmentation, and the Quality of Markets', ibid 59, Schwartz, R, and Steil, B, 'Equity Trading III: Institutional Investor Trading Practices and Preferences', ibid 81, Steil, B, 'Equity Trading IV: The ISD and the Regulation of European Market Structure', ibid 113 and Pagano, M, 'The Changing Microstructure of European Equity Markets' in Ferrarini, G (ed), *European Securities Markets. The Investment Services Directive and Beyond* (1998) 177. On the economic rationale for securities-trading markets generally see Houthakker, H, and Williamson, P, *The Economics of Financial Markets* (1996) 110–40.

securities-trading systems and the harmonized standards applicable to securities-trading markets.

XI.2 THE RATIONALE FOR REGULATING SECURITIES-TRADING MARKETS

XI.2.1 *Securities-trading Markets*

Securities-trading markets play a critical role in the secondary markets by providing a mechanism which: allows securities to be admitted to trading; creates liquidity in securities; allows buyers and sellers to deal easily and form binding contracts according to set rules; produces and discloses trading information; and provides a price-setting system in which investors can have confidence for the securities dealt in on the trading market.[2] Of these functions, the price-formation function is particularly important. It provides buyers and sellers with buy or sell prices or quotations on a continuous basis so that buyers and sellers have a reasonable expectation that they will be in a position to execute their orders at the prices quoted.[3] The extent to which and how these functions are provided by securities-trading markets depends

---

[2] While there is considerable discussion about the essential features and functions of what are variously termed markets, stock exchanges, regulated markets, exchanges, and so on, most discussions focus on 'the role of exchanges as providers of trading systems' and on trading systems 'as a forum for executing a trade': Lee, R, *What is an Exchange?: The Automation, Management and Regulation of Financial Markets* (1998) 1 (and see generally on this question). For the trading services analysis see also Fischer, D, 'Organised Exchanges and the Regulation of Dual Class Common Stock' (1987) 54 *University of Chicago LR* 119, 121–3. For a refinement of the trading-services categorization incorporating the notion of securities-trading markets as entrepreneurial firms providing trading and liquidity services and examining their regulation from that perspective see Ferrarini, G, 'Exchange Governance and Regulation: An Overview' in Ferrarini, n 1 above, 245. For a perspective based on the price-discovery mechanism and the provision of rulebooks which provide a mechanism for facilitating trades see Scott-Quinn, B, 'Networks and the Changing Structure of the European Securities Industry' in Federal Trust, *Towards an Integrated European Capital Market* (1993) Appendix 3, 39, 47–8 and, for a more general analysis, see Kitch, E, 'Competition Between Markets: Good or Bad' in Oditah, F (ed), *The Future for the Global Securities Market—Legal and Regulatory Aspects* (1996) 233, 235–8.

For a regulatory definition which attempts to capture the essential functions and features of a securities-trading market see s 3(a)(1) of the US Securities Exchanges Act, 1934 which provides that an exchange is 'any organisation, association or group of persons . . . which constitutes, maintains, or provides a market-place or facilities for bringing together purchasers and sellers of securities or for performing with respect to securities the functions commonly performed by a stock exchange as that term is generally understood, and includes the market place, and the facilities maintained by such exchange'.

[3] It has been noted (in the context of stock exchanges) that the price-formation mechanism arises as a stock exchange 'is a meeting place for demand and supply in circumstances which, since they approximate as closely as possible to perfect competition, lead to a price which can be accepted as the value of the commodity dealt in': Wymeersch, E, *Control of Securities Markets in the European Economic Community*, Collection Studies. Competition—Approximation of Legislation Series No.31 (1977) 32.

on their particular characteristics; much will depend on whether they take the form of traditional, formally organized stock exchanges and markets or whether they follow recent developments and are constituted as electronic trading systems which provide off-exchange trading services and, to varying degrees, replicate the traditional functions of organized stock exchanges and markets.

The characteristics of traditional organized markets vary widely. They are sometimes regarded as taking two main forms: exchanges which have a central, physical location and an auction or order-based market structure or model; and organized dealer markets, which operate through electronic networks but are based on intermediation of some degree and have a dealer or quote-based market model.[4] Auction markets are order-driven; a security's price is set centrally, based on the forces of supply and demand and on the interaction of all orders, by the exchange's order-book mechanism.[5] Dealer markets are quote-driven, with prices being set by market-makers who offer competing bid and offer (buy and sell) quotes in the particular security for which they are registered and in respect of which they are obliged to buy and sell securities during the time period set by the market.[6] Auction and dealer functions are often, however, blurred, with organized markets at times adopting market mechanisms which incorporate aspects of both market structures.[7] Whether organized markets adopt auction or dealer-market structures tends to be a function of investment patterns in the particular country. Where market investments are intermediated through institutional investors such as pension funds, dealer markets tend to dominate as they provide a large degree of liquidity, with market-makers available to make trades. Direct participation in the market-place tends to lead towards the

---

[4] For the exchange/organized-dealer market categorization, see IOSCO Technical Committee, Supervisory Framework for Markets Report (1999) (the IOSCO Markets Report) 1. The exchange/dealer-market categorisation is a fluid one. The London Stock Exchange, eg, has a dealer element as well as an order mechanism (see n 7 below). Indeed, the point has been made that '[e]xchanges around the globe differ profoundly in their role, functions, and governance structures, and these elements are in rapid evolution as a result of technology and competition': Gros, D, and Lanno, K, *The Euro Capital Market* (2000) 125.

[5] A range of orders can be fed into the system such as 'limit orders' which specify the size and price at which the transaction will be executed and 'at-best orders' or 'market orders', which are executed when entered at the best price then available in the system. See, eg, Houthakker and Williamson, n 1 above, 116–18.

[6] For a description of auction and dealer-market structures see the OECD's 1991 Report on Systemic Risks in Securities Markets (the OECD Systemic Risk Report) 19–20.

[7] See Röell, A, 'Competition Among European Exchanges' in Ferrarini, n 1 above, 213, 218. The London Stock Exchange, which previously was a dealer-driven market-place, has, since 1997, run an electronic order book (the Stock Exchange Electronic Trading Service or SETS) for its most liquid stocks, which, when bid and offer prices match, executes matching orders automatically. For non-SETS securities, the London Stock Exchange operates a dealer mechanism under which market makers on SEAQ and SEAQ International make two-way quotes for the securities in which they are registered. It also operates a combined service (Stock Exchange Alternative Trading System or SEATS Plus) which combines competing quotes and orders.

dominance of auction markets as they produce stable prices.[8] Organized markets tend to provide a full range of 'bundled services' including trading, price discovery and information-disclosure functions, and would also traditionally have sophisticated rule structures and admission requirements for participants and securities.[9]

Recently, electronic trading systems and communication networks (such as electronic bulletin boards), which allow buyers and sellers to enter into transactions away from traditional organized markets and to access trading systems without any form of intermediation, have challenged the established characterization of securities-trading markets.[10] These alternative trading systems (ATSs), developed by market participants, may provide many of the services normally the preserve of traditional organized markets.

XI.2.2 *The Rationale for Regulation*

The regulation of securities-trading markets is primarily directed to ensuring market integrity, efficiency, and stability and thereby investor and market confidence. The effectiveness of securities-trading markets in mediating between capital seekers and investors and in serving the economy generally is largely dependent on confidence in the operation of securities-trading markets. Regulatory regimes are typically designed to ensure that, in the interests of investor protection and confidence in the market-place: markets operate in a fair, transparent, and competitive manner, in that those that wish to access the market-place can do so without discrimination; that they are free from fraudulent and manipulative practices; that the integrity and stability of the trading process are protected; and that risks are properly identified and managed.[11] A particular concern of regulation is the protection of the integrity and efficiency of the price formation process.

The degree of regulation imposed on securities-trading markets varies according to the characteristics of the market or trading system, the sophistication of market participants, the nature of the access rights and the types of products traded.[12] It also reflects perceptions of the extent to which secu-

---

[8] OECD Systemic Risk Report, n 6 above, 19.

[9] The extent to which a market follows formal procedures and rules is another indicator of whether it is an organized market. Membership of the International Federation of Stock Exchanges (FIBV), eg, is open only to organized markets, which are defined by reference to levels of organization, regulation, and supervision.

[10] See sect. 8.4 below. They have been memorably described as 'a previously unknown type of institution, the "MONSTER" (a Market Oriented New System for Terrifying Exchanges and Regulators)': Lee, n 2 above, 1.

[11] For a typical categorization of the objectives of securities-trading market regulation see the IOSCO Markets Report, n 4 above, 2–6. From the economist's market-failure perspective, securities-trading markets can produce market failures (such as barriers to entry, fraud, and systemic risk) which require corrective regulation.

[12] IOSCO, *Objectives and Principles of Securities Regulation* (1998) (the 1998 IOSCO Principles) para 13.3.

rities-trading markets are public-interest-motivated providers of trading services or profit-driven providers of trading services. Organized markets, as the most sophisticated form of trading system, are currently the main focus for regulation. ATSs, on the other hand, are, depending on their features, in some cases exempt from regulation which specifically addresses securities markets and regulated instead as investment firms.

XI.2.3 *The Scope of Regulation*

Much of securities-trading market regulation reflects the concern to protect market efficiency and integrity and, in particular, price formation and fairness in trading. Market-conduct rules which protect the market against manipulative and price-distorting practices play an important role, as do disclosure-based rules. Reporting rules and rules on the transparency of market trades form the backbone of much of securities-trading market regulation. Generally, regulation typically involves the following elements: ensuring the competence of the operator of the market via authorization procedures which include obligations to adopt market-operating rules which pursue the objectives of market regulation; ongoing supervision of the market operator; admission of instruments to trading and the rules governing trading; admission of participants to the trading system; provision of trading information; order-management rules; execution rules; post-trade disclosure rules; supervision of the trading system and its participants; and oversight of trading disruptions.[13]

XI.3 THE EC AND SECURITIES-TRADING MARKET REGULATION

XI.3.1 *Scope of the Regime*

The EC's touch in the area of securities-trading market regulation has been a light one to date. Regulation has largely been confined to the limited liberalization and standards-harmonization provisions contained in the Investment Services Directive,[14] which are the main concern of this chapter. The securities-trading market regime also includes the general market-integrity protection and market-abuse controls contained in the EC regime, primarily in the Insider Dealing Directive[15] (see Chapter XIII below) and the

---

[13] Ibid. For an extensive discussion of the principles of market regulation see the IOSCO Markets Report, n 4 above. See also Avougleas, E, 'Financial Market Regulation and the New Market Landscape: In Search of a New Regulatory Landscape for Market Abuse' (2000) 2 *ICCLJ* 89, 95–8.

[14] Directive 93/22 on investment services in the securities field [1993] OJ L141/27 (the ISD).

[15] Directive 89/592/EEC coordinating regulations on insider dealing [1989] OJ L334/30 (the IDD).

systemic stability protections for settlement systems, which deal with the transfer of ownership post-trade, contained in the Settlement Finality Directive (see Chapter XII below).[16]

XI.3.2 *Features of the Regime*

The current ISD regime generally reflects traditional conceptions of the securities-trading market as a public-service provider of trading services, usually exercising monopoly power, and thus on the competition and, specifically, access aspects of regulation.[17] The focus on access is also a reflection of the traditional reliance on EC securities regulation as a device for market integration and, in particular, on investment firms as beneficiaries of integration. It has meant that, for the most part, the regime's attention has been directed to ensuring non-discriminatory access by investment firms to 'regulated markets' across the EC. Harmonization of the substantive operational regulation of those markets, in the interests of investor protection and the integrity of the price-formation process, has largely been sidelined; not least because the usual trigger for the reregulation post-liberalization of common standards, the internal-market passport, has not been conferred on securities-trading markets, although, as discussed in section 6.4 below, a passport has been granted to securities-trading markets with respect to remote membership. The regime does not, as a result, reveal at present an underlying rationale for regulating securities-trading markets in the internal market.

In addition, the different market models in operation across the EC have exerted a considerable influence on the development of the securities-trading market regime and generated considerable problems with respect to how the sometimes competing interests (or perceptions of these interests) of investor protection and efficiency/liquidity are to be balanced. In particular, the tension between market models has determined the approach towards market access and complicated the standards-harmonization process (as the effectiveness of a market model is sensitive to operating rules such as transparency requirements), although recently greater industry-led market-model convergence can be observed.[18]

[16] Directive 98/26/EC on settlement finality in payment and securities settlement systems [1998] OJ L166/45 (the Settlement Finality Directive).

[17] Control of monopoly powers forms a component of regulation generally. In the securities regulation sphere it plays a limited role and is most closely connected with access to trading markets or settlement systems: Goodhart, C, 'Some Regulatory Concerns' in Goodhart, C (ed), *The Emerging Framework of Financial Regulation* (1998) 215, 219. For the monopoly power analysis and its relevance to the prevailing securities-trading environment see Ferrarini, G, 'The European Regulation of Stock Exchanges: New Perspectives' (1999) 36 *CMLRev.* 569.

[18] Although, as discussed in sect. 9.7 below, greater harmonization of standards is likely to follow, the process will be eased (and more easily legitimated) if it is accompanied by market-model convergence. Some commentators are of the view that standards harmonization is inherently inappropriate in a securities-trading market environment where different market models

As market-model convergence might suggest, the shape of future EC initiatives is increasingly being formed by market developments and, in particular, by the force of the competitive pressures now prising open the market in securities-trading markets which have exposed considerable weaknesses in the ISD's current securities-trading market framework. Competition, on the foot of the ISD's liberalization and wider market developments such as technological advances, the arrival of the euro, and demutualization,[19] has emerged as the most dynamic agent for change in the trading environment. Industry movement towards greater integration of securities-trading markets across the EC appears inexorable while, in the regulatory sphere, in a classic example of regulation following market developments, the adoption of a securities-trading market passport and common supervisory standards for this competitive environment is increasingly likely. Although the Commission is committed to adopting a more sophisticated securities-trading market regime (section 9.7 below), the need for harmonization is not free of challenge, given the arrival of competition and with it the argument that, as providers of trading services subject to competitive pressures and provided with incentives to promote market integrity and investor protection, securities-trading markets should be free to engage in regulatory competition, subject to EC-level intervention only where essential to correct a market failure such as fraud or systemic instability.[20] Further harmonization should, however, benefit from the increasing maturity of EC securities regulation as a regulatory regime which is, certainly, a creature of market integration, but which also promotes distinct and articulated regulatory objectives. Indeed, the signs are that direct reference is being made to the objectives of confidence, efficiency, and transparency in designing the new harmonized system, notwithstanding its ultimate role as a market-integration device.[21]

XI.4 THE ROOTS OF THE REGIME

Initial developments in this area were concerned with access to and, to a limited extent, with the development of common standards for trading markets.

Divergences in the structure, access requirements and operational rules of securities-trading markets across the EC soon emerged as a significant

are in operation. In the transparency context, see Schaefer, S, 'Competition Between Regulated Markets in London' in Ferrarini, n 1 above, 205.

[19] The demutualization of the London Stock Exchange and its transformation into a public company vulnerable to takeover bids being a good example.

[20] For this perspective and its implications for the regulatory structure see generally Ferrarini, n 17 above.

[21] See sect. 9 below.

barrier to the integration of securities markets and to the efficient raising
and distribution of capital across the EC.[22] The 1977 Wymeersch study
reported that one or more stock exchanges or official markets (those which
restricted dealing to admitted persons and generated an official price for their
securities), operated in each Member State, while most Member States also
had over-the-counter (OTC) markets. While the former were generally subject to a high level of supervision and control, supervision over the latter
varied from a 'practically absolute absence of rules, to a pattern which is
based on extensive regulation, enforced by a market governing board and
distinguishable from the official market only in minor aspects'.[23]

The tighter regulation of official markets or stock exchanges created problems for integration. Access requirements varied widely across the EC. Some
stock exchanges required all trades to be handled by brokers who had exclusive rights to operate as intermediaries, while others permitted credit institutions to access stock exchanges directly. As admission rules were typically
discretionary, access for non-domestic firms could be problematic.[24] Wide
variations also existed in the operational rules of stock exchanges.
Significantly, practices varied with respect to 'concentration rules' or rules
requiring transactions to be executed on the designated organized market or
stock exchange.[25] The market mechanisms by which trades were executed
also varied. The predominant market mechanisms were polarized into
dealer- or quote-driven systems, of which the UK was the dominant example, and order-driven systems, which were used throughout continental
Europe.

In his 1977 study, Professor Wymeersch drew the various strands of
securities-trading market regulation across the EC together and produced
three main patterns of regulation.[26] The northern European Member States
(the UK, Ireland, and the Netherlands) allowed markets, by and large, to
adopt their own form of organization and rules and did not intervene in their
operation.[27] Consistent with this overall approach, the northern markets
(with the major exception of the Netherlands) also tended to be quote-

---

[22] See Wymeersch, n 3 above, 31–62, 87–92, 96–103, and 105–16. See also Scott-Quinn,
B, 'EC Securities Markets Regulation' in Steil, B (ed), *International Financial Market Regulation*
(1994) 121, 123–31 and Dalhuisen, J, *The New UK Securities Legislation and the EC 1992
Program* (1989) 73–8.

[23] Wymeersch, n 3 above, 31.   [24] Ibid, 54–62.

[25] While Italy, Denmark, and Luxembourg did not impose a requirement that trades be concentrated centrally on one exchange, concentration requirements were a central plank of market regulation in France. A combination of rules and market practice meant that trades tended,
in practice, to be centralized in Germany, the Netherlands, and Belgium: ibid, 89–92.

[26] Ibid, 105–16.

[27] Notwithstanding the absence of State regulation, Professor Wymeersch noted that 'the
whole regulatory machinery in these countries cannot be said to be any less comprehensive or
less incisive than the regulatory patterns which are to be found in the southern countries where
the organization and rules are established primarily by the State': ibid, 105.

driven and did not require concentration of trades. The southern European Member States (France and Italy), by contrast, were subject to a greater degree of public intervention and more likely to adopt concentration rules.[28] The dominant market mechanism in these Member States was the order-driven model. He also identified a third regulatory pattern among the central Member States (Germany, Belgium, and Luxembourg). These markets were subject to an intermediate level of public regulation which was reflected in the delegation of supervisory powers to market authorities and a residual degree of public control. This was typically expressed in the right of public authorities to review in the public interest the manner in which the delegated powers were exercised. Although these models would shift somewhat, with, in particular, Belgium moving towards a more heavily regulated pattern of regulation, they were to a large extent still in place when negotiations on the securities-trading market provisions contained in the ISD commenced, when they would collide with devastating consequences for the deadline set for the proposal's adoption.

XI.5 THE 1977 CODE OF CONDUCT

The first steps towards the supervision of securities-trading markets at EC level were taken in 1977 in the Code of Conduct Relating to Transactions in Transferable Securities which acknowledges that 'the proper working and the interpenetration of [securities] markets must be regarded as an essential aspect of the establishment of a 'common market' in capital'.[29] It does not address access but addresses the adoption of common standards which would 'encourage the interpenetration of the member countries' markets' by reducing disparities in 'the rules governing the various markets'.[30] The 1977 Code of Conduct does not express in any detail the rationale (bar market interpenetration) driving the content of the common standards. Neither, as a creature of its time and given the prevailing predominance of the trading markets as public-service providers perception, does it question the appropriateness of imposing common standards on securities-trading markets or examine the role of competition. Investor protection does, however, appear as a ground for adopting common standards for trading markets as a function of building investor confidence.[31]

The 1977 Code of Conduct makes a number of recommendations with respect to the operation of securities-trading markets. 'Securities markets'

---

[28] Although Italy did not impose concentration requirements: ibid, 89.
[29] Commission Recommendation 77/534/EEC concerning a European code of conduct relating to transactions in transferable securities [1977] OJ L212/37 (the 1977 Code of Conduct), Explanatory Memorandum, para 2.
[30] Ibid, paras 2 and 3.   [31] Ibid.

are very broadly defined as 'the official stock exchange and all the markets organized by or under the supervision of the competent authorities'. Supplementary Principle 4 adopts the concentration principle, which would subsequently prove to be so controversial, and requires that financial intermediaries should execute their orders on an organized market, unless the principal has given express instructions to the contrary.[32] Supplementary Principle 10 provides that securities markets should be sufficiently open to prevent fragmentation which could result in the same security being dealt in at the same time on different markets and at different prices. Supplementary Principle 11 addresses transparency and requires that when a security is dealt in on the market, the public should be informed not only of the different prices at which transactions take place, but also of the volume of dealings, unless the organization of the market makes it possible for the public to assess the liquidity of its investment by some other means. While the 1997 Code of Conduct's securities-trading market provisions are limited in scope, it is quite different in tenor from later developments, in that it is primarily concerned with the operation of securities-trading markets rather than with access. Developments may, as outlined in section 9.7 below, be coming full circle as the EC, albeit in very different competitive market conditions, is now moving to harmonize securities-trading markets standards.

The securities directives which followed the 1977 Code of Conduct deal with securities-trading markets from the perspective of issuer access and disclosure, although the now consolidated Admission Directive acknowledges that its harmonization is only 'partial' and that it 'constitutes a first step towards closer alignment of the rules of Member States in this field'.[33] It would not be until 1993, with the adoption of the ISD, that fundamental questions with respect to the liberalization of access to and the regulation of securities-trading markets (albeit only with respect to concentration and transparency rules) would be addressed.

---

[32] It also provides that where it is difficult or impossible to execute orders on an organized market, financial intermediaries can act as counterparties or offset orders outside the market, as long as clients' interests are not prejudiced and they can justify their actions to the competent authorities.

[33] Directive 79/279/EEC coordinating the conditions for the admission of securities to official stock exchange listing [1979] OJ L66/21, recital 9, now consolidated in Directive 2001/34/EC on admission of securities to official stock exchange listing and on information to be published on those securities [2001] OJ L184/1 (the Securities Consolidation Directive or SCD): SCD, recital 7.

XI.6 THE ISD: ACCESS LIBERALIZATION AND LIMITED STANDARDS HARMONIZATION

XI.6.1 *The Negotiations*

The ISD's securities-trading market provisions evolved significantly and grew increasingly more sophisticated and controversial as the negotiation process unfolded. The Commission's original 1988 proposal was very limited in its treatment of securities-trading markets.[34] The proposal contained market-access provisions only and did not address in detail how market access would operate.[35] It did not, for example, define what was meant by a trading market and did not clarify whether investment firms which were granted access rights were subject to the rules of the host-Member-State market. By the revised proposal,[36] the draft had not progressed to any great extent with the controversial provisions with respect to concentration and transparency still absent.

The divergences in the structure, operation, and culture of EC securities-trading markets outlined above in section 4 proved to be a major stumbling block during the negotiations on taking the Commission's proposal further in relation to access, concentration, and transparency.[37] While the specific points on which differences emerged are outlined in context in sections 6.4 and 6.5 below, the difficulties were, broadly, a result of a clash between the regulatory culture of northern Member States,[38] which, as a general rule, allowed trading markets to organize themselves as they saw fit, encouraged OTC dealing away from organized markets, and promoted competition, and that of the southern Member States[39] which imposed a greater degree of control over the operation of trading markets. More specifically, considerable difficulties arose as a result of the differing market models or mechanisms used across the EC. In particular, the split between auction/order-driven markets and dealer/quote-driven markets would be highly problematic, as would the diverging views on the desirability of OTC trading.[40] Given the

[34] [1989] OJ C43/7. Explanatory Memorandum at COM(88)778.

[35] Its limited scope and liberal treatment of the access issue caused ECOSOC to find in its comments on the proposal that organized markets were dealt with only 'in passing' [1989] OJ C298/6.

[36] [1990] OJ C42/7, Explanatory Memorandum at COM(89)629.

[37] The Commission's original proposal was presented in late 1988. It would not be until 29 June 1992 that the Council would agree on the trading market rules, the negotiations on which held up the adoption of the ISD.

[38] The UK, the Netherlands, and Germany fell into this grouping.

[39] France, Spain, Italy, which, together with Belgium, formed the 'Club Med' group.

[40] The split as regards market mechanisms at the time of the ISD negotiations is best illustrated by the differences between the Paris Bourse auction market and the London Stock Exchange's dealer mechanism.

differences in regulatory culture and market structure, in retrospect it is not surprising that the Commission's revised proposal, which liberalized access to markets but did not attempt to regulate the structure of trading markets and disregarded concentration and transparency rules, was rejected by the southern Member States. The ensuing discussions on the minimum requirements to be demanded of markets with respect to transparency and concentration as a precondition for liberalizing market access (in effect, the extent to which a particular market model could either be required or protected from competition) would dominate the ISD negotiations. Although the harmonization issue is currently receiving considerable attention in the context of the desirability of harmonization and the imposition of standards in a competitive trading environment, the fundamental question underlying the earlier ISD negotiations can also be analysed in terms of the desirability of harmonization in this area.[41]

XI.6.2 *Features of the ISD Regime*

As part of its investment-services liberalization structure and in order to enhance free movement under Article 47(2) EC, the ISD has the objective of ensuring that ISD investment firms have the same opportunities of joining or having access to regulated markets and of abolishing technical and legal restrictions on access (recital 37).

Its rules on securities-trading-markets can be divided into four broad categories. The first category introduces the concept of a 'regulated market' and imposes minimum requirements (primarily transparency and reporting requirements) designed to maintain the stability and integrity of these markets. The second category liberalizes the access by investment firms authorized under the ISD to regulated markets. The third category imposes, in the interests of market integrity and investor protection, transparency requirements on regulated markets and transaction-reporting obligations on investment firms. The fourth category addresses the concentration principle and the extent to which Member States may require that transactions must be carried out on a regulated market. There are two strands to the liberalization of regulated markets theme which underpins these four categories: liberalization of access by investment firms to regulated markets across the EC;

---

[41] Describing the Commission's original proposal as 'highly liberal' in that it liberalized access without imposing any harmonization requirements on markets, Steil has analysed the negotiations in terms of a conflict between mutual recognition and harmonization: 'whereas the Commission's mutual recognition approach would have facilitated liberalization by obliging host member States to accept application of home States' market structures in cross-border trading, the harmonization approach taken by the Council's southern members would allow host member States to block cross-border trading where home States did not adopt market structure rules which the hosts identified as essential to prudential market regulation': Steil, B, *Regional Financial Market Integration* (1998) 5.

and the conferment of a limited passport on regulated markets to extend their operations across the EC by means of remote membership mechanisms.

The ISD is primarily concerned with access and liberalization and does not deal in any detail with the supervision of regulated markets, save for the adoption of some basic requirements. Nonetheless, an admittedly largely unarticulated concern with the operation of regulated markets in the interests of investor confidence, the smooth functioning of the market-place and the integrity of the price-formation process can be inferred from the substantive transparency rules and from the inclusion within the definition of regulated market of the requirements that such market have rules which are supervised by a competent authority and that such rules are notified to Member States and the Commission.[42]

From the market-structure perspective, the compromise solutions adopted in the controversial areas of transparency and concentration also suggest a reluctance to alter market models[43] or influence moves towards an EC model of trading based on either auction or dealer markets. Finally, the ISD's model of securities-trading market regulation forms part of the ISD's investment-services market liberalization framework. Accordingly, regulated markets are defined by reference to the ISD's concept of investment services and, for example, are limited to markets on which ISD instruments are traded while the passport to access regulated markets is limited to ISD-authorized investment firms only.

XI.6.3 *Regulated Markets*

Central to the ISD's treatment of securities-trading markets is the concept of the 'regulated market'.[44] It is in respect of this market-place only that the ISD's access and operating rules apply and it is only this market that benefits from the liberalization provisions (for screen-based systems) and the protections against the prejudicial order flow-diverting concentration rules which

---

[42] Arts. 16 and 1(6).

[43] Recital 39 states, eg, that the structure of regulated markets is to be governed by national law. The reluctance to influence market structures is still a strong feature of the EC's approach to regulated markets. In its ISD Communication (Communication on Upgrading the Investment Directive (93/22/EC), COM(2000)729, at 20 the Commission included among the guiding principles for the revision of the ISD the injunctions that 'regulatory bias towards particular business models or market structures should be avoided' and that the design and application of rules must be neutral with respect to market models and technology.

[44] The original proposal did not provide a definition of what characterized a regulated market. It applied its access-liberalization rules to undefined 'stock exchanges and organized securities markets' where services similar to broking, dealing, and market-making services were provided, on the one hand, and, in a separate provision, to financial futures and option exchanges, which were also undefined, on the other: n 34 above, Art. 10(3), (4), and (6). This approach can also been seen in the Explanatory Memorandum, n 34 above, 4. This non-specific approach appeared again in Art. 13 of the revised proposal (n 36 above) before being ousted by the regulated-market concept.

Member States may otherwise apply. Member States are ultimately responsible for identifying which markets are 'regulated markets', but, in designating markets as regulated markets, they are subject to the minimum criteria set out in the ISD.

Under Article 16, each Member State is to draw up a list of the regulated markets for which it is the home Member State and forward that list, together with the relevant rules of procedures and operation of those regulated markets, to the other Member States and the Commission, which must also be informed of any changes to the list or to the rules. The home Member State of a regulated market is, under Article 1(6), the Member State in which the registered office of the body which provides trading facilities is situated or, if under its national law it has no registered office, the Member State in which that body's head office is situated.

The contrast in the treatment of investment firms and regulated markets by the ISD is immediately apparent from the definition of a regulated market. While the Article 1(13) definition of a regulated market (which encompasses traditional stock exchanges as well as other securities-trading markets)[45] has a number of elements, it is not detailed, reflecting only very basic requirements concerning admission of securities, reporting, and transparency and does not set out the defining characteristics of a trading market-place.[46]

First, the market must be a market for the instruments listed in section B of the Annex to the ISD.[47] Secondly, it must appear in the list provided

---

[45] In the UK, eg, the designated regulated markets include: the Domestic Equity Market, the European Equity Market, the Gilt Edged and Sterling Bond Market, and the Alternative Investment Market (all operated by the London Stock Exchange), the London International Financial Futures and Options Exchange (LIFFE), Tradepoint, OM London, and Jiway.

[46] Earlier attempts to grapple with a definition for and the characteristics of securities-trading markets (which were not bedevilled by the protectionist market-structure-based stances which obstructed the ISD discussion) produced conceptions of trading markets heavily based on the regularity of their operation and the existence of regulatory controls. The 1977 Code of Conduct (n 29 above) refers to the 'official stock exchange and all the markets organized by or under the supervision of the competent authorities'. A similar approach can be seen in the admission and disclosure regime. See the discussion of the meaning of 'stock exchange' in Ch. III. In 1985, the UCITS Directive (Directive 85/611/EEC on the coordination of laws, regulations and administrative provisions relating to undertakings for collective investment in transferable securities [1985] OJ L375/3) defined the range of investments in which a UCITS could invest by reference to, *inter alia*, securities 'admitted to official listing on a stock exchange' and securities 'dealt in on another regulated market in a Member State which operates regularly and is recognized and open to the public': Art. 19(1)(a) and (b). The IDD merges stock exchanges and other markets and applies to 'markets' generally, but otherwise takes a similar approach to the UCITS Directive by incorporating the concept of public access. Under Art. 1(2) it applies to transferable securities 'admitted to trading on a market which is regulated and supervised by authorities recognized by public bodies, operates regularly and is accessible directly or indirectly to the public'.

[47] These instruments are: transferable securities and units in collective-investment undertakings; money market instruments; financial-futures contracts, including equivalent cash-settled instruments; forward interest-rate agreements; interest rate, currency, and equity

for in Article 16 drawn up by the market's home Member State.[48] Thirdly, it must function regularly.[49] The fourth element of the definition concerns the operation of the market and reflects a concern with investor protection. The regulated market must be characterized by the fact that regulations issued or approved by the competent authorities define the conditions for the operation of the market, the conditions for access to the market and, where the (now consolidated) Admission Directive applies, the conditions governing admission to listing imposed in that Directive. Where the Admission Directive does not apply, the regulations must set out the conditions that must be satisfied by a financial instrument before it can effectively be dealt in on the market. With respect to these conditions, as outlined further in Chapter IV, the Commission's ground-breaking 2001 proposal to restructure the issuer-disclosure regime will, if adopted, ensure that the same disclosure requirements apply to admission to a regulated market, regardless of whether or not that regulated market is designed for officially listed securities and whether or not the Admission Directive applies. Finally, a regulated market must require compliance with the reporting and transparency rules laid down in Articles 20 and 21 of the ISD.[50]

swaps; and options to acquire or dispose of any instruments falling within section B, including equivalent cash-settled instruments and, in particular, options on currency rates and on interest rates. Accordingly, commodity derivatives exchanges, at present, fall outside the 'regulated market' definition. Current proposals to amend the definition of a regulated market as part of a wider review of the ISD's regulated-market provisions would significantly change this list: see sect. 9 below.

[48] This information is to be communicated to the other Member States and the Commission. The Commission is to publish the list of regulated markets notified to it on a yearly basis. In a sign of the changes in the securities-trading market environment which have occurred since the ISD was adopted, the Commission has announced that it is to maintain an updated list on its website given that 'as a result of reduced entry barriers and specialisation in trading segments, the list of "regulated markets" is subject to greater turnover' [2001] OJ C120/4.

[49] This provision is designed to ensure that arbitrary pricing activity and liquidity problems are avoided. See Ferrarini, G, 'Towards a European Law of Investment Services and Institutions' (1994) *21CMLRev.* 1283, 1293.

[50] The connection between qualification as a regulated market and compliance with the ISD's transparency rules led to considerable controversy. The negotiations on the characteristics of a regulated market can be read as an attempt to ensure that SEAQ International (the London Stock Exchange's screen-based system for international equity securities) would not come within the definition of a regulated market owing to the level of transparency required and would be excluded from the benefits conferred on regulated markets: Steil, n 1 above, 117. On the transparency negotiations see sect. 6.6.2 below.

XI.6.4 *Liberalization Through Access Rights*

XI.6.4.1 *The Access Passport*

(a) *The Access Rule*

At the core of the ISD's securities-trading market provisions is the passport conferred on investment firms to access regulated markets across the EC, which enhances the passport to provide investment services.[51]

Article 15 is the core provision.[52] It provides that, without prejudice to the exercise of the right of establishment and the freedom to provide services set out in Article 14,[53] host Member States are to ensure that investment firms which are authorized by the competent authorities of their home Member State to execute orders for clients and to deal for their own account can, directly or indirectly, become members of or have access to regulated markets in their host Member States where similar execution and dealing services are provided.[54] Access rights are accordingly dependent on the scope of the home-Member-State authorization.[55]

The relationship between trading on regulated markets and post-trade clearing and settlement is also addressed.[56] As in certain Member States clearing and settlement functions are performed by bodies which are separate and distinct from the markets on which the transactions are effected, host Member States are also required to ensure that such investment firms can become members of or have access to the clearing and settlement systems which are provided in the host Member State for members of its regulated markets.[57]

---

[51] An interesting connection has been drawn between the similarity of the ISD's access rules with the conditions set out in the Commission's competition rulings on whether the rules of commodity exchanges breached the Treaty's rules of competition: Ferrarini, n 2 above, 263.

[52] There are 2 country-specific exemptions from Art. 15. It does not apply to the regulation of the activities of Kursmakler in Germany or Hoekmannen in the Netherlands (Art. 15(6)). For a description of the activities of these market intermediaries see Pagano and Steil, n 1 above, 17 and 19, respectively.

[53] See further Ch. VI.

[54] The original proposal used the somewhat looser formula of requiring that host Member States ensure that investment firms authorized to carry out execution and dealing services in the home Member State 'enjoy the full range of trading privileges normally reserved to members of the stock exchanges and organized securities markets of host Member States where similar services are provided': n 34 above, Art. 10(3).

[55] In addition, Art. 15 is directed towards the host Member State. It does not directly address the blocking of access to host-Member-State exchanges by restrictive rules imposed by the home Member State, although the Treaty free-movement guarantees and the general-good rule would apply.

[56] On post trade clearing and settlement, see Ch. XII.

[57] Recital 35 provides that as a general rule any references in the ISD to access to and membership of regulated markets is to be read as including references to access to and membership of bodies performing clearing and settlement functions for regulated markets.

Member States are to abolish any national rules or laws or rules of regulated markets which limit the number of persons allowed access to the regulated markets. If access to a regulated market is limited by virtue of its legal
structure or its technical capacity, the Member State concerned is to ensure
that the market's structure and capacity are regularly adjusted.[58] Under
Article 15(3), host Member States are to offer investment firms the choice of
becoming members of or having access to their regulated markets either
directly, by setting up branches in the host Member State, or indirectly, by
setting up subsidiaries in the host Member State or by acquiring firms in the
host Member State that are already members of their regulated market or
already have access thereto. The connection between establishment and
access is broken only in Article 15(4), which addresses remote access, but
Article 15(4) applies only in the context of host-Member-State rules which
permit access without a physical presence.[59]

(b) *Electronic Markets*

Under Article 15(4), where the host-Member-State regulated market operates without any requirement for a physical presence, which would be the
case with electronic, screen-based markets, investment firms may become
members of or have access to it on the same basis without having to be
established in the host Member State. In order to enable their investment
firms to become members of or have access to host Member States' regulated
markets which operate in such a way, home Member States are to allow
these regulated markets to provide 'appropriate facilities', such as screens,
within the home Member States' territories. Investment firms may accordingly become members of the market by using trading screens in their own
places of business without being required to set up an establishment in the
market's home Member State or working though a market member located
in that Member State.

Article 15(4) can also be regarded as providing an ISD passport for
screen-based stock exchanges.[60] It has the effect of introducing a degree of
liberalization for regulated markets[61] in that it permits electronic markets to

---

[58] One example of an adjustment which may be required, may be the carrying out of periodic increases in the capital of the regulated market where access to the regulated market
depends on holding shares in its capital: Cardon de Lichtbuer, M, 'The Investment Services
Directive—An Analysis' in Wymeersch, E (ed), *Further Perspectives in Financial Integration in
Europe* (1994) 79, 93.

[59] It has been noted that Art. 15(3) and (4) seems to leave it to the host State to decide
whether a physical presence is required to access a regulated market. Usher, J, *The Law of Money
and Financial Services in the EC* (2nd edn, 2000) 105 and 143.

[60] It has been observed that Art. 15(4) is 'popularly viewed as the European "single passport" for screen-based trading systems': Steil, n 1 above, 129.

[61] Ferrarini, n 49 above, 1309.

provide trading services in another Member State without being required to comply with additional authorization or other requirements in the other Member State. In this regard, it is designed to enhance competition between regulated markets and improve liquidity and efficiency.[62] Only regulated markets benefit from this liberalizing rule.[63]

(c) *Remote Access and Notification Problems*

In its 1998 Report on the operation of certain of the ISD's provisions, including the regulated-market provisions,[64] the Commission noted that it was unclear from the ISD whether or not remote membership triggered the notification obligation which is imposed under Article 18(2) when an investment firm wishes to carry on business within the territory of another Member State for the first time, and it recommended that the interaction between remote access and the notification obligation be studied further.[65] The view has been expressed that the investment-firm passport and its notification requirements and the regulated market 'remote-access passport' are not interlinked: an investment firm using a remote-access screen does not thereby provide investment services in another Member State such that the notification obligation is triggered.[66]

(d) *Direct Access by Credit Institutions*

Whether or not credit institutions providing investment services should have direct access to regulated markets was a difficult issue during the ISD negotiations.[67] Certain Member States, particularly southern Member

---

[62] See, eg, the UK Securities and Investment Board Discussion Paper on the Implementation of the Investment Services Directive and Capital Adequacy Directive (1994) (the SIB Paper) 39.

[63] NASDAQ Europe (previously EASDAQ) is one of the more high-profile beneficiaries of Art. 15(4).

[64] Report from the Commission to the Council on the Operation of Certain Articles in the Directive, COM(1998)780 (the 1998 ISD Report).

[65] Germany also suggested that Art. 15(4) be amended to provide that when screens are installed in other Member States the competent authorities of those other Member States be notified: ibid, 7.

[66] This view has been expressed by Professor Ferrarini. See 'Securities Regulation and the Rise of Pan-European Equity Markets: An Overview' in Ferrarini, G, Hopt, K, and Wymeersch, E (eds), *Capital Markets in the Age of the Euro* (forthcoming) in which he has observed that a regulated market should be able to use the Art. 15(4) passport independently of its members offering their investment services cross-border, citing the example of iX (the failed London Stock Exchange/Deutsche Börse merger) which would have offered trading services to German banks which did not offer their services on a cross-border basis.

[67] Although the BCD II (Second Council Directive 89/646/EEC on the coordination of laws regulations and administrative procedures relating to the taking up and pursuit of the business of credit institutions and amending Directive 77/780/EEC [1989] OJ L 386/1 (now consolidated as part of the banking regime by Directive 2000/12 relating to the taking up and pursuit of the business of credit institutions [2000] OJ L126/1 (the CBD))) granted credit institutions a

States, limited access to organized markets, and, in particular, access to stock exchanges, to brokers only.[68] Specifically, certain Member States did not permit credit institutions to become members of regulated markets, except through specialized subsidiaries.[69] The original proposal reflected this position. It provided in the then Article 10(5) that '[p]ending further harmonization, host Member States which do not accept credit institutions as members of their stock exchanges or organized markets are not required to accept as members branches of investment firms [which are authorized to provide broking, dealing, or market-making services] which are credit institutions'.[70] This approach was clearly disadvantageous to universal banks. German universal banks, in particular, which already enjoyed direct market access in a number of Member States, lobbied strenuously for direct-access rights. Their argument ultimately prevailed over those of the exclusionary Member States. Those Member States had argued that, notwithstanding that universal banks already carried out securities activities and were permitted to access regulated markets directly in certain Member States, credit institution depositors would be effectively protected from the risks involved in securities transactions only by a requirement that exchange membership be obtained through a separate subsidiary.[71]

By virtue of Article 2(1), credit institutions which provide investment services and come within the scope of the ISD benefit from a direct right of access to regulated markets. Agreement on direct access had, however, been achieved only by granting a derogation (Article 15(3)) to Member States which, at the time of the adoption of the ISD, did not permit credit institutions to become members of or have access to regulated markets unless they used specialized subsidiaries, to continue to apply this restriction until 31 December 1996, as long as it was applied in a non-discriminatory fashion to credit institutions from other Member States for the purpose of access to those regulated markets.[72] This relaxation was designed to address any problems of excess capacity, which the extension of direct-access rights to

passport in respect of 'trading for own account or account of customers' in a range of financial instruments, it was completely silent on the question of access by credit institutions to securities-trading markets across the EC in pursuit of these trading activities.

[68] See O'Neill, N, 'The Investment Services Directive' in Cranston, R (ed), *The Second Market and the Law of Banking* (2nd edn, 1995) 189, 205, who described regulated markets in certain Member States prior to the adoption of the ISD as 'exclusive clubs for securities brokers'.

[69] Namely Belgium, France, Greece, Italy, Portugal, and Spain.

[70] N 34 above. This approach was criticized by ECOSOC as posing an obstacle to the freedom of establishment of credit institutions: n 35 above, 16. In the revised proposal (n 36 above) Art. 10(5) was simply deleted and direct access was introduced without the parallel introduction of a transitional period within which Member States could adjust their systems if they had previously refused direct access to credit institutions.

[71] Wouter, J, 'EC Harmonisation of National Rules Concerning Securities Offerings, Stock Exchange Listing and Investment Services' (1993) 4 *EBLRev.* 199, 224.

[72] Spain, Greece, and Portugal were given a further extension until 31 Dec 1999.

credit institutions might have triggered in those markets which previously excluded credit institutions.[73]

XI.6.4.2 *The Access Passport and Host Member State*

The access passport does not apply automatically. Access may be made subject to a number of conditions.

Under Article 15(2), Member States are to make membership of or access to a regulated market conditional on the investment firm in question complying with the requirements of the Capital Adequacy Directive[74] and on the supervision by the investment firm's home Member State of such requirements. Additional capital requirements may be imposed by the host Member State in respect of access to a regulated market only in relation to matters not covered by the CAD.[75]

Article 15(2) clarifies that access to a regulated market by a passporting investment firm is subject to the firm's compliance with: the rules of the regulated market in relation to its constitution and administration; the rules relating to transactions on the market; the professional standards imposed on staff operating on and in conjunction with the market; and the rules and procedures for clearing and settlement. Regulated markets can already rely on the ISD's general standards for investment firms and, in particular, on the review of an investment firm's fitness, propriety, and competence carried out by the investment firm's home Member State under Articles 3, 4, and 8 of the ISD. Article 15(2) also provides that the detailed arrangements for implementing these rules and procedures for passporting investment firms may be adapted as appropriate to ensure, *inter alia*, fulfilment of the ensuing obligations, as long as the ISD's underlying principle of non-discrimination is complied with.[76]

---

[73] In the 1998 ISD Report, however, the Commission noted that there were no problems in relation to direct access by credit institutions which would justify an extension of the transitional period granted to Spain, Greece, and Portugal. As all the Member States (bar France, Greece, and Sweden which did not submit a response) reported no difficulties in relation to the operation of the access rule it appears that the concerns expressed with respect to overcapacity on the introduction of direct access have been unfounded: n 64 above, 7.

[74] Directive 93/6/EEC on the capital adequacy of investment firms and credit institutions [1993] OJ L141/1 (the CAD).

[75] The SIB Paper gave the example of the capital requirements which may apply before an investment firm is accepted as a member of a clearing house (as discussed above, access to regulated markets also covers access to clearing and settlement systems) as clearing houses are exposed to risks not covered by the CAD: n 62 above, 39

[76] The Treaty freedoms and the general-good rule should act as a brake on protectionist uses of Art. 15(2). It is clear from the Explanatory Memorandum to the revised proposal that it is envisaged that host regulated markets which operate electronically can, as part of their membership rules, impose rules with respect to the operation of terminals from remote locations, including rules relating to record-keeping and inspection of records held by the investment firm from which trades originate, even where the investment firm using the screen is based in another Member State: n 36 above, 5.

XI.6.4.3 *The Access Passport and New Regulated Markets*

Under Article 15(1), the access rules set out in Article 15 do not affect the right of Member States to authorize or prohibit the creation of new markets within their territories. By contrast with Article 15(4), depending on the approach taken in defining what constitutes a 'new' regulated market, it might be argued that Article 15(5) has considerable potential to obstruct integration of securities markets if it is used for protectionist purposes.[77]

XI.6.5 *Common Standards: Concentration Rules*

XI.6.5.1 *The Concentration Problem*

Concentration rules, which effectively prohibit off-market transactions, are based on the premise that trading in listed securities which is dispersed away from the regulated market on which those securities are listed, adversely affects the price-formation process and leads to different prices in different markets in respect of the same transaction. Concentration of trades on the same market-place on which the securities are listed, the argument runs, also enhances the fair operation of the market, in that all investors can transact at the same price if they enter into transactions at the same time. Added to this argument is the assumption that regulated markets produce better prices and that non-regulated markets, being less well regulated, can pose traps for the unsophisticated retail investors.[78]

The concentration question arose in the ISD negotiations in the context of whether a Member State would be permitted to require that transactions in securities by an investment firm providing services or operating through a branch in that Member State be carried out on a regulated market. Two sharply diverging positions existed on concentration. On one side of the faultline were Member States who were in favour of centralizing securities transactions on a regulated market in order to contribute to the liquidity and transparency of the regulated market and to ensure a high level of investor protection whenever the transaction involved an investor resident in the particular Member State and a security listed on the regulated market in that Member State. In practice, trades would be centralized on the Member State's regulated market.[79] On the other side were those Member

---

[77] See the discussion in Steil, n 1 above, 129–30 and, for a different perspective, Ferrarini, n 17 above, 588

[78] The benefits of concentration have been described in terms of assuring best execution and in terms of enhancing market efficiency (with respect to price formation and liquidity) by addressing fragmentation of trading: Ferrarini, n 2 above, 262.

[79] See the discussion of the negotiations in Dassesse, M, 'The Investment Services Directive' [1992] *JIBFL* 5, 7 and in Coleman, W, and Underhill, G, 'Globalization, Regionalism and the Regulation of Securities Markets' (1995) 2 *Journal of European Public Policy* 488, 498–501. This

States[80] who wanted free competition, feared the damage the concentration rule could inflict on OTC markets or markets which did not qualify as regulated markets, and who felt that investor protection in these markets could be adequately safeguarded by the rules of conduct imposed on the investment intermediaries carrying out the trades and by adequate disclosure. The UK was a dominant member of this group, partly owing to the dealer-based structure of its market-place which meant that, unlike in an order-driven market, trades were not truly centralized and transaction prices could vary as between dealers.[81] Indeed, the premise on which the concentration principle is based can be observed most clearly in an order-driven market where, due to the use of central computer-matching systems, trades are completely centralized. The UK also argued that investors trading outside regulated markets and in the OTC markets tended almost always to be sophisticated and so not in need of the protections of centralized trading on a regulated market. The benefits of OTC markets were also raised, with the Alliance arguing that OTC markets fulfilled a valuable market service by providing a venue for the development and trying out of new products and in allowing the construction of tailor-made products for sophisticated and institutional investors. Protectionist impulses also were a strong undercurrent in the negotiations. Certain Member States sought to protect their national stock exchanges from competition with the then dominant London Stock Exchange.[82] By forcing transactions to be routed via the designated national stock exchange and subjected to the rules of that exchange,[83] concentration requirements were seen as, in effect, a way of protecting national stock exchanges from competition.

XI.6.5.2 *The Solution*

As with the transparency problem (section 6.6.2 below), the solution adopted was a compromise. The ISD does not impose a particular market model in terms of where trades should be executed, but adopts a compromise position by allowing Member States, in certain circumstances, to require that transactions in securities be carried out on a regulated market. This concession is combined with a mandatory waiver provision,

---

group of Member States, which was composed of France, Spain, Portugal, Greece, Italy, and Belgium, was known as the 'Club Med' group.

[80] The UK, Germany, Ireland, Luxembourg, and the Netherlands (the 'Alliance' group).

[81] Scott-Quinn, n 22 above, 141.

[82] France, in particular, was anxious to repatriate French share-trading, a significant proportion of which took place in London.

[83] The approach finally adopted did not provide for concentration on national recognized markets. See sect. 6.5.2 below.

which is triggered when investors wish to carry out transactions elsewhere.[84]

Specifically, under Article 14(3), a Member State may require that transactions relating to the investment services covered by the ISD must be carried out on a regulated market, but only when a number of conditions are satisfied. The reference to '*a* regulated market' (emphasis added) is designed to ensure that Member States may not avail themselves of the concentration option to direct transactions to a particular regulated market on their territory.[85] The conditions are broadly designed to ensure that concentration can be applied only in respect of domestic transactions. The investor must be habitually resident (undefined) or established in that Member State. The investment firm must carry out the transactions in question through a main establishment, through a branch situated in that Member State or under the freedom to provide services in that Member State. Finally, concentration will not be allowed if the transaction involves an instrument which is not dealt in on a regulated market in that Member State.

Under Article 14(4), however, where a Member State makes use of this ability to direct where trades must be executed, it must give investors habitually resident or established in that Member State the right not to comply with the Article 14(3) obligation and to have the transactions carried out away from a regulated market. Member States may make the exercise of this waiver by investors subject to express authorization, taking into account investors' differing needs for protection and, in particular, the ability of professional and institutional investors to act in their own best interests. The specific reference in the waiver to differentiated protection is based on the assumption that professional investors are sufficiently experienced and knowledgeable to assess the risks involved in engaging in lightly regulated off-market transactions. It also reflects a recurring theme in EC protective regulation generally that regulation should be sensitive to the different needs of retail and sophisticated investors.[86] Given that the waiver authorization

[84] During the negotiations the potential damage which the concentration requirement could have wreaked on the eurobond market was raised. While the option to waive any concentration rule imposed where the investor wishes to transact elsewhere should have a mitigating effect on concentration rules, eurobond market participants had, during the ISD negotiations, pushed for a specific exemption to be included for eurobond transactions which would have give greater protection to market participants. See Lomnicka, E, 'The Investment Services Directive' in Andenas, M, and Kenyon-Slade, S (eds), *EC Financial Market Regulation and Company Law* (1993) 81, 98.

[85] In its discussion of the operation of the concentration rule in its 1998 ISD Report the Commission supported the submission made by the UK that 'it might be helpful to re-confirm that Art. 14(3) and (4) mean that a Member State can require transactions to be carried out on a regulated market—as opposed to off market, and subject to the "opt-out" in Art. 14(4)—but do not permit a Member State to require transactions to be carried out on a particular national regulated market': 1998 ISD Report, n 64 above, 6.

[86] For a discussion of Art. 14 in the context of differentiated protection see O'Neill, N, 'Investment Services and the Single Market—Beyond 1992' [1993] *JIBFL* 17, 20. Continuing

must be given 'in conditions that do not jeopardise the prompt execution of investors' orders', it appears that the ISD favours a general advance authorization procedure which would hold good for a period of time or for the duration of the investor's relationship with a particular investment firm.[87] Credit institutions which provide investment services and come within the scope of the ISD are subject to Article 14(3) by virtue of Article 2(1).

By 31 December 1998, the Commission was to have reported on the operation of the concentration rule and, if appropriate, proposed amendments. In its report, notwithstanding the controversy which surrounded concentration during the negotiations, it found that there was no need to propose amendments to the concentration rule.[88]

XI.6.6 *Common Standards: Transparency and Reporting*

XI.6.6.1 *Transaction-reporting Obligations*

With the transaction-reporting and transparency requirements, the ISD moves more directly into imposing common operating standards on regulated markets. Transaction-reporting obligations play an important role in the detection and control of market abuse and misconduct which might prejudice investor confidence in the trading system. In order to ensure that the authorities responsible for the markets and for supervision have access to the information necessary to carry out their duties,[89] under Article 20(1)(a) Member States are to at least require, without prejudice to the reporting requirements imposed under Article 10, that investment firms[90] keep at the disposal of the authorities for at least five years the relevant data on transactions relating to the provision of investment services which they have carried out in instruments dealt in on a regulated market, whether such transactions were carried out on a regulated market or not. On- and off-market trades in all Member States are therefore covered.

Under Article 20(1)(b), home Member States are to require, at a minimum, that investment firms report on all transactions in instruments

the investor-protection theme, the point has been made that the investor waiver characterizes the concentration rule as a protective conduct rule designed to achieve best execution: Ferrarini, n 2 above, 262–3.

[87] By restricting the degree to which Member States may impose authorization requirements as a condition to granting a concentration waiver, the ISD seems to favour the arguments against concentration.

[88] 1998 ISD Report, n 64 above, 5. On the new approach proposed for concentration see sect. 9 below.

[89] In this regard, Art. 20(4) specifically provides that Member States are to ensure that the information made available under the reporting structure set out in Art. 20 is available for the purposes of collaboration between competent authorities, as required under Art. 23.

[90] Credit institutions which provide investment services and come within the scope of the ISD are subject to Art. 20 by virtue of Art. 2(1).

which are traded on any of the EC regulated markets, regardless of where in the EC the trade was actually executed and whether or not the particular trade took place on or off a regulated market, to their home-Member-State competent authorities where the transactions cover: shares or other instruments giving access to capital; bonds and other forms of securitized debt;[91] and standardized forward contracts relating to shares or standardized options on shares (Article 20(1)(b)). The reporting obligation applies only to transactions which the investment firm has carried out as agent or principal. Mere transmission of an order will not trigger the reporting obligation. Investment firms are not required to fulfil the reporting obligation directly. Article 20(3) gives Member States the option of permitting reports to be made by the investment firm, by a trade-matching system, through stock exchange authorities, or through the authorities of another regulated market.

Article 20(1)(b) specifies that the reports are to include details of the names and numbers of the instruments which are bought or sold, the dates and times of the transactions, the transaction prices, and the means of identifying the investment firms concerned. The ISD does not require that the identity of the ultimate buyers and sellers be revealed. These reports are to be made available to the relevant authority at the 'earliest opportunity'. The reporting rules set minimum standards of reporting only. Member States are permitted, as long as they do so in a non-discriminatory manner, to adopt or maintain more stringent provisions in the field governed by Article 20 with regard to substance and form in respect of the conservation and reporting of data relating to transactions carried out on a regulated market of which they are the home Member States or carried out by investment firms for which they are the home Member State.[92]

Where the investment firm carries out the transactions on a regulated market in its host Member State, the home Member State may waive its reporting requirements, but only if the investment firm is subject to equivalent requirements to report the transaction in question to the authorities in charge of the market (Article 20(2)).

---

[91] In the case of bonds and other forms of securitized debt, home Member States may permit the reporting obligation to apply only to aggregated transactions in the same instrument.

[92] Art. 20(5). Supervisory authorities do not all agree about the information which should be reported and the benefits of such disclosure in supervising investment firms: Haines, P, 'The Investment Services Directive—Progress to Date' (1995) 2 *EFSL* 30, 31.

XI.6.6.2 *Transparency*

(a) *Market Transparency*

The transparency of the market and the fairness of the price-formation process have been identified as critical to the efficient operation and supervision of organized markets. While the price-formation process depends on a number of interacting factors including the market structure adopted, liquidity provision, and the trading practices permitted on the market,[93] market transparency plays a major role in ensuring that prices reflect supply and demand and that the market is efficient. Market transparency is concerned with trading information; it is a function of the disclosure of the price, volume, and transaction information which is produced by a securities-trading market and of its availability to the market and investors on a real-time basis.[94] The ability of investors to assess the terms of a transaction in advance in relation to other transactions and to verify the trading terms afterwards with respect to other trades is a central element in ensuring fairness and allowing investors to know whether and at what prices trades can be made.[95] Investors are equipped to make such judgements by transparency requirements which ensure the disclosure of pre-trade information on the size and prices of the orders entering the market (in both auction and dealer markets—in the latter transparency is related to market-makers' quotes) and of post-trade information on the price and volume of executed transactions. In a transparent market-place, investors have a snapshot of the trading landscape, which shows all the orders entering the market and the transactions already completed.[96] More generally, confidence in the market-place is a function of the price-formation process and in the accuracy and timeliness of the information which feeds into that process.[97] Market-transparency rules also promote best execution and provide market authorities with an important mechanism for controlling market abuses.[98]

[93] See, eg, Wymeersch, n 3 above, 32.

[94] See Lindsey, R, 'Efficient Regulation of the Securities Market' in McCrudden, C (ed), *Regulation and Deregulation, Policy and Practice in the Utilities and Financial Services Industries* (1999) 295, 302. Accordingly, publication of trading information is critical. While information may be reported to the relevant market authorities, it will not be available until those authorities have published it: Pagano and Steil, n 1 above, 31.

[95] Scott-Quinn, B, n 22 above, 136. See also the 1998 IOSCO Principles, n 12 above, para 13.5.

[96] As a result, '[transparency] helps them assess whether their trades are being executed at the best prices in the market, what mark-ups their brokers are charging, whether their orders are being front-run, what the direction of trading activity is, and whether there is significant trading between, or outside, the displayed quotes': Lee, n 2 above, 256.

[97] See, eg, the discussion in Pinto, J, 'Trading and Market Making Surveillance Programme for the NASDAQ Stock Market' (1996) 4 *JFRC* 144.

[98] Market transparency as a regulatory tool is most fully developed in the USA where the SEC is a strong supporter of it, believing that it 'enhances the delivery of almost all the

(b) *The Market-model Problem*

Transparency requirements are closely connected with the market model adopted. The EC split between dealer- and order-market structures proved to be an almost fatal block to achieving agreement on a harmonized approach to transparency. In order-driven or auction markets trade information is made available as soon as a match is made on the trading screen between orders, and is then automatically reported to the market supervisor. Order markets allow for a high degree of transparency in the price-formation process as prices move in response to trades. The position is different in quote-driven or dealer markets where dealers compete with one another on price and where prices move on the basis of action by market-makers. Information on competing quotes is made available immediately, but completed transaction prices are not.[99] The market supervisor decides when this information is to be disclosed. Immediate publication of completed trade information raises two difficulties for dealers. First, in a competitive dealing market, the information a dealer holds in relation to completed trades gives that dealer, particularly where the dealer holds a large market share, a competitive advantage over other dealers with respect to pricing information. The second problem arises from the market-making function of dealers in a quote-driven market. Transparency requirements compel a dealer to declare his trading intentions. If a dealer is required to report trades immediately, this requirement may, where the dealer in order to make a market in a security does not execute a deal with a counterparty but takes a position on his own account, and particularly where a large position is taken, place the dealer at a disadvantage to other dealers; they will be immediately aware of the size of the position held and will be able to drive down the value of the position held.[100] Liquidity may suffer as a result as dealers may become less willing to take large positions in securities. In dealer-driven markets, as full transparency cannot be achieved without the sacrifice of maximum liquidity, liquidity and transparency requirements must be balanced. In effect, decisions on transparency can reveal regulatory priorities as regards investor protection, on the one hand, and liquidity and efficiency on the other.[101]

regulatory goals they view as important, including investor protection, competition, fairness, market efficiency, liquidity, market integrity and investor confidence': Lee, n 2 above, 256.

[99] The foregoing description of order and dealer markets is partly based on the analysis in Scott-Quinn, n 22 above, 136.

[100] See the analysis in Pagano and Steil, n 1 above, where the point is made that '[d]ealers' incentives to conceal information about their recent trades is so strong that even when immediate trade publication is mandated it tends to generate a variety of avoidance responses. These may, in fact, limit considerably the impact of mandatory trade publication on market transparency': n 1 above, 33.

[101] See Gros and Lannoo, n 4 above, 126.

During the negotiations a large gulf opened up between the UK and France[102] on transparency. The UK (heavily lobbied by dealers on SEAQ International) called for a light touch on transparency. It argued that pre-trade publication adequately protected investors, in that it allowed them to assess the terms of the particular transaction under consideration and that the position of market-makers and, accordingly, liquidity would be severely compromised by onerous transparency requirements. France claimed that investor protection and market integrity could be ensured only by maximum transparency in relation to trade information. It argued that retail investors were not in a position to assess whether the price of a security actually represented the value of the security and needed the protection afforded by transparency rules which would provide, as soon as possible, information on other deals in the same security for the purposes of comparison. It has been noted that another, less altruistic, agenda was also being served by the French position. The French transparency rules were, due to the pricing difficulties caused by requiring full disclosure in respect of large positions, diverting large trades in French securities to SEAQ International where the transparency requirements were less onerous.[103]

(c) *The Transparency Regime*

In attempting to achieve a compromise between the transparency approaches of order and dealer markets, the ISD has avoided the wider market-model issues raised by the transparency question. By adopting minimum rules and leaving considerable discretion with the Member States, it reveals a reluctance to engage in any harmonization which could change the structure of organized markets in the EC.[104] In dealer markets, the degree of transparency required can impact on market liquidity and, accordingly, on the activities of and business from institutional investors, whose large trading requirements demand sufficient liquidity, and, ultimately, on the market mechanism itself if the dealer mechanism becomes unworkable due to the transparency rules. The ISD's approach seems to be designed to avoid any such market restructuring and any judgement calls as to the appropriate trade-off between liquidity and transparency by taking a middle way.[105]

---

[102] On the French and UK positions see, eg, O'Neill, n 68 above, 206–7.

[103] Ibid, 206.

[104] Thus, 'while the ISD pays its respects to market transparency, it does so without sacrificing the complexities of market microstructures': Ferrarini, n 17 above, 582.

[105] That the Commission did not want to support either market mechanism seems to be borne out by the comment of one senior official that '[t]he Commission's belief is that the agreement reached in the Council will not be damaging to the operation of either quote-driven or order-driven markets': Clarotti, P, 'The Completion of the Internal Financial Market: Current Position and Outlook' in Andenas and Kenyon-Slade, n 84 above, 1, 11.

The compromise is set out in Article 21 which contains a series of transparency requirements which have 'the two-fold aim of protecting investors and ensuring the smooth operation of the markets in transferable securities' (recital 42) and are designed to enable investors to assess at any time the terms of any transaction they may be considering and to verify the conditions under which it has been carried out (Article 21(1)). Under Article 21(2), the competent authorities are to require for each instrument, at a minimum, two sets of information. First, publication is required at the start of each day's trading on the market of the weighted average price, the highest and the lowest prices, and the volume dealt in on the regulated market in question for the whole of the preceding day's trading. Secondly, for continuous order-driven[106] and quote-driven markets, the following information is required: at the end of each hour's trading on the market, publication of the weighted average price and the volume dealt in on the regulated market in question for a six-hour trading period ending so as to leave two hours' trading on the market before publication; and, every twenty minutes, publication of the weighted average price and the highest and lowest prices on the regulated market in question for a two-hour trading period ending so as to leave one hour's trading on the market before publication. None of the key terms in this formula is defined. Article 21(1) provides that the competent authorities are, for each of the regulated markets which they have listed in accordance with Article 16, to take measures to provide investors with this information. Where investors have prior access to information on the prices and quantities for which transactions may be undertaken, such information is to be available at all times during market trading hours. In addition, the terms announced for a given price and quantity must be terms on which it is possible for an investor to carry out such a transaction (Article 21(2)).

A considerable degree of discretion remains with the competent authorities in respect of the market-transparency requirements. In accordance with the requirements of Article 21(2), the competent authorities may determine the form in which and the precise time within which the information is to be made available, as well as the means by which it is to be made available, having regard to the nature, size, and needs of the market concerned and of the investors operating on that market. The competent authorities may delay or suspend publication where that proves to be justified by exceptional market conditions, or, in the case of small markets, to protect the anonymity of investors and firms. In a provision designed to minimize the adverse impact of the reporting rules on the holding of large positions, the competent authorities may also apply special conditions in the case of exceptional

---

[106] In a continuous order-driven market orders are continuously matched rather than a particular price being established at a set time.

transactions that are very large in scale compared with average transactions in the security in question on that market[107] and in the case of highly illiquid securities as long as these are defined by means of objective criteria and made public. What is meant by 'exceptional market conditions', 'small markets', 'exceptional transactions' 'very large', or 'highly illiquid' is not specified. As a result, the exceptions have the potential to be extremely porous and to prejudice the operation of a transparency regime which is already operating at a minimum level. Clarification by the Court of Justice of this legislative weakness is an unsatisfactory remedy, given the market-basis of these provisions and the limited experience of the Court to date with securities-regulation matters, not to speak of the delays involved. The competent authorities may also apply more flexible provisions, particularly as regards publication deadlines, for transactions concerning bonds and other forms of securitized debt. The main investors in these securities are likely to be institutional investors whose trading requirements typically require significant liquidity in the market and the holding of large positions by market-makers.[108]

More generally, under Article 21(3) Member States may adopt or maintain more stringent or additional provisions with regard to the substance and form in which information must be made available to investors concerning transactions carried out on regulated markets for which they are the home Member State. Those provisions must apply regardless of the Member State in which the issuer of the financial instrument is located or of the Member State on the regulated market of which the instrument was listed for the first time.

(d) *Market-model Convergence*

In light of the difficulties raised by the polarization between the order-driven and dealer-driven market mechanisms during the transparency negotiations, it is interesting to note that, since the adoption of the ISD, a trend towards electronic order-driven systems, and thus towards increased transparency, has emerged for equity trading as a result of competitive market forces. In particular, London securities markets have seen a move away from the dealer-driven market model which dominated at the time of the ISD negotiations, to a more varied range of market models. The Tradepoint sys-

---

[107] This provision was designed to allay, in part, the UK's fears.
[108] With respect to Art. 21(2), FESCO (now the Committee of European Securities Regulators) has acknowledged that while transparency requirements may need to be adjusted to reflect the features of the regulated market in question, regulated markets which exercise the Art. 21(2) derogations should be in a position to demonstrate that reliance on the derogation produces an overall benefit for market users: FESCO, *Standards for Regulated Markets under the ISD* (Dec 1999) (the FESCO Standards), 99-FESCO-C, at 13.

tem, which was introduced in 1995, is based on an auction mechanism, and in 1997, with the adoption of the SETS electronic order book, the London Stock Exchange itself adopted, for certain transactions, an order-based market model.[109]

Despite the altered trading environment and the shift in market models, and notwithstanding the failure of Article 21 to define its terms and the lack of precision with which the exceptions to the transparency rules are defined,[110] in its 1998 report on the operation of the transparency regime, the Commission could report that '[t]he transparency regime does not appear to have given rise to any particular difficulties, despite the controversy surrounding this topic during the negotiations. No amendment appears necessary'.[111] This position was to be short-lived. The Article 21 transparency regime was identified as one of the areas of the ISD which was in need of overhaul and upgrading in the Commission's ISD Communication and has been the subject of the Commission's initial proposals for review of the ISD discussed in section 9 below.[112] Whether or not this overhaul and further harmonization are warranted may be questioned in view of the fact that markets have tended to respond to competitive pressures by changing their models to allow for greater transparency, as can be seen from the London Stock Exchange's move to order-driven trading.[113]

[109] See n 7 above on the Stock Exchange Electronic Trading Service (SETS).

[110] The point has been made that '[t]he Article 21 transparency requirements are . . . so vague as to be virtually meaningless': Steil, n 1 above, 127.

[111] 1998 ISD Report, n 64 above, 10. France reported, however, that the open-outcry system operated by the MATIF did not allow all the information required by Art. 21 to be given, particularly with respect to the information required concerning the volume at which each price is traded, as this information was available only on the day following the trade. Of all the other Member States which responded to the Commission's questionnaire on the operation of the transparency rules, only Greece reported any difficulties. It indicated that its exchange was of the opinion that the information required throughout each trading session under Art. 21(2)(b) unjustifiably increased the demands made on electronic dealing systems. As long as electronic dealing systems allowed investors to see prices in a reasonable time, the Greek position was that it was not necessary to publish the weighted average price and the highest and lowest prices every 20 minutes, particularly given the additional spending involved in adjusting the relevant software. It also noted that a similar view was expressed by a majority of European exchanges at meetings held on the subject.

[112] For a criticism of the transparency requirements on the ground that the minimum requirements are not an adequate basis for an EC-wide transparency regime and a proposal for a remedial market-transparency directive see Avougleas, E, 'Market Accountability and Pre- and Post-trade Transparency: The Case for the Reform of the EU Regulatory Framework: Part 1' (1998) 19 *The Company Lawyer* 162. Part 2 is at (1998) 19 *The Company Lawyer* 202.

[113] See the analysis in Ferrarini, n 17 above, 582–3 who has argued at 583 that 'market enterprises . . . can take the right decisions about transparency because they have the appropriate incentives. Indeed, they decide, first of all, what kind of microstructure would best serve their clients' interest. The choice concerning transparency is closely connected with that regarding microstructure and the two should be treated alike from a regulatory perspective. It is also important to consider that today's competition in the trading services market puts pressure on exchanges, requiring them to look for the most efficient structures and transparency regimes. On the London Stock Exchange's move to order driven trading see Pagano, n 1 above, 192–3.

XI.6.7 *Supervision*

The ISD does not differentiate between the competent authorities responsible for the supervision of investment firms and those responsible for overseeing regulated markets. The co-operation and supervision structure which applies to the provision of services by investment firms also applies to their activities on regulated markets across the EC. The ISD's access rules and the ability of investment firms to participate in regulated markets across the EC demand a high degree of co-operation between market supervisors and regulated markets in order to ensure effective supervision of investment firms' activities in those markets and, in consequence, the protection of the regulated market against risks posed by participant investment firms.[114] The co-operation and information-exchange powers have a particular importance in that while an investment firm's home Member State is the dominant supervisor, under Article 15(2) the rules of the host regulated market are applied in respect of membership of or access to, as well as trading activities on, that regulated market. In the case of screen-based markets, where investment firms can access the market by way of a screen outside the Member State in which the market is based, that market's competent authority is likely to wish to ensure that the investment firm complies with the rules of the regulated market and, as a result, to depend on the efficacy of co-operation and information links with the investment firm's home Member State. In addition, effective supervision of regulated markets across the EC suggests that co-operation and information exchange between competent authorities in the opposite direction will also be important when the screen is initially set up in the host Member State.[115]

The generic co-operation and information-exchange procedures will also have a particular role to play in ensuring the effectiveness of the reporting obligations contained in Article 20. The home Member State is responsible for supervising the reports of all transactions covered by Article 20, regardless of where they are carried out and whether or not they are carried out on or off a regulated market, subject to the possibility of a waiver of home-Member-State reporting rules where the transactions are carried out on a regulated market in a host country and the host Member State imposes equivalent requirements. The effective tracking of market transactions across the EC, particularly off-market transactions, which is a key mechanism for detecting market abuses and insider trading, will require a high degree of co-ordination between competent authorities.[116]

---

[114] On the likelihood of a centralized securities-trading market supervisor being established see Ch. XV sect. 3.2 below.

[115] Biancheri, C, 'Cooperation Among Supervisory Authorities under the ISD' in Ferrarini, n 1 above, 363, 369.

[116] Ibid, 370.

XI.7 BEYOND THE ISD (1): COMMON STANDARDS

XI.7.1 *A Limited Regime*

By comparison with the investment-firm regime, the regulated market harmonized-standards regime is skeletal. Admittedly, many of the ISD's investment-firm standards, such as the fit-and-proper standards and the capital adequacy requirements imposed on investment firms by Article 3, feed into the regulation of regulated markets by addressing the stability and ability to meet commitments of those trading on the market-place as well as their competence and fitness to trade. Nonetheless, the detailed rules which normally underpin regulated markets and which address access conditions, governance, price formation, stability, fairness in trading, and so on are not, at present, covered.[117]

The absence of the full market-integration passport and home-country-control regime which triggered the ISD's protective and prudential rules for investment firms seems to have meant that the need to regulate in the interests of the stability and protection of the market-place as a whole was not regarded as being as critical as it was in the case of investment firms where the success of the passport regime was at stake. Difficulties in applying market-model-neutral standards and sharp North/South differences on the role of regulation would also have weighed against further harmonization beyond the already hard-fought transparency and concentration rules. Nonetheless, and even when regarding the regime in the trading-market environment of the early 1990s (since then the arguments for harmonization have become more compelling: see sections 9.4–9.5 below), the lack of common standards can be questioned. While the ISD promotes a degree of liberalization and competition in the market for regulated markets, it does not appear to address the implications of any consequent competition. In particular, where ISD-provoked competition extends to regulation which impacts on investor protection, systemic stability, or market integrity, minimum harmonized standards may be required to place a limit on competition. In terms of the investment-services market integration at the heart of the ISD (and drawing an analogy with the arguments usually raised for investor-protection harmonization), it may also be claimed that investor confidence in the integrated market-place generally, and in the provision of brokerage services specifically, was likely to have been enhanced by the adoption of common minimum standards for the fairness, transparency, and stability of regulated markets.

---

[117] The point has been made that the harmonization resulting from the ISD regulated markets regime is rather limited, given that the transparency rules have little practical effect and that the concentration rule is essentially a best-execution rule: see Ferrarini, n 66 above.

XI.7.2 *The FESCO Standards*

As in many other areas of securities regulation, the harmonization agenda
with respect to standards for regulated markets was initially set outside the
EC institutional structure by FESCO (following its transformation into the
Committee of European Securities Regulators, FESCO is now within the EC
institutional structure). In late 1999 FESCO produced harmonized standards
for markets designated as regulated markets under the ISD.[118] In a reflection
of the dominant influence confidence as a specific regulatory objective is
beginning to exert on EC securities regulation, the standards were introduced in response to FESCO's concern that the maintenance of public
confidence in ISD-regulated markets demanded more detailed regulatory
standards than those set out in the ISD. Common standards were also
thought necessary, given the freedom of regulated markets to admit members and participants from across the EC and to operate (via screens) across
the EC. A particular significance attaches to the standards, in that they
indicate an acknowledgement by EC securities regulators that common standards are necessary and because they are exerting a decisive influence on
harmonization at EC level.

The standards govern the conditions for the operation of regulated markets, the conditions for access to regulated markets, and the conditions
governing listing and/or admission to trading. The trend towards demutualization and the development of 'for profit' regulated markets is reflected in
the focus in the operation standards on governance and ownership requirements. The operation standards specifically address, for example, the management of proprietary interests in regulated markets and conflicts between
commercial objectives and regulatory responsibilities, particularly with
respect to the admission-to-listing and trading of securities and the supervision of ongoing disclosure from issuers. They also cover: management, systems and financial resources rules designed to enhance confidence in
regulated markets; trading rules which address effective price formation, the
obtaining by investors of the best price available, disclosure of price and volume information, and the prevention of disorderly markets and unfair practices by, *inter alia*, trading halts and liquidity support for thinly traded
securities;[119] transaction performance rules including timely settlement and
oversight by the regulated market of the adequacy of clearing and settlement
where those functions are carried out by a third party; and monitoring and
enforcement procedures, including data recording, complaints mechanisms,
trading termination and member removal procedures. The access conditions

---

[118] N 108 above.

[119] The FESCO standards on transparency go beyond the ISD's by imposing, eg, pre-trade
transparency.

set out membership requirements (which reflect the ISD's basic authorization criteria in that they are based on fit-and-proper and competence standards but are tailored to reflect the trading environment) and technical access arrangements. The conditions governing admission to listing and trading are based on ensuring that a proper market exists in the securities admitted to trading on the regulated market.[120] Significantly, given the current concern at the treatment of admission to listing and trading (section 9.3.1 below) the FESCO standards acknowledge the admission-to-trading/admission-to-listing dichotomy and specify that the admission-to-trading rules include a requirement that market users be able to determine easily whether a security has also been admitted to listing under the terms of the (now consolidated) Admission Directive and whether listing particulars have been prepared, and, if not, the arrangements under which the securities have been admitted to trading.

XI.7.3 *Treaty Competences and Further Harmonization*

The FESCO standards represent a considerable step forward in the regulation of regulated markets from the ISD. Whether or not the EC will ultimately adopt regulated-market standards based on FESCO's recommendations remains to be seen, although the indications are that this is likely.[121] It might be argued that if the rapidly evolving securities-trading environment continues to generate competition for trading services, the policy-maker's case for the adoption of harmonized standards as the basis for some form of trading-services passport, as a control on regulatory competition, and in order to protect investor protection and the stability and efficiency of the market-place as a whole will become increasingly compelling. Although the co-existence of divergent (if increasingly converging) market models represents a difficulty, particularly with respect to transparency requirements, certain market standards are common to all markets. Any harmonization undertaken, however, must fit within a Treaty competence. Here, as with the harmonization of investor-protection measures (Chapter IX section 12 above) problems may arise as the EC matures as a securities-market regulator and moves away from addressing the removal of barriers to free movement and, increasingly, towards general market regulation.

Harmonization in the investment-services area has been largely based on Article 47(2) and on Article 95 EC. Article 47(2) is designed to facilitate the freedom to establish (and applies to the freedom to provide services by Article 55), while Article 95 provides a basis for harmonization measures which

---

[120] The existence of a proper market is usually a function of the availability of sufficient disclosure, such that the security can be valued by potential buyers.

[121] The Commission's proposals for a new regulated market regime as set out in its ISD Working Paper are based on the FESCO regime: see sect. 9.7 below.

have as their object the establishment and functioning of the internal market. If standards harmonization is to proceed in the interests of investor confidence (per FESCO) or in order to facilitate greater integration (such as market mergers) and structural change as well to protect confidence in and the efficiency and transparency of securities trading in a competitive trading environment (per the Commission: see sections 9.4 and 9.5 below), these objectives must coincide with the legislative objectives of Articles 47(2) and 95 EC.

Reliance on Article 47(2) EC would require that the standards removed regulatory obstacles to the free movement of investment services; standards linked to the adoption of a full regulated-market passport would arguably meet this test—as long as the regulatory obstacles were real and not simply a mask for regulation. As discussed in Chapter IX in the context of whether investor-protection measures can be accommodated within Article 47(2), a need for caution can be read in the Court's statement in the *Tobacco Advertising* case that 'a mere finding of disparities between national rules and of the abstract risk of obstacles to the exercise of fundamental freedoms' would not be sufficient to justify reliance on Article 47(2) or Article 55 EC.[122] Unless the disparities between standards can be found to have a real and obstructive impact on the exercise of the Treaty free-movement guarantees, any harmonization undertaken might be vulnerable to challenge for lack of a legal basis in the Treaty.

Harmonization of standards based more generally on investor confidence, market efficiency, and transparency may be more problematic. Article 95 EC provides for legislation to be adopted in order to improve the conditions for the establishment and functioning of the common market. Measures which enhance confidence, efficiency, and transparency may be regarded as being directly linked to improving the functioning of the common market. *Tobacco Advertising* makes clear, however, that Article 95 does not grant the Community a general power of internal-market regulation.[123] The Court found that a measure adopted under Article 95 must genuinely have as its object the improvement of the conditions for the establishment and functioning of the internal market, and warned that a mere finding of disparities between national rules and of the abstract risk of obstacles to the Treaty free-movement guarantees or of distortions to competition, would not suffice. Harmonization of common standards therefore appears to face two hurdles before it can qualify as improving the functioning of the common market. First, the ends achieved—efficiency, transparency, confidence, facilitation of market restructuring/pan-EC trading/market mergers, and so on—must

---

[122] Case C–376/98 *Germany v Parliament and Council* [2000] ECR I–8419 (the *Tobacco Advertising* case). See Ch. IX sects. 12.3 and 12.4.2 above.

[123] Ibid, para 83.

genuinely improve the conditions for the establishment and functioning of the internal market. Secondly, *Tobacco Advertising* may also suggest, although it is not entirely clear, that, in addition, improvements in the functioning of the market-place are to be examined by reference to the removal of obstacles to free movement and the removals of competitive distortions.[124] As far as efficiency, transparency, and confidence as targets for Article 95 EC are concerned, a precedent may be found in the Insider Dealing Directive which, crucially, forms part of the general securities-trading-market regulatory framework. Based on Article 95 EC, its objectives are to ensure that the 'market operates smoothly' and, given that 'the smooth operation of [the secondary market] depends to a large extent on the confidence it inspires in investors', to control insider dealing which 'is likely to prejudice the smooth operation of the market'.[125] The immediate need for harmonization was a function of regulatory divergences and the fact that 'in some Member States there are no [insider dealing controls] and . . . the rules or regulations that do exist differ considerably from one Member State to another'.[126] To take, by analogy, the example of more detailed transparency harmonization, diverging transparency rules in a competitive trading environment have, as discussed in section 9.4 below, been highlighted by the Commission as a threat to market efficiency and in particular price formation by dispersing liquidity. Harmonization might come within Article 95 EC, given that the 'smooth operation of the market', identified by the Insider Dealing Directive as a legitimate target for Article 95, arguably also encompasses market efficiency and price formation. More generally, enhancing price formation and the operation of the market-place through harmonized transparency rules might be regarded as ultimately feeding into the free movement of investment services and removing competitive distortions by making trading more efficient in a uniform manner across the EC. On a more pragmatic level, while it is clear that the Court will, in the future, subject the interaction between the legal basis and the objectives of a measure to much closer scrutiny, it may be that it will be reluctant to second-guess the Commission's assessment of the extent to which a link existed between divergences in transparency rules and market efficiency, particularly given its broadly sympathetic approach to policy-makers' choices in the investment-services sphere in *Alpine Investments*.[127]

Applying the Insider Dealing Directive model to harmonization in the interests of facilitating market restructuring/pan-EC trading/market mergers, such harmonization is clearly based in the problems caused by diverging rules. A connection might be made to improving the functioning of the

---

[124] See the discussion in Ch. IX sect. 12.3 above.
[125] N 15 above, recitals 3, 4, and 6.   [126] Ibid, recital 8.
[127] Case C-384/93 *Alpine Investments v Minister van Financiën* [1995] ECR I-1141.

market-place on the grounds that such restructuring of itself enhances the functioning of the market-place and should be facilitated or, more consequentially, that the functioning of the market-place as a whole would be prejudiced were competition between markets or the development of pan-EC trading to prejudice investor protection, market stability, or efficiency. Whether this would survive a *Tobacco Advertising* ruling test or would be characterized as a manifestation of a general regulatory power beyond the competence of the internal market power will depend in large part on how the Court views the relationship between investment services 'regulation' and the functioning of the internal market.

Any standards adopted must also meet the Article 5 EC requirements on subsidiarity and proportionality. Subsidiarity requirements are likely to be met if trading markets continue to integrate, and, in particular, if pan-EC trading systems develop. Similarly, the dangers of regulatory competition in the absence of common standards should, depending on its likelihood, also provide a bulwark against failure to conform with subsidiarity arguments. Proportionality has to date usually been achieved via minimum standards. FESCO's approach (on which the Commission appears to be basing its response) is, however, quite detailed. The impact of the Lamfalussy Report and the extent to which detailed legislation will be adopted via comitology procedures will have a significant influence on the level at which standards are adopted.

XI.8　BEYOND THE ISD (2): FURTHER INTEGRATION

XI.8.1　*Benefits and Drawbacks*

Greater competition between and ultimately integration of securities-trading markets is typically regarded as bringing with it considerable efficiency gains. These include: the deepening of liquidity, which allows savings to be more effectively invested; the facilitation of competitive market-based financing by allowing issuers to obtain better prices for their securities; the strengthening of price discovery by widening the investor pool and allowing a greater volume of investors' orders to interact; and the lowering of transaction costs.[128] The arrival of the euro and the removal of currency risks has provoked greater investment on an EC-wide basis, increased institutional investors' need for liquidity (and thus interest in market consolidation)[129] and intensified demand for a cost-efficient, integrated securities-trading environment (similar pressures are being exerted in the clearing and settlement

---

[128] See, eg, the discussion in the ISD Communication, n 43 above, 5.

[129] See Targett, S, 'It's the liquidity that matters', *Financial Times Survey*, Stock and Derivatives Exchanges, 28 Mar 2001.

area: see Chapter XII below). Despite recent developments discussed in section 8.3, securities-trading markets, particularly the equity markets, are far from integrated.[130] Market pressures are now such, however, that further consolidation and integration of securities-trading markets across the EC is now regarded by many as inevitable even if the future shape of integration may be opaque.

A major restructuring of the EC trading environment is now under way. The restructuring is proceeding in two directions: increased competition between traditional exchanges and regulated markets and greater integration through alliances and mergers; and the development of alternative trading systems which provide competing trading services often on a pan-EC basis.

Depending on the form which it ultimately takes, integration could pose problems for the securities-trading system. In particular, the development of numerous pan-EC trading systems, by means of exchange alliances or through alternative trading systems, carries with it the risk of fragmenting trading in the same security across a number of different systems. Should this arise on a large scale, the EC may have replaced one set of difficulties, based on the fragmentation of securities markets on national lines, for another set, based on fragmentation of trading in the same security across different systems. If these EC-wide systems are not sufficiently connected or subject to common legal co-operation and interaction requirements, difficulties may arise with respect to investor protection and market integrity in a number of areas. These include the control of market manipulation (Chapter XIII section 11.1 below), the delivery of best execution, and the achievement of an efficient price-formation process for investors.[131]

XI.8.2 *Greater Integration and the Regulatory Structure*

XI.8.2.1 *Early Regulatory and Policy Initiatives*

The trading-market-integration discussion is not a new one. The 1966 Segré Report highlighted the narrowness of securities markets across the Community, and the consequent difficulty in buying or selling a large amount of any one security without causing significant price fluctuations and lack of liquidity, as a considerable obstacle to the creation of a European

---

[130] The fragmentation of equity markets and the associated costs are regularly raised as matters of concern. See, eg, the editorial comment of the *Financial Times*: 'Crash Start', *Financial Times*, 3 Mar 2000.

[131] It is clear from the ISD Communication (n 43 above) that fragmentation is a matter of some concern at EC level. FESCO has also identified fragmentation as a potential problem where alternative trading systems are concerned. Not all commentators believe, however, that fragmentation of trading between different suppliers of trading services is undesirable. See (published in 1993) Scott-Quinn, n 2 above, Appendix 3, 39.

capital market.[132] In particular, it noted that issuers of debt securities (the Report acknowledged that the equity market was more subject to price movements) were unlikely to access the capital market while the secondary trading market mechanism and, specifically, the price-formation process was so unsatisfactory. To counteract the narrowness problem, it suggested that action be taken to 'adapt security dealing techniques on official and unofficial markets and to create the conditions for securities to circulate as freely throughout the Community as within a domestic market'.[133]

Contemporaneously with the development of the disclosure regime and the encouragement of multiple listings by the early securities directives, the possibility of a single European securities-trading market or system was also raised.[134] In 1981, the European Parliament's Resolution on the Creation of a European Stock Exchange[135] supported the development of a European stock market system and noted that links between stock exchanges and the computerization of transactions could facilitate greater interpenetration of national markets. While it was hostile to the development of a single stock exchange (on the ground that this would be incompatible with consumer choice), it recommended that the ongoing work in the area of issuer disclosure be extended to cover removal of the obstacles represented by diverging Member State rules on access and trading methods. The Commission's 1985 White Paper on the single market took a more aggressive approach to securities-trading market integration.[136] It identified the construction of a European securities-market system as a desirable objective and, somewhat optimistically, called for the construction of a 'Community-wide trading system for securities of international interest'. The system would be based on electronic links between markets which would allow members to execute orders on the market offering the best conditions and increase the liquidity of Community markets. The White Paper also regarded 'unofficial and unsupervised markets' as a threat to more traditional stock exchanges, noting that greater links would allow stock exchanges to compete more effectively with such markets.[137] Notwithstanding these initiatives and the impetus to further integration which might have been expected with the adoption of the securities directives, securities-trading markets across the EC remained, for the most part, compartmentalized in their national markets, closed to mem-

---

[132] Report of a Group of Experts Appointed by the EEC Commission, *The Development of a European Capital Market* (1966) 238–41.

[133] Ibid, 238.

[134] For an early discussion of a possible model for an integrated securities market see Wymeersch, E, 'From Harmonization to Integration in European Securities Markets' (1981) 3 *Journal of Comparative Corporate Law and Securities Regulation* 1, 11–25.

[135] [1981] OJ C 287/29.   [136] Completing the Internal Market, COM(85)310, 29.

[137] Ibid.

bers from other Member States, in control of trading in their domestic securities, and protected from competition.[138]

XI.8.2.2 *The ISD and Integration*

As outlined above in section 6 above, the ISD does not explicitly promote the development of a single integrated trading market. Securities-trading market integration under the ISD integration model is a function of competitive market forces and market interpenetration by individual securities markets rather than of the construction of an integrated trading system.

Its regulated market provisions are, for the most part, focused not on regulated markets *per se*, but on liberalizing access by investment firms to national regulated markets both on a physical-presence basis and through remote-access mechanisms. Remote access, which has been particularly successful, with remote members now forming a large proportion of regulated market membership across the EC, is particularly significant for integration, however, in that it allows members to trade directly in the market which offers most liquidity and so generates competition for order flow between markets. In the absence of the remote-access facility, investment firms would be required either to establish in the market's home Member State or to operate through local members. Widening the membership base of regulated markets thus indirectly promotes competition between regulated markets and reduces market compartmentalization. Remote access by investment firms to national markets may also prove to be the most effective route to integrating securities-trading markets in the event that admission to listing and trading remains nationally focused. Remote access will also be critical in the event that listing and trading on a single or on multiple pan-EC trading systems become the dominant market-access pattern.[139]

Integration via the development of pan-EC electronic trading systems is also a feature of the ISD. This is clear from Article 15(4) which grants, in effect, a passport to screen-based systems to operate across the EC without further authorization, thereby promoting greater competition between and

---

[138] The situation up to the mid-1980s has been described in the following terms: '[i]n all countries, the stock exchange was a closed membership organization, with high barriers to potential entrants. Each exchange operated in isolation from the others, well sheltered from competition by national regulations, barriers to capital mobility, and high costs of telecommunications': Pagano and Steil, n 1 above, 4.

[139] The extent to which listing and trading will be carried out on a single or multiple national-market basis or on a single or multiple pan-EC trading-system basis is currently receiving considerable attention. It has been suggested that adoption of the euro and the remote membership facility will direct equity trades to the domestic exchange where liquidity will be deepest: Gros and Lannoo, n 4 above, 44, 95, and 163. For the view that multiple listings are being replaced by trading on pan-EC trading platforms see Ferrarini, n 66 above who has suggested that listings may, in consequence, migrate to the home Member State of these trading systems.

ultimately integration of securities-trading markets. The development of new pan-EC trading systems, accessed via screens in each Member State (such as EASDAQ, now NASDAQ-Europe), has been one of the most significant integration results of the adoption of the ISD.

Nonetheless, the fact remains that the ISD does not directly address the freedom of regulated markets to operate across the EC on a passport basis, although the Treaty free-movement rules, subject to the general-good qualification, would apply.[140] The Article 14(4) concentration rule and the ability of Member States to prohibit the creation of new markets in their territories under Article 15(5) also weaken the ISD's regulated-market liberalization infrastructure. The structural weaknesses of the ISD as an integration measure have recently become sharply apparent in the wake of the market developments discussed in section 8.3 below and examined further in section 9 below.[141]

XI.8.2.3 *Integration and the FSAP*

Since the adoption of the ISD, the presentation of the FSAP[142] and the conclusions of the Lisbon European Council on the need for greater integration of securities markets in the interests of economic growth and employment have refocused the attention of legislators on the integration of securities-trading markets.[143] The legislative approach appears to be to facilitate rather than influence market developments, with the FSAP highlighting the role played by market forces in developing an efficient, integrated securities-trading market. The FSAP's objectives under 'Strategic Objective 1—A Single EU Wholesale Market' include the establishment of a common legal framework for integrated securities and derivatives markets which would ensure that integration by market forces is not hindered by legal and admin-

---

[140] Whether or not securities-trading markets would use 'branch' structures is not entirely clear. See section 9.7 below.

[141] On the weaknesses of the ISD regulated-market passport see Wymeersch, E, *The Harmonisation of Securities Trading in Europe in the New Trading Environment*, WP 2000-16, Working Paper Series of the Financial Law Institute, Universiteit Gent.

[142] Commission Communication on Implementing the Framework for Financial Markets: Action Plan, COM(1999)232 (the FSAP).

[143] Prior to the adoption of the FSAP, the construction of an integrated securities-trading market was not entirely disregarded by policy-makers, as can be seen from the Commission's 1995 Communication on the Feasibility of the Creation of a European Capital Market for Smaller Entrepreneurially Managed Growing Companies, COM(95)498. In the context of the pressing investment needs of the Community's fast-growing and entrepreneurially managed companies and the, at the time, poor performance of the Community's second-tier markets, it supported the construction of a pan-EC trading market for second tier market securities and, in particular, the development of what would become NASDAQ Europe. More generally it noted at 6 that 'a pan-European market should provide substantial new business opportunities for financial institutions participating in stock market activity, including those in the regional financial centres'.

istrative obstacles. The FSAP proposals under this objective include measures on market manipulation (see Chapter XIII below) and cross-border collateral (see Chapter XII below). They also contain a commitment to presenting a Green Paper which would address the treatment of regulated markets and, specifically, the remaining obstacles to market access and remote membership and the appropriate response to new trading systems (section 9 below).

XI.8.3 *Industry Developments*

Securities-market integration is now being driven by industry developments. A marked trend away from the concentration of trading on compartmentalized and domestically-oriented national markets and towards greater competition and co-operation between securities-trading markets can now be observed.[144] Securities are regularly traded on a number of markets and trades completed on the market which offers the best price.[145] In addition to competing on price, markets can also compete on liquidity, speed of execution and transparency (in terms of confidentiality, for example).[146]

The early market attempts to connect securities-trading markets and move towards greater integration were unsuccessful, however, often because they did not provide greater trading liquidity. The 1990 Euroquote project (called PIPE or the Price and Information Project for Europe in its earlier stages), which was based on a earlier proposal for an inter-exchange information-dissemination system (IDIS),[147] was designed to provide an officially authorized integrated issuer and transaction information service to the exchanges. Its objectives included: providing an authorized, recognized source of strategic equities-market information for the European region; maximizing the visibility of European equities markets by providing a window on them on a global basis; reducing the costs associated with access to

[144] FESCO Standards, 108 above, 3.

[145] 'Trading costs have been reduced and the variety of trading mechanisms has increased substantially. Most European "blue chip" stocks are now simultaneously traded in continuous auction . . . systems and in dealer . . . markets, not to mention the hybrid systems that have emerged in some exchanges. The pressure on trading costs and the proliferation of alternative trading mechanisms are both due to an unprecedented wave of competition among European exchanges': Pagano, n 1 above, 177.

[146] Competition does not always arise where it may be expected to. When the London Stock Exchange's trading system was shut down due to a computer crash on 5 Apr 2000, investors did not transfer their business to Tradepoint even though it supplied an alternative, liquid trading venue. See Bolan, V, 'Soap gets in our eyes', *Financial Times*, 18 Sept 2000.

[147] IDIS (the Inter-Bourse Data Information Service) was an initiative of the Federation of Stock Exchanges in the European Community and was the model for the Commission's plans, outlined in the White Paper, for a Community-wide trading system: Poser, N, *International Securities Regulation. London's 'Big Bang and the European Securities Markets* (1991) 349. It was abandoned largely because the technology was not available to make the project feasible. Lee: n 2 above, 68.

information from European markets; and enhancing the quality of information available to market users. The scheme's objectives also extended beyond information to providing the basis for a common trading platform.[148] A number of intractable problems, including uncertainty on the part of certain exchange members of Euroquote as to the commercial viability of the project (including concern about competition from the Reuters information service) led to its being abandoned in 1991. Given the development of the trading environment into a competitive market for trading and liquidity services since then, and the change in the perception of exchanges as public suppliers of a services to commercially motivated competitors, it is of some interest that it has been suggested that one of the factors underlying the failure of Euroquote was its characterization as an officially authorized information source, licensed by regulated markets. While the continental exchanges were comfortable with the view of the exchange as an official body and of information licensed by a regulated market as being in some way superior to information flowing from non-regulated markets, the London Stock Exchange, in particular, was not.[149] Euroquote ultimately evolved into the more modest Eurolist system which only provided listing services (it was designed to provide simultaneous listing or a 'listing passport' for blue-chip issuers on certain EC stock exchanges for shares meeting its qualifications), did not support trading, and, having been abandoned in 1997, cannot be regarded as having been a success.

Since then competitive pressures from a number of sources have jolted securities-trading markets from their isolationist positions, increased competition for trades between markets, and produced a number of alliances.[150] Chief among these competitive pressures were: the market changes wrought by the euro; technological developments which facilitated trading link-ups;[151] increased competition between regulated markets in the wake of the ISD's liberalizing measures and the ability of new pan-EC trading systems to operate across the EC on a remote access basis; and demutualization. The demutualization trend of recent years has seen the transformation of EC securities markets from, for the most part, quasi-official bodies operating and supervising securities-trading markets into commercially motivated suppliers of securities-market services. As part of the demutualization process, traditional securities markets have also streamlined their functions by, in certain cases (such as the transfer of listing responsibility from the London

---

[148] Poser, N, *International Securities Regulation. London's 'Big Bang and the European Securities Markets* (1991) 349, 70.

[149] Ibid, 73.

[150] For an account of how competition for trading has developed and how trading mechanisms have evolved in response to greater competition since the first major market shift with the move by the London Stock Exchange into trading in international equities on SEAQ-International in 1986 see Pagano, n 1 above.

[151] For a succinct summary of the impact of automation see Lee, n 2 above, 4.

Stock Exchange to the UK Financial Services Authority), dropping the supervisory and regulatory functions which they traditionally carried out as a result of the incompatibility of those functions with the pursuit of profit and shareholder value. Competition has also come from ATSs (see section 8.4 below) and new pan-EC electronic securities-trading markets, authorized as regulated markets, such as EASDAQ (now NASDAQ Europe), which is a pan-European quote-driven screen-based market for high-growth issuers closely based on NASDAQ, which allows for Europe-wide secondary trading in its securities.[152] Its organizational model relies on the Article 15(4) passport and the freedom of regulated markets to provide remote access trading screens.

Industry developments have now moved beyond alliances to embrace full-blown mergers. The first significant step in this direction was taken in September 2000 with the launch of Euronext, formed from a merger between the Paris Bourse and the Amsterdam and Brussels stock exchanges.[153] Euronext, the first cross-border stock exchange, did not involve the construction of a new regulated market entity from the three existing markets, which continue; it is designed, however, to have a common trading platform and rule book. It operates by splitting responsibility for the various markets between the three exchanges according to the type of security. Blue-chip stocks are the responsibility of the Paris Bourse, derivatives and futures those of the Amsterdam Stock Exchange, and securities of small and medium-sized issuers those of the Brussels Stock Exchange.[154] The strategic alliance announced in early 1999 between the London Stock Exchange and Deutsche Börse, which was designed ultimately to result in the development of a common trading platform, developed in 2000 into a full-scale merger project and a proposal to create a new stock exchange, iX. The proposal involved the establishment of two iX subsidiaries in London and Frankfurt, a European blue-chip market at the London Stock Exchange and a European growth market at the Frankfurt Stock Exchange, and the use of a common trading platform by the two exchanges. While the iX proposal failed, in part due to market scepticism about whether agreement could be reached on the UK and German regulatory standards applicable and the subsequent hostile takeover bid for the London Stock Exchange by OM Gruppen, the scale of the proposal and the significance of the two

[152] EASDAQ was designated as a regulated market under Belgian law. On EASDAQ's operational structure see Averginos, Y, 'Towards a Pan-European Securities Market for SMEs: the EASDAQ and Euro.NM Models' (2000) 11 *EBLRev.* 8, Ackerly II, D, P Tamussino, P, and Williams, W, 'Easdaq—The European Stock Market for the Next Hundred Years' (1997) 12 *JIBL* 86 and Vanassche, C, 'EASDAQ—the New Pan-European Stock Market for High Growth Companies' (1996) 3 *EFSL* 258.

[153] At the time of writing, the largest exchange in continental Europe.

[154] See generally Farrow, P, 'Bringing Euronext to Life', *IFR Special Report*, issue 1379, 16 (Apr 2001).

markets involved, marked a staging post in the evolution of the EC trading environment.[155] More recently, following the 2000 launch of its pan-European exchange, Tradepoint has merged with the Swiss stock exchange to form Virt-x, which provides a pan-European market for blue-chip stocks, based on an electronic order book and using the Swiss stock exchange's trading platform, and which will support trading in all the constituents of the major European indices.[156] While the future shape of the major EC regulated markets remains to be seen, and although it is now thought that the consolidation process is slowing, at the least it can be said that the trading environment is going through a dramatic developmental stage.

XI.8.4 *Technological Developments and Alternative Trading Systems*

XI.8.4.1 *A New Form of Trading System*[157]

Technological developments facilitating electronic trading have produced a new generation of trading systems which can compete with traditional securities markets with respect to trading services, operate cross-border, reduce trading costs and provide institutional investors, in particular, with additional pools of liquidity.[158] These ATSs offer an array of services ranging from traditional broker/dealing services to order-routing services to comprehensive trading services involving sophisticated trading platforms akin to those provided by traditional organized markets. Their pan-EC operation and ability to centralize trading makes them potentially powerful agents for integration as well as a natural target for EC-level risks and regulation.

ATSs vary widely, with the term ATS often being used to refer to different forms of service provider. In general, ATSs offer to wholesale market participants trading services related to those provided by the organized markets. Operating through screen-based trading systems, they allow buyers and sellers to enter into transactions away from traditional organized markets and to access pre- and post-trade information, thereby entering into competition with the traditional organized markets' trading systems. They can take a number of forms varying from bulletin boards at which market participants indicate their trading interests and subsequently negotiate independently

---

[155] The trend towards alliance and mergers is not an isolated EC phenomenon. In 2000, 10 of the world's major exchanges including the New York Stock Exchange and Euronext agreed to form an alliance and to construct a Global Equities Market for blue-chip equities, although it remains to be seen how this will evolve.

[156] See the description at http://www.tradepoint.co.uk.

[157] See generally, Champarnaud, F, 'Facing New Regulatory Challenges: The Case of Proprietary Trading Systems' in Jeunemaître, A (ed), *Financial Markets Regulation. A Practitioner's Perspective* (1997) 84.

[158] The concentration option available to Member States under Art. 14(3) of the ISD does not appear to have hindered the ability of alternative trading systems to compete with regulated markets.

with each other to systems which match buy and sell orders at overlapping prices. Similarly, certain ATSs operate a price-formation mechanism and set trading prices, while others provide 'crossing mechanisms' which match orders at a price set on another market-place.[159]

They offer a number of advantages to the wholesale market including: cheaper trading; more demand-sensitive trading mechanisms such as out-of-hours trading; anonymity and the ability to undertake trades away from the eye of the market-place as a whole; an alternative trading location which can absorb the impact on the market of a large trade; direct access to institutional investors (traditional regulated markets normally require some form of intermediation to access the market-place); and, where the particular trading market was not already organized and centralized, greater liquidity and more efficient price formation.[160] ATSs could potentially exert considerable influence on the integration process, not only in areas in which trading markets are not already organized but also in relation to equity markets, by ultimately centralizing trading on a pan-EC basis and providing a single trading venue.[161] Although they have developed at a slower rate than in the USA, a number of ATSs are now operating in the EC securities-trading markets. One of the most advanced and successful of the ATSs is Instinet, a US-based electronic order-driven trading system owned by Reuters, which has a price-discovery mechanism. In response to the threat from ATSs some traditional organized markets are now 'unbundling' the services which they offer by carving out, for example, their listing and price-information services.[162]

XI.8.4.2 *Regulatory Concerns*

ATSs expose investors to a number of risks. Retail investors are typically not admitted to ATSs due to the increased counterparty risk they represent

[159] The various types of ATSs have sometimes been categorized as: matching systems (which display participants' orders and execute orders automatically against others in the system); crossing systems (unpriced orders are entered and executed against orders of matching interest at a price taken from another trading markets); and single-price auction systems (priced orders are entered, reviewed by a computer which establishes the price at which the largest volume of orders can be executed and all orders are matched and executed at that price). See, eg, Jennings, R, Marsh, H, Coffee, J, and Seligman, J, *Securities Regulation, Cases and Materials* (8th edn, 1998) 617.

[160] This will not be the case with equity markets which are centralized and which, conversely, are vulnerable to fragmentation by ATS trading. For certain other markets, however, such as the OTC bond markets, ATSs offer an organized trading mechanism. ATSs are now operating in the debt and standardised OTC derivative markets, where they are moving bilateral telephone trading to multilateral screen trading, as well as in equity markets, and are beginning to impact on non-standardized OTC-derivative markets: FESCO, *Proposed Standards for Alternative Trading Systems* (2001) (the FESCO ATS Common Standards Report). Fesco/01–035b. 2.

[161] FESCO, *The Regulation of Alternative Trading Systems in Europe, A Paper for the EU Commission*, Sept 2000. Fesco/00–064c (the FESCO ATS Report) 7.

[162] See the discussion in the IOSCO Markets Report, n 4 above, 13.

(Instinet, for example, is not open to retail investors), but their exclusion results in the development of prices which are not available to all investors.[163] Best execution, which is a central principle of protective regulation, may become more difficult to achieve as ATSs will, where the market is already centralized, fragment trading. Conflicts of interest can also arise where an investment firm provides execution services but also operates an ATS. More generally, ATSs pose a number of risks to the efficiency, stability, and integrity of the market-place as a whole. The fragmentation which ATSs can provoke above and beyond the existing degree of market fragmentation in the EC, by increasing the number of trading venues on which the same security trades, can compromise liquidity and damage efficient price formation. Similarly, price formation may be obstructed by the lack of transparency in certain ATSs where a large volume of trading in a security takes place on an ATS.[164] Trading activity on ATSs is subject to lower levels of supervision than trading on traditional organized markets, making it more difficult to control market manipulation. Similarly, ATS operators may not impose or enforce adequate admission standards for securities and participants or be sufficiently concerned with ensuring that trading is carried out in a fair and orderly fashion. More generally, given that ATSs provide discrete bundles of services, such as order matching and price information, which would traditionally be provided as part of the package of listing, trading, and price-discovery mechanisms provided by organized markets, there is concern that ATSs will not be concerned with ensuring that securities-trading markets are fair and orderly. ATSs may also expose the EC market-place to systemic risks where they, or their participants, do not have sufficient financial resources or where their trading mechanisms are not sufficiently bolstered against counterparty risk.

Deciding on the appropriate regulatory response to manage these risks requires a decision on whether the ATS should be treated as an investment firm, as a regulated market, or as a distinct category of market participant.[165]

---

[163] For a comprehensive review of the risks associated with ATSs see the FESCO ATS Report, n 161, above 12–14. The following discussion is based, in part, on the Report's findings.

[164] Unless an ATS qualifies under Art. 1(13) and is designated as a regulated market, it will not be subject to the ISD's transparency regime. FESCO's ATS Report identified the equity markets as an area in which transparency standards diverged significantly with ATSs generating business as a result of their lower transparency requirements, designed to reduce the market impact of large trades: n 161 above, 14.

[165] The appropriate characterization of ATSs has been the subject of considerable discussion in the USA. The approach ultimately adopted by the SEC was to allow ATSs to choose whether to register as an exchange or as a broker-dealer. The SEC retains the power to require registration as an exchange where particular trading-volume thresholds are met and treatment as an exchange is in the public interest. If the ATS chooses to register as a broker-dealer, the rules set out in the SEC's ATS regime, Regulation ATS (Securities Exchange Act Release No. 40760), apply to the ATS.

If ATSs are treated as investment firms,[166] they are subject to protective and prudential regulation which may address the investor-protection and systemic risks raised by ATSs but which may fall short with respect to the particular risks posed by the more advanced forms of trading system. Neither does the traditional protective and prudential regulation of investment firms, which is designed to deal with investor protection and systemic stability, address the market-integrity and efficiency objectives usually pursued by securities-trading market regimes. Conversely, securities-trading market regimes are not usually concerned with the investor-protection/systemic-risk implications of investment-firm activity. The variety of services provided by ATSs, which can range from information services to full-blown trading services, also demands that regulatory and supervisory arrangements be tailored accordingly.

XI.8.4.3 *The Current Regulatory Regime for ATSs*

The ISD does not address ATSs. The definition of a regulated market is skeletal. It does not provide a basis for distinguishing between ATSs and traditional regulated markets or for isolating ATSs for regulatory purposes; this flows directly from the basic problem that the ISD does not set out the characteristics of a securities-trading market but simply accepts the traditional view of a regulated market.[167] By contrast, the definition of an investment firm is, arguably, sufficiently flexible to include the trading and information services provided by ATSs. The investment-firm regime does not, however, refer to ATSs, provide a basis for distinguishing ATSs from traditional broker/dealer-based investment firms, or tailor the applicable regulatory provisions in any way. Further, while the ISD contains relatively clear and detailed capital-adequacy and operational prudential controls, its conduct-of-business regime could not, at present, be regarded as comprehensive or as sufficiently detailed to provide the basis for a common set of rules for ATSs.

XI.8.4.4 *The FESCO ATS Proposals*

In its 1999 Standards Report FESCO identified the regulation of ATSs as an area which needed further consideration, but relied on the traditional regulated market as its model for the common standards adopted. In order to support the work of the Commission in this area, it produced in 2000 a report on the regulation of ATSs which set out the risks represented by ATSs

---

[166] Among Member States, the prevailing approach is to give an ATS the option of being treated as an investment firm or a regulated market as long as it meets the relevant qualifying standards. ATSs usually, but not always, opt for the investment-firm route.

[167] FESCO ATS Report, n 161 above, 4.

and presented a series of options for how these risks could be addressed under the ISD's regulatory framework. One important product of the FESCO ATS Report was a working definition of an ATS as 'an entity which, without being regulated as an exchange, operates an automated system that brings together buying and selling interests—in the system and according to rules set by the system's operator—in a way that forms, or results in an irrevocable contract'.[168]

The FESCO ATS Report identified the main risks associated with ATSs and assessed the extent to which the current regime provided sufficient protection against those risks. It highlighted in particular the risks associated with market fragmentation (the potential damage to market efficiency as liquidity is dispersed, the greater difficulty in achieving best execution, and the prejudice to the ability of supervisors to monitor trading activity in a security across the market-place as a whole) as risks which the existing regime and its regulatory principles might not be able to address adequately. It also highlighted two governing principles critical to ensuring an effective regulatory response to ATSs: a focus on levelling the playing-field between ATSs and traditional markets; and the adoption of a consistent approach across the EC to ATSs. FESCO came up with four possible regulatory responses: maintaining the *status quo*; developing a new discrete regime for ATSs; treating ATSs as investment firms under the ISD and supplementing the ISD with FESCO standards; and constructing a new integrated 'trading system regime' in place of the current regulated market regime. Its favoured option was to treat ATSs as a service supplied by investment firms and to apply the ISD investment-firm regime, supplemented by specific ATS risk-management rules as appropriate—an approach which, as discussed in section 9.2 below, has been supported by the Commission. This analysis was followed up in 2001 with the more concrete FESCO ATS Common Standards Report which set out proposed common standards for ATSs, based on the risks identified in the earlier report, the ISD regulatory model, and the treatment of ATSs as services provided by investment firms; additional standards were regarded as necessary, given that the current ISD regime was found to be inadequate in addressing the particular risks posed by ATSs.[169] The standards have been constructed around and complement the ISD framework and, in particular Article 3 (authorization), Article 10 (operational prudential controls), Article 11 (conduct-of-business regulation), and Article 20 (reporting requirements). As well as feeding into the ISD reform process, these proposals have been designed to provide a framework for regulators in advance of any revisions made to the ISD. A core recommendation of FESCO's was that the standards be applied in a differentiated manner taking into account: the professional status of the user; the nature of the market in which the ATS-

---

[168] FESCO ATS Report, n 161 above, 5.   [169] N 160 above.

traded instruments in question were traded; the vulnerability of the instruments traded to market abuse; the significance of the ATS in the overall market for the instrument, taking into account factors such as trading volume and the ATS' impact on price formation; and the nature of the ATS, such as its degree of automation and whether it had a role in price formation. The first group of additional standards concern the authorization process and include requiring the investment firm to register their ATSs and supply the competent authority with information concerning, *inter alia*, the price-formation process, the rules of the system, the order-execution process, and governance arrangements. The disclosure standards for users of ATSs require the investment firm to: have in place an agreement setting out the nature of the relationship between the system operator and the user; provide sufficient information such that the user can use the system efficiently and understand the risks attendant on use; and provide or be satisfied that there is access to sufficient publicly available information for users to make an investment judgement. Fair and orderly trading standards have also been suggested and include the requirement that, where regulators consider it necessary to support the integrity of the broader market in a particular instrument, investment firms operating ATSs make available on a reasonable commercial basis the quote, order, and completed trade information made available to ATS users. They also include the requirement that investment firms operating ATSs put in place, when required by the national regulator, arrangements with the relevant regulator to facilitate the detection of market abuse. Standards have also been proposed with respect to ensuring the sound operation of ATSs and that parties are clear where responsibilities for settlement lie.

XI.9 THE ISD COMMUNICATION[170] AND REFORM OF THE ISD

XI.9.1 *Review of the ISD*

The recent changes to the EC securities-trading markets infrastructure outlined above have also been tracked by a general increase in cross-border securities transactions. Market-based financing is on the increase and, in the wake of the introduction of the Euro, has impacted beyond national trading markets. Investment patterns are shifting away from domestic investments to sectoral pan-EC investments with improvements in transparency and comparability. In response to the changed trading environment[171] the

---

[170] N 43 above.

[171] Which has been described in the following terms: 'investment horizons of funds and private investors are becoming more pan-European. The same financial instruments are potentially tradeable on competing exchanges and trading platforms across the EU. The same

Commission presented in November 2000 a wide-ranging Communication reviewing the ISD, identifying the major weaknesses which have emerged in the ISD's structure in the wake of market developments, and proposing revisions to its provisions.[172] Its discussion of regulated markets covered: the appropriate regulatory treatment of ATSs; a single passport for regulated markets; and the supervisory structure for regulated markets. The Communication's approach to each of these areas, which has set the basis for a more extensive discussion document issued in July 2001 (section 9.7 below), is considered at sections 9.2–9.5 below.

XI.9.2 *The Treatment of ATSs*

At the core of the Communication's discussion of ATSs was its analysis of whether they were adequately regulated and the risks they represented were appropriately managed by the ISD's investment-firm provisions under which they are, for the most part, regulated. The Commission took the view, which reflects FESCO's position, that ATSs can often be characterized for regulatory purposes with investment firms. Its initial recommendation was that a 'graduated application', based on a case-by-case assessment of the risk profile of individual ATSs, of the Article 10 organizational requirements and Article 11 conduct rules for investment firms would counter any supplementary risks to investors and the stability of the market.[173] A more considered approach to the ATS question has now been given in the 2001 ISD Working Paper discussed at section 9.7 below.

XI.9.3 *Effective Competition Between Regulated Markets*

XI.9.3.1 *Admission to Official Listing and Admission to Trading*

A key conclusion of the ISD Communication was that revisions needed to be made to the definition of a 'regulated market' in order to reflect more carefully the role played, or required to be played, by a 'regulated market' in the admission of securities to official listing and their subsequent admission to trading.[174] Article 1(13) currently defines a 'regulated market' by reference in part to the requirement for admitting securities to listing. It provides, *inter alia*, that regulated markets are characterized by the fact that rules issued or approved by competent authorities define, where the (now consolidated)

---

investment firms constitute the membership of different exchanges and serve the same national client bases. Finally, exchanges and new types of trading platforms are competing across borders for order flow and are increasingly dependent on consolidated clearing houses/central counterparty facilities': ISD Communication, n 43 above, 6.

[172] N 43 above.   [173] Ibid, 12.

[174] On the interaction between admission to listing and admission to trading see Chs. II and III above.

Admission Directive applies, the conditions governing admission to listing and, where the Directive does not apply, the conditions governing the admission to dealing or trading of financial instruments.

The extent to which a regulated market (as opposed to a designated independent competent authority) should be involved in the admission-to-listing process and in ensuring that securities admitted to official listing comply with the (now consolidated) Admission Directive is currently a matter of debate. The official listing process is the regulatory and market device used to ensure that securities are subject to extensive scrutiny before being admitted to trading. Officially listing a security also ensures that adequate disclosure is made available to the market-place as securities admitted to official listing are subject to a high level of initial and ongoing disclosure. In the EC context, admission to official listing requires compliance with the harmonized listing rules discussed in Part II which ensure minimum standards of investor protection and allow the disclosure document prepared as part of the listing process to be subject to mutual recognition procedures. Once a security has passed the qualifying listing checks and is admitted to the Official List, it is then admitted to trading.[175] Traditionally, most regulated markets undertook responsibility for overseeing admission to listing and maintained an Official List in respect of the securities dealt in on the market-place. The listing process is a cumbersome one, however, involving preparation and review of listing particulars, and places considerable burdens on a regulated market. Pressures are growing, as a result, for the admission-to-listing and the admission-to-trading function to be decoupled in the interests of greater competition. Movements to spin off the admission-to-listing function are also a consequence of the demutualization of regulated markets and conflicts between the supervisory and public-interest functions implicit in the listing process and the commercial motivation of a regulated market in generating trading business.[176] Unless the burdens of the listing process are more carefully distributed, the danger exists that regulated markets which provide listing functions will

---

[175] Tradepoint, eg, by contrast with the London Stock Exchange prior to the transfer of its listing functions, does not admit securities to listing, but admits securities to trading which have already been subject to the official listing procedure.

[176] In the context of the demutualization of the London Stock Exchange see the discussion in the Financial Services Authority, *The Transfer of the UK Listing Authority to the FSA*, Consultation Paper 37 (Dec 1999) (the FSA Transfer Paper), 3 and 10. See also the discussion of the change in the characterization of exchanges from public-interest bodies to commercial firms in Wymeersch, n 141 above. For the view that exchanges can manage the admission process see Ferrarini, n 17 above, 574–5: '[t]he argument seems to be that stock exchanges, if left to themselves, might not find the right incentives to pursue [market liquidity and prevention of systemic risk]. The public regulation of listing conditions would involve only those securities which made a sufficiently liquid market feasible being chosen. This would also contribute to the prevention of disturbances to the financial system in general. However, from an economic perspective, stock exchanges provide liquidity services and operate in a competitive setting . . . it is difficult to think of an exchange deliberately pursuing the objective of an "illiquid" market.'

unbundle listing services in the face of greater competition from other markets. The Commission accordingly recommended that the 'regulated market' definition to be clarified with respect to compliance with listing conditions.[177] The Commission's recent proposal to restructure the issuer-disclosure regime will, if adopted, have considerable impact on the disclosure aspect of the admission to official listing process in that it removes securities-trading markets from the disclosure review process and requires that independent administrative authorities ('competent administrative authorities') be relied on instead, as well as ensuring that the same disclosure regime applies to admission to official listing and to admission to trading on an ISD-regulated market.[178] The 2001 ISD Working Paper discussed in section 9.7 below goes further in dismantling the distinction between admission to trading and admission to listing.

XI.9.3.2 *The Concentration Rule*

The Communication found that the Article 14(3) concentration rule, which was designed to protect retail investors from the risks of off-market transactions, was in practice distorting competition between regulated markets, in that the rule was being applied to divert trading artificially towards a particular regulated market. These competition-restricting consequences of the concentration rule caused the Commission to suggest a change in emphasis. It recommended that investor protection be provided not via concentration requirements but instead via the imposition of controls on investment firms acting for investors and, in particular, by strict enforcement of best-execution rules.[179] This change in focus and the emphasis on best execution (which also forms a central element of the FESCO ATS regime on which the Commission also relies) also reflects the shift towards more extensive conduct-of-business regulation which can be seen in the 2001 ISD Working Paper.[180]

XI.9.4 *Common Standards*

A striking feature of the Communication is its support for an EC system of common standards for the supervision of regulated markets.[181] The moti-

---

[177] ISD Communication, n 43 above, 13–14.

[178] See Art. 19(1) of the Commission proposal on the prospectus to be published when securities are offered to the public or admitted to trading, COM(2001)280 (containing the Prospectus Proposal and the Explanatory Memorandum). See Ch. IV sect. 9.3 above.

[179] In this regard, the Commission's new position on concentration supports and is an extension of an earlier characterization of the ISD concentration rule as a rule of conduct. See Ferrarini, n 17 above, 261.

[180] See Ch. IX sect. 13.7 above.

[181] By no means is there consensus on the appropriateness of the imposition of public regulation on securities-trading markets or the automatic desirability of comprehensive EC

vation for standards harmonization is clearly the integration process; common standards are used as an integration-promoting device and in order to protect the integrated market-place from the resulting risks.

Specific reference was made to the difficulties which diverging supervisory and regulatory arrangement can cause for the integration of trading systems and to the need to 'smooth structural changes at the level of the exchanges'.[182] The relevant German and UK supervisory authorities involved in the iX proposal, for example, identified market structure, listing and disclosure, reporting and market surveillance, market-abuse rules, clearing and settlement, and takeovers as areas in which common standards were required.[183]

More generally, the Communication also pointed to the need to develop common standards and supervisory approaches in order to ensure that the regulatory objectives underlying the supervision of regulated markets (market confidence, investor protection, efficiency, transparency, integrity and stability) were met in a new regulatory environment of inter-exchange and trading-system competition and pan-EC trading. Underlying the Commission's approach was its position that the regulation of securities-trading markets can no longer be considered in an isolationist manner and at Member-State level. Two particular threats were identified: the potential for problems in one regulated market to impact on trading in other Member States; and the dangers consequent on the development of regulatory arbitrage among EC regulated markets.[184] The familiar symbiotic relationship

harmonization. See generally Ferrarini, n 17 above, for the argument for considered and market-sensitive harmonization which would be restricted to those areas where market failures are at issue. Professor Ferrarini has argued that questions of market structure, access, and transparency should be left to the markets, with harmonization being limited to those areas which concern externalities such as fraud. See also Whittaker, A, 'A European Law for Regulated Markets? Some Personal Views' in Ferrarini, n 1 above, 269 for the view that competition, supervision, and co-operation is the better way to approach the standards question. For a broad-based analysis in support of allowing exchanges to set their own standards see Mahoney, P, 'The Exchange as Regulator' (1997) 83 *Va L Rev.* 1453. The question of self-regulation by exchanges is briefly canvassed in Ch. II sect. 7.3.1 above.

[182] N 43 above, 16. In its editorial comment on the failure of the iX proposal, the *Financial Times* noted that incompatibilities between regulatory regimes (and clearing and settlement systems) posed a greater obstacle to pan-European trading than exchange rivalries, and that a new effort was needed to align regulations: Editorial comment, 'After iX', *Financial Times*, 12 Sept 2000.

[183] Financial Services Authority, Bundesaufsichtsamt für den Wertpapierhandel, Hessisches Ministerium für Wirtschaft, Verkehr und Landesentwicklung, *iX—International Exchanges-Joint Statement*, Aug 2000.

[184] Regulatory arbitrage has already been raised in the context of the Euronext system, eg. Issuers who access the Euronext trading system are, at the time of writing, subject to the regulatory regime in operation in the particular market on which they list their securities (Amsterdam, Paris, and Brussels). Concerns have been expressed that regulatory arbitrage could arise, particularly were one access market to be less rigorous than the others with respect to retail investor protection. It has been reported that Euronext is in favour of early harmonization between the three regulatory systems involved: Farrow, n 154 above, 16.

between harmonization, prejudicial regulatory competition (albeit here at the level of the trading market as well as at Member-State level), and the need to protect the stability and integrity of the market-place and EC-wide investor protection and confidence as the market-place integrates thus re-appears in the regulated-markets sphere; unlike the investment-services sphere where rule standardization was driven by the regulatory passport, here it is provoked by industry-led competition. Common trading rules were identified as essential for a unified market, as was a common model for market transparency. Divergences in transparency were identified as threatening the market-wide price-formation process, given that trading would, in the face of diverging transparency requirements and in a competitive environment, tend to concentrate where obligations were least demanding.[185] Divergences in market-membership rules were also isolated as a particular problem for integration, given the risk that, in an integrated system, arbitrage would develop between the different access points to the system. Critical to the success of the harmonization project, however, will be the extent to which it can be accommodated within the Treaty.

The Communication's specific recommendation was that the ISD be revised to include a common set of standards on orderly trading, disclosure, transparency, market integrity, and monitoring and enforcement. Emphasis was laid on the enhancement of transparency by rules on fair and orderly trading, operating conditions, and ownership structures and on building on the regulatory devices currently used in EC investment-services regulation, such as capital-adequacy requirements, large-exposure requirements, and fit-and-proper tests for management. Significantly, the FESCO Standards were identified as a 'useful reference point for further reflection'.[186]

Adoption of common standards will refocus attention on the characteristics of the regulated markets which should be subject to these common standards, in that they are vulnerable to the regulatory risks and concerns driving the harmonization project. The Communication suggested two approaches. The first limited 'regulated markets' to those which provide publicly accessible trading in equities on the ground of the heightened exposure of the economy and the retail investors to these markets. The second, broader, approach incorporated all organized systems providing for publicly accessible trading, regardless of the instruments traded. In this case, the Communication suggested that a graduated application of the common standards might be appropriate according to, amongst other considerations, the extent to which inter-professional trading took place on the market. The 2001 ISD Working Paper has now taken these proposals forward.

---

[185] But see Ferrarini, n 17 above, 582–3 for the argument that transparency levels are most efficiently set by the markets.
[186] N 43 above, 16.

XI.9.5 *Transparency*

Article 21 was also singled out as an area in need of upgrading in light of market developments. What were described as 'enormous discrepancies' were identified in the level of transparency across regulated markets.[187] Divergences were noted to be particularly marked in the transparency requirements for trading by institutional investors which, in a number of EC markets, takes place off-market and so has the potential to obstruct efficient pricing. The extent to which common standards should be adopted and applied to off-market transactions in order to protect pricing across EC markets for all investors was identified as an area for review and consideration. The Communication also expressed concerns about the effectiveness of the transparency regime in light of the fragmentation of trading due to the proliferation of different and competing trading systems and emphasized the need to protect efficient pricing. In particular, the Commission recommended that if several trading platforms develop, interaction between the separate pricing mechanisms should be encouraged, although it noted that any regulatory measures should be designed to enhance transparency and promote effective price interaction, rather than to dictate particular market structures.

XI.9.6 *The Lamfalussy Report*

The state of the regulatory framework for securities-trading markets did not escape the Lamfalussy Report's robust criticisms.[188] Among the significant gaps in the regime highlighted by the Report were: the failure of the mutual-recognition principle with respect to regulated markets; the lack of a distinction between admission to trading and admission to listing; and the absence of appropriate rules to deal with alternative trading systems. Its concerns about the efficiency of securities-trading markets were evident from the inclusion of the adoption of a single passport for 'recognized stock markets' and introduction of a clear distinction between admission to listing and trading as priorities to be brought into effect by the end of 2003.[189]

XI.9.7 *The 2001 ISD Working Paper*

XI.9.7.1 *A New Regulated Markets Regime*

Clearer indications of how the future EC securities-trading market regime might look can now be taken from the Commission's 2001 ISD Working

---

[187] Ibid, 17.
[188] Final Report of the Committee of Wise Men on the Regulation of European Securities Markets (Feb 2001).
[189] Ibid, 13.

Paper which contains the Commission's preliminary orientations on how the revisions are likely to proceed and is designed to serve as the basis for further consultations.[190] It builds, for the most part, on the ISD Communication and takes a number of the proposals canvassed by the Communication a stage further. Given the preliminary nature of these discussions, which have not, at this time, been formalized as a proposal, they will be covered here in outline only. Overall, the Working Paper suggests that a considerably expanded regulated-market regime, based on the authorization of regulated markets and on the imposition of operating rules on the lines of the FESCO Standards can be expected; the new regime would also include revised transparency rules for investment firms and markets and, significantly, admission-to-trading requirements. In addition, the Working Paper has attempted to deal more fully with the arrival of ATSs and has suggested a new regulatory characterization within which ATSs and regulated markets can be more efficiently supervised.

XI.9.7.2 *Regulated Markets, Organized Markets, and ATSs*

The first of the Commission's suggestions concerns a recasting of the concept of a regulated market in order to clarify the characterizations of ATSs, regulated markets, and investment firms and, in particular, to ensure that ATSs are subject to an appropriate regulatory regime.[191] At the core of the revisions is the retention of the ISD's current regulatory split between trading structures and investment firms, and the different approaches taken to supervision and risk management in each case, which, according to the Commission, is not fundamentally threatened by the development of new trading structures as 'most types of market operator can be accommodated within existing regulatory typology, on the basis of their core business and the functionalities that they offer'.[192] It has, however, suggested that a number of adjustments be made to the regime in order to reflect the arrival of ATSs.

Broadly speaking, the new regime would tie ATS regulation to a revised investment-firm regime. The list of investment services, and thus the definition of investment firms, would be expanded to cover specialized intermediaries providing services such as bulletin boards and price-crossing sys-

---

[190] Overview of Proposed Adjustments to the Investment Services Directive. Working Document of Services of DG Internal Market. Document 1. July 2001 (the ISD Working Paper) 5–14, 22–3, and 26–33.

[191] Ibid, 5–14.

[192] Ibid, 6. In a useful restatement of the respective objectives of supervision in each area, the Commission has stated that the investment-firm regime is directed to the management of risks in the investment-firm/client relationship, while the market regime concerns the promotion of orderly and efficient trading via rules relating to the admission of participants and securities to the markets and the application of controls on participants operating on the market.

tems.[193] A new activity of providing arranging services, for example, would bring entities providing order-matching services related to information, communication, and transmission services within the investment-firm regime. As part of the new market-conduct regime suggested by the Working Paper,[194] they would, however, be subject to specialized requirements, set out in the ISD, designed to ensure effective monitoring and supervision of order books and detect instances of market abuse, given the implications which the 'internalization' of order flows in this way has for the market as a whole. ATSs classified as investment firms would also be subject to the new conduct regime, which would be tailored to reflect their particular risk profiles. Providing arranging services, for example, would not be subject to the full-blown conduct-of-business regime, particularly with respect to suitability and best execution, although it would be subject to conduct-of-business and organizational requirements designed to address risks such as conflicts of interests or the supply of misinformation. Investment firms which operate facilities which allow for the matching of client orders would also be subject to an additional prudential requirement under the revised Article 10 regime and would be required to have in place systems approved by the competent authority which ensure appropriate execution and finalization of those transactions. Price-discovery concerns would be dealt with via the revised transparency regime (see section 9.7.3 below). A new definition of 'organized market' has been suggested in order 'to differentiate between the client order-matching services provided by investment firms on a discretionary basis and organized single-capacity trading arrangements matching multiple trading interests in financial instruments'.[195] Firms not meeting these conditions would be eligible for treatment as investment firms. This key definition is designed to restrict the organized market designation (and in consequence the regulated-market supervisory regime) to systems which 'provide a permanent venue for matching multiple interests and which play an active role in price discovery'.[196] The proposed definition is based on five criteria: the existence of formalized and non-discretionary rules and procedures for matching orders according to pre-established and transparent rules covering priority, parity, and precedence;[197] orders being matched such that transactions are completed on the system and in compliance with system rules;[198] the existence of multiple buy and sell interests on both sides of the

---

[193] These revisions to the scope of the ISD are outlined in Ch. VII sect. 10.3.2 above.

[194] See Ch. XIII sect. 11.6 below.   [195] N 190 above, 7.   [196] Ibid, 13.

[197] Thereby excluding broker order-matching systems which match orders only if a countervailing order is received and other dealing requirements fulfilled and dealer systems which match orders only where it in the interests of the dealer: ibid.

[198] Thereby excluding systems which only identify counterparties and leave completion to those counterparties: ibid.

market;[199] operation on a continuous or regular basis; and quotation of prices which reflect the interaction of supply and demand for the instruments on the system.[200] Clarification and updating of this critical definition would be carried out though Lamfalussy level 2 comitology procedures.

Where an entity qualified as an organized market, it would be required to seek authorization as a 'regulated market' in certain circumstances. The concept of regulated market is now being built on the concept that certain trading structures should be 'characterized by strict controls [such as disclosure requirements] regarding the quality and constitution of the instruments which are admitted to trading'.[201] Regulated markets would also be required to verify that instruments admitted to trading met the relevant statutory requirements. The approach the Commission has suggested is to require authorization as a regulated market where '[the market] provides for organized interaction and confrontation of multiple buy and sell interests in respect of': (1) publicly-offered transferable securities in respect of which systems are in place to ensure that the issuer has complied with initial/ongoing disclosure or other statutory requirements; (2) derivative instruments where the underlying asset is a security for which the issuer is subject to the foregoing requirements, the contract is sound, and in respect of which there is a proper market; and (3) derivatives based on rates, indices, or commodities, once conditions are such that proper market requirements are met.[202] The broader option suggested in the ISD Communication (of not limiting the regulated-market designation to equities), is, at this stage of the regime's evolution, being followed. Securities not meeting these requirements would not be admitted to trading on a regulated market. Similarly, once a security was admitted to trading on a regulated market and placed within the regulated market regime, it would no longer be permitted to trade on non-regulated markets in order to avoid simultaneous trading on markets offering varying transparency and other protections. In consequence, an organized market which provided for the trading of instruments which are admissible or admitted to trading on a regulated market would be required to seek authorization as a regulated market. The authorization process and the obligations and benefits which flow from it are discussed at section 9.7.3 below. 'Non-regulated organized markets' would continue to provide trading in instruments not admissible for trading on a regulated market and 'would be the locus for dealing in privately placed securities or

---

[199] Thereby excluding proprietary order books of banks or dealers in which, *inter alia*, the system is a counterparty for every trade but trades only when there is a benefit in doing so: n 190 above, 14.

[200] Thereby excluding systems which use a reference price taken from another venue: ibid.

[201] N 190 above, 7.

[202] The ISD Working Paper has suggested that commodity derivatives be brought within the ISD: Ch. VII sect. 10.3.2 above.

publicly offered securities where the issuer does not comply with specified levels of disclosure [and] would also be the venue for organized/formalised trading of derivative instruments based on such securities, or derivatives based on rates, indices or commodities for which certain guarantees as regards the existence of a "proper market" cannot be met'.[203]

XI.9.7.3 *A Supervisory Regime for Regulated Markets*

Tracking the approach it adopted in the ISD Communication, the Commission has suggested that authorization procedures for operation as a regulated market should be established.[204] All regulated markets would be required to be authorized by the competent authority responsible for market supervision in the country in which the market was established, in accordance with common high-level principles which would be set out in the new ISD. These high-level principles, derived, in another example of the scale of the influence being exerted by FESCO (now the Committee of European Securities Regulators) across the body of EC securities regulation, from the FESCO Standards would cover: the requirements to be met by the operator of the market; the rules of the market (concerning order-matching procedures, admission of market participants, and, in a considerable change to the current (now consolidated) Admission Directive regime, admission of instruments to trading); and the rights and obligations of market operators. These principles would be supplemented by detailed implementing measures in accordance with the Lamfalussy model. An independent competent authority would be responsible for verifying that the market operator and the regulated market complied with the requirements, although, in a recognition of practical realities and, it appears, the incentives which regulated markets now have in a competitive environment to operate stable, transparent, and efficient market-places, competent authorities would be permitted to delegate certain functions to market operators or self-regulatory organizations, while remaining ultimately responsible for compliance with the requirements. Interestingly, the Commission has suggested that it would assess whether the authorized regulated markets (the obligation on competent authorities to notify the Commission of their regulated markets would continue) complied with the ISD regime. Of perhaps more import is the suggestion that this assessment would be carried out in conjunction with the new Lamfalussy-model securities committees; this may yet come to be regarded as the opening move in a project in which the end-game is a Euro-SEC.

The suggested market-operator requirements concern the fitness and propriety of management, the identification of qualifying shareholders,

---

[203] N 190 above, 8.   [204] Ibid, 22–3 and 26–33.

conflict-of-interest management procedures, compliance arrangements, and the soundness of systems. In a major change from the very limited supervisory regime currently in place, financial resources or capital requirements would also be imposed in order to ensure that market operators held sufficient resources to cover risks and to provide for orderly market closure.

With its proposals concerning the admission-to-trading requirements for regulated markets, the ISD Working Paper has taken EC securities regulation another step down the road to obliterating the distinction between admission to official listing and admission to trading, although the Commission's thinking is sensitive to the different functions fulfilled by first- or official-tier and second-tier markets. The admission-to-trading requirements which it has suggested should be imposed on the market operator are based on the premise that a distinguishing feature of a regulated market is the existence of controls on the quality of the instruments admitted to trading which ensure that those instruments are freely negotiable and that information is readily available so that they can be fairly valued. The new regime would require the market operator to verify that, in the case of publicly offered securities, issuers complied with their disclosure requirements and other efficient trading requirements, such as minimum initial capitalization levels. Market operators would not, however, be required to assume responsibility for the disclosure of price-sensitive information but would simply be required to confirm that the issuer had arrangements in place to meet the disclosure requirements. In a major change to the current admission regime discussed in Chapter III, the revisions would also set out other requirements for the admission of any publicly offered security to trading on a regulated market, based on the now consolidated Admission Directive regime for officially listed securities but updated to reflect market practices, such that the distinction between admission to official listing and other admissions would be eliminated. As discussed in Chapter IV, the proposed new issuer-disclosure regime in its current form applies the same disclosure requirements for all public offers of securities, while the Admission Directive's ongoing disclosure-of-material-information regime already applies to regulated markets generally. Specialized criteria would be established for derivatives, including commodity derivatives, which would, *inter alia*, seek to ensure the soundness of the relevant contracts, the design of the product, and the underlying issuer. The regime would allow significant leeway beyond these basic requirements for regulated markets to set their own admission requirements in order to allow markets to specialize with respect to the nature of the issuer and the security: 'remaining criteria for the market/exchange as regards admission to trading should be left to the system as a means of positioning itself—small-cap, blue-chip, type of participant etc'.[205]

[205] N 190 above, 29. The Working Paper has also suggested that certain of the current regime's requirements 'would need to be modified to allow for the fact that there will no longer

As far as the procedures of regulated markets are concerned, the ISD Working Paper has suggested three categories of rules: clearing and settlement arrangements;[206] trading and execution; and transparency. With respect to trading and execution, in order to ensure that market participants could monitor order flow, the regulated market would be required to have clear and non-discretionary rules in place governing the order-matching process which would be subject to prior scrutiny, approved by the competent authority, and made public. The detailed content of these complex and technical rules would be left to the Member States.

The EC's transparency regime has had a controversial history. The ISD Working Paper represents another attempt to deal with the transparency of the market-place in the context of the increased fragmentation of trading brought about by ATSs.[207] The new regime is, however, sensitive to competing market interests and leaves national markets with some discretion. It is also focused on market integrity and, in particular, on the reporting of off-market transactions. At the core of the revised regime suggested by the Commission is the principle of real-time disclosure of completed transactions.[208] More specifically, major changes would be introduced with respect to the reporting of off-market transactions. FESCO's concerns that ATS trading could damage the price-formation process, given that price information concerning blocks of off-market trades would not be available to the market, have already been accepted by the Commission in its ISD Communication and are acknowledged again in the ISD Working Paper. In response,[209] a core element of the revised transparency regime is to tighten the Article 20 off-market reporting requirements by introducing a 'base-line requirement for all investment firms which match trades or conclude bilateral transactions to report price and volume data to a regulated market', such that 'the terms under which off-market transactions are concluded are integrated into the overall pricing process for that financial instrument in real-time (or as

be a semi-official regulated market status for e.g. securities which do not have a 3 year accounting history. Requirements under [the Admission Directive schedules] which would hamper the admissibility of such securities to trading would need to be revisited': ibid.

[206] See Ch. XII sect. 3.3.1 below.

[207] The EC is not alone in considering transparency questions. See the FSA Market Infrastructure Discussion Paper (2000), while in the USA, the Seligman Committee (under the aegis of the SEC) is reviewing market transparency.

[208] N 190 above, 30.

[209] 'This proposal is introduced to counter concerns relating to a possible deterioration in the efficiency of the price-discovery mechanism if details on the prices at which an undisclosed part of the market is buying and selling a given security are not made available to the market as a whole . . . [and] to ensure that growing off-market turnover in trading does not operate to the detriment of [the] overall price discovery process by ensuring that completed off-market transactions are made public to other market participants in real-time through their incorporation in an aggregated price feed': ibid, 23.

close as technically feasible)'.[210] The reporting obligation would be imposed on all off-market transactions[211] completed by investment firms concerning instruments admitted to trading on a regulated market, but would apply only to information relating to completed transactions and would not cover dealers' bid or offer positions.[212] Once an off-market reporting obligation is in place, the key question then is how the information should be disseminated so that it impacts on price formation. The Commission has suggested that the regulated market, which was the leading market or market of first quotation for the instrument in question would be required to integrate information concerning completed off-market transactions in that instrument into its price feed. Although it has acknowledged that 'in a trading environment where a security or instrument may be admitted to trading on several regulated markets in parallel, and where no market necessarily has any particular contractual relationship with the issuer, there is no straightforward answer to this question', its solution is based on the assumption that the regulated market with either the 'greatest turnover or the longest tradition of trading in the instrument would seem to be best-placed to assimilate information into a consolidated price feed which is used as a reference by the wider market'.[213] This ATS-driven reform represents a major change to the current reporting regime and a brave attempt to deal with the fragmentation problem; it remains to be seen how it will fare. More generally, if the new regime is adopted, delays will no longer be permitted for illiquid trades as under the current regime, while regulated markets will also be required to make public details of 'upstairs trading' which takes place using the systems operated by the regulated market.[214] It is hardly surprising, given the troubled history of the EC transparency regime and the commitment by the Commission to be market-model neutral in reviewing the ISD, that the ISD Working Paper has acknowledged the need to balance transparency against the need to encourage liquidity and the anonymity of counterparties to large trades, both of which have a bearing, of course, on how pre-trade transparency is managed in different markets according to their structure. Accordingly, the new regime would be based on the presumption

---

[210] N 190 above, 23.

[211] It would extend to bilateral/OTC transactions as well to transactions matched on ATSs/order books: ibid.

[212] The Commission has suggested that if a blanket reporting obligation of this nature were to be regarded as excessive, it could be scaled back by limiting it to large, price-formation-influencing trades.

[213] There are disadvantages to this approach, including the danger that particular trading markets will dominate as trading centres for particular instruments. However the Commission has stated that other alternatives, such as reporting to competent authorities or requiring investment firms to make the information public, would not feed the information into a ''reference' post-trade quotation mechanism, which could reduce comparability and real-time disclosure': n 190 above, 24.

[214] Ibid, 31.

that markets would reveal best bid and offer prices, properly structured. However, pre-trade transparency could be structured differently across the EC in order to take into account market-specific features such as different structures and types of transaction, and a number of criteria would be provided in order to assess when pre-trade transparency requirements could be eased. Detailed coverage of the transparency regime would, in accordance with the Lamfalussy model, be provided via level 2 comitology procedures.

Like the ISD Communication, the ISD Working Paper has addressed the concentration rule. The Commission has proposed that the rule be abolished, given that it can prevent firms from pursuing execution venues and terms which are more beneficial to the investor. In an attempt to respond to the investor-protection rationale for the concentration rule, it has also suggested that investment firms be required to report, on a quarterly basis, on their order-routing practices. This suggestion is designed to enhance transparency with respect to choice of venues for execution and to allow for best-execution obligations, projected to form a part of the revised ISD's conduct regime, to be supervised.

Finally, the Commission has also suggested that regulated markets have in place rules, approved by the competent authority, governing the admission of market participants.

XI.9.7.4 *Regulated Markets and Access Rights*

The ISD Working Paper has also suggested that the current remote-access regime be extended to permit regulated markets to establish trading facilities in other Member States. In order to avoid regulatory duplication, host Member States would be required to take account of the regulated market's compliance with the rules imposed by its home Member State. The Working Paper has acknowledged, however, that special arrangements may be necessary to accommodate host Member States where the regulated market sets up an order-book or order-matching system on their territory.[215]

---

[215] Some uncertainty appears to exist about the utility of the provision; the Commission has asked for feedback on the utility of adding this regime on to the remote access system and on the extent to which regulated markets might be interested in establishing branches in other Member States and exporting their trading services.

XII

The Settlement of Securities Transactions

XII.1 SECURITIES-SETTLEMENT SYSTEMS

This chapter is concerned with the post-trade custody, clearing, and settlement infrastructures which are often gathered together under the umbrella of 'securities-settlement systems'[1] and which lie behind securities-trading markets and underpin securities trading. The highly technical operational procedures and the complex private-law property and security rules attendant on settlement systems are outside the scope of a work on EC securities regulation.[2] This chapter's focus will instead be on the regulation of the settlement process and the limited action the EC has taken in this area.[3]

Custody involves the safekeeping of a security by a custodian, typically a bank or other financial institution, on behalf of its beneficial holder, in physical form where the securities trade in paper form, or, in the more common situation where the securities are immobilized or dematerialized (reflecting

---

[1] Securities-settlement systems have recently been categorized as including the 'full set of institutional arrangements for confirmation, clearance and settlement of securities trades and safekeeping of securities': IOSCO Technical Committee/BIS Committee on Payment and Settlement Systems Joint Task Force on Securities Settlement Systems, *Consultative Report on Recommendations for Securities Settlement Systems* (2001) (the Joint Task Force Report) 2. It has been observed that settlement systems 'are to payment flows and to transfers of securities what highways are to traffic': Vereecken, M, 'Reducing Systemic Risk in Payment and Securities Settlement Systems' (1998) 6 *JFRC* 107.

[2] For a discussion of custody, clearance, and settlement questions see Blair, W, Allison, A, Palmer, K, Richards-Carpenter, P, and Walker, G, *Banking and Financial Services Regulation* (2nd edn, 1998) 350–72. For an analysis of the legal questions raised by cross-border electronic transfers of securities generally see Benjamin, J, 'Cross-Border Electronic Transfers in the Securities Markets' (2001) 35 *The International Lawyer* 31.

[3] This chapter will not deal with the related infrastructure issue, the more general question of cross-border payments, which is divorced from the specific concerns of securities regulation and more concerned with banking regulation. The EC has been active in the area of cross-border credit transfers, particularly with respect to small-value credit transfers, has examined other means of cross-border payment and seeks to create an integrated, secure, cost-effective, and competitive retail payments system in the interests of the single market generally. It is particularly concerned with reducing the cost of cross-border charges, ensuring that appropriate uniform technical standards, disclosure requirements, and time limits apply and encouraging the development of an integrated automated payments infrastructure (such as the ESCB's TARGET system which delivers payments between banks within minutes but which is primarily designed for large-value payments). See, eg: the Cross-Border Credit Transfers Directive (97/5/EC [1997] OJ L307/63); the Commission's 1997 Recommendation 97/489/EC on Electronic Payment Instruments [1997] OJ L208/52; the e-money Directives (Directive 2000/28/EC [2000] OJ L 275/27 and Directive 2000/46/EC OJ (2000) 275/39); and the Commission's 2000 Communication on Retail Payments in the Internal Market, COM(2000)36.

the disadvantages and security risks attendant on physical securities),[4] through book entry or account entries. In the latter case, the custodian acts as a fiduciary, holding the securities in its own name on behalf of account holders and recording holders' rights in its accounts.[5] Many markets now have central securities depositaries or CSDs, which are central to the settlement process, in which securities are dematerialized or immobilized and trade or settle between CSD members via electronic account entries. The membership of CSDs will often include financial institutions acting as subcustodians through whose accounts with the CSD the custodian may, depending on its access rights to the CSD, indirectly hold investors' securities.

Settlement procedures, or the reciprocal cash and securities book-keeping or transaction processing mechanics through which trades in securities between sellers and buyers are ultimately carried out and which ensure that the trading bargain made on the market is performed, depend on the securities, the particular securities-trading market on which they are traded, and the clearing and settlement system concerned. These procedures usually involve computerized book-entry transfers of securities[6] although physical transfers of securities are required in some cases. Clearing is connected with settlement in that it is concerned with establishing mutual positions and matching contracts prior to settlement. While CSDs typically play a central part in the settlement process by immobilizing or dematerializing securities and providing custody and settlement services,[7] procedures which are integral to the settlement process are often carried out elsewhere. In the EC, clearing and settlement services are often provided by national CSDs,[8]

---

[4] The Joint Task Force Report has recommended that, in order to reduce settlement risk, securities should be immobilized or dematerialized and transferred by book entry to the greatest extent possible: n 1 above, 4. The problems and delays associated with paper-based settlement became obvious during the 1980s in the UK with the privatization programme. More drastically, when the stock market crashed in 1987, the failure of paper systems to provide for timely settlement left many investors exposed: Benjamin, n 2 above, 33.

[5] Goode, R, 'The Nature and Transfer of Rights in Dematerialised and Immobilised Securities' in Oditah, F, (ed), *The Future of the Global Securities Market—Legal and Regulatory Aspects* (1996) 107, 112.

[6] In a securities-settlement system, 'securities accounts are kept for the participants (mostly financial institutions and investment firms) at a settlement agent. A transfer of securities from one participant to another gives rise to the debiting of the transferor's account and to the crediting of the transferee's account. Securities transfers often given rise to a corresponding payment transfer; eg in a sales operation or a repurchase operation, the buyer will receive delivery of the securities from the seller against payment to him': Vereecken n 1 above, 109, footnotes omitted.

[7] The immobilization/dematerialization of securities and their transfer by book entry within a CSD and the concentration of custody and transfer functions in one entity has been supported by the Joint Task Force Report on grounds of efficiency, speed, cost-effectiveness, and risk management: n 1 above, 13–14.

[8] eg, the CREST system (operated by CRESTCo) provides a dematerialized settlement system to the UK and Irish markets, while Euroclear France (previously Sicovam) is the French CSD. Euroclear and Clearstream, as international CSDs (ICSDs), provide settlement facilities for internationally traded securities. Euroclear and Cedel (which merged with Deutsche Börse Clearing

although cash settlement may occur through the national payments system
rather than through accounts held at the CSD. However, confirmation
which also forms part of the settlement process and involves the confirmation of a trade and its terms, is often carried out by the relevant exchange
or market itself or its participants.[9] Central counterparties, which act as a
go-between for trading counterparties and net obligations, can also play a
part in the settlement process.[10] They benefit buyers and sellers by guaranteeing trades, taking on the risk involved in the transaction, and providing
anonymity although they have the disadvantage of leading to a concentration of risk in the counterparty and to the risk of systemic instability.
Settlement will often be carried out in a jurisdiction other than that of the
custodian of the particular securities concerned and so may require the use
of a local custodian, which participates in the relevant settlement system, to
access the settlement process.[11]

to form Clearstream) were originally established to settle trades in eurobonds, although their
remit is now expanding. Euroclear is owned and run by Euroclear Bank (since 2001 when the
operation of the Euroclear system was transferred to it from Morgan Guaranty Trust Company
of New York which previously operated the system). It has merged with what is now Euroclear
France to form the Euroclear group. For an overview of EC clearing and settlement procedures
see the description in Gros, D, and Lannoo, K, *The Euro Capital Market* (2000) 69. Virt-x (which
was formed from a merger between Tradepoint and the Swiss Stock Exchange) provides an
example of how settlement services are provided to the new exchanges which are forming as
part of the current restructuring of the trading environment. It uses a multi-settlement system
which promotes a degree of competition between three of the major settlement providers,
Euroclear, CRESTCo, and SIS (SIS Segaintersettle AG, the Swiss CSD (although it also acts as
an ICSD)). See generally 'The Hunt for Liquidity', *The Economist*, 28 July 2001, 63, 64.
Securities-trading markets may vertically integrate the clearing and settlement function with
their trading services and thereby create a 'vertical silo'. Deutsche Börse provides an example
of this with its holding in Clearstream which gives it its own clearing and settlement system.

    [9] The process has been described as follows: '[a]fter two parties agree to a trade, the terms
of the trade may first have to be confirmed by a trade comparison system, which may be run
by a specialized institution. Clearance—establishing accountability—may then be carried out
by a separate clearinghouse according to a number of different mechanisms such as trade for
trade and various forms of bilateral and multilateral netting. Settlement will then take place'.
Steil, B, 'International Securities Market Regulation' in Steil, B, (ed), *International Financial
Market Regulation* (1994) 197, 216.
    [10] Clearnet, eg, is the central counterparty for Euronext. Netting of Euronext transactions
takes place at Clearnet before settlement occurs elsewhere. The London Stock Exchange has also
introduced a central counterparty in co-operation with CRESTCo and the London Clearing
House.
    [11] For an examination of the various ways in which cross-border settlement can take place
see the Joint Task Force Report, n 1 above, 44–5. For a summary of these mechanisms see
Giddy, I, Saunders, A, and Walter, I, 'Clearing and Settlement' in Steil, B, (ed), *The European
Equity Markets. The State of the Union and an Agenda for the Millennium* (1996) 321 who at 326
have identified 5 mechanisms under which a cross-border trade may be effected: (1) direct
access to the CSD in the security's country of issue (via membership in the CSD); (2) through
a local bank or broker dealer which is a member of the CSD in question; (3) through global
custodians (international banks which manage cross-border transactions), which in turn operate through local agents as they will not have direct access to CSDs; (4) through ICSDs; and
(5) through CSD–CSD links.

XII.2 SETTLEMENT AND SECURITIES REGULATION

From the securities-regulation perspective, clearing and settlement systems are vulnerable to systemic risk and are subject to supervision in the form of risk-management controls designed to ensure their stability and integrity and shore up confidence in the market-place.[12] The systemic implications of settlement systems accordingly represent a market failure which justifies the intervention of securities regulation.[13]

Systemic risks can arise from the failure of a system adequately to address legal risk (particularly the risk that the law governing the insolvency of a system participant might prejudice the operation of the system by interfering with netting arrangements, for example, or the irrevocability of transfer orders), pre-settlement risk (the risk that a counterparty will default before final settlement),[14] settlement risk (the risk that settlement will not occur),[15]

[12] 'Weaknesses in [securities settlement systems or SSSs] can be a source of systemic disturbances to securities markets and to other payment and settlement systems. A financial or operational problem at any of the institutions that perform critical functions in the settlement process or at a major user of an SSS could result in significant liquidity pressures or credit losses for other participants. Any disruption of securities settlements has the potential to spill over to any payments systems used by the SSS or that use the SSS to transfer collateral . . . market liquidity is critically dependent on confidence in the safety and reliability of the settlement arrangement; traders will be reluctant to trade if they have significant doubts as to whether the trade will in fact settle': Joint Task Force Report, n 1 above, 1. See also the view that '[c]learance and settlement represent the "guts" of the capital markets. If the massive volume of trades cannot be properly digested, the markets may simply grind to a halt. In the worse case scenario, failures at one point in the system undermine confidence throughout the system, and liquidity problems are transformed into solvency crises'. Steil, n 9 above, 214.

[13] Ferrarini, G, 'The European Regulation of Stock Exchanges: New Perspectives' (1999) 36 *CMLRev.* 569, 593 who also warned, however, that 'too detailed rules should be avoided as the clearing and settlement systems need flexibility in order to adapt to changing circumstances'. The Joint Task Force Report also noted that trade-offs between risk reduction (beyond the minimum required for stability) and costs were to be weighed carefully: n 1 above, 7. Arguably this warning has been heeded in the EC regime, given the relatively light regulatory touch evident from the regime's limited focus on specific systemic risks and its emphasis on market-driven solutions.

[14] This is typically managed by trade confirmation rules (such as confirmation no later than trade date or T + 0 in the case of trades between direct market participants and the use of straight-through processing or STP procedures which require that trade data are entered once only and used for all settlement functions), settlement cycle requirements (such as the use of short rolling settlement cycles, such as T + 3, which reduce the time in which a counterparty can default during the settlement cycle (rolling settlement tied to trade dates, rather than settlement of all trades at the end of a particular period, is, of itself, an important protection against large exposures as it limits the number of outstanding trades)), the use and control of central counterparties, and the encouragement of securities lending as a method of speeding up settlement.

[15] Settlement risk can be addressed by a number of mechanisms including the use of book-entry transfers in preference to physical transfers of securities, delivery versus payment (DVP) mechanisms which eliminate the risk that securities are delivered but payment not received, or vice versa, the completion of final transfers by the end of the settlement day rather than deferring settlement to the next business day, and the use of collateral to cover large exposures.

operational risk (the risk of losses as a result of an internal systems failure),[16] and custody risk (the risk of loss of particular securities held in the system).[17]

XII.3 SECURITIES SETTLEMENT, SETTLEMENT SYSTEMS, AND THE EC

XII.3.1 *Scope and Features of the Regime*

A parallel can be drawn between the coverage of securities-settlement issues, on the one hand, and the regulation of the operation of securities-trading markets, on the other, by the EC securities-regulation regime. Both subjects concern the internal framework on which the integrated investment-services and securities market is built. In each case, the relevant EC regime is, at present, largely unconcerned with the adoption of harmonized operating standards. A common concern with the macro questions of stability and the management of the smooth operation of the market can, however, be observed, albeit to differing degrees, in both areas. The transparency regime applicable to regulated markets under the Investment Services Directive, for example, is, in part, directed to 'ensuring the smooth operation of the markets in transferable securities',[18] while the Settlement Finality Directive,[19] which is the centrepiece of the EC settlement regime, such as it is, builds on the strong theme of prudential regulation and protection against systemic risks which permeates the harmonized regulatory structure. Indeed, the systemic implications of securities-settlement systems are well illustrated by the inclusion of settlement systems (and payment systems) in the list of subjects in respect of which Member States must consult the ECB before adopting relevant national legislation.[20] In addition, in both cases, technical market developments, rather than harmonized rules, are driving integration, as can be seen from the development of new cross-border trading platforms and the consolidation of post-trade clearing and settlement systems.

The EC's approach to settlement systems to date has been two-pronged. First, access to clearing and settlement systems has been addressed as part the ISD's securities-trading market access system (section 3.2 below).

---

[16] Operational risk management includes the establishment of reliable contingency plans to recover operations in the event of a systems failure.

[17] This risk classification is commonly used in relation to the risk management of securities-settlement systems and is the basis of the Joint Task Force Report's recommendations. See also the discussion in Steil, n 9 above, 217–18.

[18] Directive 93/22/EEC on investment services in the securities field [1993] OJ L141/27 (the ISD): recital 42.

[19] Directive 98/26/EC on settlement finality in payment and securities settlement systems [1998] OJ L166/45 (the Settlement Finality Directive or the Directive).

[20] Art. 20 of Council Decision 98/415/EC on the Consultation of the European Central Bank by National Authorities Regarding Draft Legislative Provisions [1998] OJ L189/42.

Secondly, attention has been focused on the systemic risks represented by settlement systems and, in particular, on the management of the legal risks attached to settlement systems, particularly in relation to the insolvency of a system participant and its impact on the operation of the system.[21] This question is specifically addressed by the Settlement Finality Directive discussed in section 4 below.[22] The adoption of common standards for the risk management and supervision of clearing and settlement systems is, notwithstanding the continuing increase in cross-border settlement, still some way off.

XII.3.2 *Clearing and Settlement and the ISD*

The ISD deals with clearing and settlement indirectly, as part of its liberalization regime on the access of investment firms to regulated markets. Article 15(1) requires Member States to ensure that investment firms authorized under the ISD to provide order-execution and dealing services can, either directly or indirectly, become members of or have access to regulated markets in their host Member States. In a recognition of the link between trading and clearing and settlement and because regulated markets often outsource the clearing and settlement function (recital 35) Article 15(1) also provides that Member States are to ensure that investment firms can become members of or have access to the clearing and settlement systems which are provided for the members of the regulated market.

Difficulties have arisen with respect to access to clearing and settlement systems, in that, where remote access is granted to a regulated market in accordance with Article 15(4), such that a physical presence by the investment firm is not required, certain Member States have required remote members to rely on locally-established entities for clearing and settlement. This indirect access to clearing and settlement has resulted in an increase in costs and the obstruction of timely and efficient settlement and has been highlighted as an area in respect of which the ISD needs to be reviewed.[23]

---

[21] The operation of and access to settlement systems also implicates the Treaty competition rules, a topic which is outside the scope of this work.

[22] The Joint Task Force Report included a recommendation that securities-settlement systems should have a well-founded, clear, and transparent legal basis in the relevant jurisdictions. In particular, the Report highlighted that '[t]he reliable and predictable operation of a securities settlement system depends on (i) the laws, rules and procedures that support the holding, transfer, pledging and lending of securities and related payments; and (ii) how these laws, rules and procedures work in practice . . . if the legal framework is inadequate or its application uncertain, it can give rise to credit or liquidity risks for system participants and their customers or to systemic risks for financial markets as a whole': n 1 above, 8. The Settlement Finality Directive deals with these themes in the context of insolvency and its impact on the finality of settlement and on collateral security.

[23] Commission Communication on Upgrading the Investment Directive (93/22/EC), COM(2000)729 (the ISD Communication), 17.

XII.3.3 *Settlement and the Integrated Market-place*

XII.3.3.1 *The Regulatory Response*

Closely linked as they are to securities trading and the efficient functioning of securities markets, efficient and stable clearing and settlement systems, which provide for a smooth post-trade transfer of ownership, can clearly facilitate and encourage cross-border securities transactions.[24] Accordingly, the current initiatives to encourage and facilitate cross-border trading should also address post-trade clearing and settlement questions. A fragmented settlement infrastructure involving costly post-trade settlement charges and potentially exposing investors to systemic risk could hinder investors' ability to make cross-border investments in securities and obstruct the development of the integrated securities market.[25]

The Commission's 1998 Communication on Financial Services[26] highlighted an integrated securities (and payments) infrastructure as one of the general conditions necessary for a fully integrated financial market and called for greater interaction between national systems. At present, cross-border settlement is, for the most part, dependent on domestic settlement systems and on indirect access to these systems. While the Commission took the position that technical developments be market-driven, it stressed that the legal and operational framework for securities settlement must be able to contain systemic risks.[27] The FSAP which followed in 1999[28] returned to this theme and called for an integrated infrastructure to underpin retail and wholesale market financial transactions. In particular, although it noted the market-driven technical consolidation of securities-settlement systems and the adoption of the Settlement Finality Directive, it found that further progress with respect to the enforceability of cross-border collateral for securities transactions was needed, given the risk of invalidation of cross-border collateral arrangements and the consequent danger of higher costs and risks attaching to cross-border securities transactions.[29] The FSAP includes among its objectives the consistent and timely implementation of the

---

[24] Clearing and settlement costs have an important impact on the risk/return equation and ultimately on investment-portfolio decisions and cross-border trading. See Giddy *et al.*, n 11 above, 322.

[25] Gros and Lannoo have noted that settlement costs can 'impose an explicit and implicit tax on trading and can hinder the growth of domestic securities markets and international or cross-border trade in securities. Inefficient clearing and settlement could impede the development of a European capital market' n 8 above, 69. For an analysis of how inefficiencies in clearing and settlement can hinder equity market integration see generally Giddy *et al.*, n 11 above.

[26] Financial Services: Building a Framework for Action, COM(1998)625 (the 1998 Communication).

[27] Ibid, 18.

[28] Commission Communication on Implementing the Framework for Financial Markets: Action Plan, COM(1999)232 (the FSAP).

[29] Ibid, 6.

Settlement Finality Directive[30] and the adoption of a directive on cross-border use of collateral. While the Settlement Finality Directive focuses on settlement systems specifically, the adoption of a collateral directive (section 5 below) is designed to facilitate cross-border collateralization techniques generally by reducing the risk of legal uncertainty about the enforceability of security.

Clearing and settlements questions were given specific attention in the Commission's 2000 ISD Communication. The Communication noted that notwithstanding the blurring of functions between national CSDs and the ICSDs, cross-border settlement was 'fraught with technical and legal difficulties'.[31] While the Commission's position was not to influence the direction in which market forces will take the integration of clearing and settlement, it called for the removal of the remaining legal obstacles to the cross-border transfer and perfection of title to property, which are particularly marked with respect to bearer securities. In relation to clearing, the increased reliance on multilateral netting and central counterparties was noted and the resulting concentration of systemic risk in central counterparties highlighted as an area needing regulatory attention. Supervision of clearing houses is currently carried out at national level. The Communication suggested that the increased reliance on these entities and the systemic risk they represent might require EC-level supervision and the adoption of common risk-management standards for the regulation and supervision of clearing as well as formalised co-operation and communication procedures. Overall, while the Communication made clear that the Commission favours market-led developments as a means of consolidating the current patchwork of systems and reduce costs, it also appeared as concerned to ensure that access and competition are maintained and that appropriate risk-management policies are pursued as the market develops.[32]

The unsatisfactory state of clearing and settlement across the EC was singled out for particular attention in the 2001 Lamfalussy Report.[33] Noting that the range of factors hindering the development of a European securities markets included the large number of clearing and settlement systems which fragmented liquidity and increased costs, the Wise Men called for a

[30] Action was taken by the Commission against France, Italy, and Luxembourg due to their failure to implement the Directive on time: Financial Services Priorities and Progress, Third Report, COM(2000)692/2, 3.

[31] N 23 above, 18.

[32] At the time of writing the Commission is consulting on clearing and settlement in order to assess the obstacles to cross-border securities-market transactions and the barriers to open access and competition between settlement systems and identify the public-policy issues which might arise from future changes to the settlement infrastructure. The Giovanni group, which advises the Commission on financial-market questions is also considering clearing and settlement.

[33] Final Report of the Committee of Wise Men on the Regulation of European Securities Market, Feb 2001, 16–17.

restructuring of clearing and settlement systems. Like the Commission, they recommended, however, that consolidation and restructuring remain in the hands of the industry and suggested that market forces should determine the optimal solution to the fragmentation problem, whether that involved linkages between central securities bodies or the establishment of a single European central counterparty. Nonetheless, the Wise Men identified a number of public-policy concerns raised by integration. These included: the maintenance of competition through open and non-discriminatory access to systems and the prevention of excessive costs; the soundness of technical links; the prudential questions raised were a single central counterparty to be relied on in settlement; and the desirability of common rules for the authorization and supervision of systems. Their recommendation was that serious consideration needed to be given to whether a common regulatory framework, which took into account the link between clearing and settlement systems and the efficient functioning of securities markets and which addressed systemic questions, was needed for clearing and settlement activities.[34]

The 2001 ISD Working Paper, which sets out the Commission's preliminary orientations on the review of the ISD, also addresses clearing and settlement and reflects, in particular, the access and competition concerns of the ISD as well as the stability concerns which have emerged from more recent discussions.[35] The basic tenor of the Commission's initial thoughts as set out in the Working Paper, which acknowledges the unsatisfactory national basis of clearing and settlement,[36] is that the conditions under which market participants and regulated markets can seek access to 'post-trading infrastructures' (central counterparties and clearing and settlement systems) should be clarified, such that open access and choice are achieved and the ability of regulated markets and market participants to finalize trades efficiently enhanced. Underlying the Working Paper's proposals is a concern to ensure that access should not be unfairly impeded and that

[34] Although it remains to be seen whether harmonization will proceed in this direction, if it does, a Treaty base will have to be identified and the subsidiarity and proportionality requirements met. For a broadly analogous discussion see the examination of securities-trading market harmonisation in Ch XI sect. 7.3 above. Clearing and settlement systems arguably raise serious systemic risk concerns, a factor which may make it easier to justify harmonization in this area. See in this regard the discussion of the Supplementary Supervision Proposal for financial conglomerates, COM (2001)213, ([2001] OJ C213/227) in Ch VIII sect. 11.3.3 above.

[35] Overview of Proposed Adjustments to the Investment Services Directive. Working Document of Services of DG Internal Market. Document 1. July 2001 (the ISD Working Paper). Section 5 deals with clearing and settlement.

[36] It found that '[t]he current predominantly national configuration of [post trade] processes and systems may in particular add to the costs of cross-border transactions in financial instruments. Transactions undertaken in partner country markets must subsequently be finalised through a complex chain of clearing and settlement systems before ownership rights are ultimately transferred to the account of the purchaser. Alternatively, the purchaser is required to be a member of multiple systems with all the associated costs': ibid, 34.

where there is common ownership of trading platform/central counter-party/and clearing and settlement systems, access to these facilities is not made conditional on execution of the trades on an affiliated trading platform. Specifically, the Commission has suggested that the ISD revisions enhance the current Article 15(1) access right by providing for the following additional options: the possibility for market participants to use central counter-parties or clearing systems to novate and/or net off-market positions, subject to compliance with the membership rules of the relevant system; the possibility for a market participant to request that trades executed on a regulated market be settled in a securities-settlement system designated by the market participant rather than settled in the system designated by the regulated market (although this option would be dependent on the existence of links between the regulated market and any related central counterparty/clearing system and the chosen settlement system, as well as on the ability of the counterparty to the trade to complete the transaction through the system); and the possibility for 'regulated markets'[37] to route some or all of their confirmed trades to a recognized central counterparty in another Member State, subject to the approval of the competent authority responsible for the market.[38] The upshot of these revisions is to give investment firms increased opportunities to choose the place in which settlement occurs and to formalize the ability of regulated markets to use central counterparties in other jurisdictions. The enhanced access rights would be subject to a number of qualifications, however, including the proviso that central counterparties and clearing and settlement systems would not be required to establish links where it would not be commercially viable, the links would exceed the technical capacity of the system or where it would compromise the prudential operation of the system in another way. Access would be subject to compliance with the requirements of the relevant system on the same basis as domestic participants and competent authorities would be permitted to prevent the use of central counterparty or clearing functions in other jurisdictions in the absence of common prudential or risk-management standards. The Working Paper has not, however, in line with earlier indications, suggested that harmonized licensing/authorization requirements be applied within the revised ISD framework given that central counterparties and securities-settlement systems carry out functions and are subject to risks which are very different from those addressed by the ISD.

The Working Paper's suggestions are based on a number of assumptions. Post-trade central counterparty, clearing, and settlement facilities are recognized as constituting distinct functions which should not be equated with core investment business and banking business or brought within the ISD's core and non-core services framework; as a result, the Working Paper has

---

[37] On the Working Paper's approach to regulated markets see Ch XI sect. 9.7 above.
[38] ISD Working Paper, n 35 above, 36.

suggested that the ISD revisions include broad functional definitions of these activities (based on the Settlement Finality Directive) to make the separation clear. Central counterparties and clearing and settlement systems should operate under a single body of law in order to avoid any confusion about the jurisdiction applicable which could generate legal risk for 'potentially systemically relevant systems';[39] as discussed further in section 4 below, the Settlement Finality Directive addresses legal risk for settlement systems within its scope. Securities-trading markets should be permitted to organize their arrangements with central counterparties as they see fit and should, if they wish, be allowed to designate an exclusive central counterparty which deals with all their positions. Finally, the revisions are not designed to disrupt current ownership structures of regulated markets or trading platforms, central counterparties, and clearing and settlement systems but seek instead to ensure that joint or linked ownership of regulated markets and central counterparties does not prevent the operator of a central counterparty from providing access to another regulated market. The counterparty should make decisions with respect to access by other regulated markets on technical or commercial grounds and not based on maximizing trading on those markets with which it is affiliated.

Clearing and settlement are also addressed from the perspective of the regulated market and the extent to which the supervision of regulated markets should include their arrangements for clearing and settlement. As part of the new regime which the Commission has suggested should apply to authorized regulated markets, regulated markets would be required to have access to appropriate clearing and settlement arrangements which would ensure the timely and efficient finalization of transactions executed on the market. The Working Paper has also suggested that markets should not be required to guarantee legally the execution of trades as this would amount to a requirement to integrate vertically trading and central counterparty functions. Any such requirement would not be functionally neutral, would not be suitable for all instruments, and could limit the strategic development of individual platforms. Market operators would, therefore, be free to structure their arrangements with post-trade service providers as they wished.[40] The systems used would be subject to a requirement that they were appropriately supervised; however, authorization and supervision of post-trade systems is, at present, to remain with the Member States.

XII.3.3.2 *Technical and Market Developments*

The development of pan-European trading platforms, the growth in alternative trading systems, and alliances between traditional exchanges have all

[39] ISD Working Paper, n 35 above, 35.   [40] Ibid, 30.

contributed to facilitating cross-border securities transactions. In parallel with these developments and in response to investors' need for a similarly integrated clearing and settlement process to track cross-border trading, settlement, and clearing systems are also currently co-operating, consolidating, internationalizing and innovating.[41] Clearly, a single clearing house and settlement system for the integrated securities market would generate massive efficiency gains and cost savings; this is not a new idea—integrated clearing and settlement were promoted in 1966 by the Segré Report.[42] More immediately, as is implicit in the ISD Working Paper, the continuing fragmentation in the clearing and settlement infrastructure, which involves a network of CSDs and clearing systems scattered across the EC, is thought to be reducing the benefits attendant on the current efficiency-generating developments in the trading markets,[43] such as the alliance and merger trend and the arrival of cross-border alternative trading systems on the EC market-place.[44] Mergers and alliances between settlement-systems providers are, however, already prompting greater integration of settlement systems.[45] As is evident from the approach taken to clearing and settlement in the ISD Working Paper, central counterparties are increasingly being relied on to support efficient trading, with many regarding the establishment of a single central counterparty spanning all EC markets as being essential to a more integrated trading, clearing, and settlement system.[46]

The future shape of clearing and settlement is, at the moment, opaque. Three basic models seem to present themselves; centralization/consolidation of systems on a vertical basis and anchored to securities-trading markets which would integrate all transaction services from trading through to final

[41] HM Treasury, *Completing a Dynamic Single European Financial Services Market: A Catalyst for Economic Prosperity for Citizens and Business Across the EU* (2000), 3. The formation of Clearstream and the merger of Sicovam and Euroclear are striking examples of this trend.

[42] Report of a Group of Experts appointed by the EEC Commission, *The Development of a European Capital Market* (1966), 31 and 246–7.

[43] At the moment, between 20 and 30 institutions are involved in clearing and settlement. The costs of maintaining this system are estimated at between $1bn and $1.2 bn, as compared with $600 million in the USA where clearing and settlement is highly integrated (although, of course, comparisons with the US must be treated with caution): Van Duyn, A, 'Clearing and Settlement. Hopes for Unity are Diminished', Stocks and Derivatives Exchanges, Special Supplement to the *Financial Times*, 28 Mar 2001. See also the discussion in the Initial Report of the Committee of Wise Men on European Securities Markets, Nov 2000 (the Initial Lamfalussy Report). The Committee reported at 13 that it had been informed that a maximum of up to 1 billion euro of the current annual cross-border settlement outlay could be saved through the construction of a single settlement infrastructure.

[44] Indeed, the view has been expressed that integration is more critical with respect to clearing and settlement than with respect to trading activities. See, eg, the discussion in Boland, V, 'World's bourses jostle for position as upstarts elbow in', *Financial Times* Survey, Stock and Derivatives Exchanges, 31 Mar 2000.

[45] Work is also being carried out by the European System of Central Banks on how effective links can be made between settlement systems.

[46] The European Securities Forum, which represents many of the major participants in the wholesale securities markets, is in favour of such a development.

settlement as part of the ongoing restructuring of the securities-trading market environment (and as part of the competition for business between trading markets);[47] centralization/consolidation on horizontal basis between the settlement and clearing service providers with settlement occurring, perhaps, through ICSDs; and nationally-based settlement built on a network of enhanced links between national CSDs.[48] The national CSDs have, for example, formed the European Central Securities Depositaries Association in order to enhance co-operation between its members.[49] By contrast, the Euroclear-Sicovam merger is designed to establish a common infrastructure for clearing and settlement based on a single hub which would link all European CSDs (spokes) while other proposals emphasize the need for a single central counterparty.[50] It does appear clear that, at a minimum, the ICSDs will increasingly take on more domestic business,[51] while national CSDs are likely to become more active on a pan-EC basis.[52]

---

[47] While it might be thought that vertical integration of clearing and settlement within securities trading systems and the creation thereby of 'vertical silos', or the provision by one supplier of all trading-transaction services through to final settlement might be attractive for investors, it has been argued that vertical integration in this manner is not efficient from the costs perspective. See Giddy *et al.*, n 11 above, 326. This form of vertical integration has also the potential to create problems where the securities-trading market exercises as a result control over and access to the entire trading process, although the ISD Working Paper is clearly alive to these concerns.

[48] For an analysis of the models according to which further integration could proceed and, in particular, a discussion of the relative merits and drawbacks of centralization versus integration through a network of national CSDs see Giddy *et al.*, n 11 above, 327–33. The analysis at 335 also highlights a number of 'frictions and barriers' to greater centralization which 'largely relate to legal, contractual, payment, institutional, and regulatory differences across EU members' equity markets, all of which appear to add costs to centralizing CSD arrangements at the Euro-hub level sufficient to offset potential benefits from centralization.... Differences in settlement cycles, paper versus book-entry settlement, bearer versus registered shares, differences in tax treatment, multiple currencies and access to national payment systems are the principal issues'.

[49] Numerous links have developed between CSDs as well as between ICSDs and CSDs where they are essential in linking international and national markets. In 2000, eg, CRESTCo and the Swiss settlement system (SIS Segainsettle AG) entered into an alliance (The Settlement Network) in order to provide an integrated cross-border settlement process.

[50] An indication of the shape which might be taken by clearing and settlement systems might be taken from the European Securities Forum (ESF) settlement proposal. Its proposal for rationalizing clearing and settlement was based on: a transfer of clearing and settlement from the trading platforms; the establishment of a single central counterparty; and a rationalization of the settlement process by minimizing the number of institutions involved. In the summer of 2001, however, the ESF reported that, in light of weak securities markets and reduced revenues, its members were not prepared to support the substantial costs of establishing a single settlement system.

[51] The settlement of Irish government bond transactions, eg, was in late 2000 transferred to Euroclear from the Central Bank of Ireland.

[52] Gros and Lannoo, n 8 above, 95.

XII.4 THE SETTLEMENT FINALITY DIRECTIVE

XII.4.1 *Objectives and Treaty Basis*

The Settlement Finality Directive[53] forms part of EC securities regulation's prudential regulation framework.[54] Its objective is to reduce the systemic risk associated with payment and securities-settlement systems[55] and to minimize the disruption to a system which might be caused by insolvency proceedings by addressing the principal systemic legal risks to which systems are exposed.[56] The single-market context heightens the need to manage the systemic risks represented by settlement systems, in that cross-border

[53] The Commission's original 1996 proposal is at [1996] OJ C207/13, Explanatory Memorandum at COM(96)193. ECOSOC's 1996 comments are at [1997] OJ C56/1 and the Parliament's comments on its first reading (the proposal was adopted under the co-decision procedure) are at [1997] OJ C132/74. The Commission presented a revised proposal in 1997 ([1997] OJ C259/6, Explanatory Memorandum at COM(97)345). The Council's common position is at [1997] OJ C375/34 and Parliament's comments are at [1998] OJ C56/27. On the Directive generally see Vereecken, n 1 above.

[54] It also forms part of the wider EC insolvency regime which is outside the scope of this work. See Regulation 1346/2000 on Insolvency Proceedings [2000] OJ L160/1 (which does not apply to financial-services institutions, including credit institutions and investment firms) and Directive 2001/24/EC on the reorganisation and winding up of credit institutions [2001] OJ L125/15 (the Winding Up Directive). Broadly speaking, the Winding Up Directive adopts the home-country control principle for reorganization and winding-up proceedings. It also, however, sets out a number of exceptions to that principle for, *inter alia*, the enforcement of rights in instruments the existence or transfer of which presupposes their recording in a register, account, or central depositary system in a Member State (place where recorded, Art. 24), netting arrangements, and repurchase agreements (law of contract, Art. 25 and 26, respectively), and transactions on a regulated market (law of contract, Art. 27).

[55] The Original Proposal presented by the Commission covered only payments systems, although it noted that securities-settlement systems were under consideration and that a further proposal for settlement systems might be forthcoming: Explanatory Memorandum n 53 above, 1. ECOSOC's, the European Parliament's, and the European Monetary Institute's recommendation that securities-settlement systems be covered was incorporated in the Commission's Revised Proposal. Vereecken has explained that securities-settlement systems were included not only because the systemic risk in securities settlement systems is similar to that in payment systems, but also because payment and securities settlement systems have become increasingly interdependent due to the delivery versus payment model: 'DVP eliminates the principal risk that may arise on the settlement date in securities transactions. As principal risk is the largest source of credit risk in securities settlement, it is also the most likely source of systemic risk . . . if settlement were final in the payment leg of a DVP-transaction, whereas the delivery of the securities could be successfully challenged, the delivery versus payment principle itself would be undermined, thus reintroducing systemic risk': n 1 above, 113, footnotes omitted.

[56] Common Position, n 53 above, Statement of the Council's Reasons, para II. In its Explanatory Memorandum, the Commission noted at 1 and 2 that 'certain features of the law in a number of Member States, together with differences between Member States' laws relating to payment systems in general [reflecting the Original Proposal's limitation to payment systems], were a source of uncertainties and risk.. . . The resolution of these issues will provide a valuable foundation of certainty and serve to minimise legal risks of a systemic kind, as well as the costs which such risks entail'.

settlement and the participation of foreign institutions in settlement systems raise additional risks. In particular, legal risks in the form of conflict of laws problems can arise concerning the finality of transactions in the system and ownership rights, as the risk arises that, however robust the operation of the settlement system according to the rules of its governing law, in a cross-border insolvency involving a foreign participant, netting arrangements, the irrevocability of transfer orders, and the enforceability of collateral may be prejudiced, exacerbating the disruption caused by the insolvency of a system participant.[57]

The Directive is based on Article 95 EC which provides for the adoption of measures for the approximation of the provisions laid down by law, regulation, or administrative action which have as their object the establishment or functioning of the internal market. Article 95 does not confer a general power to regulate the internal market, however; a measure adopted under Article 95 must genuinely have as its object the improvement of the conditions for the establishment and functioning of the internal market, and a mere finding of disparities between national rules and of the abstract risk of obstacles to the Treaty free-movement guarantees or of distortions to competition will not be enough to qualify a measure for Article 95.[58] As far as securities-settlement systems are concerned, the internal-market-wide effects of these systems and their role in supporting efficient cross-border trading connects the subject matter of the Directive with the 'functioning of the internal market'. In particular, the Directive aims to protect the stability of payment and securities-settlement systems against the disruption which can be caused by the legal consequences of the insolvency of a participant in the system, such as an investment firm or credit institution (recital 4). These consequences can have domino effects through the system if other participants default on their obligations as a result of the legal consequences of the initial default, or if the operation of the system is prejudiced, and could lead to market-wide instability. Harmonizing diverging Member States' laws which impact on the insolvency of a system participant accordingly facilitates the functioning of the internal market by reducing the legal risk engendered by these different regimes and by bolstering the stability of the systems which support the internal market in investment services and the free movement of capital. In this regard, although the removal of obstacles to free movement or the levelling of competitive distortions is not directly implicated, the

---

[57] See the discussion in Ferrarini, n 13 above, 592. The Joint Task Force highlighted the main additional risks in cross-border settlement as increased custody and legal risks, the latter arising from the multiple jurisdiction context which means that 'as system operators choose the law that will govern the system and the relationship between system participants, it may introduce risks if such choices are not honoured by the courts in relevant jurisdictions': n 1 above, 45.

[58] Case C-376/98 *Germany v Parliament and Council* [2000] ECR I-8419 (the *Tobacco Advertising* case).

Directive is justified as aiming 'at contributing to the efficient and cost effective operation of cross-border payment and securities settlement arrangements in the Community, which reinforces the freedom of movement of capital in the internal market . . . [the] Directive thereby follows up the progress made towards completion of the internal market, in particular towards the freedom to provide services and liberalization of capital movements, with a view to the realisation of [EMU]' (recital 3). The Directive is not, however, limited to cross-border systems but also covers domestic systems (recital 6 and Articles 1 and 2). The link to the internal-market objectives of Article 95 EC is maintained, presumably due to the potentially wider impact of instability in, and uncertainty concerning the risk represented by, domestic systems on the wider market-place.[59] In its subsidiarity assessment, the Commission noted that the Directive set out general objectives only, leaving implementation to the Member States and that, where appropriate, institutions were free to determine the precise content of the general principles.[60]

Three specific areas which have the potential to affect systemic stability due to the legal risks they carry are targeted by the Directive through substantive and conflict-of-laws rules: settlement finality in relation to netting and transfer orders; insolvency proceedings and their impact on payment and securities-settlement systems; and the enforceability of collateral security. The management of these specific legal risks aside, there are, as outlined below, indicators in the Directive that the EC is also concerned with the regulation and supervision of systems and their internal rules generally, although the Directive does not attempt to deal with these questions.[61]

[59] This provision also reflects the 'general consensus that this directive should have the widest scope possible': Explanatory Memorandum to Original Proposal, n 53 above, 4. This is also reflected in the inclusion of systems which have non-EC participants which are essential to meet the Directive's systemic risk-control objectives given the globalization of securities transactions. See Vereecken, n 1 above, 111.

[60] Explanatory Memorandum to Original Proposal, N. 53 above 4. Ibid. A number of other approaches to the legal risk problem were canvassed by the Commission including: reliance on a model contract to be used by members of a system to remedy the legal risk difficulties (rejected as it would not address third parties and would not overrule Member States' mandatory rules); relying on a conflict-of-law rule which would designate the rules of the Member State in which the payment system was established (where that Member State recognized netting and whose bankruptcy rules did not interfere with the operation of payment systems) as those which would apply to the system and its members (rejected as being too cumbersome as it would require the courts of every Member State to interpret and apply different branches of law (insolvency, commercial, and so on) of all other Member States); and the use of a non-binding Recommendation (rejected as not being a sufficiently transparent and certain approach): n 53 above, 3.

[61] Attempts are being made to agree common standards internationally. The Joint Task Force Report sets out recommendations for the minimum requirements for the design, supervision, and operation of systems in order to 'enhance international financial stability, reduce risks, increase efficiency and provide adequate safeguards for investors': n 1 above, 2. The Joint Task Force's recommendations build on earlier standards issued by the Group of 30 in 1989 (Clearance and Settlement Systems in the World's Securities Markets). The G30 standards, which are based on 9 recommendations for efficient settlement '[f]or many years . . . provided the model for standards in the settlement industry': Benjamin, n 2 above, 33.

While the Preamble might suggest a particular concern with the stability of payment systems[62] and although the Directive is particularly important for EMU and for TARGET, which is the new EMU inter-bank payment system,[63] it has major implications for the securities-settlement systems which underpin the integrated market in securities and investment services. Recital 2 specifically refers to the importance of reducing the risk associated with participation in securities-settlement systems, although it also makes a link back to payment systems, providing that risk control is particularly important where there is a close connection between securities-settlement systems and payment systems.[64]

XII.4.2 *Scope*

Under Article 1, the Directive applies to any system, operating in any currency, governed by the law of a Member State, and to all participants in such systems. It also covers collateral security provided in connection with participation in the system or in connection with the operations of Member States' central banks.[65] The Directive's focus on protecting the EC payment and securities settlement system against systemic risks is reflected in the considerable leeway given to Member States to expand the Directive's coverage, where such expansion is warranted on grounds of systemic risk.

While the core definition of a system is set out in broad terms in Article 2(a), the definition is constructed around a series of conditions designed to ensure certain legal safeguards apply before a system can be designated as such for the purposes of the Directive.[66] A system constitutes a formal arrangement between three or more 'participants',[67] (see below) without including a possible settlement agent,[68] a possible cen-

---

[62] Recital 1 refers to the 1990 Lamfalussy Report to Governors of Central Banks of G10 countries which highlighted the systemic risks inherent in payment systems which operate on the basis of netting.

[63] In its Explanatory Memorandum to the original proposal the Commission emphasized the proposal's importance for EMU in that it supported efficient payment mechanisms and, by taking into account collateral constituted for monetary purposes (see sect. 4.5 below), it contributed to the legal framework necessary in order that the European Central Bank could develop its monetary policy: n 53 above, 2.

[64] See n 55 above.

[65] The latter inclusion of central-bank monetary operations is designed to facilitate the implementation of a single monetary policy by the ECB: recital 10.

[66] Common Position, n 53 above, Statement of the Council's Reasons, para III(B)(b)(2).

[67] Member States may, on a case-by-case basis, designate a system with two or more participants as a system for the purposes of the Directive where this is warranted on grounds of systemic risk.

[68] Defined as an entity providing to 'institutions' and/or a 'central counterparty' (see below) participating in systems settlement accounts through which transfer orders within such systems are settled and, as the case may be, extending credit to those institutions and/or central counterparties for settlement purposes: Art. 2(d). Settlement accounts are defined in Art. 2(l)

tral counterparty,[69] a possible clearing house,[70] or a possible 'indirect participant' (see below), with common rules and standardized arrangements for the execution of 'transfer orders' (see below) between the participants. It must be governed by the laws of a Member State chosen by the participants. Participants may choose the law only of a Member State in which at least one of them has its head office. The Directive's scope is thus limited to EC systems, although it is clear that systems with non-EC participants do come within its scope. Cross-border settlement through ICSDs, as well as through networks of national CSDs is caught by the Directive's broad approach to what constitutes a system. While the Directive is concerned with only one aspect of a system's operation, the control of the legal risks the system and its participants may be exposed to on the insolvency of a participant, a general concern with the supervision of payment and securities-settlement systems is evident from Article 2(a)'s final requirement, which is that the system must be designated as a system and notified to the Commission by the Member State once the Member State is satisfied about the adequacy of the rules of the system. The adequacy qualification suggests that Member States are required to review and supervise the internal rules of systems within their jurisdiction and is bolstered by Article 10(3), which provides that Member States may impose supervision or authorization requirements on systems within their jurisdiction. This limited degree of harmonization is, however, some considerable way short of the common regulatory framework envisaged by the Lamfalussy Report.

The 'transfer orders', the enforceability of which is regulated by the Directive and which form a key component of the definition of a system, are defined, first, as any instruction by a participant to place at the disposal of a recipient an amount of money (by means of a book entry on the accounts of a credit institution, central bank, or settlement agent) or any instruction which results in the assumption or discharge of a payment obligation as defined by the rules of the system. Secondly, the term 'transfer orders' covers any instruction by a participant to transfer the title to, or interest in, a security or securities[71] through a book entry on a register, or otherwise.

as accounts at a central bank, settlement agent, or central counterparty used to hold funds and securities and to settle transactions between participants in a system.

[69] A central counterparty is an entity which is interposed between the institutions in a system and which acts as the exclusive counterparty of those institutions with respect to their transfer orders: Art. 2(d).

[70] Defined as an entity responsible for the calculation of net positions of institutions, a possible central counterparty and/or a possible settlement agent. Art. 2(e). The clearing house has been described as 'the central entity, with which all parties in the system are electronically connected, to whom they direct their transfer orders and which calculates the net position of all parties vis-à-vis each other': Vereecken, n 1 above, 113.

[71] The core ISD list set out in section B of the Annex to the ISD of the instruments within its scope reappears here as the definition of securities for the purpose of the Directive. Recital 8 makes clear that Member States are permitted to designate a system as one for the purposes of

A 'participant' in a system, against whose insolvency the Directive's provisions are directed and who is, accordingly a potential source for the systemic risk addressed by the Directive, is defined in Article 2(f) by means of an exhaustive list comprised of: an 'institution', a central counterparty, a settlement agent, and a clearing house.[72] Institutions, which form the core of a system, are broadly defined in Article 2(b) by a two-pronged test. They must first come within one of four core categories: credit institutions within the terms of the banking regime;[73] investment firms within the terms of the ISD;[74] any undertaking whose head office is outside the Community but whose functions correspond to those of credit institutions and investment firms (non-EC participants who access the system by, for example, a branch or remote access, thus coming within the regime in a recognition of market realities); and public authorities and publicly guaranteed undertakings.[75] Secondly, they must participate in a system and be responsible for discharging the financial obligations arising from transfer orders within that system. Member States may broaden the scope of this definition to cover other entities which participate in a system (as long as the system is supervised in accordance with national law and executes only transfer orders which concern the transfer of title in securities and payments resulting from such orders (or is a securities-settlement system)) and which have responsibility for discharging financial obligations arising from transfer orders within the system. Their inclusion is dependent on at least three system participants being covered by the Directive's definition of 'institution' and on their inclusion being warranted on grounds of systemic risk. This provision is designed to cover participation by non-financial institutions, such as large companies, in securities-settlement systems, given that their insolvency can

the Directive where the system also deals, to a limited extent, in commodity derivatives (which are excluded, at present, from the ISD definition of securities) as long as the 'main activity' of the system is the settlement of securities. Similarly, Art. 2 provides that a Member State may designate as a system a formal arrangement within the terms of Art. 2 whose business consists of the execution of transfer orders related to the transfer of securities and which to a 'limited extent' executes orders relating to other financial instruments, where the Member State considers designation is warranted on grounds of systemic risk.

[72] In accordance with the rules of the relevant system, Art. 2(f) provides that the same participant may act as a central counterparty, a settlement agent, or a clearing house or carry out all or part of their respective tasks.

[73] Within the terms of the definition of a credit institution set out in Art. 1 of Directive 77/78/EEC on the coordination of the laws, regulations and administrative provisions relating to the taking up and pursuit of the business of credit institutions [1977] OJ L322/30 (Art. 1 of Directive 2000/12 EC relating to the taking up and pursuit of the business of credit institutions [2000] OJ L126/1 (the CBD)), but including the exclusions from the definition which are set out in A2(2) (CBD Art. 2(3).

[74] Within the terms of the definition of an investment firm set out in Art. 1(2) of the ISD, subject to the same exclusions from the ISD definition as are set out in Art. 2(2)(a)–(k), but including the exclusion set out in Art. 2(2)(l) (Italian *agenti di cambio*).

[75] Vereecken has noted that as these entities participate in a number of Member States' systems, it was important that they be included in the scope of the Directive: n 1 above, 111.

pose similar systemic risks to a system as the insolvency of a financial institution.[76] Similarly, under Article 2(g) 'indirect participants', or credit institutions with a contractual relationship with an institution participating in a system which executes transfer orders which concern only the transfer of amounts of money (or is a payment system), which contractual relationship enables the credit institution in question to pass transfer orders through the system, may also be considered as participants.[77] The Member State must decide that their inclusion is warranted on grounds of systemic risk and the indirect participant must be known to the system which it accesses via the direct participant.[78]

The wide reach of the Directive and its concern with systemic risk across the EC can be seen from the inclusion of domestic and cross-border systems, EC and non-EC participants, and the ability of Member States to extend its provisions in the interests of systemic risk management. Member States are also explicitly permitted to apply the Directive to their domestic institutions which participate directly in third-country systems and to collateral security provided in connection with participation in such systems.[79]

XII.4.3 *Settlement Finality: Transfer Orders and Netting*

As part of its strategy to reduce legal risk in payment and settlement systems, the Directive defines when transfer orders become final, in order to ensure that orders become final and irrevocable once they enter a system and that systems can operate effectively across and in all the Member States. Article 5 provides that a transfer order may not be revoked by a participant in a system, or by a third party, from the moment defined by the rules of that system. The principle of irrevocability is therefore established, but sufficient flexibility is granted so that systems can determine the point at which the order becomes irrevocable. With specific reference to protecting transfer orders against insolvency, Article 3(1) provides that transfer orders are legally enforceable and binding on third parties, even in the event of the

---

[76] This provision was introduced to take into account the situation in the UK and Sweden where commercial undertakings participate in securities-settlement systems: ibid, 112.

[77] Indirect participants do not have a direct contractual link to the system. See Vereecken, n 1 above, 112 who noted that institutions which do not meet the admission conditions imposed by settlement systems can access the system via a direct participant.

[78] This provision was added on the suggestion of ECOSOC on the ground that there would be a gap in the Directive's protection against systemic consequences were certain relationships (such as correspondent banking arrangements) excluded: n 53 above, para 6.3.

[79] Recital 7. The original proposal specifically applied to EC institutions participating in non-EC systems in order to protect the non-EC system against the systemic risk posed by an insolvent EC institution and, ultimately, to lower the admission requirements demanded of EC institutions. The provision did not survive the Council negotiations; in particular, certain Member States were concerned that this represented an attempt to apply EC rules extra-territorially: Vereecken, n 1 above, 111.

insolvency of a system participant, as long as the transfer orders were entered into the system before the opening of insolvency proceedings. Article 3(1) appears to extend to transfer orders which are individually settled on a gross basis for their initial gross amount through gross settlement systems (given that gross settlement is not expressly excluded),[80] as well as to transfer orders which are settled on a net basis. In exceptional cases, it may also be possible to insulate transfer orders which enter the system after the opening of insolvency proceedings. Where a transfer order enters the system after the opening of insolvency proceedings and is carried out on the day of the opening of the proceedings, it will still be legally enforceable and binding on third parties, but only if, after settlement, the settlement agents, central counterparties, or clearing houses can prove they were not aware, nor should have been aware, of the opening of such proceedings.[81]

Netting arrangements are widely used by payment and settlement systems. They provide that the various claims and obligations between participants in a system are set off against each other so that a final net credit or debit position is reached for each participant. Accordingly, netting reduces, and thereby brings down the cost of, the credit and liquidity exposures of participants and enhances the efficiency of securities-settlement systems. The Directive defines netting in Article 2(k) as 'the conversion into one net claim or one net obligation of claims and obligations resulting from transfer orders which a participant or participants either issue to, or receive from, one or more other participants with the result that only a net claim can be demanded or a net obligation owed'. This definition covers both bilateral and multilateral netting. In the interests of ensuring finality and protection against the adverse effects of insolvency, Article 3(1) and (2) provides that where a settlement system is based on netting, Member States are to ensure the finality of the netting of transfer orders and that it is legally enforceable and binding on third parties, even where an insolvency proceeding arises.[82]

---

[80] In a gross settlement system settlement occurs on a transaction-by-transaction basis; by contrast with net settlement systems, debits are not netted against credits. Gross settlement systems will often operate on a real time basis, such that settlement happens continuously at the time of each individual transaction (real-time gross settlement systems or RTGSs) (net systems will settle at particular intervals, usually at the end of the day, although the transactions in question are recorded in real time). RTGSs have the advantages of reducing the duration of credit and liquidity exposures, of avoiding the unwinding of payments problems which can afflict netting arrangements, and of spreading settlement obligations over time, rather than concentrating them in one time period, as occurs with netting. See Vereecken, n 1, 116 and 119.

[81] This provision was added at the common-position stage in order to avoid doubt concerning transactions entered in good faith after the opening of insolvency proceedings: Common Position (n 53 above), Statement of the Council's Reasons, para III(C)(2).

[82] At the time of the Directive's negotiation, a number of Member States' legal systems did not provide for the enforceability of netting and, in particular, multilateral netting. The problems which could follow were netting arrangements not enforceable and which were the target of the Directive's measures were described by the Commission as follows: '[i]f the liquidator of a failed participant in a payment system were on that basis to challenge this netting, this

Again, Article 3(1) protects netting arrangements as long as the transfer order to be netted was entered into the system before the opening of insolvency proceedings. Where the order is entered into the system after the opening of insolvency proceedings, the netting will be legally enforceable and binding on third parties only if, after the time of settlement, the settlement agent, the central counterparty, or the clearing house can prove that they were not aware, nor should have been aware, of the opening of such proceedings. Article 3(2) deals specifically with the impact of fraudulent preference rules. It provides that 'no law, regulation, rule or practice on the setting aside of contracts and transactions concluded before the moment of opening of insolvency proceedings . . . shall lead to the unwinding of a netting'.[83] Netting in securities-settlement systems is therefore placed on a firm legal basis across the integrated market.

Under Article 3(3), the moment at which a transfer order enters into a system is to be set by the rules of the particular system, but Article 3(3) also provides that these rules must comply with any conditions which might apply under the applicable national law. Reflecting the practice in certain Member States, Article 4 explicitly provides that Member States may provide that the opening of insolvency proceedings against a participant is not to prevent funds or securities available in the settlement account of that participant from being used to fulfil that participant's obligations in the system on the day on which insolvency proceedings open.

The finality rules on the enforceability of netting and transfer orders do not prevent a participant or any third party from exercising rights under the underlying transaction which might exist in law and concern recovery or restitution in relation to a transfer order which has entered the system (these rights may arise as a result of, for example, fraud or a technical mistake), but only for so long as the action does not lead to the unwinding of netting or the revocation of a transfer order already in the system (recital 13).

would mean that he could repudiate the net settlement debt, arrived at by netting. Instead he could insist on payments to him of all the individual underlying amounts originally due to that institution. As for the amounts due from the failed institution, they will be claims on paper in the insolvency proceedings and unlikely to be met. This phenomenon of repudiating the debt and accepting the amounts originally due is called cherry-picking. The consequence of cherry-picking is serious disruption in the payment system at best, at worst the payment system might break down (systemic risk) and cause in turn the inability of other members in the payment system to meet their obligations': n 53 above, 5. See also Steil, n 9 above, who has noted at 217–18 that '[i]f netting arrangements are not legally enforceable, the possibility of strategic behavior on the part of market participants can undermine the effective operation of the system'.

[83] Recital 12 clarifies that the finality of netting requirement does not prevent a system from testing, prior to netting, whether the relevant transfer orders comply with the rules of the system and whether settlement can take place.

XII.4.4 *Insolvency Proceedings*

Given the link between the 'opening of insolvency proceedings' and the enforceability of transfers orders and netting, the Directive defines the moment at which this occurs. Insolvency proceedings are defined in Article 2(j) as 'any collective measure provided for in the law of a Member State, or a third country, either to wind up the participant or to re-organise it, where such measure involves the suspending of, or imposing limitations on, transfers or payments'. Under Article 6(1), for the purposes of the Directive, these proceedings open at the moment the relevant judicial or administrative authority hands down its decision. In order to ensure that this decision is disclosed beyond the judicial or administrative authorities, the decision-making authority in question must, under Article 6(2), immediately notify the appropriate authority designated by the Member State. Given that this national authority is unlikely to be immediately aware of the system(s) in which the institution subject to the insolvency proceedings participates, under Article 6(3) the Member State in question must immediately inform the other Member States of this decision. While the notification procedure does not delay the time from which insolvency proceedings open under Article 6(1), notification under Article 6(2) and (3) may make it more difficult for settlement agents, central counterparties, or clearing houses to claim that they were not aware nor should have been aware of the opening of proceedings for the purposes of the enforceability of transfer orders and netting arrangements under Article 3(1).

The adverse effects of insolvency 'zero-hour' rules, which retroactively 'backdate' insolvency proceedings so that all transactions from a particular time are rendered null and void, are addressed by Article 7.[84] Article 7 in effect abolishes these rules for participants in securities-settlement and payment systems by providing that insolvency proceedings are not to have retroactive effects on the rights and obligations of a participant arising from, or in connection with, its participation in a system earlier than the moment at which insolvency proceedings were opened.

Article 8 clarifies which insolvency law is applicable to the rights and obligations of the participant in question arising from, or in connection with, participation in the system by nominating the laws of the Member State in which the system is located. Legal issues relating to participation in a system which are not covered expressly by the Directive thus benefit from a clear choice-of-law rule.[85]

---

[84] See the discussion in the Explanatory Memorandum to the original proposal, n 53 above, 6.

[85] The Commission explained that the benefit of this rule was that 'if the liquidator . . . would wish to draw on insolvency provisions "d'ordre public" to challenge a payment made through the payment system, he would have to apply the insolvency law of the Member State of location of the payment system. This approach has the advantage that the parties in a payment

XII.4.5 *Collateral Security*

XII.4.5.1 *Scope*

Collateral security is given by participants in a system as a guarantee against default and failures to meet obligations.[86] In the Directive, it is broadly defined in Article 2(m) as 'all realisable assets provided under a pledge (including money provided under a pledge), a repurchase or similar agreement, or otherwise, for the purposes of securing rights and obligations potentially arising in connection with a system, or provided to central banks of the Member States or to the future European central bank'.[87] The latter use of collateral security protects collateral security given in connection with the operations of central banks and facilitates the management of monetary policy within EMU.

XII.4.5.2 *Article 9(1)*

Article 9(1) is designed to ensure that this collateral is insulated from insolvency proceedings so that the risk of systemic problems on the default of a participant is reduced by ensuring that the collateral is available to minimize liquidity squeezes of other participants.[88] The ability of the system to settle orders, notwithstanding the default, on the basis of the security given by the participant subject to the insolvency proceedings is thus protected. Under Article 9(1), the rights of a participant to collateral security provided to it in connection with a system and the rights of central banks of the Member States or the ECB to collateral security provided to them may not be affected by insolvency proceedings against the participant or counterparty to the

system only have to examine one insolvency law, namely the insolvency law of the Member State of the location of the payment system, instead of having to examine and attempt to reconcile the insolvency law of the Member State of origin of every single participant. This would contribute to reducing legal costs and eliminating legal uncertainty': n 53 above, 7.

[86] For one definition of collateral see Benjamin, n 2 above, 34: '[c]ollateralization addresses credit risk by supporting a debt or other personal obligation (which may be defeated by the obligor's insolvency) with a right of recourse against identified assets (which should not). The purpose of collateral is to protect the collateral taker against the risk that its counterparty (the collateral giver) will become insolvent.' She has noted generally 'a new concern to manage credit exposures following the market turbulence of 1998, and the need to achieve new regulatory capital efficiencies in an increasingly competitive market': ibid. See further sect. 5 below.

[87] Recital 10 provides further guidance, stating that collateral security comprises 'all means provided by a participant to other participants in the payment and/or securities-settlement systems to secure rights and obligations in connection with that system, including repurchase agreements, statutory liens and fiduciary transfers'. The definition is not intended to affect national rules on the type of collateral security which can be used in a system.

[88] Art. 9(1) reflects a key recommendation of the Joint Task Force Report, namely that 'an individual customer's non-system creditors should be able to enforce their claims against collateral posted in the system only after the satisfaction out of the collateral of all claims owing to the system or other system participants': n 1 above, 8.

central banks of the Member States or the ECB which provided the security, and the collateral security may be realized for the satisfaction of these rights.[89]

XII.4.5.3 *Article 9(2)*

Article 9(2) deals with the vexed question of which law governs whether a valid and enforceable entitlement to collateral security, given in connection with participation in a system or to central banks of Member States or the ECB, exists and is enforceable against third parties where the securities which constitute the collateral security are held in book-entry form through possibly multiple layers of custodians and subcustodians.[90] The collateral security is thus taken over the interest in securities which is evidenced or recorded by the book entry and not over the actual securities. The significance of Article 9(2) potentially extends beyond controlling legal and thus systemic risk in settlement systems. In particular, the Article 9(2) approach is critical for cross-border transactions, where the ability to use securities as collateral free of legal risks as to the enforceability of the collateral, can lower funding costs (see section 5 below). Traditional conflict-of-law rules suggest that the *lex situs*, or the place where the collateral security is located, resolves this question. The *lex situs*, however, reflects and operates most effectively in a securities-trading environment where securities are held in physical form and transferred and pledged as security by physical delivery or by an entry on the books of the issuer. Where securities are dematerialized or immobilized and held in book-entry form, it becomes more difficult to ascertain their location. The location of securities which are recorded as a book entry on an account with Euroclear and pledged as collateral security by the opening of a pledge account with Euroclear, but which represent part of an issue of securities immobilized and deposited in the form of a global note with a French depositary, could, for example, be either Belgium, as the place where the securities are held in book-entry form with Euroclear, or France as the location of the global note. Different results

---

[89] By contrast, see the more restrictive approach taken in Art. 21(3) of the Winding Up Directive which provides that 'the adoption of reorganisation measures or the opening of winding-up procedures shall not affect the rights in re of creditors or third parties in respect of tangible or intangible, moveable or immoveable assets—both specific assets and collections of indefinite assets as a whole which change from time to time—belonging to the credit institution *which are situated within the territory of another Member State at the time of the adoption of such measures or the opening of such procedures* [emphasis added]'.

[90] This topic, which has critical repercussions for the collateralization of cross-border securities transactions and whether the collateral taken is effective and realizable in law, has recently been the subject of intense debate. See, eg, the papers from the Oxford Colloquium on Collateral and Conflict of Laws (at St John's College, Oxford) published as a Special Supplement to the *JIBFL*, Sept 1998, and J. Benjamin, *Interests in Securities* (2000).

on the enforceability of the security depending on the law applicable are clearly unacceptable from the perspective of commercial interests. Article 9(2) is designed to resolve this question. It provides that 'where securities (including rights in securities) are provided as collateral security to participants and/or central banks of the Member States or the future European Central Bank as described in [Article 9(1)], and their right (or that of any nominee, agent or third party acting on their behalf) with respect to the securities is legally recorded on a register, account or centralised deposit system located in a Member State, the determination of the rights of such entities as holders of collateral security in relation to those securities shall be governed by the law of that Member State'. The governing law under Article 9(2) with respect to proprietary rights in securities is therefore that of the place where the proprietary rights are recorded. This rule aims to ensure that, if a participant, central bank, or the ECB has a valid and effective collateral security in accordance with the laws of the Member State where the relevant registration system is located, the validity and enforceability of the security against that system and any other person claiming directly or indirectly through the system, is to be established by the laws of that Member State.[91]

XII.4.6 *Transparency, Supervision, and Review of the Directive*

In the interests of transparency and legal certainty, Article 10 requires Member States to specify the systems which are subject to the Directive's rules and notify the Commission accordingly. The Commission must also be informed of the authorities which the Member States designate as the authorities which must be notified when insolvency proceedings are opened. Similarly, the specified system must indicate to the Member State whose law is applicable to the system the participants (direct and indirect) in the system and changes to the system's participants.

In a reflection of a growing trend in the EC securities-regulation regime towards greater disclosure, Article 10 also provides that 'anyone with a legitimate interest' may require an institution to inform him of the systems within which it participates and to provide information on the main rules governing the operation of those systems. Finally on Article 10, the interest at EC level in the extent to which systems are subject to appropriate supervision and control is evident from the somewhat superfluous statement in Article 10 that Member States may impose supervision or authorization requirements on systems which come within their jurisdiction.

Under Article 12, the Commission is required to present a report to the European Parliament and the Council on the application of the Directive

---

[91] Recital 20.

and, where appropriate, present proposals for its reform. The Commission has reported that it is to launch a study early in 2002 on the Directive's impact on the operation of systems and that it plans to present the report by the end of 2002.

XII.5 THE FINANCIAL COLLATERAL ARRANGEMENTS PROPOSAL

Although more concerned with private law and not, strictly speaking, a securities-regulation measure in the way that the Settlement Finality Directive is due to its direct impact on the infrastructure of the securities-trading markets, the Commission's proposal for a financial collateral arrangements directive[92] will have an impact on transactions involving securities and on how credit risks are managed by market participants and will be considered briefly here.

The Proposal is designed to extend the foundation laid down in the Settlement Finality Directive to transactions in the financial markets generally. In its Explanatory Memorandum, the Commission highlighted the importance of the mutual acceptance and enforceability of cross-border collateral for the stability of the financial system. At present, if a participant in the EC financial market wishes to reduce credit risk by taking collateral, fifteen different legal regimes will apply to the perfection of the collateral (or govern the mechanisms which must be followed so that the collateral taker's rights over the collateral will be good as against third parties). In addition, bankruptcy rules differ across the Member States and there is uncertainty about which law governs cross-border transfers of book entry securities: '[a]s a result . . . legal uncertainty results in unnecessary systemic risks in the financial markets, there being a higher risk of invalidation of cross-border use of collateral than for domestic use of collateral'.[93] In order to ensure an integrated financial market and the smooth functioning of monetary policy, the Proposal establishes a common minimum regime for the supply of securities and cash as collateral under pledge and title transfer structures (the latter including repurchase or repo arrangements where securities are sold against cash and, at the same time, an agreement is entered into to repurchase equivalent securities at a particular price at a date in the future or on demand).

The Proposal is based on Article 95 EC and on ensuring the smooth functioning of the common market: its collateral provisions are designed to 'contribute to the integration and cost-efficiency of the financial market as well

[92] COM(2001)168 (the Proposal, including the Explanatory Memorandum): [2001] OJ C180/312.
[93] Ibid, 3.

as to the stability of the financial system . . . thereby supporting the freedom to provide services and the free movement of capital' (recital 3).[94] The Commission has explained the Proposal's contribution to the functioning of the internal market by pointing to its likelihood of increasing the opportunities for conducting cross-border business, particularly as counterparties may be more likely to deal with small and medium-sized enterprises if they have confidence in the collateral received. Stability will also be enhanced as the Proposal's strengthening of the legal regime applicable to collateral will reduce the risk that a failure by one market participant will cause other participants to default. Finally, by allowing re-use of pledged securities the Proposal is designed to enhance liquidity, reduce volatility, and facilitate the buying and selling of securities.[95]

It applies on a bilateral basis to the two parties involved in a collateral arrangement and has the following objectives: ensuring that effective and 'reasonably simple' regimes are in place for creating collateral under title-transfer or pledge structures; providing limited protection for collateral arrangements from some insolvency rules (particularly where those rules would jeopardize the validity of techniques such as the provision of top-up collateral as a result of changes in the value of the exposure or the collateral); creating legal certainty as to the conflict-of-laws treatment of book-entry securities used as collateral in cross-border transactions by extending the principle set out in Article 9(2) of the Settlement Finality Directive; ensuring that agreements permitting the collateral taker to re-use the collateral for its own purposes are recognized as effective; and restricting the imposition of burdensome formalities on the creation or enforcement of collateral arrangements.[96]

---

[94] Along with the Supplementary Supervision Proposal for financial conglomerates, COM(2001)213 ([2001] OJ C213/227) (Ch VIII sect. 11.3.3 above) it arguably reflects the wider competence which the Community legislature appears to be asserting over the functioning of the financial market-place.

[95] N 92 above, 6.   [96] Ibid, 4.

PART V

EC Securities Regulation
and the Control of Market Abuse

XIII

The Control of Market Abuse

XIII.1 INSIDER DEALING: THE RATIONALE FOR PROHIBITING INSIDER DEALING

Notwithstanding the prevalence of insider-dealing prohibitions in systems of securities-regulation and the broad acceptance by policy-makers that insider dealing should be prevented, attempts to identify a rationale for regulating insider dealing have resulted in a vast literature which embraces both economic and legal theory.[1] This discussion will not attempt to canvass all the legal and economic arguments raised by the control of insider dealing but will be limited to identifying the main features of the debate in order to identify the underlying rationale, if any, of the EC's approach to insider dealing and to assess whether it is consistently articulated in the Insider Dealing Directive.[2]

The underlying rationale for insider dealing[3] can be described as two-pronged, composed of contrasting relationship-based and market-based theories. The first rationale for insider-dealing regulation has a micro focus. It characterizes insider dealing as a breach of the fiduciary relationship of trust and confidence, where one can be established, between, typically, the insider and the company concerned.[4] The macro focus of the second theory

---

[1] For an review of the major controversies see Suter, J, *The Regulation of Insider Trading in Britain* (1989) 14–49, Hopt, K, 'The European Insider Dealing Directive' in Hopt, K, and Wymeersch, E (eds), *European Insider Dealing* (1991) 129, 129–30 and Hannigan, B, *Insider Dealing* (2nd edn, 1994) 5–13.

[2] Directive 89/592/EEC coordinating regulations on insider dealing [1989] OJ L334/30 (the Directive or the IDD).

[3] Although in reviewing the rationale for insider dealing it should be noted that in this area '[t]o cross between the doctrinal and policy discussion is to risk disorientation; in the policy debate even the settled legal rule against open trading by corporate insiders dissolves into a decidedly unsettled account of price behaviour and compensation contracts': Kraakman, R, 'The Legal Theory of Insider Trading Regulation in the United States' in Hopt and Wymeersch, n 1 above, 39, 47.

[4] Although early decisions from the federal appeals courts suggested a more market-based rationale for insider dealing (in *SEC v Texas Gulf Sulphur* 401 F 2d 833 (2d Cir 1968), eg, the court referred at 838 to 'the justifiable expectation of the securities market-place that all investors trading on impersonal exchanges have relatively equal access to material information'), the US insider-dealing regime provides the classic example of the fiduciary-based system. Difficulties in fitting the control of insider dealing within the general prohibition against any fraud or deceit 'in connection with the purchase or sale of any security' contained in Rule 10b–5 (adopted by the SEC under s 10(b) of the Securities Exchange Act, 1934) and the absence of a specific statutory provision forced the US courts into developing insider-dealing rules based on use of information in breach of a fiduciary duty owed by the dealer to the shareholders of the company (*US v Chiarella* 445 US 222 (1980), where the Supreme Court found

is on the wider securities markets and on the protection of the critical role of the effective and fair dissemination of information in the operation of the secondary-trading market-place, in particular.[5] Insider dealing is prohibited not to protect the company specifically, but to preserve investor confidence and hence the liquidity of the market-place and the efficiency with which it allocates resources.[6] If investor confidence is compromised, goes the argument, it could lead to, in the most extreme scenario, the exit of investors from the market-place.[7] While investor confidence in the market-place is notoriously difficult to assess, in the insider-dealing context it is traditionally linked to confidence about market egalitarianism or the confidence of investors in the equality of access to information in the market-place.[8] Market egalitarianism requires that in the context of impersonal markets and exchanges, investors should deal on a relatively equal basis with equal opportunities to access information and should not be unfairly disadvantaged by dealings on the part of those with special access to non-public infor-

---

at 233 that the insider dealing prohibition arose from a 'specific relationship between two parties' and *Dirks v SEC* 463 US 646 (1983) are key judgments). Allied to the fiduciary-duty analysis is the relationship-based misappropriation theory, confirmed after some controversy about its validity by the US Supreme Court in *US v O'Hagan* 117 SCt 2199 (1997), which finds insider dealing where the wrongdoer acts on the basis of information which is acquired through any fiduciary relationship and which is intended to be confidential. This theory is based on breach of a duty owed to the person from whom the information was obtained. For a review of the fiduciary approach see, eg, Loss, L, 'The Fiduciary Concept As Applied to Corporate Insiders in the United States' (1970) 33 *MLR* 34 and Jennings, R, Marsh, H, Coffee, J, and Seligman, J, *Securities Regulation: Cases and Materials* (8th edn, 1998) 1087–1129.

[5] It has been noted that '[s]ecurities trading in the secondary market has one overriding characteristic: It is affected by, and in turn produces, a continuous flow of information. New data . . . constantly causes investors to reevaluate their investment portfolios': Cox, J, Hillman, R, and Langevoort, D, *Securities Regulation, Cases and Material* (2nd edn, 1997) 653.

[6] For an exposition of the fiduciary and market approaches see Davies, P, 'The European Community's Directive on Insider Dealing: From Company Law to Securities Market Regulation' (1991) 11 *OJLS* 92, Rider, B, Abrams, C, and Ashe, M, *Guide to Financial Services Legislation* (3rd edn, 1997) 221–3 and Black, J, 'Audacious But Not Successful: A Comparative Analysis of the Implementation of Insider Dealing Regulation in EU Member States' (1998) 2 *CfiLR* 1, 3. The two approaches have been described in terms of the contrasting interests at stake: the ownership rights of the information holder and the interest of investors in the integrity of the market-place as a whole: Davies, P, 'The Take-over Bidder Exemption and the Policy of Disclosure' in Hopt and Wymeersch, n 1 above, 243, 251.

[7] 'The very preservation of any capital market depends on liquidity, which rests in turn on the investor's confidence that current quotations accurately reflect the objective value of his investment': Loss, n 4 above, 36.

[8] This rationale drives the IDD. On investor confidence in market egalitarianism generally as a rationale for regulation see Rider *et al.*, n 6 above, 216–17. For an extensive review of equal access and its parameters see Brudney, V, 'Insiders, Outsiders and Informational Advantages Under the Federal Securities Laws' (1979) 93 *Harv. LR* 322. See also the critique of equal access in Scott, K, 'Insider Trading, Rule 10-b(5), Disclosure and Corporate Privacy' (1980) 9 *J Legal Studies* 801, 805–9.

mation.[9] Investor confidence is also linked to confidence in the integrity of the price-formation process.[10]

Market-driven rationales, particularly where they rest on inchoate concepts such as investor confidence, are, however, vulnerable to attack by economists and adherents to the law and economics school on efficiency grounds, and insider dealing is no exception. The putative market benefits of insider-dealing prohibitions have been subject to voluminous economics-based criticism and support (both largely addressing dealing by corporate insiders, typically management, rather than by others in possession of price-sensitive information) since the publication of Manne's seminal 1966 work which argued against the prohibition of insider dealing on the basis of its beneficial effects on price formation.[11] As well as arguing that insider dealing is a victimless crime,[12] he argued that insider dealing ultimately moves prices in the right direction,[13] benefiting all investors, including uninformed investors, and increasing confidence in the price-formation mechanism. The stage was then set for a long-running and somewhat inconclusive debate on the impact of insider dealing on the market-place.[14] Ultimately, whatever

[9] See the extract from *SEC v Texas Gulf Sulphur* in n 4 above. Equal access has since been rejected as a basis for insider dealing by the US Supreme Court. See the discussion in Kraakman, n 3 above, 40–2. Clearly, complete equality is impossible to achieve, given the superior ability of certain (typically professional) investors legitimately to access and decode publicly available information as a result of their experience and professional expertise rather than because of any unfair access to non-public information. See Gilson, R, and Kraakman, R, 'The Mechanics of Market Efficiency' (1984) 70 *Va. LR* 549, 571.

[10] See Black, n above 6, 3 and Loss, n 4 above, 36.

[11] Manne, H, *Insider Trading and the Stock Market* (1966).

[12] The innocent party does not transact face to face with the insider, is not induced to act by the insider with whom the innocent party is randomly matched by the market, and has decided to transact based on an independent assessment of the market-place: Hannigan, n 1 above, 7.

[13] The thesis is based on the notion that buying activity by insiders with price-sensitive positive information, eg, about the company will drive the price up, reflecting more accurately the status of the company and allowing non-insiders to trade at a more accurate price.

[14] Much of the debate has focused on the interaction between efficient price formation and insider dealing. For the argument that insider-dealing prohibitions slow down the rate at which securities prices adjust to new information see Carlton, D, and Fischer, D, 'The Regulation of Insider Trading' 35 (1983) *Stanford LR* 857. For a challenge to this view, based, *inter alia*, on the argument that the inside information driving the insider's trading decision cannot be decoded by the market-place, see Gilson and Kraakman, n 9 above, 629–34. See also Rider, B, 'The Control of Insider Trading—Smoke and Mirrors' (1999) 1 *ICCLJ* 271, 283–4 who has argued that the enhanced-disclosure thesis has not, for the most part, been substantiated in practice and that, while stockwatch programmes may point to the existence of inside information, it does not follow that the information is always transferred to the market-place. The cogent point is also made at 284–6, however, that prohibitions on insider dealing can lead to the exchange and arbitrage of information and the involvement of organized crime. In the EC context, for a robust response to the price-formation argument for permitting insider dealing, based on the fact that while a positive impact on prices may be observed empirically, the fact remains that under the IDD 'essential information relevant to price is not supposed to reach the Stock Exchange slowly, indirectly and with a prior profit for insiders but immediately, directly

the uncertainties about the economic and price-formation effects of insider dealing, proponents of regulation can argue that if investors believe that they will be adversely affected by insider dealing, confidence in the market-place may be affected.[15]

The rationale underlying the control of insider dealing does have an impact on how insider dealing is characterized and prohibited. The clearest choices emerge between the micro and macro rationales. Notwithstanding the connection which can be made between both rationales not least due to their common concern, albeit differently expressed, with fairness, the beneficiary of the insider-dealing prohibition is very different in each case and the articulation of basic concepts such as 'insider' and 'inside information' and the nature of enforcement and the availability of remedies can accordingly vary considerably. For example, if investor confidence and the efficient operation of the market are the dominant objectives, the source of the inside information is largely irrelevant, although it is central if the prohibition is based on fiduciary concepts.[16] It is clear from the US relationship-based prohibition on insider dealing, however, that creative manipulation of the parameters of fiduciary relationships can bring into the prohibition on insider dealing sufficient insiders to blur the distinction in practice between both rationales.[17] Where a market-driven rationale is followed, the extent to which investor confidence in market egalitarianism or in the price-formation process is pursued will impact on the scope of the insider-dealing prohibition and, in particular, on how 'inside information' is defined.[18]

XIII.2 INSIDER DEALING: SCOPE AND FEATURES OF THE EC REGIME

The EC's insider-dealing regime consists, at present (revisions are in train: section 11.5 below), of a prohibition on insider dealing which is supple-

and with due regard to equality of opportunity, thus through timely disclosure', see Hopt, K, 'Insider Regulation and Timely Disclosure', *Forum Internationale*. No. 21 (1996) 4.

The other major feature of the debate is the extent to which insider dealing can form an appropriate component of manager compensation by providing management with an incentive to innovate and produce 'good news', and removing the requirement to renegotiate compensation contracts. See Carlton and Fischer, above.

[15] The interaction between insider dealing and investor confidence and the impact on the market are, however, difficult to assess. It has been argued that it does not have an appreciable impact on the market-place. See Hetherington, J, 'When the Sleeper Awakes: Reflections on Corporate Governance and Shareholders' Rights' (1979) 8 *Hofstra L Rev.* 183, 226–9. See also Dalhuisen, J, *The New UK Securities Legislation and the EC 1992 Program* (1989) 138.

[16] See also Davies, n 6 above, 93.   [17] See the discussion in *US v O'Hagan*, n 4 above.

[18] Black has made the point that if investor confidence in the price-formation process is the objective, information need be disclosed in advance of trading by the 'insider' in possession of the information only sufficiently widely such that it is reflected in the price. Market egalitarianism, on the other hand, suggests the widest possible dissemination of information so that all market participants have, to the extent possible, equal access to that information: n 6 above, 3–4.

mented by ancillary reporting and disclosure controls. The core measure is the IDD, although other measures impact more tangentially on the control of insider dealing, such as the ongoing disclosure regime contained in the issuer-disclosure and admission-to-official-listing regime, including, arguably, the reporting requirements imposed by the now consolidated Substantial Shareholdings Directive.[19] The failed proposed Takeover Directive[20] would, had it been adopted, also have contributed to the prohibition of insider dealing at EC level.

There are clear synergies between the market-based rationale for controlling insider dealing and the focus of EC securities regulation on, first, constructing and, secondly, protecting the efficient operation of an integrated securities and investment-services market. Similar synergies can also be observed between the market-based rationale's focus on information and its dissemination and the primacy given to information in the construction of the integrated market, as witnessed by the early securities directives and the 1977 Code of Conduct relating to transactions in transferable securities[21] and by the use of disclosure to protect investors in their dealings with investment firms. The insider-dealing regime, and, in particular, the IDD do, indeed, reflect a macro focus on the protection of the market-place. This orientation also chimes with the macro approach evident in the treatment of secondary-market regulation by the Investment Services Directive and the Capital Adequacy Directive.[22] Whatever the difficulties with the market-based rationale, the focus on the market at least allows the regime to respond to developments in the integrated market. The perception of investors about the operation of the market can, arguably, only become increasingly more important if the measures currently in preparation to encourage greater retail investor activity in the securities and investment services markets succeed.

The manner in which the IDD mediates between the market-related and company-based rationales and how it articulates the market-protection rationale in the particular context of the requirements of the integrated securities and investment-services market is not, however, entirely clear-cut and

---

[19] Directive 88/627/EEC on the information to be published when a major holding in a listed company is acquired or disposed of [1988] OJ L 348/62 (discussed in Chapter IV), now consolidated in Directive 2001/34/EC on admission of securities to official stock exchange listing and on information to be published on those securities [2001] OJ L184/1 (the Securities Consolidation Directive or SCD). It is, however, more directly addressed to ensuring that investors are aware of an issuer's ownership structure than to imposing a check on insider dealing by monitoring investment patterns (see sect. 5 below).

[20] See Ch. XIV.

[21] Commission Recommendation 77/534/EEC concerning a European code of conduct relating to transactions in transferable securities OJ (1977) L212/37 (the 1977 Code of Conduct).

[22] Directive 93/22/EEC on investment services in the securities field [1993] OJ L141/27 (the ISD) and Directive 93/3/EEC on the capital adequacy of investment firms and credit institutions [1993] OJ L141/1 (the CAD), respectively.

will be discussed further in section 4 below. What is clear is that the dominance of the wider market-place as the interest to be protected has had a critical impact on the shape of regulation.

XIII.3   INSIDER DEALING: THE ROOTS OF THE EC REGIME[23]

XIII.3.1   *A Focus on Company Insiders*

The first major appearance of insider dealing as a target for EC regulation is, as is the case with so many features of the current securities regulation framework, in the seminal 1966 Segré Report.[24] The importance the Report attached to information and the central role it granted to disclosure as a tool to support the integration of Community securities markets has already been discussed (Chapter IV above). This central theme was carried through to the Report's discussion of the operation of securities markets and of equality of access to information, albeit in the somewhat limited context of the trading activities of company directors and officers in securities of their own company. The Report found that it was necessary 'to make sure that all persons carrying out a stock-exchange operation are on an equal footing and to prevent those, who, by virtue of their office in a company, have access to information which might influence the market from using their knowledge to secure a personal advantage denied to other investors'.[25] While the Report acknowledged the 'obvious difficulties in establishing rules for so complex a matter' it recommended that two principles be followed: that restrictions placed on executives' freedom of action 'essentially aim at preventing them from using information acquired by virtue of their office to trade in the company's securities to their own advantage, before such information becomes public knowledge' and that stock exchange authorities or other administrative agencies be empowered to carry out investigations whenever price fluctuations suggested malpractice by company insiders.[26] Notwithstanding the company-relationship-based context within which insider dealing was discussed, the pull towards a market-based rationale is evident in the connection the Report made between the control of unequal access to information by company insiders and the 'good functioning of the market' and its reference to the need to make sure that persons dealing on a stock exchange do so on an 'equal footing'.[27]

Although the Report's focus on the abuser of insider information as a company insider would be broadened in subsequent Community forays into

---

[23] See generally Rider B, and Ashe, M, 'The Insider Dealing Directive' in Andenas, M, and Kenyon-Slade, S (eds), *EC Financial Market Regulation and Company Law* (1993) 209, 210–13.

[24] Report of a Group of Experts appointed by the EEC Commission, *The Development of a European Capital Market* (1966).

[25] Ibid, 249.   [26] Ibid.   [27] Ibid, 248 and 249.

insider-dealing regulation, the next appearance of insider dealing, in the 1970 draft for a European Company Statute,[28] would also reflect company-relationship-based rationales and focus on the insider as a company insider. Article 82 of the Statute, which addressed listed companies, dealt with short-swing profits made by certain insiders (board members, the auditors, and large shareholders holding more than 10 per cent) within six-month periods, by borrowing from the US securities regulation regime,[29] allowing the company to recover any such profits as a matter of right. A disclosure-of-holdings registration system was also applied to these insiders. In the context of widespread Member-State resistance to statutory prohibitions on insider dealing, particularly in Germany, and cultural attitudes which were relaxed with respect to insider dealing,[30] the draft Statute could do little more than highlight the insider-dealing problem.[31]

XIII.3.2 *A Shift of Focus*

Equality of access to information and the avoidance of market imperfections by fair and adequate disclosure are strong themes in the 1977 Code of Conduct which has a broad sphere of application covering securities markets generally, defined as 'the official stock exchange and all markets organized by or under the supervision of the competent authorities' as well as 'all transactions in transferable securities [defined as all securities which are or may be the subject of dealing on an organised market] including privately negotiated dealings between individuals in transferable securities'. In line with these themes, a number of the Code's General and Supplementary Principles can be interpreted as having a bearing on the control of insider dealing. General Principle 2, for example, requires that any person, who by virtue of his profession or duties has the duty to inform or the means of informing the public, be under a special obligation to ensure that the public is kept properly informed and that no particular class of persons attains a privileged position. General Principle 4 has perhaps a more direct connection to the abuse of inside information, stating that, when the securities of

[28] [1970] OJ C124/1. This draft was amended in 1975 (EC Bulletin, Supp. 4/75). The Regulation to Establish a European Company and the accompanying Directive concerning worker involvement were finally adopted on 8 Oct 2001.

[29] Similar rules also applied in France under a 1967/68 law which was amended in 1970: Hopt, n 1 above, 131.

[30] For the view that in Germany it was commonly held that insider trading was simply a part of doing business see Standen, D, 'Insider Trading Reforms Sweep Across Germany: Bracing for the Cold Winds of Change', 36 (1995) *Harv Int. LJ* 177, 177–8.

[31] The time lag between the USA and Europe in relation to the acceptance of the need to prohibit insider dealing has been explained by the slower development of the securities markets in continental Europe and by the time it took for the forces of financial-market globalization and the need to attract foreign investment to reach all Western European countries: Hopt, n 14 above, 4.

a company are dealt in on the 'market' (as compared with the broader definition of 'securities market' this is defined as an official stock exchange or an organized market), the members of the company's supervisory board, its directors, and others exercising control have a particular duty to avoid any action which would operate to the detriment of fair dealings in the securities concerned or prejudice the rights of other shareholders. General Principle 5 requires all persons dealing regularly on the securities markets to act fairly in accordance with the Code's objectives, even if this could result in their having to forgo short-term gains. The Supplementary Principles address insider dealing more closely, with Supplementary Principle 3, for example, providing that no person should exert pressure to obtain information which is not public and which cannot be divulged without contravening rules relating to such information. The Code specifically addresses the abuse of inside information within financial intermediaries, which may arise through the acquisition by firms of price-sensitive information as a result of the professional services they provide. Supplementary Principle 8 provides that financial intermediaries should 'endeavour to keep secret', even as between different departments or services of the same entity information which is acquired in the course of carrying out their duties which is 'not public' and which is 'price-sensitive'. It specifically requires that financial intermediaries refrain from using information in transactions which they carry out for their own account on the securities markets as well as in transactions in respect of which they advise investors and which they carry out for the account of investors. The Explanatory Memorandum to the Code expands on this principle, providing that where a financial establishment is in possession of confidential information which could be used to advise against an investment (without saying why) when the aim is to avoid a loss rather than to achieve a gain, the 'banker should be free to give such informed advice to the customer'.[32] Supplementary Principle 8 feeds into General Principle 6 which requires financial intermediaries to avoid all conflicts of interests. If a conflict arises, they should not seek to gain a direct or indirect personal advantage and should avoid any prejudice to their clients or to any persons with whom they have a fiduciary relationship. Finally, a number of important concepts central to the control of insider dealing with respect to the definition of the insider and the nature of inside information, which would later re-emerge in the IDD, appear in Supplementary Principle 9. It provides that any person who comes into possession of information which is not public and which relates to a company or to the market in its securities or to any event of general interest to the market which is price-sensitive, in the course of exercising his profession or carrying out his duties, should refrain from carrying out, directly or indirectly,

---

[32] Explanatory Memorandum, n 21 above, para III, 11 D.

any transaction in which such information is used. Supplementary Principle 9 also addresses the problem of 'tipping', providing that any such person should also refrain from giving that information to another person so that he may profit from it before the information becomes public. More generally, the importance of information is highlighted by Supplementary Principle 12 which requires prompt disclosure by a company whose securities are traded on an official stock exchange or other organized market of price-sensitive information to the public. It also appears in Supplementary Principle 13 which suggests that competent authorities should suspend dealings in a company's securities where there is a substantial risk of a leak of price-sensitive information which cannot be made public immediately for technical reasons or because its disclosure would prejudice the company. Equal access to information is specifically covered by Supplementary Principle 15 which requires that no investor or group of investors should be given more favourable treatment as regards information than other investors or the public and states explicitly that all investors should have equal access to information. The Code was, however, largely ignored by the Member States and had little impact on the control of insider dealing across the Community.[33] Nonetheless, it does reflect an important shift from the company-driven approach evident in the Segré Report and the 1970 draft European Company Statute towards a market-oriented perspective. This is best illustrated, perhaps, by Supplementary Principle 9 and underscored by the inclusion of insider-dealing provisions in a Code the 'fundamental objective' of which is 'to promote the effective functioning of securities markets'.[34]

In advance of the 1977 Code of Conduct's adoption, the Commission had already established in 1976 (under the auspices of then Directorate General XV for Financial Institutions and Taxation rather than, significantly, Directorate General III then responsible for company law harmonization)[35] a working group to review the status of insider-dealing prohibitions across the Community and to discuss the possibility of harmonizing insider-dealing rules.[36] The key recommendations of the group included: defining insiders broadly as all persons knowingly in possession of inside information (thereby moving beyond the company-relationship-based concept of insider dealing)

[33] In its comments on the proposal for the IDD, ECOSOC's support for the treatment of insider dealing via binding rules was based partly on the fact that the Code of Conduct 'has not had the success that was hoped for' [1988] OJ C35/22, para 1.2.

[34] Code of Conduct, n 21 above, Fundamental Objective para.

[35] It has been noted that this institutional allocation of responsibilities had an important influence on the IDD's ultimately following a market-based rather than a company-based approach: Hopt, n 1 above, 132. A similar institutional influence on the shape of EC securities regulation might arise if investor protection were ever either to be transferred from the Internal Market DG to the Health and Consumer Protection DG or to be dealt with outside the Internal Market DG. See further Ch. IX sect. 14.

[36] Working Paper No. 1, 'Coordination of the Rules and Regulations Governing Insider Trading', EC Commission XV/206/76-E.

and inside information as non-public price-sensitive information relating to a company or to market conditions; extending the prohibition on insider dealing to disclosure of inside information and encouraging others to act on the basis of inside information; imposing a timely disclosure-of-material information obligation on companies; and recommending that supervisory authorities be given investigatory and enforcement powers in preference to the treatment of insider dealing through voluntary, professional codes of conduct.[37]

While several of the working group's recommendations would reappear in the IDD, its work was overtaken by developments in the sphere of disclosure harmonization. The (now consolidated) Admission Directive has a bearing on the control of insider dealing, in that it established disclosure as a central principle of EC securities regulation and the harmonization of disclosure requirements as essential for market integration.[38] With respect to the control of insider dealing specifically, the principle of equal access to information is reflected in Schedule C paragraph 5(a) (which builds on Supplementary Principle 12 of the Code of Conduct) (SCD, Article 68(1)). This requires a company whose shares are admitted to official listing on a stock exchange to inform the public, as soon as possible, of any major new developments in its sphere of activity which are not public knowledge and which may, due to their effect on a company's assets or liabilities, financial position or the general course of its business, lead to substantial price movements. The ongoing disclosure theme was expanded by the now consolidated Interim Reports Directive which requires all companies whose shares are admitted to official listing to disclose specified financial information in an interim report every six months.[39] Together with the 1977 Code of Conduct, these provisions laid the basis for a market- and equal access-to-information-based approach to insider dealing.

Progress towards a directive remained painfully slow, however, not least due to continued resistance from certain Member States to a statutory treatment of insider dealing.[40] The Commission presented a proposal in 1987[41] and, after receiving the comments of the European Parliament and ECOSOC,[42]

---

[37] See Rider and Ashe, n 23 above, 211–13.

[38] Directive 79/279/EEC coordinating the conditions for the admission of securities to official stock exchange listing [1979] OJ L66/21 (the Admission Directive). Now consolidated in the SCD. See Ch. III.

[39] Directive 82/121/EEC on information to be published on a regular basis by companies the shares of which have been admitted to official stock-exchange listing [1982] OJ L48/26 (the Interim Reports Directive), now consolidated in the SCD. See Ch. IV sect. 5.3 above.

[40] Indeed, the Commission took some time to decide whether insider dealing should be addressed through a directive or a recommendation: Tridimas, T, 'Insider Trading: European Harmonisation and National Law Reform' [1991] 40 *ICLQ* 919, 920.

[41] [1987] OJ C153/8 (the Original Proposal); Explanatory Memorandum at COM(87)11.

[42] [1988] OJ C187/83 and [1988] OJ C35/22, respectively.

a lightly revised proposal in October 1988.[43] A series of insider-dealing scandals in the late 1980s, together with a movement across the Community to address insider dealing,[44] increased the pressure on Member States to respond to insider-dealing concerns, particularly given a corporate climate of increased mergers and acquisitions activity as companies restructured in order to maximize the benefits of the single market.[45] A common position was agreed by the Council in mid-1989[46] and accepted by the European Parliament later that year.[47] The IDD, which differs in a number of key respects from the Revised Proposal, was finally adopted in November 1989 and was to be adopted by the Member States by 1 June 1992. While a number of Member States had introduced insider-dealing regimes while the IDD was under negotiation, its implementation would require others to adopt new or substantially revised insider-dealing controls.[48]

XIII.4 INSIDER DEALING: THE DIRECTIVE

XIII.4.1 *Objectives and Treaty Basis*

Unusually among the securities-regulation directives which are, for the most part, based on Article 47(2) EC (investment services) and Articles 44(2)(g) and 94 EC in combination (securities and disclosure directives), the IDD[49] is based solely on Article 95 EC (at the time Article 100a EC) which broadly provides for the adoption of 'measures for the approximation of the provisions laid down by law, regulation or administrative action in Member States which have as their object the establishment and functioning of the internal market'. The Original Proposal, by contrast, based the IDD exclusively in Article 44(2)(g) EC which provides for the co-ordination of the

---

[43] [1988] OJ C277/13 (the Revised Proposal); Explanatory Memorandum at COM(88)549.

[44] The UK re-enacted the insider-dealing controls set out in Part V of the Companies Act 1980 in the Company Securities (Insider Dealing) Act 1985; Denmark adopted controls in 1986; Greece and Spain in 1988; and Belgium and the Netherlands in 1989.

[45] Fornasier, R, 'The Directive on Insider Trading', (1989–90) 13 *Fordham Int'l LJ* 149, 149.

[46] The IDD was adopted under the co-operation procedure, as required, at that time, by ex Art. 100a EC (Art. 95 EC) on which the IDD is based.

[47] [1989] OJ C291/54.

[48] On the manner in which the Directive has been implemented see Wymeersch, E, 'The Insider Trading Prohibition in the EC Member States: A Comparative Overview' in Hopt and Wymeersch, n 1 above, 65; Tridimas, n 40 above, and Black, n 6 above.

[49] There is a considerable literature on the Directive. See, eg: Fornasier. n 45 above; Tridimas, n 40 above; Ashe, M, 'The Directive on Insider Dealing' (1992) 13 *The Company Lawyer* 15; Davies, n 6 above; Hopt, n 1 above; Pingel, I, 'The EC Directive of 1989' in Gaillard, E (ed), *Insider Trading* (1992) 5; Ruiz, L, 'European Community Directive on Insider Dealing: A Model for Effective Enforcement of Prohibitions on Insider Trading in International Securities Markets' (1995) 33 *Col. J T'nal. L* 217, 235–42; Dine, J, 'European Foundation' in Rider, B, and Ashe, M, (eds), *The Fiduciary, The Insider and the Conflict* (1995) 1; and Edwards, V, *EC Company Law* (1999) 307–32.

'safeguards which, for the protection of the interests of members and others, are required by Member States of companies or firms . . . with a view to making such safeguards equivalent throughout the Community'. The proposed Directive was regarded as an 'essential supplement' to the (now consolidated) Admission Directive, the Listing Particulars Directive,[50] and the Interim Reports Directive, all of which are based on Article 44(2)(g) (together with, crucially, the general internal-market competence set out in Article 94), and as sharing their objectives of 'effective protection for investors on securities markets; . . . proper operation of the securities markets throughout the Community; . . . [and the promotion of] greater inter-penetration of national securities markets'.[51] The Revised Proposal did not explain the change in legal basis. Unlike the disclosure and listing rules contained in the afore-mentioned securities directives, however, insider-dealing rules cannot be easily characterized as 'safeguards . . . for the protection of the interests of members and others . . . required by Member States of companies'. The wider market-based view of insider dealing taken by the Original Proposal and reflected in the IDD was based on the protection of market transactions generally and was not limited to the imposition of insider-dealing controls on companies or their officers. The change of legal basis to the more general internal-market competence set out in Article 95 EC not only reflects more accurately the IDD's market orientation but the deliberate change also attests to the Commission's view of the IDD as a market-protection measure.

The essential connection between the harmonization of insider-dealing regulation and the 'establishment and functioning' of the internal market required by Article 95 EC is made through the oft-repeated, if rarely rationalized, regulators' mantra that there is a connection between insider dealing and investor confidence. The secondary market in transferable securities is identified in recital 2 of the Preamble as playing an 'important part in the financing of economic agents', while recital 3 makes a general connection between the effectiveness of the market and the adoption of measures to ensure that it operates smoothly. The smooth operation of the market is linked to the 'confidence it inspires in investors' and confidence is in turn connected with 'the assurance afforded to investors that they are placed on an equal footing and that they will be protected against the improper use of insider information' (recitals 4 and 5). By benefiting certain investors over others, insider dealing is identified as being likely to undermine investor confidence and prejudice the smooth operation of the market-place (recital

---

[50] Directive 80/390/EEC coordinating the requirements for the drawing-up, scrutiny and distribution of the listing particulars to be published for the admission of securities to official stock exchange listing [1980] OJ L100/1 (the Listing Particulars Directive), now consolidated in the SCD.

[51] Explanatory Memorandum to original proposal, n 41 above, 3–4.

6). The argument then follows that, in light of the need to combat insider dealing in the interests of investor confidence, harmonization is necessary, given the absence of insider-dealing prohibitions in some Member States and the divergences between those rules which have been adopted by the Member States (recitals 7 and 8).[52]

Two important consequences appear to flow from this reasoning. The first and more general result follows from the link made between the promotion of investor confidence and the proper functioning of the internal market in securities. This argument could, given the vague parameters of investor confidence and the uncertainties about how is can be established, grant a wide-ranging and powerful competence to the EC with respect to the securities markets under Article 95 EC (were it not to fall foul of the Court of Justice). It is also notable that the avoidance of distortions to competition is not isolated as a reason for harmonizing diverging rules, although it is normally offered as a justification under Article 95. Unlike the subsequent secondary-market investment-services measures which are predominantly designed to liberalize the provision of investment services via the passport device and which, thus far at least, re-regulate only as far as is necessary to facilitate the passport's operation, it is not a liberalization measure but is designed to regulate the single securities and investment-services market.[53] Indeed, the IDD's reasoning might support the view that the Court of Justice may be more sympathetic to general market-regulation measures designed to enhance confidence in the integrated securities and investment-services market, but which are not based on free movement or on the removal of distortions to competition, than it has shown itself to be with respect to internal-market regulation generally in the *Tobacco Advertising* ruling.[54] Secondly, the characterization of insider dealing as a threat to investor confidence owing to its impact on the 'equal footing' of investors and their confidence that they will be protected against the 'improper use' of inside information points to a treatment of insider dealing from the perspective of the protection of the market-place and market egalitarianism. The earlier attempts to deal with insider dealing from a company-relationship/fiduciary perspective appear to be cut

[52] Although the position would change during the IDD negotiations (see n 44 above) at the time of the presentation of the Original Proposal, only 4 Member States (Denmark since 1986) France (since 1967), the UK (since 1980), and Germany (since 1970)) had insider-dealing controls, with Germany's regime based on a voluntary code of conduct, while in the Netherlands the Amsterdam Stock Exchange imposed a code of conduct. The other Member States did not address insider dealing, although Belgium, Ireland, and the Netherlands were at the time preparing legislation: Explanatory Memorandum to the Original Proposal, n 41 above, 2. On the pre-IDD status of insider-dealing controls see Dalhuisen, n 15 above, 131–6.

[53] Indeed, in the context of its basis in Art. 95 EC rather than in Art. 44(2)(g) EC, it has been said of the IDD that it 'should be seen, not just as a sequel to the three previous [securities] directives . . . and thus as another new piece of the Community legislation implementing Article 54(3)(g), but rather as the first explicit step taken towards regulating the single financial market of the Community': Fornasier, n 45 above, 162.

[54] Case C-376/98 *Germany v Parliament and Council* [2000] ECR I-8419.

loose. The IDD does not, however, clarify one of the factors which it identifies as critical to investor confidence—namely 'the assurance afforded to investors that they are placed on an equal footing' beyond stating that investor confidence is prejudiced by insider dealing as certain investors are benefited more than others.[55] Whether being placed on an equal footing and avoiding disproportionate benefits to other investors requires equality of access to information or something less than that is not specified. While the link between insider-dealing prohibitions and the market-place is clearly made, the specifics of this rationale, which have a critical impact on how insiders and inside information are addressed, are not fully articulated. The Commission's Explanatory Memorandum to the Original Proposal does, however, shed some light on the IDD's rationale. It argued that the depth and liquidity of the securities markets depended on, *inter alia*, 'the assurance given to investors that prices quoted reflect all the facts and that therefore all possible measures have been taken to ensure equality of opportunity for all investors' and that insider dealing 'which enables persons with insider information to make gains at the expense of other investors . . . totally undermines equality of opportunity'.[56]

The Directive is a minimum-standards directive. Article 6 states explicitly that Member States are permitted to adopt provisions which are more stringent than those required by the Directive or additional provisions. Any such provisions must, however, apply generally.[57]

---

[55] Given the changes which the IDD went through during the negotiation process and the distance between the Directive and the initial discussion which can be tracked back to the mid 1970s, however, the point has been made that 'it is rather simplistic to attempt to discern an underlying philosophy other than pragmatism, although from the preamble to the Directive it is clear that the concept of market egalitarianism remains a guiding principle': Clarotti, P, 'A View from Brussels', in Rider and Ashe, n 49 above, 51, 54.

[56] N 41 above, 1–2.

[57] Art. 6 of the IDD was considered by the ECJ in Case C–28/99 *Criminal Proceedings against Jean Verdonck, Ronald Everaert and Edith de Baedts* [2001] ECR I–3399. Belgium had adopted a stricter interpretation of Art. 2(1) of the IDD than the IDD formula by applying the insider-dealing prohibition to those in possession of information which they knew, or ought reasonably to have known, was inside information. A special rule applied to holding companies and provided that inside information did not include information which holding companies possessed because of their role in managing companies in which they had a holding. In a preliminary reference, the Belgian court asked whether Art. 6 permitted a Member State to adopt a more stringent prohibition on insider dealing and, at the same time, to grant a specific category of persons (holding companies) an exemption from the definition of inside information contained in the national implementing law. The Court held that, while a regime specific to particular market participants would be contrary to Art. 6, if the regime simply clarified the general definition of inside information for that category of market participant, without altering the scope of the definition, it would not contravene Art. 6. It was for the national court to decide whether the holding-company rules had the effect of changing the definition of inside information for holding companies. The Court concluded that Art. 6 did not prevent the application of national rules which, with respect to the prohibition on the use of inside information, were more restrictive than those set out in the IDD, as long as the scope of the definition of inside information used in applying the national rules was the same for all natural or legal persons subject to that legislation.

XIII.4.2 *Inside Information*

XIII.4.2.1 *The Core Definition*

At the core of the IDD is Article 1(1) which defines inside information as 'information which has not been made public of a precise nature relating to one or several issuers of transferable securities or to one or several transferable securities, which, if it were made public, would be likely to have a significant effect on the price of the transferable securities or securities in question'. The three major components of this definition, which differs, if not materially, from the Original and Revised Proposal versions, are discussed at sections 4.2.2–4.2.4 below.[58]

XIII.4.2.2 *Of a Precise Nature, Relating to One or Several Issuers or to One or Several Transferable Securities*

The reference to information of a 'precise nature', while ambiguous, is designed to ensure that mere speculation, opinions, and rumours are not treated as inside information.[59] The IDD does not address when rumour hardens into concrete information.[60]

The preparatory materials, together with the IDD's market orientation, suggest a broad reading of 'relating to one or several issuers of transferable securities or to one or several transferable securities'. Indeed, the term 'relating to' implies a rather elastic control on the type of information caught by the IDD. While the text of the IDD is not explicit on this point, consistency with its objective of protecting investor confidence generally would require that inside information include market information likely to move the market as a whole, such as information on decisions on interest rates.[61]

---

[58] The Original Proposal defined inside information in Art. 6 as 'information unknown to the public of a specific nature and relating to one or more issuers of transferable securities, or to one or more transferable securities, which, if it were published, would be likely to have a material effect on the price of the transferable security or transferable securities in question'. ECOSOC's somewhat optimistic request that the Commission give concrete examples of inside information and misuse, 'as the key concepts of an insider and inside information are too vague' would fall on deaf ears: n 42 above, para 1.5.

[59] Explanatory Memorandum to Original Proposal, n 41 above, 5. This qualification is arguably increasingly important, given the rate at which rumours circulate through Internet chat rooms and bulletin boards. See also the view that 'speculation has a useful economic function': Hopt, n 1 above, 134.

[60] See Ashe, n 49 above, 16. The point has been made that rumours harden into inside information at the point when market traders take that information into account when valuing securities: Wymeersch, n 48 above, 114.

[61] Such an interpretation is supported by the Explanatory Memorandum to the Original Proposal, n 41 above, 5. It has been suggested that as Art. 1(1) of the IDD could extend to information such as 'government decisions on passing a law which will bar exports . . . or news about the pending outcome of a major case for example at the Supreme Court', and given that economic-related news is often barely distinguishable from political news: Art. 1(1) 'is

Similarly, inside information relating to an issuer can originate within or outside the issuer.[62] The potentially wide reach of this element of the definition and its reach beyond company-specific information underlines the IDD's focus on the protection of the market rather than on the misuse of information acquired from the company in a fiduciary capacity.

By the time of the IDD's adoption, numerous attempts had already been made across the EC securities-regulation structure to define 'transferable securities'. As a critical component of the key definition of inside information, it is more extensively defined in Article 1(2) than in earlier efforts. Article 1(2) sets out a list of the instruments which are encompassed within the definition of transferable securities. Shares and debt securities[63] as well as securities equivalent to shares and debt securities are included under Article 1(2)(a). Article 1(2)(b) encompasses contracts or rights to subscribe for, acquire, or dispose of the securities covered by Article 1(2)(a) while futures contracts, options, financial futures, and index contracts, each in respect of Article 1(2)(a) securities, are covered by Article 1(2)(c) and (d). 'Issuer' is neither defined nor qualified by reference to the traditional company, with securities of non-corporate issuers, such as government securities, thus being brought into the definition. Notwithstanding its breadth, however, the exclusions include units in collective-investment schemes, money-market instruments, foreign exchange and interest rate derivatives, and commodity derivatives. The emphasis on more traditional equity and equity-related securities might be regarded as sitting uneasily with the IDD's focus on the protection of the market as a whole. With the exception of units in unit trusts, however, the excluded instruments are sophisticated financial instruments which are dealt in on professional-investor-dominated markets. It might be argued that the investor whose confidence in the market-place is being promoted is the retail investor whose activities are largely confined to traditional transferable securities.

Before they come within the scope of the IDD's inside-information definition, in one of the clearest examples of the Directive's market orientation, the transferable securities must be admitted to trading on a market which is regulated and supervised by authorities recognized by public bodies, operates regularly, and is accessible directly or indirectly to the public (Article 1(2)). The breadth of definition of 'market' which has implications

---

extremely far reaching. Limits are necessary, but must be looked for elsewhere, namely in the concept of the insider and the professional prohibitions and duties imposed on them by the directive': Hopt, n 1 above, 134.

[62] The Explanatory Memorandum to the Original Proposal offers the example of information on an increase in profits as information originating within the company and knowledge of a hostile takeover bid as information originating outside the company: n 41 above, 5.

[63] Although it has been noted that insider-dealing rules 'are more important in relation to equities where prices are more sensitive to financial conditions': Wood, P, *The Law and Practice of International Finance: International Loans, Bonds and Securities Regulation* (1995) 350.

for the interpretation of a number of the IDD's provisions, is consistent with the Directive's objective of enhancing confidence in the 'secondary market in transferable securities' (recitals 2 and 4). The Community secondary market in transferable securities is not composed simply of securities admitted to the Official List in the various Member States. Second-tier secondary markets such as the London Stock Exchange's AIM and Frankfurt's *Neuer Markt* are playing an increasingly important role in the wider secondary market in transferable securities. Trading systems which are appropriately supervised and recognized also appear to come within this definition. Whether or not alternative trading systems (ATSs) which, thus far at least, operate in parallel with traditional exchanges by providing professional investors, in particular, with trading services, but which are rapidly changing the trading environment across the Community are included, particularly where they are more similar to exchanges than investment firms in their operation, is more controversial. It will depend on the extent to which ATSs are publicly supervised, recognized, and accessible to the public. Where an ATS is not regarded as a market for the purpose of Article 2(1), activities on the ATS will be caught by the IDD where the securities concerned are traded on an Article 2(1) market and the ATS can be regarded as a professional intermediary (Article 2(3)).

XIII.4.2.3 *Information which has not been Made Public*

The approach taken in determining the extent to which information must be disseminated before it shakes off the taint of 'inside information' should reveal the meaning of the IDD's rather vague objective of 'placing investors on an equal footing'. If the intent is to ensure that all investors have equal access to information, then a wide articulation of 'not been made public' would ensure the maximum availability of information.[64] A reading of the 'public' as the general public rather than as a particular section of the investment community would be appropriate. Similarly, in order to lift the restriction of having 'not been made public', reliance on forms of dissemination with a wide circulation, such as newspapers, news agencies, or stock exchange notifications, seem necessary. The IDD does not, however, make an explicit connection between the publication of information through

---

[64] It is of interest that (in the different context of the misuse of information as misconduct amounting to market abuse rather than insider dealing) the UK Financial Services Authority (FSA) has stated that 'there will always be times when certain market users have access to information that is not generally available to others. Although [such a person] may [benefit from the information] it is not necessarily against the wider interests of the market that he does so. The reality of markets is that it is impossible for every piece of information to be made known on an equal and simultaneous basis to all market participants, and the regular user has no expectation that it should be': FSA (UK Financial Services Authority), *Draft Code of Conduct*, Consultation Paper 59 (2000) (Draft Market Abuse Code Paper) 20-1.

public channels such as stock exchange notifications and whether or not information has been made public. It does deal with the specific case of investment analysts' reports. These reports are often highlighted as examples of information which can, on a broad reading, be regarded as having 'not been made public', given that they are not typically disseminated beyond the professional investment community. Recital 13 of the Preamble provides, however, that 'estimates developed from publicly available data cannot be regarded as inside information'. The position would be different were a report to be based on non-publicly available information which was disclosed at an analysts' meeting with the company. In those circumstances, the analyst would fall foul of the IDD's prohibition on disclosing inside information and on recommending or procuring a third party to trade on the basis of inside information. If, conversely, an 'equal footing' suggests that investors are trading on an equal basis in that the price-formation process on which they are relying ensures they are trading on the basis of a price which efficiently reflects the available information, 'not been made public' could be somewhat more narrowly drawn. Sectoral disclosure to an influential group of institutional investors with power to move the market price might, for example, suffice.[65]

Setting the boundaries to 'not been made public' also requires consideration not only of the disclosure process but also of how quickly information is disclosed. Yet the IDD does not specify whether a particular span of time must elapse before the information ceases to be inside information. If equality of access is the concern, it seems arguable that insiders must, once the information is disclosed or published, wait until it can be said that the information can be accessed by all investors and that they have had a reasonable opportunity to react to it. Uncertainty about when the information was assimilated by the public could be addressed by the imposition of, for example, twenty-four-hour holding periods post-disclosure during which the insider could not deal. Conversely, if the price-formation process is central, the inside block could be removed as soon as the information has impacted on the market price.[66]

Given the IDD's avowed market orientation, the vague approach to 'not been made public' is surprising. The preparatory materials are not entirely consistent with the IDD's approach and provide contrasting perspectives. The original version of this definition was wider, referring broadly to information which was 'unknown to the public'. Partly due to concerns about

---

[65] Cox *et al.*, n 5 above, 781.

[66] See Hopt, n 1 above who suggested at 134 that '[p]ossibly the best interpretation of art. 1(1) is the following: the mere fact of giving the information away to the public is not sufficient, but it is necessary that the information is available to the investing public, for example, by having appeared on the stock exchange ticker or by having been reported by public media such as television, radio or the economic press.'

the status of investment analysts' reports which, whatever the arguments which could be made on whether they had 'not been made public', would, by and large, be 'unknown' to the public,[67] the definition was amended, in line with the Parliament's suggestion, in the Revised Proposal to a formula arguably narrower than the IDD's, of information 'inaccessible or not available to the public'. It could be argued, perhaps, that the failure to adopt a more nuanced approach to 'the public' or to acknowledge the role played by publication in the price-formation process suggests an orientation towards equal footing expressed as equal access to information, rather than as equal opportunity to deal based on an efficient price formation process. This lack of clarity in a critical element of the definition of inside information is a flaw in a measure which, given its explicit reference to the need for 'penalties' to be imposed on infringement of Member-State implementing measures, foresees serious consequences for those who violate its insider-dealing prohibitions.[68]

XIII.4.2.4 *Information which, were it Made Public, would be Likely to have a Significant Effect on the Price of the Transferable Security or Securities in Question*

The IDD relies on the extent to which the information might impact on price movements as an indicator of the information's materiality. A market-based insider-dealing regime needs to use materiality or related concepts to focus insider dealing controls on information, the dissemination of which is, owing to its significance or materiality, linked to investors' perceptions of the equality of access to information or the integrity of the price-formation process. While it makes clear that the inside information must have the capacity to move the market price, the IDD avoids setting guidelines on how the assessment should be made.[69] This determination will be subjective with respect to the information and the company in question.[70] The governing terms, that

[67] See the discussion in Edwards, n 49 above, 313–14 and in Pingel, n 49 above, 6–7.

[68] ECOSOC was particularly concerned about the vagueness of the publication point where insider dealing was criminalized by Member States: n 42 above, 24.

[69] The Original and Revised Proposals both referred to a 'material effect' on prices. The Commission did not venture into explaining 'material effect' in its Explanatory Memorandum to the Original Proposal, noting only that 'all information unknown to the public is not . . . necessarily inside information [otherwise] the managers or directors or even most of the employees of a company would never be able to carry out transactions in the securities of their companies, since they always have information which has not been published': n 41 above, 5.

[70] This point has been illustrated by the example of information on management changes which could be highly price sensitive (where a company's success is linked to the performance of certain individuals) for certain companies but price-neutral for others: Rider and Ashe, n 23 above, 224. In addition, 'the impact of eventual disclosure of inside information on the market price will depend in each case on such variables as the liquidity of the company's shares and the prevailing market conditions': Wotherspoon, K, 'Insider Dealing—The New Law: Part V of the Criminal Justice Act, 1993' (1994) 57 *MLR* 419, 424.

the information 'would be likely' to have a 'significant' effect, are sufficiently vague as to give Member States considerable leeway in implementing this requirement. Some doubt exists whether the inside information, considered in isolation, must be such as to move the market price or whether it is sufficient that, when considered in relation to all other information available with respect to the security, it has an effect on prices.[71] Neither does the IDD clarify from whose perspective the price movement is significant: market professionals and retail investors may have very different positions on this.

XIII.4.3 *Insiders*

XIII.4.3.1 *Primary and Secondary Insiders*

The IDD adopts a bifurcated approach to categorizing the persons who come within the scope of the Directive's prohibition on insider dealing; insiders are categorized as primary insiders and secondary insiders (or tippees).[72]

XIII.4.3.2 *Primary Insiders*

(a) *Introduction*

Under Article 2(1), a primary insider is any person who, either by virtue of his membership of the administrative, management, or supervisory body of the issuer, his holding in the capital of the issuer, or because he has access to such information by virtue of the exercise of his employment, profession, or duties, possesses inside information. By categorizing insiders on the basis of their acquisition of inside information through a direct relationship with the issuer and on the basis of their possession of inside information from more indirect sources which do not involve a fiduciary relationship with the issuer, the definition of primary insider has a company-relationship and market orientation.

(b) *By Virtue of his Membership of the Administrative, Management, or Supervisory Bodies[73] of the Issuer*

This element of the definition covers the traditional conception of insider dealing as a wrong committed against the company. The IDD avoids the

---

[71] See Ashe, n 49 above, 17 and Wymeersch, n 48 above, 89.

[72] The point has been made, however, that, articulated to its logical conclusion, the market approach to defining the insider would mean that 'there would be no need to distinguish different categories of insider; anyone possessing inside information would be the target of the regulation. The classic distinction between "primary" and "secondary" insiders would thus be otiose': Black, n 6 above, 11.

[73] The reference to management and supervisory bodies covers the two-tier management structure common to continental company-management regimes.

potential for evasion by adopting a wide definition of 'company insiders' in preference to identifying the particular company officers subject to the insider-dealing prohibition. The use of the term 'issuer' rather than company, also brings within the prohibition on insider dealing those persons connected with the management of other entities which issue securities.

(c) *By Virtue of his Holding in the Capital of the Issuer*

Here again, the IDD adopts the company-relationship-based approach to its definition of an insider. It does not specify how large the alleged insider's holding must be before the prohibition attaches. The holding must be such, however, that 'by virtue' of that holding the person in question possesses inside information. It is unlikely that small shareholders who do not enjoy a close relationship with the company will be affected by this provision. Rather, it has in its sights large institutional shareholders who, either due to their influential relationship with the company arising from their voting power (which may in certain cases entitle them to board positions bringing them within the first category) or, for example, in the course of company briefings to institutional shareholders, acquire inside information.

(d) *Because he has Access to such Information by Virtue of the Exercise of his Employment, Profession or Duties*

This final category is clearly the widest and the one which most consistently articulates the IDD's market-protection objectives. Direct company employees are clearly caught, chiefly by the reference to duties, but arguably also by the employment criterion. So too are those not directly connected with the company (as employees would be) but in a fiduciary or confidential relationship with it (such a relationship will often be found where a profession involving the provision of legal, accounting or financial advice is exercised).[74]

More controversially, this final category of insiders could be read more widely to cover all those persons whose employment, profession, or duties are not directly performed for or are connected with the company or its securities, but who acquire the information through or 'by virtue of' the exercise of those functions. Notwithstanding its market-protection objectives and the bearing which the answer to this question has on the extent to which the market interest should be protected, the IDD is silent on whether, or the

---

[74] In its Explanatory Memorandum to the Original Proposal the Commission suggested that the definition of primary insiders (limited then to those possessing information 'in the exercise of [their] profession or duties') was designed to cover 'those who by their profession or occupation are in a fiduciary relationship with or have a duty of confidentiality towards the company whose shares are in question': n 41, 4.

degree to which, a connection back to the company or the securities in question is required.[75] It appears (given the IDD's market orientation and the wide definition of inside information as including market-related as well as issuer-related information) that those persons unconnected with the company but in possession of inside information, who acquire such information due to a direct link between the inside information and the nature of their occupation, are covered. These persons may include a stock exchange employee aware of changes to the composition of an index, an investment analyst who has received price-sensitive information from a company's investor-relations department, a civil servant in possession of market-sensitive company-taxation law-reform information, a central bank official aware of market-sensitive interest-rate changes or an employee of a rating agency aware of a forthcoming change in a company's bond rating. It might also be argued that, however tenuous, a connection could be made between these occupations and the company and its securities. The picture becomes blurred where the inside information is not related to the occupation in question and is acquired by chance, albeit in the course of that occupation.[76] While this view, which does not require a connection of any kind between the occupation and either the company, its securities, or the nature of the information, has its supporters,[77] it has been argued that the evolution of the provision from a bald definition in the Revised Proposal of an insider as one who 'in the exercise of his employment, profession or duties, acquires information' to the more nuanced IDD definition of an insider as one who 'because he has access to such information by virtue of the exercise of his employment, profession or duties' suggests that some direct connection between the inside information and the occupation in question is required and that the provision is not designed to catch those who, inadvertently, in the exercise of an unrelated occupation, simply come upon inside information.[78] Conversely, the market orientation of the IDD and its

[75] The omission of a connecting factor back to the company represents a significant extension of the approach to insiders favoured during the early preparatory work on the IDD. Early discussions supported a definition of insiders consisting of a list of specified persons such as company directors, major shareholders and professional advisers, supplemented by a clause bringing within the prohibition all person with professional or business links to the company. This clause was designed to exclude persons overhearing information, albeit in the course of their employment: Cruikshank, C, 'Insider Trading in the EEC', (1982) 10 *International Business Lawyer* 345, 347.

[76] Classic examples include the taxi-driver or waitress who overhears, or the employee of a financial printer who reads, inside information which he or she would not have had access to if he or she did not perform those particular roles.

[77] See the discussion in Tridimas (who ultimately supports the need for some degree of connection), n 40 above, 926 and Davies, n 6 above, 102.

[78] Edwards, n 49 above, 320 and Tridimas, n 40 above, 926–7. The removal of the Art. 2(1) qualification that primary insiders act with full knowledge of the facts by the new market abuse proposal, on the grounds that such insiders are aware of the confidential nature of the information to which they have access, suggests that the Commission supports the narrow interpretation (sect. 11.5.3 below).

focus on the protection of confidence suggests that a broad reading of this provision which would downplay the source of the information and the connection or lack thereof with the company, and focus more sharply on the mere possession of inside information would be appropriate. While it might be argued that those in possession of inside information who might fall outside the definition of primary insiders could still be caught by the definition of secondary insiders (see section 4.3.3 below), the scope of the prohibition on secondary insiders is narrower (see section 4.4.2 below).

XIII.4.3.3 *Secondary Insiders or Tippees*

Under Article 4, any person who 'with full knowledge of the facts possesses inside information, the direct or indirect source of which could not be other than a person referred to in Article 2', is subject to the Article 2 prohibition on insider dealing.[79]

The definition of secondary insider sits well with the IDD's market orientation in that the chain of secondary insiders is potentially a long one, given that the inside information does not have to come from a primary insider directly, be it through a direct tip or through overhearing a primary insider. All that is required is that the putative secondary insider knows that the information is inside information and that the direct or indirect source is a primary insider. If the information has been acquired through a secondary insider, the 'second generation' secondary insider will be caught as long as it can be shown that that person knew that the ultimate indirect source of the information was a primary insider.

XIII.4.4 *The Prohibition: Dealing, Disclosing, and Recommending*

XIII.4.4.1 *Primary Insiders*

(a) *Dealing*

Under Article 2(1) Member States are to prohibit a primary insider from taking advantage of inside information[80] with full knowledge of the facts by

---

[79] The notion of a secondary insider, the introduction of which represented a considerable change for some Member States from a company-relationship-based concept of insider dealing to a wider, market-driven approach, became more sophisticated during the negotiations. The Original Proposal classified a secondary insider more narrowly in Art. 3 as 'any person who has knowingly obtained inside information from a person who has acquired that information in the exercise of his profession or duties'. This definition, which suggested the active acquisition or procuring of inside information by the secondary insider from the primary insider persisted through to the Revised Proposal before the final version was adopted, which, by removing all references to obtaining information and focusing on its possession, ensured that the possession of unsolicited inside information would be caught.

[80] The point has been made by a number of commentators that the term 'taking advantage' does not imply that the insider must either make a profit or avoid a loss as a result of the insider dealing. See Edwards. n 49 above, 326 and Hopt, n 1 above, 139.

acquiring or disposing for his own account or for the account of a third party, either directly or indirectly, of transferable securities of the issuer or issuers to which that information relates. This prohibition applies under Article 2(3) to any acquisition or disposal of transferable securities effected through a professional intermediary. An exemption is available where the transaction takes place without the involvement of a professional intermediary and off market (section 4.6 below) but off-market transactions in securities which trade on an Article 2(1) market are, in principle, covered.[81]

Given the mechanics of dealing in securities and that investment firms may be in possession of inside information relating to securities while providing dealing services relating to those securities, it is not surprising that the Preamble attempts to clarify the scope of the prohibition. Recital 12 provides that 'the mere fact that marketmakers, bodies authorized to act as *contrepartie* or stockbrokers with inside information confine themselves, in the first two cases, to pursuing their normal business of buying or selling securities or, in the last, carrying out an order should not in itself be deemed to constitute use of such inside information'. While Recital 12 provides a useful clarification, it merely reinforces the qualification in Article 2(1) to the effect that dealing on the basis of inside information is prohibited only where the dealer is 'taking advantage of that information'. Recital 12 also makes clear that 'carrying out transactions with the aim of stabilizing the price of new issues or secondary offers of transferable securities should not in itself be deemed to constitute use of inside information'.

The Preamble deals specifically with a problem caused by the wide definition of inside information in Article 1(1) and the prohibition on dealing. Most securities-regulation regimes exempt the bidder for a company from insider-dealing prohibitions in order to permit the bidder, who might otherwise be prevented from dealing as a result of being in possession of sensitive information about the intention to make a bid, to purchase or trade in the target's securities up to the point at which a public announcement of the bidder's intentions with respect to the target is required.[82] Recital 11 provides, however, that 'since the acquisition or disposal of transferable securities necessarily involves a prior decision to acquire or dispose taken by the person who undertakes one or other of these operations, the carrying-out of this acquisition or disposal does not constitute in itself the use of inside information'.

The Article 2(1) reference to 'with full knowledge of the facts' implies that the prohibition bites only when the insider's decision to deal is provoked by

---

[81] Off-market transactions were brought within the IDD in order to prevent potential insiders from circumventing the IDD by trading 'off the floor' of the market: Wymeersch, n 48 above, 97 and 102.

[82] The rationale for this exemption is not linked to the investor-confidence/market-egalitarianism objectives of insider-dealing regulation but rather to the economic benefits in rewarding bidders for expending resources in researching and assessing prospective targets. See generally Davies in Hopt and Wymeersch, n 6 above.

inside information, that is, when an intention to engage in insider dealing can be identified.

Where the primary insider is a company or other type of legal person, under Article 2(2) the prohibition 'shall apply' to the natural persons who take part in the decision to carry out the transaction for the account of the legal person concerned. This provision was designed to deal with the inability in certain continental legal systems of criminal liability to be imputed to legal persons.

(b) *Disclosing and Recommending*

The core dealing prohibition is supplemented by Article 3 which extends the prohibition to disclosing and recommending activities driven by inside information. In principle, the reach of the prohibition is consistent with the macro objective of the IDD and the protection of confidence in the marketplace as a whole.

Under Article 3(a), Member States must prohibit any person subject to the Article 2 prohibition who possesses inside information from disclosing that inside information to any third party unless such disclosure is made in the normal course of the exercise of his employment, profession, or duties. No attempt is made to set parameters on the difficult question of when disclosure can be regarded as being made 'in the normal course' of the occupation in question,[83] apart from the clarification by recital 14 that the 'communication of inside information to an authority, in order to enable it to ensure that the provision of this Directive or other provisions in force are respected' is not covered. The diffuse quality of Article 3(a) fits uneasily with its uncompromising nature: unlike the dealing obligation which is qualified by intention requirements Article 3(a) is an absolute prohibition and does not contain any knowledge or intention requirements.[84] In addition, Article 3(b) provides that Member States must prohibit primary insiders from tipping or, specifically, from 'recommending or procuring a third party, on the basis of that inside information, to acquire or dispose of transferable securities admitted to trading on its securities markets as referred to in Article 1(2)'.

XIII.4.4.2 *Secondary Insiders*

Under Article 4, Member States must impose the Article 2 prohibitions on secondary insiders. Thus, secondary insiders are prohibited from dealing on

---

[83] The Commission made an attempt in its Explanatory Memorandum to the Original Proposal to clarify the disclosure prohibition, stating that '[i]nsiders should not . . . be able to communicate such information to a third party unless it is *appropriate or necessary* [emphasis added] for them to do so in the normal course of exercising their profession or duties': n 41 above, 6.

[84] See Edwards, n 49 above, 326–7.

the basis of inside information. Imposition of the prohibitions on disclosing inside information and recommending or procuring a third party, on the basis of the inside information, to deal in transferable securities is, however, under Article 6, at the discretion of the Member States. It is possible for inside information to flow, as a result, between secondary insiders although dealing on the basis of such information is prohibited.

XIII.4.5 *The IDD and Investment Firms*

Investment analysts, portfolio managers, and providers of strategic corporate advice, to name but three investment-services providers, can potentially access inside information, as defined in the IDD, with respect to a company by virtue of the exercise of their employment, profession, or duties. As a result, the prohibitions on own-account dealing, third-party-account dealing, disclosing, and recommending on the basis of this information come into play.[85] The investment analyst's exemption will apply where, although the information may not be widely available, it is based on the analyst's own research and skill and is 'developed from publicly available data' (recital 13). With specific reference to dealing, however, where individuals in an investment firm are simply in possession of inside information (where, for example, a Chinese wall is not in place and the information from another division is attributed to the alleged insider or information has been passed from another division), they will not, in their roles as stockbrokers for third parties, be prevented from carrying out an order placed by that third party.[86]

Although the IDD is silent on whether market information as to trading conditions for a particular security can be regarded as inside information,[87]

---

[85] The control of insider dealing and the transmission of inside information within multi-function investment firms and its interaction with conflict-of-interest management and duties owed to clients is a highly complex area, a full discussion of which is outside the scope of this book. Although, as outlined in sect. 3.3 above, the Code of Conduct deals briefly with these questions, they are not dealt with explicitly in the IDD. Neither does the ISD cover this area. Although it does require that conflicts of interest be addressed and requires that duties of honesty, loyalty, care and skill be imposed on investment firms, it does not address how these obligations might interact with controls on the abuse of information. See, eg, Cranston, R, 'Insider Dealing—Informational Imbalances and Financial Businesses' in Hopt and Wymeersch, n 1 above, 203, Rider, n 14 above, 305–7, Rider, B, 'Conflicts of Interest: An English Problem' in Ferrarini, G (ed.), *European Securities Markets. The Investment Services Directive and Beyond* (1998) 149 and Hopt, K, 'European Insider Dealing: Inside Information and Conflicts of Interests Between Banks—Part 1' [1999] *JIBFL* 429 (Part 2 at 499).

[86] IDD, recital 12. On whether the broker would be in breach of the prohibition where he knew that the client who placed the order did so on the basis of inside information see the analysis (finding that the broker is not in breach) in Hopt, n 85 above, 432.

[87] For a perspective on trading information see the discussion by the FSA of 'order flow information' in the context of market abuse via misuse of information (not in relation to the criminal legislation on insider dealing). It has stated that 'while trading information will be unavailable to other market users and may also be relevant in deciding the terms on which transactions should be effected, behaviour based on this information is not regarded as

it does address particular dealing practices. As outlined above, recital 12 specifies that market-makers 'pursuing their normal business of buying and selling securities' will not be deemed to be using inside information, and also provides that 'carrying out transactions with the aim of stabilizing the price of new issues or secondary offers of transferable securities should not in itself be deemed to constitute use of insider information'.

XIII.4.6 *Exemptions and Defences*

Under Article 2(3), in a further example of the IDD's market orientation, Member States are given the option not to apply the Directive's core dealing prohibition to acquisitions or disposals of transferable securities effected without the involvement of a professional intermediary outside a market as defined in Article 1(2). Where the transaction is carried out off market, but concerns securities dealt in on an Article 1(2) market, it appears that the IDD will apply, as long as it is carried out through a professional intermediary. Article 2(3) concerns purely private, off-market transactions and is consistent with the Directive's objective of ensuring investor confidence in the market-place. Article 2(4) provides that the IDD does not apply to transactions carried out by a sovereign state (or its central bank, any other body designated to that effect by the state or any person acting on their behalf) in pursuit of monetary, exchange-rate, or public-debt management policies. Member States may opt to extend this exemption to their federated states or similar local authorities in respect of the management of their public debt.

The Directive does not deal with any defences which may be offered to defend a charge of insider dealing. There is no prohibition, however, on a Member State providing for specific defences, in order to ensure consistency between the Directive and the imposition of criminal liability.[88]

XIII.4.7 *Beyond the Prohibition: Disclosure*

The Directive's focus on information and thus its place in the EC's disclosure regime[89] can be clearly seen in its inclusion of positive disclosure obligations as an antidote to insider dealing. The underlying analysis is straightforward—the quicker information reaches the public domain, the shorter the window of time within which insiders can deal. Schedule C, paragraph 5(a) of the Annex to the Admission Directive requires a company whose shares are admitted to official listing on a stock exchange to inform the public as

---

amounting to market abuse. Other users of the market would not expect to have equal access to such information . . . market users expect to be able to take advantage of their ability to understand, analyse and assess the implication of transaction flows though the market': Draft Market Abuse Code Paper, n 64 above, 28–9.

[88] See Tridimas, n 40, 923.   [89] See Ch. IV.

soon as possible of any major new developments in its sphere of activity which are not public knowledge and which may, owing to their effect on its assets and liabilities or financial position or on the general course of its business, lead to substantial movements in its share price (SCD, Article 68(1)). Under Article 7 this obligation is extended to all companies and other undertakings (Schedule C applies only to companies) whose transferable securities, whatever their nature (Schedule C is limited to shares), are admitted to trading on a market as defined in Article 1(2). The wider definition of 'market' in Article 1(2) (Schedule C currently applies only to companies whose shares are admitted to the Official List) considerably extends the disclosure obligation and emphasizes the Directive's focus on protecting the market-place as a whole.

Apart from indicating a commitment to disclosure as a regulatory tool and confidence in the effectiveness of mandatory disclosure in feeding information through to the market-place quickly (be it for equal-access or price-formation motives), Article 7, by highlighting the role of ongoing disclosure of material information in combating insider dealing, could also be read as an implicit rejection of the economic argument that insider dealing enhances the price-formation process by encouraging disclosure by insiders.

XIII.4.8 *Territorial Sphere of Application*

Given that insider dealing may have cross-border elements, and is increasingly likely to as the trading market integrates, the IDD contains rules for the allocation of jurisdiction among the different Member States which may be involved. These rules, set out in Article 5, have the net effect of giving Member States' insider-dealing regimes which implement the Directive a wide sphere of application, presumably in order the maximize the effectiveness of the IDD as a control on cross-border insider dealing and to prevent cross-border transactions, which may have contact with different Member States, from falling through any jurisdictional gaps. Indeed, recital 10 refers to the IDD's role in preventing cross-border insider dealing. The IDD's co-ordinated rules are described as having 'the advantage of making it possible, through cooperation by the competent authorities, to combat trans-frontier insider dealing more effectively'. Under Article 5, Member States are to apply the Directive's Article 2, 3, and 4 prohibitions 'at least' to actions undertaken within their territory, to the extent that the transferable securities concerned are admitted to trading on a market of 'a' Member State, not necessarily the Member State concerned.[90] Article 5 also specifies that

---

[90] As a result, '[t]his leads to the protection not only of the member State's own markets, but also of all stock exchanges and capital markets within the Community': Hopt, n 1 above, 146.

Member States are to regard a transaction as being carried out within their territory if it is carried out on a market, as defined in Article 1(2), which is situated or operates within their territory. Thus, even if the order is placed (on the basis of inside information and in breach of the Directive) in another Member State (whose insider laws will then apply), the Member State within which the market (as defined in Article 1(2)) on which the security is traded is situated or operating will also have jurisdiction to take action. The development of electronic trading may, however obscure the identification of the Member State in which the market 'is situated or operating' and result in a number of Member States having jurisdiction.[91]

XIII.4.9 *Competent Authorities and Co-operation*

Under Article 8 Member States are to designate the 'administrative authorities' or authorities competent, if necessary in collaboration with other authorities, to ensure that the Directive's requirements are applied. Competent authorities must, under Article 8(2), be given all supervisory and, in specific reference to the difficulties inherent in detecting insider dealing, investigatory powers[92] necessary for the exercise of their functions, where appropriate in collaboration with other authorities.

Given that the identification of insider dealers requires effective co-operation between authorities, in that insider dealing can involve a series of transactions some of which may be cross-border, and that investigatory powers have territorial limitations, administrative authorities are also required by Article 10(1) to co-operate with their counterparts in other Member States whenever necessary for the purpose of carrying out their duties. The need for effective co-operation is heightened, given that the Member State on whose trading market a transaction is executed in violation of the IDD has jurisdiction to take action under Article 5. That Member State will often be the one most likely to identify insider-dealing violations as they typically come to light via stockwatch programmes runs by stock exchanges. The Member State will, in order to take action, need to establish the various elements of the insider-dealing prohibition, which, while that Member State will have access to trading information, is likely to require access to additional information concerning the transaction, perhaps from the Member State in which the issuer is based or in which the order was placed.[93] The

---

[91] Ibid, 147.

[92] While the IDD does not specify the extent to which administrative authorities must be empowered to investigate insider dealing, in its Explanatory Memorandum, the Commission referred to the need to 'ascertain from financial intermediaries their clients' true identities': n 41 above, 9.

[93] See the discussion in Wymeersch, E, *The Harmonisation of Securities Trading in Europe in the New Trading Environment*, WP 2000–16, Working Paper Series of the Financial Law Institute, Universiteit Gent, 14.

development of trading on a pan-EC basis and the arrival of pan-EC markets such as Euronext (see Chapter XI section 8.3 above) will also require considerable co-operation in order that actions can be successfully taken against IDD violations, given the number of jurisdictions which may be involved in constructing the insider transaction.

Information exchange is central to the IDD co-operation system. Professional secrecy is addressed by Article 9, which provides that all persons employed or formerly employed by the competent authorities are to be bound by a professional-secrecy obligation. Information covered by professional secrecy may not be disclosed to any person or authority except by virtue of provisions laid down in law. Article 10(1) provides, however, that notwithstanding Article 9 competent authorities are to exchange any information required for the purpose of co-operating in order to carry out their duties. The exchange obligation also applies under Article 10(1) to information which relates to actions which are prohibited only by the requesting Member State under the options given to Member States by Article 5 (the conflict-of-laws rule) and the second sentence of Article 6 (power of Member States to extend the scope of the Article 2 dealing prohibition and to impose the Article 3 tipping and disclosing obligations on secondary insiders). As a result, where a Member State implements the IDD's rules in a more stringent manner than a second Member State, such that conduct which amounts to insider dealing in the first Member State is permitted in the second, the second Member State may not refuse to provide the first Member State with information on the grounds that the conduct in question is not prohibited in the second Member State.[94] Under Article 10(2)(a), competent authorities may refuse to act on a request for information where communication of the information may adversely affect the sovereignty, security, or public policy of the Member State addressed. They may also refuse to act (Article 10(2)(b)) where judicial proceedings have already been initiated in respect of the same actions and against the same persons before the authorities of the Member State addressed or where final judgment has already been passed on such persons for the same actions by the competent authorities of the Member State addressed. Authorities which receive information under Article 10(1) may use it only for the exercise of their functions within the meaning of Article 8(1) and in the context of administrative or judicial proceedings specifically relating to the exercise of these functions. Where the competent authority communicating the information consents, the receiv-

---

[94] The information-exchange procedures apply only to the IDD regime. Where Member States address the abuse of information more widely, as is the case in the market-abuse regime which applies under the Financial Services and Markets Act 2000, information exchange between Member States with diverging approaches to what constitutes market abuse will be more problematic. See Wymeersch, n 93 above, 14.

ing authority may use it for other purposes or forward it to other Member States' competent authorities (Article 10(3)).

The Directive's co-operation requirements[95] were enhanced by the establishment of FESCO (now the Committee of European Securities Regulators) in 1997.[96] Reflecting FESCO's commitment to enhancing co-operation between members, in 1999 its members signed a Multilateral Memorandum of Understanding for mutual assistance and exchange of information in order to encourage cross-border co-operation for surveillance and enforcement purposes. This initiative is designed to provide the broadest possible mutual assistance between the competent authorities of the Member States of the European Economic Area and to enhance market surveillance of financial abuse. It specifically covers investigations and enforcement in relation to insider dealing. Of particular importance is the commitment by signatory FESCO Member States that the competent authorities of FESCO Member States will conduct joint investigations, share work responsibilities, and co-ordinate follow-up actions, where appropriate.[97]

XIII.4.10 *Enforcement and the Sanctions Problem*

The difficulties which arise in enforcing insider-dealing rules are well known. Anonymous markets make detection and the imposition of sanctions difficult. Stockwatch systems typically warn supervisors only of unusual movements in particular securities. Once supervisors have been alerted, they must follow the trail back to the insider and make an evidentiary connection between the trading activity and the abuse of inside information. Supervisory authorities may have scarce resources to expend on pursuing violations. A number of elements conspire against the successful imposition of insider dealing prohibitions. These include: the complex, multi-layered nature of the insider-dealing prohibition which—and the EC is no exception here—typically requires that evidence be provided that the dealer is an 'insider' in possession of 'inside information' and engaging in the specific activity prohibited under the legislation in question or common law; the

---

[95] They also include Art. 11 which covers international co-operation and provides that the Community may, in conformity with the Treaty, conclude agreements with non-member countries on the matters governed by the IDD.

[96] See generally Ch. XV sect. 2.5.2 below.

[97] Co-operation between Member States in this area is reported to be effective owing to the prevalence of memoranda of understanding which enhance the IDD's basic co-operation requirements: Gros, D, and Lannoo, K, *The Euro Capital Market* (2000) 129. On the role of memoranda of association in the EC securities-regulation supervisory structure see further Ch. XV sect. 3.1.4 below. Insider dealing was also specifically addressed by the 1989 Council of Europe Convention on Insider Dealing which deals with establishing co-operation and information-exchange mechanisms between those States which have signed up to it. See generally Lowry, J, 'The International Approach to Insider Trading: The Council of Europe's Convention' [1990] *JBL* 460.

evidentiary and procedural requirements of the criminal law (where insider dealing is criminalized as opposed to being subject to administrative or civil sanctions); and the difficulties which can be experienced by the enforcement authorities in understanding the often complex financial context in which insider dealing must be examined.[98] Private remedies face difficult evidentiary problems as well as the conceptual difficulties inherent in applying individual remedies to a form of activity which, under the terms of the Directive at least, takes place in public, anonymous markets and is regarded as damaging the market-place as a whole, rather than particular investors or the company the inside information relates to.

In common with EC securities regulation generally, the Directive does not specify the sanctions or remedies which must be available if a Member State's implementing measures are breached. Article 13 simply provides that each Member State is to determine the penalties to be applied for infringement of the measures taken pursuant to the Directive. Sanctions are accordingly within the discretion of the Member States. Whether penalties are to be composed of civil or criminal penalties, fines or prison sentences, or private rights of action is not specified. Neither does the Directive cover the severity with which violations should be addressed, with respect to terms of imprisonment, for example, or the amount of financial penalties. The additional Article 13 requirement that penalties must be sufficient to promote compliance represents a somewhat half-hearted attempt to address ECOSOC's concerns that lack of uniformity across the EC in sanctions and penalties could hinder the effective control of insider dealing.[99]

The term 'penalties' suggests, however, that, in line with the IDD's focus on the market-place generally, its requirements are to be enforced in a public manner rather than via private rights of action,[100] although whether the criminal law is to be used rather than the civil or administrative law is not clear.[101] The evidentiary and procedural hurdles which are represented by the criminalization of insider dealing (civil penalties are typically subject to less onerous procedures) might cut against ensuring the effectiveness of the IDD and the preservation of investor confidence if the perception develops that, notwithstanding the regulation of insider dealing, enforcement and

---

[98] See Rider, B, 'Policing Insider Dealing in Britain' in Hopt and Wymeersch, n 1 above, 313, 327–9 and Rider, n 14 above.

[99] N 42 above, para 1.7. The Parliament, somewhat unrealistically, proposed that 'the Commission shall put forward proposals for harmonizing the penalties imposed in each Member State': n 42 above, 93.

[100] Although they could arguably supplement a public regime.

[101] For the view that proper implementation requires, at a minimum, public sanction, whether civil or criminal in nature: see Rider and Ashe, n 23 above, 235. It has been pointed out that the English-language text alone uses the term 'penalties' and that the use of 'sanctions' in most other language versions could accommodate remedies other than the criminal law, provided they have a deterrent effect in accordance with the Directive: Wymeersch, n 48 above, 117–18.

thus the prevention of abuse remain elusive.[102] Overall, while consistent with the general approach of EC securities regulation to questions of enforcement, sanctions, and remedies, the failure of the IDD to grapple with enforcement jars somewhat with its market-protection objectives.

XIII.4.11 *The Contact Committee*

In common with the securities directives, but unlike the later secondary-market measures, the Directive is monitored by the Contact Committee set up under Article 20 of the (now consolidated) Admission Directive (SCD, Article 108).[103] Article 12 provides that the Contact Committee is, in addition to its functions under the securities directives, to permit regular consultations on any practical problems which arise from the application of the Directive and on which exchanges of view are deemed useful (discussions on the type of penalties imposed by Member States could have a significant impact on the extent to which the EC sends a co-ordinated message on the seriousness with which it views insider dealing in the integrated securities market) and to advise the Commission, where necessary, on any additions or amendments to be made to the Directive.

Given the minimum-standards approach underlying the IDD and the lack of co-ordination with respect to penalties, co-operation mechanisms, effectively utilized, have a critical role to play in facilitating the adoption of a co-ordinated response to insider dealing across the integrated market-place.[104] For as long as enforcement remains decentralized and territorially-based, lack of co-ordination carries with it the danger of violations, always difficult to detect in any event, falling through the cracks if co-operation between agencies is not effective. The mismatch between the need to ensure the confidence of investors in the market as a whole as it integrates and the Member-State-based enforcement structure could, were insider-dealing scandals to proliferate, result in a lack of confidence in the integrated market-place as a whole. Indeed, prior to the Commission's presentation of a market abuse proposal (section 11.5 below), FESCO had recommended that any proposal incorporate amendments to the IDD which would provide for a

---

[102] See also Tridimas, n 40 above, 933–4. The observation that 'the traditional criminal law is parochial in its character and reach. Even if jurisdiction is found, the practical difficulties and costs attendant on pursuing a matter that requires evidence from another country often represent a most serious hurdle' has a particular resonance for the control of insider dealing in the integrated market: Rider, n 14 above, 279.

[103] On the contact committee structure see Ch. XV sect. 2.3.2 below.

[104] ECOSOC considered that the Contact Committee/co-operation obligation combination removed 'the need for a special European authority': n 42 above, 25. The new Committee of European Securities Regulators is likely to become the main focus for co-operation. See Ch. XV sect. 2.5.3 below.

more structured network of competent authorities, the use of preventive measures, the establishment of common powers of detection and investigation, and the introduction of administrative sanctions.[105]

XIII.5 INSIDER DEALING:
THE EC REPORTING AND DEALING CONTROLS REGIME

In addition to direct prohibition-based regulation, insider dealing can also be addressed by indirect reporting and other controls which do not specifically address the abuse of inside information but are designed to deter potential insiders who have special access to company information from insider dealing. These rules generally focus on the company insider and on disclosure and dealing rules concerning transactions in company shares or equity securities.

Disclosure rules requiring directors, company officers, and significant shareholders to report on the size of their shareholdings and on significant changes to those holdings are common to many systems of securities regulation.[106] By publicizing the trades entered into by company insiders, these reporting rules supposedly deter insiders from insider dealing, given the ease with which suspicious dealings in a company's shares can be tracked.[107] Reporting obligations may also have the indirect effect of increasing the information available to investors (thereby reinforcing the market-egalitarianism and access-to-information themes which underpin insider-dealing regimes) in that it has been observed that these filings of the trades entered into by those closest to the company (which are often reported on by the

---

[105] FESCO, Market Abuse, *FESCO's Response to the Call for Views from the Securities Regulators under the EU's Action Plan for Financial Services*, COM(1999)232 (2000), FESCO/00-0961 (the FESCO Market Abuse Report) 5.

[106] In the USA, prior to the development of the sophisticated case law on insider dealing based on Rule 10b-5, the control of insider dealing was to a large extent dependent on s 16 of the Securities Exchange Act, 1934. S 16(a) requires company directors, officers, and 10% equity security-holders to report on a monthly basis on changes to their shareholdings. In the UK, initial attempts to deal with insider dealing focused on disclosure by directors of their shareholdings. See Hannigan, n 1 above, 14 and Davies, n 6 above, 94–5 on the Cohen Committee's deliberations. The current UK insider-dealing regime is supplemented by ss 324–328 of the Companies Act 1985 which imposes an obligation on directors to report to the company on any dealings by them (and their spouse and children) in the company's shares and debentures (s 324) and an obligation on the company to disclose this information to the market-place (by keeping a register of directors' interests under s 325 and, under s 329, by notifying any exchange on which the company's shares or debentures are listed of any disclosure made by a director). Substantial shareholders are covered separately by ss 198–200 of the Companies Act 1985.

[107] For the view that a person who is prepared to abuse inside information is unlikely to be deterred by or comply with reporting obligations, particularly given the infrequency of actions being taken against breaches (in the UK) see Rider *et al.*, n 6 above, 217.

financial press) are relied on by investors, not simply as a means of check-ing for insider dealing, but also as an indication of a company's prospects and of management's faith in the company.[108]

Notwithstanding the IDD's recognition of the link between disclosure and the deterrence of insider dealing (implicit in the Article 7 ongoing material-disclosure obligation), the EC securities-regulation regime does not contain many specific reporting or disclosure obligations of this kind. By referring to reporting obligations only in the context of the transfer of holdings confer-ring control, the 1977 Code of Conduct foreshadowed the EC's approach to reporting obligations.[109] So far, the focus has been less on the deterrence of insider dealing by company insiders and more on ensuring that full disclo-sure is made of those in control of a company. While the (now consolidated) Substantial Shareholdings Directive imposes a notification obligation on all persons who enter into transactions to acquire or dispose of shareholdings which result in certain thresholds of company ownership being reached undershot, or exceeded by them, and so could draw attention to large trades in a company's shares, it is limited to shares and to large transactions by substantial shareholders and does not focus on the position of directors and officers of the company who may be engaging in smaller, illegal trades. In addition, even though the Substantial Shareholdings Directive has a certain symmetry with the Insider Dealing Directive, in that it takes as its general objective the 'increase of investors' confidence in securities markets and [ensuring] that securities markets function correctly', more specifically it is designed to ensure that 'investors [are] informed of major holdings and of changes in those holdings in Community companies the shares of which are officially listed on stock exchanges . . . within the Community' (recitals 2 and 3) (SCD, recitals 31, 33, and 34). Disclosure under the Substantial Shareholdings Directive is not, unlike disclosure under Article 7 of the IDD, primarily designed to protect the market against unfair access to informa-tion and inequality in dealings, but is rather directed to ensuring that dis-closure is made of certain legitimate trades in order that the price-formation process can accurately reflect the significance of dealings in and control over securities of the company in question.[110]

---

[108] Cox *et al.*, n 5, 813.

[109] Supplementary Principles 17 and 18 address transactions which result in the transfer of a holding conferring control.

[110] See Davies, n 6 above, 261. In its Explanatory Memorandum to the original proposal for the Substantial Shareholdings Directive, the Commission stated that the proposal would 'pro-vide investors with information on the persons liable to influence a company's management, sometimes to a considerable extent, and thus enable them to follow developments in its own-ership and gain a clearer idea of what is happening internally'. It also, however, referred to the importance of making such information public in order to 'prevent uncontrollable rumours and stop misuse of price-sensitive information': COM(85)791, 2.

Specific dealing restrictions on company insiders are another form of indirect control on insider dealing. These can range from complete prohibitions on certain types of transactions which may facilitate the use of inside information, such as dealing in options,[111] to more open-ended rules which are designed to give the company redress when profits are made within short periods of time (short-swing profits) by company insiders. The classic example of the latter is the US short-swing rule, which allows a company to recover any profits gained by a company insider (10 per cent equity security-holders, directors, and officers) from a short-swing transaction, which is defined as a purchase and sale or sale and purchase of a company security within a six-month period.[112] The company does not have to show an intent by the insider to gain from the transaction or insider dealing, although the rule is based on an underlying irrebuttable presumption that a short-swing transaction, due to its nature and timing, is based on inside information. Although the 1970 Draft European Company Statute included a short-swing profits rule,[113] it no longer appears in EC securities regulation. Given the reluctance of EC securities regulation (reflecting EC law generally) to engage with the appropriate remedies for breaches of securities regulation, and the market rather than company orientation of its approach to insider dealing, it is perhaps not surprising that the short-swing rule, which is, in essence, a company remedy against insider dealing, has not appeared since in the EC securities-regulation structure. Nonetheless, while its company focus does not fit easily within a market-based system, a short-swing rule would (assuming the willingness of a company to take action against its own members and management which cannot be guaranteed) due to its automatic application, go some way to dealing with the problem of enforcing insider-dealing prohibitions through public-law sanctions and penalties[114] and so contribute to the underlying objective of investor confidence.[115]

---

[111] In the UK, eg, ss 323 and 327 of the Companies Act 1985 prohibit directors (and their spouses and children) from dealing in options in shares or debentures.

[112] Securities Exchange Act, 1934 s 16(b).   [113] See sect. 3.1 above.

[114] See Fox, M, 'Insider Trading Deterrence Versus Managerial Incentives: A Unified Theory of Section 16(b)' (1994) 92 *Mich LR* 2088 who noted at 2092 that s 16(b) 'probably plays a larger day to day role in constraining the behavior of America's corporate executives than rule 10b-5's headline-grabbing, judge-made strictures against insider trading'. It has also been observed that while 's16(b) will impose a form of strict liability on those statutory insiders who buy and sell (or sell and buy) any equity security within any period of less than six months [and] is vulnerable to criticism that it can impose liability upon entirely innocent persons . . . the provision's very simplicity . . . has undoubtedly had a substantial deterrent effect': Jennings *et al.*, n 4 above, 1203.

[115] Blunt short-swing rules are becoming increasingly controversial, however, given the role played by management share ownership in giving incentives to management and aligning shareholder and management interests. See Fox, n 114 above.

XIII.6 INSIDER DEALING: THE EC TAKEOVERS REGIME

The price-sensitivity of takeover information has made takeovers a fertile source of insider dealing.[116] Those in possession of price-sensitive information concerning takeovers are subject to the general prohibitions of the IDD (which do not deal specifically with takeovers)[117] and those contemplating a takeover or change of control are subject to the reporting requirements of the Substantial Shareholdings Directive. The failed proposed Takeover Directive's reporting requirements, which are likely to re-appear in any attempt to revive the proposal, would also have had implications for the control of insider dealing. In particular, in order to reduce the scope for insider dealing Article 6(1) of the proposal required offerors to announce their decision to launch a bid as soon as possible and to inform the supervisory authority in question of the bid.

XIII.7 MARKET ABUSE: THE RATIONALE FOR REGULATION

While the EC has taken steps to address the problem of insider dealing, there remains a wide spectrum of egregious behaviour in the trading markets outside the scope of the insider-dealing formula, ranging from the misuse of information to manipulative trading practices, which has a detrimental effect on the integrity of the market-place, its smooth operation and investor confidence in it.

The rationale for regulating against market abuse[118] is, as it is with insider dealing, generally connected to investor confidence in the price-formation process.[119] Where the abusive behaviour results in a misleading impression being given to the market-place and to investors of the demand for and liquidity in a particular security or results in the dissemination of

---

[116] Hannigan, n 1 above, 17–19. Takeovers have been characterized as 'the locus classicus of insider trading in the UK and, indeed, other jurisdictions, notably those in North America': Davies in Hopt and Wymeersch, n 6 above, 243. On the control by the EC of insider dealing in takeovers situations see Wymeersch, n 48 above, 80–2 and Davies, above.

[117] With the exception of recital 11 which protects the bidder. See sect. 4.4.1 above.

[118] See generally Avougleas, E, 'Financial Market Regulation and the New Market Landscape: In Search of a New Regulatory Landscape for Market Abuse' (2000) 2 *ICCLJ* 89 and Rider *et al.*, n 6 above, 243–5.

[119] Nonetheless, the potential for economy-wide consequences from market manipulation was given graphic statutory form in s 2(4) of the US Securities Exchange Act, 1934. Drafted in the aftermath of the 1929 stock market crash, it provides that '[n]ational emergencies, which produce widespread unemployment and the dislocation of trade, transportation and industry and which burden interstate commerce and adversely affect the general welfare, are precipitated, intensified and prolonged by manipulation and sudden and unreasonable fluctuations of securities prices on . . . exchanges and markets'.

misleading or untrue information about the security or its issuer, the price-formation mechanism is distorted.[120] More generally, market-abuse controls seek to enhance investor confidence in the fairness, honesty, and integrity of the market-place and in its freedom from fraudulent practices.[121] Market-abuse controls are, accordingly, concerned with investors as a group and with market abuse as misconduct affecting the market as a whole. From the economist's market perspective, manipulative practices are a form of market failure which ultimately lead to an inefficient allocation of resources and damage the role of the market-place in capital allocation. Manipulative practices distort the choices made by investors on the basis of a manipulated price formation mechanism or in reliance on fraudulent practices and, ultimately, discourage investors from accessing the market-place.[122]

XIII.8 MARKET ABUSE: SCOPE

XIII.8.1 *The Range of Abusive Practices*

Market-abuse controls typically address the misuse of material information (and so supplement or include insider-dealing rules), the dissemination of false or misleading information, and practices which distort the trading price or trading volume of a security.[123] One of the difficulties inherent in tackling market abuse effectively is that it can range from relatively straightforward instances of fraudulent misrepresentation to highly complex and difficult to detect trading practices designed artificially to increase or decrease a security's trading volumes and/or distort its price or to interfere with market forces of supply and demand. Market-abuse practices are also continually evolving as new products are developed, new participants enter

---

[120] IOSCO has explained the rationale for controlling market manipulation in the following terms: '[a]nti-manipulation regulation focuses on maintaining the integrity of the market price of securities, of derivatives contracts and of the assets underlying such contracts. The rules attempt to ensure that a price is set by the unimpeded collective judgment of buyers and sellers': IOSCO Technical Committee, *Investigating and Prosecuting Market Manipulation* (2000) (the IOSCO Market Manipulation Paper) 8.

[121] The FESCO Market Abuse Report, n 105 above, 2, takes as its premise that '[m]arket integrity is a must to maintain investor confidence in the financial system and to promote the competitiveness of financial markets'. Investor confidence in the honesty of the market-place and in its being a 'clean place to do business' is the rationale underlying the FSA's approach to market abuse (a general prohibition on market abuse is contained in s 118 of the Financial Services and Markets Act 2000 (the FSMA)): Draft Market Abuse Code Paper, n 64 above, 3.

[122] Page, A, and Ferguson, R, *Investor Protection* (1992) 35. The link between the efficiency of the market's role in allocating resources and market abuse is also noted in the Draft Market Abuse Code Paper, which describes abusive conduct as that which impedes 'the proper operation of market forces and the interplay of supply and demand': n 64 above, 4.

[123] For this three-pronged classification see the FSMA, s 118. FESCO has adopted a similar classification: FESCO Market Abuse Report, n 105 above, 6.

the market-place, and, as markets become ever more interconnected, the opportunities for cross-border manipulation increase.

XIII.8.2 *Abusive Disclosure Practices*

Misuse of information (including misuse which meets or falls short of the technical elements of insider dealing) can affect confidence, as can misrepresentations and false statements concerning securities and issuers by market participants made in order to give a misleading impression. The latter can include the intentional spreading of untrue rumours concerning securities or their issuer in order to depress the market price and so enable the market abuser to buy the securities at an artificially low price.[124] Controlling the spread of manipulative false or misleading information through the Internet represents a significant challenge for regulators due to the ease and speed with which false information can be spread among a vast number of potential investors.[125]

XIII.8.3 *Market and Price Manipulation*

XIII.8.3.1 *Type of Conduct Prohibited*

Market- and price-manipulation is a particularly complex activity and encompasses a vast range of abusive conduct.[126] While difficult to define conceptually, it is often regarded as broadly covering two overlapping activities, both of which are designed to generate a gain for the perpetrator: conduct which creates an artificial and misleading impression about the real market in or price or value of a security;[127] and conduct which, by interfering with the usual forces of supply and demand, distorts the market.

---

[124] The spreading of false rumours is not a new practice. In an early and celebrated example, a purchaser of government bonds during the Napoleonic wars spread rumours that Napoleon was dead and that peace would be declared following which the bonds' value escalated and the purchaser made a huge profit: Wood, n 63 above.

[125] The dissemination of false information through Internet bulletin boards and chat rooms is increasingly coming to the attention of regulators. The SEC has recently engaged in a series of high-profile internet fraud 'sweeps' and brought fraud and manipulation actions against a range of activities designed to raise funds and boost the value of certain securities by making inflated performance claims and (in the case of private companies) false promises about initial public offerings, conducted via e-mail, electronic newsletters, websites, and electronic bulletin boards: SEC Press Release of 3 Mar 2001, 2001–34.

[126] Not all commentators are convinced of the need for controls on market manipulation. See Fischel, D, and Ross, D, 'Should the Law Prohibit "Manipulation" in Financial Markets' 105 (1991) *Harv. LR* 503 (1991) who have queried the extent to which successful manipulation is possible.

[127] Fischer and Ross take issue with manipulation controls based on price-distorting effects, given the difficulties in establishing the correct level at which a security should be trading: ibid, 509.

Price manipulation typically involves engaging in trades or a series of trades in order to create a false impression of a liquid market in particular securities or in order to maintain or position prices at an artificial level. These practices can include 'wash trades', where the beneficial interest in the security is not transferred (in that the same trader is both buyer and seller), and 'matched orders', where transactions involving buy and sell orders at the same price and quantity are entered into at the same time by different parties acting in concert. Where wash trades and matched orders are systematically undertaken at continually increasing prices, they can artificially raise a security's price. As portfolio managers, particularly collective-investment-scheme managers, engage in large trades, they can be in a position artificially to distort prices.[128] Speculative investors, in particular, are vulnerable to price manipulation and may sustain severe losses when the manipulating traders offload their securities when a particular price level is reached.

Practices which manipulate the market and the forces of supply and demand more generally include so-called 'abusive squeezes'. In an abusive squeeze, a person who exercises significant influence over the supply of a security enters into transactions under which he has the right to require others to deliver that security to him or to take delivery of it from him, and uses those deals to distort the market by setting abnormal prices for the discharge of the obligations owed to him. More generally, the market can be distorted by a trader taking advantage of a shortage in a security by controlling supply and exploiting congestion in the market-place in such a way as to create artificial prices.[129]

XIII.8.3.2 *Targeting Abusive Trading Practice*

Setting the regulatory parameters on when the market is manipulated, such that a misleading impression is given of trading conditions and of prices, is fraught with difficulties. Establishing indicators of when a security price is artificial, as evidence of manipulative conduct, represents a significant challenge for regulators.[130] Assessing whether the forces of supply and demand

---

[128] Legitimate investment strategies by professional investors can, due to the size of the trades undertaken, also lead to price manipulation concerns. See Avougleas, n 118 above, 108–10. Investment strategies which may be legitimate but which, due to their scale effects, can have a disproportionate and destabilizing impact on prices (and which were the subject of some concern following the Oct 1987 stock market crash) are discussed in the context of maintaining systemic stability in the OECD's report on *Systemic Risks in Securities Markets* (1991) at 22–4.

[129] IOSCO Market Manipulation Paper, n 120 above, 6.

[130] IOSCO has suggested that in examining whether an unusual price movement is manipulative, consideration be given to: all publicly available information; patterns of trading in similar securities; the performance of the market as a whole (whether it was a bear, bull, or flat market), and how the security performed in relation to the market; whether prior to the

have been distorted is equally complex, particularly when it comes to establishing whether the manipulator had control over the supply of the security in question. Establishing the range of persons liable to market-abuse controls can also be difficult. Where an order or a series of orders is given to a broker, it is clear that liability still remains with the party placing the orders and initiating the abusive transaction. Where the broker is aware, however, that the investor is engaging in market abuse, it may be appropriate to impose liability on the broker also. The freedom of action of intermediaries may be compromised, however, where overly onerous conditions are imposed on them with respect to monitoring investors' orders. Further, a number of trading practices which have the purpose of maintaining prices at an artificial level are legitimate. Stabilization involves trading in securities by the lead managers of a primary distribution of securities for a limited period of time after the offering in order to support the price against excessive volatility (which may arise under the initial pressure of early sell orders). It is designed to ensure that the price reflects the security's real, as opposed to speculative, value. *Prima facie*, it can be regarded as an artificial manipulation of the market price. It is usually permitted, however, albeit subject to strict controls which are designed to minimize the risk that it maintains prices at an artificial level for too long and to avoid the potential for insider dealing. These usually involve time and price controls and disclosure obligations. This dispensation is based on stabilization's contribution to the development of a stable market in the securities in question and to increasing investor confidence in new issues of securities. Market making, arbitrage activities, and hedging practices are other legitimate activities which enhance the efficiency of the market-place but may be vulnerable to a catch-all market-abuse prohibition as may be legitimate, large price-moving trades. Transparency rules play an important part in protecting legitimate conduct, as does the extent to which the conduct in question is designed to help maintain an orderly market. If the market is aware of the artificial activity engaged in by the trader, then it is not misled.

XIII.9 MARKET ABUSE: THE ENFORCEMENT PROBLEM

As with the control of insider dealing, the enforcement of market-abuse prohibitions can be problematic. If market abuse is criminalized, its enforcement becomes subject to the evidentiary and procedural hurdles of the criminal

---

manipulation the security was thinly traded; and the volatility of the security. 'The key question is whether there appears to be any logical trading patterns to the security's price and volume, or whether it seems erratic. If it is erratic, the question is whether the pattern coincides with the activities of the promoter, broker, or other participant in the potential manipulation': ibid, 13.

law. The bluntness of the criminal law renders it a cumbersome instrument for addressing the many and ever-changing ways in which market participants can engage in market abuse and for responding to technological developments which can change the nature of market abuse.

The detection of market abuse and its control is heavily dependent on action by market authorities, in particular with respect to the use of trading-surveillance programmes directed towards picking up unusual and possibly manipulative trading activity. The need for co-operation between regulatory authorities, anti-fraud agencies (where relevant), markets, and market supervisors accordingly arises.[131] Effective control of market manipulation also requires a number of mechanisms in addition to regulatory prohibitions including: the imposition of reporting requirements on traders; position limits on derivatives which reduce the possibility of unusually large exposures; and the use of trading suspensions as 'circuit-breakers' when necessary to blunt the impact of unusual market volatility.

The complexity of the supervision and enforcement process and the importance of information means that particular problems arise where the abusive activity takes place across a number of trading markets and jurisdictions unless competent authorities work in close co-operation. Derivatives raise particular problems in this regard. Where the underlying interest is trading in a different jurisdiction from the one in which the derivative interest is trading there is an increased likelihood of manipulation.[132] Supervisory authorities may not be able to monitor trading activities which are carried out from a different jurisdiction but which impact on the underlying securities and the market-place over which the authority exercises jurisdiction. Similarly, the supervisory authority responsible for the market on which the derivative interest is traded may not be aware of or have access to trading information concerning the manipulation of the underlying interest which impacts on the derivative.[133]

XIII.10 MARKET ABUSE:
SCOPE AND FEATURES OF THE EC MARKET-ABUSE REGIME

These features of market abuse and its regulation appear in the EC context, although the difficulties which arise in controlling market abuse are height-

---

[131] Davies, H, 'Financial Regulation and the Law' (1999) 3 *CfiLR* 1, 9–10.

[132] IOSCO pointed to the example of derivatives traded in one country and based on a foreign securities index and the possibility of manipulation of the foreign securities of which the index is composed via trading in the derivatives: IOSCO Market Manipulation Paper, n 120 above, 3.

[133] A number of international exchanges already share product- and trading-surveillance information under the Intermarket Surveillance Group.

ened in the complex cross-border trading environment of the integrated market-place.

The link between market abuse controls, the integrity of the market-place, and the protection of investor confidence fits naturally with the dominant underlying rationales of EC securities regulation: market construction and the protection of investor confidence and the functioning of the market-place on a macro basis. The fundamental problems of scope and enforcement are exacerbated, however, in the context of an integrated market-place. Cross-border co-operation, which may involve co-operation not just between two competent authorities in different Member States but a number of co-operation links between the various authorities responsible for the control of market abuse in each Member State, must surmount the basic problems raised by the enforcement of market-abuse controls as well as the additional problems created by cross-border trading. Clear common rules on what conduct amounts to market abuse, which aid the development of a co-ordinated response and enhance co-operation, and effective enforcement procedures, which provide an adequate level of regulation for the integrated market, must also provide a sufficient degree of flexibility so that regulation can respond to new developments. In addition to dealing with the basic difficulties involved in setting the parameters of market abuse, an appropriate EC response should also reflect the different market practices and regulatory cultures in the various Member States.

The current EC market-abuse regime is perhaps best described as interstitial. Apart from a few unconnected provisions scattered throughout the regime, EC securities regulation has yet to deal systematically with the control of market abuse and market manipulation which does not come within the IDD's definition of insider dealing, although a new market-abuse regime is in the offing, with the Commission presenting a proposal for a directive on insider dealing and market manipulation in May 2001 (section 11.5 below). Construction of the integrated market has, as a result, been undertaken in the absence of a coherent and rigorous approach to the control of abusive and manipulative disclosure, trading, and investment-services practices which could distort and damage the market-place. This is despite the fact that the risk of the occurrence of market abuse and the difficulties in controlling it are increased by the very construction of the integrated market (see section 11.1 below). As is clear from the limited treatment of securities-trading markets in the ISD at present, the EC securities-regulation regime has not engaged with the trading mechanics and practices which support and power the market-place. Neither has it dealt with the pathology of trading except to impose generic insider-dealing controls.

With respect to the regulation by the EC of the conduct of investment firms, while the ISD refers to the need to 'protect investors and the stability of the financial system' (recital 2) the substantive re-regulation it introduces to facilitate the ISD passport is directed towards institutional and market-wide prudential stability. Prohibitions on market abuse and manipulation are not covered, apart from the extent to which such prohibitions can be required by Article 11 of the ISD. Principle 1, which requires investment firms to act 'honestly and fairly in conducting its business activities in the best interests of . . . the integrity of the market', and Principle 2, which requires firms to act 'with due skill, care and diligence, in the best interests of . . . the integrity of the market', appear to require Member States to tackle market abuse by investment firms. Article 10 also has implications for the control of market abuse, in that the prudential rules which it requires Member States to impose on home-authorized investment firms include record-keeping requirements (albeit linked to compliance with prudential rules) and an obligation to maintain adequate internal-control mechanisms. While the ISD does address the regulation of regulated markets, albeit in a limited manner, it is largely concerned with ensuring market transparency.[134] Transparency is connected with market integrity and has an important bearing on the price-formation process by feeding through trading information to the market-place in a timely manner. While it may ultimately reveal market manipulation, it does not, however, prohibit or control market abuse *per se*.[135] More generally, Article 20 of the ISD provides that the home Member State must require that its investment firms provide it with certain specified information with respect to securities transactions, whether carried out on or off a regulated market-place. This information on the names and number of the instruments bought and sold, the dates and times of the transactions, the prices, and the means of identifying the investment firm concerned is important in tracking insider dealing and market abuse.[136]

The disclosure regime set out in the securities directives (and in Article 7 of the IDD) contributes to the integrity of the market-place and the price-formation process by ensuring a steady flow of information from the issuer of securities to the market-place which includes financial statements, interim reports, disclosure of substantial shareholdings and material information (see Chapter IV above). Only the (now consolidated) Admission Directive, which is limited to securities admitted to official listing, deals with market abuse, if only tangentially. Article 14(1) provides that the competent authorities responsible for admitting a security to the official list 'may decide to suspend the listing of a security where the smooth operation of the market is, or may be, temporarily jeopardized or where protection of investors

---

[134] See Ch. XI sect. 6.6.2 above.

[135] 'Disclosure and transparency requirements focus on generating and maintaining [the] integrity of the price formation process, and manipulation prohibitions focus on preventing harm to that integrity': IOSCO Market Manipulation Paper, n 120 above, 8.

[136] On Art. 20 of the ISD see Ch. XI sect. 6.6.1 above.

so requires' (SCD, Article 18(2)). Under Article 14(2) (SCD, Article 18(2)), competent authorities may proceed to delist a security 'where they are satisfied that, owing to special circumstances, normal regular dealings in a security are no longer possible'. The competent authorities required to be set up under the Admission Directive are more concerned with admission to listing, however, than with regulating trading practices and their powers are linked to the admission of securities to official listing on a stock exchange (Article 9(1) and (2)) (SCD, Articles 11(1) and 105) and thus to the relationship between the issuer and the market, rather than that between market participants and the trading market.

The failed proposed Takeover Directive contained provisions designed to control market abuse in the often febrile atmosphere of a takeover battle. Principle 3(1)(d) provided that 'false markets' were not be created in the securities of the offeree company, the offeror company, or any other company concerned by the bid. Notably, given the difficulties in this area, the principle attempted to define a false market by referring to an artificial rise or fall in the price of securities and disruption in the normal functioning of the market. Article 8(1) required Member States to ensure that rules were in force which required a bid to be made public in such a way as to ensure market transparency and integrity for the securities of the offeree company, of the offeror, or of any other company affected by the bid. In particular, the publication or dissemination of false or misleading information was to be avoided.

Paradoxically, the most extensive coverage at EC level of market abuse and market manipulation is still to be found, twenty-four years later, in the largely symbolic 1977 Code of Conduct; until further harmonization is undertaken it provides the most comprehensive EC treatment of market abuse. Market abuse and market manipulation were natural targets for a measure which acknowledges the link between 'the proper working' of securities markets and market integration and which is designed to 'establish standards of ethical behaviour on a Community-wide basis, so as to promote the effective functioning of securities markets (i.e. by creating the best possible conditions for matching supply and demand for capital), and to safeguard the public interest'.[137] As noted in section 3.2 above, the Code extends beyond trading on official stock exchanges and applies to all 'securities markets', defined as 'the official stock exchange and all the markets organized by or under the supervision of the competent authorities and also all transactions in transferable securities . . . including privately negotiated dealings between individuals in transferable securities'. General Principle 5, which imposes a general obligation on 'persons dealing regularly on the

---

[137] 1977 Code of Conduct, n 21 above. Explanatory Memorandum para 1, and Fundamental Objective, para 2, respectively.

securities markets' to act fairly in accordance with Code's objectives, is supplemented by a number of trading rules set out in the Supplementary Principles which further illustrate the fair-dealing principle. Supplementary Principle 1 reiterates the fair-dealing requirement but links it to investor confidence, providing that all persons dealing regularly on the securities markets have a duty to promote investors' confidence in market fairness 'by observance of the best standards of commercial probity and professional conduct'. Supplementary Principle 2 specifically addresses market manipulation and provides that financial intermediaries (defined as 'all persons professionally concerned in transactions in transferable securities') 'should not engage in manipulation which could distort the normal operation of the marketplace'. More generally, Supplementary Principle 3 prohibits all persons from inciting another, whether a professional trader or not, to breach the law or the principles of good conduct which apply to the securities markets and from pressurizing others to carry out irregular or dishonest transactions. The core market-abuse principle is arguably Supplementary Principle 7 which addresses price manipulation in some detail. It provides that '[a]ny attempt or manipulation by persons acting separately or in concert with others, which aims or results in the rise or fall in the price of securities by fraudulent means, is contrary to the fundamental objective of this code'. The spreading of rumours and false information (described as the publication or diffusion of information which is false, exaggerated, or tendentious) is explicitly included in price manipulation, as are any 'other devices aimed at disrupting the markets' normal operation'. Financial intermediaries and the management of companies whose securities are dealt in on the securities market who become aware of any manipulation are charged with taking 'the necessary steps to thwart it' and of informing the relevant competent authorities and the company concerned without delay.

XIII.11 MARKET ABUSE: MOVES TOWARDS A NEW EC REGIME

XIII.11.1 *The Need for Action*

The extent to which investor confidence in the integrated market as an honest and fair place in which to do business is buttressed by effective market-abuse controls is becoming an ever more pressing question as the structure of trading markets continues to evolve rapidly. A common approach to the control and enforcement of market abuse is increasingly seen as necessary, given the extent to which national trading markets are integrating and trading is taking place on an EC-wide basis. Securities-trading markets are integrating through alliances and mergers and moving towards common trading platforms, remote exchange membership and cross-border trading are increasing, as are the numbers of market participants and the variety of investment products,[138] new trading markets and systems are competing with traditional exchanges for businesses, and online trades are on the increase. Alternative trading systems (ATSs) pose a particular challenge to the control of market abuse across the EC. Competition between traditional securities-trading markets and between those markets and ATSs has the effect of fragmenting, to a greater extent than previously, the market in particular instruments. This fragmentation places demands on supervision and on the control of market manipulation.[139] Trading activity on one market-place can also impact on another market-place as securities are traded in more than one market-place.[140]

In this cross-border trading environment, the integrity of the integrating and evolving EC securities market demands a co-ordinated approach to market abuse which harmonizes the basic components of market abuse, the principles of its regulation, and the treatment of violations. Wide variations exist across the Member States, however, with respect to the definition of market abuse and the types of sanctions imposed.[141] Considerable divergences exist between Member States and markets with respect to stabilization,[142] which could have markedly beneficial results for the integrated market as a whole,[143] and the treatment of large market-moving trades. Not

---

[138] The development of new derivative products can increase the scope for the same manipulation to affect a number of markets: FESCO Market Abuse Report, n 105 above, 4.

[139] In its report on ATSs FESCO noted that the market fragmentation associated with ATSs, greater competition between traditional securities-trading markets, and the development of pan-European trading carried the risk of 'the ability to monitor overall trading in the market for an investment instrument being impaired, with implications for effective deterrence and policing of market abuse': FESCO, *The Regulation of Alternative Trading Systems in Europe. A Paper for the EU Commission* (2000), Fesco/00-064c, 15.

[140] It has been noted that 'large trades, which have . . . been effected on the market of a Member State, where such trades are less strictly regulated, may have an appreciable effect on the price of the same security also listed on the market of another Member State': Avgouleas, n 118 above, 81.

[141] It has been observed that '[t]he current approaches in Member States are very diverse with different systems and different powers existing across the EEA. Criteria vary among jurisdictions regarding concepts used to define infringements and to impose sanctions, as well as the persons subject to the Market Abuse regime. The range of criminal sanctions varies and many jurisdictions have few administrative sanctions available in this area, except with regard to regulated entities': FESCO Market Abuse Report, n 105 above, 3.

[142] FESCO has been active in this area and has, as 'it is necessary to align stabilisation rules to make sure that all parties involved are covered by similar safe harbour rules' produced suggested common standards for regulating stabilization (and allotment) practices: FESCO, *Stabilisation and Allotment, A European Supervisory Approach*, Consultative Paper (2000), Fesco/00-099b (FESCO Stabilisation Paper). The non-binding standards are designed to ensure that a European entity engaging in stabilization can do so according to its home rules even where the stabilization occurs in another FESCO member State and to provide for a safe harbour from charges of market abuse (as defined in the FESCO Market Abuse Report, n 105 above).

[143] FESCO has described the benefits of stabilization as considerable, pointing out that 'new, particularly small and medium sized companies are encouraged to access the capital market,

only does the lack of a uniform approach towards determining which trading strategies are legitimate and which amount to manipulation hinder the development of pan-European markets, confidence in the integrity of the integrated market-place as a whole may be threatened if market-abuse rules were ever to become an instrument of competition. Indeed, from the market-failure perspective, the external effects of market abuse across the market-place support the argument for harmonization.[144] Effective enforcement of market-abuse controls in a cross-border trading environment requires the establishment of a network of competent authorities with clearly defined powers to control market abuse and effective co-operation between and surveillance by market authorities across the EC. A common understanding of what conduct amounts to manipulation enhances supervision and enforcement, as competent authorities have a clearer understanding of what trading and other information is significant and should be requested from or given to other Member States' authorities in order to facilitate enforcement.

XIII.11.2 *The FSAP*

The 1999 Financial Services Action Plan (FSAP) contains a commitment to the adoption of a directive designed to address market manipulation and enhance market integrity 'by reducing the possibility for institutional investors and intermediaries to rig markets'. It should also establish 'common disciplines for trading floors in order to enhance investor confidence in an embryonic single securities market'.[145] The familiar macro themes of the smooth functioning of the market and investor confidence, linked together by their impact on market integration, were thus highlighted from the outset as key influences on the new regime.

---

established issuers will be more comfortable raising funds from the securities markets through capital increases. Investors will feel more confident making an investment, where there is an expectation, that at least for a limited period of time, an orderly market will be actively encouraged . . . Eventually Stabilisation may also contribute to lower cost of funding': ibid, 8.

[144] See generally Avgouleas, n 118 above, who has argued, in the context of self-regulation by exchanges of market-abuse rules, that, disclosure-based rules apart, competitive exchange regulation of price manipulation would achieve sub-optimal results. The dangers of regulatory competition between trading-market regimes was also adverted to in the Commission's Communication on Upgrading the Investment Services Directive 93/22/EEC, COM(2000)729 (the ISD Communication), 15. The question of self-regulation by exchanges is briefly considered in Ch. II sect. 7.3 above.

[145] Communication from the Commission, Implementing the Framework for Financial Markets: Action Plan, COM(1999)232 (the FSAP), 18. The proposed directive comes under Strategic Objective 1—A Single Wholesale Market, and, specifically, within the group of measures designed to establish a common framework for integrated securities and derivatives markets.

XIII.11.3 *The Lamfalussy Report*

Support for clear EC-wide regulation of market abuse was provided by the Lamfalussy Report which highlighted the absence of regulation in this area as one of the factors hindering the development of the integrated securities market.[146] More significantly perhaps, the Lamfalussy Report's recommendation for a new law making model based on the adoption of high-level principles (level 1 measures) according to the standard Treaty law-making procedures and the adoption of technical implementing measures (level 2 measures) by means of comitology procedures involving law-making by the Commission supervised by a European Securities Committee and aided by a Committee of European Securities Regulators (CESR), has significant implications for the structure of the next generation of securities-regulation measures.[147] Indeed, one of the striking features of the proposed market-abuse regime is that, although work on the new regime predates the Lamfalussy Report, together with the proposed new disclosure regime, it provides the first example of a measure prepared in accordance with the level 1/level 2 formula. The new CESR is also likely to have a significant impact on convergence in regulatory and enforcement practices.

XIII.11.4 *FESCO and the Emergence of a Market-abuse Regime*

FESCO (now the CESR) has exerted considerable influence on the development of the proposed market-abuse regime. Its 1999 Multilateral MoU already deals with co-operation between FESCO member States with respect to the investigation and enforcement of market manipulation and other fraudulent or manipulative practices in the securities field. It has been engaging in a market-abuse project, the main purpose of which is to develop common standards in respect of insider dealing, market manipulation, and the dissemination of false and misleading information. Most significantly, its 2000 Report on Market Abuse[148] contained a number of proposals recommended for adoption by the Commission when formulating the proposed market-manipulation regime.

FESCO's central recommendation was that a common approach was necessary, given the disparities between national regimes and the development of a competitive, cross-border trading environment,[149] and that a directive 'should define market abuse and establish a common legal framework to seek to prevent, detect, investigate and sanction market manipulation and the dissemination of false misleading information'.[150] Its rationale for the

---

[146] Final Report of the Committee of Wise Men on the Regulation of European Securities Market, Feb 2001 (the Lamfalussy Report), 10 and 12.

[147] The Lamfalussy law-making model is examined in Ch. XV sect. 2.5.3 below.

[148] N 105 above.   [149] Ibid, 4.   [150] Ibid.

control of market abuse was linked to investor confidence: '[e]nhancing
investors' confidence in the integrity of the financial system is essential to
support the development of efficient and competitive financial markets in
Europe. Market Abuse undermines that confidence and prejudices the
smooth operation of the market. Investors will avoid trading in such markets and the cost of capital for European companies will rise.'[151]

In order to ensure sufficient flexibility for market regulators to respond
effectively to the rapidly evolving trading environment, the Report proposed
that a general definition of market abuse be adopted and that the detailed
rules necessary to control market abuse be agreed by consultation between
national competent authorities. FESCO's approach was thus heavily dependent on co-operation between competent authorities. The market-abuse
definition had three elements: the misuse of material information; the dissemination of false or misleading information; and behaviour which abnor-
mally or artificially affects, or is likely to affect, the formation of prices or
volumes of financial instruments. FESCO also recommended that any
definition of market abuse not require a manipulative intent on the part of
the abuser. The scope of the proposed market-abuse regime extended beyond
regulated markets (as defined in the ISD) to include all off-market transactions and all primary market activity in instruments which would be admitted to trading on a regulated market. The securities protected from market
abuse were widely defined as the instruments listed in the ISD together with
commodity derivatives. At the core of the FESCO recommendations was that
the proposed directive include preventative measures, to be enforced by the
competent authorities, which would prevent abuse from occurring. These
would include: requirements such as Chinese walls and internal codes of
conduct; specific requirements imposed on authorized market professionals
such as a general duty of care not to engage in transactions on behalf of
investors if the professional reasonably believes the transaction will amount
to market abuse and front-running rules on the conditions under which
research issued by the professional can be used; and specific requirements
imposed on issuers of listed instruments such as disclosure obligations.

The FESCO Report also set out a number of proposals on how effective
enforcement and co-operation between competent authorities might be
achieved. The key recommendation was that, in order to enhance competent authorities' ability to respond to changing market conditions and practices and to avoid inconsistent implementation of the regime's core
principles, Member States identify a single competent authority under a duty
to co-operate with its counterparts in other Member States in order to agree
on a harmonized market-abuse regime. Competent authorities were to have
the power to: detect and investigate breaches, and settle and impose admin-

---

[151] N 105 above 2.

istrative sanctions; issue implementing rules and guidance, including preventive measures; and issue technical rules and guidance which respond to
the particular features of the national market. They were also required to
co-operate with their counterparts to the extent necessary to achieve a uniform regime and in the enforcement of specific cases and to establish a formal co-operation network. Given the increase in the powers of competent
authorities envisaged by FESCO, it also recommended that they be subject to
accountability controls set out in the directive. In a significant extension of
the treatment of enforcement by the IDD, the Report also recommended that
competent authorities have specific detection powers (including the ability,
directly or indirectly, to monitor the price-formation process and the dissemination of information to the market) and powers of investigation
(including the ability to obtain records, interview persons, carry out inspections, search premises, and sequester funds). Finally, in another material
change from the IDD's approach, FESCO recommended that a consistent
approach be taken to the imposition of administrative sanctions,[152] that
harmonized sanctions, including fines and withdrawals of authorization, be
adopted, and, given the power of disclosure as deterrent, that the imposition
of sanctions be disclosed to the market-place.

In another illustration of the influence wielded by FESCO (which is being
channelled into the new CESR), the new regime closely tracks the FESCO
recommendations.

XIII.11.5 *The Proposed Market-abuse Regime*

XIII.11.5.1 *Objective, Main Features, and Treaty Basis*

At the end of May 2001 the Commission presented a proposal for a new
market-abuse regime.[153] While it introduces controls on market manipulation and represents a new departure for EC securities regulation in this
respect, it also restructures and consolidates the current regime by bringing
together the IDD regime (which (as recommended by FESCO) it at the same
time updates and enhances) and the new market-manipulation system
within a single market-abuse directive.[154] An integrated approach has been
adopted in order to reflect the basic premise that market abuse consists of
insider dealing and market manipulation, the control of both of which is
concerned with market integrity (recital 9). It also addresses concerns that
the IDD does not reflect changes in the market-place since its adoption. In

---

[152] 'In a single market, it cannot be acceptable for the same wrong to incur a heavy penalty
in one country, a light penalty in another country and no penalty in a third country': ibid, 15.
[153] Proposal for a Directive on insider dealing and market manipulation (market abuse) (the
Market Abuse Proposal or the Proposal), COM(2001)281 (including the Explanatory
Memorandum): [2001] OJ C240/265.
[154] The IDD will be repealed when the Proposal comes into force.

addition, given that any market-manipulation measure would contain higher standards than those in the IDD with respect to implementation and enforcement in light of market developments and the current push to complete the single market in securities, confusion and inconsistencies could arise and loopholes develop (which could undermine public confidence and prejudice the smooth functioning of the markets) were the two measures not integrated and a common framework not established for the allocation of responsibilities, enforcement, and co-operation (recital 10). The Proposal has four key elements. The first of these is the imposition of two core prohibitions: the prohibition of insider dealing and the prohibition of market manipulation, both of which are widely drawn. Secondly, the scope of the regime is set by broad definitions of the markets and securities covered. Thirdly, both prohibitions are subject to a common (and in the case of the IDD regime significantly upgraded) enforcement regime which includes provisions on administrative and criminal sanctions. Finally, the new Proposal introduces a supervisory co-operation system which again represents an advance on the IDD. A particular (and likely to be controversial) innovation is the introduction of operating controls on the dissemination of information by issuers and market professionals and on the acceptance of orders by the latter in order to enhance the effectiveness of the new market-abuse regime.

Like the proposal for a new issue-disclosure regime which was presented at the same time, the Proposal provides for the adoption of technical, implementing, level 2 measures via comitology procedures (Article 17) and so reflects the Lamfalussy decision-making model, albeit to a much lesser extent than the disclosure proposal, a feature which may result in it having an easier legislative passage than its sister measure.[155] As the regime is at the time of writing at the earliest stage of its legislative journey and given that it is likely to change as the legislative and lobbying process gets underway, it will be considered here in outline only.[156]

The Commission's Explanatory Memorandum makes explicit the rationale for market-abuse regulation in the EC context and links it squarely to eco-

---

[155] On the difficulties which the Lamfalussy model may create for the proposed disclosure regime see Ch. IV sect. 9.3 above.

[156] Market reaction thus far has not been entirely favourable. Concerns have been expressed that the new regime is too broadly based and extends over an overly wide range of markets and products and, more generally, that the market was not adequately consulted: 'Labouring with Lamfalussy', *The Economist*, 16 June 2001, 83, and Boland, V, 'Battle looms over Brussels plan for capital markets regulations', *Financial Times*, 11 June 2001. It appears that the Commission has acknowledged some inadequacies in the consultation process. It notes in the Explanatory Memorandum that in view of the need for urgent action in the market-abuse area and given that it had consulted with Member States' governments, regulators, and the financial industry, it decided to present the Proposal rather than to delay it by using more formal consultative procedures. While this does not augur well for the success of the Lamfalussy model which emphasizes transparency and consultation, the Commission has committed to engage in consultations as and when level 2 implementing measures are adopted: Explanatory Memorandum to the Proposal, n 153 above, para 1.

nomic growth (as does recital 2 of the Proposal). In one of its many recent reiterations of the importance of market-based finance, the Commission highlights the role played by markets in transferable securities in financing and the wider economy and, in particular, their role in guaranteeing or collateralizing bank loans[157] and in the financing of high-growth undertakings. It finds that the 'smooth functioning of financial markets and public confidence in them are prerequisites for sustained economic growth and wealth'.[158] Market abuse is declared to increase the cost of finance for companies, damage the integrity of the market-place and public confidence, and, ultimately, undermine economic growth and European economic policy. The new regime has, in consequence, a threefold aim: to ensure the integrity of European markets; to put in place common market-abuse standards; and, tracking the IDD's governing rationale, to enhance investor confidence.[159] The IDD's focus on the protection of the market-place is thus retained. The need for a new regime is justified by reference to the lack of a common approach to market manipulation which has resulted in a variety of approaches to market abuse (with certain Member States not addressing market manipulation), leading to confusion among market participants, competitive distortions, and obstructions to the development of a single market based on a level playing-field.[160] New products and technologies, cross-border trading, the Internet and other market developments are also highlighted as increasing the likelihood of manipulation. In light of these factors, the Commission finds that the protection of the integrated market-place demands a 'common legal framework . . . on the prevention, detection, investigation and punishment of market abuse'.[161]

Harmonization of market abuse must, of course, be accommodated within a Treaty competence. The new regime is based on Article 95 EC which provides for the adoption of measures 'for the approximation of the provisions laid down by law, regulation or administrative action in Member States which have as their object the establishment and functioning of the internal market'. Investor confidence and its impact on the smooth functioning of the market-place has been claimed as a competence by the Community legislature in other securities-regulation measures under Article 95, with respect to the construction of the internal market (the IDD) and, where free

---

[157] On the measures which are being taken to support cross-border collateralization given its importance in the supply of credit to undertakings and thus economic development, see Ch. XII sect. 5 above.

[158] Explanatory Memorandum to the Proposal, n 153 above, para 1.

[159] The investor-confidence argument appears to be based on the premise that market abuse distorts the principle that investors should be placed on an equal footing and disadvantages investors who may, as a result, leave the market-place: ibid, para 1(a). The equal-footing argument also underpins the IDD's basis in investor confidence. See sect. 4.1 above.

[160] Recital 8 and Explanatory Memorandum to the Proposal, n 153 above, para 1(b).

[161] Ibid.

movement is more directly concerned, under Article 47(2) EC (the Investor Compensation Schemes Directive).[162] The new regime follows the IDD model. Although a direct connection is not made between Article 95, the establishment/functioning of the internal market, and the objectives of the proposed directive, recital 2 reflects the smooth functioning of the market-place and investor-confidence-generating/internal-market-functioning role which has been claimed for Article 95, declaring that 'an integrated and efficient financial market requires market integrity. The smooth functioning of securities markets and public confidence in markets are prerequisites for economic growth and wealth. Market abuse harms the integrity of financial markets and public confidence in securities and derivatives' (recital 2). The need for a co-ordinated response to market abuse in the context of cross-border trading and in light of the diverging approaches across the Member States to its control should meet the *Tobacco Advertising*[163] ruling's require-ment that harmonization genuinely have as its object the improvement of the conditions for the establishment and functioning of the internal market. Although the new regime does not directly address the removal of obstacles to free movement or distortions to competition (although this role could be found where, for example, confusion exists about the scope of market abuse controls across the Community),[164] it is concerned with protecting the inte-grated market-place against new integration risks. Control of these risks should, it is suggested, given the particular investor-protection and market-integrity needs of the integrated investment-services and securities market-place, be accommodated within Article 95's 'functioning of the market-place' requirement (see also the discussion of the Supplementary Supervision proposal for financial conglomerates in Chapter VIII section 11.3.3 above). The requirements of the subsidiarity and proportionality prin-ciples must also be met, although the development of cross-border and pan-EC trading should support the need for EC-level action. In this regard, recital 21 notes that the prevention of market abuse in the form of insider dealing and market manipulation cannot be sufficiently achieved by the Member States and, by reason of the scale and effects of the measure, is better achieved by the Community. The level at which harmonization takes place also impacts on both of these principles. While market abuse involves a wide array of practices, a detailed definition of market abuse, for example, would, in all likelihood, fail to catch all practices and might fall foul of the sub-sidiarity principle which favours more open-textured harmonization.[165] The

---

[162] Directive 97/9/EC on investor-compensation schemes [1997] OJ L84/22.

[163] Case C-376/98 *Germany v Parliament and Council* [2000] ECR I-8419.

[164] The Explanatory Memorandum does note that differences in national market-abuse regimes can lead to competitive distortions and 'hinder the development of a single European financial market based on a level playing field': n 153 above, para 1(b).

[165] Protocol on the Application of the Principles of Subsidiarity and Proportionality annexed to the Amsterdam Treaty, paras 6 and 7.

new regime is, however, pitched at a minimum level (recital 21) as can be seen most clearly with the general definition of market manipulation (see section 11.5.4 below).

XIII.11.5.2 *Scope and Exemptions*

The scope of the new regime is considerably wider than that of the IDD and reflects the development of new products, particularly derivatives, and new trading venues. The Proposal applies to any financial instrument admitted, or going to be admitted, to trading on a regulated market, irrespective of whether the transaction itself actually takes place on that market (Article 9). Underlining the macro market focus and taking the reach of the regime beyond what may be regarded as the markets on which retail investors are most likely to be active, financial instruments are broadly defined by reference to the ISD's list of instruments with the additional inclusion of commodity derivatives; this definition also reflects the new, broader approach to the definition of a regulated market (Chapter XI section 9.7 above). This definition, like the key definitions of inside information, market manipulation, and regulated market, is to be revised by the Commission in accordance with level 2 comitology procedures in order to reflect technical market developments and to ensure uniform application across the Member States. The IDD's market focus can also be seen in the admitted-to-trading restriction, but this is now defined by reference to regulated markets which are defined in relation to the ISD in order to ensure consistency between the two directives and to avoid confusion. The new regime is not, however, limited to conduct which takes place on a regulated market. Given that the current restructuring of the securities-trading market environment is resulting in trades occurring away from regulated markets and on alternative trading systems (ATSs) in particular, its scope extends to systems such as unregulated markets, trading platforms, and price-information services, as well as to off-market transactions, where they are used to manipulate or engage in insider dealing with respect to an instrument admitted or going to be admitted to trading on a regulated market.[166] A more sophisticated approach to the protection of the market is thus evident.

Member States are to apply the new regime at least to actions undertaken within their territory whenever the financial instruments concerned are admitted or going to be admitted, to trading in a Member State (Article 10). The Explanatory Memorandum makes clear that Member States will be permitted to apply the new rules to actions where only certain elements are undertaken within their territories, as would be the case where prohibited actions were taken by remote members of a domestic exchange or where

---

[166] Explanatory Memorandum to the Proposal, n 153 above, para 2.

inside information was transmitted in a third country but impacted on financial instruments on a domestic regulated market.

As is the case with the IDD at present (Article 2(4)), the new regime will
not apply to transactions carried out in pursuit of monetary, exchange-rate,
or debt-management policies by a Member State, the European System of
Central Banks, and national central banks (Article 7). Unlike the IDD, however, the Proposal establishes a framework within which an exemption
regime for stabilization (and buy-back programmes)[167] can be addressed in
some detail. The exemption regime is based on the premise that while stabilization and buy-back activities can fulfil valuable economic functions,
they must be carried out in a transparent manner in order to avoid insider
dealing or misleading the market-place. Under Article 8, the prohibitions set
out in the new regime will not apply to trading in own shares in buy-back
programmes or to the stabilization of financial instruments, as long as the
trading is carried out under 'agreed conditions'. These conditions are to be
established by the Commission under level 2 comitology procedures.[168]

XIII.11.5.3 *Core Prohibition (1): Insider Dealing*

Articles 2–4 of the Proposal contain the prohibition on insider dealing. It
tracks the IDD regime for the most part. However, the definition of inside
information is revised to reflect the scope of the new regime; in particular,
the range of instruments subject to the prohibition is increased to include
money-market and foreign-exchange/interest-rate instruments and commodity derivatives. In addition, the qualification that primary insiders must 'act
with full knowledge of the facts' (IDD, Article 2(1)) is removed, given that
such insiders are, per the Commission, aware of the confidential nature of
the information which they have access to often on a daily basis. The restriction of the insider-dealing prohibition to transactions carried out through a
professional intermediary (IDD, Article 2(3)) is also removed, bringing direct
transactions between parties which are based on inside information within
the scope of the insider-dealing prohibition, as long as the instruments in
question are admitted, or going to be admitted, to trading on a regulated
market. The effect of this revision, together with the more sophisticated range
of instruments covered, suggests that while the market orientation of the IDD
has been retained, the new regime, tracking the proposed changes to the ISD
concept of a regulated market, takes an expansive view of the market which

---

[167] In a buy-back programme, shares are traded in order to strengthen an issuer's equity
capital.

[168] FESCO is again likely to have laid the foundations for these conditions with its
Stabilisation Paper, n 142 above, which, with respect to stabilization, is designed to establish
common standards so that investment firms can carry out stabilization activities on the basis
of one set of rules, regardless of the market on which the issue is stabilized.

is to be protected and, in particular, is designed to encompass the professional sector of the market-place as well as the segment which has most consequence for retail investors. The IDD's investor-confidence/equal-footing-based rationale for controlling insider dealing (section 4.1 above) is also retained, with the Explanatory Memorandum noting that market abuse, including insider dealing, can 'undermine the general principle that all investors must be placed on an equal footing' and that '[t]rades based on [inside] information lead to unjustified economic advantages to the expense of "outsiders"'. The new regime appears to link the 'equal footing' for all investors argument more tightly to equality of access to information, however, by setting out additional information-dissemination obligations in Article 6 and controlling selective disclosure to a greater extent and more explicitly than does the current IDD regime.

XIII.11.5.4 *Core Prohibition (2): Market Manipulation*

The new prohibition on market manipulation is contained in Article 5 which simply requires Member States to prohibit natural and legal persons from engaging in market manipulation. In defining this critical term, the Commission has opted for a general definition which is designed to be sufficiently flexible to adapt to market developments and contain new abusive practices as they emerge, but clear enough for market participants to be sure of the parameters of the prohibition and to tailor their conduct accordingly.[169] In line with the approach commonly taken, market manipulation has been defined in terms of trading practices (Article 1(2)(a)) and the dissemination of false or misleading information (Article 1(2)(b)). Under Article 1(2)(a) market manipulation covers '[t]ransactions or orders to trade, which give, or are likely to give, false or misleading signals as to the supply, demand or price of financial instruments, or which secure, by one or more persons acting in collaboration, the price of one or several financial instruments at an abnormal or artificial level, or which employ fictitious devices or any other form of deception or contrivance'. Clearly room for confusion exists here, notably with respect to what is meant by certain key phrases such as 'likely to give', 'misleading signals', and 'abnormal or artificial level'. As suggested by FESCO, the prohibition is characterized in terms of the nature of the orders or trading practices in question, and is not qualified by reference to the intention of the alleged manipulator. This omission of any references to intention is designed to ensure that the market-manipulation prohibition applies to behaviour and is not dependent on the intention or

---

[169] In this regard, it is designed to 'encourage and guide the responsible behaviour' of market participants rather than to set out detailed rules on what behaviour is not permitted: Explanatory Memorandum to the Proposal, n 153 above, para 2.

aim of the alleged manipulators.[170] The effectiveness of the prohibition and of enforcement should, as a result, be enhanced. Under Article 1(2)(b), manipulation via the abuse of information covers '[d]issemination of information through the media, including the Internet, or by any other means, which gives, or is likely to give, false or misleading signals as to the supply, demand or price of financial instruments, including the dissemination of rumours and false or misleading news'. In order to elaborate on this general catch-all definition, a non-exhaustive list of the typical methods used for market manipulation is annexed to the Proposal.[171] The Commission is to adopt amendments to these examples in accordance with comitology (level 2) procedures.

Member States are expressly permitted to adopt specific provisions for persons acting for journalistic purposes in the normal course of the exercise of their profession.

XIII.11.5.5 *Information Dissemination and Preventive Measures*

A striking feature of the Proposal is its emphasis on preventive measures and, in particular, its attempts to ensure in a proactive fashion that information is properly disseminated and the potential for abuse minimized via operational controls (Article 6). In this respect, it represents a step up from Article 7 of the IDD and tracks a key element of the FESCO Market Abuse Report. Article 6 does not, however, cover all the FESCO recommendations, particularly those specific to investment firms; Chinese wall rules and internal codes of conduct, for example, are not expressly mentioned. It is clear from the Annex, section B, examples, however, that front-running research or trading securities in advance of a trade recommendation amounts to market manipulation.

A general issuer disclosure obligation is imposed by Article 6(1) which requires Member States to ensure that issuers of financial instruments inform the public as soon as possible of inside information. More specifically, under Article 6(2) issuers must make complete and effective disclosure of information which is selectively disclosed to a third party in the normal exercise of his employment, profession, or duties; this must be done 'promptly'

---

[170] N 153 above, para 2.

[171] Section B of the Annex contains a number of examples of 4 categories of market manipulation. These are: (1) trade-based actions intended to create a false impression of activity (the examples include 'wash trades' and 'pumping and dumping' (where the price of an instrument is pushed to an artificially high level and the manipulator then sells its own instruments on a massive scale)); (2) trade-based actions intended to create a shortage (the examples include 'abusive squeezes'); (3) time-specific trade-based actions (the examples include trading at the close of the market in an attempt to alter the closing price and misleading those who act on closing prices); and (4) information-related actions (such as 'scalping' or buying instruments for one's own account before recommending it to others). The latter has significant implications for investment firms with respect to their proprietary trading business.

where the disclosure has not been intentional. The Article 6(2) requirement does not apply if the party receiving the information owes a duty of trust and confidence to the issuer or agrees to keep the information confidential or if the primary business of the entity which receives the information is the supply of mandatory credit ratings, as long as the information is solely for the purpose of developing a credit rating which will be publicly available.[172] Member States must also require that issuers establish a regularly updated list of those persons working for them who have access to inside information. Issuers may delay disclosure at their own risk so as not to prejudice their legitimate interests as long as the omission would not be likely to mislead the public and, significantly, the issuer is able to ensure the confidentiality of the information in question (Article 6(3)).[173] Underlying the issuer disclosure rules is the principle that prompt and fair disclosure to the public enhances market integrity and that selective disclosure can lead to a loss of investor confidence (recital 12).

These disclosure and operational controls extend beyond the issuer to market professionals[174] in two rules which are likely to prove controversial. First, Member States are to require that natural or legal persons responsible for producing or disseminating research or other relevant information to distribution channels or to the public take reasonable care to ensure that information is fairly presented and that they disclose their interests or indicate conflicts of interests in the financial instruments to which that information relates (Article 6(4)).[175] Secondly, those persons or entities which professionally arrange transactions in financial instruments are to refrain from entering into transactions and must reject orders on behalf of clients where they reasonably suspect that a transaction would be based on inside information or would constitute market manipulation (Article 6(5)).[176] The

---

[172] This very specific exemption protects the commercially important relationship between debt issuers and rating agencies which use company information to issue ratings on the creditworthiness of the issuer. The market typically demands that issuers of public debt, particularly large issuers who access the international market-place, provide a debt rating from a rating agency. Rating agencies will generally be in receipt of sensitive information particularly with respect to the medium-term strategy of the issuer.

[173] The Explanatory Memorandum gives the example of discussions on a potential takeover bid: n 153 above, para 2.

[174] Recital 12 provides that 'professional economic actors must contribute to market integrity'.

[175] This provision appears to reflect the current controversy in the investment-analysis industry on the extent to which analysts' reports are objective when the investment firm for which the analysts work also acts as broker or corporate-finance adviser to the issuer in question.

[176] This requirement may meet with some resistance given that it imposes an additional burden on investment firms. Indeed, the Commission has noted the potential 'negative consequences on short term brokerage revenues' in its impact-assessment form (annexed to the Proposal), although it has referred by way of counterbalance to the benefits to the industry which would follow on a general increase in investor confidence.

technical requirements on how information is to be disclosed to the public
in accordance with the Article 6(1) and (2) obligations and on how research
should be fairly presented and conflicts of interests disclosed in accordance
with Article 6(4) are to be adopted by the Commission by way of level 2
comitology procedures.

XIII.11.5.6 *Competent Authorities, Co-operation, and Enforcement*

(a) *The Competent Authorities*

One of the defining features of the Proposal, and a sharp point of difference
between it and the IDD, is its relatively sophisticated and rigorous approach
to supervision, enforcement, and co-operation between supervisors, which
seems to reflect FESCO's focus on rendering market-abuse controls effective
and to address the charge of inadequate enforcement which is frequently
levelled against the EC regime. The Proposal represents a considerably more
aggressive foray into the structure and power of competent authorities than
has been seen up to now in EC securities regulation. In line with the emphasis placed on effective enforcement by the Lamfalussy decision-making
model,[177] the Proposal may mark a rebalancing of EC securities regulation,
which has traditionally been focused on rule harmonization, to reflect a
more balanced engagement between harmonization and the enforcement of
common standards.

The first indication of a more prescriptive approach to the structure and
powers of national competent authorities (as discussed further in Chapter XV
considerable leeway has been given up to now to Member States on how
they organize the competent authorities which support and supervise the
harmonized rule structure) appears in Article 11. Member States must designate a single (hitherto Member States could split functions between
authorities) 'administrative authority', independent of the market-place and
free from conflicts of interests (recital 17), competent to ensure that the new
regime's provisions are applied.[178] Supervision of market manipulation by
exchanges (in certain Member States there are, at present, no public supervisory authorities in this area with supervision being carried out by the
exchanges) will, as a result, no longer be permitted.[179] Under Article 12, the
competent authority must have, in a reiteration of the traditional formula,

[177] Levels 3 and 4 of the Lamfalussy model concern enforcement. See Ch. XV sect. 2.5.3
below.

[178] One particular problem in controlling market abuse across the Community is the variety of agencies involved in policing market abuse, even within a single Member State. This fragmentation has led to confusion and generates costs for the market-place. Requiring that a single
administrative authority be designated should respond 'to a need for efficiency and clarity and
. . . enhance co-operation between competent authorities': Explanatory Memorandum to the
Proposal, n 153 above, para 2.

[179] Ibid.

all the supervisory and investigatory powers that are necessary for the exercise of its functions; these powers are to be exercised directly or, where appropriate, in collaboration with judicial and other authorities. Article 12 departs from the typical EC securities-regulation formula by setting out in some detail the powers which must be conferred on the competent authority. This reflects the new focus on ensuring the effectiveness of common standards via consistent and adequate supervision and enforcement. These powers must include the right to: have access to and receive copies of any document; demand information and require the testimony (where necessary) of any person; carry out on-site inspections; require telephone and data traffic records; request the freezing and/or the sequestration of assets; and request temporary prohibitions of professional activity.

As is the case with most EC securities-regulation measures, decisions taken by the competent authorities must be subject to the right to apply to courts (Article 15).

(b) *Co-operation*

While the new regime requires that competent authorities be subject to professional secrecy obligations (Articles 12 and 14), it also sets out in Article 16 co-operation procedures which are a considerable advance on the IDD regime and are designed to enhance cross-border co-operation and enforcement in light of the increase in cross-border trading activities and the need to deter cross-border-based market-abuse schemes. The general principle, common to EC securities regulation generally, is that competent authorities are to co-operate whenever necessary to carry out their duties (Article 16(1)). This provision also specifies that competent authorities are to grant assistance to other competent authorities and exchange information and co-operate in investigative activities. Article 16(2)–(5) sets out in some detail the extent of the basic co-operation obligation. Article 16(2) concerns the supply of information and requires the requested authority to take the necessary measures to supply the required information immediately. If it cannot, it must explain why to the requesting competent authority. Refusals can be made where communication might adversely affect the sovereignty, security, or public policy of the Member State addressed or where judicial proceedings have been initiated in respect of the same action and against the same persons before the authorities of the State addressed or where final judgment has been passed on such persons by the competent authorities of the State addressed. Restrictions are placed on the uses to which the information requested can be put by the requesting authority (it can be used only in the exercise of the authority's functions within the scope of the new regime and in the context of related administrative and judicial proceedings), unless the requested authority consents otherwise. In order to prevent abusive behaviour from slipping though jurisdictional loopholes where a Member State's competent authority becomes aware of abusive behaviour but does not have jurisdiction to act, Article 16(3) requires a competent authority, where it is convinced that prohibited activities are being or have been carried out on the territory of another Member State, to notify the competent authority concerned. The notified authority is to take appropriate action and inform the first authority of the outcome and, to the extent possible, of significant interim developments. Article 16(4) concerns investigations and establishes the basic principle that a competent authority of one Member State may request that an investigation be undertaken by the competent authority of another Member State on that State's territory. Article 16(4) also specifies that the requesting Member State may ask that its personnel be permitted to accompany the staff of the requested State's competent authority on the investigation, although the investigation is to remain under the overall control of the Member State on whose territory it is carried out. Competent authorities may refuse to agree to an investigation request under the same conditions as apply to information request refusals. The Commission is to adopt level 2 implementing measures on the procedures according to which information is to be exchanged and cross-border inspections carried out (Article 16(5)).

(c) *Sanctions*

The sanctions regime is also more sophisticated than the IDD regime and, in its current form, moves EC securities regulation significantly closer to developing a sanctions policy, even though sanctions are traditionally regarded as the preserve of the Member States. Ensuring the effectiveness of the new common standards and their ability to protect the integrity of the Community market-place lies at the heart of the new sanctions regime. At present, notwithstanding the integration of securities markets, sanctions policies for market abuse vary widely across the EC; the same conduct can trigger a heavy penalty in one Member State, a light one in another, and escape sanction in a third.[180] While detailed harmonization of sanctions is acknowledged to be outside the scope of the new regime, Article 14 attempts to impose a more tightly drawn general sanctions obligation on Member States in order to promote convergence in sanctions policies. Under Article 14(1) Member States are to ensure that the 'appropriate measures' be taken against those responsible (both natural and legal persons) where the provisions of the new regime are not complied with. The new regime also prescribes that these appropriate measures must include 'administrative and criminal sanctions' and be 'effective, proportionate and dissuasive'. In a

---

[180] N 153 above, para 2.

move on from the more general sanctions requirement imposed by the IDD, administrative measures become mandatory.[181] Under Article 14(2), Member States must impose sanctions for failure to comply with an investigation carried out under Article 12. Reflecting the growing reliance on disclosure as a regulatory and enforcement mechanism across the securities-regulation regime and its dominance in the FSAP, Article 14(3) provides that Member States are to ensure that competent authorities may disclose to the public the sanctions which are imposed for breaches of the new regime, unless disclosure would jeopardize the financial markets or cause disproportionate damage to the parties involved.

Given the reach of the Proposal and its focus on enforcement, it also reflects a concern for procedural and fundamental rights which has hitherto been dormant in EC securities regulation. The new Proposal is declared in recital 24 to respect fundamental rights and observe the principles recognized in particular by the Charter of Fundamental Rights of the European Union. An awareness of fundamental rights runs through the Explanatory Memorandum in particular, with the Commission noting that Member States' sanctions policies must comply with human rights and fundamental freedoms and linking the right to apply to the courts under Article 15 to the principle of legal certainty and the right to a fair trial required by the European Convention on Human Rights.

XIII.11.6 *The 2001 ISD Working Paper*

In addition to the Market Abuse Proposal, the Commission has also suggested that the current Article 11-based market-integrity regime for investment firms contained in the ISD be upgraded. In its 2001 ISD Working Paper,[182] it has suggested that a new provision be added to the ISD which would require competent authorities to ensure that investment firms behave in accordance with EC rules which seek to protect the integrity of the market. Competent authorities would be required to ensure that investment firms, their management, and employees did not: use information not publicly available to their own advantage or to the advantage of others; behave in such a way as to distort the price-discovery process or disseminate misleading information; or otherwise act in a manner detrimental to the interests of the market, other participants, or investors. Competent authorities would also be required to ensure that investment firms implemented effective internal procedures for preventing and detecting abusive practices by management, employees and clients. The competent authority responsible for the new market-integrity

---

[181] The Commission's rationale for this requirement is based in part on the speed with which administrative sanctions can be imposed by comparison with criminal sanctions: ibid.

[182] Overview of Proposed Adjustments to the Investment Services Directive, Working Document of Services of DG Internal Market, Document 1, July 2001 (the ISD Working Paper).

obligations would be that of the Member State of the investment firm's initial authorization, although, reflecting the co-operation structure proposed by the Market Abuse Proposal, this allocation of jurisdiction would be without prejudice to involvement of other competent authorities.

Reflecting FESCO's position that ATS regulation should address the risk of market manipulation and insider dealing occurring,[183] investment firms carrying out ATS-type services, particularly order-matching services, would be subject to a special regime requiring them, *inter alia*, to have procedures in place which would detect whether a client was using their systems to perpetrate market abuse and to report suspicious activity immediately to the competent authority.

While these suggested revisions would bolster the proposed market-abuse regime, they also mark moves towards a more integrated and coherent approach to EC securities regulation, with greater efforts now being expended on interlocking related measures and the treatment of different groups of market actors (investors, traditional investment firms, ATSs, and securities-trading markets) in the interests of the efficient regulation of the market as a whole. In this respect, the Working Paper is an indicator of a regulatory regime of increasing maturity and sophistication.

[183] FESCO, *Proposed Standards for Alternative Trading Systems* (2001) (the FESCO ATS Common Standards Report), Fesco/01-035b.

PART VI

EC Securities Regulation and Takeovers

PART VI

Securities Regulation and Takeovers

XIV

EC Securities Regulation and Takeovers

XIV.1 TAKEOVERS AND REGULATION

Takeovers are but one way of bringing about a change of control in a company, but they are unique in that they permit a change in control to take place without the approval of the incumbent board of directors and without the permission of a large number of the shareholders.[1] They involve the acquisition of control by one company (the offeror or bidder) of another company (the offeree or target) through an offer to purchase the target's voting securities.[2] Where the offer to purchase the voting securities is not accompanied by a recommendation from the target board of directors to accept the offer, the bid is termed hostile. Takeover offers are generally conditional on the bidder acquiring sufficient voting rights to obtain control of the target. The consideration may be in cash or in securities of the bidder or of another company and is usually set at a premium to the current market price.

Takeover activity can act as an economic stimulant. Although the literature on the benefits of takeover activity is vast and contains numerous and diverging schools of thought, many would hold the view that it is socially useful and efficient that companies whose management is seen to be underperforming and whose underperformance is reflected in a low share price, be subject to a change of management through a hostile bid. Takeovers, in this sense, exert an important discipline on incumbent managers.[3] If

[1] See Sealy, L, 'The Draft Thirteenth EC Directive on Take-overs' in Andenas, M, and Kenyon-Slade, S (eds), *EC Company Law and Financial Market Regulation* (1993) 135, 136.

[2] In a takeover bid by share offer, the target is not dissolved as a result of the takeover but becomes a subsidiary of the bidder. Legal mergers or assets mergers, which are more common in continental Europe, are another form of corporate reorganization which involves the dissolution of the company being taken over and the transfer of its assets and liabilities to another company. In the EC, these mergers are regulated by the Third Company Law Directive 78/855/EEC concerning mergers of public limited companies [1978] OJ L295/36.

[3] A full discussion of the theories underlying the market for corporate control is outside the scope of this ch. One of the most influential pieces in the area is the classic study by Manne which argued that an efficient capital market will lower the market value of a company's shares to reflect weak management, thereby facilitating its takeover by a more efficient management. The threat of a takeover therefore gives managers an incentive to perform: Manne, H, 'Mergers and the Market for Corporate Control' (1965) 73 *JPE* 110. See also Easterbrook, F, and Fischel, D, 'The Proper Role of a Target's Management in Responding to a Takeover Offer' (1981) 94 *Harv. LR* 1161 who argue in that piece that incumbent management should play a passive role during a takeover bid and should be prohibited from taking defensive action. The principal challenges to this theory are succinctly summarized in Cranston, R, 'The Rise and Rise of the Hostile Takeover' in Hopt, K, and Wymeersch, E (eds), *European Takeovers—Law and Practice* (1992) 77, 88. The analysis points to the fact that bidders may not act in an economically rational

takeovers are seen as beneficial, the dilemma then arises whether or not they should be subject to regulation. Regulation which makes takeover activity more burdensome may be criticized as hampering a beneficial activity.[4]

Takeover regulation is primarily a creature of company law and corporate governance. It is covered here, as it also traditionally comes within the purview of securities regulation, although the fundamental objectives of securities regulation are supplanted by a focus on investor protection expressed as a concern to protect the position of minority shareholders in a change of control and to ensure their fair treatment.[5] Nonetheless, the focus on transparency in the EC's most recent attempt to deal with takeover regulation also reflects securities regulation's preoccupation with market integrity. In addition, the dominant securities-regulation regulatory device, disclosure, runs through the EC initiatives in this area. Disclosure has been relied on as a mechanism for ensuring fair treatment for shareholders, supporting the integrity of the market-place against the abuse of takeover-related information, and feeding takeover information through to the market-place and the price-formation process. The link between takeover regulation and securities regulation can also be seen in the connection

manner in that they may knowingly pay more for a company than it is worth in the general upheaval surrounding a takeover, that companies may not be efficiently valued by the stock markets, and that hostile takeovers may not actually improve economic performance. The school of thought which opposes unhindered takeover activity holds that the threat of hostile takeovers (which ultimately generate only private gains) distracts management from long-term strategic thinking and results in a detrimental focus on short-term goals. See, eg, Lipton, M, 'Takeover bids in the Target's Boardroom: A response to Professors Easterbrook and Fischel' (1980) 55 *NYUL Rev.* 1231.

[4] One US study found that after the adoption of the Williams Act, 1968 (which regulates US takeovers at a federal level via disclosure and procedural requirements) the costs of launching and completing a takeover bid increased (measured by an increase in the average cash premium paid), with the result that the volume and productivity of cash takeovers decreased, incurring large social costs: Jarrell, G, and Bradley, M, 'The Economic Effects of Federal and State Regulations of Cash Tender Offers' (1980) 23 *J L and Econ.* 371.

[5] Given that takeover regulation is a somewhat ancillary component of securities regulation and that it pursues, for the most part, different objectives from the investor-confidence/systemic-stability/market-integrity objectives which dominate securities regulation generally, this ch. is limited to a discrete review of the EC's approach to takeover regulation in the interests of completeness. It will not discuss in any detail the underlying rationales for takeover regulation and the link between regulation and the market for corporate control or the EC's approach to corporate governance in general. For an analysis of takeover regulation from the governance perspective see, eg, Ferrarini, G, *Share Ownership, Takeover Law and the Contestability of Corporate Control*, WP1-2001, Working Paper Series of the Centre for Law and Finance, University of Genoa (forthcoming in *Company Law Reform in OECD Countries: A Comparative Outlook of Current Trends*, Conference Proceedings), Bradley, C, 'Corporate Control: Markets and Rules' (1990) 53 *MLR* 170 and Coffee, J, 'Regulating the Market for Corporate Control: A Critical Assessment of the Tender Offer's Role in Corporate Governance' (1984) 84 *Col. LR* 1145. On corporate governance and harmonization see Hopt, K, 'Common Principles of Corporate Governance in Europe' in Markesinis, B, *The Clifford Chance Millennium Lectures. The Coming Together of the Common Law and the Civil Law* (2000) 105.

between the interpenetration of securities markets across the EC and the consequent diversification of shareholder bases across the Community and the need to ensure equivalent protections for investors as shareholders in the event of a takeover.[6]

The second reason for covering takeover regulation in a book on EC securities regulation concerns the volatile political and institutional climate on which the development of EC securities regulation as a whole is dependent. EC securities regulation is not developed in a vacuum. The lamentable history of the EC's attempts to agree on minimum standards for the regulation of takeovers illustrates with alarming clarity the dependence of EC securities regulation as a system on the complexities and vagaries of the inter-institutional and, it appears, increasingly national-interests-captive law-making process. On 4 July 2001, the Commission's proposal for a takeover directive, after a twelve-year legislative odyssey during which the proposal had been completely recast once and subject to numerous fundamental revisions, finally collapsed, having failed to gain the approval of the European Parliament as required under the final stage of the particular Treaty law-making process in issue, the co-decision procedure.[7] This procedure, which since the Maastricht and Amsterdam revisions to the Treaty, has dominated internal market (and thus securities-regulation) law-making is dependent in large part on dialogue between the Council (the forum for Member State interests and the most powerful law-maker in the institutional structure) and the Parliament (an emerging influence on law-making since the adoption of the co-decision procedure which effectively gives it a veto on legislation at certain stages of the co-decision process). While the chasm between those Member States which support, in principle, a market for corporate control and those which regard hostile takeover activity as undesirable, disruptive, and a threat to national industries, meant that agreement on takeover standards had been in doubt for as long as the proposal had been discussed, the final collapse of the proposal was, nonetheless, unexpected. The competing national interests and diverging national perspectives which dogged the progress of the proposal through the Council since its initial presentation by the Commission in 1989,[8] appeared to have been overcome in June 2000. At that point, some eleven years into the legislative process, the Council, after difficult and lengthy negotiations which almost foundered on the question of the ability of companies to defend themselves against hostile takeovers, adopted a common position on the proposal, which, in a key

---

[6] In addition, as with securities regulation generally, takeover regulation has been connected to improving the functioning and stability of the financial market: Commission, *Progress on Financial Services*, Second Report, COM(2000)336, 2.

[7] The co-decision procedure is outlined in Ch. XV sect. 2.2.1 below.

[8] The main points of conflict which arose and the legislative history are discussed in sects. 3 and 4 below.

provision, prohibited target companies from taking defensive action without shareholder approval.[9] As it is entitled to under the co-decision procedure, the Parliament proposed amendments to the Council's common position.[10] These amendments were largely concerned with employees' rights, rather than with the defensive-action problem, although, as discussed further in section 4 below, attempts were also made to change the nature and scope of the ban on defensive measures. The Commission sought to broker a compromise between the Parliament and the Council in the Conciliation Committee, which was then convened under the rules of co-decision. By now it had become clear that Germany, which had been hostile to the proposal's treatment of takeover defences, had turned against the proposal in the face of lobbying from a number of large German companies concerned about their vulnerability to attack from Anglo-American predators in particular.[11] The Commission unexpectedly managed to broker a compromise, however, in early June 2001.[12] The agreed text did not concede the basic point on takeover defences but did allow Member States four rather than three years in which to implement the new regime and gave them an additional fifth year to implement the defensive action rules. It also required hostile bidders to inform employees of potential job losses and contained a declaration by the Commission that it would re-examine three contentious areas: how the equitable price required in a mandatory bid was to be determined; the equal treatment of shareholders; and the right of majority shareholders to acquire the shares of the minority. The Commission also committed to making an annual report to the Council and Parliament on take-over bid activity across the Community, once the proposal was in force, which would examine whether imbalances were being generated by regulatory differences between the Member States. As required by the co-decision procedure, agreement on the compromise text was then required from the Parliament (by an absolute majority) and the Council (by a qualified majority). The internal vote by the Parliament's delegation on whether to accept the Commission's compromise did not augur well for its adoption; agreement was reached only after an eight to six vote in which all the German representatives voted against the compromise and all the British representa-

---

[9]   Common Position No 1/2001 [2001] OJ C23/1.

[10]   At a plenary session of the Parliament in Dec 2000. For a discussion of the amendments see the Commission's opinion at COM(2001)77.

[11]   See Betts, P, and Hargreaves, D, 'No way in', *Financial Times*, 3 May 2001. Volkswagen, eg, was reported as being concerned that it could become a takeover target given the consolidation taking place in the global car industry: reported in 'Sugaring the Pill', *The Economist*, 9 June 2001, 88, 89. BASF was also reported as lobbying against the proposal. See Mortished, C, and Fletcher, M, 'MEPs throw out takeover rules Bill', *The Times*, 5 July 2001 who also reported that the level of opposition from German industry was instrumental in changing the German government's position on the Proposal.

[12]   MEMO/01/216.

tives supported it.[13] Discussions in and lobbying of the Parliament focused primarily on the defensive-action provision, with German, Italian, and Spanish MEPs reported as lobbying against the proposal.[14] Ironically, after twelve years of discussions the final vote was tied, which was enough to defeat the proposal.

The history of the proposal serves as a stark reminder of the influence which the Parliament can wield on law-making and of the impact of national interests. While the fate of the proposal can be read as a signal of the damage a resurgence of national interests and a volatile Parliament could inflict on the FSAP[15] it might also be suggested that harmonization is only ever realistic where Member States are broadly *ad idem* on the basic principles on which harmonization is sought. Not only is the desirability of prohibitions on takeover defences a far from universally held view,[16] more generally, local market sentiment and practices are a powerful brake on harmonization.[17]

The evolution of the takeover regime also illustrates the other factors which can shape EC securities regulation. National interests aside, the imprints of the subsidiarity principle, the traditional focus of the Parliament on non-producer interests (in this case employees' rights), the sensitivity of Member States to attempts to alter their supervisory structures (in this case the resistance by the UK to any measures which might have prejudiced the position of the Takeover Panel), and market developments (the successful $190 billion hostile takeover of Mannesmann by Vodafone in 1999/2000 might be regarded as crystallizing industry opposition to the proposal in certain quarters) can all be seen in the progress of the takeover proposal.

Although the collapse of the proposal provoked immediate recriminations and generated considerable controversy,[18] it has been reported that the Commission will present another proposal in due course. It seems unlikely that, as far as content is concerned, any such proposal would differ considerably from the version which failed in July 2001, which was a minimum-

[13] 'Sugaring the Pill', n 11 above.
[14] See Hargreaves, D, and Norman, P, 'Distressing signals for the single market', *Financial Times*, 5 July 2001 who reported that these MEPs were concerned that 'national champions' would be vulnerable to takeovers.
[15] 1999 Commission Communication on Implementing the Framework for Financial Markets; Action Plan COM(1999)232 (the FSAP).
[16] See n 68 below.
[17] Betts and Hargreaves, n 11 above, eg, noted that while Member States are beginning to adopt a broadly similar approach to takeover regulation they still retain national and cultural characteristics. They pointed to the example of the Netherlands which has a thriving corporate sector but has traditionally given 'bullet-proof' protection to its companies from predators.
[18] Commissioner Bolkestein, who was responsible for the legislation, eg, found that the rejection was a serious set-back to the EU's plans to become the world's most competitive economy: reported in Dombey, D, 'EU rejects chance to set cross-border takeover rules', *Financial Times*, 5 July 2001. The *Financial Times* also noted that the defeat sent a signal that the Community was not committed to opening up its capital markets. Hargreaves and Norman, n 14 above.

standards measure only, although clearly it remains to be seen whether the more controversial provisions, and chiefly the defensive measures prohibition, will resurface. A Group of High Level Experts was established in September 2001 to advise on takeover-rule harmonization and, in particular, on the creation of a level playing-field for shareholder rights, what is meant by an 'equitable price' for shares in a takeover, and the 'squeeze-out' procedure which allows a majority shareholder to buy out the minority. The form of any new proposal is a different matter; the Commission may proceed down the non-binding Recommendation route, although this would fit uneasily with the focus on formal, binding level 1 and level 2 measures in the wake of the Lamfalussy Report.[19] It may be that market developments and the extent to which continental markets, influenced by shareholder value-seeking institutional investors, move towards accepting the market for corporate control will be decisive. The provisions of the Council's June 2000 common position are, however, discussed at some length in this chapter, not only as part of this chapter's analysis of how the takeover rules harmonization project has evolved but also in order to outline one model for EC takeover regulation which may yet reappear.

XIV.2 TAKEOVERS AND THE EC

It is only in the last thirty-five years or so that takeover bids have been used a method of corporate re-organization in the Community.[20] Takeover bids do not occur with equal frequency in all Member States due to varying legal, cultural, and structural conditions. The greatest number of takeover bids occurs in the UK, where a combination of widely held shareholdings of listed shares, an absence of bearer shares allowing easy identification of shareholders, and controls on the use of frustrating techniques by offeree boards are all conducive to allowing market forces efficiently to determine the outcome of bids.[21] In addition, takeovers are generally regarded in the UK as a healthy incentive to management to perform. In other Member States, by contrast, hostile takeovers can be regarded as disruptive, expensive, and time-consuming and are discouraged. Certain Member States also have relatively illiquid equities markets dominated by large, often family-based, shareholders. In addition, a common continental European practice is for

---

[19] Final Report of the Committee of Wise Men on the Regulation of European Securities Markets, Feb 2001 (the Lamfalussy Report).

[20] The same comment can be made in respect of the USA where hostile takeovers, in particular, were relatively unknown until the 1960s.

[21] See the discussion of takeover bids in the UK by the House of Lords Select Committee on the European Communities Report on Takeover Bids. House of Lords, Session 1995-96, 13th Report (the HL Takeover Report) paras 1-27.

companies to establish networks of cross-participation in other undertakings in the same or related industries. This pattern of cross-shareholdings makes transfers of control without the approval of the major shareholders difficult.[22] Such intimate capital markets also discourage aggressive takeover activity. Other technical barriers to takeover activity include governance rules which allocate power between management, shareholders, and employees and rules limiting voting power.[23] Continental equity markets are, however, currently undergoing seismic structural changes which are likely to alter the takeover landscape significantly. Continental takeover activity has grown in recent years, as European investors have taken on board the Anglo-American doctrine that shareholder value should be elevated above all other considerations. Not only have European fund managers become more demanding of companies they invest in, but credit institutions, traditionally the largest shareholder constituency in continental Europe, are in turn under pressure to maximize the value of the capital they invest in their corporate clients and are being given incentives to do so by tax reforms. Among the most high-profile examples of this change in culture in recent years have been the fiercely contested bid by the UK company Vodafone for the German company Mannesmann in 1999/2000 and the hostile takeover by Olivetti of Telecom Italia in 1999.

The market-integration theme which underpins EC securities regulation generally emerges again in the takeovers area although the focus shifts to corporate governance. In particular, 'differences in style and forms of governance can limit cross-border investment and hinder the creation of European corporations'.[24] While the Commission has acknowledged that there is no single model of corporate governance (including takeover regulation) which would facilitate increased integration of wholesale markets, it is promoting agreement on common principles which could underpin the market-place. More specifically, an environment in which takeovers occur freely and without the burden of differing legislative and structural barriers could contribute to improving the competitive position of the Community

[22] It has been observed (in 1992) that 'in Continental economies transfers of control cannot usually take place except as a consequence of transactions between the controlling shareholder and the bidder, most of the time involving a transfer of a substantial amount of shares of the company, or of shares in a company that held its controlling interest. In these usual cases, the takeover bid is a consequence, almost a by-product, of a previously agreed-upon control transfer': Wymeersch, E, 'Problems of the Regulation of Takeover Bids in Western Europe: A Comparative Survey' in Hopt and Wymeersch, n 3 above, 95, 101. The *Financial Times* cited in 2001 a study by the European Economic Review which revealed the average concentration of voting power in the UK as 9.9% but in excess of 50% in Germany, Austria, and Italy: Betts and Hargreaves, n 11 above.

[23] On the technical and structural (economic conditions) obstacles to takeovers in Europe and their impact on the market for corporate control see Ferrarini, n 5 above, 6–12.

[24] Commission Communication on Financial Services, *Building a Framework for Action*, COM(1998)625 (the 1998 Communication), 7.

generally by allowing the creation of corporate structures which, due to their economies of scale, can face international challenges.[25]

The Community has not legislated specifically to remove the many technical barriers which exist to the creation of a single market in corporate control in order to encourage Community-wide takeover activity. Numerous technical barriers to cross-border takeover activity exist in the form of accounting divergences, shareholder identification where bearer shares are issued, variations in voting rights, and restrictions on the acquisitions of shares (via 'golden share' rules)[26] to highlight but a few.[27] Since the late 1980s, however, the Commission has been engaged in trying to secure agreement on a directive which would set minimum principles for the conduct of takeovers and secure equivalent protection for shareholders in takeover bids. Given the prevailing economic conditions and the evolving corporate culture, agreement on the proposed takeover directive (section 4 below) was highlighted in the 1998 Communication as being key to the development of common principles of corporate governance while, in 1999, the FSAP described its adoption, which forms part of the FSAP, as amounting to 'an immediate and tangible contribution to the functioning of the single financial market' and called for 'a clear signal of the political commitment to make progress as urgently as possible'.[28] While cross-border takeover activity might not be actively stimulated by any future successful attempts at harmonization based on the proposed takeover directive model, takeover harmonization is, at least, unlikely to hamper such activity.

---

[25] See the comments of ECOSOC on the 1989 Proposal for a 13th directive on company law concerning takeover and other general bids [1989] OJ C298/56, para 1.4.

[26] Variations in voting rights are particularly striking, with the 'one share one vote' principle far from the general rule. Multiple voting rights, capped voting rights, and shares without a right to vote are all evident to varying degrees across the Community. A useful table setting out the variations in voting rights across the Community is set out in Gros, D, and Lannoo, K, *The Euro Capital Market* (2000) 120. The failure of the EC's proposed takeover regime to ban shares carrying special voting rights was identified as a weakness by some opponents of the regime. Golden shares (or controls on the acquisition of holdings in privatized companies) are particularly contentious. These typically require potential purchasers of shareholdings in privatized companies to seek Government authorization before an acquisition can be made. In his 3 July 2001 Opinion in Joined Cases C-367/98 *Commission v Portugal*, C-483/99 *Commission v France*, and C-503/99 *Commission v Belgium*. Ruiz-Járabo Colomer AG found that golden shares did not breach the freedom to establish or the movement of capital (as argued by the Commission) as long the restrictions did not discriminate against citizens from other Member States.

[27] A useful source of these problems is the DTI-commissioned report by Coopers & Lybrand, *Barriers to Takeovers in the European Community* (1989). It highlighted difficulties in identifying takeover targets as a result of varying disclosure requirements, regulatory deterrents and post acquisition difficulties. See also Hopt, K, 'European Takeover Regulation: Barriers to and Problems of Harmonising Takeover Law in the European Community' in Hopt and Wymeersch, n 3 above, 165 and Ferrarini, n 5 above, 7–12.

[28] N 15 above, 2.

Ultimately, however, changes in practice and perspective will be necessary before the single market for corporate control becomes a reality.[29]

XIV.3 EARLY ATTEMPTS AT HARMONIZATION

XIV.3.1 *The 1977 Code of Conduct*

Elements of takeover regulation appear briefly in the 1977 Commission Recommendation concerning a Code of Conduct Relating to Transactions in Transferable Securities.[30] General Principle 3 reflects a major principle of takeover regulation by providing that equality of treatment be guaranteed to all holders of securities of the same type issued by the same company. It also provides that any act resulting directly or indirectly in the transfer of a holding, conferring *de jure* or *de facto* control of a company whose securities are dealt in on the market, should have regard to the right of all shareholders to be treated in the same fashion. Supplementary Principle 17 provides that transfers of controlling holdings should not be carried out in a 'surreptitious fashion'. It also recommends that shareholders of a company control of which has changed hands should be offered the opportunity to dispose of their securities on identical conditions, unless they have the benefit of alternative safeguards which can be regarded as equivalent. The proviso on equivalent safeguards was added to reflect the alternative German approach of controlling the powers of dominant shareholders (section 4.8.2 below).[31] Supplementary Principle 18 trenchantly states that any acquisition or attempted acquisition of a controlling holding made without the public being informed is against the objectives of the Code. These early expressions of the principles of disclosure, minority protection, and equivalent treatment have since evolved to become the cornerstones of the EC's approach to takeovers.

XIV.3.2 *Moves Towards a Takeover Directive*[32]

The first incarnation of the Community's many attempts to deal with takeover regulation would not be presented by the Commission until

---

[29] Adoption of the proposal would, however, have coincided with an increase in global mergers and acquisitions activity in recent years. By the end of the first quarter of 2000, eg, global mergers and acquisitions activity reached $1,166 billion, a record figure: Skapinker, M, 'Marrying in Haste', *Financial Times*, 12 April 2000.

[30] Commission Recommendation 77/534/EEC [1977] OJ L212/37. The genesis of EC takeover-regulation harmonization, however, arguably lies back in 1974 with Professor Pennington's Report on *Takeover and other Bids*: COM Doc XI/56/74.

[31] 1977 Code of Conduct, n 30 above. Explanatory Memorandum III, C.

[32] Directive 88/627/EEC on the information to be published when a major holding in a listed company is acquired or disposed of [1988] OJ L348/62 (the Substantial Shareholdings Directive

January 1989 (the 1989 Proposal)[33] although the Commission suggested in its White Paper on the Internal Market that a directive be proposed in 1987.[34] It has since been described, somewhat ruefully, by the Commission itself as 'an ambitious text'.[35] Adopted under Article 44 EC (then Article 54 EC), it was designed to establish equivalent protection for shareholders.[36] A strong theme of market transparency and adequate disclosure ran throughout its requirements.[37] In an omission reminiscent of another contemporaneous and notorious exclusion, the failure to define 'public offer' in the EC's public-offer disclosure regime, it did not, however, define 'takeover bid'.[38] The 1989 Proposal applied to offers for all public companies, regardless of whether the company was publicly quoted. While its detailed provisions were designed to ensure respect for the basic principle set out in Article 3 that shareholders in the same position be treated equally, it did not contain any other general principles. This omission generated much criticism on the

or SSD (now consolidated in Directive 2001/34/EC on admission of securities to official stock exchange listing and on information to be published on those securities [2001] OJ L184/1 (the Securities Consolidation Directive or SCD)) also has implications for takeover regulation due to the potential impact of its notification obligations on the development of a market for corporate control (see Ch. IV.5.4). See the discussion in Ferrarini, n 5 above, 3–5.

[33] [1989] OJ C64/8; Explanatory Memorandum at COM(88)823. An unofficial draft was presented in 1987: COM DOC XV/63/87. On the 1989 Proposal see Klein, D, 'The European Community's Proposed Directive on Takeover Bids and Its Impact on Shareholders' Rights' (1990) 16 *Brooklyn J Int'l. L* 561 and Cooke, V, 'Does the European Community Have a Fatal Attraction for Hostile Takeovers? A Comparison of the European Commission's Proposed Directive on Takeover Bids and the United States Experience' (1990) 47 *Washington and Lee Review* 663.

[34] COM(85)310, 35.

[35] In its Explanatory Memorandum to the 1996 Proposal for a 13th Directive on Company Law Concerning Takeover Bids, COM(95)655, 2. The 1989 Proposal followed many of the provisions of the detailed City Code on Take-overs and Mergers, the non-statutory code which, as issued and applied by the self-regulatory Panel on Take-overs and Mergers, forms the basis of UK takeover regulation (the City Code and the Takeover Panel, respectively).

[36] At the time of the Commission's adoption of the 1989 Proposal takeover regulation varied significantly across the EC. Various forms of non-statutory regulation were in place in the UK (since 1968), the Netherlands (since 1970), Italy (since 1972), Germany (since 1979), and Denmark (since 1988). Although Belgium had adopted a statute which contained a basis for takeover regulation in 1964, statutory regulation was not introduced until later in 1989. Spain and Portugal both introduced takeover statutes in 1989 and 1986, respectively. In France, a non-statutory system was in existence from 1972 but this was replaced in 1989 by a statutory regime. See generally Wymeersch, n 22 above, 95.

[37] The detailed disclosure requirements can be explained by the stance of many of the Member States during initial negotiations that regulation in this area was linked to the preceding securities directives, in that it should primarily involve prospectus requirements in order to provide the investor with adequate information with respect to a decision to sell securities. See further Berger, K, 'The Proposed EC Takeover Directive: Balancing Investor Protection with the Need for Regulatory Flexibility' (1991) 6 *JIBL* 11.

[38] In its Explanatory Memorandum, however, the Commission referred to a takeover bid as 'an offer made to holders of securities carrying voting rights in a company or convertible into securities carrying such voting rights . . . to acquire their securities for consideration in cash or other securities, the purpose of the offer usually being to acquire control of the company or to consolidate the offeror's existing control': n 33 above, 4.

ground that implementation of the Proposal's provisions, which although detailed were not comprehensive, was open to varying interpretations, as Member States were not guided in the application and implementation of the Proposal by general principles. Member States were required to designate authorities[39] to supervise compliance with the Proposal's rules. Neither the supervisory authorities nor the Member States were given many opportunities to derogate from its requirements or to apply its provisions flexibly. Detailed provision was made for disclosure, including rules on the publication of the intention to make an offer, the offer document and its content, and the outcome of the bid. Specific rules applied to the use of defence tactics by the offeree board. In particular, directors were prohibited from issuing securities or convertible securities carrying voting rights and from engaging in 'transactions which do not have the character of current operations concluded under normal conditions' and which were not authorized by the supervisory authority, unless, in each case, the action was authorized by the general meeting. The conduct of the bid was also subject to detailed regulation. One of the most controversial provisions, Article 4, introduced a mandatory-bid requirement and provided that in order to secure minority shareholder protection, an offeror was required to launch an offer for all the remaining securities of a company on acquisition of a particular percentage of voting rights, which could not be set by the Member States at more than one third of the voting rights (see further section 4.8.2 below). Concert-party provisions were introduced to ensure that the mandatory-bid rule could not be circumvented. Supervisory authorities were, however, given the power to grant exemptions to the mandatory-bid requirement, given concerns that the rule could impact severely on smaller companies and make takeover bids, particularly agreed bids, prohibitively and unnecessarily expensive. While ECOSOC[40] and the Parliament[41] suggested extensive amendments, they were broadly supportive of the 1989 Proposal.

In 1990 the Commission presented a revised proposal (the '1990 Proposal').[42] In some respects it represented an unhappy marriage of the detailed approach of the 1989 Proposal and the more flexible approach which was to come. Its most significant amendment was the addition of a

---

[39] In what seems to have been an attempt to deal with non-statutory regimes, Art. 6 provided that the supervisory body could delegate all or part of its powers to 'other authorities or to associations or private bodies'.

[40] [1989] OJ C298/56. [41] [1990] OJ C38/41.

[42] [1990] OJ C240/7; Explanatory Memorandum at COM(90)416. For an analysis of the proposal see Wouters, J, 'Towards a Level Playing Field for Takeovers in the European Community: An Analysis of the Proposed Thirteenth Directive in Light of the American Experience' (1993) 30 *CMLRev.* 267. See also Berger, n 37 above, Sealy, n 1 above; and Kenyon-Slade, S, and Andenas, M, 'The Proposed Thirteenth Directive on Take-overs: Unravelling the United Kingdom's Self-Regulatory Success?' in Andenas and Kenyon-Slade, n 1 above, 149.

series of general principles to guide the supervisory authority in carrying out its functions and, in particular, when granting exemptions. They were designed to introduce flexibility while ensuring legal certainty. These principles included: the equal treatment of all shareholders in the same position; ensuring that all persons to whom the bid was addressed had sufficient time and all the necessary information to make a decision on the bid; ensuring that the directors of the offeree refrained from taking defensive measures; preventing the creation of false markets; and ensuring that the affairs of the offeree were not impeded for an unreasonable time. These principles did not, however, replace the detailed rules reflecting these principles which carried over from the 1989 Proposal.[43] Other amendments included: providing a definition of 'takeover bid';[44] restricting the scope of the Proposal to offers for securities listed on an exchange in at least one Member State; specifying the circumstances in which an exemption could be granted to the mandatory-bid obligation; clarifying that the obligation to make a mandatory bid arose on the actual acquisition of control and not on the formation of an intention to acquire control; and clarifying that shareholder approval for defensive measures was to be obtained during the currency of the bid and that a general meeting could therefore be called during the bid.

In a forerunner of subsequent developments, ECOSOC presciently suggested at this point that a radically different approach be taken.[45] Given the need for flexibility in the fast-changing environment of takeover bids and the rapid evolution of financial and legal takeover strategies, it was concerned at the failure of the 1990 Proposal to grant a general power to the supervisory authorities to suspend the detailed rules in particular cases, while always operating within a framework of immutable general principles. It suggested that any takeover proposal be limited to a statement of general principles. Detailed rules should, it suggested, be included in the form of an appendix, which would act as a guideline for Member States in implementing the general principles.

Negotiations on the 1990 Proposal stalled, not least due to a slow-down in the EC economies and a decrease in mergers and acquisitions activity, which removed any urgency to introduce harmonized legislation. More fundamentally, intractable disagreements arose on three fronts. The use of the obligation to mount a full mandatory bid as the only means of protecting minority shareholders in a bid proved objectionable to Germany and the

---

[43] Leading to concerns in the UK that the precedence of the City Code's general principles over its detailed rules which allowed the Takeover Panel to operate flexibly but in the spirit of the Code would be threatened by a requirement that formal rules take priority: Sealy, n 1 above, 143.

[44] Broadly defined as an offer made to the holders of the securities of a company to acquire all or part of those securities by payment in cash or in exchange for other securities.

[45] [1991] OJ C102/49.

Netherlands in particular.[46] The provisions dealing with restrictions on the power of the board of directors to frustrate the bid were, in an augury of things to come, also problematic. More generally, Germany and the Netherlands were broadly against any harmonization which would lead to a market for corporate control, preferring cross-ownership and bank share-holdings as alternative forms of regulation of changes of control.[47] Equally fundamentally, the UK questioned the need for any legally binding takeover measures, given the absence of parallel measures to remove the structural and cultural obstacles to takeovers in certain Member States. It also expressed grave concerns with respect to the increased litigation risk and potential damage to the effectiveness of the UK self-regulatory system which it felt might follow from placing takeover regulation on a statutory footing. In June 1991 negotiations in the Council working group were suspended.[48]

XIV.3.3 *A Change in Approach*

Nonetheless, the Commission did not abandon takeover regulation. Its efforts were given a new direction and impetus by the Maastricht Treaty and its for-malization of the subsidiarity principle, which fortuitously coincided with an increase in takeover activity in certain Member States. In 1992 at the European Council in Edinburgh, and again at the Essen European Council in 1994, the Commission committed itself to revising the 1990 proposal. In 1993 it began a series of consultations with the Member States in order to obtain their views on how to proceed in the area of takeovers. These consultations revealed that the Member States preferred a framework directive which would set out general principles, and that they did not want the detailed harmoniza-tion provided by the 1990 Proposal. At the same time, a number of Member States began to provide for takeover regulation, both statutory and non-statutory, and often based in part on the 1989 and 1990 Proposals, to the extent that the Commission at one point described its earlier abortive propos-als as having had the practical effect of a recommendation.[49]

---

[46] The prevailing view was that majority shareholders tended not to exploit minority share-holders and, in any event, due to the remedies available against oppressive behaviour, could not risk behaving in an exploitative and oppressive fashion.

[47] See Andenas, M, 'European Take-over Regulation and the City Code' (1996) 17 *The Company Lawyer* 150.

[48] The Netherlands, which was strongly opposed to both Proposals, held the presidency of the Council for the second 6 months of 1991 making significant progress difficult at that time. It would be misleading to leave the impression that all Member States were opposed to the early proposals. With the adoption of its takeover statute in 1989, Belgian law conformed broadly with the 1990 Proposal's requirements.

[49] HL Takeover Report, n 21 above, Evidence of the Commission, para 9. Spain, France, and Belgium all adopted takeover statutes in 1989. For a comparative review of takeover regula-tion across the Community in the early 1990s see Berger, D, 'A Comparative Analysis of Takeover Regulation in the European Community', (1993) 55 *Law and Contemporary Problems*

In February 1996, the Commission presented an entirely new proposal, which adopted a framework approach to takeover regulation (the 1996 Proposal).[50] Following the comments of the Parliament and ECOSOC,[51] the Commission presented a revised proposal in November 1997, which formed the basis of the regime which failed to gain the support of the Parliament and collapsed in July 2001.[52] The most controversial changes to the 1996 Proposal, which were instigated by the Parliament, concerned a greater consideration of employment interests and an extension of the application of the disclosure principle from shareholders to employees. Although the mandatory-bid rule and the principle of offeree board neutrality required strenuous negotiation, as did the provisions concerning the relationship between the takeover regime and review by the courts, after resolution of a dispute between the UK and Spain concerning the treatment of Gibraltar, a common position was adopted by the Council in June 2000.[53] As noted above, the Parliament was consulted on the common position and proposed a number of additional amendments, some of which were accepted by the Commission, although the majority were rejected.[54] A compromise was ultimately brokered between the Parliament and the Council in the Conciliation Committee, notwithstanding, as outlined in section 1 above, growing resistance to the common position from the German government following heavy lobbying against the regime from certain German corporates. Even though the length of the proposed takeover regime's gestation period had, by the Conciliation Committee stage, passed into legend, and despite the fact that most institutional hurdles had by then been cleared, national interests, it appears, led to the failure by the Parliament to adopt the harmonized regime on its vote on the compromise solution. The discussion of the EC's failed takeover regime which follows is based on the Council's common position (referred to throughout as the Proposed Directive), although reference is made to the amendments suggested by the Parliament and the Commission's compromise.

53; 'Constraints on Cross Border Takeovers and Mergers—A Catalogue of Disharmony', A Report by the Section on Business Law (International Bar Association) for the International Capital Markets Group, *International Business Lawyer*, Feb 1991, 51 and Wymeersch, n 22 above.

[50] [1996] OJ C162/5; Explanatory Memorandum, COM(95)655. While the original 1989 Proposal contained 23 Arts., the 1996 Proposal shrank to a mere 12.

[51] [1997] OJ C222/20 and [1996] OJ C295/1, respectively.

[52] [1997] OJ C378/10; COM(97)565. See generally Clausen, N, and Sørensen, K, 'The Regulation of Takeover Bids in Europe: The Impact of the Proposed 13th EC Company Law Directive on the Present Regulation in the EU Member States' (1999) 1 *ICCLJ* 169.

[53] [2001] OJ C23/1.

[54] COM(2001)77. While some of the amendments were uncontroversial, the revision to the frustrating action ban struck at the core of the common position (sect. 4.6.1 below). Other amendments concerned employees and sought to give them a voice in the bid procedure and to supplement the disclosure made to them.

XIV.4 THE PROPOSED THIRTEENTH COMPANY LAW DIRECTIVE

XIV.4.1 *Objectives*

The Proposed Directive was designed to 'protect the interests of holders of securities of companies governed by the law of a Member State when these companies are subject to a takeover bid or to a change of control' (recital 2). Although the Proposed Directive was based on Article 44 EC generally, and thus in the power of the Community to adopt directives to attain the freedom to establish, recital 1 based the Proposal more directly in Article 44(2)(g) EC (and underlined the Proposed Directive's connection with shareholder protection) by referring to the necessity to co-ordinate certain safeguards which Member States required of companies for the protection of members and others in order to make such safeguards equivalent throughout the Community. By providing a clarification of the major takeover rules, the Proposed Directive might also have contributed to preventing the corporate restructuring which is currently in train across the Community from being distorted by cultural and governance variations. In this regard, recital 13 stated that the Proposed Directive would create 'Community-wide clarity and transparency in respect of legal issues to be settled in the event of takeover bids and to prevent patterns of corporate restructuring within the Community from being distorted by arbitrary differences in governance and management cultures'.[55] The minimum degree of harmonization introduced by the Proposed Directive (section 4.2 below) would, however, have limited its impact on the market for corporate control.[56]

Accordingly, although takeovers have implications for a wide group of economic actors and financial interests, such as employees, creditors, and local communities, the primary (albeit not exclusive) focus of the Proposed Directive was on the protection of shareholders.[57] It appears that individual

---

[55] These were stated to be the main goals of the Proposed Directive in the Council's Statement of Reasons to the Common Position, n 53 above, III. In its response to the Parliament's amendments to the Common Position, the Commission supported this wider objective of the Proposed Directive and referred to its objective of harmonizing 'national rules on takeover bids, particularly regarding the transparency of the procedure, in order to facilitate restructuring in Europe': n 54 above, 3.

[56] Nonetheless, while divergences remain, structural barriers are still in place, and approaches to corporate governance differ, the basic principles of takeover regulation have tended to converge across Continental Europe, following the UK model. See Hopt, n 5 above, 110–13.

[57] Detractors of takeovers and of regulation which encourages takeover activity point to the adverse consequences a change in management and a likely aggressive new focus on maximizing profits may have for employees, suppliers, the environment, and, if new management takes on more debt or risk, creditors and debt-holders. See, for example, Coffee, J, 'Shareholders versus Managers: Strains in the Corporate Web' (1986) 85 *Mich. LR* 1. In its evidence to the House of Lords Select Committee the Law Society of Scotland suggested that, as a successful

shareholder protection and the right of individual shareholders to participate
in the outcome of a bid were the dominant regulatory concerns, given the
emphasis on disclosure, timely publication of information, minority protection, and on prohibiting frustrating action. The collective interests of shareholders were also reflected, however, in provisions such as the requirement
that the offeree board act in the best interests of the company as a whole.

In order to achieve its objectives, the Proposed Directive provided minimum guidelines on the conduct of bids, set a minimum level of disclosure,
and sought to ensure that certain minimum shareholder safeguards, including the mandatory-bid mechanism and the imposition of a neutrality
principle on offeree boards in order to control the use of defensive measures,
were in place in all the Member States. While the mandatory-bid and the
defensive-measures rules are interventionist devices, transparency and disclosure requirements also permeated the regime. In this respect, the
Proposed Directive represented a logical fit with the regulatory philosophy,
evident in the preceding securities directives, that securities markets across
the EC should, in the interests of investor protection and market integrity,
be transparent and that investors should take investment decisions, whether
to buy or sell, on the basis of adequate disclosure; it also chimed with the
trend towards greater reliance on disclosure as a regulatory control on the
investor/investment-firm relationship.

XIV.4.2 *Subsidiarity and Structure*

One of the most commented on features of the Proposed Directive was its
framework nature which was driven by political exigencies as much as by
the subsidiarity principle. The Proposed Directive was a framework measure,
which consisted of common principles and general requirements and was
designed to be implemented through more detailed rules 'according to
[Member States'] national systems and their cultural contexts' (recital 4).
The particular sensitivity of the takeover sphere to cultural conditions was
thus explicitly acknowledged. With respect to its subject matter, compliance
with the subsidiarity principle was deemed to be met as, per recital 3, only
action at Community level could ensure an adequate level of protection for
holders of securities across the Community and provide minimum guidelines
for the conduct of bids, given that Member States acting alone were not in
a position to establish the same level of protection for cross-border takeovers.

The Proposed Directive covered the same areas as the 1990 Proposal with
the critical difference that it did so through minimum principles and requirements. To take one example, while the 1990 Proposal set out detailed rules

takeover may result in the liquidation of the offeree, it was important that regulation provide
for appropriate consideration of the impact of a takeover on employee and creditor interests:
HL Takeover Report, n 21 above, 28, para 73.

concerning the revision of takeover bids, the Proposed Directive simply provided in Article 10(b) that Member States were to introduce rules concerning revisions. The preparatory legislative materials reveal that the Commission was determined to preserve the framework nature of the Proposal. Many of the amendments suggested by Parliament and ECOSOC were rejected as not being suitable for a framework directive or as being more appropriately dealt with by the Member States.[58] Throughout, the Proposed Directive avoided setting detailed prescriptive requirements; the most notorious example is arguably the failure to define 'control' for the purposes of the mandatory bid requirements, but others would include the omission of rules on the pricing of offers. While the argument can be and has been raised that the Proposed Directive was, as a result, toothless, it did introduce a mandatory-bid requirement for all Member States (Article 5), eliminate the possibility of a mandatory-bid alternative (Article 5), outlaw the taking of defensive measures without shareholder approval (Article 9(1)), place controls on the type of consideration which could be offered (Article 5), and introduce concert-party requirements (Article 2).[59]

Nonetheless, its effectiveness can be challenged, given that takeover requirements would have continued to diverge across the Community, although common core principles would have been established. The general principles set out in Article 3 with which Member States must comply might, however, have provided some protection against those divergences which might have threatened the Proposed Directive's common core.

XIV.4.3 *Scope*

The Proposed Directive applied in Article 1(1) to 'the laws, regulations, administrative provisions, codes of practice or other arrangements of the

---

[58] One such example was the Parliament's suggestion that the Common Position be amended to specify the specific information required on the bidder's intentions with regard to the future business of the offeree under Art. 6(3). This was rejected by the Commission on the ground that 'excessively detailed lists' had no place in a framework directive: n 54 above, para III.1.4.

[59] Although the framework approach reflected the subsidiarity principle, nonetheless, in its assessment of the 1996 Proposal which also adopted a framework approach, the House of Lords Select Committee found that, contrary to Art. 5 EC, it did not solve any problems which could not have been addressed by the Member States and did not produce any clear benefits. It doubted whether 'a big stick of a directive is needed for Member States to act' in the area of takeover regulation given the evidence of 'soft harmonization' driven by market forces: HL Takeover Report, n 21, paras 94–96. The Takeover Panel also attacked the takeover regime on subsidiarity grounds prior to the adoption of the common position, arguing that the use of vague minimal principles meant that no real harmonization was achieved by the directive and that action at Community level was accordingly inappropriate. For a defence of the regime's compliance with the subsidiarity principle (based on the 1996 Proposal), see the argument that rule harmonization must not be confused with the objective of the Proposal which is harmonization of equivalence of protection: Dine, J, 'Subsidiarity, Datafin and the DTI' (1996) 17 *The Company Lawyer* 248, 251.

Member States, including arrangements established by organisations officially authorized to regulate the markets . . . relating to takeover bids for the securities of a company governed by the law of a Member State'. Its provisions were limited to bids for the securities of publicly quoted companies as the securities in question were to be admitted to trading on a regulated market, as defined by the Investment Services Directive.[60]

The Proposed Directive did not apply to takeover bids for securities issued by companies the object of which is the collective investment of capital provided by the public, and which operate on the principle of risk spreading, and the units of which are, at the holder's request, repurchased or redeemed, directly or indirectly, out of the assets of those companies (Article 1(2)). This exclusion was designed to take UCITs, outside the takeover regime as UCITS shareholders already benefit from specific protection.

A takeover bid was broadly defined in Article 2(a) as a public offer, other than an offer by the offeree company itself, to the holders of the securities (securities were briefly defined in Article 2(e) as transferable securities carrying voting rights in a company) of a company to acquire all or part (thereby covering partial bids)[61] of such securities. This basic definition had, at least, the merit of simplicity. The definition of takeover also emphasized that a bid could be mandatory (section 4.8 below) or voluntary and, in a qualification added at the common position stage, was to follow or have as its objective the acquisition of control. Substantial acquisitions, short of control, which are often dealt with through separate rules, fell outside the Proposed Directive as a result.

Offeree company was defined as a company whose securities were the subject of the bid (Article 2(b)) while offeror covered any natural person or legal entity in public or private law making a bid (Article 2(c)). Under Article 2(f) 'parties to the bid' covered the offeror, the members of the offeror's board if the offeror was a company, holders of securities of the offeree company, and the members of the board of the offeree company or persons acting in concert with such parties. The definition of 'persons acting in concert' was an addition to the 1997 Proposal which had considerable significance for the mandatory-bid rule (which had a control trigger) and which was included in the interests of legal certainty: concert parties were defined as natural persons or legal entities who co-operated with the offeror or the offeree company on the basis of an agreement, either express or tacit, oral or written, and aimed respectively at obtaining control of the offeree company or frustrating the successful outcome of a bid (Article 2(d)). Persons controlled by another person in accordance with the Substantial

---

[60] Directive 93/22/EC on investment services in the securities field [1993] OJ L141/27 (the ISD).

[61] Although mandatory bids could not to be made in the form of partial bids: Art. 5(1).

Shareholdings Directive[62] (Article 8) were also deemed to be acting in concert with such persons and with each other.

XIV.4.4 *General Principles*

As did the 1990 Proposal, the Proposed Directive set out in Article 3 a number of general principles which were to be respected in the implementing rules to be adopted by the Member States. Member States were also to ensure that rules would be in place which satisfied the minimum requirements set out in the Proposed Directive. As befitted the Proposed Directive's status as a framework measure, Article 3(2)(b) provided that Member States might impose additional conditions and more stringent provisions than those required by the Proposed Directive to regulate bids.

Equivalent treatment of shareholders was at the heart of the Proposed Directive and can be seen in specific requirements such as the disclosure obligations and the minority protection rules. Principle 3(1)(a) required that all holders of securities of an offeree company of the same class be given equivalent treatment. In particular, and in order to stress the need for minority protection, if a person acquired control of a company, the other holders of securities were to be protected. The use of equivalent treatment rather than equal treatment was designed to allow the supervisory authority to ensure that the different circumstances of security-holders were taken into account. The Proposed Directive's emphasis on disclosure and transparency was reflected by Principle 3(1)(b) which provided that holders of securities of an offeree company were to have sufficient time and information to enable them to reach a properly informed decision on the bid. Under Principle 3(1)(c), the offeree company's board was to act in the interests of the company as a whole and was not to deny the holders of securities the opportunity to decide on the merits of the bid.[63] Principle 3(1)(d) set out that false markets were not to be created in the securities of the offeree company, the offeror company, or any other company concerned by the bid. The Principle attempted to define a false market by referring to an artificial rise or fall in the price of securities and disruption in the normal functioning of the market. Principle 3(1)(e) was designed to prevent tactical bids which could be prejudicial to shareholders. It provided than an offeror was to announce a bid only after ensuring that it could fulfil in full any cash consideration, if so offered, and having taken all reasonable measures to secure the implementation of any other type of consideration. Finally, Principle 3(1)(f) sought to prevent the offeree company from being held in

---

[62] N 32 above.

[63] The Parliament had amended the 1997 Proposal to include a direct reference to the need to consider safeguarding jobs. This end was achieved via Art. 9 which required the offeree board to give an opinion on the implications of the takeover for employment: sect. 4.6.2 below.

a permanent state of siege by bidders and provided that an offeree company was not to be hindered in the conduct of its affairs for longer than was reasonable by a bid for its securities.

XIV.4.5 *Disclosure and the Offer Document*

XIV.4.5.1 *Disclosure and Takeovers*

A dominant theme of EC securities regulation generally, disclosure was also prominent in the Proposed Directive. Reflecting General Principles 3(1)(b) and 3(1)(d), the Proposed Directive set out minimum disclosure and transparency requirements which were to serve individual investor-protection interests as well as, by limiting the opportunities for insider dealing and channelling information through to the market-place (the Proposal being directed towards regulated markets), the wider market-integrity and efficiency objectives promoted by securities regulation.

Disclosure requirements were at the core of the Proposed Directive's shareholder-protection structure. Disclosure in the context of takeovers of publicly quoted companies is usually justified by reference to the fact that the market price for the target's shares does not reflect any information with respect to changes of management and the consequences that are likely to follow on a change of control. The market price is, in fact, usually based on the performance of the incumbent management. As a result, specific disclosure is required concerning the intentions of the bidder in order to allow the shareholder to make a rational decision. Disclosure as a regulatory device for protecting shareholders is therefore neutral with respect to the intrinsic worth of takeovers. It simply allows shareholders to exercise an informed choice with respect to the future of the target. Disclosure also minimizes the incentive to take insider profits, given that share prices tend (although obviously not always) to rise in the wake of a takeover, by publicizing the intentions of bidders.

XIV.4.5.2 *Disclosing the Bid*

Article 6(1) required that Member States were to ensure that rules would be in force requiring that the decision to make a bid be made public without delay and that the supervisory authority be informed of the bid. In order to reflect the position in certain Member States, Member States were to require that the supervisory authority be informed before the decision was made public. As soon as the bid was publicly announced, the board of the offeree company was required to inform the employees' representatives or, in the absence of such representation, the employees themselves.

XIV.4.5.3 *The Offer Document*

Article 6(2) provided that Member States were to ensure that rules would be in force requiring the offeror to draw up an offer document and make it public 'in good time'. The document was to contain, in a formula familiar from the securities directives, 'the information necessary to enable the addressees of the bid to reach a properly informed decision on the bid'.

Article 6(3) set out minimum content requirements for the offer document; these were to be supplemented by more detailed disclosure regimes at Member-State level. It required that the offer document state, at least: the terms of the bid; the identity of the offeror and, where the offeror was a company, its type, name, and registered office; the securities or class or classes of securities for which the bid was made; the consideration offered for each security or class of securities and, in the case of mandatory bids (section 4.8 below), the basis of the valuation used in determining it, with particulars of the way in which that consideration was to be given; the maximum and minimum percentages or quantities of securities which the offeror undertook to acquire; details of any existing holdings of the offeror, and of persons acting in concert with him, in the offeree company; and all the conditions to which the offer was subject, including the period for acceptance of the bid. Details were also to be given of the offeror's intention with regard to the future business and undertakings of the offeree company, its employees, and its management, including any material change in the conditions of employment. Where the consideration offered by the offeror included securities, information was to be given about those securities, and details also given of the financing for the bid.[64] Finally, disclosure was to be made of the identity of persons acting in concert with the offeror or with the offeree company together with, in the case of companies, their type, name, and registered office, and their relationship with the offeror and, where possible, with the offeree company.[65]

The disclosure requirements also included under Article 7 a requirement which placed a condition on Member States with respect to the conduct of the bid. Member States were to provide that the period for acceptance of the bid, which was to be specified in the offer document, could not be less than four weeks nor more than ten weeks from the date of publication of the offer document. This requirement dovetailed with the disclosure philosophy in attempting to ensure that shareholders had a minimum period of time in which to reflect on the information disclosed and within which to make a

---

[64] This requirement reflected the general principle in Art. 3(1)(e) that the bidder's financing arrangements be sound.

[65] Clausen and Sørensen have noted that disclosure requirements are not only relevant to the shareholder's assessment of whether to accept the bid, but also impact on any assessment of the company's future value. In this regard, the offer document fulfils the same function as listing particulars or other public-offer prospectuses and serves the same purposes of investor protection and market protection that underpin the securities directives: n 52 above, 202–3.

rational decision with respect to their shareholdings. Member States could provide that the ten-week period be prolonged on the condition that the offeror gave at least two weeks' prior notice of its intention to close the bid. Under Article 7(2) Member States were permitted to provide for rules modifying the prescribed period in 'specific appropriate cases'. They could also authorize the supervisory authority to grant a derogation from the prescribed period in order to allow the offeree company to organize a general meeting to consider the bid; this might have been necessary if the board wished to seek an authorization to take defensive action, for example.

Under Article 6(4), Member States were to ensure that rules would be in force requiring parties to a bid to provide the supervisory authorities of their Member States at any time on request with all information in their possession concerning the bid which was necessary for the authorities to discharge their functions.

XIV.4.5.4 *Pre-vetting and Publication*

Minimum requirements applied to the publication and distribution of the offer document, although the Member States were given considerable discretion in this area. The Proposed Directive did not explicitly require that the offer document be pre-vetted or approved by the supervisory authority before publication. Under Article 6(2), however, the offer document (which was to be made public) was to be communicated to the supervisory authority before it was made public. Although it is unlikely that pre-vetting was implicit in this communication requirement, anxiety had been expressed in the UK that a pre-vetting requirement might be implied, which would have involved a radical change in the work of the Takeover Panel which does not vet or approve offer documents.[66] Any pre-vetting obligation would have imposed an onerous obligation on supervisory authorities in the already charged atmosphere of a takeover bid and was surely not envisaged by a prior communication requirement which must have been designed more as a means of ensuring that the offer document was prepared and the supervisory authority appropriately informed in the event that difficulties arose in the course of the bid. A pre-vetting requirement would also be out of kilter with the general tenor of the EC capital-raising regime. Only listing particulars are subject to prior approval. The other major disclosure documents in the EC system, interim reports and public-offer prospectuses which have not been prepared in accordance with the Listing Particulars Directive,[67] are not, for the present at least, subject to pre-vetting requirements.

[66] See the evidence of the Company Law Committee of the Law Society, HL Takeover Report, n 21 above, 65.
[67] Directive 80/390/EEC coordinating the requirements for the drawing up, scrutiny and distribution of the listing particulars to be published for the admission of securities to official stock exchange listing [1980] OJ L100/1 (now consolidated in the SCD).

Where the offer document was made subject to prior approval, in an addition to the 1997 Proposal, the Proposed Directive contained a mutual-recognition mechanism which provided for the recognition of approved offer documents in other Member States on whose markets the securities of the offeree company were trading without further approval procedures and free of any additional information requirements. It appears that the minimum disclosure requirements were regarded in the negotiations as representing a satisfactory common minimum level on which to base an offer document 'passport'. The passport mechanism provided for the imposition of translation requirements. It also permitted other supervisory authorities to require that the offer document include information specific to the market of the Member State(s) on whose markets the securities of the offeree company were admitted to trading concerning the formalities to be complied with for accepting the bid and for receiving the consideration and concerning tax arrangements. This practical mechanism had the potential, had it been adopted, to enhance the cross-border legal environment for takeovers considerably.

The offeree company board was required to communicate the offer document, once the offer was made public, to the employees' representatives or, in their absence, the employees themselves. Article 8(2) provided that rules were to be in force which provided for the disclosure of all information or documents required in such a manner as to ensure that they were both readily and promptly available to the holders of securities, at least in those Member States where the securities of the offeree company were admitted to trading on a regulated market, and to the representatives of the employees of the offeree company or, where there were no such representatives, to the employees themselves. The Conciliation Committee compromise bolstered employees' rights further by including a requirement that the offeror was to inform the employees or their representatives at the same time as it informed the management of the offeree of the impact of the takeover on employment, employment conditions, and the location of employees.

XIV.4.5.5 *False Markets*

Finally, tracking General Principle 3(1)(d), the disclosure rules specifically addressed the problem of false markets being created in the course of a takeover bid. Under Article 8(1), Member States were to ensure that rules would be in place requiring a bid to be made public in such a way as to ensure market transparency and integrity for the securities of the offeree company, of the offeror, or of any other company affected by the bid. In particular, such rules were to address the avoidance of the publication or dissemination of false or misleading information. More generally, the danger of insider dealing occurring in the context of a takeover was mitigated by the obligation to disclose the bid and prepare and publish an offer document.

XIV.4.6 *Obligations of the Offeree Board*

XIV.4.6.1 *Frustrating Action*

Article 9(1) was one of the few provisions in the Proposed Directive which had a direct bearing on the removal of barriers to takeover activity across the Community. It addressed the extent to which defensive action could be taken by the board of directors against a hostile bid.[68] Consensus on the appropriate treatment of defensive action proved difficult to achieve, as certain Member States allowed the use of such tactics while others, such as the UK and France, placed severe restrictions on the powers of offeree boards to take frustrating action.[69]

In common with the 1989 and 1990 Proposals, the Proposed Directive's stance on frustrating action was to ensure that the final response to the bid lay with the shareholders and, accordingly, market forces, by prohibiting the taking of frustrating action by the board of the offeree company once the bid had been notified to them unless shareholder approval was given; it imposed, in effect, a neutrality principle. Article 9(1) was a specific expression of the general principle set out in Article 3(1)(c) that the board of the company was to act in the interests of the company as a whole and was not to deny the holders of securities the opportunity to decide on the merits of the bid. It also reflected a core corporate-governance principle: the general meeting of shareholders should decide on the outcome of the bid and directors should accordingly be accountable to the body of shareholders.

In line with its framework structure, the Proposed Directive did not define 'frustrating action', although it did refer specifically to issues of shares.[70] Article 9(1) provided that, at the latest after receiving notification of the bid and until the result of the bid was made public or the bid lapsed, the board of the offeree company was to abstain from completing any action, other than seeking alternative bids, which might have resulted in the frustration of the offer. In particular, the offeree company was to abstain from the issuing of shares which might have resulted in a lasting impediment to the offeror obtaining control. It appears that the identification of one form of

---

[68] The extent to which the target management should be passive in the face of a takeover is closely related to the question of the desirability of takeover activity and its impact on shareholder welfare, and has generated a considerable literature, particularly in the USA. See generally, eg, Ferrarini, n 5 above, 13–23; Davies, P, 'The Regulation of Defensive Tactics in the United Kingdom and the United States' in Hopt and Wymeersch, n 3 above, 195; Easterbrook and Fischel, n 3 above; and Bebchuk, L, 'Tender Offers' (1982) 95 *Harv. LR* 1028.

[69] The Netherlands, eg, took the stance during negotiations that rather than banning defensive measures, provision should be made to allow majority shareholders to appeal against their imposition in certain circumstances.

[70] The Commission stated in its Explanatory Memorandum to the 1996 Proposal that, in general, frustrating actions are those which are not carried out in the normal course of a company's business or are not in conformity with normal market practices: n 50 above, 8.

defensive action in this way was not designed to imply that the neutrality principle was limited to share issues only. Boards were, however, permitted to search for white knights, or alternative bids.[71] As the ban applied only from the time at which the offer was notified, the Proposed Directive did not deal with action taken by a target board which had reason to believe that a bid was imminent. In that sense, the prohibition in Article 9(1) might have been triggered too late to provide effective protection for shareholders.[72]

Circumstances may arise, however, where it may be in the best interests of the company that frustrating action is taken and, indeed, where the board would have a duty to the company to do so. As a result, the ban was not absolute. The board could take frustrating action if it had the prior authorization of the general meeting of the shareholders given for that purpose. This authorization was to be given during the period for acceptance of the bid.

The Proposed Directive did, as a compromise, explicitly authorize one form of defensive action under Article 9(2).[73] Member States could allow the board of the offeree company to increase the share capital during the period for acceptance of the bid on condition that prior authorization had been received from the general meeting of shareholders not earlier than eighteen months before the beginning of the period for the acceptance of the bid. Full recognition was to be given to the right of pre-emption of all shareholders provided for in the Second Company Law Directive.[74] As a result, shares could not be issued to particular shareholders only (typically the controlling shareholder), but were to be offered to all.

XIV.4.6.2 *Consideration of the Offer*

Under Article 9(1)(b) the board of the offeree company was required to draw up and make public a document setting out its opinion on the bid (be it

[71] For the argument that any resistance which triggers a bidding war is undesirable see Easterbrook and Fischel, n 3 above.

[72] It has been noted that the controlling or significant shareholder would not have been prevented by Art. 9 from introducing protective techniques in advance of a bid: Wymeersch, E, 'The Proposal for a 13th Company Law Directive on Takeovers: a Multijurisdictional Survey, Part 2' (1997) 4 *EFSL* 2, 4. The Commission accepted an amendment by the Parliament to the common position to the effect that the ban would come into play from the time when, by whatever means, the existence of bid became known to management: n 54 above, para 3.1.

[73] In its amendments to the common position, the Parliament proposed considerable changes to the frustrating action rule which cut against the core principle underlying Art. 9(1). In particular, the Parliament added a provision to Art. 9(2) setting out other situations in which the supervisory authorities or the courts could authorize defensive measures. The Commission rejected this revision as being incompatible with the spirit of the rule whereby only holders of securities were to determine the company's future as well as with the independence of the competent authority. The Commission also pointed to the likelihood of prejudicial delays were the courts to become involved: n 54 above, para 3.1.5.

[74] Directive 77/91/EEC [1977] OJ L26/1.

positive or negative), together with the reasons on which it was based. The opinion was also to include the board's views on the effects of implementation on all the interests of the company, including employment. This obligation formed part of the Proposed Directive's disclosure framework, supplementing the information on the basis of which shareholders could make an informed decision.

XIV.4.7 *Conduct of the Bid*

In contrast to the 1989 Proposal, the Proposed Directive did not set out specific rules on the conduct of the bid. Instead Article 10 simply required Member States to ensure that rules were in force which would govern: the lapse of the bid; revision of bids; competing bids; disclosure of the results of the bids; and the irrevocability of the bid and the conditions permitted. Member States had therefore a large discretion in the content of these conduct rules, although they were to respect the general principles set out in Article 3 in their adoption.

XIV.4.8 *Minority Shareholder Protection and Mandatory Bids*

XIV.4.8.1 *The Mandatory Bid*

The Proposed Directive's regulatory devices were not, however, confined to largely non-interventionist disclosure and procedural requirements. In providing for equivalent treatment, the Proposed Directive moved beyond simply providing shareholders with equivalent access to information so that all could make an informed choice, but moved into regulating the offer itself by means of the mandatory-bid device.[75]

Actual control of a company with a widely dispersed shareholding may be acquired by the purchase of significantly less than an outright majority of the shares. Accordingly, by paying a premium price for a selective part of the shareholding, a bidder can obtain control. In such a situation, the remaining shareholders who have not benefited from the premium may suffer a reduction in the value of their shareholdings,[76] and find themselves locked into the company following a change in control which they do not support. They may then be coerced into selling their holdings to the new

---

[75] The mandatory bid has been described as 'the severest intrusion on market freedom imposed by take-over regulation': Tridimas, T, 'Self Regulation and Investor Protection in the United Kingdom: The Take-over Panel and the Market for Corporate Control' (1991) 10 *Civil Justice Quarterly* 24, 32.

[76] One reason for a reduction in share value, where the successful bidder is a group, may be a change in management strategy resulting in the target being run for the benefit of the new group in which it now finds itself and the diversion of profits and earnings away from the target.

controllers at a price less than that at which they value their shareholdings. Shareholder choice is then distorted. As shareholders targeted by a takeover tend to be widely dispersed and passive in monitoring the bidder or the target's intentions, in the interests of the equivalent treatment of shareholders[77] many systems of regulation protect minority shareholders during and after a change of control.[78]

The mandatory-bid rule is one way of achieving this protection. It requires a person who has obtained control to share the control premium among all shareholders by launching an offer for all the remaining shares of the target. It is designed to ensure that minority shareholders, who may not be in favour of the change in control, have an exit from the company at a non-discriminatory price. It prevents the acquisition of companies at a price which does not reflect the real value of the control acquired. Due to the expense and time involved in a mandatory bid, its imposition also has the effect of discouraging purely speculative acquisitions of controlling interests which can have an adverse effect on the value of the minority holdings thereby created. A requirement to launch a mandatory bid may, however, have counter-productive effects in that its high costs can deter investment in companies.[79]

XIV.4.8.2 *The Proposed Directive's Mandatory-bid Rule*

(a) *Mandatory Requirement*

The design of the mandatory-bid rule[80] and the extent to which it was a mandatory requirement for Member States went through a number of formulations. The earlier Proposals were based on the premise that the

---

[77] The point has been made that it is not entirely clear why equal treatment should be insisted on if its consequence, in practice, is the deterrence of productive takeover activity. See Alhauge, E, 'Towards a European Sale of Control Doctrine' (1993) 41 *Am. J Comp. L* 627 who cites at 643 Pareto's principle that uneven gains should be allowed as long as some persons are better off and none are worse off. The latter may not always occur in a takeover, however.

[78] The Proposed Directive focused on regulating sales of controlling shareholdings from the perspective of the bidder and imposed obligations on the bidder which were designed to protect all shareholders. For a discussion of sale of control issues from the alternative perspective of imposing fiduciary obligations on the sellers of controlling blocks of shares see Alhauge, n 77 above.

[79] For a critique of the standard rationales offered for the imposition of a mandatory bid requirement see Wymeersch, E, 'The Mandatory Bid: A Critical View' in Hopt and Wymeersch, n 3 above, 351, 356–67. The counter-arguments include that a mandatory-bid rule is predicated on the intention of the bidder to freeze out the minority and strip the target of its assets, which may not in fact exist at the time and which, in any event, could be dealt with after the acquisition. Mandatory bids may also prevent minority shareholders from maximizing the price for their holdings as, once the mandatory bid has been triggered by the acquisition of control, it is unlikely that other bidders will counter-offer.

[80] For a comparative analysis see the discussion (in the context of the 1997 Proposal) in Clausen and Sørensen, n 52 above, 188–99.

mandatory bid was the only way of ensuring minority protection. They required a mandatory bid to be launched whenever control was acquired. This compulsory imposition of a mandatory-bid rule was highly contentious. In particular, certain Member States pointed to the expense involved in launching a mandatory bid and felt that it could undermine the market for corporate control while minority protection could be achieved through alternative means.[81] The 1997 Proposal adopted a middle way: where control of a company was acquired, Member States were to ensure that rules or other mechanisms or arrangements were in force which either obliged that person to make a mandatory bid or to offer 'other appropriate and at least equivalent means in order to protect the minority shareholders of that company'. Member States accordingly had the option of ensuring minority protection either through a full mandatory bid, a partial mandatory bid, or other equivalent means. The salient features of the mandatory bid are that it protects minority shareholders by providing an exit route at a non-discriminatory price. Other forms of minority protection focus on ensuring that the minority shareholder can continue to participate in the company on fair and equal terms. The controversial option was introduced largely to address German concerns.[82] Germany strongly resisted the imposition of a mandatory bid as the only form of minority protection, as it provides for minority-shareholder protection through alternative methods, one of which is its *Konzernrecht* or Law of Corporate Groups. It contains specific provisions concerning dominating influences, or majority shareholdings, in groups of companies. In particular, in groups of affiliated companies where the group structure is formalized and contractual, minority shareholders of a dependent company are entitled to certain payments, paid at least once a year, which represent an indemnity to minority shareholders for their lack of control. Minority shareholders also have a right to withdraw from the company

---

[81] Not all Member States were opposed in principle to mandatory bids; France, Belgium, Italy, Spain, Portugal and the UK all provided for mandatory bids. Variations existed in the threshold of shareholdings at which the obligation arose and how shareholdings were aggregated for the purposes of determining control, the percentage of shares subject to the mandatory offer, and the price of the mandatory offer. In continental Europe the mandatory bid was particularly important in imposing disclosure, transparency, and equal treatment in a context where, due to the practice of control transfers through sales of controlling shareholdings, such elements might otherwise have been missing. See generally Wymeersch, n 79 above, who at 360–4 countered this rationale for the mandatory bid by arguing that its imposition and its disadvantages contribute to diverting control transfers to the negotiating table and away from the public-takeover market. In some cases mandatory-bid provisions seem to have been triggered by the earlier Proposals. In 1991 Spain adopted a mandatory-bid rule requiring a bid for all shares to be made when 25% of the shareholding was acquired. Germany and the Netherlands, which relied on alternative company-law devices to protect minority shareholders, were the fiercest opponents of the mandatory-bid rule. The UK also criticized the mandatory-bid provisions, but on the ground that they were not sufficiently detailed to provide adequate minority protection.

[82] Explanatory Memorandum to 1996 Proposal, n 50 above, 5.

where they are no longer able to defend their own financial interests, where those interests diverge from the interests of the majority shareholders.[83]

In a return to the original approach, however, the Proposed Directive made the full mandatory bid compulsory for all Member States (Article 5). A transitional period of one year from the implementation deadline of the Proposed Directive was put in place, during which Member States, which at the time of the adoption of the Directive provided for 'other appropriate and at-least-equivalent means in order to protect the minority shareholders' could continue to apply these means (Article 5(3)). The means employed were to be specific to the transfer of control and include specific financial compensation for minority shareholders. Article 5 of the Proposed Directive was driven by the rationale that the full mandatory bid was the only means of protecting minority shareholders. The earlier 'other equivalent means' option was dropped following agreement by a majority of Member States, including Germany, that the mandatory bid was the best way of delivering shareholder protection.[84] Article 5(4) provided, however, that these other equivalent means could be used in addition to the mandatory bid. Member States could, in addition to the mandatory-bid rule, provide, under Article 5(4), for 'further instruments aiming at the protection of the interests of holders of securities' as long as they did not hinder the normal course of the mandatory bid.[85]

(b) *The Control Trigger*

By contrast with the 1989 and 1990 Proposals which defined control by reference to a 33.33 per cent holding of voting rights, what constituted control for the purposes of triggering the mandatory-bid mechanism was not defined. Article 5(1) applied the mandatory-bid rule to a 'natural person or legal entity' who, as a result of his own acquisition or the acquisition by persons acting in concert with him, held securities of a company within the

---

[83] The Netherlands also objected to the mandatory-bid rule. It argued that majority shareholders tended not to exploit minority shareholders and, in any event, due to the Dutch remedies available against oppressive behaviour, could not risk behaving in an exploitative and oppressive fashion. These protections included the right to request a court to reverse a decision of a shareholders' meeting and the ability of minority shareholders to call for an investigation into the company's affairs. See the comments of Timmermans, L, in Wymeersch, E (ed), 'The Proposal for a 13th Company Law Directive on Takeovers: a Multijurisdictional Survey part 1' (1996) 3 *EFSL* 301.

[84] For the argument that the protections of the German rules on groups are not 'equivalent' to those provided by a mandatory bid requirement see Hopt, K, 'Company Law in the European Union: Harmonisation and/or Subsidiarity' 1 (1999) *ICCLJ* 41, 54–5.

[85] The Conciliation Committee compromise would have committed the Commission to a re-examination of the treatment of minority shareholders and in particular to an assessment of 'squeeze-outs' or the right of the majority to remove minority shareholders. The High Level Expert Group is considering this question.

scope of the Proposed Directive which, when added to any existing holdings and the holdings of persons acting in concert with him, directly or indirectly, gave him 'a specified percentage of voting rights[86] in that company, conferring on him control of that company'. The percentage of voting rights which conferred control and its method of calculation was to be set by the Member State where the company had its registered office. The failure to define the threshold at which control was deemed to exist was severely criticized during the negotiations.[87] Had the Proposed Directive been adopted, it could well have resulted in major discrepancies in the treatment of minority shareholders across the Community.[88] The Commission justified the omission by reference to the difficulties which had arisen in finding agreement on a threshold during negotiations on the earlier proposals. The definition of concert parties (section 4.3 above) did, however, address the possibility that bidders could evade the minority-shareholder protections by acting in concert with other parties to acquire control where Member States did not already provide for concert party rules.

(c) *Conduct of the Mandatory Bid*

Article 5 contained little substantive detail on the operation of the mandatory bid.[89] A full mandatory bid was to be launched to all holders of securities. Recital 7 to the Proposed Directive made clear, however, that the 'further instruments' which Member States could provide for under Article 5(4) could include the obligation to make a partial bid where the offeror did not acquire control of the company.

Minority protection is little served by a mandatory bid unless the price of the offer reflects the equal-treatment principle which is the rationale for the mandatory-bid rule. Article 5 did not specifically address the price at which the mandatory bid was to be conducted, except to provide that the bid was to be made at 'an equitable price' which ensured equal treatment for share-

---

[86] The mandatory-bid rule did not apply to acquisitions of securities which did not carry voting rights in ordinary general meetings. Member States could extend the mandatory-bid obligation to the acquisition of securities which only carried voting rights in specific circumstances or which did not carry voting rights (Recital 8).

[87] See, eg, the HL Takeover Report, n 21, above para 112 which described it as a 'significant and unacceptable omission in a harmonizing measure'.

[88] ECOSOC also expressed concern that the ability of Member States to set the control threshold could result in minority protection rules being used as protectionist measures: n 51 above, para 3.3.3.

[89] For an example of a detailed mandatory-bid rule see Rule 9 of the Takeover Code, the specific provisions of which include: the threshold at which the bid obligation triggers; concert-party provisions; restrictions on the conditions which may be placed on the offer; and rules on the consideration for the offer. Rule 9 also contains extensive notes on the mandatory-bid rule and its application.

holders.[90] The Proposed Directive did not require that a cash consideration be made available although a cash consideration would have granted shareholders the option of leaving the company, protected the target shareholders against a decrease in the value of the share consideration, and reduced the risk of manipulation of those shares. Conversely, however, cash alternatives are costly while share-only considerations increase liquidity in those shares and market-place liquidity. Article 5(1) represented a compromise and provided that where the consideration offered did not consist of 'liquid securities admitted to trading on a regulated market', an alternative cash consideration was to be made available. This provision was designed to enhance the protection of minority shareholders and prevent them from being locked into an illiquid investment. Liquid securities, conversely, allow shareholders to leave the company and realize their investment when they wish.

Under Article 5(2), where a voluntary bid was made in accordance with the Proposed Directive to all holders of securities for all their holdings and control obtained, the obligation to launch a bid then fell away. This provision reflected the reality that in such circumstances minority shareholders were protected by the full voluntary bid conducted in accordance with the equivalent treatment principle.

XIV.4.9 *The Supervisory Authority*

XIV.4.9.1 *Designation of Competent Authorities*

Clearly any attempt, however attenuated, to harmonize takeover regulation is dependent on the existence of a network of supervisory authorities competent to supervise the implementing rules. Under Article 4(1), Member States were to designate the authority (or authorities) which were to supervise the entire course of the bid. The Commission was to be informed of these designations, together with any divisions of functions.

The authorities designated could be either public authorities or associations or private bodies recognized either by national law or by public

---

[90] This provision reflected the Proposed Directive's framework structure and diverging approaches across the Member States. To take one example, the UK Takeover Code provides, *inter alia*, that the price at which a mandatory bid is conducted must be not less than the highest price which the bidder has paid for any shares in the target in the 3-month (and, in certain circumstances, 12-month) period preceding the offer. The Commission stated that 'Member States proved unable to choose a more precise definition—in spite of two years of negotiation—from among the various national definitions applied because they could not decide what might be best for all of them. It was therefore deemed expedient to leave this matter to the discretion of the competent supervisory authorities': n 54 above, para 3.1.2. In the Conciliation Committee compromise, however, the Commission committed to re-examine the 'equitable price' question and to bring forward proposals if appropriate. The High Level Expert Group is considering this question.

authorities expressly empowered for that purpose by national law. In a clear acknowledgment of the position of the unique self-regulatory status of the UK Takeover Panel (see further section 4.9.5 below), recital 11 provided that supervision could be exercised by self-regulatory bodies.

Member States were also to ensure that the supervisory authorities exercised their functions impartially and independently of all parties to the bid.

XIV.4.9.2 *Cross-border Bids*

Article 4(2) set out a series of steps for determining which supervisory authority was competent to supervise a particular takeover bid. The governing principle was that the competent supervisory authority would be that of the Member State in which the offeree was admitted to trading. In the first instance, jurisdiction was given under Article 4(2)(a) to the supervisory authority of the Member State in which the offeree company had its registered office, as long as its securities were admitted to trading on a regulated market in that Member State. If that was not the case, either Article 4(2)(b) or (c) governed which supervisory authority was competent to supervise the bid. Underlying the somewhat byzantine scheme for determining the competent supervisory authority where the offeree was not admitted to trading in its Member State of registration was the principle that a distinction be maintained between the market rules of the Member States in which the offeree's securities were admitted to trading and the home rules of the Member State in which it was registered. Procedural matters, including the price to be paid, were assigned to the former, while questions of company law and, in particular, disclosure to employees, were assigned to the latter.[91]

Under Article 4(2)(b), if the securities of the offeree company were not admitted to trading on a regulated market in the Member State in which the company had its registered office, the supervisory authority responsible for the bid was to be that of the Member State on whose regulated market the securities of the company were admitted to trading. If the securities were admitted to trading on a regulated market in more than one Member State, the competent supervisory authority was to be that of the Member State on whose regulated market the securities were first admitted. Under Article 4(2)(c), if the securities of the offeree company were first admitted to trading on regulated markets within more than one Member State simultaneously, the offeree company was to determine the competent authority for supervising the bid by notifying those regulated markets and their supervisory authorities on the first trading day. If the securities of the offeree company were already admitted to trading on regulated markets in more than

---

[91] This distinction, according to the Commission, 'corresponds to economic realities': Commission Communication to the Parliament concerning the Common Position, SEC(2000) 1300, para 3.3.

one Member State at the deadline for the Proposed Directive's implementation, and were admitted simultaneously, the supervisory authorities of these Member States were to agree on who was to be the competent authority for supervising the bid within four weeks of that deadline. Otherwise the competent authority was to be determined by the offeree company on the first trading day following this four-week period. Member States were to ensure that rules would be in force requiring the decisions made under Article 4(2)(c) to be made public.

Where Article 4(2)(b) and (c) applied and a company was admitted to trading outside its Member State of registration, Article 4(2)(e) attempted to resolve conflict-of-laws problems which might otherwise have arisen. Matters relating to the consideration offered in the case of a bid (particularly the price), matters relating to the procedure of the bid (particularly the information on the offeror's decision to make a bid), the contents of the offer document, and the disclosure of the bid were to be dealt with in accordance with the rules of the Member State of the competent authority (Article 4(2(e)). In matters relating to the information to be provided to the employees of the offeree company and in matters relating to company law (particularly the threshold of voting rights which conferred control, any derogations from the obligation to launch a bid as well as the conditions under which the offeree board could take frustrating action), however, the applicable rules and the competent authority were those of the Member State in which the offeree company had its registered office (Article 4(2)(e)).

XIV.4.9.3 *Confidentiality and Co-operation*

As might be expected, the supervisory authorities were subject to secrecy and confidentiality constraints. Under Article 4(3), each Member State was to ensure that all persons who were or had been employed by the supervisory authorities were bound by professional-secrecy obligations. Information covered by professional secrecy was not to be divulged to any person or authority except by virtue of provisions laid down in law.

Under Article 4(4), the supervisory authorities and other authorities supervising capital markets (in particular the ISD, SSD (now consolidated in the SCD), and Insider Dealing Directive[92] competent authorities) were to co-operate and supply each other with information where necessary, particularly where the bid had a cross-border element in that the company's registered office was in a different Member State from that where its securities were admitted to trading on a regulated market. Co-operation was to include the ability to serve the legal documents necessary to enforce measures as well as such other assistance as might reasonably have been

---

[92] Directive 89/592/EEC coordinating regulations on insider dealing [1989] OJ L334/30.

requested by the supervisory authorities concerned for the purposes of investigating any actual or alleged breaches of the rules made under the Proposed Directive.

XIV.4.9.4 *Powers*

In terms of their powers, Article 4(5) required that the supervisory authorities have all the powers necessary for the performance of their functions. These powers were to include responsibility for ensuring that the parties to a bid comply with the rules implementing the Proposed Directive. In a reflection of the Proposed Directive's framework approach and given that the granting of derogations is common practice among the Member States, Member States were permitted to provide in their implementing rules that their supervisory authorities could, in particular types of cases and on the basis of a reasoned decision, in specific appropriate cases grant derogations from these rules. More generally, recital 10 of the Preamble emphasized the need for flexibility and provided that 'takeover regulation should be flexible and capable of dealing with new circumstances as they arise, and should accordingly provide for the possibility of exceptions and derogations'.

Sanctions or remedies were not, in line with EC securities regulation generally, expressly addressed. Member States were simply required under Article 12 to determine the sanctions to be applied in the case of infringements. These were to be sufficient to promote compliance with the Proposed Directive's requirements.

XIV.4.9.5 *Judicial Review and Litigation Risk*

Article 4(6) represented the most recent of a series of attempts to deal with the bedevilled question of litigation risk or the extent to which decisions of supervisory authorities can be challenged before the courts and, in particular, to address the concerns of the UK that adoption of the Proposed Directive would have increased the possibility of delaying litigation during the course of a takeover bid and prejudiced the unique position of the self-regulatory Takeover Panel. Resolution of this question dogged the negotiations from the outset.[93]

---

[93] The Takeover Panel does not have any statutory authority and the City Code does not have the force of law. Nonetheless the Panel is widely regarded as an effective regulator of takeover bids. The Panel has frequently stated that its status allows it to respond with speed and flexibility to rapidly changing takeover situations. Rulings of the Panel are subject to judicial review, but the courts have acknowledged the special status of the Panel and the environment within which it operates. They will review its interpretations of the Code only where there is real injustice or the interpretation is either perverse or in conflict with principles of equity (*R v Takeover Panel, ex parte Datafin* [1987] 1 QB 815 and *R v Panel on Takeovers and Mergers, ex parte Guinness plc* [1989] 1 All ER 511). Its position must now be considered in light of the Financial Services and Markets Act 2000.

The UK consistently expressed its opposition to harmonized takeover regulation throughout

For the most part, this question was ultimately left to the Member States with Article 4(6) designed to clarify that the Proposed Directive did not create *inter partes* rights, which was a particular concern of the UK Takeover Panel, and that Member States had a discretion as regards how disputes were handled, whether via the courts or through an administrative appeals procedure.[94] Article 4(6) provided that the Proposed Directive did 'not affect the powers of the Member States to designate judicial or other authorities responsible for dealing with disputes and for deciding on irregularities committed in the bid procedure'. It also stated that the Proposed Directive did not affect the power of Member States to regulate whether and under which circumstances parties to a bid were entitled to bring administrative or judicial proceedings. In particular, it confirmed that the Proposed Directive did not affect the power which courts may have in a Member State to decline to hear legal proceedings and to decide whether such proceedings affect the outcome of a bid. It appears that this provision was designed to ensure that a court would be permitted to refuse to entertain actions which were purely tactical in nature, and, in consequence, address a major concern of the UK Takeover Panel. Finally, Article 4(6) provided that the Proposed Directive did not affect the powers of the Member States to determine the legal position concerning the liability of supervisory authorities or concerning litigation between the parties to a bid. Member States could, as a result, protect the position of supervisory authorities and insulate them from damages claims.

XIV.4.10 *Contact Committee*

Given its open-textured nature and the sensitivity of its provisions it is not surprising that the Proposed Directive would, on its adoption, have been placed under the supervision of the Contact Committee set up under Article

the various stages of the takeover regime's development. At the heart of this opposition was the concern that adoption of a directive on takeovers would prejudice the special position of the Panel by placing it on a statutory footing and so exposing it to increased litigation risk, but would not bring any advantages to an already widely admired and practical system of takeover regulation. A major concern was that the imposition of a statutory framework, based on a directive, would add a layer of European law to the self-regulatory structure and lead to litigation concerning the interpretation and application of the Proposed Directive's requirements in both the national courts and the European Court of Justice. In particular, the extent to which the Proposed Directive conferred rights on individuals which could then be exercised against the Panel in the courts was a matter of concern. The experience of the USA and Australia, where litigation is routinely used as a delaying tactic in hostile takeover bids, was frequently adverted to. Among the reports on and discussions of this hard-fought battle see: HL Takeover Report, n 21 above; Department of Trade and Industry, Consultative Document, *Proposal for a Thirteenth Directive on Company Law Concerning Take-over Bids* (1996); Dine, n 59 above; Andenas, M, 'European Takeover Directive and the City' (1997) 18 *The Company Lawyer* 101 and Edwards, V, *EC Company Law* (1999) 393–9.

[94] Common Position, n 53 above; Statement of the Council's Reasons, III.

20 of the (now consolidated) Admissions Directive (SCD, Article 108).[95] Article 11 provided that the Contact Committee would facilitate the harmonized application of the Proposed Directive through regular meetings which would, in particular, deal with practical problems arising in connection with its application. It was also to advise the Commission, if necessary, on additions or amendments. Article 11(2) clarified that the Contact Committee was not to appraise the merits of decisions taken by the supervisory authorities in individual cases. Particular emphasis was placed in the Preamble on the Committee's role in monitoring the mutual recognition of offer documents mechanism and the implementation of the Proposed Directive with respect to cross-border takeovers.

XIV.4.11 *Revision of the SSD*

The Proposed Directive would, had it been adopted, have amended Article 1 of the SSD (SCD, Article 85(1)), so that its requirements would apply in respect of shares admitted to trading on a regulated market within the meaning of the ISD, rather than, as at present, simply to 'shares . . . which are officially listed on a stock exchange or exchanges situated or operating within one or more Member States'. This revision was designed to ensure that the SSD and the Proposed Directive would have had the same scope.

---

[95] Directive 79/279/EEC coordinating the conditions for the admission of securities to official stock exchange listing [1979] OJ L66/21. On the Contact Committee structure see Ch. XV sect. 2.3.2 below.

PART VII

The Institutional Structure of EC Securities Regulation

XV

Rule-making and Market Supervision

XV.1 INTRODUCTION

The preceding chapters have examined the regulatory and supervisory systems adopted by the EC and designed to underpin the single securities and investment-services market-place. These systems are based on a combination of harmonized rules, which impose, by and large, minimum standards, and the mutual recognition of Member States' regulatory regimes. Supervision and enforcement take place at national level through national competent authorities which are subject to legal obligations to co-operate with the authorities of other Member States.

The extent to which the EC's rule-making procedures accommodate rapid identification of the appropriate regulatory responses to the problems and challenges raised by the integration and evolution of EC securities and investment-services markets is an important element of the debate on the institutional structure of EC securities regulation; so too is the extent to which the structure can ensure the consistent implementation of rules across the market-place. In particular, there is considerable concern that the glacial pace and cumbersome institutional structure of EC rule-making are seriously prejudicing the timely delivery of the FSAP[1] and achievement of the economy-wide benefits of integration (section 2 below). The institutional debate is also concerned with whether the supervision of an integrated securities and investment-services market, which operates under a discrete, if minimal, rule framework and is subject to system-wide risks, by a structure of national supervisors connected by co-operation obligations can be effective or whether the centralization of operational supervisory functions is an inexorable consequence of an integrated market-place (section 3 below).

XV.2 RULE-MAKING AND THE INSTITUTIONAL STRUCTURE

XV.2.1 Introduction

The speed at which new risks and regulatory challenges are emerging (with respect to, for example, stock exchange alliances, the development of alternative trading systems (ATSs), and the use of e-commerce) coupled with the

---

[1] 1999 Commission Communication on Implementing the Framework for Financial Markets: Action Plan, COM(1999)232 (the FSAP).

need to update and refine the current regulatory system in order to achieve the benefits of integration, evident from the FSAP and the Lamfalussy Report,[2] means that it is imperative that the process of developing and amending legislation is sufficiently responsive, flexible, and close to the market-place. In addition, as the directive is the dominant legislative instrument used in the securities-regulation sphere and given that, reflecting the requirements of the subsidiarity principle, Member States are responsible for the detailed implementation of harmonized EC securities and investment-services rules,[3] the exercise of effective centralised supervision over the implementation process is a critical component of the rule-making process. So too are mechanisms which monitor the extent to which directives are implemented consistently across the integrated market-place and assess whether open-textured or opaque provisions are leading to divergences in how a particular directive is being applied. At present, the harmonization regime is, of course, generally limited to minimum standards, is, in many areas (notably investor protection), unsophisticated and inconsistent, and does not extend across the full panoply of securities and investment-services regulation. Although the mutual recognition principle as developed by the Court of Justice mitigates the impact of a failure to harmonize, the availability of the general-good justification, combined with the uneven state of harmonization, represents a continuing reminder of the dominance of national rules in the integrated market and a challenge to the rule-making process.

The institutional structure for rule-making has two dimensions: the Treaty-based institutional structure which supports EC law-making in general and the additional elements which are grafted on to this structure in the securities and investment-services sphere. The structure is perhaps best described as being in a state of transition. It has become increasingly apparent that longstanding inter-institutional tensions and procedural logjams are exercising a disproportionate and prejudicial influence on law-making. An uneasy resolution may be forthcoming as a result of a new law-making model designed to streamline the process whereby securities-regulation measures are adopted.

---

[2] Final Report of the Committee of Wise Men on the Regulation of European Securities Markets, Feb 2001 (the Lamfalussy Report).

[3] Art. 249 EC provides that directives are binding on Member States as regards the result to be achieved but that the choice of form and method of implementation is left to the Member States. The forms of legislation which can be used in the securities-regulation regime, such as directives and regulations, and the subsidiarity principle are outlined in Ch. I sects. 2 and 4 above.

XV.2.2 *The General Institutional Structure*

XV.2.2.1 *Law-making by the Council, and the Council and Parliament Acting Together*

Under Article 249 EC, EC legislation may be adopted by the Parliament acting jointly with the Council, the Council acting alone, and the Commission. Commission law-making powers are very limited, although, as outlined in section 2.2.2 below, the Council can delegate law-making powers to the Commission, subject to the supervision of the Commission under the comitology process.

Not only is the adoption of EC securities-regulation measures vulnerable, in principle, to obstruction by national interests, given the sensitivity of financial market regulation and the ever-growing importance of the securities and investment-services sector economically and socially (as public savings are increasingly channelled towards the securities markets), it also faces highly complex and formal legislative procedures. The particular procedure which must be followed and the EC institutions involved are set out in the Treaty and depend on the Treaty competence on which the measure in question is based. Law-making is an inter-institutional process, with the Commission having the power of legislative initiative and the Council and European Parliament sharing law-making powers to varying degrees, depending on the particular procedure followed.

As discussed in more detail with respect to the discrete elements of the regime in earlier chapters, EC securities-regulation measures must have a basis in a specific competence granted to the EC and set out in the Treaty. Securities-regulation rules have, for the most part, been based on Article 44(2)(g) EC (directives designed to co-ordinate the safeguards required by Member States of companies or firms), Articles 47(2) and 55 EC (directives designed to co-ordinate Member States' rules on the taking-up and pursuit of activities as self-employed persons), Article 94 EC (directives for the approximation of Member States' rules which directly affect the establishment or functioning of the common market) and Article 95 EC (measures for the approximation of Member States' rules which have as their object the establishment and functioning of the internal market).[4] The Commission has the power of legislative initiative in relation to measures adopted under all of these competences. The legislative procedure for the adoption of Article 94 measures requires that the Council, acting unanimously, adopt the measures in question after consulting the Parliament and the Economic and

---

[4] The residual competence, Art. 308 EC, which activates when action by the Community is necessary to attain, in the course of the operation of the common market, one of the objectives of the Community when the Treaty has not provided the necessary powers, has not played a role in the development of the regime to date.

Social Committee (ECOSOC). After a series of Treaty amendments, the other Treaty legislative competences all share the same legislative procedure—the co-decision procedure which is set out in Article 251 EC. Most securities-regulation measures therefore are proposed by the Commission and adopted by the Council and the Parliament under the co-decision procedure.

The co-decision procedure, which was introduced by the Maastricht Treaty, gives the Parliament considerably greater powers in the legislative process as compared to those which it previously exercised and, in particular, allows it to exercise a veto over legislation. Co-decision involves a number of institutions and stages and can be summarized, very broadly, as follows: the legislative proposal is submitted to the Council by the Commission following informal consultations by the Commission of relevant interest groups; the opinion of the Parliament and ECOSOC is sought on the proposal, which may then be amended by the Commission and is submitted to the Council; the Council may then adopt the proposal but only if it accepts all of the Parliament's amendments or if there have been no amendments; if it is not adopted, the Council adopts a 'common position' which is submitted to the Parliament; if, within three months, Parliament approves the common position or does not act, the measure is deemed to be approved; if the common position is rejected by the Parliament by an absolute majority, the measure fails; if amendments are suggested by the Parliament within the three-month time limit, the measure returns to the Council and Commission for their opinion; if the amendments are approved by the Council within three months the act is deemed to be adopted; if not all the amendments are approved the measure goes to a Conciliation Committee composed of representatives of the Council and of the Parliament and attempts are made (with the assistance of the Commission) to reach an agreement; if agreement on a text is reached within six weeks, the Council and Parliament have six weeks to approve the text; finally, if agreement on a text cannot be reached or if the Council or Parliament do not approve the text within the six-week period, the measure fails.[5] It is hardly surprising, given the complexity of

---

[5] For a full discussion of the complex procedures involved in co-decision see Weatherill, S, and Beaumont, P, *EU Law* (3rd edn, 1999) 133–9. The progress of the ill-fated proposed Takeover Directive illustrates the complexities of the procedure, the need for inter-institutional dialogue, and the extent to which national interests can influence the fate of legislation even outside the Council where such interests are traditionally paramount. In the last stages of the co-decision process and before the final collapse of the current incarnation of the proposed Takeover Directive (the process started 12 years ago), the Parliament approved the Council's hard-fought common position but amended it in such a way as to threaten one of the core provisions, the ban on taking frustrating action without general-meeting approval. Although a compromise was brokered between both institutions and the Commission in the Conciliation Committee, it failed, following heavy lobbying by German, Italian and Spanish MEPs, in particular, to win the support of the Parliament on the final vote (which resulted in a tie). Ironically, although difficulties in the Council have, in the 12 years that the proposed Takeover Directive has been under discussion, slowed its progress, in the end it was a flexing of legislative muscle (and, it appears, of national interests) by the EC's newest law-maker, the

this procedure, which can take three to four years to complete, that the law-making process has been criticized as slow, cumbersome, and ill-equipped to cope with the need to respond rapidly and effectively to developments in EC securities markets.

XV.2.2.2 *Law-making by the Commission: The Comitology Process*

The comitology process provides a quicker and less cumbersome mechanism for adopting rules. Article 202 EC permits the Commission to adopt legislation under a delegation of powers from the Council in order to implement rules adopted by the Council, subject to any requirements the Council may impose on the exercise of these powers. Where law-making functions are delegated to the Commission, institutional controls in the form of comitology procedures are imposed in order to ensure that the law-making process is sufficiently transparent and that there is full accountability towards the Council and the Parliament (towards the latter where the Commission's implementing powers concern a basic measure adopted under the co-decision procedure). Accountability towards and communications with the Parliament are particularly sensitive when law-making powers are delegated, given that the adoption of comitology procedures, in cases where the implementing measure would otherwise be adopted under the co-decision process, has the effect of removing the Parliament from the law-making process. Parliament has only recently succeeded in strengthening its position as a law-maker under the co-decision process: since the Amsterdam Treaty, the co-decision procedure has become the standard method for adopting single-market legislation. As a nascent influence on legislation, the Parliament is careful to protect its position. Finding a politically acceptable and institutionally balanced relationship between the Commission, comitology committees, and the Parliament, which since the collapse of the Proposed Takeover Directive has emerged aggressively as a force to be reckoned with in the law-making process, represents one of the greatest challenges to the current proposals, chief among them those contained in the Lamfalussy Report, to accelerate and streamline the securities-regulation law-making process by relying on variants of the comitology process (section 2.5.3 below).

The comitology process is based on the supervision of the Commission by various comitology committees. The varying degrees of supervision which

Parliament, which finally killed off the Directive on 4 July 2001. Amidst the recriminations and the confusion which followed the events of 4 July 2001 one compelling fact has emerged: the Parliament has been revealed as a critical and volatile influence on the securities-regulation law-making process and as an institution which can reflect national interests with devastating results. Whether or not the Parliament's action augurs badly for the success of FSAP remains to be seen (see sect. 2.5.3 below). On the tortured history of the proposed Takeover Directive see further Ch. XIV.

can be exercised by these committees depend on the type of committee designated to supervise the Commission and the procedures under which that committee operates in accordance with framework Decision 99/468/EC.[6] The procedures vary according to whether the committee is an advisory, management, or regulatory committee. The greatest degree of control over the Commission is exercised by regulatory committees and the weakest by advisory committees with management committees operating in the middle ground (the advisory committee procedures are set out in Article 3, the management committee procedures in Article 4, and the regulatory committee procedures in Article 5). Article 2(b) of the Comitology Decision provides that the regulatory committee procedure is designed to be used with respect to the adoption by the Commission of measures of general scope which are designed to implement or apply 'essential' provisions of basic instruments. It is also to be used with respect to the adoption by the Commission of measures designed to adapt or update 'non-essential' provisions of basic instruments.[7] Management committees are designed to be used with respect to the management of common EC policies or programmes with substantial budgetary implications, while advisory committees are to be used in any case where it is considered appropriate (Article 2(a) and (c), respectively). Regulatory committees can significantly obstruct Commission proposals with which they do not agree.[8] They first deliver an opinion on the Commission's proposal. If the Commission's measure accords with the committee's opinion, the measure may be adopted by the Commission. If not, the Commission may not adopt the measure, but must submit the proposal to the Council. At the same time, in order to maintain the institutional balance, the Parliament must be informed and, if it considers that a proposal submitted by the Commission under a basic measure adopted under the co-decision procedure exceeds the implementing powers granted to the Commission in that basic measure, inform the Council to that effect. The Council may adopt the proposal under a qualified majority (as set out in Article 205(2) EC) within three months of the referral of the proposal. If

---

[6] Council Decision 99/468/EC Laying Down the Procedures for the Exercise of Implementing Powers Conferred on the Commission [1999] OJ L184/23 (the Comitology Decision). This framework Decision replaces Decision 87/373/EC [1987] OJ L197/33. On the Decision see generally Lenaerts, K, and Verhoeven, A, 'Towards a legal framework for executive rule-making in the EU? The contribution of the new comitology decision' (2000) 37 *CMLRev*. 645.

[7] The references to implementing and applying 'essential' provisions and adapting 'non-essential' provisions reflect the controls the Court of Justice has placed on the delegation of law-making functions. In particular, a delegation of law-making with respect to the adoption of general principles, rather than detailed implementing rules, is not permitted, although the Court has taken a relaxed approach to the categorization of measures as implementing measures: Case 25/70 *Einfuhr- und Vorratsstelle v Köster* [1970] ECR 1161.

[8] By contrast, advisory committees simply advise the Commission. Management committees exercise greater control, but the Commission may still adopt a proposal if the management committee opposes it, although the Council may ultimately adopt a different measure.

during that period the Council indicates that it opposes the proposal, the Commission may present an amended proposal. The Commission's original proposal may be adopted only if the Council neither adopts the proposal nor indicates its opposition during the three-month period. Use of a regulatory committee has recently been proposed in the sphere of accounting disclosure and with respect to financial conglomerates.

Law-making through comitology procedures considerably increases the influence of the Commission. In the securities-regulation sphere, this would place decision-making in the hands of an institution enthusiastically committed to integration and delivery of the FSAP,[9] but perhaps less sensitive to retail-investor-protection interests. These interests are often protected, as legislation develops, by interventions from the Parliament under the co-decision process.[10] As outlined further in section 2.5.3 below, the comitology model of delegated decision-making, or at least the Lamfalussy Report's variant of it, may yet have a seismic impact on how EC securities-regulation measures are adopted in the future, both with respect to the speed of law-making and the institutional influences on the development of EC securities regulation.

XV.2.2.3 *The Commission and Member-State Compliance with EC Rules*

Compliance by Member States (and their competent authorities) with the EC securities and investment-services regime is the responsibility of the Commission in its role as guardian of the Treaty and in accordance with its duty to ensure that the provisions of the Treaty are applied under Article 211 EC. The Article 226 EC enforcement procedure allows the Commission to take enforcement action against Member States who breach EC law. This

---

[9] Although the Commission's ability to steer through the FSAP in the face of Member-State and inter-institutional tensions (as witnessed by the proposed Takeover Directive's fate) has been questioned. See Hargreaves, D, and Norman, P, 'Distressing Signals for the Single Market', *Financial Times*, 5 July 2001. More generally, the Commission itself has acknowledged that communication, management, workload, and operational problems can hinder its effectiveness: Reforming the Commission, A White Paper—Part I. COM(2000)200 (Commission Reform White Paper).

[10] See, eg, the Parliament's comments on the Commission's original proposal for a distance marketing directive [1998] OJ C385/10, in which it amended the proposal to require communication of contractual terms and conditions prior to contract conclusion. This approach was subsequently adopted by the Commission in its revised proposal [2000] OJ C177/21). More generally, it has called for a greater focus on consumer protection in financial-services measures. See its comments on the Commission's Green Paper on Financial Services: Meeting Consumers' Expectations, COM(96)209 [1997] OJ C65/76 para 3.4.1. From the integrationist perspective, however, since 4 July 2001 and the collapse of the proposed Takeover Directive it might be argued that the Parliament's more marked institutional focus on retail interests must now be measured against the risk that it will serve as a focus for obstructive national interests and that a downgrading of the Parliament's newly acquired influence via co-decision might also reduce the risk of national interests blocking the liberalization and integration process.

can lead to a judgment by the Court of Justice against the Member State and, ultimately, substantial fines. The reliance on directives in constructing the securities-regulation regime has meant that the success of the regime is dependent on Member States implementing directives correctly and on time; it is clear from the Commission's reports on the application of Community law, however, that a significant number of breaches of the securities and investment-services regime arise from failure to implement directives in time.[11] Delayed implementation of key directives has obstructed the integration of securities and investment-services markets and been a source of costs for market participants.[12] Although the foundation elements of the securities and investment-service regime are now, for the most part, in place across the Member States, the Commission is committed to ensuring that implementing delays are kept to a minimum.[13] As discussed further below (section 2.5.3 below), the Lamfalussy Report has also called for more stringent monitoring of compliance with EC requirements and for more resources to be given to enforcement. While enforcement is ultimately the Commission's responsibility, in monitoring Member-State compliance it maintains regular contacts with the national authorities through the institutional committees discussed in the next section.

XV.2.3 *The Securities Regulation Structure*

XV.2.3.1 **Introduction**

While the Commission alone has the power of legislative initiative,[14] a particular feature of EC securities regulation is the existence of committees which, to varying degrees, advise and assist the Commission in the preparation of new proposals and in the development of regulatory policy and which facilitate the effective implementation of securities-regulation measures.[15] In addition, in certain cases the Commission has power to enact

[11] For a discussion of infringements in the financial services area generally see the 16th Annual Report on Monitoring the Application of Community Law [1999] OJ C354/1 (the 16th Monitoring Report) para 2.1.4.2.

[12] Communication from the Commission, *Financial Services: Building a Framework for Action*, COM(1998)625 (the 1998 Communication) 4. See also the discussion of the Investment Services Directive (Directive 93/22/EC on investment services in the securities field [1993] OJ L141/27) in Ch. VII sect. 10.2 above.

[13] See, eg, the attention directed towards ensuring timely implementation of Directive 98/26/EC on settlement finality in payment and securities settlement systems [1998] OJ L166/45: Report from the Commission on Financial Services Priorities and Progress, Third Report, COM(2000)692/2 (the 3rd Progress Report), 3.

[14] Although the Council and Parliament may request the Commission to present proposals.

[15] For an overview of these committees see the Commission document on Institutional Arrangements for the Regulation and Supervision of the Financial Sector (2000) (the Institutional Arrangements Paper) 32–45.

securities-regulation measures under delegated law-making powers, subject to supervision by comitology committees.

XV.2.3.2 *Contact Committees*

The securities directives are monitored by a Securities Contact Committee, composed of persons appointed by the Member States and representatives of the Commission.[16] It fulfils a critical function with respect to the implementation of the directives by undertaking consultations on any practical problems arising from their application and by facilitating the establishment of a concerted attitude between Member States on the adoption of more stringent or additional conditions at national level where the adoption of such conditions is permitted by the directives. It also advises the Commission on whether any amendments to the directives are needed. Meetings of the Committee are to be convened by its chairman (a Commission representative), either at the chairman's initiative or at the request of a Member State's delegation.[17] The Committee's rules of procedure are drawn up by the Committee itself.[18] The influence of the Contact Committee on law-making is heavily circumscribed and its place in the law-making

---

[16] Art. 20 of Directive 79/279/EEC coordinating the conditions for the admission of securities to official stock exchange listing [1979] OJ L66/21 (the Admissions Directive) (now consolidated in Directive 2001/34/EC on admission of securities to official stock exchange listing and on information to be published on those securities [2001] OJ L184/1 (the Securities Consolidation Directive or SCD)) provided for the establishment of a Contact Committee. Its functions were subsequently enlarged to cover advising on Directive 80/390/EEC coordinating the requirements for the drawing up, scrutiny and distribution of the listing particulars to be published for the admission of securities to official stock exchange listing [1980] OJ L100/1 (the LPD) (LPD, Art. 26) (now consolidated in the SCD), Directive 82/121/EEC on information to be published on a regular basis by companies the shares of which have been admitted to official stock exchange listing (the IRD) (IRD, Art. 11) (now consolidated in the SCD), Directive 88/627/EEC on the information to be published when a major holding in a listed company is acquired or disposed of [1988] OJ L348/62 (the SSD) (SSD, Art. 16) (now consolidated in the SCD), Directive 89/592/EEC coordinating regulations on insider dealing [1989] OJ L334/31 (the IDD) (IDD, Art. 12) and Directive 89/298/EEC coordinating the requirements for the drawing-up, scrutiny and distribution of the prospectus to be published when transferable securities are offered to the public [1989] OJ L124/8 (the POD) (POD, Art. 25). A separate Contact Committee was established in relation to Directive 85/611/EEC on the coordination of laws, regulations and administrative provisions relating to undertakings for collective investment in transferable securities [1985] OJ L375/3 (the UCITS Directive). The now defunct proposed Takeover Directive would, had it been adopted, have been monitored by the Admissions Directive Contact Committee. The SCD Contact Committee regime is set out in Art. 108.

[17] Admission Directive Art. 20(4) (SCD, Art. 108(1)) and UCITS Directive Art. 53(4).

[18] Admission Directive Art. 20(4) (SCD, Art. 108(1)) and UCITS Art. 53(4). The Commission has reported that the Securities Contact Committee has never adopted rules of procedure and that its members have never been formally appointed by the Member States. Members are instead nominated on a case-by-case basis depending on the agenda of the meeting called by the Commission: Institutional Arrangements Paper, n 15 above, 32.

institutional structure limited, however, in that its role is advisory only.[19] It is also notable that the Contact Committee advisory model does not explicitly provide for the involvement of representatives from industry and other interest groups.[20]

XV.2.3.3 *The Banking Advisory Committee*

In order to assess the committee structure underpinning the investment-services regime, the sophisticated consultation and advisory structure applicable to the banking regime should be highlighted. Article 11 of the BCD I[21] provides for the establishment of a Banking Advisory Committee (the BAC). Its functions are to assist the Commission in ensuring the proper implementation of the banking regime, to carry out the specific tasks required of it across the banking regime, and to assist the Commission in the preparation of new proposals concerning further co-ordination in the sphere of credit institutions. Its composition is carefully delineated, certainly by comparison with the Contact Committee requirements. Under Article 11(4) (CBD, Article 57(4)) it is to be composed of not more than three representatives from each Member State and from the Commission, although representatives may be accompanied by advisers, with the prior agreement of the Commission. Notably, qualified persons and experts can also be invited by the BAC. It is to meet at regular intervals and whenever the situation demands. In addition, the Commission may ask the BAC to hold an emergency meeting if it considers that the situation so requires (BCD I, Article 11(5)) (CBD, Article 57(5)). Article 11(6) (CBD, Article 57(6)) explicitly provides that the BAC's discussions and the outcomes thereof are confidential unless the Committee decides otherwise. Its activities include advising on the preparation of new measures (the Commission has never proposed measures which were not in accordance with the majority view of the BAC), advising the Commission on the need to adjust prudential rules, establishing solvency ratios for credit

[19] Although the Securities Contact Committee does exert a very limited supervisory/comitology function in that under Art. 21 of the Admission Directive (SCD, Art. 109) it exercises a comitology role in relation to the adoption by the Commission of revisions to the minimum foreseeable market-capitalization requirement demanded of companies under the Admission Directive by Sch A(1) para 2 (SCD, Art. 43). At the time of the Commission's Institutional Arrangements paper (n 15 above), this function had never been exercised: Institutional Arrangements Paper, n 15 above, 36.

[20] As far back as 1974, in its comments on the proposal for what would become the now consolidated LPD, ECOSOC noted that the Contact Committee should include industry representatives such as representatives of issuers, banks, stock exchanges, and investors [1974] OJ C125/1, para 2.4.2.

[21] Directive 77/780/EEC on the coordination of laws, regulations and administrative procedures relating to the taking up and pursuit of the business of credit institutions [1977] OJ L322/30 (the BCD I) (now consolidated in Directive 2000/12 relating to the taking up and pursuit of the business of credit institutions [2000] OJ L126/1 (the Consolidated Banking Directive or CBD)). Art. 57 of the CBD parallels Art. 11.

institutions, assisting the Commission in the proper implementation of the banking regime (including considering how measures have been implemented, assessing whether implementation has been consistent and whether there is a need for further convergence)[22] and following up on the implementation process (by, for example, assessing the need for particular derogations or transitional periods to remain in operation). The banking regime also requires national competent authorities to inform the BAC where certain decisions are taken. More generally, the BAC also acts as a sounding board for banking supervisors across the Community.[23]

XV.2.3.4 *Law-making, Comitology, and the BAC*

The BAC, in its alternative guise as a comitology committee, also plays a key role in facilitating the extent to which amendments to legislation can be flexibly adopted by the Commission under a delegation of law-making powers rather than being subject, as is usual, to adoption by the Council or the Council/Parliament, with all the delays and complexities the legislative process can entail. Technical adaptations may be made to specified aspects of the banking regime by the Commission in accordance with the comitology procedures set out in the Comitology Decision.[24] Where the proposed measure is an amendment to the regime which comes within the scope of the technical adaptation power, the Commission can enact the measure much more quickly with the assistance of a committee and according to the regulatory committee procedure set out in the Comitology Decision. In practice, although the BAC and the regulatory committee which oversees the technical adaptation process are constitutionally separate entities, the composition of the regulatory committee coincides with that of the BAC (the chairmanship simply switches to the Commission).[25]

[22] In this regard the BAC is assisted by a working group which examines questions arising from the interpretation of the banking regime. The views of this group, once endorsed by the BAC, are an important point of reference (while not legally binding) on the operation of the banking regime.

[23] For a review of the BAC's functions see the Institutional Arrangements Paper, n 15 above, 5–7.

[24] These comitology functions were, prior to the CBD's consolidation of the banking rules, scattered across the banking regime. See, eg, Art. 22 of the 2nd Council Directive 89/646/EEC on the coordination of laws, regulations and administrative procedures relating to the taking up and pursuit of the business of credit institutions and amending Directive 77/780/EEC [1989] OJ L 386/1 (the BCD II) on the extent to which the BCD II was subject to comitology. The technical adaptation power for the banking regime as a whole is now contained in Art. 60 of the CBD.

[25] For an example of a committee which fulfils comitology and other functions without the need for an alter-ego as required by the BAC model see the Insurance Committee established under Directive 91/675/EEC on the setting up of an insurance committee [1991] OJ L374/32. This Committee fulfils comitology and advisory/policy functions. The BAC's position is anomalous in that, predating by some time the original comitology process, it is chaired by a Member State's representative. Comitology rules require, however, that the Commission chairs comitology committees.

XV.2.3.5 *Law-making, Comitology, and the Search for a Securities Committee*

It took until June 2001 for a committee similar in function to the BAC and exercising advisory and comitology functions to be established for investment-services and securities measures. While the new committee structure (section 2.5.3 below) reflects recent developments in the area, notably the Lamfalussy Report's law-making proposals, the establishment of a Securities Committee, has, for some considerable time, been a goal of the Commission, even if the shape of the proposed Committee has changed over time.

Although the Investment Services Directive refers to the setting up of, variously, a 'securities market committee'[26] and a 'transferable securities committee',[27] it does not establish any such committee.[28] Not only does the ISD not provide for the establishment of a securities advisory committee on the lines of the BAC, but it does not contain a procedure parallel to that contained in the banking regime empowering the Commission to adopt technical adaptations to the ISD with the assistance of a securities committee acting as a regulatory committee, akin to the *alter ego* of the BAC. It provides instead in Article 29 that 'pending the adoption of a further Directive laying down provisions adapting this Directive to technical progress in the areas specified'[29] the Council, in accordance with the requirements of Article 29, is to adopt any technical adaptations necessary.[30] The technical

---

[26] Directive 93/22/EEC on investment services in the securities field [1993] OJ L141/27 (the ISD), recital 44.

[27] Art. 7(1).

[28] Functions which under the banking regime are fulfilled by the BAC are, in certain cases, fulfilled by the Council. Art. 7(1) of the ISD requires, eg, that notifications of authorizations of direct or indirect subsidiaries of parent undertakings governed by the law of a third country and acquisitions by such parent undertakings of holdings in Community investment firms be made to the Commission which in turn informs the Council 'until such time as a committee on transferable securities is set up by the Council acting on a proposal from the Commission'. In the banking regime, the BAC is informed.

[29] Recital 44 provides that the Commission is to make the technical adaptations necessary after referring the matter to the committee to be set up in the securities markets field.

[30] The Commission's original and revised proposals for the ISD [1989] OJ C43/7 and [1990] OJ C42/7, did contain in Arts. 20 and 23, respectively, provisions empowering the Commission to adopt technical adaptations, assisted by a committee composed of representatives of the Commission and the Member States. Both proposals also envisaged that this committee would fulfil certain other information-dissemination and notification functions under the ISD. The ultimate exclusion of the securities-committee/comitology provisions from the ISD arose as a result of difficulties in finding agreement on the division of responsibilities between the BAC/comitology committee and any securities committee to be established under the ISD, given that credit institutions which provided investment services could come within the remit of both committees. In order to expedite the adoption of the ISD, the Council decided to put on one side the securities-committee provisions and to retain for itself on a temporary basis the powers, comitology-based and otherwise, which would otherwise have been exercised by the securities committee. See the Commission's Explanatory Memorandum to its proposal amending the ISD to provide for technical adaptation by the Commission and a Securities Committee, COM(95)360, 2 and Carbon de Lichtbuer, M, 'The Investment Services Directive—An Analysis' in Wymeersch, E (ed), *Further Perspectives in Financial Integration in Europe* (1994) 79, 106.

adaptations specified in Article 29 include adapting the terminology of the ISD Annex to take into account developments in financial markets, clarifying definitions in order to ensure uniform application of the ISD and in order to take into account developments in financial markets, and aligning the terminology of the ISD in accordance with subsequent investment firm and related measures. A similar provision is contained in the Capital Adequacy Directive.[31] It appears clear from the ISD, however, that, in a sign of things which were to come, the Securities Committee it envisaged was not to be limited to advising in relation to investment-services-specific measures but was to have a similar advisory role in relation to the other securities directives.[32]

In 1995 the Commission presented a proposal to amend the ISD to provide for the establishment of a Securities Committee and to empower the Commission to adopt technical adaptations to the ISD, assisted by the Securities Committee.[33] Although the Council reached a common position on this proposal in 1997, it was abandoned. Establishment of a Securities Committee in order to contribute to the elaboration of legislation in the securities field forms part of the FSAP. Its functions were originally projected to reflect the Commission's perspective on the needs of the overall Community regulatory framework[34] but, since the adoption of the FSAP, the Lamfalussy Report has, as outlined in section 2.5.3 below, intervened to change the law-making context, to cast new light on the functions which should be fulfilled by a Securities Committee, and to prompt the Commission to proceed speedily to establish a new committee structure.

Although the gap has now been filled, the failure for so long to establish a Securities Committee has resulted in a marked difference, hitherto, between the institutional structure for the development of banking legislation, on the one hand, and investment-services and securities measures, on the other, which was highlighted in the FSAP as a significant impediment to the development and implementation of legislation for the investment-services and securities markets.[35] Apart from failing to provide for the

[31] Directive 93/6/EEC on the capital adequacy of investment firms and credit institutions [1993] OJ L141/1 (the CAD), Art. 10.

[32] Recital 43 provides that 'examination of the problems arising in the areas covered by the Council Directives on investment services and securities, as regards both the application of existing measures and the possibility of closer cooperation in the future, requires cooperation between national authorities and the Commission within a committee'. The remit of the Securities Committee recently established by the Commission cuts across the securities and investment-services sectors. See sect. 2.5.3 below.

[33] The Commission proposal and explanatory memorandum are at COM(95)360.

[34] Report from the Commission on Progress on Financial Services, Second Report, COM(2000)336 (the 2nd Progress Report), 21.

[35] FSAP, n 1 above, 11. Not all commentators have faith in the ability of a Securities Committee to enhance the development of EC securities and investment-services law. For the view that a committee appointed from the Member States would be too removed from the market-place and overly political see Scott-Quinn, B, 'EC Securities Market Regulation' in Steil,

oversight of Commission implementing powers, the regime has also long
lacked an umbrella advisory body. The Contact Committees, which until
June 2001 were the only formal advisory bodies established under the EC
securities and investment-services regime, have specific functions in relation
to particular directives only. They do not have a mandate to advise on issues
which affect the EC regime horizontally, such as the impact of e-
commerce.[36] The Commission does, however, benefit on an informal basis
from the advisory function fulfilled by the High Level Securities Supervisors
Committee, an informal working group which was established by the
Commission in 1985 to advise with respect to broad policy questions. Since
1996 advice has also been given by the Giovanni Group of financial-market
participants which advises the Commission on financial-market issues generally. More recently, FESCO (the Forum of European Securities Commissions
and now the Committee of European Securities Regulators: section 2.5.2
below), which at least up to its transformation into the Committee of
European Securities Regulators, was independent of the Community institutional structure, was available to provide advice on policy questions and
played a decisive role in the development of EC securities-regulation policy.

The pressure to establish a committee exercising comitology, as well as
advisory, powers has been growing for some time. In its pre-FSAP 1998
Communication, the Commission suggested that the legislative process be
streamlined and speeded up by confining the scope of new legislative measures to setting out fundamental objectives only and by adopting detailed
rules on the implementation of those objectives in Commission decisions,
which could be more flexibly adopted and amended under the comitology
procedure.[37] The far-reaching recommendations of the Lamfalussy Report
with respect to law-making are also dependent on the establishment of some
form of Securities Committee. As discussed at section 2.5.3 below, the
Commission has now taken action in this area. However, recent proposals
from the Commission reveal that the lack of a dedicated securities committee does not necessarily prevent the application of the comitology process in
the securities-regulation area (section 2.5.4 below).

XV.2.4 *The Representation of Investor Interests*

The pace of market integration and, in particular, the ongoing consolidation
in the investment-services industry is increasing not only the market power

B (ed), *International Financial Market Regulation* (1994) 121, 153. The novel structure of the
new committee model, which is based on a dual-committee format which incorporates a
Member States' committee and an experts' or regulators' committee, may reduce the risk of this
occurring. See further at sect. 2.5.3 below.

[36] Lannoo, K, 'Supervising in Harmony' *FRR*, Oct 1999, 26.
[37] 1998 Communication, n 12 above, 3.

of investment intermediaries but also, arguably, their lobbying power and influence over the development of EC securities regulation.[38] These interest groups have an interest in reducing regulatory costs and will have a natural tendency to call for deregulation rather than the re-regulation implicit in the harmonization of protective measures.[39] The ability of investors, particularly retail investors, to influence the development of legislation is thus becoming a significant question. The Treaty does not provide for investor involvement in law-making. ECOSOC, whose opinion is sought on investment-services proposals, is not required to include investor groups, although it must, under Article 257 EC, include 'representatives of the general public' which could include retail investors.[40] The Parliament, which is closely involved in securities-regulation measures under the co-decision process, while not directly representing investor interests, has taken pro-consumer/investor stances when examining investment-services measures.[41] Article 95(3) EC (which brings consumer-protection interests to bear on internal-market law-making) has, however, more directly influenced investor participation. Retail investors' interests can be represented through the Consumer Committee,[42] which was established after the introduction of Article 95(3) and whose members include representatives of European consumer groups (such as the Bureau Européen des Unions des Consommateurs (BEUC) which has been an outspoken advocate for retail consumers of investment services),[43] consumer experts, and national consumer groups. In addition,

[38] On the imbalance between consumer and industry interests in the standard-setting process see McGee, A, and Weatherill, S, 'The Evolution of the Single Market—Harmonisation or Liberalisation' (1990) 53 *MLR* 578. There is a considerable economics literature on how interest groups can influence decision-making, much of which flows from the arguments made in the seminal article: Stigler, G, 'The Theory of Economic Regulation' (1971) 2 *Bell J Econ. & Management Sci.* 3. For an investment services example see Langevoort, D, 'The SEC as a Bureaucracy: Public Choice, Institutional Rhetoric and the Process of Policy Formation' (1990) 47 *Washington and Lee LR* 527.

[39] One study has concluded that '[interest groups outside the financial-services sector including investors] are at best on the margins of banking and securities policy communities. Rarely do they figure at the core of policy networks formulating and implementing financial services' policy. The danger in this situation is that policy will follow too closely the interests of financial services firms and not serve well the broader public interest': Coleman, W, *Financial Services, Globalization and Domestic Policy Change* (1996) 237. Concerns about the influence of market intermediaries were raised some years ago with respect to the Commission's White Paper on the Internal Market, in respect of which the point was made that '[i]t is ominous that much of the discussion in the White Paper and in the subsequent debate focuses on the interests of the current range of financial institutions rather than on the interests of the consumers who support—and indeed pay for—the whole system either directly or indirectly': Mitchell, J, 'The Integration of Personal Financial Services within the European Community: A Consumer Perspective' in Castello Branco, M, and Pelkmans, J (eds), *Internal Market for Financial Services* (1987) 125.

[40] Van Crombugghe, N, 'Consumer Protection and Free Movement of Financial Services' in Campbell, D (ed), *Financial Services in the New Europe* (1992) 349, 357.

[41] See n 10 above.   [42] [1995] OJ L162/37.

[43] It was consulted, eg, during the preparation of the original Distance Marketing Proposal: Impact Assessment Form, Proposal for a Distance Marketing Directive (COM(98)486), para 6.

Article 5 EC on subsidiarity has been interpreted by the Protocol on the Application of the Principles of Subsidiarity and Proportionality attached to the Amsterdam Treaty as requiring the Commission to consult widely before proposing legislation. Subsidiarity 'as a feature of institutional culture'[44] may thus have a significant impact on investor participation. Indeed, as part of the process of reforming the legislative process in the financial-services sphere, the Commission has constituted 'Forum Groups' consisting of market experts, industry representatives and, significantly, consumer groups to advise it on the implications of its proposals.[45] The new emphasis on consultation and transparency in the wake of the Lamfalussy Report should also facilitate the extent to which investor interest can be fed through to the law-making process.

XV.2.5 *The Rise of Comitology*

XV.2.5.1 *Initial Initiatives to Enhance Delivery of the FSAP*

The Commission is likely to continue as the dominant influence on the development of the regulatory structure underpinning EC securities and investment-services markets given its power of legislative initiative. However, both the process by which the Commission identifies policy objectives and interacts with other bodies in developing the regulatory framework and the ability of the legislative procedure to deliver regulation at EC level effectively have recently been the subject of high-level discussions in order to ensure that the FSAP can be delivered on time.

In the 1998 Communication and the FSAP the lengthy delays in adopting financial-services measures and, in particular, the three to four years typically needed to complete the co-decision procedure were criticized. In the FSAP, the Commission reviewed in some detail the EC's approach to rule-making, both as regards the procedures followed and the form of legislation, in light of the broader and more challenging policy objectives set for EC securities regulation in the FSAP. It identified three weaknesses in particular. First, a piecemeal and reactive approach was followed in designing legislation which was inadequate in an era of financial conglomeration which required a cross-sectoral approach to regulation. Secondly, the decision-making process was often protracted. Finally, the adoption of overly detailed, inflexible, and prescriptive measures carried the danger of stultifying market structures and behaviour. In order to address these concerns it proposed a number of initiatives including: the establishment of a forum to forge con-

---

[44] Beaumont and Weatherill, n 5 above, 31.
[45] In its Nov 1999 Progress Report at 3 it reported 'modest but tangible progress in terms of . . . the mobilisation of input from market practitioners and other important constituencies (consumers, users)'.

sensus on emerging challenges which would consist of representatives of the national ministries responsible for regulation; the initiation of discussions with the Parliament at an early stage on the policy objectives of proposed measures; and the creation of a high-level forum to take soundings from bodies representing the principal interest groups. It also proposed that input from national supervisory authorities be integrated at an early stage in the development of Commission measures.[46]

XV.2.5.2 *FESCO*

FESCO's influence on the pace and substance of harmonization has been one of the most striking features of the recent evolution of EC securities regulation. Frustrated at the failure to establish a Securities Committee, European securities regulators took the initiative by establishing a forum for co-operation and policy development, FESCO,[47] in 1997. Its Charter objectives were to foster the fair and efficient realization of the European single market in financial services by close co-operation; to develop common European regulatory standards regarding the supervision of financial services and markets (particularly by building on EC directives); and to enhance market surveillance and enforcement in the EEA by mutual assistance and cross-border co-operation. It operated through six working groups (European Public Offers, Standards for Investor Protection, Market Abuse, Primary Market Practices, Alternative Trading Systems, and FESCOPOL; the last dealing with information exchange and market surveillance). These working groups broadly reflected FESCO's concerns: supporting the development of efficient and competitive financial markets in Europe; safeguarding investors' rights in the provision of financial services; ensuring the integrity of exchanges; harmonizing disclosure rules for companies; protecting investors from fraud; combating market abuse; and fighting financial fraud.

FESCO's activities were limited by its informal structure, the consensus-driven nature of its operation, and the non-binding status of its recommendations. Nonetheless, it has been a prime mover in keeping the momentum going with respect to achievement of the FSAP, particularly in the wholesale-markets area, by adopting common standards which its members are committed to implement in their home jurisdictions. These common standards are increasingly being used by the Commission as the basis for FSAP measures and, in particular, as templates for the detailed technical rules required for level 2 law-making under the Lamfalussy model (see section 2.5.3 below). With regard to the provision of investment services, it has fulfilled an important 'gap-filling' role in relation to the ISD, proposing in 1999 common standards with respect to the assessment of the fitness and

---

[46] FSAP, n 1 above, 13–15.   [47] Forum of European Securities Commissions.

propriety of investment firms in order, *inter alia*, to 'improve mutual understanding of how the relevant minimum standards laid down in the ISD are
applied and developed'.[48] Its influential report on the harmonization of conduct-of-business principles and its ongoing work (in its new incarnation as
the Committee of European Securities Regulators) in this area is set to have
a far-reaching impact on investor protection and conduct-of-business regulation.[49] FESCO was also active in the area of the regulation of market
manipulation, producing in 2000 a report setting out its recommendations
on how harmonization should be approached by the Commission and on
which the Commission has based its 2001 proposal for a market-abuse
regime.[50] Its activities have extended beyond the investment-services sphere
to issuer transactions and, in particular, include important initiatives concerning a single disclosure passport for issuers.[51] Finally, in the area of market regulation, it appears that its Standards for Regulated Markets will form
the core of the EC's approach to market regulation.[52]

FESCO performed a valuable function in achieving consensus between
market supervisors and, in effect, allowed for a form of controlled regulatory
competition to set common standards to take place in areas in which the EC
has not acted. As well as being able to draw directly on the expertise and
experience of supervisors, it also had the necessary flexibility to adapt its
standards as market conditions changed. Its activities have, however, now
been drawn into the EC's law-making structure and its associated institutional checks and balances as a result of the other critical factor impinging
on the Parliament's influence on the shape of EC securities regulation—the
landmark Lamfalussy Report. FESCO has now been formally reconstituted
within the EC institutional structure (and, perhaps, its exposure to the

[48] FESCO, *European Standards on Fitness and Propriety to Provide Investment Services* (1999).
99-FESCO-A, 2.

[49] FESCO, *Standards and Rules for Harmonizing Core Conduct of Business Rules For Investor
Protection*, Consultative Paper (2001), FESCO/00-124b. A second consultation paper was issued
in Oct 2001: CESR, Standards and Rules for Harmonizing Core Conduct of Business Rules for
Investor Protection (2001), CESR/01/04. The ISD Working Paper has suggested that the stan-
dards will form the basis of the new ISD conduct-of-business regime: Overview of Proposed
Adjustments to the Investment Services Directive, Working Document of Services of DG Internal
Market, Document 1, July 2001 (the ISD Working Paper). See Ch. IX.13.7.

[50] FESCO, *Market Abuse, FESCO's Response to the Call for View from the Securities Regulators
under the EU's Action Plan for Financial Services*, COM(1999)232 (2000), FESCO/00-0961 (the
Market Abuse Report). FESCO issued a follow-up paper in Aug 2001: FESCO, *Measures to
Promote Market Integrity* FESCO/01-052.

[51] FESCO, *A 'European Passport' for Issuers*, Consultation Paper (2000), FESCO/99-098e and
A 'European Passport' for Issuers. A Report for the EU Commission (2000), FESCO/00-138b. Both
of these documents have exerted a considerable influence on the Commission's recent initiative
in this area. See Ch. IV sect. 9.2.3 above. FESCO has also produced a report on *Market Conduct
Standards for Participants in and Offering* (1999). 99-FESCO-B.

[52] FESCO, *Standards for Regulated Markets under the ISD* (Dec 1999), 99-FESCO-C; ISD
Working Paper, n 49 above, 26–33.

influence of the Commission adversely heightened) as the Committee of European Securities Regulators.

XV.2.5.3 *The Lamfalussy Report and the Rise of Comitology*

(a) *A New Law-making Model*

The securities and investment-services rule-making process and, in particular, its ability to deliver the FSAP came under close scrutiny with the appointment in the summer of 2000 of the Committee of Wise Men under the chairmanship of Baron Lamfalussy to investigate the regulation of EC securities markets. As well as indicating the major weaknesses in the regulatory structure and highlighting the critical legislative priorities, the Lamfalussy Report contained practical recommendations for sweeping changes to the process whereby legislation is adopted. Significantly, although the changes will, if fully implemented, drastically alter the way in which securities and investment-services measures are adopted, they do not require Treaty revisions and work within the current comitology structure. In particular, they rely heavily on the regulatory committee model.

The Lamfalussy Report reads as a dismal indictment of the legislative process. In particular, the Committee noted that while the participants in the single market in securities and investment services welcomed the FSAP, considerable concerns existed about whether the legislative process was equipped to respond with the required urgency; indeed the Report's trenchant conclusion was that 'the chances of delivering the FSAP on time are close to zero'.[53] The process of adopting legislation was criticized as being too slow, with the average time taken for the co-decision procedure, even where political agreement existed, amounting to two years in general and to longer in the financial-services area: specific reference was made to the (now failed) proposed Takeover Directive and its notorious twelve-year gestation period. The Commission's attempts to improve the consultation process were noted, but the failure to adopt an agreed consultation mechanism criticised. Neither the Council nor the Parliament escaped censure, with the Council criticized, in particular, for its tendency to over-complicate legislation 'often in an attempt to try to fit 15 sets of national legislation into one Community framework'.[54] Over-reliance on directives, attributed to subsidiarity pressures, was identified as leading to uneven and delayed implementation of EC rules. The Wise Men's conclusion was that the legislative process was too slow and too rigid to respond to changing market conditions, inclined to produce ambiguous texts, and unable to distinguish between core essential framework principles and detailed implementing rules. Their response was to propose a mechanism which might facilitate

---

[53] N 2 above, 12.   [54] Ibid, 14.

achievement of the FSAP, while respecting the democratic processes at national and Union levels, maintaining the present institutional balance in the Union, and conforming to the present structure of the Treaties, taking into account the requirements of subsidiarity and proportionality.[55]

The Lamfalussy Report's ambitious recommendation is based on a rethink of both the form which legislation should take and the manner in which it is adopted. At the core of the Report is the realization that securities-market legislation is comprised of two layers: basic political choices which can be articulated as broad, but sufficiently precise, framework rules; and detailed technical measures, which conform to and implement the objectives of the framework rules. A four-level regulatory approach based on this duality is set out in some detail in the report.

Level 1 involves the adoption of framework principles, in the form of regulations or directives and in accordance with the usual legislative procedures, and is designed to speed up the co-decision legislative process, as the institutions involved are required only to agree on basic principles. Framework principles were characterized by the Report as principles reflecting key political choices which specified the nature and extent of the technical implementing measures required. The Report gave the example of a level 1 measure designed to expand on the conduct-of-business regime contained in Article 11 of the ISD which would include as framework principles the basic components of conduct-of-business rules such as due diligence, acting honestly, adequate disclosure, home-country control, and the necessity to differentiate between professional and retail investors. Implementing measures would set out the detailed rules needed to implement these principles. Critical to the success of the Report's proposal is that, in order to protect the institutional balance and ensure adequate democratic safeguards, level 1 measures clearly set out the substantive content of the implementing rules delegated to the level 2 procedure. The use of regulations as an alternative to directives was suggested in order to improve the transparency, speed, and accuracy of transposition and implementation. The Report also recommended that the process according to which the Commission would develop level 1 proposals include rigorous consultation procedures (involving market participants, issuers and consumers/investors, national regulators, and the Parliament) and transparency mechanisms.[56]

---

[55] N 2 above, 7–8, 14–15, and 20.

[56] The Commission's first foray into level 1 law-making has been less than auspicious in this regard. It was criticized by the market-place on the presentation of its May 2001 proposals for an issuer passport and a market-abuse directive, both of which are drawn up (to different degrees) as level 1 measures, for not consulting sufficiently widely, and, in effect, not meeting the transparency standards which underpin the Lamfalussy proposals: Boland, V, 'Battle looms over Brussels plan for capital markets regulation', *Financial Times*, 11 June 2001. Clearer evidence of a move towards greater transparency in law-making can be seen, however, in the detailed pre-proposal consultations launched by the Commission on market transparency

Level 2 involves the implementation of these framework principles and the adaptation of measures to reflect new developments in supervision and on financial markets using comitology procedures, national regulators, and the Commission. At the heart of level 2 is the establishment of a Securities Committee (SC), with regulatory and supervisory functions akin to a comitology committee, and a Securities Regulatory Committee (SRC), with advisory functions. The SRC would, after full consultation of the markets and users which would be carried out according to defined procedures, forward its technical advice on the implementing rules to the Commission which would then forward a proposal for implementing rules based on this advice to the SC. At all stages the Parliament would be fully informed. The SC (which would also advise the Commission on level 1 proposals and on level 2 mandates for the SRC) would then vote on the proposal according to the rules applicable to regulatory committees under the Comitology Decision. Of particular significance for expediting level 2 proposals are the time limits and guillotines applicable to Commission law-making under the regulatory committee procedures. Membership of the key SC would be comprised of Member States' nominees and the SC would be chaired by the Commission. The SRC membership would build on the FESCO structure and comprise the heads of national securities regulators. A striking and, from the participation of investors perspective, heartening feature of the level 2 procedure is the detail with which the Lamfalussy Report sets out the consultation procedures which must be followed by the SRC before it proffers its technical advice.[57] These procedures, which also reflect the trend which can be observed throughout EC securities regulation towards a more investor-protection-sensitive regime, represent an attempt to address the failure of the Initial Lamfalussy Report's[58] exposition of the four-level approach to set out institutionalized and transparent procedures for involving market practitioners and consumers in the legislative process which had emerged as a concern during the consultations on that Report. A possible procedure was suggested by the Report involving: initial public consultation, for no longer than three months, on the basis of a concept release outlining the problem and the options available; subsequent release of a draft proposal for consultation

(*Towards an EU Regime on Transparency Obligations of Issuers whose Securities are Admitted to Trading on a Regulated Market*, Consultation Document of the Services of the Internal Market Directorate General, MARKT/11.07.2001) and on reform of the ISD (Commission Communication on Upgrading the Investment Services Directive 93/22/EC, COM(2000)729 and the ISD Working Paper, n 49 above). Although greater transparency in the securities-regulation sphere reflects the Lamfalussy model, it also forms part of a generalized move towards better involvement and more openness in Community law-making which forms a central element of the Commission's July 2001 White Paper on European Governance, COM(2001)428 (the European Governance White Paper).

[57] N 2 above, 32–3.
[58] Initial Report of the Committee of Wise Men on the Regulation of European Securities Markets, Nov 2000 (the Initial Lamfalussy Report).

with markets and end users; the use of hearings, round tables, and mandatory reliance on the Internet; and attachment of a summary of public comments to the SRC's final recommendations to the Commission.

Level 3 is designed to enhance the consistency with which level 1 and level 2 measures are transposed and implemented by the Member States. The SRC is at the core of the level 3 recommendations. The Report envisaged that it would: produce guidelines for detailed regulations to be adopted at national level; issue interpretive recommendations and common standards for matters not covered at EC level; review regulatory practices in order to ensure best practice; and conduct peer reviews of regulatory practices. Level 4 is concerned with enforcement at the level of Member-State compliance with Community rules. While the Report acknowledged the key role of the Commission in this regard, it suggested that the private-sector and national regulatory bodies be more proactive in bringing infringements to the attention of the Commission. It also suggested that the Commission be bolder in enforcing Member-State compliance with EC law and that more care be given to checking the implementation process.

(b) *The Fate of the Lamfalussy Model*

While the Lamfalussy Report received a cautious welcome from the marketplace,[59] the implications of the proposal for the Parliament's position have generated considerable inter-institutional tensions. At the heart of the Parliament's difficulties with the Report is its concern about its removal from the level 2 process and its fear that the SC would become too powerful. In order to protect its position it sought a right of appeal against Commission decisions. The possibility of a parliamentary veto over measures was rejected by the Lamfalussy Report as not being envisaged in the Treaty. The Report attempted to assuage the Parliament's concerns by pointing to the close contact which would be maintained by both committees with the Parliament. It also emphasized that under its proposals, the Parliament would have time before the Commission makes a proposal to the SC and after the SC votes on it to check that the proposal and the decision conform with the scope of the implementing power given by the level 1 decision. Finally, the Report noted that if the Parliament were to consider that the Commission's proposal did not conform with the scope of the implementing power under the level 1 decision, it would pass a resolution to that effect. The Commission would then be required to reconsider its proposal, taking the Parliament's position into account.[60]

---

[59] Norman, P, and Bolland, V, 'Caution over the pace of market regulation', *Financial Times*, 16 February 2001.

[60] N 2 above, 34. The Report's conclusion at 34 was that 'it is in everybody's interest that the European Parliament be given an adequate role in the procedure . . . [w]ere Parliament not

The Report was endorsed by the March 2001 Stockholm European Council which resolved that the four-level approach should be implemented in order to make the law-making process more effective and transparent and to improve the quality of securities regulation measures.[61] The Resolution emphasized, however, that transparency and legal certainty as well as the 'prerogatives of the institutions concerned and the current institutional balance' must be respected.[62] While it encouraged the use of level 2 measures in order to ensure that technical rules keep pace with market and regulatory developments, it did address the most controversial aspect of the Lamfalussy model, the critical faultline between level 1 and level 2 measures, and emphasized that the level 1/level 2 split was to be determined in a clear and transparent manner.[63] The Resolution also recommended that Regulations be used at level 1 where this would accelerate the legislative process. The inter-institutional tensions provoked by the Report which emerged initially in the Parliament can be seen in the Resolution's overt references to the institutional balance but also in its attempts to safeguard the Council's ascendancy. The Resolution placed a brake on the Commission's exercise of implementing powers, noting that in order to find a balanced solution to measures which are acknowledged to be 'particularly sensitive' the Commission 'has committed itself . . . to avoid going against predominant views which might emerge within the Council'.[64] In a similar vein, the Commission also 'commits itself to expeditiously re-examine' draft measures which the Parliament believes exceed the bounds of the implementing power granted in the relevant level 1 measure.[65] If the political will necessary to implement this new approach fully can be found, and this will only be tested on a case-by-case as the foundation level 1 measures are negotiated and as the extent to which the Parliament will agree to a transfer of rule-making powers to level 2 procedures becomes apparent, it could significantly enhance the speedy achievement of the FSAP.

The Commission has acted quickly to implement the Lamfalussy proposals. As outlined in Chapters IV section 9.3 and XIII section 11.5 above, respectively, the May 2001 Prospectus Proposal and Market Abuse

to be satisfied, the consequences would be felt the next time co-decision legislation (Level 1) conferring implementing powers on the Securities Committee is proposed. This point would no doubt not be lost on the Commission or on the Securities Committee'.

[61] Presidency Conclusions, Stockholm European Council, 23 and 24 Mar 2001, Annex 1, Resolution on More Effective Securities Market Regulation (the Stockholm Resolution), para 1. Agreement on the wording of the Resolution required some negotiation, given the inter-institutional interests at stake and also the concerns of some Member States that the Commission's approach to market regulation (which in some quarters is seen as being Anglocentric) would become too dominant.

[62] Ibid, Introduction.   [63] Ibid, para 2.

[64] Ibid, para 5. Although the Resolution does note that this commitment does not constitute a precedent.

[65] Ibid.

Proposal[66] provide for the adoption of detailed technical requirements under level 2 procedures, although the level of detail contained on both these level 1 measures does not seem to reflect the Lamfalussy model's characterization of level 1 measures as framework measures. Further, the Commission has adopted decisions on the establishment of a European Securities Committee (ESC)[67] and a Committee of European Securities Regulators (CESR),[68] as per the Lamfalussy model. The ESC is established as an advisory body in the first instance (Article 2); if the Lamfalussy proposals are a success, it will also be called on to act as a regulatory comitology committee as and when required in the future by level 1 measures which will set out the scope of the measures which can be adopted as level 2 rules and under comitology procedures (recital 11). The current proposal for a public-offers disclosure regime, for example, envisages that detailed disclosure rules are to be adopted under comitology procedures.[69] The sensitivity of the Parliament to the Lamfalussy law-making model is evident in the reassurance given to the Parliament in the Explanatory Memorandum that the Commission will inform the Parliament on a regular basis of the ESC's proceedings when it acts as a comitology committee. The Commission has also committed itself to send ESC meeting agendas, the results of votes, the summary records of meetings, and the list of authorities to whom Member-State representatives belong to the Parliament at the same time and on the same terms as to members of the ESC.[70] As far as its general advisory functions are concerned, the ESC is to 'serve as a body for reflection, debate and advice for the Commission in the field of securities' (recital 9). It is to be consulted by the Commission on policy questions generally and not solely with respect to the measures which the Commission may propose as level 1 measures; under Article 2 it is to advise the Commission on policy issues as well as on legislative proposals which the Commission may adopt in the field of securities. In this regard, it is designed to take on the functions of the informal High Level Securities Supervisors Committee. Its procedural framework is very similar to that of the BAC. Under Article 3, the ESC is comprised of 'high level representatives of the Member States' and is to be chaired by a Commission representative (the Commission is also to provide the secretariat (Article 5)); the ESC may

---

[66] Commission proposal on the prospectus to be published when securities are offered to the public or admitted to trading, COM(2001)280 (the Prospectus Proposal) and Commission Proposal for a Directive on insider dealing and market manipulation (market abuse) (the Market Abuse Proposal), COM(2001)281.

[67] Commission Decision 2001/528/EC establishing the European Securities Committee [2001] OJ L191/45 (the ESC Decision), Proposal and Explanatory Memorandum at COM(2001)1493.

[68] Commission Decision 2001/527/EC establishing the Committee of European Securities Regulators [2001] OJ L191/43 (the CESR Decision), Proposal and Explanatory Memorandum at COM(2001)1501.

[69] See further Ch. IV sect. 9.3.2 above.

[70] N 67 above, Explanatory Memorandum to the ESC Proposal, 4.

invite experts and observers to attend meetings (Article 3). Like the BAC, it may set up working groups (Article 4). It is to adopt its own rules of procedure (Article 5). Care has been taken to ensure that close links are maintained between the ESC and the CESR; the chairperson of the CESR will participate at meetings of the ESC as an observer (Article 3). The legal basis for the establishment of the ESC (and the CESR which has the same basis) is of some interest; as well as relying on Article 49 EC, which is the foundation free movement of services provision and provides for the prohibition of restrictions on the freedom to provide services within the Community, the Commission has also called in aid the free movement of capital provisions and, in particular, Article 56 EC which prohibits, within the framework set out in the capital and payments chapter of the Treaty, all restrictions on the free movement of capital between the Member States. It also prohibits all restrictions on payments between Member States.[71] The capital provisions, which appeared, of course, in their current form only in the Maastricht Treaty, have not figured heavily in the securities and investment-services regime to date although the Settlement Finality Directive[72] is justified in part by reference to its reinforcement of the free movement of capital. The CESR is, like the ESC, also designed to serve as an independent advisory body for 'reflection, debate and advice' for the Commission (Article 1 and recital 8). Under Article 2, its function is to advise the Commission, either at the request of the Commission or on its own initiative, particularly with respect to the preparation of draft implementing measures in the field of securities. While the CESR is designed to act as a general advisory body and although the proposed Decision does not use the language of level-based decision-making, it is clear from the Explanatory Memorandum that the CESR is to assist in the preparation of level 2 implementing measures.[73] The Decision does not refer to the CESR's role in level 3 but this function is referred to in recital 9 which calls on the CESR, in line with the Stockholm Resolution,[74] to contribute to the 'consistent and timely implementation' of legislation at Member-State level and to secure 'more effective cooperation between national supervisory authorities, carrying out peer reviews and promoting best practice'. Article 3 addresses the composition of the CESR and provides that it is to be composed of 'high-level representatives from the national public authorities competent in the field of securities'; each Member State is to designate a representative and the chairperson is to be elected from CESR members. Like the ESC, the CESR is to adopt its own rules of procedures (Article 7), it may invite experts and observers to attend its

[71] On the Treaty free movement of capital rules see Ch. I sect. 8 above.
[72] Directive 98/26/EC on settlement finality in payment and securities settlement systems [1998] OJ L166/45 (the Settlement Finality Directive or the Directive). See Ch. XII.
[73] Explanatory Memorandum to the CESR Proposal, n 68 above, 4.
[74] N. 61 above, para 6.

meetings (Article 3) and it may set up working groups (Article 4).[75] The need to maintain close links between the Commission, as the dominant player in the level 2 process, and the CESR is affirmed by Article 3, which provides that the Commission is to be present at all meetings of the CESR and is to designate a high-level representative to participate in CESR debates, and Article 4, which requires the CESR to maintain 'close operational links' between it and the Commission.[76] Unlike the ESC, the CESR is, in line with the Lamfalussy model, subject to specific transparency and consultation requirements. Article 5 requires that before the CESR presents the Commission with its opinion on securities matters, it must consult 'extensively and at an early stage' with market participants, and, in another illustration of the renewed focus on retail investor interests in EC securities regulation, with consumers and end users, 'in an open and transparent manner'.[77] This transparency of the critical level 2 process should be further enhanced by Article 6, which requires the CESR to present an annual report to the Commission. The work previously carried out by FESCO has now transferred to the CESR.[78] In a creative restructuring of the law-

---

[75] Perhaps it is unfair to infer a pro-market bias from the Commission's stated hope that the CESR will establish a market participants' group and its silence on the subject of an investor-interests working group: Explanatory Memorandum to the CESR Proposal, n 68 above, 4. The operational arrangements of the CESR suggest, however, that investor interests will not be disregarded. See n 78 below.

[76] The Explanatory Memorandum has made clear that the Commission is to exert the dominant influence on the CESR's work, noting that it will play a key role in the CESR's operations, 'giving [it] mandates to discharge within defined time limits' and that it will inform it 'of ongoing political priorities' and 'contribute to discussions of emerging ideas': ibid.

[77] This provision reflects in part the European Council's general exhortation to the Commission 'to make use of early, broad and systematic consultation with the institutions and all interested parties in the securities area, in particular strengthening its dialogue with consumers and market practitioners' as well as its specific recommendation that the CESR should consult in an open and transparent manner, in line with the Lamfalussy model, and have the confidence of market participants: Stockholm Resolution, n 61 above, paras 2 and 4.

[78] FESCO agreed on a Charter of the Committee of European Securities Regulators (FESCO/01-070e—the CESR Charter) (which was adopted by the CESR in Sept 2001 (CESR/01-002)) which is designed to set out the operational arrangements of the CESR and to 'reflect the wish of the network of national securities regulators, that have successfully worked within FESCO in the last three years, to go a step further and fully play the role assigned to them in the Lamfalussy Report, the March Resolution of the European Parliament [on the Lamfalussy Report] and the recent decision of the European Commission': Wittich, G, FESCO Chairman, FESCO Press Release, 19 June 2001, FESCO/01-095. Art. 9.3 of the Charter provides that '[a]ll understandings, standards, commitments and work agreed within [FESCO] will be taken over by the [CESR] with the same consequences for the present and future members'. While it is based on the CESR's establishing Decision, the Charter also provides, *inter alia*, that: competent authorities from Member States which are not EU members will also participate in the CESR (but not in its decision-making processes); the annual report prepared for the Commission will, in a commitment reflecting inter-institutional relations, be sent to the Council and Parliament; CESR members will keep national ESC members informed of their discussions and make all necessary arrangements so that they can speak for the national competent authorities as a whole; and the CESR will develop mechanisms to promote consistent regulatory practices. It will meet at least 4 times a year and establish expert and/or permanent

making environment, FESCO's expertise and influence is accordingly institutionalized within the EC's law-making structures, although care has been
taken to ensure that regulatory co-operation remains protected by confidentiality constraints.[79] Considerable emphasis has been placed on the level 3
functions to be fulfilled by the CESR. According to the CESR Charter, the
CESR will encourage and review common implementation and application
of EC rules, issue guidelines, recommendations, and standards on regulatory
practice to be introduced by CESR members on a voluntary basis, and undertake reviews of regulatory practices within the single market.[80]

The mechanisms needed for law-making under the Lamfalussy model are
accordingly being established by an apparently committed and enthusiastic
Commission (which is, it must be noted, the main beneficiary of the
Lamfalussy Report's re-ordering of legislative power and influence). Whether
or not the new model will work will depend on how the Parliament and the
Council, as the primary law-makers, react to the Commission's level 1 proposals and, in particular, on their readiness to agree on the scope of level 1
transfers of rule-making to level 2 procedures. The Council's position has
already received special attention in the Stockholm Resolution. It appears
that the Parliament's support cannot be presumed. Not only has it already
displayed considerable resistance to the Lamfalussy model and concerns
about its transparency, its rejection of the proposed Takeover Directive in
July 2001 after twelve years of negotiations has revealed it to be a law-
maker of some volatility, independent of both the Commission and the
Council (and, it seems, of its own representatives who brokered the compromise solution which was ultimately rejected). More generally, the collapse of the proposed Takeover Directive might also mark a return to the
dominance of national interests[81] which would, were they to obstruct

groups. As far as transparency is concerned, the working procedures set out in the Charter
reveal a commitment to consult market participants, consumers, and end users and suggest the
use of concept releases, consultative papers, public hearings, Internet consultations, as well as
public disclosure of the results of consultations.

[79] The Commission will be excluded from CESR discussions which involve confidential matters relating to individuals and firms: CESR Charter, n 78 above, Art. 3.1.

[80] Ibid, Art. 4.3.

[81] It has been reported that the Parliament's failure to adopt the proposed Takeover Directive
was as a result, in part, of lobbying led by German MEPs who were responding to German opposition to the Directive's prohibition on the taking of action to frustrate a takeover bid (although
the German government finally came round to supporting the proposed Takeover Directive during the final Council discussions, it appears that it changed position at the 11th hour when the
discussions had moved to the Parliament following heavy lobbying from German corporates
who feared their greater vulnerability to takeovers). Similar concerns were raised by Italian and
Spanish MEPs. In a reference to the German position, the internal market Commissioner, Fritz
Bolkentein, stated after the vote that '[f]ourteen out of fifteen Member States clearly wanted the
directive. It is tragic to see how Europe's broader interests can be frustrated by certain narrow
interests', reported in Mortished, C, and Fletcher, M, 'MEPs throw out takeover rules bill', *The
Times*, 5 July 2001. The same report also noted concerns in Brussels that signs are emerging
of a growing resistance to opening up the internal market. See also Hargreaves and Norman,

agreement in the Council and Parliament, stymie the achievement of the FSAP more effectively than any institutional and procedural weaknesses in the legislative procedures themselves.[82]

(c) A Conceptual Framework for Law-making

A caveat can be sounded: while the legislative procedures on which the regime depends must be effective, these procedures do not operate in a vacuum. There is little point in constructing a mechanism which delivers regulation speedily and efficiently without, at the same time, considering the objectives of and rationale underlying this new generation of legislation. In light of the general reluctance of the securities-regulation regime to engage with an assessment of the rationales for regulation beyond the market-integration imperative, even as the regime increasingly pushes at the boundaries of what traditionally comes under the market-integration umbrella, it is hoped that the attention of policy-makers will not be directed solely to the mechanics of law-making set out in the Report but also to its 'conceptual framework for European securities legislation'[83] which represents a new departure for EC securities regulation. The principles suggested by the Report include: maintaining confidence in European securities markets; maintaining high levels of prudential supervision; contributing to the efforts of prudential supervisors to ensure systemic stability; ensuring appropriate levels of consumer protection proportionate to the different degrees of risk involved; respecting the subsidiarity and proportionality principles; promoting competition and ensuring compliance with the Treaty competition rules; ensuring that regulation is efficient as well as encouraging innovation; and taking account of the European, as well as the wider international dimension of, securities markets. A more considered articulation of these principles, always within the limits of the com-

n 9 above who noted that the defeat of the proposed Takeover Directive 'sends a signal to the outside world that Europe is not serious about opening up its capital markets' and referred to Commissioner Bolkenstein's view that it is an important setback to the liberalizing agenda. They also observed that 'this year's [2001] economic slow down has highlighted how many of [the liberalizing] objectives threaten long-cherished national interests and revived corporatist instincts, particularly in Germany'. The influential *Financial Times* Lex column was also concerned about the signal the defeat sent about the seriousness of the Community's commitment to liberalization: *Financial Times*, Lex Column, 18 July 2001. For a discussion of the coalition of interests which led to the defeat of the proposed Takeover Directive see further Ch. XIV.

[82] At the time of writing, the Commission's prognosis on the progress of the FSAP was gloomy. In its Nov 2001 Fifth Report on the FSAP it expressed concern at the pace of law-making and warned that timely delivery of the FSAP was under threat: *Financial Services: Europe Must Deliver On Time*: COM(2001)712.

[83] N 2 above, 22.

petences conferred by the Treaty, can only enhance the effectiveness and consistency of the regime.[84]

XV.2.5.4 *A General Move Towards Comitology*

Whatever the ultimate impact of the Wise Men's proposals, greater reliance on comitology procedures is already under consideration in the securities-regulation sphere. Comitology procedures have been proposed in the accounting area, albeit as a particular response to the institutional problems involved in adopting non-EC-derived IAS as the common standard for EC publicly listed companies.[85] Notably, the IAS proposal also adopts a bifurcated committee approach: it relies on a regulatory comitology to supervise the Commission in its adoption of IAS and on an expert technical committee to provide the Commission with technical advice and expertise. More traditional comitology procedures are followed in the Supplementary Supervision Proposal for financial conglomerates which provides for its provisions to be clarified by the Commission via the comitology process and under the regulatory committee procedure. It establishes a specific Financial Conglomerates Committee in this regard.[86] In addition, the new UCITS regime grants regulatory committee powers to the UCITS Contact Committee.[87]

There is also some evidence of a generalized move towards level 1 type legislation, although level 1 type legislation without the level 2 process envisaged by the Lamfalussy Report is likely to create more difficulties with respect to the consistency of implementation than it will resolve problems with legislative log-jams. The Commission has expressed a preference for confining new financial-services legislation to prescribing basic principles, suggesting that more detailed guidance where necessary could be provided in the form of more flexible communications and recommendations.[88] Indeed, several of the initiatives being undertaken under the FSAP to help attain open and secure retail markets are not, at the moment, being considered in the form of detailed directives.[89]

---

[84] The signs are that notice is being taken of these principles. The Stockholm Resolution recommended that the new approach to law-making take full account of the principles: n 61 above, para 1. They are also referred to in the Commission's Explanatory Memorandum to the ESC Proposal, n 67 above, 3 and to the Proposed CESR Decision, n 68 above, 3 and in the CESR Charter, n 78 above, Art. 5.7.

[85] See the discussion of the Accounting Regulatory Committee in Ch. IV sect. 10.5 above.

[86] COM(2001)213. See Ch. VIII sect. 11.3.3 above.

[87] See Ch. V sect. 8.2.9 above.

[88] 1998 Communication, n 12 above, 3. Relying on communications to achieve legislative objectives can be a precarious path to take, as was made clear in Case C–57/95 France v Commission [1997] ECR I–1627.

[89] Communications form an important part of the FSAP.

XV.2.5.5 *The European Central Bank and Law-making*

Further in the background, the possibility always exists that the European
Central Bank (ECB) will come to play a role in the development of EC securities regulation, if only in the prudential-supervision sphere. Article 25 of
the Protocol to the Statute of the European System of Central Banks and the
European Central Bank grants the ECB an advisory role in relation to prudential supervision. It provides that the ECB 'may offer advice to and be consulted by the Council, the Commission and the competent authorities of the
Member States on the scope and implementation of Community legislation
relating to the prudential supervision of credit institutions and to the stability of the financial system'. Article 105(4) EC provides that the ECB is to be
consulted 'on any proposed Community acts in its field of competence',
which has been interpreted as including rules applicable to financial institutions where they materially influence the stability of financial institutions
and markets.[90] The ECB is also empowered under Article 105(4) to 'submit
opinions to the appropriate Community institutions or bodies . . . on matters in its field of competence'. Apart from this somewhat nebulous involvement in rule-making, Article 105(6) (section 3.3.3 below) sets out the
possibility for 'specific tasks' to be given to the ECB 'concerning *policies*
[emphasis added] relating to the prudential supervision of credit institutions
and other financial institutions with the exception of insurance undertakings'. If Article 105(6) is activated at some future point, it may be that the
ECB will be given specific rule-making powers with respect to prudential
regulation.[91]

XV.2.5.6 *A Specialized Law-making Agency?*

The concentration of rule-making functions and/or the supervision of
Member States' implementation obligations (and market supervision powers:
sections 3.2 and 3.3 below) in a distinct Community agency with specialized personnel in order to enhance the rule-adoption process and make rule
implementation as consistent as possible, has a certain appeal.[92] The attractions of such a model would, arguably, be enhanced were the agency to be
concerned with technical market rules (or, conversely, with establishing

---

[90] Council Decision 98/415/EC [1998] OJ L189/42, Art. 2(1).

[91] It has been suggested that Art. 105(6) EC could have considerable consequences for the
scope and application of the 'general-good' justification: Usher, J, *The Law of Money and
Financial Services in the European Community* (2nd edn, 2000) 222. See also Andenas, M, and
Hadjiemmanuil, C, 'Banking Supervision, the Internal Market and European Monetary Union'
in Andenas, M, Gormley, L, Hadjiemmanuil, C, and Harden, I (eds), *European Economic and
Monetary Union: The Institutional Framework* (1997) 373, 402.

[92] Might it be argued, however, that the more specialized and market aware the body the
greater the likelihood of regulatory capture? See n 150 below.

broad policy guidelines for areas not harmonized at Community level)[93] and/or charged with monitoring implementation, co-ordinating the rules of national markets, and promoting convergence through co-operation and consultation rather than with setting high-level rules.[94] Such a development would, however, represent a new direction for European agencies (the ECB and the European Investment Bank were established by the Maastricht Treaty and are distinct Community institutions rather than agencies exercising delegated powers). While ten agencies have been established,[95] usually under the residual law-making power given to the Community in order to pursue its objectives by Article 308 EC,[96] they have been concerned with implementing Community policies (and, in particular, with ensuring compliance with Community policies by certifying and controlling private conduct) and producing information.[97] Hitherto, agencies have either not exercised delegated decision-making functions, or, where they have, those decisions have been formally adopted by Community institutions.[98]

[93] In support of a structure based on the Art. 105(6) EC model and involving the setting of policy guidelines see Wymeersch, E, *The Harmonisation of Securities Regulation in Europe in the New Trading Environment*, Working Paper 2000-16, Working Paper Series of the Financial Law Institute, Universiteit Gent, 4.

[94] The attractions of the Community agency model have been summarized as follows by one commentator: '[they] facilitate the use of scientific and/or technical experts who are not part of the normal bureaucratic structure, offer greater staffing flexibility, reduce the workload of the administration so as to enable it to concentrate on strategic policy, insulate the resolution of technical regulatory issues from day-to-day political changes and contribute to greater transparency and accountability. The very fact that a clearly identified agency, instead of an obscure Commission division or an equally obscure committee, carries out clearly defined tasks should, in principle, create greater transparency . . . [they can] encourage uniform interpretation and implementation of Community law where they form the nucleus in networks of national authorities and promote administrative integration, whilst they could play an important role in the international arena too': Vos, E, 'Reforming the European Commission: What Role To Play For EU Agencies' (2000) 37 *CMLRev.* 1113, 1119 (footnotes omitted). Although the Lamfalussy model does require considerable Commission involvement, the ESC and the CESR structure, anchored by transparency and consultation obligations, might also deliver some of these benefits.

[95] More may be expected, given that the Commission is in favour of greater delegation (or 'externalization') of certain of its functions so that it can refocus its activities on its core responsibilities and policy priorities. See the Commission Reform White Paper, n 9 above, 10–12.

[96] See n 4 above. For an examination of the role of Art. 308 EC in the establishment of agencies see Vos, n 94 above, 1121–3 who has noted that Art. 308 EC cannot be used to change the institutional structure of the Community and its balance of powers: 'agency powers must not encroach upon those of the Treaty institutions': at 1122.

[97] See the analysis in Chiti, E, 'The Emergence of a Community Administration: the Case of European Agencies' (2000) 37 *CMLRev.* 309. An example of the former is the Office for Harmonization in the Internal Market (Trade Marks and Designs), while the European Environment Agency is an example of the latter.

[98] de Búrca, G, 'The Institutional Development of the European Union: A Constitutional Analysis' in Craig, P, and de Búrca, G (eds), *The Evolution of EU Law* (1998) 55, 75–7. Although considerable constitutional difficulties exist (see below), in principle, the supervision of EC securities markets, rather than the securities-regulation rule-making process, may ultimately be affected by the Commission's suggestion, made as part of its consultation on reforming European governance, that additional autonomous 'regulatory agencies' be created which

Delegations of existing competences under the Treaty are, however, subject to restrictions. The delegation to independent agencies of powers already conferred on the institutions of the Community under the Treaties is possible only where the delegation involves clearly defined executive powers, rather than discretionary powers, and the exercise of the delegated powers can be subject to review in light of objective criteria set by the delegating authority.[99] An alternative rule-making model might be to transfer rule-making/convergence-supervision/policy-guideline powers to a newly constituted institution by an amendment to the Treaty, as was the case with the establishment of the ECB and the European Investment Bank. The indications so far are that such a move is unlikely. Nonetheless, the issue is unlikely to disappear. Among the final comments of the Lamfalussy Report was the somewhat, given its political ramifications, apocalyptic warning that if, by 2004, the Report's law-making proposals were shown not to have any prospect of success 'it might be appropriate to consider a Treaty change, including the creation of a single EU regulatory authority for financial services generally in the Community'.[100]

XV.3 SUPERVISION, ENFORCEMENT, AND THE INSTITUTIONAL STRUCTURE

XV.3.1 *The Current Model*

XV.3.1.1 *The Need for Supervisory Co-operation*

As outlined in earlier chapters, the supervision of compliance by market participants with the harmonized rule structure underpinning the EC securities

---

would be granted power to take 'individual decisions in application of regulatory measures': European Governance White Paper, n 56 above, 24.

[99] Case 9/56 *Meroni v High Authority* [1957-8] ECR 133. For a discussion of the constitutional limitations on delegations of powers by Community institutions to agencies see Lenaerts, K, 'Regulating the Regulatory Process' (1993) 18 *ELR* 23. The *Meroni* standard has been challenged by Vos who has noted that its focus on hierarchy-based controls on rule-making is out of date, given the greater attention given by modern administrative law to procedural requirements, transparency, and other indicia of administrative legitimacy and that discretionary powers could be delegated were they to be accompanied by a reinforcement of the controls to which agencies are subject: n 94 above, 1123-4. As part of its proposal to create additional agencies and to define the criteria for the creation of agencies, the Commission has restated the parameters within which the creation of regulatory agencies must be undertaken: (1) agencies may be granted the power to take individual decisions in specific areas but cannot be granted power to adopt general regulatory measures; (2) they cannot be given responsibilities in areas in respect of which the Treaty has conferred a direct decision-making power on the Commission; (3) they cannot be granted decision-making powers in areas where they would be required to mediate between conflicting public interests, exercise political discretion, or carry out complex economic assessments; and (4) they must be subject to effective supervision and control: European Governance White Paper, n 56 above, 24.

[100] N 2 above, 41.

and investment-services markets is entrusted to national competent authorities, in co-operation with the competent authorities of other Member States, and is carried out according to the co-operation mechanisms and rules allocating supervisory jurisdiction set out in the relevant directives.

The institutional structure and co-operation mechanisms of the EC supervisory regime could be regarded as a microcosm of the larger supervisory co-ordination and co-operation mechanisms which form an essential element of international securities regulation. Co-operation between domestic regulators on an international level is regularly highlighted as being essential for the effective regulation of domestic markets, given the ever-increasing globalization of markets, the growth of financial conglomerates, and the increasingly international dimension to the activities of market participants.[101] Effective supervision must now accommodate co-operation and co-ordination between the various nationally-based supervisors who are responsible for the activities of a market participant, cross-border and domestic, in order that a co-ordinated approach can be taken to the supervision of the participant. Domestic systemic stability is not just a function of domestic regulation but is also dependent on international developments while international systemic stability demands that domestic supervisors co-ordinate in supervising internationally active market participants.[102] Effective control of fraud and market abuse often requires supervisors to liaise with supervisors in other jurisdictions as transactions in the same instrument are increasingly carried out on different market-places. Investor protection is now pursued in domestic market-places in which securities of foreign issuers and foreign collective-investment schemes are marketed to investors. The Internet is continually testing the limits of traditional, territorially-based supervision. In this environment, formalized co-operation and information-exchange mechanisms have emerged as essential regulatory tools,[103] and convergence of supervisory standards and practices has been identified as central to ensuring the application of consistent standards. IOSCO has been the instigator of an impressive number of initiatives designed to enhance supervisory co-operation, many of which are based on information exchange.[104] Information exchange was also at the heart of the

---

[101] See the discussion of international supervisory co-operation in Blair, W, Allison, A, Palmer, K, Richards-Carpenter, P, and Walker, G, *Banking and Financial Services Regulation* (2nd edn, 1998) 398–415. Reference is made in that discussion at 398 to the 'fundamental global market but local control conflict'.

[102] See the Group of 30 Report on Global Institutions, National Supervision and Systemic Risk (1997) discussed in Coakley, J, 'Trends in Financial Services and Influences on Approaches to Regulation' in McCrudden, C (ed), *Regulation and Deregulation. Policy and Practice in the Utilities and Financial Services Industries* (1999) 343, 352–3.

[103] See the IOSCO Objectives and Principles of Securities Regulation (1998) para 9.3.

[104] See, eg, its 1994 Resolution on Commitment to Basic IOSCO Principles of High Regulatory Standards and Mutual Co-operation and Assistance and its 1998 Guidance on Information Exchange.

1998 Report of the G-7 Finance Ministers on Financial Stability—
Supervision of Global Financial Institutions which included Ten Key
Principles on Information Sharing.[105] IOSCO also strives to enhance mutual
understanding between supervisors and promotes convergence in supervisory standards and practices.[106]

A broad parallel can be drawn between the need for co-operation at international level to ensure effective supervision and, in particular, the containment of systemic risk as market participants operate on an international
basis, and the imperative that EC competent authorities co-operate in order
to police EC securities markets and the provision of pan-EC investment services effectively. However, the unique combination of liberalization, the
passport mechanism, mutual recognition, and the home- and host-Member-
State control device places particular demands on nationally based supervision structures and co-operation mechanisms which are not made at
international level. The EC market-place demands sophisticated and formalized supervisory and co-operation mechanisms which reflect not only the
allocation of supervisory jurisdiction set out in the liberalizing directives but
also the particular risks, both to investors and the system as a whole, inherent in the integrated market-place. Nonetheless, the fundamental emphasis
on information exchange evident at international level also underlines the
EC regime while, of course, the convergence of standards is a core feature of
the directives which underpin the internal market in securities and investment services.

The effectiveness of the current decentralized supervision and enforcement structure has recently come under scrutiny as integration deepens and
cross-border activity increases. Although the primary focus of EC securities
regulation to date has been on the construction of the integrated market-
place via common standards, all the indications are that attention is, certainly in the prudential supervision sphere, shifting to the effectiveness of the
supervisory and enforcement systems which underpin this market-place.[107]
The Lamfalussy Report has been one of the major catalysts in this paradigm
shift. Level 3 of its model for legislative reform addresses co-operation
between regulators and calls for greater consistency in regulatory practices.

---

[105] The principles are based on: authorization to share and gather information; cross-sector
information-sharing; information about systems and controls; information about individuals;
information-sharing between exchanges; confidentiality; formal agreements, and written
requests; reciprocity requirements; the passing on of exchanged information to other supervisory agencies; and the removal of laws preventing supervisory information exchange.

[106] See, eg, its joint work (with the Basel Committee on Banking Supervision and the
International Association of Insurance Supervisors) on financial conglomerates; its 1998
Objectives and Principles of Securities Regulation; and its 1998 International Disclosure
Standards for Cross-Border Offerings and Initial Listings by Foreign Issuers.

[107] See, eg, the 2000 Commission Communication on Upgrading the Investment Services
Directive, COM(2000)729, 7 (the ISD Communication), 6.

Part of the CESR's mandate in this regard is to conduct peer reviews and compare and review regulatory practices in order to set standards of best practice and ensure effective enforcement across the market-place. Level 4 is directed towards bolstering the enforcement of common standards. While the Lamfalussy model is primarily focused on the Commission's role in this regard and on the Member States' obligation to implement legislation, it also noted the role of regulators and the private sector in improving enforcement.

XV.3.1.2 *Competent Authorities*

An important aspect of the EC securities and investment-services regime has been the requirement imposed on Member States to establish competent authorities to oversee the various directives.[108]

While there is a lively debate on the respective benefits and disadvantages of self-regulation versus public regulation and as to the extent to which both forms should be combined,[109] by and large the directives currently in force have not directly addressed this question, although a striking feature of two of the most high-profile proposals presented in the wake of the Lamfalussy Report and as part of the FSAP (the Market Abuse Proposal and the Prospectus Proposal) has been the prescriptive approach taken to the form which the competent authorities must take. The extent to which competent authorities must take a particular form varies as between the directives.[110] While the pre-consolidation Admission Directive simply contained an obligation to 'designate the national authority or authorities competent to decide on the admission of securities',[111] the UCITS Directive requires that the

[108] As early as 1966, the Segré Report, albeit in the limited sphere of issuer disclosure, suggested that the establishment of supervisory agencies in countries which did not already have them would be an appropriate way to regulate the stock markets and encourage greater investment in securities by enhancing investor confidence: Report by a Group of Experts Appointed by the EEC Commission, *The Development of a European Capital Market* (1966) 235.

[109] This has been a matter of considerable debate in the UK due to the evolution of the regulatory regime from a system heavily based on self-regulation to one characterized by strong central control by a public authority, the Financial Services Authority (the FSA). See, eg: Ogus, A, *Regulation. Legal Form and Economic Theory* (1994) 107–11; Page, A, and Ferguson, R, *Investor Protection* (1992) 82–4; and Llewellyn, D, 'Consumer Protection in Retail Investment Services: Protection Against What' (1995) 3 *JFRC* 43, 51–2.

[110] The competent authority provisions of each directive and any particular features they have specific to the type of powers exercised by the particular competent authority (such as Art. 18(4) of the LPD and Art. 9(7) of the IRD (SCD, Art. 105(3)) which, in light of the fears of certain national authorities that they would be liable in respect of their decisions in relation to listing particulars and their supervision of interim disclosure, provide that liability questions are to be dealt with by national law) are dealt with in the relevant earlier chapters.

[111] Art. 9(1). The new codified obligation for the official-listing-disclosure regime as a whole in SCD, Art. 105(1) reflects the LPD, IRD, and SSD, however, and refers to the appointment of 'one or more competent authorities for the purposes of the Directive'. The POD refers to the LPD (and thus SCD, Art. 105(1)) where the prospectus is based on that directive and does not require the designation of a competent authority otherwise.

competent authorities designated be 'public authorities or bodies appointed by public authorities' (Article 49(2)). The IDD suggests public control and provides in Article 8 that Member States are to designate the 'administrative authorities' or authorities competent, if necessary in collaboration with other authorities, to ensure that the IDD's requirements are applied. The ISD takes a more encyclopædic approach and requires that competent authorities be 'either public authorities, bodies recognized by national law or bodies recognized by public authorities expressly empowered for that purpose by national law',[112] while, somewhat perplexingly given its sister status to the ISD, the CAD requires rather differently that competent authorities 'must be public authorities or bodies officially recognized by national law or by public authorities as part of the supervisory system in operation in the Member State concerned' (Article 9(2)). The now failed proposed Takeover Directive was particularly controversial, of course, and provided expressly that supervision could be exercised by self-regulatory bodies in order to accommodate the self-regulatory UK Takeover Panel.[113] Overall, these provisions allow the Member States some flexibility in the form which competent authorities take and are sensitive to the prevalence of self-regulation as the supervisory mechanism of choice in certain Member States, at the outset of the harmonization programme, in any event. In the case of the cornerstone ISD, for example, supervision through self-regulatory structures appears to be possible as long as the competent authorities hold their powers by way of a delegation from public authorities and that, as a result, their rules and decisions can be indirectly tracked back to a public authority and that, under Article 26, their decisions are subject to review by the courts.[114] Self-regulatory bodies must also have the powers demanded by the particular directives in question. Nonetheless, despite the possibility of supervision though self-regulation, EC harmonization has resulted in an increase across the integrated market in the involvement of public authorities in regulation and a general decrease in self-regulation.[115] This trend is now being mir-

---

[112] The ISD competent authorities also manage the compensation scheme regime. Directive 97/7/EC on investor compensation schemes [1997] OJ L84/22 (the ICSD).

[113] This reference is made in the common position which was adopted by the Council with a view to adopting a Directive on company law concerning takeover bids [2001] OJ C23/1. See further Ch. XIV sect. 4.9.1 above.

[114] Backstop court review of decisions taken in pursuant of a directive's requirements is also envisaged in Art. 15 of the Admission Directive (SCD, Art. 19), Art. 51(2) of the UCITS Directive, and, controversially, was included in the proposed Takeover Directive where it was subject to special controls to minimize litigation risk (on which see further Ch. XIV sect. 4.9.5 above). It also appears in the Market Abuse Proposal and the Prospectus Proposal. On whether directives can be implemented via self-regulation and supervision by self-regulatory bodies see (in the context of the Takeover Panel and the failed proposed Takeover Directive) Tison, M, 'Financial Regulation and EC Directives' [1993] *LMCLQ* 60, 74–8.

[115] Wymeersch, E, 'The Implementation of the ISD and the CAD' in Ferrarini, G (ed), *European Securities Markets: the Investment Services Directive and Beyond* (1998) 6–10 and 38–40. See also Coleman, W, and Underhill, G, 'Globalization, Regionalism and the Regulation

rored at EC level as the indications are that EC securities regulation is becoming more prescriptive of the form which competent authorities take and that, in line with a renewed focus on enforcement, public control is in the ascendant. The changes proposed to be made to how the disclosure regime is supervised illustrate this trend. The open-textured approach of the official-listing regime accommodates, at the moment, self-regulation via the securities-trading markets.[116] This approach has been the subject of some controversy recently, with the transformation of securities-trading markets from quasi-public-interest bodies to commercially motivated entities as demutualization has taken hold and competition between securities-trading markets has exploded. If the Commission's Prospectus Proposal is successful, the disclosure review required when an issuer applies for admission to trading on a 'regulated market' (or on a public offer of securities) will be removed from the securities-trading markets (where they still exercise this function) and carried out by independent 'competent administrative authorities' (see Chapter IV section 9.3.6 above). The Market Abuse Proposal which was presented at the same time has followed this public-control approach, although by requiring that Member States designate 'administrative authorities' it reflects the original IDD formula. It additionally requires, however, that Member States designate a single authority only in the interests of effective supervision.[117]

All of these authorities are, typically, required to have such powers as may be necessary for the exercise of their duties,[118] although the IDD makes specific reference in Article 8(2) to the need for the relevant authorities to have all the 'supervisory and investigatory powers' necessary to exercise their functions. This should not pose any particular problems for public authorities, but demands that self-regulatory authorities have appropriate supervisory and enforcement powers. More recently, however, reflecting the heightened focus on enforcement, a move towards greater prescription of the

of Securities Markets' (1995) 2 *J of European Public Policy* 488, 501–3. For a detailed review of the forms of supervision, public and private, across the Community in the late 1970s prior to the harmonization programme see Wymeersch, E, *Control of Securities Markets in the European Economic Community*, Collection Studies, Competition—Approximation of Legislation Series, No. 31 (1977) 38–53 and 105–16. The supervision structure which Professor Wymeersch revealed was one of great diversity, although three patterns could then be observed: the dominance of self-regulation based predominantly on the exchanges and broker-dealer associations (UK, Ireland, and the Netherlands); public or government regulation, mediated by a degree of self regulation particularly at the level of the exchanges (France and Italy); and intermediate regulation, characterized by government intervention in certain areas (Belgium, Luxembourg, and Germany).

[116] For this view of the Admission Directive see Wymeersch in Ferrarini, n 115 above, 7.

[117] N 66 above, Art. 11. See Ch. XIII sect. 11.5.6 above.

[118] The CAD is more specific, referring in Art. 9(3) to 'all the powers necessary for the performance of their tasks, and in particular that of overseeing the constitution of trading books'. The ISD refers simply in Art. 22(3) to 'all powers necessary for the performance of their functions'.

powers which must be exercisable by competent authorities can be observed. The Commission's proposal to restructure the disclosure regime sets out in some detail the powers which the competent authority must have (Chapter IV section 9.3.6 above) as does the Market Abuse Proposal (Chapter XIII section 11.5.6 above). Whatever its weaknesses the EC supervisory structure has at least advanced some way since the adoption of the 1977 Code of Conduct Relating to Transactions in Transferable Securities which merely provides that 'there should be in each Member State at least one body (supervisory authority, professional association, etc.) responsible for supervising the implementation of the code at national level'.[119]

XV.3.1.3 *Competent Authorities and Co-operation*

The EC securities and investment-services regime directives, as discussed in earlier chapters, require competent authorities to co-operate in order to carry out their tasks under the directives and specify particular information-exchange mechanisms. Information exchange, assistance in obtaining records, assistance in interviewing, where necessary, and help in accessing national judicial mechanisms, such as injunctions, all facilitate effective supervision under the split supervisor model, although information exchange is the dominant form of co-operation in the directives.[120] The Market Abuse Proposal contains more sophisticated co-operation mechanisms, however, which address investigations as well as more traditional information exchange procedures (Chapter XIII section 11.5.6 above).

Co-operation between these competent authorities is important on a number of fronts. First, effective supervision of the rules governing the liberalized market, where supervision is split between home-Member-State and host-Member-State authorities under the dominant mutual-recognition model, requires that supervisors collaborate and communicate.[121] In many

---

[119] Commission Recommendation 77/534/EEC concerning a European Code of Conduct Relating to Transactions in Transferable Securities [1977] OJ L212/37: Explanatory Memorandum, IV, para 14.

[120] This is true even of the IDD, the subject matter of which might have suggested more formalized co-operation mechanisms with respect to the gathering of evidence and the bringing of enforcement actions. Art. 10 is slightly more nuanced than most co-operation provisions, however, and could act as the basis for more extensive co-operation in that it provides that the competent authorities are to co-operate whenever necessary for the performance of their duties, 'making use of the powers mentioned in Article 8(2)'. Art. 8(2) refers to 'all supervisory and investigatory powers that are necessary' for the exercise of the competent authority's functions under the Directive, where appropriate in collaboration with other authorities. The ISD is more detailed than most directives, however, in that it provides for the conduct of on-the-spot verifications of information in Art. 24.

[121] See, eg, the observation at 38 in the Introduction to Bratton, W, McCahery, J, Picciotto, S, and Scott, C (eds), *International Regulatory Competition and Coordination* (1996) that 'enforcement [of harmonized financial services rules] remains decentralised, and the Commission has a minimal role, so there is a complex and perhaps unstable interaction between the roles and responsibilities of the EC institutions and the home and host states'.

cases, the information which a competent authority requires to exercise effective control is generated outside the competent authority's jurisdiction.[122] The premise that co-operation between national authorities is essential to manage institutional prudential risk on an EC-wide basis, for example, underlies the prudential supervision mechanisms set up in the ISD and the CAD.

Secondly, optimal supervision of the EC investment-services and securities markets also requires that national supervisors communicate in order to agree on common standards and practices when applying the typically (thus far, at least) open-textured minimum EC rules. Divergences in the standards and supervisory practices applied by national supervisors have the potential to weaken the supervisory structure. The Commission has suggested that it can play a role by issuing interpretive communications,[123] but it has also called on national supervisors to co-operate in this regard. Level 3 of the Lamfalussy model also addresses this question and institutionalizes co-operation via the CESR. Such co-operation is also necessary in the application of rules which are not fully harmonized at present, as is the case with the conduct-of-business regime contained in the ISD, and in unharmonized areas such as (until the Market Abuse Proposal is adopted) the control of market abuse.[124]

Finally, co-operation also enhances the ability of supervisors to identify and address new risks as they emerge. In this regard, the effective supervision of financial conglomerates which straddle the insurance, banking, securities, and investment-services sectors and which are forming an increasingly more important part of the securities and investment-services landscape represents a significant challenge for the decentralized co-operation-based supervision structure.[125]

XV.3.1.4 *Memoranda of Understanding, Contact Committees, and FESCO*

Co-operation between supervisors is often strengthened by the conclusion of Memoranda of Understanding (MoU) between competent authorities. MoU are typically bilateral and establish a structure setting out the practical procedures according to which information can be requested and exchanged (such as the type of information which may be requested, any time limits

---

[122] Bergsträsser, S, 'Cooperation between Supervisors' in Ferrarini, n 115 above, 373, 373.

[123] Such as its 1997 Communication on the Freedom to Provide Services and the Interest of the General Good in the Second Banking Directive [1997] OJ C209/6.

[124] FESCO has observed that, in the area of market abuse it is important that competent authorities 'act together to develop co-ordinated implementing rules and guidance. The latter are increasingly important for FESCO members in order to maintain a high level of market integrity and investor confidence irrespective of the domestic or cross border nature of the financial markets': FESCO Market Abuse Report, n 50 above, 4.

[125] See further Ch. VIII sect. 11.3.3 above.

applicable, the agencies to which the request may be directed, the uses to which the information may be put, and the preservation of the rights of persons affected by the request in the requested Member State) and subject to which confidentiality of information is maintained. They may also set out the procedures under which investigations can be carried out or establish co-operation and information mechanisms designed to facilitate enforcement actions.[126] The co-operation procedures contained in the directives have, to a large extent, taken the pressure from Member States to enter into bilateral MoU in recent years,[127] although in areas where the harmonized system has not had an impact thus far, a classic example being the supervision of financial conglomerates, supervisory co-ordination via MoU obligations has resulted in the development of what has been termed 'contractually organized supervision'.[128]

Co-operation is also assisted by an informal, *ad hoc*, institutional structure in that the Contact Committee which assists the Commission in relation to the operation and amendment of the securities directives has also become a focal point for co-operation between supervisory authorities.[129] As previously outlined, the absence of a Securities Committee, which would otherwise have provided a forum for co-operation and communication for investment-services and securities supervisors,[130] was a factor leading to the establishment of FESCO. In 1999 its members signed a multilateral MoU for mutual assistance and the exchange of information in order to encourage cross-border co-operation for surveillance and enforcement purposes.[131] In addition to facilitating the completion of co-operation agreements between supervisors, it also provided a forum whereby the nature and extent of the actual co-operation in practice between supervisors could be monitored. The Commission has already explicitly acknowledged the importance of FESCO's role in deepening supervisory co-operation and mutual understanding in the area of conduct-of-business regulation and supervision.[132] In the future, the

---

[126] On the features of Memoranda of Understanding see IOSCO Technical Committee, *Principles for Memorandum of Understanding* (1991) and see generally Bergsträsser, n 122 above.

[127] Ibid, 379.   [128] Wymeersch, n 93 above, 3.

[129] 1998 Communication, n 12 above, 15.

[130] The BAC has, since its inception, acted as a forum for co-operation and communication between banking supervisors. In addition, the Groupe de Contact, which is an informal group of banking supervisors and does not have official status, acts as a forum for the discussion of supervisory policies and the exchange of information on prudential issues relating to individual banks. It also plays an important role in rule development by carrying out surveys of existing banking practices and rules which form the basis for future harmonization. More recently, the Banking Supervision Sub-Committee of the ECB has emerged as an important forum for encouraging the exchange of information between supervisors and alerting them to potential problems.

[131] Before the establishment of the CESR, a dedicated FESCO working group composed of senior officials responsible for surveillance activities and information exchange at each member competent authority (FESCOPOL) facilitated the sharing of information and the co-ordination of supervision and enforcement activities.

[132] 1998 Communication, n 12 above, 4 and ISD Communication, n 107 above, 8.

CESR is likely to be the core mechanism for encouraging communication between supervisors.

While the various Contact Committees constituted under the EC securities and investment-services directives and FESCO have acted as a vehicle for encouraging greater co-operation between national supervisors, they play an advisory role only and are not actively involved in supervision. It is made clear, for example under Article 53(2) of the UCITS Directive, that the Contact Committee set up under Article 53 to advise the Commission on the operation of the directive must not appraise the merits of decisions taken in individual cases by the competent authorities responsible for the authorization and supervision of UCITSs.[133] Similarly, the CESR as currently constituted is a forum for consultation and is not designed to intervene directly in the supervision of the integrated market.

XV.3.2 *Beyond Co-operation*

XV.3.2.1 *Centralized Supervision: The Choices*

Decentralized supervision by national supervisors linked by co-operation obligations represents but one model for the supervision of EC securities and investment-services markets. One of the debates of the hour centres on whether or not, with a basic common rule framework in place and with deepening integration, the current decentralized and nationally-focused institutional structure will evolve, via the informal bodies through which supervisors currently co-operate, into a structure based on supervision by a central-market supervisor or single regulator exercising investigative and enforcement powers, with comparative reference being most typically made to the US Securities and Exchange Commission (SEC).[134]

---

[133] A similar provision applies to the Contact Committee set up under Art. 20 of the Admission Directive by Art. 20(2) of that directive (SCD, Art. 108(2)) and Art. 25(2) of the POD (with respect to its activities under the POD) which provide that it shall not be the function of the Committee to appraise the merits of the decisions taken by the competent authorities in individual cases.

[134] Although it is being aired with ever-increasing frequency as the EC securities-regulation regime becomes more sophisticated and the market-place more integrated, this question has been a remarkably persistent theme of EC securities regulation. As early as 1966, the Segré Report suggested, in the context of the establishment of a common disclosure policy, that there was a case for considering the establishment at Community level of an agency similar to the US SEC. Examining how disclosure could be supervised it stated that '[a] first solution that comes to mind is the establishment of an agency at Community level, to be competent for issues floated within the territory of the Community and to be endowed with powers similar to those of the Securities and Exchange Commission in the US, the Banking Commission in Belgium or the Bank Control Commissariat in Luxembourg'. It went on to say, however, that 'this solution would not be practicable as soon as would be necessary. Although the setting of a larger market would make such a solution appear more logical, the establishment of such agencies in the countries which still lack them could also be envisaged: this might indeed be the most appropriate way of 'moralizing' the stock exchange . . . and at the same time of making

Any move towards more centralized supervision could involve a number of different supervisory models[135] which could vary as a function of the particular market sectors, securities offerings, investment services, trading markets, and so on, over which supervision was exercised. Greater co-ordination and centralization could range from a simple enhancement of co-operation through the adoption of more extensive multilateral memoranda of understanding to the establishment of a more formal committee structure which would oversee supervisory co-operation and manage the network of multilateral or bilateral memoranda of understanding. More drastically, it could (taking the CESR a stage further) involve the establishment of a new high-level co-ordinating body in the form of an independent agency which would formally co-ordinate supervision between national supervisors, set operational rules in accordance with the subsidiarity principle, and act as the central hub of a network of national enforcement bodies.

The most revolutionary option would involve the transfer of national market supervision and enforcement powers to a new central supervisor.[136]

investment in securities a sounder proposition than it all too often is at the present time': n 108 above, 235. For another relatively early perspective, see Buxbaum, R, and Hopt, K, *Legal Harmonisation and the Business Enterprise* (1988) at 267 who were of the prescient opinion that the establishment of a securities commission was highly unlikely given political sentiment.

[135] It has been observed that 'no provision has been made for the creation of common institutions to supervise the financial sector or to regulate capital markets. A truly integrated capital market will sooner or later call for a common institutional framework . . . Although this does not necessarily imply that the euro zone requires a single supervisory authority, strengthened forums for cooperation between different national and European bodies are indispensable': Gros, D, and Lannoo, K, *The Euro Capital Market* (2000) p. xvii.

[136] On the ability of the EC to establish independent agencies see sect. 2.5.6 above. Given its limitations, the agency model is unlikely to serve as the basis for a new supervisor. The constitutional difficulties are most likely to be met by a Treaty amendment setting up a new institution and conferring on it market-supervision powers. An amendment may be necessary, as it not clear whether the residual Art. 308 EC power (which is the only power which could be used here; the other general power, Art. 95 EC, requires a connection with rule harmonization) could contain the establishment of a new market supervisor. Art. 308 EC is limited by the requirement that the measure adopted be 'necessary to attain, in the course of the operation of the common market, one of the objectives of the Community'. Although the objectives of the Community, set out in Art. 2 EC, are extremely wide (the establishment of a single regulator could, eg, be contained within 'the harmonious, balanced and sustained development of economic activities'), leading one commentary to refer to the 'potentially unlimited legislative power' of Art. 308 EC (Beaumont and Weatherill, n 5 above, 156), the Court appears to be scaling back the reach of Art. 308 EC. In addition to Art. 308-specific judgments such as Opinion 2/94 [1996] ECR I-1759 (in which the Court found that Art. 308 EC cannot widen the scope of the Community's powers beyond the general framework created by the Treaty and, in particular Arts. 2 and 3 EC which (admittedly widely) set out the objectives and tasks of the Community), account should be taken of what seems to be a growing scepticism on the part of the Court as to the extent to which Treaty provisions can be manipulated to accommodate 'necessary' Community action (as witnessed by the *Tobacco Advertising* ruling (Case C-376/98 *Germany v Parliament and Council* [2000] ECR I-8419)). For an argument supporting reliance on Art. 308EC see Thieffry, G, 'Towards a European Securities Commission' *IFLR*, Oct 1999, 14. In addition, given the influence which such a body would exercise over the EC securities and investment-services markets and their participants and the potential for economy-wide effects to be felt as a result of its decisions, it would also raise concerns about governance and,

As discussed in section 2.5.6 above, rule-making, as well as supervision, could fall within the remit of such a body. Indeed, the Lamfalussy Report might suggest that any move towards centralization is more likely to be in the rule-making sphere than in the supervision sphere. A move towards centralized supervision by a dedicated body might, however, reflect the current trend away from self-regulation towards stronger public control, as witnessed recently in the UK with the establishment of the Financial Services Authority. Given the coverage of EC securities and investment-service regulation, the remit of a central supervisor could cover some or all of the following: the supervision of the offer of securities and, in particular, disclosure to the market-place; the secondary-trading markets and their participants, leading, depending on the path taken by the securities-trading markets, to the overseeing of, in due course, an integrated securities-trading platform; the prudential regulation of investment firms; and protective supervision, involving the protection of investors in the secondary markets.

XV.3.2.2 *The Case for Centralized Supervision*[137]

(a) *Supervision as an Instrument of Competition*

Member States currently display a wide range of supervisory structures and techniques in supervising their investment-services and securities markets. The mutual recognition and home-country device means that the home-Member-State supervisor is dominant. This combination of home-Member-State control and differences in supervisory structures and techniques for supervision from Member State to Member State raises the possibility of the structure and form of supervision becoming a tool in the competition between Member States for securities and investment business, which could hinder the effectiveness of supervision in the integrated securities and investment-services market.[138] This problem could be minimized by a greater degree of alignment between the supervisors of their supervisory practices, however, via by the ESC/CESR structure.

in particular, accountability. The ECB, eg, which was established under a Treaty amendment, is subject to independence requirements and accountability controls (such as reporting requirements, appearances before the European Parliament, and requirements as to participation by the ECB in meetings of other EC institutions and vice versa). See, eg, the discussion in Smits, R, *The European Central Bank. Institutional Aspects* (1997) 152–69 and 169–78.

[137] On the potential for a Euro-SEC for transactions on the securities markets generally see Wymeersch, E, 'From Harmonization to Integration in European Securities Markets' (1981) 3 *J of Comparative Corporate Law and Securities Regulation* (an early perspective based on securities market integration), Lee, R, 'Should There Be A European Securities Commission: A Framework for Analysis' 3 (1992) *EBLRev.* 102, Garzaniti, L, and Pope, D, 'Single Market Making: EC Regulation of Securities Markets' (1993) 14 *The Company Lawyer* 43, 51–4, Taylor, M, 'A European SEC', *FRR*, Sept 1998, Thieffry, n 136 above and Lannoo, K, *Does Europe Need an SEC? Securities Market Regulation in the EU* (1999).

[138] On this see Lannoo, n 36 above, 26.

(b) *Weaknesses in the Member-State Model*

The more common argument made in favour of a greater degree of co-ordination, however, is that home-country supervision (which is set to become the supervisory model for the entire regime once greater harmonization is achieved), supported by the current co-operation arrangements, is not adequately adapted to cope with the increasing volume of cross-border investment and securities business.[139] Neither is it adapted to deal with the changing structure of the market as witnessed by the rise of cross-border alliances between exchanges, the development of new trading systems and clearing and settlement mechanisms, and the increasing number of financial conglomerates as industry consolidation continues. The ability of the decentralized supervisory structure to monitor pan-EC trading effectively and to control market abuse is often raised as a particular problem.[140] A structure which is based on the willingness and ability of competent authorities to comply with their co-operation obligations could be seen as an overly diffuse and unstable form of supervision which does not ensure that supervisors are presented with a complete picture. This is particularly the case in the supervision of investment-services firms where supervisors may not have an adequate perspective on all of a firm's cross-border activities. Unless information-exchange and co-operation procedures are solid and effective, this structure could be overly complex to result in effective cooperation.

The weakness, in principle, of a co-operation-based supervisory structure is exacerbated by the number of supervisors across the Community and the variety of ways in which they are organized and operate.[141] Clear lines of communication and co-operation can be difficult to establish where the supervisory community is crowded with a range of different actors with different powers and responsibilities. Co-operation is often required between different competent authorities at national level as well as at EC level.[142] Institutional rivalries can develop between supervisors both nationally and

---

[139] Greater centralization of supervision and risk management following on market integration is not of course simply a feature of the securities and investment-services market-place. The point has been made generally that '[t]he spillover effect of market integration . . . has involved the Community in developing an active policy on product safety regulation and the management of risks "Post-Maastricht", therefore, greater Community activity in various areas entails a fundamental shift of powers from national to Community level': Vos, n 94 above, 1113.

[140] Supervisors are also of the view that co-operation between investment-services and securities supervisors is not sufficiently developed: Lannoo, K, 'Securities Committee Still Stuck', *FRR*, Mar 1998, 21.

[141] The proliferation of supervisors provoked the Lamfalussy Report to note that 'there are about 40 public bodies in the European Union dealing with securities markets regulation and supervision. Competences are mixed. Responsibilities are different. The result at European level is fragmentation and often confusion': n 2 above, 15.

[142] In France, eg, different bodies supervise securities markets and investment firms. The Market Abuse Proposal represents a recent attempt to rationalize the number of national authorities involved in supervision.

at EC level which hinder co-operation. Supervision and enforcement run the risk of being uneven and inconsistent across the EC where supervisory authorities are staffed and supported to varying degrees and enforcement procedures vary.[143]

(c) *The Special Case of Prudential Supervision*

The need for a centralized supervisor is most frequently raised in the context of the co-ordination of prudential supervision of investment firms and credit institutions.[144] The high degree of harmonization in the area of prudential supervision, combined with the link between prudential supervision and systemic risk, has focused attention on the adequacy of the institutional structure of prudential supervision, given increases in cross-border activity and heightened competition between financial institutions.[145]

In particular, prudential supervision is often identified as a target for more co-ordinated supervision as the failure of an investment firm (particularly a market maker) or credit institution could pose a threat to the stability of the EC market-place as a whole.[146] Co-ordinated prudential supervision would accordingly focus on those rules, such as capital adequacy rules, which are designed with systemic stability in mind. An initial response would be simply to strengthen co-operation between supervisors; this approach is currently being taken with respect to financial conglomerates. The case in principle for a more drastic centralization of prudential supervision draws support from the danger that enforcement of prudential requirements by national supervisors could be weak, leading to wider systemic problems which strong centralized enforcement by a central agency might be able to avoid. In addition, the Commission has noted that '[a]s financial institutions organize themselves on a cross-border basis, their nationality may become less clear and ascertaining which supervisors should assume responsibility in the event of a solvency crisis could become difficult'.[147] These difficulties

---

[143] See Andenas and Hadjiemmanuil, n 91 above, 386.

[144] See, eg, Vigneron, P, Steinfeld, P, and Counye, D, 'European Regulatory Lessons of the BCCI Collapse—the Case for Strengthening Financial Supervision' [1993] *YBEL* 263, 290 ff. The prospect of an agency with responsibility only for the prudential aspect of supervision is not unheard of. The Australian approach has been to split the supervision of systemic stability, other prudential supervision (such as the protection of client funds), and market integrity and conduct-of-business regulation between three different supervisors: Gros and Lannoo, n 135 above, 146–7.

[145] Increased competition leads to a greater focus on profits and may result in riskier behaviour leading to an increase in systemic risk: Plender, J, 'Crisis in the Making' [1999] *JIBFL* 227.

[146] See, eg, Heremans, D, 'Economic Aspects of the Second Banking Directive and of the Proposal for a Directive on Investment Services in the Securities Field' in Stucyk, J (ed), *Financial and Monetary Integration in the European Economic Community, Legal, Institutional and Economic Aspects* (1993) 37, 45.

[147] 1998 Communication, n 12 above, 16.

are aggravated in the case of financial conglomerates, where responsibilities for prudential supervision could be spread across a number of different supervisors. A centralized agency for prudential supervision of those participating in investment-services markets (investment firms or credit institutions) which was also responsible for the prudential supervision of credit institutions and insurance companies would respond to the need to take into account the trend towards financial conglomeration and the risks it poses. The threat which investment firms pose in terms of systemic risk is, however, questionable, as compared to credit institutions which provide investment-services or credit institutions carrying out traditional banking functions only. This uncertainty is likely to act as a significant brake on any discussion of the extent to which investment-services firms should be subject to centralized prudential supervision.

(d) *The Special Case of Securities-trading Markets*

The recent move towards securities-trading markets alliances, the development of cross-border trading, the growth of ATSs, and, in particular, mergers between regulated markets has been charged with placing a considerable new strain on the decentralized supervisory structure particularly with respect to the control of market abuse. In addition, given that the securities directives can be regarded as providing a disclosure code which ensures the dissemination of disclosure to the market-place and thus enhances confidence in the price-formation process across EC markets,[148] the absence of a single authority which ensures that price-sensitive information is, in practice, disseminated to all markets at the same time and in an efficient manner is arguably a significant weakness in the disclosure structure.[149] Looking further ahead, if securities-trading markets were to consolidate to such a degree that the integrated market would be underpinned by a small number of pan-EC trading systems supported by a consolidated clearing and settlement system, delivery of investor confidence, market integrity, and systemic stability objectives would be most effectively carried out by a single regulator with investigatory and enforcement powers.

XV.3.2.3 *The Case Against Centralized Supervision*[150]

(a) *The Subsidiarity Principle*

The case against a greater degree of supervisory co-ordination can be made most compellingly with respect to the most drastic option. The establishment

---

[148] See Ch. IV.

[149] Federal Trust, *Towards an Integrated European Capital Market* (1993) 20.

[150] The EC context aside, more general considerations as to the desirability of greater centralization also come into play. In particular, the risk of regulatory capture arising arguably

of a single authority with responsibility for supervising offers of securities and/or the provision of investment services and the securities-trading markets would require a significant transfer of power from the Member States to the authority which fits uneasily with the principle of subsidiarity. Although the subsidiarity principle would not appear to apply, strictly speaking, to a Treaty amendment to establish a single regulator, the principle is unlikely to be disregarded.[151] Compliance with the subsidiarity principle would require that the setting up of a single authority and the nature of its competences would achieve objectives which could not be sufficiently achieved by the Member States and, by reason of the scale and effects of the activities pursued by the authority, would be better achieved at Community level. The extensive local market expertise and experience of national supervisors would make it difficult to justify a complete transfer of their powers to a central authority, given that a substantial proportion of securities and investment-services activity is still carried out domestically. In particular, whatever arguments can be made in respect of prudential supervision on market-wide systemic grounds or in relation to the supervision of an integrated securities-trading market, effective investor protection or protective supervision is, at the moment, best directed towards tracking the current home-bias of retail investors towards securities traded on their domestic exchanges. This domestic focus may change, however, particularly if the provision of investment services on-line continues to develop.[152]

(b) *The Incomplete Rule Framework*

EC securities regulation is as yet still some way from achieving the degree of harmonization which would make centralized supervision a realistic option. Not only are large areas of securities regulation, such as marketing and conduct-of-business regulation, still not harmonized, the absence of fully harmonized regimes with respect to the laws and procedures underlying taxation and company law makes the central regulation of investment firms established in different Member States currently impracticable. Notably, the

increases in a centralized supervision or law-making model. Regulatory capture risk concerns the risk that a supervisor/regulator becomes captured by the industry or sector it regulates in that it fails to differentiate between the interests of the regulated sector and the general good promoted by the regulation in question. See, eg, Kay, J, and Vickers, J, 'Regulatory Reform: An Appraisal' in Majone, G (ed), *Deregulation or Re-regulation. Regulatory Reform in Europe and the United States* (1990) 221, 232–3.

[151] The Protocol to the Amsterdam Treaty on the application of the principles of subsidiarity and proportionality has been described as contributing to the subsidiarity principle's 'shaping as a workable basis for guiding institutional and constitutional choices': Beaumont and Weatherill. n 5 above, 30.

[152] A change in supervisory structure might also be required were cross-border investment services and securities services drastically to increase in volume or were consolidation in the investment industry to lead to the dominance of large pan-European investment firms.

Initial Lamfalussy Report relied on the incomplete state of harmonization as an argument against the establishment, for the time being at least, of a central regulator. In their Initial Report, the Wise Men briefly considered the case, in principle, for a single regulatory authority.[153] They concluded that, given the current state of the development of the securities and investment-services markets, the gaps still existing in the basic harmonized legal infrastructure of the single market, and the need for speedy action to address the immediate problems faced by the integration programme, establishment of a dedicated regulatory agency was not a realistic option.[154]

(c) *Distance from the Market-place*

This argument is an aspect of the subsidiarity argument. While certain aspects of the supervision of the securities and investment-services markets such as prudential supervision or oversight of disclosure documents could, arguably, be carried out at a distance, supervision of the investment-firm/investor relationship and of trading on regulated markets demands that the supervisor be close to the market-place. In the case of the investor/investment-firm relationship and the supervision of protective regulation, effective supervision is dependent on proximity to the market in which the relationship is conducted.[155] Similarly, the supervision of regulated markets and securities trading requires daily supervision and close proximity to the market in question. In both cases, local supervision, supplemented by strong co-operation between competent authorities across the EC where cross-border elements arise, might be regarded as the most effective use of supervisory resources.

(d) *Market Conditions*

More practically, while the integration of national investment-services and securities markets is proceeding overall, the various sectors of the market are behaving different. The integration of the retail investment-services market, for example, is sluggish, as compared with the wholesale sector. The different structural conditions which exist across the EC suggest that national

---

[153] N 58 above.   [154] Ibid, 26.

[155] 'If . . . a European equivalent of the SEC sought to apply a pan-European system of investor protection to safeguard the transactions of individual investors in each country, it could well prove a cumbersome and bureaucratic creature ill-suited to dealing with very different local circumstances. Retail transactions . . . 'are in the foreseeable future likely to be more conveniently supervised by national regulators' and 'a central regulatory body . . . would be likely to prove remote, bureaucratic and almost certainly ineffective. In retail transactions generally the principle of subsidiarity should prevail', Federal Trust, n 149 above, 10 and 18. See also the view of Buxbaum and Hopt (expressed in 1988) that national supervisors 'are in line with national traditions, both in structure and style, and know the nuances of their respective domestic capital markets': n 134 above, 266.

supervisory structures which can best respond to those conditions are still the most appropriate model for supervision. The degree to which individuals invest in equities or purchase units in collective-investment schemes is much more pronounced in the UK than in continental Europe, for example, due in part to different approaches to pension provision. Credit institutions are the dominant providers of investment services in certain continental European States, whereas investment firms represent a considerable sector of the market in the UK and Ireland. More fundamentally, the importance of the securities markets in financing investment still varies across the EC. Politically, any move towards centralized supervision would be highly sensitive.

Given all of these variables, allowing greater co-ordination to evolve organically through the interaction of national supervisors, be it through the medium of the CESR or other committees, might be the least traumatic and most market-sensitive way to develop an institutional structure for the supervision of the investment-services and securities markets.[156]

XV.3.3 *Centralized Supervision: The Possibilities*

XV.3.3.1 *The Commission's Perspective*

In its 1998 Communication, although the Commission recognized that the *ad hoc* nature of co-operation needed to be upgraded, its position was that structured co-operation between national supervisory bodies, rather than the creation of new EU-level arrangements, was sufficient to ensure market-wide stability. It suggested that in order to enhance the quality of supervision, a blueprint or supervisor's charter be developed defining the responsibilities and mechanisms for co-ordination between all the different national and EU-level bodies involved in financial supervision.[157]

(a) *Prudential and Conduct of Business Regulation*

The Commission appears reluctant to address the possibility of centralized supervision of investment-services providers, with respect either to prudential or conduct regulation. That it has given scant attention to centralized supervision of conduct and investor protection is not surprising, given that the challenge faced here is the more basic one of establishing harmonized standards. But even in the more developed area of prudential regulation, an assessment of the merits and demerits of centralized supervision does not

---

[156] In this regard it is worth noting the comment by Padoa-Schioppa, T, a member of the ECB's executive board, that 'co-operation among the banking supervisors . . . will allow a sort of euro area collective supervisor to emerge that can act as effectively as if there were a single supervisor', cited in Plender, n 145 above, 228.

[157] N 12 above, 3 and 16.

appear to be on the agenda. The Commission regards increased co-operation as central to the control of prudential risk and has, uncontroversially, called for enhanced co-operation between sector supervisors in order to deal effectively with challenge of conglomeration.[158] The relatively high degree of co-operation between supervisors with respect to prudential regulation may be an explanatory factor.

(b) *Securities-trading Markets Supervision*

Co-operation and co-ordination between securities-markets supervisors is significantly less developed, leading the Commission to highlight, in the 1998 Communication, the supervision of securities markets as an area in which the present co-operation arrangements were unable to keep pace with the acceleration in market integration.[159] A similar opinion is expressed in the FSAP where it noted that, as cross-border trade in securities becomes more of a reality, market integrity concerns may ultimately require the establishment of a single authority to oversee securities markets.[160] Some industry-level support does appear to exist for a Euro-Sec supervisor in the area of securities-market supervision, at least with respect to the wholesale markets and, specifically, with respect to standardizing the market-conduct rules and practices applicable to issuers and intermediaries active in the wholesale market.[161] It may be that the new committee structure will meet these concerns, particularly given the moves towards greater harmonization of securities-trading market regulation and market-conduct rules discussed in earlier chapters.

XV.3.3.2 *The Lamfalussy Report: Enhanced Co-operation*

The Lamfalussy Report suggests that discussions on the various possibilities for centralized supervision are very much a secondary priority as compared to the need to complete the legislative framework for the single market in securities and investment services and to enhance co-operation between supervisors. While the Initial Lamfalussy Report highlighted the supervision structure as a weakness in the EU regulatory framework,[162] it did not sup-

---

[158] 1998 Communication, n 12 above, 16 and FSAP, n 1 above, 11.
[159] N 12 above, 3.   [160] N 1 above, 11.
[161] See the report in *The Economist*, 21 Aug 1999, 70: 'No Sec's please, we're European'. For a similar view see the report by the Federal Trust, n 149 above, which recommended at 19 and 24 the establishment of a Euro-Sec for the wholesale securities markets, whose powers would be mainly limited to co-ordinating supervisory practices and supervisors' rule books.
[162] It noted that '[t]here is no single template for supervision. Cooperation between securities regulators for dealing with cross-border practices and trading is only lightly covered. The investigative powers of national authorities and sanctions are not defined at EU level': Initial Lamfalussy Report, n 58 above, 15.

port centralizing supervision. The final Report also downplayed the possibility of a central supervisor, although the establishment of a single market authority was not ruled out in the event that the Report's law-making proposals do not succeed.

XV.3.3.3 *The Potential Role of the ECB*[163]

The establishment of the institutions of EMU has given a new dimension to the central supervisor question, at least with respect to prudential supervision. Given the debate on centralized prudential supervision, it might have been thought that the Treaty provisions governing the European Central Bank (ECB) and the European System of Central Banks (ECSB)[164] might, in some way, involve the new institutions of EMU in prudential supervision on an executive, operational basis. This is not the case. The prudential supervision functions which have been granted to the ECB and the ESCB under the Treaty and the Protocol on the Statute of the ESCB and the ECB reflect the decision at the time of the negotiations not to alter the structure of prudential supervision by the Member States.[165]

The prudential-supervision provisions make clear that the ESCB is not to act as a separate competent authority. Prudential supervision is not listed among the 'basic tasks' of the ESCB which are listed in Article 105(2) EC and are concerned with the operation of monetary policy and the maintenance of price stability.[166] Article 105(5) and Article 3(3) of the Protocol on the Statute of the ESCB and the ECB provide that the ESCB is simply to 'contribute' to the smooth conduct of policies pursued by the competent authorities relating to the prudential supervision of credit institutions and the stability of the financial system. These provisions apply only to Member States which are members of EMU and so are limited in terms of

---

[163] See generally Smits, n 136 above, 327–62, Avgerinos, Y, 'European System of Central Banks: Monetary Policy, Independence, Banking Supervision and Future Perspectives', [1999] *JIBFL* 144; Andenas and Hadjiemmanuil, n 91 above; and Lastra, R, *Central Banking and Banking Regulation* (1996) 239–43.

[164] The ESCB is comprised of the ECB and the national central banks of the Member States of EMU.

[165] Smits has noted that '[t]he internal market legislation had only just been adopted, or was still under discussion, and the new arrangements had not yet been proven in practice. With that state of affairs, a case for the radical departure from the concept agreed for establishing the internal banking market could hardly be made. Thus, the continued role of the present-day supervisory agencies was not questioned, nor the idea that the State bodies should be predominant in banking supervision': n 136 above, 334.

[166] Under Art. 105(2) EC the basic tasks to be fulfilled by the ESCB are: the definition and implementation of the Community's monetary policy; the conduct of foreign-exchange operations; the holding and management of the official foreign reserves of Member States; and the promotion of the smooth operation of payment systems.

their potential impact on EC-wide prudential supervision.[167] The role played by the ESCB in this regard is typically described in terms of being a co-ordinating and advisory function.[168] Operational prudential supervision remains within the remit of the Member States. As outlined in section 2.5.5 above, the ECB also plays an advisory role in the development of legislation in the prudential sphere.

The seeds of some form of centralized executive prudential supervision of the investment-services markets through the ECB or an agency related to it may be contained in Article 105(6) EC. The controversy about the extent to which the ECB should be involved in prudential supervision was resolved by the adoption of Article 105(6) which is an enabling clause which permits the allocation of additional tasks to the EC in the future.[169] It provides that the Council may, acting unanimously on a proposal from the Commission and after consulting the ECB and after receiving the assent of the European Parliament, confer upon the ECB specific tasks concerning policies relating to the prudential supervision of credit institutions and other financial institutions, with the exception of insurance undertakings.[170] Although 'financial institutions' is not a defined term, the specific exclusion of insurance undertakings and the reference to financial institutions rather than simply to credit institutions suggests that the definition could include a wide range of investment-services providers. The significance which these 'specific tasks' might hold for the current structure of prudential supervision can perhaps be inferred from the degree of agreement which is needed among the institutions of the Community before any tasks can be conferred on the ECB. Significantly, Article 105(6) applies to all Member States, including those Member States which do not fulfil the conditions for entry into EMU

---

[167] Arts. 122(3) and 43(1) of the Protocol. UK Opt Out Protocol, Arts. 5 (re Art. 105(5) EC) and 8 (re Art. 3(3) of the Protocol). The uneven application of Arts. 105(5) EC and 3(3) of the Protocol reveals how the nature of the ECB's role in prudential supervision is complicated by the monetary split of the EC into EMU Member States, Member States with a derogation, and opt-out Member States. Member States with a derogation are those Member States which do not meet the conditions for EMU membership. They are subject to a special regime under the Treaty EMU provisions and the Protocol, a number of the provisions of which do not apply to them. The extent to which provisions are inapplicable is governed by Art. 122(3) (with respect to the Treaty) and by Art. 43 of the Protocol (with respect to the Protocol). Denmark and the UK each negotiated an opt-out from EMU. The effect of Denmark's opt-out, however, is that it is treated as a Member State with a derogation: Art. 2, Denmark Protocol. The special position of the UK is set out in detail in its Protocol (hereafter UK Protocol).

[168] The exact scope of Art. 105(5) EC has been a matter of some debate, particularly with respect to whether it implies that the ESCB can engage in rule-making. See, eg, Smits, n 136 above, 339–43 and Andenas and Hadjiemmanuil, n 91 above, 401–2.

[169] Art. 105(6) EC is reflected in Art. 25(2) of the Protocol which provides that the ECB 'may perform specific tasks concerning policies relating to the prudential supervision of credit institutions and other financial institutions with the exception of insurance undertakings'.

[170] Insurance undertakings were excluded as they do not normally come within the supervisory remit of central banks.

(Member States with a derogation)[171] and those Member States which have opted out of EMU.[172]

Although it has been suggested that Article 105(6) EC might lead to more direct involvement of the ECB in prudential supervision,[173] whether or not Article 105(6) has the potential to involve the ECB more directly in the prudential supervision of investment-services providers must be questionable. Together, the references to prudential supervision in the Treaty and in the Protocol appear to relegate the role of the ECB in prudential supervision to a secondary one at best, with the emphasis on advising with respect to legislation and assisting competent authorities in their role as prudential supervisors.[174] Whatever the arguments in favour of combining monetary functions and prudential supervision of credit institutions in central banks in order to enhance the stability of the financial system generally,[175] investment firms are not as central to the structure of the financial system nor as prone to systemic risk as are credit institutions. The recent trend to take prudential supervision of credit institutions away from central banks[176] also suggests that any changes to prudential supervision engendered by Article 105(6) EC might involve the establishment by the ECB of a separate agency to deal with any matters of prudential supervision which may be entrusted to it. The utility of any such agency in a securities and investment-services

---

[171] Art. 122(3) EC does not identify Art. 105(6) EC as one of the provisions which do not apply to Member States with a derogation. Similarly, Art. 43.1 of the Protocol does not include Art. 25(2) in the list of Protocol Arts. which do not apply to Member States with a derogation.

[172] The UK Protocol does not specify that Art. 105(6) EC does not apply to the UK.

[173] Smits has noted that Art. 105(6) EC 'seems to imply a supervisory function separate from the competences of [national central banks] and other supervisory agencies. This may be read as a task alongside the supervisory tasks of these authorities as well as an overseeing role, more far-reaching than the coordinating one which the [ESCB] is to play from the outset': n 136 above, 356. He predicted that Art. 105(6) EC might give the ECB a role in the licensing and ongoing supervision of financial-market operators which he acknowledged at 358 'would be a major departure from current law and practice under which only national bodies are competent for the authorization and day-to-day supervision of financial market operators'. For the view that Art. 105(6) EC is designed to confer rule- and policy-making competencies see Andenas and Hadjiemmanuil, n 91 above, 402.

[174] The role of the ECB in prudential supervision has been described as 'only an advisory and coordinating role in the prudential supervision of banks': Gros and Lannoo, n 135 above, 133. In a similar vein Andenas and Hadjiemmanuil observed that 'the drafting of the relevant [prudential supervision] provisions of the EC Treaty and the Statute of the ESCB is characterized by considerable imprecision and limiting spirit. Instead of figuring among the basic tasks of the ESCB, prudential supervision is treated as a separate, supplementary function': n 91 above, 397.

[175] See Lastra, n 163 above, 148–50.

[176] In 1997, eg, the Bank of England lost its role in prudential supervision, which was transferred to the Financial Services Authority. Similar moves are afoot in Ireland where the central bank which currently supervises monetary and regulatory matters is to be restructured in the form of two subsidiaries operated by the new umbrella Central Bank of Ireland and Financial Services Authority, the Irish Monetary Authority and the Irish Financial Services Regulatory Authority, both of which will operate under the supervision of a board drawn from both entities.

market in which financial conglomerates with significant insurance operations are likely to play an increasingly more important role can be questioned, however, given the exclusion of insurance undertakings from Article
105(6). More generally, Article 105(6), while applicable to all Member
States, is weakened by the monetary split in the Community. The problem
arises with respect to which of the ECB's governing bodies would exercise
the functions allocated to the ECB under Article 105(6). The General Council
of the ECB is the only part of the ECB's decision-making structure where the
central banks of Member States which do not participate in EMU are represented.[177] The other decision-making bodies, the Governing Council and the
Executive Board, are limited to the central banks of Member States which
are members of EMU.[178] The General Council's functions are limited, however, and do not extend to the performance of tasks under Article 105(6),
resulting, until the membership of EMU parallels that of the EC, in a mismatch between the Member States potentially subject to supervisory control
by the ECB and the Member States who are permitted to participate in the
exercise of that supervision.[179] Finally, compliance with the subsidiarity
doctrine could also prove problematic for any transfer of powers to the ECB.
The nature and extent of the supervisory powers transferred are likely to be
critical.

The significance of the ECB for the supervision of securities and investment-services markets lies less in the extent to which the current constitutional structure might be manipulated to encompass supervision of the
investment-services markets, however, and rather more in the precedent
it establishes of centralized policy-setting, advisory, and co-ordination
functions.

XV.4 CENTRALIZATION AND DECENTRALIZATION: THE NEW MODEL

Predicting the future shape of the institutional structure of EC securities and
investment-services markets supervision and rule-making is a somewhat
academic exercise, given the current pace of change. At the very least, it

---

[177] The General Council consists of the President and Vice-President of the ECB and the governors of the central banks of all the Member States.

[178] The Governing Body consists of the Executive Board plus the governors of the central
banks of Member States participating in EMU. The Executive Board is comprised of the President
and Vice-President of the ECB and 4 other members who are all to be 'persons of recognized
standing and professional experience in monetary and banking matters': Art. 112(2)(b) EC.

[179] Smits has made the point that the unanimous vote of all the Member States in the
Council which is necessary to activate Art. 105(6) is unlikely to be forthcoming while the
Community remains split for monetary purposes, as non-participating Member States would be
voting for a change in supervisory methods over which they would have little control: n 136
above, 360.

seems clear that co-operation and co-ordination between national competent authorities and between those authorities and the EC institutions (including the ECB,[180] the existing system of Contact Committees, and the CESR) must be enhanced and greater consistency achieved in supervisory practices and in the implementation of EC rules.

The institutional model (encompassing both rule-making and enforcement) which seems to be emerging is some distance removed from amounting to a centralized market supervisor or a Euro-SEC. The Lamfalussy Report's model, with its emphasis on more extensive centralized decision-making supported by widespread consultation, and its reliance on the decentralized *status quo* as far as supervision is concerned, albeit supported by more intensive co-ordination of rule implementation and greater convergence in regulatory practices via the CESR, is at least a workable compromise. It may yet mark the emergence of a strengthened two-tier institutional structure. In a reflection of the still immature (if fast developing) state of the securities and investment-services regime, what does appear to be clear, as far as institutional change is concerned, is a focus on rule-making rather than on direct market supervision. It may be, however, that if the FSAP is delivered, the sophistication of the EC securities-regulation regime and the deeper integration of the market-place which should follow will place the central supervisor debate in a very different market context.

---

[180] In particular with respect to prudential supervision and systemic stability issues.

Index